山东统计年鉴

SHANDONG STATISTICAL YEARBOOK

2022

(总第 34 期 No. 34)

山　东　省　统　计　局
国家统计局山东调查总队　编

Compiled by

Shandong Provincial Bureau of Statistics

Survey Office of the National Bureau of Statistics in Shandong

图书在版编目（CIP）数据

山东统计年鉴. 2022 = Shandong Statistical Yearbook 2022 : 汉英对照 / 山东省统计局, 国家统计局山东调查总队编. -- 北京 : 中国统计出版社, 2022.10
ISBN 978-7-5037-9899-3

Ⅰ.①山… Ⅱ.①山… ②国… Ⅲ. ①统计资料－山东－2022－年鉴－汉、英 Ⅳ. ①C832.52-54

中国版本图书馆 CIP 数据核字(2022)第 148235 号

山东统计年鉴 2022

作　　者/ 山东省统计局　国家统计局山东调查总队
责任编辑/ 高媛媛
责任校对/ 张圣红　辛　超　赵善胜　张　静
装帧设计/ 程潇濛
出版发行/ 中国统计出版社有限公司
地　　址/ 北京市丰台区西三环南路甲 6 号
邮政编码/ 100073
电　　话/ 邮购（010）63376909　书店（010）68783171
网　　址/ http://www.zgtjcbs.com
印　　刷/ 济南百思特印业有限公司
经　　销/ 新华书店
开　　本/ 890mm×1240mm　1/16
字　　数/ 1900 千字
印　　张/ 40.5
版　　别/ 2022 年 10 月第 1 版
版　　次/ 2022 年 10 月第 1 次印刷
定　　价/ 460.00 元　Price:460.00 yuan (RMB)

本书附同版本 CD-ROM 一张，光盘内容以书面文字为准。
如有印装差错，由本社发行部调换。

《山东统计年鉴 2022》
编辑委员会

Shandong Statistical Yearbook 2022

EDITORIAL BOARD AND STAFF

编 辑 说 明

一、《山东统计年鉴》是一部全面反映山东省国民经济和社会发展情况的资料性年刊，是认识和研究山东省情、制定政策、指导国民经济发展的重要资料和历史性工具书。

二、《山东统计年鉴 2022》共包括特载、统计表和附录三大部分。特载部分包括政府工作报告、统计公报和统计工作综述，综合反映全省经济社会发展概况和山东省统计工作情况。

统计表部分收录了 2021 年度山东省国民经济和社会发展方面的统计数据，共有二十二篇：第一篇，综合；第二篇，国民经济核算；第三篇，人口；第四篇，就业、工资和社会保障；第五篇，固定资产投资；第六篇，对外经济和旅游；第七篇，能源；第八篇，财政和金融；第九篇，价格指数；第十篇，居民生活；第十一篇，城市建设；第十二篇，资源和环境；第十三篇，农业；第十四篇，工业；第十五篇，建筑业；第十六篇，服务业；第十七篇，运输和邮电；第十八篇，批发和零售业、住宿和餐饮业；第十九篇，教育和科技；第二十篇，文化、体育和卫生；第二十一篇，公共管理和社会服务；第二十二篇，各县（市、区）主要经济指标。

各篇章插页后附有简要说明，概括介绍各篇主要内容和资料来源；各篇章最后附有主要统计指标解释，简要介绍指标的概念、统计方法、统计口径和统计范围。

附录部分包括全国各省（市、自治区）主要经济指标、部分国际统计资料和山东省统计局工作大事记等。

三、本年鉴所列各项指标，《政府工作报告》和《统计公报》使用的数字为快报数或初步统计数；其他各部分为正式年报数据。凡与本年鉴数字不符的一律以本年鉴为准。

四、本年鉴的编辑，已根据现行国家统计制度，对统计指标概念、口径、范围、计算方法、计算价格等，作了统一调整，并分别在各部分的主要指标解释或表末加以注释；各表中价值量指标，凡未加说明的，均按当年价格计算。部分数据合计数或相对数由于单位取舍不同而产生的计算误差均未作机械调整。

五、《山东统计年鉴》公开出版以来，受到了广大读者的关心与支持，对此深表谢意。本年鉴编辑中难免存在不足之处，恳请广大读者提出宝贵意见，以便改进、提高。

PREFACE

I. *Shandong Statistical Yearbook* is an annual publication, which covers very comprehensive data and reflects various aspects of Shandong's social and economic development. It can also work as an important and historical reference book which will play a great role in comprehending and studying the basic conditions of Shandong, making policies, and guiding the development of society and economy.

II. The yearbook contains the following three parts: part one feature, part two statistics and part three appendixes. Feature mainly includes Government Work Report, Shandong Statistics Communique and Summary of Shandong Statistical Undertaking, comprehensively reflecting the development of society and economy and showing the achievements in statistics of Shandong Province.

Part 2 contains the following twenty-two chapters, 1. General Survey; 2. National Accounts; 3. Population; 4. Employment, Wages and Social Security ; 5. Investment in Fixed Assets; 6. Foreign Trade and Tourism; 7. Energy; 8. Government Finance and Banking; 9. Price Indices; 10. People's Livelihood; 11. City Construction; 12. Natural Resources and Environment; 13. Agriculture; 14. Industry; 15. Construction; 16.Service Enterprises; 17. Transport, Post and Telecommunication Services; 18. Wholesale, Retail, Hotels and Catering Services; 19. Education, Science and Technology; 20. Culture,Sports and Health;21.Public Management and Social Services;22. Main Indicators of Counties (Cities and Districts at County Level).

In brief introduction at the beginning of each chapter, main coverage of this chapter, data sources and statistical coverage are concerned. In addition, explanatory notes on main statistical indicators are provided at the end of each chapter, giving a brief explanation of statistical indicators, such as definition, statistical methods, statistical coverage and statistical scope.

Appendix contains the main economic indicators of some other provinces (municipality), international statistics and Events of Shandong Provincial Bureau of Statistics.

III. Data used in Government Work Report and Shandong Statistics Communiqué are preliminary statistics. data in other chapters is official annual data. Data in Shandong Statistical Yearbook are all verified and should be based on this standard.

IV. In *Shandong Statistical Yearbook*, statistical definitions, statistical coverage, statistical methods and prices are adjusted according to the current state statistical standards, and all changes have been noted at the end of the table or in the explanatory notes. Data in value terms are calculated at current prices if there are no notes. Statistical discrepancies on totals and relative figures due to rounding are not adjusted.

V. After this yearbook was published, it has received lots of concerns and support from readers whom we should thank. Because of our ability, it is inevitable that there are shortcomings in this book, so we welcome all candid comments and criticism from our readers to perfect this book and to offer readers better service.

目录 Contents

第一篇 综　合
CHAPTER 1 General Survey

简要说明
Brief Introduction

1-1 行政区划(2021年底) 3
Divisions of Administrative Areas (Year-end of 2021)

1-2 国民经济和社会发展主要指标 4
Main Indicators on National Economic and Social Development

1-3 国民经济和社会发展主要指标增长速度 16
Growth Rates of Main Indicators on National Economic and Social Development

1-4 全省经济和社会发展结构指标 28
Composition Indicators on National Economic and Social Development

1-5 平均每天社会经济活动 30
Selected Indicators on Average Daily Social and Economic Activities

1-6 国民经济和社会发展主要指标占全国的比重(2021年) 31
Proportion of Main Economic and Social Indicators to the Whole Country (2021)

1-7 按行业分法人单位数 32
Number of Corporate Units by Sector

1-8 按机构类型分法人单位数 33
Number of Corporate Units by Status of Organization

1-9 按地区分法人单位数 33
Number of Corporate Units by Region

主要统计指标解释 34
Explanatory Notes on Main Statistical Indicators

第二篇 国民经济核算
CHAPTER 2 National Accounts

简要说明
Brief Introduction
2-1 主要年份地区生产总值 ……41
Gross Domestic Product in Major Years
2-2 主要年份地区生产总值指数 ……42
Indices of Gross Domestic Product in Major Years
2-3 主要年份地区生产总值构成 ……44
Composition of Gross Domestic Product in Major Years
2-4 地区生产总值 ……45
Gross Domestic Product
2-5 三次产业对经济增长的贡献率及拉动百分点……46
Share and Contribution of the Three Industries to the Increase of GDP
2-6 各市生产总值(2021年) ……47
Gross Domestic Product by Region(2021)
2-7 各市生产总值构成(2021年) ……48
Composition of Gross Domestic Product by Region(2021)
主要统计指标解释 ……49
Explanatory Notes on Main Statistical Indicators

第三篇 人 口
CHAPTER 3 Population

简要说明
Brief Introduction
3-1 主要年份总人口 ……55
Population in Major Years
3-2 主要年份人口出生率、死亡率、自然增长率 ……56
Birth Rate, Death Rate and Natural Growth Rate of Population in Major Years
3-3 人口年龄结构、抚养比和性别比 ……57
Age Composition and Dependency Ratio of Population
3-4 各市人口数和总户数(2021年) ……57
Population and Households by Region (2021)
3-5 七次人口普查主要数据 ……58
Major Data of All Previous Provincial Population Census
主要统计指标解释 ……59
Explanatory Notes on Main Statistical Indicators

第四篇 就业、工资和社会保障
CHAPTER 4 Employment , Wages and Social Security

简要说明
Brief Introduction
4-1 就业基本情况……63
Employment
4-2 按三次产业分的年底就业人员数 ……64
Number of Employed Persons at the Year-end by Three Industries

4-3 按登记注册类型和行业分城镇非私营单位就业人员数(2021年底) 65
Number of Employed Persons in Urban Non-private units at the Year-end by Status of Registration and Sector(2021)
4-4 各市年底就业人员数(2021年底) 66
Number of Employed Persons at the Year-end by Region（2021）
4-5 按登记注册类型和行业分城镇非私营单位就业人员工资总额(2021年)......68
Total Wages Bill of Employed Persons in Urban Non-private units by Status of Registration and Sector(2021)
4-6 各市按行业分城镇非私营单位就业人员工资总额(2021年)......69
Total Wages Bill of Employed Persons in Urban Non-private units by Sector and Region (2021)
4-7 按登记注册类型和行业分城镇非私营单位就业人员平均工资(2021年) 71
Average Earning of Employed Persons in Urban Non-private units by Status of Registration and Sector(2021)
4-8 各市按行业分城镇非私营单位就业人员平均工资(2021年) 72
Average Earning of Employed Persons in Urban Non-private units by Sector and Region (2021)
4-9 各市按行业分城镇私营单位就业人员平均工资(2021年)......73
Average Wage of Staff and Workers in Urban Non-private units by Sector and Region(2021)
4-10 各市城镇登记失业人员及失业率......75
Registered Urban Unemployed Persons and Unemployment Rate by Region
4-11 主要年份年末离休、退休、退职人员人数 75
Numbers of Retired and Resigned Persons at Year-end in Major Years
4-12 离休、退休人员数(2021年底) 76
Numbers of Retired and Resigned Persons at Year-end(2021)
4-13 各市离休、退休人员数(2021年底)......76
Numbers of Retired and Resigned Persons at Year-end by Region(2021)
4-14 离休、退休人员保险福利费用(2021年) 77
Social Insurance and Welfare Funds for Retired Persons(2021)
4-15 各市离休、退休保险福利费用(2021年) 77
Social Insurance and Welfare Funds for Retired Persons by Region(2021)
4-16 社会保险基金收支及累计结余 78
Revenue, Expenses and Balance of Social Insurance Fund
4-17 主要年份年末社会保险参保人数 79
Number of Persons Participated in Social Insurance in Major Years
4-18 各市社会保险参保人数(2021年底) 79
Number of Persons Participated in Social Insurance at Year-end by Region(2021)
4-19 职工养老保险基本情况 80
Basic Statistics on Pension Insurance in Urban Areas
4-20 各市居民基本养老保险情况(2021年)......80
Statistics on Residents Old-age Insurance by Region(2021)
主要统计指标解释 81
Explanatory Notes on Main Statistical Indicators

第五篇 固定资产投资
CHAPTER 5 Investment in Fixed Assets

简要说明
Brief Introduction
5-1 1978-2017年全社会固定资产投资总额 87
Total Investments in Fixed Assets from 1978 to 2017
5-2 1978-2021年全社会固定资产投资构成 88
Composition of Total Investments in Fixed Assets from 1978 to 2021

5-3 按产业分固定资产投资总额 89
Total Investment in Fixed Assets by Three Strata of Industry
5-4 固定资产投资(2021年) 90
Total Investments in Fixed Assets (2021)
5-5 固定资产投资项目情况(2021年) 91
Investment Projects in Fixed Assets(2021)
5-6 按行业分的固定资产投资增长速度(2021年) 92
The growth of Investments in Fixed Assets by Sector(2021)
5-7 按行业分的固定资产投资构成(2021年) 95
Composition of Investments in Fixed Assets by Sector(2021)
5-8 各市固定资产投资增长速度......98
The growth of Total Investments in Fixed Assets by Region
5-9 各市民间固定资产投资增长速度 98
The growth of Non-government Investments in Fixed Assets by Region
5-10 各市房地产开发投资和销售情况（2021年）......99
General Scale of Investment Actually Completed by Enterprises for Real Estate Development and Floor Space of Commercialized Buildings Sold(2021)
5-11 按登记注册类型分的房地产开发投资情况(2021年) 100
Investment in Real Development by Registration Status (2021)
5-12 按登记注册类型分的房地产开发财务情况(2021年) 102
Financial Indicators of Real Estate Development by Registration Status (2021)
5-13 房地产开发企业(单位)施工、销售和待售情况(2021年) 104
Construction and Sale of Buildings Made by Real Estate Enterprises(2021)
主要统计指标解释 106
Explanatory Notes on Main Statistical Indicators

第六篇 对外经济和旅游
CHAPTER 6 Foreign Trade and Tourism

简要说明
Brief Introduction
6-1 1978-2021年人民币对主要外币年平均汇价(中间价) 113
Average Exchange Rate of RMB Yuan Against Main Convertible Currencies from 1978 to 2021(Middle Rate)
6-2 1984-2021年海关进出口情况 114
Basic Statistics on Imports and Exports from 1984 to 2021
6-3 进出口主要分类情况 115
Imports and Exports by Category
6-4 按主要国家(地区)分海关进出口商品总值(2021年) 116
Total Value of Import and Export Commodities by Countries or Regions(2021)
6-5 海关进出口商品分类金额(2021年) 117
Imports and Exports Value by Category of Commodities(2021)
6-6 各市进口总值 118
Import Value by Region
6-7 各市出口总值 118
Export Value by Region
6-8 各市外商投资企业进口总值 119
Import Value of Foreign-funded Enterprises by Region

6-9 各市外商投资企业出口总值 119
Export Value of Foreign-funded Enterprises by Region
6-10 1979-2021年利用外资情况 120
Statistics on Utilization of Foreign Capitals from 1979 to 2021
6-11 按主要国家(地区)分外商直接投资......121
Foreign Direct Investment by Countries or Regions
6-12 按行业分外商直接投资(2021年)......122
Foreign Direct Investment by Sector(2021)
6-13 按方式分外商直接投资 124
Basic Statistics on Foreign Direct Investments by Form
6-14 各市外商直接投资 124
Foreign Direct Investment by Region
6-15 境外投资情况......125
Overseas Investment
6-16 各市境外投资情况 125
Overseas Investment by Region
6-17 按主要国别(地区)分境外投资情况 126
Overseas Investment by Countries or Regions
6-18 1982-2021年对外承包工程和劳务合作情况 129
Statistics on Contracted Projects and Labor Services Cooperation with Foreign Countries 1982 to 2021
6-19 对外承包工程和劳务合作情况 130
Statistics on Contracted Projects and Labour Cooperation with Foreign Countries or Regions
6-20 旅游业情况 130
Tourism
6-21 1995-2021年国内旅游情况 131
Domestic Tourism 1995 to 2021
6-22 按主要国家分接待外国旅游人数......132
Number of Foreigner Tourists by Country
6-23 接待入境游客构成......133
Structure of Foreigner Tourists
6-24 各市接待入境游客人数 133
Number of Foreigner Tourists by Region
6-25 各市入境旅游外汇收入 134
Foreign Exchange Earnings by Region
6-26 入境旅游外汇收入及构成 134
Foreign Exchange Earnings and Its Composition
主要统计指标解释 135
Explanatory Notes on Main Statistical Indicators

第七篇 能 源
CHAPTER 7 Energy

简要说明
Brief Introduction
7-1 主要年份一次能源生产总量 141
Primary Energy Output in Major Years
7-2 1979-2021年能源生产、能源消费弹性系数 142
Elasticity Ratio of Energy Production and Energy Consumption from 1979 to 2021

7-3 一次能源生产量及构成 143
Primary Energy Output and Composition
7-4 能源消费量及构成......143
Total Consumption and Composition of Energy
7-5 按行业分能源消费量 (2021年) 144
Energy Consumption by Sector (2021)
7-6 平均每天各种能源消费量 146
Average Daily Energy Consumption by Type of Energy
7-7 平均每人年生活用能源 146
Annual Per Capita Energy Consumption for Non-Production Purpose
7-8 分品种生活能源年消费总量 147
Annual Energy Consumption for Non-Production Purpose by Category
7-9 综合能源平衡表......147
Overall Energy Balance Sheet
7-10 石油平衡表 148
Petroleum Balance Sheet
7-11 煤炭平衡表 149
Coal Balance Sheet
7-12 电力平衡表 150
Electricity Balance Sheet
7-13 各市万元GDP能耗......151
Energy Consumption per 10 000-yuan GDP by Region
7-14 各市规模以上工业万元增加值能耗......152
Energy Consumption per 10 000-yuan Value Added of Industrial Enterprises above the Designated Size by Region
7-15 各市万元GDP电耗......153
Electricity Consumption per 10 000-yuan GDP by Region
7-16 各市电力消费量(2021年) 154
Electricity Consumption by Region(2021)
主要统计指标解释 155
Explanatory Notes on Main Statistical Indicators

第八篇 财政和金融
CHAPTER 8 Government Finance and Banking

简要说明
Brief Introduction
8-1 主要年份一般公共预算收入 159
General Public Budget Revenue in Major Years
8-2 1950-2006年地方财政支出 160
Total Local Government Budgetary Expenditure from 1950 to 2006
8-3 1979-2006年财政支出中用于文、教、科、卫的支出 161
Expense on Culture, Education, Science and Health from 1979 to 2006
8-4 一般公共预算收入 162
General Public Budget Revenue
8-5 一般公共预算支出 163
General Public Budget Expenditure
8-6 各市一般公共预算收入(2021年) 163
General Public Budget Revenue by Region (2021)

8-7 各市一般公共预算支出(2021年) 165
General Public Budget Expenditure by Region (2021)
8-8 主要年份金融机构人民币存款余额 166
RMB Deposits of Financial Institutions in Major Years
8-9 主要年份金融机构人民币贷款余额 167
RMB Loans of Financial Institutions in Major Years
8-10 金融机构本外币信贷收支情况(2021年) 168
RMB and Foreign Currencies Credit Funds Balance Sheet of Financial Institution (2021)
8-11 金融机构人民币信贷收支情况(2021年) 169
RMB Credit Funds Balance Sheet of Financial Institution (2021)
8-12 金融机构分行业本外币贷款情况(2021年) 170
Loans of RMB and Foreign Currencies of Financial institutions by sector(2021)
8-13 各市金融机构本外币存贷款余额(2021年) 170
RMB and Foreign Currencies Deposits and Loans of Financial Institutions by Region(2021)
8-14 1997-2021年保险费收入和赔款给付 171
Premium and Payment of Insurance Companies 1997 to 2021
8-15 人身保险公司主要业务指标(2021年) 171
Major Business Indicators of Life Insurance Companies(2021)
8-16 财产保险公司主要业务指标(2021年) 172
Major Business Indicators of Insurance Companies(2021)
8-17 各市保险业务情况(2021年) 172
Basic Statistics on Insurance by Region (2021)
8-18 山东省证券期货市场基本情况 173
Basic Situation of Securities and Futures Markets of Shandong Province
8-19 各市证券期货市场基本情况(2021年) 174
Basic Situation of Securities and Futures Markets by Region (2021)
主要统计指标解释 175
Explanatory Notes on Main Statistical Indicators

第九篇 价格指数
CHAPTER 9 Price Indices

简要说明
Brief Introduction
9-1 居民消费价格指数 179
Consumer Price Indices
9-2 居民消费和商品零售价格总指数(2021年) 179
General Consumer and Retail Price Indices(2021)
9-3 历年居民消费价格总指数 180
General Consumer Price Indices over the Years
9-4 历年城市居民消费价格总指数 181
General Urban Consumer Price Indices over the Years
9-5 历年农村居民消费价格总指数 182
General Rural Consumer Price Indices over the Years
9-6 历年商品零售价格总指数 183
General Retail Price Indices over the Years
9-7 历年农业生产资料价格总指数 184
General Price Indices of Means of Agricultural Production over the Years

9-8 居民消费价格分类指数(2021年) 185
Consumer Price Indices by Category (2021)
9-9 商品零售价格分类指数(2021年) 187
Retail Indices by Category (2021)
9-10 农产品生产者价格指数 189
Producer Price Indices for Farm Products
9-11 工业生产者价格指数......190
Price Indices for Industrial Producer
9-12 工业生产者出厂价格指数 191
Producer Price Indices for Industrial Products
9-13 工业生产者出厂价格指数(2021年) 192
Producer Price Indices for Industrial Products(2021)
9-14 工业生产者购进价格指数(2021年) 194
Industrial Producer Purchasing Price Indices(2021)
9-15 各市住宅销售价格指数(2021年) 195
Price Indices for Real Estate(2021)
主要统计指标解释 196
Explanatory Notes on Main Statistical Indicators

第十篇 居民生活
CHAPTER 10 People's Livelihood

简要说明
Brief Introduction
10-1 居民人均可支配收入和指数 201
Per Capita Disposable Income of Households and Index
10-2 居民人均消费支出和指数......202
Per Capita Expense on Consumption of Households and Index
10-3 主要年份城镇居民家庭基本情况......203
Basic Conditions of Urban Households of Major Years
10-4 主要年份城镇居民人均可支配收入......204
Per Capita Disposable Income of Urban Households of Major Years
10-5 主要年份城镇居民人均消费支出......205
Per Capita Consumption Expenditure of Urban Households of Major Years
10-6 主要年份农村居民家庭基本情况......206
Basic Conditions of Rural Households of Major Years
10-7 主要年份农村居民人均可支配收入......207
Per Capita Disposable Income of Rural Households of Major Years
10-8 主要年份农村居民人均消费支出......208
Per Capita Consumption Expenditure of Rural Households of Major Years
10-9 调查户和调查人口基本情况(2021年)......209
Condition of Households Surveyed and Residents Surveyed(2021)
10-10 全体居民人均可支配收入......210
Per Capita Disposable Income of All Households
10-11 城镇居民人均可支配收入......211
Per Capita Disposable Income of Urban Households

10-12 农村居民人均可支配收入……212
Per Capita Disposable Income of Rural Households
10-13 全体居民人均消费支出……213
Per Capita Expense on Consumption of All Households
10-14 城镇居民人均消费支出……213
Per Capita Expense on Consumption of Urban Households
10-15 农村居民人均消费支出……214
Per Capita Expense on Consumption of Rural Households
10-16 居民家庭能源消费数量和金额(2021年)……214
Energy consumption of Households(2021)
10-17 居民家庭人均食品消费数量(2021年)……215
Per Capita Food Consumption of Households(2021)
10-18 居民家庭住房和耐用消费品拥有情况(2021年)……216
Household Ownership of Housing and Durables Consumer Goods(2021)
10-19 社区基础设施和居民享有的基本社会服务情况(2021年)……218
Community Infrastructure and Basic Social Services(2021)
10-20 各市全体居民人均收支情况(2021年)……219
Per Capita Income and Consumption Expenditure of All Households by Region(2021)
10-21 各市城镇居民人均收支情况(2021年)……220
Per Capita Income and Consumption Expenditure of Urban Households by Region(2021)
10-22 各市农村居民人均收支情况(2021年)……221
Per Capita Income and Consumption Expenditure of Rural Households by Region(2021)
主要统计指标解释……222
Explanatory Notes on Main Statistical Indicators

第十一篇 城市建设
CHAPTER 11 City Construction

简要说明
Brief Introduction
11-1 城市基础设施……227
Basic Statistics on Urban Infrastructure
11-2 城市设施水平(2021年)……228
Basic Statistics on Urban Infrastructure by City(2021)
11-3 城市供水(2021年)……229
Urban Water Supply by City (2021)
11-4 城市公共交通(2021年)……230
Public Transportation by City (2021)
11-5 城市市政设施(2021年)……231
Infrastructure by City (2021)
11-6 城市园林绿化(2021年)……233
Parks, Gardens and Green Areas by City (2021)
11-7 城市燃气供热情况(2021年)……234
Gas Supply and Heating by City(2021)
主要统计指标解释……235
Explanatory Notes on Main Statistical Indicators

第十二篇 资源和环境
CHARPTER 12 Natural Resources and Environment

简要说明
Brief Introduction
12-1 人口和自然资源(2021年) 239
Population and Natural Resources (2021)
12-2 主要湖泊、河流基本情况 240
Basic Statistics on Major Lakes and Rivers
12-3 主要山脉高度 240
Height of Major Mountains
12-4 各市平均气温(2021年) 241
Monthly Average Temperature by Region (2021)
12-5 各市降水量(2021年) 242
Monthly Precipitation by Region (2021)
12-6 各市日照时数(2021年) 243
Monthly Sunshine Hours by Region (2021)
12-7 各市土地利用情况(2020年) 244
Land Use by Region (2020)
12-8 各市湿地面积(2020年) 244
Area of Wetlands by Region (2020)
12-9 造林面积情况 245
Area of Afforestation
12-10 供水用水情况 246
Water Supply and Water Use
12-11 水资源情况 247
Water Resources
12-12 1981-2021年主要污染物排放及处理情况 248
Discharge and Treatment of Major Pollutants from 1981 to 2021
12-13 各市主要污染物排放情况(2016年) 249
Discharge of Major Pollutants by Region (2016)
12-14 各市主要污染物排放情况(2017年) 250
Discharge of Major Pollutants by Region (2017)
12-15 各市主要污染物排放情况(2018年) 251
Discharge of Major Pollutants by Region (2018)
12-16 各市主要污染物排放情况(2019年) 252
Discharge of Major Pollutants by Region (2019)
12-17 各市主要污染物排放情况(2020年) 253
Discharge of Major Pollutants by Region (2020)
12-18 各市主要污染物排放情况(2021年) 254
Discharge of Major Pollutants by Region (2021)
12-19 各市工业固体废物产生及利用处置情况(2016年) 255
Generation、Treatment and Utilization of Industrial Solid Wastes by Region(2016)
12-20 各市工业固体废物产生及利用处置情况(2017年) 255
Generation、Treatment and Utilization of Industrial Solid Wastes by Region (2017)
12-21 各市工业固体废物产生及利用处置情况(2018年) 256
Generation、Treatment and Utilization of Industrial Solid Wastes by Region (2018)

12-22 各市工业固体废物产生及利用处置情况(2019年) 256
Generation、Treatment and Utilization of Industrial Solid Wastes by Region (2019)
12-23 各市工业固体废物产生及利用处置情况(2020年) 257
Generation、Treatment and Utilization of Industrial Solid Wastes by Region (2020)
12-24 各市工业固体废物产生及利用处置情况(2021年) 257
Generation、Treatment and Utilization of Industrial Solid Wastes by Region (2021)
主要统计指标解释 258
Explanatory Notes on Main Statistical Indicators

第十三篇 农 业
CHAPTER 13 Agriculture

简要说明
Brief Introduction
13-1 主要年份农林牧渔业总产值 265
Gross Output Value of Farming, Forestry, Animal Husbandry and Fishery in Major Years
13-2 主要年份农林牧渔业总产值指数(以1952年为100) 266
Indices of Farming, Forestry, Animal Husbandry and Fishery in Major Years(1952=100)
13-3 农林牧渔业总产值 267
Gross Output Value of Farming, Forestry, Animal Husbandry and Fishery
13-4 各市农林牧渔业总产值(2021年) 268
Gross Output Value of Farming, Forestry, Animal Husbandry and Fishery by Region(2021)
13-5 主要年份粮、棉、油产量 269
Output of Grain, Cotton and Oil-bearing Crops in Major Years
13-6 1978-2021年畜牧业生产情况 270
Production of Animal Husbandry from 1978 to 2021
13-7 1978-2021年渔业生产情况 272
Output of Fishery from 1978 to 2021
13-8 农作物播种面积和产量 274
Sown Area and Output of Farm Crops
13-9 各市农作物播种面积和产量(2021年) 275
Sown Area and Output of Farm Crops by Region(2021)
13-10 各市茶叶、水果生产情况(2021年) 280
Production of Tea and Fruits by Region(2021)
13-11 各市林业生产情况(2021年) 281
Production of Forestry by Region(2021)
13-12 各市畜牧业生产情况(2021年) 281
Production of Animal Husbandry by Region(2021)
13-13 各市水产品产量和养殖面积(2021年) 283
Output and Breeding Area of Aquatic Products by Region (2021)
13-14 主要农业机械年末拥有量......285
Major Agricultural Machinery at the Year-end
13-15 各市主要农业机械年末拥有量(2021年)......286
Number of Major Agricultural Machinery at the Year-end by Region(2021)
13-16 各市地类面积(2020年)......287
Land Category Area by Region (2020)

13-17 各市灌溉面积 288
Irrigated Area by Region
13-18 各市农村电气化和农业化学化情况(2021年) 288
Rural Electrification and Agriculture Chemicals by Region (2021)
主要统计指标解释 290
Explanatory Notes on Main Statistical Indicators

第十四篇 工 业
CHAPTER 14 Industry

简要说明
Brief Introduction
14-1 规模以上工业企业主要经济指标(2021年) 295
Main Economic Indicators of Industrial Enterprises above Designated Size(2021)
14-2 规模以上国有控股工业企业主要经济指标(2021年) 299
Main Economic Indicators of State-holding Industrial Enterprises above Designated Size (2021)
14-3 规模以上外商投资和港澳台商投资工业企业主要经济指标(2021年) 303
Main Economic Indicators of Industrial Enterprises above Designated Size with Funds from Foreign Countries (Territories),Hong Kong,Macao and Taiwan(2021)
14-4 规模以上非公有制工业企业主要经济指标(2021年) 307
Main Economic Indicators of Non-public Industrial Enterprises above Designated Size(2021)
14-5 规模以上工业企业主要财务分析指标(2021年) 311
Main Financial Indicators of Industrial Enterprises above Designated Size(2021)
14-6 规模以上国有控股工业企业主要财务分析指标(2021年) 313
Main Financial Indicators of State-holding Industrial Enterprises above Designated Size(2021)
14-7 规模以上非公有制工业企业主要财务分析指标(2021年) 315
Main Financial Indicators of Non-public Industrial Enterprises above Designated Size(2021)
14-8 2008-2021年规模以上工业增加值 317
Value Added of Industry Enterprises above Designated Size From 2008 to 2021
14-9 按行业分规模以上工业增加值构成 318
Its Composition of Industry Enterprises above Designated Size by Sector
14-10 各市规模以上工业企业主要经济指标(2021年) 320
Main Economic Indicators of Industrial Enterprises above Designated Size by Region(2021)
14-11 各市规模以上国有控股工业企业主要经济指标(2021年) 321
Main Economic Indicators of State-holding Industrial Enterprises above Designated Size by Region(2021)
14-12 各市规模以上外商和港澳台商投资工业企业主要经济指标(2021年) 322
Main Economic Indicators of Industrial Enterprises with Funds from Foreign Countries (Territories), Hong Kong,Macao and Taiwan by Region(2021)
14-13 各市规模以上非公有制工业企业主要经济指标(2021年) 323
Main Economic Indicators of Non-public Industrial Enterprises above Designated Size by Region(2021)
14-14 各市规模以上工业企业主要财务分析指标(2021年) 324
Main Financial Indicators of Industrial Enterprises above Designated Size by Region(2021)
14-15 各市规模以上国有控股工业企业主要财务分析指标(2021年) 325
Main Financial Indicators of State-holding Industrial Enterprises above Designated Size by Region(2021)
14-16 规模以上工业主要产品产量(2021年) 326
Output of Major Industrial Products above Designated Size(2021)
主要统计指标解释 331
Explanatory Notes on Main Statistical Indicators

第十五篇 建筑业
CHAPTER 15 Construction

简要说明
Brief Introduction
15-1 主要年份建筑业总产值 339
Gross Output Value of Construction Enterprises in Major Years
15-2 主要年份计算建筑业劳动生产率的平均人数 340
Average Number of Employed Persons in Construction Enterprises for calculating the Labor Productivity in Major Years
15-3 建筑业企业生产指标(2021年) 341
Main Production Indicators of Construction Enterprises (2021)
15-4 建筑业主要财务指标(2021年) 345
Major Financial Indicators of Construction Enterprises (2021)
15-5 各市建筑业主要生产指标(2021年) 351
Main Production Indicators of Construction Enterprises by Region (2021)
15-6 各市建筑业主要财务指标(2021年) 352
Financial Indicators of Construction Enterprises by Region (2021)
主要统计指标解释 353
Explanatory Notes on Main Statistical Indicators

第十六篇 服务业
CHAPTER 16 Service Enterprises

简要说明
Brief Introduction
16-1 规模以上服务业企业主要财务状况(2021年)......357
Main Financial Indicators of Service Enterprises above the Designated(2021)
16-2 规模以上服务业企业分登记注册类型财务状况(2021年)......358
Financial Indicators of Service Enterprises above Designated Size by Registration Type(2021)
16-3 规模以上服务业企业分控股情况财务状况(2021年)......362
Financial Indicators of Service Enterprises above Designated Size by Holding Type(2021)
16-4 规模以上服务业企业分行业财务状况(2021年)......363
Financial Indicators of Service Enterprises above Designated Size by Sector(2021)
16-5 各市规模以上服务业企业财务状况(2021年)......365
Financial Indicators of Service Enterprises above Designated Size by Region(2021)
主要统计指标解释 367
Explanatory Notes on Main Statistical Indicators

第十七篇 运输和邮电
CHAPTER 17 Transport, Post and Telecommunication Services

简要说明
Brief Introduction
17-1 主要年份运输线路长度 371
Length of Transport Routes in Major Years
17-2 主要年份旅客运量及周转量 372
Passenger Traffic and Turnover Volume in Major Years

17-3 主要年份货物运量及周转量......373
Freight Traffic and Turnover Volume in Major Years
17-4 沿海主要港口货物吞吐量......374
Volume of Freight Handled in Major Coastal Ports
17-5 交通运输企业主要技术经济指标......374
Major Technical and Economic Indicators of Transportation Enterprises
17-6 1978-2021年邮政基本情况......375
Basic Conditions of Post Services from 1978 to 2021
17-7 1978-2021年电信业务总量......376
Business Volume of Telecommunication Services from 1978 to 2021
17-8 邮电业务基本情况......377
Basic Conditions of Post and Telecommunication Services
17-9 各市邮电业务基本情况(2021年)......377
Basic Conditions of Post and Telecommunication Services by Region(2021)
17-10 各市公路情况(2021年)......378
Basic Conditions of Highways by Region (2021)
17-11 各市地方交通旅客运输量(2021年)......378
Passenger Transport Volume of Local Traffic by Region(2021)
17-12 各市地方交通货物运输量(2021年)......379
Freight Transport Volume of Local Traffic by Region(2021)
17-13 各市民用汽车拥有量(2021年)......379
Possession of Private Vehicles by Region(2021)
17-14 各市私人汽车拥有量(2021年)......380
Possession of Private Vehicles by Region(2021)
17-15 各市公路营业性运输车辆(2021年)......381
Transport Vehicles in Operation by Region(2021)
17-16 按行业分企业信息化及电子商务情况(2021年)......382
Informatization and E-Commerce of Enterprises by Industrial Sector(2021)
17-17 各市企业信息化及电子商务情况(2021年)......384
Informatization and E-Commerce of Enterprises by Region (2021)
主要统计指标解释......386
Explanatory Notes on Main Statistical Indicators

第十八篇 批发和零售业、住宿和餐饮业
CHAPTER 18 Wholesale, Retail, Hotels and Catering Services

简要说明
Brief Introduction
18-1 批发和零售业情况......393
Basic Conditions of Wholesale and Retail Trades
18-2 限额以上批发和零售业商品购进、销售、库存总额(2021年)......394
Total Purchases,Sales and Inventory of Enterprises above Designated Size of Wholesale and Retail Trades(2021)
18-3 限额以上批发和零售业企业财务状况(2021年)......398
Financial Indicators of Enterprises above Designated Size of Wholesale and Retail Trades(2021)
18-4 各市限额以上批发和零售业商品购进、销售、库存总额(2021年)......406
Total Purchases,Sales and Inventory of Enterprises above Designated Size of Wholesale and Retail Trades by Region(2021)

18-5 各市限额以上批发和零售业财务状况(2021年)......407
Financial Indicators of Enterprises above Designated Size of Wholesale and Retail Trades by Region(2021)
18-6 限额以上住宿和餐饮业情况......408
Basic Conditions of Hotels and Catering Services
18-7 限额以上住宿和餐饮业经营情况(2021年)......409
Business of Hotels and Catering Services above Designated Size(2021)
18-8 各市限额以上住宿和餐饮业经营情况(2021年)......413
Business of Hotels and Catering Services above Designated Size by Region (2021)
18-9 限额以上住宿和餐饮业财务状况(2021年)......414
Financial Indicators of Enterprises above Designated Size of Hotels and Catering Services(2021)
18-10 各市限额以上住宿和餐饮业财务状况(2021年)......422
Financial Indicators of Enterprises above Designated Size of Hotels and Catering Services by Region(2021)
18-11 亿元以上商品交易市场情况(2021年)......423
Basic Statistics on Commodity Exchange Markets of Turnover above 100 Million Yuan (2021)
18-12 亿元以上商品交易市场成交情况(2021年)......425
Basic Statistics on Commodity Exchange Markets of Turnover above 100 Million Yuan(2021)
18-13 各市亿元以上商品交易市场情况(2021年)......426
Basic Statistics on Commodity Exchange Markets of Turnover above 100 Million Yuan by Region(2021)
18-14 连锁门店及配送中心分布情况(2021年)......427
Distribution of Stores and Distribution Centers of chain stores of Wholesale and Retail Trades and Hotel and Catering Services(2021)
18-15 批发和零售业连锁经营情况(2021年)......428
Business of chain operation of Wholesale and Retail Trade(2021)
18-16 住宿和餐饮业连锁经营情况(2021年)......432
Business of chain operation of Hotels and Catering Services(2021)
18-17 主要年份社会消费品零售总额......436
Retail Sale of Consumer Goods in Major Years
18-18 各市社会消费品零售总额(2021年)......437
Retail Sale of Consumer Goods by Region(2021)
主要统计指标解释......438
Explanatory Notes on Main Statistical Indicators

第十九篇 教育和科技
CHAPTER 19 Education, Science and Technology

简要说明
Brief Introduction
19-1 各级各类学校基本情况(2021年)......445
Basic Statistics on Education Institutions (2021)
19-2 主要年份普通高等教育基本情况......446
Basic Statistics on Higher Education in Major Years
19-3 主要年份中等专业教育基本情况......447
Basic Statistics on Vocational Secondary Education in Major Years
19-4 主要年份普通中学基本情况......448
Basic Statistics on Senior and Junior Secondary Education in Major Years
19-5 主要年份技工学校基本情况......449
Basic Statistics on Technical Schools in Major Years
19-6 主要年份小学基本情况......450
Basic Statistics on Primary Schools in Major Years

19-7 1985-2021年成人高等教育基本情况 451
Basic Statistics on Adult Education from 1985 to 2021
19-8 研究生教育基本情况 452
Basic Statistics on Postgraduate Education
19-9 各市中等职业学校基本情况(2021年) 453
Basic Statistics on Secondary Vocational Schools by Region (2021)
19-10 各市普通中学情况(2021年) 453
Basic Statistics on Secondary Schools by Region (2021)
19-11 各市小学基本情况(2021年) 454
Basic Statistics on Primary Schools by Region (2021)
19-12 各市幼儿园基本情况(2021年) 454
Basic Statistics on Kindergartens by Region(2021)
19-13 各市特殊教育基本情况(2021年) 455
Basic Statistics on Special Education by Region(2021)
19-14 各市中小学教职工情况(2021年) 456
Basic Statistics on Teachers and Staff of Primary and Secondary Schools by Region (2021)
19-15 各市普通中小学专任教师学历情况(2021年) 457
Basic Statistics on Education of Teachers and Staff of Primary and Secondary Schools by Region (2021)
19-16 各市幼儿园、特殊教育专任教师学历情况(2021年) 458
Basic Statistics on Education of Teachers and Staff of Kindergartens and Special Education(2021)
19-17 1978-2021年重要科技成果数量 459
Major Achievements in Science and Technology from 1978 to 2021
19-18 科技成果情况 460
Basic Statistics on Science and Technology
19-19 各市国内三种专利授权数(2021年) 461
Patents Granted by Region(2021)
19-20 R&D经费支出情况(2021年) 462
Basic Statistics On Expenditure on R&D(2021)
19-21 R&D人员情况(2021年) 464
Basic Statistics On R&D Personnel(2021)
19-22 R&D人员折合全时当量情况(2021年) 465
Basic Statistics On Full-time Equivalent of R&D Personnel(2021)
19-23 规模以上工业企业R&D经费支出情况(2021年) 466
Expenditures of Industrial Enterprises above Designated Size on R&D(2021)
19-24 规模以上工业企业R&D人员情况(2021年) 470
Basic Statistics On R&D Personnel of Industrial Enterprises above Designated Size(2021)
19-25 规模以上工业企业R&D人员折合全时当量情况(2021年) 474
Full-time Equivalent of R&D Personnel of Industrial Enterprises above Designated Size(2021)
19-26 按行业分规模以上工业企业新产品开发及生产情况(2021年) 476
New Products Development and Production of Industrial Enterprises above Designated Size by Industrial Sector(2021)
19-27 高技术制造业R&D活动及新产品开发情况 477
Statistics on R&D Activities and New Products Development in High-tech Manufacturing Industry
19-28 高技术制造业基本情况 478
Statistics on Production and Management in High-tech Manufacturing Industry
主要统计指标解释 479
Explanatory Notes on Main Statistical Indicators

第二十篇 文化、体育和卫生
CHAPTER 20 Culture, Sports and Health

简要说明

Brief Introduction

20-1 主要年份文化、文物事业基本情况 483

Number of Institutions for Culture and Cultural Relics of Major Years

20-2 文化、文物机构人员情况(2021年) 485

Number of Institution and Personnel in Culture and Culture Relics (2021)

20-3 各市文化、文物事业基本情况(2021年) 485

Basic Statistics on Culture and Cultural Relics by Region (2021)

20-4 电影基本情况 486

Basic Statistics on Film

20-5 广播电视基本情况 486

Basic Statistics on Radio and Television Stations

20-6 图书、期刊和报纸出版情况(2021年) 487

Number of Books, Magazines and Newspapers Published (2021)

20-7 档案馆基本情况(2021年) 488

Statistics on Archive Institution(2021)

20-8 等级运动员、教练员、裁判员发展人数 489

Basic Statistics on Athletes, Coaches and Referees

20-9 分项目分技术等级运动员发展人数 (2021年) 490

Certified Athletes by Type of Sports and Technical Grade(2021)

20-10 体育系统机构人员情况 (2021年) 491

Number of Institutions and Engaged Persons of Physical Education System(2021)

20-11 卫生总费用 491

Total Health Expenditure

20-12 卫生事业基本情况 492

Basic Statistics of Health Institutions

20-13 医院工作状况 493

Basic Statistics of Hospitals above County Level

20-14 各类医疗卫生机构基本情况(2021年) 494

Basic Statistics on Medical Institutions(2021)

20-15 各市卫生事业基本情况(2021年) 495

Statistics on Health Service by Region(2021)

主要统计指标解释 496

Explanatory Notes on Main Statistical Indicators

第二十一篇 公共管理和社会服务
CHAPTER 21 Public Management and Social Services

简要说明

Brief Introduction

21-1 民政事业基本情况 501

Basic Statistics on Civil Affairs

21-2 婚姻登记情况 502

Basic Statistics on Marriages and Divorces

21-3 养老服务机构和设施情况(2021年) 503
Statistics on Old-age Care Institutions and Facilities(2021)
21-4 律师、公证工作基本情况 504
Basic Statistics on Lawyers and Notarization
21-5 各市交通事故情况 (2021年) 504
Basic Statistics on Traffic Accidents by Region (2021)
21-6 火灾事故情况 (2021年)......505
Basic Statistics on Fire Accidents(2021)
21-7 各市火灾事故情况 (2021年)......505
Basic Statistic on Fires by Region(2021)
21-8 人民检察院审查批准、决定逮捕犯罪嫌疑人和提起公诉被告人情况 (2021年)......506
Arrests of Criminal Suspects and Defendants under Public Prosecution Approved by People's Procuratorate (2021)
21-9 人民法院审理一审案件情况......506
First Trial Cases by Courts
21-10 各市测绘持证单位个数和人员情况(2021年)......507
Basic Statistics on Surveying and Mapping Departments by Region(2021)
21-11 残疾人事业基本情况 508
Basic Statistics on the Work for Persons with Disabilities
21-12 产品质量监督抽查情况(2021年) 509
Results of Sampling Check on the Quality of Products(2021)
21-13 各市质量强省建设情况(2021年) 510
Statistics on Quality Province by Region(2021)
21-14 各市标准化工作情况(2021年) 511
Statistics on Standardization by Region(2021)
主要统计指标解释......512
Explanatory Notes on Main Statistical Indicators

第二十二篇 各县（市、区）主要经济指标
CHAPTER 22 Main Indicators of Counties (Cities and Districts at County Level)

简要说明
Brief Introduction
22-1 各县(市、区)主要经济指标(2021年) 517
Major Economic Indicators of Counties(Cities and Districts at County Level,2021)

附 录
APPENDICES

附录1 全国各省(市、自治区)主要经济指标 530
Main Economic Indicators of the Whole Country by Region
附录2 国际统计资料 560
International Statistical Data
附录3 统计公报和统计工作 602
Shandong Statistics Communique and Shandong Statistical Undertaking

第1篇

综　合

General Survey

简 要 说 明

一、本篇资料的主要内容

本篇资料是对全省乡镇以上行政区划、分行业法人单位数和国民经济、社会发展的综合反映，主要包括行政区划、法人单位数和平均每天社会经济活动、国民经济主要比例关系、国民经济和社会发展主要指标占全国的比重、国民经济和社会发展主要指标及其增长速度等资料。

二、本篇资料的来源

1.“行政区划一览表”主要包括2021年底各（地级）市、各县（市、区）和乡镇级的行政区划资料，数据来源于省民政厅。

2.法人单位情况由省统计局普查中心整理提供。

3.国民经济和社会发展综合部分来源于本年鉴各篇章中的资料，由省统计局综合处加工整理。

Brief Introduction

I. Main Content

Data in this chapter cover the main indicators on divisions of administrative areas, corporate units and national economy and social development, including divisions of administrative areas, number of corporate units and average daily social and economic activities, ratio, and percentage of main indicators of Shandong to the whole nation and growth rate.

II. Source of Data

(1) Data on divisions of administrative areas are provided by Shandong Provincial Department of Civil Affairs.

(2) Data on corporate units situation are provided and compiled by the Census Center of Shandong Provincial Bureau of Statistics.

(3) Data on general survey of economy and society are based on those of different chapters and compiled by the Division of Comprehensive Statistics of Shandong Provincial Bureau of Statistics.

1-1　行政区划(2021年底)

Divisions of Administrative Areas (Year-end of 2021)

单位：个　　　　(unit)

地　区　Region		县级单位数 Numbers of Counties	市辖区 Districts under the Jurisdiction of Cities	县级市 Cities at County Level	县 County	乡镇级单位数 Numbers of Towns	街道办事处 Street Communities	乡 Townships	镇 Towns
全　省	**Total**	**136**	**58**	**26**	**52**	**1825**	**696**	**57**	**1072**
济南市	Jinan	12	10		2	161	132		29
青岛市	Qingdao	10	7	3		144	108		36
淄博市	Zibo	8	5		3	88	31		57
枣庄市	Zaozhuang	6	5	1		65	21		44
东营市	Dongying	5	3		2	40	15	2	23
烟台市	Yantai	11	5	6		153	65	6	82
潍坊市	Weifang	12	4	6	2	120	61		59
济宁市	Jining	11	2	2	7	156	49	4	103
泰安市	Tai'an	6	2	2	2	88	20	6	62
威海市	Weihai	4	2	2		72	24		48
日照市	Rizhao	4	2		2	55	16	4	35
临沂市	Linyi	12	3		9	156	30	6	120
德州市	Dezhou	11	2	2	7	134	29	14	91
聊城市	Liaocheng	8	2	1	5	135	32	5	98
滨州市	Binzhou	7	2	1	4	91	29	4	58
菏泽市	Heze	9	2		7	167	34	6	127

1-2　国民经济和社会发展主要指标

类　　别		Category		2000	2010
一、人　口		**Population**			
年末常住人口	（万人）	Total Population at the Year-end	(10 000 persons)	8997	9579
按性别分		**By Sex**			
男	（万人）	Male	(10 000 persons)	(4562)	(4839)
女	（万人）	Female	(10 000 persons)	(4413)	(4697)
按农村城镇分		**Agricultural and Non-agricultural Population**			
农村人口	（万人）	Agricultural Population	(10 000 persons)	5564	4817
城镇人口	（万人）	Non-agricultural Population	(10 000 persons)	3433	4762
人口密度	（人/平方公里）	Population Density	(persons/sq.km)	574	610
二、就业人员和劳动工资		**Employment and Wages**			
年末就业人员	（万人）	Year-end Employed Persons	(10 000 persons)	5387	5940
第一产业	（万人）	Primary Industry	(10 000 persons)	2807	2257
第二产业	（万人）	Secondary Industry	(10 000 persons)	1293	1853
第三产业	（万人）	Tertiary Industry	(10 000 persons)	1287	1830
乡村就业人员	（万人）	Rural Employed Persons	(10 000 persons)	3394	3166
城镇就业人员	（万人）	Urban Employed Persons	(10 000 persons)	1993	2774
职工年末人数	（万人）	Number of Staff and Workers at the Year-end	(10 000 persons)	790.1	919.9
#国有单位	（万人）	State-owned Units	(10 000 persons)	542.1	422.4
城镇集体单位	（万人）	Urban Collective-owned Units	(10 000 persons)	103.9	54.6
工资总额	（亿元）	Total Wages Bill	(100 million yuan)	695.1	3166.7
#国有单位	（亿元）	State-owned Units	(100 million yuan)	524.4	1683.5
城镇集体单位	（亿元）	Urban Collective-owned Units	(100 million yuan)	58.8	147.1
平均工资	（元）	Average Wage	(yuan)	8772	33321
#国有单位	（元）	State-owned Units	(yuan)	9655	38490
城镇集体单位	（元）	Urban Collective-owned Units	(yuan)	5585	25626
三、国民经济核算		**National Accounting**			
地区生产总值	（亿元）	Gross Domestic Product	(100 million yuan)	8278.06	33922.49
第一产业	（亿元）	Primary Industry	(100 million yuan)	1252.08	3411.34
第二产业	（亿元）	Secondary Industry	(100 million yuan)	4120.19	17733.08
第三产业	（亿元）	Tertiary Industry	(100 million yuan)	2905.79	12778.07
人均地区生产总值	（元）	Per Capita GDP	(yuan)	9260	35599
四、固定资产投资		**Investment in Fixed Assets**			
全社会固定资产投资额	（亿元）	Total Investment in Fixed Assets	(100 million yuan)	2542.65	23276.69
国有经济	（亿元）	State-Owned Units	(100 million yuan)	1153.65	3648.45
集体经济	（亿元）	Collective-Owned Units	(100 million yuan)	679.48	2627.32
个体经济	（亿元）	Individuals Economy	(100 million yuan)	353.93	6505.00
其他经济	（亿元）	Others	(100 million yuan)	355.59	10495.92
房地产开发投资	（亿元）	Investment in Real Development	(100 million yuan)	223.29	3249.37

注：1.2000和2010年年末常住人口为人口普查数，2020年为根据第七次人口普查数据推算数，其余年份均为人口抽样调查数，括号内为公安户籍人口数。
2.根据第七次人口普查结果，对全省2011—2019年年末总人口及相关指标、人均地区生产总值数据进行了修订。
3.根据第七次人口普查结果，对全省2000—2019年年末就业人员及相关指标数据进行了修订。
4.2010年起，工资总额、平均工资数据为城镇单位就业人员口径。
5.根据第四次经济普查结果，对全省2000—2018年生产总值及相关数据进行了修订。

Main Indicators on National Economic and Social Development

2011	2012	2013	2014	2015	2016	2017	2018	2019	2020	2021
9665	9708	9746	9808	9866	9973	10033	10077	10106	10165	10170
(4870)	(4868)	(4883)	(4960)	(4999)	(5049)	(5089)	(5130)	(5153)	(5162)	(5169)
(4721)	(4712)	(4729)	(4787)	(4823)	(4872)	(4919)	(4966)	(4995)	(5011)	(5023)
4749	4657	4536	4436	4245	4076	3934	3884	3854	3756	3667
4916	5051	5210	5372	5621	5897	6099	6193	6252	6409	6503
613	616	619	620	624	630	634	636	637	643	644
5915	5892	5840	5798	5773	5728	5693	5621	5561	5510	5475
2165	2068	1974	1879	1795	1707	1623	1535	1446	1372	1316
1881	1915	1916	1919	1922	1907	1907	1877	1852	1840	1850
1869	1909	1951	2000	2055	2114	2163	2209	2263	2298	2309
3076	2981	2873	2771	2656	2538	2437	2338	2258	2165	2089
2839	2911	2967	3027	3117	3191	3256	3283	3303	3345	3386
1006.0	1060.2	1237.6	1210.0	1178.0	1155.5	1130.3	1065.4	1000.1	1027.8	1039.1
424.4	431.8	397.6	386.2	374.6	372.1	369.6	345.4	330.6	360.8	367.3
58.4	60.5	55.5	48.3	44.5	44.2	38.9	26.7	17.5	17.6	17.2
3956.1	4628.2	6098.9	6545.4	7054.6	7531.7	8059.3	8260.5	8688.9	9597.4	10457.7
1885.8	2125.1	2184.5	2334.1	2677.1	2940.3	3191.7	3212.7	3378.2	3952.3	4291.5
182.1	216.3	247.7	232.8	235.4	242.3	234.4	164.9	104.7	112.4	118.5
37618	41904	46998	51825	57270	62539	68081	73593	81446	87749	94768
43469	47894	52811	58485	69050	76903	83845	89598	98587	106784	113670
29683	34001	41416	45015	50191	53790	58002	57237	56301	61845	67351
39064.93	42957.31	47344.33	50774.84	55288.79	58762.46	63012.10	66648.87	70540.48	72798.17	83095.90
3768.55	4047.06	4454.11	4662.81	4902.82	4830.25	4832.71	4950.52	5116.99	5364.35	6029.03
19926.11	21275.89	22615.89	23588.02	24814.88	25565.04	26925.59	27523.67	28171.78	28456.66	33187.16
15370.27	17634.36	20274.33	22524.01	25571.09	28367.17	31253.80	34174.68	37251.71	38977.16	43879.71
40581	44348	48673	51933	56205	59239	62993	66284	69901	71825	81727
26769.73	31255.96	36789.07	42495.55	48312.46	53322.49	55202.73				
3783.31	3949.65	4757.31	5455.94	6304.58	7497.32	9568.25				
2715.00	3129.27	3113.17	3380.39	3125.74	1545.38	1496.62				
8234.50	9879.75	12827.66	16215.47	20268.78	22191.42	22328.55				
12036.92	14297.30	16090.93	17443.75	18613.36	22088.37	21809.31				
4106.75	4708.31	5444.53	5817.95	5892.16	6323.38	6637.25	7552.97	8614.89	9450.49	9819.75

a) Data of 2000 and 2010 are based on the national census,that of 2020 are calculated according to the data of the Seventh National Census,and others are based on the sample surveys.Data in the brackets are taken from the annual of the Public Security Departments.

b) According to the Seventh National Census,the data of Total population,GDP per capita from 2011 to 2019 of Shandong Province have been revised.

c) According to the Seventh National Census,the data of Employed Persons from 2000 to 2019 of Shandong Province have been revised.

d) Since 2010,data of total wages bill and average wage refer to the range of employed persons in urban.

e) According to the Fourth National Economic Census, the data of GDP from 2000 to 2018 have been revised.

1-2 续表 1

类别		Category		2000	2010
五、能 源		**Energy**			
能源生产总量	(万吨标煤)	Total Energy Production	(10 000 tons of SCE)	9648.75	16055.71
原 煤		Coal		5741.96	11913.14
原 油		Crude Oil		3822.49	3980.08
天然气		Natural Gas		83.54	129.01
一次电力		Primary Electricity		0.76	33.48
六、财 政		**Government Finance**			
一般公共预算收入	(亿元)	General Public Budget Revenue	(100 million yuan)	463.68	2749.38
#税收收入		Tax Revenue		392.90	2149.90
#增值税		Value Added Tax		89.69	378.23
营业税		Business Tax		87.66	631.51
企业所得税		Company Income Tax		81.87	293.31
个人所得税		Personal Income Tax		24.75	81.01
资源税		Resource Tax		6.22	33.29
城市维护建设税		Urban Maintenance and Development Tax		27.62	130.74
房产税		Tax on Real Estates		15.56	64.65
城镇土地使用税		Urban Land Using Tax		8.82	137.69
土地增值税		Land Value-added Tax		0.74	66.19
车船税		Tax on Vehicle and License		3.19	23.27
行政事业性收费收入		Income from Administrative Work Fees		30.57	203.02
一般公共预算支出	(亿元)	Expenditure for General Public Budget	(100 million yuan)	613.08	4145.03
#一般公共服务支出		Expenditure for General Public Service Expenditure			544.31
教育支出		Expenditure for Education			770.45
社会保障和就业支出		Expenditure for Social Security and Employment			416.77
卫生健康支出		Expenditure for Health			250.77
农林水支出		Expenditure for Farming、Forestry and Irrigation Affairs			465.98
七、金 融		**Financial Intermediation**			
金融机构人民币存款余额	(亿元)	RMB Deposits	(100 million yuan)	7471.20	41104.96
#住户存款		Household Deposits		4466.72	19648.21
金融机构人民币贷款余额	(亿元)	RMB Loans	(100 million yuan)	6209.05	30722.64
八、价格指数		**Price Indices**			
居民消费价格总指数	(上年=100)	Consumer Price Index	(preceding year=100)	100.2	102.9
商品零售价格总指数	(上年=100)	Retail Price Index	(preceding year=100)	98.6	102.7
工业生产者出厂价格指数	(上年=100)	Producer Price Indices for Industrial Products	(preceding year=100)	105.9	107.2
工业生产者购进价格指数	(上年=100)	Industrial Producer Purchasing Price Indices	(preceding year=100)	104.7	109.3
九、居民生活		**People's Livelihood**			
全体居民生活		**All Households Livelihood**			
年末人均住房建筑面积	(平方米)	Per Capita Space of Living House at Year-end	(sq.m)		
人均可支配收入	(元)	Annual Per Capita Disposable Income of All Households	(yuan)	4095	12922
人均消费支出	(元)	Annual Per Capita Consumption Expenditure of All Households	(yuan)	2982	8560
农村居民生活		Rural's Livelihood			
年末人均住房建筑面积	(平方米)	Per Capita Space of Living House at Year-end	(sq.m)	23.6	34.7
人均可支配收入	(元)	Annual Per Capita Disposable Income of Rural Households	(yuan)	2663	7034
人均消费支出	(元)	Annual Per Capita Consumption Expenditure of Rural Households	(yuan)	1743	4472

注：1.2009年开始，一次电力包含水电、风电、核电、生物质发电和太阳能光伏发电，2000年数据为水电。
2.2014年及以前住户存款数据为储蓄存款口径数据。
3.从2013年起，全省实施城乡住户调查一体化改革，根据国家统一规定，2018年，按照新指标口径对居民收支调查历史数据进行修正。

continued

2011	2012	2013	2014	2015	2016	2017	2018	2019	2020	2021
15997.81	16973.80	15165.08	15220.40	14693.06	13616.76	13710.27	13102.01	12539.10	12205.72	11543.68
11585.87	12528.16	10722.56	10699.80	10277.40	9404.96	9623.27	8827.54	7820.68	7422.75	6322.85
3973.65	3963.94	3894.94	3876.09	3751.91	3301.96	3192.79	3203.20	3177.70	3170.31	3158.22
64.33	75.71	65.11	62.89	57.70	56.23	49.72	52.80	56.10	63.43	68.42
53.35	79.19	116.19	133.13	161.90	229.07	305.89	484.11	742.71	817.13	1142.09
3455.93	4059.43	4559.95	5026.83	5529.33	5860.18	6098.63	6485.40	6526.71	6559.93	7284.46
2603.13	3050.20	3533.49	3965.76	4203.12	4212.59	4419.40	4897.92	4849.29	4757.62	5475.99
413.82	438.12	489.56	596.96	594.98	1129.75	1705.96	1902.12	1958.67	1814.47	2030.31
765.72	896.64	1068.33	1135.92	1252.40	650.45					
398.56	441.64	445.95	483.01	498.72	503.24	620.30	677.38	696.20	686.55	867.43
96.58	95.11	104.59	115.18	143.12	143.15	186.73	215.30	147.47	182.06	243.40
38.36	91.11	92.62	119.57	103.81	95.18	99.56	119.75	119.98	108.27	126.15
179.60	198.88	217.84	231.33	243.71	250.83	261.82	306.46	290.13	283.97	324.72
74.02	100.83	111.75	122.49	133.86	143.36	157.81	168.25	166.73	165.57	188.96
158.46	211.69	229.16	264.69	358.75	393.74	398.18	396.84	337.27	299.89	302.53
105.67	145.21	205.91	257.74	259.51	293.15	367.18	390.79	404.28	433.38	487.11
29.72	35.86	40.26	46.65	53.31	61.00	69.37	75.85	78.10	82.30	94.43
278.82	305.29	284.12	302.20	296.74	328.25	320.28	303.52	307.22	308.32	336.99
5002.07	5904.52	6688.80	7177.31	8250.01	8755.21	9258.40	10100.96	10739.76	11233.52	11713.16
618.48	705.51	749.96	725.33	738.11	783.56	857.51	943.35	1061.95	1118.07	1136.11
1047.90	1311.80	1399.67	1461.05	1690.62	1825.99	1890.00	2006.50	2156.14	2283.84	2411.09
501.54	596.48	681.98	763.53	904.64	992.66	1131.96	1253.99	1444.63	1657.53	1863.39
360.36	422.91	485.86	605.67	701.43	790.19	829.27	885.15	912.07	1045.50	1092.72
564.00	673.82	748.14	772.84	964.42	943.44	953.59	998.50	1075.98	1065.29	1026.95
46345.41	54301.53	62077.88	67498.29	74524.16	83414.88	88531.71	94298.18	102676.38	116155.37	127871.85
22173.27	26343.31	29796.08	33178.56	37320.02	41350.93	44035.84	48434.98	55232.15	64258.40	72255.34
35179.00	42899.91	44761.26	50058.64	55437.00	61726.88	67575.96	74879.40	83702.97	95411.56	108436.77
105.0	102.1	102.2	101.9	101.2	102.1	101.5	102.5	103.2	102.8	101.2
104.7	101.6	101.4	101.0	100.2	101.3	100.8	102.2	102.2	102.0	101.4
106.0	98.4	98.4	98.4	95.2	98.5	105.5	103.7	99.7	98.1	110.3
109.2	99.2	98.4	98.2	95.0	98.0	107.3	103.6	99.2	97.5	109.5
		37.9	38.7	38.5	39.6	39.9	39.6	39.9	40.0	41.3
15077	17127	19008	20864	22703	24685	26930	29205	31597	32886	35705
9853	10902	11897	13329	14578	15926	17281	18780	20427	20940	22821
36.3	38.4	39.6	40.3	40.9	42.1	42.5	43.2	43.5	43.4	44.0
8395	9506	10687	11882	12930	13954	15118	16297	17775	18753	20794
5489	6304	6877	7962	8748	9519	10342	11270	12309	12660	14299

a) Since 2009, Primary Electricity includes that generated by hydro power, wind power, nuclear power, bio-energy and solar PV power. Data of 2000 refer to hydro power.

b) Data of Household Deposits before 2014 refers to Urban and Rural Household Savings Deposits .

c)An integrated household survey programme has been implemented since 2013,instead of the two separate urban and rural household surveys.In 2018 according to national uniform regulation,the historical data of residents' income and expenditure are revised according to the new survey programme.

1-2 续表 2

类　　别	Category	2000	2010
城镇居民生活	**Urban's Livelihood**		
年末人均住房建筑面积 (平方米)	Per Capita Space of Living House at Year-end (sq.m)	13.8	32.1
人均可支配收入 (元)	Annual Per Capita Disposable Income of Urban Households (yuan)	6417	18971
人均消费支出 (元)	Annual Per Capita Consumption Expenditure of Urban Households (yuan)	4991	12761
十、农林牧渔业	**Farming,Forestry,Animal Husbandry and Fishery**		
农林牧渔业总产值 (亿元)	Gross Output Value of Farming Forestry, Animal Husbandry and Fishery (100 million yuan)	2294.35	6573.77
农　业	Farming	1300.44	3588.42
林　业	Forestry	47.62	86.53
牧　业	Animal Husbandry	599.17	1796.52
渔　业	Fishery	347.12	829.77
农林牧渔专业及辅助性活动	Output Value of Farming,Forestry,Animal Husbandry and Fishery professions and auxiliary activities		272.52
农业生产情况	**Farming**		
粮食总产量 (万吨)	Total Output of Grain (10 000 tons)	3837.7	4502.8
粮食单产 (千克/公顷)	Grain (kilogram/hectare)	4938	6043
棉花总产量 (万吨)	Total Output of Cotton (10 000 tons)	59.0	59.0
棉花单产 (千克/公顷)	Cotton (kilogram/hectare)	1085	945
油料总产量 (万吨)	Total Output of Oil-bearing Crops (10 000 tons)	356.9	347.7
油料单产 (千克/公顷)	Oil-bearing Crops (kilogram/hectare)	3730	4317
肉类总产量 (万吨)	Total Output of Grain (10 000 tons)	500.0	754.0
猪存栏 (万头)	Number of Pigs (10 000 heads)	2401.8	2871.6
牛存栏 (万头)	Number of Cattles (10 000 heads)	779.9	440.3
羊存栏 (万只)	Number of Sheep and Goats (10 000 heads)	2260.1	1926.9
家禽存栏 (万只)	Number of Poultry (10 000 heads)	47789.9	58214.0
猪出栏 (万头)	Slaughtered Pigs (10 000 heads)	3213.2	4425.5
牛出栏 (万头)	Slaughtered Cattle (10 000 heads)	322.2	413.0
羊出栏 (万只)	Slaughtered Sheep (10 000 heads)	2375.7	2707.4
家禽出栏 (万只)	Slaughtered Poultry (10 000 heads)	91195.0	169549.8
禽蛋产量 (万吨)	Poultry Eggs (10 000 tons)	301.0	384.8
奶类产量 (万吨)	Milk (10 000 tons)	62.7	231.0
水产品总产量 (吨)	Total Aquatic Products (tons)	6306551	7838259
海水产品 (吨)	Seawater Aquatic Products (tons)	5375169	6463345
海洋捕捞 (吨)	Catching in Ocean (tons)	2780483	2350888
海水养殖 (吨)	Seawater Aquiculture (tons)	2594685	3962643
淡水产品产量 (吨)	Freshwater Aquatic Products (tons)	931382	1374914
捕捞量 (吨)	Catching (tons)	81214	130896
养殖量 (吨)	Freshwater Aquiculture (tons)	850168	1244018
水产品养殖面积 (万亩)	Aquiculture Area (10 000 mu)	788.4	1136.5
海　水 (万亩)	Seawater Aquiculture Area (10 000 mu)	420.7	751.4
淡　水 (万亩)	Freshwater Aquiculture Area (10 000 mu)	367.6	385.1
十一、工　业	**Industry**		
全部工业增加值 (亿元)	Value Added of Industry Enterprises (100 million yuan)	3620.06	15449.95
十二、建筑业	**Industry**		
建筑业增加值 (亿元)	Value Added of Construction Enterprises (100 million yuan)	500.13	2283.13

continued

2011	2012	2013	2014	2015	2016	2017	2018	2019	2020	2021
33.2	33.4	36.4	37.3	36.4	37.5	37.6	36.8	37.1	37.3	39.3
21678	24496	26882	29222	31545	34012	36789	39549	42329	43726	47066
14164	15349	16646	18323	19854	21495	23072	24798	26731	27291	29314
7311.11	7817.84	8577.06	8988.18	9283.92	9075.60	9140.36	9397.39	9671.67	10190.58	11468.01
3737.04	3829.19	4335.77	4556.10	4662.61	4387.51	4403.23	4678.26	4914.43	5168.36	5814.56
99.96	107.01	120.30	131.53	139.92	147.48	165.09	181.63	197.70	214.20	219.94
2205.73	2328.69	2410.56	2478.81	2602.08	2620.29	2501.37	2432.67	2412.06	2571.87	2904.24
973.24	1227.81	1347.03	1420.85	1447.28	1409.65	1475.96	1425.91	1397.42	1432.08	1652.60
295.14	325.14	363.40	400.90	432.03	510.66	594.70	678.92	750.06	804.06	876.68
4701.3	4815.8	4883.4	5038.3	5147.4	5332.3	5374.3	5319.5	5357.0	5446.8	5500.7
6172	6214	6099	6087	6123	6261	6356	6329	6444	6577	6584
60.8	51.4	43.4	44.2	33.9	32.9	20.7	21.7	19.6	18.3	14.0
1043	1012	923	1122	1042	1179	1185	1184	1158	1281	1273
343.7	341.8	341.6	329.6	318.7	317.1	318.3	310.9	289.0	290.9	285.9
4367	4404	4386	4355	4302	4310	4389	4370	4236	4366	4420
763.1	822.6	838.2	836.8	845.5	837.1	866.0	854.7	704.0	728.0	819.3
2998.2	3101.2	3167.0	3179.5	3147.3	3086.8	3040.3	2985.6	2176.5	2933.9	3151.0
438.3	433.7	424.3	410.5	407.6	391.9	401.5	380.6	364.2	278.7	279.8
1887.9	1850.3	1797.9	1765.0	1767.9	1693.1	1754.0	1801.4	1837.4	1501.7	1466.4
63790.2	70959.8	70261.3	69911.9	71816.0	78056.1	76604.5	75614.9	78864.3	83642.4	84578.1
4387.8	4800.8	5043.0	5245.7	5156.4	5093.2	5180.7	5082.3	3176.4	3344.8	4401.7
390.0	385.3	382.6	372.4	370.2	360.8	361.6	363.4	345.9	275.7	280.0
2546.5	2493.4	2472.1	2530.6	2527.1	2540.8	2629.8	2682.4	2701.1	2491.6	2373.4
181519.0	199140.7	195931.9	182274.9	192052.0	214261.0	220423.3	217200.2	231299.1	252670.8	263535.7
401.6	402.4	396.6	388.4	424.3	441.1	445.1	447.4	450.6	482.2	456.6
235.8	248.6	237.7	244.7	240.7	233.8	231.3	232.5	234.5	241.6	288.4
8138280	7885248	8084522	8464587	8722448	8899622	8680030	8614032	8232724	8286092	8544248
6647212	6524046	6654179	7085761	7352063	7541952	7371727	7360685	7062086	7180937	7403008
2512437	2161603	2087829	2286654	2356409	2414112	2180891	2149830	2091101	2039543	2029166
4134775	4362443	4566350	4799107	4995654	5127840	5190836	5210855	4970985	5141394	5373842
1491068	1361202	1430344	1378826	1370385	1357670	1308303	1253347	1170638	1105155	1141240
135378	112783	115167	90661	83086	93900	83730	82821	89290	95634	95733
1355690	1248419	1315177	1288165	1287299	1263770	1224573	1170526	1081348	1009521	1045507
1174.4	1205.2	1240.4	1252.7	1269.2	1259.3	1250.4	1173.4	1138.3	1116.9	1147.8
768.2	785.6	820.2	822.7	844.8	907.2	915.6	856.3	842.3	870.5	912.6
406.2	419.6	420.1	429.9	424.4	352.1	334.8	317.1	296.1	246.4	235.3
17280.78	18421.90	19475.30	20178.23	21156.50	21695.98	22515.81	22613.01	22755.13	22986.45	27243.55
2645.33	2853.99	3188.60	3476.06	3731.63	3909.44	4441.01	5024.90	5532.77	5574.19	6094.45

1-2　续表 3

类　　别	Category	2000	2010
十三、交通运输邮电	**Transport,Posts and Telecommunications**		
铁路通车里程 (公里)	Length of Railways (km)	2672	3833
公路通车里程 (公里)	Length of Highways (km)	70686	229858
#晴雨通车 (公里)	Length of Highways Operating under All Weathers (km)	70038	228906
内河通航里程 (公里)	Length of Navigable Inland Waterways (km)	1476	1150
客运量 (万人)	Passenger Traffic (10 000 persons)	66128	248720
铁　路	Railways	3840	6041
公　路	Highways	61466	240044
水　路	Waterways	822	2635
客运周转量 (百万人公里)	Passenger Turnover (million passenger-km)	54873	164471
铁　路	Railways	22180	42135
公　路	Highways	32358	121151
水　路	Waterways	335	1185
货运量 (万吨)	Freight Traffic (10 000 tons)	92483	298055
铁　路	Railways	11253	18056
公　路	Highways	76778	264366
水　路	Waterways	4452	15633
货运周转量 (百万吨公里)	Freight Turnover (million ton-km)	403315	1174705
铁　路	Railways	79964	144775
公　路	Highways	40575	621680
水　路	Waterways	282776	408250
沿海主要港口货物吞吐量 (万吨)	Volume of Freight Handled in Major Coastal Ports (10000 tons)	16025	86421
邮政局总计 (处)	Number of Post & Telecommunications Offices (unit)	3011	2840
函　件 (万件)	Number of Letters (10 000 pcs)	32878	53963
电信业务总量 (亿元)	Business Volume of Telecommunication Services (100 million yuan)	186.5	1920.9
邮政业务总量 (亿元)	Business Volume of Post Services (100 million yuan)	74.2	52.5
互联网宽带接入用户 (万户)	Number of Mobile Telephone (10 000 subscribers)		
移动电话用户 (万户)	Number of Mobile Telephone (10 000 subscribers)	501.0	6190.4
民用汽车拥有量 (万辆)	Number of Private Vehicles (10 000 subscribers)	112.3	842.7
十四、国内贸易	**Domestic Trade**		
社会消费品零售总额 (亿元)	Total Retail Sales of Consumer Goods (100 million yuan)	2988.30	12028.30
商品零售	Retail Sales		10829.15
餐饮收入	Catering Income		1199.15
十五、对外贸易和旅游	**Foreign Economy and Trade,Tourism**		
对外贸易	Foreign Economy and Trade		
海关进出口总值 (万美元)	Total Value of Imports and Exports (10 000 USD)	2498998	18895058
海关出口总值 (万美元)	Total Exports (10 000 USD)	1552905	10424695
#一般贸易	General Trade	746563	4973019
来料加工装配贸易	Processing and Assembling with Customer's Materials	293008	750340
进料加工贸易	Processing and Assembling with Import Materials	507050	4230872
海关进口总值 (万美元)	Total Imports (10 000 USD)	946093	8470390

注：1.交通运输部2014年修订了公路、水运运输量统计试行方案，统计口径发生了变化。
2.表中2000年邮电业务总量按1990年不变价格计算，2001—2010年按2000年不变价格计算。2011—2015年邮电业务总量按2010年价格计算；2016—2020年，按2015年价格计算；2021年按2020年价格计算。2012年起，邮政业务量由山东邮政管理局提供，包括快递业务量，2012年以前数据由山东省邮政公司提供。
3.2019年起，公路货运量采用全国公路货运量专项调查数据。与往年数据不可比。
4.2020年起，铁路客货运量、周转量为济南局、北京局、郑州局在山东省内数据，口径为国家铁路；铁路通车里程含地方铁路。

continued

2011	2012	2013	2014	2015	2016	2017	2018	2019	2020	2021
4177	4306	4397	4546	4863	4882	5115	5676	5972	6881	7198
233189	244586	252785	259514	263447	265720	270590	275642	280325	286814	288143
232264	243779	252066	259031	262986	265265	270150	275344	280186	286741	283469
1150	1150	1150	1150	1150	1150	1150	1150	1150	1117	1117
250469	264935	269391	73582	59625	62727	64536	66613	67317	30096	28350
6609	7650	8484	9508	10666	11904	13388	14525	15722	9797	12164
241457	254711	258327	62052	46960	48823	49111	50044	49581	19475	15139
2403	2574	2580	2022	1999	2000	2037	2044	2014	824	1047
172751	183196	189285	114056	112745	116882	122676	126935	127981	59517	70560
45872	50951	54995	61734	64444	68442	73365	76302	77287	43191	52392
125691	130995	133137	51141	47137	47240	48104	49357	49256	15931	17783
1188	1250	1153	1181	1164	1200	1207	1276	1439	395	385
314962	330270	344401	260983	258444	281557	322564	349481	304732	308627	333420
19711	19814	19043	16792	15786	16745	17853	18710	20850	23189	22895
279380	296752	311812	230018	227934	249752	288052	312807	266124	267230	291196
15871	13704	13546	14172	14724	15060	16659	17964	17758	18208	19329
1258364	1099119	1026088	817690	833415	879552	962225	995988	1007631	1034063	1200214
152606	149384	138910	123808	107728	113668	121363	126468	143456	156609	168212
662435	705922	749888	571138	587699	607143	665022	685968	674620	678440	751761
443323	243813	137290	122744	137988	158741	175840	183552	189555	199014	280241
96188	106655	118137	128593	134218	142856	151571	161512	161064	168881	178158
2851	2856	2861	2870	2870	2878	2880	2873	2889	3005	2979
46014	45663	42389	29233	18787	10328	6978	6369	6263	4341	3796
723.6	797.6	863.7	1067.8	1253.1	863.4	1494.8	3651.9	5786.6	7200.1	1002.0
47.6	94.1	117.4	145.8	205.5	301.6	392.9	528.4	718.0	993.7	642.8
1154.1	1364.1	1465.1	1523.9	1625.7	2366.5	2588.7	2884.8	3186.1	3445.6	3863.7
7118.0	7588.9	8333.4	8664.1	9413.8	9594.5	9943.9	10569.6	10785.5	10907.1	11248.5
968.6	1122.3	1277.4	1407.2	1553.6	1750.5	1952.9	2148.3	2351.0	2537.1	2736.8
13939.83	15785.25	17703.85	19706.36	21550.95	23482.07	25527.94	27480.28	29251.18	29248.05	33714.54
12506.44	14181.87	15926.53	17744.99	19346.19	20996.37	22794.81	24421.00	25895.16	26118.91	29886.32
1433.39	1603.38	1777.32	1961.37	2204.76	2485.70	2733.13	3059.28	3356.02	3129.14	3828.22
23599191	24554487	26715854	27711549	24174867	23420733	26305670	29239097	29628464	31844703	45386886
12578809	12873171	13450998	14474545	14406069	13715826	14710207	16013984	16143995	18903512	27184375
6466907	6875045	7603996	8373918	9042024	8653875	9428956	11047764	11256710	13853845	19567326
842878	867657	866031	802064	739933	716557	651868	601424	605165	497612	553192
4737751	4566215	4392892	4734553	4183875	3904404	4151643	3918203	3496008	3466764	4257732
11020382	11681316	13264856	13237004	9768798	9704906	11595464	13225113	13484469	12941191	18202512

a)The pilot statistical investigation program on passenger highway and turnover was revised in 2014,and the statistical scope was adjusted.

b) Business volume of postal service and telecommunication service of 2000 was calculated at 1990 constant prices, and that from 2001 to 2010 was calculated at 2000 constant prices,and that from 2011 to 2015 was calculated at 2010 constant prices,and that from 2016 to 2020 was calculated at 2015 constant prices, and that of 2021 was calculated at 2020 constant prices. The data of business volume of postal service before 2012 come from Shandong Post Company, since 2012, they are from Shandong Post Bureau, including business volume of courier companies above designated size.

c) The road freight volume adopts the special survey data of national road freight volume since 2019,and not comparable with the previous.

d) Since2020, the railway passenger and freight volume and turnover refer to the data of Jinan Bureau,Beijing Bureau and Zhengzhou Bureau in Shan-dong Province,the caliber is national railway,and the data of railways length includes the local railways.

1-2 续表 4

类　　别		Category		2000	2010
利用外资		**Utilization of Foreign Capital**			
新设外商直接投资企业数	(个)	Number of newly established Companies by foreign direct investment	(unit)	2728	1632
实际使用外商直接投资	(万美元)	Direct Foreign Investments	(10 000 USD)	297119	916833
对外承包工程和劳务合作		**Foreign Contracted Projects Labor Cooperation**			
合同个数	(个)	Number of Contracts	(unit)	1250	3075
合同金额	(万美元)	Contracted Value	(10 000 USD)	61601	1092504
营业额	(万美元)	Value of Business	(10 000 USD)	45229	602415
年末在外人数	(人)	Population in Foreign Countries and Regions	(person)	35028	102149
旅　游		**Tourism**			
接待海外旅游人数	(万人次)	International Tourists	(10 000 person-times)	72.3	366.8
外国人		Foreigners		48.0	277.9
港澳台胞		Compatriots from Hong Kong Macao and Taiwan		24.3	88.9
旅游外汇收入	(万元)	Foreign Exchange Earnings	(10 000 yuan)	260839	1458866
旅游外汇收入	(万美元)	Foreign Exchange Earnings	(10 000 USD)	31513	215506
人民币对主要外币年平均汇价(中间价)		**Average Exchange Rate of RMB Yuan Against Main Convertible Currencies (Middle Rate)**			
100美元	(人民币元)	100 US Dollars	(RMB yuan)	827.84	676.95
100日元	(人民币元)	100 Japanese Yen	(RMB yuan)	7.69	7.73
100港元	(人民币元)	100 Hong Kong Dollars	(RMB yuan)	106.18	87.13
100欧元	(人民币元)	100Euros	(RMB yuan)		897.25
十六、教　育		**Education**			
普通高等学校		**Regular Institutions of Higher Education**			
学校数	(所)	Number of Schools	(unit)	58	133
招生数	(人)	New Enrollment	(person)	124817	495722
在校学生数	(人)	Total Enrollment	(person)	303826	1631373
毕业生数	(人)	Graduates	(person)	49687	444003
教职工数	(人)	Teachers and Staff	(person)	54910	139100
#专任教师	(人)	Full-time Teachers	(person)	24764	91413
中等专业学校基本情况		**Secondary Professional Schools**			
学校数	(所)	Number of Schools	(unit)	243	640
招生数	(人)	New Enrollment	(person)	93493	426954
毕业生数	(人)	Graduates	(person)	103629	439337
在校学生数	(人)	Total Enrollment	(person)	333184	1131621
教职工数	(人)	Teachers and Staff	(person)	37241	78769
#专任教师	(人)	Full-time Teachers	(person)	20409	55465
普通中学基本情况		**Regular Senior Secondary Schools**			
学校数	(所)	Number of Schools	(unit)	4575	3645
招生数	(万人)	New Enrollment	(10 000 persons)	234.18	164.12
毕业生数	(万人)	Graduates	(10 000 persons)	167.96	156.89
在校学生数	(万人)	Total Enrollment	(10 000 persons)	678.60	501.07
教职工数	(人)	Teachers and Staff	(person)	430754	438787
#专任教师	(人)	Full-time Teachers	(person)	350353	372082
技工学校基本情况		**Technical Schools**			
学校数	(所)	Number of Schools	(unit)	279	209
招生数	(人)	New Enrollment	(person)	48008	136995
毕业生数	(人)	Graduates	(person)	66546	133615
在校学生数	(人)	Total Enrollment	(person)	137718	397719
教职工数	(人)	Teachers and Staff	(person)	24484	18183
#专任教师	(人)	Full-time Teachers	(person)	14066	14962

注:1.2004年起实行新的外商投资统计制度,取消对外借款部分、外商直接投资数据为商务部反馈数。2008年实际使用外资采用全口径统计方式。2019年起，实际使用外资采用商务部通报口径，不包含股东贷款、投资性公司投资，合同外资不再统计。
2.2010年起，中等专业学校数据改为中等职业学校口径。
3.因疫情管控影响暂停入境旅游数据核算。

continued

2011	2012	2013	2014	2015	2016	2017	2018	2019	2020	2021
1433	1333	1405	1352	1509	1477	1479	2156	2517	3060	3064
1116022	1235267	1405315	1519511	1630090	1682556	1785731	2051636	1468933	1764763	2151578
948287	988209	1078349	1237694	1344383	1355479	1393003	1548846	1364140	1051092	1181608
819857	898864	940828	1021544	1120799	1195427	1278651	1314181	1256300	1030379	1016257
108662	103736	98988	115328	116100	119655	130384	125224	133849	89162	71218
424.2	469.9	452.7	445.7	460.8	485.5	494.4	513.1	521.3	52.8	
312.3	342.2	327.4	325.7	335.9	352.7	353.1	366.1	370.9	44.2	
111.9	127.7	125.3	120.0	124.9	132.8	141.3	147.0	150.4	8.6	
1647486	1845554	1691487	1667300	1804062	2034836	2143055	2226223	2354552	144162	
255076	292365	273120	271424	289651	306345	317405	336420	341314	20900	
645.88	631.25	619.32	614.28	622.84	664.23	675.18	661.74	689.85	689.76	645.15
8.11	7.90	6.33	5.82	5.15	6.12	6.02	5.99	6.33	6.46	5.87
82.97	81.38	79.85	79.22	80.34	85.58	86.64	84.43	88.05	88.93	83.00
900.11	810.67	822.19	816.51	691.41	734.26	763.03	780.16	772.55	787.55	762.93
139	137	140	142	143	144	145	145	146	152	153
497292	498621	527539	580763	595646	624408	612660	629065	741661	729927	780954
1645589	1658490	1698545	1796665	1900612	1995880	2015345	2040793	2183944	2291481	2429912
472882	474266	475858	464076	474195	509142	571220	585871	577980	605379	617855
142698	142370	142240	143939	147035	150345	154311	158526	164932	172041	177805
94621	96058	98685	101380	104724	107748	110807	112717	117609	124215	129888
591	560	525	460	435	428	401	398	391	397	400
444703	404670	363547	319143	294033	288180	261190	245355	267223	297527	293603
386564	380451	378626	354032	320353	286687	248347	250210	259891	233426	221047
1177130	1147012	1031585	948167	857264	809826	793357	750142	730164	777416	839144
74232	71449	66810	64188	62319	60613	60408	59304	58249	58824	60026
53569	52430	50243	49274	48926	48244	48659	48269	48099	49169	53576
3569	3522	3464	3461	3446	3504	3560	3671	3791	3920	4019
161.83	159.88	158.53	153.58	151.12	160.35	164.39	164.26	176.10	187.62	187.58
157.80	153.20	156.04	153.73	156.01	157.62	151.42	148.46	157.56	166.72	163.43
501.58	492.64	488.48	486.06	479.93	482.41	494.85	509.93	528.13	548.68	570.76
462765	464942	466088	471653	475798	484579	502004	515123	536931	558935	586421
376760	376819	382340	386923	390059	397471	410339	419903	435808	453428	471988
208	213	207	203	194	194	194	181	181	181	194
149407	154546	144165	128007	131550	133600	129109	135184	151122	173803	169851
123404	113066	121782	108046	98154	89629	103815	96351	91679	95962	104221
381503	401207	369922	329473	318182	335348	332634	329897	355409	405418	442034
24379	29909	30860	29404	29228	29133	29294	29388	29438	29943	32647
21050	21451	23977	23000	22613	22908	22565	22525	22294	23573	26284

a) Since 2004,foreign loads is canceled according to the new statistical system on foreign investments, data of foreign direct investments come from Ministry of Commerce.In 2008 the foreign capital actually utilized is changed to the actual received foreign capital.From 2019,Actual use of foreign capital uses Bulletin of the Ministry of Commerce,does not contain shareholder loan and the investment from investment companies,and contract foreign investment is no longer counted.

b) Data of secondary professional schools refer to the caliber of secondary vocational school since 2010 .

c) The accounting of inbound tourism data has been suspended due to the impact of COVID-19.

1-2　续表 5

类　　别		Category		2000	2010
小学基本情况		**Regular Primary Schools**			
学校数	(所)	Number of Schools	(unit)	26017	12405
招生数	(万人)	New Enrollment	(10 000 persons)	104.5	111.3
毕业生数	(万人)	Graduates	(10 000 persons)	195.1	110.3
在校学生数	(万人)	Total Enrollment	(10 000 persons)	774.9	629.3
教职工数	(人)	Teachers and Staff	(person)	440161	417504
#专任教师	(人)	Full-time Teachers	(person)	408200	387453
成人高等学校基本情况		**Adult Institutions of Higher Education**			
学校数	(所)	Number of Schools	(unit)	40	18
招生数	(人)	New Enrollment	(person)	82423	133191
毕业生数	(人)	Graduates	(person)	70810	110347
在校学生数	(人)	Total Enrollment	(person)	219977	388741
教职工数	(人)	Teachers and Staff	(person)	14090	4225
#专任教师	(人)	Full-time Teachers	(person)	7084	2946
十七、科　技		**Science**			
重要科技成果		**Major Scientific Achievements**			
成果数量	(项)	Number of Achievements	(unit)	3728	2367
#农　业	(项)	Agricultural	(unit)	575	391
工　业	(项)	Industry	(unit)	1289	751
国际领先先进水平	(项)	Internationally Advanced	(unit)	599	676
国内领先先进水平	(项)	Nationally Advanced	(unit)	2861	1316
专利情况		**Patent Applications**			
申请量	(件)	Number of Patent Applications Examined	(unit)	10019	80856
授权量	(件)	Number of Patent Applications Granted	(unit)	6962	51490
#发明专利	(件)	Inventions	(unit)		4106
十八、卫生、文化事业基本情况		**Public Health and Culture**			
卫生机构数	(个)	Number of Health Institutions	(unit)	17118	16496
#医院(卫生院)	(个)	Hospitals and Township Hospitals	(unit)	3150	3099
卫生机构床位数	(万张)	Number of Beds in Health Institutions	(10 000 units)	21.5	38.2
卫生技术人员数	(万人)	Medical Technical Personnel	(10 000 persons)	31.5	44.1
#执业(助理)医师	(万人)	Licensed (Assistant) Doctors	(10 000 persons)	14.5	17.8
注册护士	(万人)	Registered Nurse	(10 000 persons)	9.2	15.6
文化(艺术)馆		**Cultural(Arts) Centers**			
机构数	(个)	Number of Institutions	(unit)	159	158
人　数	(人)	Number of Employed Persons	(person)	3055	3055
文化站		**Cultural Stations**			
机构数	(个)	Number of Institutions	(unit)	2422	1855
人　数	(人)	Number of Employed Persons	(person)	3304	4543
艺术表演团体		**Arts Performance Troupes**			
机构数	(个)	Number of Institutions	(unit)	118	119
人　数	(人)	Number of Employed Persons	(person)	5943	6268
剧场(院)		**Theaters and Music Halls**			
机构数	(个)	Number of Institutions	(unit)	105	91
人　数	(人)	Number of Employed Persons	(person)	2473	1904
图书馆		**Libraries**			
机构数	(个)	Number of Institutions	(unit)	133	149
人　数	(人)	Number of Employed Persons	(person)	2506	2680
博物馆		**Museums**			
机构数	(个)	Number of Institutions	(unit)	59	114
人　数	(人)	Number of Employed Persons	(person)	1633	2456

注：1.自2011年，医疗卫生机构数含村卫生室，自2013年，含部分计划生育技术服务机构。
2.2017年以前，专利申请量是指国家知识产权局受理的专利申请数量；从2017年开始，是指国家知识产权局受理的按规定缴足申请费、符合进入初步审查阶段条件的专利申请数量。2021年起，国家知识产权局不再发布专利申请量数据。

continued

2011	2012	2013	2014	2015	2016	2017	2018	2019	2020	2021
12047	11573	11151	10770	10404	10027	9738	9674	9646	9619	9458
119.4	109.6	115.7	124.7	124.4	123.9	127.0	129.6	127.9	129.6	137.9
106.8	106.2	103.3	101.0	98.9	107.2	111.0	111.5	117.8	125.2	125.7
644.1	627.7	626.0	648.5	674.6	691.3	708.5	726.0	738.6	743.3	755.8
393612	387203	383692	378886	379239	386405	391838	392333	396465	400114	410021
386280	382562	387312	389080	396368	408856	421877	430702	442729	454285	468276
17	17	11	11	11	11	11	11	11	11	11
147677	166515	165522	178737	163012	179199	157559	233966	292911	414972	451062
144703	120404	128297	147592	161377	167440	279185	181058	158662	223507	280241
386481	428180	459803	485274	484493	502274	375102	426995	556026	742379	906118
3951	4286	2843	2259	2200	1604	1580	1479	1257	1248	1140
2731	2917	1982	1544	1493	1082	1048	970	785	777	702
2379	2393	2332	2955	3011	3016	2537	1791	2552	2342	2908
305	338	297	440	385	421	363	232	316	338	329
723	853	866	1095	1019	919	796	451	807	673	754
647	609	681	817	967	762	610	416	735	485	638
1296	1349	1067	1146	1212	1095	973	682	957	988	1002
109599	128614	155170	158619	193220	212911	204861	238795	263407	369349	
58843	75522	76976	72818	98101	98093	100522	132382	146481	238778	329838
5856	7454	8913	10538	16881	19404	19090	20338	20652	26745	36345
68275	68840	75475	77066	77435	77050	79099	81512	83661	84870	85716
3135	3188	3426	3491	3556	3643	4108	4219	4203	4202	4194
41.6	47.3	49.0	50.0	51.9	54.3	58.5	60.8	63.0	64.7	67.4
48.2	53.0	59.8	60.4	61.9	64.3	68.9	73.9	78.3	81.4	85.3
18.6	20.0	23.2	23.1	23.7	24.5	26.5	29.0	31.5	32.9	34.3
17.1	19.2	24.0	24.6	25.4	26.9	29.4	32.3	34.1	35.6	37.6
160	158	159	158	157	157	157	157	157	158	158
3086	3033	3062	3047	3034	3006	2978	2950	2864	2887	2974
1828	1821	1807	1811	1814	1816	1815	1819	1815	1821	1821
4643	4987	4915	5181	5534	5262	5334	5329	5581	5628	6194
116	104	103	104	104	103	105	105	104	103	101
6163	5722	5557	5728	5368	5651	5689	5539	5665	5381	5237
93	93	93	93	92	93	100	106	93	87	82
2134	2083	1719	1734	1632	1602	1821	1902	1732	1712	1618
150	150	153	153	154	154	154	154	154	154	153
2697	2647	2760	2730	2750	2828	2877	2843	2816	2904	2995
120	178	194	243	312	393	485	517	541	577	629
2787	4353	4748	5369	6310	7152	7976	8059	8319	8871	10114

a) Since 2011,the number of health institutions includes village clinics, and since 2013, it includes family planning technical services institutions.

b) Before 2017, the amount of patent application refers to the number of patent applications accepted by the State Intellectual Property Office; from 2017, it refers to the amount of application fees paid by the State Intellectual Property Office and the number of patent applications that have entered the preliminary examination stage.Since 2021, the State Intellectual Property Office has stopped publishing data on the amount of patent application

1-3 国民经济和社会发展主要指标增长速度

单位:%

类　　别	Category	2000	2010
一、人　口	**Population**		
年末总人口	Population at the Year-end	1.3	1.24
按性别分	**By Sex**		
男	Male	(0.6)	(1.0)
女	Female	(0.6)	(0.9)
按农村城镇分	**Agricultural and Non-agricultural Population**		
农村人口	Agricultural Population		-1.7
城镇人口	Non-agricultural Population		4.2
人口密度	Population Density	1.2	1.2
二、就业人员和劳动工资	**Employment and Wages**		
年末就业人员	Year-end Employed Persons	1.4	1.6
第一产业	Primary Industry	-0.2	-2.0
第二产业	Secondary Industry	3.8	4.0
第三产业	Tertiary Industry	2.4	4.0
乡村就业人员	Rural Employed Persons	-6.9	-0.4
城镇就业人员	Urban Employed Persons	19.4	4.1
职工年末人数	Number of Staff and Workers at the Year-end	-2.4	3.4
#国有单位	State-owned Units	-4.3	2.2
城镇集体单位	Urban Collective-owned Units	-12.8	0.4
工资总额	Total Wages Bill	12.1	17.3
#国有单位	State-owned Units	10.2	15.2
城镇集体单位	Urban Collective-owned Units	-2.2	20.3
平均工资	Average Wage	14.6	13.3
#国有单位	State-owned Units	15.1	11.5
城镇集体单位	Urban Collective-owned Units	12.0	15.5
三、国民经济核算	**National Accounting**		
地区生产总值	Gross Domestic Product	9.5	10.4
第一产业	Primary Industry	2.4	3.1
第二产业	Secondary Industry	10.8	11.7
第三产业	Tertiary Industry	10.6	10.3
人均地区生产总值	Per Capita GDP	8.5	9.4
四、固定资产投资	**Investment in Fixed Assets**		
全社会固定资产投资额	Total Investment in Fixed Assets	14.4	22.3
国有经济	State-Owned Units	10.6	18.2
集体经济	Collective-Owned Units	6.9	13.8
个体经济	Individuals Economy	13.9	24.3
其他经济	Others	52.7	24.9
房地产开发投资	Investment in Real Development	28.6	33.8

注：1.年末总人口及农村、城镇人口2011–2019年增速根据第七次人口普查修订数计算；括号内为根据公安户籍人口数计算。
2.就业人员及相关指标2005–2019年增速根据第七次人口普查修订数计算。
3.2010年起，工资总额、平均工资增速为城镇单位就业人员口径。
4.根据第四次经济普查结果，对全省2000–2018年生产总值及相关数据进行了修订。

Growth Rates of Main Indicators on National Economic and Social Development

(%)

2011	2012	2013	2014	2015	2016	2017	2018	2019	2020	2021
0.90	0.44	0.39	0.64	0.59	1.08	0.60	0.44	0.29	0.58	0.05
(0.6)	(0.0)	(0.3)	(1.6)	(0.8)	(1.0)	(0.8)	(0.8)	(0.4)	(0.2)	(0.1)
(0.5)	-(0.2)	(0.4)	(1.2)	(0.8)	(1.0)	(1.0)	(1.0)	(0.6)	(0.3)	(0.2)
-1.4	-1.9	-2.6	-2.2	-4.3	-4.0	-3.5	-1.3	-0.8	-2.6	-2.4
3.2	2.7	3.1	3.1	4.6	4.9	3.4	1.5	1.0	2.5	1.5
0.5	0.5	0.5	0.2	0.6	1.0	0.6	0.3	0.2	0.9	0.2
-0.4	-0.4	-0.9	-0.7	-0.4	-0.8	-0.6	-1.3	-1.1	-0.9	-0.6
-4.1	-4.5	-4.6	-4.8	-4.4	-4.9	-4.9	-5.4	-5.8	-5.1	-4.1
1.5	1.8	0.03	0.2	0.2	-0.8	-0.01	-1.6	-1.4	-0.6	0.5
2.2	2.1	2.2	2.5	2.7	2.8	2.4	2.1	2.5	1.5	0.5
-2.8	-3.1	-3.6	-3.5	-4.2	-4.4	-4.0	-4.0	-3.4	-4.1	-3.5
2.4	2.5	1.9	2.0	3.0	2.3	2.1	0.8	0.6	1.3	1.2
5.4	5.4	16.7	-2.2	-2.6	-1.9	-2.2	-5.7	-6.1	2.8	1.1
-3.0	1.7	-7.9	-2.9	-3.0	-0.7	-0.7	-2.6	-4.3	9.1	1.8
3.5	3.6	-8.3	-13.0	-7.9	-0.7	-12.0	-25.4	-34.5	0.6	-2.3
24.9	17.0	31.8	7.3	7.8	6.8	7.0	2.5	5.2	10.5	9.0
12.0	12.7	2.8	6.8	14.7	9.8	8.5	0.7	5.2	17.0	8.6
23.8	18.8	14.5	-6.0	1.1	2.9	-3.3	-29.7	-36.5	7.3	5.5
12.9	11.4	12.2	10.3	10.5	9.2	8.9	8.1	10.7	7.7	8.0
12.9	10.2	10.3	10.7	18.1	11.4	9.0	6.9	10.0	8.3	6.4
15.8	14.5	21.8	8.7	11.5	7.2	7.8	-1.3	-1.6	9.8	8.9
10.7	9.7	9.4	8.5	7.8	7.4	7.3	6.3	5,3	3.5	8.3
3.7	4.5	3.5	3.8	4.2	3.8	3.6	2.7	1.1	2.7	7.5
11.5	10.3	9.8	8.8	7.1	6.2	6.0	4.1	2.6	3.2	7.2
11.5	10.1	10.3	9.2	9.6	9.3	9.3	8.9	8.2	3.8	9.2
9.6	9.0	8.9	7.9	7.1	6.5	6.4	5.8	4.9	3.0	7.9
21.8	20.2	17.7	15.5	13.7	10.4	7.2	4.1	-8.3	3.3	5.1
3.7	12.0	21.8	14.7	15.6	18.9	30.8	3.1	8.4	-12.4	2.7
3.3	21.6	0.7	8.6	-7.5	-50.6	-2.1	-37.0	-16.8	-54.2	2.2
26.6	25.8	31.1	26.4	25.0	9.5	4.9	16.7	-29.8	4.0	13.6
14.7	50.1	13.7	8.4	6.7	18.7	-1.3	-4.2	4.9	12.4	0.9
26.4	14.6	15.6	6.9	1.3	7.3	5.0	13.8	14.1	9.7	3.9

a) The growth rate on Total population,ural and urban population from 2011 to 2019 are calculated according to the data of the Seventh National Census.Data in the brackets are based on the data from the are based on the sample surveys.

b) The growth rate of employed persons and related indicators from 2005 to 2019 is calculated according to the data of the Seventh National Census.

c) Since 2010,data of total wages bill and average wage refer to the range of employed persons in urban.

d) According to the Fourth National Economic Census, the data of GDP from 2000 to 2018 have been revised.

1-3 续表 1

单位:%

类　　别	Category	2000	2010
五、能　源	**Energy**		
能源生产总量	Total Energy Production	-6.5	10.0
原　煤	Coal	-10.6	14.3
原　油	Crude Oil	0.4	-1.5
天然气	Natural Gas	-6.2	7.5
一次电力	Primary Electricity		113.8
六、财　政	**Government Finance**		
一般公共预算收入	General Public Budget Revenue	14.6	25.0
#税收收入	Tax Revenue	14.6	25.0
#增值税	Value Added Tax	14.7	16.6
营业税	Business Tax	11.0	34.2
企业所得税	Company Income Tax	29.6	33.1
个人所得税	Personal Income Tax	31.9	25.3
资源税	Resource Tax	4.1	1.5
城市维护建设税	Urban Maintenance and Development Tax	16.0	19.9
房产税	Tax on Real Estates	15.4	11.7
城镇土地使用税	Urban Land Using Tax	22.8	13.9
土地增值税	Land Value-added Tax	111.9	51.0
车船税	Tax on Vehicle and License	64.2	31.5
行政事业性收费收入	Income from Administrative Fees	43.9	18.3
一般公共预算支出	General Public Budget Expenditure	11.5	26.8
#一般公共服务支出	Expenditure for General Public Services		11.1
教育支出	Expenditure for Education		25.6
社会保障和就业支出	Expenditure for Social Safety Net and Employment Effort		21.6
卫生健康支出	Expenditure for Health Care		32.5
农林水支出	Expenditure for Agriculture, Forestry and Water Conservancy		26.2
七、金　融	**Financial Intermediation**		
金融机构人民币存款余额	RMB Deposits	13.8	18.5
#住户存款	Household Deposits	8.7	15.0
金融机构人民币贷款余额	RMB Loans	9.3	18.3
八、价格	**Price Indices**		
居民消费价格	Consumer Price	0.2	2.9
商品零售价格	Retail Price	-1.4	2.7
工业生产者出厂价格	Producer Price for Industrial Products	5.9	7.2
工业生产者购进价格	Industrial Producer Purchasing Price	4.7	9.3
九、居民生活	**People's Livelihood**		
全体居民生活	**All Households Livelihood**		
年末人均住房建筑面积	Per Capita Space of Living House at Year-end		
人均可支配收入	Annual Per Capita Disposable Income of All Households		13.4
人均消费支出	Annual Per Capita Consumption Expenditure of All Households		9.8
农村居民生活	**Rural's Livelihood**		
年末人均住房建筑面积	Per Capita Space of Living House at Year-end	-5.8	1.4
人均可支配收入	Annual Per Capita Disposable Income of Rural Households	4.3	14.3
人均消费支出	Annual Per Capita Consumption Expenditure of Rural Households	4.9	8.2

注：1.2009年开始，一次电力包含水电、风电、核电、生物质发电和太阳能光伏发电,2000年数据为水电。
2.2014年及以前住户存款数据为储蓄存款口径数据。
3.从2013年起,全省实施城乡住户调查一体化改革,根据国家统一规定,2018年,按照新指标口径对居民收支调查历史数据进行修正。

continued

(%)

2011	2012	2013	2014	2015	2016	2017	2018	2019	2020	2021
-0.4	6.1	-10.7	0.4	-3.5	-7.3	0.7	-4.4	-4.3	-2.7	-5.4
-2.7	8.1	-14.4	-0.2	-3.9	-8.5	2.3	-8.3	-11.4	-5.1	-14.8
-0.2	-0.2	-1.7	-0.5	-3.2	-12.0	-3.3	0.3	-0.8	-0.2	-0.4
-50.1	17.7	-14.0	-3.4	-8.2	-2.5	-11.6	6.2	6.3	13.1	7.9
59.4	48.4	46.7	14.6	21.6	41.5	33.5	58.3	53.4	10.0	39.8
25.7	17.5	12.3	10.2	10.0	8.5	6.6	6.3	0.6	0.5	11.0
21.1	17.2	15.8	12.2	6.0	4.6	9.1	10.8	-1.0	-1.9	15.1
9.4	5.9	11.7	21.9	-0.3	32.8	5.4	11.5	3.0	-7.4	11.9
21.3	17.1	19.1	6.3	10.3	-20.9					
35.9	10.8	1.0	8.3	3.3	0.9	23.3	9.2	2.8	-1.4	26.3
19.2	-1.5	10.0	10.1	24.3	持平	30.4	15.3	-31.5	23.5	33.7
15.2	137.5	1.7	29.1	-13.2	-8.3	4.6	20.3	0.2	-9.8	16.5
37.4	10.7	9.5	6.2	5.4	2.9	4.4	17.1	-5.3	-2.1	14.4
14.5	36.2	10.8	9.6	9.3	7.1	10.1	6.6	-0.9	-0.7	14.1
15.1	33.6	8.3	15.5	35.5	9.8	1.1	-0.3	-15.0	-11.1	0.9
59.6	37.4	41.8	25.2	0.7	13.0	25.3	6.4	3.5	7.2	12.4
27.7	20.6	12.3	15.9	14.3	14.4	13.7	9.3	3.0	5.4	14.7
37.3	9.5	-6.9	6.4	-1.8	10.6	-2.4	-5.2	1.2	0.4	9.3
20.7	18.0	13.3	7.3	14.9	6.1	5.2	9.1	6.3	4.6	4.3
13.6	14.1	6.3	-3.3	1.8	6.3	9.4	9.9	12.6	5.3	1.6
36.0	25.2	6.7	4.4	15.7	7.4	3.5	6.1	7.5	5.9	5.6
20.3	18.9	14.3	12.0	18.5	9.9	14.0	10.9	15.2	14.7	12.4
43.7	17.4	14.9	24.7	15.8	12.7	4.9	6.5	3.0	14.6	4.5
21.0	19.5	11.0	3.3	24.8	-2.3	1.1	4.5	7.8	-1.0	-3.6
12.7	17.2	14.3	8.7	9.4	11.9	6.1	6.2	8.9	13.1	10.1
12.9	18.8	13.1	11.4	8.9	10.8	6.5	9.9	14.0	16.3	12.4
14.5	21.9	4.3	11.8	10.7	11.3	9.5	10.4	11.8	14.0	13.7
5.0	2.1	2.2	1.9	1.2	2.1	1.5	2.5	3.2	2.8	1.2
4.7	1.6	1.4	1.0	0.2	1.3	0.8	2.2	2.2	2.0	1.4
6.0	-1.6	-1.6	-1.6	-4.8	-1.5	5.5	3.7	-0.3	-1.9	10.3
9.2	-0.8	-1.6	-1.8	-5.0	-2.0	7.3	3.6	-0.8	-2.5	9.5
			2.1	-0.5	2.9	0.5	-0.6	0.9	0.05	3.4
16.7	13.6	11.0	9.8	8.8	8.7	9.1	8.4	8.2	4.1	8.6
15.1	10.6	9.1	12.0	9.4	9.2	8.5	8.7	8.8	2.5	9.0
4.6	5.8	2.9	1.7	1.6	2.9	1.0	1.6	0.8	-0.3	1.5
19.3	13.2	12.4	11.2	8.8	7.9	8.3	7.8	9.1	5.5	10.9
22.7	14.8	9.1	15.8	9.9	8.8	8.6	9.0	9.2	2.9	12.9

a) Since 2009, Primary Electricity includes that generated by hydro power, wind power, nuclear power, bio-energy and solar PV power. Data of 2000 refer to hydro power.

b) Data of Household Deposits before 2014 refers to Urban and Rural Household Savings Deposits .

c)An integrated household survey programme has been implemented since 2013,instead of the two separate urban and rural household surveys.In 2018 according to national uniform regulation,the historical data of residents' income and expenditure are revised according to the new survey programme.

1-3 续表 2

单位:%

类别	Category	2000	2010
城镇居民生活	**Urban's Livelihood**		
年末人均住房建筑面积	Per Capita Construction Area of Buildings	5.0	0.9
人均可支配收入	Annual Per Capita Disposable Income of Urban Households	11.3	11.6
人均消费支出	Annual Per Capita Consumption Expenditure of Urban Households	11.0	9.0
十、农林牧渔业	**Farming,Forestry,Animal Husbandry and Fishery**		
农林牧渔业总产值	**Gross Output Value of Farming Forestry,Animal Husbandry and Fishery**	**3.9**	**3.6**
农　业	Farming	4.0	2.5
林　业	Forestry	6.2	9.9
牧　业	Animal Husbandry	5.4	3.9
渔　业	Fishery	0.5	4.9
农林牧渔专业及辅助性活动	Output Value of Farming,Forestry,Animal Husbandry and Fishery professions and auxiliary activities		9.9
农业生产情况	**Farming**		
粮食总产量	Total Output of Grain	-10.1	1.4
粮食单产	Grain	-6.3	-0.7
棉花总产量	Total Output of Cotton	50.5	-25.3
棉花单产	Cotton	1.2	-17.9
油料总产量	Total Output of Oil-bearing Crops	11.4	-0.4
油料单产	Oil-bearing Crops	3.2	-0.7
肉类总产量	Total Output of Grain	-4.7	3.2
猪存栏	Number of Pigs	-6.2	0.9
牛存栏	Number of Cattles	-20.2	-2.7
羊存栏	Number of Sheep and Goats	-10.9	-0.6
家禽存栏	Number of Poultry	-10.4	6.3
猪出栏	Slaughtered Pigs	-1.1	4.2
牛出栏	Slaughtered Cattle	-17.6	-3.2
羊出栏	Slaughtered Sheep	-16.3	-4.2
家禽出栏	Slaughtered Poultry	-9.0	5.2
禽蛋产量	Poultry Eggs	-13.8	2.0
奶类产量	Milk	2.3	4.9
水产品总产量	Total Aquatic Products	0.5	4.0
海水产品	Seawater Aquatic Products	-1.2	3.2
海洋捕捞	Catching in Ocean	-7.4	-4.0
海水养殖	Seawater Aquiculture	6.5	3.9
淡水产品产量	Freshwater Aquatic Products	11.2	8.1
捕捞量	Catching	1.5	2.0
养殖量	Freshwater Aquiculture	12.2	8.8
水产品养殖面积	Aquiculture Area	9.1	10.4
海　水	Seawater Aquiculture Area	25.2	13.5
淡　水	Freshwater Aquiculture Area	-4.9	4.9
十一、工　业	**Industry**		
全部工业增加值	Value Added of Industry Enterprises	10.9	11.6
十二、建筑业	**Industry**		
建筑业增加值	Value Added of Construction Enterprises	10.1	11.9

continued

(%)

2011	2012	2013	2014	2015	2016	2017	2018	2019	2020	2021
3.4	0.8	8.8	2.5	-2.5	3.2	0.3	-2.2	0.9	0.5	5.2
14.3	13.0	9.7	8.7	8.0	7.8	8.2	7.5	7.0	3.3	7.6
11.0	8.4	8.5	10.1	8.4	8.3	7.3	7.5	7.8	2.1	7.4
3.8	**4.7**	**3.8**	**4.0**	**4.3**	**4.4**	**4.0**	**3.0**	**0.8**	**3.0**	**8.6**
3.9	2.5	4.4	4.6	4.7	5.0	4.4	3.9	3.1	3.4	4.3
9.3	3.4	9.0	9.7	8.1	9.5	9.9	9.3	9.2	6.3	1.7
2.5	7.7	2.1	2.4	3.1	2.6	3.7	-0.1	-4.6	2.3	19.2
4.4	4.1	3.3	2.7	3.2	2.0	-0.5	0.8	-2.5	1.3	5.9
7.2	7.7	9.5	9.3	8.5	15.8	12.5	13.5	9.3	5.3	8.2
4.4	2.4	1.4	3.2	2.2	3.6	0.8	-1.0	0.7	1.7	1.0
2.1	0.7	-1.9	-0.2	0.6	2.2	1.5	-0.4	1.8	2.1	0.1
3.0	-15.4	-15.5	1.8	-23.3	-3.0	-37.1	4.8	-9.7	-6.6	-23.4
10.3	-2.9	-8.8	21.5	-7.1	13.1	0.6	-0.1	-2.2	10.6	-0.6
-1.1	-0.6	-0.1	-3.5	-3.3	-0.5	0.4	-2.3	-7.1	0.7	-1.7
1.1	0.9	-0.4	-0.7	-1.2	0.2	1.8	-0.4	-3.1	3.1	1.2
1.2	7.8	1.9	-0.2	1.0	-1.0	3.5	-1.3	-17.6	3.4	12.5
4.4	3.4	2.1	0.4	-1.0	-1.9	-1.5	-1.8	-27.1	34.8	7.4
-0.5	-1.1	-2.2	-3.2	-0.7	-3.9	2.4	-5.2	-4.3	-23.5	0.4
-2.0	-2.0	-2.8	-1.8	0.2	-4.2	3.6	2.7	2.0	-18.3	-2.4
9.6	11.2	-1.0	-0.5	2.7	8.7	-1.9	-1.3	4.3	6.1	1.1
-0.9	9.4	5.0	4.0	-1.7	-1.2	1.7	-1.9	-37.5	5.3	31.6
-5.6	-1.2	-0.7	-2.7	-0.6	-2.5	0.2	0.5	-4.8	-20.3	1.6
-5.9	-2.1	-0.9	2.4	-0.1	0.5	3.5	2.0	0.7	-7.8	-4.7
7.1	9.7	-1.6	-7.0	5.4	11.6	2.9	-1.5	6.5	9.2	4.3
4.4	0.2	-1.4	-2.1	9.2	4.0	0.9	0.5	0.7	7.0	-5.3
2.1	5.4	-4.4	3.0	-1.6	-2.9	-1.0	0.5	0.8	3.0	19.4
3.8	-3.1	2.5	4.7	3.0	2.0	-2.5	-0.8	-4.4	0.6	3.1
2.8	-1.9	2.0	6.5	3.8	2.6	-2.3	-0.1	-4.1	1.7	3.1
6.9	-14.0	-3.4	9.5	3.1	2.4	-9.7	-1.4	-2.7	-2.5	-0.5
4.3	5.5	4.7	5.1	4.1	2.6	1.2	0.4	-4.6	3.4	4.5
8.4	-8.7	5.1	-3.6	-0.6	-0.9	-3.6	-4.2	-6.6	-5.6	3.3
3.4	-16.7	2.1	-21.3	-8.4	13.0	-10.8	-1.1	7.8	7.1	0.1
9.0	-7.9	5.3	-2.1	-0.1	-1.8	-3.1	-4.4	-7.6	-6.6	3.6
3.3	2.6	2.9	1.0	1.3	-0.8	-0.7	-6.2	-3.0	-1.9	2.8
2.2	2.3	4.4	0.3	2.7	7.4	0.9	-6.5	-1.6	3.4	4.8
5.5	3.3	0.1	2.3	-1.3	-17.1	-4.9	-5.3	-6.6	-16.8	-4.5
12.2	10.8	10.1	8.8	6.9	6.1	6.2	4.5	2.0	3.4	8.6
6.4	7.0	9.6	9.2	8.1	6.0	4.4	4.2	6.5	1.5	1.8

1-3 续表 3

单位:%

类　　别	Category	2000	2010
十三、交通运输邮电	**Transport,Posts and Telecommunications**		
铁路通车里程	Length of Railways	持平	5.9
公路通车里程	Length of Highways	4.2	1.4
#晴雨通车	Length of Highways Operating under All Weathers	4.5	1.6
内河通航里程	Length of Navigable Inland Waterways	持平	13.6
客运量	Passenger Traffic	11.4	6.2
铁　路	Railways	4.6	4.0
公　路	Highways	12.1	6.2
水　路	Waterways	-4.8	14.9
客运周转量	Passenger Turnover	5.9	3.6
铁　路	Railways	7.8	10.9
公　路	Highways	12.2	1.2
水　路	Waterways	-19.1	18.9
货运量	Freight Traffic	15.3	4.8
铁　路	Railways	6.6	-7.9
公　路	Highways	13.4	5.1
水　路	Waterways	14.1	17.7
货运周转量	Freight Turnover	26.7	7.2
铁　路	Railways	8.7	7.9
公　路	Highways	14.8	2.8
水　路	Waterways	70.9	14.4
沿海主要港口货物吞吐量	Volume of Freight Handled in Major Coastal Ports	15.2	18.3
邮政局总计	Number of Post & Telecommunications Offices	-31.8	-0.8
函　件	Number of Letters	-6.4	3.6
电信业务总量	Business Volume of Telecommunication Services	32.1	21.1
邮政业务总量	Business Volume of Post Services		
互联网宽带接入用户	Number of Mobile Telephone		
年末移动电话用户	Number of Mobile Telephone	101.2	15.9
民用汽车拥有量	Number of Private Vehicles	14.4	18.7
十四、国内贸易	**Domestic Trade**		
社会消费品零售总额	**Total Retail Sales of Consumer Goods**	**12.4**	**16.9**
商品零售	Retail Sales		
餐饮收入	Catering Income		
十五、对外贸易和旅游	**Foreign Economy and Trade,Tourism**		
对外贸易	Foreign Economy and Trade		
海关进出口总值	Total Value of Imports and Exports	36.8	36.3
海关出口总值	Total Exports	34.1	31.0
#一般贸易	General Trade	37.9	36.7
来料加工装配贸易	Processing and Assembling with Customer's Materials	34.0	7.5
进料加工贸易	Processing and Assembling with Import Materials	28.4	28.4
海关进口总值	Total Imports	41.4	43.5

注：1.交通运输部2014年修订了公路、水运运输量统计试行方案，统计口径发生了变化。

2.表中2000年邮电业务总量按1990年不变价格计算，2001—2010年按2000年不变价格计算。2011—2015年邮电业务总量按2010年价格计算；2016—2020年，按2015年价格计算；2021年按2020年价格计算。2012年起，邮政业务量由山东邮政管理局提供，包括快递业务量，2012年以前数据由山东省邮政公司提供。

3.2019年起，公路货运量采用全国公路货运量专项调查数据。与往年数据不可比。

4.2020年起，铁路客货运量、周转量为济南局、北京局、郑州局在山东省内数据，口径为国家铁路；铁路通车里程含地方铁路。

continued

(%)

2011	2012	2013	2014	2015	2016	2017	2018	2019	2020	2021
9.0	3.1	2.1	3.4	7.0	0.4	4.8	11.0	5.2		4.6
1.4	4.9	3.4	2.7	1.5	0.9	1.8	1.9	1.7	2.3	0.5
1.5	5.0	3.4	2.8	1.5	0.9	1.8	1.9	1.8	2.3	-1.1
持平	持平	持平	持平	持平	持平	持平	持平	持平	-2.9	持平
0.7	5.8	1.7	-1.0	-19.0	5.2	2.9	3.2	1.1	-55.9	-5.8
9.4	15.7	10.9	12.1	12.2	11.6	12.5	8.5	8.2	-41.0	24.2
0.6	5.5	1.4	-3.1	-24.3	4.0	0.6	1.9	-0.9	-60.7	-22.3
-8.8	7.1	0.2	11.8	-1.1	0.1	1.8	0.3	-1.5	-59.1	27.1
5.0	6.0	3.3	5.5	-1.1	3.7	5.0	3.5	0.8	-55.4	18.6
8.9	11.1	7.9	12.3	4.4	6.2	7.2	4.0	1.3	-47.9	21.3
3.7	4.2	1.6	-1.7	-7.8	0.2	1.8	2.6	-0.2	-67.7	11.6
0.3	5.2	-7.8	7.3	-1.5	3.1	0.6	5.7	12.7	-72.5	-2.5
5.7	4.9	4.3	0.1	-1.0	8.9	14.6	8.3		1.2	8.0
9.2	0.5	-3.9	-11.8	-6.0	6.1	6.6	4.8	11.4	10.2	-1.3
5.7	6.2	5.1	1.0	-0.9	9.6	15.3	8.6		0.4	9.0
1.5	3.5	-1.2	2.7	3.9	2.3	10.6	7.8	-1.1	2.5	6.2
7.1	-12.7	-6.6	0.9	1.9	5.6	9.4	3.5	1.2	1.9	16.1
5.4	-2.1	-7.0	-10.9	-13.0	6.0	6.8	4.2	13.4	3.9	7.4
6.6	6.6	6.2	3.9	2.9	3.3	9.5	3.1	-1.7	0.6	10.8
8.6	5.5	2.1	1.3	12.4	15.0	10.8	4.4	3.3	5.0	40.8
11.3	10.9	10.8	8.9	4.4	6.4	6.1	6.6	-0.3	4.9	5.5
0.4	0.2	0.2	0.3	持平	0.3	0.1	-0.2	0.6	4.0	-0.9
-14.7	-0.8	-7.2	-31.0	-35.7	-45.0	-32.4	-8.7	-1.7	-30.7	-12.6
14.8	10.2	8.3	23.6	17.3	49.3	73.1	144.3	58.5	24.4	30.1
	15.6	24.8	24.2	41.0	46.7	30.3	34.5	35.9	38.4	30.3
	18.2	7.4	4.0	6.7	45.6	9.4	11.4	10.4	8.1	12.1
15.0	6.6	9.8	4.0	8.7	1.9	3.6	6.3	2.0	1.1	3.1
14.9	15.9	13.8	10.2	10.4	12.7	11.6	10.0	9.4	7.9	7.9
15.9	**13.2**	**12.2**	**11.3**	**9.4**	**9.0**	**8.7**	**7.6**	**6.4**	**持平**	**15.3**
15.5	13.4	12.3	11.4	9.0	8.5	8.6	7.1	6.0	0.8	14.4
19.5	11.9	10.8	10.4	12.4	12.7	10.0	11.9	9.7	-6.2	22.4
24.9	4.1	8.8	3.7	-12.8	-3.1	12.3	11.2	1.3	7.5	42.5
20.7	2.4	4.5	7.6	-0.5	-4.8	7.2	8.9	0.8	17.1	43.8
30.0	6.3	10.6	10.1	8.0	-4.3	9.0	17.2	1.9	23.1	41.2
12.3	2.9	-0.2	-7.4	-7.7	-3.2	-9.0	-7.7	0.6	-17.8	11.2
12.0	-3.6	-3.8	7.8	-11.6	-6.7	6.3	-5.6	-10.8	-0.8	22.8
30.1	6.0	13.6	-0.2	-26.2	-0.7	19.5	14.1	2.0	-4.0	40.7

a)The pilot statistical investigation program on passenger highway and turnover was revised in 2014,and the statistical scope was adjusted.

b) Business volume of postal service and telecommunication service of 2000 was calculated at 1990 constant prices, and that from 2001 to 2010 was calculated at 2000 constant prices,and that from 2011 to 2015 was calculated at 2010 constant prices,and that from 2016 to 2020 was calculated at 2015 constant prices, and that of 2021 was calculated at 2020 constant prices. The data of business volume of postal service before 2012 come from Shandong Post Company, since 2012, they are from Shandong Post Bureau, including business volume of courier companies above designated size.

c) The road freight volume adopts the special survey data of national road freight volume since 2019,and not comparable with the previous .

d) Since2020, the railway passenger and freight volume and turnover refer to the data of Jinan Bureau,Beijing Bureau and Zhengzhou Bureau in Shan -dong Province,the caliber is national railway,and the data of railways length includes the local railways.

1-3 续表 4

单位:%

类别	Category	2000	2010
利用外资	**Utilization of Foreign Capital**		
新设外商直接投资企业数	Number of newly established Companies by foreign direct investment	58.9	11.2
实际利用外商直接投资	Direct Foreign Investments	20.4	14.5
对外承包工程和劳务合作	**Foreign Contracted Projects Labor Cooperation**		
合同个数	Number of Contracts (unit)	12.0	28.3
合同金额	Contracted Value	-9.0	17.2
营业额	Value of Business	-28.9	18.3
年末在外人数	Population in Foreign Countries and Regions	13.1	5.9
旅　游	**Tourism**		
接待海外旅游人数	International Tourists	16.3	18.3
外国人	Foreigners	14.9	15.2
港澳台胞	Compatriots from Hong Kong Macao and Taiwan	23.5	29.1
旅游外汇收入(人民币)	Foreign Exchange Earnings(RMB)	18.8	21.0
旅游外汇收入(美元)	Foreign Exchange Earnings(USD)	18.8	22.1
人民币对主要外币年平均汇价（中间价）	**Average Exchange Rate of RMB Yuan Against Main Convertible Currencies (Middle Rate)**		
100美元	100 US Dollars	0.0	-0.9
100日元	100 Japanese Yen	-8.5	5.9
100港元	100 Hong Kong Dollars	-0.4	-1.1
100欧元	100Euros		-5.8
十六、教　育	**Education**		
普通高等学校	**Regular Institutions of Higher Education**		
学校数	Number of Schools	11.5	3.9
招生数	New Enrollment	51.5	-1.1
毕业生数	Graduates	0.2	2.9
在校学生数	Total Enrollment	42.2	2.4
教职工数	Teachers and Staff	10.7	1.7
专任教师	Full-time Teachers	16.5	1.9
中等专业学校	**Secondary Professional Schools**		
学校数	Number of Schools	-3.2	
招生数	New Enrollment	-23.6	
毕业生数	Graduates	-2.9	
在校学生数	Total Enrollment	-3.2	
教职工数	Teachers and Staff	-5.2	
专任教师	Full-time Teachers	-4.2	
普通中学	**Regular Senior Secondary Schools**		
学校数	Number of Schools	-0.2	-2.8
招生数	New Enrollment	5.4	2.4
毕业生数	Graduates	1.9	-1.1
在校学生数	Total Enrollment	9.4	0.3
教职工数	Teachers and Staff	3.9	-0.8
专任教师	Full-time Teachers	4.9	-0.1
技工学校	**Technical Schools**		
学校数	Number of Schools	-7.6	6.6
招生数	New Enrollment	-5.7	-6.8
毕业生数	Graduates	-6.9	-4.8
在校学生数	Total Enrollment	-14.7	0.4
教职工数	Teachers and Staff	-15.2	-27.2
专任教师	Full-time Teachers	-3.2	-22.8

注:1.2004年起实行新的外商投资统计制度,取消对外借款部分,外商直接投资数据为商务部反馈数。2008年实际使用外资采用全口径统计方式。2019年起，实际使用外资采用商务部通报口径，不包含股东贷款、投资性公司投资，合同外资不再统计。
2.2010年起，中等专业学校数据改为中等职业学校口径。

continued

(%)

2011	2012	2013	2014	2015	2016	2017	2018	2019	2020	2021
-12.2	-7.0	5.4	-3.8	11.6	-2.1	0.1	45.8	16.7	21.6	0.1
21.7	10.7	13.8	8.1	7.3	3.2	6.1	14.9	18.6	20.1	21.9
-13.2	4.2	12.1	14.8	8.6	0.8	2.8	11.2	-11.9	-22.9	12.4
36.1	9.6	4.5	8.6	9.7	6.7	7.0	2.8	-4.4	-18.0	-1.4
6.4	-4.5	2.3	16.5	0.7	3.1	9.0	-4.0	6.9	-33.4	-20.1
15.7	10.8	-3.7	-1.6	3.4	5.4	1.8	3.8	1.6	-89.9	
12.4	9.6	-4.3	-0.5	3.1	5.0	0.1	3.7	1.3	-88.1	
25.8	14.1	-1.8	-4.3	4.1	6.3	6.4	4.0	2.3	-94.3	
12.9	12.0	-8.3	-1.4	8.2	12.8	5.3	3.9	5.8	-93.9	
18.4	14.6	-6.6	-0.6	6.7	5.8	3.6	6.0	1.5	-93.9	
-4.6	-2.3	-1.9	-0.8	1.4	6.6	1.6	-2.0	4.2	-0.01	-6.5
4.9	-2.5	-19.9	-8.1	-11.4	18.8	-1.6	-0.6	5.8	2.0	-9.1
-4.8	-1.9	-1.9	-0.8	1.4	6.5	1.2	-2.6	4.3	1.0	-6.7
0.3	-9.9	1.4	-0.7	-15.3	6.2	3.9	2.2	-1.0	1.9	-3.1
4.5	-1.4	2.2	1.4	0.7	0.7	0.7	持平	0.7	4.1	0.7
0.3	0.3	5.8	10.1	2.6	4.8	-1.9	2.7	17.9	-1.6	7.0
6.5	0.3	0.3	-2.5	2.2	7.4	12.2	2.6	-1.3	4.7	2.1
0.9	0.8	2.4	5.8	5.8	5.0	1.0	1.3	7.0	4.9	6.0
2.6	-0.2	-0.1	1.2	2.2	2.3	2.6	2.7	4.0	4.3	3.4
3.5	1.5	2.7	2.7	3.3	2.9	2.8	1.7	4.3	5.6	4.6
-7.7	-5.2	-6.3	-12.4	-5.4	-1.6	-6.3	-0.7	-1.8	1.5	0.8
4.2	-9.0	-10.2	-12.2	-7.9	-2.0	-9.4	-6.1	8.9	11.3	-1.3
-12.0	-1.6	-0.5	-6.5	-9.5	-10.5	-13.4	0.8	3.9	-10.2	-5.3
4.0	-2.6	-10.1	-8.1	-9.6	-5.5	-2.0	-5.4	-2.6	6.4	7.9
-5.8	-3.7	-6.5	-3.5	-3.4	-2.7	-0.3	-1.8	-1.8	1.0	2.0
-3.4	-2.1	-4.2	-1.9	-0.7	-1.4	0.9	-0.8	-0.4	2.2	9.0
-2.1	-1.3	-1.6	-0.1	-0.4	1.7	1.6	3.1	3.3	3.4	2.5
-1.4	-1.2	-0.8	-3.1	-1.6	6.1	2.5	-0.1	7.2	6.5	持平
0.6	-2.9	1.9	-1.5	1.5	1.0	-3.9	-2.0	6.1	5.8	-2.0
0.1	-1.8	-0.8	-0.5	-1.3	0.5	2.6	3.0	3.6	3.9	4.0
5.5	0.5	0.2	1.2	0.9	1.8	3.6	2.6	4.2	4.1	4.9
1.3	0.02	1.5	1.2	0.8	1.9	3.2	2.3	3.8	4.0	4.1
-0.5	2.4	-2.8	-1.9	-4.4	持平	持平	-6.7	持平	持平	7. 2
9.1	3.4	-6.7	-11.2	2.8	1.6	-3.4	4.7	11.8	15.0	-2.3
-7.6	-8.4	7.7	-11.3	-9.2	-8.7	15.8	-7.2	-4.8	4.7	8.6
-4.1	5.2	-7.8	-10.9	-3.4	5.4	-0.8	-0.8	7.7	14.1	9.0
34.1	22.7	3.2	-4.7	-0.6	-0.3	0.6	0.3	0.2	1.7	9.0
40.7	1.9	11.8	-4.1	-1.7	1.3	-1.5	-0.2	-1.0	5.7	11.5

a)Since 2004,foreign loads is canceled according to the new statistical lations on foreign investments, data of foreign direct investments come from the Ministry of Commerce.In 2008 the foreign capital actually utilized is changed to the actual received foreign capital.From 2019,Actual use of foreign capital uses Bulletin of the Ministry of Commerce,does not contain shareholder loan and the investment from investment companies,and contract fo-reign investment is no longer counted.

b)Data of secondary professional schools refer to the caliber of secondary vocational school since 2010 .

1-3 续表 5

单位:%

类　　别	Category	2000	2010
小　学	**Regular Primary Schools**		
学校数	Number of Schools	-11.7	-3.5
招生数	New Enrollment	-10.0	9.4
毕业生数	Graduates	1.9	0.7
在校学生数	Total Enrollment	-11.0	0.4
教职工数	Teachers and Staff	-2.4	-0.8
专任教师	Full-time Teachers	-2.5	-0.6
成人高等学校	**Adult Institutions of Higher Education**		
学校数	Number of Schools	持平	-14.3
招生数	New Enrollment	-5.4	-2.1
毕业生数	Graduates	14.9	5.0
在校学生数	Total Enrollment	-0.5	3.0
教职工数	Teachers and Staff	-1.7	-32.3
专任教师	Full-time Teachers	-0.7	-28.9
十七、科　技	**Science**		
重要科技成果	**Major Scientific Achievements**		
成果数量	Number of Achievements	1.1	0.1
#农　业	Agricultural	3.2	27.8
工　业	Industry	1.5	-11.5
国际领先先进水平	Internationally Advanced	-19.5	-10.0
国内领先先进水平	Nationally Advanced	4.5	-6.8
专利情况	**Patent Applications**		
申请量	Number of Patent Applications Examined	16.7	20.9
授权量	Number of Patent Applications Granted	6.5	49.2
#发明专利	Inventions		43.3
十八、卫生、文化事业	**Public Health and Culture**		
卫生机构数	Number of Health Institutions	17.2	9.3
#医院(卫生院)	Hospitals and Township Hospitals	持平	2.5
卫生机构床位数	Number of Beds in Health Institutions	0.7	10.1
卫生技术人员数	Medical Technical Personnel	2.3	8.6
#执业(助理)医师	Licensed (Assistant) Doctors	4.3	5.3
注册护士	Registered Nurse	2.3	12.5
文化(艺术)馆	**Cultural (Arts) Centers**		
机构数	Number of Institutions	0.6	持平
人　数	Number of Employed Persons	-4.4	-1.9
文化站	**Cultural Stations**		
机构数	Number of Institutions	-2.8	-0.6
人　数	Number of Employed Persons	0.3	-1.1
艺术表演团体	**Arts Performance Troupes**		
机构数	Number of Institutions	0.9	0.8
人　数	Number of Employed Persons	-2.2	-0.2
剧场(院)	**Theaters and Music Halls**		
机构数	Number of Institutions	-1.9	11.0
人　数	Number of Employed Persons	-2.8	16.1
图书馆	**Libraries**		
机构数	Number of Institutions	持平	-0.7
人　数	Number of Employed Persons	-1.9	0.4
博物馆	**Museums**		
机构数	Number of Institutions	3.5	2.7
人　数	Number of Employed Persons	-1.8	6.5

注：1.自2011年，医疗卫生机构数含村卫生室，自2013年，含部分计划生育技术服务机构。
2.2017年以前，专利申请量是指国家知识产权局受理的专利申请数量；从2017年开始，是指国家知识产权局受理的按规定缴足申请费、符合进入初步审查阶段条件的专利申请数量。2021年起，国家知识产权局不再发布专利申请量数据。

continued

(%)

2011	2012	2013	2014	2015	2016	2017	2018	2019	2020	2021
-2.9	-3.9	-3.6	-3.4	-3.4	-3.6	-2.9	-0.7	-0.3	-0.3	-1.7
7.3	-8.2	5.6	7.8	-0.2	-0.4	2.5	2.1	-1.4	1.4	6.4
-3.1	-0.6	-2.7	-2.2	-2.1	8.3	3.6	0.5	5.6	6.3	0.5
2.4	-2.5	-0.3	3.6	4.0	2.5	2.5	2.5	1.7	0.6	1.7
-5.7	-1.6	-0.9	-1.3	0.1	1.9	1.4	0.1	1.1	0.9	2.5
-0.3	-1.0	1.2	0.5	1.9	3.2	3.2	2.1	2.8	2.6	3.1
-5.6	持平	-35.3	持平	持平	持平	持平	持平	持平	持平	持平
10.9	12.8	-0.6	8.0	-8.8	9.9	-12.1	48.5	25.2	41.7	8.7
31.1	-16.8	6.6	15.0	9.3	3.8	66.7	-35.1	-12.4	40.9	25.4
-0.6	10.8	7.4	5.5	-0.2	3.7	-25.3	13.8	30.2	33.5	22.1
-6.5	8.5	-33.7	-20.5	-2.6	-27.1	-1.5	-6.4	-15.0	-0.7	-8.7
-7.3	6.8	-32.1	-22.1	-3.3	-27.5	-3.1	-7.4	-19.1	-1.0	-9.7
0.5	0.6	-2.5	26.7	1.9	0.2	-15.9	-29.4	42.5	-8.2	24.2
-22.0	10.8	-12.1	48.1	-12.5	9.4	-13.8	-36.1	36.2	7.0	-2.7
-3.7	18.0	1.5	26.4	-6.9	-9.8	-13.4	-43.3	78.9	-16.6	12.0
-4.3	-5.9	11.8	20.0	18.4	-21.2	-19.9	-31.8	76.7	-34.0	31.5
-1.5	4.1	-20.9	7.4	5.8	-9.7	-11.1	-29.9	40.3	3.2	1.4
35.5	17.3	20.6	2.2	21.8	10.2		16.6	10.3	40.2	
14.3	28.3	1.9	-5.4	34.7	持平	2.5	31.7	10.7	63.0	38.1
42.6	27.3	19.6	18.2	60.2	14.9	-1.6	6.5	1.5	29.5	35.9
	0.8	9.6	2.1	0.5	-0.5	2.7	3.1	2.6	1.4	1.0
1.2	1.7	7.5	1.9	1.9	2.4	12.8	2.7	-0.4	持平	-0.2
8.9	13.8	3.4	2.1	3.8	4.5	7.8	4.0	3.5	2.7	4.2
9.2	10.0	12.8	1.0	2.5	3.9	7.2	7.1	6.0	4.0	4.8
4.5	7.8	15.7	-0.4	2.6	3.4	8.0	9.6	8.7	4.5	4.1
9.8	12.1	25.3	2.3	3.4	5.8	9.2	9.9	5.8	4.2	5.8
1.3	-1.3	0.6	-0.6	-0.6	持平	持平	持平	持平	0.6	持平
1.0	-1.7	1.0	-0.5	-0.4	-0.9	-0.9	-0.9	-2.9	0.8	3.0
-1.5	-0.4	-0.8	0.2	0.2	0.1	-0.1	0.2	-0.2	0.3	持平
2.2	7.4	-1.4	5.4	6.8	-4.9	1.4	-0.1	4.7	0.8	10.1
-2.5	-10.3	-1.0	1.0	持平	-1.0	1.9	持平	-1.0	-1.0	-1.9
-1.7	-7.2	-2.9	3.1	-6.3	5.3	0.7	-2.6	2.3	-5.0	-2.7
2.2	持平	持平	持平	-1.1	1.1	7.5	6.0	-12.3	-6.5	-5.7
12.1	-2.4	-17.5	0.9	-5.9	-1.8	13.7	4.4	-8.9	-1.2	-5.5
0.7	持平	2.0	持平	0.7	持平	持平	持平	持平	持平	-0.6
0.6	-1.9	4.3	-1.1	0.7	2.8	1.7	-1.2	-0.9	3.1	3.1
5.3	48.3	9.0	25.3	28.4	26.0	23.4	6.6	4.6	6.7	9.0
13.5	56.2	9.1	13.1	17.5	13.3	11.5	1.0	3.2	6.6	14.0

a) Since 2011,the number of health institutions includes village clinics,and since 2013 ,it includes family planning technical services institutions.

b) Before 2017, the amount of patent application refers to the number of patent applications accepted by the State Intellectual Property Office; from 2017,it refers to the amount of application fees paid by the State Intellectual Property Office and the number of patent applications that have entered the preliminary examination stage.Since 2021, the State Intellectual Property Office has stopped publishing data on the amount of patent applications

1-4 全省经济和社会发展结构指标

Composition Indicators on National Economic and Social Development

单位:% (%)

项目	Item	2015	2016	2017	2018	2019	2020	2021
一、地区生产总值比例	**Structure of Gross Domestic Product**							
第一产业	Primary Industry	8.9	8.2	7.7	7.4	7.3	7.4	7.3
第二产业	Secondary Industry	44.9	43.5	42.7	41.3	39.9	39.1	39.9
第三产业	Tertiary Industry	46.2	48.3	49.6	51.3	52.8	53.5	52.8
二、常住人口比例	**Structure of Population**							
按性别分	Sexual Structure							
男	Male	50.5	50.7	50.7	50.2	49.8	50.7	50.8
女	Female	49.5	49.3	49.3	49.8	50.2	49.3	49.2
按年龄分	Age							
0-14岁	Aged 0-14	16.6	16.4	17.2	18.1	18.0	18.8	18.4
15-64岁	Aged 15-64	71.2	70.4	68.8	66.9	66.2	66.1	65.7
65岁及以上	Aged 65 and Over	12.2	13.2	14.0	15.0	15.8	15.1	15.9
按农村城镇分	Agricultural and Non-agricultural Structure							
农村人口	Agricultural Structure	43.03	40.87	39.21	38.54	38.14	36.95	36.06
城镇人口	Non-agricultural Structure	56.97	59.13	60.79	61.46	61.86	63.05	63.94
三、社会就业人员比例	**Structure of Employment**							
第一产业	Primary Industry	31.1	29.8	28.5	27.3	26.0	24.9	24.0
第二产业	Secondary Industry	33.3	33.3	33.5	33.4	33.3	33.4	33.8
第三产业	Tertiary Industry	35.6	36.9	38.0	39.3	40.7	41.7	42.2
四、农林牧渔业总产值比例	**Structure of Gross Output Value of Agriculture**							
农　业	Farming	50.2	48.3	48.2	49.8	50.8	50.7	50.7
林　业	Forestry	1.5	1.6	1.8	1.9	2.0	2.1	1.9
牧　业	Animal Husbandry	28.0	28.9	27.4	25.9	24.9	25.2	25.3
渔　业	Fishery	15.6	15.5	16.1	15.2	14.4	14.1	14.4
农林牧渔专业及辅助性活动	Farming,Forestry,Animal Husbandry and Fishery professions and auxiliary activities	4.7	5.6	6.5	7.2	7.8	7.9	7.6
五、全社会固定资产投资比例	**Structure of Investment in Fixed Assets**							
国有经济	State-owned Units	13.0	14.1	17.3	20.1	23.8	20.2	19.7
集体经济	Collective-owned Units	6.5	2.9	2.7	1.2	1.1	0.5	0.5
个体经济	Self-employed Units	42.0	41.6	40.4	39.1	29.9	30.1	32.5
其他经济	Others	38.5	41.4	39.5	39.6	45.2	49.3	47.3
六、社会消费品零售总额比例	**Structure of Total Retail Sales of Consumer Goods**							
城镇	Urban	79.9	79.8	79.7	79.5	79.4	82.2	83.3
乡村	Rural	20.1	20.2	20.3	20.5	20.6	17.8	16.7
七、人民生活	**People's Living Conditions**							
城乡居民收入比(农村居民收入为1)	Urban and Rural Income Ratio(Rural Income as 1)	2.44	2.44	2.43	2.43	2.38	2.33	2.26
城镇居民人均消费支出	Of Per Capita Consumption Expenditure of Urban Households							
食品烟酒	Food, Tobacco and Liquor	27.8	27.6	26.8	26.3	26.1	26.8	26.2
交通通信	Transport and Communications	13.8	14.0	14.2	14.5	14.1	13.5	14.7
教育文化娱乐	Education, Cultural and Recreation	10.8	11.2	11.4	11.7	11.9	11.7	12.5
医疗保健	Health Care and Medical Services	7.1	7.5	7.7	7.9	8.2	8.4	8.2
农村居民人均消费支出	Of Per Capita Consumption Expenditure of Rural Households							
食品烟酒	Food, Tobacco and Liquor	30.4	29.8	28.6	28.1	27.8	29.4	29.6
交通通信	Transport and Communications	15.9	16.2	16.5	16.6	16.2	16.7	17.0
教育文化娱乐	Education, Cultural and Recreation	10.4	10.6	11.0	11.2	11.6	10.2	10.5
医疗保健	Health Care and Medical Services	10.5	10.8	10.9	10.7	10.9	11.2	10.5

注：表中2015-2019年常住人口比例、就业人员比例根据第七次人口普查结果进行了修订。

a)According to the Seventh National Census, the data of Structure of Population and Employment between 2015 to 2019 have been revised.

1-4 续表 continued

单位:% (%)

项 目	Item	2015	2016	2017	2018	2019	2020	2021
八、一般公共预算收入与地区生产总值之比	**Proportion of General Public Budget Revenue to GDP**	**10.0**	**10.0**	**9.7**	**9.7**	**9.3**	**9.0**	**8.8**
九、一般公共预算收入比例	**Of General Public Budget Revenue**							
税收收入	Tax Revenue	76.0	71.9	72.5	75.5	74.3	72.5	75.2
国内增值税	Domestic Value-added Tax	10.8	19.3	28.0	29.3	30.0	27.7	27.9
企业所得税	Corporate Income Tax	9.0	8.6	10.2	10.4	10.7	10.5	11.9
个人所得税	Individual Income Tax	2.6	2.4	3.1	3.3	2.3	2.8	3.3
十、一般公共预算支出比例	**Of of General Public Budget Expenditure**							
一般公共服务支出	Expenditure for General Public Service	8.9	8.9	9.3	9.3	9.9	10.0	9.7
科学技术支出	Expenditure for Science and Technology	1.9	1.9	2.1	2.3	2.8	2.7	3.2
教育支出	Expenditure for Education	20.5	20.9	20.4	19.9	20.1	20.3	20.6
社会保障和就业支出	Expenditure for Social Safety Net and Employment Effort	11.0	11.3	12.2	12.4	13.5	14.8	15.9
十一、交通运输	**Structure of Transport**							
货运量比例	Structure of Freight Traffic							
铁路	Railways	6.1	5.9	5.5	5.4	6.8	7.5	6.9
公路	Highways	88.2	88.7	89.3	89.5	87.3	86.6	87.3
水运	Waterways	5.7	5.3	5.2	5.1	5.8	5.9	5.8
铁路网密度(公里/万平方公里)	Railway Density (km/10 000 sq.km)	308	309	324	359	378	436	456
公路网密度(公里/万平方公里)	Highway Density (km/10 000 sq.km)	16683	16827	17130	17450	17746	18157	18241
十二、邮电通信业	**Postal and Telecommunication Services**							
电话普及率(含移动电话)(部/百人)	Popularization Rate of Telephone (Include Mobile Telephone) (set/100 persons)	106.7	105.9	107.9	113.3	118.5	118.4	121.5
移动电话普及率(部/百人)	Popularization Rate of Mobile Telephone (set/100 persons)	95.4	96.2	99.1	104.9	106.7	107.3	110.6
十三、R&D经费支出比例	**Structure of R&D Expenditure**							
#基础研究	Basic Research	2.1	2.3	2.3	3.0	3.8	3.0	3.8
应用研究	Applied Research	5.4	5.7	5.7	6.8	6.6	6.6	6.1
试验发展	Experimental Development	92.5	91.9	92.0	90.3	89.5	90.4	90.1
#政府资金	Government Funds	7.8	6.9	7.0	8.3	9.8	8.6	8.9
企业资金	Enterprises Funds	90.2	91.0	91.1	88.9	88.7	90.3	90.0
十四、卫生	**Public Health**							
卫生技术人员	**Structure of Medical Technical Personnel**							
#执业(助理)医师	Licensed (Assistant) Doctors	38.3	38.1	38.4	39.3	40.3	40.5	40.2
注册护士	Registered Nurses	41.1	41.8	42.6	43.7	43.6	43.7	44.1
每万人口执业(助理)医师数 (人)	Number of Licensed (Assistant) Doctors per 10 000 Population (person)	24.0	24.6	26.4	28.8	31.2	32.4	33.7
每万人口医疗卫生机构床位数 (张)	Number of Beds of Hospitals and Health Centers per 10 000 Population (bed)	52.6	54.4	58.3	60.4	62.3	63.7	66.3

1-5 平均每天社会经济活动

Selected Indicators on Average Daily Social and Economic Activities

指标名称	Item	2016	2017	2018	2019	2020	2021
一、全省每天创造的财富	**Daily Production**						
地区生产总值 (万元)	Gross Domestic Product (10 000 yuan)	1605532	1726359	1825996	1932616	1994470	2276600
农林牧渔业总产值 (万元)	Gross Output Value of Farming, Forestry, Animal Husbandry and Fishery (10 000 yuan)	247967	250421	257463	264977	279194	314192
建筑业总产值 (万元)	Gross Output Value of Construction (10 000 yuan)	275613	314460	353378	390939	409515	449645
一般公共预算收入 (万元)	General Public Budget Revenue (10 000 yuan)	160114	167086	177682	178814	179724	199574
原盐 (吨)	Salt (ton)	43296	38556	30652	29364	24611	20351
布 (万米)	Cloth (10 000 m)	3249	3318	1841	1216	1126	1148
发电量 (万千瓦时)	Electricity (10 000 kW·h)	147720	156911	161155	161568	159080	170146
原油 (万吨)	Crude Oil (10 000 tons)	6.29	6.12	6.14	6.13	6.08	6.06
粗钢 (吨)	Steel (ton)	195822	195833	196636	174164	219000	209570
汽车 (辆)	Motor Vehicles (unit)	3441	3844	3734	3113	3173	2940
二、全省每天消费量	**Daily Consumption**						
社会消费品零售额 (万元)	Total Retail Sails of Consumer Goods (10 000 yuan)	641587	699396	752884	801402	801316	923686
三、其他经济活动	**Other Daily Economic Activities**						
铁路、公路和水路客运人数 (万人)	Passenger Traffic (10 000 persons)	171.4	176.8	182.5	184.4	82.5	77.7
铁路、公路和水路货运量 (万吨)	Freight Traffic (10 000 tons)	769.3	883.7	957.5	834.9	845.6	913.5
住宅竣工面积 (平方米)	Floor Space of Residential Buildings Completed (sq.m)	173720	175519	220742	211908	196508	235526
四、全省人口变动和婚姻	**Daily Population Changes and Marriages**						
出生人口 (人)	Birth (person)	4849	4795	3644	3233	2384	2056
死亡人口 (人)	Death (person)	1918	2027	1973	2055	2027	2050
结婚对数 (对)	Marriages (couples)	1835	1718	1645	1464	1337	1268
离婚对数 (对)	Divorces (couples)	695	747	752	780	711	513

注：1.2020年起，铁路客货运量、周转量为济南局、北京局、郑州局在山东省内数据，口径为国家铁路。
2.平均每天出生人口和死亡人口数按常住人口计算。

a) The railway passenger and freight volume and turnover refer to the data of Jinan Bureau, Beijing Bureau and Zhengzhou Bureau in Shandong Province,the caliber is national railway.

b) Data on average daily births and deaths refers to permanent resident population.

1-6 国民经济和社会发展主要指标占全国的比重(2021年)
Proportion of Main Economic and Social Indicators to the Whole Country(2021)

指标名称		Item		山东 Shandong	全国 China	山东占全国比重(%) Proportion of Shandong to China (%)
一、人口与就业		**Population and Employment**				
年末总人口	(万人)	Population at the Year-end	(10 000 persons)	10170	141260	7.2
就业人员	(万人)	Employment	(10 000 persons)	5475	74652	7.3
二、生产总值	**(亿元)**	**Gross Domestic Product**	**(100 million yuan)**	**83095.9**	**1143669.7**	**7.3**
第一产业	(亿元)	Primary Industry	(100 million yuan)	6029.0	83085.5	7.3
第二产业	(亿元)	Secondary Industry	(100 million yuan)	33187.2	450904.5	7.4
第三产业	(亿元)	Tertiary Industry	(100 million yuan)	43879.7	609679.7	7.2
三、人均地区生产总值	**(元)**	**Per Capita Gross Domestic Product**	**(yuan)**	**81727**	**80976**	
四、农林牧渔业总产值	**(亿元)**	**Gross Output Value of Farming, Forestry, Animal Husbandry and Fishery**	**(100 million yuan)**	**11468.0**	**147013.4**	**7.8**
五、主要工农业产品产量		**Output of Major Farm and Industrial Products**				
粮食	(万吨)	Grain	(10 000 tons)	5500.7	68284.7	8.1
棉花	(万吨)	Cotton	(10 000 tons)	14.0	573.1	2.4
油料	(万吨)	Oil-bearing Crops	(10 000 tons)	285.9	3613.2	7.9
肉类	(万吨)	Meat	(10 000 tons)	819.3	8990.0	9.1
水产品	(万吨)	Aquatic products	(10 000 tons)	854.4	6463.7	13.2
原油	(万吨)	Crude Oil	(10 000 tons)	2210.7	19888.1	11.1
原盐	(万吨)	Salt	(10 000 tons)	742.8	5706.5	13.0
纱	(万吨)	Yarn	(10 000 tons)	375.5	2873.7	13.1
布	(亿米)	Cloth	(100 million m)	41.9	502.0	8.3
农用化肥	(万吨)	Chemical Fertilizer	(10 000 tons)	397.4	5543.6	7.2
水泥	(万吨)	Cement	(10 000 tons)	16444.7	237810.8	6.9
平板玻璃	(万重量箱)	Plate Glass	(10 000 weight cases)	9074.9	101920.7	8.9
粗钢	(万吨)	Steel	(10 000 tons)	7649.3	103524.3	7.4
汽车	(万辆)	Motor Vehicles	(10 000 units)	107.3	2652.8	4.0
家用电冰箱	(万台)	Household Refrigerators	(10 000 units)	888.8	8992.1	9.9
彩色电视机	(万台)	Color Television Sets	(10 000 units)	1986.7	18496.5	10.7
六、房地产开发投资	**(亿元)**	**Investment in Real Estate Development**	**(100 million yuan)**	**9819.7**	**147602.08**	**6.7**
七、财政金融		**Finance and Financial Intermediation**				
地方一般公共预算收入	(亿元)	General Public Budget Revenue	(100 million yuan)	7284.5	111077.1	6.6
地方一般公共预算支出	(亿元)	General Public Budget Expenditure	(100 million yuan)	11713.2	211271.5	5.5
住户本外币存款余额	(亿元)	RMB Savings and Deposit of Urban and Rural Households at the Year-end	(100 million yuan)	72609.8	1033117.5	7.0
八、国内贸易		**Domestic Trade**				
社会消费品零售总额	(亿元)	Total Retail Sales of Consumer Goods	(100 million yuan)	33714.5	440823.2	7.6
九、外贸外经旅游		**Foreign Trade and Tourism**				
进出口总额	(亿美元)	Total Value of Imports and Exports	(100 million USD)	4538.7	60514.9	7.5
出口总额	(亿美元)	Exports	(100 million USD)	2718.4	33639.6	8.1
十、价格指数		**Price Indices**				
商品零售价格指数	(上年=100)	Retail Price Indices	(preceding year=100)	101.4	101.6	
居民消费价格指数	(上年=100)	Consumer Price Indices	(preceding year=100)	101.2	100.9	
工业生产者出厂价格指数	(上年=100)	Producer Price Indices for Industrial Products	(preceding year=100)	110.3	108.1	
十一、人民生活		**People's Livelihood**				
城镇单位就业人员平均工资	(元)	Average Wage of Employed Persons in Urban Units	(yuan)	94768	106837	
全体居民人均可支配收入	(元)	Disposable Income of All Households	(yuan)	35705	35128	
城镇居民人均可支配收入	(元)	Disposable Income of Urban Households	(yuan)	47066	47412	
农村居民人均可支配收入	(元)	Disposable Income of Rural Households	(yuan)	20794	18931	
十二、教育、卫生		**Education and Health Care**				
研究生在校生数	(万人)	Total Enrollment of Institutions of Higher Education	(10 000 persons)	14.9	333.2	4.5
医院床位数	(万张)	Number of Hospital Beds	(10 000 beds)	67.4	741.2	9.1
卫生技术人员数	(万人)	Number of Medical Technical Personnel	(10 000 persons)	85.3	1124.2	7.6

1-7 按行业分法人单位数

Number of Corporate Units by Sector

单位:个 (unit)

行 业	Sector	2018	2019	2020	2021
总 计	**Total**	**1801301**	**2309350**	**2842426**	**3261425**
农、林、牧、渔业	Agriculture,Forestry,Animal Husbandry and Fishing	24243	125306	160524	176239
采矿业	Mining	2358	2558	2795	2759
制造业	Manufacturing	310428	354724	416009	454353
电力、燃气及水的生产和供应业	Production and Supply of Electric Power and Heat Power	6280	6939	7884	9284
建筑业	Construction	124512	185126	245179	299765
批发和零售业	Wholesale and Retail Trade	598403	728791	906404	1063075
交通运输、仓储和邮政业	Traffic,Transport,Storage and Post	52848	66140	82583	94666
住宿和餐饮业	Hotels and Catering Services	28234	34177	41439	49281
信息传输、软件和信息技术服务业	Information Transfer, Software and Information Technology Services	58722	81022	105443	130317
金融业	Financial Intermediation	5783	8144	9842	11655
房地产业	Real Estate	51380	62011	73834	84202
租赁和商务服务业	Leasing and Business Services	171491	232003	297319	356897
科学研究和技术服务业	Scientific Research and Technical Service	93529	119160	153680	188504
水利、环境和公共设施管理业	Management of Water Conservancy,Environment and Public Facilities	10758	14663	20713	26329
居民服务、修理和其他服务业	Households Services, Repair and Other Services	33873	39141	47685	54892
教 育	Education	43057	52077	63276	65006
卫生和社会工作	Health and Social Work	18784	20243	22428	20417
文化、体育和娱乐业	Culture,Sports and Entertainment	37583	43350	50216	55878
公共管理、社会保障和社会组织	Public management,Social Security and Social Organization	129035	133775	135173	117906
国际组织	International Organization				

1-8　按机构类型分法人单位数

Number of Corporate Units by Status of Organization

单位:个　(unit)

机构类型	Organization Status	2015	2016	2017	2018	2019	2020	2021
合　计	**Total**	**1269917**	**1652065**	**2014790**	**1801301**	**2309350**	**2842426**	**3261425**
企　业	Enterprises	1048470	1344176	1675975	1547260	1982468	2483474	2928948
事业单位	Institutions	40919	44903	48350	50681	47378	47480	39744
机　关	Agencies & Organizations	12411	12826	12304	12465	12213	12417	10835
社会团体	Social Groups	15919	18819	20929	13337	17384	18876	14015
民办非企业单位	Private Non-enterprise Units	16098	19740	24624	28723	34781	39907	34220
基金会	Foundation	81	99	115	116	153	185	195
居委会	Neighborhood Committee	7507	7323	7048	7307	7463	7424	6905
村委会	Village Committee	73947	73909	73453	71411	73870	73589	67156
农民专业合作社	Professional Farmers Cooperatives		110936	136031	58750	122477	148883	151584
其他组织机构	Others	54565	19334	15961	11251	11163	10191	7823

1-9　按地区分法人单位数

Number of Corporate Units by Region

单位:个　(unit)

地　区	Region	2015	2016	2017	2018	2019	2020	2021
全省总计	**Total**	**1269917**	**1652065**	**2014790**	**1801301**	**2309350**	**2842426**	**3261425**
济 南 市	Jinan	119575	144859	162066	200414	285944	363089	421843
青 岛 市	Qingdao	230230	302471	345793	359226	427061	504379	553871
淄 博 市	Zibo	68198	89514	115280	97597	114573	134612	150309
枣 庄 市	Zaozhuang	37887	47322	60639	38717	62031	79353	91359
东 营 市	Dongying	28465	39590	49073	39374	51023	63279	75052
烟 台 市	Yantai	118699	151831	168440	182515	200567	231694	257964
潍 坊 市	Weifang	115593	154860	194938	174232	229327	276417	304145
济 宁 市	Jining	101533	123715	153557	130348	177396	214475	248556
泰 安 市	Tai'an	56600	69235	79894	65349	72766	92032	115482
威 海 市	Weihai	51595	69610	86039	64510	78757	92520	106762
日 照 市	Rizhao	29516	37205	48228	52880	69645	86002	95960
莱 芜 市	Laiwu	17200	22005	28270	29883			
临 沂 市	Linyi	92164	121410	167916	109478	178389	241088	294325
德 州 市	Dezhou	51189	64949	83694	70831	91383	111800	120371
聊 城 市	Liaocheng	46442	59745	80289	60844	90489	123109	152017
滨 州 市	Binzhou	44869	61010	76260	58839	85354	110797	128797
菏 泽 市	Heze	60162	92734	114414	66264	94645	117780	144612

注：根据行政区划调整，2019年起，莱芜市并入济南市，以下表同。
a)According to administrative division adjustment,Laiwu City merged into Jinan City from 2019.The same applies to tables following.

主要统计指标解释

行政区划 指国家对行政区域的划分。根据宪法规定，我国的行政区域划分如下：(1)全国分为省、自治区、直辖市；(2)省、自治区分为自治州、县、自治县、市；(3)自治州分为县、自治县、市；(4)县、自治县分为乡、民族乡、镇；(5)直辖市和较大的市分为区、县；(6)国家在必要时设立的特别行政区。

国民经济行业分类 自2017年统计年报开始使用新的《国民经济行业分类》(GB/T4754-2017)，该分类是由国家统计局组织修订，经原国家质量监督检验检疫总局和国家标准化管理委员会批准，于2017年6月30日发布。这次修订是在2011年分类标准的基础上，参照联合国《所有经济活动的国际标准产业分类》(ISIC/Rev.4)进行的。修订后的《国民经济行业分类》(GB/T4754-2017)共有门类20个，大类97个，中类473个，小类1380个。大类增加1个，中类增加41个，小类增加286个。

企业(单位)登记注册类型 是以在工商行政管理机关登记注册的各类企业为划分对象，以工商行政管理部门对企业登记注册的类型为依据，将企业登记注册类型分为内资企业、港澳台商投资企业和外商投资企业三大类。内资企业包括国有企业、集体企业、股份合作企业、联营企业、有限责任公司、股份有限公司、私营公司和其他企业；港澳台商投资企业和外商投资企业分别包括合资经营企业、合作经营企业、独资经营企业和股份有限公司。对不在工商行政管理部门进行登记注册的行政机关、事业单位和社会团体，主要按其经费来源和管理方式进行划分。

国有企业 指企业全部资产归国家所有，并按《中华人民共和国企业法人登记管理条例》规定登记注册的非公司制的经济组织。不包括有限责任公司中的国有独资公司。

集体企业 指企业资产归集体所有，并按《中华人民共和国企业法人登记管理条例》规定登记注册的经济组织。

股份合作企业 指以合作制为基础，由企业职工共同出资入股，吸收一定比例的社会资产投资组建，实行自主经营，自负盈亏，共同劳动，民主管理，按劳分配与按股分红相结合的一种集体经济组织。

联营企业 指两个及两个以上相同或不同所有制性质的企业法人或事业单位法人，按自愿、平等、互利的原则，共同投资组成的经济组织。联营企业包括国有联营企业、集体联营企业、国有与集体联营企业和其他联营企业。

有限责任公司 指根据《中华人民共和国公司登记管理条例》规定登记注册，由两个以上、五十个以下的股东共同出资，每个股东以其所认缴的出资额对公司承担有限责任，公司以其全部资产对其债务承担责任的经济组织。有限责任公司包括国有独资公司以及其他有限责任公司。

股份有限公司 指根据《中华人民共和国公司登记管理条例》规定登记注册，其全部注册资本由等额股份构成并通过发行股票筹集资本，股东以其认购的股份对公司承担有限责任，公司以其全部资产对其债务承担责任的经济组织。

私营企业 指由自然人投资设立或由自然人控股，以雇佣劳动为基础的营利性经济组织。包括按照《公司法》《合伙企业法》《私营企业暂行条例》规定登记注册的私营有限责任公司、私营股份有限公司、私营合伙企业和私营独资企业。

其他企业 指上述企业之外的其他内资经济组织。

与港澳台商合资经营企业 指港澳台地区投资者与内地企业依照《中华人民共和国中外合资经营企业法》及有关法律的规定，按合同规定的比例投资设立、分享利润和分担风险的企业。

与港澳台商合作经营企业 指港澳台地区投资者与内地企业依照《中华人民共和国中外合作经营企业法》及有关法律的规定，依照合作合同的约定进行投资或提供条件设立、分配利润和分担风险的企业。

港澳台商独资经营企业 指依照《中华人民共和国外资企业法》及有关法律的规定，在内地由港澳台地区投资者全额投资设立的企业。

港澳台商投资股份有限公司 指根据国家有关规定，经原外经贸部依法批准设立，其中港、澳、台商的股本占公司注册资本的比例达25%以上的股份有限公司。凡其中港、澳、台商的股本占公司注册资本的比例小于25%的，属于内资企业中的股份有限公司。

中外合资经营企业 指外国企业或外国人与中国内地企业依照《中华人民共和国中外合资经营企业法》及有关法律的规定，按合同规定的比例投资设立、分享利润和分担风险的企业。

中外合作经营企业 指外国企业或外国人与中国内地企业依照《中华人民共和国中外合作经营企业法》及有关法律的规定，依照合作合同的约定进行投资或提供条件设立、分配利润和分担风险的企业。

外资企业 指依照《中华人民共和国外资企业法》及有关法律的规定，在中国内地由外国投资者全额投资设立的企业。

外商投资股份有限公司 指根据国家有关规定，经原外经贸部依法批准设立，其中外资的股本占公司注册资本的比例达25%以上的股份有限公司。凡其中外资股本占公司注册资本的比例小于25%的，属于内资企业中的股份有限公司。

行政机关、事业单位和社会团体 参照企业登记注册类型，主要按其经费来源和管理方式划分。具体规定如下：

⑴行政机关：包括国家机关和政党机关，原则上均列为“国有”。但有特殊规定的，如供销社等，则列为“集体”。

⑵事业单位：包括经国家机构编制部门和有关业务主管部门批准成立的各类事业单位，不包括实行企业化管理的事业单位。事业单位的划分办法如下：

①由国家财政预算拨款或列入财政预算外资金管理以及经费主要来源于国有主管部门或国有上级单位的事业单位，列为“国有”。

②经费主要来源于集体单位的事业单位，列为“集体”。

③公民个人(或个人合伙)开办的事业单位，列为“私营”。

④上述以外的其他事业单位，如果其经费来源不明确，按管理方式进行归类。

⑶社会团体：包括经民政部门批准成立以及未纳入社会团体管理条例范围的工会、妇联等各类社会团体。社会团体的划分办法如下：

①未纳入民政部社会团体管理条例范围的工会、妇联、共青团、青联、工商联、科协、侨联等社会团体，国家拨款设立的基金会或基金管理组织以及经费主要来源于国有业务主管部门或国有上级单位的社会团体，列为“国有”。

②经费主要来源于集体单位的社会团体，列为“集体”。

③公民个人(或个人合伙)开办的社会团体，划为“私营”。

④上述以外的其他社会团体，如果其经费来源不明确，改按管理方式进行归类。

Explanatory Notes on Main Statistical Indicators

Divisions of Administrative Areas refers to the division of administrative areas by the state. The Constitution of the People Republic of China stipulates that the administrative areas in China are divided as: 1) The whole country is divided into provinces, autonomous regions and municipalities directly under the central government; 2) Provinces and autonomous regions are divided into autonomous prefectures, counties, autonomous counties and cities; 3) Autonomous prefectures are divided into counties, autonomous counties and cities; 4) Counties and autonomous counties are divided into townships, nationality townships and towns; 5) Municipalities and large cities are divided into districts and counties, 6) The state shall, when necessary, establish special administrative regions.

Industrial Classification of the National Economy The new Industrial Classification of the National Economy (GB/T 4754-2017) is used in **Industrial Classification of the National Economy** starting from the compilation of 2017 annual statistics. This Classification is revised and organized by the National Bureau of Statistics, promulgated by the National Administration of Quality Supervision, Inspection and Quarantine and Standardization Administration of the People's Republic of China on June 30, 2017. This revision is taking into consideration of the International Standards of the Industrial Classification of All Economic Activities (ISIC/Rev.4) of the United Nations, and based on the the Classification Standard in 2011. The revised version of the Industrial Classification of the National Economy (GB/T 4754-2017) is composed of 20 major divisions, 97 divisions, 473 major groups and 1380 groups, added 1 division, 41 major groups and 286 groups.

Registration Status of Enterprises are classified into 3 categories, namely domestic funded enterprises, enterprises with investment from Hong Kong, Macau and Taiwan, and enterprises with foreign investment, in the light of the registration status of an enterprise in industrial and commercial administration agencies. Domestic-funded enterprises include state-owned enterprises, collective-owned enterprises, cooperative enterprises, joint ownership enterprises, limited liability corporations, share-holding corporations Ltd., private enterprises and other enterprises. Included in the enterprises with investment from Hong Kong, Macau and Taiwan and enterprises with foreign investment are joint-venture enterprises, cooperative enterprises, sole investment enterprises and share holding corporations Ltd. For government agencies, institutions and social organizations which are not requested to be registered in industrial and commercial administration agencies, they are classified mainly by their sources of funds and way of management.

State-owned Enterprises refer to non-corporation economic units where the entire assets are owned by the state and which have registered in accordance with the Regulation of the People' s Republic of China on the Management of Registration of Corporate Enterprises. Excluded from this category are sole state funded corporations in the limited liability corporations.

Collective-owned Enterprises refer to economic units where the assets are owned collectively and which have registered in accordance with the Regulation of the People' s Republic of China on the Management of Registration of Corporate Enterprises.

Cooperative Enterprises refer to a form of collective economic units (enterprises) where capitals come mainly from employees as their shares, with certain proportion of capital from the outside, where production is organized on the basis of independent operation, independent accounting for profits and losses, joint work, democratic management, and a distribution system that integrates remuneration according to work with dividend according to capital share.

Joint Ownership Enterprises refer to economic units established by two or more corporate enterprises or corporate institutions of the same or different ownership, through joint investment on the basis of equality, voluntary participation and mutual benefits. They include state joint ownership enterprises, collective joint ownership enterprises, joint state-collective enterprises, other joint ownership enterprises.

Limited Liability Corporations refer to economic units established with investment from 2-50 investors and registered in accordance with the Regulation of the People' s Republic of China on the Management of Registration of Corporations, each investor bearing limited liability to the corporation depending on its share of investment, and the corporation bearing liability to its debt to the maximum of its total assets. Limited liability corporations include exclusive state funded limited liability corporations and other limited liability corporations.

Share-holding Corporations Ltd. refer to economic units registered in accordance with the Regulation of the People' s Republic of China on the Management of Registration of Corporations, with total registered capitals divided into equal shares and raised through issuing stocks. Each investor bears limited liability to the corporation depending on the holding of shares, and the corporation bears liability to its debt to the maximum of its total assets.

Private Enterprises refer to profit-making economic units invested and established by natural persons, or controlled by natural persons using employed labour. Included in this category are private limited liability corporations, private share-holding corporations Ltd., private partnership enterprises and private-funded enterprises registered in accordance with the Corporation Law, Partnership Enterprises Law and Interim Regulations on Private Enterprises.

Other Domestic-funded Enterprises refer to domestic funded economic units other than those mentioned above.

Cooperative Enterprises with Funds from Hong Kong Macau and Taiwan established by investors from Hong

Kong, Macau and Taiwan with enterprises in the mainland of China in accordance with the Law of the People' s Republic of China on Sino-foreign Cooperative Enterprises and other relevant laws, where the investment or provision of facilities, and the share of profits and risks is stipulated in the cooperative contract.

Enterprises with Sole (exclusive) Investment from Hong Kong, Macau and Taiwan refer to enterprises established in the mainland of China with exclusive investment from investors from Hong Kong, Macau and Taiwan in accordance with the Law of the People's Republic of China on Foreign Funded Enterprises and other relevant laws.

Share-holding Corporations Ltd. with Investment from Hong Kong, Macau and Taiwan refer to share holding corporations Ltd. established with the approval from the former Ministry of Foreign Trade and Economic Relations in line with relevant state regulations, where the share of investment from Hong Kong, Macau or Taiwan businessmen exceeds 25% of the total registered capital of the corporation. In case the share of investment from Hong Kong, Macau or Taiwan is less than 25% of the total registered capital, the enterprise is to be classified as domestic-funded share-holding corporation Ltd.

Joint-venture Enterprises with Foreign Investment refer to enterprises jointly established by foreign enterprises or foreigners with enterprises in the mainland of China in accordance with the Law of the People' s Republic of China on Sino-foreign Joint Venture Enterprises and other relevant laws, where the share of investment, profits and risks is stipulated in the contract.

Cooperation Enterprises with Foreign Investment refer to enterprises jointly established by foreign enterprises or foreigners with enterprises in the mainland of China in accordance with the Law of the People' s Republic of China on Sino foreign Cooperative Enterprises and other relevant laws, where the investment or provision of facilities, and the share of profits and risks is stipulated in the cooperative contract.

Enterprises with Sole (exclusive) Foreign Investment refer to enterprises established in the mainland of China with exclusive investment from foreign investors in accordance with the Law of the People' s Republic of China on Foreign Funded Enterprises and other relevant laws.

Share-holding Corporations Ltd. with Foreign Investment refer to share-holding corporations Ltd. established with the approval from the Ministry of Foreign Trade and Economic Relations in line with relevant state regulations, where the share of investment from foreign investors exceeds 25% of the total registered capital of the corporation. In case the share of foreign investment is less than 25% of the total registered capital, the enterprise is to be classified as domestic funded share holding corporation Ltd.

Government Agencies, Institutions and Social Organizations are classified into following categories by source of funds and way of management taking reference of the registration status of enterprises:

(1) Government agencies: include state and party agencies, classified in principle as state owned. There are exceptions, such as supply and marketing cooperatives which are classified as collective-owned.

(2) Institutions: include institutions of various types established with the approval by organization and staffing departments of the government, but exclude institutions where enterprise management system is introduced. Institutions are further classified as follows:

(a) Institutions whose main budget is listed in the government budget appropriations or extra budget funds, or allocated from the budget of their competent government agencies. Such institutions are classified as state owned.

(b) Institutions whose budget mainly comes from collective units. Such institutions are classified as collective owned.

(c) Social organizations established by individual or a group of citizens, which are classified as private.

(d) Institutions other than those mentioned above whose source of budget is not clear. Such institutions are classified by way of management.

(3) Social organizations: include social organizations established with the approval from the Ministry of Civil Affairs, and organizations that are not covered by social organization management regulations such as trade unions, women federations etc.. Social organizations are further classified as follows:

(a) Social organizations that are not covered by social organization management regulations of the Ministry of Civil Affairs such as trade unions, women federations, communist youth leagues, youth associations, industrial and commerce associations, scientists associations, overseas Chinese associations, etc., foundations and fund management organizations established with funds from the state, and social organizations whose funds mainly come from the budget of their competent government agencies. Such institutions are classified as state owned.

(b) Social organizations whose budget mainly comes from collective units. Such institutions are classified as collective owned.

(c) Social organizations established by individual or a group of citizens, which are classified as private.

(d) Social organizations other than those mentioned above whose source of budget is not clear. Such organizations are classified by way of management.

第
2
篇

国民经济核算

National Accounts

简 要 说 明

一、本篇资料的主要内容

本篇资料从宏观上反映了经济发展的总体状况和发展水平，主要包括地区生产总值及其增长、结构、三次产业对经济增长的贡献等方面的资料。

根据国家统计局统一要求，支出法地区生产总值历史数据修订工作正在进行中，故暂时无法提供按支出法计算的地区生产总值及居民消费水平等数据。

二、本篇资料的来源

本篇资料来源于国民经济核算统计报表，由省统计局核算处整理提供。

Brief Introduction

I. Main Content

Data in the chapter reflect the overall situation and development of economy on the macro level, including growth rate and components of GDP, share of the three industries to the increase of GDP and household consumption expenditure.

According to the unified work arrangement of the National Bureau of Statistics, the work of revising the historical data of GDP by Expenditure Approach is in progress, so data of GDP by Expenditure Approach and the Resident Consumption Level can't be provided temporarily.

II. Source of Data

Data in this chapter are prepared according to the data of national accounts and compiled by the Division of National Accounts of Shandong Provincial Bureau of Statistics.

2-1 主要年份地区生产总值

Gross Domestic Product in Major Years

单位:亿元 (100 million yuan)

年 份 Year	地 区 生产总值 Gross Domestic Product	第一产业 Primary Industry	第二产业 Secondary Industry	第三产业 Tertiary Industry	#工 业 Industry	#建筑业 Construction	人均地区生产总值(元) Per Capita GDP (yuan)
1952	43.81	29.55	7.27	6.99	6.82	0.45	91
1955	57.78	35.52	11.42	10.84	10.81	0.61	113
1957	61.39	31.95	17.59	11.85	16.62	0.97	116
1962	64.38	30.42	16.91	17.05	15.90	1.01	120
1965	86.25	42.24	28.96	15.05	25.99	2.97	152
1970	126.31	52.23	53.71	20.37	50.16	3.55	199
1975	166.19	65.54	75.31	25.34	69.76	5.55	240
1978	225.45	75.06	119.35	31.04	108.53	10.82	316
1979	251.60	91.12	127.68	32.80	114.67	13.01	350
1980	292.13	106.43	146.11	39.59	130.55	15.56	402
1981	346.57	132.21	155.41	58.95	138.09	17.32	472
1982	395.38	154.07	166.05	75.26	147.10	18.95	531
1983	459.83	185.57	178.75	95.51	159.15	19.60	611
1984	581.56	222.13	239.27	120.16	214.20	25.07	765
1985	680.46	235.96	293.07	151.43	259.42	33.65	887
1986	742.05	252.73	313.21	176.11	274.80	38.41	956
1987	892.29	287.31	384.57	220.41	341.31	43.26	1131
1988	1117.66	331.94	497.10	288.62	435.51	61.59	1395
1989	1293.94	359.14	579.65	355.15	513.97	65.68	1595
1990	1511.19	425.29	635.98	449.92	568.25	67.73	1815
1991	1810.54	521.85	745.90	542.79	663.90	82.00	2122
1992	2196.53	534.62	999.11	662.80	889.59	109.52	2557
1993	2770.37	596.63	1355.71	818.03	1201.67	154.04	3212
1994	3844.50	775.03	1891.43	1178.04	1692.10	199.33	4441
1995	4953.35	1010.13	2355.78	1587.44	2098.06	257.73	5701
1996	5883.80	1200.17	2784.09	1899.54	2475.99	308.10	6746
1997	6537.07	1195.00	3147.37	2194.70	2796.02	351.35	7461
1998	7021.35	1215.81	3408.06	2397.49	3008.45	399.61	7968
1999	7493.84	1221.00	3644.32	2628.52	3197.16	447.16	8483
2000	8278.06	1252.08	4120.19	2905.79	3620.06	500.13	9260
2001	9076.22	1340.46	4466.74	3269.02	3911.03	555.71	10063
2002	10076.52	1369.15	5037.63	3669.74	4364.37	673.26	11120
2003	10903.23	1456.98	5720.01	3726.24	4995.68	724.33	11977
2004	13308.08	1748.22	7327.61	4232.25	6497.70	829.91	14540
2005	15947.51	1928.17	8841.13	5178.21	7875.58	965.55	17308
2006	18967.80	2098.26	10568.49	6301.05	9467.48	1101.01	20443
2007	22718.06	2451.01	12529.41	7737.64	11233.13	1296.28	24329
2008	27106.22	2876.20	14911.50	9318.52	13310.80	1600.70	28861
2009	29540.80	3076.19	15919.67	10544.94	13998.52	1921.15	31282
2010	33922.49	3411.34	17733.08	12778.07	15449.95	2283.13	35599
2011	39064.93	3768.55	19926.11	15370.27	17280.78	2645.33	40581
2012	42957.31	4047.06	21275.89	17634.36	18421.90	2853.99	44348
2013	47344.33	4454.11	22615.89	20274.33	19475.30	3188.60	48673
2014	50774.84	4662.81	23588.02	22524.01	20178.23	3476.06	51933
2015	55288.79	4902.82	24814.88	25571.09	21156.50	3731.63	56205
2016	58762.46	4830.25	25565.04	28367.17	21695.98	3909.44	59239
2017	63012.10	4832.71	26925.59	31253.80	22515.81	4441.01	62993
2018	66648.87	4950.52	27523.67	34174.68	22613.01	5024.90	66284
2019	70540.48	5116.99	28171.78	37251.71	22755.13	5532.77	69901
2020	72798.17	5364.35	28456.66	38977.16	22986.45	5574.19	71825
2021	83095.90	6029.03	33187.16	43879.71	27243.55	6094.45	81727

注:1. 本表按当年价格计算。
2. 根据第四次经济普查结果，对全省2000—2018年生产总值进行了修订。
3. 2021年数据为初步核算数(以下相关表同)。
4. 根据第七次人口普查结果，对全省2011—2019年人均生产总值进行了修订(以下相关表同)。

a) Data in this table are calculated at current prices.
b) According to the Fourth National Economic Census, the data of GDP from 2000 to 2018 of Shandong have been revised.
c) The data of 2021 come form the number of preliminary accounting(the same as in the following tables).
d)According to the Seventh National Census,the data of GDP per capita from 2011 to 2019 of Shandong have been revised(the same as in the following tables).

2-2 主要年份地区生产总值指数

Indices of Gross Domestic Product in Major Years

(以1952年为100) (1952=100)

年 份 Year	地 区 生产总值 Gross Domestic Product	第一产业 Primary Industry	第二产业 Secondary Industry	第三产业 Tertiary Industry	#工 业 Industry	#建筑业 Construction
1952	100.0	100.0	100.0	100.0	100.0	100.0
1955	127.4	115.6	155.2	147.0	157.1	127.3
1957	137.4	101.6	261.9	154.6	264.5	222.5
1962	113.4	69.6	214.8	184.4	213.0	238.4
1965	171.1	107.1	404.7	197.9	385.5	679.0
1970	251.6	129.1	752.8	261.0	747.3	825.5
1975	361.5	154.4	1364.7	310.7	1372.4	1222.2
1978	466.1	174.3	1945.2	379.7	1904.6	2547.8
1979	496.9	188.7	2067.8	395.2	2001.7	3066.1
1980	557.7	207.2	2315.5	470.1	2230.1	3612.1
1981	589.9	220.6	2388.6	524.9	2326.7	3369.6
1982	656.3	244.3	2522.3	667.6	2440.2	3786.0
1983	747.4	283.3	2712.8	825.9	2644.2	3803.4
1984	877.3	335.1	3191.5	951.8	3085.0	4824.9
1985	977.4	342.3	3780.2	1094.0	3612.6	6280.4
1986	1038.4	340.0	4184.8	1189.3	4029.1	6546.0
1987	1182.0	365.0	4898.3	1391.9	4786.5	6703.9
1988	1330.2	364.1	6007.7	1526.1	5850.6	8493.7
1989	1383.0	361.7	6431.1	1568.0	6348.5	7929.7
1990	1455.6	381.0	6890.7	1578.2	6856.4	7761.3
1991	1668.4	435.0	7852.0	1830.7	7881.5	8192.2
1992	1950.5	435.6	10095.2	2129.1	10201.7	9881.3
1993	2347.5	462.2	12928.1	2553.8	13124.4	12085.4
1994	2728.7	495.9	15178.6	3081.3	15432.8	13962.6
1995	3110.0	540.3	17316.2	3604.3	17555.3	16412.5
1996	3484.8	575.9	19711.9	4053.9	19965.0	18865.3
1997	3871.4	578.6	22218.1	4639.7	22500.5	21290.6
1998	4287.6	611.3	24899.0	5159.4	25218.7	23828.6
1999	4717.3	640.1	27902.2	5639.3	28300.6	26321.9
2000	5164.9	655.1	30913.4	6235.7	31374.3	28976.9
2001	5650.4	679.9	34004.5	6920.0	34524.3	31789.3
2002	6272.0	696.5	38736.5	7636.1	39113.1	37653.9
2003	6949.4	734.4	43967.8	8314.1	44593.1	41416.4
2004	7818.0	784.7	50992.2	9086.7	52513.4	42711.3
2005	8803.1	821.9	58393.5	10205.3	60374.9	47310.5
2006	9885.9	862.4	66431.1	11485.2	68961.9	52054.1
2007	11062.3	895.8	75125.0	12936.9	78460.7	55838.7
2008	12135.4	938.2	82158.3	14473.5	86163.7	58781.6
2009	13324.6	976.1	91377.0	15793.2	94658.2	72879.4
2010	14710.4	1006.3	102047.6	17417.1	105682.9	81575.7
2011	16284.4	1044.0	113741.2	19420.7	118589.2	86765.1
2012	17864.0	1091.4	125476.1	21387.1	131379.7	92815.2
2013	19543.2	1129.5	137729.1	23587.1	144601.3	101726.2
2014	21204.4	1172.2	149816.6	25748.1	157319.4	111049.5
2015	22858.3	1220.9	160408.1	28212.8	168215.0	120084.1
2016	24554.6	1267.8	170359.5	30833.1	178426.6	127264.4
2017	26352.1	1312.9	180536.8	33693.5	189478.4	132822.5
2018	28013.0	1347.8	188000.6	36697.4	197929.8	138455.7
2019	29483.7	1362.1	192953.8	39713.3	201840.0	147443.8
2020	30500.9	1398.3	199064.2	41224.4	208778.9	149686.1
2021	33021.6	1502.5	213324.6	45008.6	226633.9	152327.4

注：本表按可比价格计算。

a) Data in this table are calculated at constant prices.

2-2 续表 continued

(以上年为100) (preceding year=100)

年 份 Year	地 区 生产总值 Gross Domestic Product	第一产业 Primary Industry	第二产业 Secondary Industry	第三产业 Tertiary Industry	#工 业 Industry	#建筑业 Construction	人均地区 生产总值 Per Capita GDP
1955	109.5	110.4	104.5	112.2	104.7	101.6	107.0
1957	96.5	87.5	110.8	101.9	112.9	83.0	95.2
1962	97.4	106.8	79.8	108.2	80.7	70.7	95.1
1965	122.0	126.6	130.0	102.5	125.7	180.2	120.4
1970	115.7	103.5	126.1	117.4	127.1	114.9	112.6
1975	129.2	110.6	159.8	104.7	163.6	113.1	127.8
1978	110.1	94.0	125.4	100.8	123.5	152.1	109.1
1979	106.6	108.2	106.3	104.1	105.1	120.3	105.8
1980	112.2	109.8	112.0	118.9	111.4	117.8	111.0
1981	105.8	106.5	103.2	111.7	104.3	93.3	104.7
1982	111.3	110.8	105.6	127.2	104.9	112.4	109.7
1983	113.9	116.0	107.6	123.7	108.4	100.5	112.7
1984	117.4	118.3	117.6	115.3	116.7	126.9	116.2
1985	111.4	102.1	118.4	114.9	117.1	130.2	110.4
1986	106.2	99.3	110.7	108.7	111.5	104.2	105.0
1987	113.8	107.3	117.0	117.0	118.8	102.4	112.0
1988	112.5	99.7	122.6	109.6	122.2	126.7	110.8
1989	104.0	99.3	107.0	102.7	108.5	93.4	102.7
1990	105.3	105.3	107.1	100.6	108.0	97.9	102.6
1991	114.6	114.2	114.0	116.0	115.0	105.6	111.8
1992	116.9	100.2	128.6	116.3	129.4	120.6	116.1
1993	120.4	106.1	128.1	120.0	128.6	122.3	119.9
1994	116.2	107.3	117.4	120.7	117.6	115.5	115.8
1995	114.0	108.9	114.1	117.0	113.8	117.5	113.6
1996	112.1	106.6	113.8	112.5	113.7	114.9	111.6
1997	111.1	100.5	112.7	114.4	112.7	112.9	110.6
1998	110.8	105.7	112.1	111.2	112.1	111.9	110.1
1999	110.0	104.7	112.1	109.3	112.2	110.5	109.4
2000	109.5	102.4	110.8	110.6	110.9	110.1	108.5
2001	109.4	103.8	110.0	111.0	110.0	109.7	108.4
2002	111.0	102.5	113.9	110.3	113.3	118.4	110.5
2003	110.8	105.4	113.5	108.9	114.0	110.0	110.3
2004	112.5	106.8	116.0	109.3	117.8	103.1	111.9
2005	112.6	104.7	114.5	112.3	115.0	110.8	111.8
2006	112.3	104.9	113.8	112.5	114.2	110.0	111.5
2007	111.9	103.9	113.1	112.6	113.8	107.3	111.2
2008	109.7	104.7	109.4	111.9	109.8	105.3	109.1
2009	109.8	104.0	111.2	109.1	109.9	124.0	109.2
2010	110.4	103.1	111.7	110.3	111.6	111.9	109.4
2011	110.7	103.7	111.5	111.5	112.2	106.4	109.6
2012	109.7	104.5	110.3	110.1	110.8	107.0	109.0
2013	109.4	103.5	109.8	110.3	110.1	109.6	108.9
2014	108.5	103.8	108.8	109.2	108.8	109.2	107.9
2015	107.8	104.2	107.1	109.6	106.9	108.1	107.1
2016	107.4	103.8	106.2	109.3	106.1	106.0	106.5
2017	107.3	103.6	106.0	109.3	106.2	104.4	106.4
2018	106.3	102.7	104.1	108.9	104.5	104.2	105.8
2019	105.3	101.1	102.6	108.2	102.0	106.5	104.9
2020	103.5	102.7	103.2	103.8	103.4	101.5	103.0
2021	108.3	107.5	107.2	109.2	108.6	101.8	107.9

2-3 主要年份地区生产总值构成

Composition of Gross Domestic Product in Major Years

单位:% (%)

年 份 Year	地 区 生产总值 Gross Domestic Product	第一产业 Primary Industry	第二产业 Secondary Industry	第三产业 Tertiary Industry	#工 业 Industry	#建筑业 Construction
1952	100	67.4	16.6	16.0	15.6	1.0
1955	100	61.5	19.7	18.8	18.7	1.0
1957	100	52.0	28.7	19.3	27.1	1.6
1962	100	47.2	26.3	26.5	24.7	1.6
1965	100	49.0	33.5	17.5	30.1	3.4
1970	100	41.4	42.5	16.1	39.7	2.8
1975	100	39.4	45.3	15.3	42.0	3.3
1978	100	33.3	52.9	13.8	48.1	4.8
1979	100	36.2	50.8	13.0	45.6	5.2
1980	100	36.4	50.0	13.6	44.7	5.3
1981	100	38.2	44.8	17.0	39.8	5.0
1982	100	39.0	42.0	19.0	37.2	4.8
1983	100	40.3	38.9	20.8	34.6	4.3
1984	100	38.2	41.1	20.7	36.8	4.3
1985	100	34.7	43.0	22.3	38.1	4.9
1986	100	34.1	42.2	23.7	37.0	5.2
1987	100	32.2	43.1	24.7	38.3	4.8
1988	100	29.7	44.5	25.8	39.0	5.5
1989	100	27.8	44.8	27.4	39.7	5.1
1990	100	28.1	42.1	29.8	37.6	4.5
1991	100	28.8	41.2	30.0	36.7	4.5
1992	100	24.3	45.5	30.2	40.5	5.0
1993	100	21.5	49.0	29.5	43.4	5.6
1994	100	20.2	49.2	30.6	44.0	5.2
1995	100	20.4	47.6	32.0	42.4	5.2
1996	100	20.4	47.3	32.3	42.1	5.2
1997	100	18.3	48.1	33.6	42.7	5.4
1998	100	17.3	48.5	34.2	42.8	5.7
1999	100	16.3	48.6	35.1	42.6	6.0
2000	100	15.1	49.8	35.1	43.7	6.0
2001	100	14.8	49.2	36.0	43.1	6.1
2002	100	13.6	50.0	36.4	43.3	6.7
2003	100	13.4	52.4	34.2	45.8	6.6
2004	100	13.1	55.1	31.8	48.8	6.2
2005	100	12.1	55.4	32.5	49.4	6.1
2006	100	11.1	55.7	33.2	49.9	5.8
2007	100	10.8	55.1	34.1	49.4	5.7
2008	100	10.6	55.0	34.4	49.1	5.9
2009	100	10.4	53.9	35.7	47.4	6.5
2010	100	10.1	52.2	37.7	45.5	6.7
2011	100	9.6	51.1	39.3	44.2	6.8
2012	100	9.4	49.5	41.1	42.9	6.6
2013	100	9.4	47.8	42.8	41.1	6.7
2014	100	9.2	46.4	44.4	39.7	6.8
2015	100	8.9	44.9	46.2	38.3	6.7
2016	100	8.2	43.5	48.3	36.9	6.7
2017	100	7.7	42.7	49.6	35.7	7.0
2018	100	7.4	41.3	51.3	33.9	7.5
2019	100	7.3	39.9	52.8	32.3	7.8
2020	100	7.4	39.1	53.5	31.6	7.7
2021	100	7.3	39.9	52.8	32.8	7.3

注:本表按当年价格计算。

a)Data in this table are calculated at current prices.

2-4 地区生产总值

Gross Domestic Product

单位:亿元 (100 million yuan)

分　组	Sector	2020	2021	2020年为2019年 % 2019=100	2021年为2020年 % 2020=100
地区生产总值	**Gross Domestic Product**	**72798.17**	**83095.90**	**103.5**	**108.3**
第一产业	Primary Industry	5364.35	6029.03	102.7	107.5
第二产业	Secondary Industry	28456.66	33187.16	103.2	107.2
第三产业	Tertiary Industry	38977.16	43879.71	103.8	109.2
农林牧渔业	Agriculture, Forestry, Animal Husbandry and Fishery	5750.08	6449.47	102.8	107.5
工　业	Industry	22986.45	27243.55	103.4	108.6
建筑业	Construction	5574.19	6094.45	101.5	101.8
批发和零售业	Wholesale and Retail Trades	9810.75	11549.95	102.0	112.8
交通运输、仓储和邮政业	Transport, Storage and Postal Services	3478.58	4166.77	101.4	110.2
住宿和餐饮业	Hotels and Catering Services	1071.02	1258.87	90.0	113.1
信息传输、软件和信息技术服务业	Information Transmission, Software and Information Technology	1758.15	2011.94	116.9	116.0
金融业	Financial Intermediation	4522.30	4938.59	106.7	105.6
房地产业	Real Estate	4225.93	4524.48	102.1	105.9
租赁和商务服务业	Leasing and Business Services	2055.73	2197.35	101.0	106.5
科学研究和技术服务业	Scientific Research and Technical Services	1445.16	1568.26	108.1	108.2
水利、环境和公共设施管理业	Management of Water Conservancy, Environment and Public Facilities	370.00	382.14	111.7	101.1
居民服务、修理和其他服务业	Service to Households, Repair and Other Services	1357.81	1556.67	101.3	117.6
教　育	Education	2668.80	2856.42	107.4	106.8
卫生和社会工作	Financial Intermediation	1574.94	1687.72	107.2	105.2
文化、体育和娱乐业	Culture, Sports and Recreation	424.24	479.98	91.2	109.0
公共管理、社会保障和社会组织	Public Management,Social Security and Social Organization	3724.04	4129.29	107.3	105.0
人均地区生产总值　（元）	**Per Capita GDP　(yuan)**	**71825**	**81727**	**103.0**	**107.9**

注：本表绝对数按当年价格计算，指数按可比价格计算。

a)Data in this table are calculated at current prices.Indices are calculated at constant prices.

2-5 三次产业对经济增长的贡献率及拉动百分点

Share and Contribution of the Three Industries to the Increase of GDP

单位:% (%)

年 份 Year	贡献率 Share			地区生产总值增长率 Increase Rate of Gross Domestic Product	拉动百分点(个) Contribution (unit)		
	第一产业 Primary Industry	第二产业 Secondary Industry	第三产业 Tertiary Industry		第一产业 Primary Industry	第二产业 Secondary Industry	第三产业 Tertiary Industry
1980	25.6	53.4	21.0	12.2	3.1	6.5	2.6
1981	42.0	25.2	32.8	5.8	2.4	1.5	1.9
1982	36.2	22.4	41.4	11.3	4.1	2.5	4.7
1983	43.3	23.3	33.4	13.9	6.0	3.2	4.7
1984	40.3	41.0	18.7	17.4	7.0	7.1	3.3
1985	7.3	65.4	27.3	11.4	0.8	7.5	3.1
1986	-3.7	73.7	30.0	6.2	-0.2	4.6	1.8
1987	17.6	55.3	27.1	13.8	2.4	7.6	3.8
1988	-0.6	83.2	17.4	12.5	-0.1	10.4	2.2
1989	-4.6	89.3	15.3	4.0	-0.2	3.6	0.6
1990	27.0	70.3	2.7	5.3	1.4	3.7	0.2
1991	27.2	40.2	32.6	14.6	4.0	5.9	4.7
1992	0.3	70.7	29.0	16.9		12.0	4.9
1993	7.2	63.4	29.4	20.4	1.5	12.9	6.0
1994	9.5	52.5	38.0	16.2	1.5	8.5	6.2
1995	12.5	49.8	37.7	14.0	1.7	7.0	5.3
1996	10.2	56.8	33.0	12.1	1.2	6.9	4.0
1997	0.8	57.6	41.6	11.1	0.1	6.4	4.6
1998	8.4	57.3	34.3	10.8	0.9	6.2	3.7
1999	7.2	62.1	30.7	10.0	0.7	6.2	3.1
2000	3.6	59.8	36.6	9.5	0.3	5.7	3.5
2001	6.1	52.9	41.0	9.4	0.6	4.9	3.9
2002	3.2	63.3	33.5	11.0	0.4	6.9	3.7
2003	6.7	64.2	29.1	10.8	0.7	7.0	3.1
2004	6.9	67.2	25.9	12.5	0.9	8.4	3.2
2005	4.5	62.5	33.0	12.6	0.6	7.8	4.2
2006	4.9	62.0	33.1	12.3	0.6	7.6	4.1
2007	3.7	61.7	34.6	11.9	0.4	7.4	4.1
2008	5.1	54.8	40.1	9.7	0.5	5.3	3.9
2009	4.1	64.8	31.1	9.8	0.4	6.4	3.0
2010	2.8	64.4	32.8	10.4	0.3	6.7	3.4
2011	3.5	56.0	40.5	10.7	0.4	6.0	4.3
2012	4.4	56.0	39.6	9.7	0.4	5.5	3.8
2013	3.3	55.0	41.7	9.4	0.3	5.2	3.9
2014	3.8	54.8	41.4	8.5	0.3	4.7	3.5
2015	4.3	48.3	47.4	7.8	0.3	3.8	3.7
2016	4.6	37.5	57.9	7.4	0.3	2.8	4.3
2017	4.2	36.2	59.6	7.3	0.3	2.7	4.3
2018	3.5	28.7	67.8	6.3	0.2	1.8	4.3
2019	1.6	21.5	76.9	5.3	0.1	1.1	4.1
2020	5.9	38.4	55.7	3.5	0.2	1.3	2.0
2021	6.6	33.9	59.5	8.3	0.6	2.8	4.9

注:本表按可比价格计算。
a) Data in this table are calculated at constant prices.

2-6 各市生产总值(2021年)

Gross Domestic Product by Region(2021)

单位:亿元 (100 million yuan)

地 区	Region	地区生产总值 Gross Domestic Product		第一产业增加值 Value-added of Primary Industry		第二产业增加值 Value-added of Secondary Industry	
		2021	2021年为2020年% 2020=100	2021	2021年为2020年% 2020=100	2021	2021年为2020年% 2020=100
全 省	**Total**	**83095.90**	**108.3**	**6029.03**	**107.5**	**33187.16**	**107.2**
济南市	Jinan	11432.22	107.2	408.77	107.1	3964.06	103.6
青岛市	Qingdao	14136.46	108.3	470.06	106.7	5070.33	106.9
淄博市	Zibo	4200.62	109.4	180.58	107.3	2073.06	110.1
枣庄市	Zaozhuang	1951.57	108.3	185.83	107.8	795.40	106.6
东营市	Dongying	3441.72	108.5	181.88	108.2	1988.43	109.5
烟台市	Yantai	8711.75	108.0	626.14	107.5	3598.50	106.7
潍坊市	Weifang	7010.60	109.7	628.36	107.6	2831.38	110.0
济宁市	Jining	5069.96	108.5	583.79	107.6	2034.56	108.2
泰安市	Tai'an	2996.66	106.1	327.35	107.1	1166.47	102.0
威海市	Weihai	3463.93	107.5	349.17	107.4	1355.13	107.7
日照市	Rizhao	2211.96	106.8	194.68	107.4	903.55	100.8
临沂市	Linyi	5465.50	108.7	484.14	107.1	2116.75	109.1
德州市	Dezhou	3488.72	108.3	366.92	107.7	1435.00	107.9
聊城市	Liaocheng	2642.52	108.4	374.21	107.5	968.47	109.9
滨州市	Binzhou	2872.11	108.3	279.30	108.1	1212.01	108.0
菏泽市	Heze	3976.67	108.8	390.92	107.7	1653.26	108.9

注:本表绝对额按当年价格计算,速度按可比价格计算。
a)Absolute figure in this table are calculated at current prices while growth rate at constant prices.

2-6 续表 continued

单位:亿元 (100 million yuan)

地 区	Region	第三产业增加值 Value-added of Tertiary Industry		工业增加值 Value-added of Industry		人均地区生产总值(元) Per Capita GDP (yuan)
		2021	2021年为2020年% 2020=100	2021	2021年为2020年% 2020=100	2021
全 省	**Total**	**43879.71**	**109.2**	**27243.55**	**108.6**	**81727**
济南市	Jinan	7059.39	109.2	2746.00	105.7	123075
青岛市	Qingdao	8596.07	109.2	3884.07	108.8	138849
淄博市	Zibo	1946.98	108.8	1762.21	110.7	89238
枣庄市	Zaozhuang	970.34	109.7	648.40	108.3	50613
东营市	Dongying	1271.41	107.0	1912.22	109.5	156852
烟台市	Yantai	4487.11	109.0	3100.77	107.3	122818
潍坊市	Weifang	3550.86	109.8	2339.05	110.5	74606
济宁市	Jining	2451.61	108.8	1743.36	108.8	60728
泰安市	Tai'an	1502.84	109.0	784.91	107.0	54917
威海市	Weihai	1759.63	107.3	1164.69	109.0	118925
日照市	Rizhao	1113.73	111.7	734.22	101.2	74434
临沂市	Linyi	2864.61	108.7	1764.66	110.6	49585
德州市	Dezhou	1686.80	108.8	1292.49	109.4	62223
聊城市	Liaocheng	1299.84	107.6	835.41	110.3	44485
滨州市	Binzhou	1380.80	108.6	1093.77	108.2	73078
菏泽市	Heze	1932.49	109.0	1415.93	109.5	45366

2-7 各市生产总值构成(2021年)

Composition of Gross Domestic Product by Region(2021)

单位:% (%)

地区	Region	地区生产总值 Gross Domestic Product	第一产业 Primary Industry	第二产业 Secondary Industry	第三产业 Tertiary Industry
全省	**Total**	**100.0**	**7.3**	**39.9**	**52.8**
济南市	Jinan	100.0	3.6	34.7	61.7
青岛市	Qingdao	100.0	3.3	35.9	60.8
淄博市	Zibo	100.0	4.3	49.4	46.3
枣庄市	Zaozhuang	100.0	9.5	40.8	49.7
东营市	Dongying	100.0	5.3	57.8	36.9
烟台市	Yantai	100.0	7.2	41.3	51.5
潍坊市	Weifang	100.0	9.0	40.4	50.6
济宁市	Jining	100.0	11.5	40.1	48.4
泰安市	Tai'an	100.0	10.9	38.9	50.2
威海市	Weihai	100.0	10.1	39.1	50.8
日照市	Rizhao	100.0	8.8	40.8	50.4
临沂市	Linyi	100.0	8.9	38.7	52.4
德州市	Dezhou	100.0	10.5	41.1	48.4
聊城市	Liaocheng	100.0	14.2	36.6	49.2
滨州市	Binzhou	100.0	9.7	42.2	48.1
菏泽市	Heze	100.0	9.8	41.6	48.6

注:本表按当年价格计算。

a)Data in this table are calculated at current prices.

主要统计指标解释

国内生产总值（GDP） 指一个国家（或地区）所有常住单位在一定时期内生产活动的最终成果。

国内生产总值有三种表现形态，即价值形态、收入形态和产品形态。

从价值形态看，它是所有常住单位在一定时期内生产的全部货物和服务价值超过同期中间投入的全部非固定资产货物和服务价值的差额，即所有常住单位的增加值之和；

从收入形态看，它是所有常住单位在一定时期内创造并分配给常住单位和非常住单位的初次收入分配之和；

从产品形态看，它是所有常住单位在一定时期内最终使用的货物和服务价值与货物和服务净出口价值之和。

在实际核算中，国内生产总值有三种计算方法，即生产法、收入法和支出法。三种方法分别从不同的方面反映国内生产总值及其构成。

①生产法 是从生产过程中生产的货物和服务总产品价值入手，剔除生产过程中投入的中间产品的价值，得到增加价值的一种方法，公式为：

增加值＝总产出－中间投入

总产出 是一定时期内一个国家（或地区）常住单位生产的所有货物和服务的价值。既包括新增价值，也包括转移价值。

中间投入 是常住单位在生产或提供货物与服务过程中，消耗和使用的所有非固定资产货物和服务的价值。中间投入也称为中间消耗。

增加值 是指常住单位生产过程创造的新增价值和固定资产的转移价值。按生产法计算它等于总产出减去中间投入。

②收入法 收入法也称分配法，按收入法计算国内生产总值是从生产过程创造收入的角度，对常住单位的生产活动成果进行核算。按照这种计算方法，增加值由劳动者报酬、生产税净额、固定资产折旧和营业盈余四个部分组成。

用公式表示为：

增加值＝劳动者报酬+生产税净额+固定资产折旧+营业盈余

国民经济各部门的增加值之和等于国内生产总值。

劳动者报酬 指劳动者因从事生产活动所获得的全部报酬。它包括劳动者获得的各种形式工资、奖金和津贴，既包括货币形式的，也包括实物形式的，它还包括劳动者所享受的公费医疗和医疗卫生费、上下班交通补贴和单位直接支付的社会保险费等。

生产税净额 生产税减生产补贴后的差额。

生产税指政府对生产单位生产、销售和从事经营活动以及因从事生产活动使用某些生产要素，如固定资产、土地、劳动力所征收的各种税、附加费和规费。具体包括销售税金及附加、增值税、管理费中开支的各种税、应交纳的养路费、排污费和水电费附加、烟酒专卖上缴政府的专项收入等。

生产补贴与生产税相反，是政府对生产单位的单方面收入转移，因此视为负生产税处理，包括政策亏损补贴、粮食系统价格补贴、外贸企业出口退税收入等。

固定资产折旧 指一定时期内为弥补固定资产损耗按照核定的固定资产折旧率提取的固定资产折旧，或按国民经济核算统一规定的折旧率虚拟计算的固定资产折旧。它反映了固定资产在当期生产中的转移价值。各种类型企业和企业化管理的事业单位的固定资产折旧指实际计提并计入成本费用中的折旧费；不计提折旧的单位，如政府机关、非企业化管理的事业单位和居民住房的固定资产折旧则是按照统一规定的折旧率和固定资产原值计算的虚拟折旧。

营业盈余 是指常住单位创造的增加值扣除劳动者报酬、生产税净额和固定资产折旧后的余额。它相当于企业的营业利润加上生产补贴，但要扣除从利润中开支的工资和福利等。

③支出法 支出法是从最终使用角度来反映国内生产总值最终去向的一种方法。最终使用包括货物和服务的最终消费支出、资本形成总额、货物和服务净出口三部分。

最终消费 指常住单位在一定时期内对于货物和服务的全部最终消费支出，也就是常住单位为满足物质、文化和精神生活的需要，从本国经济领土和国外购买的货物和服务的支出；不包括非常住单位在本国经济领土内的消费支出。最终消费分为居民消费和政府消费。

居民消费 指常住住户对货物和服务的全部最终消费支出。居民消费按市场价格计算，即按居民支付的购买者价格计算。购买者价格是购买者取得货物所支付的价值，包括购买者支付的运输和商业费用。

居民消费除了直接以货币形式购买货物和服务的消费之外，还包括以其他方式获得的货物和服务的消费支出，即所谓的虚拟消费支出。居民虚拟消费支出包括以下几种类型：单位以实物报酬及实物转移的形式提供给劳动者的货物和服务；住户生产并由本住户消费的货物和服务，其中的服务仅指住户的自有住房服务；金融机构提供的金融媒介服务；保险公司提供的保险服务。

政府消费 指政府部门为全社会提供公共服务的消费支出和免费或以较低价格向住户提供的货物和服务的净支出。前者等于政府服务的产出价值减去政府单位所获得的经营收入的价值，政府服务的产出价值等于它的经常性业务支出加上固定资产折旧；后者等于政府部门免费或以较低价格向住户提供的货物和服务的市场价值减去向住户收取的价值。

资本形成总额 指常住单位在一定时期内获得减去处置的固定资产和存货的净额，包括固定资本形成总额和存货增加两部分。

固定资本形成总额 指常住单位购置、转入和自产自用的固定资产价值，扣除销售和转出的价值，包括有形固定资产形成总额和无形固定资产形成总额。有形固定资产形成总额包括一定时期内完成的建筑工程、安装工程和设备工器具购置（减处置）价值，商品房销售增值，土地改良形成的固定资产，新增役、种、奶、毛、娱乐用牲畜和新增经济林木价值。无形固定资产形成总额包括矿藏勘探、计算机软件、娱乐和文学艺术品原件等获得减处置的价值。

存货增加 指常住单位存货实物量变动的市场价值，即期末价值减期初价值的差额。存货增加可以是正值，也可以是负值；正值表示存货上升，负值表示存货下降。它包括生产单位购进的原材料、燃料和储备物资等存货，以及生产单位生产的产成品、在制品等存货等。

货物和服务净出口 指货物和服务出口减货物和服务进口的差额。出口包括常住单位向非常住单位出售或无偿转让的各种货物和服务的价值；进口包括常住单位从非常住单位购买或无偿得到的各种货物和服务的价值。由于服务活动的提供与使用同时发生，因此服务的进出口业务并不发生出入境现象，一般把常住单位从国外得到的服务作为进口，非常住单位从本国得到的服务作为出口。货物的出口和进口都按离岸价格计算。

三次产业 三次产业的划分是世界上较为常用的产业结构分类，但各国的划分不尽一致。根据《国民经济行业分类》（GB/T 4754—2017）和《三次产业划分规定》，我国的三次产业划分是：

第一产业 指农、林、牧、渔业（不含农、林、牧、渔专业及辅助性活动）。

第二产业 指采矿业（不含开采专业及辅助性活动），制造业（不含金属制品、机械和设备修理业），电力、热力、燃气及水生产和供应业，建筑业。

第三产业 即服务业，是指除第一产业、第二产业以外的其他行业。

当年价格 指报告期的实际价格，如工业品的出厂价格，农产品的收购价格，商业的零售价格等。按当年价格计算，是指一些以货币表现的物量指标，如工农业总产值、国内生产总值等，按照当年的实际价格来计算总量。使用当年价格计算的数字，是为了使国民经济各项指标互相衔接，便于考察当年社会经济效益，便于对生产流通、生产和分配、生产和消费进行经济核算和综合平衡。

按当年价格计算的价值指标，在不同年份之间进行对比时，因为包含有各年间价格变动的因素，不能确切地反映实物量的增减变动。必须消除价格变动因素后，才能真实反映经济发展动态。因此，在计算增长速度时都使用按可比价格计算的数字。

可比价格 指计算各种总量指标所采用的扣除了价格变动因素的价格，可进行不同时期总量指标的对比。按可比价格计算总量指标有两种方法：一种是直接用产品产量乘某一年的不变价格计算；另一种是用价格指数进行换算。

不变价格 指以同类产品某一时期的平均价格作为固定价格，用于计算各时期的产品价值。按不变价格计算的产品价值消除了价格变动因素，不同时期对比可以反映生产的发展速度。新中国成立后，随着工农业产品价格水平的变化，国家统计局先后八次制定了全国统一的工业产品不变价格和农业产品不变价格。从 1949 年到 1957 年使用 1952 年工（农）业产品不变价格，从 1957 年到 1971 年使用 1957 年不变价格，从 1971 年到 1981 年使用 1970 年不变价格，从 1981 年到 1990 年使用 1980 年不变价格，从 1991 年到 2000 年使用 1990 年不变价格，从 2001 年到 2005 年使用 2000 年不变价格，从 2006 年开始使用 2005 年不变价格，从 2011 年开始使用 2010 年不变价格，从 2016 年开始使用 2015 年不变价格，从 2021 年开始使用 2020 年不变价格。

Explanatory Notes on Main Statistical Indicators

Gross Domestic Product refers to the final products at market prices produced by all residents in a country (or a region) during a certain period of time.

Gross domestic product is expressed in three different forms, i.e. value, income, and products respectively.

GDP in its value form refers to the total value of all goods and services produced by all resident units during a certain period of time, minus the total value of input of goods of non-fixed assets and services; in other term, it is the sum of the value-added of all resident units.

GDP in the form of income includes the income created by all resident units and distributed to resident and non-resident units.

GDP in the form of products refers to the value of all goods and services for final consumption by all resident units minus the net exports of goods and services during a given period of time.

In the practice of national accounting, gross domestic product is calculated with three approaches, i.e. production approach, income approach and expenditure approach, which reflect gross domestic product and its composition from different aspects.

Production Approach focuses on the total value of goods and services produced in production activities. GDP by Production Approach equals the value of total output minus that of input consumed in production process.

GDP by Production Approach = gross output − intermediate input

Gross Output refers to the total value of goods and service produced by all residents in a given period,including newly-produced goods and service, and intermediate input.

Intermediate Input refers to non-fixed assets and paid service consumed during production process when goods and service are produced. Intermediate input is also called intermediate consumption.

Value-added refers to the value of newly-produced goods and service and that of consumed fixed assets. By production approach, it equals gross output minus intermediate input.

Income Approach (also known as distribution approach): refers to the method measuring the final results of production activities o from the perspective of income made by all residents. GDP of income approach includes laborers' remuneration,net taxed on production, depreciation of fixed assets and operating surplus.

GDP by income approach = laborers' remuneration+ net taxed on production+depreciation of fixed assets+operating surplus.

The sum of value added made by different industries is GDP.

Laborers' Remuneration refers to the whole payment of various forms earned by the laborers' from the productive activities they are engaged in. It includes wages, bonuses and allowances the laborers' earned in monetary form and in kind. It also includes the free medical services provided to the laborers' and the medicine expenses, traffic subsidies and social insurance, housing fund paid by the employers.

Net Taxes on Production refers to the difference of the taxes on production minus the subsidies on production.

Taxes on production refers to the various taxes, extra charges and fees levied on the production units on their production, sale and business activities as well as on the use of some factors of production, such as fixed assets, land and labor force in the production activities they are engaged in.

In contrast to the taxes on production, the subsidies on production refer to the unilateral government transfer to the production units and are therefore regarded as negative taxes on production.They include subsidies on the loss due to implementation of government policies, price subsidies, etc.

Depreciation of Fixed Assets refers to the depreciation of fixed assets of a given period, drawn in accordance with the stipulated depreciation rate for the purpose of compensating the wear loss of the fixed assets or the depreciation of fixed assets calculated in a fictitious way in accordance with the stipulated unified depreciation rate in the national economic accounting system. It reflects the value of transfer of the fixed assets in the production of the current period. The depreciation of fixed assets in various enterprises and institutions managed as enterprises refers to the depreciation expenses actually drawn. In government agencies and institutions not managed as enterprises which do not draw the depreciation expenses, as well as for the houses of residents, the depreciation of fixed assets is the imputed depreciation, which is calculated in accordance with the stipulated unified depreciation rate. In principle, the depreciation of fixed assets should be calculated on the basis of the re-purchased value of the fixed assets.

Operating Surplus refers to the balance of the value added created by the resident units deducting the laborers' remuneration, net taxes on production and the depreciation of fixed assets. It is equivalent to the business profit of the enterprises plus subsidies on production, but the wages and welfare expenses paid from the profits should be deducted.

GDP by Expenditure Approach refers to the method of measuring the final results of production activities of a country (region) during a given period from the perspective of final use. It includes final consumption expenditure, total capital formation and net export of goods and services.

Final Consumption Expenditure refers to the total expenditure on goods and services in a given period, which means the total expenditure of resident units for purchases of goods and services from domestic economic territory and abroad to meet the requirements of material, cultural and spiritual life. It excludes the expenditure of non-resident units on consumption in the economic territory of the country. The final consumption expenditure is broken down into household consumption expenditure and government consumption expenditure.

Household consumption refers to the consumption expenditure made by household on goods and services. It is calculated at market price which is the purchasers'price. Purchasers'price means the money the purchasers paid for goods, including transportation fees and operating fees.

In addition to the consumption of goods and services bought by the households directly with money, the households consumption expenditure also includes expenditure on goods and services obtained by the households in other ways, i.e. the so-called imputed consumption expenditure, which includes the following: (a) the goods and services provided to the households by the employer in the form of payment in kind and transfer in kind; (b) goods and services produced and consumed by the households themselves, in which the services refer only to the owner-occupied housing and domestic and individual services provided by the paid household workers; (c) financial intermediate services provided by financial institutions; (d) insurance services provided by insurance companies.

Government Consumption Expenditure refers to the expenditure on the consumption of the public services provided by the government to the whole society and the net expenditure on the goods and services provided by the government to the households free of charge or at low prices. The former equals to the output value of the government services minus the value of operating income obtained by the government departments. The latter equals to the market value of the goods and services provided by the government free of charge or at low prices to the households minus the value received by the government from the households.

Total Capital Formation refers to the fixed assets acquired minus those disposed of and the net value of inventory, including the total fixed capital formation and the increase in inventory.

Total Fixed Capital Formation refers to the value of fixed assets acquired minus those disposed of during a given period. Fixed assets are the assets produced through production activities with specified unit value which could be used for over one year, excluding natural assets. Total fixed capital formation can be categorized into total tangible capital formation and total intangible capital formation. The total tangible capital formation include the value of the construction projects, installation projects completed and the equipment,apparatus and instruments purchased as well as the value of land improved, the value of draught animals, breeding stock, animals for milk, wool and for recreational purpose, and the newly increased forest with economic value during a given period. The total intangible capital formation includes the prospecting of minerals, the acquisition of computer software, artistic works artistic minus the disposal of them.

Increase in Inventory refers to the market value of the change in inventory of resident units during a given period, i.e. the difference of value between the beginning and the end of the period minus the current gains due to the change in prices. The increase in inventory can be positive or negative. A positive value indicates the increase in inventory while a negative value indicates the decrease in stock. The inventory includes the raw materials, fuels and reserve materials purchased by the production units as well as the inventory of finished products, semi-finished products, work-in-progress, etc.

Net Export of Goods and Services refers to the difference of the exports of goods and services minus the imports of goods and services. The imports include the value of various goods and services sold or gratuitously transferred by the resident units to the non-resident units. The imports include the value of various goods and services purchased or gratuitously acquired by the resident units from the non-resident units. Because the provision of services and the use of them happen simultaneously, the acquisition of services by the resident units from abroad is usually treated as import while the acquisition of services by non-resident units in this country is usually treated as export. The export and import of goods are calculated at FOB.

Three Strata of Industry Classification of economic activities into three strata of industries is a common practice in the world, although the grouping varies to some extent from country to country. In China, according to Industrial Classification for National Economic Activities (GB/T 4754—2017) and Rules on Division of Three Strata of Industries, economic activities are categorized into the following three strata of industries:

Primary industry refers to agriculture, forestry, animal husbandry and fishery industries (not including services in support of agriculture, forestry, animal husbandry and fishery industries).

Secondary industry refers to mining and quarrying (not including support activities for mining), manufacturing (not including repair service of metal products, machinery and equipment), production and supply of electricity, heat, gas and water, and construction.

Tertiary industry refers to all other economic activities not included in the primary or secondary industries.

Current Price refers to the actual price during the reporting period, such as Ex-factory Price of Industrial Products, purchasing price of agricultural produces and retail price. Some indicators calculatedat current price are volume indicators in the value form, such as total value of output of industrial and agricultural industries and GDP, etc. Data calculated at current price are useful when it comes to evaluating the economic development and analyzing different aspects of economy, such as production, circulation,distribution and consumption.

When the different indicators calculated at current price are compared, it is in evitable that price changes will affect the comparison. Therefore, the change in volume cannot be showed. In order to eliminate the effect of price and reflect economic development, growth rate is calculated at current price.

Constant Price refers to the price without the effect of price change. By using constant price, total amount indices of different periods can be compared. There are two methods in which total amount indices are obtained, one using current price of some year to multiply the physical volume of certain products and the other using price index.

Fixed Price refers to the average price of similar products in a given period, with which the product value of different period can be calculated. The product value calculated at fixed price can show the growth rate of production in different period. Since 1949, NBS has framed the united industrial and agricultural fixed price 8 times, including the fixed price of 1952 used from 1949 to 1957, the fixed price of 1957 used from 1957 to 1971, the fixed price of 1970 used from 1971 to 1981, the fixed price of 1980 used from 1981 to 1990, the fixed price of 1990 used from 1991 to 2000, the fixed price of 2000 used from 2001 to 2005, the fixed price of 2005 used from 2006, the fixed price of 2010 used from 2011,the fixed price of 2015 used from 2016, and the fixed price of 2020 used from 2021.

第3篇 人　口

Population

简 要 说 明

一、本篇资料的主要内容

本篇资料主要反映了全省人口方面的基本情况，包括全省 16 个市的主要人口统计数据、历年人口数、农村和城镇人口数、人口出生率、死亡率、自然增长率。另外，还对中华人民共和国成立以来开展的 7 次人口普查主要数据进行了比较。

二、本篇资料的来源

本篇资料分别来源于国家开展的人口普查、人口抽样调查和省公安厅的户籍登记资料，由省统计局人口处（社科处）整理提供。

Brief Introduction

I. Main Content

Data in this chapter show the basic condition of population, such as the basic condition of 16 cities, population, rural and urban population, birth rate, death rate and natural growth rate. Furthermore, relevant figures obtained from seven national population censuses have been compared.

II. Source of Data

Data in this chapter are from national population censuses, national sample survey. Some are derived from household registration provided by Shandong Provincial Department of Public Security. The data above are compiled by the Division of Urbanization,Population and Employment Statistics（by the Division of Social,Science and Culture Industry Employment Statistics）of Shandong Provincial Bureau of Statistics.

3-1 主要年份总人口

Population in Major Years

单位:万人 (10 000 persons)

年 份 Year	总人口 Total	按性别分 Grouped by Sex		按农村、城镇分 Grouped by Rural and Urban		人口密度 Density of Population (人/平方公里) (Person/sq.km)
		男 Male	女 Female	农村人口 Rural Population	城镇人口 Urban Population	
1949	(4549)	(2199)	(2350)	(4289)	(260)	290
1952	(4827)	(2392)	(2435)	(4538)	(289)	308
1955	(5174)	(2587)	(2587)	(4796)	(378)	330
1957	(5373)	(2694)	(2679)	(4936)	(437)	343
1962	(5426)	(2718)	(2708)	(5015)	(411)	346
1965	(5711)	(2866)	(2845)	(5258)	(453)	364
1970	(6441)	(3241)	(3200)	(5966)	(475)	411
1975	(6971)	(3524)	(3447)	(6408)	(563)	445
1976	(7038)	(3561)	(3477)	(6455)	(583)	449
1977	(7099)	(3592)	(3507)	(6507)	(592)	453
1978	(7160)	(3624)	(3536)	(6533)	(627)	457
1979	(7232)	(3660)	(3572)	(6570)	(661)	462
1980	(7296)	(3694)	(3602)	(6605)	(691)	466
1981	(7395)	(3750)	(3645)	(6659)	(736)	472
1982	(7494)	(3806)	(3688)	(6720)	(774)	478
1983	(7564)	(3847)	(3717)	(6753)	(811)	483
1984	(7637)	(3887)	(3750)	(6701)	(936)	487
1985	7711(7695)	(3922)	(3773)	(6676)	(1017)	492
1986	7818(7776)	(3967)	(3810)	(6797)	(979)	499
1987	7958(7889)	(4029)	(3860)	(6844)	(1045)	508
1988	8061(8009)	(4092)	(3917)	(6702)	(1307)	514
1989	8160(8181)	(4181)	(4000)	(6698)	(1483)	521
1990	8493(8424)	(4299)	(4125)	(6846)	(1578)	542
1991	8570(8534)	(4352)	(4182)	(6884)	(1650)	547
1992	8610(8580)	(4373)	(4207)	(6819)	(1761)	549
1993	8642(8620)	(4392)	(4228)	(6724)	(1896)	551
1994	8671(8653)	(4407)	(4246)	(6574)	(2079)	553
1995	8705(8701)	(4429)	(4272)	(6531)	(2170)	556
1996	8738(8747)	(4452)	(4295)	(6484)	(2263)	558
1997	8785(8810)	(4483)	(4327)	(6500)	(2310)	561
1998	8838(8872)	(4513)	(4359)	(6575)	(2296)	564
1999	8883(8922)	(4537)	(4385)	(6600)	(2322)	567
2000	8997(8975)	(4562)	(4413)	(6566)	(2409)	574
2001	9041(9024)	(4584)	(4440)	(6507)	(2517)	577
2002	9082(9069)	(4607)	(4463)	(6435)	(2634)	580
2003	9125(9108)	(4624)	(4484)	(6275)	(2833)	582
2004	9180(9163)	(4652)	(4512)	(6212)	(2951)	586
2005	9248(9212)	(4676)	(4537)	(6066)	(3147)	589
2006	9309(9282)	(4707)	(4575)	(6055)	(3228)	592
2007	9367(9346)	(4739)	(4606)	(5909)	(3436)	596
2008	9417(9392)	(4761)	(4632)	(5860)	(3532)	599
2009	9470(9449)	(4792)	(4658)	(5902)	(3548)	603
2010	9579(9536)	(4839)	(4697)	(5698)	(3839)	610
2011	9665(9591)	(4870)	(4721)	(5646)	(3945)	613
2012	9708(9580)	(4868)	(4712)	(5559)	(4021)	616
2013	9746(9612)	(4883)	(4729)	(5482)	(4130)	619
2014	9808(9747)	(4960)	(4787)	(5462)	(4285)	620
2015	9866(9822)	(4999)	(4823)	(5120)	(4702)	624
2016	9973(9921)	(5049)	(4872)	(5056)	(4865)	630
2017	10033(10009)	(5089)	(4919)	(4984)	(5024)	634
2018	10077(10096)	(5130)	(4966)	(4953)	(5143)	636
2019	10106(10148)	(5153)	(4995)	(5080)	(5068)	637
2020	10165(10172)	(5162)	(5011)	(5047)	(5125)	643
2021	10170(10191)	5162(5169)	5008(5023)	3667	6503	644

注:1.1990、2000和2010年为人口普查数,其余年份均为人口抽样调查数,括号内为公安户籍人口数。2006年之前的农村、城镇人口分别为公安户籍统计的农业、非农业人口。

2.根据第七次人口普查结果,对全省2011—2019年年末总人口进行了修订。

3.2020年为根据第七次人口普查数据推算年末人口数。

a) Data of 1990、2000 and 2010 are based on the national population census,and others are based on the sample surveys.Data in the brackets are from the annual reports of the Public Security Departments.Before 2006,the rural and urban population are changed to the agriculture and non-agricultural population from the Public Security Departments.

b) According to the Seventh National Census, the data of total population from 2011 to 2019 of Shandong have been revised.

c) Data of 2020 are calculated according to the data of the Seventh National Census.

3-2 主要年份人口出生率、死亡率、自然增长率

Birth Rate,Death Rate and Natural Growth Rate of Population in Major Years

年 份 Year	出生率 (‰) Birth Rate (‰)	死亡率 (‰) Death Rate (‰)	自然增长率 (‰) Natural Growth Rate (‰)	出生人口数 (万人) Population of Birth (10 000 persons)	死亡人口数 (万人) Population of Death (10 000 persons)	自然增长人数 (万人) Population of Natural Growth (10 000 persons)
1949	(28.10)	(12.20)	(15.90)			
1952	(31.50)	(12.20)	(19.30)			
1955	(37.30)	(13.70)	(23.60)	(191)	(70)	(121)
1957	(35.80)	(12.10)	(23.70)	(190)	(64)	(126)
1962	(38.10)	(12.40)	(25.70)	(204)	(66)	(138)
1965	(35.50)	(10.20)	(25.30)	(201)	(58)	(143)
1970	(33.89)	(7.34)	(26.55)	(215)	(47)	(168)
1975	(21.56)	(7.53)	(14.03)	(149)	(52)	(97)
1976	(18.46)	(7.63)	(10.83)	(129)	(53)	(76)
1977	(16.96)	(7.24)	(9.72)	(120)	(51)	(69)
1978	(16.80)	(6.50)	(10.30)	(119)	(46)	(73)
1979	(16.94)	(6.15)	(10.79)	(122)	(44)	(78)
1980	(13.91)	(6.40)	(7.51)	(101)	(47)	(54)
1981	(16.48)	(6.41)	(10.07)	(121)	(47)	(74)
1982	(17.05)	(6.10)	(10.95)	(127)	(45)	(82)
1983	15.10(12.76)	6.73(5.87)	8.37(6.89)	114(96)	51(44)	63(52)
1984	13.80(12.99)	5.80(6.03)	8.00(6.96)	104(99)	44(46)	60(53)
1985	15.12(11.75)	6.64(5.90)	8.48(5.85)	116(90)	51(45)	65(45)
1986	19.90(14.71)	7.28(5.86)	12.62(8.85)	156(114)	57(46)	99(68)
1987	23.35(17.43)	7.07(5.64)	16.28(11.79)	184(137)	56(44)	128(93)
1988	17.54(17.95)	6.04(5.95)	11.50(12.00)	140(143)	48(47)	92(96)
1989	16.88(18.87)	5.70(5.51)	11.18(13.36)	137(153)	46(45)	91(108)
1990	18.21(26.10)	6.96(6.02)	11.25(20.08)	152(217)	58(50)	94(167)
1991	15.40(16.39)	6.54(5.73)	8.86(10.66)	131(139)	56(49)	75(90)
1992	11.43(10.95)	6.88(6.02)	4.55(4.93)	98(94)	59(52)	39(42)
1993	10.49(9.47)	6.76(5.84)	3.73(3.63)	90(81)	58(50)	32(31)
1994	9.69(9.31)	6.67(5.99)	3.02(3.32)	84(80)	58(52)	26(28)
1995	9.82(9.66)	6.47(5.83)	3.35(3.83)	85(84)	56(51)	29(33)
1996	10.60(10.33)	6.76(6.04)	3.84(4.29)	92(90)	59(53)	33(37)
1997	11.28(10.84)	6.65(5.90)	4.63(4.94)	99(95)	58(52)	41(43)
1998	11.58(11.52)	6.12(5.95)	5.46(5.57)	102(102)	54(53)	48(49)
1999	11.08(10.23)	6.27(5.72)	4.81(4.51)	98(91)	55(51)	43(40)
2000	10.75(11.38)	6.29(6.70)	4.46(4.68)	97(102)	56(60)	40(42)
2001	11.12(9.93)	6.24(5.46)	4.88(4.47)	100(89)	56(49)	44(40)
2002	11.17(10.20)	6.62(5.86)	4.55(4.34)	101(92)	60(53)	41(39)
2003	11.42(9.31)	6.64(6.07)	4.78(3.24)	104(85)	61(55)	43(30)
2004	12.50(10.59)	6.49(5.60)	6.01(4.99)	114(97)	59(51)	55(46)
2005	12.14(10.17)	6.31(5.85)	5.83(4.32)	112(94)	58(54)	54(40)
2006	11.60(9.59)	6.10(5.62)	5.50(3.97)	108(89)	57(52)	51(37)
2007	11.11(10.05)	6.11(6.47)	5.00(3.58)	104(94)	57(60)	47(33)
2008	11.25(10.13)	6.16(6.81)	5.09(3.32)	106((95)	58(64)	48(31)
2009	11.70(10.96)	6.08(6.11)	5.62(4.86)	110(103)	57(58)	53(46)
2010	11.65(15.82)	6.26(8.58)	5.39(7.24)	111(150)	60(81)	51(69)
2011	11.50(11.97)	6.10(7.07)	5.40(4.90)	110(114)	59(68)	51(47)
2012	11.90(11.74)	6.95(8.33)	4.95(3.40)	115(113)	67(80)	48(33)
2013	11.41(12.19)	6.40(6.23)	5.01(5.95)	111(117)	59(60)	52(57)
2014	14.23(22.74)	6.84(6.39)	7.39(16.35)	139(220)	67(62)	72(158)
2015	12.55(14.59)	6.67(6.16)	5.88(8.43)	124(143)	66(60)	58(83)
2016	17.89(15.56)	7.05(5.41)	10.84(10.15)	177(154)	70(53)	107(101)
2017	17.54(20.59)	7.40(11.88)	10.14(8.71)	175(205)	74(118)	101(87)
2018	13.26(14.93)	7.18(6.46)	6.08(8.47)	133(150)	72(65)	61(85)
2019	11.77(12.13)	7.50(6.46)	4.27(5.67)	118(123)	75(65)	43(58)
2020	8.56(9.87)	7.25(7.12)	1.31(2.75)	87(100)	74(72)	13(28)
2021	7.38	7.36	0.02	75.04	74.83	0.20

注:1990、2000年为普查数，2010年、2020年为人口普查推算数据，其余年份均为人口抽样调查数，括号内为当年前往公安机关申报登记数。

a)Data of 1990 and 2000 are based on the national population census,data of 2010 and 2020 are calculated according to the national population census. others are based on the sample surveys. Data in the brackets are registration data of the public security department.

3-3 人口年龄结构、抚养比和性别比

Age Composition and Dependency Ratio of Population

单位：% (%)

年 份 Year	总人口性别比(以女性为100) Sex Ratio of Total Population (female=100)	各年龄段所占比重 The Proportion of Total Population By Age			总抚养比 Gross Dependency Ratio	少儿抚养比 Children Dependency Ratio	老年抚养比 Old Dependency Ratio
		0-14岁 Aged 0-14	15-64岁 Aged 15-64	65岁及以上 Aged 65 and Over			
1982	102.9	31.0	63.4	5.6	57.7	48.9	8.8
1990	103.5	26.6	67.2	6.2	48.8	39.6	9.2
1995	103.7	24.6	68.0	7.4	47.1	36.2	10.9
2000	102.5	20.8	71.1	8.1	40.6	29.3	11.4
2001	102.7	20.4	71.4	8.2	40.1	28.6	11.5
2002	102.4	18.8	72.7	8.5	37.6	25.9	11.7
2003	100.4	18.4	72.6	9.1	37.8	25.3	12.5
2004	100.7	17.1	73.7	9.2	35.8	23.2	12.5
2005	102.0	15.9	74.1	9.9	34.9	21.5	13.4
2006	100.8	15.3	74.7	10.0	33.9	20.5	13.4
2007	101.4	15.0	74.8	10.2	33.7	20.1	13.6
2008	100.2	15.6	74.1	10.3	34.9	21.0	13.8
2009	102.3	15.7	73.9	10.4	35.4	21.2	14.1
2010	102.3	15.7	74.4	9.9	34.4	21.1	13.3
2011	102.0	15.7	74.3	10.0	34.6	21.1	13.5
2012	101.4	16.1	73.5	10.4	36.0	21.8	14.2
2013	101.2	16.1	72.9	11.0	37.1	22.1	15.0
2014	101.1	16.4	72.0	11.6	38.9	22.8	16.1
2015	102.1	16.6	71.2	12.2	40.4	23.3	17.1
2016	102.8	16.4	70.4	13.2	42.0	23.3	18.8
2017	102.7	17.2	68.8	14.0	45.3	25.0	20.3
2018	100.8	18.1	66.9	15.0	49.5	27.0	22.5
2019	99.2	18.0	66.2	15.8	51.1	27.2	23.9
2020	102.7	18.8	66.1	15.1	51.3	28.4	22.9
2021	103.1	18.4	65.7	15.9	52.3	28.1	24.2

注：1982、1990、2000、2010和2020年数据为人口普查数据；2001－2004年为抽样调查样本数据；其他年份为抽样调查估算数据。

a)Data of 1982、1990、2000、2010 and 2020 are taken from the national population census.Data of 2001-2004 are taken from Population Sample Survey. Others are estimated on population sample survey.

3-4 各市人口数和总户数(2021年)

Population and Households by Region (2021)

地 区	Region	年末总人口(万人) Total year-end Population (10 000 persons)	按性别分(万人) Grouped by Sex (10 000 persons)		按农村、城镇分(万人) Grouped by Rural and Urban (10 000persons)		平均家庭户规模(人/户) Average Family Size(person/household)
			男 Male	女 Female	农村人口 Rural Population	城镇人口 Urban Population	
全省总计	**Total**	**10169.99(10191.48)**	**(5168.95)**	**(5022.53)**	**3667.30**	**6502.69**	**2.50**
济 南 市	Jinan	933.61(816.61)	(404.03)	(412.57)	240.78	692.83	2.50
青 岛 市	Qingdao	1025.67(846.2)	(416.66)	(429.54)	234.16	791.51	2.42
淄 博 市	Zibo	470.88(434.04)	(215.37)	(218.66)	119.46	351.42	2.49
枣 庄 市	Zaozhuang	385.31(426.44)	(222.89)	(203.55)	153.97	231.34	2.80
东 营 市	Dongying	219.5(198.34)	(98.47)	(99.87)	62.54	156.96	2.43
烟 台 市	Yantai	708.28(649.34)	(322.1)	(327.24)	228.00	480.28	2.21
潍 坊 市	Weifang	940(920.31)	(463.22)	(457.08)	327.12	612.88	2.60
济 宁 市	Jining	833.65(894.52)	(461.19)	(433.33)	323.54	510.11	2.64
泰 安 市	Tai'an	543.49(569.36)	(287.45)	(281.91)	191.26	352.23	2.40
威 海 市	Weihai	291.46(256.47)	(126.68)	(129.79)	83.30	208.16	2.13
日 照 市	Rizhao	297.17(309.55)	(157.42)	(152.13)	113.13	184.04	2.37
临 沂 市	Linyi	1101.95(1201.46)	(621.2)	(580.26)	485.19	616.76	2.53
德 州 市	Dezhou	560(596.08)	(302.17)	(293.91)	255.36	304.64	2.45
聊 城 市	Liaocheng	592.79(648.31)	(333.25)	(315.06)	272.86	319.93	2.58
滨 州 市	Binzhou	393.01(397.35)	(200.5)	(196.85)	156.36	236.65	2.63
菏 泽 市	Heze	873.24(1027.1)	(536.33)	(490.77)	420.29	452.95	2.61

注：年末总人口根据人口抽样调查数据推算，括号内为公安户籍统计数字。

a) Data on total year-end population are estimated on the basis of the annual national sample survey of population.Data in the brackets are taken from the annual reports of public security departments.

3-5 七次人口普查主要数据

Major Data of All Previous Provincial Population Census

指　　标	Item	第一次人口普查 The First (1953.7.1)	第二次人口普查 The Second (1964.7.1)	第三次人口普查 The Third (1982.7.1)	第四次人口普查 The Fourth (1990.7.1)
一、总人口　(万人)	**Total (10 000 persons)**	**4887.65**	**5549.62**	**7441.91**	**8439.21**
按性别分	By Sex				
男	Male	2431.14	2790.45	3773.74	4291.32
女	Female	2456.52	2759.17	3668.16	4147.89
二、总户数　(万户)	**Total Households (10 000 units)**	**1109.77**	**1277.08**	**1739.04**	**2197.56**
家庭户　(万户)	Households (10 000 units)			1733.55	2187.44
平均家庭户规模(人)	Average Household Size (person)			4.20	3.75
三、民　族	**Nationalities**				
民族个数　(个)	The number of Nationalities (unit)	17	32	39	54
汉族人口　(万人)	Total Population of Han Nationality (10 000 persons)	4862.40	5520.04	7401.14	8388.62
少数民族人口(万人)	Total Population of Minority Nationalities (10 000 persons)	25.24	29.55	40.74	50.59
四、市镇人口　(万人)	**Population of City and Town (10 000 persons)**	**357.92**	**717.57**	**1419.05**	**2307.67**
五、平均预期寿命(岁)	**Life Expectancy (year old)**			**69.2**	**70.6**
六、各种文化程度人口	**Population by Education**				
大　学　(万人)	University and Above (10 000 persons)			26.32	82.29
高　中　(万人)	Senior Middle Schools (10 000 persons)			438.72	603.36
初　中　(万人)	Junior Middle Schools (10 000 persons)			1316.97	2125.47
小　学　(万人)	Primary Schools (10 000 persons)			2510.81	3061.20
文盲半文盲　(万人)	Illiterate or Semiliterate (10 000 persons)			2045.72	1425.61
七、6岁及以上人口平均受教育年限　(年)	**Years of education of Population Aged 6 and Over (year)**			**4.9**	**6.2**
八、就业人口　(万人)	**Economically Active Population(10 000 persons)**			**4009.79**	**5077.21**

3-5 续表 continued

指　　标	Item	第五次人口普查 The Fifth (2000.11.1)	第六次人口普查 The Sixth (2010.11.1)	第七次人口普查 The Seventh (2020.11.1)
一、总人口　(万人)	**Total (10 000 persons)**	**8997.18**	**9579.27**	**10152.75**
按性别分	By Sex			
男	Male	4554.21	4844.69	5143.29
女	Female	4442.97	4734.58	5009.45
二、总户数　(万户)	**Total Households (10 000 units)**	**2732.04**	**3079.47**	**3704.55**
家庭户　(万户)	Households (10 000 units)	2670.93	3010.55	3518.42
平均家庭户规模(人)	Average Household Size (person)	3.22	2.98	2.70
三、民　族	**Nationalities**			
民族个数　(个)	The number of Nationalities (unit)	56	56	56
汉族人口　(万人)	Total Population of Han Nationality (10 000 persons)	8933.90	9506.68	10062.25
少数民族人口(万人)	Total Population of Minority Nationalities (10 000 persons)	63.27	72.59	90.50
四、市镇人口　(万人)	**Population of City and Town (10 000 persons)**	**3432.59**	**4762.07**	**6401.43**
五、平均预期寿命(岁)	**Life Expectancy (year old)**	**73.9**	**76.5**	**79.2**
六、各种文化程度人口	**Population by Education**			
大　学　(万人)	University and Above (10 000 persons)	300.08	832.87	1460.35
高　中　(万人)	Senior Middle Schools (10 000 persons)	994.64	1332.26	1455.28
初　中　(万人)	Junior Middle Schools (10 000 persons)	3297.35	3846.80	3632.42
小　学　(万人)	Primary Schools (10 000 persons)	2946.97	2391.22	2405.46
文盲半文盲　(万人)	Illiterate or Semiliterate (10 000 persons)	765.43	475.73	330.83
七、6岁及以上人口平均受教育年限　(年)	**Years of education of Population Aged 6 and Over (year)**	**7.5**	**8.8**	**9.4**
八、就业人口　(万人)	**Economically Active Population(10 000 persons)**	**5477.41**	**5902.34**	**5510.00**

主要统计指标解释

人口数 指一定时点、一定地区范围内有生命的个人总和。

城镇人口和乡村人口 普查的城镇人口是指居住在城镇范围内的全部常住人口；乡村人口是除上述人口以外的全部人口。公安机关登记的城镇人口是指户口登记在城镇的人口，其统计口径是以居民常住户口所在地的城乡性质划分的。

出生率(又称粗出生率) 指在一定时期内(通常为一年)一定地区的出生人数与同期内平均人数(或期中人数)之比，用千分率表示。本资料中的出生率指年出生率，其计算公式为：

$$出生率=\frac{年出生人数}{年平均人数}\times 1000‰$$

式中：出生人数指活产婴儿，即胎儿脱离母体时(不管怀孕月数)，有过呼吸或其他生命现象。年平均人数指年初、年底人口数的平均数，也可用年中人口数代替。

死亡率(又称粗死亡率) 指在一定时期内(通常为一年)一定地区的死亡人数与同期内平均人数(或期中人数)之比，用千分率表示。本资料中的死亡率指年死亡率，其计算公式为：

$$死亡率=\frac{年死亡人数}{年平均人数}\times 1000‰$$

人口自然增长率 指在一定时期内(通常为一年)人口自然增加数(出生人数减死亡人数)与该时期内平均人数(或期中人数)之比，用千分率表示。计算公式为：

$$人口自然增长率=\frac{本年出生人数-本年死亡人数}{年平均人数}\times 1000‰$$

$$=人口出生率-人口死亡率$$

总抚养比 也称总负担系数。是指人口总体中非劳动年龄人口数与劳动年龄人口数之比。通常用百分比表示。说明每100名劳动年龄人口要负担多少名非劳动年龄人口。用于从人口角度反映人口与经济发展的基本关系。

计算公式为：

$$GDR=\frac{P_{0\sim14}+P_{65+}}{P_{15\sim64}}\times 100\%$$

其中：GDR 为总抚养比；

$P_{0\sim14}$ 为0~14岁少年儿童人口数；

P_{65+} 为65 岁及以上的老年人口数；

$P_{15\sim64}$ 为15~64 岁劳动年龄人口数。

老年人口抚养比 也称老年人口抚养系数。是指某人口总体中老年人口数与劳动年龄人口数之比。通常用百分比表示。用以表明每100名劳动年龄人口要负担多少名老年人。老年人口抚养比是从经济角度反映人口老化社会后果的指标之一。

计算公式为：

$$ODR=\frac{P_{65+}}{P_{15\sim64}}\times 100\%$$

其中：ODR 为老年人口抚养比；

P_{65+} 为65岁及以上的老年人口数；

$P_{15\sim64}$ 为15~64岁的劳动年龄人口数。

少年儿童抚养比 也称少年儿童抚养系数。是指某人口总体中少年儿童人口与劳动年龄人口数之比。通常用百分比表示。用以反映每100名劳动年龄人口要负担多少名少年儿童。

计算公式为：

$$CDR=\frac{P_{0\sim14}}{P_{15\sim64}}\times 100\%$$

其中：CDR 为少年儿童抚养比；

$P_{0\sim14}$ 为0- 14岁少年儿童人口数；

$P_{15\sim64}$ 为15~64岁劳动年龄人口数。

Explanatory Notes on Main Statistical Indicators

Total Population refers to the total number of people alive at a certain point of time within a given area.

Urban Population and Rural Population Urban population refer to all people residing in cities and towns, while rural population refer to population other than urban population. Urban population data of public security department only include persons whose household registration in urban.

Birth Rate (or Crude Birth Rate) refers to the ratio of the number of births to the average population (or mid period population) during a certain period of time (usually a year), expressed in ‰. Birth rate in the chapter refers to annual birth rate. The following formula is used:

$$\text{Birth Rate} = \frac{\text{Number of Births}}{\text{Annual Average Population}} \times 1000‰$$

Number of births in the formula refers to live births, i.e. when a baby has breathed or showed any vital phenomena regardless of the length of pregnancy.

Annual average number of population is the average of the number of population at the beginning of the year and that at the end of the year. Sometimes it is substituted by the mid year population.

Death Rate (or Crude Death Rate) refers to the ratio of the number of deaths to the average population (or mid period population) during a certain period of time (usually a year), expressed in ‰. Death rate in the chapter refers to annual death rate. The following formula is used:

$$\text{Death Rate} = \frac{\text{Number of Deaths}}{\text{Annual Average Population}} \times 1000‰$$

Natural Growth Rate of Population refers to the ratio of natural increase in population (number of births minus number of deaths) in a certain period of time (usually a year) to the average population (or mid period population) of the same period, expressed in ‰. The following formula is applied:

$$\frac{\text{Natural Growth}}{\text{Rate of Population}} = \frac{\text{Number of Births} - \text{Number of Deaths}}{\text{Annual Average Population}} \times 1000‰$$

Natural Growth Rate of Population = Birth Rate－Death

Gross Dependency Ratio also called gross dependency coefficient, refers to the ratio of non-working-age population to the working-age population ,express in %. Describing in general the number of non-working-age population that every 100 people at working ages will take care of, this indicator reflects the basic relation between population and economic development from the demographic perspective. The gross dependency ratio is calculated with the following formula:

$$GDR = \frac{P_{0\sim14} + P_{65+}}{P_{15\sim64}} \times 100\%$$

Where: GDR is the gross dependency ratio,

$P_{0\sim14}$ is the population of children aged 0-14;

P_{65+} is the elderly population aged 65 and over ;

$P_{15\sim64}$ is the working –age population aged 15-64.

Old Dependency Ratio also called old dependency coefficient,refers to the ratio of the elderly population to the working-age population, express in %.It describes the number of the elderly population that every 100 people at working ages will take care of. Old dependency ratio is one of the indicators reflecting the social implication of population aging from the economic perspective. The old dependency ratio is calculated with the following formula:

$$ODR = \frac{P_{65+}}{P_{15\sim64}} \times 100\%$$

Where: ODR is the old dependency ratio,

P_{65+} is the elderly population aged 65 and over;

$P_{15\sim64}$ is the working –age population aged 15-64.

Children Dependency Ratio also called children dependency coefficient, refers to the ratio of the children population to the working-age population ,express in %.It describes the number of children population that every 100 people at working ages will take care of. The children dependency ratio is calculated with the following formula:

$$CDR = \frac{P_{0\sim14}}{P_{15\sim64}} \times 100\%$$

Where:CDR is the children dependency ratio;

$P_{0\sim14}$ is the children population aged 0-14;

$P_{15\sim64}$ is the working-age population aged 15-64.

第
4
篇

就业、工资和社会保障

Employment, Wages and Social Security

简 要 说 明

一、本篇资料的主要内容

本篇资料反映全省劳动经济方面的基本情况，包括就业人员及职工人数，城镇登记失业人数，就业人员工资总额，平均工资等。

二、本篇资料的来源

1.就业基本情况及分组资料、工资总额、平均工资等资料取自《劳动工资统计报表制度》。

2.城镇登记失业人员及失业率、社会保障等资料由省人力资源和社会保障厅、省医疗保障局根据其相关统计制度整理提供。

3.本篇资料由省统计局人口处（社科处）整理提供。

Brief Introduction

I. Main Content

Data in this chapter show the basic conditions of Shandong’s labor economy, including number of employed persons, number of registered unemployed persons in urban areas, total wage bills and average wages of employed persons, etc.

II. Source of Data

(1) Data on basic conditions of employment,data by groups, total wage bills and average wages of employed persons are collected and compiled through The Reporting Form System on Labour Wage Statistics.

(2) Data on registered unemployed persons in urban areas and unemployment rate and social securities are provided by Shandong Provincial Department of Human Resource and Social Security,Medical Insurance Bureau.

(3) Data in this chapter are prepared and compiled by the Division of Urbanization,Population and Employment Statistics（by the Division of Social,Science and Culture Industry Employment Statistics）of Shandong Provincial Bureau of Statistics.

4-1 就业基本情况
Employment

类　别	Category	2017	2018	2019	2020	2021
就业人员合计　(万人)	**Total Number of Employed Persons　(10 000 persons)**	**5693**	**5621**	**5561**	**5510**	**5475**
第一产业	Primary Industry	1622.5	1534.5	1445.9	1372.0	1316.0
第二产业	Secondary Industry	1907.2	1877.4	1851.8	1840.3	1850.0
第三产业	Tertiary Industry	2163.3	2209.1	2263.3	2297.7	2309.0
就业人员构成　(合计=100)	**Composition of Employed Persons　(total=100)**					
第一产业	Primary Industry	28.5	27.3	26.0	24.9	24.0
第二产业	Secondary Industry	33.5	33.4	33.3	33.4	33.8
第三产业	Tertiary Industry	38.0	39.3	40.7	41.7	42.2
按城乡分就业人员	**Number of Employed Persons by Urban and Rural Areas**					
城镇就业人员　(万人)	Urban Employed Persons　(10 000 persons)	3256.4	3282.7	3303.2	3344.6	3386.0
#国有单位	State-owned Units	384.9	359.9	345.4	372.8	381.4
城镇集体单位	Urban Collective-owned Units	41.0	29.0	18.7	18.6	17.9
股份合作单位	Cooperative Units	6.5	4.6	1.8	2.5	1.9
联营单位	Joint Ownership Units	0.7	0.5	0.5	0.8	0.9
有限责任公司	Limited Liability Corporations	471.5	461.6	424.2	420.9	426.0
股份有限公司	Share-holding Corporations Ltd.	144.1	148.1	147.3	153.6	149.9
港澳台投资单位	Units with Funds from Hong Kong,Macao & Taiwan	36.6	33.4	31.9	33.4	39.7
外商投资单位	Foreign Funded Units	91.1	77.5	76.2	73.9	67.2
乡村就业人员　(万人)	Rural Employed Persons　(10 000 persons)	2436.6	2338.3	2257.8	2165.4	2089.0
城镇非私营单位在岗职工人数(万人)	**Number of Staff and Workers on the job of Urban Non private units　(10 000 persons)**	**1130.3**	**1065.4**	**1000.1**	**1027.8**	**1039.1**
国有单位	State-owned Units	369.6	345.4	330.6	360.8	367.3
城镇集体单位	Urban Collective-owned Units	38.9	26.7	17.5	17.6	17.2
其他单位	Units of Other Types of Ownership	721.7	693.2	652.0	649.4	654.6
城镇非私营单位女性就业人员(万人)	**Urban Employed Female Persons of Urban Non private units　(10 000 persons)**	**430.2**	**410.6**	**406.7**	**426.8**	**435.3**
城镇累计新增就业人数　(万人)	**Number of Newly Employed Persons in Urban Areas　(10 000 persons)**	**128.3**	**136.8**	**138.3**	**122.7**	**124.2**
就业转失业人员再就业　(万人)	**Number of reemployed Persons　(10 000 persons)**	**58.1**	**54.5**	**51.7**	**48.0**	**45.1**
#困难群体再就业	Reemployed Persons in Difficult Groups	8.8	10.1	11.6	7.5	8.9
城镇登记失业人数　(万人)	**Number of Registered Unemployed Persons in Urban Areas　(10 000 persons)**	**45.7**	**46.5**	**44.2**	**46.7**	**42.3**
城镇登记失业率　(%)	**Registered Unemployment Rate in Urban Areas　(%)**	**3.4**	**3.4**	**3.3**	**3.1**	**2.9**

注：2000—2019年就业人员相关数据根据第七次全国人口普查修订(以下相关表同)。

a)According to the Seventh National Census, the data of Employed Persons from 2000 to 2019 of Shandong have been revised(the same as in the following tables).

4-2 按三次产业分的年底就业人员数

Number of Employed Persons at the Year-end by Three Industries

年 份 Year	就业人员 (万人) Total Employed Persons (10 000 Persons)	第一产业 Primary Industry	第二产业 Secondary Industry	第三产业 Tertiary Industry	构成(合计=100) Composition in Percentage(Total=100) 第一产业 Primary Industry	第二产业 Secondary Industry	第三产业 Tertiary Industry
1949	1859.3						
1952	1897.2						
1955	1959.7						
1957	2150.4						
1962	1981.2						
1965	2146.0						
1970	2606.0						
1975	2925.0						
1978	2969.8	2350.9	366.6	252.3	79.2	12.3	8.5
1980	3117.5	2458.1	382.5	276.9	78.9	12.3	8.9
1981	3192.4	2508.2	389.0	295.2	78.6	12.2	9.3
1982	3270.0	2520.8	442.2	307.0	77.1	13.5	9.4
1983	3795.1	2950.8	465.8	378.5	77.8	12.3	10.0
1984	3563.7	2509.1	528.8	525.8	70.4	14.8	14.8
1985	3561.1	2438.6	705.3	417.2	68.5	19.8	11.7
1986	3651.2	2431.1	776.0	444.1	66.6	21.3	12.2
1987	3765.7	2422.6	848.2	494.9	64.3	22.5	13.1
1988	3887.1	2474.5	905.1	507.5	63.7	23.3	13.1
1989	3940.3	2527.6	902.6	510.1	64.2	22.9	13.0
1990	4043.2	2585.7	922.5	535.0	64.0	22.8	13.2
1991	4219.3	2708.0	958.7	552.6	64.2	22.7	13.1
1992	4302.6	2705.1	1000.8	596.7	62.9	23.3	13.9
1993	4379.3	2689.9	1070.4	619.0	61.4	24.4	14.1
1994	4382.1	2541.6	1098.0	742.5	58.0	25.1	16.9
1995	5207.4	2832.3	1305.5	1069.6	54.4	25.1	20.5
1996	5227.4	2788.0	1286.1	1153.3	53.3	24.6	22.1
1997	5256.0	2812.5	1311.9	1131.6	53.5	25.0	21.5
1998	5287.6	2837.3	1245.8	1204.5	53.7	23.6	22.8
1999	5314.7	2811.7	1245.7	1257.3	52.9	23.4	23.7
2000	5386.7	2806.5	1292.8	1287.4	52.1	24.0	23.9
2001	5430.9	2791.5	1336.0	1303.4	51.4	24.6	24.0
2002	5510.2	2755.1	1394.1	1361.0	50.0	25.3	24.7
2003	5541.0	2687.4	1446.2	1407.4	48.5	26.1	25.4
2004	5622.4	2642.5	1529.3	1450.6	47.0	27.2	25.8
2005	5689.2	2582.9	1587.3	1519.0	45.4	27.9	26.7
2006	5756.3	2527.0	1640.5	1588.7	43.9	28.5	27.6
2007	5803.6	2460.7	1688.9	1654.0	42.4	29.1	28.5
2008	5815.1	2378.4	1732.9	1703.8	40.9	29.8	29.3
2009	5844.7	2302.8	1782.6	1759.3	39.4	30.5	30.1
2010	5940.0	2257.2	1853.3	1829.5	38.0	31.2	30.8
2011	5915.0	2164.9	1881.0	1869.1	36.6	31.8	31.6
2012	5892.0	2068.1	1914.9	1909.0	35.1	32.5	32.4
2013	5840.0	1973.9	1915.5	1950.6	33.8	32.8	33.4
2014	5798.0	1878.6	1919.1	2000.3	32.4	33.1	34.5
2015	5773.0	1795.4	1922.4	2055.2	31.1	33.3	35.6
2016	5728.0	1706.9	1907.4	2113.6	29.8	33.3	36.9
2017	5693.0	1622.5	1907.2	2163.3	28.5	33.5	38.0
2018	5621.0	1534.5	1877.4	2209.1	27.3	33.4	39.3
2019	5561.0	1445.9	1851.8	2263.3	26.0	33.3	40.7
2020	5510.0	1372.0	1840.3	2297.7	24.9	33.4	41.7
2021	5475.0	1316.0	1850.0	2309.0	24.0	33.8	42.2

4-3 按登记注册类型和行业分城镇非私营单位就业人员数(2021年底) Number of Employed Persons in Urban Non-private units at the Year-end by Status of Registration and Sector(2021)

单位:万人 (10 000 persons)

类别	Category	总计 Total	在岗职工 Staff and Workers	国有单位 State-owned Units	城镇集体单位 Urban Collective-owned Units
总计	**Total**	**1108.3**	**1039.1**	**381.4**	**17.9**
按企、事业和机关分	**Grouped by Enterprises,institutions and Agencies**				
企业	Enterprises	765.2	707.6	61.0	11.2
政府	Government	327.5	316.6	317.8	5.5
民间非营利组织	Civil Nonprofit Organization	15.1	14.5	2.4	1.1
其他	Others	0.4	0.4	0.1	
按国民经济行业分	**Grouped by Sector**				
农、林、牧、渔业	Agriculture,Forestry,Animal Husbandry and Fishing	1.0	1.0	0.4	0.1
采矿业	Mining	27.5	26.7	2.3	
制造业	Manufacturing	276.3	273.6	4.0	1.2
电力、热力、燃气及水的生产和供应业	Production and Supply of Electric, Heat, Gas and Water	28.4	28.1	12.4	0.1
建筑业	Construction	139.3	125.0	9.1	6.5
批发和零售业	Wholesale and Retail Trade	44.0	43.2	2.0	0.6
交通运输、仓储和邮政业	Traffic,Transport,Storage and Post	45.5	44.7	7.5	0.2
住宿和餐饮业	Hotels and Catering Services	11.9	11.4	2.1	0.1
信息传输、软件和信息技术服务业	Information Transfer, Software and Information Technology Services	21.0	20.8	2.0	
金融业	Financial Intermediation	65.9	33.9	5.8	
房地产业	Real Estate	28.5	27.3	1.4	0.5
租赁和商务服务业	Leasing and Business Services	24.7	23.6	4.4	0.5
科学研究和技术服务业	Scientific Research and Technical Service	22.6	21.9	7.1	0.3
水利、环境和公共设施管理业	Management of Water Conservancy,Environment and Public Facilities	15.8	13.7	5.4	0.2
居民服务、修理和其他服务业	Households Services, Repair and Other Services	3.5	3.3	0.9	0.2
教育	Education	133.5	130.6	111.3	4.3
卫生和社会工作	Health and Social Work	76.0	72.3	64.6	2.6
文化、体育和娱乐业	Culture,Sports and Entertainment	8.0	7.7	4.8	0.1
公共管理、社会保障和社会组织	Public management,Social Security and Social Organization	134.9	130.1	133.9	0.3
国际组织	International Organization				

4-4 各市年底就业人员数(2021年底)

Number of Employed Persons at the Year-end by Region（2021）

单位:万人 (10 000 persons)

地 区	Region	总 计 Total	城 镇 非 私营单位 Urban Non-private Units	农、林、牧、渔业 Agriculture, Forestry, Animal Husbandry and Fishing	采矿业 Mining	制造业 Manufacturing	电力、热力、燃气及水的生产和供应业 Production and Supply of Electric Heat, Gas and Water	建筑业 Construction	批发和零售业 Wholesale and Retail Trade
全省合计	**Total**	**5475.0**	**1108.3**	**1.0**	**27.5**	**276.3**	**28.4**	**139.3**	**44.0**
济 南 市	Jinan	470.8	158.7	0.1	1.3	26.0	1.8	28.8	8.8
青 岛 市	Qingdao	527.7	147.7	0.1		45.0	2.2	12.2	8.6
淄 博 市	Zibo	227.0	68.3	0.1	0.3	16.5	1.2	19.2	1.8
枣 庄 市	Zaozhuang	197.2	34.0		2.4	5.7	0.6	5.4	0.7
东 营 市	Dongying	123.3	36.7	0.1	8.0	8.0	0.5	3.2	1.1
烟 台 市	Yantai	429.1	86.5	0.1	2.9	31.8	1.7	6.2	3.7
潍 坊 市	Weifang	527.6	96.0	0.1	0.1	34.6	1.2	7.2	3.6
济 宁 市	Jining	425.4	75.8	0.1	8.3	12.8	1.4	7.4	2.4
泰 安 市	Tai'an	295.0	57.1		2.9	10.2	0.9	19.4	1.7
威 海 市	Weihai	173.3	48.5	0.1		21.1	1.0	2.5	2.2
日 照 市	Rizhao	164.8	32.0			8.8	0.5	3.3	1.6
临 沂 市	Linyi	617.7	73.0	0.1	0.1	15.1	1.1	9.6	3.5
德 州 市	Dezhou	323.2	41.9		0.1	11.1	0.8	3.7	1.4
聊 城 市	Liaocheng	283.6	41.3			8.0	0.6	4.3	0.8
滨 州 市	Binzhou	210.5	42.2		0.1	16.1	1.8	2.5	1.1
菏 泽 市	Heze	479.4	49.1	0.1	1.0	4.9	0.5	4.6	0.9

4-4 续表 1 continued

单位:万人 (10 000 persons)

地 区	Region	交通运输、仓储和邮政业 Traffic, Transport, Storage and Post	住宿和餐饮业 Hotels and Catering Services	信息传输、软件和信息技术服务业 Information Transfer, Software and Information Technology Services	金融业 Financial Intermediation	房地产业 Real Estate	租赁和商务服务业 Leasing and Business Services	科学研究和技术服务业 Scientific Research and Technical Service
全省总计	**Total**	**45.5**	**11.9**	**21.0**	**65.9**	**28.5**	**24.7**	**22.6**
济 南 市	Jinan	7.2	2.6	9.5	10.0	6.2	5.2	7.1
青 岛 市	Qingdao	9.0	3.0	2.8	11.3	5.1	3.4	5.5
淄 博 市	Zibo	1.2	0.3	1.5	3.9	1.0	1.7	0.9
枣 庄 市	Zaozhuang	0.9	0.2	0.3	2.6	0.6	0.4	0.4
东 营 市	Dongying	0.9	0.3	0.5	1.3	0.7	3.0	1.1
烟 台 市	Yantai	4.0	1.0	1.0	5.0	2.3	1.4	1.5
潍 坊 市	Weifang	1.8	0.8	1.2	3.2	2.3	1.4	1.1
济 宁 市	Jining	1.4	0.8	0.7	5.3	1.6	1.5	0.9
泰 安 市	Tai'an	1.0	0.5	0.8	3.6	1.1	0.8	0.5
威 海 市	Weihai	1.4	0.8	0.3	3.1	1.9	1.1	0.6
日 照 市	Rizhao	2.9	0.2	0.3	1.2	0.8	1.0	0.4
临 沂 市	Linyi	1.5	0.5	0.5	5.0	1.9	1.6	0.8
德 州 市	Dezhou	0.9	0.3	0.4	3.4	0.8	0.9	0.5
聊 城 市	Liaocheng	1.0	0.2	0.3	3.0	0.7	0.4	0.4
滨 州 市	Binzhou	1.1	0.3	0.3	1.3	0.9	0.4	0.4
菏 泽 市	Heze	1.0	0.2	0.4	2.7	0.6	0.6	0.6

4-4 续表 2 continued

单位:万人 (10 000 persons)

地 区	Region	水利、环境和公共设施管理业 Management of Water Conservancy, Environment and Public Facilities	居民服务、修理和其他服务业 Households Services, Repair and Other Services	教 育 Education	卫生和社会工作 Health and Social Work	文化、体育和娱乐业 Culture,Sports and Entertainment	公共管理、社会保障和社会组织 Public management, Social Security and Social Organization	国际组织 International Organization
全省总计	**Total**	**15.8**	**3.5**	**133.5**	**76.0**	**8.0**	**134.9**	
济 南 市	Jinan	1.9	0.8	16.4	10.4	2.1	12.5	
青 岛 市	Qingdao	2.2	0.5	14.2	8.6	1.3	12.6	
淄 博 市	Zibo	1.1	0.1	6.3	4.4	0.4	6.5	
枣 庄 市	Zaozhuang	0.5	0.1	4.3	2.1	0.2	6.3	
东 营 市	Dongying	0.3	0.1	2.2	1.6	0.2	3.7	
烟 台 市	Yantai	0.8	0.2	7.8	5.4	0.5	9.3	
潍 坊 市	Weifang	2.8	0.2	13.8	6.8	0.5	13.4	
济 宁 市	Jining	0.8	0.2	11.2	6.4	0.5	12.1	
泰 安 市	Tai'an	0.7	0.1	5.3	3.9	0.3	3.5	
威 海 市	Weihai	0.5	0.2	4.1	2.8	0.3	4.6	
日 照 市	Rizhao	0.5	0.1	3.4	1.9	0.2	5.1	
临 沂 市	Linyi	1.2	0.3	12.7	7.0	0.5	10.1	
德 州 市	Dezhou	0.6	0.2	6.3	3.1	0.4	7.1	
聊 城 市	Liaocheng	0.6	0.2	8.7	3.8	0.2	8.1	
滨 州 市	Binzhou	0.3	0.2	5.4	2.3	0.2	7.5	
菏 泽 市	Heze	1.1	0.1	11.4	5.6	0.3	12.5	

4-5 按登记注册类型和行业分城镇非私营单位就业人员工资总额(2021年)

Total Wages Bill of Employed Persons in Urban Non-private units by Status of Registration and Sector(2021)

单位:万元 (10 000 yuan)

类别	Category	总计 Total	在岗职工 Staff and Workers	国有单位 State -owned Units	城镇集体单位 Urban Collective -owned Units
总计	**Total**	**104576542**	**101043007**	**42914881**	**1185385**
按企、事业和机关分	**Grouped by Enterprises,institutions and Agencies**				
企业	Enterprises	66692226	63685825	6749851	599064
政府	Government	36976875	36479234	35973589	524346
民间非营利组织	Civil Nonprofit Organization	876279	846995	180057	60244
其他	Others	31160	30953	11384	1731
按国民经济行业分	**Grouped by Sector**				
农、林、牧、渔业	Agriculture,Forestry,Animal Husbandry and Fishing	67520	66739	32709	4378
采矿业	Mining	3101580	3058407	205476	1376
制造业	Manufacturing	22945484	22752617	372083	81953
电力、热力、燃气及水的生产和供应业	Production and Supply of Electric, Heat, Gas and Water	3501653	3488210	1787589	4247
建筑业	Construction	10442413	9479794	818317	323432
批发和零售业	Wholesale and Retail Trade	3308369	3257000	211147	31463
交通运输、仓储和邮政业	Traffic,Transport,Storage and Post	4899284	4860378	832656	13000
住宿和餐饮业	Hotels and Catering Services	627919	615765	117419	5319
信息传输、软件和信息技术服务业	Information Transfer, Software and Information Technology Services	2425001	2412896	260841	296
金融业	Financial Intermediation	6813086	5344459	791623	1826
房地产业	Real Estate	2333645	2296289	112915	23896
租赁和商务服务业	Leasing and Business Services	1978914	1942493	365580	28570
科学研究和技术服务业	Scientific Research and Technical Service	2661188	2592414	914336	20152
水利、环境和公共设施管理业	Management of Water Conservancy,Environment and Public Facilities	812949	768825	411333	9532
居民服务、修理和其他服务业	Households Services, Repair and Other Services	207176	199699	73348	9154
教育	Education	14421459	14302639	12860860	380845
卫生和社会工作	Health and Social Work	8746220	8528170	7835044	203739
文化、体育和娱乐业	Culture,Sports and Entertainment	803061	787842	525881	8551
公共管理、社会保障和社会组织	Public management,Social Security and Social Organization	14479621	14288371	14385723	33658
国际组织	International Organization				

4-6 各市按行业分城镇非私营单位就业人员工资总额(2021年)

Total Wages Bill of Employed Persons in Urban Non-private units by Sector and Region (2021)

单位:万元 (10 000 yuan)

地 区	Region	总 计 Total	农、林、牧、渔业 Agriculture, Forestry, Animal Husbandry and Fishing	采矿业 Mining	制造业 Manufacturing	电力、热力、燃气及水的生产和供应业 Production and Supply of Electric Heat, Gas and Water	建筑业 Construction	批发和零售业 Wholesale and Retail Trade
全省合计	**Total**	**104576542**	**67520**	**3101580**	**22945484**	**3501653**	**10442413**	**3308369**
济南市	Jinan	18110031	7206	129922	2645630	197892	2825241	741244
青岛市	Qingdao	17004166	5376	552	4231177	240911	1058263	790504
淄博市	Zibo	5895112	4305	33037	1436630	159818	1382668	129640
枣庄市	Zaozhuang	2658503	1347	214072	386274	51571	321140	46385
东营市	Dongying	4018627	3925	1281374	673057	50598	216374	80518
烟台市	Yantai	8202532	4851	310446	2685361	224667	386429	271797
潍坊市	Weifang	8374400	7333	6156	2770649	112187	672719	267493
济宁市	Jining	6388602	5880	765100	933278	141450	461860	134397
泰安市	Tai'an	4255118	1893	218216	698466	83727	1233274	103177
威海市	Weihai	3889719	6441		1513196	100101	170136	144740
日照市	Rizhao	2880578	2500	1044	759944	53695	217650	93744
临沂市	Linyi	6113039	6333	15089	1096862	104993	560861	227062
德州市	Dezhou	3235898	1721	7092	901943	83521	253441	85334
聊城市	Liaocheng	3278689	1615		507791	54629	272762	52225
滨州市	Binzhou	3701463	3527	8536	1262549	165871	167485	73225
菏泽市	Heze	3655000	3267	110943	300213	36234	242107	66883

4-6 续表 1 continued

单位:万元 (10 000 yuan)

地 区	Region	交通运输、仓储和邮政业 Traffic, Transport, Storage and Post	住宿和餐饮业 Hotels and Catering Services	信息传输、软件和信息技术服务业 Information Transfer,Software and Information Technology Services	金融业 Financial Intermediation	房地产业 Real Estate	租赁和商务服务业 Leasing and Business Services	科学研究和技术服务业 Scientific Research and Technical Service
全省合计	**Total**	**4899284**	**627919**	**2425001**	**6813086**	**2333645**	**1978914**	**2661188**
济南市	Jinan	840574	135195	1106895	1446071	504862	514864	953077
青岛市	Qingdao	1034815	186308	415119	1414212	638670	316792	750030
淄博市	Zibo	97584	13441	172674	350325	60800	92807	86863
枣庄市	Zaozhuang	59358	8595	32774	160696	39703	31790	40151
东营市	Dongying	88729	17848	50825	135808	50029	372822	115898
烟台市	Yantai	479182	50503	114855	508048	185285	112587	173397
潍坊市	Weifang	135790	40579	91310	348105	163650	75520	87944
济宁市	Jining	112994	36365	69853	413345	105049	80975	79235
泰安市	Tai'an	74895	20719	82925	324851	69930	34835	50672
威海市	Weihai	116923	41003	40271	257732	117706	59674	48511
日照市	Rizhao	259125	8953	27762	97308	52122	46125	35332
临沂市	Linyi	130468	23430	58459	460221	140759	96801	72300
德州市	Dezhou	76821	14866	42523	284883	63921	47391	35726
聊城市	Liaocheng	86431	9676	33704	306356	42605	34431	51225
滨州市	Binzhou	84795	12943	36756	140909	54247	27816	37294
菏泽市	Heze	87985	7496	48296	164217	44305	33685	43534

4-6 续表 2 continued

单位:万元 (10 000 yuan)

地 区	Region	水利、环境和公共设施管理业 Management of Water Conservancy, Environment and Public Facilities	居民服务、修理和其他服务业 Households Services, Repair and Other Services	教 育 Education	卫生和社会工作 Health and Social Work	文化、体育和娱乐业 Culture, Sports and Entertainment	公共管理、社会保障和社会组织 Public management, Social Security and Social Organization	国际组织 International Organization
全省合计	**Total**	**812949**	**207176**	**14421459**	**8746220**	**803061**	**14479621**	
济南市	Jinan	128299	51531	2115045	1630630	262651	1873202	
青岛市	Qingdao	139942	38856	2155460	1389496	164444	2033239	
淄博市	Zibo	38369	4440	723420	417421	34867	656002	
枣庄市	Zaozhuang	28623	6896	382070	202661	16732	627665	
东营市	Dongying	24585	5477	231299	193526	12995	412940	
烟台市	Yantai	55825	12003	949054	558771	38207	1081264	
潍坊市	Weifang	82940	9421	1336552	704915	37138	1423997	
济宁市	Jining	45583	11417	1144263	715676	39890	1091992	
泰安市	Tai'an	44947	5913	527551	353733	18293	307103	
威海市	Weihai	25319	9384	440185	308526	27937	461935	
日照市	Rizhao	35022	2877	373351	199970	22649	591406	
临沂市	Linyi	44478	12441	1265571	671403	41758	1083750	
德州市	Dezhou	31514	7019	502201	269360	24121	502498	
聊城市	Liaocheng	31496	11401	738873	416840	16795	609833	
滨州市	Binzhou	18494	11806	558889	247489	20449	768382	
菏泽市	Heze	37512	6295	977675	465803	24136	954413	

4-7 按登记注册类型和行业分城镇非私营单位就业人员平均工资(2021年)

Average Earning of Employed Persons in Urban Non-private units by Status of Registration and Sector(2021)

单位:元 (yuan)

类别	Category	总计 Total	在岗职工 Staff and Workers	国有单位 State-owned Units	城镇集体单位 Urban Collective-owned Units
总计	**Total**	**94768**	**98094**	**113670**	**67351**
按企、事业和机关分	**Grouped by Enterprises,institutions and Agencies**				
企业	Enterprises	87159	90591	109902	54543
政府	Government	114408	116721	114722	95856
民间非营利组织	Civil Nonprofit Organization	59336	59773	74990	53764
其他	Others	86933	87356	75741	66326
按国民经济行业分	**Grouped by Sector**				
农、林、牧、渔业	Agriculture,Forestry,Animal Husbandry and Fishing	66054	66562	78950	59416
采矿业	Mining	113104	115253	84363	60334
制造业	Manufacturing	83162	83264	93122	65970
电力、热力、燃气及水的生产和供应业	Production and Supply of Electric, Heat, Gas and Water	122998	123841	140892	55560
建筑业	Construction	76278	77683	87800	51048
批发和零售业	Wholesale and Retail Trade	75628	75805	106724	53034
交通运输、仓储和邮政业	Traffic,Transport,Storage and Post	106536	107658	110521	53894
住宿和餐饮业	Hotels and Catering Services	53297	54790	56736	41647
信息传输、软件和信息技术服务业	Information Transfer, Software and Information Technology Services	116084	116551	127014	92500
金融业	Financial Intermediation	97701	157609	137793	175606
房地产业	Real Estate	81054	83125	78534	47136
租赁和商务服务业	Leasing and Business Services	80887	83219	85124	61607
科学研究和技术服务业	Scientific Research and Technical Service	120830	121713	130806	73963
水利、环境和公共设施管理业	Management of Water Conservancy,Environment and Public Facilities	51780	56383	76284	49881
居民服务、修理和其他服务业	Households Services, Repair and Other Services	60785	62217	82843	54523
教育	Education	109680	111138	117171	89945
卫生和社会工作	Health and Social Work	117288	120120	123511	78537
文化、体育和娱乐业	Culture,Sports and Entertainment	100855	102834	109841	81812
公共管理、社会保障和社会组织	Public management,Social Security and Social Organization	108681	111073	108718	99493
国际组织	International Organization				

4-8 各市按行业分城镇非私营单位就业人员平均工资(2021年)
Average Earning of Employed Persons in Urban Non-private units by Sector and Region (2021)

单位:元 (yuan)

地区	Region	总计 Total	农、林、牧、渔业 Agriculture, Forestry, Animal Husbandry and Fishing	采矿业 Mining	制造业 Manufacturing	电力、热力、燃气及水的生产和供应业 Production and Supply of Electric Heat, Gas and Water	建筑业 Construction	批发和零售业 Wholesale and Retail Trade
全省合计	**Total**	**94768**	**66054**	**113104**	**83162**	**122998**	**76278**	**75628**
济南市	Jinan	114596	84756	99321	101929	110346	98619	85375
青岛市	Qingdao	116477	69573	54373	94413	113909	93571	92353
淄博市	Zibo	87266	81333	101397	87731	109645	76299	68007
枣庄市	Zaozhuang	79027	48282	88235	68754	79492	60239	62102
东营市	Dongying	109295	69953	155993	84793	104105	69348	71693
烟台市	Yantai	94524	69965	107787	83707	133362	64164	73830
潍坊市	Weifang	86567	74408	55855	80643	95291	79337	72109
济宁市	Jining	84863	53909	96170	73123	104535	63074	60707
泰安市	Tai'an	75769	52433	75752	69559	94220	65794	60491
威海市	Weihai	80128	66761		71851	101129	66625	66861
日照市	Rizhao	90223	56274	98168	85959	118288	68324	57490
临沂市	Linyi	84363	67429	90054	73865	99580	59794	67045
德州市	Dezhou	78045	52271	101289	81652	112934	70293	60560
聊城市	Liaocheng	80297	53530		63633	88498	67488	65870
滨州市	Binzhou	86504	63899	77342	74905	93343	66387	68181
菏泽市	Heze	74482	57535	116475	62185	69251	53680	69774

4-8 续表 1 continued

单位:元 (yuan)

地区	Region	交通运输、仓储和邮政业 Traffic, Transport, Storage and Post	住宿和餐饮业 Hotels and Catering Services	信息传输、软件和信息技术服务业 Information Transfer,Software and Information Technology Services	金融业 Financial Intermediation	房地产业 Real Estate	租赁和商务服务业 Leasing and Business Services	科学研究和技术服务业 Scientific Research and Technical Service
全省合计	**Total**	**106536**	**53297**	**116084**	**97701**	**81054**	**80887**	**120830**
济南市	Jinan	116497	53393	118024	138617	80540	101969	134599
青岛市	Qingdao	114457	62953	149555	121891	121628	92586	145469
淄博市	Zibo	82998	45606	103770	80573	62683	54420	105036
枣庄市	Zaozhuang	66342	39898	101031	59834	67482	64488	97103
东营市	Dongying	97687	57459	109525	98543	70208	123791	105882
烟台市	Yantai	119372	49127	109947	95266	78829	80410	120969
潍坊市	Weifang	76446	50576	78968	104599	69812	55543	83693
济宁市	Jining	64824	45984	100474	74534	69146	54347	88237
泰安市	Tai'an	75898	44939	101406	86091	61971	48463	107414
威海市	Weihai	85247	50430	128055	77375	60368	57264	84958
日照市	Rizhao	88215	50264	92857	79619	67416	50654	92951
临沂市	Linyi	83774	51079	117539	83042	74548	57947	95268
德州市	Dezhou	81868	48431	97884	81054	76532	54483	72303
聊城市	Liaocheng	82182	47434	126298	95118	61848	96873	118345
滨州市	Binzhou	79723	50883	108972	106774	62039	70772	94036
菏泽市	Heze	83370	43659	114992	52014	68267	58675	77077

4-8 续表 2 continued

单位:元 (yuan)

地 区	Region	水利、环境和公共设施管理业 Management of Water Conservancy, Environment and Public Facilities	居民服务、修理和其他服务业 Households Services, Repair and Other Services	教 育 Education	卫生和社会工作 Health and Social Work	文化、体育和娱乐业 Culture, Sports and Entertainment	公共管理、社会保障和社会组织 Public management, Social Security and Social Organization	国际组织 International Organization
全省合计	**Total**	**51780**	**60785**	**109680**	**117288**	**100855**	**108681**	
济 南 市	Jinan	66393	62968	129571	160913	127906	151763	
青 岛 市	Qingdao	63178	81068	154351	165553	130475	161618	
淄 博 市	Zibo	35774	44323	115172	99273	95111	104069	
枣 庄 市	Zaozhuang	56387	60413	88665	98081	71873	104673	
东 营 市	Dongying	93002	86599	103828	125226	83615	111750	
烟 台 市	Yantai	67526	56229	122229	105314	84056	117662	
潍 坊 市	Weifang	29352	59437	98499	104108	76693	108038	
济 宁 市	Jining	57185	70646	104211	114279	75081	89879	
泰 安 市	Tai'an	72562	74952	100659	93008	61736	88620	
威 海 市	Weihai	55553	48619	110321	110124	80666	102665	
日 照 市	Rizhao	73415	46667	111927	106202	92483	116906	
临 沂 市	Linyi	36944	43333	102422	99036	91323	107600	
德 州 市	Dezhou	52697	46449	80818	89870	65934	73477	
聊 城 市	Liaocheng	54737	55161	87226	107540	89828	77851	
滨 州 市	Binzhou	60222	61149	105386	107489	105948	103044	
菏 泽 市	Heze	36712	49177	87640	85546	72426	75943	

4-9 各市按行业分城镇私营单位就业人员平均工资(2021年)

Average Wage of Staff and Workers in Urban Non-private units by Sector and Region(2021)

单位:元 (yuan)

地 区	Region	总 计 Total	农、林、牧、渔业 Agriculture, Forestry, Animal Husbandry and Fishing	采矿业 Mining	制造业 Manufacturing	电力、热力、燃气及水的生产和供应业 Production and Supply of Electric, heat,gas and water	建筑业 Construction	批发和零售业 Wholesale and Retail Trade
全省合计	**Total**	**56521**	**47861**	**67649**	**57092**	**65941**	**61552**	**53522**
济 南 市	Jinan	60914	50296	72520	56460	62652	68964	58174
青 岛 市	Qingdao	63631	52279	62075	60761	66192	73974	61193
淄 博 市	Zibo	55989	41163	80101	54740	67454	65394	57886
枣 庄 市	Zaozhuang	50540	47337	53420	57769	59175	53872	43698
东 营 市	Dongying	61533	49190	60766	72689	75271	53754	62342
烟 台 市	Yantai	56073	53775	48361	57543	66989	53769	54234
潍 坊 市	Weifang	56006	40672	50629	60637	67685	53150	50485
济 宁 市	Jining	52327	40958	66566	55993	61972	61858	47068
泰 安 市	Tai'an	55836	39204	82876	52039	39667	70275	45206
威 海 市	Weihai	55870	53091	58654	58256	58348	56058	55398
日 照 市	Rizhao	56661	46883	77889	63271	83396	59436	42638
临 沂 市	Linyi	56320	47018	54867	56626	63084	58511	50289
德 州 市	Dezhou	52294	40146		55692	62339	54814	42505
聊 城 市	Liaocheng	49476	56223		51327	63819	52042	48845
滨 州 市	Binzhou	55912	46930	52475	56943	72456	57834	56484
菏 泽 市	Heze	48627	41179	70778	49045	61732	52169	45747

4-9 续表 1 continued

单位:元 (yuan)

地　区	Region	交通运输、仓储和邮政业 Traffic, Transport, Storage and Post	住宿和餐饮业 Hotels and Catering Services	信息传输、软件和信息技术服务业 Information Transfer, Software and Information Technology Services	金融业 Financial Intermediation	房地产业 Real Estate	租赁和商务服务业 Leasing and Business Services	科学研究和技术服务业 Scientific Research and Technical Service
全省合计	**Total**	**56825**	**44509**	**70067**	**71694**	**55824**	**54720**	**63193**
济南市	Jinan	60686	48308	82043	81436	64988	59379	65592
青岛市	Qingdao	63157	46026	90503	89323	65914	61975	72462
淄博市	Zibo	56933	41654	71300	86578	54177	51743	66524
枣庄市	Zaozhuang	48916	37335	41775	61718	53873	43993	43092
东营市	Dongying	67275	42091	64874	66387	50545	57921	59476
烟台市	Yantai	55890	53150	70287	58219	56891	52968	68230
潍坊市	Weifang	60200	40041	51868	81322	49269	49297	52252
济宁市	Jining	47898	41523	53150	74433	48170	47332	48469
泰安市	Tai'an	43590	34796	40349	48976	48570	40181	53209
威海市	Weihai	62967	45459	52740	70273	46858	59822	59001
日照市	Rizhao	58503	49590	63574		59404	65051	49619
临沂市	Linyi	54330	42281	52214	66662	62701	64423	75359
德州市	Dezhou	52125	39782	50913	62579	64424	46279	66016
聊城市	Liaocheng	45259	40078	40906	71796	51366	43675	51748
滨州市	Binzhou	59694	37100	55618	66786	48155	52888	59634
菏泽市	Heze	53425	39198	41030	55662	49937	45683	52236

4-9 续表 2 continued

单位:元 (yuan)

地　区	Region	水利、环境和公共设施管理业 Management of Water Conservancy, Environment and Public Facilities	居民服务、修理和其他服务业 Households Services, Repair and Other Services	教育 Education	卫生和社会工作 Health and Social Work	文化、体育和娱乐业 Culture, Sports and Entertainment	公共管理、社会保障和社会组织 Public management, Social Security and Social Organization	国际组织 International Organization
全省合计	**Total**	**35606**	**42462**	**47869**	**58229**	**50325**		
济南市	Jinan	38477	41152	52988	61539	50211		
青岛市	Qingdao	44518	48408	59516	69715	64287		
淄博市	Zibo	28415	38615	40047	50686	38049		
枣庄市	Zaozhuang	27721	42388	36021	49211	47363		
东营市	Dongying	41017	45685	45244	46830	46834		
烟台市	Yantai	27002	44060	51211	64559	51046		
潍坊市	Weifang	25894	38381	46395	57298	48168		
济宁市	Jining	28757	44463	45467	46965	44148		
泰安市	Tai'an	28830	39087	39572	57936	43954		
威海市	Weihai	40427	47104	50270	45908	55469		
日照市	Rizhao	52591	54331	38961	48680	46224		
临沂市	Linyi	43839	46766	43896	64157	52733		
德州市	Dezhou	52051	36748	41242	52527	39632		
聊城市	Liaocheng	31957	31916	45424	48232	37556		
滨州市	Binzhou	36241	47047	46238	55834	49812		
菏泽市	Heze	35694	35607	47559	53361	39222		

4-10 各市城镇登记失业人员及失业率

Registered Urban Unemployed Persons and Unemployment Rate by Region

地 区	Region	失业人员(万人) Unemployment(10 000 persons)							登记失业率(%) Unemployment Rate(%)						
		2015	2016	2017	2018	2019	2020	2021	2015	2016	2017	2018	2019	2020	2021
全省总计	**Total**	**43.7**	**45.8**	**45.7**	**46.5**	**44.2**	**46.7**	**42.3**	**3.4**	**3.5**	**3.4**	**3.4**	**3.3**	**3.1**	**2.9**
济南市	Jinan	3.2	3.4	3.2	3.5	3.5	3.6	3.5	2.0	2.2	2.1	2.1	2.0	2.0	2.0
青岛市	Qingdao	7.5	8.0	7.8	7.4	8.3	8.7	7.8	3.0	3.2	3.1	2.9	3.0	3.0	2.7
淄博市	Zibo	3.0	3.2	3.4	3.4	2.8	3.0	3.2	2.8	2.7	2.9	2.4	2.2	2.3	2.8
枣庄市	Zaozhuang	1.9	1.9	1.9	2.6	2.0	2.2	1.9	2.3	2.4	2.4	3.0	2.2	2.3	2.1
东营市	Dongying	1.0	1.2	1.3	1.4	1.4	1.4	1.0	2.2	2.4	2.5	2.5	2.6	2.7	1.9
烟台市	Yantai	5.4	5.7	5.5	5.0	4.4	4.8	4.4	3.2	3.2	3.3	2.9	2.2	2.5	2.4
潍坊市	Weifang	3.9	3.9	3.9	4.0	3.8	3.5	3.3	2.9	2.9	2.9	2.9	2.7	2.5	2.3
济宁市	Jining	3.1	3.3	3.3	3.1	3.3	3.0	2.2	3.0	3.1	3.1	3.0	3.1	2.3	1.8
泰安市	Tai'an	2.1	2.6	2.5	2.4	2.2	2.3	2.0	2.1	2.5	2.4	2.2	2.0	2.1	1.9
威海市	Weihai	0.8	0.8	1.0	1.0	0.9	1.2	1.4	1.5	1.5	1.7	1.8	1.8	2.4	2.3
日照市	Rizhao	1.1	1.2	1.3	1.6	1.0	1.1	0.9	2.0	2.2	2.2	2.3	1.7	2.0	1.6
莱芜市	Laiwu	0.7	0.7	0.7	0.7				2.5	2.6	2.6	2.7			
临沂市	Linyi	2.6	2.6	2.7	2.8	3.0	3.4	3.2	2.4	2.3	2.3	2.3	2.2	2.4	2.2
德州市	Dezhou	1.9	1.8	1.7	2.0	1.9	2.0	1.8	2.8	2.6	2.5	2.4	2.4	2.5	2.2
聊城市	Liaocheng	2.6	2.6	2.5	2.6	2.3	2.5	2.3	3.0	3.1	3.0	3.1	2.7	3.0	2.7
滨州市	Binzhou	1.2	1.2	1.2	1.5	1.3	1.7	1.6	2.2	2.1	2.1	2.6	1.8	2.5	2.3
菏泽市	Heze	1.8	1.7	1.7	1.8	2.2	2.2	1.7	3.2	3.1	3.1	2.7	3.1	2.8	2.5

注：根据行政区划调整，2019年起，莱芜市并入济南市，以下表同。
a)According to administrative division adjustment,Laiwu City merged into Jinan City from 2019.The same applies to tables following.

4-11 主要年份年末离休、退休、退职人员人数

Numbers of Retired and Resigned Persons at Year-end in Major Years

单位：人 (person)

年 份 Year	总 计 Total	离休人员 Retired Veterans	退休人员 Retired Persons	领取定期生活费的退职人员 Resigned Persons
2000	1803820	144063	1592549	67208
2001	1880547	141761	1684005	54781
2002	2005227	130318	1830820	44089
2003	2121128	124002	1948428	48698
2004	2244567	118302	2077937	48328
2005	2487619	114650	2372969	
2006	2617076	104437	2512563	
2007	2821703	99016	2722687	
2008	3050455	93560	2956895	
2009	3260326	88574	3171752	
2010	3450734	79974	3370760	
2011	3730537	71844	3623657	35036
2012	4163329	68132	4058431	36766
2013	4591639	62261	4492295	37083
2014	5115111	56939	5020415	37757
2015	5543745	49531	5454932	39282
2016	6073980	28093	6008374	37513
2017	6387821	20093	6330627	37101
2018	6771167	17504	6715388	38275
2019	7111822	14915	7060702	36205
2020	7541440	12804	7486120	42516
2021	7889902	10804	7830758	48340

注：本表不包括民政部门支付离休、退休、退职费的人数。
a)Data in this table exclude the number of retired or resigned people whose pensions are paid by civil affair departments.

4-12 离休、退休人员数(2021年底)

Numbers of Retired and Resigned Persons at Year-end(2021)

单位：人 (person)

类别	Category	离休、退休退职人员 Retired and Resigned Persons	离休人员 Retired Veterans	退休人员 Retired Persons
总计	**Total**	**7889902**	**10804**	**7830758**
一、执行企业养老保险制度	**According to the Enterprise Pension Insurance System**	**6543318**	**10804**	**6485069**
(一)企业	Enterprise	4180142	10789	4138953
1. 内资企业	Domestic Funded Enterprises	4093899	10737	4054959
国有企业	State-owned Enterprises	1927814	7643	1907592
集体企业	Collective Owned Enterprises	926053	1431	918776
其他企业	Others	1240032	1663	1228591
2. 港、澳、台及外资企业	Enterprises with Investment from Hong Kong, Macao and Taiwan	86243	52	83994
(二)事业	Institutions	10944	3	10626
(三)机关	Government Agencies	3215	7	3140
(四)其他人员	Others	2349017	5	2332350
二、执行机关事业单位养老保险制度	**According to the Government Agencies and Institutions Pension Insurance System**	**1346584**		**1345689**
(一)机关	Government Agencies	303554		303445
(二)事业	Institutions	1042998		1042212
(三)其他单位	Others	32		32

4-13 各市离休、退休人员数(2021年底)

Numbers of Retired and Resigned Persons at Year-end by Region(2021)

单位：人 (person)

地区	Region	离休、退休退职人员 Retired and Resigned Persons	离休人员 Retired Veterans	退休人员 Retired Persons
全省总计	**Total**	**7889902**	**10804**	**7830758**
济南市	Jinan	761308	1412	756847
青岛市	Qingdao	1177285	1206	1171906
淄博市	Zibo	492962	617	481040
枣庄市	Zaozhuang	208762	201	206674
东营市	Dongying	73726	74	73493
烟台市	Yantai	801190	1007	795493
潍坊市	Weifang	621417	711	616076
济宁市	Jining	412327	459	409746
泰安市	Tai'an	344051	305	342127
威海市	Weihai	483621	259	482134
日照市	Rizhao	243628	108	235536
临沂市	Linyi	435048	450	434553
德州市	Dezhou	258355	273	257299
聊城市	Liaocheng	253677	232	253407
滨州市	Binzhou	224051	239	222494
菏泽市	Heze	277571	263	277160

注：各市数据不包括省直管企业参保离退休人数。
a)Municipal data exclude the number of retired and resigned persons in provincial enterprises.

4-14 离休、退休人员保险福利费用(2021年)
Social Insurance and Welfare Funds for Retired Persons(2021)

单位:万元 (10 000 yuan)

类别	Category	总计 Total	离休金 Pensions for Retired Veterans	退休金 Pensions for Retired Persons
总计	**Total**	**33205064**	**131730**	**32048378**
一、执行企业养老保险制度	**According to the Enterprise Pension Insurance System**	**24045514**	**131730**	**22902929**
(一)企业	Enterprise	17671955	131578	16793629
1. 内资企业	Domestic Funded Enterprises	17288009	130954	16423185
国有企业	State-owned Enterprises	9130253	91816	8687396
集体企业	Collective Owned Enterprises	3368364	18318	3197925
其他企业	Others	4789392	20820	4537864
2. 港、澳、台及外资企业	Enterprises with Investment from Hong Kong, Macao and Taiwan	383946	624	370444
(二)事业	Institutions	24597	25	22347
(三)机关	Government Agencies	11728	81	10825
(四)其他人员	Others	6337234	46	6076128
二、执行机关事业单位养老保险制度	**According to the Government Agencies and Institutions Pension Insurance System**	**9159550**		**9145449**
(一)机关	Government Agencies	2121449		2117548
(二)事业	Institutions	7037901		7027701
(三)其他单位	Others	200		200

4-15 各市离休、退休保险福利费用(2021年)
Social Insurance and Welfare Funds for Retired Persons by Region(2021)

单位:万元 (10 000 yuan)

地区	Region	总计 Total	离休金 Pensions for Retired Veterans	退休金 Pensions for Retired Persons
全省总计	**Total**	**33205064**	**131730**	**32048378**
济南市	Jinan	3407775	14785	3206016
青岛市	Qingdao	4881467	19489	4763226
淄博市	Zibo	1955517	7434	1878045
枣庄市	Zaozhuang	871207	2865	859614
东营市	Dongying	328015	639	323936
烟台市	Yantai	3131341	11651	3105744
潍坊市	Weifang	2504850	8290	2378248
济宁市	Jining	1808795	9087	1724165
泰安市	Tai'an	1313239	3918	1300927
威海市	Weihai	1563679	2431	1435819
日照市	Rizhao	774697	1401	718925
临沂市	Linyi	1640682	7537	1632933
德州市	Dezhou	1044082	3383	1035461
聊城市	Liaocheng	1029937	2990	977900
滨州市	Binzhou	792483	3269	743386
菏泽市	Heze	1121210	2247	1088572

注：各市数据不包括省直管企业离退休费用。
a)Municipal data exclude the costs of retired and resigned persons in provincial enterprises.

4-16 社会保险基金收支及累计结余

Revenue, Expenses and Balance of Social Insurance Fund

单位：亿元 (100 million yuan)

年份 Year	合计 Total	基本养老保险 Basic Pension Insurance	失业保险 Unemployment Insurance	基本医疗保险 Basic Medical Care Insurance	工伤保险 Work Injury Insurance	生育保险 Maternity Insurance
基金收入 Revenue						
2005	474.9	360.5	23.5	82.1	5.0	3.8
2006	592.9	441.1	31.3	108.2	7.3	5.0
2007	782.9	591.8	36.5	137.7	10.4	6.5
2008	938.4	687.5	45.5	183.0	13.3	9.1
2009	1109.4	825.7	41.8	215.4	16.8	9.7
2010	1283.0	943.5	43.1	264.2	20.5	11.7
2011	1645.9	1191.1	65.5	343.1	28.4	17.8
2012	1883.4	1316.6	83.2	425.8	34.7	23.1
2013	2114.7	1489.0	57.3	500.3	40.0	28.1
2014	2589.5	1672.7	68.6	770.5	45.1	32.6
2015	3206.9	2105.6	71.6	942.7	51.0	36.0
2016	3502.4	2242.5	92.4	1081.5	50.2	35.8
2017	3663.7	2289.3	67.6	1195.2	58.9	52.7
2018	4460.9	2728.1	74.1	1530.5	64.1	64.1
2019	4579.2	2784.7	82.1	1582.7	56.9	72.8
2020	4164.5	2491.2	58.3	1585.1	29.9	
2021	5541.2	3454.3	104.3	1921.5	61.1	
基金支出 Expenses						
2005	379.0	296.2	14.0	63.2	3.3	2.3
2006	450.9	352.1	13.3	77.7	4.8	3.0
2007	571.1	443.9	13.6	102.0	7.3	4.3
2008	690.7	530.5	14.7	131.2	8.7	5.6
2009	840.5	622.7	22.4	177.0	11.7	6.7
2010	1027.1	749.3	31.4	222.2	15.1	9.1
2011	1223.9	886.9	25.9	279.3	20.1	11.7
2012	1475.6	1059.0	35.3	336.0	28.0	17.3
2013	1783.9	1270.5	46.3	413.5	31.3	22.3
2014	2365.8	1557.7	49.3	692.3	35.0	31.5
2015	2791.4	1845.2	57.3	820.4	38.4	30.1
2016	3202.3	2090.3	70.0	956.7	39.4	45.9
2017	3622.9	2358.7	65.2	1094.6	42.2	62.2
2018	4081.1	2656.5	64.5	1253.7	47.8	58.6
2019	4512.4	2954.7	77.7	1362.6	53.8	63.6
2020	4879.7	3232.8	134.0	1457.1	55.8	
2021	5539.5	3544.4	102.4	1827.6	65.1	
累计结余 Balance at Year-end						
2005	410.0	293.7	40.2	64.1	6.3	5.7
2006	552.2	382.7	58.3	94.6	8.8	7.8
2007	756.9	523.4	81.3	130.4	11.8	10.0
2008	1004.6	680.4	112.1	182.2	16.4	13.5
2009	1273.4	883.4	131.5	220.6	21.4	16.5
2010	1529.2	1077.6	143.2	262.5	26.9	19.0
2011	1951.4	1381.9	182.9	326.3	35.2	25.1
2012	2359.8	1639.5	230.7	416.7	41.9	31.0
2013	2693.3	1857.9	241.7	506.3	50.6	36.8
2014	2959.3	1973.0	261.0	626.8	60.6	37.9
2015	3378.0	2233.4	275.3	752.4	73.1	43.8
2016	3678.8	2385.7	297.8	877.6	83.9	33.8
2017	3718.8	2315.7	300.1	979.2	100.6	23.2
2018	4098.7	2387.2	309.8	1256.1	116.9	28.7
2019	4126.8	2217.2	252.2	1492.7	119.7	45.0
2020	3411.7	1475.7	176.5	1665.7	93.8	
2021	3413.1	1385.6	178.4	1759.2	89.9	

注：基本养老保险不包含居民养老保险；自2014年起，基本医疗保险包括职工基本医疗保险和居民基本医疗保险。自2020起，生育保险和职工基本医疗保险合并实施，基金合并运行。

a)Basic Pension Insurance doesn't include that for residents. Since 2014, Basic Medical Care Insurance includes employee and residents medical care insurance. Since 2020, maternity insurance and basic medical insurance for employees will be implemented together, and the fund will be operated together.

4-17 主要年份年末社会保险参保人数

Number of Persons Participated in Social Insurance in Major Years

单位:万人 (10 000 persons)

年份 Year	职工基本养老保险 Urban Basic Pension Insurance	企业基本养老保险 Enterprise's Pension Insurance	机关事业养老保险 Institution and Government Agency's Pension Insurance	医疗保险 Medical Care Insurance	失业保险 Unemployment Insurance	工伤保险 Work Injury Insurance	生育保险 Maternity Insurance
2000	972.2	757.6	214.6	255.5	715.0	279.4	325.5
2001	1022.2	793.9	228.3	490.2	700.2	285.5	331.8
2002	1043.0	805.0	238.0	625.6	701.2	278.2	323.2
2003	1135.9	883.5	252.4	691.1	719.1	281.8	336.5
2004	1218.7	958.1	260.6	771.9	747.5	476.7	390.8
2005	1302.5	1027.4	275.1	861.5	771.1	578.7	461.2
2006	1368.0	1086.2	281.8	996.1	789.7	647.3	488.8
2007	1455.7	1165.4	291.6	1115.9	814.9	745.0	563.3
2008	1565.8	1266.1	299.7	1266.2	864.1	865.0	638.0
2009	1661.0	1352.1	308.9	2540.2	899.5	1064.6	703.0
2010	1773.0	1459.5	313.5	2770.6	931.2	1211.2	774.1
2011	1907.1	1589.4	317.6	2947.8	964.9	1276.1	857.8
2012	2063.2	1739.8	323.4	3101.2	1009.8	1339.6	919.0
2013	2259.6	1931.7	327.8	3647.9	1089.6	1371.9	974.4
2014	2370.2	2037.5	332.7	3988.0	1154.3	1421.5	1046.5
2015	2477.5	2138.5	339.0	9235.8	1203.8	1473.5	1111.3
2016	2576.4	2224.2	352.2	9188.8	1222.9	1510.9	1139.1
2017	2660.9	2303.4	357.6	9295.7	1268.3	1569.1	1186.6
2018	2762.7	2399.5	363.2	9437.1	1318.5	1633.0	1235.4
2019	2868.0	2494.0	374.1	9569.6	1366.0	1710.7	1298.8
2020	3046.3	2655.3	391.0	9697.8	1466.1	1822.1	1534.3
2021	3226.7	2823.1	403.6	9732.4	1542.7	1921.9	1607.5

注：城镇职工社会基本养老保险参保人数包含离退休人数；2009年起，医疗保险参保人数包含城镇居民医疗保险。2015年起，医疗保险参保人数中含新农合并入人员。

a) Number of persons participated in urban basic pension insurance include retirees.Since 2009,number of persons participated in medical care insurance include urban residents participated in medical care insurance. Since 2015,number or persons participated in medical care insurance included the new rural co-operative medical system incorporated into the personnel.

4-18 各市社会保险参保人数(2021年底)

Number of Persons Participated in Social Insurance at Year-end by Region(2021)

单位:万人 (10 000 persons)

地区	Region	城镇职工基本养老保险 Urban Basic Pension Insurance	企业基本养老保险 Enterprise's Pension Insurance	机关事业养老保险 Institution and Government Agency's Pension Insurance	医疗保险 Medical Care Insurance	失业保险 Unemployment Insurance	工伤保险 Work Injury Insurance	生育保险 Maternity Insurance
全省总计	**Total**	**3226.7**	**2823.1**	**403.6**	**9732.4**	**1542.7**	**1921.9**	**1607.5**
济南市	Jinan	472.7	441.9	30.8	843.1	226.9	293.5	235.8
青岛市	Qingdao	503.6	464.5	39.1	911.9	271.3	315.0	319.7
淄博市	Zibo	191.8	172.8	19.0	429.6	104.1	136.9	90.4
枣庄市	Zaozhuang	86.7	72.2	14.5	373.4	42.3	44.7	39.7
东营市	Dongying	68.9	59.6	9.3	177.6	36.2	70.3	31.9
烟台市	Yantai	294.5	265.0	29.4	647.3	132.4	160.5	137.1
潍坊市	Weifang	243.2	209.2	34.0	904.5	121.5	187.1	127.6
济宁市	Jining	183.5	152.0	31.5	822.1	91.9	106.1	96.4
泰安市	Tai'an	137.7	118.9	18.8	527.1	69.9	90.3	69.2
威海市	Weihai	143.3	131.5	11.7	257.3	63.1	67.0	79.2
日照市	Rizhao	82.8	72.6	10.2	285.0	31.5	49.3	40.6
临沂市	Linyi	188.3	154.5	33.8	1080.7	82.8	115.6	106.4
德州市	Dezhou	110.6	88.7	21.9	531.8	50.4	68.8	53.9
聊城市	Liaocheng	95.1	72.2	22.8	579.7	46.4	65.5	50.1
滨州市	Binzhou	98.7	84.6	14.1	381.2	46.9	64.3	41.1
菏泽市	Heze	133.3	98.1	35.2	921.9	48.0	76.3	50.7

注:各市养老、失业保险人数不包括省直管企业人数。

a)Municipal data on pension insurance exclude the staff and workers of provincial enterprise.

4-19 职工养老保险基本情况

Basic Statistics on Pension Insurance in Urban Areas

类别	Category	2016	2017	2018	2019	2020	2021
一、年末参保人数 （万人）	**Number of People Insured (10 000 persons)**	**2576.4**	**2660.9**	**2762.7**	**2868.0**	**3046.3**	**3226.7**
职工 （万人）	Employed People (10 000 persons)	1969.0	2022.2	2085.6	2156.8	2292.1	2437.7
#企业 （万人）	Enterprises (10 000 persons)	1722.3	1775.3	1838.7	1904.9	2031.0	2168.8
离休、退休、退职人数 （万人）	Retired and Resigned Persons (10 000 persons)	607.4	638.8	677.1	711.2	754.1	789.0
二、基金收支情况	**Revenue and Expenses**						
基金收入 （亿元）	Revenue (100 million yuan)	2242.5	2289.3	2728.1	2784.7	2491.2	3454.3
基金支出 （亿元）	Expenses (100 million yuan)	2090.3	2358.7	2656.5	2954.7	3232.8	3544.4
三、企业养老金社会化发放人情况	**Payment of Pension Insurance**						
养老金实发人数 （万人）	People Receiving Pension Insurance (10 000 persons)	501.9	528.1	560.7	589.0	624.3	654.3
#社会化发放人数 （万人）	People Receiving Socialized Pension Insurance (10 000 persons)	501.9	528.1	560.7	589.0	624.3	654.3
社会化发放率 (%)	Rate of Socialized Pension Insurance (%)	100.0	100.0	100.0	100.0	100.0	100.0

4-20 各市居民基本养老保险情况(2021年)

Statistics on Residents Old-age Insurance by Region(2021)

地区	Region	参保人数(人) Contributors at Year-end (person)	达到领取待遇年龄参保人数 Number of Participants Who Have Reached the Prescribed Age of Benefit Entilement	基金收支情况(亿元) Revenue and Expense(100 million yuan) 基金收入 Revenue	基金支出 Expenses	累计结余 Balance at Year-end
全省总计	**Total**	**46140950**	**15725316**	**598.1**	**383.0**	**1506.0**
济南市	Jinan	3083759	1052872	55.3	30.0	137.5
青岛市	Qingdao	2793066	1038718	55.8	45.0	106.4
淄博市	Zibo	1464622	647064	22.0	17.4	57.2
枣庄市	Zaozhuang	1964651	584377	25.0	12.4	47.4
东营市	Dongying	747153	280349	14.0	8.8	45.4
烟台市	Yantai	3183572	1245307	62.3	38.0	208.7
潍坊市	Weifang	4741369	1638033	81.1	37.7	188.7
济宁市	Jining	4496221	1368200	42.4	28.9	127.0
泰安市	Tai'an	2741739	969443	24.6	19.5	50.3
威海市	Weihai	910111	380384	16.1	12.6	48.4
日照市	Rizhao	1400317	489594	34.5	10.1	55.3
临沂市	Linyi	5557230	1921338	47.3	37.7	125.2
德州市	Dezhou	3075874	976745	27.5	20.1	66.9
聊城市	Liaocheng	3062163	978236	30.7	22.0	96.2
滨州市	Binzhou	2126621	675285	20.6	14.5	50.7
菏泽市	Heze	4792482	1479371	38.9	28.3	94.7

主要统计指标解释

就业人员 指在16周岁及以上，从事一定社会劳动并取得劳动报酬或经营收入的人员。这一指标反映了一定时期内全部劳动力资源的实际利用情况，是研究我国基本国情国力的重要指标。

单位就业人员 指在各级国家机关、政党机关、社会团体及企业、事业单位中工作，取得工资或其他形式的劳动报酬的全部人员。包括在岗职工、再就业的离退休人员、民办教师以及在各单位中工作的外方人员和港澳台方人员、兼职人员、借用的外单位人员和第二职业者。不包括离开本单位仍保留劳动关系的职工。单位就业人员反映了各单位实际参加生产或工作的全部劳动力。

城镇登记失业人员 指报告期末，公共就业和人才交流服务机构登记在册的城镇失业人员总数。期末领取失业保险金的城镇户籍人员，应全部统计为登记失业人员。

城镇登记失业率 指报告期末，城镇登记失业人员期末实有人数占期末从业人员总数与城镇登记失业人员期末实有人数之和的比重。其中，期末从业人员总数，是指截至报告期末，辖区内城镇劳动年龄人口中就业人员及离岗职工总数，不包括聘用的离退休人员，台、港、澳和外籍人员及使用的农村劳动力。计算公式为：

$$\text{城镇登记失业率}=\frac{\text{城镇登记失业人员期末实有人数}}{\text{期末从业人员总数}+\text{城镇登记失业人员期末实有人数}}\times100\%$$

国有单位 指资产归国家所有的经济组织。包括按《中华人民共和国企业法人登记管理条例》规定登记注册的非公司制的经济组织，以及中央、地方各级国家机关、事业单位和社会团体。

集体单位 指生产资料归集体所有，并按《中华人民共和国企业法人登记管理条例》规定登记注册的经济组织。

其他单位 包括股份合作单位、联营单位、有限责任公司、股份有限公司、港澳台商投资单位以及外商投资单位等其他登记注册类型单位。

在岗职工 指在本单位工作并由单位支付工资的人员，以及有工作岗位，但由于学习、病伤产假等原因暂未工作，仍由单位支付工资的人员。

工资总额 指各单位在一定时期内直接支付给本单位全部职工的劳动报酬总额。工资总额的计算原则应以直接支付给职工的全部劳动报酬为根据。各单位支付给职工的劳动报酬以及其他根据有关规定支付的工资，不论是计入成本的还是不计入成本的，不论是按国家规定列入计征奖金税项目的，还是未列入计征奖金税项目的，不论是以货币形式支付的还是以实物形式支付的，均包括在工资总额内。

平均工资 指企业、事业、机关单位的职工在一定时期内平均每人所得的货币工资额。它表明一定时期职工工资收入的高低程度，是反映职工工资水平的主要指标。计算公式为：

$$\text{平均工资}=\frac{\text{报告期实际支付的全部职工工资总额}}{\text{报告期全部职工平均人数}}$$

基本养老保险

1.（参保）职工人数：指报告期末按照国家法律、法规和有关政策规定参加基本养老保险并在社保经办机构已建立缴费记录档案的职工人数，包括中断缴费但未终止养老保险关系的职工人数，不包括只登记未建立缴费记录档案的人数。

2.（参保）离退休人员人数：指报告期末参加基本养老保险的离休、退休和退职人员的人数。

3.基本养老保险基金收入：指根据国家有关规定，由纳入基本养老保险范围的缴费单位和个人按国家规定的缴费基数和缴费比例缴纳的养老保险基金，以及通过其他方式取得的形成基金来源的收入。包括单位和职工个人缴纳的基本养老保险费、基本养老保险基金利息收入、上级补助收入、下级上解收入、转移收入、财政补贴和其他收入。

4.基本养老保险基金支出：指按照国家政策规定的开支范围和开支标准从养老保险基金中支付给参加基本养老保险的离休、退休、退职人员个人的养老金、丧葬抚恤补助，以及由于保险关系转移、上下级之间调剂资金等原因而发生的支出。包括离休金、退休金、退职金、各种补贴、医疗费、死亡丧葬补助费、抚恤救济费、社会保险经办机构管理费、补助下级支出、上解上级支出、转移支出、其他支出等。

5.基本养老保险基金累计结余：指截至报告期末基本养老保险基金收支相抵后的累计余额。

离休、退休、退职人员 指正式办理了离休、退休、退职手续，并享受相应的离休、退休、退职待遇的人员。

基本医疗保险

1.参保人数：指报告期末按国家有关规定参加基本医疗保险的人数。包括参加职工基本医疗保险和城乡居民基本医疗保险人数。

2.基金收入：指根据国家有关规定，由纳入基本医疗保险范围的缴费单位和个人，按国家规定的缴费基数和缴费比例缴纳的基金，以及通过其他方式取得的形成基金来源的款项，包括：单位缴纳的社会统筹基金收入、个人缴纳的个人账户基金收入、财政补贴收入、利息收入、其他收入。

3.基金支出：指按照国家政策规定的开支范围和开支标准从社会统筹基金中支付给参加基本医疗保险的职工和退休人员的医疗保险待遇支出，和从个人账户基金中支付给参加基本医疗保险的职工和退休人员的医疗费用支出，以及其他支出。包括：住院医疗费用支出、门急诊医疗费用支出、个人账户基金支出、其他支出。

4.基金累计结余：指截至报告期末基本医疗保险的社会

统筹和个人账户基金累计结余金额。包括银行存款、财政专户、债券投资和其他。

失业保险

1.参保人数：指报告期末按照国家法律、法规和有关政策规定参加了失业保险的城镇企业事业单位的职工及地方政府规定参加失业保险的其他人员的人数。

2.失业保险基金收入：指按照规定从企业、事业及其他单位筹集的失业保险费及其他并入失业保险基金收入的总额。包括单位和个人缴纳的失业保险费、失业保险基金利息收入、上级补助收入、下级上解收入、转移收入、财政补贴和其他收入。

3.失业保险基金支出：指报告期内为保障失业人员和下岗职工基本生活、促进其再就业等支出的基金总额。包括失业救济金、医疗费、死亡丧葬补助费、抚恤救济费、转业训练费支出、失业保险经办机构管理费、补助下级支出、上解上级支出、转移支出和其他支出。

4.基金累计结余：指截至报告期末失业保险基金收支相抵后的累计余额。

工伤保险

1.参加保险人数：指报告期末依据国家有关规定参加工伤保险的职工人数。

2.享受保险待遇人数：指劳动者因工负伤致残、死亡或因患职业病致残，根据有关规定享受工伤保险待遇职工或供养直系亲属人数。包括伤残人数、职业病人数、因工死亡人数、供养直系亲属人数。

3.基金收入：指根据国家有关规定，由参加工伤保险的单位按国家规定的缴费基数和缴费比例缴纳的工伤保险基金，以及通过其他形式取得的形成基金来源的款项。包括：单位缴纳的社会统筹基金收入、财政补贴收入、利息收入、其他收入。

4.基金支出：指按照国家政策规定的开支范围和开支标准从工伤保险基金中支付给参加工伤保险的人员及供养直系亲属工伤保险待遇支出及其他支出。包括工伤医疗费、伤残补助金、工亡补助金、护理费、丧葬补助费、工伤预防费用、职业康复费用和其他支出。

5.基金累计结余：指截至报告期末工伤保险基金累计结余金额。包括银行存款、财政专户、债券投资和其他。

生育保险

1.参保人数：指报告期末依据有关规定参加生育保险的职工人数。

2.基金收入：指根据国家有关规定，由参加生育保险的单位按照国家规定的缴费基数和缴费比例缴纳的生育保险基金，以及通过其他方式取得的形成基金来源的款项，包括：单位缴纳的基金收入、利息收入和其他收入。

3.基金支出：指按照国家政策规定的开支范围和开支标准，从生育保险基金中支付给参加生育保险的职工，因妊娠、分娩和计划生育手术而享受的待遇及其他支出。包括：生育津贴、医疗费用支出及其他支出。

4.基金累计结余：指截至报告期末生育保险基金累计结余金额。包括银行存款、财政专户、债券投资和其他。

离休、退休、退职人员保险福利费用 指离休、退休、退职人员实际得到的生活费用总额，包括从社会保险经办机构和单位得到的费用。

1.离休金：指按规定支付给离休人员的生活费用。

2.退休金：指按规定支付给退休人员的生活费用。

3.退职生活费：指按规定支付给退职人员的生活费用。

4.医疗卫生费：指单位直接支付给离休、退休、退职人员的医疗费、住院费以及住院伙食补助等费用。

5.其他：指离休金、退休金、退职生活费和医疗卫生费以外的其他保险福利费用，如丧葬抚恤救济费、生活补贴、物价补贴、冬季取暖补贴等。

Explanatory Notes on Main Statistical Indicators

Employed Persons refer to the persons aged 16 and over who are engaged in social working and receive remuneration payment or earn business income. This indicator reflects the actual utilization of total labour force during a certain period of time and is often used for the research on China' s economic situation and national power.

Persons Employed in Units refer to all the persons working in government agencies of various levels, political and party organizations, social organizations, enterprises and institutions, and receiving wages or other forms of payment. They include fully employed staff and workers, re employed retirees, teachers in schools run by the local people, foreigners and Chinese compatriots from Hong Kong, Macao, and Taiwan working in various units, part time employees, employees of other units working temporarily at current posts, and employees holding the second job, but exclude staff and workers who have left their working units while keeping their labour contract (employment relation) unchanged. This indicator reflects the total number of laborers actually engaged in production or other operations in various units.

Registered Urban Unemployed Persons refer to the total number of urban unemployed registered by public employment and personnel exchange service agencies at the end of the reporting period. The urban household registration personnel who receive unemployment insurance compensation at the end of the reporting period shall be all counted as registered unemployed persons.

Registered Urban Unemployment Rate refers to the ratio of the actual number of registered urban unemployed persons to the total number of employees and the total number of registered urban unemployed persons at the end of the period. Total number of employees refers to the number of persons employed and laid-off workers in the working-age population in urban units at the end of the reporting period(minus the rural labor force, retirees, and Hong Kong, Macao, Taiwan or foreign employees they employ). The formula is as follows:

Registered urban unemployment rate=number of registered urban unemployed persons÷(number of employees in urban units + number of registered urban unemployed persons) ×100%.

State owned Units refer to economic units whose assets are owned by the state. Included are non corporation units registered according to Regulation of the People Republic of China on the Registration of Enterprises and Corporations,state organs, institutions and social organizations at the central and local levels.

Collective Owned Units refer to economic units registered according to Regulation of the People Republic of China on the Registration of Enterprises and Corporations where the means of production are collectively owned.

Units of Other Types of Ownership refer to units registered with other types of ownership, including cooperative units, joint ownership units, limited companies, share holding corporations, units invested by entrepreneurs from Hong Kong, Macao, and Taiwan, and foreign invested units.

Fully Employed Staff and Workers refer to persons who work in, and receive wages from their working units, as well as persons who have their work posts, but are temporarily absent from work for reasons of study or on sick, injury or maternal leave and still receive wages from their working units.

Total Wages Bill refer to the total remuneration payment to staff and workers in various units during a certain period of time. The calculation of total wages is based on the total remuneration payment to the staff and workers. Therefore, all the wages and salaries and other payments to staff and workers are included in the total wages regardless of their sources, category, and forms (in kind or cash). (Total wages of staff and workers in this yearbook include only total wages of fully employed staff and workers, excluding the living allowances distributed to those who have left their working units while keeping their labour contract/employment relation unchanged).

Average Wage refers to the average wage in money terms per person during a certain period of time for staff and workers in enterprises, institutions, and government agencies, which reflects the general level of wage income during a certain period of time and is calculated as follows:

Average Wage=Total Wages of Staff and Workers at Reference Time/Average Number of Staff and Workers at Reference Time.

Basic Pension Insurance

1.Number of staff and workers covered refer to staff and workers participating in basic pension insurance programme in line with national laws, regulations and related policies by the end of reference period, who have already had payment records in social security management agencies, including those who interrupt payment without terminating the insurance programme. Those who have registered in the programme with no payment records are not included.

2. Number of retirees participating in basic pension insurance programme refer to number of retirees participating in basic pension insurance programme by the end of reference period.

3. Revenue of basic pension insurance refer to payments made by employers and individuals participating in pension insurance programs in accordance with the basis and proportion stipulated in state regulations, and income from other sources that become source of pension insurance fund, including the premium paid by employers and staff and works, interest income, subsidies from higher level agencies, income as transfer from subordinate agencies, transferred income, government financial subsidies and other income.

4. Expenses of basic pension insurance refer to payment made to those retired and resigned people covered in pension insurance program in terms of pension or compensation within the scope and standards of expenditure according to related national policies, and expenditure occurred due to shift of the insurance relationship or adjustment of funds among agencies, including pension for resigned people, pension for retired people, pension for people quitting jobs, various subsidies, medical fees, funeral subsidies, compensation pension, management fees for social security agencies, expenses on subsidies to lower subordinates, expenses as transfer to agencies at higher level, transferred expenditure and other expenditure.

5. Balance of basic pension insurance refers to the balance of basic pension insurance at the end of the reference period after deducting expenses from revenue.

Retired or Resigned Personnel refers to people who have formally completed formalities for their retirement or quitting work and enjoy the corresponding retirement treatments.

Basic Medical Care Insurance

1. Number of participants refers to people participating in the basic medical care insurance programme according to related regulations by the end of reference period, including the number of people participating in the basic medical care insurance for staff and workers and the number of people participating in the basic medical care insurance for urban and rural residents.

2. Revenue of insurance programme refer to payments made by employers and individuals participating in medical care insurance programs in accordance with the basis and proportion stipulated in state regulations, and income from other sources that become source of medical insurance fund, including income of social comprehensive funds paid by employers, income from individual accounts, government financial subsidies, interest income and other income.

3. Expenses of insurance programme refer to payment made from social comprehensive funds to those retired and resigned people covered in basic medical care insurance within the scope and standards of expenditure according to related national policies, and medical care payment made from individual accounts to staff and workers and retirees, and other expenses, including medical expenses of hospital inpatients, medical expenses for outpatients and emergency patients, payment from individual accounts and other expenditure.

4. Balance of basic medical care insurance refer to the balance of medical care insurance of social comprehensive funds and individual accounts at the end of the reference period, including bank savings, special fiscal accounts, investment in bonds and others.

Unemployment Insurance

1. Number of people covered refers to staff and workers in urban enterprises or institutions who have participated in unemployment insurance programme in line relevant policies and regulations, and other people who have participated according to local government regulations, by the end of reference period.

2. Revenue of unemployment insurance refer to payments made by employers and individuals participating in unemployment insurance programme in accordance with relevant regulations and other income contributed to this programme, including unemployment insurance premium made by employers and individuals, interest income, subsidies from higher level agencies, income as transfer from subordinate agencies, transferred income, government financial subsidies and other income.

3. Expenses of unemployment insurance refer to total expenses during the reference period to guarantee the basic livelihood of unemployed people and laid off staff and workers and to encourage their re employment. Included are unemployment relief, medical fees, funeral subsidies, compensation pension, training expenses, management fees for unemployment insurance agencies, subsidies to lower level agencies, expenses as transfer to higher level agencies, transferred expenditure and other expenditure.

4. Balance of unemployment insurance refer to the balance of unemployment revenue deducting unemployment expenses at the end of the reference period.

Work Injury Insurance

1. Number of people covered refers to staff and workers who have participated in work injury insurance programme in line with relevant national regulations.

2. Number of beneficiaries refers to staff and workers and their direct dependents who can, in line with relevant regulations, benefit from work injury insurance, as a result of work injury leading to disability or death of the staff/worker, or occupational disease leading to disability. Included in this category are number of injured and disabled people, number of people with occupational diseases, number of deaths at work places, and number of direct dependents.

3. Revenue of work injury insurance refer to payments made by employers participating in work injury insurance programs in accordance with the basis and proportion stipulated in state regulations, and income from other sources that become source of work injury insurance fund, including income of social comprehensive funds paid by employers, government financial subsidies, interest income and other income.

4. Expenses of work injury insurance refer to payments made from work injury insurance funds to those who participated in the work injury insurance programme and their direct dependents within the scope and standards of expenditure according to related national policies, and other expenditure, including medical fees for work injury, injury and disability subsidies, death subsidies, nursing fees, funeral subsidies, injury prevention fees, rehabilitation fees for occupational diseases and other expenditure.

5. Balance of work injury insurance refer to the balance of the work injury funds at the end of the reference period, including bank savings, special fiscal account, investment in bonds and others.

Maternity Insurance

1. Number of people covered refers to staff and workers who have participated in maternity insurance programme according to relevant regulation at the end of the reporting period.

2. Revenue of maternity insurance refers to payments made by employers participating in maternity insurance programs in accordance with the basis and proportion stipulated in state regulations, and income from other sources that become source of maternity insurance fund, including income of funds paid by employers, interest income and other income.

3. Expenses of maternity insurance refer to payments made from maternity insurance funds to staff and workers who participated in maternity insurance programme within the scope and standards of expenditure according to related national policies, expenses paid for pregnancy, child delivery or surgeries related to family planning, and other expenditure, including allowance for child bearing, medical fees and other expenditure.

4. Balance of the maternity insurance refers to the balance of the maternity insurance funds at the end of reference period, including bank savings, special fiscal account, investment in funds and others.

Insurance and Welfare Funds for Retirees refer to the total payment for living expenses actually received by retirees, including payment received from social insurance management agencies and units.

1. Pensions for retired veteran cadres refer to living expenses paid to retired veteran cadres according to related regulations.

2. Pensions for retirement refer to living expenses paid to retired staff and workers according to related regulations.

3. Living allowances for resigned staff and workers refer to living expenses paid to resigned staff and workers according to related regulation.

4. Medical care expenses refer to medical fees, hospitalization cost and per diem subsidies during hospitalizations paid by employers directly to retirees.

5. Others refer to insurance and welfare payments other than the above mentioned payments, including funeral subsidies, living allowances, price subsidies and heating subsidies during winter.

第5篇

固定资产投资

Investment in Fixed Assets

简 要 说 明

一、本篇资料的主要内容

本篇资料主要反映了全省固定资产投资方面的情况，主要包括固定资产投资的规模、结构、资金来源和投资的效果等方面的资料。2011 年，固定资产投资项目统计起点由 50 万元提高到 500 万元，名称统一规范为“固定资产投资”，其中包括城镇、非农户 500 万元及以上项目投资、房地产开发投资；“全社会固定资产投资”包括“固定资产投资加农户固定资产投资”。

二、本篇资料的来源

本篇资料来源于固定资产投资统计年报，由省统计局投资处整理提供。

三、内容修订

为进一步贯彻新发展理念，更好地反映经济结构和质量的变化，反映投资对优化供给结构的关键性作用。本篇资料对固定资产投资表式进行了改版，内容以各分组固定资产投资比上年增长速度为主，通过速度变化反映固定资产投资形势及政策效应。

Brief Introduction

I. Main Content

Data in this chapter show the basic conditions of investment in fixed assets of Shandong Province, mainly including the total investment in fixed assets, the structure of investment, the resources of investment and the results of investment, etc.Since 2011, the statistical criteria of fixed assets investment projects had been increased from 500 thousand to 5 million yuan. Investment in fixed assets include urban area and non-farmers 5 million and above project investments, real estate development investment; the total investment include investment in fixed assets and farmer investment in fixed assets.

II. Source of Data

Data in this chapter are based on the yearly report on investment in fixed assets and provided by the Division of Investment and Construction Statistics of Shandong Provincial Bureau of Statistics.

III. Revision of Content

In order to further implement the New Development Principles, better reflect the changes in economic structure and quality, and reflect the key role of investment in optimizing the supply structure. This chapter revises the fixed assets investment form. The content is mainly about the growth rate of fixed assets investment in each group compared with the preceding year, reflecting the situation of fixed assets investment and policy effects through the change of speed.

5-1 1978-2017年全社会固定资产投资总额

Total Investments in Fixed Assets from 1978 to 2017

单位:亿元 (100 million yuan)

年 份 Year	全社会固定资产投资额 Total Investment	国有经济 State-owned Units	集体经济 Collective-owned Units	#城 镇 Urban	个体经济 Self-employed Units	#农 村 Rural	其他经济 Others
1978	41.87	29.27	8.42	1.78	4.18	3.98	
1979	61.35	31.62	18.97	1.55	10.76	10.41	
1980	69.97	35.83	22.24	3.12	11.90	11.47	
1981	79.60	29.63	32.08	3.27	17.89	17.28	
1982	85.00	43.29	23.38	4.38	18.33	17.46	
1983	96.46	49.11	19.19	3.76	28.16	26.48	
1984	140.15	67.09	25.29	5.01	47.77	44.43	
1985	194.33	100.42	30.21	8.64	63.70	58.51	
1986	223.08	121.95	43.09	11.95	58.04	52.32	
1987	297.77	155.65	78.75	17.84	63.37	56.05	
1988	369.82	192.20	100.97	35.46	76.65	64.83	
1989	305.54	162.30	69.68	19.68	73.56	62.00	
1990	335.66	185.44	71.51	18.63	78.71	67.47	
1991	439.82	234.04	104.73	25.06	101.05	85.73	
1992	601.50	343.17	186.43	42.27	71.90	54.19	
1993	892.48	476.26	245.90	49.90	105.44	83.05	64.88
1994	1108.00	537.59	318.42	56.42	118.45	92.30	133.54
1995	1320.97	611.92	383.97	51.62	140.54	113.13	184.55
1996	1558.01	691.76	484.79	79.79	202.65	166.14	178.81
1997	1792.22	773.30	569.70	60.15	241.76	198.68	207.46
1998	2056.97	938.73	610.20	66.70	274.20	227.00	233.84
1999	2222.17	1043.13	635.55	82.72	310.64	228.43	232.85
2000	2542.65	1153.65	679.48	108.63	353.93	254.11	355.59
2001	2807.79	1157.44	688.61	134.92	384.06	263.35	577.68
2002	3509.29	1237.16	812.65	196.78	487.31	285.64	972.17
2003	5328.44	1615.57	1177.00	321.79	733.64	296.03	1802.23
2004	7629.04	1762.29	2455.86	383.83	772.28	116.36	2638.61
2005	10541.87	1853.29	1042.41	620.23	2736.61	1491.55	4909.56
2006	11136.06	1855.41	1063.61	713.49	3096.56	1186.20	5120.48
2007	12537.02	1838.55	1269.64	857.34	3566.49	1141.34	5862.34
2008	15435.93	2431.54	1811.23	1333.23	4360.90	1304.02	6832.27
2009	19030.97	3086.82	2308.54	1717.74	5235.29	1586.71	8400.32
2010	23276.69	3648.45	2627.32	1841.40	6505.00	1822.99	10495.92
2011	26769.73	3783.31	2715.00		8234.50		12036.92
2012	31255.96	3949.65	3129.27		9879.75		14297.30
2013	36789.07	4757.31	3113.17		12827.66		16090.93
2014	42495.55	5455.94	3380.39		16215.47		17443.75
2015	48312.46	6304.58	3125.74		20268.78		18613.36
2016	53322.49	7497.32	1545.38		22191.42		22088.37
2017	55202.73	9568.25	1496.62		22328.55		21809.31

注:1.2011年起，集体经济和个体经济不再细分城镇和农村(下表同)。
2.2011年起，固定资产投资项目统计起点由50万元提高到500万元，名称统一规范为“固定资产投资”，其中包括城镇、非农户500万元及以上项目投资和房地产开发投资；“全社会固定资产投资”包括“固定资产投资加农户固定资产投资”(下表同)。

a)Collective-owned Units and Self-employed Units had no longer divided into urban and rural unit since 2011.(The same applies to tables following).
b)Since 2011, the statistical criteria of fixed assets investment projects had been increased from 500 thousand to 5 million yuan. Investment in fixed assets include urban area and non-farmers 5 million and above project investments, real estate development and investment.Total investment include investment in fixed assets and farmer investment in fixed assets.(The same applies to tables following).

5-2 1978-2021年全社会固定资产投资构成

Composition of Total Investments in Fixed Assets from 1978 to 2021

单位:% (%)

年 份 Year	全社会固定资产投资额 Total Investment	国有经济 State-owned Units	集体经济 Collective-owned Units	#城 镇 Urban	个体经济 Self-employed Units	#农 村 Rural	其他经济 Others
1978	100.0	69.9	20.1	4.2	10.0	9.5	
1979	100.0	51.5	30.9	2.5	17.6	17.0	
1980	100.0	51.2	31.8	4.5	17.0	16.4	
1981	100.0	37.2	40.3	4.1	22.5	21.7	
1982	100.0	50.9	27.5	5.1	21.6	20.5	
1983	100.0	50.9	19.9	3.9	29.2	27.5	
1984	100.0	47.9	18.0	3.6	34.1	31.7	
1985	100.0	51.7	15.5	4.5	32.8	30.1	
1986	100.0	54.7	19.3	5.4	26.0	23.5	
1987	100.0	52.3	26.4	6.0	21.3	18.8	
1988	100.0	52.0	27.3	9.6	20.7	17.5	
1989	100.0	53.1	22.8	6.4	24.1	20.3	
1990	100.0	55.2	21.3	5.6	23.5	20.1	
1991	100.0	53.2	23.8	5.7	23.0	19.5	
1992	100.0	57.1	31.0	7.0	11.9	9.0	
1993	100.0	53.4	27.6	5.6	11.8	9.3	7.2
1994	100.0	48.5	28.7	5.1	10.7	8.3	12.1
1995	100.0	46.3	29.1	3.9	10.6	8.6	14.0
1996	100.0	44.4	31.1	5.1	13.0	10.7	11.5
1997	100.0	43.1	31.8	3.4	13.5	11.1	11.6
1998	100.0	45.6	29.7	3.3	13.3	11.0	11.4
1999	100.0	46.9	28.6	3.7	14.0	10.3	10.5
2000	100.0	45.4	26.7	4.3	13.9	10.0	14.0
2001	100.0	41.2	24.5	4.8	13.7	9.4	20.6
2002	100.0	35.3	23.1	5.6	13.9	8.1	27.7
2003	100.0	30.3	22.1	6.0	13.8	5.6	33.8
2004	100.0	23.1	32.2	5.0	10.1	1.5	34.6
2005	100.0	17.6	9.9	5.9	25.9	14.1	46.6
2006	100.0	16.7	9.5	6.4	27.8	10.7	46.0
2007	100.0	14.7	10.1	6.8	28.4	9.1	46.8
2008	100.0	15.8	11.7	8.6	28.3	8.4	44.3
2009	100.0	16.2	12.1	9.0	27.5	8.3	44.1
2010	100.0	15.7	11.3	7.9	27.9	7.8	45.1
2011	100.0	14.1	10.1		30.8		45.0
2012	100.0	12.6	10.0		31.6		45.7
2013	100.0	12.9	8.5		34.9		43.7
2014	100.0	12.8	8.0		38.2		41.0
2015	100.0	13.0	6.5		42.0		38.5
2016	100.0	14.1	2.9		41.6		41.4
2017	100.0	17.3	2.7		40.4		39.5
2018	100.0	20.1	1.2		39.1		39.6
2019	100.0	23.8	1.1		29.9		45.2
2020	100.0	20.2	0.5		30.1		49.3
2021	100.0	19.7	0.5		32.5		47.3

5-3 按产业分固定资产投资总额

Total Investment in Fixed Assets by Three Strata of Industry

单位:亿元 (100 million yuan)

年 份 Year	固定资产投资额 Investment in Fixed Assets	按产业分 Grouped by Three Strata of Industry			构成(%) Grouped by Structure		
		第一产业 Primary Industry	第二产业 Secondary Industry	第三产业 Tertiary Industry	第一产业 Primary Industry	第二产业 Secondary Industry	第三产业 Tertiary Industry
2000	2542.7	77.1	1176.7	1288.8	3.0	46.3	50.7
2001	2807.8	95.0	1289.8	1423.1	3.4	45.9	50.7
2002	3509.3	131.7	1650.6	1727.0	3.8	47.0	49.2
2003	5328.4	167.5	2799.5	2361.5	3.1	52.5	44.3
2004	7629.0	249.7	4577.1	2802.3	3.3	60.0	36.7
2005	10541.9	308.4	6653.5	3579.6	2.9	63.1	34.0
2006	11136.1	291.7	6908.7	3935.6	2.6	62.0	35.3
2007	12537.0	360.4	7508.2	4668.4	2.9	59.9	37.2
2008	15435.9	563.2	8182.1	6690.6	3.6	53.0	43.3
2009	19031.0	614.8	9615.4	8800.8	3.2	50.5	46.2
2010	23276.7	551.8	11332.4	11392.5	2.4	48.7	48.9
2011	25927.1	533.3	12425.3	12968.5	2.1	47.9	50.0
2012	30319.8	679.6	14432.3	15207.9	2.2	47.6	50.2
2013	35875.9	644.8	17204.1	18027.0	1.8	48.0	50.2
2014	41599.1	705.3	21287.7	19606.1	1.7	51.2	47.1
2015	47381.5	898.3	24092.7	22390.4	1.9	50.8	47.3
2016	52364.5	973.6	27425.7	23965.1	1.9	52.4	45.8
2017	54236.0	1029.6	26876.3	26330.1	1.9	49.6	48.5
2018					1.7	39.5	58.8
2019					1.7	30.1	68.2
2020					2.3	31.3	66.4
2021					1.9	32.4	65.7

注：2000-2010年数据为全社会固定资产投资口径，2011年起数据为固定资产投资口径(不含农户固定资产投资)。

a) Caliber of 2000-2010 data are total fixed investment, from 2011 data are fixed asset investment(excluding rural households).

5-4 固定资产投资(2021年)

Total Investments in Fixed Assets (2021)

单位:% (%)

类 别	Category	增长速度 The growth		构成 Grouped by Structure	
		固定资产投资 Investment in Fixed Assets	#房地产开发投资 Investment in Real Estate Development	固定资产投资 Investment in Fixed Assets	#房地产开发投资 Investment in Real Estate Development
总 计	**Total**	**6.0**	**3.9**	**100.0**	**100.0**
按登记注册类型分	**Registration Status**				
内 资	Domestic Fund	5.7	2.7	94.2	92.7
国 有	State-owned		-32.6	11.9	1.0
集 体	Collective-owned	2.0	-21.2	0.4	0.5
股份合作	Cooperative	-57.1	-97.1		
联 营	Joint Ownership Units	-14.3			
有限责任	Limited Liability	4.0	-1.3	44.4	53.7
股份有限	Share-holding Corporations Ltd.	-16.3	-31.5	2.6	0.9
私营	Private	13.0	12.3	33.0	35.9
其 他	Others	6.4	208.2	1.9	0.7
港澳台商投资	Fund from Hong Kong,Macao and Taiwan	17.8	22.3	3.2	5.7
合资经营	Joint Venture	16.1	20.7	1.8	3.3
合作经营	Collaborative Operation	144.9	2790.0		0.1
独 资	Solely Foreign-owned	5.9	-1.7	1.0	1.8
股 份	Share-holding	68.0		0.2	0.2
其 他	Others	85.9	283.1	0.1	0.3
外商投资	Fund from Overseas	4.8	23.6	2.5	1.6
合资经营	Joint Venture	-23.6	-2.7	1.3	1.0
合作经营	Collaborative Operation	-11.8			
外 资	Foreign Funded	29.4	111.4	0.6	0.5
股 份	Share-holding	271.4	503.2	0.5	0.1
其 他	Others	48.6	-100.0		
个体经营	Self-employed	11.3		0.1	
按建设性质分	**Investment by Type of Construction**				
新 建	New Construction	14.2		65.5	
扩 建	Expansion	-0.8		11.1	
改建和技术改造	Reconstruction and Technical Transformation	-6.7		21.1	
单纯建造生活设施	Housing	-33.4		0.1	
迁 建	Removal and Reconstruction	3.9		1.6	
恢 复	Resumption	-47.9		0.1	
单纯购置	Purchase only	-0.8		0.5	

注：本表固定资产投资不含农户投资，下表同。

a)Data in this table of investment in fixed asset does not include farmers investment.The same applies to tables following.

5–5 固定资产投资项目情况(2021年)

Investment Projects in Fixed Assets(2021)

单位：% (%)

类别	Category	增长速度 The growth		构成 Grouped by Structure	
		总计 Total	地方项目 Local Investment	总计 Total	地方项目 Local Investment
计划总投资	**Total planned investment**	**16.9**	**19.4**		
自开始建设累计完成投资	**Completed Investment from Beginning**	**29.2**	**33.1**		
本年完成投资	**Investment Completed This Year**	**6.9**	**7.8**	**100.0**	**100.0**
#住宅投资	Residential Buildings	6.4	5.4	3.4	3.4
按构成分	**Investment by Structure**				
建筑安装工程	Construction and Installation	11.1	12.6	73.4	73.9
设备工器具购置	Purchase of Equipment and Instruments	-7.8	-9.0	14.7	14.2
#购置旧设备	Purchase of Second-hand Equipment	-21.7	-21.2	0.1	0.1
其他费用	Others	2.8	2.9	11.9	12.0
#旧建筑物购置费	Purchase of Used Buildings	-21.7	-28.7	0.2	0.2
#建设用地费	Cost of Construction Land	15.8	15.3	8.0	8.2
本年新增固定资产	**Newly Increased Real Estate**	**23.6**	**23.6**		
施工项目个数	**Number of Projects Under Construction**	**8.6**	**8.6**	**100.0**	**100.0**
#本年新开工	Started This Year	-4.7	-4.9	50.0	50.0
本年投产项目个数	**Number of Projects Put into Use**	**-0.6**	**-1.2**		
本年资金来源合计	**Total Fund of Different Sources**	**7.2**	**8.9**		
上年末结余资金	Fund Left Last Year	120.5	131.3		
本年资金来源小计	Total Fund of This Year	5.1	6.7	100.0	100.0
国家预算内资金	State Budgetary Appropriations	-18.9	-18.2	7.0	7.0
国内贷款	Domestic Loans	-2.0	-2.0	9.0	8.2
债　券	Stock	4.9	4.9	0.3	0.3
利用外资	Overseas Funds	-14.2	-11.7	0.4	0.5
自筹资金	Self-raised Fund	7.6	9.3	75.6	76.2
其他资金来源	Others	23.2	24.3	7.7	7.9
本年各项应付款合计	**Total of Account Payable**	**13.5**	**15.4**	**100.0**	**100.0**
#工程款	for Projects	19.0	20.3	44.2	44.1

注：本表固定资产投资不含房地产开发投资和农户投资。
a)Data in this table of investment in fixed asset does not include investment in real estate development and farmers investment.

5-6 按行业分的固定资产投资增长速度(2021年)

The growth of Investments in Fixed Assets by Sector(2021)

单位:% (%)

类 别	Category	固定资产投资额 Investments in Fixed Assets	计 划 总投资 Total planned investment	施工项目 Number of Project under Cons -truction	新开工项目 Started This Year
总 计	**Provincial Total**	**6.0**	**16.9**	**8.6**	**-4.7**
(一)农、林、牧、渔业	**Farming, Forestry, Animal Husbandry and Fishery**	**-14.9**	**-7.1**	**-8.2**	**-20.9**
农 业	Farming	-18.6	-9.4	-9.4	-16.4
林 业	Forestry	-36.2	-31.6	-36.8	-27.9
畜牧业	Animal Husbandry	-20.2	-9.1	-6.9	-29.2
渔 业	Fishery	50.9	50.2	5.6	-3.9
农林牧渔业及辅助性活动	Services for Farming, Forestry, Animal Husbandry and Fishery	-14.9	-17.9	-5.9	-17.7
(二)采矿业	**Mining**	**0.7**	**8.0**	**-28.3**	**-37.7**
煤炭开采和洗选业	Mining and Washing of Coal	-54.0	1.1	-16.7	-31.9
石油和天然气开采业	Extraction of Petroleum and Natural Gas	24.7	34.1	5.9	
黑色金属矿采选业	Mining and Dressing of Ferrous Metal Ores	100.3	13.9	28.0	9.5
有色金属矿采选业	Mining and Dressing of Nonferrous Metals Ores	-32.7	-28.6	-52.5	-64.5
非金属矿采选业	Mining and Dressing of Nonmetal Ores	-40.0	-13.6	-35.1	-60.5
开采专业及辅助性活动	Mining Specialties and Auxiliary Activities	-47.4	-19.9		-40.0
其他采矿业	Mining and Dressing of Other Ores	-58.0	-19.6	-50.0	-100.0
(三)制造业	**Manufacture**	**13.1**	**15.0**	**14.9**	**2.6**
农副食品加工业	Processing of Farm and Sideline Food	29.4	57.3	22.2	15.8
食品制造业	Manufacture of Food	21.1	41.4	30.6	19.9
酒、饮料和精制茶制造业	Manufacture of Wine, Drinks and Refined Tea	4.6	-2.9	11.5	7.7
烟草制品业	Tobacco Products	56.1	463.2	50.0	25.0
纺织业	Textile Industry	23.8	37.9	10.6	-6.1
纺织服装、服饰业	Manufacture of Textile Wearing Apparel and Finery	11.5	16.7	20.3	25.0
皮革、毛皮、羽毛及其制品和制鞋业	Manufacture of Leather, Fur, Feather & Its Products and Footwear	48.3	32.6	42.2	53.6
木材加工及木、竹、藤、棕、草制品业	Timber Processing, Bamboo, Cane, Palm Fiber & Straw Products	81.6	23.9	37.9	28.8
家具制造业	Manufacture of Furniture	40.8	39.3	24.8	24.7
造纸及纸制品业	Papermaking and Paper Products	-3.8	42.0	16.5	7.9
印刷和记录媒介复制业	Printing, Reproduction of Recording Media	6.3	10.9	38.1	43.2
文教、工美、体育和娱乐用品制造业	Manufacture of Culture, Education,Arts and crafts, Sport and Entertainment Goods	28.0	12.2	33.5	64.6
石油、煤炭及其他燃料加工业	Processing of Oil, Coal and Other Fuel	-5.9	2.8	-2.2	-23.0
化学原料和化学制品制造业	Manufacture of Raw Chemical Materials	24.0	7.4	14.1	-12.4
医药制造业	Manufacture of Medicines	11.4	8.3	5.9	-15.2
化学纤维制造业	Manufacture of Chemical Fibers	13.0	11.9	17.4	32.1
橡胶和塑料制品业	Manufacture of Rubber and Plastic	31.6	38.2	20.8	6.4
非金属矿物制品业	Nonmetal Mineral Products	-0.7	4.3		-13.3
黑色金属冶炼及压延加工业	Smelting and Pressing of Ferrous Metals	-8.9	-12.0	-3.6	-8.7
有色金属冶炼及压延加工业	Smelting and Pressing of Nonferrous Metals	-23.9	-1.3	-7.7	-19.2
金属制品业	Manufacture of Metal Products	1.8	13.4	13.8	5.7

注：计划总投资、施工及新开工项目个数等指标不含房地产企业开发数据(下表同)。

a) Data of total planned investment , number of project under construction and new started exclude those developed by real estate companies.(The sam applies to tables following).

5-6 续表 1 continued

单位:% (%)

类　别	Category	固定资产投资 Investments in Fixed Assets	计　划总投资 Total planned investment	施工项目 Number of Project under Cons -truction	新开工项　目 Started This Year
通用设备制造业	Manufacture of General Purpose Machinery	7.0	22.6	18.6	0.6
专用设备制造业	Manufacture of Special Purpose Machinery	26.4	29.0	14.1	-3.6
汽车制造业	Manufacture of Automotive	9.1	13.0	13.5	7.6
铁路、船舶、航空航天和其他运输设备制造业	Manufacture of Railroad,Marine,Aerospace and Other Transportation Equipment	12.0	3.3	14.3	-18.8
电气机械及器材制造业	Manufacture of Electrical Machinery & Equipment	30.9	15.7	28.3	34.1
计算机、通信和其他电子设备制造业	Manufacture of Computer, Communications and Other Electronic Equipment	-3.6	35.1	8.7	27.5
仪器仪表制造业	Manufacture of Measuring Instrument	-3.6	35.1	8.7	27.5
其他制造业	Other Manufacture	3.4	-22.7	10.0	-10.3
废弃资源综合利用业	Comprehensive Utilization of Waste	-16.6	5.4	9.6	5.4
金属制品、机械和设备修理业	Metal Products, Machinery and Equipment Repair Industry	216.7	366.5	68.8	21.4
(四)电力、热力、燃气及水的生产和供应业	**Production and Supply of Electric, Heat, Gas and Water**	**-6.9**	**9.9**	**13.8**	**16.0**
电力、热力生产和供应业	Production and Supply of Electric Power and Heating Power	-9.2	4.3	20.4	38.0
燃气生产和供应业	Production and Supply of Gas	41.6	121.6	-1.4	-18.5
水的生产和供应业	Production and Supply of Tap Water	-9.9	15.1	4.9	-13.5
(五)建筑业	**Construction**	**155.7**	**11.1**	**-42.9**	**-33.3**
房屋建筑业	Building Construction	-17.9	-44.9	-66.7	-100.0
土木工程建筑业	Civil Engineering Construction	392.3	189.8	50.0	
建筑安装业	Construction Installment	-100.0	-100.0	-100.0	-100.0
建筑装饰和其他建筑业	Construction Decoration and Others	-100.0	-100.0	-100.0	-100.0
(六)批发和零售业	**Wholesale and Retail Trade**	**-32.4**	**-19.5**	**-12.4**	**-30.8**
批发业	Wholesale	-17.6	-12.3	-12.7	-38.9
零售业	Retail Trade	-39.8	-23.2	-12.1	-24.0
(七)交通运输、仓储和邮政业	**Transport, Storage and Postal Services**	**-3.2**	**20.8**	**-4.8**	**-19.5**
铁路运输业	Railway Transport	29.8	9.2	-4.6	-52.0
道路运输业	Road Transport	-13.4	26.8	-15.3	-32.0
水上运输业	Waterway Transport	-4.9	-6.3	2.8	-14.3
航空运输业	Air Transport	-25.3	12.6	10.7	-46.2
管道运输业	Pipeline Transport	22.8	14.2	25.8	28.6
多式联运和运输代理业	Multimodal transport and Transportation agency	206.9	70.7	9.1	-23.5
装卸搬运和仓储业	Loading and Unloading and Storage	4.8	25.3	28.2	25.6
邮政业	Postal Services	151.7	20.5	-18.8	-30.0
(八)住宿和餐饮业	**Accommodations and Catering Services**	**-1.8**	**-2.8**	**6.9**	**5.4**
住宿业	Accommodations	-4.1	-6.5	5.4	4.2
餐饮业	Catering Services	10.5	44.0	13.0	8.8
(九)信息传输、软件和信息技术服务业	**Information Transmission, Computer Services and Software**	**-5.7**	**7.3**	**14.7**	**-0.8**
电信、广播电视和卫星传输服务	Telecommunications, Radio and Television and Satellite Transmission Services	-27.7	36.9	20.7	-6.8
互联网和相关服务	Internet and related Services	7.2	2.4	16.8	13.5
软件和信息技术服务业	Software and Information Technology Services	-6.6	7.6	9.2	-11.2
(十)金融业	**Finance**	**-18.8**	**2.3**	**22.5**	**-9.1**
货币金融服务	Monetary and Financial Services	131.8	43.3	68.4	45.5
资本市场服务	Capital Market Services	-79.8	-66.9	-50.0	-50.0

5-6 续表 2 continued

单位:% (%)

类别	Category	固定资产投资 Investments in Fixed Assets	计划总投资 Total planned investment	施工项目 Number of Project under Cons-truction	新开工项目 Started This Year
保险业	Insurance				
其他金融业	Others	-7.6	42.8		-85.7
(十一)房地产业	**Real Estate**	**9.3**	**31.6**	**30.6**	**27.9**
(十二)租赁和商务服务业	**Leasing and Business Services**	**39.9**	**44.9**	**23.0**	**4.6**
租赁业	Leasing Services	-46.8	1.4	20.0	66.7
商务服务业	Business Services	41.9	45.5	23.0	4.2
(十三)科学研究和技术服务	**Scientific Research and Technical Services**	**3.2**	**25.8**	**-5.5**	**-19.8**
研究与试验发展	Research and Experimental Development	1.6	37.9	-4.0	-30.9
专业技术服务业	Special Technical Services	-16.3	19.8	-20.9	-17.4
科技推广和应用服务业	Science and Technology Promotion and Application Services	18.5	16.3	7.7	-14.4
(十四)水利、环境和公共设施管理业	**Management of Water Conservancy, Environment and Public Facilities**	**-8.8**	**9.6**	**-7.7**	**-21.1**
水利管理业	Management of Water Conservancy	-33.4	16.0	-23.5	-51.4
生态保护和环境治理业	Ecological Protection and Environmental Management	-3.2	30.6	4.9	-0.5
公共设施管理业	Management of Public Facilities	-3.0	6.6	-6.1	-16.5
土地管理业	Management of Land	-58.9	-23.1		-27.3
(十五)居民服务、修理和其他服务业	**Households services, Repair and Other Services**	**-25.7**	**24.6**	**-2.2**	**-16.3**
居民服务业	Services to Households	-25.0	26.7	-4.9	-15.8
机动车、电子产品和日用产品修理业	Motor Vehicles, Electronics and Household Products Repair	39.8	133.3	-20.0	-40.0
其他服务业	Other Services	-50.3	3.8	31.6	
(十六)教　育	**Education**	**20.8**	**37.3**	**30.9**	**12.7**
教　育	Education	20.8	37.3	30.9	12.7
(十七)卫生和社会工作	**Health and Social Work**	**13.1**	**27.0**	**11.0**	**-16.2**
卫　生	Health Care	25.0	25.3	19.8	-14.0
社会工作	Social Work	-19.8	32.4	-7.4	-21.2
(十八)文化、体育和娱乐业	**Culture, Sports and Recreation**	**-12.8**	**-6.8**	**-3.0**	**-23.0**
新闻和出版业	News and Publication	36.1	0.9		
广播、电视、电影和影视录音制作业	Radio, Television, Film and Video Recording Production	-3.1	-16.9	-3.6	-7.7
文化艺术业	Culture and Arts	-23.8	6.5	-3.6	-4.8
体　育	Sports	-24.1	-23.5	5.4	-22.2
娱乐业	Recreation	-5.3	-7.0	-4.3	-30.5
(十九)公共管理、社会保障和社会组织	**Public Management,Social Security and Social Organizations**	**5.3**	**30.0**	**2.9**	**-29.1**
中国共产党机关	CPC Agencies	-14.3	-73.7	-20.0	-66.7
国家机构	Government Agencies	6.1	39.9	-1.2	-33.3
人民政协、民主党派	CPPCC and Democratic Parties	-73.2	-73.1		-100.0
社会保障	Social Security	-88.7	-92.7	-50.0	-100.0
群众团体、社会团体和其他成员组织	Mass Organizations, Social Organizations and Other Organizations	229.7	162.1	100.0	300.0
基层群众自治组织	Self-governing Mass Organizations at the Grass-roots Level	16.1	104.6	57.9	40.0
(二十)国际组织	**International Organizations**				
国际组织	International Organizations				

5-7 按行业分的固定资产投资构成(2021年)

Composition of Investments in Fixed Assets by Sector(2021)

单位:% (%)

类　别	Category	固定资产投资 Investments in Fixed Assets	计　划总投资 Total planned investment	施工项目 Number of Project under Cons -truction	新开工项　目 Started This Year
总　计	**Provincial Total**	**100.0**	**100.0**	**100.0**	**100.0**
(一)农、林、牧、渔业	**Farming, Forestry, Animal Husbandry and Fishery**	**2.3**	**2.9**	**5.8**	**6.2**
农　业	Farming	0.7	0.9	2.2	2.5
林　业	Forestry		0.1	0.2	0.2
畜牧业	Animal Husbandry	0.8	0.9	2.1	2.0
渔　业	Fishery	0.2	0.4	0.3	0.4
农林牧渔业及辅助性活动	Services for Farming, Forestry, Animal Husbandry and Fishery	0.5	0.5	1.1	1.1
(二)采矿业	**Mining**	**0.8**	**0.5**	**0.6**	**0.6**
煤炭开采和洗选业	Mining and Washing of Coal	0.1	0.1	0.1	0.2
石油和天然气开采业	Extraction of Petroleum and Natural Gas	0.6	0.2	0.1	0.1
黑色金属矿采选业	Mining and Dressing of Ferrous Metal Ores	0.1		0.1	0.1
有色金属矿采选业	Mining and Dressing of Nonferrous Metals Ores	0.1		0.1	0.1
非金属矿采选业	Mining and Dressing of Nonmetal Ores	0.1	0.1	0.1	0.1
开采专业及辅助性活动	Mining Specialties and Auxiliary Activities				
其他采矿业	Mining and Dressing of Other Ores				
(三)制造业	**Manufacture**	**27.5**	**33.9**	**47.9**	**51.7**
农副食品加工业	Processing of Farm and Sideline Food	1.1	1.1	2.8	3.5
食品制造业	Manufacture of Food	1.0	1.1	2.4	2.7
酒、饮料和精制茶制造业	Manufacture of Wine, Drinks and Refined Tea	0.2	0.2	0.4	0.5
烟草制品业	Tobacco Products				
纺织业	Textile Industry	0.5	0.6	1.5	1.8
纺织服装、服饰业	Manufacture of Textile Wearing Apparel and Finery	0.2	0.1	0.5	0.6
皮革、毛皮、羽毛及其制品和制鞋业	Manufacture of Leather, Fur, Feather & Its Products and Footwear	0.1	0.1	0.2	0.2
木材加工及木、竹、藤、棕、草制品业	Timber Processing, Bamboo, Cane, Palm Fiber & Straw Products	0.3	0.2	0.8	1.1
家具制造业	Manufacture of Furniture	0.2	0.2	0.5	0.6
造纸及纸制品业	Papermaking and Paper Products	0.3	0.5	0.7	0.7
印刷和记录媒介复制业	Printing, Reproduction of Recording Media	0.1	0.2	0.5	0.6
文教、工美、体育和娱乐用品制造业	Manufacture of Culture, Education,Arts and crafts, Sport and Entertainment Goods	0.3	0.3	0.7	0.9
石油、煤炭及其他核燃料加工业	Processing of Oil, Coal and Other Fuel	0.5	0.6	0.5	0.5
化学原料和化学制品制造业	Manufacture of Raw Chemical Materials and Chemica Products	5.0	6.6	4.3	4.1
医药制造业	Manufacture of Medicines	1.8	2.3	2.4	2.4
化学纤维制造业	Manufacture of Chemical Fibers	0.3	0.4	0.4	0.4
橡胶和塑料制品业	Manufacture of Rubber and Plastic	0.9	0.9	2.2	2.6
非金属矿物制品业	Nonmetal Mineral Products	2.3	2.5	5.3	5.5
黑色金属冶炼及压延加工业	Smelting and Pressing of Ferrous Metals	0.8	1.2	0.5	0.5
有色金属冶炼及压延加工业	Smelting and Pressing of Nonferrous Metals	0.6	0.8	0.9	0.8
金属制品业	Manufacture of Metal Products	1.2	1.4	2.9	3.3

注：计划总投资、施工及新开工项目个数等指标不含房地产企业开发数据(下表同)。

a) Data of total planned investment, number of project under construction and new started exclude those developed by real estate companies.(The same applies to tables following).

5-7 续表 1 continued

单位:% (%)

类别	Category	固定资产投资额 Investments in Fixed Assets	计划总投资 Total planned investment	施工项目 Number of Project under Cons -truction	新开工项目 Started This Year
通用设备制造业	Manufacture of General Purpose Machinery	2.3	2.6	5.1	5.4
专用设备制造业	Manufacture of Special Purpose Machinery	2.3	2.6	4.5	4.6
汽车制造业	Manufacture of Automotive	1.2	1.3	1.8	2.0
铁路、船舶、航空航天和其他运输设备制造业	Manufacture of Railroad,Marine,Aerospace and Other Transportation Equipment	0.7	0.8	0.8	0.6
电气机械及器材制造业	Manufacture of Electrical Machinery & Equipment	1.0	1.8	2.0	2.2
计算机、通信和其他电子设备制造业	Manufacture of Computer, Communications and Other Electronic Equipment	1.9	2.9	2.0	1.9
仪器仪表制造业	Manufacture of Measuring Instrument	0.2	0.3	0.5	0.6
其他制造业	Other Manufacture	0.1	0.1	0.2	0.1
废弃资源综合利用业	Comprehensive Utilization of Waste	0.2	0.2	0.6	0.6
金属制品、机械和设备修理业	Metal Products, Machinery and Equipment Repair Industry			0.1	0.1
(四)电力、热力、燃气及水的生产和供应业	**Production and Supply of Electric, Heat, Gas and Water**	**4.1**	**5.8**	**5.8**	**6.2**
电力、热力生产和供应业	Production and Supply of Electric Power and Heating Power	2.9	4.4	3.7	4.3
燃气生产和供应业	Production and Supply of Gas	0.3	0.4	0.4	0.4
水的生产和供应业	Production and Supply of Tap Water	0.9	1.0	1.7	1.5
(五)建筑业	**Construction**				
房屋建筑业	Building Construction				
土木工程建筑业	Civil Engineering Construction				
建筑安装业	Construction Installment				
建筑装饰和其他建筑业	Construction Decoration and Others				
(六)批发和零售业	**Wholesale and Retail Trade**	**0.4**	**0.6**	**1.0**	**0.9**
批发业	Wholesale	0.2	0.2	0.4	0.4
零售业	Retail Trade	0.3	0.4	0.5	0.6
(七)交通运输、仓储和邮政业	**Transport, Storage and Postal Services**	**8.8**	**13.9**	**5.7**	**5.1**
铁路运输业	Railway Transport	1.7	2.2	0.2	0.1
道路运输业	Road Transport	5.0	8.7	3.5	3.0
水上运输业	Waterway Transport	0.6	0.9	0.3	0.2
航空运输业	Air Transport	0.2	0.6	0.1	
管道运输业	Pipeline Transport	0.1	0.1	0.1	0.1
多式联运和运输代理业	Multimodal transport and Transportation agency	0.2	0.3	0.1	0.1
装卸搬运和仓储业	Loading and Unloading and Storage	1.0	1.2	1.4	1.6
邮政业	Postal Services				
(八)住宿和餐饮业	**Accommodations and Catering Services**	**0.5**	**0.6**	**0.8**	**0.8**
住宿业	Accommodations	0.4	0.5	0.6	0.6
餐饮业	Catering Services	0.1	0.1	0.2	0.2
(九)信息传输、软件和信息技术服务业	**Information Transmission, Computer Services and Software**	**1.2**	**1.9**	**1.5**	**1.5**
电信、广播电视和卫星传输服务	Telecommunications, Radio and Television and Satellite Transmission Services	0.2	0.2	0.3	0.4
互联网和相关服务	Internet and related Services	0.5	0.9	0.6	0.6
软件和信息技术服务业	Software and Information Technology Services	0.5	0.9	0.5	0.5
(十)金融业	**Finance**	**0.1**	**0.2**	**0.1**	**0.1**
货币金融服务	Monetary and Financial Services			0.1	0.1
资本市场服务	Capital Market Services				

5-7 续表 2 continued

单位:% (%)

类 别	Category	固定资产投资额 Investments in Fixed Assets	计划总投资 Total planned investment	施工项目 Number of Project under Cons-truction	新开工项目 Started This Year
保险业	Insurance				
其他金融业	Others	0.1	0.2		
(十一)房地产业	**Real Estate**	**35.0**	**10.5**	**5.2**	**3.2**
(十二)租赁和商务服务业	**Leasing and Business Services**	**3.7**	**6.6**	**3.0**	**2.6**
租赁业	Leasing Services		0.1		
商务服务业	Business Services	3.7	6.6	2.9	2.6
(十三)科学研究和技术服务	**Scientific Research and Technical Services**	**2.2**	**3.1**	**2.0**	**1.6**
研究与试验发展	Research and Experimental Development	1.1	1.4	0.6	0.4
专业技术服务业	Special Technical Services	0.3	0.5	0.6	0.6
科技推广和应用服务业	Science and Technology Promotion and Application Services	0.7	1.2	0.9	0.7
(十四)水利、环境和公共设施管理业	**Management of Water Conservancy, Environment and Public Facilities**	**6.6**	**9.1**	**10.6**	**11.2**
水利管理业	Management of Water Conservancy	0.8	1.1	1.3	1.1
生态保护和环境治理业	Ecological Protection and Environmental Management	0.7	1.0	1.1	1.2
公共设施管理业	Management of Public Facilities	5.1	6.9	8.0	8.8
土地管理业	Management of Land		0.1	0.2	0.1
(十五)居民服务、修理和其他服务业	**Households services, Repair and Other Services**	**0.2**	**0.4**	**0.5**	**0.5**
居民服务业	Services to Households	0.2	0.4	0.4	0.4
机动车、电子产品和日用产品修理业	Motor Vehicles, Electronics and Household Products Repair				
其他服务业	Other Services		0.1	0.1	0.1
(十六)教 育	**Education**	**2.6**	**2.8**	**4.1**	**3.4**
教 育	Education	2.6	2.8	4.1	3.4
(十七)卫生和社会工作	**Health and Social Work**	**1.9**	**3.3**	**2.4**	**1.8**
卫 生	Health Care	1.5	2.4	1.7	1.3
社会工作	Social Work	0.4	0.9	0.6	0.5
(十八)文化、体育和娱乐业	**Culture, Sports and Recreation**	**1.8**	**3.6**	**2.3**	**1.8**
新闻和出版业	News and Publication				
广播、电视、电影和影视录音制作业	Radio, Television, Film and Video Recording Production	0.1	0.1	0.1	0.1
文化艺术业	Culture and Arts	0.4	0.7	0.5	0.5
体 育	Sports	0.3	0.3	0.3	0.3
娱乐业	Recreation	1.0	2.5	1.3	1.0
(十九)公共管理、社会保障和社会组织	**Public Management,Social Security and Social Organizations**	**0.3**	**0.3**	**0.8**	**0.7**
中国共产党机关	CPC Agencies				
国家机构	Government Agencies	0.3	0.3	0.7	0.6
人民政协、民主党派	CPPCC and Democratic Parties				
社会保障	Social Security				
群众团体、社会团体和其他成员组织	Mass Organizations, Social Organizations and Other Organizations				
基层群众自治组织	Self-governing Mass Organizations at the Grass-roots Level			0.1	0.1
(二十)国际组织	**International Organizations**				
国际组织	International Organizations				

5-8 各市固定资产投资增长速度
The growth of Total Investments in Fixed Assets by Region

单位:% (%)

地 区	Region	2018	2019	2020	2021
全省总计	**Total**	**4.1**	**-8.4**	**3.6**	**6.0**
济 南 市	Jinan	9.6	12.6	4.0	11.5
青 岛 市	Qingdao	7.9	21.6	3.2	4.1
淄 博 市	Zibo	6.6	-44.6	7.5	22.1
枣 庄 市	Zaozhuang	-19.8	-15.8	3.2	6.5
东 营 市	Dongying	-10.0	-32.6	8.9	12.5
烟 台 市	Yantai	6.0	5.0	2.9	0.2
潍 坊 市	Weifang	4.4	-23.2	4.5	16.0
济 宁 市	Jining	7.1	-3.6	3.2	12.4
泰 安 市	Tai'an	5.8	-23.3	2.9	-29.4
威 海 市	Weihai	7.5	-15.0	2.9	6.0
日 照 市	Rizhao	6.3	-16.5	3.2	3.0
莱 芜 市	Laiwu	7.2			
临 沂 市	Linyi	7.8	-23.5	4.0	11.4
德 州 市	Dezhou	7.3	-13.6	-2.9	-19.6
聊 城 市	Liaocheng	-4.3	-41.2	6.8	12.9
滨 州 市	Binzhou	-16.8	-23.5	7.8	15.3
菏 泽 市	Heze	8.0	8.1	7.5	15.8

注：根据行政区划调整，2019年起，莱芜市并入济南市，以下表同。
a)According to administrative division adjustment,Laiwu City merged into Jinan City from 2019.The same applies to tables following.

5-9 各市民间固定资产投资增长速度
The growth of Non-government Investments in Fixed Assets by Region

单位:% (%)

地 区	Region	2018	2019	2020	2021
全省总计	**Total**	**4.1**	**-18.0**	**6.9**	**8.2**
济 南 市	Jinan	8.5	-10.9	3.9	24.9
青 岛 市	Qingdao	21.8	20.9	13.0	8.3
淄 博 市	Zibo	15.8	-45.3	7.8	24.1
枣 庄 市	Zaozhuang	-21.3	-32.3	2.7	-2.2
东 营 市	Dongying	-9.6	-45.7	7.0	26.6
烟 台 市	Yantai	2.9	6.4	3.6	0.8
潍 坊 市	Weifang	8.9	-31.8	11.8	12.7
济 宁 市	Jining	2.6	-8.8	10.3	10.2
泰 安 市	Tai'an	-6.4	-33.0	-4.1	-21.6
威 海 市	Weihai	7.1	-21.9	-5.9	8.9
日 照 市	Rizhao	-3.6	-13.7	26.6	6.1
莱 芜 市	Laiwu	5.9			
临 沂 市	Linyi	9.5	-36.9	8.3	17.2
德 州 市	Dezhou	12.3	-18.8	-2.9	-15.6
聊 城 市	Liaocheng	-5.7	-47.2	0.9	5.0
滨 州 市	Binzhou	-21.5	-29.9	7.2	10.7
菏 泽 市	Heze	4.5	-5.2	15.5	6.5

5-10 各市房地产开发投资和销售情况(2021年)

General Scale of Investment Actually Completed by Enterprises for Real Estate Development and Floor Space of Commercialized Buildings Sold(2021)

地区	Region	本年完成投资(万元) Investment Completed This Year (10 000 yuan)	#住宅 Residential Buildings	商品房销售面积(平方米) Floor Space of Commercialized Buildings Sold(sq.m)	#住宅 Residential Buildings	商品房销售额(万元) Total Sale of Commercialized Buildings Sold(10 000 yuan)	#住宅 Residential Buildings
全省总计	**Total**	**98197496**	**76945048**	**142728495**	**126320491**	**121556183**	**110441422**
济南市	Jinan	19280018	13513858	15481974	13001987	19569740	17216533
青岛市	Qingdao	19818480	14810338	16445197	14196327	22672959	20392399
淄博市	Zibo	4142393	3169781	5285363	4773218	4456485	4057179
枣庄市	Zaozhuang	3102663	2552449	5538991	5113039	4299731	4002750
东营市	Dongying	1931627	1670005	3041199	2723467	2264313	2034364
烟台市	Yantai	8030960	6965507	10561536	9879743	8765691	8231697
潍坊市	Weifang	8752202	7279714	15957161	13866718	10261744	9387925
济宁市	Jining	5849020	4969547	12308159	11482079	8591199	8103915
泰安市	Tai'an	2811655	2356478	4499967	4245226	3398255	3247654
威海市	Weihai	3824927	3181158	5184628	4650142	4298229	3941661
日照市	Rizhao	2105262	1330529	2997994	2834995	2756954	2650605
临沂市	Linyi	7035815	5602959	16228321	13487322	12404571	10881841
德州市	Dezhou	3295863	2845215	7364535	6861745	4936062	4716786
聊城市	Liaocheng	3219551	2530529	7312945	5751949	4945081	4254189
滨州市	Binzhou	1567677	1347848	4769450	4346013	2887787	2693986
菏泽市	Heze	3429383	2819133	9751075	9106521	5047382	4627938

5-11 按登记注册类型分的房地产开发投资情况(2021年)

类　别		Category		总计 Total	内资企业 Domestic Funded	国有企业 State-owned Enterprises
计划总投资	**(万元)**	**Intended Investment**	**(10 000 yuan)**	**691799013**	**648103846**	**4665095**
自开始建设累计完成投资	**(万元)**	**Cumulative Investment**	**(10 000 yuan)**	**392033957**	**368847912**	**2703031**
本年完成投资	**(万元)**	**Investment Completed in Current Year**	**(10 000 yuan)**	**98197496**	**91012468**	**1000253**
按构成分		**Grouped by Use of Funds**				
建筑工程	(万元)	Construction	(10 000 yuan)	62163197	57745152	453337
安装工程	(万元)	Installation	(10 000 yuan)	5542063	5287446	41750
设备工器具购置	(万元)	Purchase of Equipment and Instruments	(10 000 yuan)	918619	876196	7516
其他费用	(万元)	Others	(10 000 yuan)	29573617	27103674	497650
#旧建筑物购置费	(万元)	Purchase of Used Building	(10 000 yuan)	60003	59993	1773
土地购置费	(万元)	Purchase of Land	(10 000 yuan)	24755318	22586149	466554
按工程用途分		**Grouped by Use of Buildings**				
住　宅	(万元)	Residential Buildings	(10 000 yuan)	76945048	71089826	785328
#90平方米以下住宅	(万元)	Residential Buildings below 90sq.m	(10 000 yuan)	6559278	5969030	23829
144平方米以上住宅	(万元)	Residential Buildings above 144sq.m	(10 000 yuan)	18044500	17048344	137019
办公楼	(万元)	Office Buildings	(10 000 yuan)	4101338	3720561	3352
商业营业用房	(万元)	Buildings for Business	(10 000 yuan)	7160856	6751689	63563
其　他	(万元)	Others	(10 000 yuan)	9990254	9450392	148010
本年新增固定资产	**(万元)**	**Newly Increased Fixed Assets**	**(10 000 yuan)**	**47267424**	**43428883**	**183106**
到位资金情况		**Funds in Place**				
上年末结余资金	(万元)	Fund Left from Last Year	(10 000 yuan)	46025503	42418963	611560
本年资金来源小计	(万元)	Fund of All Sources in Current Year	(10 000 yuan)	132721708	122617163	2602848
国内贷款	(万元)	Domestic Loans	(10 000 yuan)	12371390	11239133	261581
#银行贷款	(万元)	from Banks	(10 000 yuan)	10479481	9431435	250631
非银行金融机构贷款	(万元)	from Other Financial Departments	(10 000 yuan)	1891909	1807698	10950
利用外资	(万元)	Foreign Investment	(10 000 yuan)	101429	6081	421
自筹资金	(万元)	Self-Raising Funds	(10 000 yuan)	41289759	38003288	897434
定金及预付款	(万元)	Earnest Money and Advance Charge	(10 000 yuan)	54517698	50059595	1240838
个人按揭贷款	(万元)	Mortgage Loans	(10 000 yuan)	20590982	19594669	137776
其他到位资金	(万元)	Others	(10 000 yuan)			
本年各项应付款合计	(万元)	Account Payable	(10 000 yuan)	33130971	31033148	957646
#工程款	(万元)	Payment for Construction	(10 000 yuan)	20501105	19100584	801669
待开发土地面积	**(平方米)**	**Space of Land to be Developed**	**(sq.m)**	**44639456**	**43159434**	**539810**
本年购置土地面积	**(平方米)**	**Space of Land Purchased in Current Year**	**(sq.m)**	**19063421**	**17921328**	**467498**
本年土地成交价款	**(万元)**	**Value of Commercial Land**	**(10 000 yuan)**	**10306199**	**9481266**	**318434**

Investment in Real Development by Registration Status(2021)

集体企业 Collective-owned Enterprises	股份合作企业 Cooperative Enterprises	联营企业 Joint-owned Enterprises	有限责任公司 Limited Liability Corporations	股份有限公司 Share-holding Corporations Limited	私营企业 Private Enterprises	其他企业 Other Enterprises	港澳台商投资企业 Enterprises with Funds from Hong Kong, Macao and Taiwan	外商投资企业 Foreign Funded Enterprises
3305429	**204917**		**326565532**	**7147082**	**273097797**	**3291466**	**33225302**	**10469865**
1428750	**57620**		**184690445**	**4046739**	**157414290**	**982749**	**17394377**	**5791668**
446366	**5358**		**48434965**	**895663**	**35260432**	**639010**	**5621135**	**1563893**
241236	1278		29970750	555712	23338914	237650	3405193	1012852
13475			2639486	60534	2306098	16647	174903	79714
892			403065	3393	430626	226	33074	9349
190763	4080		15421664	276024	9184794	384487	2007965	461978
			23109	4581	26626	325		10
160707			12984033	235132	7483298	340450	1772658	396511
301382	5348		37484125	751674	28284569	564259	4549114	1306108
47132	5348		3243146	31277	2181401		353724	236524
123582			9115597	81459	6643502	304552	760961	235195
15990			2032269	1833	1105196	2	310012	70765
6939			3521217	86742	2727174	23215	315407	93760
122055	10		5397354	55414	3143493	51534	446602	93260
76113			**22139094**	**448655**	**18844779**	**288703**	**3197763**	**640778**
75601	44268	5938	25465312	606199	12572838	8811	2782407	824133
659644	78106	102684	68201527	1392910	42905739	27960	7582764	2521781
2190	27463		6758408	67379	2651940		625793	506464
2190	21000		5558908	64779	2148632		551793	496253
	6463		1199500	2600	503308		74000	10211
			3530		2130		92048	3300
20056	10000		19930041	564733	13983057	9583	2763888	522583
420573	14807	93297	29448673	483978	17015241	18377	3246688	1211415
196031	25836	9387	10598592	244603	8196525		746095	250218
48922	21317	12600	17014161	497160	10968638		1627195	470628
43377	13035	10255	10497804	275975	6829568		1090224	310297
	253660		**22272583**	**955603**	**16369401**		**1043355**	**436667**
62549			**8416140**	**219588**	**7928348**		**814936**	**327157**
44831			**5358792**	**109503**	**3098930**		**719537**	**105396**

5-12 按登记注册类型分的房地产开发财务情况(2021年)

单位:万元

类别	Category	总计 Total	内资企业 Domestic Funded	国有企业 State-owned Enterprises
一、期初存货	**Initial Inventory**	**348558045**	**330473465**	**8896101**
二、期末资产负债	**Property debt at the End**			
流动资产合计	Total Liquid Liabilities	669610004	631762090	16909557
#应收账款	Accounts receivable	19290806	17584500	788923
存　货	Inventory	379508826	359627345	9867706
固定资产原价	Fixed Asset Value	20050076	18994472	286120
累计折旧	Accumulated Depreciation	3869482	3567425	54279
#本年折旧	in Current Year	733337	699276	8240
资产总计	Assets	793743461	753110412	21592121
负债合计	Liabilities	664502711	637577141	16099825
所有者权益合计	Owners' Equity	129240750	115533271	5492296
#实收资本	Paid-up Capital	75267539	62854921	1242216
三、损益及分配	**Net Income or Loss and Distribution**			
营业收入	Revenues from Business	110215933	103982112	1960435
#主营业务收入	Revenues from Principal Business	100106569	94130800	1844354
土地转让收入	Revenues from Land Transfer	673680	670342	12902
商品房屋销售收入	Revenues from Commercial Housing Sales	95272746	89441601	1761401
自持物业收入	Self Holding Property Income	950229	839765	7974
#房屋出租收入	Housing Rental Income	561660	453823	6205
其他收入	Others	3209914	3179093	62077
营业成本	Business Cost	88756619	83861571	1505490
#主营业务成本	Main Business Cost	81159925	76534273	1406617
营业税金及附加	Business Tax and Extra Charges	4816742	4539619	151203
其他业务利润	Other Operating Profits	228525	227194	641
销售费用	Sales Expenses	4029684	3686594	47370
管理费用	Management Expenses	3740349	3546538	57747
财务费用	Financial Expenses	2446208	2404562	55614
营业利润	Business Profits	7864047	7341708	218979
营业外收入	Non-operating Income	620802	605531	53463
营业外支出	Non-operating Expenses	625522	606384	18541
利润总额	Total Profits	7804240	7294835	253395
所得税费用	Income Tax Payable	2237375	2058235	70101
应交增值税	Value-added Tax Payable	4192439	3906532	53943
四、人工成本	**Labor costs**			
本年应付工资总额	Wages Payable in Current Year	2603060	2394990	47896

 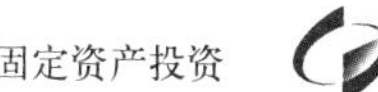

Financial Indicators of Real Estate Development by Registration Status(2021)

(10 000 yuan)

集体企业 Collective-owned Enterprises	股份合作企业 Cooperative Enterprises	联营企业 Joint-owned Enterprises	有限责任公司 Limited Liability Corporations	股份有限公司 Share-holding Corporations Limited	私营企业 Private Enterprises	其他企业 Other Enterprises	港澳台商投资企业 Enterprises with Funds from Hong Kong, Macao and Taiwan	外商投资企业 Foreign Funded Enterprises
2224100	**445483**	**126931**	**206487855**	**3705059**	**108493263**	**94674**	**14385715**	**3698865**
3799887	718966	100016	405001594	9742891	195192171	297009	28928347	8919567
82159	2899	3998	10075837	332637	6297444	603	1490521	215785
2730309	471507	62155	225406054	4576527	116420105	92983	14911210	4970271
94847	1000	132	13840893	509444	4249577	12460	1020316	35287
40131	560	72	1908898	87403	1473268	2814	287631	14426
4527	40	67	432342	8554	244728	776	32133	1929
4008245	735586	100078	496419358	14407226	215537626	310173	31153925	9479124
4081401	686973	130232	410255648	11723746	194398598	200720	20097703	6827866
-73156	48614	-30154	86163710	2683481	21139028	109453	11056221	2651258
61394	65498	1000	44555843	966064	15949907	13000	10180746	2231872
201530	70	58157	61191015	1585708	38957492	27707	5258076	975745
193391	70	58157	55035369	1545414	35426340	27707	5060393	915375
			520613	31330	105497		3304	35
184317		58157	51673897	1349034	34387089	27707	4924049	907097
8323			395734	28091	399644		103417	7047
8323			219780	27087	192429		100896	6941
751	70		2445125	136959	534111		29624	1197
174972	122	83097	48828020	1304925	31950360	14585	4175134	719914
166998		83097	44027860	1263590	29571994	14118	3950692	674960
6402	946	46	2945885	57825	1376620	691	218441	58682
165			79279	22993	124116		1563	-233
22739	1213	1197	2200809	41117	1370063	2086	280756	62335
37027	1199	505	1878847	71279	1497718	2215	147958	45853
4498	3046	4209	1735538	36196	565656	-195	36557	5090
-43639	-6059	-30772	4800221	234437	2160211	8330	460135	62204
728	67	10	347381	18496	185269	117	11584	3688
672	31	25	344929	15753	226374	58	18586	551
-42647	-6024	-30787	4806256	237337	2068915	8389	449487	59919
3666	-30		1357633	30586	594129	2151	143803	35336
24037	1565	918	2260813	54554	1508001	2703	241864	44043
7209	1384	372	1356457	53587	926481	1604	159119	48951

5-13 房地产开发企业(单位)施工、销售和待售情况(2021年)

类 别		Category		合 计 Total
房屋施工面积	**(平方米)**	**Floor Space Under Construction**	**(sq.m)**	**827716679**
#新开工面积	(平方米)	Recently-started Projects	(sq.m)	165720958
房屋竣工面积	**(平方米)**	**Floor Space Completed**	**(sq.m)**	**113736815**
#不可销售面积	(平方米)	Space of Floor not Ready for Sale	(sq.m)	6451503
商品住宅竣工套数	**(套)**	**Number of Commercial Buildings Completed**	**(unit)**	
竣工房屋价值	**(万元)**	**Value of Buildings Completed**	**(10 000 yuan)**	**35608190**
出租房屋面积	**(平方米)**	**Floor Space of Buildings to Lease**	**(sq.m)**	**996278**
商品房销售面积	**(平方米)**	**Floor Space of Commercial Buildings Sold**	**(sq.m)**	**142728495**
#现房销售面积	(平方米)	Floor Space of Complete Departments	(sq.m)	14389937
期房销售面积	(平方米)	Floor Space of Forward Delivery Housing	(sq.m)	128338558
商品房销售额	**(万元)**	**Total Sale of Commercial Building**	**(10 000 yuan)**	**121556183**
#现房销售额	(万元)	Sale of Complete Departments	(10 000 yuan)	9875262
期房销售额	(万元)	Sale of Forward Delivery Housing	(10 000 yuan)	111680921
商品住宅销售套数	**(套)**	**Number of Commercial Buildings Sold**	**(unit)**	
#现房销售套数	(套)	Complete Departments	(unit)	
期房销售套数	(套)	Forward Delivery Housing	(unit)	
待售面积	**(平方米)**	**Floor Space of Waiting For Sale**	**(sq.m)**	**27652607**
#待售1-3年(含1年)	(平方米)	1 to 3 years	(sq.m)	13832174
待售3年以上(含3年)	(平方米)	more than 3 years	(sq.m)	5838121

Construction and Sale of Buildings Made by Real Estate Enterprises(2021)

住 宅 Residential Buildings	按户型面积分 #90平方米及以下住宅 Below or Equal 90 sq.m	按户型面积分 144平方米以上住宅 Above 144 sq.m	办公楼 Office Buildings	商业营业用房 Buildings for Business	其 他 Others
607126199	**58824186**	**131882224**	**29596124**	**64582864**	**126411492**
125008177	6725439	25640282	4291669	10278531	26142581
85966904	**10055744**	**21085364**	**2680803**	**7795506**	**17293602**
3174623	954874	264603	141495	480648	2654737
709801	**139331**	**116338**			
27442141	**2801526**	**7526017**	**1018065**	**2691188**	**4456796**
21135	**21135**		**450645**	**429243**	**95255**
126320491	**7539005**	**27478197**	**2406850**	**5403849**	**8597305**
11164435	1524739	2796764	508652	1364518	1352332
115156056	6014266	24681433	1898198	4039331	7244973
110441422	**5827214**	**28809542**	**2592938**	**5231154**	**3290669**
7687054	825802	2507489	556636	1094494	537078
102754368	5001412	26302053	2036302	4136660	2753591
1019878	**103667**	**162461**			
95008	22709	15910			
924870	80958	146551			
16309313	**2576365**	**4391462**	**1620185**	**5891832**	**3831277**
8956621		513076	513076	2175418	2187059
2234832		602557	602557	2418292	582440

主要统计指标解释

全社会固定资产投资 是以货币形式表现的在一定时期内全社会建造和购置固定资产的工作量以及与此有关的费用的总称。该指标是反映固定资产投资规模、结构和发展速度的综合性指标,又是观察工程进度和考核投资效果的重要依据。全社会固定资产投资按登记注册类型可分为国有、集体、个体、联营、股份制、外商、港澳台商、其他等。

房地产开发投资 指各种登记注册类型的房地产开发公司、商品房建设公司及其他房地产开发法人单位和附属于其他法人单位实际从事房地产开发或经营活动的单位统一开发的包括统代建、拆迁还建的住宅、厂房、仓库、饭店、宾馆、度假村、写字楼、办公楼等房屋建筑物和配套的服务设施，土地开发工程（如道路、给水、排水、供电、供热、通讯、平整场地等基础设施工程）的投资；不包括单纯的土地交易活动。

计划总投资 是指在建的建设工程按照总体设计（或按设计概算或预算）规定的内容全部建成计划需要的总投资。

固定资产投资的资金来源 根据固定资产投资的资金来源不同，分为国家预算内资金、国内贷款、利用外资、自筹资金和其他资金。

(1)国家预算内资金：分为财政拨款和财政安排的贷款两部分。包括中央财政的基本建设基金(分经营性基金和非经营性基金两部分)、专项支出(如煤代油专项等)、收回再贷、贴息资金，财政安排的挖潜改造和新产品试制支出、城建支出、商业部门简易建筑支出、不发达地区发展基金等资金中用于固定资产投资的资金；地方财政中由国家统筹安排的资金等。

(2)国内贷款：指报告期固定资产投资单位向银行及非银行金融机构借入的用于固定资产投资的各种国内借款，包括银行利用自有资金及吸收的存款发放的贷款、上级主管部门拨入的国内贷款、国家专项贷款(包括煤代油贷款、劳改煤矿专项贷款等)、地方财政专项资金安排的贷款、国内储备贷款、周转贷款等。

(3)利用外资：指报告期收到的用于固定资产建造和购置的国外资金(包括设备、材料、技术在内)。包括对外借款(外国政府、国际金融组织贷款、出口信贷、外国银行商业贷款、对外发行债券和股票)、外商直接投资及外商其他投资。不包括我国自有外汇资金(国家外汇、地方外汇、留成外汇、调剂外汇和中国银行自有资金发行的外汇贷款等)。计算利用外资时，需要折算成人民币，折算中所使用的外汇汇率按现汇计算，即按使用外汇时的汇率计算。

(4)自筹资金：指固定资产投资单位报告期收到的，由各地区、各部门及企、事业单位筹集用于固定资产投资的预算外资金，包括中央各部门、各级地方和企、事业单位的自筹资金。

(5)其他资金：指在报告期收到的除以上各种资金之外其他用于固定资产投资的资金，包括企业或金融机构通过发行各种债券筹集到的资金、群众集资、个人资金、无偿捐赠的资金及其他单位拨入的资金等。

固定资产投资按国民经济行业分 根据建设项目建成投产后的主要产品或主要用途及社会经济活动性质来确定国民经济行业。一般情况下，一个建设项目或一个企业、事业单位只能属于一种国民经济行业。

固定资产投资按建设性质分 根据整个建设项目情况来确定。建设项目的性质一般分为新建、扩建、改建和技术改造、迁建、恢复。房地产开发单位投资不划分建设性质。

(1)新建：一般指从无到有“平地起家”开始建设的企业、事业和行政单位或建设项目。现有企业、事业、行政单位一般不属于新建。但如有的单位原有基础很小，经过建设后新增的固定资产价值超过该企、事业、行政单位原有固定资产价值(原值)三倍以上的也应作为新建。

(2)扩建：指在厂内或其他地点，为扩大原有产品的生产能力(或效益)或增加新的产品生产能力，而增建主要的生产车间(或主要工程)、分厂、独立的生产线。行政、事业单位在原单位增建业务用房(如学校增建教学用房、医院增建门诊部、病房等)也作为扩建。

现有企、事业单位为扩大原有主要产品生产能力或增加新的产品生产能力,增建一个或几个主要生产车间(或主要工程)、分厂，同时进行一些更新改造工程的，也应作为扩建。

(3)改建和技术改造：指现有企业、事业单位，对原有设施进行技术改造或更新(包括相应配套的辅助性生产、生活福利设施)的建设项目。现有企业、事业单位为适应市场变化的需要,而改变企业的主要产品种类(如军工企业转产民用品等)的建设项目，应作为改建。原有产品生产作业线由于各工序(车间)之间能力不平衡，为填平补齐充分发挥原有生产能力而增建不增加本企业主要产品设计能力的车间，也应作为改建。技术改造是指企业、事业单位在现有基础上，用先进的技术代替落后的技术，用先进的工艺和装备代替落后的工艺和装备，以改变企业落后的技术经济面貌，实现以内涵为主的扩大再生产，达到提高产品质量、促进产品更新换代、节约能源、降低消耗、扩大生产规模、全面提高社会经济效益的目的。技术改造具体包括以下内容：机器设备和工具的更新改造；生产工艺改革、节约能源和原材料的改造；厂房建筑和公共设施的改造；劳动条件和生产环境的改造等。

固定资产投资按构成分 固定资产投资活动按其工作内容和实现方式分为建筑安装工程，设备、工具、器具购置，其他费用三个部分。

(1)建筑安装工程(建筑安装工作量)：指各种房屋、建筑物的建造工程和各种设备、装置的安装工程。包括各种房屋建造工程；各种用途设备基础和各种工业窑炉的砌筑工程及金属结构工程；为施工而进行的各种准备工作和临时工程以及完工后的清理工作等；铁路、道路的铺设，矿井的开凿及石油管道的架设等；水利工程；防空地下建筑等特殊工程；列入房屋工程预算内的暖气、卫生、通风、照明、煤气等设备的价值及装设油饰工程；列入建筑工程预算内的各种管道(蒸汽、压缩空气、石油、给排水等管道)、电力、电讯电缆导线等的敷设工程；以及各种机械设备的安装工程；为测定安装工程质量，对设备进行的试运工作；房地产开发单位进行的商品房屋开发建设工程、土地开发工程。

在安装工程中，不包括被安装设备本身的价值。

(2)设备、工具、器具购置：指建设单位或企、事业单位购置或自制的，达到固定资产标准的设备、工具、器具的价值。新建单位及扩建单位的新建车间，按照设计或计划要求购置或自制的全部设备、工具、器具，不论是否达到固定资产标准均计入“设备、工具、器具购置”中。

(3)其他费用：指在固定资产建造和购置过程中发生的，除上述几项内容以外的各种应分摊计入固定资产的费用。

施工项目 指报告期内进行过建筑或安装施工活动的项目。凡是报告期内施过工的建设项目，不论施工时间长短，均作为施工项目统计。施工项目个数可以反映一定时期固定资产投资的实际规模，与同期全部建成投产项目个数相比，可以从建设速度的角度反映固定资产投资的效果。根据建设项目施工活动的不同性质，施工项目又分为：本年正式施工项目、本年收尾项目和以前年度全部停缓建项目。

全部建成投产项目 工业项目指设计文件规定形成生产能力的主体工程及其相应配套的辅助设施全部建成，经负荷试运转，证明具备生产设计规定合格产品的条件，并经过验收鉴定合格或达到竣工验收标准，与生产性工程配套的生活福利设施可以满足近期正常生产的需要，正式移交生产的建设项目。非工业项目指设计文件规定的主体工程和相应的配套工程全部建成，能够发挥设计规定的全部效益，经验收鉴定合格或达到竣工验收标准，正式移交使用的建设项目。

新增固定资产 指报告期内已经完成建造和购置过程，并已交付生产或使用单位的固定资产价值。该指标是表示固定资产投资成果的价值指标，也是反映建设进度，计算固定资产投资效果的重要指标。

商品房销售面积 指报告期内出售商品房屋的合同总面积(即双方签署的正式买卖合同中所确定的建筑面积)。由现房销售建筑面积和期房销售建筑面积两部分组成。

商品房销售额 指报告期内出售商品房屋的合同总价款(即双方签署的正式买卖合同中所确定的合同总价)。该指标与商品房销售面积同口径，由现房销售额和期房销售额两部分组成。

Explanatory Notes on Main Statistical Indicators

Total Investment in Fixed Assets in the Whole Country refers to the volume of activities in construction and purchases of fixed assets and related fees, expressed in monetary terms. It is a comprehensive indicator which shows the size, structure and growth of the investment in fixed assets, providing basis for observing the progress of construction projects and evaluating results of investment. Total investment in fixed assets in the whole country includes, by type of ownership, the investment by the state owned units, collective units, individuals, joint ownership units, share holding units, as well as investment by businessmen from foreign countries and from Hong Kong, Macao and Taiwan, and by other units.

Investment in Real Estate Development refers to the investment by the real estate development companies, commercial buildings construction companies and other real estate development units of various types of ownership in the construction of house buildings, such as residential buildings, factory buildings, warehouses, hotels, guesthouses, holiday villages, office buildings, and the complementary service facilities and land development projects, such as roads, water supply, water drainage, power supply, heating, telecommunications, land leveling and other projects of infrastructure. It excludes the activities in pure land transactions.

Total planned investment refers to total investment needed to complete all the items of a project under construction as laid out in the overall design (or the budget estimate or budget of the design).

Sources of Funds for Investment in Fixed Assets include fund from state budget, domestic loans, foreign investment, self raised funds, and others depending on the source of investment.

(1) Fund from state budget consists of budgetary appropriation and loans from state budget. More specifically, it includes, from the budget of the central government, capital construction fund (operation fund and non-operational fund), special expenses (e.g. expenses on substituting petroleum with coal), loans from repayment, discount fund, expenses on innovation and trial production of new products, expenses on urban construction, expenses on temporary construction by trade departments, development fund for less developed areas, as well as local budgetary fund transferred from the central budget.

(2) Domestic loans refer to loans of various forms borrowed by investing units from banks and non-bank financial institutions during the reference period for the purpose of investment in fixed assets, including loans issued by banks from their self owned funds and deposit, loans appropriated by higher responsible authorities, special loans by government (including loan for substituting petroleum with coal, special loan for reform through labour coal mines), loans arranged by local government from special funds, domestic reserve loan, and working loan, etc.

(3) Foreign Investment refers to foreign funds received during the reference period for the construction and purchase of investment in fixed assets (covering equipment, materials and technology), including foreign borrowings (loans from foreign governments and international financial institutions, export credit, commercial loans from foreign banks, issue of bonds and stocks overseas), foreign direct investment and other foreign investment. Excluded in this category are capitals in foreign exchanges owned by China (foreign exchanges owned by the central and local governments, foreign exchanges retained by enterprises, foreign exchanges by enterprises through regulating mechanism, loans in foreign exchanges issued by the Bank of China with its own fund, etc.). In calculating the utilization of foreign capitals, foreign currencies are converted into Chinese Renminbi applying the current exchange rate when the foreign capitals are actually used.

(4) Self-raised funds refer to extra budgetary funds for investment in fixed assets received by investing units from central government ministries, local governments, enterprises and institutions, including their self raised funds.

(5) Others refer to funds for investment in fixed assets received from the sources other than those listed above, including capitals raised through issuing bonds by enterprises or financial institutions, funds raised from individuals and through donations, and funds transferred from other units.

Investment in Fixed Assets by Sector The classification of construction projects by sector is determined by the major products or the purpose of the projects when they are put into production or use, and by the nature of their social economic activities. In general, one project or one enterprise or institution can only be classified into one sector.

Investment in Fixed Assets by Type of Construction The construction projects in general can be classified, by the type of construction, into new construction, expansion, reconstruction and technical transformation, moving and restoration. However, investment by type of construction is not applied to investment by real estate development units.

(1) New construction in general refers to newly constructed enterprises, institutions, administrative agencies or independent projects from scratch. Construction in the existing enterprises, institutions or agencies is not considered as new construction. In case the assets of the existing unit is quite small, and the value of newly added fixed assets exceeds the original value of assets by three times, the expansion will be considered as new construction.

(2) Expansion refers to construction of new major production workshop, branch factory or independent production line within a factory or in other locations, for the purpose of increasing the production capacity (or improving efficiency) of the original products. Newly constructed houses for the operation of institutions and administrative organizations (such as the newly constructed buildings for teaching in schools, buildings for clinics or wards in hospitals, etc.) are also

classified as expansion.

Also included in the expansion are investments by existing enterprises or institutions in building major production line(s) or branch factory(ies) along with some work on innovation, for the purpose of expending the production capacity of original products or producing new products.

(3) Reconstruction refers to construction projects by existing enterprises or institutions in innovation or technical transformation of the old facilities (including auxiliary production equipment and welfare facilities).Also considered as reconstruction is the construction of new workshops by the existing enterprises or institutions to change the variety of products to meet the market demand (such as the production of civil products by defence industries), or to bring the designed production capacity into full play through a more balanced production process on production lines. Technical transformation refers to replacement of old technology or equipment by new technology or equipment, in order to expand the reproduction through improvement of technology contents in production, to improve product quality, to promote new products, to save energy and reduce consumption and to improve overall social economic efficiency. Contents of technical transformation include: updating of machinery, equipment and tools; reforming production process by using energy or materials saving technology; construction of factory workshops and transformation of public facilities; improvement of working conditions and environment, etc.

Investment in Fixed Assets by Structure By their contents, investment activities are classified into 3 categories, i.e. construction and installation, purchase of equipment and instrument, and other expenses.

(1) Construction and installation (work volume of construction and installation) refers to the construction of various houses and buildings and installation of various kinds of equipment and instruments. They include construction of various houses; equipment foundations, industrial kilns and stoves, and metal structure work; preparation works for project construction, and clearing up works post project construction; pavement of railways and roads, drilling of mines and putting up of oil pipes; construction of projects of water conservancy; construction of underground air raid shelters and construction of other special projects; value of equipment for heating, sanitation, ventilation, lighting, gas, painting, etc. that are covered by the budget of housing projects; laying out of various pipelines (for steam, compressed air, petroleum, tap water and sewage) and lines for electric power and for communications; installation of various machinery equipment, testing operation for pre testing the quality of installation projects, and land and other development work conducted by real estate developers for commercial housing. The value of equipment installed is not included in the value of installation projects.

(2) Purchase of equipment and instruments refers to the total value of equipment, tools, and instruments purchased or self produced which come up to standards for fixed assets by the construction units or investing enterprises or institutions. Equipment, tools and instruments purchased or self produced for new workshops by newly established or expanded units are categorized as "purchase of equipment and instruments" no matter whether they come up to the standards for fixed assets.

(3)Other expenses refer to expenses occurring during the construction or purchase of fixed assets other than those mentioned above.

Projects under Construction refer to projects with construction and installation activities undertaken in the reference period. All projects that have construction activities undertaken during the reference period are reported as projects under construction irrespective of the length of construction work. The number of projects under construction can reflect the actual size of investment in fixed assets during a given period, and when compared with the number of projects completed and put into use during the same period, it demonstrates the results of investment in fixed assets. Depending on the nature of construction activities, projects under construction can also be classified into projects under construction in current year, winding up projects in current year and stopped or suspended projects in previous years (with preservation work in current year).

Projects Completed and Put into Use Industrial projects refer to the major projects and accessory facilities completed which result in forming production capacity and have been checked and accepted while the living and welfare facilities have been completed and can ensure normal production and formally put into production. Non industrial projects refer to the major projects and accessory facilities completed which possess the designed capacity and have been checked, accepted and formally put into production.

Newly Increased Fixed Assets refer to the newly increased value of fixed assets, constructed or purchased, that have been transferred to the investors. This is an indicator that demonstrates the results of investment in fixed assets in monetary terms, and an important indicator to reflect the speed of construction and to calculate the efficiency of investment.

Area of Commercial Housing Sold refers to total contracted area of commercial housing (i.e. area of floor space as designated in the formal contracts signed by both sides) during the reference time. It constitutes floor space of completed housing and floor space of future housing.

Value of Commercial Housing Sold refer to total value of contracts (i.e. value of sales/purchase for selling/purchase of commercial housing as designated in the contracts signed by both sides) during the reference time. It has the same coverage as the area of commercial housing sold, constituting completed housing and floor space of future housing.

第6篇

对外经济和旅游

Foreign Trade and Tourism

简 要 说 明

一、本篇资料的主要内容

本篇资料反映了全省外经外贸和旅游的基本情况，主要包括进出口、利用外资、境外投资、对外承包工程和劳务合作、人民币外汇牌价、旅游业基本情况等方面的内容。

二、本篇资料的来源

1.进出口数据来源于海关统计，进出口商品价值，出口按离岸价（FOB）、进口按到岸价（CIF）统计。

2.利用外资、对外承包工程和劳务合作、境外投资等资料来源于省商务厅。

3.历年人民币对主要外币的年平均汇价资料来源于国家外汇管理局，是根据当年国家外汇管理局提供的每日汇价进行加权平均计算而得出的当年年平均汇价。

4.旅游资料来源于省文化和旅游厅财务处。

本篇资料由省统计局贸易处整理提供。

Brief Introduction

I. Content

Data in this chapter show the basic conditions of foreign trade and tourism, mainly including imports and exports, utilization of foreign capitals, overseas direct investments, contracted projects, labor services cooperation, exchange rate of RMB to other currencies and tourism, etc.

II. Source of Data

(1)Data on foreign trade are based on the statements made by the Administration of Customs. Exports are calculated at FOB, imports at CIF.

(2)Data on utilization of foreign capitals, contracted projects and labor services cooperation are provided by the Bureau of Commerce of Shandong Province.

(3)Average exchange rates of RMB yuan to other currencies over the years come from the State Administration of Exchange Control. The annual average exchange rate is calculated as the weighted mean of the daily exchange rates provided by the State Administration of Exchange Control.

(4)Data on tourism are provided by the Division of Finance of the Culture and Tourism of Shandong Province.

Data in this chapter are prepared and compiled by the Division of Trade and External Economic Relations Statistics of Shandong Provincial Bureau of Statistics.

6-1 1978-2021年人民币对主要外币年平均汇价(中间价)

Average Exchange Rate of RMB Yuan Against Main Convertible Currencies from 1978 to 2021(Middle Rate)

单位:人民币元 (RMB yuan)

年 份 Year	100美元 100 US Dollars	100日元 100 Japanese Yen	100港元 100 Hong Kong Dollars	100欧元 100Euros
1978	168.36	0.81	36.16	
1979	155.49	0.71	31.35	
1980	149.84	0.66	30.15	
1981	170.51	0.77	30.41	
1982	189.26	0.76	31.15	
1983	197.57	0.83	27.36	
1984	232.70	0.98	29.71	
1985	293.67	1.25	37.57	
1986	345.28	2.07	44.22	
1987	372.21	2.58	47.74	
1988	372.21	2.91	47.70	
1989	376.51	2.74	48.28	
1990	478.32	3.32	61.39	
1991	532.33	3.96	68.45	
1992	551.46	4.36	71.24	
1993	576.20	5.20	74.41	
1994	861.87	8.44	111.53	
1995	835.10	8.92	107.96	
1996	831.42	7.64	107.51	
1997	828.98	6.86	107.09	
1998	827.91	6.35	106.88	
1999	827.83	7.29	106.66	
2000	827.84	7.69	106.18	
2001	827.70	6.81	106.08	
2002	827.70	6.62	106.07	800.58
2003	827.70	7.15	106.24	936.13
2004	827.68	7.66	106.23	1029.00
2005	819.17	7.45	105.30	1019.53
2006	797.18	6.86	102.62	1001.90
2007	760.40	6.46	97.46	1041.75
2008	694.51	6.74	89.19	1022.27
2009	683.10	7.30	88.12	952.70
2010	676.95	7.73	87.13	897.25
2011	645.88	8.11	82.97	900.11
2012	631.25	7.90	81.38	810.67
2013	619.32	6.33	79.85	822.19
2014	614.28	5.82	79.22	816.51
2015	622.84	5.15	80.34	691.41
2016	664.23	6.12	85.58	734.26
2017	675.18	6.02	86.64	763.03
2018	661.74	5.99	84.43	780.16
2019	689.85	6.33	88.05	772.55
2020	689.76	6.46	88.93	787.55
2021	645.15	5.87	83.00	762.93

6-2　1984-2021年海关进出口情况

Basic Statistics on Imports and Exports from 1984 to 2021

单位:万美元 (10 000 USD)

年　份 Year	进出口总值 Total Value of Imports and Exports	出口总值 Total Value of Exports	一般贸易 General Trade	来料加工装配贸易 Processing and Assembling Trade with Sent Materials	进料加工贸易 Processing Trade with Imported Materials	其他贸易 Other Trades	进口总值 Total Value of Imports
1984	352012	207786					144226
1985	414448	234652					179796
1986	382840	191926					190914
1987	355294	289938	264633	2566	19232	3507	65356
1988	573361	309773	261451	3796	40458	4068	263588
1989	616511	327015	266337	6274	49047	5357	289496
1990	428522	341719	274898	8660	53152	5009	86803
1991	483200	375230	293951	13681	63430	4168	107970
1992	778140	433752	330729	18598	79452	4973	344388
1993	728586	420360	292058	23834	96748	7720	308226
1994	962927	587011	371013	40640	168470	6888	375916
1995	1395007	816101	460278	77503	270177	8143	578906
1996	1616394	918298	449683	130565	331035	6339	698096
1997	1753631	1085888	483895	185156	410664	6173	667743
1998	1661740	1034705	458607	172262	396013	7823	627035
1999	1827094	1157909	541405	218625	394880	2999	669185
2000	2498998	1552905	746563	293008	507050	6284	946093
2001	2896313	1812899	913253	310013	579125	10508	1083414
2002	3394175	2111511	1089063	341530	669958	10960	1282664
2003	4465752	2657285	1400709	392861	845249	18466	1808467
2004	6078136	3587286	1799792	483369	1252126	51999	2490850
2005	7688876	4625113	2310122	594991	1668351	51649	3063763
2006	9528817	5864717	3013461	655916	2083042	112298	3664100
2007	12261798	7524374	3800924	679014	2863332	181104	4737424
2008	15814480	9317486	4739880	722044	3573434	282128	6496994
2009	13860378	7956530	3637582	697915	3296132	324901	5903848
2010	18895085	10424695	4973019	750340	4230872	470464	8470390
2011	23599191	12578809	6466907	842878	4737751	531273	11020382
2012	24554487	12873171	6875045	867657	4566215	564254	11681316
2013	26715854	13450998	7603966	866031	4392892	588109	13264856
2014	27711549	14474545	8373918	802064	4734553	564010	13237004
2015	24174867	14406069	9042024	739933	4183875	440237	9768798
2016	23420733	13715826	8653875	716557	3904404	440990	9704906
2017	26305670	14710207	9428956	651868	4151643	477739	11595464
2018	29239097	16013984	11047764	601424	3918203	446592	13225113
2019	29628464	16143995	11256710	605165	3496008	786112	13484469
2020	31844703	18903512	13853845	497612	3466764	1085291	12941191
2021	45386886	27184375	19567326	553192	4257732	2806124	18202512

6-3 进出口主要分类情况

Imports and Exports by Category

单位:亿美元 (100 million USD)

类 别	Category	2010	2015	2016	2017	2018	2019	2020	2021
一、进出口总值	**Total Value of Imports and Exports**	**1889.5**	**2417.5**	**2342.1**	**2630.6**	**2923.9**	**2962.8**	**3184.5**	**4538.7**
出口额	Exports	1042.5	1440.6	1371.6	1471.0	1601.4	1614.4	1890.4	2718.4
进口额	Imports	847.0	976.9	970.5	1159.5	1322.5	1348.4	1294.1	1820.3
二、出口商品	**Exported Goods**								
初级产品	Primary Goods	138.5	159.7	172.9	179.6	189.6	194.9	195.8	229.1
工业制品	Manufactured Goods	903.6	1279.6	1198.0	1290.7	1412.3	1419.5	1693.5	2489.3
三、进口商品	**Imported Goods**								
初级产品	Primary Goods	360.6	508.0	551.7	757.1	904.4	967.4	896.1	1257.6
工业制品	Manufactured Goods	434.9	458.8	421.4	418.0	418.4	387.8	416.1	562.7
四、纺织服装进出口总值	**Total Value of Imports and Exports of Textile Apparel**	**188.5**	**228.8**	**221.4**	**227.0**	**243.8**	**231.3**	**274.2**	**329.3**
出口额	Exports	173.3	212.5	206.5	213.2	230.4	219.7	264.3	318.0
进口额	Imports	15.2	16.3	14.9	13.8	13.4	11.6	9.9	11.3
五、农产品进出口总值	**Total Value of Imports and Exports of Agricultural Products(By-products)**	**250.6**	**313.7**	**298.0**	**310.9**	**323.5**	**334.7**	**352.5**	**410.6**
出口额	Exports	127.0	153.1	162.9	170.1	174.2	178.9	181.7	191.7
进口额	Imports	123.6	160.7	135.1	140.8	149.3	155.8	170.8	219.0
六、机电产品进出口总值	**Total Value of Imports and Exports of Mechanical and Electrical Products**	**725.0**	**871.8**	**786.0**	**835.6**	**867.6**	**846.5**	**1076.3**	**1535.0**
出口额	Exports	450.7	576.3	524.9	572.4	602.6	603.6	809.5	1172.2
进口额	Imports	274.3	295.6	261.1	263.1	265.0	242.9	266.8	362.8
七、高新技术产品进出口总值	**Total Value of Imports and Exports of High and New-tech Products**	**329.1**	**352.8**	**293.7**	**293.0**	**300.0**	**266.7**	**316.1**	**440.0**
出口额	Exports	175.8	177.1	147.8	146.2	153.6	133.3	153.6	202.4
进口额	Imports	153.3	175.8	145.9	146.9	146.3	133.4	162.5	237.6
八、外商投资企业进出口总值	**Total Value of Imports and Exports of**	**962.8**	**926.2**	**824.6**	**841.6**	**857.7**	**749.1**	**707.6**	**908.0**
出口额	Exports	565.7	561.3	504.8	508.1	515.8	456.8	438.0	581.9
进口额	Imports	397.1	364.9	319.8	333.5	341.9	292.3	269.6	326.1
九、一般贸易进出口总值	**Total Value of Imports and Exports under General Trades**	**974.4**	**1493.7**	**1478.7**	**1717.3**	**1972.1**	**1989.1**	**2180.9**	**3020.7**
出口额	Exports	497.3	904.2	865.4	942.9	1104.8	1125.7	1385.4	1956.7
进口额	Imports	477.0	589.5	613.3	774.4	867.4	863.4	795.5	1064.0
十、加工贸易进出口总值	**Total Value of Imports and Exports under Processing Trades**	**756.4**	**744.7**	**683.5**	**699.2**	**657.3**	**573.3**	**555.2**	**700.6**
出口额	Exports	498.1	492.4	462.1	480.4	452.0	410.1	396.4	481.1
进口额	Imports	258.3	252.3	221.4	218.9	205.4	163.2	158.7	219.5
来料加工贸易进出口总值	Total Value of Imports and Exports under Processing Trades with Sent Materials	118.3	113.2	112.9	101.0	95.2	94.0	79.0	94.9
出口额	Exports	75.0	74.0	71.7	65.2	60.1	60.5	49.8	55.3
进口额	Imports	43.3	39.2	41.2	35.9	35.0	33.5	29.2	39.6
进料加工贸易进出口总值	Total Value of Imports and Exports under Processing Trades with Imported Materials	638.1	631.5	570.7	598.2	562.2	479.3	476.2	605.6
出口额	Exports	423.1	418.4	390.4	415.2	391.8	349.6	346.7	425.8
进口额	Imports	215.0	213.1	180.2	183.0	170.4	129.7	129.5	179.9

6-4 按主要国家(地区)分海关进出口商品总值(2021年)

Total Value of Import and Export Commodities by Countries or Regions(2021)

单位:万美元 (10 000 USD)

国别(地区)	Country(Region)	进出口总值 Total Value of Imports and Exports	出口总值 Total Value of Exports	进口总值 Total Value of Imports
合　计	**Total**	**45386886**	**27184375**	**18202512**
亚　洲	**Asia**	**20844976**	**12901304**	**7943672**
东　盟	Asean	6676534	3727756	2948778
香　港	Hong kong	961016	951270	9746
日　本	Japan	2812333	2158248	654085
韩　国	Republic of Korea	4166740	2701713	1465028
台　湾	Taiwan	1068831	311025	757806
马来西亚	Malaysia	2286600	684378	1602222
印度尼西亚	Indonesia	776803	524216	252587
新加坡	Singapore	508434	321693	186741
印　度	India	941646	713172	228474
泰　国	Thailand	1056553	575925	480627
非　洲	**Africa**	**2938230**	**1679187**	**1259043**
南　非	South Africa	292049	218450	73599
欧　洲	**Europe**	**8221120**	**5154465**	**3066656**
欧　盟	EU	4466337	3423866	1042471
英　国	United Kingdom	861384	725863	135521
德　国	Germany	1042301	706572	335729
法　国	France	339797	263608	76189
意大利	Italy	415257	314875	100383
荷　兰	Netherlands	805220	714164	91056
西班牙	Spain	397383	308319	89063
瑞　典	Sweden	103028	63238	39791
瑞　士	Switzerland	54883	25139	29744
俄罗斯	Russia	1991216	738035	1253181
比利时	Belgium	246802	222083	24719
拉丁美洲	**Latin America**	**5091012**	**1966192**	**3124821**
阿根廷	Argentina	145628	82885	62744
巴　西	Brazil	2488316	403785	2084531
智　利	Chile	666656	216510	450146
墨西哥	Mexico	641692	583936	57756
巴拿马	Panama	66501	60787	5714
北美洲	**North America**	**5936847**	**4744416**	**1192432**
美　国	United States	5167042	4212724	954319
加拿大	Canada	756707	531602	225105
大洋洲	**Oceanic**	**2352181**	**738811**	**1613369**
澳大利亚	Australia	2050264	608827	1441437
新西兰	New Zealand	246180	82338	163842

注:进口国别指原产国,出口国别指最终消费国。

a)The importing country refers to country of origin and the exporting country refers to country of final consumption.

6-5 海关进出口商品分类金额(2021年)
Imports and Exports Value by Category of Commodities(2021)

单位:万美元 (10 000 USD)

商 品 类 别	Category	出 口 Export	进 口 Import
总 计	**Total**	**27184375**	**18202512**
一、活动物;动物产品	Live Animals & Animal Products	336584	883260
二、植物产品	Plant Products	701575	927274
三、动植物油脂、蜡及分解产品;食用油	Animal and Vegetable Oils; Fats and Wax; Edible Oils and Fats	7788	71337
四、食品饮料酒醋;烟草及代用品	Food; Beverages; Liquor and Vinegar; Tobacco and Tobacco Substitutes	801650	155491
五、矿产品	Minerals	372119	9369433
六、化学工业及其相关工业产品	Chemicals and Related Products	2357532	543234
七、塑料及其制品;橡胶及其制品	Plastics and Related Products; Rubber and Related Products	2668787	909329
八、皮及皮制品;旅行用品;动物肠线	Leather and Leather Products; Travel Articles; Animal Casing	320471	51478
九、木及软木制品、编结材料制品	Wood and Wooden Products; Plaited Products	501646	277560
十、木浆及纤维状纤维素浆;废纸纸板及制品	Paper Pulp and Cellulose Pulp; Paper and Waste Paper; Paperboard and Related Products	279707	420738
十一、纺织原料及纺织制品	Textile Materials and Products	2971936	254198
十二、鞋帽伞杖鞭及零件;羽毛人发制品	Footwear; Headgear; Umbrellas; Canes; Whips; Feather and Wigs and Related Products	619937	23321
十三、石料膏泥棉云母及制品;陶瓷玻璃	Gypsum; Cement; Asbestos; Mica; Ceramic Glass	948200	38395
十四、珍珠宝石贵金属及制品;仿首饰	Pearls and Precious Stones; Precious Metal and Related Products; Artificial Jewelry	196229	49984
十五、贱金属及制品	Base Metals and Related Products	3056691	641131
十六、机械、电气设备、电视机及音响设备	Machinery; Electric Equipment; TV Sets and Audio	5755820	3002909
十七、车辆,航空器,船舶及运输设备	Locomotives; Vehicles; Aircraft; Ship and Related Transportation Equipment	1752514	127209
十八、照相计量医疗精密仪器及设备,零附件	Photographic, Measuring and Medical Instruments and Equipment; Related Parts and Accessories	293298	385340
十九、武器弹药及其零件、附件	Weapons and Ammunition; Related Parts and Accessories	3958	14
二十、杂项制品	Miscellaneous Products	3119968	34317
二十一、艺术品,收藏品及古物	Works of Art, Collectibles and Antiques	2404	734
二十二、特殊交易品及未分类商品	Special Transactions Goods and Products Not Otherwise Classified	96761	35830

6-6 各市进口总值

Import Value by Region

单位:万美元 (10 000 USD)

地　区	Region	2010	2012	2013	2014	2015	2016	2017	2018	2019	2020	2021
全省总计	**Total**	**8470390**	**11681316**	**13264856**	**13237004**	**9768798**	**9704906**	**11595464**	**13225113**	**13484469**	**12941191**	**18202512**
济南市	Jinan	338077	341237	408513	443894	391559	350402	379949	463640	695984	904029	1184182
青岛市	Qingdao	2316976	3241127	3595284	3411137	2487228	2311566	2953121	3250313	3649250	3659830	5529787
淄博市	Zibo	267156	421339	375846	334093	184217	267096	451785	807562	672788	574169	731713
枣庄市	Zaozhuang	16510	19205	30477	28668	19188	13080	17748	10649	10544	20531	36591
东营市	Dongying	524370	731888	734502	716119	794434	1051990	1443459	1905102	1866571	1281659	2319009
烟台市	Yantai	1830134	1944322	1983808	2334823	2134194	1907065	1974377	1942911	1702423	1813701	2578564
潍坊市	Weifang	305563	400365	455585	545743	593745	647520	752393	890728	952781	993774	1243063
济宁市	Jining	216172	191947	189611	196240	200202	205097	255957	311351	256535	229387	299040
泰安市	Tai'an	66296	93837	111785	124246	53469	39068	51570	50248	54662	96445	151491
威海市	Weihai	498919	646678	644731	521511	431693	609922	809153	724569	698916	648185	833309
日照市	Rizhao	1116594	2141712	2916013	2998036	1105077	819816	824426	743880	937008	982816	1171661
莱芜市	Laiwu	168635	139196	175308	129828	91300	72516	54134	59062			
临沂市	Linyi	194120	398994	477219	509646	268604	270149	257005	215443	224314	253860	272864
德州市	Dezhou	61408	85025	151165	128026	96771	92607	95686	157768	205904	203171	276119
聊城市	Liaocheng	234233	374313	418645	336790	253633	268550	329540	368833	292517	254647	254284
滨州市	Binzhou	253989	344896	474668	341746	450673	494963	592241	778990	814833	708364	877287
菏泽市	Heze	61237	165234	121695	136457	212811	283487	352919	544064	449439	316623	443547

注：根据行政区划调整，2019年起，莱芜市并入济南市(以下表同)。
a)According to administrative division adjustment,Laiwu City merged into Jinan City from 2019.The same applies to tables following.

6-7 各市出口总值

Export Value by Region

单位:万美元 (10 000 USD)

地　区	Region	2010	2012	2013	2014	2015	2016	2017	2018	2019	2020	2021
全省总计	**Total**	**10424695**	**12873171**	**13450998**	**14474545**	**14406069**	**13715826**	**14710207**	**16013984**	**16143995**	**18903512**	**27184375**
济南市	Jinan	405065	571423	548093	606119	599604	734449	750622	855195	934788	1089566	1818852
青岛市	Qingdao	3388997	4079090	4195962	4577696	4532685	4246549	4459296	4795545	4943258	5608922	7613630
淄博市	Zibo	403077	531938	524998	559843	578724	523697	549162	632460	605733	710361	1121684
枣庄市	Zaozhuang	74567	93923	94656	115373	140271	121770	130190	149161	200853	364322	431650
东营市	Dongying	275753	498199	580290	609488	496787	455879	492935	558417	497315	663184	859141
烟台市	Yantai	2547962	2835914	2947468	2940357	2804476	2484594	2566322	2675220	2510602	2842338	3788619
潍坊市	Weifang	869581	1096820	1160420	1232904	1298380	1234913	1396149	1570247	1637051	1757251	2882746
济宁市	Jining	229866	319613	333417	326913	343461	336635	348655	331002	410928	561337	752084
泰安市	Tai'an	92614	122221	136696	173108	174881	161578	173000	188253	191794	211879	299116
威海市	Weihai	891721	1065926	1070238	1137218	1262087	1167064	1258820	1382187	1336251	1686362	2312664
日照市	Rizhao	221080	387622	387918	478865	413386	422266	515035	615483	590263	496514	622842
莱芜市	Laiwu	103202	73382	75095	92056	98413	97606	103086	108868			
临沂市	Linyi	282591	389726	463548	569408	605650	592273	727522	806213	982973	1440346	2445332
德州市	Dezhou	133596	186760	202646	222717	220674	224347	264983	284894	295105	358361	516721
聊城市	Liaocheng	128938	184919	200303	238553	253684	292520	345107	369527	300099	328837	567329
滨州市	Binzhou	254980	282876	354250	378169	363203	376194	398407	461493	452084	473651	715575
菏泽市	Heze	121105	152819	175000	215759	219703	243491	230915	229820	254895	310280	436390

6-8 各市外商投资企业进口总值

Import Value of Foreign-funded Enterprises by Region

单位:万美元 (10 000 USD)

地区	Region	2010	2012	2013	2014	2015	2016	2017	2018	2019	2020	2021
济南市	Jinan	98172	85119	137608	121857	59933	71494	78449	87785	79017	94474	151190
青岛市	Qingdao	946037	941800	935831	963393	839443	737077	817862	937447	947372	852617	1026872
淄博市	Zibo	73952	88517	72702	73356	54431	50150	52439	51745	52905	36709	42736
枣庄市	Zaozhuang	9145	6859	6137	7045	7476	6962	6447	1924	2964	6647	14482
东营市	Dongying	225175	259554	199707	194742	156487	193733	228643	156866	90661	36951	50840
烟台市	Yantai	1523651	1408391	1318853	1600465	1481398	1220765	1215986	1082135	718017	778277	940833
潍坊市	Weifang	119937	139381	153361	157793	135743	138059	116589	128191	101739	98588	115730
济宁市	Jining	182080	134841	138489	136729	124541	90107	104127	121811	92426	66528	74558
泰安市	Tai'an	3546	4938	4583	3722	8807	5891	5378	4383	8082	12163	39678
威海市	Weihai	356285	353942	332885	310320	270964	245756	255345	248512	248222	236627	316854
日照市	Rizhao	200410	462024	560543	582506	309894	280355	235303	275238	223917	165105	202274
莱芜市	Laiwu	4746	703	4158	4086	5872	6743	6945	6309			
临沂市	Linyi	81620	141203	195419	178341	53095	28245	31840	25895	32560	56064	49889
德州市	Dezhou	8884	11957	14373	12673	9985	24016	32370	41173	46482	52431	71011
聊城市	Liaocheng	41743	43793	54378	44011	29577	21758	46088	31927	39541	27252	35888
滨州市	Binzhou	83601	42249	129309	73674	89302	67496	89019	205538	222045	159863	114960
菏泽市	Heze	17199	22938	20673	10837	12258	9354	12206	12273	14775	15436	13371

6-9 各市外商投资企业出口总值

Export Value of Foreign-funded Enterprises by Region

单位:万美元 (10 000 USD)

地区	Region	2010	2012	2013	2014	2015	2016	2017	2018	2019	2020	2021
济南市	Jinan	131488	152160	160182	169035	175359	159112	202975	218474	248186	259217	424111
青岛市	Qingdao	1676534	1764622	1660659	1727138	1623387	1414566	1463348	1532797	1351204	1274682	1656008
淄博市	Zibo	212442	261842	248033	245167	218869	199297	209282	228176	206778	199979	223702
枣庄市	Zaozhuang	22546	30954	29827	39001	37026	29547	28975	29809	30150	32151	47156
东营市	Dongying	62815	60123	46084	51501	28559	22994	24500	25899	28463	35406	59756
烟台市	Yantai	2170903	2077348	1967676	2166016	1938415	1793586	1741082	1713560	1366005	1314798	1729801
潍坊市	Weifang	301865	381763	392609	420019	381747	378298	357239	364546	328763	313047	418144
济宁市	Jining	81702	125593	125724	126494	112577	82944	79997	81521	73227	66960	101834
泰安市	Tai'an	22570	23355	22901	23294	20907	23017	20971	16956	15921	13819	24537
威海市	Weihai	566264	607243	570564	571512	523011	454534	475067	462686	453624	407412	481934
日照市	Rizhao	108232	235944	243267	321319	237924	176171	135927	154932	177644	153215	212654
莱芜市	Laiwu	15125	8037	9245	12908	12661	11381	9091	7824			
临沂市	Linyi	123593	157795	172855	175650	141064	133516	132507	124813	104141	120611	172618
德州市	Dezhou	38784	49103	54410	49228	41164	46288	56796	64002	76540	85473	127715
聊城市	Liaocheng	27318	21974	18049	18274	20572	21007	28798	30939	27631	28732	44817
滨州市	Binzhou	61757	51299	51793	49035	40845	41792	41611	45778	34979	35055	42514
菏泽市	Heze	32385	39775	49986	63063	58844	60196	73012	54866	44569	39354	51950

6-10 1979-2021年利用外资情况

Statistics on Utilization of Foreign Capitals from 1979 to 2021

单位:万美元 (10 000 USD)

年 份 Year	新设企业数(个) Number of Newly Established Companies	#外商直接投资 Foreign Direct Investments	合同外资金额 Total Amount of Contracted Foreign Capital	#外商直接投资 Foreign Direct Investments	实际使用外资金额 Total Amount of Foreign Capital Actually Utilized	#外商直接投资 Foreign Direct Investments
1979	49		1278		1276	
1980	46		1254		1245	
1981	40	1	1296	10	1296	10
1982	60		1348		1327	
1983	51		2010		1831	
1984	100	16	15283	10470	1642	40
1985	232	32	10994	4925	6375	559
1986	109	37	13377	5927	11743	1939
1987	151	53	30520	3890	10219	2381
1988	458	203	59553	26020	14231	3908
1989	485	240	55272	17855	31498	13132
1990	674	366	55164	23283	31123	15084
1991	1187	801	102358	65481	46789	17950
1992	4651	4109	471994	391961	137684	97335
1993	8012	7229	754863	705116	226068	184319
1994	4747	3650	624570	526217	340137	253566
1995	5035	2709	532980	462521	326698	260719
1996	2223	2175	633894	539797	339426	259041
1997	1681	1597	454145	328037	358447	250044
1998	1434	1366	367072	221866	361036	222262
1999	1745	1717	421333	311087	374464	246878
2000	2733	2728	561066	507435	381243	297119
2001	3058	3047	715880	672040	424886	362093
2002	4072	4065	1186072	1130680	652124	558603
2003	5305	5305	1989296	1341413	1125985	709371
2004	5890	5890	2144647	2028958	982105	870064
2005	6415	6415	2884398	2749510	1101441	897072
2006	4030	4030	1645089	1624175	1020966	1000069
2007		2717		1173880		1101159
2008		1527		1014959		820246
2009		1468		871045		801007
2010		1632		1363381		916833
2011		1433		1579081		1116022
2012		1333		1655717		1235267
2013		1405		1770879		1405315
2014		1352		1595327		1519511
2015		1509		2004467		1630090
2016		1477		2115351		1682556
2017		1479		2740567		1785731
2018		2156		2850735		2051636
2019		2517				1468933
2020		3060				1764763
2021		3064				2151578

注:2003年实际利用外资金额是全口径数据包括对外借款,合同外资个数和合同外资金额不包括对外借款部分。2004年起实行新的外商投资统计制度,取消对外借款部分,外商直接投资数据为商务部反馈数。2008年起实际使用外资采用全口径统计方式。2019年起，实际使用外资采用商务部通报口径，不包含股东贷款、投资性公司投资，合同外资不再统计。

a)In 2003,data of total amount of foreign capital actually utilized are including foreign loads.And Data of projects for contracted foreign capital and total amount of contracted foreign capital are excluding foreign loads.Since 2004,foreign loads is canceled according to the new statistical system on foreign investments.Data of foreign direct investments come from the Ministry of Commerce.In 2008 the foreign capital actually utilized is received foreign capital.From 2019,Actual use of foreign capital uses Bulletin of the Ministry of Commerce，does not contain shareholder loan,the changed to the actual investment of investment company,and contract foreign investment is no longer counted.

6-11 按主要国家(地区)分外商直接投资

Foreign Direct Investment by Countries or Regions

单位:万美元 (10 000 USD)

国家(地区)	Country(Region)	新设企业数(个) Number of Newly Established Companies (unit)		实际使用外商投资金额 Total Amount of Foreign Capital Actually Utilized	
		2020	2021	2020	2021
总计	**Total**	**3060**	**3064**	**1764763**	**2151578**
韩国	Republic of Korea	621	635	87895	70646
香港地区	Hong Kong	1230	1338	1351694	1624833
美国	United States	104	92	23085	9583
日本	Japan	125	194	31459	111206
台湾省	Taiwan	180	158	12115	11071
英属维尔京群岛	Virgin Islands	14	20	45735	48678
新加坡	Singapore	94	120	101550	149059
英国	United Kingdom	47	40	12442	16090
加拿大	Canada	67	56	9248	4552
澳大利亚	Australia	61	32	11026	7463
法国	France	15	16	756	3650
德国	Germany	46	33	12519	7704
毛里求斯	Mauritius			160	808
马来西亚	Malaysia	22	11	373	433
萨摩亚	Samoa	3	1	10836	1256
意大利	Italy	13	6	2102	7371
荷兰	Netherlands	7	8	18115	1888
开曼群岛	Cayman Islands	3	7	7764	27735
泰国	Thailand	10	5	287	5408
澳门	Macao	14	20	4576	13882
瑞士	Switzerland	4	5	108	631
巴拿马	Panama		1		
百慕大	Bermuda	1		4750	1000
俄罗斯	Russia	30	21	97	17
菲律宾	Philippines	1	2	1661	
丹麦	Denmark	3	1	824	254
印度尼西亚	Indonesia	7	4	112	1798
奥地利	Austria	4	3	3345	876
西班牙	Spain	2	2	5	
新西兰	New Zealand	9	4	27	151
卢森堡	Luxembourg				472
瑞典	Sweden	4	2	23	117
比利时	Belgium	5	2	255	200
欧洲联盟	The European Union	115	91	38045	35862
东南亚联盟	Southeast Asian Union	149	146	104243	157674

6-12 按行业分外商直接投资(2021年)
Foreign Direct Investment by Sector(2021)

行业	Sector	新设企业数(个) Number of Newly Established Companies(unit)		
		本年新增 Newly Added in the Year	比上年增长(%) Growth Rate (%)	2021年止累计 Accumulative number end to 2021
总计	**Total**	**3064**	**0.1**	**82883**
第一产业	**Primary Industry**	**31**	**-50.0**	**2566**
第二产业	**Secondary Industry**	**1075**	**56.9**	**57190**
采矿业	Mining	4	-33.3	246
制造业	Manufacturing	920	62.0	54734
电力、热力、燃气及水的生产和供应业	Production and Supply of Electric, Heat, Gas and Water	116	93.3	803
建筑业	Construction	43	-23.2	1422
第三产业	**Tertiary Industry**	**1958**	**-15.4**	**23127**
交通运输、仓储和邮政业	Transport, Storage and Post	48	9.1	990
信息传输、计算机服务和软件业	Information Transmission, Computer Services and Software	127	-38.7	1044
批发和零售业	Wholesale and Retail Trade	839	-7.5	8369
住宿和餐饮业	Hotels and Catering Services	43		1722
金融业	Financial Intermediation	33	-48.4	720
房地产业	Real Estate	54	-73.3	2879
租赁和商务服务业	Leasing and Business Services	385	14.9	3736
居民服务和其他服务业	Services to Households and Other Services	18	-5.3	327
科学研究和技术服务业	Scientific Research, Technical Service and Geologic Prospecting	304	-4.7	1869
水利、环境和公共设施管理业	Management of Water Conservancy, Environment and Public Facilities	13	-65.8	225
教育	Education	19	-53.7	209
文化、体育和娱乐业	Culture, Sports and Entertainment	42	-25.0	818
卫生和社会工作	Health, Social Work	18	63.6	155
公共管理、社会保障和社会组织	Public Management,Social Security and Social Organizations	2		5

6−12 续表 continued

行　　业	Sector	实际使用外资金额 Total Amount of Foreign Capital Actually Utilized		
		本　　年 (万美元) This Year (10000 USD)	比上年增　长 (%) Growth Rate (%)	2021年止累计 (亿美元) Accumulative number end to 2021 (100 million USD)
总　　计	**Total**	**2151578**	**21.9**	**2797.6**
第一产业	**Primary Industry**	**3214**	**-67.6**	**66.9**
第二产业	**Secondary Industry**	**845184**	**65.6**	**1701.7**
采矿业	Mining	22720	884.4	21.0
制造业	Manufacturing	654848	73.1	1535.7
电力、热力、燃气及水的生产和供应业	Production and Supply of Electric, Heat, Gas and Wate	110574	60.2	107.7
建筑业	Construction	58872	-3.2	37.2
第三产业	**Tertiary Industry**	**1303180**	**4.7**	**1029.0**
交通运输、仓储和邮政业	Transport, Storage and Post	36170	-42.5	84.2
信息传输、计算机服务和软件业	Information Transmission, Computer Services and Software	101765	11.5	43.1
批发和零售业	Wholesale and Retail Trade	377227	71.9	175.5
住宿和餐饮业	Hotels and Catering Services	1632	-88.4	20.1
金融业	Financial Intermediation	69437	3.9	84.5
房地产业	Real Estate	171888	-57.5	355.7
租赁和商务服务业	Leasing and Business Services	338168	67.1	124.7
居民服务和其他服务业	Services to Households and Other Services	9041	600.9	6.8
科学研究和技术服务业	Scientific Research, Technical Service and Geologic Prospecting	134638	-11.6	98.6
水利、环境和公共设施管理业	Management of Water Conservancy, Environment and Public Facilities	11762	59.7	11.1
教　育	Education	111	-85.2	2.1
文化、体育和娱乐业	Culture, Sports and Entertainment	9493	-24.3	15.0
卫生和社会工作	Health, Social Work	7765	382.9	2.6
公共管理、社会保障和社会组织	Public Management,Social Security and Social Organizations	31414		3.1

6-13 按方式分外商直接投资

Basic Statistics on Foreign Direct Investments by Form

单位:万美元 (10 000 USD)

类别	Category	新设企业数(个) Number of Newly Established Companies(unit)					实际使用外资金额 Total Amount of Foreign Capital Actually Utilized				
		2017	2018	2019	2020	2021	2017	2018	2019	2020	2021
外商直接投资	**Foreign Direct Investments**	**1479**	**2156**	**2517**	**3060**	**3064**	**1785731**	**2051636**	**1468933**	**1764763**	**2151578**
合资经营企业	Sino-foreign Joint-ventures enterprises	500	771	1021			523682	495124	551829		
合作经营企业	Sino-foreign Cooperative Operation enterprises	11	12	6			22112	29364	1364		
外资企业	Foreign Investment Enterprises	960	1366	1472			1189814	1493011	770140		
外商投资股份制企业	Foreign Investment Share Enterprises	8	7	10			50123	34137	143156		
合作开发	Cooperative Development								2000		
其他	Others			8					444		

注：2020年起，《外商投资法》实施，不再区分合资、合作、独资企业。

a)Since 2020, the foreign investment law has been implemented, and there will be no distinction between joint venture, cooperative and wholly-owned enterprises.

6-14 各市外商直接投资

Foreign Direct Investment by Region

单位:万美元 (10 000 USD)

地区	Region	新设企业数(个) Number of Newly Established Companies (unit)		实际使用外资 Amount of Foreign Capital Actually Utilized	
		2020	2021	2020	2021
全省总计	**Total**	**3060**	**3064**	**1764763**	**2151578**
济南市	Jinan	203	330	192456	265840
青岛市	Qingdao	870	908	585297	616898
淄博市	Zibo	91	83	37812	82044
枣庄市	Zaozhuang	117	85	30495	45236
东营市	Dongying	64	60	44493	64315
烟台市	Yantai	482	386	228263	264914
潍坊市	Weifang	292	214	108326	132349
济宁市	Jining	132	152	81239	112838
泰安市	Tai'an	80	64	68251	40696
威海市	Weihai	329	343	135822	144963
日照市	Rizhao	42	58	46664	51922
临沂市	Linyi	173	162	93156	137548
德州市	Dezhou	39	46	26584	45256
聊城市	Liaocheng	62	78	20844	45578
滨州市	Binzhou	37	34	36058	51418
菏泽市	Heze	47	61	29003	49763

6-15 境外投资情况
Overseas Investment

类别	Category	境外投资项目(个) Overseas Investment Projects (unit)		备案核准中方投资总额(万美元) Approved and Registered Total Amount of Chinese Investment (10 000 USD)	
		2021	2021年止累计 Accumulative number end to 2021	2021	2021年止累计 Accumulative number end to 2021
总计	**Total**	**255**	**7061**	**383988**	**10694048**
贸易性企业	Trade Enterprises	103	2892	40105	1358590
非贸易性企业	Non-trade Enterprises	122	3372	343883	9335459
资源开发企业	Resource Development	5	480	13313	1739617

6-16 各市境外投资情况
Overseas Investment by Region

单位:万美元 (10 000 USD)

地区	Region	企业数(个) Number of Enterprises(unit)		备案核准投资额 Approved and Registered Amount of Investment		对外实际投资额 Actual amount of Overseas Investment	
		2020	2021	2020	2021	2020	2021
全省总计	**Total**	**308**	**255**	**651812**	**383988**	**835470**	**698331**
济南市	Jinan	79	59	138854	38902	191321	174208
青岛市	Qingdao	61	67	130103	134115	103217	116857
淄博市	Zibo	18	17	12426	14100	51398	25843
枣庄市	Zaozhuang	2	2	590	110	210	165
东营市	Dongying	10	11	5305	3770	18306	24951
烟台市	Yantai	28	20	103111	37836	169456	124129
潍坊市	Weifang	22	19	140023	20517	48134	80020
济宁市	Jining	18	7	43889	25270	95828	55224
泰安市	Tai'an	13	7	1435	10954	5525	6837
威海市	Weihai	20	16	26230	9685	48790	34464
日照市	Rizhao	5	3	6020	32	10449	1166
临沂市	Linyi	11	13	13039	87149	1985	7557
德州市	Dezhou	11	8	17555	1725	10469	16270
聊城市	Liaocheng	6	2	4126	152	19067	750
滨州市	Binzhou	2	3	9007	55	54040	20154
菏泽市	Heze	2	1	99	-385	7274	9739

6-17 按主要国别(地区)分境外投资情况
Overseas Investment by Countries or Regions

单位:万美元 (10 000 USD)

国别(地区)	Country(Region)	项目数(个) Number of Projects(unit)		备案核准中方投资额 Approved and Registered Amount of Chinese Investment	
		2020	2021	2020	2021
总计	**Total**	**308**	**255**	**651812**	**383988**
亚洲小计	**Subtotal of Asia**	**170**	**148**	**256942**	**291987**
阿富汗	Afghanistan				
阿联酋	UAE	3	3	-3188	30
澳门	Macao		1		1000
巴基斯坦	Pakistan	2	4	6905	702
巴林	Bahrain				
朝鲜	Korea DPR				
东帝汶	East Timor	2		15	
菲律宾	Philippine	2			
哈萨克斯坦	Kazakhstan	2	1	37	
韩国	Republic of Korea	12	15	11413	2099
吉尔吉斯斯坦	Kyrgyzstan				
柬埔寨	Cambodia	2	1	5417	35225
卡塔尔	Qatar				
科威特	Kuwait		1		
老挝	Laos	2	1	1332	
马来西亚	Malaysia	5	3	554	542
蒙古	Mongolia	1	1	1604	10
孟加拉国	Bangladesh	2	3	-720	115
缅甸	Myanmar	1		300	
日本	Japan	16	6	2757	3802
沙特阿拉伯	Saudi Arabia	1	3	250	6322
斯里兰卡	Sri Lanka	3	2	30900	170
塔吉克斯坦	Tajikistan				
中国台湾	Taiwan,China				1147
泰国	Thailand	7	3	26734	7629
土库曼斯坦	Turkmenistan				
乌兹别克斯坦	Uzbekistan	1	1	20	14
香港	Hong Kong	61	69	61138	32179
新加坡	Singapore	24	15	52785	36174
叙利亚	Syria				
也门	Yemen				
伊朗	Iran				
以色列	Israel		1		
印度	India	3	1	25081	
印度尼西亚	Indonesia	5	3	24943	81683
约旦	Jordan				
越南	Vietnam	11	6	8636	82877
伊拉克	Iraq	1			
马尔代夫	Maldives		1		15
阿曼	Oman				
格鲁吉亚	Georgia				
尼泊尔	Nepal		1		220
土耳其	Turkey	1	2	30	32
非洲小计	**Subtotal of Africa**	**39**	**39**	**29421**	**17459**
阿尔及利亚	Algeria		1		98
埃及	Egypt	1	1		
埃塞俄比亚	Ethiopia	4		550	
安哥拉	Angola	2		1000	
贝宁	Benin				
博茨瓦纳	Botswana		1		10

6-17 续表 1 continued

单位:万美元 (10 000 USD)

国别(地区)	Country(Region)	项目数(个) Number of Projects(unit)		备案核准中方投资额 Approved and Registered Amount of Chinese Investment	
		2020	2021	2020	2021
布基纳法索	Burkina Faso	1			
赤道几内亚	Eq.Guinea				
多哥	Togo	1	1	20	20
厄立特里亚	Eritrea				
佛得角	Cape Verde				
冈比亚	Gambia				
刚果(布)	Congo Rep				
刚果(金)	Congo DR				
几内亚	Guinea	2	5	1200	3234
几内亚(比绍)	Guinea-Bissau				
加纳	Ghana	1	4	500	9190
加蓬	Gabon				
津巴布韦	Zimbabwe				
喀麦隆	Cameroon				
科特迪瓦	Cote D'Ivoire	2	1	12461	
肯尼亚	Kenya	2	5	165	668
莱索托	Lesotho				
利比里亚	Liberia				
利比亚	Libya				
马里	Mali				
马达加斯加	Madagascar		2		3
毛里求斯	Mauritius	1		2200	
毛里塔尼亚	Mauritania	1		100	
摩洛哥	Morocco				
马拉维	Malawi		1		
莫桑比克	Mozambique	3	2	903	62
纳米比亚	Namibia			-40	
南非	South Africa	2	2	39	43
南苏丹	South Sudan	2	1		770
尼日利亚	Nigeria	4	1	10076	2000
尼日尔	Niger	1	2		100
塞内加尔	Senegal				
塞拉利昂	Sierra Leone				
塞浦路斯	Cyprus				
塞舌尔	Seychelles		1		5
苏丹	Sudan	1		50	
坦桑尼亚	Tanzania	2	4	92	193
突尼斯	Tunisia				
乌干达	Uganda	1	1		1000
赞比亚	Zambia	3	2	106	62
中非	Central Africa				
乍得	Chad	2	1		
吉布提	Djibouti				
欧洲小计	**Subtotal of Europe**	**48**	**25**	**167959**	**24205**
阿塞拜疆	Azerbaijan				
奥地利		1		1527	
白俄罗斯	Belorussia				
保加利亚	Bulgaria	1		11088	
比利时	Belgium	2	1	362	46
波黑	Bosnia and Herzegovina	1	3		
波兰	Poland	1		6000	-398
德国	Germany	10	2	62455	-4599
丹麦	Denmark			-2080	
俄罗斯	Russia	9	5	26756	848
法国	France	3		19552	305
芬兰	Finland				
荷兰	Netherlands		2		361
捷克	Czech	1		114	

6-17 续表 2 continued

单位:万美元 (10 000 USD)

国别(地区)	Country(Region)	项目数(个) Number of Projects(unit)		备案核准中方投资额 Approved and Registered Amount of Chinese Investment	
		2020	2021	2020	2021
拉托维亚	Latvia				
立陶宛	Lithuania				
卢森堡	Luxembourg				
罗马尼亚	Romania	2		4232	
挪威	Norway				
葡萄牙	Portugal				
瑞典	Sweden	2	1	1605	-127
瑞士	Switzerland	1	1	100	2283
斯洛伐克	Slovakia				
塞浦路斯	Cyprus				
乌克兰	Ukraine	1		800	
西班牙	Spain	3		1123	
希腊	Greece	1		550	
匈牙利	Hungary	1		300	
亚美尼亚	Armenia		1		
意大利	Italy	2	1	30088	24358
英国	United Kingdom	5	4	3136	7249
塞尔维亚	Serbia		4		-6121
爱尔兰	Ireland				
斯洛文尼亚	Slovenia	1		250	
拉丁美洲小计	**Subtotal of Latin America**	**19**	**12**	**43049**	**13422**
阿根廷	Argentina	2		3342	335
安提瓜和巴布达	Antigua and Barbuda				
巴巴多斯	Barbados				
巴拉圭	Paraguay				
巴拿马	Panama				
巴西	Brazil	3	2	400	112
玻利维亚	Bolivia	1			
多米尼加	Dominican Rep.				
厄瓜多尔	Ecuador	1		100	
圭亚那	Guyana	1	1	500	15
哥伦比亚	Colombia	2	2	7	600
哥斯达黎加	Costa Rica				
古巴	Cuba				
秘鲁	Peru			300	
开曼群岛	Cayman Islands	2	1	30413	2000
苏里南	Surinam				
圣卢西亚	Saint Lucia				
特立尼达和多巴哥	Trinidad and Tobago	1		500	
危地马拉	Guatemala				
委内瑞拉	Venezuela				
乌拉圭	Uruguay				
英属安圭拉	Anguilla				
英属维尔京群岛	British Virgin Islands	2	3	6	5
智利	Chile	1		10	
牙买加	Jamaica				
墨西哥	Mexico	3	3	7470	10355
北美洲小计	**Subtotal of North America**	**24**	**27**	**107046**	**26970**
百慕大群岛	Bermuda		1	61193	6200
加拿大	Canada	8	10	21428	5821
美国	United States	16	16	24425	14949
大洋洲小计	**Subtotal of Oceanic**	**8**	**4**	**47394**	**9945**
澳大利亚	Australia	8	3	44094	5350
巴布亚新几内亚	Papua New Guinea				
斐济	Fiji				
新西兰	New Zealand		1	3300	4595
所罗门	Solomon				
汤加	Tonga				
萨摩亚	Samoa				

6-18 1982-2021年对外承包工程和劳务合作情况

Statistics on Contracted Projects and Labor Services Cooperation with Foreign Countries 1982 to 2021

年 份 Year	合同个数 (个) Number of Contracts (unit)	合同金额 (万美元) Contracted Value (10 000 USD)	营业额 (万美元) Turnover (10 000 USD)	年末在外人数 (人) Number of Persons outside the Country at Year-end (person)	派出人数 (人) Number of Persons Sent out(person)
1982	1	421	421		
1983	1	1286	40	408	
1984	1	451	664	783	
1985	4	645	852	1147	
1986	26	1099	876	1597	
1987	33	802	999	1239	
1988	34	502	987	865	
1989	69	1389	1000	1179	
1990	91	3377	1712	1462	
1991	123	5952	3017	2326	
1992	192	8747	3882	3571	
1993	299	20250	6959	7254	
1994	411	31882	12222	10288	
1995	672	38604	18274	16217	
1996	880	52005	28933	23355	
1997	966	57654	36315	26626	
1998	1296	73703	46508	29121	
1999	1116	67729	63615	30979	
2000	1250	61601	45229	35028	
2001	1580	104622	55913	36489	
2002	1380	134098	83133	43554	
2003	1322	124243	99213	52077	
2004	1879	146590	151568	62705	
2005	2171	164091	174518	71610	37797
2006	2513	392134	232293	83974	41369
2007	2642	540344	301928	93797	45212
2008	2880	754137	358867	90623	45269
2009	2397	932312	509083	96421	46296
2010	3075	1092504	602415	102149	47300
2011		948287	819857	108662	48836
2012		988209	898864	103736	51425
2013		1078349	940828	98988	52591
2014		1237694	1021544	115328	59941
2015		1344383	1120799	116100	60764
2016		1355479	1195427	119655	68673
2017		1393003	1278651	130384	71570
2018		1548846	1314181	125224	57878
2019		1364140	1256300	133849	62734
2020		1051092	1030379	89162	31484
2021		1181608	1016257	71218	31406

注：2011年起，商务部不再对外公布对外劳务合作合同数(下表同)。
a)The Commerce Department had no longer published data refer to Contracts of Labor Cooperation since 2011.The same applies to tables following.

6-19 对外承包工程和劳务合作情况

Statistics on Contracted Projects and Labour Cooperation with Foreign Countries or Regions

项目		Item		2016	2017	2018	2019	2020	2021
一、承包工程合同个数	**（个）**	**Number of Contracted Projects**	**(unit)**	**306**	**417**	**484**	**504**	**475**	**296**
二、合同金额	**（万美元）**	**Contracted Value**	**(10 000 USD)**	**1355479**	**1393003**	**1548846**	**1364140**	**1051092**	**1181608**
承包工程	（万美元）	Contracted Projects	(10 000 USD)	1266500	1295541	1439085	1269937	1010672	1122204
劳务合作	（万美元）	Labor Cooperation	(10 000 USD)	88979	97462	109761	94203	40420	59404
三、营业额	**（万美元）**	**Turnover**	**(10 000 USD)**	**1195427**	**1278651**	**1314181**	**1256300**	**1030379**	**1016257**
承包工程	（万美元）	Contracted Projects	(10 000 USD)	1093045	1175577	1219211	1147941	942980	931382
劳务合作	（万美元）	Labor Cooperation	(10 000 USD)	102382	103074	94970	108359	87399	84875
四、年末在国外人数	**（人）**	**Number of Persons outside the Country at year end**	**(person)**	**119655**	**130384**	**125224**	**133849**	**89162**	**71218**
承包工程	（人）	Contracted Projects	(person)	30546	35470	30885	33449	31177	23532
劳务合作	（人）	Labor Cooperation	(person)	89109	94914	94339	100400	57985	47686
五、派出人数	**（人）**	**Number of Persons Sent out**	**(person)**	**68673**	**71570**	**57878**	**62734**	**31484**	**31406**
承包工程	（人）	Contracted Projects	(person)	24730	25216	21618	21192	13663	12344
劳务合作	（人）	Labor Cooperation	(person)	43943	46354	36260	41542	17821	19062

6-20 旅 游 业 情 况

Tourism

类别		Category		2020	2021
旅行社总数	（个）	Total Number of Travel Agencies	(unit)	2685	2729
星级饭店总数	（个）	Total Number of Star-rated Hotels	(unit)	539	492
A级旅游景区总数	（个）	The total number of A-grade scenic spot	(unit)	1227	1193
接待入境游客	（万人次）	Number of International Tourists Arrival to China	(10 000 person-time)	52.8	
外国人	（万人次）	Foreigners	(10 000 person-time)	44.2	
港澳台胞	（万人次）	Hong Kong, Macao and Taiwan Compatriots	(10 000 person-time)	8.6	
港澳同胞	（万人次）	Compatriots from Hong Kong and Macao	(10 000 person-time)	4.8	
台湾同胞	（万人次）	Compatriots from Taiwan	(10 000 person-time)	3.8	
国内旅游人数	（万人次）	Number of Domestic Tourists	(10 000 person-time)	57669.6	73052.2
旅游总收入	（亿元）	Total Tourism Consumption	(100 million yuan)	6019.7	8278.6
入境旅游收入	（亿美元）	International Tourism Earnings	(100 million USD)	2.1	
国内旅游收入	（亿元）	Domestic Tourism Earnings	(100 million yuan)	6005.3	8278.6

注：因疫情管控影响，2021年暂停入境旅游数据核算（以下相关表同）。

a) The accounting of inbound tourism data of 2021 has been suspended due to the impact of COVID-19(The same applies to following revelant tables).

6-21　1995-2021年国内旅游情况
Domestic Tourism 1995 to 2021

年　份 Year	国内游客人数 (万人次) Number of Domestic Tourists (10 000 person-time)	国内旅游收入 (亿元) Domestic tourism revenue (100 million yuan)	人均花费 (元) Per Capita Expenditure (yuan)
1995	4655	157.68	338.7
1996	5151	187.43	363.9
1997	5488	213.02	388.2
1998	5844	245.83	420.7
1999	6429	285.17	443.6
2000	7007	386.49	551.6
2001	8086	462.64	572.2
2002	9573	571.53	597.0
2003	8918	542.78	608.6
2004	11749	767.65	653.4
2005	14097	974.59	691.3
2006	16775	1214.82	724.2
2007	20343	1550.76	762.3
2008	24046	1908.53	793.7
2009	28882	2331.70	807.3
2010	34990	2915.80	833.3
2011	41696	3573.70	857.1
2012	48739	4335.03	889.4
2013	54262	5014.74	924.2
2014	59577	5711.20	958.6
2015	65045	6505.11	1000.1
2016	70716	7399.61	1046.4
2017	77966	8491.46	1089.1
2018	85899	9661.50	1124.7
2019	93288	10851.33	1163.2
2020	57670	6005.32	1041.3
2021	73052	8278.60	1133.2

6-22 按主要国家分接待外国旅游人数
Number of Foreigner Tourists by Country

单位：人 (person)

国别	Country	2010	2015	2016	2017	2018	2019	2020
总计	**Total**	**2778699**	**3358553**	**3525019**	**3530595**	**3661207**	**3708645**	**442477**
亚洲	**Asia**	**2159102**	**2377625**	**2509292**	**2481664**	**2557490**	**2607694**	**298913**
印度	India	23932	32543	32988	34063	35155	35409	2499
印度尼西亚	Indonesia	24835	29906	28879	31381	37032	37805	2999
日本	Japan	566511	357727	375306	391238	409105	419598	55197
马来西亚	Malaysia	40230	62694	65075	68583	69984	89236	5502
蒙古	Mongolia	7064	12356	11725	11697	12457	12563	120
菲律宾	Philippines	42487	34364	36647	37430	41513	41486	3803
新加坡	Singapore	70126	95077	99340	102910	108786	111907	8901
韩国	Republic of Korea	1292880	1580582	1683278	1606678	1643098	1671997	201703
泰国	Thailand	13387	22422	22939	27869	32471	33208	5798
非洲	**Africa**	**15843**	**43580**	**42524**	**49292**	**56100**	**60647**	**8514**
欧洲	**Europe**	**331858**	**484332**	**488489**	**516169**	**535336**	**532784**	**65092**
英国	United Kingdom	62730	82032	88529	89610	93672	93170	12835
德国	Germany	63694	80739	85920	88434	92920	92580	11408
法国	France	40839	66841	71390	72451	75637	73500	5473
意大利	Italy	24532	34034	34587	37851	38082	37709	3065
荷兰	Netherlands	6376	6190	5483	5778	5595	5201	6737
瑞典	Sweden	8498	9018	9539	10361	10150	10287	2698
瑞士	Switzerland	8358	11031	11913	12696	13089	12246	2072
俄罗斯	Russia	63036	102785	109069	121093	131870	134413	10202
美洲	**America**	**191175**	**281514**	**296476**	**314376**	**323872**	**318799**	**48148**
加拿大	Canada	39869	54636	53104	56149	60628	62376	6618
美国	United States	133305	196761	211042	221693	219419	207074	39721
大洋洲	**Oceanic**	**58310**	**93197**	**100238**	**104235**	**112397**	**111976**	**9748**
澳大利亚	Australia	40738	57523	62747	66456	69576	68795	7297
新西兰	New Zealand	12588	17359	19590	21362	25167	26870	2018
其他	**Others**	**22411**	**78305**	**88000**	**64859**	**76012**	**76386**	**12062**

6−23 接待入境游客构成

Structure of Foreigner Tourists

单位:% (%)

指 标	Indicator	2010	2011	2012	2013	2014	2015	2016	2017	2018	2019
总 计	**Total**	**100.0**	**100.0**	**100.0**	**100.0**	**100.0**	**100.0**	**100.0**	**100.0**	**100.0**	**100.0**
按性别分	**by Sex**	**100.0**	**100.0**	**100.0**	**100.0**	**100.0**	**100.0**	**100.0**	**100.0**	**100.0**	**100.0**
男	Male	67.8	68.7	69.9	67.7	68.9	70.4	68.2	67.8	68.0	68.1
女	Female	32.2	31.3	30.1	32.3	31.1	29.6	31.8	32.2	32.0	31.9
按年龄分	**by Age**	**100.0**	**100.0**	**100.0**	**100.0**	**100.0**	**100.0**	**100.0**	**100.0**	**100.0**	**100.0**
14岁以下	14 and under	1.6	1.5	2.2	1.9	1.8	2.2	2.5	2.6	2.7	2.6
15～24岁	15-24	9.1	9.6	10.0	9.3	9.2	10.5	10.5	10.1	10.2	10.3
25～44岁	25-44	51.5	50.3	51.6	46.8	48.3	49.7	49.4	49.5	49.6	49.5
45～64岁	45-64	31.8	32.1	29.8	36.1	35.2	32.0	31.9	31.7	31.5	31.4
65岁以上	65 and over	6.0	6.5	6.5	5.9	5.5	5.6	5.7	6.1	6.0	6.2
按来鲁目的分	**by Purpose of Coming to Shandong**	**100.0**	**100.0**	**100.0**	**100.0**	**100.0**	**100.0**	**100.0**	**100.0**	**100.0**	**100.0**
从事经济商务活动	Business	46.3	47.7	54.4	46.5	47.7	49.8	48.3	48.5	48.7	48.6
从事文化学术交流	Cultural and Academic Exchanges	7.7	6.3	8.2	7.9	8.1	6.1	6.9	6.7	6.8	6.9
探亲访友	Visiting relatives and Friends	4.4	4.5	6.2	6.4	5.9	5.2	6.6	6.2	6.0	6.1
旅游观光	Sightseeing	39.6	39.8	26.5	31.2	35.9	35.7	35.3	35.5	35.7	35.7
其 它	Others	2.1	1.8	4.6	8.1	2.4	3.2	2.9	3.1	2.8	2.7

注：因新冠肺炎疫情影响，2020−2021年未开展入境游客问卷调查，相关数据无法获取（以下相关表同）。

a) Because of COVID-19, survey by questionnaire of inbound tourists had not been carried out in 2020-2021, relevant data can't be obtained(The same applies to following revelant tables).

6−24 各市接待入境游客人数

Number of Foreigner Tourists by Region

单位:万人次 (10 000 person-time)

地 区	Region	2015	外国人 Foreigner	2016	外国人 Foreigner	2017	外国人 Foreigner	2018	外国人 Foreigner	2019	外国人 Foreigner	2020	外国人 Foreigner
全省总计	**Total**	**460.8**	**335.9**	**485.5**	**352.7**	**494.4**	**353.1**	**513.1**	**366.1**	**521.3**	**370.9**	**52.8**	**44.2**
济 南 市	Jinan	33.3	20.5	35.2	21.7	37.5	23.3	39.8	24.7	45.7	28.5	10.9	8.8
青 岛 市	Qingdao	133.8	99.6	141.0	104.2	144.4	105.7	153.6	111.9	170.3	125.8	18.8	15.7
淄 博 市	Zibo	19.6	11.3	20.3	11.6	21.0	11.7	21.5	11.8	20.0	11.2	0.5	0.5
枣 庄 市	Zaozhuang	3.1	1.4	3.4	1.4	3.4	1.5	3.6	1.7	4.4	2.4	0.3	0.1
东 营 市	Dongying	5.8	3.7	6.0	3.8	6.2	3.8	6.4	4.0	6.5	4.1	0.1	0.1
烟 台 市	Yantai	57.4	45.2	61.3	48.3	63.8	50.5	63.8	50.6	65.0	52.3	12.0	10.8
潍 坊 市	Weifang	33.4	27.2	34.8	28.3	34.8	28.0	36.7	29.4	26.6	17.4	2.2	1.2
济 宁 市	Jining	32.1	18.2	34.6	19.6	32.8	17.9	33.0	18.9	28.4	14.2	0.9	0.7
泰 安 市	Tai'an	37.0	19.0	38.5	19.7	39.5	16.9	40.1	16.4	40.0	17.0	0.8	0.4
威 海 市	Weihai	46.2	43.2	48.5	45.4	49.2	45.7	50.7	47.1	51.9	48.0	5.2	5.1
日 照 市	Rizhao	27.0	25.6	28.3	26.8	27.6	26.0	28.2	26.5	28.3	26.7	0.4	0.3
莱 芜 市	Laiwu	0.7	0.6	0.8	0.5	0.8	0.4	0.8	0.5				
临 沂 市	Linyi	17.5	9.8	18.2	10.2	18.7	10.3	19.3	10.7	18.4	11.3	0.3	0.3
德 州 市	Dezhou	2.3	1.1	2.1	1.0	2.2	1.1	2.5	1.2	2.7	1.6	0.1	0.04
聊 城 市	Liaocheng	5.5	4.7	5.8	5.0	5.8	5.0	5.9	5.0	6.0	4.9	0.04	0.03
滨 州 市	Binzhou	4.7	4.5	4.9	4.7	5.1	4.9	5.6	5.3	5.2	4.9	0.2	0.1
菏 泽 市	Heze	1.4	0.4	1.5	0.4	1.6	0.4	1.8	0.5	1.9	0.5	0.03	0.02

注：根据行政区划调整，2019年起，莱芜市并入济南市，以下表同。

a)According to administrative division adjustment,Laiwu City merged into Jinan City from 2019.The same applies to the relevant following tables .

6-25 各市入境旅游外汇收入

Foreign Exchange Earnings by Region

单位:万美元 (10 000 USD)

地 区	Region	2005	2010	2014	2015	2016	2017	2018	2019	2020
全省总计	**Total**	**78023**	**215506**	**271424**	**289651**	**306345**	**317405**	**336420**	**341314**	**20900**
济南市	Jinan	4175	11354	17058	18419	19609	20841	22285	27493	3322
青岛市	Qingdao	41493	60104	82284	91798	98055	102074	116381	156772	12521
淄博市	Zibo	982	9206	9412	9565	9858	10135	10529	9117	97
枣庄市	Zaozhuang	113	824	816	720	810	823	767	630	31
东营市	Dongying	77	3128	5055	5188	5277	5489	5144	4559	44
烟台市	Yantai	13207	37707	47242	51859	55260	58512	61273	49217	2112
潍坊市	Weifang	1055	16238	21630	21976	22474	24419	25003	8570	303
济宁市	Jining	2603	17118	13508	14615	15247	15849	14821	8137	116
泰安市	Tai'an	3740	18380	22508	23559	24328	24174	24299	16896	124
威海市	Weihai	7086	19151	24221	25134	27207	27293	27668	30762	1756
日照市	Rizhao	1908	9795	12786	11808	12363	12018	11780	13070	262
莱芜市	Laiwu	25	314	475	482	654	674	670		
临沂市	Linyi	648	7717	9755	9807	10111	9944	10328	9580	78
德州市	Dezhou	446	1752	563	517	536	548	416	563	52
聊城市	Liaocheng	342	1580	2539	2516	2701	2582	2793	3336	11
滨州市	Binzhou	85	898	1289	1375	1491	1659	1897	2171	65
菏泽市	Heze	38	239	284	311	363	370	366	440	6

6-26 入境旅游外汇收入及构成

Foreign Exchange Earnings and Its Composition

单位:万美元 (10 000 USD)

类 别	Category	2016		2017		2018		2019	
		数额 Value	比重 (%) Proportion	数额 Value	比重 (%) Proportion	数额 Value	比重 (%) Proportion	数额 Value	比重 (%) Proportion
总 计	**Total**	**306345.1**	**100.0**	**317404.6**	**100.0**	**336419.6**	**100.0**	**341313.6**	**100.0**
长途交通	Long Distance Transportation	88104.9	28.8	91793.4	28.9	98200.9	29.2	100414.4	29.4
#民 航	Civil Aviation	70735.1	23.1	73542.6	23.2	78890.4	23.5	80788.9	23.7
铁 路	Railway	3706.8	1.2	3777.1	1.2	4003.4	1.2	4198.2	1.2
汽 车	Highway	7873.1	2.6	8443.0	2.7	8545.1	2.5	8293.9	2.4
轮 船	Waterway	5789.9	1.9	6030.7	1.9	6762.0	2.0	7133.5	2.1
游 览	Visiting	27142.2	8.9	28058.5	8.8	28965.7	8.6	28602.1	8.4
住 宿	Accommodation	37190.3	12.1	39136.0	12.3	41278.7	12.3	42288.8	12.4
餐 饮	Food and Beverage	27417.9	9.0	27772.9	8.8	29571.3	8.8	30138.0	8.8
购 物	Shopping	67794.2	22.1	71289.0	22.5	79361.4	23.6	83314.6	24.4
娱 乐	Entertainment	20494.5	6.7	21234.4	6.7	22371.9	6.7	22117.1	6.5
邮电通讯	Post and Communication Services	11518.6	3.8	11870.9	3.7	12783.9	3.8	13243.0	3.9
市内交通	Local Transportation	9466.1	3.1	9776.1	3.1	10193.5	3.0	10410.1	3.1
其他服务	Other Services	17216.6	5.6	16473.3	5.2	13692.3	4.1	10785.5	3.2

注：因新冠肺炎疫情影响，2020—2021年未开展入境游客问卷调查，相关数据无法获取。

a) Because of COVID-19, survey by questionnaire of inbound tourists had not been carried out in 2020-2021, relevant data can't be obtained.

主要统计指标解释

进出口总额 指实际进出我国国境的货物总金额。包括对外贸易实际进出口货物，来料加工装配进出口货物，国家间、联合国及国际组织无偿援助物资和赠送品，华侨、港澳台同胞和外籍华人捐赠品，租赁期满归承租人所有的租赁货物，进料加工进出口货物，边境地方贸易及边境地区小额贸易进出口货物(边民互市贸易除外)，中外合资企业、中外合作经营企业、外商独资经营企业进出口货物和公用物品，到、离岸价格在规定限额以上的进出口货样和广告品(无商业价值、无使用价值和免费提供出口的除外)，从保税仓库提取在中国境内销售的进口货物，以及其他进出口货物。该指标可以观察一个国家在对外贸易方面的总规模。我国规定出口货物按离岸价格统计，进口货物按到岸价格统计。

商品经营单位所在地进、出口额 指所在地海关注册登记的有进出口经营权的企业实际进、出口额。

商品目的地进口额和商品货源地出口额 目的地进口额指进口货物的消费、使用或最终抵运地的实际进口额；货源地出口额指出口货物的产地或原始发货地的实际出口额。

利用外资 指我国各级政府、部门、企业和其他经济组织通过对外借款、吸收外商直接投资以及用其他方式筹措的境外现汇、设备、技术等。

对外借款 指通过对外正式签订借款协议，从境外筹措的资金，包括外国政府贷款、国际金融组织贷款、外国银行商业贷款、出口信贷以及对外发行债券等。1996年及以前还包括对外发行股票。该指标是我国利用外资的重要部分。

外商直接投资 指外国企业和经济组织或个人(包括华侨、港澳台胞以及我国在境外注册的企业)按我国有关政策、法规，用现汇、实物、技术等在我国境内开办外商独资企业、与我国境内的企业或经济组织共同举办中外合资经营企业、合作经营企业或合作开发资源的投资(包括外商投资收益的再投资)，以及经政府有关部门批准的项目投资总额内企业从境外借入的资金。

外商其他投资 指除对外借款和外商直接投资以外的各种利用外资的形式。包括企业在境内外股票市场公开发行的以外币计价的股票（目前主要是在香港证券市场发行的H股和在境内证券市场发行的B股）发行价总额，国际租赁进口设备的应付款，补偿贸易中外商提供的进口设备、技术、物料的价款，加工装配贸易中外商提供的进口设备、物料的价款。

对外直接投资 指我国国内投资者以现金、实物、无形资产等方式在国外及港澳台地区设立、购买国（境）外企业，并以控制该企业的经营管理权为核心的经济活动。

对外承包工程 指各对外承包公司以招标议标承包方式承揽的下列业务：(1)承包国(境)外工程项目；(2)承包我国对外经济援助项目；(3)承包我国驻外机构工程项目；(4)企业自带设备,以收取设备使用费、技术服务费等形式承揽和实施的国外及港澳台地区工程项目；(5)企业为实施承包工程项目出口的大型成套和机电设备,并负责安装和调试；(6)企业为境外投资建设项目提供咨询和管理服务,开展相关规划、咨询、勘察、设计、造价、监理、项目管理和运营维护等活动。对外承包工程的营业额是以货币表现的本期内完成的对外承包工程的工作量，包括以前年度签订的合同和本年度新签订的合同在报告期内完成的工作量。

对外劳务合作 对外劳务合作指组织劳务人员赴其他国家或地区为国外的企业或机构工作的经营性活动。劳务合作营业额按报告期内雇主提交的结算数(包括工资、加班费和奖金等)统计。

旅游总收入 是指相关方为游客支付的一切旅游费用。包括行、游、住、食、购、娱以及为亲友、家人购买纪念品、礼品等方面的支出，不包括商业目的而购买的房、地、车、船及贵重物品等资本性或交易性的投资、馈赠亲友的现金及给公共机构的捐赠。

旅游者人数

(1)入境国际旅游者人数：指来中国参观、访问、旅行、探亲、访友、休养、考察、参加会议和从事经济、科技、文化、教育、宗教等活动的外国人、华侨、港澳同胞和台湾同胞的人数。不包括外国在我国的常驻机构，如使领馆、通讯社、企业办事处的工作人员；来我国常住的外国专家、留学生以及在岸逗留不过夜人员。

(2)出境居民人数：指大陆居民因公务活动或私人事务短期出境的人数。公务活动出境居民人数包括在国际交通工具上的中国服务员工，因私出境居民人数不包括在国际交通工具上的中国服务员工。

(3)国内旅游者人数：指我国大陆居民和在我国常住1年以上的外国人、华侨、港澳台同胞离开常住地在境内其他地方的旅游设施内至少停留一夜，最长不超过6个月的人数。

国际旅游(外汇)收入 指入境旅游的外国人、华侨、港澳同胞和台湾同胞在中国大陆旅游过程中发生的一切旅游支出，其对于国家来说就是国际旅游(外汇)收入。

国际旅行社 指经营对外招徕并接待外国人、华侨、港澳同胞和台湾同胞来中国、归国或回内地旅游业务的旅行社。

国内旅行社 指负责经营招徕、组团、接待国内旅客的旅游业务，以及不对外招徕，负责经营接待国际旅行社或其它涉外部门组织的外国人、华侨、港澳同胞和台湾同胞来中国、归国或回内地的旅游业务的旅行社。

Explanatory Notes on Main Statistical Indicators

Total Imports and Exports at Customs refer to the real value of commodities imported into and exported from the boundary of China. They include the actual imports and exports through foreign trade, imported and exported goods under the processing and assembling trades and materials, supplies and gifts as aid given gratis between governments and by the United Nations and other international organizations, and contributions donated by overseas Chinese, compatriots in Hong Kong and Macao and Chinese with foreign citizenship, leasing commodities owned by tenant at the expiration of leasing period, the imported and exported commodities processed with imported materials, commodities trading in border areas (excluding mutual exchange goods), the imported and exported commodities and articles for public use of the Sino foreign joint ventures, cooperative enterprises and ventures exclusively with foreign own investment. Also included are import or export of samples and advertising goods for whose CIF or FOB value are beyond the permitted ceiling (excluding goods of no trading or use value and free commodities for export), imported goods sold in China from bonded warehouses and other imported or exported goods. The indicator of the total imports and exports at customs can be used to observe the total size of external trade in a country. In accordance with the stipulation of the Chinese government, imports are calculated at CIF, while exports are calculated at FOB.

Import and Export Value by Location of Foreign Trade Managing Units refers to actual value of imports and exports carried out by corporations which have been registered by the local customhouse and are vested with right to run import export business.

Import and Export Value of Commodities by Destination and Origin of goods in China: The former indicator refers to the value of import commodities of the places of their consumption, utilization or the places of their final destination. The latter indicator refers to the value of export commodities of the places of their origin or the places of the commodities dispatched.

Utilization of Foreign Capitals refers to remittance, equipment and technology financed from abroad, by loans, foreign direct investment and other forms undertaken by the Chinese governments at all levels, by various departments, enterprises and other economic units.

Foreign Borrowings refer to funds borrowed from abroad through formal signing of borrowing agreements with foreign institutions, including loans of foreign governments, loans of international financial institutions, commercial loans of foreign banks, export credit, and funds raised by Chinese bonds (and shares before 1996) issued abroad. It is an important part of China' s utilization of foreign capitals.

Foreign Direct Investment refers to the investments inside China by foreign enterprises and economic organizations or individuals (including overseas Chinese, compatriots from Hong Kong, Macao and Taiwan, and Chinese enterprises registered abroad), following the relevant policies and laws of China, for the establishment of ventures exclusively with foreign own investment, Sino foreign joint ventures and cooperative enterprises or for cooperative exploration of resources with enterprises or economic organizations in China. It includes the re investment of the foreign entrepreneurs with the profits gained from the investment and the funds that enterprises borrow from abroad in the total investment of projects which are approved by the relevant department of the government.

Other Investment by Foreign Entrepreneurs refers to all forms of utilization of foreign capitals other than foreign borrowings and foreign direct investment. It includes the total value of stock shares in foreign currencies issued by enterprises at domestic or foreign stock exchanges (now mainly consisting of H shares issued at Hong Kong Security Market and B shares issued at domestic security markets), rent payable for the imported equipment through international leasing arrangement, cost of imported equipment, technology and materials provided by foreign counterparts in compensation trade and processing and assembly trade.

Overseas Direct Investment refers to enterprises set up or bought by domestic investors in foreign countries and in Hong Kong, Macao and Taiwan, and the economic activities centering on operation and management of those enterprises are under the control of domestic investors. The statistical scope covers various corporation type enterprises and non-corporation type enterprises receiving direct investment from domestic investment entities.

Contracted Projects with Foreign Countries refer to the following business contracted by foreign contracting companies in the form of bidding and negotiation:(1) Contractor projects abroad; (2) to contract Chinese foreign economic aid projects; (3) to contract for domestic institutions; (4) Engineering projects contracted and implemented in foreign countries and Hong Kong, Macao and Taiwan regions by the enterprise's own equipment in the form of collecting equipment usage fee and technical service fee; (5) The enterprise shall be responsible for the installation and commissioning of large complete sets of mechanical and electrical equipment exported for the implementation of the contracted project; (6) The enterprise provides consulting and management services for overseas investment construction projects, and carries out related activities such as planning, consulting, investigation, design, cost, supervision, project management, operation and maintenance.The turnover of foreign contracted projects is the workload of foreign contracted projects completed in the current period expressed in currency, including the workload completed in the reporting period of contracts signed in the previous year and new contracts signed in the current year.

Servicc Cooperation with Foreign Countries refers to the economic activities of organizing labor personnel to go to other countries or regions to work for foreign enterprises or institutions. Thc business income of labour service cooperation is the income in the form of wages and salaries, overtime pay, bonuses and other remuneration received from the employers during the reference period.

Total Income form Tourism refers to all travel expenses paid by the relevant party for the tourists. Including transportation, sighting, accommodation, food, shopping, entertainment, and the purchase of souvenirs, gifts, etc. for relatives and friends, family, etc.Not including capital or transactional investments, cash for friends and relatives, and donations to public institutions for houses, land, cars, boats and valuables purchased for commercial purposes, etc.

Number of Tourists

(1) International tourists refer to foreigners, overseas Chinese, Chinese compatriots from Hong Kong, Macao and Taiwan coming to China for sight seeing, visits, tours, family reunions, vacations, study tours, conferences and other activities of a business, scientific and technological, cultural, educational and religious nature. It does not include representatives and employees of resident institutions of foreign countries in China such as embassies, consulates, news agencies and offices of foreign companies and organizations, nor does it include long-term foreign experts or students residing in China, or persons in transition without spending a night in China.

(2) Chinese residents going abroad refer to Chinese residents going abroad for short terms for either public business or private purposes. Chinese employees working on international transport carriers are included in those going abroad for public business purpose, not in those for private purpose.

(3) Domestic tourists refer to residents of the mainland of China who stay for one night at least but no more than 6 months at tourist facilities in other places than their permanent residence within the territory of the Chinese mainland, including foreigners, overseas Chinese and Chinese compatriots from Hong Kong, Macao and Taiwan who have resided in China for over one year.

Foreign Exchange Earnings from International Tourism refer to the total expenditures of foreigners, overseas Chinese, Chinese compatriots from Hong Kong, Macao and Taiwan during their stay in the mainland of China, which are earnings of foreign exchange from international tourism from the point of view from China.

International Travel Agencies refer to travel agencies engaged in the promotion, solicitation, organization and reception of tours to the mainland of China by foreigners, overseas Chinese, Chinese compatriots from Hong Kong, Macao and Taiwan.

Domestic Travel Agencies refer to travel agencies engaged in the promotion, solicitation, organization and reception of domestic tourists, and in the reception of foreigners, overseas Chinese, Chinese compatriots from Hong Kong, Macao and Taiwan organized by international travel agencies or other departments concerned, without their own promotion and solicitation programmes.

第7篇

能　源

Energy

简 要 说 明

一、本篇资料的主要内容

本篇资料反映了全省能源生产和消费状况，主要包括能源生产、消费及品种构成，能源生产和消费弹性系数，生活用能源消费量，综合能源平衡表和主要能源品种的单项平衡表，全省各市主要发展约束性指标，以及全省各市电力消费情况。

二、本篇资料的来源

本篇数据主要来源于全省能源平衡表，以及全省节能核算表和省电力部门，由省统计局能源处编制提供。

三、关于数据口径与计算的说明

1．一次能源生产量与能源产品产量统计数字一致。

2．能源生产与消费弹性系数分别以能源生产、消费增长速度与国内生产总值增长速度相比求得。GDP 按可比价格计算。

3．能源平衡表中，进口量和出口量采用海关统计数据。

4．电力折算成标准煤时，有当量、等价两种折标系数。电力折算标准煤的当量系数为 1.229 吨标准煤/万千瓦时，等价系数按平均发电煤耗计算。

5．煤炭包括原煤、洗精煤、其他洗煤和煤制品（即型煤），不包括焦炭。煤品包括煤炭、焦炭、焦炉煤气、高炉煤气、转炉煤气和其他焦化产品。

6．煤品占能耗总量的比重，不包括入鲁火电所占能耗总量的比重。

7．依据 2018 年第四次全国经济普查资料，对 2015 年至 2017 年能源历史数据进行了调整。

Brief Introduction

I. Main Content

Data in this chapter show the energy production and consumption of Shandong Province, including mainly energy production and consumption and their composition, the elasticity ratio of energy production and consumption, the consumption of energy for residential use, overall balance sheet of energy and balance sheets by different types of energy, main binding indicators on development of Shandong, and the energy consumption grouped by sector.

II. Source of Data

Data in this chapter are mainly based on the energy balance sheet of the whole province, provincial energy saving accounting table,and power sector. The data are provided by the Division of Energy Statistics of Shandong Provincial Bureau of Statistics.

III. Notes on Coverage and Calculation of Data

(1) The data on production of primary energy are the same as the corresponding data on output of energy products.

(2) The elasticity ratio of energy production is calculated as the quotient of the growth rate of energy production divided by the growth rate of GDP; and the elasticity ratio of energy consumption is calculated as the quotient of the growth rate of energy consumption divided by the growth rate of GDP.

(3) In the energy balance sheet, data on imports and exports are from Customs statistics. The refueling by Chinese ships and airplanes abroad is included in imports.

(4) The coefficient for conversion of electric power into the standard coal equivalent is calculated on the basis of heat value equivalent. the coefficient for the conversion of electric power into the standard coal equivalent is calculated on the basis of the heat value equivalent. One kilowatt is equal to 0.1229 kg SCE. The coefficient is calculated according to the average consumption of coal for generating electricity.

(5) Coal includes crude coal, fine washed coal, other washed coal and coal products, and it excludes coke. Coal products include coal, coke, coke oven gas, blast furnace gas, converter gas and other coking products.

(6) The proportion of coal consumption in total energy consumption includes the proportion of thermal power transmitted into Shandong Province.

(7) Based on the fourth national economic census data in 2018, some energy historical data from 2015 to 2017 are adjusted.

7-1 主要年份一次能源生产总量

Primary Energy Output in Major Years

单位：万吨标煤 (10 000 tons of SCE)

年 份 Year	能源生产总量 Total Energy Production	原 煤 Coal	原 油 Crude Oil	天然气 Natural Gas	一次电力 Primary Electricity
1949	120.79	120.79			
1952	258.58	258.58			
1955	342.73	342.73			
1956	386.58	386.58			
1957	440.37	440.37			
1962	1041.29	1041.17	0.01		0.11
1965	1362.94	1242.89	119.81		0.24
1970	2383.80	1716.18	667.59		0.03
1975	4555.04	2036.54	2388.62	128.62	1.26
1976	5013.70	2382.91	2500.65	128.88	1.26
1977	5387.37	2727.99	2502.71	155.88	0.79
1978	5901.83	2928.71	2781.49	190.46	1.17
1979	6075.07	3170.21	2697.14	205.49	2.23
1980	5873.37	3064.71	2616.94	189.00	2.72
1981	5392.54	2950.42	2301.75	138.72	1.65
1982	5505.80	3040.71	2335.21	129.41	0.47
1983	5898.00	3132.28	2625.00	139.79	0.93
1984	6696.54	3258.96	3288.36	148.17	1.05
1985	7531.89	3516.00	3861.74	151.89	2.26
1986	8046.80	3642.79	4215.52	185.94	2.55
1987	8511.34	3798.47	4514.38	197.24	1.25
1988	8918.29	3970.94	4757.61	188.73	1.01
1989	9038.69	4067.83	4765.07	205.35	0.44
1990	9262.21	4282.54	4786.70	191.39	1.58
1991	9269.98	4282.53	4793.22	191.25	2.98
1992	9508.88	4535.86	4780.24	191.92	0.86
1993	9875.38	4519.97	5171.83	182.08	1.50
1994	10624.66	5560.85	4887.14	173.78	2.89
1995	10757.67	6305.32	4294.76	156.04	1.55
1996	10697.72	6392.56	4159.57	144.62	0.97
1997	10620.51	6496.14	4002.01	121.67	0.69
1998	10436.05	6412.17	3901.51	122.09	0.28
1999	10322.39	6425.10	3807.55	89.01	0.73
2000	9648.75	5741.96	3822.49	83.54	0.76
2001	11550.26	7634.32	3811.52	103.34	1.08
2002	13241.75	9333.02	3816.52	91.07	1.14
2003	14384.08	10476.85	3808.65	98.36	0.22
2004	14394.61	10461.78	3820.50	111.84	0.49
2005	13995.62	10021.63	3849.36	123.03	1.60
2006	14083.40	10042.24	3935.89	103.46	1.82
2007	14616.67	10526.28	3990.22	99.22	0.95
2008	14615.32	10500.62	3998.91	113.05	2.74
2009	14600.08	10424.07	4040.38	119.97	15.66
2010	16055.71	11913.14	3980.08	129.01	33.48
2011	15997.81	11585.87	3973.65	64.33	53.35
2012	16973.80	12528.16	3963.94	75.71	79.19
2013	15165.08	10722.56	3894.94	65.11	116.19
2014	15220.40	10699.80	3876.09	62.89	133.13
2015	14693.06	10277.40	3751.91	57.70	161.90
2016	13616.76	9404.96	3301.96	56.23	229.07
2017	13710.27	9623.27	3192.79	49.72	305.89
2018	13102.01	8827.54	3203.20	52.80	484.11
2019	12539.10	7820.68	3177.70	56.10	742.71
2020	12205.72	7422.75	3170.31	63.43	817.13
2021	11543.68	6322.85	3158.22	68.42	1142.09

注：1.本表使用当量折标系数折算标准煤。
2.2009年开始，一次电力包含水电、风电、核电、生物质发电和太阳能光伏发电，1949-2008年数据为水电。

a)Data of standard coal equivalent is calculated on the basis of heat value equivalent.

b)Since 2009, Primary Electricity includes that generated by hydro power, wind power, nuclear power, bio-energy and solar PV power, and data of 1949-2008 refer to hydro power.

7-2 1979-2021年能源生产、能源消费弹性系数
Elasticity Ratio of Energy Production and Energy Consumption from 1979 to 2021

年 份 Year	能源生产弹性系数 Elasticity Ratio of Energy Production				能源消费弹性系数 Elasticity Ratio of Energy Consumption			
	能源生产比上年增长(%) Growth Rate of Energy Production over	电力生产比上年增长(%) Growth Rate of Electricity Production over Preceding	能源生产弹性系数 Elasticity Ratio of Energy Production	电力生产弹性系数 Elasticity Ratio of Electricity Production	能源消费比上年增长(%) Growth Rate of Energy Consumption over	电力消费比上年增长(%) Growth Rate of Electricity Consumption over	能源消费弹性系数 Elasticity Ratio of Energy Consumption	电力消费弹性系数 Elasticity Ratio of Electricity Consumption
1979	1.69	9.68	0.15	0.84		11.03		0.95
1980	-3.33	8.78		0.55	0.62	5.96	0.03	0.40
1981	-8.17	4.58		0.25	-12.23	6.13		0.33
1982	2.12	4.62	0.15	0.33	21.98	6.06	1.56	0.43
1983	7.11	7.26	0.44	0.44	-13.50	7.43		0.46
1984	13.53	8.33	0.51	0.31	7.34	12.43	0.27	0.47
1985	12.46	10.83	0.73	0.63	-12.67	8.70		0.51
1986	6.83	14.46	0.75	1.59	7.34	11.02	0.81	1.22
1987	5.79	10.62	0.29	0.52	13.68	9.68	0.68	0.48
1988	4.78	14.41	0.19	0.57	5.73	8.04	0.23	0.32
1989	1.36	10.58	0.09	0.67	4.84	7.17	0.31	0.45
1990	2.46	6.33	0.15	0.38	3.46	9.76	0.21	0.58
1991	0.52	11.20	0.03	0.57	3.05	9.75	0.15	0.49
1992	2.14	14.06	0.16	0.66	1.92	13.92	0.09	0.65
1993	-0.14	7.85		0.30	-1.07	7.77		0.29
1994	8.27	10.95	0.21	0.28	13.09	10.50	0.33	0.29
1995	6.13	9.09	0.21	0.31	10.58	9.48	0.36	0.32
1996	-2.77	7.28		0.38	3.12	7.51	0.16	0.39
1997	1.52	7.68	0.13	0.66	-0.02	7.38		0.64
1998	-1.81	-7.09			12.70	-1.19	1.10	
1999	-1.01	14.84		0.58	0.22	14.57	0.87	0.53
2000	-6.52	9.91		0.55	-9.17	10.12		0.56
2001	1.71	9.86	0.17	0.98	10.41	10.94	1.03	1.09
2002	4.68	13.19	0.40	1.14	18.06	12.42	1.56	1.07
2003	8.49	11.75	0.62	0.86	18.74	13.47	1.36	0.98
2004	0.07	17.50	0.01	1.15	21.30	17.50	1.39	1.14
2005	-2.78	16.58		1.11	20.08	16.58	1.32	1.09
2006	0.64	15.24	0.04	1.04	10.96	15.24	0.74	1.04
2007	3.79	14.23	0.27	1.00	8.66	14.26	0.61	1.00
2008	-0.01	3.89		0.32	4.48	5.04	0.37	0.42
2009	-0.10	3.95		0.33	5.73	7.85	0.48	0.66
2010	9.97	6.29	0.80	0.50	7.54	12.15	0.60	0.97
2011	-0.36	2.64	-0.03	0.24	6.68	10.21	0.62	0.94
2012	6.10	4.20	0.63	0.43	4.73	4.38	0.48	0.45
2013	-10.66	8.82	-1.12	0.92	4.74	7.60	0.50	0.80
2014	0.36	3.90	0.04	0.45	3.29	3.44	0.38	0.40
2015	-3.86	5.48	-0.49	0.69	3.95	5.18	0.50	0.65
2016	-7.33	9.66	-0.99	1.30	2.05	9.34	0.28	1.26
2017	0.69	6.22	0.09	0.85	-0.10	6.37	-0.01	0.87
2018	-4.44	2.70	-0.70	0.43	1.20	4.51	0.19	0.72
2019	-4.30	0.26	-0.79	0.05	1.99	3.80	0.37	0.70
2020	-2.66	-1.54	-0.75	-0.43	1.79	1.96	0.30	0.55
2021	-5.42	6.96	-0.65	0.84	5.88	6.21	0.71	0.75

注：本表2005年以来数据均依据能源平衡表，能源生产、消费增速分别采用当量值和等价值，电力生产量包括一次电力和火电，电力消费量指全省电力消费量。

a)The data of the table prior to 2005 are calculated according to Overall Energy Balance Sheet . Growth rate of energy production adopt heat equivalen value, and that of energy consumption adopt heat value equivalent.The production of electricity include primary electricity and thermal power.The consumption of electricity refers to the whole provincial consumption.

7-3　一次能源生产量及构成

Primary Energy Output and Composition

类　　别	Category	2016	2017	2018	2019	2020	2021
能源生产总量(折标准煤)	**Total Energy Production**	**13957.81**	**14137.56**	**13735.61**	**13499.51**	**13213.36**	**13030.87**
(万吨标准煤)	**(10 000 tons of SCE)**						
构　成	Composition						
原　煤　(%)	Coal　(%)	67.38	68.07	64.27	57.93	56.18	48.52
原　油　(%)	Crude Oil　(%)	23.66	22.58	23.32	23.54	23.99	24.24
天然气　(%)	Natural Gas　(%)	0.40	0.35	0.38	0.42	0.48	0.53
电　力　(%)	Electricity　(%)	4.08	5.19	8.14	12.62	13.81	20.18
其　他　(%)	Others　(%)	4.47	3.81	3.89	5.50	5.54	6.54

注：本表使用等价折标系数折算标准煤。

a)Data of standard coal equivalent are calculated on the basis of the consumed heat value equivalent.

7-4　能源消费量及构成

Total Consumption and Composition of Energy

类　　别	Category	2016	2017	2018	2019	2020	2021
能源消费量(折标准煤)	**Energy Consumption**	**40137.9**	**40097.7**	**40580.5**	**41390.0**	**42132.9**	**44611.1**
(万吨标准煤)	**(10 000 tons of SCE)**						
构　成	Composition						
煤　品　(%)	Coal　(%)	73.92	72.70	69.32	67.28	66.38	63.01
油　品　(%)	Crude Oil　(%)	15.81	16.15	17.54	15.52	14.21	16.02
天然气　(%)	Natural Gas　(%)	3.27	3.79	4.24	5.01	5.79	5.72
一次电力　(%)	Primary Electricity　(%)	1.42	1.83	2.75	4.11	4.33	5.89
电力净调入(+)　(%)	Net Input of Electricity (+)　(%)	4.02	4.19	4.89	6.36	7.55	7.53
其　他　(%)	Others　(%)	1.54	1.34	1.26	1.72	1.74	1.83

注：本表使用等价折标系数折算标准煤。2020年数据已修订。

a) Data of standard coal equivalent are calculated on the basis of the consumed heat value equivalent.Data of 2020 have been revised.

7-5 按行业分能源消费量（2021年）

行业	Sector	能源消费总量（万吨标准煤）Total Energy Consumption (10 000 sce)
消费总量	**Total Consumption**	**44611.1**
农、林、牧、渔业	**Agriculture, Forestry, Animal Husbandry and Fishery**	**583.1**
工业	**Industry**	**34029.4**
采矿业	**Mining**	**938.5**
煤炭开采和洗选业	Mining and Washing of Coal	394.9
石油和天然气开采业	Extraction of Petroleum and Natural Gas	310.1
黑色金属矿采选业	Mining and Processing of Ferrous Metal Ores	75.8
有色金属矿采选业	Mining and Processing of Non-Ferrous Metal Ores	53.2
非金属矿采选业	Mining and Processing of Nonmetal Ores	58.9
开采专业及辅助性活动	Professional and Support Activities for Mining	30.1
其他采矿业	Mining of Other Ores	15.5
制造业	**Manufacturing**	**30263.2**
农副食品加工业	Processing of Food from Agricultural Products	720.7
食品制造业	Manufacture of Foods	472.8
酒、饮料和精制茶制造业	Manufacture of Liquor, Beverages and Refined Tea	73.7
烟草制品业	Manufacture of Tobacco	8.1
纺织业	Manufacture of Textile	761.0
纺织服装、服饰业	Manufacture of Textile, Wearing Apparel and Accessories	45.2
皮革、毛皮、羽毛及其制品和制鞋业	Manufacture of Leather, Fur, Feather and Related Products and Footwear	36.2
木材加工和木、竹、藤、棕、草制品业	Processing of Timber, Manufacture of Wood, Bamboo, Rattan, Palm, and Straw Products	268.7
家具制造业	Manufacture of Furniture	30.6
造纸和纸制品业	Manufacture of Paper and Paper Products	1109.0
印刷和记录媒介复制业	Printing and Reproduction of Recording Media	32.3
文教、工美、体育和娱乐用品制造业	Manufacture of Articles for Culture, Education, Arts and Crafts, Sport and Entertainment Activities	29.4
石油、煤炭及其他燃料加工业	Processing of Petroleum, Coal and Other Fuels	3125.1
化学原料和化学制品制造业	Manufacture of Raw Chemical Materials and Chemical Products	7311.3
医药制造业	Manufacture of Medicines	338.3
化学纤维制造业	Manufacture of Chemical Fibers	123.4
橡胶和塑料制品业	Manufacture of Rubber and Plastics Products	804.1
非金属矿物制品业	Manufacture of Non-metallic Mineral Products	2704.6
黑色金属冶炼和压延加工业	Smelting and Pressing of Ferrous Metals	5108.2
有色金属冶炼和压延加工业	Smelting and Pressing of Non-ferrous Metals	4792.4
金属制品业	Manufacture of Metal Products	1006.2
通用设备制造业	Manufacture of General Purpose Machinery	445.5
专用设备制造业	Manufacture of Special Purpose Machinery	125.2
汽车制造业	Manufacture of Automobiles	235.2
铁路、船舶、航空航天和其他运输设备制造业	Manufacture of Railway, Ship, Aerospace and Other Transport Equipments	84.5
电气机械和器材制造业	Manufacture of Electrical Machinery and Apparatus	148.0
计算机、通信和其他电子设备制造业	Manufacture of Computers, Communication and Other Electronic Equipment	140.7
仪器仪表制造业	Manufacture of Measuring Instruments and Machinery	10.6
其他制造业	Other Manufacture	100.5
废弃资源综合利用业	Utilization of Waste Resources	67.5
金属制品、机械和设备修理业	Repair Service of Metal Products, Machinery and Equipment	4.2
电力、热力、燃气及水生产和供应业	**Production and Supply of Electricity, Gas and Water**	**2827.7**
电力、热力生产和供应业	Production and Supply of Electric Power and Heat Power	2671.4
燃气生产和供应业	Production and Supply of Gas	17.2
水的生产和供应业	Production and Supply of Water	139.1
建筑业	**Construction**	**535.3**
交通运输、仓储和邮政业	**Transport, Storage and Post**	**2181.8**
批发和零售业、住宿和餐饮业	**Wholesale and Retail Trades, Hotels and Catering Services**	**1073.3**
其他	**Others**	**1613.1**
居民生活	**Household Consumption**	**4595.1**

Energy Consumption by Sector (2021)

煤炭 (万吨) Coal (10 000 tons)	焦炭 (万吨) Coke (10 000 tons)	原油 (万吨) Crude Oil (10 000 tons)	汽油 (万吨) Gasoline (10 000 tons)	煤油 (万吨) Kerosene (10 000 tons)	柴油 (万吨) Diesel Oil (10 000 tons)	燃料油 (万吨) Fuel Oil (10 000 tons)	天然气 (亿立方米) Natural Gas (100 million cu.m)	电力 (亿千瓦小时) Electricity (100 million kW·h)
39429.7	**4387.8**	**14875.6**	**738.3**	**103.4**	**1318.4**	**1790.6**	**233.7**	**7397.7**
24.7			**4.5**		**108.9**			**142.3**
38569.6	**4387.8**	**14875.6**	**48.8**	**0.1**	**260.5**	**1758.4**	**158.1**	**5600.9**
583.2	**23.5**	**254.0**	**1.0**		**20.6**		**3.1**	**182.0**
566.1			0.1		1.4		0.1	56.6
1.9		254.0	0.6		2.4		2.9	62.9
8.3	23.5				1.7			16.6
					1.4			18.0
6.9					1.0			18.7
			0.3		12.6			3.7
								5.5
15700.0	**4256.6**	**14621.5**	**46.4**	**0.1**	**234.3**	**1757.6**	**150.3**	**4607.7**
259.0	2.8		0.3		0.9	0.2	7.3	115.9
182.6	15.1		0.1		0.2		3.2	69.0
19.7	3.4					0.2	1.1	12.7
							0.1	2.1
56.8	4.5		0.2		0.3		4.5	203.5
0.6			0.2		0.1		0.4	11.7
0.8					0.1		0.2	10.3
0.1					0.3		1.2	71.8
					0.1		0.1	10.4
597.0	16.2		0.1		1.4	0.5	4.1	167.2
			0.1		0.1	0.1	0.3	8.9
0.8			0.1		0.1		0.5	6.5
3804.5	18.2	14029.2	20.1		189.5	1208.3	17.1	168.6
3585.0	526.8	592.3	21.7		11.2	535.9	24.4	735.2
94.1	2.8		0.1		0.1	0.1	2.6	55.7
18.6	1.5						0.6	24.1
72.1	4.3		0.4		0.8	0.1	2.4	198.4
1383.6	34.7		0.2		13.5	10.1	37.2	329.8
2406.1	3334.5		0.1		4.8		9.9	466.2
3103.1	116.8		0.1		2.8	1.8	12.9	1287.8
71.5	151.7		0.3		0.8		9.9	255.5
	16.2		0.6	0.1	1.9		1.8	142.7
3.9			0.5		1.3		1.7	29.8
29.5	3.4		0.4		2.2		4.0	57.3
			0.2		1.2	0.1	0.5	25.9
			0.3		0.2		1.2	45.9
3.5			0.1		0.1		1.0	42.4
			0.1				0.1	3.4
								34.5
7.0	3.8				0.2	0.1	0.3	12.8
					0.1			1.4
22286.4	**107.6**	**0.2**	**1.4**		**5.7**	**0.8**	**4.7**	**811.2**
22286.4	107.6	0.2	1.2		5.6	0.8	4.3	758.0
			0.1				0.4	4.8
			0.1					48.4
0.4			**15.0**		**63.5**	**2.5**	**0.4**	**74.8**
0.2			**155.0**	**103.2**	**812.3**	**29.7**	**9.8**	**154.3**
213.5			**24.2**		**33.8**		**13.6**	**210.1**
143.0			**45.3**		**23.5**		**7.7**	**434.5**
478.3			**445.5**		**15.9**		**44.2**	**780.8**

7-6 平均每天各种能源消费量
Average Daily Energy Consumption by Type of Energy

类 别	Category	2016	2017	2018	2019	2020	2021
合 计 （吨标准煤）	**Total (tons of SCE)**	**1099668**	**1098568**	**1111795**	**1133973**	**1154327**	**1222222**
煤 炭 （吨）	Coal (ton)	1155079	1150783	1159438	1181726	1062747	1080265
焦 炭 （吨）	Coke (ton)	101873	91332	96151	99163	130847	120213
原 油 （吨）	Crude Oil (ton)	279546	314717	357136	373482	403428	407552
燃料油 （吨）	Fuel Oil (ton)	123595	128395	65107	57433	63601	49056
汽 油 （吨）	Gasoline (ton)	17923	17972	18906	19371	18454	20229
煤 油 （吨）	Kerosene (ton)	3157	3096	3295	3450	2762	2832
柴 油 （吨）	Diesel Oil (ton)	32818	36186	34897	36601	35677	36120
液化石油气 （吨）	Liquefied Petroleum (ton)	12049	10041	5248	6057	14635	21821
电 力 （万千瓦时）	Electricity (10 000 kW·h)	162186	172525	180302	187159	190824	202677

注：1.本表使用等价折标系数折算标准煤。2.汽油、柴油、燃料油消费量含炼油再投入量。3.2020年数据已修订。
a) Data of standard coal equivalent is calculated on the basis of the consumed heat value equivalent.
b) Data on consumption of fuel oil include those for refining oil.
c) Data of 2020 have been revised.

7-7 平均每人年生活用能源
Annual Per Capita Energy Consumption for Non-Production Purpose

类 别	Category	2016	2017	2018	2019	2020	2021
合 计 （千克标准煤）	**Total (kgce)**	**362.3**	**371.2**	**396.6**	**416.8**	**436.7**	**451.9**
煤 炭 （千克）	Coal (kg)	66.4	56.5	53.2	47.6	49.5	47.0
汽 油 （千克）	Gasoline (kg)	39.6	40.6	43.0	43.1	41.2	43.8
液化石油气 （千克）	Liquefied Petroleum (kg)	5.4	5.3	5.5	5.5	5.3	5.7
电 力 （千瓦小时）	Electricity (kW·h)	560.1	604.4	666.3	694.1	714.4	768.0

注：本表使用等价折标系数折算标准煤。
a)Data of standard coal equivalent is calculated on the basis of the consumed heat value equivalent.

7-8 分品种生活能源年消费总量

Annual Energy Consumption for Non-Production Purpose by Category

类　　别	Category	2016	2017	2018	2019	2020	2021
合　　计　（万吨标准煤）	**Total (10 000 tons of SCE)**	**3585.3**	**3714.2**	**3976.7**	**4192.4**	**4439.1**	**4595.1**
煤　　炭　（万吨）	Coal (10 000 tons)	657.4	565.1	533.1	478.7	503.5	478.3
汽　　油　（万吨）	Gasoline (10 000 tons)	391.6	406.0	431.0	433.5	418.8	445.5
液化石油气　（万吨）	Liquefied Petroleum (10 000 tons)	53.8	53.3	54.7	55.1	53.4	57.7
电　　力　（亿千瓦小时）	Electricity (100 million kW·h)	554.4	604.8	668.1	698.2	726.2	780.8

注：本表使用等价折标系数折算标准煤。

a)Data of standard coal equivalent is calculated on the basis of the consumed heat value equivalent.

7-9 综合能源平衡表

Overall Energy Balance Sheet

单位：万吨标准煤 (10 000 tons of SCE)

项　　目	Item	2017	2018	2019	2020	2021
可供消费的能源总量	**Total Energy for Consumption**	**40097.7**	**40580.5**	**41390.0**	**42132.9**	**44611.1**
一次能源生产量	Primary Energy Output	14137.6	13735.6	13499.5	13213.4	13030.9
外省(区、市)调入量	Allocation from Other Provinces	32185.0	31537.2	36082.7	31841.3	34130.4
进口量	Imports	13910.6	13118.8	14622.4	16554.2	14572.4
本省(区、市)调出量(-)	Allocation to Other Provinces(-)	-17722.0	-16853.7	-22325.9	-19785.4	-16164.4
出口量(-)	Exports(-)	-2375.8	-253.1	-49.1	-2.6	-94.3
年初年末库存差额	Stock Changes in the Year	42.1	-704.3	-439.7	312.0	-864.4
能源消费总量	**Total Energy Consumption**	**40097.7**	**40580.5**	**41390.0**	**42132.9**	**44611.1**
在总量中:	Consumption by sector					
1.农林牧渔业	1.Agriculture,Forestry,Animal Husbandry and Fishery	540.0	550.1	599.7	574.6	583.1
2.工　业	2.Industry	31139.0	31146.2	31293.7	32111.3	34029.4
3.建筑业	3.Construction	430.0	437.3	481.4	500.6	535.3
4.交通运输、仓储和邮政业	4.Transport,Storage and Post	2124.2	2188.3	2381.8	2037.9	2181.8
5.批发、零售业和住宿、餐饮业	5.Wholesale and Retail Trades,Hotels and Catering Services	882.2	928.2	986.7	978.3	1073.3
6.其他行业	6.Other Sectors	1268.0	1353.6	1454.4	1491.2	1613.1
7.生活消费	7.Household Consumption	3714.2	3976.7	4192.4	4439.1	4595.1
在总量中:	Consumption by Usage					
(一) 终端消费	(I)End-use Consumption	37842.3	38243.9	40359.4	41584.6	43678.7
#工业	Industry	28883.5	28809.5	30263.1	31563.0	33097.0
(二) 加工转换损失量	(II)Losses During the Process of Energy Conversion	2255.5	2336.6	1030.6	548.4	932.5
炼焦	Coking	324.9	395.1	3.0	341.0	327.0
炼油	Petroleum Refining	2024.9	2508.4	1622.5	804.2	1171.9
(三) 损失量	(III)Energy Losses					
平衡差额	**Balance**					

注：本表使用等价折标系数折算标准煤。2020年数据已修订。

a) Data of standard coal equivalent are calculated on the basis of the consumed heat value equivalent.Data of 2020 have been revised.

7-10 石油平衡表

Petroleum Balance Sheet

单位：万吨 (10 000 tons)

项　　目	Item	2017	2018	2019	2020	2021
一、可供量	**Total Energy Available for Consumption**	**4040.3**	**4229.3**	**4102.8**	**4163.3**	**4832.4**
原油产量	Crude Output	2234.9	2242.1	2237.8	2219.2	2210.7
外省(区、市)调入量	Allocation from Other Provinces	5631.5	4508.4	3272.2	3215.5	3676.8
进口量	Imports	8382.5	8502.6	9558.2	11028.0	9742.0
本省(区、市)调出量(－)	Allocation to Other Provinces(-)	-10241.6	-10776.8	-10771.9	-11880.1	-10563.1
出口量(－)	Exports(-)	-1651.5	-75.4		-1.8	-6.5
年初年末库存差额	Stock Changes in the Year	-261.4	-171.5	-193.5	-417.5	-228.0
年初库存量	Stock of early Year	939.7	1201.1	1372.6	1566.1	1983.6
年末库存量(－)	Stock of Year end(-)	-1201.1	-1372.6	-1566.1	-1983.6	-2211.6
二、消费量	**Total Energy Consumption**	**4040.3**	**4229.3**	**4102.8**	**4163.3**	**4832.4**
在总量中：	Consumption by sector					
1.农林牧渔业	1.Agriculture,Forestry,Animal Husbandry and Fishery	127.2	134.3	134.8	108.9	114.3
2.工　业	2.Industry	1842.1	1902.8	1744.4	2173.5	2738.1
3.建筑业	3.Construction	198.9	200.6	206.8	212.1	213.4
4.交通运输、仓储和邮政业	4.Transport,Storage and Post	1250.8	1340.1	1360.4	1041.6	1101.7
5.批发、零售业和住宿、餐饮业	5.Wholesale and Retail Trades, Hotels and Catering Services	66.3	70.5	72.2	66.2	72.8
6.其他行业	6.Other Sectors	75.6	75.3	75.8	73.6	73.0
7.生活消费	7.Household Consumption	479.5	505.6	508.5	487.3	519.1
在总量中：	Consumption by Usage					
1.终端消费	1.End-use Consumption	3147.3	3406.9	3410.7	3560.6	4148.5
#工业	Industry	949.0	1080.4	1052.3	1570.9	2054.3
2.加工转换损失	2.Losses During the Process of Energy Conversion	893.1	822.4	692.1	602.6	683.9
火力发电	Thermal Power	17.2	18.0	21.9	30.1	25.8
供　热	Heating	52.4	46.6	37.1	33.0	36.2
炼油损耗	Petroleum Refining	823.5	757.9	633.1	536.5	616.1
制　气	Gas Production				3.1	5.7
3.损 失 量	3.Other Losses					
三、平衡差额	**Balance**					

注：2020年数据已修订。
a)Data of 2020 has been revised.

7-11 煤炭平衡表
Coal Balance Sheet

单位：万吨 (10 000 tons)

项　目	Item	2017	2018	2019	2020	2021
一、可供量	**Total Energy Available for Consumption**	**42003.6**	**42319.5**	**43133.0**	**38790.3**	**39429.7**
原煤生产量	Raw coal output	13159.6	12556.5	11918.1	10944.6	9312.0
外省(区、市)调入量	Allocation from Other Provinces	29478.8	31339.3	38410.1	29785.1	32274.3
进口量	Imports	1409.4	1538.8	1244.8	1188.2	959.0
本省(区、市)调出量(－)	Allocation to Other Provinces(-)	-2532.2	-2435.3	-8073.7	-4532.7	-2188.8
出口量(－)	Exports(-)	-114.4	-79.1	-99.9		-10.5
年初年末库存差额	Stock Changes in the Year	602.4	-600.7	-266.5	1405.1	-916.3
年初库存量	Stock of early Year	3528.6	2926.2	3526.9	3793.3	2388.2
年末库存量(－)	Stock of Year end(-)	-2926.2	-3526.9	-3793.3	-2388.2	-3304.5
二、消费量	**Total Energy Consumption**	**42003.6**	**42319.5**	**43133.0**	**38790.3**	**39429.7**
在总量中：	Consumption by sector					
1.农林牧渔业	1.Agriculture,Forestry,Animal Husbandry and Fishery	60.2	50.2	45.6	40.6	24.7
2.工　业	2.Industry	40774.8	41251.3	42168.2	37858.7	38569.6
3.建筑业	3.Construction	9.8	1.2			0.4
4.交通运输、仓储和邮政业	4.Transport,Storage and Post	16.1	16.1	15.0	12.0	0.2
5.批发、零售业和住宿、餐饮业	5.Wholesale and Retail Trades, Hotels and Catering Services	341.5	281.5	254.8	224.8	213.5
6.其他行业	6.Other Sectors	236.1	186.1	170.8	150.8	143.0
7.生活消费	7.Household Consumption	563.1	533.1	478.7	503.5	478.3
在总量中：	Consumption by Usage					
1.终端消费	1.End-use Consumption	8113.7	6626.7	7083.9	6638.6	6496.0
#工业	Industry	6884.9	5558.5	6119.1	5706.9	5636.0
2.用于加工转换	2.Energy Conversion	33889.9	35692.8	36049.1	32151.7	32933.6
火力发电	Thermal Power	21174.2	21313.7	20515.8	18498.7	19361.8
供　热	Heating	5818.4	7119.8	8128.3	8243.6	8688.6
洗煤损耗	Losses in Coal Washing and Dressing	938.0	991.4	468.0	732.2	360.1
炼　焦	Coking	5878.7	6108.2	6762.9	4464.0	4324.3
制　气	Gas Production	81.7	146.9	170.6	200.9	185.8
型煤加工损耗	Losses in briquette Processing	-1.0	12.8	3.5	12.3	13.0
3.损失量	3.Other Losses					
三、平衡差额	**Balance**					

7-12 电力平衡表

Electricity Balance Sheet

单位：亿千瓦小时 (100 million kwh)

项　　目	Item	2017	2018	2019	2020	2021
一、可供量	**Total Energy Available for Consumption**	**6297.2**	**6581.0**	**6831.3**	**6965.1**	**7397.7**
生产量	Output	5727.2	5882.1	5897.2	5806.4	6210.3
火力发电	Hydropower	5478.4	5488.2	5292.9	5141.6	5281.0
水力发电、核发电、其他发电	Hydro,Nuclear and other Power	248.9	393.9	604.3	664.9	929.3
外省(区、市)调入量	Allocation from Other Provinces	572.2	710.9	941.4	1165.7	1197.1
进口量	Imports					
本省(区、市)调出量(-)	Allocation to Other Provinces(-)	-2.3	-12.0	-7.3	-7.1	-9.7
出 口 量(-)	Exports(-)					
二、消费量	**Total Energy Consumption**	**6297.2**	**6581.0**	**6831.3**	**6965.1**	**7397.7**
在总量中：	Consumption by sector	6297.2	6581.0	6831.3	6965.1	7397.7
1.农林牧渔业	1.Agriculture,Forestry,Animal Husbandry and Fishery	110.1	121.3	136.7	141.5	142.3
2.工　业	2.Industry	5016.6	5145.6	5280.6	5352.2	5600.9
3.建筑业	3.Construction	45.7	50.8	60.7	65.7	74.8
4.交通运输、仓储和邮政业	4.Transport,Storage and Post	100.2	109.9	123.3	135.2	154.3
5.批发、零售业和住宿、餐饮业	5.Wholesale and Retail Trades,Hotels and Catering Services	140.1	158.3	174.3	173.7	210.1
6.其他行业	6.Other Sectors	279.8	327.1	357.5	370.7	434.5
7.生活消费	7.Household Consumption	604.8	668.1	698.2	726.2	780.8
在总量中：	Consumption by Usage	6297.2	6581.0	6831.3	6965.1	7397.7
1. 终端消费	1.End-use Consumption	6297.2	6581.0	6831.3	6965.1	7397.7
#工业	Industry	5016.6	5145.6	5280.6	5352.2	5600.9
2. 输配电损失量	2.Losses in Transmission					
三、平衡差额	**Balance**					

7-13 各市万元GDP能耗

Energy Consumption per 10 000-yuan GDP by Region

地 区	Region	2017 比2016年上升或下降(±%) Increased or Decreased Compared with 2016	2018 比2017年上升或下降(±%) Increased or Decreased Compared with 2017	2019 比2018年上升或下降(±%) Increased or Decreased Compared with 2018	2020 比2019年上升或下降(±%) Increased or Decreased Compared with 2019	2021 比2020年上升或下降(±%) Increased or Decreased Compared with 2020
全省总计	**Total**	**-6.91**	**-4.80**	**-3.09**	**-2.41**	**-2.20**
济南市	Jinan	-14.20	-8.87	-7.38	-4.75	-0.96
青岛市	Qingdao	-3.86	-2.58	-6.60	-4.66	1.04
淄博市	Zibo	-7.83	-4.76	-5.83	-0.81	-7.56
枣庄市	Zaozhuang	-7.49	-2.87	-2.43	-4.75	-3.85
东营市	Dongying	-4.12	-2.48	-3.73	-5.32	1.94
烟台市	Yantai	-6.14	-3.43	-3.16	4.53	9.08
潍坊市	Weifang	-3.75	-3.96	3.49	-6.15	-5.61
济宁市	Jining	-3.96	-2.15	-4.39	-1.47	-3.90
泰安市	Tai'an	-8.29	-2.20	-4.62	-1.52	3.72
威海市	Weihai	-5.50	-4.33	-7.03	-5.48	-3.40
日照市	Rizhao	-4.21	-3.91	-2.57	-3.25	-5.98
临沂市	Linyi	-7.77	-5.34	-4.30	-3.15	-0.80
德州市	Dezhou	-8.47	-3.52	-5.54	4.41	-3.60
聊城市	Liaocheng	-4.03	-10.59	8.48	-1.29	-4.89
滨州市	Binzhou	3.76	-6.28	-9.25	-6.69	-8.17
菏泽市	Heze	-5.95	-3.92	-9.07	-2.42	-5.86

注:1.本表使用等价折标系数折算标准煤。2.本表数据包含原料能。
3.根据行政区划调整，2019年起，莱芜市并入济南市，以下表同。
a) Data of standard coal equivalent is calculated on the basis of the consumed heat value quivalente.
b) The invoved energy consumption for the calculation of the data in this table includes energy used as raw material.
c)According to administrative division adjustment,Laiwu City merged into Jinan City from 2019.The same applies to tables following.

7-14 各市规模以上工业万元增加值能耗

Energy Consumption per 10 000-yuan Value Added of Industrial Enterprises above the Designated Size by Region

地　区	Region	2017	2018	2019	2020	2021
		比2016年上升或下降(±%) Increased or Decreased Compared with 2016	比2017年上升或下降(±%) Increased or Decreased Compared with 2017	比2018年上升或下降(±%) Increased or Decreased Compared with 2018	比2019年上升或下降(±%) Increased or Decreased Compared with 2019	比2020年上升或下降(±%) Increased or Decreased Compared with 2020
全省总计	**Total**	**-9.89**	**-5.35**	**-1.16**	**-6.86**	**-5.57**
济南市	Jinan	-25.14	-21.37	-5.07	-9.63	-0.42
青岛市	Qingdao	-6.56	-2.59	-5.64	-8.82	3.84
淄博市	Zibo	-6.55	-6.09	4.19	-4.41	-13.30
枣庄市	Zaozhuang	-4.90	-3.12	-0.45	-6.52	-8.01
东营市	Dongying	-5.43	-2.26	-2.11	-8.77	-1.24
烟台市	Yantai	-7.63	-4.17	-1.41	-4.65	11.13
潍坊市	Weifang	-0.77	-4.76	9.92	-13.93	-10.95
济宁市	Jining	-6.38	-5.00	-9.42	-11.74	-8.08
泰安市	Tai'an	-7.74	-3.80	-3.66	-4.71	3.78
威海市	Weihai	-9.22	-5.83	-9.28	-10.95	-2.81
日照市	Rizhao	-5.90	5.78	2.51	-7.39	-1.90
莱芜市	Laiwu	-3.14	-7.07			
临沂市	Linyi	-10.06	-6.50	4.93	-3.49	-9.88
德州市	Dezhou	-9.34	-5.52	-3.85	-0.64	-6.87
聊城市	Liaocheng	-17.80	-10.86	-3.97	-3.77	-12.52
滨州市	Binzhou	-16.21	-3.33	-9.73	-10.23	-11.78
菏泽市	Heze	-6.84	-3.94	2.06	-9.09	-17.29

注：1.本表使用当量折标系数折算标准煤。2.本表数据包含原料能。

a) Data of standard coal equivalent is calculated on the basis of the consumed heat value equivalent.

b) The invoved energy consumption for the calculation of the data in this table includes energy used as raw material.

7-15 各市万元GDP电耗

Electricity Consumption per 10 000-yuan GDP by Region

地 区	Region	2017 比2016年上升或下降(±%) Increased or Decreased Compared with 2016	2018 比2017年上升或下降(±%) Increased or Decreased Compared with 2017	2019 比2018年上升或下降(±%) Increased or Decreased Compared with 2018	2020 比2019年上升或下降(±%) Increased or Decreased Compared with 2019	2021 比2020年上升或下降(±%) Increased or Decreased Compared with 2020
全省总计	**Total**	**-6.14**	**2.50**	**-3.07**	**-1.67**	**-1.77**
济南市	Jinan	-7.45	-2.90	-3.88	-0.45	2.18
青岛市	Qingdao	1.73	0.39	-0.39	-1.07	7.07
淄博市	Zibo	-8.06	-1.66	-2.82	-1.20	-2.54
枣庄市	Zaozhuang	0.26	9.25	-2.17	-1.90	-1.31
东营市	Dongying	-3.05	1.78	0.56	-3.17	-0.58
烟台市	Yantai	-0.95	1.99	-0.90	-2.93	-2.36
潍坊市	Weifang	1.50	2.19	4.42	-0.25	-2.12
济宁市	Jining	-4.28	5.88	0.90	-1.63	-0.76
泰安市	Tai'an	-7.87	3.63	-2.95	1.73	7.18
威海市	Weihai	-0.29	1.35	1.42	-1.98	2.73
日照市	Rizhao	1.77	8.14	3.94	1.29	-11.67
临沂市	Linyi	2.73	3.17	-2.39	-2.96	3.02
德州市	Dezhou	-10.55	8.42	2.92	0.54	3.94
聊城市	Liaocheng	-19.83	9.96	-1.61	-1.09	-7.15
滨州市	Binzhou	-13.39	3.18	-10.60	-3.92	-7.28
菏泽市	Heze	-1.56	6.81	-0.26	-1.35	0.11

注：电力数据为国网山东电力公司数据。
a) The invoved data of electricity energy for the calculation of the data in this table come from by Shandong Electric Power Corporation.

7-16 各市电力消费量(2021年)
Electricity Consumption by Region(2021)

单位:亿千瓦时 (100 million kW·h)

地区	Region	全社会用电量 Electricity Consumption	#第一产业 Primary Industry Electricity Consumption	第二产业 Secondary Industry Electricity Consumption	第三产业 Tertiary Industry Electricity Consumption	工业用电 Industrial Electricity Consumption	#城乡居民生活用电 Household Electricity Consumption
全省总计	**Total**	**7382.5**	**104.7**	**5659.0**	**837.9**	**5585.6**	**780.8**
济南市	Jinan	475.3	3.3	267.0	118.4	256.6	86.5
青岛市	Qingdao	552.7	8.3	309.3	143.8	298.0	91.3
淄博市	Zibo	425.3	2.3	351.0	34.0	348.4	38.0
枣庄市	Zaozhuang	186.4	1.4	132.5	25.3	130.4	27.3
东营市	Dongying	363.8	5.0	316.9	23.4	315.2	18.5
烟台市	Yantai	595.2	13.6	467.6	60.3	463.1	53.8
潍坊市	Weifang	690.5	15.6	529.4	74.1	521.9	71.3
济宁市	Jining	389.7	6.0	263.7	60.3	260.0	59.7
泰安市	Tai'an	244.9	3.4	174.3	32.6	171.8	34.6
威海市	Weihai	152.2	4.0	92.9	30.8	89.7	24.6
日照市	Rizhao	257.6	5.6	205.8	23.9	203.7	22.3
临沂市	Linyi	559.7	9.4	401.3	68.6	395.2	80.5
德州市	Dezhou	283.0	7.1	202.6	35.5	198.4	37.8
聊城市	Liaocheng	656.8	7.3	572.6	36.4	569.2	40.6
滨州市	Binzhou	1240.5	5.9	1177.0	26.1	1174.0	31.6
菏泽市	Heze	280.1	6.5	166.5	44.4	161.3	62.6

注：本表数据为国网山东电力公司数据。
a) Data in this table are provided by Shandong Electric Power Corporation.

主要统计指标解释

能源生产总量　指一定时期内，一个地区一次能源生产量的总和。该指标是观察一个地区能源生产水平、规模、构成和发展速度的总量指标。一次能源生产量包括原煤、原油、天然气、水电、核能及其他动力能(如风能、太阳能、生物质能、地热能等)发电量，不包括非商品类的低热值燃料生产量、生物质能、太阳能等的利用，以及由一次能源加工转换而成的二次能源产量。

能源消费总量　指一定时期内，一个地区物质生产部门、非物质生产部门和生活消费的各种能源的总和。该指标是观察能源消费水平、构成和增长速度的总量指标。能源消费总量包括煤品和油品、天然气、电力和其他能源，不包括非商品类的低热值燃料、生物质能和太阳能等的利用。能源消费总量分为终端能源消费量、能源加工转换损失量和能源损失量三部分。

(1)终端能源消费量：指一定时期内，一个地区生产和生活消费的各种能源在扣除了用于加工转换二次能源消费量和损失量以后的数量。

(2)能源加工转换损失量：指一定时期内，一个地区投入加工转换的各种能源数量之和与产出各种能源产品之和的差额。该指标是观察能源在加工转换过程中损失量变化的指标。

(3)能源损失量：指一定时期内，能源在输送、分配、储存过程中发生的损失和由客观原因造成的各种损失量，不包括各种气体能源放空、放散量。

能源生产弹性系数　是研究能源生产增长速度与国民经济增长速度之间关系的指标。计算公式：

$$能源生产弹性系数=\frac{能源生产总量年平均增长速度}{国民经济年平均增长速度}$$

国民经济年平均增长速度，可根据不同的目的或需要，用国民生产总值、国内生产总值等指标来计算，本年鉴是采用国内生产总值指标计算的。

电力生产弹性系数　是研究电力生产增长速度与国民经济增长速度之间关系的指标。一般来说，电力的发展应当快于国民经济的发展，也就是说电力应超前发展。计算公式为：

$$电力生产弹性系数=\frac{电力生产量年平均增长速度}{国民经济年平均增长速度}$$

能源消费弹性系数　反映能源消费增长速度与国民经济增长速度之间比例关系的指标。计算公式为：

$$能源消费弹性系数=\frac{能源消费量年平均增长速度}{国民经济年平均增长速度}$$

电力消费弹性系数　反映电力消费增长速度与国民经济增长速度之间比例关系的指标。计算公式为：

$$电力消费弹性系数=\frac{电力消费量年平均增长速度}{国民经济年平均增长速度}$$

Explanatory Notes on Main Statistical Indicators

Total Energy Production refers to the total production of primary energy by all energy producing enterprises in the region in a given period of time. It is a comprehensive indicator to show the capacity, scale, composition and development of energy production of the country. The production of primary energy includes that of coal, crude oil, natural gas, and electricity generated by hydropower, nuclear energy and other means such as wind power, solar power, bio-energy and geothermal power. However, it excludes the production of noncommercial fuels of low calorific value, bio-energy, solar energy and the secondary energy converted from the primary energy.

Total Domestic Energy Consumption refers to the total consumption of energy of various kinds by material production sectors, non material production sectors and households in the country in a given period of time. It is a comprehensive indicator to show the scale, composition and development of energy consumption. The total energy consumption includes that of coal, crude oil and their products, natural gas, electricity and other energy resources. However, it excludes the consumption of noncommercial fuel of low calorific value, bio-energy and solar energy. Total domestic energy consumption can be divided into three parts: final energy consumption, loss during the process of energy conversion, and energy loss.

(1)Final Energy Consumption: It refers to the total energy consumption by material production sectors, non material production sectors and households in the region in a given period of time, but excludes the consumption in conversion of the primary energy into the secondary energy and the loss in the process of energy conversion.

(2)Loss During the Process of Energy Conversion: It refers to the total input of various kinds of energy for conversion, minus the total output of various kinds of energy in the region in a given period of time. It is an indicator to show the loss that occurs during the process of energy conversion.

(3)Energy Loss: It refers to the total of the loss of energy during the course of energy transport, distribution and storage and the loss caused by any objective reason in a given period of time. The loss of various kinds of gas due to gas discharges and stocktaking is excluded.

Elasticity Ratio of Energy Production is an indicator to show the relationship between the growth rate of energy production and the growth rate of the national economy. The formula is:

$$\text{Elasticity Ratio of Energy Production} = \frac{\text{Average Annual Growth Rate of Energy Production}}{\text{Average Annual Growth Rate of National Economy}}$$

The average annual growth rate of the national economy can be shown by the gross national product, gross domestic product and other indicators, depending upon the purposes or needs. The gross domestic product is used in calculation of the ratio in this chapter.

Elasticity Ratio of Electricity Production is an indicator to show the relationship between the growth rate of electricity production and the growth rate of the national economy. Generally speaking, the growth rate of electricity production should be higher than that of the national economy.

Its formula is:

$$\text{Elasticity Ratio of Electricity Production} = \frac{\text{Average Annual Growth Rate of Electricity Production}}{\text{Average Annual Growth Rate of National Economy}}$$

Elasticity Ratio of Energy Consumption is an indicator to show the relationship between the growth rate of energy consumption and the growth rate of the national economy. The formula is:

$$\text{Elasticity Ratio of Energy Consumption} = \frac{\text{Average Annual Growth Rate of Energy Consumption}}{\text{Average Annual Growth Rate of National Economy}}$$

Elasticity Ratio of Electricity Consumption is an indicator to show the relationship between the growth rate of electricity consumption and the growth rate of the national economy. The formula is:

$$\text{Elasticity Ratio of Electricity Consumption} = \frac{\text{Average Annual Growth Rate of Electricity Consumption}}{\text{Average Annual Growth Rate of National Economy}}$$

第
8
篇

财政和金融

Government Finance and Banking

简 要 说 明

一、本篇资料的主要内容

本篇资料反映了全省财政收支、金融和保险、证券方面的情况，主要包括财政收入、财政支出、金融机构存贷款、保险机构、保险业务开展和山东省辖区证券市场等方面的资料。

二、本篇资料的来源

1.财政部分的资料来源于省财政厅。根据财政部2019年《财政收支分类科目》，财政支出科目变动较大，与往年不可比。

2.金融方面的资料来源于中国人民银行济南分行。

3.保险方面的资料来源于中国银保监会山东监管局。

4.证券方面的资料来源于中国证监会山东监管局。

5.本篇资料由省统计局综合处整理。

Brief Introduction

I. Main Content

Data in this chapter show the conditions of local government budgetary finance, banking and insurance,and securities, including government revenue and expenditure, credit funds, cash income and expenses, statistics on insurance companies and basic situation of securities markets in Shandong province.

II. Source of Data

（1）Data on local government finance are provided by Shandong Provincial Department of Finance. Because of reform of Government Revenue and Expenditure Classification Items issued by the Ministry of Finance of China in 2019,data on items cannot be compared with those of preceding years.

（2）Data on banking are provided by Jinan Branch of the People's Bank of China.

（3）Data on insurance are provided by China Bank and Insurance Regulatory Commission of Shandong Bureau.

（4）Data on securities are provided by China Securities Regulatory Commission of Shandong Bureau.

（5）Data in this chapter are prepared and compiled by the Division of Comprehensive Statistics of Shandong Provincial Bureau of Statistics.

8-1 主要年份一般公共预算收入

General Public Budget Revenue in Major Years

单位:万元 (10 000 yuan)

年 份 Year	一般公共预算收入 General Public Budget Revenue	税收收入 Tax Revenue	增值税 Value Added Tax	营业税 Business Tax	企业所得税 Corporate Income Tax	个人所得税 Individual Income Tax	城市维护建设税 City Maintenance and Construction Tax	房产税 House Property Tax	印花税 Stamp Tax
1950	44253	35209							
1952	76284	62545							
1955	89333	79914							
1957	107262	92112							
1962	125506	96577							
1965	164766	100184							
1970	309438	167361							
1975	459668	233132							
1976	496749	270119							
1977	559590	313898							
1978	641286	327465							
1979	569948	322814							
1980	481097	335362							
1981	511850	368177	471			3			
1982	492888	416477	3001			5			
1983	504050	428911	12980			8			
1984	536022	484039	21457	13611		15			
1985	675316	638230	45950	101566		216	30811		
1986	621535	567351	86294	131137		498	37058	440	
1987	727901	652813	108184	159799		515	41417	10663	
1988	826814	825681	192216	216442		371	51037	11012	362
1989	1009416	973118	223717	274118		452	59324	14781	7451
1990	1091082	1058745	241241	291283	84831	687	63936	19110	5754
1991	1285184	1145170	264599	315116	89766	744	71381	26116	5994
1992	1393225	1287334	312552	367710	76817	980	77163	27263	6175
1993	1943978	1908554	545599	458562	85753	1566	90282	32420	6515
1994	1346611	1264642	363371	311355	163942	22983	117238	38577	7115
1995	1790025	1635139	416401	405456	256396	55930	140782	49773	9273
1996	2416742	2156333	518976	515829	365781	89493	172075	61064	10053
1997	3044232	2648693	617844	622148	484919	126801	202164	80812	13373
1998	3523912	3019024	701402	752239	468054	46780	131149	226211	107540
1999	4044829	3429430	782176	789669	631666	187585	238123	134879	19983
2000	4636788	3929022	896895	876638	818659	247492	276205	155591	22440
2001	5731793	4883422	1002918	926921	1491110	369925	290458	165321	26963
2002	6102242	4950266	1112319	1176414	783934	310934	307978	209770	37256
2003	7137877	5582820	1260824	1447077	664382	260262	444019	244706	46613
2004	8283306	6274331	1160390	1764502	860624	319637	549266	267768	62914
2005	10731250	8264612	1930040	2177928	1108282	388938	659514	327950	92515
2006	13562526	10357905	2428345	2717252	1482753	458361	784298	387000	123031
2007	16753980	13083516	2907862	3397121	1985020	568145	924642	443522	159005
2008	19570541	15335324	3337763	3960900	2299728	611251	1041367	472576	203026
2009	21986324	17203455	3244846	4706109	2203040	646665	1090776	578637	238728
2010	27493842	21498997	3782348	6315107	2933058	810098	1307440	646535	337443
2011	34559267	26031329	4138174	7657247	3985551	965805	1796032	740189	411070
2012	40594301	30502010	4381207	8966409	4416434	951065	1988839	1008346	465851
2013	45599463	35334906	4895590	10683275	4459540	1045930	2178411	1117476	528630
2014	50268273	39657605	5969647	11359162	4830098	1151842	2313253	1224873	605607
2015	55293253	42031178	5949766	12523983	4987224	1431225	2437121	1338572	594147
2016	58601836	42125903	11297486	6504453	5032373	1431522	2508344	1433639	612587
2017	60986324	44194025	17059602		6202953	1867335	2618202	1578095	747811
2018	64853959	48979231	19021182		6773754	2152981	3064603	1682525	809162
2019	65267095	48492909	19586652		6962049	1474723	2901252	1667267	743334
2020	65599306	47576242	18144737		6865544	1820627	2839694	1655720	836298
2021	72844608	54759900	20303130		8674330	2434028	3247197	1889612	1095060

注:1.本表中1994年以来的财政收入及分组均系新口径数,与历史资料不可比。
2.2016开始,增值税和营业税均系新口径数,与历史资料不可比。

a)Data from 1994 are based on new grouping method,so they cannot compare with other data.

b)Since 2016,Data of Value-added Tax and business Tax are based on new method,so they cannot compare with other data.

8-2 1950-2006年地方财政支出

Total Local Government Budgetary Expenditure from 1950 to 2006

单位:万元 (10 000 yuan)

年份 Year	地方财政支出 Expenditure of Local Government	#基本建设 Expenditure for Capital Construction	#城市维护费 Expenditure on City Maintenance	#支援农业支出 Expenditure for Agriculture	#文教科学卫生事业费 Expenditure for Culture, Education, Science and Health	#行政管理费 Expenditure for Government Administration
1950	10281	556	79	266		4704
1951	15965	3221	490	364		7357
1952	31886	8860	245	735		8332
1953	32272	5719	263	433		9548
1954	33657	6505	245	1447		9381
1955	31143	4023	209	1954		9868
1956	47155	13244	107	3484		12695
1957	49164	10522	201	4770		11790
1958	120740	75087	67	4468		12461
1959	158857	78459	22	16116		14162
1960	239314	98855	82	23717		14571
1961	135988	19073	69	27392		13612
1962	63594	6560	334	9526		11753
1963	79714	10271	1018	12029		13054
1964	89615	17557	1535	12620		13212
1965	95407	18711	1807	10048		13144
1966	104100	24115	1690	10425		13691
1967	102007	33442	1669	9728		12064
1968	88752	31016	1719	7476		12264
1969	113952	49590	1756	7683		12669
1970	142528	70447	1805	8389		14245
1971	159105	67943	1743	11247		17779
1972	188907	82551	1621	15603		19336
1973	194872	66635	2419	21980		18541
1974	191061	56996	2005	24284		18435
1975	212560	52389	2194	26906		21241
1976	214205	48383	2579	29119		22899
1977	226136	48648	2610	32399		24449
1978	319044	83503	3750	40221		26553
1979	316239	69982	9535	41812	77298	31908
1980	300736	46680	9484	38422	90951	39017
1981	255341	32150	13144	28754	94093	39200
1982	294482	32395	17044	37525	110039	45512
1983	324119	39875	18184	38058	122536	52391
1984	389763	51801	22063	39512	144038	69508
1985	512953	55562	39340	42453	174126	70091
1986	679384	63375	47595	49892	208135	79655
1987	752168	48880	48156	57550	219751	83423
1988	940725	59630	63024	78301	278458	114421
1989	1136714	55472	75062	102293	324427	98493
1990	1238530	78060	76532	111848	354574	107220
1991	1320610	73926	80209	116383	390775	121071
1992	1456988	85542	89276	141474	457972	158948
1993	1883646	115922	104912	163489	536522	208572
1994	2187683	100904	121656	176277	721820	269520
1995	2758656	179597	163339	224793	832336	315337
1996	3589836	248334	226014	276556	1032168	402325
1997	4233342	239629	281070	367611	1182892	456970
1998	4878175	318452	367382	377198	1325393	501269
1999	5500034	325120	351390	402651	1453237	544497
2000	6130774	295068	388802	411914	1677928	622058
2001	7537781	409608	485770	478933	1936046	743144
2002	8606484	440415	547982	557939	2290732	900217
2003	10106395	636760	685165	618116	2553316	1123337
2004	11893716	600330	885953	731073	3091148	1312928
2005	14662271	704835	1179667	895847	3751654	1629489
2006	18334400	821963	1470287	1083756	4542846	1929519

8-3 1979-2006年财政支出中用于文、教、科、卫的支出

Expense on Culture,Education,Science and Health from 1979 to 2006

单位:万元 (10 000 yuan)

年份 Year	合计 Total	文体广播事业费 Operating Expenses for Culture,Sports and Broadcast	教育事业费 Operating Expenses for Education	科学事业费 Operating Expenses for Science	卫生经费 Operating Expenses for Health	科技三项经费 Science and Technology Promotion Funds
1979	80348	9219	43077	4141	20098	3813
1980	93350	9974	53296	4060	23290	2730
1981	95577	9791	54453	4094	24965	2274
1982	111630	11702	62804	4335	29737	3052
1983	125430	14353	67656	5040	33667	4714
1984	145710	18779	77533	6738	37382	5278
1985	175562	22631	97565	6513	44117	4736
1986	209611	29869	114757	8056	50910	6019
1987	225197	30555	125465	7053	56678	5446
1988	284003	39108	161889	10205	67256	5545
1989	333489	43029	187894	10535	82969	9062
1990	363035	48165	202060	11646	92703	8461
1991	401036	54145	225118	12757	98755	10261
1992	470129	61127	271681	14629	110310	12382
1993	568801	70133	337052	16678	129131	15807
1994	738553	84780	464330	22340	150028	17075
1995	856648	112065	523754	22551	173966	24312
1996	1066333	124463	670721	27256	209728	34165
1997	1229252	154418	753374	34974	240126	46360
1998	1388027	150517	886208	35703	252965	62634
1999	1532952	159272	999902	35491	258572	79715
2000	1770387	175745	1181042	38543	282598	92459
2001	2051303	206502	1377529	45428	306587	115257
2002	2427593	274203	1627761	53056	335712	136861
2003	2693986	307350	1791484	58375	396107	140670
2004	3091148	366895	2048284	65970	452199	157800
2005	3751654	449415	2487484	76471	544085	194199
2006	4542846	519674	2922839	90544	733206	276583

8-4 一般公共预算收入

General Public Budget Revenue

单位:万元 (10 000 yuan)

类别	Category	2017	2018	2019	2020	2021
一般公共预算收入	**General Public Budget Revenue**	**60986324**	**64853959**	**65267095**	**65599306**	**72844608**
一、税收收入	**Tax Revenue**	**44194025**	**48979231**	**48492909**	**47576242**	**54759900**
增值税	Value Added Tax	17059602	19021182	19586652	18144737	20303130
企业所得税	Corporate Income Tax	6202953	6773754	6962049	6865544	8674330
个人所得税	Individual Income Tax	1867335	2152981	1474723	1820627	2434028
资源税	Resource Tax	995617	1197478	1199824	1082741	1261539
城市维护建设税	City Maintenance and Construction Tax	2618202	3064603	2901252	2839694	3247197
房产税	House Property Tax	1578095	1682525	1667267	1655720	1889612
印花税	Stamp Tax	747811	809162	743334	836298	1095060
城镇土地使用税	Urban land Use Tax	3981763	3968395	3372743	2998933	3025349
土地增值税	Land Appreciation Tax	3671771	3907890	4042826	4333819	4871132
车船税	Tax on vehicles and Boat Operation	693744	758480	781048	822964	944339
耕地占用税	Farm Land Occupation Tax	1632367	1192855	972500	976708	974605
契　税	Deed Tax	3125176	4285778	4555154	5028331	5886643
烟叶税	Tobacco Leaf Tax	19589	17077	21266	23489	23594
环境保护税	Environmental Tax		147071	193865	134127	118411
其他税收收入	Other Tax			18406	12510	10931
二、非税收入	**Non-tax Revenue**	**16792299**	**15874728**	**16774186**	**18023064**	**18084708**
专项收入	Special Program Receipts	3103868	3519647	3474406	3601058	3789355
行政事业性收费收入	Charge of Administrative and Institutional Units	3202844	3035195	3072246	3083218	3369904
罚没收入	Penalty Receipts	1802335	1949593	2087842	2251619	2997949
国有资本经营收入	Operating Income from Government Capital	306582	255264	713007	709745	373656
国有资源(资产)有偿使用收入	Income from Use of State-owned Resources (Assets)	7556093	6480027	6435974	7435801	6191908
其他收入	Other Non-tax Receipts	820577	635002	990711	941623	1361936

8-5 一般公共预算支出
General Public Budget Expenditure

单位:万元 (10 000 yuan)

类 别	Category	2017	2018	2019	2020	2021
一般公共预算支出	**General Public Budget Expenditure**	**92583984**	**101009606**	**107397560**	**112335163**	**117131607**
一般公共服务支出	Expenditure for General Public Services	8575099	9433490	10619500	11180676	11361128
公共安全支出	Expenditure for Public Security	5660530	6449501	6332058	6316573	6351953
教育支出	Expenditure for Education	18899972	20065026	21561355	22838368	24110936
科学技术支出	Expenditure for Science and Technology	1957718	2327392	3057556	2986162	3723197
文化旅游体育与传媒支出	Expenditure for Culture, Tourism, Sport and Media	1418993	1535220	1895034	1701115	1803572
社会保障和就业支出	Expenditure for Social Safety Net and Employment Effort	11319595	12539881	14446327	16575296	18633891
卫生健康支出	Expenditure for Health	8292714	8851487	9120675	10455012	10927223
城乡社区支出	Expenditure for Urban and Rural Community Affairs	10759203	11097209	10702489	10538645	10873296
农林水支出	Expenditure for Agriculture, Forestry and Water Conservancy	9535911	9984950	10759789	10652864	10269455
交通运输支出	Expenditure for Transportation	3673120	4127928	3777587	3758935	3262570
资源勘探工业信息等支出	Expenditure for Affairs of ResourceExploration and Industrial Information	1986534	2268809	2161059	2594688	2589794
商业服务业等支出	Expenditure for Affairs of Commerce and Services	839616	1021953	558267	742788	847941
自然资源海洋气象等支出	Expenditure for Natural Ocean and Weather	1446349	1291748	1355145	1311128	1362818
住房保障支出	Expenditure for Affairs of Housing Security	3098883	3438172	2392927	2516290	2806846

注：2019年起，文化体育与传媒支出更名为文化旅游体育与传媒支出，医疗卫生与计划生育支出更名为卫生健康支出，国土海洋气象等支出更名为自然资源海洋气象等支出。

a)Since 2019,Expenditure for Culture, Sport and Media renames to Expenditure for Culture,Tourism,Sport and Media.Expenditure for Medical and Health Care,and Family Planning renames to Expenditure for Health.Expenditure for Affairs of of Land,Ocean and Weather renames to Expenditure for Natural Ocean and Weather

8-6 各市一般公共预算收入(2021年)
General Public Budget Revenue by Region (2021)

单位:万元 (10 000 yuan)

地 区	Region	一般公共预算收入 General Public Budget Revenue	税收收入 Tax Revenue	增值税 Value Added Tax	企业所得税 Corporate Income Tax	个人所得税 Individual Income Tax	资源税 Resource Tax
全省总计	**Total**	**72844608**	**54759900**	**20303130**	**8674330**	**2434028**	**1261539**
济南市	Jinan	10076073	7764785	2680312	1320640	427753	65976
青岛市	Qingdao	13682971	10168782	3629995	1922765	676918	26465
淄博市	Zibo	3689765	2730749	1191171	392260	138074	58915
枣庄市	Zaozhuang	1589062	1224693	457405	133176	34788	66240
东营市	Dongying	2618341	1849614	651862	224728	59843	29769
烟台市	Yantai	6466386	4812753	1606748	764014	395566	136117
潍坊市	Weifang	6569006	4995734	1921299	613050	151484	74336
济宁市	Jining	4405237	3318043	1126838	475231	91489	202228
泰安市	Tai'an	2305436	1730827	742937	215123	53727	58842
威海市	Weihai	2668789	1988041	668240	229193	77093	14321
日照市	Rizhao	1874860	1515513	552107	348000	45465	23758
临沂市	Linyi	4094785	3345201	1305289	403681	89788	58111
德州市	Dezhou	2340858	1799352	709472	240221	54091	19673
聊城市	Liaocheng	2303156	1738130	681562	257601	48326	22798
滨州市	Binzhou	2873060	2161562	957046	362756	37722	25004
菏泽市	Heze	2838888	2186184	816140	229535	51901	96112

8-6 续表 1 continued

单位:万元 (10 000 yuan)

地 区	Region	城市维护建设税 City Maintenance and Construction Tax	房产税 House Property Tax	城镇土地使用税 Urban Land Use Tax	土 地增值税 Land Appreciation Tax	耕 地占用税 Farm Land Occupation Tax	契 税 Contract Tax	其他各项税收收入 Other Tax Revenue
全省总计	**Total**	**3247197**	**1889612**	**3025349**	**4871132**	**974605**	**5886643**	**2192335**
济 南 市	Jinan	472017	274078	253968	1016281	54257	893405	306098
青 岛 市	Qingdao	654071	418030	318782	1153501	57883	968082	342290
淄 博 市	Zibo	206347	94874	165007	112036	41784	223581	106700
枣 庄 市	Zaozhuang	82631	30245	55634	82586	27590	207325	47073
东 营 市	Dongying	166477	76486	292251	70398	26513	146768	104519
烟 台 市	Yantai	235792	182592	312789	474618	69505	455633	179379
潍 坊 市	Weifang	320586	176214	385402	404416	150621	557604	240722
济 宁 市	Jining	158712	98388	177222	297436	173299	401538	115662
泰 安 市	Tai'an	116382	48492	86369	121197	40077	180548	67133
威 海 市	Weihai	99396	141725	206526	154470	40692	284657	71728
日 照 市	Rizhao	83711	46563	88355	79436	24349	126482	97287
临 沂 市	Linyi	180740	86671	184027	304174	45279	511958	175483
德 州 市	Dezhou	97576	55862	121848	171288	21173	233553	74595
聊 城 市	Liaocheng	101618	47932	80031	158814	22808	237626	79014
滨 州 市	Binzhou	157195	67535	171089	92042	35058	161118	94997
菏 泽 市	Heze	113946	43925	126049	178439	143717	296765	89655

8-6 续表 2 continued

单位:万元 (10 000 yuan)

地 区	Region	非税收入 Non-tax Revenue	专项收入 Special Program Receipts	行政事业性收费收入 Charge of Administrative and Institutional Units	罚没收入 Penalty Receipts	国有资本经营收入 Operating Income from Government Capital	国有资源(资产)有偿使用收入 Income from Use of State-owned Resources (Assets)	其他收入 Other Non-tax Receipts
全省总计	**Total**	**18084708**	**3789355**	**3369904**	**2997949**	**373656**	**6191908**	**1361936**
济 南 市	Jinan	2311288	593365	519433	225083	42480	789345	141582
青 岛 市	Qingdao	3514189	1109311	669505	437704	76699	681105	539865
淄 博 市	Zibo	959016	202267	86804	190571		421793	57581
枣 庄 市	Zaozhuang	364369	66201	76813	133640	1405	63475	22835
东 营 市	Dongying	768727	199152	98747	72967		354707	43154
烟 台 市	Yantai	1653633	223748	160302	159927	22268	1018735	68653
潍 坊 市	Weifang	1573272	283345	300153	318383	66222	562558	42611
济 宁 市	Jining	1087194	146204	151952	160711	4850	567806	55671
泰 安 市	Tai'an	574609	102891	105632	98094		236638	31354
威 海 市	Weihai	680748	88847	162950	91658	109565	221535	6193
日 照 市	Rizhao	359347	77780	73822	106145	18493	61603	21504
临 沂 市	Linyi	749584	168245	180869	246644	58	115029	38739
德 州 市	Dezhou	541506	88770	79734	111999		230586	30417
聊 城 市	Liaocheng	565026	99270	170888	132830	7465	121188	33385
滨 州 市	Binzhou	711498	141762	224890	200576	5251	106693	32326
菏 泽 市	Heze	652704	132896	116892	219270	18900	115027	49719

8-7 各市一般公共预算支出(2021年)

General Public Budget Expenditure by Region (2021)

单位:万元 (10 000 yuan)

地区	Region	一般公共预算支出 General Public Budget Expenditure	一般公共服务支出 Expenditure for General Public Service	公共安全支出 Expenditure for Public Security	教育支出 Expenditure for Education	科学技术支出 Expenditure for Science and Technology	文化旅游体育与传媒支出 Expenditure for Culture, Tourism, Sport and Media	社会保障和就业支出 Expenditure for Social Safety Net and Employment Effort	卫生健康支出 Expenditure for Health
全省总计	**Total**	**117131607**	**11361128**	**6351953**	**24110936**	**3723197**	**1803572**	**18633891**	**10927223**
济南市	Jinan	12927074	1333132	629098	2131020	411774	122465	2038253	1117061
青岛市	Qingdao	17067635	1991186	1095451	3088039	513252	252504	2431109	1244611
淄博市	Zibo	5226768	589365	342093	1073189	105260	92326	809550	484979
枣庄市	Zaozhuang	2738792	314443	167842	648041	24046	31554	602163	354646
东营市	Dongying	3011302	396079	162857	610382	57943	44372	293934	261739
烟台市	Yantai	8029313	789088	445979	1367916	311999	138807	1540352	783199
潍坊市	Weifang	8798370	791897	431150	2024365	231351	184200	1347853	807034
济宁市	Jining	7272310	835597	374576	1688587	76960	141057	1076421	829075
泰安市	Tai'an	4281902	375300	182454	918945	37279	53479	812840	484368
威海市	Weihai	3434977	347243	178255	854521	66588	44424	454233	314193
日照市	Rizhao	2705827	302874	155528	610481	76675	38610	496885	337408
临沂市	Linyi	8066215	758689	409476	1988972	92706	135308	1436485	1037735
德州市	Dezhou	4933640	436990	262115	901688	97515	77836	879404	545370
聊城市	Liaocheng	4879894	516261	238951	1044708	18298	62605	780569	578118
滨州市	Binzhou	4781796	450849	209491	755793	258731	106830	680983	470118
菏泽市	Heze	6331229	593371	259081	1276354	26699	67646	1288286	876079

8-7 续表 continued

单位:万元 (10 000 yuan)

地区	Region	节能环保支出 Expenditure for Environment Protection	城乡社区支出 Expenditure for Urban and Rural Community Affairs	农林水支出 Expenditure for Agriculture, Forestry and Water Conservancy	交通运输支出 Expenditure for Transportation	资源勘探工业信息等支出 Expenditure for Affairs of Resource Exploration and Industrial Information	商业服务业等支出 Expenditure for Affairs of Commerce and Services	金融支出 Expenditure for Financial Affairs	自然资源海洋气象等支出 Expenditure for Natural, Ocean and Weather	住房保障支出 Expenditure for Affairs of Housing Security
全省总计	**Total**	**2667867**	**10873296**	**10269455**	**3262570**	**2589794**	**847941**	**1153317**	**1362818**	**2806846**
济南市	Jinan	395348	2933964	672251	136479	210372	80329	31878	162125	295116
青岛市	Qingdao	177057	2448340	852668	370748	814641	200009	308021	132927	461246
淄博市	Zibo	191857	308272	391834	104781	212876	82643	18495	53446	113272
枣庄市	Zaozhuang	40221	108878	190477	52115	35670	9668	385	18291	43677
东营市	Dongying	69955	351218	239703	87815	87926	27672	25330	67800	41078
烟台市	Yantai	149628	756179	499474	148917	319351	32475	160755	98550	118484
潍坊市	Weifang	252489	977930	794984	157356	123472	56404	96165	95476	83237
济宁市	Jining	233346	551338	722827	185744	108825	29833	6415	82170	90442
泰安市	Tai'an	72491	371920	461441	75856	94714	24719	963	39585	76159
威海市	Weihai	69313	173030	437067	78803	44826	28589	10738	62691	121413
日照市	Rizhao	44450	132436	216728	75514	18037	18072	4364	32588	59526
临沂市	Linyi	155239	358452	876536	196071	66532	24916	48954	66495	217849
德州市	Dezhou	166238	325949	483805	112074	65202	89793	10208	65403	246890
聊城市	Liaocheng	274897	333584	497146	154304	60967	16081	3882	38986	133799
滨州市	Binzhou	153115	497842	516731	103043	74585	9887	24543	63064	239665
菏泽市	Heze	137975	231802	750027	155117	163335	24621	981	103088	278174

8-8 主要年份金融机构人民币存款余额

RMB Deposits of Financial Institutions in Major Years

单位:亿元 (100 million yuan)

年份 Year	存款余额 Deposits	住户存款 Household Deposits	非金融企业存款 Non-financial Corporate Deposits	广义政府存款 General Government Deposits	非银行业金融机构存款 Non-bank Financial Intermediary Deposits
1952	2.8				
1955	6.7				
1957	6.7				
1962	14.8				
1965	17.4				
1970	54.0				
1975	72.2				
1976	76.5				
1977	78.2				
1978	90.0				
1979	65.6				
1980	87.9				
1981	113.6				
1982	123.1				
1983	155.5				
1984	233.3				
1985	278.8				
1986	351.6				
1987	470.2				
1988	591.3				
1989	724.7				
1990	934.1				
1991	1163.6				
1992	1448.3				
1993	1816.6				
1994	2522.5				
1995	3424.4				
1996	4293.8				
1997	4969.8				
1998	5755.5				
1999	6563.0				
2000	7471.2				
2001	8501.7				
2002	10247.8				
2003	12438.2				
2004	14514.3				
2005	17103.5				
2006	19634.0				
2007	22072.2				
2008	26930.2				
2009	34697.8				
2010	41105.0				
2011	46345.4				
2012	54301.5				
2013	62077.9				
2014	67498.3				
2015	74524.2	37320.0	22717.8	11470.9	2870.2
2016	83414.9	41350.9	26654.7	12672.0	2639.7
2017	88531.7	44035.8	27913.9	14356.5	2122.6
2018	94298.2	48435.0	28023.0	15777.7	1810.9
2019	102676.4	55232.1	30462.8	15106.9	1757.3
2020	116155.4	64258.4	34625.1	14800.8	2357.8
2021	127871.8	72255.3	37601.8	15129.3	2758.7

8-9 主要年份金融机构人民币贷款余额

RMB Loans of Financial Institutions in Major Years

单位:亿元 (100 million yuan)

年 份 Year	贷款余额 Loans	住户贷款 Household Loans	中长期贷款 Medium and Long-term Loans	企(事)业单位贷款 Loans to Non-financial Enterprises and Government Departments & Organizations	短期贷款 Short-term Loans	中长期贷款 Medium and Long-term Loans	非银行业金融机构贷款 Non-bank Financial Intermediary Loans
1952	1.6						
1955	14.0						
1957	16.9						
1962	41.5						
1965	39.0						
1970	66.9						
1975	91.8						
1976	102.9						
1977	120.9						
1978	133.7						
1979	124.9						
1980	180.2						
1981	206.4						
1982	235.4						
1983	265.0						
1984	366.7						
1985	446.5						
1986	554.9						
1987	667.8						
1988	803.1						
1989	941.3						
1990	1166.8						
1991	1428.0						
1992	1720.6						
1993	2079.1						
1994	2520.4						
1995	3128.9						
1996	3680.2						
1997	4456.7						
1998	5106.8						
1999	5679.9						
2000	6209.0						
2001	7017.7						
2002	8536.6						
2003	10467.1						
2004	11782.8						
2005	13381.7						
2006	15709.6						
2007	17545.1						
2008	20053.9						
2009	25961.3						
2010	30722.6						
2011	35179.0						
2012	40021.5						
2013	44761.3						
2014	50058.6						
2015	55437.0	13980.4	9798.3	41328.7	22592.3	15814.0	2.1
2016	61726.9	16496.6	12477.7	45096.4	22982.4	18282.5	7.1
2017	67576.0	20070.2	15656.9	47357.9	23349.6	21619.1	26.4
2018	74879.4	24226.3	19079.3	50507.6	22587.6	24333.5	5.0
2019	83703.0	29431.7	23048.9	54147.0	21850.1	27638.4	22.0
2020	95411.6	35015.0	27384.9	60298.6	23051.5	31910.2	
2021	108436.8	40300.8	31210.0	68019.5	24295.8	36975.6	

注：自2020年起，“非金融企业及机关团体贷款”更名为“企(事)业单位贷款”。

a) Since 2020,"Non-financial Corporate and Institution Loans" was changed its name to "Loans to Non-financial Enterprises and Government Departments & Organizations".

8-10 金融机构本外币信贷收支情况(2021年)

RMB and Foreign Currencies Credit Funds Balance Sheet of Financial Institution (2021)

单位:亿元 (100 million yuan)

类 别	Category	2021年末余额 2021 Year-end	比年初增减额 Increase/ Decrease from Year Beginning
各项存款	**Deposits in Various Forms**	**130482.1**	**12132.7**
境内存款	Domestic Deposits	130018.1	12003.3
住户存款	Household Deposits	72609.8	7993.2
活期存款	Demand Deposits	19421.5	840.6
定期及其他存款	Fixed and Other Deposits	53188.3	7152.6
非金融企业存款	Non-financial Corporate Deposits	39511.7	3327.0
活期存款	Demand Deposits	14816.5	385.0
定期及其他存款	Fixed and Other Deposits	24695.2	2942.0
广义政府存款	General Government Deposits	15131.9	282.0
财政性存款	Fiscal Deposits	1269.9	100.0
机关团体存款	Non-profit Institution Deposits	13861.9	182.0
非银行业金融机构存款	Non-bank Financial Intermediary Deposits	2764.7	401.0
境外存款	Overseas Deposits	464.0	129.4
各项贷款	**Loans in Various Forms**	**111035.4**	**13154.8**
境内贷款	Domestic Loans	109686.2	13263.5
住户贷款	Household Loans	40301.9	5286.1
短期贷款	Short-term Loans	9091.8	1460.2
消费贷款	Consumption Loans	3177.3	411.9
经营贷款	Business Loans	5914.5	1048.3
中长期贷款	Medium and Long-term Loans	31210.1	3825.9
消费贷款	Consumption Loans	27688.8	3236.9
经营贷款	Business Loans	3521.3	589.0
企（事）业单位贷款	Loans to Non-financial Enterprises and Government Departments & Organizations	69384.3	7977.4
短期贷款	Short-term Loans	25447.5	1534.5
中长期贷款	Medium and Long-term Loans	37188.3	5039.4
票据融资	Bill Financing	6048.2	1333.3
融资租赁	Financial Leases	544.1	46.0
各项垫款	Advances	156.2	24.2
非银行业金融机构贷款	Non-bank Financial Intermediary Loans		
境外贷款	Overseas Loans	1349.2	-108.7

8-11 金融机构人民币信贷收支情况(2021年)

RMB Credit Funds Balance Sheet of Financial Institution (2021)

单位:亿元 (100 million yuan)

类别	Category	2021年末余额 2021 Year-end	比年初增减额 Increase/ Decrease from Year Beginning
各项存款	**Deposits in Various Forms**	**127871.8**	**11716.5**
境内存款	Domestic Deposits	127745.0	11703.0
住户存款	Household Deposits	72255.3	7999.9
活期存款	Demand Deposits	19208.3	836.3
定期及其他存款	Fixed and Other Deposits	53047.1	7163.6
非金融企业存款	Non-financial Corporate Deposits	37601.8	3007.8
活期存款	Demand Deposits	13720.3	236.5
定期及其他存款	Fixed and Other Deposits	23881.5	2771.2
广义政府存款	General Government Deposits	15129.3	294.4
财政性存款	Fiscal Deposits	1269.9	100.0
机关团体存款	Non-profit Institution Deposits	13859.3	194.4
非银行业金融机构存款	Non-bank Financial Intermediary Deposits	2758.7	400.9
境外存款	Overseas Deposits	126.8	13.5
各项贷款	**Loans in Various Forms**	**108436.8**	**13025.2**
境内贷款	Domestic Loans	108320.2	13006.8
住户贷款	Household Loans	40300.8	5285.9
短期贷款	Short-term Loans	9090.7	1460.1
消费贷款	Consumption Loans	3176.2	411.8
经营贷款	Business Loans	5914.5	1048.3
中长期贷款	Medium and Long-term Loans	31210.0	3825.9
消费贷款	Consumption Loans	27688.7	3236.9
经营贷款	Business Loans	3521.3	589.0
企（事）业单位贷款	Loans to Non-financial Enterprises and Government Departments & Organizations	68019.5	7720.9
短期贷款	Short-term Loans	24295.8	1280.2
中长期贷款	Medium and Long-term Loans	36975.6	5029.4
票据融资	Bill Financing	6048.2	1333.3
融资租赁	Financial Leases	544.1	46.0
各项垫款	Advances	155.7	31.9
非银行业金融机构贷款	Non-bank Financial Intermediary Loans		
境外贷款	Overseas Loans	116.5	18.4

8-12 金融机构分行业本外币贷款情况(2021年)
Loans of RMB and Foreign Currencies of Financial institutions by sector (2021)

单位:亿元 (100 million yuan)

行业	Sector	2021年末余额 2021 Year-end	比年初增减额 Increase/Decrease from Year Beginning
贷款总计	**Total**	**105282.6**	**11928.7**
农、林、牧、渔业	Agriculture,Forestry,Animal Husbandry and Fishing	769.5	78.9
采矿业	Mining	2042.0	246.5
制造业	Manufacturing	14652.9	588.1
电力、燃气及水的生产和供应业	Production and Supply of Electric Power and Heat Power	3912.0	557.9
建筑业	Construction	4629.7	700.1
批发和零售业	Wholesale and Retail Trade	6205.9	784.4
交通运输、仓储和邮政业	Traffic,Transport,Storage and Post	7396.7	1254.4
住宿和餐饮业	Hotels and Catering Services	285.9	-18.6
信息传输、软件和信息技术服务业	Information Transfer, Software and Information Technology Services	337.2	45.2
金融业	Financial Intermediation	1124.0	81.4
房地产业	Real Estate	4226.7	-136.7
租赁和商务服务业	Leasing and Business Services	9183.8	1516.6
科学研究和技术服务业	Scientific Research and Technical Service	349.6	61.6
水利、环境和公共设施管理业	Management of Water Conservancy,Environment and Public Facilities	7094.9	736.4
居民服务、修理和其他服务业	Households Services, Repair and Other Services	114.6	14.7
教　育	Education	483.4	114.8
卫生和社会工作	Health and Social Work	543.3	61.9
文化、体育和娱乐业	Culture,Sports and Entertainment	260.5	68.2
公共管理、社会保障和社会组织	Public management,Social Security and Social Organization	19.2	-4.5
国际组织	International Organization		

8-13 各市金融机构本外币存贷款余额(2021年)
RMB and Foreign Currencies Deposits and Loans of Financial Institutions by Region(2021)

单位:亿元 (100 million yuan)

地区	Region	各项存款 Total Deposits		#住户存款 Household Deposits		各项贷款 Total Loans	
		余额 Year-end	比年初增减 Increase/Decrease from Year Beginning	余额 Year-end	比年初增减 Increase/Decrease from Year Beginning	余额 Year-end	比年初增减 Increase/Decrease from Year Beginning
全省总计	**Total**	**130482.1**	**12132.7**	**72609.8**	**7993.2**	**111035.4**	**13154.8**
济南市	Jinan	23437.0	2372.0	8620.5	972.9	23313.2	2593.0
青岛市	Qingdao	22374.9	1867.7	9152.9	994.5	24089.1	3024.3
淄博市	Zibo	6167.6	555.1	4004.0	457.4	4287.7	407.8
枣庄市	Zaozhuang	2590.8	180.9	1831.9	168.1	2011.2	280.9
东营市	Dongying	4610.5	487.7	2451.6	296.0	3412.7	79.0
烟台市	Yantai	11013.5	1015.7	6470.3	636.4	7477.1	815.2
潍坊市	Weifang	11217.8	1141.3	6913.3	732.4	8873.0	1298.9
济宁市	Jining	7257.7	689.6	4838.0	494.9	5600.9	817.9
泰安市	Tai'an	4947.9	345.2	3478.7	407.4	3579.9	442.5
威海市	Weihai	5246.0	513.3	3274.2	367.0	4048.3	651.7
日照市	Rizhao	3306.1	178.9	2010.8	189.3	3365.5	391.2
临沂市	Linyi	8960.3	767.7	5894.7	681.6	8170.0	1161.3
德州市	Dezhou	4777.0	480.7	3459.7	399.7	2903.0	368.1
聊城市	Liaocheng	4898.8	532.5	3484.3	383.5	3135.4	249.6
滨州市	Binzhou	3767.0	324.4	2273.3	276.8	3067.6	163.4
菏泽市	Heze	5619.7	580.4	4451.0	537.2	3457.3	435.0

8-14 1997-2021年保险费收入和赔款给付

Premium and Payment of Insurance Companies 1997 to 2021

年 份 Year	保险费收入 (万元) Premium (10 000 yuan)	赔款及给付支出 (万元) Settled Claim and Payment (10 000 yuan)	简单赔付率 (%) Simple Payment Rate (%)
1997	785298	317889	40.5
1998	837500	294648	35.2
1999	956496	365490	38.2
2000	1110622	402204	36.2
2001	1533204	409588	26.7
2002	2238236	456801	20.4
2003	2835306	561804	19.8
2004	3171584	656966	20.7
2005	3408050	766254	22.5
2006	3962203	1209078	30.5
2007	5017177	1717385	34.2
2008	6739812	1983902	29.4
2009	7928870	2283924	28.8
2010	10300687	2286398	22.2
2011	10360352	2712276	26.2
2012	11280360	3245582	28.8
2013	12804211	4416570	34.5
2014	14549297	5189703	35.7
2015	17876030	6221728	34.8
2016	23021888	7868526	34.2
2017	27380627	8312832	30.4
2018	29598304	9299333	31.4
2019	32388907	9034125	27.9
2020	34824927	10364798	29.8
2021	32783125	11403123	34.8

注：2021年末数据不含四家风险处置机构（以下相关表同）。
a)The data of 2021 excludes four risk disposal institutions. The same applies to the relevant following tables.

8-15 人身保险公司主要业务指标(2021年)

Major Business Indicators of Life Insurance Companies (2021)

单位:万元 (10 000 yuan)

类 别	Category	保费收入 Premium Income	赔款支出 Indemnity Expenditure	年金给付 Total Annuity Payment	满期给付 Total Mature Payment	死伤医疗给付 Payment for Death,Injury and Medical Treatment
总 计	**Total**	**23351990**	**1134212**	**827151**	**2081334**	**1110535**
一、人寿保险	**Life Insurance**	**16831326**		**827151**	**1644756**	**264071**
(一)非分红产品	Non-dividend Insurance	9114544		394122	215408	154830
定期寿险	Time Insurance	63710			24	15520
两全寿险	Endowment Insurance	1411279		89254	200958	47673
终身寿险	WLL	3180367			755	60980
年 金	Total Annuity Payment	4459189		304867	13670	30657
(二)分红产品	Dividend Insurance	7650989		433030	1420229	96026
定期寿险	Time Insurance					
两全寿险	Endowment Insurance	4516180		144311	1308741	54049
终身寿险	WLL	885634			4	21131
年 金	Total Annuity Payment	2249175		288719	111484	20846
(三)投资连接产品	Investment Link Insurance	1243			3953	299
(四)万能产品	Universal Life Insurance	64551		-1	5166	12915
二、意外伤害保险	**Accident Injury Insurance**	**426186**	**118971**			
一年期以内	Within-One-year Period Business	58990	23596			
一年期及一年期以上	One-year Period and more Business	367196	95375			
三、健康保险	**Health Insurance**	**6094478**	**1015241**		**436578**	**846464**
一年期(及一年期以内)	Within-One-year Period Business	1393592	1015241			
一年期以上	One-year Period Business	4700886			436578	846464

8-16 财产保险公司主要业务指标(2021年)

Major Business Indicators of Insurance Companies(2021)

单位:万元 (10 000 yuan)

类 别	Category	保费收入 Premium	赔款支出 Payment
总 计	**Total**	**9431135**	**6249892**
机动车辆及第三者责任险	Motor Vehicle and Third Party Liability	5796929	4190239
企财险	Enterprise Property insurance	261071	136909
家财险	Family Property Insurance	60406	21001
工程险	Project Insurance	56872	42862
责任险	Liability Insurance	558887	280300
信用险	Credit Insurance	143960	82517
保证保险	Guarantee Insurance	478107	258975
船舶险	Ship Insurance	28076	17657
货运险	Freight Transport Insurance	98551	44330
特殊风险保险	Peculiar Risk Insurance	29866	8934
农业保险	Agriculture Insurance	564273	376985
健康险	Health Insurance	933459	663685
意外伤害险	Accident Injury Insurance	375521	92500
其 他	Other Property Insurance	45158	32998

8-17 各市保险业务情况(2021年)

Basic Statistics on Insurance by Region (2021)

单位:亿元 (100 million yuan)

地 区	Region	保费收入 Premium	财产险公司 Property Insurance Company	人身险公司 Life Insurance Company	赔款与给付 Claim and Payment	财产险公司 Property Insurance Company	人身险公司 Life Insurance Company
全省总计	**Total**	**3278.3**	**943.1**	**2335.2**	**1140.3**	**625.0**	**515.3**
济 南 市	Jinan	595.3	131.8	463.5	212.4	90.9	121.6
青 岛 市	Qingdao	461.8	156.4	305.4	162.4	99.6	62.8
淄 博 市	Zibo	196.6	39.9	156.7	56.5	25.0	31.4
枣 庄 市	Zaozhuang	87.2	26.2	60.9	34.0	17.5	16.5
东 营 市	Dongying	101.6	30.9	70.7	30.2	17.9	12.2
烟 台 市	Yantai	265.7	59.4	206.4	89.1	41.5	47.6
潍 坊 市	Weifang	267.0	79.4	187.7	95.3	52.9	42.3
济 宁 市	Jining	207.8	69.3	138.5	73.6	44.4	29.2
泰 安 市	Tai'an	129.4	31.9	97.5	43.1	20.9	22.2
威 海 市	Weihai	111.9	27.4	84.5	37.9	19.3	18.6
日 照 市	Rizhao	74.4	26.9	47.5	25.5	15.9	9.6
临 沂 市	Linyi	282.1	95.2	186.9	99.1	65.4	33.7
德 州 市	Dezhou	127.6	40.6	87.0	42.7	26.1	16.6
聊 城 市	Liaocheng	116.6	41.7	74.9	41.3	28.9	12.4
滨 州 市	Binzhou	111.3	37.6	73.7	40.9	25.8	15.1
菏 泽 市	Heze	144.2	48.3	95.9	54.3	30.9	23.4

8-18 山东省证券期货市场基本情况

Basic Situation of Securities and Futures Markets of Shandong Province

项　　目		Item		2020	2021
上市公司数	(家)	Number of Listed Companies	(unit)	229	270
#发行A股公司数	(家)	A Shares	(unit)	227	268
发行B股公司数	(家)	B Shares	(unit)	5	5
A、B股均发行公司数	(家)	Number of Listed Companies (A Shares and B Shares)	(unit)	3	3
境内、外均发行公司数	(家)	Companies Listed Overseas and Domestic	(unit)	12	12
ST公司数	(家)	Number of ST Listed Companies	(unit)	4	3
*ST公司数	(家)	*ST Listed Companies	(unit)	5	4
证券公司数	(家)	No.of Securities Companies	(unit)	2	3
证券公司分公司数	(家)	No.of Branches of Securities Companies	(unit)	124	133
证券公司营业部数	(家)	No.of Securities Business Department	(unit)	572	561
期货公司数	(家)	No.of Futures Broker Companies	(unit)	3	4
期货公司分公司数	(家)	No.of Branches of Futures Broker Companies	(unit)	66	79
期货公司营业部数	(家)	No.of Trading Offices of Futures Broker Companies	(unit)	95	91
证券投资咨询机构数	(家)	No.of Securities Investment Consultative Institutions	(unit)	13	13
证券投资者资金开户数	(万户)	No.of Opening Account of Securities Investors	(10 000 households)	1237.1	1441.7
上市公司当年境内募集资金总额	(亿元)	Total Domestic Capital Volume Collected by Listed Companies	(100 million yuan)	739.0	671.3
首次公开发行	(亿元)	IPO	(100 million yuan)	154.0	270.5
配股	(亿元)	Share Right Issued	(100 million yuan)	19.6	
增发	(亿元)	Adding the Share Issue	(100 million yuan)	186.9	363.2
可转债	(亿元)	Transferable Loans	(100 million yuan)	241.5	34.6
公司债	(亿元)	Corporate Bond	(100 million yuan)	60.0	3.0
市价总值	(亿元)	Total Market Value	(100 million yuan)	32375.4	39294.9
证券营业部代理证券交易额	(亿元)	Trading Volume of Securities Business Department	(100 million yuan)	196299.7	228655.8
期货经营机构代理交易额	(亿元)	Trading Volume of Agency by Futures Managerial Institutions	(100 million yuan)	207736.4	313654.0
全国中小企业股份转让系统挂牌公司	(家)	Listed Company on National SME Share Transfer System	(unit)	506	433
交易所公司债券发行金额	(亿元)	Issued Volume of Corporate Bonds Listed on the Exchange	(100 million yuan)	2875.7	3106.2
私募基金管理人登记数	(家)	Registration No.of Private investment fund managers	(unit)	707	836

注：证券营业部、期货公司营业数为已开业家数。

a)The number of securities business department(trading offices of futures broker companies) refers to those that has been opened.

8-19 各市证券期货市场基本情况(2021年)

Basic Situation of Securities and Futures Markets by Region (2021)

单位:家 (unit)

地 区	Region	上市公司 Number of Listed Companies	拟上市公司 Number of Listed Companies in plan	新三板挂牌公司 Number of New third board Listed Companies	证券公司 No.of Securities Companies	证券公司分公司 No.of Branches of Securities Companies
全省总计	**Total**	**270**	**166**	**433**	**3**	**133**
济南市	Jinan	43	28	113	1	61
青岛市	Qingdao	58	38	65	2	37
淄博市	Zibo	29	15	27		3
枣庄市	Zaozhuang	4	2	11		1
东营市	Dongying	6	10	16		2
烟台市	Yantai	45	17	47		9
潍坊市	Weifang	29	13	23		3
济宁市	Jining	10	8	19		2
泰安市	Tai'an	4	4	17		2
威海市	Weihai	12	7	35		2
日照市	Rizhao	2	4	6		1
临沂市	Linyi	5	3	9		3
德州市	Dezhou	10	7	14		2
聊城市	Liaocheng	4	4	17		2
滨州市	Binzhou	7	4	10		1
菏泽市	Heze	2	2	4		2

8-19 续表 continued

单位:家 (unit)

地 区	Region	证券公司营业部 No. of Securities Business Department	期货公司 No. of Futures Broker Companies	期货公司分公司 No. of Branches of Futures Broker Companies	期货公司营业部 No. of Trading Offices of Futures Broker Companies	私募基金管理人 No. of Private investment fund managers
全省总计	**Total**	**561**	**4**	**79**	**91**	**836**
济南市	Jinan	90	1	53	21	205
青岛市	Qingdao	119	1	19	26	441
淄博市	Zibo	40	1	2	6	19
枣庄市	Zaozhuang	14				9
东营市	Dongying	24			4	8
烟台市	Yantai	56	1	3	10	41
潍坊市	Weifang	49		1	2	25
济宁市	Jining	24			4	8
泰安市	Tai'an	22			1	16
威海市	Weihai	27			1	11
日照市	Rizhao	9		1	8	12
临沂市	Linyi	33			7	16
德州市	Dezhou	11			1	8
聊城市	Liaocheng	20				6
滨州市	Binzhou	14				7
菏泽市	Heze	9				4

主要统计指标解释

一般公共预算收入 指国家财政参与社会产品分配所取得的收入，是实现国家职能的财力保证。财政收入所包括的内容几经变化，目前主要包括：

（1）税收收入：包括增值税、企业所得税、个人所得税、资源税、城市维护建设税、房产税、印花税、城镇土地使用税、土地增值税、车船税、耕地占用税、契税、烟叶税、环境保护税等。

（2）非税收入：包括专项收入、行政事业性收费收入、罚没收入、国有资本经营收入、国有资源(资产)有偿使用收入等。

一般公共预算支出 国家财政将筹集起来的资金进行分配使用，以满足经济建设和各项事业的需要，主要包括：

（1）一般公共服务支出：反映政府提供一般公共服务的支出。

（2）公共安全支出：反映政府维护社会公共安全方面的支出，有关事务包括武装警察、公安、国家安全、检察、法院、司法、监狱、强制隔离戒毒、国家保密、缉私警察等。

（3）教育支出：反映政府教育事务支出。有关具体教育事务包括教育行政管理、学前教育、小学教育、初中教育、普通高中教育、普通高等教育、初等职业教育、中专教育、技校教育、职业高中教育、高等职业教育、广播电视教育、留学生教育、特殊教育、干部继续教育、教育机关服务等。

（4）科学技术支出：反映政府用于科学技术方面的支出。

（5）文化旅游体育与传媒支出：反映政府在文化旅游、文物、体育、广播电视、新闻出版等方面的支出。

（6）社会保障和就业支出：反映政府在社会保障与就业方面的支出。有关事项包括社会保障与就业管理事务、民政管理事务、财政对社会保险基金的补助、补充全国社会保障基金、行政事业单位离退休、企业改革补助、就业补助、抚恤、退役安置、社会福利、残疾人事业、城市居民最低生活保障、其他城镇社会救济、农村社会救济、自然灾害生活补助、红十字事务等。

（7）卫生健康支出：反映政府医疗卫生方面的支出。具体包括医疗卫生管理事务支出、医疗服务支出、医疗保障支出、疾病预防控制支出、卫生监督支出、妇幼保健支出、农村卫生支出等。

（8）城乡社区支出：反映政府城乡社区事务支出。具体包括：城乡社区管理事务支出、城乡社区规划与管理支出、城乡社区公共设施支出、城乡社区住宅支出、城乡社区环境卫生支出、建设市场管理与监督支出等。

（9）农林水支出：反映政府农林水事务方面的支出。具体包括农业、林业、水利、扶贫支出、农业综合开发支出等。

存　款 指企业、机关、团体或居民根据资金必须收回的原则，把货币资金存入银行或其他信贷机构保管并取得一定利息的一种信用活动形式。根据存款对象或性质的不同可划分为企业存款、财政存款、机关团体存款、基本建设存款、储蓄存款、农村存款、委托存款、其他存款等科目。它是银行信贷资金的主要来源。

贷　款 指银行或其他信贷机构根据资金必须归还的原则，按一定利率，为企业、个人等提供资金的一种信用活动形式。我国银行贷款分为短期贷款、中期流动资金贷款、中长期贷款、信托贷款、融资租赁、委托贷款、票据融资、各项垫款等。

保险公司 在中国境内的、经过保险监督管理部门批准设立，并依法登记注册的各类商业保险公司。

保险金额 指保险人承担赔偿或者给付保险金责任的最高限额。

保　费 指投保人为取得保险人在约定范围内所承担赔偿责任而支付给保险人的费用。

赔　款 指保险人根据保险合同的规定，向被保险人支付的赔偿保险责任损失的金额。

给　付 包括死伤医疗给付、满期给付和年金给付。死伤医疗给付是指保险人根据人寿保险及长期健康保险合同的规定，因被保险人在保险期内发生保险责任范围内的保险事故支付给被保险人(或受益人)的金额。满期给付是指被保险人生存期满，保险人按人寿保险合同规定支付给被保险人的满期保险金额。年金给付是指保险人因年金保险业务的被保险人生存至规定的年龄，按保险合同约定支付给被保险人的金额。

Explanatory Notes on Main Statistical Indicators

General Public Budget Revenue refers to the revenue of the government finance by means of participating in the distribution of the social products, which is the financial resources for ensuring the government to function. The contents of government revenue have been changed several times. Now it includes the following main items:

(1) Various tax revenues including value added tax, enterprise income tax, personal income tax, resources tax, fixed assets investment direction regulating tax, tax on city maintenance and construction, real estate tax, stamp tax, tax on use of urban land, land value added tax, vehicle and vessel tax, tax on occupancy of cultivated land, property tax, tobacco leaf tax.

(2) Non-tax Revenues including special revenues, revenues from Administrative and institutional fees, penalty and confiscatory revenues , revenues from state-owned capital operation,revenues from paid use of state-owned resources.

General Public Budget Expenditure refers to the distribution and use of the funds the government finance has raised, so as to meet the needs of economic construction and various causes. It includes the following main items:

(1) Expenditure for general public services: It reflects the expenditure from the government for general public services.

(2) Expenditure for public security: It reflects the expenditure from the government towards safeguarding the public security, including the related affairs of armed police, public security, state security, procuratorial administration,law court, judicial administration, jail , reeducation through labor, state confidentiality, anti-smuggling Patrol,etc.

(3) Expenditure for education: It reflects the expenditure from the government on education, including the related affairs of educational administration management, preschool education, primary education, junior secondary educate, regular senior secondary educate, regular higher education, primary vocational education, specialized secondary educate, technical educate, vocational senior secondary educate, vocational higher education, radio and television education, foreign student educate, special education, cadre continuing education, education institution services,etc.

(4) Expenditure for science and technology: It reflects the expenditure from the government on science and technology.

(5) Expenditure for culture, sport and media: It reflects the expenditure from the government on culture, cultural relics, sport, radio and television, publication, etc.

(6)Expenditure for social Safety net and employment effort:It reflects the expenditure from the government on social security and employment, including the related affairs of management of social security and employment, civil administration, subsidies to social insurance funds, supplement to national social security funds, retirees of government agencies and institutions, subsidies to enterprises reform, subsidies to employment, pension, settling down demobilized servicemen,social security, disabled person administration, minimum living allowance in urban area, other social relief in urban area, social relief in rural area, subsidies to natural disaster, Red Cross business,etc.

(7)Expenditure for medical and health care,and family planning: It reflects the expenditure from the government on health care, including expenditure on management of health care, medical services, medical security, disease control and prevention, public health supervision, rural health care,etc.

(8) Expenditure for urban and rural community affairs: It reflects the expenditure from the government on urban and rural community affairs, including expenditure on management of urban and rural community affairs, plan and management of urban and rural community, public utility of urban and rural community, residential buildings of urban and rural community, environmental sanitation of urban and rural community, management and supervision of markets construction, etc.

(9) Expenditure for agriculture, forestry and water conservancy: It reflects the expenditure from the government on agriculture, forest and irrigation, including expenditure on agriculture, forest, irrigation, poverty alleviation, comprehensive development of agriculture, etc.

Deposit is a form of credit by which enterprises, institutions, organizations or households can put money into banks and other credit institutions for safekeeping and interest earning under the principle of free withdrawal. According to different depositors, deposits are divided into enterprise deposits, treasury deposits, deposits of government agencies and organizations, capital construction deposits, savings deposits, rural saving deposits, entrusted deposits and other deposits. Deposits are major sources of the credit funds of banks.

Loan is a form of credit by which banks and other credit institutions provide funds at certain interest rate to enterprises and individuals in the light of the principle of unconditional repayment. Loans from Chinese banks include circulating capital loans, fixed assets loans, loans to urban and rural individuals engaged in industrial and commercial business and agricultural loans.

Insurance Companies refers to commercial insurance companies of various forms registered by law and established in China with the approval of insurance regulatory agencies.

Amount Insured refers to the maximum that the insurant will get for the claim of the case insured.

Premium is the fee paid by the insurant to the insurer to obtain the obligation of compensation from the insurance within the agreed terms.

Settled Claim is the compensation paid by the insurer to the insurant in accordance with the insurance contract.

Payment includes payment for death, injury or medical treatment, mature payment. and annuity payment. Payment for death, injury or medical treatment refers to the money paid to the insurant (or the beneficiary) in accordance with the life or health insurance contract when the insurant encounters accidents within the insured period covered in the contract. Mature payment refers to the mature payment to the insurant in accordance with the life insurance contract at the end of the insured period. Annuity payment refers to the amount that the insurer pays to the insured in accordance with the insurance contract as the insured of the annuity insurance business survives to the prescribed age.

第
9
篇

价格指数

Price Indices

简 要 说 明

一、本篇资料的主要内容

本篇资料反映了全省生产、流通与消费等环节的价格变动状况。主要包括居民消费、商品零售、工业生产者出厂、工业生产者购进、住宅销售等价格指数。

二、本篇资料的来源

1.居民消费和商品零售价格指数来源于消费价格统计调查年报，由国家统计局山东调查总队消费价格调查处整理提供。

2.工业生产者出厂、工业生产者购进、住宅销售等价格指数来源于生产价格统计调查年报，由国家统计局山东调查总队生产价格调查处整理提供。

3.农产品生产者价格指数来源于农产品生产者价格调查年报，由国家统计局山东调查总队农业调查处整理提供。

Brief Introduction

I. Main Content

Data on the price indices in this chapter show the changing trend in production, circulation and consumption, including mainly consumer price indices of residents, retail price indices, producer price indices for industrial products, purchasing price indices for industrial producers and price indices of residential sales.

II. Source of Data

(1) Data on consumer price indices of residents and retail price indices are based on yearly report on consumer price and are provided by the Division of Consumer Price Survey of the National Bureau of Statistics in Shandong.

(2) Data on producer price indices of industrial products, industrial producer purchasing price indices and real estate price indices are based on yearly report on production price and are provided by the Division of Production Price Survey of the National Bureau of Statistics in Shandong.

(3)Data on producer price index of agricultural products are based on yearly report on producer price of agricultural products and provided by the Division of Agriculture Statistics of Shandong Provincial Bureau of Statistics.

9-1 居民消费价格指数

Consumer Price Indices

(上年=100) (Preceding Year=100)

类　别	Category	2020	2021
居民消费价格指数	**Consumer Price Index**	**102.8**	**101.2**
城　市	Urban Areas	102.5	101.3
农　村	Rural Areas	103.6	101.0
服务项目价格指数	**Services Price Index**	**100.4**	**101.0**
消费品价格指数	**Consumer Goods Price Index**	**104.2**	**101.4**
食品烟酒	Food, Tobacco, Liquor	109.5	100.9
粮　食	Grain	102.4	101.1
食用油	Edible Oil	101.6	108.2
菜及食用菌	Vegetables and Edible Mushrooms	109.3	108.0
鲜　菜	Fresh Vegetables	109.9	109.0
畜肉类	Livestock Meat	140.5	83.1
禽肉类	Poultry	102.5	98.1
水产品	Aquatic Products	104.7	110.3
蛋　类	Eggs	90.7	112.8
衣着	Clothing	100.6	100.1
居住	Residence	99.7	101.1
生活用品及服务	Daily Necessities and Services	99.9	99.8
交通通信	Transportation Communication	96.2	104.5
教育文化娱乐	Education Culture Recreation	101.2	101.3
医疗保健	Health Care	101.5	100.1
其他用品及服务	Other Supplies and Services	104.6	98.5
商品零售价格指数	**Retail Price Index**	**102.0**	**101.4**
城　市	Urban Areas	101.9	101.4
农　村	Rural Areas	102.6	101.5

9-2 居民消费和商品零售价格总指数(2021年)

General Consumer and Retail Price Indices(2021)

类　别	Category	居民消费价格总指数 General Consumer Price Indices			商品零售价格总指数 General Retail Price Indices		
		全 省 Provincial Indices	城 市 Urban Indices	农 村 Rural Indices	全 省 Provincial Indices	城 市 Urban Indices	农 村 Rural Indices
以1950年价格为100	1950=100	788.1	788.7		586.9	556.0	553.8
以1952年价格为100	1952=100	695.2	696.9		488.0	487.3	502.0
以1957年价格为100	1957=100	640.4	648.7		444.6	400.3	460.2
以1965年价格为100	1965=100	630.9	631.5		424.3	434.0	439.3
以1970年价格为100	1970=100	647.1	648.3		430.9	445.9	446.5
以1978年价格为100	1978=100	646.4	647.9	639.3	431.4	443.9	447.4
以1980年价格为100	1980=100	611.7	620.7	601.3	412.3	431.4	427.9
以1985年价格为100	1985=100	527.1	526.2	512.3	372.3	385.3	388.6
以1990年价格为100	1990=100	323.8	336.4	316.8	232.7	232.8	246.1
以1995年价格为100	1995=100	176.6	174.2	183.5	138.0	132.5	150.8
以2000年价格为100	2000=100	158.5	151.3	169.5	137.5	132.1	150.2
以上年价格为100	Preceding Year=100	101.2	101.3	101.0	101.4	101.4	101.5

9–3 历年居民消费价格总指数

General Consumer Price Indices over the Years

年 份 Year	以1950年为100 1950=100	以1952年为100 1952=100	以1978年为100 1978=100	以1990年为100 1990=100	以1995年为100 1995=100	以上年为100 Preceding Year=100
1952	113.2					102.2
1955	120.8	106.7				99.9
1957	122.9	108.5				101.0
1962	132.2	116.8				100.5
1965	124.8	110.3				97.8
1970	121.7	107.4				98.9
1975	121.5	107.3				100.2
1976	121.7	107.5				100.2
1977	121.5	107.3				99.8
1978	121.9	107.6				100.3
1979	122.8	108.4	100.7			100.7
1980	128.9	113.8	105.7			105.0
1981	131.2	115.8	107.6			101.8
1982	132.4	116.8	108.6			100.9
1983	135.6	119.6	111.2			102.4
1984	137.6	121.4	112.9			101.5
1985	149.6	132.0	122.7			108.7
1986	156.3	137.9	128.2			104.5
1987	169.1	149.2	138.7			108.2
1988	200.7	177.1	164.7			118.7
1989	235.5	207.7	199.1			117.3
1990	243.5	214.8	199.7			103.4
1991	255.4	225.3	209.5	104.9		104.9
1992	272.8	240.6	223.7	112.0		106.8
1993	307.4	271.2	252.2	126.3		112.7
1994	379.4	334.6	311.2	155.8		123.4
1995	446.1	393.5	365.9	183.2		117.6
1996	489.0	431.3	401.1	200.8	109.6	109.6
1997	502.6	443.3	412.3	206.4	112.7	102.8
1998	499.6	440.7	409.8	205.2	112.0	99.4
1999	496.1	437.6	406.9	203.8	111.2	99.3
2000	497.1	438.5	407.7	204.2	111.4	100.2
2001	506.0	446.4	415.0	207.9	113.4	101.8
2002	502.5	443.2	412.1	206.4	112.6	99.3
2003	508.0	448.1	416.6	208.7	113.8	101.1
2004	526.3	464.3	431.6	216.2	117.9	103.6
2005	535.2	472.1	439.0	219.9	119.9	101.7
2006	540.6	476.9	443.4	222.1	121.1	101.0
2007	564.4	497.9	462.9	231.9	126.4	104.4
2008	594.3	524.2	487.4	244.2	133.1	105.3
2009	594.3	524.2	487.4	244.2	133.1	100.0
2010	611.5	539.4	501.6	251.3	137.0	102.9
2011	642.2	566.5	526.7	263.9	143.9	105.0
2012	655.7	578.4	537.8	269.4	146.9	102.1
2013	670.2	591.1	549.6	275.4	150.2	102.2
2014	682.9	602.4	560.1	280.6	153.0	101.9
2015	691.1	609.6	566.8	284.0	154.8	101.2
2016	705.6	622.4	578.7	289.9	158.1	102.1
2017	716.2	631.7	587.4	294.3	160.5	101.5
2018	734.1	647.5	602.1	301.6	164.5	102.5
2019	757.6	668.3	621.3	311.3	169.7	103.2
2020	778.8	687.0	638.7	320.0	174.5	102.8
2021	788.1	695.2	646.4	323.8	176.6	101.2

9-4 历年城市居民消费价格总指数

General Urban Consumer Price Indices over the Years

年 份 Year	以1930–1936年平均价格为100 Average Price (1930-1936)=100	以1952年为100 1952=100	以1978年为100 1978=100	以1980年为100 1980=100	以1990年为100 1990=100	以1995年为100 1995=100	以上年为100 Preceding Year=100
1949	260.9						
1952	302.2						102.2
1955	322.5	106.7					99.9
1957	328.0	108.5					101.0
1962	352.9	116.8					100.5
1965	333.5	110.3					97.8
1970	324.9	107.4					98.9
1975	324.2	107.3					100.2
1976	324.9	107.5					100.2
1977	324.3	107.3					99.8
1978	325.2	107.6					100.3
1979	329.7	109.1	101.4				101.4
1980	339.3	112.3	104.3				102.9
1981	346.4	114.6	106.5	102.1			102.1
1982	347.4	115.0	106.9	102.4			100.3
1983	345.3	114.3	106.2	101.8			99.4
1984	350.5	116.0	107.8	103.3			101.5
1985	381.4	126.2	117.3	112.4			108.8
1986	400.5	132.5	123.2	118.0			105.0
1987	436.9	144.6	134.4	128.8			109.1
1988	526.9	174.4	162.1	155.3			120.6
1989	609.6	201.7	187.5	179.7			115.7
1990	625.5	207.0	192.4	184.4			102.6
1991	664.3	219.8	204.3	195.8	106.2		106.2
1992	721.4	238.7	221.9	212.6	115.3		108.6
1993	826.7	273.6	254.3	243.7	132.1		114.6
1994	1036.7	343.1	318.9	305.6	165.7		125.4
1995	1210.9	400.7	372.5	356.9	193.6		116.8
1996	1338.0	442.8	411.6	394.4	213.9	110.5	110.5
1997	1380.8	457.0	424.8	407.0	220.7	114.0	103.2
1998	1376.7	455.6	423.5	405.8	220.0	113.7	99.7
1999	1376.7	455.6	423.5	405.8	220.0	113.7	100.0
2000	1393.2	461.1	428.6	410.7	222.6	115.1	101.2
2001	1408.5	466.2	433.3	415.2	225.0	116.4	101.1
2002	1390.2	460.1	427.7	409.8	222.1	114.9	98.7
2003	1399.9	463.3	430.7	412.7	223.7	115.7	100.7
2004	1439.1	476.3	442.7	424.2	230.0	118.9	102.8
2005	1454.9	481.5	447.6	428.9	232.5	120.2	101.1
2006	1469.5	486.3	452.1	433.2	234.8	121.4	101.0
2007	1525.3	504.8	469.3	449.7	243.7	126.0	103.8
2008	1597.0	528.5	491.4	470.8	255.2	131.9	104.7
2009	1596.1	528.2	491.1	470.6	255.0	131.8	99.9
2010	1637.6	542.0	503.8	482.8	261.6	135.3	102.6
2011	1714.1	567.3	527.4	505.3	273.9	141.8	104.7
2012	1750.1	579.2	538.5	515.9	279.6	144.8	102.1
2013	1786.9	591.4	549.8	526.7	285.5	147.8	102.1
2014	1824.4	603.8	561.3	537.8	291.5	150.9	102.1
2015	1850.0	612.2	569.2	545.3	295.6	153.0	101.4
2016	1890.7	625.7	581.7	557.3	302.1	156.4	102.2
2017	1920.9	635.7	591.0	566.3	306.9	158.9	101.6
2018	1967.0	651.0	605.2	579.8	314.3	162.7	102.4
2019	2028.0	671.2	624.0	597.8	324.0	167.8	103.1
2020	2078.7	687.9	639.6	612.8	332.1	172.0	102.5
2021	2105.7	696.9	647.9	620.7	336.4	174.2	101.3

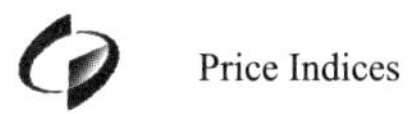

9-5 历年农村居民消费价格总指数

General Rural Consumer Price Indices over the Years

年 份 Year	以1978年为100 1978=100	以1980年为100 1980=100	以1985年为100 1985=100	以1990年为100 1990=100	以1995年为100 1995=100	以上年为100 Preceding Year=100
1979	100.4					100.4
1980	106.2					105.8
1981	107.9	101.6				101.6
1982	109.1	102.7				101.1
1983	113.0	106.4				103.6
1984	114.7	108.0				101.5
1985	124.7	117.4				108.7
1986	129.8	122.2	104.1			104.1
1987	139.4	131.2	111.8			107.4
1988	163.1	153.5	130.8			117.0
1989	194.0	182.5	155.5			118.9
1990	201.7	189.8	161.7			104.0
1991	209.8	197.4	168.2	104.0		104.0
1992	219.5	206.5	175.9	108.8		104.6
1993	242.9	228.6	194.7	120.4		110.7
1994	295.7	278.2	236.9	146.5		121.7
1995	348.6	328.0	279.3	172.7		117.9
1996	379.9	357.5	304.4	188.2	109.0	109.0
1997	389.1	366.1	311.7	192.7	111.6	102.4
1998	385.2	362.4	308.6	190.8	110.5	99.0
1999	379.8	357.3	304.3	188.1	109.0	98.6
2000	377.1	354.8	302.2	186.8	108.2	99.3
2001	386.2	363.3	309.5	191.3	110.8	102.4
2002	385.8	362.9	309.2	191.1	110.7	99.9
2003	391.6	368.3	313.8	194.0	112.4	101.5
2004	409.6	385.2	328.2	202.9	117.5	104.6
2005	419.4	394.5	336.1	207.8	120.3	102.4
2006	423.6	398.4	339.5	209.9	121.6	101.0
2007	446.1	419.5	357.5	221.0	128.0	105.3
2008	473.8	445.5	379.7	234.7	135.9	106.2
2009	474.1	445.8	380.0	234.9	136.0	100.1
2010	490.7	461.4	393.2	243.1	140.8	103.5
2011	519.5	488.7	416.4	257.4	149.1	105.9
2012	529.9	498.5	424.7	262.6	152.1	102.0
2013	543.1	510.9	435.3	269.1	155.9	102.5
2014	551.3	518.6	441.9	273.2	158.2	101.5
2015	556.2	523.3	445.8	275.6	159.6	100.9
2016	566.3	532.7	453.9	280.6	162.5	101.8
2017	574.2	540.1	460.2	284.5	164.8	101.4
2018	589.7	554.7	472.6	292.2	169.2	102.7
2019	610.9	574.7	489.7	302.7	175.3	103.6
2020	632.9	595.4	507.3	313.6	181.6	103.6
2021	639.3	601.3	512.3	316.8	183.5	101.0

9-6 历年商品零售价格总指数

General Retail Price Indices over the Years

年 份 Year	以1930-1936年平均价格为100 Average Price (1930-1936)=100	以1952年为100 1952=100	以1978年为100 1978=100	以1980年为100 1980=100	以1990年为100 1990=100	以1995年为100 1995=100	以上年为100 Preceding Year=100
1949	257.0						
1952	303.6						100.4
1955	325.6	107.2					100.2
1957	333.5	109.8					101.7
1962	359.9	118.5					100.4
1965	349.4	115.1					97.6
1970	343.8	113.3					99.2
1971	343.5	113.2					99.9
1972	342.5	112.8					99.7
1973	342.2	112.7					99.9
1974	341.8	112.6					99.9
1975	342.2	112.7					100.1
1976	342.5	112.8					100.1
1977	342.2	112.7					99.9
1978	343.5	113.2					100.4
1979	349.0	115.0	101.6				101.6
1980	359.5	118.5	104.6				103.0
1981	365.6	120.5	106.4	101.7			101.7
1982	367.8	121.2	107.1	102.3			100.6
1983	363.0	119.7	105.6	101.0			98.7
1984	367.0	121.0	106.8	102.1			101.1
1985	398.2	131.3	115.9	110.8			108.5
1986	416.1	137.2	121.1	115.8			104.5
1987	450.6	148.6	131.2	125.4			108.3
1988	536.3	176.8	156.1	149.2			119.0
1989	626.9	206.7	182.5	174.4			116.9
1990	636.9	210.0	185.4	177.2			101.6
1991	668.1	220.3	194.5	185.9	104.9		104.9
1992	709.5	233.9	206.6	197.4	111.4		106.2
1993	782.6	258.0	227.8	217.7	122.9		110.3
1994	941.5	310.4	274.1	261.9	147.8		120.3
1995	1075.2	354.5	313.0	299.1	168.8		114.2
1996	1150.6	378.9	334.9	320.1	180.6	107.0	107.0
1997	1159.8	381.9	337.6	322.7	182.0	107.9	100.8
1998	1126.2	370.8	327.8	313.3	176.7	104.8	97.1
1999	1093.5	360.0	318.3	304.2	171.6	101.8	97.1
2000	1078.2	355.0	313.8	299.9	169.2	100.4	98.6
2001	1078.2	355.0	313.8	299.9	169.2	100.4	100.0
2002	1065.3	350.7	310.0	296.3	167.2	99.2	98.8
2003	1067.4	351.4	310.7	296.9	167.5	99.4	100.2
2004	1097.3	361.3	319.4	305.2	172.2	102.2	102.8
2005	1103.9	363.4	321.3	307.0	173.2	102.8	100.6
2006	1110.5	365.6	323.2	308.9	174.3	103.4	100.6
2007	1150.5	378.8	334.8	320.0	180.6	107.1	103.6
2008	1206.9	397.4	351.2	335.7	189.4	112.3	104.9
2009	1199.3	394.9	349.0	333.6	188.3	111.6	99.4
2010	1231.6	405.5	358.4	342.6	193.3	114.7	102.7
2011	1288.9	424.3	375.1	358.5	202.3	120.0	104.7
2012	1309.6	431.1	381.1	364.2	205.6	121.9	101.6
2013	1327.9	437.1	386.4	369.3	208.4	123.6	101.4
2014	1341.2	441.5	390.3	373.0	210.5	124.8	101.0
2015	1343.8	442.4	391.1	373.8	211.0	125.1	100.2
2016	1361.3	448.1	396.1	378.6	213.7	126.7	101.3
2017	1372.2	451.7	399.3	381.7	215.4	127.7	100.8
2018	1402.4	461.7	408.1	390.1	220.1	130.5	102.2
2019	1433.3	471.8	417.1	398.6	225.0	133.4	102.2
2020	1461.9	481.2	425.4	406.6	229.5	136.1	102.0
2021	1482.4	488.0	431.4	412.3	232.7	138.0	101.4

注：本表已根据现行价格调查统计制度予以调整，均不包括农业生产资料部分。

a)The data in this form have been adjusted according to current statistical system of price survey.Means of agricultural production are excluded.

9-7 历年农业生产资料价格总指数
General Price Indices of Means of Agricultural Production over the Years

年 份 Year	以1950年为100 1950=100	以1952年为100 1952=100	以1978年为100 1978=100	以1990年为100 1990=100	以1995年为100 1995=100	以上年为100 Preceding Year=100
1952	97.0					102.2
1955	103.8	107.0				94.1
1957	103.4	106.7				99.7
1962	106.8	110.1				99.3
1965	92.7	95.5				96.8
1970	84.2	86.8				99.9
1975	79.2	81.6				100.0
1976	79.2	81.6				100.0
1977	79.2	81.6				100.0
1978	78.5	80.9				99.1
1979	78.6	81.0	100.1			100.1
1980	78.6	81.0	100.1			100.0
1981	79.9	82.4	101.8			101.7
1982	80.8	83.3	102.9			101.1
1983	82.9	85.5	105.6			102.6
1984	88.9	91.7	113.2			107.2
1985	92.5	95.5	117.8			104.1
1986	94.4	97.5	120.3			102.1
1987	99.9	103.2	127.3			105.8
1988	114.6	118.4	146.0			114.7
1989	135.5	139.9	172.6			118.2
1990	139.8	144.4	178.1			103.2
1991	142.6	147.3	181.7	102.0		102.0
1992	144.6	149.4	184.2	103.4		101.4
1993	161.4	166.7	205.6	115.4		111.6
1994	200.3	206.9	255.1	143.2		124.1
1995	267.0	275.8	340.1	190.9		133.3
1996	281.7	291.0	358.8	201.4	105.5	105.5
1997	272.1	281.1	346.6	194.6	101.9	96.6
1998	261.8	270.4	336.5	187.2	98.0	96.2
1999	249.0	257.2	320.0	178.0	93.2	95.1
2000	245.8	253.9	315.8	175.7	92.0	98.7
2001	250.2	258.5	321.5	178.9	93.7	101.8
2002	251.0	259.3	322.5	179.4	94.0	100.3
2003	257.0	265.5	330.2	183.7	96.2	102.4
2004	283.2	292.6	363.9	202.5	106.0	110.2
2005	300.7	310.7	386.4	215.0	112.6	106.2
2006	309.8	320.0	398.0	221.5	116.0	103.0
2007	331.8	342.7	426.3	237.2	124.2	107.1
2008	395.8	408.8	508.6	283.0	148.2	119.3
2009	381.2	393.7	489.8	272.5	142.7	96.3
2010	392.6	405.5	504.4	280.7	147.0	103.0
2011	436.2	450.6	560.4	311.9	163.4	111.1
2012	461.9	477.2	593.5	330.3	173.0	105.9
2013	467.5	482.9	600.6	334.3	175.1	101.2
2014	465.1	480.5	597.6	332.6	174.2	99.5
2015	461.9	477.1	593.4	330.3	173.0	99.3
2016	456.8	471.9	586.9	326.6	171.1	98.9
2017	460.9	476.1	592.2	329.6	172.7	100.9
2018	492.7	509.0	633.0	352.3	184.6	106.9
2019	530.1	547.7	681.1	379.1	198.6	107.6
2020	559.8	578.3	719.3	400.3	209.7	105.6

注：自2021年起，不再统计农业生产资料价格指数。

a) Since the year of 2021, The Statistics of Price Indices of Agricultural Production Means has been no longer carried out.

9-8 居民消费价格分类指数(2021年)

Consumer Price Indices by Category(2021)

(上年=100) (preceding year=100)

商品类别	Category	全省 Provincial Indices	城市 Urban Indices	农村 Rural Indices
居民消费价格指数	**Consumer Price Index**	**101.2**	**101.3**	**101.0**
服务价格指数	Services Price Index	101.0	101.1	100.7
消费品价格指数	Consumer Goods Price Index	101.4	101.4	101.2
非食品价格指数	Non-food Price Index	101.5	101.5	101.5
扣除鲜菜鲜果价格指数	Deducting Fruit Vegetable Price Index	101.0	101.1	100.7
一、食品烟酒	**Food, Tobacco, Liquor**	**100.9**	**101.1**	**100.1**
1.食品	Food	100.0	100.3	99.3
(1)粮 食	Grain	101.1	101.8	99.8
(2)薯 类	Tuber	99.8	101.5	95.2
(3)豆 类	Beans	108.4	108.8	107.5
(4)食用油	Edible Oil	108.2	108.5	107.5
(5)菜及食用菌	Vegetables and Edible Mushrooms	108.0	107.1	111.1
(6)畜肉类	Livestock Meat	83.1	83.8	80.9
(7)禽肉类	Poultry	98.1	97.7	99.6
(8)水产品	Aquatic Products	110.3	110.4	109.7
(9)蛋 类	Eggs	112.8	111.4	116.2
(10)奶 类	Milk	101.8	101.8	102.1
(11)干鲜瓜果类	Dried and Fresh Melons and Fruits	103.4	103.4	103.3
(12)糖果糕点类	Candy and Cakes	101.1	102.3	97.6
(13)调味品	Condiment	101.7	102.3	100.3
(14)其他食品类	Other Foods	99.7	99.8	99.5
2.茶及饮料	Tea and Beverages	100.8	101.2	99.7
3.烟 酒	Tobacco and Liquor	101.4	101.0	102.3
(1)卷 烟	Cigarette	100.7	100.5	101.2
(2)酒 类	Liquor	102.1	101.5	103.7
4.在外餐饮	Outside Catering	103.5	103.7	102.5
二、衣 着	**Clothing**	**100.1**	**100.2**	**99.7**
1.服 装	Garments	100.3	100.4	99.9
(1)男式服装	Men's Clothing	100.7	100.9	99.5
(2)女式服装	Women's Clothing	100.0	100.2	99.6
(3)儿童服装	Children's Clothing	100.3	99.9	102.0
(4)衣着材料及配件	Clothing Material and Accessories	100.5	100.7	99.9
(5)衣着服务费	Clothing service fee	101.3	101.6	100.8
2.鞋 类	Footwear	99.3	99.4	98.9
(1)鞋	Shoes	99.3	99.4	98.9
(2)鞋类服务	Footwear Services	101.4	101.7	99.9
三、居 住	**Residence**	**101.1**	**101.0**	**101.6**
1.租赁房房租	Rental Housing Rent	100.7	100.6	102.1
2.住房保养维修及管理	Housing Maintenance	102.4	102.0	103.9
(1)住房装潢材料	Housing Decoration Materials	101.8	101.4	103.4
(2)住房维修管理费	Housing Maintenance Management Fee	102.9	102.4	104.2
3.水电燃料	Water, Electricity and Fuels	101.9	101.5	103.0
(1)水	Water	100.0	100.0	100.0
(2)电	Electricity	100.0	100.0	100.0
(3)燃 气	Gas	105.5	103.3	111.2
(4)其他水电燃料类	Other Water Electricity Fuel	102.7	102.3	103.8
4.自有住房	Self-owned House	100.6	100.6	100.4

9-8 续表 continued

(上年=100) (preceding year=100)

商品类别	Category	全省 Provincial Indices	城市 Urban Indices	农村 Rural Indices
四、生活用品及服务	**Daily Necessities and Services**	**99.8**	**99.8**	**100.0**
1.家具及室内装饰品	Furniture and Interior Decorations	101.0	101.0	100.6
(1)家具	Furniture	100.9	101.0	100.6
(2)室内装饰品	Interior Decorations	101.2	101.1	101.4
2.家用器具	Household Appliances	100.2	100.2	100.2
(1)大型家用器具	Large Household Appliances	99.9	99.9	99.8
(2)小家电	Small Household Appliances	101.9	101.7	102.7
3.家用纺织品	Home Textiles	99.4	99.3	99.6
(1)床上用品	Bedding Article	99.4	99.3	99.7
(2)窗帘门帘	Curtain	99.8	99.7	100.1
(3)其他家用纺织品	Other Household Textiles	98.7	98.9	97.6
4.家庭日用杂品	The Family Daily Sundry Goods	99.4	99.3	99.8
(1)洗涤卫生用品	Washing Sanitary Articles	99.9	100.3	98.7
(2)厨具餐具茶具	Kitchenware, Tableware, Tea Set	96.2	96.1	96.5
(3)其他家庭日用杂品	Other Household Articles For Daily Use	100.4	99.8	102.5
5.个人护理用品	Personal Care Products	97.5	97.3	98.4
(1)化妆品	Cosmetics	96.2	96.0	97.5
(2)其他护理用品类	Other Nursing Products	99.6	99.6	99.8
6.家庭服务	Family Services	102.6	102.6	103.0
五、交通通信	**Transport Communication**	**104.5**	**104.7**	**104.0**
1.交通	Transport	105.7	105.8	105.2
(1)交通工具	Transport Tools	99.3	99.1	99.7
(2)交通工具用燃料	Transport Fuels	117.5	117.4	117.9
(3)交通工具使用和维修	Vehicle Use and Maintenance	102.2	102.3	102.2
(4)交通费	Travelling Expenses	106.9	107.6	104.0
2.通信	Signal Communication	100.7	100.9	100.0
(1)通信工具	Communication Tools	102.4	102.4	102.5
(2)通信服务	Communication Services	99.7	100.1	98.5
(3)邮递服务	Mailing Service	99.7	99.4	100.6
六、教育文化娱乐	**Education Culture Recreation**	**101.3**	**101.3**	**101.1**
1.教育	Education	101.0	101.0	101.0
(1)教育用品	Educational Supplies	101.4	101.4	101.4
(2)教育服务	Education Services	101.0	101.0	101.0
2.文化娱乐	Culture and Entertainment	101.7	101.8	101.3
(1)文娱耐用消费品	Recreational Consumer Durables	99.8	99.5	100.8
(2)其他文娱用品	Other Entertainment Products	100.6	100.6	100.8
(3)文化娱乐服务	Cultural and Recreational Services	105.4	106.1	101.5
(4)旅游	Tourism	100.0	99.7	102.6
七、医疗保健	**Health Care**	**100.1**	**100.1**	**100.1**
1.药品及医疗器具	Drugs and Medical Devices	99.9	99.8	100.3
(1)中药	Traditional Chinese Medicine	101.7	101.9	101.2
(2)西药	West Medicine	99.2	98.9	99.9
(3)滋补保健品	Western Medicine	100.9	101.1	99.6
(4)医疗卫生器具	Medical and Health Equipment	97.0	95.6	102.1
(5)保健器具	Healthcare Apparatus	100.4	100.5	99.9
2.医疗服务	Medical Services	100.2	100.2	100.0
(1)综合医疗类	Comprehensive Health Care	100.1	100.4	99.5
(2)诊断类	Diagnostic	99.8	99.8	99.9
(3)治疗类	Therapeutic	100.7	100.6	100.8
(4)康复类	Rehabilitation	100.6	100.6	100.8
(5)中医医疗服务类	Chinese Medicine Services	100.7	100.7	100.6
(6)其他医疗服务	Other Medical Services	100.7	100.9	100.1
八、其他用品及服务	**Other Supplies and Services**	**98.5**	**98.5**	**98.4**
1.其他用品	Other Products	98.6	98.3	99.8
(1)首饰手表	Jewelry Watches	98.0	97.6	100.0
(2)母婴用品	Maternal and Infant Products	98.7	98.9	98.5
(3)其他杂项用品	Other Miscellaneous Supplies	99.9	99.6	100.8
2.其他服务	Other Services	98.4	98.7	96.6
(1)在外住宿	Accommodation Outside	106.9	107.7	100.9
(2)美容美发洗浴	Hairdressing Bath	101.9	101.9	101.8
(3)养老服务	Pension Services	101.0	100.7	102.0
(4)金融及保险服务	Finance and Insurance Service	94.8	95.3	92.7
(5)中介法律及其他服务	Intermediary Law and Other Service	100.3	100.4	100.3

9-9 商品零售价格分类指数(2021年)
Retail Indices by Category(2021)

(上年=100) (preceding year=100)

商品类别	Category	全省 Provincial Indices	城市 Urban Indices	农村 Rural Indices
商品零售价格总指数	**Retail Index**	**101.4**	**101.4**	**101.5**
一、食　品	**Food**	**100.8**	**101.1**	**99.5**
1.粮　食	Grain	100.8	101.8	98.3
2.薯　类	Tuber	99.6	101.0	95.1
3.豆　类	Beans	107.9	108.0	107.8
4.食用油	Edible Oil	108.2	108.4	107.8
5.菜及食用菌	Vegetables and Edible Mushrooms	107.8	107.1	110.5
6.畜肉类	Livestock Meat	83.0	83.9	80.0
7.禽肉类	Poultry	98.3	97.9	99.9
8.水产品	Aquatic Products	110.5	110.4	110.9
9.蛋　类	Eggs	112.4	111.3	115.4
10.奶　类	Milk	101.7	101.9	100.9
11.干鲜瓜果类	Dried and Fresh Melons and Fruits	103.3	103.3	103.1
12.糖果糕点类	Candy and Cakes	101.3	102.2	97.9
13.调味品	Flavoring	101.7	102.2	100.2
14.其他食品类	Other Foods	99.8	99.7	100.3
15.餐饮业零售	Restaurant Retail	103.6	103.7	102.7
二、饮料、烟酒	**Beverages,Tobacco and Liquor**	**101.2**	**101.0**	**101.9**
1.茶及饮料	Tea and Beverages	100.9	101.1	99.5
2.卷　烟	Cigarette	100.7	100.5	101.4
3.酒　类	Liquor	101.8	101.4	103.8
三、服装、鞋帽	**Garments,Footwear and Hats**	**100.2**	**100.3**	**99.4**
1.服　装	Garments	100.4	100.5	99.8
(1)男士服装	Men's Clothing	100.7	101.0	99.3
(2)女士服装	Women's Clothing	100.2	100.4	99.2
(3)儿童服装	Children's Clothing	100.4	99.9	103.0
2.鞋帽袜	Footwear and Hats	99.4	99.6	98.5
(1)鞋	Shoes	99.2	99.5	98.2
(2)袜　子	Socks	100.7	100.8	100.2
(3)帽　子	Hats	100.7	100.6	101.4
3.其他衣着配件	Others	100.1	100.7	97.1
四、纺织品	**Textiles**	**99.4**	**99.4**	**99.2**
1.服装材料	Clothing Material	101.5	102.5	98.4
2.床上用品	Bed Articles	99.0	98.9	99.3

9-9 续表 continued

(上年=100) (preceding year=100)

商品类别	Category	全 省 Provincial Indices	城 市 Urban Indices	农 村 Rural Indices
五、家用电器及音像器材	**Household Appliances, Music and Video Equipment**	**100.0**	**99.9**	**100.4**
1.家庭设备	Household Facilities	99.9	99.8	100.1
2.文娱用耐用消费品	Durable Consumer Goods for Cultural and Recreational Use	98.8	98.5	100.0
3.专业音像器材	Professional Music and Video Equipment	115.0	115.3	113.6
六、文化办公用品	**Cultural and Office Appliances**	**100.6**	**100.3**	**101.7**
七、日用品	**Articles for Daily Use**	**99.5**	**99.4**	**99.9**
1.日用百货	General Merchandise for Daily Use	100.4	100.6	100.0
2.厨具餐具茶具	Kitchenware, Tableware, Tea Set	96.0	96.0	95.7
3.清洗用品	Washing Products	99.8	99.8	99.6
4.其它日用品	Other Articles for Daily Use	99.6	99.3	100.9
八、体育娱乐用品	**Sports and Recreation Articles**	**100.3**	**100.2**	**100.9**
1.体育户外用品	Sports Articles	99.7	99.7	99.5
2.娱乐用品	Recreation Articles	100.4	100.3	101.1
九、交通、通信用品	**Transportation and Communication Articles**	**99.6**	**99.5**	**99.9**
1.交通运输机械	Transport machinery	99.0	98.9	99.5
2.通信器材	Communication Equipment	102.6	102.6	102.5
十、家　具	**Furniture**	**101.0**	**101.1**	**100.6**
十一、化妆品	**Cosmetics**	**96.6**	**96.4**	**97.8**
十二、金银饰品	**Gold, Silver and Jewelry**	**97.4**	**97.0**	**99.5**
十三、中西药品及医疗保健用品	**Traditional Chinese and Western Medicines and Health Care Articles**	**100.1**	**99.9**	**100.6**
1.医疗卫生器具	Medical Apparatus and Articles	96.4	95.0	104.0
2.中　药	Traditional Chinese Medicine	101.7	101.9	101.2
3.西　药	Western Medicines	99.4	99.2	100.2
4.保健器具及用品	Health Care Appliances and Supplies	100.9	101.1	99.7
十四、书报杂志及电子出版物	**Books, Newspapers, Magazines and Electronic Publications**	**101.0**	**101.0**	**101.2**
1.教材及参考书	Teaching Materials and Reference Books	101.6	101.7	101.4
2.书报杂志	Books, Newspapers and Magazines	101.2	101.3	100.5
3.计算机办公软件	Computer Office Software	98.9	98.6	101.1
十五、燃　料	**Fuels**	**116.7**	**116.6**	**117.2**
1.煤炭及制品	Coal and Products	127.5	128.6	123.0
2.石油及制品	Petroleum and Products	116.0	115.8	116.9
十六、建筑材料及五金电料	**Building Materials and Hardware**	**101.7**	**101.3**	**102.8**
1.建筑装潢材料	Building Decoration Materials	102.0	101.5	103.5
2.五金水暖	Plumbing Hardware	100.9	100.9	100.9

9-10 农产品生产者价格指数

Producer Price Indices for Farm Products

(上年＝100) (preceding year=100)

指标	Item	2016	2017	2018	2019	2020	2021
农产品生产者价格指数	**Producers' Price Indices for Farm Products**	**102.8**	**98.6**	**100.5**	**112.2**	**108.7**	**104.2**
种植业产品	**Planting Products**	**98.5**	**99.3**	**101.2**	**106.1**	**107.9**	**110.7**
#谷物	Cereal	89.9	100.5	103.2	99.0	108.0	117.0
#小麦	Wheat	98.6	104.6	98.0	95.0	102.5	106.5
稻谷	Rice	102.7	101.3	99.8	91.0	102.4	102.3
玉米	Corn	82.3	97.5	107.9	102.7	113.0	126.7
大豆	Beans	91.8	101.6	92.9	99.1	106.4	128.7
油料	Oil-bearing Crops	102.7	92.3	85.7	108.8	112.2	108.6
棉花	Cotton	92.7	116.5	99.2	100.1	103.7	122.4
蔬菜	Vegetable	111.5	95.1	102.8	115.9	112.4	103.1
水果	Fruit	93.2	103.8	96.8	118.0	105.5	103.0
林业产品	**Forestry Products**	**98.7**	**101.2**	**101.4**	**100.3**	**104.8**	**101.5**
畜牧业产品	**Animal Husbandry Products**	**109.7**	**90.7**	**97.3**	**132.2**	**115.2**	**89.5**
活猪	Live Pig	126.7	84.2	84.0	162.7	146.3	62.9
活牛	Live Cattle and Buffaloes	95.8	101.2	110.1	112.0	113.8	103.5
活羊	Live Sheep and Goats	94.5	104.6	110.4	114.7	106.9	105.6
肉禽	Live Poultry	97.9	94.5	102.7	105.5	87.6	108.4
蛋类	Eggs	90.8	89.7	122.8	105.2	80.2	124.9
奶类	Milk	93.1	99.3	100.2	104.1	98.9	108.5
渔业产品	**Fishery Products**	**103.3**	**106.8**	**103.1**	**101.3**	**101.8**	**110.7**
海水养殖鱼类	Seawater Fish	87.1	127.4	120.7	102.2	81.3	124.6
淡水养殖鱼类	Freshwater Fish	104.0	103.6	107.8	96.9	106.2	117.3

9-11 工业生产者价格指数
Price Indices for Industrial Producer

年 份 Year	以1988年为100 (1988=100)		以上年为100 (preceding year=100)	
	工业生产者出厂价格指数 Producer Price Indices for Industrial Products	工业生产者购进价格指数 Industrial Producer Purchasing Price Indices	工业生产者出厂价格指数 Producer Price Indices for Industrial Products	工业生产者购进价格指数 Industrial Producer Purchasing Price Indices
1988	100.0	100.0		
1989	123.8	136.7	123.8	136.7
1990	129.6	144.1	104.7	105.4
1991	133.5	154.2	103.0	107.0
1992	146.5	171.0	109.7	110.9
1993	180.1	230.3	123.0	134.7
1994	223.7	279.4	124.2	121.3
1995	261.8	316.2	117.0	113.2
1996	272.5	334.3	104.1	105.7
1997	275.8	336.3	101.2	100.6
1998	264.7	318.1	96.0	94.6
1999	257.3	297.1	97.2	93.4
2000	272.5	311.1	105.9	104.7
2001	270.1	311.1	99.1	100.0
2002	266.8	307.0	98.8	98.7
2003	276.2	324.5	103.5	105.7
2004	293.8	369.3	106.4	113.8
2005	304.7	391.1	103.7	105.9
2006	311.7	407.9	102.3	104.3
2007	322.0	427.5	103.3	104.8
2008	349.7	483.5	108.6	113.1
2009	329.1	461.7	94.1	95.5
2010	352.6	504.6	107.2	109.3
2011	373.7	550.9	106.0	109.2
2012	367.7	546.5	98.4	99.2
2013	361.8	537.8	98.4	98.4
2014	356.0	528.1	98.4	98.2
2015	338.9	501.7	95.2	95.0
2016	333.8	491.7	98.5	98.0
2017	352.2	527.6	105.5	107.3
2018	365.2	546.6	103.7	103.6
2019	364.1	542.2	99.7	99.2
2020	357.3	528.4	98.1	97.5
2021	394.1	578.7	110.3	109.5

9-12 工业生产者出厂价格指数
Producer Price Indices for Industrial Products

(上年=100) (preceding year=100)

类 别	Category	2016	2017	2018	2019	2020	2021
总指数	**Total Price Indices**	**98.5**	**105.5**	**103.7**	**99.7**	**98.1**	**110.3**
轻工业	Light Industry	99.0	101.4	101.2	100.6	99.4	102.3
以农产品为原料	Agricultural Products as Raw Materials	99.1	101.3	101.5	100.9	99.5	103.2
以非农产品为原料	Non-agricultural Products as Raw Materials	98.5	101.5	100.5	99.3	99.0	100.5
重工业	Heavy Industry	98.3	107.2	104.6	99.3	97.6	113.2
采 掘	Mining	100.9	120.5	109.8	101.7	92.9	125.6
原 料	Raw Materials	95.9	110.2	106.7	97.2	94.4	118.4
加 工	Processing	99.2	104.9	103.1	100.2	99.5	108.0
生产资料	Means of Production	98.0	106.9	104.4	98.9	97.1	112.6
采 掘	Mining	100.9	120.5	109.8	101.7	92.9	125.6
原 料	Raw Materials	95.9	110.5	106.7	97.0	94.1	118.5
加 工	Processing	98.8	104.7	103.1	99.6	98.6	107.6
生活资料	Consumer Goods	100.0	100.6	101.0	102.3	101.5	101.0
食 品	Food	100.9	99.9	100.4	104.3	103.3	102.2
衣 着	Clothing	100.1	101.9	101.7	100.9	99.0	99.9
一般日用品	Articles for Daily Use	99.9	101.6	101.9	99.5	100.0	99.8
耐用消费品	Durable Consumer Goods	96.4	100.5	101.3	101.1	99.2	99.6
按工业部门分	**by Industrial Department**						
冶金工业	Metallurgical Industry	102.7	114.8	103.7	102.9	102.3	119.3
电力工业	Power Industry	96.2	99.8	97.7	98.2	98.9	101.1
煤炭及炼焦工业	Coal Industry	100.3	131.7	109.3	98.4	88.5	133.4
石油工业	Petroleum Industry	88.4	115.4	115.0	94.3	83.9	124.1
化学工业	Chemical Industry	97.5	105.6	104.3	97.5	96.2	113.6
机械工业	Machine Building Industry	98.7	101.1	101.6	99.7	99.8	101.5
建筑材料工业	Building Materials Industry	99.2	109.5	109.8	102.2	98.5	100.7
森林工业	Timber Industry	99.0	102.2	103.1	102.4	100.6	101.3
食品工业	Food Industry	99.9	99.9	100.7	104.1	103.9	103.2
纺织工业	Textile Industry	97.2	101.6	101.2	97.3	92.5	104.9
缝纫工业	Tailoring Industry	99.5	101.7	101.4	100.6	99.2	99.7
皮革工业	Leather Industry	101.4	100.5	103.0	102.5	98.4	100.0
造纸工业	Paper Industry	99.6	108.2	106.1	93.7	95.4	105.1
文教艺术用品工业	Industry of Cultural, Educational& Handicrafts Articles	100.7	102.5	101.8	99.3	99.0	98.3
其它工业	Others	100.6	103.2	100.0	98.5	100.9	107.3

9-13 工业生产者出厂价格指数(2021年)

Producer Price Indices for Industrial Products(2021)

(上年=100) (preceding year=100)

类 别	Category	全年平均 Annual Average	一季度 1st Quarter	二季度 2nd Quarter	三季度 3rd Quarter	四季度 4th Quarter
总指数	**Total Price Indices**	**110.3**	**103.2**	**111.4**	**112.2**	**114.5**
(一)核心指数	**Core Indices**	**108.8**	**103.9**	**109.5**	**110.4**	**111.5**
(二)高技术	**High Technology**	**99.8**	**99.5**	**99.5**	**100.2**	**100.1**
(三)能源	**Energy**	**120.0**	**100.5**	**123.4**	**125.0**	**133.2**
(四)按轻重工业分	**By Light and Heavy Industry**					
1.轻工业	Light Industry	102.3	101.0	102.4	102.6	103.3
(1)以农产品为原料	Agricultural Products as Raw Materials	103.2	101.6	103.6	103.5	104.2
(2)以非农产品为原料	Non-agricultural Products as Raw Materials	100.5	99.9	100.1	100.7	101.3
2.重工业	Heavy Industry	113.2	103.9	114.7	115.7	118.5
(1)采掘	Mining	125.6	109.6	133.1	127.8	133.5
(2)原料	Raw Materials	118.4	104.0	121.0	122.2	127.2
(3)加工	Processing	108.0	103.4	108.3	109.6	110.4
(五)按生产生活资料分	**By Means of Production and Consumer Goods**					
1.生产资料	Means of Production	112.6	103.7	114.0	115.0	117.7
(1)采掘	Mining	125.6	109.6	133.1	127.8	133.5
(2)原料	Raw Materials	118.5	104.1	121.2	122.4	127.2
(3)加工	Processing	107.6	103.0	108.0	109.3	110.3
2.生活资料	Consumer Goods	101.0	101.0	101.0	100.7	101.3
(1)食品	Food	102.2	102.4	102.8	101.4	102.3
(2)衣着	Clothing	99.9	99.0	99.6	100.4	100.5
(3)一般日用品	Articles for Daily Use	99.8	101.6	99.4	99.0	99.2
(4)耐用消费品	Durable Consumer Goods	99.6	96.3	98.7	101.6	102.0
(六)按初级中间最终产品分	**By Primary 、Intermediate and Final Products**					
1.初级产品	Primary Products	125.6	109.6	133.1	127.8	133.5
(1)矿产品	Minerals	125.6	109.6	133.1	127.8	133.5
(2)废料	Scrap					
2.中间产品	Intermediate Products	111.1	103.3	112.2	113.3	115.7
3.最终产品	Final Products	106.2	100.4	106.5	107.6	110.3
(1)最终投资品	Investment Goods	108.8	100.3	109.4	111.1	114.7
(2)最终消费品	Consumer Goods	101.1	100.6	101.0	100.8	101.9
(七)按工业部门分	**By Industrial Department**					
1.冶金工业	Metallurgical Industry	119.3	111.9	122.7	121.2	121.3
2.电力工业	Power Industry	101.1	99.4	100.8	100.8	103.6
3.煤炭及炼焦工业	Coal Industry	133.4	122.1	132.4	140.0	139.3
4.石油工业	Petroleum Industry	124.1	96.8	130.4	131.1	143.2
5.化学工业	Chemical Industry	113.6	105.1	114.1	117.0	118.1
6.机械工业	Machine Building Industry	101.5	100.2	101.5	102.1	102.3
7.建筑材料工业	Building Materials Industry	100.7	97.2	98.7	100.3	106.7
8.森林工业	Timber Industry	101.3	100.6	101.4	100.5	102.7
9.食品工业	Food Industry	103.2	103.5	103.8	102.4	102.9
10.纺织工业	Textile Industry	104.9	98.1	102.3	107.9	111.7
11.缝纫工业	Tailoring Industry	99.7	98.9	99.4	100.2	100.3
12.皮革工业	Leather Industry	100.0	98.8	101.8	101.1	98.6
13.造纸工业	Paper Industry	105.1	99.5	107.9	106.5	106.9
14.文教艺术用品工业	Industry of Cultural, Educational & Handicrafts Articles	98.3	96.9	97.9	98.8	99.7
15.其它工业	Others	107.3	104.6	106.3	107.6	110.5

9-13 续表 continued

(上年=100) (preceding year=100)

类　　别	Category	全年平均 Annual Average	一季度 1st Quarter	二季度 2nd Quarter	三季度 3rd Quarter	四季度 4th Quarter
(八)按工业行业分	**by Industrial Sector**					
煤炭开采和洗选业	Mining and Washing of Coal	129.9	113.8	125.4	137.1	143.6
石油和天然气开采业	Extraction of Petroleum and Natural Gas	149.9	102.3	200.8	153.2	169.7
黑色金属矿采选业	Mining of Ferrous Metal Ores	123.1	135.3	143.9	125.6	92.2
有色金属矿采选业	Mining of Non-ferrous Metal Ores	94.7	105.6	94.8	88.2	91.6
非金属矿采选业	Mining and Processing of Nonmetal Ores	108.9	99.8	104.8	112.4	118.9
开采专业及辅助性活动	Mining Specialties and Auxiliary Activities					
其他采矿业	Mining of Other Ores					
农副食品加工业	Processing of Food from Agricultural Products	103.5	104.3	104.7	102.6	102.6
食品制造业	Manufacture of Foods	103.4	102.5	103.5	103.1	104.6
酒、饮料和精制茶制造业	Manufacture of Wine, Drinks and Refined Tea	100.0	99.4	99.3	100.7	100.5
烟草制品业	Manufacture of Tobacco	101.4	101.9	102.1	101.8	100.0
纺织业	Manufacture of Textile	104.9	98.1	102.3	107.9	111.7
纺织服装、服饰业	Manufacture of Textile Wearing Apparel and Finery	99.7	98.9	99.4	100.2	100.3
皮革、毛皮、羽毛及其制品和制鞋业	Manufacture of Leather, Fur, Feather & Its Products and Footwear	100.0	98.8	101.8	101.1	98.6
木材加工及木 竹、藤、棕、草制品业	Timber Processing, Bamboo, Cane, Palm Fiber & Straw Products	101.5	100.9	101.5	100.6	103.0
家具制造业	Manufacture of Furniture	100.3	99.2	100.6	100.3	101.1
造纸及纸制品业	Manufacture of Paper and Paper Products	105.1	99.5	107.9	106.5	106.9
印刷和记录媒介复制业	Printing, Reproduction of Recording Media	95.9	94.4	95.1	96.6	97.5
文教、工美、体育和娱乐用品制造业	Manufacture of Culture, Education,Arts and crafts, Sport and Entertainment Goods	102.8	104.2	103.0	102.0	102.2
石油、煤炭及其他燃料加工业	Processing of Oil, Coal and Other Fuel	124.5	99.1	128.7	131.9	141.9
化学原料和化学制品制造业	Manufacture of Chemical Raw Material and Chemical Products	121.6	108.1	122.8	127.4	128.5
医药制造业	Manufacture of Medicines	100.3	102.2	100.2	99.2	99.6
化学纤维制造业	Manufacture of Chemical Fiber	107.9	103.2	108.0	109.1	111.5
橡胶和塑料制品业	Manufacture of Rubber and Plastic	101.2	98.9	100.9	101.9	103.3
非金属矿物制品业	Manufacture of Non-metallic Mineral Products	102.9	98.5	100.7	102.8	109.4
黑色金属冶炼及压延加工业	Manufacture and Processing of Ferrous Metals	129.3	116.9	136.2	133.6	130.4
有色金属冶炼及压延加工业	Manufacture & Processing of Non-ferrous Metals	116.3	110.3	118.2	117.0	119.6
金属制品业	Manufacture of Metal Products	108.0	101.7	107.0	111.1	112.2
通用设备制造业	Manufacture of General Purpose Machinery	100.7	100.0	101.0	101.1	100.9
专用设备制造业	Manufacture of Special Purpose Machinery	101.0	100.1	100.9	100.8	102.1
汽车制造业	Manufacture of Automotive	101.4	101.4	101.6	101.3	101.3
铁路、船舶、航空航天和其他运输设备制造业	Manufacture of Railroad,Marine,Aerospace and Other Transportation Equipment	100.3	100.0	100.3	100.4	100.5
电气机械及器材制造业	Manufacture of Electrical Machinery & Equipment	104.7	102.0	104.8	105.6	106.4
计算机、通信和其他电子设备制造业	Manufacture of Computer, Communications and Other Electronic Equipment	99.1	97.0	98.6	100.7	100.1
仪器仪表制造业	Manufacture of Measuring Instrument	101.0	100.4	100.8	100.8	101.9
其他制造业	Other Manufacture					
废弃资源综合利用业	Comprehensive Utilization of Waste					
金属制品、机械和设备修理业	Metal Products, Machinery and Equipment Repair Industry					
电力、热力生产和供应业	Production and Supply of Electric Power and Heat Power	101.1	99.4	100.8	100.8	103.6
燃气生产和供应业	Production and Supply of Gas	103.8	100.0	103.6	102.9	108.9
水的生产和供应业	Production and Supply of Water	100.0	100.0	100.0	100.0	100.0

9-14 工业生产者购进价格指数(2021年)
Industrial Producer Purchasing Price Indices(2021)

(上年=100) (preceding year=100)

类 别	Category	全年平均 Annual Average	一季度 1st Quarter	二季度 2nd Quarter	三季度 3rd Quarter	四季度 4th Quarter
总指数	**Total Price Indices**	**109.5**	**103.1**	**110.6**	**111.4**	**113.0**
一、按初级中间最终产品分	**By Primary and Intermediate Products**					
1.初级产品	Primary Products	118.0	107.9	119.5	120.3	124.3
(1)农产品	Farm Produce	106.8	108.8	108.8	104.8	104.8
(2)矿产品	Minerals	128.8	107.0	130.3	135.6	143.5
(3)废料	Scrap	110.9	108.9	113.3	110.8	110.8
2.中间产品	Intermediate Products	108.4	102.4	109.5	110.3	111.4
二、九大类原材料购进价格指数	**By Nine Categories of Raw Material**					
1.燃料、动力类	Fuel and Power	120.1	98.5	121.0	125.1	138.1
2.黑色金属材料类	Ferrous Metals	121.6	114.4	126.6	126.3	119.2
(1)钢材	Steel	116.0	106.6	118.4	120.8	118.3
(2)其它	Others	141.9	145.8	158.4	145.1	121.9
3.有色金属材料及电线类	Nonferrous Metals	114.1	108.8	116.5	115.0	116.2
4.化工原料类	Raw Chemical Materials	116.4	105.5	118.6	120.5	121.2
5.木材及纸浆类	Timber and Paper Pulp	109.2	102.9	112.3	112.3	109.6
6.建筑材料及非金属类	Building Materials and Nonmetal Ores	101.3	95.0	99.5	103.6	107.4
7.其它工业原材料及半成品类	Other Industrial Raw Materials and Semi-finished Products	103.5	100.7	102.8	104.8	105.8
8.农副产品类	Agricultural Products	101.5	105.5	105.6	99.1	96.0
9.纺织原料类	Textile Materials	105.7	102.0	104.6	106.6	109.4

9-15 各市住宅销售价格指数(2021年)

Price Indices for Real Estate(2021)

(上月=100) (Last Month=100)

类 别	Category	1月 January	2月 February	3月 March	4月 April	5月 May	6月 June
新建商品住宅	**New Commercial Residential Buildings**						
济 南	Jinan	100.2	100.4	100.5	100.8	101.0	101.5
青 岛	Qingdao	100.2	100.3	100.5	100.7	100.8	100.7
烟 台	Yantai	99.8	100.3	100.5	100.6	100.4	100.3
济 宁	Jining	100.7	100.6	100.8	100.7	101.0	100.8
二手住宅	**Second-hand House**						
济 南	Jinan	100.4	99.8	100.1	100.6	100.5	100.5
青 岛	Qingdao	99.9	100.3	100.4	100.5	100.4	100.3
烟 台	Yantai	100.4	100.3	100.5	100.5	100.3	100.3
济 宁	Jining	100.6	100.5	100.3	100.4	100.6	100.5

注：2021年，其他市数据暂不发布。
a)The data on other cities will not be released temporarily in 2021.

9-15 续表 continued

(上月=100) (Last Month=100)

类 别	Category	7月 July	8月 August	9月 September	10月 October	11月 November	12月 December
新建商品住宅	**New Commercial Residential Buildings**						
济 南	Jinan	100.7	100.6	100.4	99.6	99.5	100.0
青 岛	Qingdao	101.0	100.8	100.0	99.8	99.7	99.9
烟 台	Yantai	100.6	99.9	99.8	99.5	99.7	99.7
济 宁	Jining	100.7	100.1	100.4	99.9	99.6	99.5
二手住宅	**Second-hand House**						
济 南	Jinan	100.4	100.2	99.7	99.8	99.5	99.9
青 岛	Qingdao	100.3	100.1	99.9	99.9	99.6	99.7
烟 台	Yantai	100.6	100.1	99.9	99.8	99.8	99.9
济 宁	Jining	99.8	99.8	100.2	99.8	100.0	99.3

主要统计指标解释

居民消费价格指数 是反映一定时期内城乡居民所购买的生活消费品和服务项目价格变动趋势和程度的相对数，是对城市居民消费价格指数和农村居民消费价格指数进行综合汇总计算的结果。通过该指数可以观察和分析消费品的零售价格和服务项目价格变动对城乡居民实际生活费支出的影响程度。

城市居民消费价格指数 是反映一定时期内城市居民家庭所购买的生活消费品价格和服务项目价格变动趋势和程度的相对数。通过该指数可以观察和分析消费品的零售价格和服务项目价格变动对城镇居民收入和消费支出的影响。

农村居民消费价格指数 是反映一定时期内农村居民家庭所购买的生活消费品价格和服务项目价格变动趋势和程度的相对数。该指数可以观察农村消费品的零售价格和服务项目价格变动对农村居民收入和生活消费支出的影响。

商品零售价格指数 是反映一定时期内城乡商品零售价格变动趋势和程度的相对数。商品零售价格的变动与国家的财政收入、市场供需的平衡、消费与积累的比例关系有关。因此，该指数可以从一个侧面对上述经济活动进行观察和分析。

农产品生产价格指数 是反映一定时期内，农产品生产者出售农产品价格水平变动趋势及幅度的相对数。该指数可以客观反映全国农产品生产价格水平和结构变动情况，满足农业与国民经济核算需要。其中某代表品生产价格指数是通过对全部有出售该产品行为的调查单位的个体指数进行几何平均求得的，类价格指数是通过对其所属的类（或代表品）的价格指数进行加权平均求得的。季度累计价格指数的计算方法与分季指数的计算方法相同。

工业生产者价格指数 包括工业生产者出厂价格指数和工业生产者购进价格指数。

工业生产者出厂价格指数 反映工业企业产品第一次出售时的出厂价格的变化趋势和变动幅度。

工业生产者购进价格指数 反映工业企业作为中间投入产品的购进价格的变化趋势和变动幅度。

住宅销售价格指数 反映商品住宅价格总体变化趋势和变化幅度的相对数。各市住宅销售价格指数是由新建商品住宅价格指数和二手住宅价格指数组成。

Explanatory Notes on Main Statistical Indicators

Consumer Price Indices reflect the trend and degree of changes in prices of consumer goods and services purchased by urban and rural households during a given period. They are obtained by combining Consumer Price Indices of Urban Household and Consumer Price Indices of Rural Household. The Indices enable the observation and analysis of the degree of impact of the changes in the prices of retailed goods and services on the actual living expenses of urban and rural residents.

Urban Consumer Price Indices reflect the trend and degree of changes in prices of consumer goods and services purchased by urban households during a given period. It can be used to observe and analyze the impact of price changes in consumer goods and services on urban household income and consumption expenditure.

Rural Consumer Price Indices reflect the trend and degree of changes in prices of consumer goods and services purchased by rural households during a given period. It can be used to observe the impact of change in retail prices of consumer goods and service prices on rural household income and consumption expenditure on living.

Retail Price Indices reflect the trend and degree of change in retail prices of commodities during a given period. The change in retail prices of commodities is related to government revenue, the equilibrium of market supply and demand, and the ratio of consumption to accumulation. Therefore, the retail price indices are useful from an oblique perspective for observing and analyzing the changes of the above economic activities.

Indices of Producers' Prices for Farm Products reflect the trend and degree of changes in producers' prices received by farmers when they sell farm products during a given period. These indices depict the change in the level and structure of producers' prices of farm products of the country and meet the needs of agriculture statistics and national account statistics. The producers' price index of a given product is calculated through geometrical mean of individual indices of all surveyed units who sell such product, and the indices of a product category is obtained through weighted mean of price indices of all products in the category. Method for calculating accumulative quarterly indices is the same as for calculating the distinctive quarterly indices.

Producer Price Indices for Industrial Products reflect the trend and degree of changes in general ex-factory prices of all manufactured goods for first sale during a given period.

Industrial Producer Purchasing Price Indices reflect changes in the level and degree of purchasing prices such as intermediate input such as raw materials, fuels and power.

Price Indices for Real Estate reflect the trend and degree of changes in prices of real estate during a given period, including price indices for selling houses and buildings.

第10篇

居民生活

People's Livelihood

简 要 说 明

一、本篇资料的主要内容

本篇资料反映了全省居民、城镇居民、农村居民的家庭收支、就业、居住、耐用消费品拥有、生产和生活等方面的情况。

二、本篇资料的来源

本篇资料中历年城乡居民收支相关资料来源于城镇住户调查年报和农村住户调查年报，自2013年起，全省实施城乡住户调查一体化改革，居民收支相关资料来源于住户收支与生活状况调查年报，指标名称和口径范围有所调整，由国家统计局山东调查总队居民收支调查处整理提供。

Brief Introduction

I. Content

Data in this chapter show the basic conditions of the people's livelihood in Shandong Province, including income and expenditure of the households, employment, housing condition, consumption and possession of the major consumer goods, etc.

II. Source of Data

Data in this chapter over the years are collected by the sample survey on urban and rural households. Since 2013, Integrated Household Survey has been launched, so data of 2013 collected by annual survey of household incomes and living conditions may different from those of previous years due to the change of indexes and statistics scopes. All data are prepared and provided by the Division of Household Income and Expenditure Survey of the National Bureau of Statistics in Shandong.

10-1 居民人均可支配收入和指数
Per Capita Disposable Income of Households and Index

年 份	全省居民人均可支配收入 Per Capita Disposable Income of Households		城镇居民人均可支配收入 Per Capita Disposable Income of Urban Households		农村居民人均可支配收入 Per Capita Disposable Income of Rural Households	
	绝对数（元） Value (yuan)	指数（2005=100） Index(2005=100)	绝对数（元） Value (yuan)	指数（1978=100） Index(1978=100)	绝对数（元） Value (yuan)	指数（1978=100） Index(1978=100)
1978			391	100.0	115	100.0
1979			420	105.8	160	138.8
1980			448	109.7	210	172.5
1981			495	118.7	252	203.2
1982			525	125.3	300	239.6
1983			537	128.9	361	277.9
1984			639	150.9	395	299.9
1985			748	162.4	408	284.9
1986			854	176.7	449	301.4
1987			987	187.3	518	323.4
1988			1163	183.2	584	311.8
1989			1349	183.7	631	283.1
1990	895		1466	194.5	680	293.9
1991			1688	210.8	764	317.4
1992			1974	227.0	803	319.0
1993			2515	252.4	953	342.0
1994			3444	275.6	1320	389.2
1995			4264	292.1	1715	429.3
1996			4890	303.2	2086	479.1
1997			5191	311.7	2292	514.1
1998			5361	322.9	2454	556.3
1999			5766	347.4	2552	586.9
2000	4095		6417	382.1	2663	616.2
2001			6995	411.9	2810	634.7
2002			7473	445.7	2955	668.3
2003			8212	486.3	3159	703.7
2004			9191	529.6	3519	749.4
2005	6860	100.0	10422	594.2	3946	820.6
2006	7795	112.5	11780	664.9	4387	903.5
2007	9085	125.6	13726	746.0	5009	980.3
2008	10411	136.7	15628	811.6	5671	1045.0
2009	11398	149.7	17006	883.8	6154	1132.8
2010	12922	165.0	18971	961.6	7034	1250.6
2011	15077	183.3	21678	1050.1	8395	1409.4
2012	17127	204.0	24496	1162.5	9506	1564.4
2013	19008	221.5	26882	1248.5	10687	1716.1
2014	20864	238.8	29222	1329.7	11882	1880.8
2015	22703	256.7	31545	1416.1	12930	2027.5
2016	24685	273.4	34012	1494.0	13954	2149.2
2017	26930	293.9	36789	1591.1	15118	2295.3
2018	29205	310.9	39549	1670.7	16297	2410.1
2019	31597	325.8	42329	1734.2	17775	2537.8
2020	32886	329.9	43726	1747.7	18753	2584.4
2021	35705	354.0	47066	1857.8	20794	2837.6

注：1.本表2013—2021年人均可支配收入来源于住户收支与生活状况调查，1978—2012年数据是根据历史数据按住户收支与生活状况调查可比口径推算获得。可支配收入绝对数按当年价计算，指数按可比价计算。

a) The data of year 2013-2021 are compiled on the basis of the household survey on income and expenditure and living conditions, the data of year 1978-2012 are reckoned at comparable coverage by the household survey on income and expenditure and living conditions. The absolute amounts of disposable income are calculated at annual price, the index is calculated at comparable prices.

10-2 居民人均消费支出和指数
Per Capita Expense on Consumption of Households and Index

年 份	全省居民人均消费支出 Per Capita Expense on Consumption of Households		城镇居民人均消费支出 Per Capita Expense on Consumption of Urban Households		农村居民人均消费支出 Per Capita Expense on Consumption of Rural Households	
	绝对数（元） Value (yuan)	指数（2005=100） Index(2005=100)	绝对数（元） Value (yuan)	指数（1978=100） Index(1978=100)	绝对数（元） Value (yuan)	指数（1978=100） Index(1978=100)
1978			340	100.0	94	100.0
1979			367	106.5	128	135.6
1980			396	111.7	165	165.2
1981			450	124.3	202	199.1
1982			455	125.3	230	224.2
1983			473	131.0	264	248.4
1984			521	142.2	287	266.1
1985			670	168.1	322	274.7
1986			751	179.5	365	299.1
1987			813	178.1	406	309.8
1988			1026	186.4	482	314.4
1989			1161	182.3	513	281.4
1990	734		1229	188.1	547	288.5
1991			1407	202.8	613	310.9
1992			1599	212.2	656	318.1
1993			1947	225.5	724	317.1
1994			2635	243.4	996	358.4
1995			3285	259.8	1338	408.4
1996			3771	269.9	1653	462.9
1997			4041	280.3	1626	444.7
1998			4136	287.8	1587	438.4
1999			4497	312.9	1662	465.6
2000	2982		4991	343.2	1743	491.7
2001			5209	354.3	1865	513.8
2002			5539	381.7	1945	536.4
2003			5994	410.2	2066	561.3
2004			6577	437.8	2301	597.7
2005	4740	100.0	7333	482.8	2619	664.4
2006	5443	113.7	8309	541.6	2992	751.5
2007	6249	125.0	9464	594.3	3426	817.2
2008	7128	135.4	10752	644.9	3835	861.4
2009	7794	148.1	11711	702.8	4132	927.4
2010	8560	158.1	12761	746.4	4472	969.8
2011	9853	173.3	14164	791.5	5489	1124.2
2012	10902	187.8	15349	840.1	6304	1265.8
2013	11897	200.5	16646	892.3	6877	1347.2
2014	13329	220.4	18323	962.0	7962	1536.7
2015	14578	238.2	19854	1028.0	8748	1673.3
2016	15926	254.9	21495	1089.0	9519	1788.6
2017	17281	272.5	23072	1150.5	10342	1916.4
2018	18780	288.9	24798	1207.6	11270	2033.5
2019	20427	304.5	26731	1262.6	12309	2143.8
2020	20940	303.6	27291	1257.6	12660	2128.3
2021	22821	327.0	29314	1333.1	14299	2379.4

注：1.本表2013—2021年人均消费支出来源于住户收支与生活状况调查，1978—2012年数据是根据历史数据按住户收支与生活状况调查可比口径推算获得。消费支出绝对数按当年价计算，指数按可比价计算。

a) The data of year 2013-2021 are compiled on the basis of the household survey on income and expenditure and living conditions, the data of year 1978-2012 are reckoned at comparable coverage by the household survey on income and expenditure and living conditions. The absolute amounts of expense on consumption are calculated at annual price, the index is calculated at comparable prices.

10-3 主要年份城镇居民家庭基本情况
Basic Conditions of Urban Households of Major Years

年 份 Year	调查户数（户） Number of Households Surveyed (household)	平均每户家庭人口（人） Average Household Size (person)	平均每户就业人口（人） Average Number of Employed Persons per Household (person)	平均每一就业者负担人数（人） Number of Dependents per Employee (person)	人均可支配收入（元） Per Capita Disposable Income (yuan)	人均消费支出（元） Per Capita Consumption Expenditure (yuan)	人均住房建筑面积（平方米） Per Capita Construction Area of Building (sq.m)
1978	380	4.37	2.20	1.99	391	340	5.40
1980	380	4.35	2.50	1.74	448	396	5.70
1981	380	4.19	2.45	1.71	495	450	6.10
1982	430	4.07	2.42	1.68	525	455	6.11
1983	430	3.97	2.37	1.68	537	473	6.65
1984	430	3.93	2.35	1.67	639	521	6.90
1985	900	3.57	2.10	1.70	748	670	7.77
1986	1630	3.54	2.05	1.72	854	751	9.15
1987	1730	3.53	2.05	1.72	987	813	9.61
1988	1830	3.51	2.06	1.71	1163	1026	9.96
1989	2080	3.43	2.01	1.71	1349	1161	10.25
1990	2180	3.38	2.00	1.69	1466	1229	10.05
1991	2180	3.31	1.98	1.67	1688	1407	10.49
1992	2180	3.26	1.98	1.65	1974	1599	10.80
1993	2080	3.24	1.96	1.65	2515	1947	11.20
1994	2080	3.21	1.96	1.64	3444	2635	11.88
1995	2050	3.19	1.96	1.63	4264	3285	12.35
1996	2050	3.16	1.99	1.59	4890	3771	12.13
1997	2100	3.17	2.01	1.58	5191	4041	12.70
1998	2300	3.14	1.98	1.59	5361	4136	12.82
1999	2400	3.12	1.93	1.62	5766	4497	13.10
2000	2500	3.10	1.87	1.66	6417	4991	13.75
2001	2450	3.06	1.82	1.68	6995	5209	14.17
2002	2650	3.02	1.78	1.70	7473	5539	24.57
2003	2650	2.98	1.77	1.68	8212	5994	25.67
2004	2650	2.95	1.77	1.67	9191	6577	26.39
2005	2800	2.91	1.69	1.72	10422	7333	28.49
2006	3000	2.91	1.71	1.70	11780	8309	29.29
2007	3050	2.87	1.68	1.71	13726	9464	29.80
2008	3300	2.87	1.64	1.75	15628	10752	31.33
2009	3300	2.86	1.64	1.74	17006	11711	31.80
2010	3300	2.86	1.67	1.71	18971	12761	32.09
2011	3300	2.83	1.69	1.67	21678	14164	33.18
2012	3300	2.83	1.69	1.67	24496	15349	33.44
2013	3661	2.79	1.63	1.71	26882	16646	36.39
2014	3679	2.83	1.69	1.67	29222	18323	37.30
2015	3738	2.86	1.70	1.68	31545	19854	36.36
2016	3776	2.81	1.65	1.70	34012	21495	37.51
2017	3767	2.82	1.63	1.73	36789	23072	37.61
2018	4070	2.95	1.57	1.88	39549	24798	36.80
2019	4080	2.96	1.55	1.91	42329	26731	37.14
2020	4080	2.93	1.50	1.95	43726	27291	37.31
2021	4080	3.08	1.71	1.80	47066	29314	39.27

注：1.住房建筑面积指标2001年以前为人均居住面积，2002年以后为人均建筑面积。
2.从2013年起，全省实施城乡住户调查一体化改革，根据国家统一规定，2018年，按照新指标口径对居民收支调查历史数据进行修正（以下相关表同）。

a)Data before 2001 on construction area of building means per capita living space, data after 2002 per capita floor space.b)An integrated household survey institution has been implemented since 2013,including both urban and rural households.According to national uniform regulations,In 2018, the historical data of residents' income and expenditure surveys were revised according to the new indicators.(The same applies to tables following).

10-4 主要年份城镇居民人均可支配收入

Per Capita Disposable Income of Urban Households of Major Years

单位:元/人 (yuan/person)

年 份 Year	可支配收入 Disposable Income	工资性收入 Income of Wages and Salaries	经营净收入 Net Business Income	财产净收入 Net income from Properties	转移净收入 Net Income from Transfer
1978	391				
1979	420				
1980	448				
1981	495	464			31
1982	525	489			36
1983	537	505			31
1984	639	595			43
1985	748	654	6		88
1986	854	718	7		129
1987	987	852	4		131
1988	1163	977	4		182
1989	1349	1092	6	12	239
1990	1466	1234	6	16	211
1991	1688	1370	6	16	296
1992	1974	1680	5	27	262
1993	2515	2124	13	37	341
1994	3444	2941	2	54	447
1995	4264	3651	10	67	536
1996	4890	4316	4	103	467
1997	5191	4617	7	119	447
1998	5361	4716	18	118	508
1999	5766	4977	29	115	645
2000	6417	5432	79	128	779
2001	6995	5771	101	182	941
2002	7473	6456	170	102	744
2003	8212	7079	255	156	723
2004	9191	7874	342	178	798
2005	10422	8350	565	249	1258
2006	11780	9568	652	398	1162
2007	13726	10559	856	593	1718
2008	15628	11269	1408	716	2236
2009	17006	11934	1635	912	2525
2010	18971	12847	2099	1355	2670
2011	21678	14204	2789	1679	3006
2012	24496	16036	3193	1926	3341
2013	26882	17427	3653	2137	3666
2014	29222	18866	4036	2271	4049
2015	31545	20386	4375	2475	4309
2016	34012	21812	4778	2740	4681
2017	36789	23431	5194	3034	5131
2018	39549	25041	5584	3337	5588
2019	42329	26611	6046	3575	6097
2020	43726	27250	6097	3793	6586
2021	47066	28019	7995	3921	7131

10-5 主要年份城镇居民人均消费支出
Per Capita Consumption Expenditure of Urban Households of Major Years

单位：元/人 (yuan/person)

年份 Year	消费支出 Consumption Expenditure	食品烟酒 Food,tobacco and Liquor	衣 着 Clothing	居 住 Residence	生活用品及服 务 Supplies and Services	交通通信 Transport and Communi -cations	教育文化娱乐 Recreation, Education and Cultural	医疗保健 Health care and Medical Services	其他用品及服务 Miscellaneous Goods and Services
1978	340								
1979	367								
1980	396								
1981	450	248	72	19	40	10	41	3	19
1982	455	263	73	20	37	12	34	3	13
1983	473	284	71	23	38	13	31	2	11
1984	521	312	85	24	41	12	31	3	13
1985	670	339	103	32	72	11	86	5	21
1986	751	378	106	59	85	13	77	5	28
1987	813	433	121	38	97	14	72	7	30
1988	1026	524	155	39	156	19	86	11	36
1989	1161	603	158	48	145	19	121	16	50
1990	1229	636	186	46	141	23	125	23	48
1991	1407	734	229	60	151	28	124	23	59
1992	1599	816	267	79	166	38	141	32	59
1993	1947	898	349	125	186	59	206	48	76
1994	2635	1213	474	180	248	95	250	72	104
1995	3285	1489	571	224	309	169	294	107	122
1996	3771	1651	658	262	324	194	397	147	137
1997	4041	1662	674	325	344	236	475	180	144
1998	4136	1639	580	326	429	255	530	188	189
1999	4497	1665	602	393	548	270	593	220	205
2000	4991	1727	642	442	558	348	699	324	251
2001	5209	1773	663	522	518	401	755	330	247
2002	5539	1886	698	573	393	519	892	411	166
2003	5994	1986	717	727	453	607	883	447	174
2004	6577	2219	738	836	448	753	922	488	174
2005	7333	2377	800	1103	487	834	958	579	196
2006	8309	2549	923	1300	507	1075	1095	625	234
2007	9464	2937	1016	1677	627	1195	1065	704	244
2008	10752	3350	1107	2135	753	1239	1117	786	267
2009	11711	3562	1206	2310	824	1497	1156	872	284
2010	12761	3743	1324	2670	844	1834	1197	869	280
2011	14164	4271	1494	3026	933	1876	1302	924	338
2012	15349	4583	1606	3325	1035	2005	1391	993	411
2013	16646	4858	1612	3929	1147	2049	1565	1083	403
2014	18323	5298	1801	4016	1431	2377	1770	1188	442
2015	19854	5527	1943	4058	1477	2748	2141	1416	543
2016	21495	5929	1978	4473	1576	3002	2399	1610	527
2017	23072	6180	2034	4895	1736	3284	2622	1781	540
2018	24798	6529	2008	5302	1901	3605	2903	1966	584
2019	26731	6965	2042	5883	2083	3762	3171	2184	640
2020	27291	7319	2013	5973	2149	3688	3204	2298	647
2021	29314	7693	2097	6199	2319	4309	3666	2404	628

10-6 主要年份农村居民家庭基本情况

Basic Conditions of Rural Households of Major Years

年 份 Year	调查户数(户) Number of Households Surveyed (household)	平均每户常住人口(人) Average Number of Permanent Residents Per Household (person)	平均每户整半劳力(人) Average Number of Full/Semi Labour Force Per Household (person)	人均住房建筑面积(平方米) Per Capita Space of Living House at Year-end (sq.m)	人均可支配收入(元) Per Capita Disposable Income (yuan)	人均消费支出(元) Per Capita Consumption Expenditure (yuan)
1978	715	5.77	2.54	9.81	115	94
1979	732	5.65	2.67	9.91	160	128
1980	825	5.64	2.70	10.98	210	165
1981	827	5.49	2.63	10.03	252	202
1982	1529	5.13	2.54	10.64	300	230
1983	1438	5.05	2.85	12.50	361	264
1984	1558	4.96	2.86	14.54	395	287
1985	4000	4.72	2.84	15.13	408	322
1986	4200	4.68	2.85	15.74	449	365
1987	4200	4.60	2.86	16.48	518	406
1988	4200	4.54	2.86	17.34	584	482
1989	4200	4.46	2.85	17.96	631	513
1990	4200	4.40	2.82	18.48	680	547
1991	4200	4.34	2.77	19.87	764	613
1992	4200	4.26	2.75	19.31	803	656
1993	4200	4.17	2.77	20.64	953	724
1994	4200	4.10	2.76	21.15	1320	996
1995	4200	4.07	2.78	21.56	1715	1338
1996	4200	4.01	2.68	22.32	2086	1653
1997	4200	3.95	2.65	23.16	2292	1626
1998	4200	3.90	2.64	23.91	2454	1587
1999	4200	3.84	2.60	25.07	2552	1662
2000	4200	3.79	2.60	23.61	2663	1743
2001	4200	3.73	2.54	24.60	2810	1865
2002	4200	3.71	2.58	25.59	2955	1945
2003	4200	3.67	2.62	26.53	3159	2066
2004	4200	3.66	2.67	26.92	3519	2301
2005	4200	3.66	2.69	29.64	3946	2619
2006	4200	3.64	2.69	30.69	4387	2992
2007	4200	3.62	2.69	31.69	5009	3426
2008	4200	3.60	2.68	32.98	5671	3835
2009	4200	3.57	2.68	34.24	6154	4132
2010	4200	3.54	2.67	34.71	7034	4472
2011	4200	3.51	2.53	36.31	8395	5489
2012	4200	3.41	2.51	38.43	9506	6304
2013	3398	3.15	2.30	39.56	10687	6877
2014	3404	3.13	2.28	40.25	11882	7962
2015	3441	3.13	2.28	40.91	12930	8748
2016	3470	3.11	2.24	42.10	13954	9519
2017	3469	3.10	2.22	42.54	15118	10342
2018	3114	3.11	2.17	43.21	16297	11270
2019	3120	3.11	2.15	43.55	17775	12309
2020	3120	3.10	2.18	43.41	18753	12660
2021	3120	3.10	2.14	44.04	20794	14299

注：1.1978年至1980年的住房建筑面积中包括生产用房。
a)The space of production house is included in the space of living house from 1978 to 1980.

10-7 主要年份农村居民人均可支配收入
Per Capita Disposable Income of Rural Households of Major Years

单位：元/人 (yuan/person)

年 份 Year	可支配收入 Disposable Income	工资性收入 Income of Wages and Salaries	经营净收入 Net Business Income	财产净收入 Net income from Properties	转移净收入 Net Income from Transfer
1978	115	82	21	7	5
1979	160	109	37	3	10
1980	210	141	45	10	14
1981	252	165	57	11	18
1982	300	220	60	10	11
1983	361	55	286	8	13
1984	395	63	314	4	14
1985	408	81	309	6	12
1986	449	91	339	7	13
1987	518	112	385	6	15
1988	584	144	416	9	16
1989	631	161	444	9	17
1990	680	168	486	9	17
1991	764	181	551	9	23
1992	803	228	537	15	23
1993	953	226	688	9	30
1994	1320	295	961	17	47
1995	1715	409	1231	29	47
1996	2086	523	1467	48	49
1997	2292	686	1495	30	81
1998	2454	723	1604	49	78
1999	2552	780	1610	68	94
2000	2663	828	1699	57	80
2001	2810	926	1738	32	114
2002	2955	999	1773	44	138
2003	3159	1021	1934	60	144
2004	3519	1081	2228	61	149
2005	3946	1305	2369	95	177
2006	4387	1497	2549	117	224
2007	5009	1722	2878	131	279
2008	5671	1964	3172	146	388
2009	6154	2134	3368	173	479
2010	7034	2410	3794	203	627
2011	8395	3031	4324	210	829
2012	9506	3573	4649	219	1064
2013	10687	4189	4979	242	1276
2014	11882	4713	5431	287	1451
2015	12930	5139	5856	326	1608
2016	13954	5569	6267	359	1760
2017	15118	6069	6730	391	1928
2018	16297	6550	7194	429	2124
2019	17775	7165	7799	456	2355
2020	18753	7591	8095	485	2582
2021	20794	10430	7066	499	2798

10-8 主要年份农村居民人均消费支出

Per Capita Consumption Expenditure of Rural Households of Major Years

单位：元/人 (yuan/person)

年 份 Year	消费支出 Consumption Expenditure	食品烟酒 Food,tobacco and Liquor	衣 着 Clothing	居 住 Residence	生活用品及服 务 Supplies and Services	交通通信 Transport and Communications	教 育 文教娱乐 Education, Culture and Recreation	医疗保健 Health Care and Medical Services	其他用品及服 务 Miscellaneous Goods and Services
1978	94	58	13	11	10	1	1		
1979	128	78	17	15	13	1	2	1	
1980	165	99	24	21	11	3	4	2	1
1981	202	113	27	32	19	4	4	3	1
1982	230	116	31	47	22	4	6	3	1
1983	264	134	35	50	25	6	8	5	2
1984	287	149	35	57	24	5	11	5	2
1985	322	168	36	66	24	5	14	7	1
1986	365	182	39	86	26	6	16	8	1
1987	406	202	42	97	28	6	21	10	1
1988	482	238	49	115	36	8	24	11	1
1989	513	259	54	113	37	6	31	13	1
1990	547	297	53	106	34	6	33	17	1
1991	613	333	61	105	40	10	41	21	2
1992	656	358	62	106	39	14	48	26	3
1993	724	416	60	99	41	15	60	25	10
1994	996	577	75	151	53	20	76	31	12
1995	1338	749	102	209	74	43	106	40	16
1996	1653	872	131	265	98	59	144	64	20
1997	1626	872	131	216	98	64	149	71	24
1998	1587	801	116	240	92	78	156	84	21
1999	1662	809	112	250	106	90	183	89	24
2000	1743	762	114	295	114	100	212	117	27
2001	1865	775	118	354	91	131	231	113	52
2002	1945	800	124	327	95	153	267	125	53
2003	2066	841	127	331	91	183	307	136	50
2004	2301	935	130	354	109	217	318	152	86
2005	2619	1000	147	426	134	285	405	182	40
2006	2992	1083	180	521	156	340	444	214	55
2007	3426	1231	201	646	193	407	467	222	60
2008	3835	1383	222	759	237	436	464	270	65
2009	4132	1428	234	888	269	512	449	289	63
2010	4472	1574	266	779	319	621	479	367	67
2011	5489	1828	345	1054	407	723	558	487	87
2012	6304	2004	390	1310	403	903	589	610	93
2013	6877	2190	421	1319	437	1004	684	711	112
2014	7962	2465	489	1547	524	1226	801	776	134
2015	8748	2662	540	1627	553	1393	912	919	142
2016	9519	2833	576	1767	604	1545	1013	1027	153
2017	10342	2960	585	1974	690	1710	1141	1129	152
2018	11270	3162	622	2214	762	1873	1266	1205	166
2019	12309	3423	671	2421	838	1999	1429	1343	184
2020	12660	3722	689	2435	818	2112	1291	1413	181
2021	14299	4232	787	2693	925	2428	1499	1506	230

10-9 调查户和调查人口基本情况(2021年)
Condition of Households Surveyed and Residents Surveyed(2021)

指标名称		Indicator		全体居民 All Household	城镇居民 Urban Household	农村居民 Rural Household
一、调查户基本情况		**Basic Statistics on Households Surveyed**				
(一)调查样本住户数	(户)	Number of Households Surveyed	(household)	7200	4080	3120
(二)户主文化程度		Education of Head of Household				
1.未上过学	(%)	Can not Read	(%)	0.6	0.5	0.7
2.小学	(%)	Primary School	(%)	8.6	6.0	12.0
3.初中	(%)	Junior High School	(%)	56.0	43.4	72.7
4.高中	(%)	Senior High School	(%)	19.3	24.5	12.4
5.大学专科	(%)	Junior College	(%)	9.0	14.3	1.9
6.大学本科	(%)	Bachelor	(%)	5.9	10.2	0.3
7.研究生	(%)	Graduate	(%)	0.6	1.0	
(三)农业经营户比例	(%)	Proportion of Farming Households	(%)	31.2	13.5	54.5
二、期末户均调查人口	**(人)**	**Average Number of Residents Surveyed**	**(person)**	**3.2**	**3.2**	**3.3**
三、期末常住成员情况		**Condition of Permanent Residents**				
(一)户均常住成员	(人)	Average Number of Permanent Residents Per Household	(person)	3.1	3.1	3.1
其中：在校学生人数		Total Enrollment		0.6	0.6	0.7
(二)性别		Sex				
1.男性	(%)	Male	(%)	50.3	50.4	50.1
2.女性	(%)	Female	(%)	49.7	49.6	49.9
四、常住从业人员情况		**Employment of Permanent Residents**				
(一)户均常住从业人数	(人)	Average Number of Employed Permanent Residents Per Household	(person)	1.8	1.7	1.9
(二)就业状况		Employment				
1.雇主	(%)	Employer	(%)	0.7	1.1	0.2
2.公职人员	(%)	Public Officials	(%)	1.1	2.0	0.1
3.事业单位人员	(%)	Institution staff	(%)	4.7	8.3	0.4
4.国有企业雇员	(%)	Employees of State-owned Enterprises	(%)	3.0	5.1	0.4
5.其他雇员	(%)	Other Employees	(%)	58.7	61.9	54.9
6.农业自营	(%)	Agricultural Operations	(%)	20.1	7.7	35.0
7.非农自营	(%)	Non-Agricultural Operations	(%)	11.6	13.9	8.9
(三)主要从事行业		Sector Employment				
1.第一产业	(%)	Primary Industry	(%)	22.0	9.1	37.5
2.第二产业	(%)	Second Industry	(%)	32.1	29.0	35.8
3.第三产业	(%)	Tertiary Industry	(%)	45.9	61.9	26.7

10-10 全体居民人均可支配收入
Per Capita Disposable Income of All Households

单位：元/人 (yuan/person)

指标名称	Indicator	2020	2021
可支配收入	**Disposable Income**	**32886**	**35705**
一、工资性收入	**Income of Wages and Salaries**	**18716**	**20413**
(一)工资	Wage	17965	19723
(二)实物福利	Benefits in kind	70	95
(三)其他	Others	682	595
二、经营净收入	**Net Business Income**	**6964**	**7593**
(一)第一产业净收入	Net Income from Primary Industry	2244	2371
1.农业	Farming	1804	2031
2.林业	Forestry	117	91
3.牧业	Animal Husbandry	295	218
4.渔业	Fishery	29	30
(二)第二产业净收入	Net Income from Second Industry	887	985
(三)第三产业净收入	Net Income from Tertiary Industry	3833	4237
三、财产净收入	**Net Income from Properties**	**2357**	**2441**
(一)利息净收入	Net Income from Interest	138	157
(二)红利收入	Income from Bonus	136	150
(三)储蓄性保险净收益	Income from Savings Insurance	7	6
(四)转让承包土地经营权租金净收入	Net Income from Land Management Rights Transfer	113	123
(五)出租房屋净收入	Net Income from Renting Houses	369	426
(六)出租其他资产净收入	Net Income from Renting Other assets	10	19
(七)自有住房折算净租金	Income from Net Rent Equivalent to the value of Owned housing	1513	1487
(八)其他	Others	72	74
四、转移净收入	**Net Income from Transfer**	**4848**	**5257**
(一)转移性收入	Income from Transfer	6804	7346
1.养老金或离退休金	Old-age Pensions	5292	5572
2.社会救济和补助	Relief and Pensions	75	67
3.惠农补贴	Subsidies for Agriculture from The Government	105	117
4.政策性生活补贴	Policy-living Allowance	95	94
5.报销医疗费	Allowance of Medical Expense	321	392
6.家庭外出从业人员寄回带回收入	Sent Back by Non-permanent Resident	519	632
7.赡养收入	Alimony Income	249	288
8.其他经常转移收入	Others	95	116
9.从政府和组织得到的实物产品和服务折价	Equivalent Monetary value of Physical products and services from The Government and other Organizations	53	67
(二)转移性支出	Expenditure for Transfers	1956	2089
1.个人所得税	Personal Income Tax	129	143
2.社会保障支出	Social Security Expenditure	1505	1593
3.外来从业人员寄给家人的支出	Sent to Family by Outland Employees	61	55
4.赡养支出	Alimony Expense	179	194
5.其他经常转移支出	Others	82	103

10-11 城镇居民人均可支配收入
Per Capita Disposable Income of Urban Households

单位：元/人 (yuan/person)

指 标 名 称	Indicator	2020	2021
可支配收入	**Disposable Income**	**43726**	**47066**
一、工资性收入	**Income of Wages and Salaries**	**27250**	**28019**
(一)工资	Wage	26002	26884
(二)实物福利	Benefits in kind	97	127
(三)其他	Others	1151	1008
二、经营净收入	**Net Business Income**	**6097**	**7995**
(一)第一产业净收入	Net Income from Primary Industry	411	702
1.农业	Farming	321	592
2.林业	Forestry	15	23
3.牧业	Animal Husbandry	68	79
4.渔业	Fishery	7	8
(二)第二产业净收入	Net Income from Second Industry	1050	1289
(三)第三产业净收入	Net Income from Tertiary Industry	4636	6004
三、财产净收入	**Net Income from Properties**	**3793**	**3921**
(一)利息净收入	Net Income from Interest	175	211
(二)红利收入	Income from Bonus	198	220
(三)储蓄性保险净收益	Income from Savings Insurance	4	8
(四)转让承包土地经营权租金净收入	Net Income from Land Management Rights Transfer	44	59
(五)出租房屋净收入	Net Income from Renting Houses	629	726
(六)出租其他资产净收入	Net Income from Renting Other assets	15	17
(七)自有住房折算净租金	Income from Net Rent Equivalent to the value of Owned housing	2674	2621
(八)其他	Others	55	60
四、转移净收入	**Net Income from Transfer**	**6586**	**7131**
(一)转移性收入	Income from Transfer	9516	10252
1.养老金或离退休金	Old-age Pensions	8320	8741
2.社会救济和补助	Relief and Pensions	77	60
3.惠农补贴	Subsidies for Agriculture from The Government	21	41
4.政策性生活补贴	Policy-living Allowance	123	124
5.报销医疗费	Allowance of Medical Expense	325	453
6.家庭外出从业人员寄回带回收入	Sent Back by Non-permanent Resident	306	393
7.赡养收入	Alimony Income	173	221
8.其他经常转移收入	Others	113	141
9.从政府和组织得到的实物产品和服务折价	Equivalent Monetary value of Physical products and services from The Government and other Organizations	58	77
(二)转移性支出	Expenditure for Transfers	2930	3121
1.个人所得税	Personal Income Tax	222	245
2.社会保障支出	Social Security Expenditure	2217	2342
3.外来从业人员寄给家人的支出	Sent to Family by Outland Employees	106	93
4.赡养支出	Alimony Expense	274	291
5.其他经常转移支出	Others	111	150

10-12　农村居民人均可支配收入
Per Capita Disposable Income of Rural Households

单位：元/人　　(yuan/person)

指标名称	Indicator	2020	2021
可支配收入	**Disposable Income**	**18753**	**20794**
一、工资性收入	**Income of Wages and Salaries**	**7591**	**10430**
(一)工资	Wage	7487	10326
(二)实物福利	Benefits in kind	34	52
(三)其他	Others	70	52
二、经营净收入	**Net Business Income**	**8095**	**7066**
(一)第一产业净收入	Net Income from Primary Industry	4635	4561
1.农业	Farming	3738	3920
2.林业	Forestry	250	181
3.牧业	Animal Husbandry	590	401
4.渔业	Fishery	57	60
(二)第二产业净收入	Net Income from Second Industry	674	586
(三)第三产业净收入	Net Income from Tertiary Industry	2786	1919
三、财产净收入	**Net Income from Properties**	**485**	**499**
(一)利息净收入	Net Income from Interest	89	86
(二)红利收入	Income from Bonus	56	59
(三)储蓄性保险净收益	Income from Savings Insurance	11	2
(四)转让承包土地经营权租金净收入	Net Income from Land Management Rights Transfer	203	206
(五)出租房屋净收入	Net Income from Renting Houses	29	32
(六)出租其他资产净收入	Net Income from Renting Other assets	5	22
(七)其他	Others	93	92
四、转移净收入	**Net Income from Transfer**	**2582**	**2798**
(一)转移性收入	Income from Transfer	3269	3533
1.养老金或离退休金	Old-age Pensions	1344	1412
2.社会救济和补助	Relief and Pensions	73	77
3.惠农补贴	Subsidies for Agriculture from The Government	214	217
4.政策性生活补贴	Policy-living Allowance	59	55
5.报销医疗费	Allowance of Medical Expense	316	311
6.家庭外出从业人员寄回带回收入	Sent Back by Non-permanent Resident	796	947
7.赡养收入	Alimony Income	349	376
8.其他经常转移收入	Others	71	83
9.从政府和组织得到的实物产品和服务折价	Equivalent Monetary value of Physical products and services from The Government and other Organizations	46	55
(二)转移性支出	Expenditure for Transfers	686	735
1.个人所得税	Personal Income Tax	9	10
2.社会保障支出	Social Security Expenditure	577	610
3.外来从业人员寄给家人的支出	Sent to Family by Outland Employees	2	5
4.赡养支出	Alimony Expense	55	67
5.其他经常转移支出	Others	44	42

10-13 全体居民人均消费支出

Per Capita Expense on Consumption of All Households

单位：元/人　　(yuan/person)

指 标 名 称	Indicator	2020	2021
消费支出	**Expense on Household Consumption**	**20940**	**22821**
#服务性消费支出	Service Consumption	8507	9027
一、食品烟酒	Food,Tobacco and liquor	5757	6196
二、衣着	Clothing	1438	1530
三、居住	Residence	4437	4683
四、生活用品及服务	Supplies and Services	1571	1716
五、交通通信	Transport and Communications	3004	3496
六、教育文化娱乐	Recreation,Education and Cultural	2374	2729
七、医疗保健	Health care	1914	2016
八、其他用品及服务	Others	445	456

10-14 城镇居民人均消费支出

Per Capita Expense on Consumption of Urban Households

单位：元/人　　(yuan/person)

指 标 名 称	Indicator	2020	2021
消费支出	**Expense on Household Consumption**	**27291**	**29314**
#服务性消费支出	Service Consumption	11430	12038
一、食品烟酒	Food,Tobacco and liquor	7319	7693
二、衣着	Clothing	2013	2097
三、居住	Residence	5973	6199
四、生活用品及服务	Supplies and Services	2149	2319
五、交通通信	Transport and Communications	3688	4309
六、教育文化娱乐	Recreation,Education and Cultural	3204	3666
七、医疗保健	Health care	2298	2404
八、其他用品及服务	Others	647	628

10-15 农村居民人均消费支出

Per Capita Expense on Consumption of Rural Households

单位：元/人 (yuan/person)

指标名称	Indicator	2020	2021
消费支出	**Expense on Household Consumption**	**12660**	**14299**
#服务性消费支出	Service Consumption	4695	5075
一、食品烟酒	Food,Tobacco and liquor	3722	4232
二、衣着	Clothing	689	787
三、居住	Residence	2435	2693
四、生活用品及服务	Supplies and Services	818	925
五、交通通信	Transport and Communications	2112	2428
六、教育文化娱乐	Recreation,Education and Cultural	1291	1499
七、医疗保健	Health care	1413	1506
八、其他用品及服务	Others	181	230

10-16 居民家庭能源消费数量和金额(2021年)

Energy consumption of Households(2021)

指标名称	Indicator	全体居民 All Households		城镇居民 Urban Households		农村居民 Rural Households	
		数量 Amount	金额(元/人) Money (yuan/person)	数量 Amount	金额(元/人) Money (yuan/person)	数量 Amount	金额(元/人) Money (yuan/person)
一、生活用电 （度）	**Electricity Consumption (kW·h)**	**509.8**	**289.1**	**542.1**	**308.7**	**467.4**	**263.4**
二、生活用燃料	**Living With Fuel**						
(一)燃气	Gas						
1.罐装液化石油气 (公斤/人)	Bottled LPG (kg/person)	5.0	31.0	3.3	21.0	7.1	44.1
2.管道煤气 (立方米/人)	Gas Pipeline (Cum/person)	1.1	3.6	1.3	4.1	0.7	2.9
3.管道天然气 (立方米/人)	Natural gas pipeline (Cum/person)	26.5	72.7	33.8	94.6	16.9	44.0
(二)燃料用油	Fuel Oil						
1.汽油 (升/人)	Gasoline (Liters/person)	0.07	0.49	0.09	0.58	0.06	0.38
2.柴油 (升/人)	Diesel Oil (Liters/person)	0.09	0.42	0.07	0.38	0.10	0.47
(三)其他燃料	Other Fuels						
1.煤炭 (公斤/人)	Coke (kg/person)	95.3	124.2	56.0	75.5	146.7	188.1
2.柴 (公斤/人)	Firewood (kg/person)	0.005	0.320	0.002	0.059	0.008	0.663
3.草 (公斤/人)	Grass (kg/person)	0.001	0.001	0.001	0.002		
4.沼气 (立方米/人)	Biogas (Cum/person)	0.001	0.003			0.002	0.006

10-17 居民家庭人均食品消费数量(2021年)
Per Capita Food Consumption of Households(2021)

单位：公斤/人 (kg/person)

指 标 名 称	Indicator	全体居民 All Households	城镇居民 Urban Households	农村居民 Rural Households
一、粮食	**Grain**	**139.3**	**121.5**	**162.6**
(一)谷物	Cereal	127.9	110.5	150.8
1.大米	Wheat	14.0	14.0	13.9
2.面粉	Rice	104.3	87.8	125.9
3.玉米	Corn	3.9	2.9	5.1
4.其他谷物及制品	Others	5.8	5.7	5.9
(二)薯类	Tubers	2.2	2.2	2.3
1.红薯	Sweet Potato	0.6	0.6	0.7
2.马铃薯	Potato	1.2	1.1	1.3
3.其他薯类及制品	Others	0.4	0.4	0.4
(三)豆类	Beans	9.1	8.8	9.4
1.大豆	Soybean	0.5	0.3	0.7
2.其他豆类	Others	8.6	8.5	8.7
二、食用油	**Cooking oil**	**8.3**	**7.4**	**9.4**
(一)食用植物油	Edible vegetable oil	8.2	7.4	9.3
(二)食用动物油	Edible animal oil	0.0	0.0	0.1
三、蔬菜及食用菌	**Vegetables and Mushroom**	**98.1**	**101.2**	**93.9**
(一)鲜菜	Fresh Vegetables	94.1	97.0	90.2
(二)干菜及菜制品	Dried Vegetables and Products	1.6	1.6	1.6
(三)鲜菌	Fresh Mushrooms	2.3	2.5	2.1
(四)干菌及制品	Dry Bacteria and Products	0.1	0.2	0.1
四、肉禽及制品	**Products of Meat and Poultry**	**37.8**	**38.5**	**36.9**
(一)肉类	Meat	28.5	29.5	27.2
1.猪肉	Pork	21.0	21.0	21.0
2.牛肉	Beef	1.1	1.5	0.7
3.羊肉	Mutton	1.1	1.4	0.8
4.其他肉类及制品	Other meat and Processed Products	5.2	5.6	4.7
(二)禽类	Poultry	9.3	8.9	9.7
1.鸡	Chickens	5.9	5.5	6.5
2.鸭	Ducks	0.1	0.1	0.1
3.鹅	Gooses	0.1	0.1	0.1
4.其他禽类及制品	Other Poultry and Processed Products	3.2	3.2	3.1
五、水产品	**Aquatic Products**	**11.9**	**14.1**	**9.0**
(一)鱼类	Fish	6.4	7.2	5.5
(二)虾蟹贝类	Shrimp,Shellfish and Crab	3.9	5.0	2.3
(三)藻类	Algae	0.2	0.3	0.2
(四)其他水产品及制品	Others	1.4	1.7	1.0
六、蛋类	**Eggs and Products**	**21.3**	**20.6**	**22.3**
(一)鲜蛋	Fresh Eggs	21.0	20.2	22.0
(二)蛋制品	Egg Products	0.3	0.4	0.3
七、奶类	**Milk and Dairy Products**	**17.1**	**19.9**	**13.3**
(一)鲜奶	Fresh Milk	12.4	14.4	9.8
(二)酸奶	Yoghurt	3.5	4.2	2.7
(三)奶粉	Milk Powder	0.4	0.5	0.2
(四)其他奶制品	Other Milk Products	0.7	0.8	0.6
八、干鲜瓜果类	**Dried and Fresh Melons and Fruits**	**80.6**	**83.3**	**77.1**
(一)鲜瓜果	Fresh Melons and Fruits	73.5	76.0	70.2
(二)瓜果制品	Processed Products of melons and Fruits	1.9	2.1	1.6
(三)坚果类	Nuts and Processed Products	5.3	5.3	5.3
九、糖果糕点类	**Candy and Pastry**	**8.6**	**8.6**	**8.5**
(一)食糖	Sugar	0.8	0.7	0.9
(二)糖果	Candy	0.8	0.8	0.7
(三)糕点	Pastry	6.5	6.5	6.5
(四)其他糖果糕点	Others	0.6	0.6	0.5

10-18　居民家庭住房和耐用消费品拥有情况(2021年)
Household Ownership of Housing and Durables Consumer Goods(2021)

单位：%　　　　(%)

指标名称	Indicator	全体居民 All Households	城镇居民 Urban Households	农村居民 Rural Households
一、现住房情况	**Housing Condition**			
(一)人均住房建筑面积　(平方米)	Per Capita Construction Area of Building　(sq.m)	41.3	39.3	44.0
(二)按居住空间样式分的户数比重	Proportion of Housing Style			
1.单栋楼房	Single Building Housing	9.2	8.7	9.9
2.单栋平房	Single Bungalow	54.1	29.3	86.7
3.单元房	Units Housing	36.3	61.5	3.2
4.筒子楼或连片平房	Tube-shaped Apartment or Contiguous Bungalow	0.4	0.5	0.2
5.其他	Others			
(三)按主要建筑材料分的户数比重	Proportion of Housing Building Materials			
1.钢筋混凝土	Reinforced Concrete	38.1	55.9	14.7
2.砖混材料	Brick and Concrete Materials	42.2	35.1	51.6
3.砖瓦砖木	Brick and Wood Materials	19.6	9.0	33.7
4.竹草土坯	Bamboo,Grass, Adobe Materials			
5.其他	Others			
(四)按房屋来源分的户数比重	Proportion of Housing Source			
1.租赁住房	Leasehold	1.9	3.1	0.3
2.自建住房	Self-built	61.3	35.9	94.8
3.购买商品房	Commercial Housing	22.1	37.8	1.5
4.购买房改住房	Reform Housing	3.6	6.2	
5.购买保障性住房	Indemnificatory Housing	0.7	1.0	0.3
6.拆迁安置房	Resettlement Housing	9.3	14.6	2.3
7.继承或获赠住房	Inheritance or Gift Housing	0.5	0.3	0.6
8.其他	Others	0.7	1.0	0.2
(五)住房外道路为硬化路面的户比重	Proportion of Hardening Road Near Housing	97.0	98.6	94.9
二、生活设施状况	**Living Condition**			
(一)饮用水状况	Drinking Water Condition			
1.取水位置	Water Intake Location			
①住宅内管道取水	Residential Pipeline Water Intake	85.5	92.2	76.5
②住宅内其他方式取水	Other Residential Water Intake Method	1.9	1.8	2.1
③院内管道取水	Courtyard Pipeline Water Intake	11.3	5.1	19.5
④院内其他方式取水	Other Courtyard Water Intake Method	0.8	0.6	1.0
⑤其他位置取水	Others	0.6	0.4	0.8
2.主要饮用水来源	Source of Drinking Water			
①经过净化处理的自来水	Tap Water	92.2	97.1	85.7
②受保护的井水和泉水	Protected Wells and Springs	7.6	2.8	14.0
③不受保护的井水和泉水	Non-Protected Wells and Springs			
④江河湖泊水	Rivers and Lakes Water			
⑤其他饮用水来源	Others(%)	0.2	0.1	0.4

10-18 续表 continued

单位：% (%)

指标名称	Indicator	全体居民 All Households	城镇居民 Urban Households	农村居民 Rural Households
3.获取饮用水存在的主要困难	Major Difficulty on Obtaining Drinking Water			
①单次取水往返时间超过半小时	Round-trip Time More Than Half Hour			
②间断或定时供水	Intermittent or Regular Supply	0.2	0.2	0.2
③当年连续缺水超过15天	Water over More than 15 days			
④获取饮用水无困难	No Difficulty	99.8	99.8	99.8
4.饮用前家里采取的主要处理措施	Treatment of Drinking Water			
①煮沸	Boiling	97.0	95.9	98.4
②加漂白剂/氯等	Add bleach / chlorine			0.0
③使用水过滤器	Water Filter	2.3	3.4	1.0
④其他处理措施	Others	0.6	0.7	0.5
⑤没有任何水处理措施	No Treatment			
(二)住宅内厕所状况	Toilet Condition			
1.水冲式卫生厕所	Flushing Sanitary Toilet	89.5	94.2	83.4
2.水冲式非卫生厕所	Flushing Non-Sanitary Toilet	0.3	0.3	0.3
3.卫生旱厕	Sanitary toilet	8.8	4.6	14.2
4.普通旱厕	Ordinary Toilet	1.4	0.9	2.1
5.无厕所	No Toilet			
(三)主要炊用能源	Major Source of Cooking			
1.天然气、煤气、液化石油气	Natural Gas, Coal Gas, Liquefied Petroleum Gas	74.7	85.4	60.6
2.煤炭	Coal	2.4	1.0	4.3
3.电	Electricity	19.8	11.8	30.4
4.沼气	Biogas	0.02	0.03	
5.其他	Others	3.0	1.7	4.8
三、每百户耐用消费品拥有情况	**Number of Durable Consumer Goods Owned by Per 100 Households**			
(一)家用汽车 (辆)	Automobiles (unit)	52.4	63.1	38.2
(二)摩托车 (辆)	Motorcycles (unit)	21.3	13.6	31.6
(三)电冰箱(柜) (台)	Refrigerators (unit)	103.9	104.6	102.9
(四)洗衣机 (台)	Washing Machines (unit)	99.5	100.8	97.7
(五)热水器 (台)	Water Heaters (unit)	96.6	99.6	92.7
(六)空调 (台)	Air Conditioner (unit)	135.8	157.1	107.7
(七)彩色电视机 (台)	Color TV Sets (unit)	104.8	104.8	104.9
(八)照相机 (台)	Cameras (unit)	9.0	14.8	1.5
(九)计算机 (台)	Computers (unit)	49.7	63.3	31.7
其中：接入互联网的计算机 (台)	Computers With Internet Access (unit)	44.6	57.2	28.1
(十)中高档乐器 (架)	High-grade Instruments (unit)	4.8	7.8	0.7
(十一)固定电话 (线)	Fixed-line Phones (unit)	5.4	6.3	4.3
(十二)移动电话 (部)	Mobile Phones (unit)	242.0	244.2	239.1
其中：接入互联网的移动电话 (部)	Mobile Phones With Internet Access (unit)	198.1	201.5	193.7
(十三)健身器材 (组)	Fitness Equipment (unit)	4.5	7.2	0.9
(十四)空气净化器(含新风系统) (台)	Air Purifier (Including Central Ventilation System) (unit)	5.9	9.6	0.9
(十五)吸尘器 (台)	Dust Collector (unit)	11.1	18.3	1.4

10-19 社区基础设施和居民享有的基本社会服务情况(2021年)
Community Infrastructure and Basic Social Services(2021)

单位：% (%)

指标名称	Indicator	全体居民 All Households	城镇居民 Urban Households	农村居民 Rural Households
一、社区基础设施情况和基本公共服务	**Community Infrastructure and Basic Social Services**			
(一)社区通公路的户比重	Proportion of Community Access Roads	100.0	100.0	100.0
(二)社区能便利地乘坐公共汽车的户比重	Proportion of Communities Through Bus	99.0	99.6	98.3
(三)社区通电的户比重	Proportion of Community Having Powered	100.0	100.0	100.0
(四)社区通电话的户比重	Proportion of Community Having Phone	100.0	100.0	100.0
(五)社区能接收有线电视信号的户比重	Proportion of Communities Can Receive TV signals	100.0	100.0	100.0
(六)社区饮用水经过了集中净化处理的户比重	Proportion of Community Drinking Purification water	99.6	100.0	99.1
(七)社区主要饮用水水源无化学污染的户比重	Proportion of Community Water Source Free of Chemical Contamination	100.0	100.0	100.0
(八)社区开通了管道燃气的户比重	Proportion of Community Open Gas Pipeline	53.4	74.6	25.5
(九)社区有集中供暖的户比重	Proportion of Community Have Central Heating	37.1	62.3	3.7
(十)按进社区道路状况分的户比重	Proportion of Road Into the Community			
1.水泥或柏油路面	Cement or Asphalt Road	100.0	100.0	100.0
2.沙石或石板等硬质路面	Hardening Road			
3.其他	Others			
(十一)按社区内主要道路状况分的户比重	Proportion of Community Road Conditions			
1.水泥或柏油路面	Cement or Asphalt Road	100.0	100.0	100.0
2.沙石或石板等硬质路面	Hardening Road			
3.其他	Others			
(十二)社区主要道路有路灯的户比重	Proportion of Community Main Road Have Streetlights	99.0	99.4	98.5
(十三)社区内垃圾能集中处理的户比重	Proportion of Community Can Focus Process Garbage	100.0	100.0	100.0
(十四)社区有健身器材的户比重	Proportion of Community With Fitness Equipment	99.4	99.6	99.2
(十五)社区有绿化园林景观的户比重	Proportion of Community Have Green Landscape	67.9	80.7	51.0
(十六)社区有卫生站(室)的户比重	Proportion of Community Have Health Stations	94.2	96.5	91.2
(十七)按上幼儿园便利程度分的户比重	Proportion of Classification by Kindergarten			
1.社区内有，且便利	Community kindergarten,Convenience	45.4	51.6	37.3
2.社区内无，但入园较便利	No Community kindergarten,Convenience	53.5	48.1	60.5
3.不便利	No Convenience	1.1	0.3	2.2
(十八)按上小学便利程度分的户比重	Proportion of Classification by Primary school and Convenience			
1.社区内有，且便利	Community Primary school,Convenience	45.0	52.0	35.4
2.社区内无，但入学较便利	No Community Primary school,Convenience	53.9	47.8	62.4
3.不便利	No Convenience	1.1	0.2	2.2
(十九)社区本年度未发生盗窃或其他刑事案件的户比重	Proportion of Community Without Theft or Other Criminal Cases	96.7	95.3	98.6
(二十)社区有安全保卫的户比重	Proportion of Community with Security	76.7	82.9	68.5
(二十一)行政村拥有合法行医证的医生的户比重	Proportion of Village have Legitimate Doctor	56.7	36.3	83.7
(二十二)行政村有合格接生员的户比重	Proportion of Village Have Qualified Midwives	8.5	7.7	9.4
二、社会保障	**Social Securities**			
参加医疗保险或享受公费医疗的人数比重	Proportion of Participated Medical Insurance or Public Health Services			
1.新型农村合作医疗	New Rural Cooperative Medical	19.7	13.9	27.4
2.城镇职工基本医疗保险	Urban Basic Medical Insurance	21.0	32.8	5.4
3.城乡居民基本医疗保险	Resident Basic Medical Insurance	58.2	51.8	66.7
4.公费医疗	Public Health Services	0.1	0.1	
5.商业医疗保险	Commercial Medical Insurance	4.0	5.4	2.3
6.其他医疗保险	Others	0.5	0.6	0.2
7.没有参加任何医疗保险	No Medical Insurance	0.6	0.8	0.3

10-20 各市全体居民人均收支情况(2021年)

Per Capita Income and Consumption Expenditure of All Households by Region(2021)

单位:元/人 (yuan/person)

地 区	Region	可支配收入 Disposable Income	工资性收入 Income of Wages and Salaries	经营净收入 Net Business Income	财产净收入 Net Income from Properties	转移净收入 Net Income from Transfer	消费支出 Expense on Household Consumption
济南市	Jinan	46725	27050	4728	6887	8060	30016
青岛市	Qingdao	51223	30491	9701	4319	6712	32878
淄博市	Zibo	42265	28905	4893	3618	4849	27389
枣庄市	Zaozhuang	29772	19662	6053	1281	2776	17910
东营市	Dongying	45808	30183	5881	4002	5742	28197
烟台市	Yantai	42629	23804	9638	3266	5921	28021
潍坊市	Weifang	37103	20205	9524	2886	4488	23033
济宁市	Jining	31845	21546	4932	1676	3690	19034
泰安市	Tai'an	33505	21469	6235	2016	3785	20277
威海市	Weihai	44612	26523	7300	3023	7765	27599
日照市	Rizhao	31059	20690	6420	1632	2317	17950
临沂市	Linyi	31528	17356	10776	1537	1859	16352
德州市	Dezhou	25826	15387	7150	1262	2027	17099
聊城市	Liaocheng	24512	15143	5995	1269	2105	15630
滨州市	Binzhou	32374	19528	6299	2137	4410	21031
菏泽市	Heze	23854	9875	6946	1421	5611	16703

10-20 续表 continued

单位:元/人 (yuan/person)

地 区	Region	食品烟酒 Food, Tobacco and liquor	衣着 Clothing	居住 Residence	生活用品及服务 Supplies and Services	交通通信 Transport and Communications	教育文化娱乐 Recreation, Education and Cultural	医疗保健 Health care	其他用品及服务 Others
济南市	Jinan	7360	1728	8835	2113	3986	3199	2178	617
青岛市	Qingdao	9204	2973	7707	2192	4873	3363	1789	777
淄博市	Zibo	6861	2337	5680	2066	3874	4043	2024	504
枣庄市	Zaozhuang	5374	1464	3636	1443	2417	2071	1132	373
东营市	Dongying	6498	2560	6141	1750	5699	3158	1818	572
烟台市	Yantai	8525	2489	5719	1768	4197	2642	1936	744
潍坊市	Weifang	5511	1399	4630	1589	4248	3089	2152	417
济宁市	Jining	5138	1264	3479	1506	2939	2783	1540	384
泰安市	Tai'an	5126	1461	4277	1555	2647	2664	2093	452
威海市	Weihai	6987	2100	5403	1794	5138	2309	2972	895
日照市	Rizhao	5268	1145	3190	1059	3422	2401	1091	373
临沂市	Linyi	4409	1313	3602	1204	2885	1698	994	247
德州市	Dezhou	4955	1144	4316	953	2495	1561	1406	271
聊城市	Liaocheng	4613	1120	3219	836	1865	2163	1499	317
滨州市	Binzhou	5669	1525	4227	1457	3381	2640	1671	462
菏泽市	Heze	4829	1240	3550	1069	2174	2036	1565	240

10-21 各市城镇居民人均收支情况(2021年)

Per Capita Income and Consumption Expenditure of Urban Households by Region(2021)

单位:元/人 (yuan/person)

地 区	Region	可支配收入 Disposable Income	工资性收入 Income of Wages and Salaries	经营净收入 Net Business Income	财产净收入 Net Income from Properties	转移净收入 Net Income from Transfer	消费支出 Expense on Household Consumption
济南市	Jinan	57449	33546	3146	9732	11025	36866
青岛市	Qingdao	60239	36222	9416	5706	8895	38574
淄博市	Zibo	50096	33637	5451	4843	6164	31675
枣庄市	Zaozhuang	37843	26720	5397	2179	3547	22030
东营市	Dongying	56625	39173	4617	4809	8026	33526
烟台市	Yantai	53169	31299	9303	4581	7987	34178
潍坊市	Weifang	46616	25783	10015	4407	6411	28498
济宁市	Jining	41256	28189	4352	2754	5961	24051
泰安市	Tai'an	41741	27870	5454	3242	5175	24696
威海市	Weihai	54264	33139	7676	4280	9169	33752
日照市	Rizhao	39380	26888	6960	2666	2865	23559
临沂市	Linyi	42606	23680	14030	2591	2304	20367
德州市	Dezhou	31927	20495	7122	2244	2066	19091
聊城市	Liaocheng	32262	23452	4929	2301	1580	19012
滨州市	Binzhou	41566	26552	5823	3435	5755	26513
菏泽市	Heze	31872	15268	7498	2928	6178	20319

10-21 续表 continued

单位:元/人 (yuan/person)

地 区	Region	食品烟酒 Food, Tobacco and liquor	衣着 Clothing	居住 Residence	生活用品及服务 Supplies and Services	交通通信 Transport and Communications	教育文化娱乐 Recreation, Education and Cultural	医疗保健 Health care	其他用品及服务 Others
济南市	Jinan	8654	2173	11339	2634	4773	3969	2534	792
青岛市	Qingdao	10727	3596	9152	2571	5556	3972	2079	920
淄博市	Zibo	7740	2837	6769	2460	4350	4739	2155	626
枣庄市	Zaozhuang	6517	1871	4651	1836	2873	2547	1278	459
东营市	Dongying	7699	3327	7420	2206	6180	3707	2257	731
烟台市	Yantai	10142	3232	7166	2226	5008	3228	2233	944
潍坊市	Weifang	6467	1854	5634	2016	5579	3852	2574	523
济宁市	Jining	6458	1688	4705	1996	3266	3488	1915	534
泰安市	Tai'an	5929	1969	5258	1786	3274	3316	2507	657
威海市	Weihai	8372	2638	6756	2249	6422	2852	3279	1185
日照市	Rizhao	6854	1511	3866	1353	4671	3300	1488	517
临沂市	Linyi	5333	1831	4298	1479	3992	2053	1046	337
德州市	Dezhou	5402	1433	4371	1031	2795	2120	1585	353
聊城市	Liaocheng	5366	1620	4254	999	2278	2490	1601	405
滨州市	Binzhou	7093	2125	5549	1902	3967	3348	1885	643
菏泽市	Heze	5439	1421	4992	1384	2451	2376	1926	329

10-22 各市农村居民人均收支情况(2021年)

Per Capita Income and Consumption Expenditure of Rural Households by Region(2021)

单位:元/人 (yuan/person)

地 区	Region	可支配收入 Disposable Income	工资性收入 Income of Wages and Salaries	经营净收入 Net Business Income	财产净收入 Net Income from Properties	转移净收入 Net Income from Transfer	消费支出 Expense on Household Consumption
济南市	Jinan	22580	12423	8291	482	1383	14591
青岛市	Qingdao	26125	14536	10495	458	636	17021
淄博市	Zibo	23010	17271	3522	603	1614	16850
枣庄市	Zaozhuang	19553	10725	6883	144	1801	12692
东营市	Dongying	22255	10608	8633	2245	769	16593
烟台市	Yantai	24574	10966	10213	1013	2381	17472
潍坊市	Weifang	24007	12527	8847	791	1841	15511
济宁市	Jining	20747	13713	5616	405	1013	13119
泰安市	Tai'an	21769	12348	7347	269	1804	13979
威海市	Weihai	25692	13554	6563	560	5015	15537
日照市	Rizhao	20154	12566	5712	278	1598	10598
临沂市	Linyi	17783	9509	6739	228	1307	11370
德州市	Dezhou	19020	9690	7181	166	1984	14878
聊城市	Liaocheng	17512	7639	6958	336	2579	12576
滨州市	Binzhou	20539	10485	6911	464	2678	13975
菏泽市	Heze	16872	5179	6466	108	5118	13554

10-22 续表 continued

单位:元/人 (yuan/person)

地 区	Region	食品烟酒 Food, Tobacco and liquor	衣着 Clothing	居住 Residence	生活用品及服务 Supplies and Services	交通通信 Transport and Communications	教育文化娱乐 Recreation, Education and Cultural	医疗保健 Health care	其他用品及服务 Others
济南市	Jinan	4446	725	3197	941	2214	1466	1378	223
青岛市	Qingdao	4965	1237	3685	1138	2972	1668	980	377
淄博市	Zibo	4700	1107	3002	1098	2704	2334	1701	205
枣庄市	Zaozhuang	3926	950	2351	947	1841	1468	947	263
东营市	Dongying	3884	889	3356	757	4653	1965	862	227
烟台市	Yantai	5755	1215	3242	983	2809	1637	1427	403
潍坊市	Weifang	4195	772	3247	1001	2416	2039	1570	271
济宁市	Jining	3582	764	2033	928	2553	1952	1099	208
泰安市	Tai'an	3982	738	2880	1227	1754	1734	1504	160
威海市	Weihai	4273	1046	2752	904	2621	1246	2369	328
日照市	Rizhao	3189	665	2303	675	1785	1224	572	185
临沂市	Linyi	3264	670	2739	862	1511	1258	930	136
德州市	Dezhou	4455	821	4255	865	2160	937	1206	179
聊城市	Liaocheng	3933	668	2284	689	1491	1867	1406	238
滨州市	Binzhou	3834	753	2526	884	2626	1727	1395	230
菏泽市	Heze	4297	1082	2294	796	1933	1739	1251	162

主要统计指标解释

可支配收入 指居民可用于最终消费支出和储蓄的总和，即居民可以用来自由支配的收入。可支配收入既包括现金，也包括实物收入。按照收入的来源，可支配收入包含四项，分别为：工资性收入、经营净收入、财产净收入、转移净收入。计算公式为：

可支配收入 ＝ 工资性收入 ＋ 经营净收入 ＋ 财产净收入 ＋ 转移净收入

其中：经营净收入 ＝ 经营收入 － 经营费用 － 生产性固定资产折旧-生产税净额（生产税-生产补贴）

财产净收入 ＝ 财产性收入 － 财产性支出

转移净收入 ＝ 转移性收入 － 转移性支出

工资性收入 指就业人员通过各种途径得到的全部劳动报酬和各种福利，包括受雇于单位或个人、从事各种自由职业、兼职和零星劳动得到的全部劳动报酬和福利。

经营净收入 指住户或住户成员从事生产经营活动所获得的净收入，是全部经营收入中扣除经营费用、生产性固定资产折旧和生产税之后得到的净收入。

财产净收入 指住户或住户成员将其所拥有的金融资产、住房等非金融资产和自然资源交由其他机构单位、住户或个人支配而获得的回报并扣除相关的费用之后得到的净收入。财产净收入包括利息净收入、红利收入、储蓄性保险净收益、转让承包土地经营权租金净收入、出租房屋净收入、出租其他资产净收入和自有住房折算净租金等。

转移性收入 指国家、单位、社会团体对住户的各种经常性转移支付和住户之间的经常性收入转移。包括政府、非行政事业单位、社会团体对居民转移的养老金或退休金、社会救济和补助、惠农补贴、政策性生活补贴、救灾款、经常性捐赠和赔偿以及报销医疗费等；住户之间的赡养收入、经常性捐赠和赔偿以及农村地区（村委会）在外（含国外）工作的本住户非常住成员寄回带回的收入等。转移性收入不包括住户之间的实物馈赠。

转移性支出 指调查户对国家、单位、住户或个人的经常性或义务性转移支付。包括缴纳的税款、各项社会保障支出、赡养支出、经常性捐赠和赔偿支出以及其他经常转移支出等。

消费支出 指住户用于满足家庭日常生活消费需要的全部支出，包括用于消费品的支出和用于服务性消费的支出。根据用途不同，消费支出可划分为食品烟酒、衣着、居住、生活用品及服务、交通通信、教育文化娱乐、医疗保健、其他用品及服务八大类。根据来源不同，消费支出可划分为现金消费支出、实物消费支出（含自产自用、来自单位、来自政府和其他社会组织）。

食品烟酒 指用于各种食品和烟草、酒类的支出，包括食品和烟酒两个中类。

衣着 指与居民穿着有关的支出，包括服装、服装材料、鞋类、其他衣类及配件、衣着相关加工服务的支出。

居住 指与居住有关的支出，包括房租、水、电、燃料、物业管理等方面的支出，也包括自有住房折算租金。

生活用品及服务 指家庭及个人的各类生活品及家庭服务。包括家具及室内装饰品、家用器具、家用纺织品、家庭日用杂品、个人用品和家庭服务。

交通通信 指用于交通和通信工具及相关的各种服务费、维修费和车辆保险等支出。

教育文化和娱乐 指用于教育和文化娱乐方面的支出。

医疗保健 指用于医疗和保健的药品、用品和服务的总费用。包括医疗器具及药品，以及医疗服务。

其他用品及服务 指无法直接归入上述各类支出的其他用品与服务支出。

就业者负担人数 指家庭人口与就业人口之比。

农村整、半劳动力 整劳动力指男子 18 周岁到 50 周岁，女子 18 周岁到 45 周岁；半劳动力指男子 16 周岁到 17 周岁，51 周岁到 60 周岁；女子 16 周岁到 17 周岁，46 周岁到 55 周岁，同时具有劳动能力的人。虽然在劳动年龄之内，但已丧失劳动能力的人，不应算为劳动力；超过劳动年龄，但能经常参加劳动，计入半劳动力数内。

Explanatory Notes on Main Statistical Indicators

Disposable Income refer to the households income sum that can be used for final consumption expenditure and savings. Disposable income includes cash and real income. According to sources of income, disposable income includes the wage income, net operating income, net property income, and net transfer income. The formula for computing:

Disposable income = the wage income+ net operating income+net property income+net transfer income

Net operating income =
income - operating costs - depreciation of productive fixed assets - net taxes on production (production tax - production subsidies)

Net property income = income from property - property expenditure

The transfer of net income = income from transfer - transfer expenditure

Wage Income refers to income and all kinds of welfare obtained by laborers employed by different establishments, working independently or part time.

Net Operating Income refers to the net income from operation run by the members of households, and it equals to total income minus operating costs and depreciation of productive fixed assets and taxes on production.

Net Property Income refers to the net income obtained from the financial assets, non-financial assets such as housing and natural resources provided by its owners to other establishments, households or individuals. It includes net interest income, bonus, net income from saving insurance, net income from the transfer of the right to land contractual management, income from house renting, income from renting of other assets and net rental income of home ownership.

Income from Transfer refers to the current transaction between government, establishments, social organization and households, and to the income transaction between households. It includes annuity, pension, social relief, agricultural subsidy, disaster relief fund, and medical expense, which are provided by governments, institutions, social organizations. It also includes supporting expense, regular donations, and income provided by non-permanent population. It does not include donations between households.

Transfer Expenditure refers to the regular or obligatory expenditure provided by the households to governments, institutions, other households or residents. It includes taxes, social security expenditure, supporting expenditure, regular donation and compensation expenditure, etc.

Expense on Service Consumption refers to the consumption of all expenditure needs to meet the family daily life, including those for the consumer spending and for service consumption expenditure. According to different purposes, consumption can be divided into tobacco and food, clothing, housing, daily necessities and services, transportation and communication, education, culture and entertainment, health care, the other services. According to different sources, consumption can be divided into cash consumption, real consumer spending (including self occupied, from the unit, from the government and other social organizations).

Tobacco and Food refers to all kinds of expenditure on foods, tobaccos and beverages, including food and tobacco.

Clothing refers to the expenditure on clothes, clothing materials, shoes, accessories and charges for making clothes.

Housing refers to the expenditure related to residing, including rent, the expenditure of water, fuel, power and real estate management and net rental income of home ownership.

Daily Necessities and Services refers to the expenditure on daily necessities and home service, including the expenditures on furniture, decoration, appliance, textile, personal items and home service.

Transportation and Communication refers to the expenditure on transportation, communication, related service, maintenance, and vehicle insurance.

Education, Culture and Entertainment refers to the expenditure on education, culture and entertainment.

Health Care refers to the expenditure on health care, medicine, related products and service.

Other Services refers to the expenditure on the service that cannot be included in the services mentioned above.

Number of Dependents per Employee refers to the ratio between number of persons in households and the number of dependents.

Rural Full/Semi Labor Force Full labor force refers to persons capable of work, aged 18-50 for males and 18-45 for females. Semi labor force refers to persons capable of work, aged 16-17 and 51-60 for males and 16-17 and 46-55 for females. Persons at their working ages but not capable of work are not to be included as labor force. Persons not at working ages but participating regularly in work are included in semi labor force. For staff and workers as resident population of the household, they are included as full or semi labor force of the household if they are in the labor force.

第 11 篇

城市建设

City Construction

简 要 说 明

一、本篇资料的主要内容

本篇资料反映了全省各城市基础设施基本情况，包括设施水平、供水、公共交通、道路桥梁、排水、园林绿化、燃气、供热等方面的资料。

二、本篇资料的来源

本篇资料来源于省住房城乡建设厅和省交通运输厅，由山东省统计局综合处和服务业处整理提供。

Brief Introduction

I. Content

Data in this chapter show the basic conditions of public facilities of main cities in Shandong, including infrastructure, water supply, public communications, roads, bridges, drainage, urban greenery, gas and heating, etc.

II. Source of Data

Data in this chapter are provided by the Housing and Urban-Rural Development and Transportation Department of Shandong Province. Data in this chapter are prepared and compiled by the Division of Comprehensive Statistics and the Division of Comprehensive Service Statistics of Shandong Provincial Bureau of Statistics.

11-1 城市基础设施

Basic Statistics on Urban Infrastructure

指 标 名 称	Item	2018	2019	2020	2021
一、设施水平	**Urban Facilities**				
城市人口密度 (人/平方公里)	Population Density (person/sq.km)	1622	1665	1665	1716
人均日生活用水量 (升)	Per Capita Daily Water Consumption (litre)	126.6	125.5	119.4	126.1
供水普及率 (%)	Coverage Rate of Water Supply (%)	99.4	99.7	99.8	99.9
燃气普及率 (%)	Coverage Rate of Natural Gas Supply (%)	99.2	99.1	99.3	99.3
人均城市道路面积 (平方米)	Per Capita Area of Roads (sq.m)	25.3	25.3	25.6	26.5
建成区排水管道密度 (公里/平方公里)	Built-up Area Density of Sewage Pipelines (km/sq.km)	11.5	11.8	11.3	11.8
人均公园绿地面积 (平方米)	Per Capita Public Green Areas (sq.m)	17.6	17.6	17.7	17.9
建成区绿化覆盖率 (%)	Coverage Rate of Urban Green Areas (%)	41.8	41.8	41.7	43.0
二、供水情况	**Water Supply**				
供水总量 (万立方米)	Volume of Water Supply (10 000 cu.m)	394788	392093	379082	398912
#生产运营用水 (万立方米)	For Productive Use (10 000 cu.m)	166016	156581	155140	159236
用水人口 (万人)	Population Using Water (10 000 persons)	3673	3853	3983	4081
三、公共交通	**Public Transportation**				
公共汽电车客运总量 (万人次)	Volume of Passenger Traffic (Buses and Trolley Buses,etc.) (10 000 person-times)	385805	403854	226711	308625
公共汽电车运营车数 (辆)	Number of Operating Vehicles (Buses and Trolley Buses,etc.) (unit)	53298	56657	54799	67125
出租汽车数 (辆)	Number of Taxis (unit)	62138	62852	61872	70263
四、市政设施	**Infrastructure by City**				
道路面积 (万平方米)	Area of Roads (10 000 sq.m)	93397	97663	102269	108259
#人行道面积 (万平方米)	Area of Sidewalks (10 000 sq.m)	18473	18964	20348	21627
道路长度 (公里)	Length of Roads (km)	45633	48149	49986	53058
路灯盏数 (盏)	Number of Streetlights (unit)	2008130	2061918	2119319	2199036
桥梁数 (座)	Number of Bridges (unit)	5708	5855	5821	5956
污水年排放量 (万吨)	Volume of Waste Water Discharged (10 000 tons)	340919	354337	341815	364625
污水年处理量 (万吨)	Volume of Waste Water Treated (10 000 tons)	332217	346414	335873	358769
五、园林绿化	**Parks,Gardens and Green Areas**				
园林绿地面积 (公顷)	Garden Green Area (ha)	243368	252338	262968	272462
公园绿地面积 (公顷)	Park Green Area (ha)	65179	67884	70508	73314
绿化覆盖面积 (公顷)	Coverage of Green Area (ha)	279143	289833	299506	308569
#建成区绿化覆盖面积 (公顷)	Coverage of Urban Green Area (ha)	215930	226228	235167	244015
公园个数 (个)	Number of Parks (unit)	1214	1200	1299	1420
公园面积 (公顷)	Area of Parks (ha)	40554	41450	47635	50067

11-2 城市设施水平(2021年)

Basic Statistics on Urban Infrastructure by City (2021)

城市名称	City	城市人口密度(人/平方公里) Population Density (person/sq.km)	人均日生活用水量(升) Per Capita DailyWater Consumption (litre)	供水普及率(%) Coverage Rate of Water Supply (%)	燃气普及率(%) Coverage Rate of Gas Supply (%)	人均城市道路面积(平方米) Per Capita Area of Roads (sq.m)	人均公园绿地面积(平方米) Per Capita Public Green Areas (sq.m)	建成区绿化覆盖率(%) Coverage Rate of Urban Green Areas (%)
全　省	**Total**	**1716**	**126.1**	**99.9**	**99.3**	**26.5**	**17.9**	**43.0**
济南市	Jinan	2714	142.0	100.0	100.0	20.8	12.7	41.7
青岛市	Qingdao	1878	144.7	100.0	100.0	19.9	18.0	43.1
胶州市	Jiaozhou	755	134.5	100.0	100.0	18.9	12.8	44.9
平度市	Pingdu	683	83.1	100.0	100.0	27.9	13.6	43.2
莱西市	Laixi	757	121.5	100.0	100.0	24.9	14.5	44.6
淄博市	Zibo	2732	119.3	100.0	100.0	31.4	18.8	45.2
枣庄市	Zaozhuang	2076	100.7	100.0	99.9	28.2	15.0	43.1
滕州市	Tengzhou	3318	135.9	100.0	100.0	21.0	14.8	41.5
东营市	Dongying	790	206.8	100.0	100.0	34.3	26.6	42.7
烟台市	Yantai	2306	134.6	99.3	98.0	29.4	18.6	43.7
龙口市	Longkou	2858	82.3	100.0	100.0	32.2	18.8	44.9
莱阳市	Laiyang	1017	132.8	99.6	100.0	17.2	17.3	41.0
莱州市	Laizhou	1086	98.5	100.0	100.0	20.1	15.8	41.1
招远市	Zhaoyuan	1454	154.0	100.0	100.0	23.5	21.4	33.4
栖霞市	Qixia	5657	70.6	98.2	96.5	15.9	12.8	36.7
海阳市	Haiyang	897	84.2	99.7	99.7	19.8	17.1	42.7
潍坊市	Weifang	1471	110.6	100.0	100.0	28.2	18.7	42.6
青州市	Qingzhou	1256	107.7	100.0	100.0	29.2	15.3	41.5
诸城市	Zhucheng	1536	128.8	100.0	100.0	24.7	23.5	44.8
寿光市	Shouguang	1858	81.1	100.0	100.0	16.6	16.3	43.0
安丘市	Anqiu	894	114.6	100.0	100.0	33.8	20.6	44.4
高密市	Gaomi	1489	136.6	100.0	100.0	25.4	17.6	39.0
昌邑市	Changyi	1679	105.3	100.0	100.0	24.5	21.3	42.0
济宁市	Jining	1844	113.3	100.0	99.0	37.6	20.0	43.5
曲阜市	Qufu	3327	84.9	100.0	99.5	26.6	17.3	42.5
邹城市	Zoucheng	3720	128.0	100.0	100.0	19.0	14.4	41.1
泰安市	Tai'an	1895	100.4	100.0	100.0	28.2	23.2	45.1
新泰市	Xintai	1131	105.0	100.0	100.0	25.5	18.5	44.9
肥城市	Feicheng	2257	130.7	100.0	100.0	25.0	18.3	43.9
威海市	Weihai	1624	117.4	100.0	100.0	41.9	26.1	46.0
荣成市	Rongcheng	898	93.2	100.0	100.0	31.1	26.0	46.0
乳山市	Rushan	1668	107.1	100.0	100.0	30.1	18.7	45.8
日照市	Rizhao	2300	135.6	100.0	99.9	22.9	18.0	43.9
临沂市	Linyi	1884	122.5	100.0	96.6	28.0	21.2	42.5
德州市	Dezhou	1475	118.1	100.0	100.0	30.2	25.5	43.3
乐陵市	Leling	2620	57.3	100.0	100.0	30.5	13.1	39.0
禹城市	Yucheng	3345	95.2	96.2	98.9	27.1	11.3	39.6
聊城市	Liaocheng	1883	92.6	100.0	100.0	24.7	12.6	42.5
临清市	Linqing	1249	75.3	100.0	92.6	30.3	13.8	37.0
滨州市	Binzhou	855	181.3	100.0	100.0	40.6	31.5	45.8
邹平市	Zouping	1480	68.3	100.0	100.0	39.4	18.6	39.6
菏泽市	Heze	2070	137.3	98.1	90.4	38.0	15.3	41.7

注：设市城市为市本级数据。
a)The data of cities are from Municipal level.

11-3 城市供水(2021年)

Urban Water Supply by City (2021)

城市名称	City	综合生产能力(万立方米/日) Production Capacity of Water Supply (10 000 cu.m/day)	地下水 Groundwater	供水管道长度(公里) Length of Water Supply Pipelines (km)	供水总量(万立方米) Volume of Water Supply (10 000 cu.m)	生产运营用水 For Productive Use	公共服务用水 For Public Service	居民家庭用水 For Households Use	用水人口(万人) Population with Access to Tap Water (10 000 persons)
全　省	**Total**	**1957.2**	**552.6**	**62838.8**	**398912.2**	**159235.8**	**49194.3**	**138376.5**	**4080.7**
济 南 市	Jinan	291.4	113.2	6593.9	49951.7	6027.3	15047.7	18949.2	656.6
青 岛 市	Qingdao	210.1	3.9	8303.6	55561.2	17572.3	8611.9	21988.5	580.2
胶 州 市	Jiaozhou	19.7	6.0	743.8	5605.3	1916.7	1380.8	1712.4	63.1
平 度 市	Pingdu	12.8	5.8	737.0	3773.0	1729.0	181.0	1311.0	49.2
莱 西 市	Laixi	10.9	1.9	583.6	2870.9	1001.0	316.8	1168.2	33.9
淄 博 市	Zibo	182.5	88.0	3208.8	30787.4	18058.3	1448.7	7726.0	210.9
枣 庄 市	Zaozhuang	48.1	34.8	1904.9	9502.7	4074.2	631.9	3415.8	110.1
滕 州 市	Tengzhou	24.0	19.0	1150.0	5355.0	2014.6	503.0	1925.0	49.0
东 营 市	Dongying	107.0		1899.8	16918.8	7356.8	3091.9	4319.4	98.4
烟 台 市	Yantai	111.6	18.9	4921.0	20460.5	6391.3	3108.6	9234.7	251.3
龙 口 市	Longkou	8.0		396.0	1757.7	627.9	193.2	699.5	29.7
莱 阳 市	Laiyang	12.4	0.4	363.1	2303.8	538.4	491.6	962.1	30.0
莱 州 市	Laizhou	10.5		743.8	2318.7	386.0	35.1	1402.3	40.0
招 远 市	Zhaoyuan	8.4	2.0	512.0	1997.8	805.6	265.8	861.7	20.1
栖 霞 市	Qixia	3.7	1.0	156.9	704.4	212.0	120.6	310.9	16.8
海 阳 市	Haiyang	11.9		480.3	1224.6	319.4	64.6	653.9	23.5
潍 坊 市	Weifang	86.0	16.2	2523.2	19968.0	10927.1	323.5	6723.0	174.5
青 州 市	Qingzhou	18.2	15.2	817.5	3680.0	1894.9	326.9	1153.3	37.7
诸 城 市	Zhucheng	25.0	4.2	371.2	7957.0	4869.0	621.4	1735.2	50.1
寿 光 市	Shouguang	29.5	10.6	762.9	9736.0	7727.0	51.9	1752.9	61.0
安 丘 市	Anqiu	29.5	0.6	525.8	5206.2	2660.8	508.1	1514.0	48.4
高 密 市	Gaomi	37.6	13.1	820.0	8787.9	5363.8	379.1	1091.2	29.5
昌 邑 市	Changyi	13.5	10.9	122.8	3733.9	2808.5	187.7	586.8	20.2
济 宁 市	Jining	64.5	48.5	1286.0	15719.2	5709.0	2039.5	4683.4	163.0
曲 阜 市	Qufu	11.0	11.0	417.0	1401.9	528.4	103.2	577.0	22.0
邹 城 市	Zoucheng	14.5	14.5	483.6	3707.0	1530.0	525.0	1106.0	36.4
泰 安 市	Tai'an	32.3	17.0	4763.2	5977.1	1131.0	1370.3	2711.8	111.4
新 泰 市	Xintai	17.5	1.0	667.1	3010.3	523.7	288.1	1854.9	56.1
肥 城 市	Feicheng	7.2	7.2	295.6	2303.6	507.8	102.5	1364.5	31.0
威 海 市	Weihai	53.7	0.6	3393.5	8403.7	2597.4	1425.8	3105.3	105.7
荣 成 市	Rongcheng	18.1	0.1	789.1	2681.3	847.5	120.2	1367.8	44.2
乳 山 市	Rushan	12.8	0.5	614.6	1964.5	621.5	81.0	836.0	23.5
日 照 市	Rizhao	55.7		1898.5	10269.0	4101.8	986.8	3570.0	92.8
临 沂 市	Linyi	88.3	17.3	2546.7	18923.6	7837.4	392.5	9393.1	218.9
德 州 市	Dezhou	61.2	0.4	1899.5	15262.9	10298.7	346.4	3477.6	88.7
乐 陵 市	Leling	6.5	1.0	111.7	767.5	137.9	113.0	434.8	26.2
禹 城 市	Yucheng	12.0	9.0	410.8	2421.3	1480.1	71.7	599.1	19.3
聊 城 市	Liaocheng	28.1	24.6	1614.0	7665.1	1391.6	849.2	3470.6	127.8
临 清 市	Linqing	13.7	2.9	301.0	1201.1	173.5	42.4	856.3	32.7
滨 州 市	Binzhou	65.7		1387.3	10667.0	5042.6	1603.6	2921.1	68.4
邹 平 市	Zouping	36.0	6.0	149.9	5821.9	4655.8	87.2	676.6	30.6
菏 泽 市	Heze	46.4	25.4	1168.2	10581.6	4838.4	754.2	4173.9	98.3

注：设市城市为市本级数据。
a)The data of cities are from Municipal level.

11-4 城市公共交通(2021年)

Public Transportation by City(2021)

城市名称	City	公共汽电车 Bus and Trolley Bus				巡游出租汽车数(辆) Number of Cruise taxi (unit)
		运营车数(辆) Number of Operating Vehicles (unit)	标准运营车数(标台) Number of Standard Operating Vehicles (unit)	运营线路总长度(公里) Length of Operation Lines (km)	客运总量(万人次) Volume of Passenger Traffic (10 000 person -times)	
全　省	**Total**	**67125**	**73982**	**187331**	**308625**	**70263**
济南市	Jinan	8833	10741	15852	58701	10386
青岛市	Qingdao	10891	13364	24650	88262	11638
胶州市	Jiaozhou	1051	1174	1765	4055	
平度市	Pingdu	904	840	2977	1475	
莱西市	Laixi	301	336	2210	2099	
淄博市	Zibo	2887	3234	11107	11665	6519
枣庄市	Zaozhuang	2598	2772	6928	9100	1540
滕州市	Tengzhou	1184	1311	2556	5221	
东营市	Dongying	1518	1694	7650	5329	3360
烟台市	Yantai	4004	4585	11239	26699	5410
龙口市	Longkou	307	356	1255	1525	
莱阳市	Laiyang	252	253	451	847	
莱州市	Laizhou	127	130	218	612	
招远市	Zhaoyuan	234	266	1099	660	
栖霞市	Qixia	237	233	1711	257	
海阳市	Haiyang	270	257	1491	538	
潍坊市	Weifang	4766	5256	12650	15864	4876
青州市	Qingzhou	418	402	648	1232	
诸城市	Zhucheng	557	594	2251	2493	
寿光市	Shouguang	566	552	2056	744	
安丘市	Anqiu	383	393	777	450	
高密市	Gaomi	273	268	1170	355	
昌邑市	Changyi	309	306	664	502	
济宁市	Jining	6787	6996	15856	19146	4551
曲阜市	Qufu	352	312	1326	1028	
邹城市	Zoucheng	1067	1124	1641	2581	
泰安市	Tai'an	4123	4121	12199	9578	2111
新泰市	Xintai	815	774	2984	1991	
肥城市	Feicheng	345	336	875	918	
威海市	Weihai	2194	2534	10867	17604	2487
荣成市	Rongcheng	466	538	2740	3007	
乳山市	Rushan	280	299	2800	780	
日照市	Rizhao	1641	1875	7512	7085	1401
临沂市	Linyi	3825	3822	10052	10616	4632
德州市	Dezhou	2650	2619	10471	4411	4248
乐陵市	Leling	207	160	1052	80	
禹城市	Yucheng	286	301	1465	339	
聊城市	Liaocheng	3614	3530	7460	8822	2624
临清市	Linqing	460	466	944	582	
滨州市	Binzhou	2301	2310	9194	5655	1637
邹平市	Zouping	530	566	1115	2362	
菏泽市	Heze	4493	4532	13643	10090	2843

11−5 城市市政设施(2021年)
Infrastructure by City (2021)

城市名称	City	道路长度(公里) Length of Roads (km)	道路面积(万平方米) Area of Roads (10 000 sq.m)	人行道面积(万平方米) Area of Sidewalks (10 000 sq.m)	路灯盏数(盏) Number of Streetlights (unit)	桥梁数(座) Number of Bridges (unit)
全　省	**Total**	**53057.8**	**108259.4**	**21626.8**	**2199036**	**5956**
济南市	Jinan	7592.9	13644.5	2742.4	190385	940
青岛市	Qingdao	6351.8	11545.8	2517.1	194489	797
胶州市	Jiaozhou	792.7	1194.2	176.5	25131	114
平度市	Pingdu	768.0	1370.7	252.9	13331	34
莱西市	Laixi	518.1	844.8	153.5	24303	24
淄博市	Zibo	2708.3	6630.8	1309.2	107437	286
枣庄市	Zaozhuang	1519.1	3105.6	713.7	55342	152
滕州市	Tengzhou	629.1	1027.8	230.6	24212	45
东营市	Dongying	1620.8	3376.1	730.0	79189	317
烟台市	Yantai	3704.4	7429.6	1429.4	164338	219
龙口市	Longkou	496.9	955.6	250.6	21976	16
莱阳市	Laiyang	345.9	518.7	139.8	7737	26
莱州市	Laizhou	329.9	802.2	118.7	17854	13
招远市	Zhaoyuan	296.2	471.8	102.6	10594	56
栖霞市	Qixia	142.5	271.2	51.6	10405	32
海阳市	Haiyang	213.1	465.1	167.3	12034	47
潍坊市	Weifang	2275.8	4921.5	1161.2	107913	138
青州市	Qingzhou	620.0	1100.8	258.6	55367	27
诸城市	Zhucheng	640.9	1237.5	236.3	29268	39
寿光市	Shouguang	601.7	1010.5	118.7	33247	9
安丘市	Anqiu	835.6	1634.2	142.5	23896	87
高密市	Gaomi	445.2	747.3	207.8	24952	64
昌邑市	Changyi	271.3	494.5	127.2	9501	29
济宁市	Jining	2336.5	6123.7	1120.5	98513	217
曲阜市	Qufu	260.1	583.4	130.8	22422	32
邹城市	Zoucheng	392.9	692.0	163.0	19950	39
泰安市	Tai'an	1448.7	3139.5	468.8	39922	218
新泰市	Xintai	577.7	1428.6	167.9	19693	38
肥城市	Feicheng	323.8	773.6	80.4	16994	38
威海市	Weihai	1779.7	4425.1	741.9	95086	463
荣成市	Rongcheng	706.3	1372.1	186.9	34120	106
乳山市	Rushan	376.1	705.5	130.0	22498	90
日照市	Rizhao	1046.0	2124.3	401.7	58323	109
临沂市	Linyi	2878.1	6129.0	919.6	176132	182
德州市	Dezhou	1396.2	2676.5	1030.5	84789	203
乐陵市	Leling	392.3	799.0	199.0	15230	10
禹城市	Yucheng	185.5	544.4	75.0	9270	66
聊城市	Liaocheng	1350.2	3160.2	632.3	96734	214
临清市	Linqing	444.7	991.7	315.8	7845	30
滨州市	Binzhou	1237.2	2775.2	478.9	73353	214
邹平市	Zouping	538.4	1207.6	188.2	14521	55
菏泽市	Heze	1667.6	3807.5	857.5	50740	121

注：设市城市为市本级数据。
a)The data of cities are from Municipal level.

11-5 续表 continued

城市名称	City	排水管道长度 (公里) Length of Sewage Pipelines (km)	污水年排放量 (万立方米) Volume of Waste Water Discharged (10 000 m^3)	污水处理总量 (万立方米) Volume of Waste Water Treated Yearly (10 000 m^3)	生活垃圾清运量 (万吨) Volume of Garbage Disposal (10 000 tons)	生活垃圾无害化处理量 (万吨) Volume of Garbage Harmless Diposed (10 000 tons)
合　计	**Total**	**72793.2**	**364625**	**358769**	**1769.0**	**1769.0**
济南市	Jinan	8760.8	48952	48572	287.6	287.6
青岛市	Qingdao	10212.9	53632	52693	303.6	303.6
胶州市	Jiaozhou	869.3	5493	5410	35.7	35.7
平度市	Pingdu	812.3	3584	3506	39.5	39.5
莱西市	Laixi	761.3	2829	2776	24.2	24.2
淄博市	Zibo	3952.5	24210	23842	61.2	61.2
枣庄市	Zaozhuang	1495.5	7006	6890	32.1	32.1
滕州市	Tengzhou	618.1	4552	4465	16.5	16.5
东营市	Dongying	2924.4	14940	14649	43.8	43.8
烟台市	Yantai	4678.5	15975	15688	118.1	118.1
龙口市	Longkou	602.5	1493	1453	11.8	11.8
莱阳市	Laiyang	357.9	1865	1825	9.3	9.3
莱州市	Laizhou	352.4	2009	1959	13.2	13.2
招远市	Zhaoyuan	465.4	1646	1614	7.8	7.8
栖霞市	Qixia	147.0	619	589	2.9	2.9
海阳市	Haiyang	402.8	1041	1019	9.9	9.9
潍坊市	Weifang	3049.8	17972	17700	80.6	80.6
青州市	Qingzhou	864.3	3128	3081	17.2	17.2
诸城市	Zhucheng	770.6	7130	7022	15.0	15.0
寿光市	Shouguang	906.5	9716	9569	28.9	28.9
安丘市	Anqiu	998.1	4486	4418	13.9	13.9
高密市	Gaomi	671.9	8310	8169	15.4	15.4
昌邑市	Changyi	338.3	3200	3149	6.3	6.3
济宁市	Jining	2822.5	15280	15048	60.0	60.0
曲阜市	Qufu	345.8	1390	1359	6.9	6.9
邹城市	Zoucheng	374.3	3670	3605	11.6	11.6
泰安市	Tai'an	1720.8	10131	9963	47.7	47.7
新泰市	Xintai	626.8	2709	2655	25.8	25.8
肥城市	Feicheng	331.5	2601	2562	9.9	9.9
威海市	Weihai	3148.9	7659	7516	54.2	54.2
荣成市	Rongcheng	1343.7	2271	2227	19.6	19.6
乳山市	Rushan	828.4	1723	1691	9.3	9.3
日照市	Rizhao	2915.5	9908	9745	34.8	34.8
临沂市	Linyi	4030.6	16909	16655	108.3	108.3
德州市	Dezhou	1773.2	12234	12040	45.9	45.9
乐陵市	Leling	306.9	652	642	8.2	8.2
禹城市	Yucheng	291.4	2058	2017	6.1	6.1
聊城市	Liaocheng	2119.4	6719	6605	34.4	34.4
临清市	Linqing	391.8	1021	1000	8.4	8.4
滨州市	Binzhou	2083.6	9067	8914	37.0	37.0
邹平市	Zouping	534.2	4949	4859	10.6	10.6
菏泽市	Heze	1790.9	9886	9607	36.0	36.0

注：设市城市为市本级数据。

a)The data of cities are from Municipal level.

11−6 城市园林绿化(2021年)

Parks, Gardens and Green Areas by City (2021)

城市名称	City	绿化覆盖面积(公顷) Coverage of Green Area (ha)	建成区 Urban Green Area	园林绿地面积(公顷) Garden Green Area (ha)	公园绿地面积(公顷) Park Green Area (ha)	公园个数(个) Number of Parks (unit)	公园面积(公顷) Area of Parks (ha)
全 省	**Total**	**308569.1**	**244014.6**	**272461.6**	**73314.4**	**1420**	**50067.0**
济 南 市	Jinan	33378.5	33101.9	29872.0	8360.3	164	3944.6
青 岛 市	Qingdao	46779.8	32831.1	42660.6	10465.0	236	7943.1
胶 州 市	Jiaozhou	4057.1	4018.1	3740.0	807.5	21	632.5
平 度 市	Pingdu	3302.2	3088.2	2801.5	667.5	29	581.9
莱 西 市	Laixi	1966.1	1859.9	1684.4	492.1	9	342.9
淄 博 市	Zibo	22605.0	13347.0	20227.5	3966.3	48	1759.7
枣 庄 市	Zaozhuang	9642.0	6753.7	7613.9	1647.8	49	1250.8
滕 州 市	Tengzhou	2932.7	2663.0	2669.0	723.2	25	407.8
东 营 市	Dongying	10556.4	7126.7	9912.0	2621.9	56	2557.5
烟 台 市	Yantai	18106.5	17376.2	16252.0	4709.8	60	2228.3
龙 口 市	Longkou	2514.6	2121.1	2130.1	557.8	9	203.0
莱 阳 市	Laiyang	2529.0	1780.6	1656.5	521.7	3	113.0
莱 州 市	Laizhou	2249.7	2221.8	2065.6	631.7	38	277.1
招 远 市	Zhaoyuan	1189.2	1189.2	1159.6	429.2	12	392.4
栖 霞 市	Qixia	702.5	627.5	602.4	217.4	4	41.0
海 阳 市	Haiyang	1582.0	1469.4	1464.5	401.0	6	382.7
潍 坊 市	Weifang	12646.6	8296.8	11674.7	3255.3	60	2390.0
青 州 市	Qingzhou	3126.9	2238.8	2191.4	578.0	17	530.4
诸 城 市	Zhucheng	3808.2	2443.8	3305.6	1178.7	14	621.0
寿 光 市	Shouguang	4243.5	2031.5	3748.6	992.3	20	815.0
安 丘 市	Anqiu	3980.7	2842.0	3441.9	997.2	18	823.1
高 密 市	Gaomi	2414.2	2168.0	1956.7	518.7	5	184.0
昌 邑 市	Changyi	1936.0	1386.1	1486.1	428.8	4	360.2
济 宁 市	Jining	12869.3	10819.7	10434.1	3259.1	50	2055.2
曲 阜 市	Qufu	1484.1	1146.2	1307.4	379.7	25	380.0
邹 城 市	Zoucheng	2186.1	2012.5	1927.9	524.0	16	524.0
泰 安 市	Tai'an	7746.5	7376.3	7395.3	2578.2	39	1861.6
新 泰 市	Xintai	3255.2	3138.2	3048.5	1037.0	20	976.0
肥 城 市	Feicheng	2447.7	2189.7	2134.3	566.0	6	460.2
威 海 市	Weihai	10630.5	9079.7	9587.5	2757.4	55	1255.4
荣 成 市	Rongcheng	3103.7	2711.6	2844.7	1146.8	22	1062.6
乳 山 市	Rushan	2049.6	1675.6	1768.6	438.6	13	245.0
日 照 市	Rizhao	5948.7	5531.4	5349.9	1673.3	53	1096.4
临 沂 市	Linyi	15334.8	11124.4	13503.8	4644.8	46	4352.1
德 州 市	Dezhou	8361.2	7275.6	7411.5	2257.3	39	1626.3
乐 陵 市	Leling	1551.6	1346.6	1187.4	343.6	15	353.7
禹 城 市	Yucheng	1972.1	1517.8	1677.0	226.0	9	168.0
聊 城 市	Liaocheng	10423.7	6638.6	9447.9	1610.2	31	1167.0
临 清 市	Linqing	2288.7	1163.1	1915.1	450.2	8	192.6
滨 州 市	Binzhou	7600.2	6943.1	6791.8	2152.3	49	2342.2
邹 平 市	Zouping	3280.5	2338.1	2251.5	570.0	3	294.0
菏 泽 市	Heze	9785.7	7004.0	8160.9	1530.9	14	873.0

注：设市城市为市本级数据。

a)The data of cities are from Municipal level.

11-7 城市燃气供热情况(2021年)
Gas Supply and Heating by City (2021)

城市名称	City	天然气供气量(万立方米) Total Natural Gas Supply (10 000 cu.m)	居民家庭用量 Residential Use	液化石油气供气量(吨) Total Liquefied Petroleum Gas Supply (ton)	居民家庭用量 Residential Use	集中供热面积(万平方米) Heating Area (10 000 sq.m)	住宅 Houses
全 省	**Total**	**1304043.1**	**308535.7**	**268776.2**	**173674.5**	**172858.9**	**145771.3**
济南市	Jinan	172066.0	77652.0	23930.0	11953.0	29397.4	24622.5
青岛市	Qingdao	147284.3	36993.0	31287.0	12403.7	27103.2	22857.8
胶州市	Jiaozhou	18843.0	3947.7	5120.0	4730.0	2350.0	2107.0
平度市	Pingdu	11843.0	1916.6	3897.0	3857.0	1659.0	1481.0
莱西市	Laixi	10703.0	3920.0	6942.0	5527.0	1375.8	1314.7
淄博市	Zibo	207987.2	17343.9	20650.4	11820.0	9391.4	8221.0
枣庄市	Zaozhuang	12663.7	4083.0	8064.0	6445.0	4265.8	3948.1
滕州市	Tengzhou	28852.1	4306.0			3132.0	2909.0
东营市	Dongying	45229.8	13563.8	1268.0	689.9	6106.9	4647.0
烟台市	Yantai	42963.2	10338.2	35229.0	12226.0	13000.3	9432.4
龙口市	Longkou	44397.0	2120.0	2262.5	2150.0	1420.0	1235.0
莱阳市	Laiyang	5743.4	1043.3	1600.0	1200.0	1117.0	951.0
莱州市	Laizhou	3412.0	1065.0	3248.0	3132.0	818.3	666.9
招远市	Zhaoyuan	2943.1	884.8	990.0	548.0	833.9	714.2
栖霞市	Qixia	2900.0	700.0	2560.0	2230.0	235.4	210.6
海阳市	Haiyang	2226.0	1083.1	1990.0	1200.0	576.3	519.4
潍坊市	Weifang	55900.0	10669.0	9000.0	8930.0	10147.0	8489.0
青州市	Qingzhou	11400.0	2027.5	1500.0	605.0	2056.2	1911.4
诸城市	Zhucheng	15294.0	2231.0	6800.0	6780.0	1374.0	1370.0
寿光市	Shouguang	13626.0	2430.0	2650.0	2640.0	1680.0	1350.0
安丘市	Anqiu	7341.4	1375.5	5588.4	5521.0	925.0	866.0
高密市	Gaomi	17621.9	4040.0	569.0	167.0	861.5	747.9
昌邑市	Changyi	3719.0	3012.6	1820.0	1796.0	496.6	490.8
济宁市	Jining	44007.0	16854.8	626.3	624.0	5230.9	4184.7
曲阜市	Qufu	7246.1	1615.6			1319.1	1177.0
邹城市	Zoucheng	5553.0	4800.6	470.0	162.0	1761.3	1615.6
泰安市	Tai'an	42730.7	5267.4	1351.0	94.5	4523.5	3947.5
新泰市	Xintai	8039.5	1990.4	3260.0	2532.5	970.0	908.0
肥城市	Feicheng	6391.9	4549.2	424.5	145.4	891.0	803.6
威海市	Weihai	17616.4	5435.8	16093.0	8764.0	9536.8	7012.0
荣成市	Rongcheng	7625.7	2124.2	9245.0	4563.0	1440.0	1188.1
乳山市	Rushan	2550.3	1323.3	180.0		802.0	766.0
日照市	Rizhao	29242.6	7018.8	8147.4	8060.2	2865.9	2485.0
临沂市	Linyi	89850.4	12406.1	17993.4	16756.7	7935.9	7521.1
德州市	Dezhou	30724.0	9271.0	5510.0	5350.0	3409.5	2805.4
乐陵市	Leling	4405.0	1327.0	3191.0	3187.0	380.0	371.0
禹城市	Yucheng	8871.5	2626.9	2600.0	305.2	1125.8	999.1
聊城市	Liaocheng	44367.0	5028.5	5667.0	2380.0	2905.1	2677.7
临清市	Linqing	4580.0	2206.0	1427.1	1427.0	740.4	660.6
滨州市	Binzhou	27698.9	8623.4	5334.1	5331.5	4448.5	3598.0
邹平市	Zouping	20840.7	3519.0	6350.0	3890.0	652.0	542.0
菏泽市	Heze	16743.8	5801.7	3941.0	3551.0	1598.4	1446.5

注：设市城市为市本级数据。
a)The data of cities are from Municipal level.

主要统计指标解释

供水普及率 指报告期末城区内用水人口与总人口的比率。计算公式：

$$供水普及率=\frac{城区用水人口}{城区人口+城区暂住人口}\times100\%$$

燃气普及率 指报告期末城区内使用燃气的人口与总人口的比率。计算公式：

$$燃气普及率=\frac{城区用气人口}{城区人口+城区暂住人口}\times100\%$$

供水综合生产能力 指按供水设施取水、净化、送水、出厂输水干管等环节设计能力计算的综合生产能力。计算时，以四个环节中最薄弱的环节为主确定能力。

年末供水管道长度 指从送水泵至各类用户引入管之间所有管道的长度。不包括新安装尚未使用、水厂内以及用户建筑物内的管道。

全年供水总量 指报告期供水企业（单位）供出的全部水量。包括有效供水量和漏损水量。

生产运营用水 指在城区范围内生产、运营的农、林、牧、渔业、工业、建筑业、交通运输业等单位在生产、运营过程中的用水。

公共服务用水 指为城区社会公共生活服务的用水，包括行政事业单位、部队营区和公共设施服务、社会服务业、批发零售贸易业、旅馆饮食业以及社会服务业等单位的用水。

居民家庭用水 指城市范围内所有居民家庭的日常生活用水，包括城市居民、农民家庭、公共供水站用水。

全年供气总量 指全年燃气企业(单位)向用户供应的燃气数量。包括销售量和损失量。

供热面积 指供热企业(单位)向城市各类房屋建筑物、构筑物及其附属设施供热的全部建筑面积。

年末道路长度 指道路长度和与道路相通的桥梁、隧道的长度，按车行道中心线计算。

道路面积 指道路实际铺装面积和与道路相通的广场、桥梁、隧道的铺装面积。

城市桥梁 指为跨越天然或人工障碍物而修建的构筑物，包括跨河桥、立交桥、人行天桥以及人行地下通道等。

城市排水管道长度 指所有市政排水总管、干管、支管、检查井及连接井进出口等长度之和。

年末运营车数 指年末公交企业(单位)用于运营业务的全部车辆数。以企业(单位)固定资产台账中已投入运营的车辆数为准。

绿化覆盖面积 指城市中的乔木、灌木、草坪等所有植被的垂直投影面积。

园林绿地面积 指报告期末用作园林和绿化的各种绿地面积。包括公园绿地、防护绿地、广场用地内绿地、附属绿地和区域绿地的面积。其中：公园绿地是指城市中向公众开放，以游憩为主要功能，兼具生态、景观、文教和应急避险等功能，有一定游憩和服务设施的绿地。

Explanatory Notes on Main Statistical Indicators

Coverage Rate of Urban Population with Access to Tap Water refers to the ratio of the urban population with access to tap water to the total urban population at the end of reference period. The formula is:

$$\frac{\text{Coverage of urban population}}{\text{with access to tap water}} = \frac{\text{Urban population with access to tap water}}{\text{Urban population}} \times 100\%$$

Percentage of Urban Population with Access to Gas refers to the ratio of use of gas in urban area population and the total population. at the end of the reference period. The formula is:

$$\frac{\text{Coverage rate of urban}}{\text{population with access to gas}} = \frac{\text{Urban population with access to gas}}{\text{Urban population}} \times 100\%$$

Production Capacity of Water Supply refers to the designed overall production capacity of water facilities, covering the four segments of water collection, purification, conveyance, and outflow through trunk pipelines. Increased capacity through transformation and innovation projects is included as well. The capacity is determined mainly on the weakest of the above-mentioned four segments.

Length of Water Supply Pipelines refers to the total length of all pipelines between the water pumps and the user water meters, excluding pipelines newly installed but not in use yet, pipeline in the water factory, and pipeline in the users' buildings.

Total Volume of Urban Water Supply refers to the total volume of water supplied by water-works (units) during the reference period, including both the effective water supply and loss during the water supply.

Consumption of Water for Production Use refers to water consumption in the process of production and operation by production and operation units of agriculture, forestry, animal husbandry, fisheries, manufacturing, construction, transport, etc. in urban areas.

Consumption of water for public service use refers to water consumption for public service in the urban areas, including water consumption of administrative institutions, military barracks, public facilities, wholesale and retail, accommodation and catering industries and social service industry, etc.

Consumption of water for household use refers to consumption of water for daily life of all households in cities, including households of urban residents and farmers, and public water supply stations.

Volume of Gas Supply refers to the total volume of gas provided to users by gas-producing enterprises (units) during the reporting period, including the volume sold and the volume lost.

Area of Heat-supply Service refers to the total area of buildings, structures and their affiliated facilities with heat supply provided by heating enterprises (units).

Length of Paved Roads refers to the length of roads with paved surface, including bridges and tunnels connected with roads. Length of the roads is measured by the central lines.

Area of Road refers to the actual pavement area of the road and the pavement area of squares, bridges and tunnels connected with the road.

Urban Bridges refer to bridges built to cross over natural or man-made barriers, including bridges over rivers, overpasses for traffic and for pedestrians, underpasses for pedestrians, etc.

Length of Urban Sewage Pipes refers to the total length of general drainage, trunks, branch and inspection wells, connection wells, inlets and outlets, etc.

Number of Vehicles under Operation at the Year-end refers to the total number of vehicles under operation by public transport enterprises (units) at the end of the year, based on the records of operational vehicles by the enterprises (units).

Area of Green coverage refers to the vertical projection area of all trees in the city such as trees, shrubs, lawns, etc.

Garden green area refers to a green area for gardening and greening. Including parks, green space in square land, protective green, the accessory Greenbelt and regional green areas at the end of referenced period.Park Green Land refers to the green land which is open to the public for relaxation and has service facilities and is used for ecological protection, landscaping and disaster reduction. It is an important part of construction land, urban green space and municipal public facilities.

第
12
篇

资源和环境

Natural Resources and Environment

简 要 说 明

一、本篇资料的主要内容

本篇资料主要反映了全省资源和环境保护事业发展状况，资源部分主要包括自然资源、湖泊、河流、山脉和气候以及土地利用和水资源状况，环境保护部分主要包括工业废水、废气、固体废物等工业污染物排放及处理情况和工业污染治理项目建设情况。

二、本篇资料的来源

1．自然资源和湖泊、河流、山脉等表，由省统计局综合处根据年鉴积累资料整理。

2．气象资料主要包括各市平均气温、降水量、日照等方面的资料，数据来源于省气象局，由省统计局综合处整理提供。

3．湿地、造林资料和土地利用情况来源于省自然资源厅，由省统计局能源处整理提供。

4．水资源资料来源于省水利厅，由省统计局能源处整理提供。

5．环境保护资料来源于省生态环境厅，由省统计局能源处整理提供。

Brief Introduction

I. Content

Data in this chapter reflect natural resources of Shandong and development in environment protection. Resources mainly include natural resources, lakes, rivers, mountains and climate. Environment protection mainly shows treatment and discharge of industrial waste water, solid waste and waste gas, construction of projects for pollution treatment.

II. Source of Data

(1) Data on natural resources, lakes, rivers, and mountains are prepared by the Division of Comprehensive Statistics of Shandong Provincial Bureau of Statistics.

(2) Data on climate mainly include average temperature, precipitation and sunshine hours. The data are provided by the Meteorological Bureau of Shandong Province and prepared by the Division of Comprehensive Statistics of Shandong Provincial Bureau of Statistics.

(3) Data on wetland and plantation and land use are provided by the Department of Nature and Resources of Shandong Province and prepared by the Division of Energy Statistics of Shandong Provincial Bureau of Statistics.

(4) Data on water resource are provided by the Department of Water Resources of Shandong Province and prepared by the Division of Energy Statistics of Shandong Provincial Bureau of Statistics.

(5) Data on environment protection are provided by the Ecological Environment Department of Shandong Province and prepared by the Division of Energy Statistics of Shandong Provincial Bureau of Statistics.

12-1 人口和自然资源(2021年)

Population and Natural Resources (2021)

项　　目		Item		2021
一、人　口		**Population**		
年末总人口	(万人)	Total Population(year-end)	(10 000 persons)	10169.99
人口密度	(人/平方公里)	Density of Population	(person/sq.km)	644
二、土　地（2020年）		**Land(2020)**		
全省土地面积	(万平方公里)	Land Area	(10 000 sq.km)	15.8
农用地		Land for Agriculture Use		11.7
耕地		Cultivated Land		6.4
园地		Garden Land		1.3
牧草地		Grazing and Pasture Land		
建设用地		Land for Construction		3.2
城镇村及工矿用地		Land for Urban Village, Mining and Manufacturing		2.8
交通用地		Land for Transport Facilities		0.3
水利设施用地		Land for Water Conservancy Facilities		0.1
三、矿　产		**Mineral Resources**		
已发现矿产种类	(种)	Mineral Resources Discovered	(kind)	148
已探明储量的矿产种类	(种)	Number of Mineral Resources with Insured Reserves	(kind)	91
能源矿产	(种)	Energy Resources	(kind)	7
金属矿产	(种)	Metal Mineral	(kind)	27
非金属矿产	(种)	Nonmetal Mineral	(kind)	54
水气矿产	(种)	Water and Gas	(kind)	3
四、水文、水利		**Water Resources**		
水资源总量	(亿立方米)	Average Volume of Water Resources	(100 million cu.m)	525.33
地表水资源量	(亿立方米)	Surface Water Volume	(100 million cu.m)	381.84

12-2 主要湖泊、河流基本情况
Basic Statistics on Major Lakes and Rivers

湖泊名	Names of Lakes	面积（平方公里） Area of Lakes (sq.km)	河流名	Names of Rivers	面积（平方公里） Drainage Area (sq.km)	河长（公里） Length (km)
小　计	Total	1494.6	徒骇河	Tuhaihe River	13136.6	446.5
微山湖	Weishan Lake	531.7	沂　河	Yihe River	10909.9	287.5
昭阳湖	Zhaoyang Lake	337.1	马颊河	Majiahe River	10638.4	448.0
独山湖	Dushan Lake	144.6	小清河	Xiaoqinghe River	10498.8	233.0
南阳湖	Nanyang Lake	211.0	大汶河	Dawenhe River	9069.0	211.0
东平湖	Dongping Lake	167.0	潍　河	Weihe River	6493.2	233.0
麻大湖	Mada Lake	110.0	沭　河	Shuhe River	6161.4	263.0
白云湖	Baiyun Lake	16.2	大沽河	Daguhe River	4161.9	179.9
青沙湖	Qingsha Lake	11.1	弥　河	Mihe River	3847.5	206.0

12-3 主要山脉高度
Height of Major Mountains

山　名	Mountain Range	标高（米） Height of Mountain Peak (m)	山　名	Mountain Range	标高（米） Height of Mountain Peak (m)
泰　山	Taishan Mountains	1532	马耳山	Maer Mountains	707
蒙　山	Mengshan Mountains	1156	龙须崮	Longxvgu Mountains	707
崂　山	Laoshan Mountains	1133	凤凰山	Fenghuang Mountains	648
鲁　山	Lushan Mountains	1108	四海山	Sihai Mountains	625
沂　山	Yishan Mountains	1032	鏊子崮	Aozigu Mountains	616
徂徕山	Culai Mountains	1028	黑　山	Heishan Mountains	612
昆嵛山	Kunyu Mountains	923	珂楼埠山	Keloubu Mountains	577
九顶山	Jiuding Mountains	834	大　山	Dashan Mountains	560
艾　山	Aishan Mountains	814	伟德山	Weide Mountains	554
牙　山	Yashan Mountains	806	招虎山	Zhaohu Mountains	550
大泽山	Daze Mountains	737	孟良崮	Menglianggu Mountains	536
摩天岭	Motianling Mountains	735	布　山	Bushan Mountains	447

12-4 各市平均气温(2021年)

Monthly Average Temperature by Region(2021)

单位:摄氏度 (℃)

城市名	City	一 月 Jan.	二 月 Feb.	三 月 Mar.	四 月 Apr.	五 月 May	六 月 June
济南市	Jinan	0.8	7.5	10.7	15.0	21.4	27.3
青岛市	Qingdao	0.6	4.9	8.3	12.4	16.9	21.8
淄博市	Zibo	-1.4	5.6	9.5	13.9	20.0	26.2
枣庄市	Zaozhuang	1.0	7.1	10.6	14.8	21.1	26.6
东营市	Dongying	-1.2	5.2	9.3	14.1	19.8	25.4
烟台市	Yantai	-1.0	3.8	7.5	12.3	17.2	22.7
潍坊市	Weifang	-1.1	5.2	9.1	13.8	19.7	25.0
济宁市	Jining	1.5	7.9	11.2	15.3	21.6	27.4
泰安市	Tai'an	-0.7	5.6	10.2	14.7	20.9	25.9
威海市	Weihai	-0.2	4.3	7.7	12.7	17.2	22.8
日照市	Rizhao	0.7	5.6	8.6	12.9	18.2	22.5
临沂市	Linyi	0.4	6.0	9.6	14.1	19.8	25.2
德州市	Dezhou	-2.6	4.8	9.2	14.2	19.9	26.0
聊城市	Liaocheng	-0.9	6.3	9.6	14.4	20.1	26.5
滨州市	Binzhou	-2.3	4.3	8.9	13.8	19.4	25.4
菏泽市	Heze	1.2	8.1	10.8	15.3	21.6	27.7

12-4 续表 continued

单位:摄氏度 (℃)

城市名	City	七 月 July	八 月 Aug.	九 月 Sept.	十 月 Oct.	十一月 Nov.	十二月 Dec.	全年平均 Annual Average
济南市	Jinan	27.5	25.8	22.6	14.8	9.3	3.9	15.6
青岛市	Qingdao	25.3	25.7	23.3	16.7	11.2	4.7	14.3
淄博市	Zibo	27.6	25.5	22.3	13.9	8.0	1.9	14.4
枣庄市	Zaozhuang	27.2	26.1	23.6	16.7	9.5	3.3	15.6
东营市	Dongying	28.0	26.1	23.2	14.7	8.6	2.5	14.6
烟台市	Yantai	25.5	24.5	22.1	15.6	9.5	2.9	13.6
潍坊市	Weifang	27.7	25.9	23.0	15.1	9.0	2.9	14.6
济宁市	Jining	28.1	26.3	23.2	15.6	9.7	4.0	16.0
泰安市	Tai'an	27.3	25.5	22.5	14.6	8.2	1.7	14.7
威海市	Weihai	25.4	25.0	22.4	16.2	10.2	3.7	14.0
日照市	Rizhao	25.3	25.4	23.2	16.5	10.9	4.5	14.5
临沂市	Linyi	26.2	25.3	22.7	16.1	10.0	3.9	14.9
德州市	Dezhou	27.1	25.0	21.9	13.2	7.2	1.3	13.9
聊城市	Liaocheng	27.5	25.7	22.4	14.5	8.5	2.6	14.8
滨州市	Binzhou	27.5	25.3	22.4	14.0	7.6	1.4	14.0
菏泽市	Heze	27.8	25.9	23.1	15.1	9.4	3.8	15.8

12-5 各市降水量(2021年)

Monthly Precipitation by Region(2021)

单位:毫米 (millimeter)

城市名	City	一 月 Jan.	二 月 Feb.	三 月 Mar.	四 月 Apr.	五 月 May	六 月 June
济南市	Jinan	1.8	26.5	26.7	41.3	20.6	64.5
青岛市	Qingdao	2.3	24.9	35.4	62.2	55.2	28.5
淄博市	Zibo	2.8	16.5	26.7	60.0	14.8	140.0
枣庄市	Zaozhuang	9.5	45.3	33.4	35.5	68.6	111.2
东营市	Dongying	3.5	8.4	26.6	60.5	17.2	99.3
烟台市	Yantai	26.0	5.7	46.5	88.8	53.4	71.9
潍坊市	Weifang	4.3	18.7	33.0	74.1	51.3	77.8
济宁市	Jining	6.4	65.4	20.8	31.4	29.4	114.5
泰安市	Tai'an	4.8	44.7	24.1	33.7	15.1	131.6
威海市	Weihai	21.3	3.4	50.0	103.2	49.2	80.8
日照市	Rizhao	2.8	37.1	34.3	78.4	44.2	91.3
临沂市	Linyi	5.3	29.5	32.0	50.2	39.1	157.5
德州市	Dezhou		17.0	22.2	15.9	24.6	71.1
聊城市	Liaocheng	0.1	45.5	16.1	26.6	21.7	129.5
滨州市	Binzhou	1.8	8.6	25.1	47.4	16.3	85.9
菏泽市	Heze	1.4	71.7	15.7	30.0	37.0	118.4

12-5 续表 continued

单位:毫米 (millimeter)

城市名	City	七 月 July	八 月 Aug.	九 月 Sept.	十 月 Oct.	十一月 Nov.	十二月 Dec.	全 年 Annual Total
济南市	Jinan	391.2	149.0	190.1	51.7	77.2	2.8	1043.4
青岛市	Qingdao	203.1	168.7	159.3	50.6	55.8	1.0	847.0
淄博市	Zibo	172.9	132.6	212.6	79.5	49.1	2.5	910.0
枣庄市	Zaozhuang	359.1	255.3	157.4	8.6	45.0	0.5	1129.4
东营市	Dongying	241.9	95.5	184.5	134.1	96.2	1.2	968.9
烟台市	Yantai	189.0	155.1	182.2	109.8	57.2	17.1	1002.7
潍坊市	Weifang	142.8	134.5	131.0	82.1	45.3	3.0	797.9
济宁市	Jining	259.8	332.2	218.5	42.2	42.4	1.6	1164.6
泰安市	Tai'an	200.0	241.3	340.7	56.7	42.3	0.7	1135.7
威海市	Weihai	153.6	168.7	125.2	64.3	79.7	16.8	916.2
日照市	Rizhao	244.4	183.2	208.9	43.9	37.3		1005.8
临沂市	Linyi	293.7	198.4	170.8	8.0	45.7		1030.2
德州市	Dezhou	228.5	110.8	197.1	80.1	49.4	2.6	819.3
聊城市	Liaocheng	301.7	130.3	291.3	54.0	56.7	3.7	1077.2
滨州市	Binzhou	229.6	172.2	117.9	102.8	73.8	0.5	881.9
菏泽市	Heze	136.5	299.9	325.4	33.2	63.4	2.4	1135.0

12-6 各市日照时数(2021年)

Monthly Sunshine Hours by Region(2021)

单位:小时 (hour)

城市名	City	一 月 Jan.	二 月 Feb.	三 月 Mar.	四 月 Apr.	五 月 May	六 月 June
济南市	Jinan	213.0	206.5	194.0	208.3	282.9	224.8
青岛市	Qingdao	156.5	166.2	212.9	199.0	241.0	163.6
淄博市	Zibo	178.0	190.9	160.1	169.1	229.0	174.1
枣庄市	Zaozhuang	161.3	174.2	157.8	143.8	212.7	172.8
东营市	Dongying	194.0	199.5	188.3	190.3	256.6	195.1
烟台市	Yantai	227.3	196.4	193.1	205.4	229.7	196.9
潍坊市	Weifang	200.2	205.8	199.8	200.6	261.6	198.9
济宁市	Jining	211.3	206.7	247.6	169.6	235.4	201.4
泰安市	Tai'an	243.8	235.2	246.9	193.3	258.4	213.7
威海市	Weihai	149.6	197.6	205.9	217.0	246.0	212.5
日照市	Rizhao	242.8	240.5	285.7	276.2	317.6	292.1
临沂市	Linyi	186.4	197.3	189.1	161.8	220.5	173.8
德州市	Dezhou	187.2	191.4	163.4	204.5	259.2	201.7
聊城市	Liaocheng	202.8	200.0	151.3	187.8	262.7	214.8
滨州市	Binzhou	241.2	227.2	193.8	199.2	271.6	213.5
菏泽市	Heze	180.3	187.3	150.9	171.7	235.6	201.4

12-6 续表 continued

单位:小时 (hour)

城市名	City	七 月 July	八 月 Aug.	九 月 Sept.	十 月 Oct.	十一月 Nov.	十二月 Dec.	全 年 Annual Total
济南市	Jinan	167.6	192.9	160.7	149.4	201.0	208.9	2410.0
青岛市	Qingdao	175.1	186.9	169.7	164.3	186.3	191.4	2212.9
淄博市	Zibo	140.7	152.6	150.5	116.4	166.3	181.9	2009.6
枣庄市	Zaozhuang	116.1	141.0	140.4	133.5	174.8	182.1	1910.5
东营市	Dongying	182.2	187.9	175.4	165.8	191.6	189.0	2315.7
烟台市	Yantai	173.8	178.4	167.3	167.9	144.4	163.0	2243.6
潍坊市	Weifang	190.8	199.7	167.8	167.8	189.7	206.9	2389.6
济宁市	Jining	158.4	158.1	143.1	124.8	155.9	157.8	2170.1
泰安市	Tai'an	167.0	171.8	170.0	148.5	198.5	203.3	2450.4
威海市	Weihai	193.7	166.7	177.0	171.2	137.5	165.2	2239.9
日照市	Rizhao	292.4	286.6	256.2	259.1	243.1	251.1	3243.4
临沂市	Linyi	139.9	156.5	155.7	150.6	190.6	199.6	2121.8
德州市	Dezhou	149.5	188.6	159.6	144.5	191.0	200.9	2241.5
聊城市	Liaocheng	162.5	189.0	152.8	128.1	185.5	204.5	2241.8
滨州市	Binzhou	187.4	203.3	169.5	163.7	196.5	193.4	2460.3
菏泽市	Heze	154.5	164.5	163.2	119.0	178.9	183.1	2090.4

12-7 各市土地利用情况(2020年)

Land Use by Region(2020)

单位:公顷 (hectare)

地　区	Region	农用地 Land for Agriculture Use	建设用地 Land for Construction	城镇村及工矿用地 Land for Urban Village, Mining and Manufacturing	交通用地 Land for Transport Facilities	水利设施用　地 Land for Water Conservancy Facilities	未利用地(不含裸岩石砾地) unutilized land (excluding exposed rock land)
全省总计	**Total**	11697673	3192850	2830831	271816	90203	886712
济南市	Jinan	757429	216727	189766	19391	7570	47214
青岛市	Qingdao	811447	256730	226313	25472	4945	56198
淄博市	Zibo	438400	130061	115254	12167	2641	25986
枣庄市	Zaozhuang	343050	97578	87863	6994	2721	12687
东营市	Dongying	477709	151363	132248	11345	7770	196622
烟台市	Yantai	1091902	229957	204527	23128	2302	68028
潍坊市	Weifang	1161529	354460	318917	30150	5392	100391
济宁市	Jining	766355	222108	189474	19561	13073	124891
泰安市	Tai'an	590784	141283	126933	11963	2387	40278
威海市	Weihai	453347	92674	81615	10458	601	36161
日照市	Rizhao	418767	100316	86657	12630	1029	17312
临沂市	Linyi	1337329	325916	295451	26667	3798	52445
德州市	Dezhou	818158	199689	170486	16631	12573	17924
聊城市	Liaocheng	670227	184501	162869	14411	7221	8069
滨州市	Binzhou	629481	229884	207935	13507	8441	58359
菏泽市	Heze	931760	259604	234522	17341	7740	24148

注：数据来源于2020年度国土变更调查。（以下相关表同）

a) The data in this table come from the 2020 National Land Changing Survey.(The same applies to the following relevant tables.)

12-8 各市湿地面积(2020年)

Area of Wetlands by Region (2020)

地　区	Region	湿地面积(千公顷) Area of Wetlands (1 000 hectares)	沿海滩涂 coastal beach	内陆滩涂 Inland tidal flat	沼泽地 swamps
全省总计	**Total**	**246778.5**	**199806.0**	**46918.7**	**53.9**
济南市	Jinan	406.7		406.7	
青岛市	Qingdao	23606.2	23028.1	578.1	
淄博市	Zibo	926.1		926.1	
枣庄市	Zaozhuang	149.9		149.9	
东营市	Dongying	123265.5	91072.1	32193.5	
烟台市	Yantai	16822.3	16463.5	358.8	
潍坊市	Weifang	37730.2	35421.6	2308.6	
济宁市	Jining	1158.1	0.1	1104.1	53.9
泰安市	Tai'an	727.0		727.0	
威海市	Weihai	14215.0	13773.9	441.1	
日照市	Rizhao	3669.8	3369.6	300.1	
临沂市	Linyi	1234.9		1234.9	
德州市	Dezhou	263.5		263.5	
聊城市	Liaocheng	84.6		84.6	
滨州市	Binzhou	22094.0	16677.1	5416.9	
菏泽市	Heze	424.8		424.8	

12-9 造林面积情况

Area of Afforestation

单位:公顷　　(hectare)

年份 Year 地区 Region		造林总面积 Total Area of Afforestation	按造林方式分 By Approach 人工造林 Manual Planting	按林种用途分 By Function of Forest 用材林 Timber Forests	经济林 By-product Forests	防护林 Protection Forests	薪炭林 Fuel Forests	特种用途林 Forests for Special Purpose
2000		153389	153389	18007	100769	34268	63	282
2001		135259	135259	19019	84039	32155		46
2002		152597	152597	43671	80066	27670	1098	92
2003		344079	344079	192653	92130	57709	1039	548
2004		262711	262711	134193	53536	74441	233	308
2005		141141	141141	47470	42674	49559	633	805
2006		134423	134423	40421	34252	59193	7	550
2007		156738	156738	49409	26971	68046	66	254
2008		185575	184928	69516	25947	89726	20	366
2009		182171	180529	42463	26172	113067		469
2010		205131	198998	36101	37856	129877		1297
2011		219028	219028	34598	51154	130896		2380
2012		197956	195875	25178	49195	122277		1306
2013		220473	219129	32569	63604	122536		1764
2014		224972	223560	43411	66219	113208		2134
2015		221207	206552	41627	60372	102643		1910
2016		146684	115179	19229	35812	59264		874
2017		142195	92306	20805	27941	42713		847
2018		147481	118745	30886	36323	49814		1722
2019			125393	38972	35641	49924		856
2020			102830	27904	21614	52369	97	846
2021			7137	1108	232	5769		28
济南市	Jinan		2931	114		2817		
青岛市	Qingdao		17			17		
淄博市	Zibo		272			272		
枣庄市	Zaozhuang		297	2	32	263		
东营市	Dongying		128	61	4	63		
烟台市	Yantai		200			200		
潍坊市	Weifang		196	20	9	167		
济宁市	Jining		1019	341	27	623		28
泰安市	Tai'an		121			121		
威海市	Weihai							
日照市	Rizhao		422	71	16	335		
临沂市	Linyi		767	212	75	480		
德州市	Dezhou							
聊城市	Liaocheng		201	134		67		
滨州市	Binzhou		154	20		134		
菏泽市	Heze		412	133	69	210		

12-10 供水用水情况

Water Supply and Water Use

年份 地区	Year Region	供水总量(亿立方米) Water Supply (100 millioncu.m)	地表水 Surface Water	地下水 Ground-water	其他 Others	用水总量(亿立方米) Water Use (100 millioncu.m)	农业 Agriculture	工业 Industry	生活 Consumption	生态 Ecological Protection
2000		249.46	114.40	131.81	3.25	244.09	179.84	43.65	20.61	
2001		251.61	115.60	133.71	2.30	252.73	187.40	41.92	23.08	0.34
2002		252.39	117.66	132.96	1.77	244.73	192.87	36.59	14.98	0.29
2003		219.34	104.12	113.95	1.27	215.70	162.54	27.96	23.92	1.38
2004		214.88	106.28	107.40	1.20	211.30	160.14	24.81	24.67	1.68
2005		211.02	106.70	102.67	1.65	207.65	161.73	18.38	25.17	2.37
2006		225.53	119.77	103.90	1.86	222.24	175.07	18.93	25.62	2.62
2007		219.55	115.59	101.98	1.98	219.55	164.81	24.12	27.42	3.20
2008		219.89	115.51	101.23	3.15	219.89	162.76	24.69	28.71	3.73
2009		219.99	119.62	97.05	3.33	219.99	161.60	24.70	29.77	3.94
2010		222.47	127.15	91.31	4.01	222.47	159.65	26.84	31.34	4.64
2011		224.05	127.33	89.34	7.38	224.05	154.26	29.72	32.89	7.17
2012		221.79	126.12	89.26	6.41	221.79	154.23	28.10	32.81	6.66
2013		217.94	124.94	86.86	6.15	217.94	149.72	28.86	33.31	6.06
2014		214.52	121.26	85.99	7.28	214.52	146.72	28.64	33.39	5.78
2015		212.77	122.00	83.11	7.65	212.77	143.29	29.59	32.99	6.89
2016		213.99	123.26	82.34	8.39	213.99	141.50	30.64	34.22	7.64
2017		209.47	121.08	79.71	8.68	209.47	134.03	28.85	34.57	12.02
2018		212.66	125.66	78.29	8.71	212.66	133.46	32.53	36.05	10.62
2019		225.26	137.05	78.67	9.54	225.26	138.23	31.87	37.29	17.87
2020		222.50	135.67	74.96	11.87	222.50	134.04	31.91	37.47	19.08
2021		210.13	128.90	66.84	14.40	210.13	115.75	32.64	40.31	21.43
济南市	Jinan	18.68	10.59	5.92	2.17	18.68	7.66	2.83	5.21	2.98
青岛市	Qingdao	10.62	7.61	2.10	0.90	10.62	2.55	2.17	5.02	0.87
淄博市	Zibo	9.77	4.74	4.40	0.63	9.77	3.80	3.31	1.79	0.87
枣庄市	Zaozhuang	5.84	1.70	3.60	0.55	5.84	2.34	1.33	1.43	0.74
东营市	Dongying	13.39	12.58	0.73	0.08	13.39	5.64	2.56	1.43	3.76
烟台市	Yantai	10.07	6.16	3.56	0.36	10.07	5.86	1.38	2.74	0.10
潍坊市	Weifang	16.45	8.57	6.90	0.98	16.45	8.30	2.70	3.59	1.86
济宁市	Jining	20.89	10.88	8.02	1.99	20.89	14.39	2.48	3.10	0.92
泰安市	Tai'an	9.58	3.64	4.59	1.36	9.58	5.79	1.03	1.85	0.92
威海市	Weihai	4.50	3.51	0.82	0.18	4.50	2.02	0.86	1.15	0.48
日照市	Rizhao	5.97	4.30	1.06	0.60	5.97	2.31	1.55	1.39	0.71
临沂市	Linyi	17.22	12.45	4.09	0.68	17.22	9.91	2.13	3.87	1.30
德州市	Dezhou	17.36	12.24	4.42	0.70	17.36	11.72	1.67	1.75	2.23
聊城市	Liaocheng	16.22	9.12	6.40	0.70	16.22	12.35	1.74	1.63	0.51
滨州市	Binzhou	15.14	12.90	1.25	0.98	15.14	7.84	3.42	1.53	2.35
菏泽市	Heze	18.42	7.91	8.98	1.53	18.42	13.26	1.51	2.81	0.83

注：自2021年起，原地下水水源供水量中的微咸水调整至其他水源供水量。

a) Since 2021, the volume of brackish water of groundwater has been adjusted to other water supply resources.

12-11 水资源情况
Water Resources

年 份 地 区	Year Region	水资源总量(亿立方米) Total Amount of Water Resources (100 millioncu.m)	地表水资源量 Surface Water Resources	地下水资源与地表水资源不重复量 Unduplicated Measurement Between Surface Water and Groundwater
2003		489.69	349.29	140.40
2004		349.46	234.51	114.55
2005		415.86	295.85	120.01
2006		199.78	109.56	90.22
2007		387.11	280.19	106.93
2008		328.71	228.96	99.75
2009		284.95	173.80	111.16
2010		309.12	199.08	110.04
2011		347.61	237.49	110.12
2012		274.08	182.17	91.90
2013		291.70	191.07	100.64
2014		148.44	76.61	71.83
2015		168.44	84.30	84.14
2016		220.32	121.18	99.14
2017		225.61	139.14	86.47
2018		343.25	230.58	112.67
2019		195.21	119.66	75.54
2020		375.30	259.83	115.46
2021		525.33	381.84	143.49
济南市	Jinan	39.42	26.17	13.25
青岛市	Qingdao	21.12	16.67	4.46
淄博市	Zibo	25.49	16.71	8.78
枣庄市	Zaozhuang	27.66	21.55	6.11
东营市	Dongying	13.03	12.04	0.99
烟台市	Yantai	38.65	34.51	4.14
潍坊市	Weifang	28.79	20.41	8.38
济宁市	Jining	44.42	27.62	16.80
泰安市	Tai'an	30.12	23.46	6.66
威海市	Weihai	20.86	18.27	2.59
日照市	Rizhao	18.48	16.38	2.10
临沂市	Linyi	78.13	69.28	8.85
德州市	Dezhou	32.15	17.47	14.68
聊城市	Liaocheng	31.89	15.55	16.34
滨州市	Binzhou	20.22	14.29	5.94
菏泽市	Heze	54.90	31.47	23.43

12-12 1981-2021年主要污染物排放及处理情况

Discharge and Treatment of Major Pollutants from 1981 to 2021

单位:万吨 (10 000 tons)

年 份 Year	废水排放量 Volume of Waste Water Discharged	# 工 业 Industry	二氧化硫排放量 Volume of Sulphur Dioxide Discharged	氮氧化物排放量 Volume of Nitrogen Oxides Discharged	颗粒物排放量 Volume of Particulate Emissions	一般工业固体废物产生量 Volume of Common Industrial Solid Waste generated	一般工业固体废物综合利用量 Volume of Common Industrial Solid Waste Utilized
1981	104790	87673	119		77	2522	639
1982	105942	82641	120		97	2615	723
1983	110938	88168	122		85	2559	716
1984	129033	106275	142		117	2743	760
1985	131898	105375	160		120	2748	765
1986	127277	98913	171		129	2860	847
1987	132770	93811	173		116	2848	894
1988	144346	97136	191		128	3325	968
1989	137165	91360	189		130	3610	1117
1990	136573	87631	193		121	3880	1337
1991	137051	88728	204		121	3837	2169
1992	137721	86412	226		125	3941	2410
1993	142322	86350	228		135	4201	2353
1994	147979	87316	225		130	4263	2871
1995	158681	96214	232		130	4484	2899
1996	204200	101018				4652	2824
1997	246100	130918	247		108	5131	3448
1998	234048	117069	226		92	5109	3777
1999	224100	107975	183		71	5166	3877
2000	229000	110324	180		67	5407	4173
2001	235271	115233	172		65	6215	5224
2002	230709	106668	169		62	6559	5704
2003	245782	115933	184		62	6786	6054
2004	264014	128706	182		52	7922	7191
2005	280377	139071	200		62	9175	8683
2006	302637	144365	196		58	11011	10397
2007	334255	166574	182		46	11935	11615
2008	358910	176977	169		44	12988	12173
2009	386731	182673	159		42	14138	13826
2010	436371	208257	154		39	16038	15297
2011	443331	187245	183	179	78	19533	18298
2012	479100	183634	175	174	70	18343	17073
2013	494570	181179	164	165	70	18172	17134
2014	514423	180022	159	159	121	19199	18380
2015	550230	185493	153	142	108	19797	18308
2016	361471	156599	73	142	62	26350	22314
2017	357803	142495	42	120	48	28484	23152
2018	371738	145052	34	115	39	29995	23831
2019	374309	144039	28	109	37	32129	25230
2020	376378	133359	19	62	24	24989	19612
2021	371082	133854	17	66	22	25233	20028

注：1.2011年以前，颗粒物排放量为烟尘排放量，从2014年起颗粒物排放量包含无组织排放的颗粒物。
2.根据"二污普"结果，对2016-2019年污染源统计初步数据进行了更新，2021年数据为初步统计数据。

a) Before 2011，the volume of Particulate Emissions refers to that of soot and dust discharged, since 2014, the volume of Particulate Emissions inclu-des particulate matter discharged not through pipes.

b) The data on contaminants of 2016 to 2019 have been revised according to the results of the second national survey on pollution sources, and data of 2021 are Preliminary statistical results.

12-13 各市主要污染物排放情况(2016年)

Discharge of Major Pollutants by Region (2016)

地 区	Region	废水排放量(万吨) Volume of Waste Water Discharged (10 000 tons)	工业 Industry	生活 Daily Life	化学需氧量排放量(吨) Volume of COD Discharged (ton)	工业 Industry	生活 Daily Life	氨氮排放量(吨) Volume of Ammonia Nitrogen Discharged (ton)	工业 Industry	生活 Daily Life
全省总计	**Total**	**361471**	**156599**	**204872**	**338002**	**66972**	**230002**	**28813**	**3414**	**24980**
济南市	Jinan	27961	6894	21067	21754	2656	19096	1731	150	1581
青岛市	Qingdao	34099	7351	26748	14476	1650	12782	1363	57	1304
淄博市	Zibo	23516	12160	11356	15574	6300	9224	676	303	371
枣庄市	Zaozhuang	14397	7167	7230	16580	2483	14097	1212	180	1032
东营市	Dongying	15479	9271	6208	9533	4018	5515	714	285	429
烟台市	Yantai	19329	8365	10964	19414	3373	16010	1502	128	1372
潍坊市	Weifang	39881	22321	17560	23578	9081	14455	2446	506	1938
济宁市	Jining	30355	14023	16332	22935	3617	19299	2080	117	1960
泰安市	Tai'an	16081	6290	9791	17598	2506	15044	1932	87	1842
威海市	Weihai	10927	1995	8932	5446	2607	2816	304	76	228
日照市	Rizhao	13012	7972	5040	7364	3471	3827	837	78	753
临沂市	Linyi	29799	11461	18339	24437	6924	17499	2888	360	2524
德州市	Dezhou	20671	7285	13386	28423	2844	25560	3687	129	3556
聊城市	Liaocheng	18863	7073	11790	17784	2837	14900	1957	202	1752
滨州市	Binzhou	27907	19653	8254	20004	6509	13476	1463	384	1073
菏泽市	Heze	19194	7318	11876	32522	6096	26402	3636	371	3265

注：1.按照国家统一部署，根据"二污普"结果，对2016-2019年污染源初步统计数据进行了更新。（以下相关表同）
2.表中各市化学需氧量、氨氮排放量数据不含农业源排放量，全省数据含农业源排放量。（以下相关表同）

a)According to the unified national deployment, the preliminary statistics of pollution sources in 2016 to 2019 are revised based on the results of the second national survey on pollution sources.(The same applies to the following relevant tables.)

b)The volume of COD and Ammonia Nitrogen Discharged in each regions does not include agricultural source emission, while that of the whole prov -ince do.(The same applies to the following relevant tables.)

12-13 续表 continued

地 区	Region	二氧化硫排放量(吨) Volume of Sulphur Dioxide Discharged (ton)	工业 Industry	生活 Daily Life	氮氧化物排放量(吨) Volume of Nitrogen Oxides Discharged (ton)	工业 Industry	生活 Daily Life	颗粒物排放量(吨) Volume of Soot and Dust Discharged (ton)	工业 Industry	生活 Daily Life
全省总计	**Total**	**729757**	**663871**	**65840**	**1417763**	**773679**	**40543**	**622649**	**452253**	**157501**
济南市	Jinan	43084	37995	5078	64727	61687	2985	50475	39644	10825
青岛市	Qingdao	25533	16956	8577	33728	29242	4487	35493	16355	19138
淄博市	Zibo	69291	66122	3167	90110	88095	2007	47628	40160	7466
枣庄市	Zaozhuang	23752	20972	2779	34728	33775	950	30828	23587	7240
东营市	Dongying	33277	31556	1703	29717	28421	1262	12679	8738	3936
烟台市	Yantai	39974	34084	5889	44567	40933	3597	40977	26903	14065
潍坊市	Weifang	53148	48341	4806	67159	63956	3199	40805	30530	10273
济宁市	Jining	34975	29261	5713	50805	47364	3436	51585	35996	15589
泰安市	Tai'an	18483	14040	4442	27302	24499	2801	26922	16992	9931
威海市	Weihai	14109	11429	2680	16458	14201	2257	15007	11223	3783
日照市	Rizhao	25724	23884	1839	48846	47463	1381	40819	34930	5890
临沂市	Linyi	58829	52329	6499	72656	68532	4116	87450	69300	18140
德州市	Dezhou	32000	29680	2315	33034	30979	2030	22293	17190	5094
聊城市	Liaocheng	61359	59384	1975	39488	38460	1026	20878	16702	4176
滨州市	Binzhou	142073	138829	3243	123325	121404	1919	42017	33833	8183
菏泽市	Heze	54144	49009	5135	37756	34666	3090	43943	30170	13773

注：2016年各市氮氧化物和颗粒物排放量不含机动车，全省氮氧化物和颗粒物排放量含机动车。（以下相关表同）

a) The volume of Nitrogen Oxides, Soot and Dust Discharged in each regions in 2016 does not include vehicle emission, while that of the whole prov -ince do.(The same applies to the following revelant tables.)

12−14 各市主要污染物排放情况(2017年)

Discharge of Major Pollutants by Region (2017)

地 区	Region	废 水 排放量 (万吨) Volume of Waste Water Discharged (10 000 tons)	工 业 Industry	生 活 Daily Life	化学需氧量排放量 (吨) Volume of COD Discharged (ton)	工 业 Industry	生 活 Daily Life	氨氮排放量 (吨) Volume of Ammonia Nitrogen Discharged (ton)	工 业 Industry	生 活 Daily Life
全省总计	**Total**	**357803**	**142495**	**215308**	**316890**	**56718**	**229937**	**25555**	**2771**	**22509**
济 南 市	Jinan	28398	5694	22704	20167	1709	18457	1464	113	1351
青 岛 市	Qingdao	35326	5742	29584	12782	1383	11372	1280	39	1239
淄 博 市	Zibo	21196	10380	10817	13720	4184	9488	342	131	206
枣 庄 市	Zaozhuang	13677	6198	7479	15853	1871	13982	1099	198	902
东 营 市	Dongying	15620	9310	6310	7538	3376	4161	420	224	196
烟 台 市	Yantai	23298	7466	15832	17578	2590	14943	1314	77	1235
潍 坊 市	Weifang	39070	20800	18270	22354	8006	14319	2181	442	1737
济 宁 市	Jining	31454	14656	16798	26702	3763	22935	1829	145	1683
泰 安 市	Tai'an	15368	4942	10426	16609	1927	14672	1523	75	1444
威 海 市	Weihai	8880	1446	7434	5400	2624	2763	248	61	187
日 照 市	Rizhao	12727	7086	5641	6221	2951	3222	730	61	665
临 沂 市	Linyi	30082	10971	19111	23195	6171	16998	2578	378	2193
德 州 市	Dezhou	21220	6931	14289	28337	2690	25634	3388	108	3279
聊 城 市	Liaocheng	16180	6630	9550	17778	2236	15511	1854	149	1701
滨 州 市	Binzhou	26363	17563	8799	21922	5966	15949	1718	288	1429
菏 泽 市	Heze	18943	6679	12264	30826	5270	25532	3346	281	3062

12−14 续表 continued

地 区	Region	二氧化硫排放量 (吨) Volume of Sulphur Dioxide Discharged (ton)	工 业 Industry	生 活 Daily Life	氮氧化物排放量 (吨) Volume of Nitrogen Oxides Discharged (ton)	工 业 Industry	生 活 Daily Life	颗粒物排放量 (吨) Volume of Soot and Dust Discharged (ton)	工 业 Industry	生 活 Daily Life
全省总计	**Total**	**416328**	**362859**	**53331**	**1195164**	**521467**	**34010**	**483351**	**348025**	**122877**
济 南 市	Jinan	25987	21811	4113	51809	49268	2453	37309	29636	7664
青 岛 市	Qingdao	16356	8978	7378	24283	20219	4065	29222	13858	15364
淄 博 市	Zibo	31680	29346	2333	53657	52160	1477	31659	26837	4820
枣 庄 市	Zaozhuang	12242	9814	2421	20715	19279	1418	19427	13687	5736
东 营 市	Dongying	19070	17136	1901	23139	21894	1160	10964	7503	3450
烟 台 市	Yantai	26024	21362	4659	27362	24513	2808	33362	23250	10107
潍 坊 市	Weifang	34058	29502	4544	54926	51806	3101	38101	26951	11148
济 宁 市	Jining	20624	17035	3588	28580	26381	2190	39318	31209	8109
泰 安 市	Tai'an	11859	8145	3714	21139	18712	2425	23142	14039	9102
威 海 市	Weihai	6685	4748	1937	7207	6014	1193	10323	6173	4149
日 照 市	Rizhao	16496	15029	1467	49549	48438	1110	34550	30477	4073
临 沂 市	Linyi	31954	26041	5911	51973	48037	3913	65872	50477	15393
德 州 市	Dezhou	16889	14092	2782	20840	18901	1875	15084	9782	5292
聊 城 市	Liaocheng	38815	36695	2120	28659	27437	1221	19138	14854	4284
滨 州 市	Binzhou	78831	76531	2299	69221	67537	1681	32647	26147	6500
菏 泽 市	Heze	28759	26596	2163	22789	20869	1919	30831	23144	7687

12-15 各市主要污染物排放情况(2018年)

Discharge of Major Pollutants by Region (2018)

地区	Region	废水排放量(万吨) Volume of Waste Water Discharged (10 000 tons)	工业 Industry	生活 Daily Life	化学需氧量排放量(吨) Volume of COD Discharged (ton)	工业 Industry	生活 Daily Life	氨氮排放量(吨) Volume of Ammonia Nitrogen Discharged (ton)	工业 Industry	生活 Daily Life
全省总计	**Total**	**371738**	**145052**	**226687**	**292047**	**54401**	**227962**	**24847**	**2634**	**22105**
济南市	Jinan	28714	4770	23944	19756	1433	18323	1497	111	1386
青岛市	Qingdao	38889	6373	32515	12912	1388	11512	1197	40	1156
淄博市	Zibo	22283	10139	12144	12542	3221	9290	303	90	212
枣庄市	Zaozhuang	14693	6738	7955	15504	1912	13591	1159	224	935
东营市	Dongying	16239	9335	6904	7219	3332	3887	433	231	201
烟台市	Yantai	21659	9313	12346	17175	2611	14510	1317	65	1251
潍坊市	Weifang	40745	21453	19292	21949	8036	13884	2164	421	1742
济宁市	Jining	31771	13857	17914	26562	3898	22662	1840	137	1703
泰安市	Tai'an	15900	5106	10794	17674	1919	15748	1495	77	1417
威海市	Weihai	12155	1473	10682	5069	2154	2902	285	45	240
日照市	Rizhao	12646	6962	5684	6319	2789	3515	727	64	662
临沂市	Linyi	30864	10689	20174	23256	6362	16878	2641	377	2263
德州市	Dezhou	21704	7216	14488	27488	2844	24626	3181	113	3067
聊城市	Liaocheng	14576	5994	8581	17213	2309	14879	1705	158	1546
滨州市	Binzhou	27870	19007	8863	21314	5645	15648	1566	227	1337
菏泽市	Heze	21032	6627	14405	30670	4549	26107	3241	255	2986

12-15 续表 continued

地区	Region	二氧化硫排放量(吨) Volume of Sulphur Dioxide Discharged (ton)	工业 Industry	生活 Daily Life	氮氧化物排放量(吨) Volume of Nitrogen Oxides Discharged (ton)	工业 Industry	生活 Daily Life	颗粒物排放量(吨) Volume of Soot and Dust Discharged (ton)	工业 Industry	生活 Daily Life
全省总计	**Total**	**341254**	**295709**	**45478**	**1145150**	**455216**	**31984**	**385657**	**267415**	**107522**
济南市	Jinan	20948	16672	4261	43841	41128	2674	31345	22497	8846
青岛市	Qingdao	12079	6346	5733	20015	16413	3602	23355	10821	12534
淄博市	Zibo	24622	22150	2461	44662	42870	1703	24865	19203	5649
枣庄市	Zaozhuang	9872	7807	2058	19999	18710	1266	14036	9099	4935
东营市	Dongying	15232	13680	1537	23525	22460	1037	8957	6105	2845
烟台市	Yantai	22416	18088	4326	25813	22981	2800	27175	17689	9482
潍坊市	Weifang	27000	23260	3737	50309	47513	2791	25290	19294	5994
济宁市	Jining	20385	17287	3097	29066	26934	2123	28303	20396	7906
泰安市	Tai'an	9090	5990	3100	17512	15321	2190	17086	8927	8159
威海市	Weihai	4505	2758	1747	7412	6201	1211	9663	5428	4235
日照市	Rizhao	13215	11922	1293	40882	39649	1232	26580	22088	4492
临沂市	Linyi	30370	25759	4609	54497	51052	3426	59161	46475	12685
德州市	Dezhou	17061	14625	2426	21180	19269	1862	15233	10717	4508
聊城市	Liaocheng	31548	30411	1137	22244	21496	748	12115	9758	2357
滨州市	Binzhou	64228	62291	1936	48122	46564	1554	24695	19222	5471
菏泽市	Heze	18683	16661	2020	18426	16657	1767	27118	19695	7423

12-16 各市主要污染物排放情况(2019年)
Discharge of Major Pollutants by Region (2019)

地区	Region	废水排放量(万吨) Volume of Waste Water Discharged (10 000 tons)	工业 Industry	生活 Daily Life	化学需氧量排放量(吨) Volume of COD Discharged (ton)	工业 Industry	生活 Daily Life	氨氮排放量(吨) Volume of Ammonia Nitrogen Discharged (ton)	工业 Industry	生活 Daily Life
全省总计	**Total**	**374309**	**144039**	**230271**	**275674**	**52729**	**221014**	**23356**	**2505**	**20805**
济南市	Jinan	29261	5120	24140	19131	1425	17705	1447	78	1369
青岛市	Qingdao	42090	6536	35554	12764	1434	11320	1106	38	1068
淄博市	Zibo	22825	9952	12873	11475	2819	8647	293	88	203
枣庄市	Zaozhuang	15791	7682	8109	14673	1835	12838	1122	186	936
东营市	Dongying	17433	9547	7886	6800	3234	3566	407	214	193
烟台市	Yantai	21422	9713	11708	16250	2418	13787	1280	57	1220
潍坊市	Weifang	40431	20842	19589	20344	6991	13344	2001	377	1624
济宁市	Jining	30563	12035	18529	26100	3986	22112	1814	150	1664
泰安市	Tai'an	15660	4856	10804	17922	1833	16088	1280	87	1193
威海市	Weihai	8855	1397	7458	4902	2307	2583	345	70	274
日照市	Rizhao	12815	6954	5861	6433	2755	3667	633	69	564
临沂市	Linyi	31400	10608	20792	23555	7139	16409	2644	413	2230
德州市	Dezhou	21193	7219	13975	25969	2520	23444	2953	111	2840
聊城市	Liaocheng	14915	6102	8813	14932	2513	12411	1564	162	1401
滨州市	Binzhou	28175	19174	9002	20809	5298	15503	1458	198	1259
菏泽市	Heze	21481	6302	15179	31818	4222	27589	2973	207	2766

12-16 续表 continued

地区	Region	二氧化硫排放量(吨) Volume of Sulphur Dioxide Discharged (ton)	工业 Industry	生活 Daily Life	氮氧化物排放量(吨) Volume of Nitrogen Oxides Discharged (ton)	工业 Industry	生活 Daily Life	颗粒物排放量(吨) Volume of Soot and Dust Discharged (ton)	工业 Industry	生活 Daily Life
全省总计	**Total**	**281511**	**241076**	**40384**	**1093288**	**415801**	**29976**	**371582**	**266986**	**97220**
济南市	Jinan	17124	13353	3765	41533	38022	3479	31258	22404	8853
青岛市	Qingdao	10246	5334	4911	17326	14024	3299	21288	10136	11149
淄博市	Zibo	20377	18194	2179	39195	37564	1602	22228	16993	5232
枣庄市	Zaozhuang	8701	6958	1738	19213	18129	1063	12179	7965	4212
东营市	Dongying	13949	12580	1356	24955	24010	919	9160	6640	2515
烟台市	Yantai	17697	13711	3980	24833	22142	2653	29481	20643	8835
潍坊市	Weifang	23581	20303	3276	46452	43880	2567	25154	19721	5433
济宁市	Jining	20625	17763	2861	27155	25128	2019	31581	24197	7383
泰安市	Tai'an	8616	5819	2797	15212	13224	1986	15434	7985	7449
威海市	Weihai	4409	2768	1641	6524	5401	1122	9116	5082	4034
日照市	Rizhao	9803	8588	1213	35632	34448	1182	25689	21417	4272
临沂市	Linyi	30591	26605	3985	54605	51504	3085	58013	46532	11480
德州市	Dezhou	15350	13114	2231	18391	16720	1629	14684	10658	4021
聊城市	Liaocheng	24821	23944	877	18448	17787	659	11625	9811	1814
滨州市	Binzhou	37306	35641	1664	38076	36724	1341	18034	13242	4791
菏泽市	Heze	18314	16401	1908	18471	17095	1372	29310	23560	5748

12-17 各市主要污染物排放情况(2020年)
Discharge of Major Pollutants by Region (2020)

地 区	Region	废水排放量(万吨) Volume of Waste Water Discharged (10 000 tons)	工 业 Industry	生 活 Daily Life	化学需氧量排放量(吨) Volume of COD Discharged (ton)	工 业 Industry	生 活 Daily Life	氨氮排放量(吨) Volume of Ammonia Nitrogen Discharged (ton)	工 业 Industry	生 活 Daily Life
全省总计	**Total**	**376378**	**133359**	**242533**	**1534845**	**46419**	**522414**	**53121**	**1883**	**37384**
济 南 市	Jinan	46493	5886	40577	49922	1744	48172	3016	54	2961
青 岛 市	Qingdao	30655	5695	24897	40793	2710	38073	2313	76	2236
淄 博 市	Zibo	20256	9946	10231	29673	2708	26957	1166	100	1064
枣 庄 市	Zaozhuang	10829	6190	4620	31327	1514	29811	1644	60	1584
东 营 市	Dongying	18721	8372	10341	14938	3337	11600	1170	197	973
烟 台 市	Yantai	28573	6315	22198	30982	1794	29161	2954	48	2905
潍 坊 市	Weifang	43290	18516	24734	43658	6605	37046	4293	373	3920
济 宁 市	Jining	21221	13638	7575	48811	2882	45926	4718	106	4612
泰 安 市	Tai'an	16640	5755	10883	30168	1678	28488	2507	108	2398
威 海 市	Weihai	5870	1596	4263	15333	2508	12794	783	70	713
日 照 市	Rizhao	12753	7799	4933	26942	3036	23899	1837	52	1785
临 沂 市	Linyi	29023	6078	22910	52566	2700	49850	3173	134	3035
德 州 市	Dezhou	19002	5980	12995	38893	1866	37019	3124	59	3064
聊 城 市	Liaocheng	19198	5609	13576	36041	2366	33647	1752	93	1657
滨 州 市	Binzhou	29825	20013	9768	31861	6249	25607	2244	200	2043
菏 泽 市	Heze	24028	5971	18033	47098	2723	44363	2586	153	2433

12-17 续表 continued

地 区	Region	二氧化硫排放量(吨) Volume of Sulphur Dioxide Discharged (ton)	工 业 Industry	生 活 Daily Life	氮氧化物排放量(吨) Volume of Nitrogen Oxides Discharged (ton)	工 业 Industry	生 活 Daily Life	颗粒物排放量(吨) Volume of Soot and Dust Discharged (ton)	工 业 Industry	生 活 Daily Life
全省总计	**Total**	**193272**	**152865**	**40315**	**624689**	**287363**	**18236**	**244161**	**131517**	**108087**
济 南 市	Jinan	15920	11356	4519	52729	25382	2384	25871	13414	12147
青 岛 市	Qingdao	4831	3317	1514	48233	9453	1040	10471	5858	4091
淄 博 市	Zibo	15714	9374	6338	34065	19036	2399	22923	5785	16950
枣 庄 市	Zaozhuang	4585	3078	1500	21276	9073	510	10294	6152	4006
东 营 市	Dongying	10503	10180	308	29389	19187	114	4422	3470	822
烟 台 市	Yantai	20596	17295	3300	38939	15921	1184	24556	15386	8820
潍 坊 市	Weifang	14554	10949	3604	59292	25865	1517	20412	10280	9652
济 宁 市	Jining	11720	6467	5250	51982	13724	1589	19950	5485	14004
泰 安 市	Tai'an	9971	8518	1451	27759	13839	828	10903	6821	3907
威 海 市	Weihai	5570	3845	1725	16974	5602	641	6058	1262	4612
日 照 市	Rizhao	11750	9684	2063	41809	29563	957	18949	13259	5532
临 沂 市	Linyi	16829	14490	2338	75336	32604	1511	21250	14298	6309
德 州 市	Dezhou	11228	8976	2250	24282	12466	1175	16797	10580	6047
聊 城 市	Liaocheng	8595	7357	1238	31235	15230	989	9101	5567	3357
滨 州 市	Binzhou	19590	18081	1500	40853	27166	791	12073	7847	4032
菏 泽 市	Heze	11319	9897	1418	30537	13251	607	10132	6053	3798

注：2020年各市氮氧化物和颗粒物排放量含机动车。

a)The volume of Nitrogen Oxides, Soot and Dust Discharged in each regions in 2020 include vehicle emission.

12-18 各市主要污染物排放情况(2021年)

Discharge of Major Pollutants by Region (2021)

地区	Region	废水排放量(万吨) Volume of Waste Water Discharged (10 000 tons)	工业 Industry	生活 Daily Life	化学需氧量排放量(吨) Volume of COD Discharged (ton)	工业 Industry	生活 Daily Life	氨氮排放量(吨) Volume of Ammonia Nitrogen Discharged (ton)	工业 Industry	生活 Daily Life
全省总计	**Total**	**371082**	**133854**	**236825**	**1562795**	**41921**	**477179**	**46436**	**1372**	**28502**
济南市	Jinan	49649	6084	43528	44799	1557	43238	2568	52	2515
青岛市	Qingdao	30841	6514	24274	41152	2015	39122	2024	48	1976
淄博市	Zibo	22009	11742	10261	20214	2701	17512	955	73	882
枣庄市	Zaozhuang	11187	6533	4634	24085	1766	22315	843	52	791
东营市	Dongying	19769	7973	11795	15035	3035	12000	925	167	758
烟台市	Yantai	31552	7200	24295	28046	1710	26316	2500	47	2453
潍坊市	Weifang	34251	15053	19162	40004	4690	35307	1442	115	1326
济宁市	Jining	20128	13002	7115	47648	3277	44365	3972	89	3882
泰安市	Tai'an	14019	6473	7538	30710	1903	28805	1401	100	1300
威海市	Weihai	5739	1506	4205	13017	583	12395	664	21	642
日照市	Rizhao	12602	7999	4582	20602	2980	17613	1698	69	1629
临沂市	Linyi	36044	6522	29493	46942	2906	44023	2936	138	2796
德州市	Dezhou	17598	6569	11007	36411	2321	34086	2498	73	2425
聊城市	Liaocheng	17874	5234	12617	34125	1692	32432	1708	62	1646
滨州市	Binzhou	23934	19678	4209	32535	6454	26077	1964	147	1816
菏泽市	Heze	23887	5770	18111	43908	2330	41573	1782	118	1664

12-18 续表 continued

地区	Region	二氧化硫排放量(吨) Volume of Sulphur Dioxide Discharged (ton)	工业 Industry	生活 Daily Life	氮氧化物排放量(吨) Volume of Nitrogen Oxides Discharged (ton)	工业 Industry	生活 Daily Life	颗粒物排放量(吨) Volume of Soot and Dust Discharged (ton)	工业 Industry	生活 Daily Life
全省总计	**Total**	**165340**	**125102**	**40168**	**658734**	**244099**	**19073**	**215851**	**102853**	**107774**
济南市	Jinan	13601	9458	4141	51934	22763	2390	22555	11047	11148
青岛市	Qingdao	5777	2897	2880	70774	8387	1754	11156	2724	7763
淄博市	Zibo	10669	4850	5813	31350	15963	2255	20030	4278	15550
枣庄市	Zaozhuang	4197	2692	1500	20248	8095	510	9317	5176	4006
东营市	Dongying	7845	7532	300	28799	16870	112	3203	2256	803
烟台市	Yantai	18485	15478	3000	43954	14926	1108	18030	9626	8021
潍坊市	Weifang	9933	6327	3604	53891	17944	1654	17047	6876	9665
济宁市	Jining	10930	6052	4875	53014	13151	1479	17640	4158	13005
泰安市	Tai'an	10748	8558	2186	43888	11500	1145	12689	6356	5876
威海市	Weihai	4914	3184	1730	17579	5187	643	5918	1102	4624
日照市	Rizhao	9046	7169	1875	39103	20095	900	17167	11946	5032
临沂市	Linyi	14077	12301	1775	70570	27924	1415	17930	12471	4815
德州市	Dezhou	7127	4871	2250	22783	9954	1153	16013	9791	6045
聊城市	Liaocheng	7930	6505	1425	30391	14945	1185	7984	3954	3870
滨州市	Binzhou	19603	18090	1500	50808	23733	791	10826	6509	4032
菏泽市	Heze	10458	9139	1313	29649	12662	578	8346	4584	3518

注：2021年数据为初步统计数据；各市氮氧化物和颗粒物排放量数据含机动车排放源。

a) The data of 2021 come from the number of preliminary statistics, vehicle emission source is included in the Volume of Nitrogen Oxides , Soot and Dust Discharged in each regions.

12—19　各市工业固体废物产生及利用处置情况(2016年)

Generation、Treatment and Utilization of Industrial Solid Wastes by Region(2016)

单位：万吨　　(10 000 tons)

地 区	Region	一般工业固体废物产生量 Total Volume of Industrial Solid Waste Produced	一般工业固体废物综合利用量 Total Volume of Industrial Solid Waste Utilized	一般工业固体废物处置量 Volume of Industrial Solid Waste Treated	危险废物产生量 Hazardous Waste Produced	危险废物利用处置量 Hazardous Waste Utilized and Treated
全省总计	**Total**	**26349.7**	**22314.3**	**1322.3**	**516.7**	**465.7**
济南市	Jinan	2939.2	2625.2	69.1	53.7	53.5
青岛市	Qingdao	764.5	730.8	26.6	6.9	5.9
淄博市	Zibo	1625.5	1319.8	197.4	98.3	96.8
枣庄市	Zaozhuang	1077.3	1073.8	3.0	5.8	5.8
东营市	Dongying	390.7	329.1	21.0	16.4	14.6
烟台市	Yantai	2977.2	2347.4	395.1	185.8	173.2
潍坊市	Weifang	1632.1	1426.6	34.9	29.0	26.9
济宁市	Jining	1857.6	1787.0	86.7	3.6	3.1
泰安市	Tai'an	1347.5	1074.0	15.8	2.0	1.9
威海市	Weihai	341.0	334.1	4.5	1.2	1.0
日照市	Rizhao	1353.2	1295.5	49.8	7.0	6.9
临沂市	Linyi	1840.3	1773.6	10.8	32.3	18.4
德州市	Dezhou	1149.1	1017.1	95.2	11.2	10.5
聊城市	Liaocheng	1691.5	1447.8	212.6	2.3	2.3
滨州市	Binzhou	4812.4	3213.6	91.0	43.4	27.6
菏泽市	Heze	550.6	518.8	8.8	18.1	17.3

注：按照国家统一部署，以第二次全国污染源普查成果为基准，对2016—2019年污染源统计初步数据进行更新，更新指标不含“一般工业固体废物贮存量”。(以下相关表同)

a)According to the unified national deployment,the preliminary statistics of pollution sources in 2016 to 2019 are revised based on the results of the second national survey on pollution sources,data on stock of Common Industrial Solid Waste have not been revised.(The same applies to the relevant following tables)

12—20　各市工业固体废物产生及利用处置情况(2017年)

Generation、Treatment and Utilization of Industrial Solid Wastes by Region(2017)

单位：万吨　　(10 000 tons)

地 区	Region	一般工业固体废物产生量 Total Volume of Industrial Solid Waste Produced	一般工业固体废物综合利用量 Total Volume of Industrial Solid Waste Utilized	一般工业固体废物处置量 Volume of Industrial Solid Waste Treated	危险废物产生量 Hazardous Waste Produced	危险废物利用处置量 Hazardous Waste Utilized and Treated
全省总计	**Total**	**28484.0**	**23151.7**	**1650.3**	**854.0**	**726.0**
济南市	Jinan	2804.7	2405.0	399.1	73.1	73.1
青岛市	Qingdao	720.5	687.5	27.8	16.5	17.2
淄博市	Zibo	1905.2	1412.1	63.2	98.0	94.0
枣庄市	Zaozhuang	1188.1	1163.6	22.6	30.0	29.0
东营市	Dongying	481.5	393.2	26.6	43.0	45.4
烟台市	Yantai	2785.5	1883.1	651.2	251.4	135.2
潍坊市	Weifang	1803.8	1440.8	253.9	34.4	32.4
济宁市	Jining	2039.8	2008.8	21.2	13.6	14.5
泰安市	Tai'an	1393.2	961.4	4.2	7.6	7.4
威海市	Weihai	387.0	360.1	11.8	3.5	2.6
日照市	Rizhao	1572.0	1520.8	66.2	15.4	15.4
临沂市	Linyi	2186.8	2115.0	50.5	108.7	106.2
德州市	Dezhou	903.4	888.5	15.2	14.5	14.8
聊城市	Liaocheng	2080.4	1743.7	5.4	21.4	20.3
滨州市	Binzhou	5733.1	3679.1	21.4	79.9	74.6
菏泽市	Heze	499.0	489.1	10.0	43.0	43.6

12-21 各市工业固体废物产生及利用处置情况(2018年)

Generation、Treatment and Utilization of Industrial Solid Wastes by Region(2018)

单位：万吨 (10 000 tons)

地 区	Region	一般工业固体废物产生量 Total Volume of Industrial Solid Waste Produced	一般工业固体废物综合利用量 Total Volume of Industrial Solid Waste Utilized	一般工业固体废物处置量 Volume of Industrial Solid Waste Treated	危险废物产生量 Hazardous Waste Produced	危险废物利用处置量 Hazardous Waste Utilized and Treated
全省总计	**Total**	**29995.4**	**23830.8**	**1723.3**	**832.7**	**774.8**
济南市	Jinan	2607.5	2236.6	29.7	75.8	75.7
青岛市	Qingdao	783.8	738.2	30.5	14.7	13.5
淄博市	Zibo	2036.9	1455.7	142.9	94.3	91.0
枣庄市	Zaozhuang	1224.9	1095.8	127.9	21.4	21.5
东营市	Dongying	556.8	456.7	74.9	37.4	38.1
烟台市	Yantai	3241.1	2185.9	459.7	260.1	209.6
潍坊市	Weifang	1807.1	1535.1	33.6	31.2	30.5
济宁市	Jining	2094.5	2044.0	51.6	14.7	17.5
泰安市	Tai'an	1376.4	959.2	18.7	13.2	13.2
威海市	Weihai	368.9	354.1	4.7	2.0	2.0
日照市	Rizhao	2250.8	2149.8	71.8	33.2	32.9
临沂市	Linyi	2445.1	2296.3	89.7	59.0	59.1
德州市	Dezhou	1029.1	921.1	77.7	15.7	15.8
聊城市	Liaocheng	2232.8	1665.5	333.9	14.1	13.8
滨州市	Binzhou	5370.1	3208.8	159.7	91.8	86.4
菏泽市	Heze	569.7	528.1	16.2	54.2	54.1

12-22 各市工业固体废物产生及利用处置情况(2019年)

Generation、Treatment and Utilization of Industrial Solid Wastes by Region(2019)

单位：万吨 (10 000 tons)

地 区	Region	一般工业固体废物产生量 Total Volume of Industrial Solid Waste Produced	一般工业固体废物综合利用量 Total Volume of Industrial Solid Waste Utilized	一般工业固体废物处置量 Volume of Industrial Solid Waste Treated	危险废物产生量 Hazardous Waste Produced	危险废物利用处置量 Hazardous Waste Utilized and Treated
全省总计	**Total**	**32128.7**	**25230.4**	**2299.0**	**985.6**	**1046.1**
济南市	Jinan	2693.0	2168.0	385.6	71.1	71.1
青岛市	Qingdao	824.1	714.1	84.8	17.6	18.3
淄博市	Zibo	2102.2	1463.4	230.6	97.6	97.7
枣庄市	Zaozhuang	1331.4	1233.7	11.3	15.8	15.7
东营市	Dongying	642.0	510.7	68.9	39.6	40.3
烟台市	Yantai	3606.9	2331.1	756.7	254.2	313.1
潍坊市	Weifang	1940.0	1622.1	105.6	32.7	35.8
济宁市	Jining	2250.7	2154.0	102.3	20.5	20.6
泰安市	Tai'an	1592.2	1060.8	7.0	22.0	21.4
威海市	Weihai	405.4	407.3	9.4	2.3	2.1
日照市	Rizhao	2906.3	2636.7	92.3	92.2	91.8
临沂市	Linyi	2445.5	2164.3	148.8	63.8	64.6
德州市	Dezhou	1091.0	948.4	91.2	19.8	20.4
聊城市	Liaocheng	2337.4	2105.4	6.8	19.2	19.7
滨州市	Binzhou	5332.7	3137.8	186.1	146.6	141.5
菏泽市	Heze	627.8	572.6	11.7	70.7	71.8

12-23 各市工业固体废物产生及利用处置情况(2020年)

Generation、Treatment and Utilization of Industrial Solid Wastes by Region(2020)

单位：万吨 (10 000 tons)

地区	Region	一般工业固体废物产生量 Total Volume of Industrial Solid Waste Produced	一般工业固体废物综合利用量 Total Volume of Industrial Solid Waste Utilized	一般工业固体废物处置量 Volume of Industrial Solid Waste Treated	一般工业固体废物贮存量 Volume of Industrial Wastes in Solid Stocks	危险废物产生量 Hazardous Wastes Produced	危险废物利用处置量 Hazardous Waste Utilized and Treated
全省总计	**Total**	**24989.4**	**19611.7**	**1586.6**	**3990.8**	**933.3**	**1052.1**
济南市	Jinan	2263.4	2169.4	117.0	6.8	59.8	67.2
青岛市	Qingdao	716.9	625.7	78.4	16.0	17.7	17.9
淄博市	Zibo	1737.0	1021.6	360.4	366.9	79.9	84.7
枣庄市	Zaozhuang	612.6	508.1	105.7	1.2	15.5	15.4
东营市	Dongying	551.2	464.1	102.8	2.6	39.0	39.8
烟台市	Yantai	2830.7	1961.0	151.1	733.7	249.0	320.8
潍坊市	Weifang	1540.9	1444.9	35.0	69.7	52.1	57.1
济宁市	Jining	1599.4	1505.8	103.5	0.3	27.1	27.5
泰安市	Tai'an	936.8	677.7	155.0	112.3	18.4	18.4
威海市	Weihai	312.5	275.5	54.8	2.5	3.6	3.9
日照市	Rizhao	1867.1	1757.6	49.0	89.0	84.7	84.3
临沂市	Linyi	1855.2	1739.7	117.1	5.2	46.4	55.5
德州市	Dezhou	849.6	770.9	79.2	2.2	17.9	20.0
聊城市	Liaocheng	2221.9	1667.1	35.1	521.8	30.8	30.8
滨州市	Binzhou	4625.6	2568.1	27.8	2060.4	135.8	153.3
菏泽市	Heze	468.8	454.5	14.6	0.3	55.7	55.3

注：2020年危险废物综合利用量、处置量指标改为危险废物利用处置量。

a)In 2020, the comprehensive utilization and disposal volume of hazardous waste are adjustmented to the Hazardous Waste Utilized and Treated.

12-24 各市工业固体废物产生及利用处置情况(2021年)

Generation、Treatment and Utilization of Industrial Solid Wastes by Region(2021)

单位：万吨 (10 000 tons)

地区	Region	一般工业固体废物产生量 Total Volume of Industrial Solid Waste Produced	一般工业固体废物综合利用量 Total Volume of Industrial Solid Waste Utilized	一般工业固体废物处置量 Volume of Industrial Solid Waste Treated	一般工业固体废物贮存量 Volume of Industrial Waste in Solid Stocks	危险废物产生量 Hazardous Waste Produced	危险废物利用处置量 Hazardous Waste Utilized and Treated
全省总计	**Total**	**25233.4**	**20027.5**	**1625.3**	**3993.6**	**967.1**	**1008.2**
济南市	Jinan	2411.5	2320.6	126.6	8.1	93.7	94.0
青岛市	Qingdao	828.5	737.8	81.3	10.5	23.8	23.7
淄博市	Zibo	1702.5	949.7	421.0	345.5	100.9	100.9
枣庄市	Zaozhuang	693.5	680.5	14.9	1.7	22.3	22.3
东营市	Dongying	712.2	831.7	93.6	19.9	53.0	54.1
烟台市	Yantai	2166.2	1603.0	118.3	456.4	145.8	185.5
潍坊市	Weifang	1670.6	1315.9	97.6	274.1	64.0	65.9
济宁市	Jining	1514.4	1420.4	97.6	0.4	27.2	27.3
泰安市	Tai'an	1117.4	826.4	110.9	190.1	23.0	22.3
威海市	Weihai	308.9	304.0	23.0	5.6	6.7	6.8
日照市	Rizhao	1573.0	1447.9	75.2	70.9	65.3	65.7
临沂市	Linyi	1937.0	1773.5	148.4	23.3	56.1	55.1
德州市	Dezhou	984.7	876.7	118.2	2.4	28.5	27.5
聊城市	Liaocheng	2317.5	1752.1	57.4	513.1	39.5	39.9
滨州市	Binzhou	4793.8	2697.0	30.1	2071.5	159.6	159.2
菏泽市	Heze	501.7	490.4	11.1	0.3	57.7	58.0

注：2021年数据为初步统计数据。

a) Data of 2021 are preliminary statistical results.

主要统计指标解释

自然资源 指人类可以直接从自然界获得，并用于生产和生活的物质资源。自然资源一般可以分成可再生资源和非再生资源两大类。可再生资源指在较短时间内可以再生、可以循环利用的资源，包括土地资源、水资源、气候资源、生物资源和海洋资源等。非再生资源指在使用后不能再生的资源，包括矿产资源和地热能源。

土地资源 土地指陆地的表层部分，它主要由岩石、岩石的风化物和土壤构成。土地资源按利用类型可以分为农用地、建筑用地和未利用地。农用地包括耕地、园地、林地、牧草地和水面。建筑用地包括居民点及工矿用地、交通用地和水利设施用地。未利用地指农用地和建筑用地以外的土地，包括滩涂、荒漠、戈壁、冰川和石山等。

耕地面积 指经过开垦用以种植农作物并经常进行耕耘的土地面积。包括种有作物的土地面积、休闲地、新开荒地和抛荒未满三年的土地面积。

森林资源 指森林、林木、林地以及依托森林、林木、林地生存的野生动物、植物和微生物。林木指树木和竹子。森林指以乔木为主体的植物群落，是集生的乔木及与共同作用的植物、动物、微生物和土壤、气候等的总体。

森林面积 指由乔木树种构成，郁闭度0.2以上(含0.2)的林地或冠幅宽度10米以上的林带的面积，即有林地面积。森林面积包括天然起源和人工起源的针叶林面积、阔叶林面积、针阔混交林面积和竹林面积，不包括灌木林地面积和疏林地面积。

水资源 水在自然界中以固体、液体和气态三种聚集状态存在，分布于海洋、陆地(包括土壤)以及大气之中，通过水循环形成水资源。水资源包括经人类控制并直接可供灌溉、发电、给水、航运、养殖等用途的地表水和地下水，以及江河、湖泊、井、泉、潮汐、港湾和养殖水域等。水资源是发展国民经济不可缺少的重要自然资源。

地表水和地下水 陆地上的水因空间分布不同，分为地表水和地下水。地表水指分别存在于河流、湖泊、沼泽、冰川和冰盖等水体中水分的总称，又称陆地水。地下水指储存在地面以下饱和岩土孔隙、裂隙及溶洞中的水。

水资源总量 指评价区内降水形成的地表和地下产水总量，即地表产流量与降水入渗补给地下水量之和，不包括过境水量。

地表水资源量 指评价区内河流、湖泊、冰川等地表水体中可以逐年更新的动态水量，即当地天然河川径流量。

地下水资源量 指评价区内降水和地表水对饱水岩土层的补给量，包括降水入渗补给量和河道、湖库、渠系、渠灌田间等地表水体的入渗补给量。

内陆水域总面积 指江、河、湖泊、池塘、塘堰、水库等各种流水或蓄水的水面占地面积。

海　洋 是海和洋的统称。洋为地球表面上相连接的广大咸水水体的主体部分。海为地球表面相连接的广大咸水水体被陆地、岛礁、半岛包围或分隔的边缘部分。

海水可养殖面积 指利用滩涂、浅海、港湾进行鱼、虾、蟹、贝、藻等海水经济动植物的人工养殖的水面面积。

径　流 指陆地上接受降水后扣除损耗外，从地表和地下向流域出口断面汇集的水流。径流可分为地表径流、地下径流和壤中流。地表径流指沿地表向河流、湖泊、沼泽、海洋等汇集的水流；地下径流指沿潜水层或隔水层间的含水层，向河流、湖泊、沼泽、海洋等汇集的地下水水流。

径流量 指在一定时段内通过河流某一过水断面的水量，用以反映一个国家或地区水资源的丰歉程度。计算公式为：

径流量=降水量−蒸发量

矿产资源 矿产指由地质作用形成，富集于地壳中或出露于地表达到工农业利用要求的有用矿物。矿产是一种重要的自然资源，是社会发展的重要物质基础。

矿产基础储量 基础储量是查明矿产资源的一部分。它能满足现行采矿和生产所需的指标要求，是控制的、探明的并通过可行性或预可行性研究认为属于经济的、边界经济的部分，用未扣除设计、采矿损失的数量表示。

气　温 指空气的温度，我国一般以摄氏度(℃)为单位表示。气象观测的温度表是放在离地面约1.5米处通风良好的百叶箱里测量的，因此，通常说的气温指的是离地面1.5米处百叶箱中的温度。其统计计算方法为：

月平均气温是将全月各日的平均气温相加，除以该月的天数而得。

年平均气温是将12个月的月平均气温累加后除以12而得。

相对湿度 指空气中实际所含水蒸气密度和同温度下饱和水蒸气密度的百分比值。其统计方法与气温相同。

降水量 指从天空降落到地面的液态或固态(经融化后)水，未经蒸发、渗透、流失而在地面上积聚的深度。其统计计算方法为：

月降水量是将全月各日的降水量累加而得。

年降水量是将12个月的月降水量累加而得。

日照时数 指太阳实际照射地面的时间。其统计方法与降水量相同。

工业废水排放量 指报告期内经过企业厂区所有排放口排到企业外部的工业废水量。包括生产废水、外排的直接冷却水、废气治理设施废水、超标排放的矿井地下水和与工业废水混排的厂区生活污水，不包括独立外排的间接冷却水（清浊不分流的间接冷却水应计算在内）。

城镇生活污水排放量 指城镇居民每年排放的生活污水。用人均系数法测算。测算公式为：

$$\frac{\text{生活污水}}{\text{排放量}}=\frac{\text{城镇生活污水}}{\text{排放系数}}\times\frac{\text{市镇非}}{\text{农业人口}}\times 365$$

城镇生活污水中化学需氧量(COD)产生量 指城镇居民每年排放的生活污水中的 COD 的产生量。用人均系数法测算。测算公式为：

$$\frac{\text{城镇生活污水}}{\text{中}COD\text{排放量}}=\frac{\text{城镇生活污水中}}{COD\text{产生系数}}\times\frac{\text{市镇非}}{\text{农业人口}}\times 365$$

化学需氧量（COD） 测量有机和无机物质化学分解所消耗氧的质量浓度的水污染指数。

工业废气排放量 指报告期内企业厂区内燃料燃烧和生产工艺过程中产生的各种排入大气的含有污染物的气体的总量，以标准状态(273K，101325Pa)计算。测算公式为：

$$\frac{\text{工业废气}}{\text{排放量}}=\frac{\text{燃料燃烧过程}}{\text{中废气排放量}}+\frac{\text{生产工艺过程}}{\text{中废气排放量}}$$

二氧化硫排放量 指报告期内企业在燃料燃烧和生产工艺过程中排入大气的二氧化硫总质量。工业中二氧化硫主要来源于化石燃料（煤、石油等）的燃烧，还包括含硫矿石的冶炼或含硫酸、磷肥等生产的工业废气排放。

氮氧化物排放量 指报告期内企业在燃料燃烧和生产工艺过程中排入大气的氮氧化物总质量。

烟（粉）尘排放量 指报告期内企业在燃料燃烧和生产工艺过程中排入大气的烟尘及工业粉尘的总质量之和。烟尘或工业粉尘排放量可以通过除尘系统的排风量和除尘设备出口烟尘浓度相乘求得。

一般工业固体废物产生量 指未被列入《国家危险废物名录》或者根据国家规定的危险废物鉴别标准（GB5085）、固体废物浸出毒性浸出方法（GB5086）及固体废物浸出毒性测定方法（GB／T 15555）鉴别方法判定不具有危险特性的工业固体废物。

一般工业固体废物综合利用量 指报告期内企业通过回收、加工、循环、交换等方式，从固体废物中提取或者使其转化为可以利用的资源、能源和其他原材料的固体废物量（包括当年利用的往年工业固体废物累计贮存量）。如用作农业肥料、生产建筑材料、筑路等。综合利用量由原产生固体废物的单位统计。

一般工业固体废物处置量 指报告期内企业将工业固体废物焚烧和用其他改变工业固体废物的物理、化学、生物特性的方法，达到减少或者消除其危险成分的活动，或者将工业固体废物最终置于符合环境保护规定要求的填埋场的活动中，所消纳固体废物的量。

一般工业固体废物贮存量 指报告期内企业以综合利用或处置为目的，将固体废物暂时贮存或堆存在专设的贮存设施或专设的集中堆存场所内的量。

危险废物 指列入国家危险废物名录或根据国家规定的危险废物鉴别标准和鉴别方法认定的，具有爆炸性、易燃性、易氧化性、毒性、腐蚀性、易传染疾病等危险特性之一的废物。

危险废物产生量 指报告期内调查对象实际产生的危险废物的量。危险废物指列入国家危险废物名录或者根据国家规定的危险废物鉴别标准和鉴别方法认定的，具有爆炸性、易燃性、易氧化性、毒性、腐蚀性、易传染性疾病等危险特性之一的废物。

危险废物利用处置量 指调查年度调查对象从危险废物中提取物质作为原材料或者燃料的活动中消纳危险废物的量，以及将危险废物焚烧和用其他改变危险废物物理、化学、生物特性的方法，达到减少或者消除其危险成分的活动，或者将危险废物最终置于符合环境保护规定要求的填埋场的活动中，所消纳危险废物的量。包括本单位自行处置利用的本单位产生和接收外单位危险废物量

Explanatory Notes on Main Statistical Indicators

Natural Resources refers to material resources that could be obtained from the nature by human being and used for production and living. Natural resources in general can be classified as renewable resources and non-renewable resources. Renewable resources refer to resources that could be renewed and recycled during a relatively short period of time, including land resource, water resource, climate resource, biology resource and marine resource. Non-renewable resources include resources that could not be renewed, such as minerals and geothermal resource.

Land Resources refers to the surface of the earth, consisting of mainly rocks and its weathering and earth. Land resource can be classified, by its utilization, as land for agriculture, land for construction and unused land. Land for agriculture includes cultivated land, plantation land, forestland, grassland and waters. Land for construction includes land for residential purpose, for manufacturing and mining, for transportation and for water-conservancy projects. Unused land refers to land other than land for agriculture and construction, including beaches, deserts, Gobi, glaciers and rock mountains.

Area of Cultivated Land refers to area of land reclaimed for the regular cultivation of various farm crops, including crop-cover land, fallow, newly reclaimed land and land laid idle for less than 3 years.

Forest Resource refers to forests, trees, forestland and wild animals, plants and microorganism that live on forest and trees. Trees include trees and bamboo. Forest refers to the population of clusters of trees and other plants, animals and microorganism as well as the earth and climate that have interactions with the trees.

Forest Area refers to the area of forest where trees and bamboo grow with canopy density above 0.2, including land of natural woods and planted woods, but excluding bush land and thin forest land. It reflects the total areas of afforestation.

Water Resource refers to water that exists in the nature in solid, liquid and gaseous states, is distributed in the ocean, land (including earth) and air, and constitutes the water resource through the circulation of water. Water resource includes the surface water and underground water that is controlled by the human being for irrigation, power-generation, water supply, navigation and cultivation. It also includes rivers, lakes, wells, springs, tides, gulf and water area for cultivation. Water resource as an important natural resource is indispensable for the development of the national economy.

Surface Water and Underground Water Water on earth can be divided into surface water and underground water according to its distribution. Surface water refers to moisture exists in rivers, lakes, swamps, glaciers, icecaps and so on. It is also called land water. The underground water refers to water deposited underground in the cranny and the hole of saturated rock soil and in the water-eroded cave.

Total Water Resources refers to total volume of water resources measured as run-off for surface water from rainfall and recharge for groundwater in a given area, excluding transit water.

Surface Water Resources refers to total renewable resources which exist in rivers, lakes, glaciers and other collectors from rainfall and are measured as run-off of rivers.

Groundwater Resources refers to replenishment of aquifers with rainfall and surface water.

Inland Water Area refers to water area of rivers, lakes, ponds, reservoir, etc.

Ocean is the general name for sea and ocean. Ocean refers to the main body of large salt water connected with the earth. Sea refers to the edge areas of the salt water on the earth that are comparted or surrounded by land, island, reef or peninsula.

Marine Cultivatable Areas refer to water areas in beach, shallow sea and lough that are used to breed marine cash propagation, such as fish, shrimp, crab, shellfish, alga and so on.

Runoff refers to the water gathered at the way out of the cross section of drainage area either from the surface or underground after deducting the wastage of the precipitation on the land. Runoff can be divided into surface runoff, underground runoff and within soil runoff. Surface runoff refers to water flow to the rivers, lakes, swamps, and seas on the surface of the earth. Underground runoff refers to water flow to rivers, lakes, swamps, and seas through the water-bearing stratum of confined layer or unconfined layer.

Volume of Runoff refers to the total volume of water running through a certain cross section of a river during a certain period of time, reflecting the water resource condition in a country or a region. The formula for calculating volume or runoff is as follows:

Runoff =Precipitation-Evaporation

Mineral Resources refer to useful minerals that can be used for industrial or agricultural purposes enriched in lithosphere or on earth due to the geological process. Minerals are important natural resources, and important material base for social development.

Ensured Mineral Reserves refer to the actual mineral reserves, which equal to the proven mineral reserves (including industrial reserves and prospective reserves) minus extracted parts and underground losses.

Temperature refers to the air temperature. China uses centigrade as the unit. The thermometry used for weather observation is put in a breezy shutter, which is 1.5 meters high from the ground. Therefore, the commonly used temperature refers to the temperature in the breezy shutter 1.5 meters away from the ground. The calculation method is as follows:

Monthly Average Temperature is the summation of average daily temperature of one month divided by the actual days of that particular month.

Annual Average Temperature is the summation of monthly average of a year divided by 12 months.

Relative Humidity refers to the ratio of actual water vapor pressure to the saturation water vapor density under the current temperature. The statistical method is the same as that of temperature.

Volume of Precipitation refers to the deepness of liquid state or solid state (thawed) water falling from the sky to the ground that has not been evaporated, infiltrated or run off. The calculation method is as follows:

Monthly precipitation is the summation of daily precipitation of a month.

Annual precipitation is the summation of 12 months precipitation of a year.

Sunshine Hours refer to the actual hours of sun irradiating the earth. The calculation method is the same as that of the precipitation.

Industrial Waste Water Discharged Refers to the volume of industrial waste water discharged through all of the drainage system to the outside of factory complex by enterprises during the report period. It includes discharged waste water from production, direct cooling water, waste gas treatment facilities, mine groundwater beyond the standard and domestic sewage mixed with industrial waste water, does not include independently discharged indirect cooling water (voicing split-less indirect cooling water should be taken into account).

Urban Non industrial Waste Water Discharge refers to annual discharge of non-industrial waste water by urban households. It is estimated by per ca pita coefficient using the formula:

$$\frac{\text{Urban non-industrial}}{\text{waste water discharge}} = \frac{\text{urban non-industrial waste}}{\text{water discharge coefficient}} \times \frac{\text{urban non-agricultural}}{\text{population}} \times 365$$

Volume of Chemical Oxygen Demand (COD) Generated by Urban Non-industrial Waster Water refers to chemical oxygen demand generated through the annual discharge of non-industrial waste water by urban households. It is estimated as:

$$\begin{array}{c}\text{Volume of chemical oxygen}\\ \text{demand (cod) generated}\\ \text{by urban non-industrial}\\ \text{waster water}\end{array} = \begin{array}{c}\text{Coefficient of COD}\\ \text{generated through urban}\\ \text{non-industrial waste water}\end{array} \times \begin{array}{c}\text{urban}\\ \text{non-agricultural}\\ \text{population}\end{array} \times 365$$

Chemical Oxygen Demand (COD) refers to index of water pollution measuring the mass concentration of oxygen consumed by the chemical breakdown of organic and inorganic matter.

Industrial Waste Air Emission refers to discharge into atmosphere of waste air containing pollutants generated from fuel burning and production process in enterprises within a given period of time. It is calculated at standard status (273K, 101325Pa) as:

$$\frac{\text{Industrial waste}}{\text{air emission}} = \frac{\text{emission through}}{\text{fuel burning}} + \frac{\text{emission through}}{\text{production process}}$$

SO_2 Emission refers to the total volume of SO_2 discharged into air during the process of fuel combustion and industrial production in enterprises in a given time, and is mainly caused by the combustion of fossil fuel, ore smelting and the production of sulphuric acid and phosphate fertilizers.

Nitrogen Oxides Emission refers to the total volume of nitrogen oxides discharged into air during the process of fuel combustion and industrial production.

Industrial Soot and Dust Emission refers to volume of soot and dust in smoke emitted in process of fuel burning and industrial production in premises of enterprises in the report period. It is calculated by multiplying exhaust volume of dust removal system by dust concentration.

Common Industrial Solid Wastes Produced refers to the industrial solid wastes not listed in the 《National Catalogue of Hazardous Wastes》, or not regarded as hazardous according to the national hazardous waste identification standards (GB5085),solid waste-extraction procedure for leaching toxicity (GB5086), or solid waste-extraction procedure for leaching toxicity (GB/T 15555).

Common Industrial Solid Wastes Comprehensively Utilized refers to volume of solid wastes from which useful materials can be extracted or which can be converted into usable resources, energy or other materials by means of reclamation, processing, recycling and exchange (including utilizing in the year the stocks of industrial solid wastes of the previous year) during the report period, e.g. Examples of such utilization include fertilizers, building materials and road materials. The information shall be collected by the producing units of the wastes.

Common industrial Solid Wastes Disposed refers to the quantity of solid wastes which are burnt or specially disposed using other methods to alter the physical, chemical and biological properties and thus to reduce or eliminate hazards, or placed ultimately in the sites meeting the requirements for environmental protection during the report period.

Stock of Common Industrial Solid Wastes refers to the volume of sold wastes placed in special facilities or special sites by enterprises for purposes of utilization or disposal during the report period.

Hazardous Wastes refers to those included in the national hazardous wastes catalog or specified as any one of the following properties in the national hazardous wastes identification standards: explosive, ignitable, oxidizable, toxic, corrosive or liable to cause infectious diseases or lead to other dangers.

Hazardous Wastes Produced refers to the volume of

actual hazardous wastes produced by surveyed samples throughout the year of the survey. Hazardous wastes refers to those included in the national hazardous wastes catalog or specified as any one of the following properties in light of the national hazardous wastes identification standards and methods: explosive, ignitable, oxidizable, toxic, corrosive, or liable to cause infectious diseases or lead to other dangers.

Hazardous Wastes Reused and Disposed refers to the amount of hazardous wastes that are used to extract materials as raw materials or fuel over the year of the survey, and the amount of hazardous wastes which are incineration or specially disposed using other methods to change its physical, chemical, and biological properties to reduce or eliminate the hazards, or placed ultimately in the sites following the requirements for environmental protection over the year of the survey. It includes the hazardous wastes generated by the enterprise itself and received from other enterprises.

第13篇

农　业

Agriculture

简要说明

一、本篇资料的主要内容

本篇资料反映了全省农业生产和农村经济的基本情况，主要包括农林牧渔业总产值、耕地、主要农产品产量、农业机械年末拥有量、农村电气化和农业化学化情况以及农田水利建设等方面的统计资料。

二、本篇资料的来源

1．地类面积资料、林业生产资料来源于省自然资源厅，由省统计局农村处整理提供。

2．灌溉面积资料来源于省水利厅，由省统计局农村处整理提供。

3．渔业生产资料、农业机械资料来源于省农业农村厅，由省统计局农村处整理提供。

4．粮食生产情况、畜牧业生产情况由山东调查总队农业调查处、农村调查处整理提供。

5．其余资料来源于农村综合统计年报，由省统计局农村处整理提供。

三、本篇资料的统计范围和统计口径

本篇资料的统计范围包括省内所属的各种经济类型、各个系统的全部农林牧渔业生产单位以及各非农行业附属的农林牧渔业生产活动单位。军委系统的农业生产（除军马外）也包括在内，但不包括农业科学试验机构进行的农业生产。

Brief Introduction

I. Content

Data in this chapter show the basic conditions of agricultural production and rural economy, mainly including agricultural output, cultivated land, output of main agricultural produces, agricultural machinery, electrification and chemistry in rural areas and basic construction on irrigation and drainage.

II. Source of Data

1. Data on land and forestry production are provided by the Department of Nature and Resources of Shandong Province.

2. Data on irrigated area are provided by the Water Resources Department of Shandong Province.

3. Data on fishery production means and agricultural machinery are provided by the Department of Agriculture and Rural of Shandong Province.

4. Data on grain output and animal husbandry output are provided by the Division of Agriculture Survey and the Division of Countryside Survey of the National Bureau of Statistics in Shandong.

5. Other data in this chapter are based on the statistical reporting summary tables of countryside statistics.

III. Scope and Coverage of Statistics

The coverage of the comprehensive statistical reporting includes all productive units of farming, forestry, animal husbandry and fishery and those related non-agricultural affiliated units with various ownership and the activities of horse raising for military purpose and those undertaken by agricultural research institutions are excluded.

13-1 主要年份农林牧渔业总产值

Gross Output Value of Farming,Forestry, Animal Husbandry and Fishery in Major Years

单位:亿元 (100 million yuan)

年 份 Year	农林牧渔业总产值 Gross Output Value of Farming, Forestry,Animal Husbandry and Fishery	农 业 Farming	种植业 Planting	林 业 Forestry	牧 业 Animal Husbandry	渔 业 Fishery	农林牧渔专业及辅助性活动 Farming,Forestry, Animal Husbandry and Fishery professions and auxiliary activities
1949	20.07	18.01	16.01	0.12	1.66	0.28	
1952	40.00	35.05	31.16	0.25	3.98	0.72	
1955	44.97	40.05	35.40	0.66	3.37	0.89	
1957	36.44	31.21	30.36	0.87	3.54	0.82	
1962	38.32	32.77	32.71	0.26	4.09	1.20	
1965	50.49	42.88	42.79	0.55	5.76	1.30	
1970	66.78	55.75	55.62	0.90	8.14	1.99	
1975	93.43	75.85	75.64	2.65	12.33	2.60	
1976	100.36	80.37	80.12	2.60	14.24	3.15	
1977	99.27	78.83	78.40	2.10	14.72	3.62	
1978	102.22	84.77	83.71	1.81	12.19	3.45	
1979	135.92	113.34	111.33	2.04	16.61	3.93	
1980	160.91	128.81	126.22	4.52	23.43	4.15	
1981	198.50	155.62	151.83	4.91	33.04	4.94	
1982	218.51	171.58	167.98	7.22	34.12	5.59	
1983	259.50	208.75	202.87	8.48	36.21	6.06	
1984	310.11	245.19	236.64	8.60	48.20	8.12	
1985	335.42	248.17	236.62	11.07	62.82	13.36	
1986	361.19	269.51	255.92	12.67	62.84	16.17	
1987	413.18	313.76	299.05	12.11	64.15	23.16	
1988	494.53	331.59	313.98	14.80	108.07	40.07	
1989	547.66	366.24	347.61	14.28	124.71	42.43	
1990	645.75	419.50	397.85	20.45	150.19	55.61	
1991	779.18	491.76	471.53	22.19	186.52	78.71	
1992	815.62	462.58	437.03	23.73	215.73	113.58	
1993	944.99	526.66	511.48	28.24	239.90	150.19	
1994	1282.25	660.13	649.84	36.78	348.78	236.56	
1995	1678.16	931.89	922.96	41.81	433.62	270.84	
1996	1962.12	1090.64	1078.05	49.97	512.60	308.91	
1997	2058.32	1137.19	1107.33	49.86	550.58	320.69	
1998	2174.54	1219.85	1184.65	45.91	583.40	325.38	
1999	2202.95	1254.87	1232.44	44.93	572.95	330.20	
2000	2294.35	1300.44	1280.12	47.62	599.17	347.12	
2001	2453.96	1401.34	1385.22	47.22	654.71	350.69	
2002	2526.05	1420.88	1402.81	48.25	698.44	358.48	
2003	2902.45	1599.32		53.70	831.34	370.04	48.05
2004	3453.91	1891.73		59.49	1022.84	426.09	53.76
2005	3741.81	2033.95		57.57	1125.04	465.52	59.73
2006	4058.62	2283.29		65.48	1025.37	522.94	161.54
2007	4752.65	2589.46		81.98	1317.06	577.31	186.83
2008	5583.98	2863.29		102.24	1715.47	679.12	223.87
2009	5953.15	3170.05		101.27	1699.51	735.75	246.58
2010	6573.77	3588.42		86.53	1796.52	829.77	272.52
2011	7311.11	3737.04		99.96	2205.73	973.24	295.14
2012	7817.84	3829.19		107.01	2328.69	1227.81	325.14
2013	8577.06	4335.77		120.30	2410.56	1347.03	363.40
2014	8988.18	4556.10		131.53	2478.81	1420.85	400.90
2015	9283.92	4662.61		139.92	2602.08	1447.28	432.03
2016	9075.60	4387.51		147.48	2620.29	1409.65	510.66
2017	9140.36	4403.23		165.09	2501.37	1475.96	594.70
2018	9397.39	4678.26		181.63	2432.67	1425.91	678.92
2019	9671.67	4914.43		197.70	2412.06	1397.42	750.06
2020	10190.58	5168.36		214.20	2571.87	1432.08	804.06
2021	11468.01	5814.56		219.94	2904.24	1652.60	876.68

注：本表按当年价格计算，2007至2017年数据系与第三次农业普查衔接数据。

a)Data are calculated at current prices.Data from 2007 to 2017 are consistent with those obtained from the Third Agricultural Census.

13-2 主要年份农林牧渔业总产值指数(以1952年为100)

Indices of Farming,Forestry,Animal Husbandry and Fishery in Major Years(1952=100)

年 份 Year	农林牧渔业总产值 Indices of Farming,Forestry, Animal Husbandry and Fishery	农 业 Farming	种植业 Planting	林 业 Forestry	牧 业 Animal Husbandry	渔 业 Fishery	农林牧渔专业及辅助性活动 Farming,Forestry, Animal Husbandry and Fishery professions and auxiliary activities
1949	57.7	59.1	59.1	56.9	48.0	44.2	
1952	100.0	100.0	100.0	100.0	100.0	100.0	
1955	108.1	109.9	109.3	256.9	81.3	118.4	
1957	94.2	92.1	100.8	360.8	91.9	118.4	
1962	65.5	63.9	71.8	70.6	70.0	114.3	
1965	99.8	96.7	108.6	174.5	114.3	142.9	
1970	123.5	117.7	132.1	264.7	151.2	204.8	
1975	163.2	151.2	169.6	745.1	216.5	252.4	
1976	166.9	152.6	171.1	692.2	237.8	291.8	
1977	164.8	149.4	167.1	556.9	245.5	334.7	
1978	177.1	160.6	178.2	680.4	253.4	383.7	
1979	193.9	177.1	195.7	637.3	287.2	338.8	
1980	212.1	190.0	209.7	680.4	347.4	375.5	
1981	218.8	198.2	218.1	627.5	352.9	336.1	
1982	239.2	215.3	236.9	1043.1	373.1	383.0	
1983	273.7	253.2	275.9	988.2	386.1	399.3	
1984	326.0	302.4	326.8	1109.8	462.2	449.7	
1985	338.2	306.5	326.8	1427.5	520.9	491.8	
1986	339.2	304.4	321.2	1380.4	539.2	566.0	
1987	366.3	331.7	350.4	1364.7	551.7	681.6	
1988	378.6	324.4	337.3	1325.5	703.9	887.8	
1989	383.5	321.8	333.9	1259.2	768.7	959.7	
1990	404.2	335.6	345.3	1235.3	823.3	1150.7	
1991	452.3	370.2	384.0	1315.6	922.9	1393.5	
1992	455.9	345.4	352.9	1380.1	985.7	1721.0	
1993	510.6	381.0	399.8	1526.4	1080.3	2103.1	
1994	578.0	411.1	436.2	1770.6	1295.3	2523.7	
1995	629.4	441.9	471.1	1839.7	1463.7	2720.5	
1996	675.3	478.1	507.4	2141.6	1551.5	2902.8	
1997	707.0	490.1	506.4	2154.4	1716.0	2975.4	
1998	777.0	589.3	562.1	2068.2	1915.1	3121.2	
1999	819.7	615.2	599.2	2072.3	2045.3	3345.9	
2000	851.7	639.8	625.6	2200.8	2155.7	3362.6	
2001	885.8	666.0	655.6	2064.4	2315.2	3315.5	
2002	895.5	649.4	637.2	1971.5	2472.6	3391.8	
2003	944.8	691.6		2121.3	2613.5	3449.5	111.5
2004	998.7	732.4		2138.3	2772.9	3601.3	108.0
2005	1050.6	761.0		2059.2	2975.3	3842.6	109.2
2006	1105.2	802.1		2279.5	3106.2	3992.5	118.8
2007	1141.7	829.4		2457.3	3131.0	4180.1	110.8
2008	1199.9	859.3		2798.9	3315.7	4426.7	113.3
2009	1251.5	882.5		3076.0	3488.1	4701.2	110.1
2010	1296.6	904.6		3380.5	3624.1	4931.6	109.9
2011	1345.9	939.9		3694.9	3714.7	5148.6	107.2
2012	1409.2	963.4		3820.5	4000.7	5359.7	107.7
2013	1462.7	1005.8		4164.3	4084.7	5536.6	109.5
2014	1521.2	1052.1		4568.3	4182.7	5686.1	109.3
2015	1586.6	1101.5		4938.3	4312.4	5868.1	108.5
2016	1656.4	1156.6		5407.4	4424.5	5985.5	115.8
2017	1722.7	1207.5		5942.7	4588.2	5955.6	112.5
2018	1774.4	1254.6		6495.4	4583.6	6003.2	113.5
2019	1788.6	1293.5		7093.0	4372.8	5847.1	109.3
2020	1842.8	1337.9		7540.6	4473.4	5923.1	105.3
2021	2000.5	1395.7		7667.2	5332.7	6273.8	108.2

注：本表按可比价格计算；农林牧渔专业及辅助性活动指数以上年为100。

a)Data are calculated at constant prices.Indices of Farming,Forestry,Animal Husbandry and Fishery professions and auxiliary activities in preceding year is considered as 100.

13-3 农林牧渔业总产值
Gross Output Value of Farming,Forestry,Animal Husbandry and Fishery

单位:亿元 (100 million yuan)

类 别	Category	2020	2021	2021为 2020% 2020=100
农林牧渔业总产值	**Gross Output Value of Farming,Forestry, Animal Husbandry and Fishery**	**10190.58**	**11468.01**	**108.6**
一、农业产值	**Output Value of Farming**	**5168.36**	**5814.56**	**104.3**
1.谷物及其他作物	Cereal and Other Corps	1871.71	1714.93	81.1
#粮食	Grain	1235.17	1369.73	101.3
油料	Oil	139.25	147.73	99.2
棉花	Cotton	88.30	11.42	12.6
2.蔬菜园艺作物	Vegetable Gardening Crops	1908.42	2536.81	126.4
#蔬菜(含菜用瓜)	Vegetables	1796.23	2379.48	106.4
3.水果坚果饮料	Fruit and Nut Beverages	1281.69	1424.90	101.8
#水果坚果(含果用瓜)	Fruit and Nut	1245.31	1293.91	101.3
4.中药材	Chinese Herbal Medicines	106.55	137.91	147.6
二、林业产值	**Output Value of Forestry**	**214.20**	**219.94**	**101.7**
1.林木的培育和种植	Trees Cultivation and Planting	80.07	70.80	90.8
2.竹木采运	Bamboo Logging and Transport	51.82	56.79	107.2
3.林产品	Forestry Products	82.31	92.35	108.8
三、牧业产值	**Output Value of Animal Husbandry**	**2571.87**	**2904.24**	**119.2**
1.牲畜饲养	Livestock Feeding	491.03	745.59	137.6
2.猪的饲养	Pig Feeding	959.95	966.11	140.5
3.家禽的饲养	Poultry Feeding	937.12	1127.07	104.9
#肉禽	Poultry for Eating	522.57	680.98	109.0
禽蛋	Egg of Poultry	414.55	446.09	95.7
4.狩猎和捕捉动物	Animal Hunting and Trapping	2.09	1.26	56.4
5.其他畜牧业	Other Animal Husbandry	181.66	64.21	31.2
四、渔业产值	**Output Value of Fishery**	**1432.08**	**1652.60**	**105.9**
1.海水产品	Seawater Aquatic Products	1210.23	1410.65	106.2
2.内陆水域水产品	Inland waterways Aquatic Products	221.85	241.95	104.2
五、农林牧渔专业及辅助性活动产值	**Output Value of Farming,Forestry,Animal Husbandry and Fishery professions and auxiliary activities**	**804.06**	**876.68**	**108.2**

注:本表绝对数按当年价格计算,速度按可比价格计算。

a)Absolute data in the table are calculated at current prices, the speed are calculated at constant price.

13-4 各市农林牧渔业总产值(2021年)
Gross Output Value of Farming,Forestry,Animal Husbandry and Fishery by Region(2021)

单位:万元 (10 000 yuan)

地 区	Region	农林牧渔业总产值 Output Value of Farming,Forestry, Animal Husbandry and Fishery	农业产值 Output Value of Farming	林业产值 Output Value of Forestry	牧业产值 Output Value of Animal Husbandry	渔业产值 Output Value of Fishery	农林牧渔专业及辅助性活动产值 Output Value of Services to Farming, Forestry,Animal Husbandry and Fishery professions and auxiliary activities
全省总计	**Total**	**114680094**	**58145565**	**2199350**	**29042367**	**16526030**	**8766782**
济南市	Jinan	7584102	5019841	344086	1709854	81991	428330
青岛市	Qingdao	8970590	4228955	41462	1836006	2247619	616548
淄博市	Zibo	3350604	2184719	168315	752452	64551	180567
枣庄市	Zaozhuang	3590296	2291677	22930	729380	144713	401596
东营市	Dongying	3542841	1103573	30142	1108316	963517	337293
烟台市	Yantai	11768971	5125753	235729	2150882	3422054	834553
潍坊市	Weifang	11835250	6303503	85798	3379901	1065301	1000747
济宁市	Jining	11161811	6189841	158780	2882031	1012418	918741
泰安市	Tai'an	6360658	3702070	109025	1708235	227630	613698
威海市	Weihai	6451217	1123653	14236	685577	4325332	302419
日照市	Rizhao	3769784	1240811	52984	1063390	1103666	308933
临沂市	Linyi	9079971	4948622	435863	2861238	339681	494567
德州市	Dezhou	7671137	3694462	187370	2628894	146947	1013464
聊城市	Liaocheng	7119080	4544346	58370	1802989	196694	516681
滨州市	Binzhou	5553869	2242047	118339	1661040	1006470	525973
菏泽市	Heze	6869913	4201692	135921	2082182	177446	272672

13-5 主要年份粮、棉、油产量

Output of Grain,Cotton and Oil-bearing Crops in Major Years

年 份	粮 食 Grain		棉 花 Cotton		油 料 Oil-bearing Crops	
Year	总产量 (万吨) Gross Output (10 000 tons)	单 产 (千克/公顷) Output Per Hectare (kg/hectare)	总产量 (万吨) Gross Output (10 000 tons)	单 产 (千克/公顷) Output Per Hectare (kg/hectare)	总产量 (万吨) Gross Output (10 000 tons)	单 产 (千克/公顷) Output Per Hectare (kg/hectare)
1949	870.0	795	8.1	180	55.6	1170
1952	1199.0	1035	16.9	240	84.5	1470
1955	1276.0	1110	20.9	285	106.1	1485
1957	1126.0	990	17.4	225	70.0	945
1962	910.0	915	3.9	105	42.4	1875
1965	1332.0	1350	19.9	300	67.1	1395
1970	1465.0	1575	27.3	390	78.5	1575
1975	2170.5	2355	24.1	390	84.2	1515
1976	2241.5	2460	15.8	255	58.5	1065
1977	2099.0	2370	14.9	240	67.7	2025
1978	2288.0	2595	15.4	255	95.9	1785
1979	2472.0	2835	16.7	315	109.1	1800
1980	2384.0	2820	53.7	735	143.0	2160
1981	2312.5	2835	67.5	720	142.1	2010
1982	2375.0	3090	96.0	720	142.5	2190
1983	2700.0	3465	122.5	825	152.0	2460
1984	3040.0	3885	172.5	1005	182.0	2790
1985	3137.7	3930	106.2	915	267.9	2745
1986	3250.0	3840	94.1	930	207.6	2355
1987	3393.7	4125	124.4	1020	234.3	2940
1988	3225.0	3990	113.7	825	197.8	2505
1989	3250.0	4035	102.5	780	150.0	1995
1990	3570.0	4380	102.8	690	212.1	2910
1991	3916.9	4845	135.1	870	233.1	3285
1992	3589.3	4533	67.7	455	166.3	2380
1993	4100.0	4992	41.0	539	268.4	3434
1994	4091.1	5015	55.9	705	338.3	3781
1995	4245.0	5220	47.1	707	315.0	3580
1996	4332.7	5260	37.2	773	309.3	3767
1997	3852.2	4766	35.4	894	240.9	2977
1998	4264.8	5244	41.3	996	335.6	3908
1999	4269.0	5271	39.2	1072	320.5	3614
2000	3837.7	4938	59.0	1085	356.9	3730
2001	3720.6	5201	78.1	1062	377.3	3743
2002	3292.7	4763	72.2	1086	340.4	3458
2003	3435.5	5355	87.7	994	361.8	3572
2004	3516.7	5570	109.8	1036	369.7	3913
2005	3917.4	5837	84.6	1000	363.9	4044
2006	4093.0	5848	102.3	1149	328.2	4136
2007	4107.8	5896	95.1	1112	368.8	4190
2008	4353.9	6086	94.0	1172	374.7	4283
2009	4442.7	6088	79.0	1151	349.2	4349
2010	4502.8	6043	59.0	945	347.7	4317
2011	4701.3	6172	60.8	1043	343.7	4367
2012	4815.8	6214	51.4	1012	341.8	4404
2013	4883.4	6099	43.4	923	341.6	4386
2014	5038.3	6087	44.2	1122	329.6	4355
2015	5147.4	6123	33.9	1042	318.7	4302
2016	5332.3	6261	32.9	1179	317.1	4310
2017	5374.3	6356	20.7	1185	318.3	4389
2018	5319.5	6329	21.7	1184	310.9	4370
2019	5357.0	6444	19.6	1158	289.0	4236
2020	5446.8	6577	18.3	1281	290.9	4366
2021	5500.7	6584	14.0	1273	285.9	4420

注：本表2007至2017年数据系与第三次农业普查衔接数据。

a)Data from 2007 to 2017 are consistent with those obtained from the Third Agricultural Census.

13-6 1978-2021年畜牧业生产情况

Production of Animal Husbandry from 1978 to 2021

年 份 Year	肉类总产量 (万吨) Output of Meat (10 000 tons)	猪存栏 (万头) Stocked Pigs (10 000 heads)	牛存栏 (万头) Stocked Cattle (10 000 heads)	羊存栏 (万只) Stocked Sheep (10 000 heads)	家禽存栏 (万只) Stocked Poultry (10 000 heads)
1978	60.80	1992.00	227.60	756.40	6766.00
1979	65.18	2117.60	221.50	925.80	7204.00
1980	90.10	2112.50	217.80	1041.30	7997.00
1981	96.26	1901.10	213.70	1025.60	8075.00
1982	94.98	1726.20	213.60	989.50	9115.00
1983	94.54	1562.70	222.10	901.80	10216.80
1984	104.38	1681.50	232.60	753.90	14688.90
1985	128.62	1812.80	258.00	783.30	16548.20
1986	141.78	1668.90	292.50	985.30	15120.70
1987	141.02	1547.00	344.60	1404.10	16916.30
1988	171.47	1688.60	416.00	1436.40	21582.10
1989	195.63	1604.10	472.40	1491.30	20471.30
1990	221.61	1576.70	511.80	1528.10	23974.60
1991	241.49	1599.40	501.40	1591.20	24136.80
1992	250.67	1602.60	531.90	1655.20	25810.80
1993	286.61	1603.70	603.00	1703.50	27188.70
1994	338.77	1701.50	681.30	1799.80	35118.60
1995	394.42	1718.10	714.10	1866.10	34613.80
1996	405.52	1723.60	740.10	1877.20	37485.00
1997	460.64	2209.70	811.90	2038.60	41833.00
1998	497.90	2485.90	911.80	2322.00	48484.00
1999	524.49	2560.48	977.25	2536.22	53332.00
2000	499.99	2401.81	779.90	2260.06	47789.90
2001	531.49	2500.29	778.54	2357.24	50263.73
2002	559.66	2602.80	787.88	2466.79	53236.24
2003	591.00	2686.09	804.31	2543.26	55031.28
2004	621.72	2761.01	771.51	2667.51	56875.64
2005	657.78	2771.96	750.45	2645.96	54641.26
2006	698.32	2508.52	632.71	2368.26	52100.31
2007	660.00	2686.01	557.46	2281.96	49627.42
2008	704.52	2786.69	498.53	2033.94	55864.43
2009	730.91	2845.80	452.59	1939.09	54789.42
2010	754.03	2871.65	440.32	1926.95	58214.00
2011	763.07	2998.20	438.27	1887.90	63790.18
2012	822.56	3101.21	433.66	1850.33	70959.78
2013	838.18	3167.00	424.28	1797.90	70261.33
2014	836.81	3179.54	410.53	1765.01	69911.92
2015	845.50	3147.33	407.65	1767.89	71816.01
2016	837.11	3086.81	391.93	1693.10	78056.12
2017	866.01	3040.33	401.48	1754.05	76604.46
2018	854.70	2985.60	380.60	1801.41	75614.88
2019	704.02	2176.50	364.23	1837.44	78864.33
2020	728.02	2933.93	278.71	1501.65	83642.36
2021	819.26	3151.04	279.76	1466.35	84578.07

注：本表2006至2017年数据系与第三次农业普查衔接数据。

a)Data from 2006 to 2017 are consistent with those obtained from the Third Agricultural Census.

13-6 续表 continued

年 份 Year	猪出栏 (万头) Slaughtered Pigs (10 000 heads)	牛出栏 (万头) Slaughtered Cattle (10 000 heads)	羊出栏 (万只) Slaughtered Sheep (10 000 heads)	家禽出栏 (万只) Slaughtered Poultry (10 000 heads)	禽蛋产量 (万吨) Output of Poultry Eggs (10 000 tons)	奶类产量 (万吨) Output of Milk (10 000 tons)
1978	901.20	4.60	142.40		22.50	6.83
1979	1047.50	6.70	228.60		23.67	6.95
1980	1241.60	8.80	377.50		25.62	6.80
1981	1296.80	11.50	460.70		29.47	5.24
1982	1213.20	10.60	521.60		34.30	8.77
1983	1159.20	18.90	616.30		41.07	11.43
1984	1284.00	18.40	519.10		62.28	13.34
1985	1482.60	27.60	558.30	8283.10	72.50	13.26
1986	1681.20	32.30	617.60	9234.50	69.66	15.81
1987	1514.00	49.80	842.10	11397.30	79.14	17.28
1988	1619.60	69.00	1219.00	15904.00	102.97	19.53
1989	1845.40	82.80	1348.40	16701.20	109.43	21.24
1990	1936.20	110.10	1416.40	22769.00	124.25	22.53
1991	1983.50	119.50	1348.70	30792.70	149.14	23.65
1992	2046.00	140.90	1366.10	33467.90	154.30	25.17
1993	2092.90	177.10	1411.00	42837.30	184.07	28.05
1994	2185.70	213.10	1668.20	64716.70	240.75	32.45
1995	2453.00	248.40	2034.10	71286.50	247.15	36.98
1996	2500.90	272.40	2051.80	73508.00	267.30	41.14
1997	2801.10	334.50	2269.30	82549.00	294.30	45.82
1998	3123.20	354.90	2518.90	91299.00	322.00	53.98
1999	3248.13	391.10	2838.80	100246.00	349.06	61.29
2000	3213.24	322.25	2375.73	91195.00	301.04	62.72
2001	3370.69	359.63	2530.15	99493.75	311.58	80.48
2002	3566.19	380.13	2646.54	105550.38	328.33	103.92
2003	3765.90	396.47	2731.23	113458.25	349.11	132.05
2004	4060.41	413.21	2869.43	122660.64	355.83	167.92
2005	4263.54	425.73	3002.98	145089.38	363.20	196.66
2006	4389.90	436.57	3026.24	151090.90	353.89	219.67
2007	3680.17	440.30	3001.42	140913.62	359.90	207.06
2008	3972.95	439.30	2941.33	155662.06	364.98	217.95
2009	4245.45	426.49	2827.01	161151.11	377.12	220.25
2010	4425.46	413.01	2707.40	169549.81	384.84	230.97
2011	4387.82	390.04	2546.51	181519.01	401.64	235.83
2012	4800.79	385.34	2493.35	199140.72	402.44	248.55
2013	5043.03	382.59	2472.15	195931.87	396.59	237.69
2014	5245.73	372.37	2530.64	182274.92	388.38	244.74
2015	5156.44	370.19	2527.12	192051.95	424.28	240.73
2016	5093.23	360.84	2540.84	214260.99	441.12	233.75
2017	5180.69	361.57	2629.76	220423.34	445.15	231.32
2018	5082.26	363.37	2682.36	217200.22	447.44	232.52
2019	3176.44	345.93	2701.14	231299.11	450.63	234.49
2020	3344.79	275.71	2491.58	252670.83	482.19	241.57
2021	4401.74	280.03	2373.39	263535.68	456.64	288.37

13-7 1978-2021年渔业生产情况

Output of Fishery from 1978 to 2021

单位：吨 (tons)

年 份 Year	水产品总产量 Total Aquatic Products	海水产品 Seawater Aquatic Products	海洋捕捞 Ocean Fishing	海水养殖 Mariculture
1978	740283	691451	501504	189947
1979	627531	581165	432700	148465
1980	619591	570854	416814	154040
1981	589905	540408	407194	133214
1982	657698	611824	477729	134095
1983	674813	623122	465382	157740
1984	754572	693277	525027	168250
1985	814047	729568	531977	197591
1986	914411	806086	599376	206710
1987	1106641	983119	717588	265531
1988	1355865	1220408	809820	410588
1989	1539905	1403323	899265	504058
1990	1677973	1522059	1032683	489376
1991	1981169	1779214	1138436	640778
1992	2481648	2251437	1384628	866809
1993	3192828	2896171	1555657	1340514
1994	3506539	3053106	1608172	1444934
1995	3440763	2956402	1461525	1494876
1996	5299159	4683795	2337772	2346023
1997	5512326	4840507	2686824	2153683
1998	5875574	5116993	3003764	2113228
1999	6277843	5440155	3003387	2436767
2000	6306551	5375169	2780483	2594685
2001	6196988	5266599	2511170	2755430
2002	6277536	5403654	2457272	2946382
2003	6378795	5456872	2421393	3035479
2004	6486528	5528613	2440631	3087982
2005	6648983	5655207	2421396	3233811
2006	6837469	5783299	2359570	3423729
2007	7133795	5986873	2451596	3535277
2008	7303048	6094766	2481256	3613510
2009	7535939	6263895	2449591	3814304
2010	7838259	6463345	2350888	3962643
2011	8138280	6647212	2512437	4134775
2012	7885248	6524046	2161603	4362443
2013	8084522	6654179	2087829	4566350
2014	8464587	7085761	2286654	4799107
2015	8722448	7352063	2356409	4995654
2016	8899622	7541952	2414112	5127840
2017	8680030	7371727	2180891	5190836
2018	8614032	7360685	2149830	5210855
2019	8232724	7062086	2091101	4970985
2020	8286092	7180937	2039543	5141394
2021	8544248	7403008	2029166	5373842

注：本表2012至2017年数据系与第三次农业普查衔接数据。

a)Data from 2012 to 2017 are consistent with those obtained from the Third Agricultural Census.

13－7 续表 continued

年 份 Year	淡水产品产量(吨) Freshwater Aquatic Products (ton)	捕捞量 Fishing Output	养殖量 Breeding Output	水产品养殖面积(万亩) Water Area for Breeding Aquatics (10 000 mu)	海 水 Seawater	淡 水 Freshwater
1978	48832	32507	16325	202.30	26.80	175.50
1979	46366	30968	15398	193.29	26.54	166.75
1980	48737	32436	16301	203.21	28.50	174.71
1981	49497	31489	18008	182.24	28.66	153.58
1982	45874	29696	16178	176.15	35.18	140.97
1983	51691	31713	19978	160.05	32.31	127.74
1984	61295	34438	26857	165.10	37.70	127.40
1985	84479	37370	47109	215.14	49.58	165.56
1986	108325	38641	69684	243.14	56.70	186.44
1987	123522	34103	89419	257.65	70.87	186.78
1988	135457	29354	106103	234.90	104.27	180.63
1989	136582	26847	109735	246.73	103.72	143.01
1990	155914	31545	124369	273.52	105.01	168.51
1991	201955	41772	160183	304.04	112.54	191.50
1992	230211	41074	189137	312.30	115.89	196.41
1993	296657	50088	246569	400.16	223.76	176.40
1994	453433	58373	395060	466.56	197.36	269.21
1995	484362	55428	428933	497.39	197.81	299.58
1996	615364	67222	548142	564.54	242.45	322.09
1997	671819	73221	598598	618.91	274.04	344.87
1998	758582	80336	678246	649.80	283.22	366.58
1999	837689	80002	757687	722.78	336.14	386.65
2000	931382	81214	850168	788.35	420.71	367.64
2001	930389	79991	850397	829.39	434.99	394.40
2002	873882	71142	802740	802.51	439.15	363.36
2003	921923	91019	830904	930.91	537.52	393.38
2004	957915	93484	864431	1014.34	598.02	416.32
2005	993776	110887	882889	1033.11	611.09	422.02
2006	1054170	117390	936780	840.03	564.62	275.42
2007	1146922	114368	1032554	884.99	609.26	275.73
2008	1208282	129643	1078639	993.45	639.33	354.12
2009	1272044	128342	1143702	1029.30	662.10	367.20
2010	1374914	130896	1244018	1136.51	751.42	385.09
2011	1491068	135378	1355690	1174.40	768.19	406.21
2012	1361202	112783	1248419	1205.16	785.56	419.60
2013	1430344	115167	1315177	1240.35	820.23	420.12
2014	1378826	90661	1288165	1252.66	822.73	429.93
2015	1370385	83086	1287299	1269.23	844.80	424.43
2016	1357670	93900	1263770	1259.25	907.20	352.05
2017	1308303	83730	1224573	1250.38	915.57	334.81
2018	1253347	82821	1170526	1173.38	856.29	317.10
2019	1170638	89290	1081348	1138.34	842.25	296.09
2020	1105155	95634	1009521	1116.93	870.53	246.40
2021	1141240	95733	1045507	1147.82	912.56	235.26

13-8 农作物播种面积和产量

Sown Area and Output of Farm Crops

类别	Category	2020			2021		
		播种面积(公顷) Sown Area (hectare)	总产量(吨) Total Output (ton)	单产(千克/公顷) Output per Hectare (kg/hectare)	播种面积(公顷) Sown Area (hectare)	总产量(吨) Total Output (ton)	单产(千克/公顷) Output per Hectare (kg/hectare)
农作物总播种面积	**Total Sown Area of Crops**	**10889085**			**10948594**		
一、粮食作物合计	**Grain**	**8281540**	**54468131**	**6577**	**8355135**	**55007457**	**6584**
(一)夏收粮食	Summer Harvest Grain	3935380	25691959	6528	3995465	26372037	6600
1.谷物	Cereals	3934700	25689965	6529	3994317	26368240	6601
#小麦	Wheat	3934430	25688535	6529	3994033	26366607	6602
2.夏杂豆	Beans	680	1994	2932	1148	3797	3307
(二)秋收粮食	Autumn Harvest Grain	4346160	28776171	6621	4359670	28635420	6568
1.谷物	Cereals	4019762	27070687	6734	4045673	26999872	6674
(1)稻谷	Rice	112479	987676	8781	113041	974748	8623
(2)玉米	Corn	3871090	25954006	6705	3897005	25895220	6645
(3)谷子	Millet	33164	119660	3608	32733	120821	3691
(4)高粱	Chinese Sorghum	2348	7119	3031	2219	6855	3089
(5)其他	Others	681	2225	3269	674	2228	3305
2.豆类合计	Beans	192356	564948	2937	186390	544871	2923
#大豆	Soybean	188672	554949	2941	182823	535057	2927
3.薯类(按折粮计算)	Tubers	134042	1140536	8509	127608	1090676	8547
二、油料作物合计	**Oil-bearing Crops**	**666403**	**2909458**	**4366**	**646763**	**2858894**	**4420**
#花生果	Peanuts	650856	2866416	4404	631741	2818214	4461
油菜籽	Rapeseeds	8580	22012	2566	9263	23948	2585
芝 麻	Sesame	659	1486	2256	713	1702	2387
三、棉花	**Cotton**	**142900**	**183000**	**1281**	**110184**	**140253**	**1273**
四、生麻	**Fiber Crops**	**27**	**57**	**2112**	**25**	**40**	**1559**
#生 大 麻	Hemp	27	57	2112	17	29	1710
五、甜菜	**Beetroots**	**5**	**120**	**22500**	**8**	**180**	**22500**
六、烟叶	**Tobacco**	**18182**	**47242**	**2598**	**17974**	**46998**	**2615**
#烤烟	Flue-cured Tobacco	18035	46773	2593	17881	46682	2611
七、中草药材	**Medical Materials**	**54265**			**56913**		
八、蔬菜及食用菌	**Vegetable and Mushroom**	**1487342**	**84347078**	**56710**	**1524684**	**88010797**	**57724**
九、瓜果类	**Melon**	**211468**	**11090839**	**52447**	**208717**	**11186717**	**53598**
#西瓜	Watermelon	141495	7613614	53808	136939	7501654	54781
十、其他农作物	**Other Farm Crops**	**26952**			**28192**		
#青饲料	Fresh Feed	8744			16178		

13-9 各市农作物播种面积和产量(2021年)
Sown Area and Output of Farm Crops by Region(2021)

地 区	Region	农作物总播种面积(公顷) Total Sown Area of Farm Crops (hectare)	一、粮食作物合计 Grain Crops			(一)夏收粮食 Summer Harvest Grain		
			播种面积(公顷) Sown Area (hectare)	总产量(吨) Total Output (ton)	单 产(千克/公顷) Output per Hectare (kg/hectare)	播种面积(公顷) Sown Area (hectare)	总产量(吨) Total Output (ton)	单 产(千克/公顷) Output per Hectare (kg/hectare)
全省总计	**Total**	**10948594**	**8355135**	**55007457**	**6584**	**3995465**	**26372037**	**6600**
济 南 市	Jinan	620432	483616	2930705	6060	219510	1392481	6344
青 岛 市	Qingdao	667938	480070	3127743	6515	227582	1429566	6282
淄 博 市	Zibo	253506	217303	1447669	6662	96233	656322	6820
枣 庄 市	Zaozhuang	401145	284130	1830839	6444	139883	896181	6407
东 营 市	Dongying	285377	254253	1365193	5369	107974	673151	6234
烟 台 市	Yantai	443852	302746	1833379	6056	121506	746945	6147
潍 坊 市	Weifang	981139	685252	4358638	6361	327863	2099630	6404
济 宁 市	Jining	966708	719699	4868125	6764	346365	2321263	6702
泰 安 市	Tai'an	530183	371876	2572384	6917	166592	1164899	6993
威 海 市	Weihai	195243	121844	726690	5964	47136	265242	5627
日 照 市	Rizhao	210295	130781	871096	6661	51876	338232	6520
临 沂 市	Linyi	987579	645029	4180241	6481	291442	1807736	6203
德 州 市	Dezhou	1199657	1068769	7616021	7126	542864	3801316	7002
聊 城 市	Liaocheng	990772	812698	5679749	6989	412272	2832452	6870
滨 州 市	Binzhou	662252	587997	3721976	6330	281316	1876419	6670
菏 泽 市	Heze	1552515	1189073	7877009	6624	615053	4070202	6618

13-9 续表 1 continued

地 区	Region	1.谷 物 Cereals			#小 麦 Wheat			2.夏杂豆 Beans		
		播种面积(公顷) Sown Area (hectare)	总产量(吨) Total Output (ton)	单 产(千克/公顷) Output per Hectare (kg/hectare)	播种面积(公顷) Sown Area (hectare)	总产量(吨) Total Output (ton)	单 产(千克/公顷) Output per Hectare (kg/hectare)	播种面积(公顷) Sown Area (hectare)	总产量(吨) Total Output (ton)	单 产(千克/公顷) Output per Hectare (kg/hectare)
全省总计	**Total**	**3994317**	**26368240**	**6601**	**3994033**	**26366607**	**6602**	**1148**	**3797**	**3307**
济 南 市	Jinan	219510	1392481	6344	219510	1392481	6344			
青 岛 市	Qingdao	227582	1429566	6282	227582	1429566	6282			
淄 博 市	Zibo	96233	656322	6820	96233	656322	6820			
枣 庄 市	Zaozhuang	139883	896181	6407	139883	896181	6407			
东 营 市	Dongying	107974	673151	6234	107974	673151	6234			
烟 台 市	Yantai	121506	746945	6147	121506	746945	6147			
潍 坊 市	Weifang	326715	2095833	6415	326715	2095833	6415	1148	3797	3307
济 宁 市	Jining	346365	2321263	6702	346365	2321263	6702			
泰 安 市	Tai'an	166592	1164899	6993	166592	1164899	6993			
威 海 市	Weihai	47136	265242	5627	47136	265242	5627			
日 照 市	Rizhao	51876	338232	6520	51876	338232	6520			
临 沂 市	Linyi	291442	1807736	6203	291158	1806103	6203			
德 州 市	Dezhou	542864	3801316	7002	542864	3801316	7002			
聊 城 市	Liaocheng	412272	2832452	6870	412272	2832452	6870			
滨 州 市	Binzhou	281316	1876419	6670	281316	1876419	6670			
菏 泽 市	Heze	615053	4070202	6618	615053	4070202	6618			

13-9 续表 2 continued

地 区	Region	(二)秋收粮食 Autumn Harvest Grain 播种面积(公顷) Sown Area (hectare)	总产量(吨) Total Output (ton)	单 产(千克/公顷) Output per Hectare (kg/hectare)	1.谷 物 Cereals 播种面积(公顷) Sown Area (hectare)	总产量(吨) Total Output (ton)	单 产(千克/公顷) Output per Hectare (kg/hectare)	(1)稻 谷 Rice 播种面积(公顷) Sown Area (hectare)	总产量(吨) Total Output (ton)	单 产(千克/公顷) Output per Hectare (kg/hectare)
全省总计	**Total**	**4359670**	**28635420**	**6568**	**4045673**	**26999872**	**6674**	**113041**	**974748**	**8623**
济南市	Jinan	264106	1538224	5824	247841	1439717	5809	806	6260	7771
青岛市	Qingdao	252488	1698178	6726	241337	1637141	6784	426	3010	7066
淄博市	Zibo	121069	791347	6536	116962	769319	6577	390	3283	8422
枣庄市	Zaozhuang	144247	934658	6480	130638	861199	6592	1803	14004	7768
东营市	Dongying	146279	692042	4731	134666	669590	4972	23519	133879	5692
烟台市	Yantai	181240	1086434	5994	163176	969662	5942	133	1030	7745
潍坊市	Weifang	357389	2259007	6321	346597	2198205	6342	1512	11026	7294
济宁市	Jining	373334	2546862	6822	310154	2261148	7290	40044	389976	9739
泰安市	Tai'an	205284	1407485	6856	175512	1261426	7187	67	724	10752
威海市	Weihai	74709	461448	6177	64124	399513	6230	621	4585	7379
日照市	Rizhao	78906	532864	6753	67974	453056	6665	2059	19081	9265
临沂市	Linyi	353588	2372505	6710	291458	1964071	6739	38062	358000	9406
德州市	Dezhou	525904	3814705	7254	520163	3789373	7285			
聊城市	Liaocheng	400426	2847297	7111	393080	2820053	7174	7	48	7184
滨州市	Binzhou	306680	1845557	6018	298188	1817334	6095	546	3478	6372
菏泽市	Heze	574020	3806806	6632	543802	3689065	6784	3046	26364	8656

13-9 续表 3 continued

地 区	Region	(2)玉 米 Corn 播种面积(公顷) Sown Area (hectare)	总产量(吨) Total Output (ton)	单 产(千克/公顷) Output per Hectare (kg/hectare)	(3)谷 子 Millet 播种面积(公顷) Sown Area (hectare)	总产量(吨) Total Output (ton)	单 产(千克/公顷) Output per Hectare (kg/hectare)	(4)高 粱 Chinese Sorghum 播种面积(公顷) Sown Area (hectare)	总产量(吨) Total Output (ton)	单 产(千克/公顷) Output per Hectare (kg/hectare)
全省总计	**Total**	**3897005**	**25895220**	**6645**	**32733**	**120821**	**3691**	**2219**	**6855**	**3089**
济南市	Jinan	236414	1395596	5903	10398	37289	3586	121	282	2324
青岛市	Qingdao	240140	1631325	6793	618	2322	3754	61	166	2706
淄博市	Zibo	114108	758561	6648	2368	7127	3009	96	348	3638
枣庄市	Zaozhuang	127975	843807	6594	832	3297	3960	16	50	3144
东营市	Dongying	110463	533957	4834	87	227	2620	597	1527	2557
烟台市	Yantai	161426	962635	5963	1458	5453	3739	28	83	2933
潍坊市	Weifang	338814	2162652	6383	5392	21429	3974	765	2738	3578
济宁市	Jining	268903	1867097	6943	1207	4075	3377			
泰安市	Tai'an	173492	1253157	7223	1903	7392	3885	37	110	2957
威海市	Weihai	63502	394928	6219						
日照市	Rizhao	63591	424527	6676	2277	9302	4085	9	32	3516
临沂市	Linyi	248973	1589491	6384	4258	16058	3771	82	250	3056
德州市	Dezhou	520038	3788817	7286	117	526	4496	8.4	30.4	3612
聊城市	Liaocheng	392454	2818224	7181	600	1728	2880	19	53	2833
滨州市	Binzhou	297103	1812070	6099	100	373	3745	358	1126	3144
菏泽市	Heze	539608	3658377	6780	1117	4224	3781	21	62	2867

13-9 续表 4 continued

地 区	Region	(5)其他谷物 Other Cereals 播种面积(公顷) Sown Area (hectare)	总产量(吨) Total Output (ton)	单 产(千克/公顷) Output per Hectare (kg/hectare)	2.豆 类 Beans 播种面积(公顷) Sown Area (hectare)	总产量(吨) Total Output (ton)	单 产(千克/公顷) Output per Hectare (kg/hectare)	#大 豆 Soybean 播种面积(公顷) Sown Area (hectare)	总产量(吨) Total Output (ton)	单 产(千克/公顷) Output per Hectare (kg/hectare)
全省总计	**Total**	**674**	**2228**	**3305**	**186390**	**544871**	**2923**	**182823**	**535057**	**2927**
济 南 市	Jinan	102	290	2838	7486	20500	2738	7108	19522	2747
青 岛 市	Qingdao	90	317	3512	4965	13894	2798	4965	13894	2798
淄 博 市	Zibo				1951	5671	2906	1673	4877	2915
枣 庄 市	Zaozhuang	11	41	3626	9200	30766	3344	8858	29730	3356
东 营 市	Dongying				11327	20053	1770	11204	19794	1767
烟 台 市	Yantai	131	462	3531	8030	26110	3251	7830	25566	3265
潍 坊 市	Weifang	114	361	3165	5036	16728	3321	4914	16390	3335
济 宁 市	Jining				46867	134051	2860	46765	133782	2861
泰 安 市	Tai'an	13	42	3217	20578	60731	2951	20396	60206	2952
威 海 市	Weihai				4517	11054	2447	4491	11003	2450
日 照 市	Rizhao	38	115	3015	3711	12309	3317	3188	10806	3389
临 沂 市	Linyi	83	273	3310	18101	52925	2924	17666	51753	2929
德 州 市	Dezhou				4750	15886	3344	4711	15805	3355
聊 城 市	Liaocheng				6155	17359	2820	6029	17010	2821
滨 州 市	Binzhou	81	288	3544	8080	24955	3089	7976	24670	3093
菏 泽 市	Heze	10	37	3741	25636	81880	3194	25048	80247	3204

13-9 续表 5 continued

地 区	Region	3.薯类(按折粮薯类计算) Tubers 播种面积(公顷) Sown Area (hectare)	总产量(吨) Total Output (ton)	单 产(千克/公顷) Output per Hectare (kg/hectare)	二、油 料 Oil-bearing Crops 播种面积(公顷) Sown Area (hectare)	总产量(吨) Total Output (ton)	单 产(千克/公顷) Output per Hectare (kg/hectare)	#花 生 果 Peanuts 播种面积(公顷) Sown Area (hectare)	总产量(吨) Total Output (ton)	单 产(千克/公顷) Output per Hectare (kg/hectare)
全省总计	**Total**	**127608**	**1090676**	**8547**	**646763**	**2858894**	**4420**	**631741**	**2818214**	**4461**
济 南 市	Jinan	8779	78007	8886	17541	65957	3760	16207	62930	3883
青 岛 市	Qingdao	6187	47142	7620	69380	339452	4893	69376	339448	4893
淄 博 市	Zibo	2155	16358	7589	4135	14546	3518	4131	14535	3518
枣 庄 市	Zaozhuang	4410	42693	9681	19456	80491	4137	17672	76377	4322
东 营 市	Dongying	285	2399	8408	522	1851	3544	499	1808	3621
烟 台 市	Yantai	10033	90663	9036	92648	415594	4486	92639	415557	4486
潍 坊 市	Weifang	5756	44074	7657	36817	179443	4874	36767	179328	4877
济 宁 市	Jining	16312	151663	9297	36422	148309	4072	35978	147481	4099
泰 安 市	Tai'an	9194	85327	9281	45511	189755	4169	44921	188359	4193
威 海 市	Weihai	6068	50881	8384	49003	199130	4064	49003	199130	4064
日 照 市	Rizhao	7221	67499	9348	51147	219133	4284	51145	219129	4284
临 沂 市	Linyi	44029	355509	8074	158543	723131	4561	157501	720825	4577
德 州 市	Dezhou	991	9446	9536	2851	12443	4364	2086	9656	4629
聊 城 市	Liaocheng	1192	9885	8293	7777	34408	4424	7235	32958	4555
滨 州 市	Binzhou	412	3268	7922	2154	7655	3554	1936	7158	3697
菏 泽 市	Heze	4582	35862	7826	52857	227598	4306	44645	203535	4559

13-9 续表 6 continued

地 区	Region	#油菜籽 Rapeseeds 播种面积(公顷) Sown Area (hectare)	总产量(吨) Total Output (ton)	单 产(千克/公顷) Output per Hectare (kg/hectare)	#芝 麻 Sesame 播种面积(公顷) Sown Area (hectare)	总产量(吨) Total Output (ton)	单 产(千克/公顷) Output per Hectare (kg/hectare)	三、棉 花 Cotton 播种面积(公顷) Sown Area (hectare)	总产量(吨) Total Output (ton)	单 产(千克/公顷) Output per Hectare (kg/hectare)
全省总计	**Total**	**9263**	**23948**	**2585**	**713**	**1702**	**2387**	**110184**	**140253**	**1273**
济南市	Jinan	1058	2359	2229	147	263	1796	3257	3810	1170
青岛市	Qingdao							57	79	1389
淄博市	Zibo	4	11	3000				898	1163	1295
枣庄市	Zaozhuang	1628	3893	2391	41	47	1153	963	1199	1245
东营市	Dongying	23	43	1854				10410	10915	1049
烟台市	Yantai							2	2	1331
潍坊市	Weifang	6	14	2250	43	99	2317	3797	4339	1143
济宁市	Jining	433	796	1838	2	3	1589	19868	25558	1286
泰安市	Tai'an	546	1319	2416	1	1	1406	3002	3764	1254
威海市	Weihai									
日照市	Rizhao	2	4	1714				163	197	1207
临沂市	Linyi	1022	2165	2120	2	3	1964	1997	2506	1255
德州市	Dezhou	125	312	2507				17001	23433	1378
聊城市	Liaocheng	268	705	2632	2	3	1425	3383	4356	1288
滨州市	Binzhou	150	364	2433	38	77	2041	15384	17167	1116
菏泽市	Heze	3999	11963	2991	439	1206	2747	30002	41764	1392

13-9 续表 7 continued

地 区	Region	四、烟 叶 Tobacco 播种面积(公顷) Sown Area (hectare)	总产量(吨) Total Output (ton)	单 产(千克/公顷) Output per Hectare (kg/hectare)	#烤 烟 Cigarettes 播种面积(公顷) Sown Area (hectare)	总产量(吨) Total Output (ton)	单 产(千克/公顷) Output per Hectare (kg/hectare)	五、中药材播种面积(公顷) Sown Area of Medical Materials (hectare)
全省总计	**Total**	**17974**	**46998**	**2615**	**17881**	**46682**	**2611**	**56913**
济南市	Jinan	647	1560	2413	627	1491	2377	5026
青岛市	Qingdao	355	853	2401	349	841	2411	1027
淄博市	Zibo	344	778	2261	344	777	2260	2490
枣庄市	Zaozhuang							884
东营市	Dongying							143
烟台市	Yantai							302
潍坊市	Weifang	6023	16576	2752	6023	16576	2752	3505
济宁市	Jining							4175
泰安市	Tai'an	7	21	2837	5	12	2199	5087
威海市	Weihai							2825
日照市	Rizhao	2630	6922	2632	2566	6698	2610	3324
临沂市	Linyi	7967	20287	2547	7967	20287	2547	15089
德州市	Dezhou							1313
聊城市	Liaocheng							1595
滨州市	Binzhou							1697
菏泽市	Heze							8431

13-9 续表 8 continued

地 区	Region	六、蔬菜及食用菌 Vegetable and Edible Fungi		#马铃薯 Potato		七、瓜果类 Melon	
		播种面积(公顷) Sown Area (hectare)	总产量(吨) Total Output (ton)	播种面积(公顷) Sown Area (hectare)	总产量(吨) Total Output (ton)	播种面积(公顷) Sown Area (hectare)	总产量(吨) Total Output (ton)
全省总计	**Total**	**1524684**	**88010797**	**133655**	**6823761**	**208717**	**11186717**
济南市	Jinan	97352	6917627	6035	280298	9994	505365
青岛市	Qingdao	109039	6617749	24482	1186353	7745	393121
淄博市	Zibo	26490	1949616	922	38768	1790	100913
枣庄市	Zaozhuang	92295	5480114	41417	2341480	3232	160711
东营市	Dongying	14397	772924	45	2679	3918	195980
烟台市	Yantai	41855	2451274	3315	154550	6115	276062
潍坊市	Weifang	198936	13065619	16655	838645	39808	2428137
济宁市	Jining	168503	7540066	9598	473492	17841	947646
泰安市	Tai'an	101353	5693489	16314	835375	1424	73675
威海市	Weihai	19332	981340	2184	86164	2218	122061
日照市	Rizhao	19256	1160547	1615	76995	2029	108423
临沂市	Linyi	140547	8254267	7932	338896	16422	928099
德州市	Dezhou	103151	6527889	766	39520	4933	288834
聊城市	Liaocheng	149001	9123586	734	45311	15959	918130
滨州市	Binzhou	34111	1752401	368	19449	15285	708547
菏泽市	Heze	209065	9722288	1273	65786	60002	3031013

13-9 续表 9 continued

地 区	Region	#西 瓜 Watermelon		#香瓜(甜瓜) Muskmelon		八、其他农作物播种面积(公顷) Sown Area of Other Farm Crops (hectare)	#青饲料播种面积 Fresh Feed Succulence
		播种面积(公顷) Sown Area (hectare)	总产量(吨) Total Output (ton)	播种面积(公顷) Sown Area (hectare)	总产量(吨) Total Output (ton)		
全省总计	**Total**	**136939**	**7501654**	**46870**	**2439897**	**28192**	**16178**
济南市	Jinan	5394	294690	2415	122158	3000	2935
青岛市	Qingdao	3246	205977	2456	115000	266	260
淄博市	Zibo	1107	71867	216	11308	57	57
枣庄市	Zaozhuang	2287	122885	510	22169	184	137
东营市	Dongying	3094	149299	721	42901	1734	1676
烟台市	Yantai	2815	152332	540	24522	185	136
潍坊市	Weifang	24052	1460496	7403	399587	7000	414
济宁市	Jining	11697	661367	5013	235598	200	158
泰安市	Tai'an	715	43497	467	21651	1906	1560
威海市	Weihai	1085	64290	284	12798	20	
日照市	Rizhao	1087	64495	96	4777	964	653
临沂市	Linyi	6541	402251	5714	333531	1985	350
德州市	Dezhou	4121	238905	654	44352	1640	1548
聊城市	Liaocheng	7257	411513	8296	491902	359	145
滨州市	Binzhou	13353	623366	1754	79032	5616	5525
菏泽市	Heze	49089	2534424	10331	478611	3076	623

13-10 各市茶叶、水果生产情况(2021年)
Production of Tea and Fruits by Region(2021)

单位:吨 (ton)

地 区	Region	茶叶产量 Output of Tea	园林水果产量 Output of Garden Fruits	苹果 Apple	梨 Pear	葡萄 Grape	桃 Peach	杏 Apricot	红枣 Jujube
全省总计	**Total**	**28536**	**19139178**	**9772090**	**1233162**	**1228899**	**4493589**	**173963**	**608030**
济南市	Jinan	590	618972	192585	41635	33287	201225	34662	9667
青岛市	Qingdao	4955	805227	260743	123488	165403	166550	10894	1658
淄博市	Zibo	7	1024022	491498	17367	74027	321490	2429	957
枣庄市	Zaozhuang	26	294164	25668	16310	16567	134815	7055	12256
东营市	Dongying	10	73973	40281	9123	12669	5359	253	4958
烟台市	Yantai	514	7435358	6060957	386130	407206	174085	9575	1758
潍坊市	Weifang	1819	1007647	199706	41401	95299	371184	2219	31134
济宁市	Jining	7	388606	74370	25999	101367	130412	12991	8513
泰安市	Tai'an	1338	587833	169648	30401	22041	160604	31316	2621
威海市	Weihai	686	1199922	1062040	34105	33854	27161	249	169
日照市	Rizhao	16314	453139	134541	13666	8571	252870	1059	762
临沂市	Linyi	2267	3144290	472691	41102	106020	2252491	31146	13839
德州市	Dezhou		303566	64155	45699	21346	53467	3337	99899
聊城市	Liaocheng		503783	213706	108888	56032	85123	3032	2937
滨州市	Binzhou		780013	59808	223396	11074	49000	17657	412951
菏泽市	Heze		518663	249692	74453	64136	107754	6089	3951

13-10 续表 continued

单位:公顷 (hectare)

地 区	Region	柿子(吨) Persimmon (ton)	山楂(吨) Hawthorn (ton)	其他(吨) Others (ton)	年末实有果园面积 Orchard Area at the Year-end	#苹果园 Apple	梨园 Pear	葡萄园 Grape	桃园 Peach
全省总计	**Total**	**104924**	**322036**	**1202484**	**610553**	**243246**	**37536**	**36235**	**140820**
济南市	Jinan	26255	31458	48197	38347	12033	2112	1135	9694
青岛市	Qingdao	1797	2208	72487	31824	8085	3700	4838	6725
淄博市	Zibo	8422	8755	99078	32135	11955	704	2173	9766
枣庄市	Zaozhuang	3450	3926	74117	15128	867	537	665	5472
东营市	Dongying	3	18	1311	3291	1755	399	384	337
烟台市	Yantai	7466	720	387461	179722	132869	9536	10906	4876
潍坊市	Weifang	23515	114314	128874	35856	5485	1134	2783	12408
济宁市	Jining	2519	6180	26256	16633	2786	813	3002	5165
泰安市	Tai'an	4047	33729	133427	32538	7153	1419	834	7192
威海市	Weihai	805	130	41409	33839	26477	1298	1520	1264
日照市	Rizhao	5852	1203	34615	20260	4055	462	398	7929
临沂市	Linyi	14751	111226	101024	93067	12568	1241	2748	60524
德州市	Dezhou	692	2671	12299	11061	1981	1258	629	1588
聊城市	Liaocheng	356	4742	28967	16897	6602	3489	1830	2542
滨州市	Binzhou	1910	314	3902	33673	1649	7338	415	1393
菏泽市	Heze	3083	444	9060	16283	6927	2095	1975	3943

13-11 各市林业生产情况(2021年)

Production of Forestry by Region(2021)

地 区	Region	主要林产品产量(吨) Output of Major Forestry Products(ton)		营林情况(公顷) Forestation(hectare)	
		核桃 Walnut	板栗 Chestnut	当年人工造林面积 Forested Area in the Year	森林抚育面积 Laid out Area of Forest Tending
全省总计	**Total**	**130729**	**256957**	**7137**	**199618**
济南市	Jinan	27585	27934	2931	3426
青岛市	Qingdao	578	1548	17	5713
淄博市	Zibo	5571	3924	272	5193
枣庄市	Zaozhuang	7282	7362	297	5616
东营市	Dongying	40		128	14519
烟台市	Yantai	2066	8031	200	3868
潍坊市	Weifang	10900	36584	196	12294
济宁市	Jining	12280	10293	1019	18434
泰安市	Tai'an	41908	41862	121	3366
威海市	Weihai	308	4547		8642
日照市	Rizhao	1045	19753	422	6454
临沂市	Linyi	18183	95117	767	927
德州市	Dezhou	520			45207
聊城市	Liaocheng	1260		201	19269
滨州市	Binzhou	508	2	154	27283
菏泽市	Heze	695		412	19407

13-12 各市畜牧业生产情况(2021年)

Production of Animal Husbandry by Region(2021)

地 区	Region	大牲畜年末存栏(万头) Stocked Large Livestock at Year-end (10000 hcads)	#牛 Cattle	猪年末存栏(万头) Stocked Pigs at Year-end (10000 heads)	羊年末存栏(万只) Stocked Sheep and Goats at Year-end (10000 heads)	家禽年末存栏(万只) Stocked Poultry at Year-end (10000 heads)	兔年末存栏(万只) Stocked Hare at Year-end (10000 heads)
全省总计	**Total**	**284.61**	**279.76**	**3151.04**	**1466.35**	**84578.07**	**565.41**
济南市	Jinan	17.18	17.16	131.95	73.56	2763.07	4.74
青岛市	Qingdao	15.46	15.37	177.90	19.99	4551.93	16.18
淄博市	Zibo	11.84	11.78	44.54	44.29	1360.21	20.84
枣庄市	Zaozhuang	3.76	3.51	79.05	56.28	1536.78	36.38
东营市	Dongying	17.56	17.54	118.17	173.40	2413.22	3.89
烟台市	Yantai	12.61	12.56	303.14	42.66	6342.82	1.30
潍坊市	Weifang	18.07	17.86	374.10	66.85	13130.67	21.35
济宁市	Jining	23.09	22.95	222.37	143.28	3558.83	24.88
泰安市	Tai'an	12.49	12.48	106.70	69.53	3732.30	20.21
威海市	Weihai	2.46	2.44	85.49	4.75	2046.95	0.01
日照市	Rizhao	6.00	5.89	113.93	22.45	3432.93	38.87
临沂市	Linyi	29.45	28.68	374.47	198.64	12744.76	283.89
德州市	Dezhou	41.05	40.69	329.51	88.26	5681.81	11.00
聊城市	Liaocheng	9.79	7.80	168.77	90.93	9622.01	39.75
滨州市	Binzhou	38.55	38.30	178.85	85.99	5050.13	1.47
菏泽市	Heze	25.26	24.76	342.07	285.48	6609.66	40.65

13-12 续表 1 continued

地 区	Region	牛 当年出栏 (万头) Slaughtered Cattle in the Year (10000 heads)	猪 当年出栏 (万头) Slaughtered Pigs in the Year (10000 heads)	羊 当年出栏 (万只) Slaughtered Sheep and Goats in the Year (10000 heads)	家禽 当年出栏 (万只) Slaughtered Poultry in the Year (10000 heads)	兔 当年出栏 (万只) Slaughtered Hare in the Year (10000 heads)
全省总计	**Total**	**280.03**	**4401.74**	**2373.39**	**263535.68**	**1963.09**
济南市	Jinan	13.75	192.00	126.84	5257.10	12.36
青岛市	Qingdao	6.87	262.24	38.29	20305.86	92.55
淄博市	Zibo	12.10	69.30	83.00	3739.60	113.54
枣庄市	Zaozhuang	4.99	101.96	91.81	4144.52	123.50
东营市	Dongying	11.63	127.48	273.28	8763.53	12.50
烟台市	Yantai	13.14	442.73	84.01	22410.56	3.10
潍坊市	Weifang	17.47	492.96	125.08	49828.11	75.33
济宁市	Jining	23.25	323.85	212.78	7446.96	83.88
泰安市	Tai'an	8.00	150.17	121.65	11219.16	63.76
威海市	Weihai	2.72	112.20	7.44	5829.21	
日照市	Rizhao	5.57	140.74	39.42	9710.36	199.92
临沂市	Linyi	33.99	531.43	311.65	39167.48	762.76
德州市	Dezhou	35.72	458.73	162.28	15533.23	50.28
聊城市	Liaocheng	8.37	246.45	151.21	32507.09	254.88
滨州市	Binzhou	57.97	240.90	124.81	15370.71	7.61
菏泽市	Heze	24.50	508.59	419.82	12302.18	107.12

13-12 续表 2 continued

单位:吨 (ton)

地 区	Region	肉类总产量 Output of Meat	#牛肉 Beef	#猪肉 Pork	#羊肉 Mutton	#禽肉 Poultry Meat	奶类产量 Output of Milk	#牛奶 Cow Milk
全省总计	**Total**	**8192628**	**613000**	**3558560**	**330100**	**3649074**	**2883705**	**2882554**
济南市	Jinan	273576	28807	154189	18642	71686	420987	420987
青岛市	Qingdao	505481	14311	213246	5581	270847	332484	332484
淄博市	Zibo	149309	25431	55346	10538	55269	133917	133891
枣庄市	Zaozhuang	165025	10929	82276	11956	57581	31828	31828
东营市	Dongying	295476	24671	102672	39799	128111	376014	376014
烟台市	Yantai	719813	27972	361745	10009	319962	153224	152540
潍坊市	Weifang	1145643	37728	395059	16627	694844	191480	191250
济宁市	Jining	464046	51403	264249	32346	114275	138706	138706
泰安市	Tai'an	313618	16894	120666	15066	159337	252583	252538
威海市	Weihai	183970	5461	89444	1320	87725	41374	41374
日照市	Rizhao	270718	12231	113285	5205	137471	65820	65820
临沂市	Linyi	1096354	71493	427684	39633	544276	128468	128345
德州市	Dezhou	678516	78368	372259	21422	203863	265579	265579
聊城市	Liaocheng	654265	17980	200949	23468	404061	80787	80753
滨州市	Binzhou	564986	137984	196509	17771	212423	89378	89378
菏泽市	Heze	711833	51338	408981	60716	187343	181075	181066

13-12 续表 3 continued

单位:吨 (ton)

地 区	Region	羊毛产量 Output of Wool	山羊毛 Goat Wool	绵羊毛 Sheep Wool	禽蛋产量 Poultry Eggs	蚕茧产量 Output of Cocoon	# 桑蚕茧 Cocoon	# 柞蚕茧 Oak Cocoon
全省总计	**Total**	**5762**	**378**	**5384**	**4566425**	**11089**	**11076**	**14**
济 南 市	Jinan	61	12	49	305052	2	2	
青 岛 市	Qingdao	15		14	290067	1	1	
淄 博 市	Zibo	77	40	37	130597	71	71	
枣 庄 市	Zaozhuang	42	4	38	94745			
东 营 市	Dongying	3271	1	3270	61299			
烟 台 市	Yantai	28	2	26	225551	4	2	2
潍 坊 市	Weifang	285	2	283	381871	737	737	
济 宁 市	Jining	438	102	336	402617			
泰 安 市	Tai'an	344	47	297	144956	509	505	4
威 海 市	Weihai	1		1	188762	5		5
日 照 市	Rizhao	46	6	39	149522	842	838	3
临 沂 市	Linyi	253	107	146	452038	8430	8430	
德 州 市	Dezhou	58	3	54	483381			
聊 城 市	Liaocheng	471	1	470	530664			
滨 州 市	Binzhou	199	1	197	258083			
菏 泽 市	Heze	173	47	126	467219	489	489	

13-13 各市水产品产量和养殖面积(2021年)

Output and Breeding Area of Aquatic Products by Region (2021)

地 区	Region	水产品总产量(吨) Total Aquatic Products (ton)	海水产品 Seawater Aquatic products	海洋捕捞 Ocean Fishing	海水养殖 Seawater Cultured	淡水产品产量 Freshwater Aquatic Products
全省总计	**Total**	**8544248**	**7403008**	**2029166**	**5373842**	**1141240**
济 南 市	Jinan	14068				14068
青 岛 市	Qingdao	1012560	996374	198082	798292	16186
淄 博 市	Zibo	19698				19698
枣 庄 市	Zaozhuang	68275				68275
东 营 市	Dongying	510546	419890	66782	353108	90656
烟 台 市	Yantai	1800948	1793035	480623	1312412	7913
潍 坊 市	Weifang	490522	466421	103421	363000	24101
济 宁 市	Jining	275689				275689
泰 安 市	Tai'an	83919				83919
威 海 市	Weihai	2613844	2591888	637802	1954086	21956
日 照 市	Rizhao	456085	437464	157432	280032	18621
临 沂 市	Linyi	123285				123285
德 州 市	Dezhou	60376				60376
聊 城 市	Liaocheng	61611				61611
滨 州 市	Binzhou	530088	360568	47656	312912	169520
菏 泽 市	Heze	85366				85366
省属远洋捕捞企业	Provincial Ocean Fishing Enterprises	6543	6543	6543		

注：本表全省水产品产量数据含远洋产量。

a)The total output of aquatic products of the whole province in this table includes ocean going aquatic products.

13-13 续表 continued

地 区	Region	内陆捕捞 Landlocked Fishing	内陆养殖 Landlocked Cultured	水产品养殖面积（公顷） Breeding Area of Aquatic Products (hectare)	海水养殖 Seawater Cultured	内陆养殖 Landlocked Cultured
全省总计	**Total**	**95733**	**1045507**	**765213**	**608376**	**156837**
济南市	Jinan	1187	12881	4336		4336
青岛市	Qingdao	184	16002	37254	34286	2968
淄博市	Zibo	732	18966	2675		2675
枣庄市	Zaozhuang	3014	65261	9241		9241
东营市	Dongying	2422	88234	107092	93049	14043
烟台市	Yantai	2448	5465	203968	201138	2830
潍坊市	Weifang	3263	20838	64407	60389	4018
济宁市	Jining	41897	233792	34155		34155
泰安市	Tai'an	17700	66219	9289		9289
威海市	Weihai		21956	109794	107228	2566
日照市	Rizhao	2223	16398	42047	37206	4841
临沂市	Linyi	10697	112588	24952		24952
德州市	Dezhou	642	59734	5796		5796
聊城市	Liaocheng	1671	59940	4838		4838
滨州市	Binzhou	2690	166830	90471	75080	15391
菏泽市	Heze	4963	80403	14898		14898
省属远洋捕捞企业	Provincial Ocean Fishing Enterprises					

13-14 主要农业机械年末拥有量

Major Agricultural Machinery at the Year-end

类 别	单位	Category	Unit	2020	2021
农业机械总动力	**(万千瓦)**	**total power of agricultural machinery**	**(10000 kW)**	**10964.66**	**11186.07**
一、拖拉机及配套机械		**Tractors and related machinery**			
拖拉机	(万台)	Tractor	(10000 units)	248.00	245.01
	(万千瓦)		(10000 kW)	4423.73	4496.39
#大中型(22.1千瓦以上)	(万台)	Large and Medium-sized(14.7 kW and above)	(10000 units)	50.41	51.68
	(万千瓦)		(10000 kW)	2577.73	2672.36
拖拉机配套农具	(万部)	Tractor Supporting Tools	(10000 units)	440.95	440.14
#与58.8千瓦及以上拖拉机配套	(万部)	Large and Medium-sized	(10000 units)	59.24	60.49
二、种植业机械		**Farming Machinery**			
机引犁	(万台)	Mechanical Power Plow	(10000 units)	137.98	137.72
旋耕机	(万台)	Rotary Tiller	(10000 units)	36.69	37.58
免耕播种机	(万台)	No-tillage Seeder	(10000 units)	18.18	18.60
精量播种机	(万台)	Precision Seeder	(10000 units)	36.59	37.71
农用水泵	(万台)	Agricultural Water-pump	(10000 units)	295.59	295.28
节水灌溉类机械	(万套)	Water-saving Irrigation Machinery	(10000 units)	54.37	54.68
谷物联合收割机	(万台)	Combine Harvester	(10000 units)	33.05	33.61
	(万千瓦)		(10000 kW)	1728.76	1818.91
#玉米联合收割机	(万台)	Corn Combine Harvester	(10000 units)	13.95	14.24
秸秆粉碎还田机	(万台)	Straw crushing Machinery	(10000 units)	14.70	15.11
机动脱粒机	(万台)	Thresher	(10000 units)	40.19	40.27
三、畜牧机械	**(万台)**	**Animal Husbandry Machinery**	**(10000 units)**	**27.40**	**34.62**
	(万千瓦)		(10000 kW)	155.33	182.07
四、水产机械	**(万台)**	**Fishery Machinery**	**(10000 units)**	**16.97**	**17.46**
	(万千瓦)		(10000 kW)	111.12	111.01
五、农产品初加工机械		**Agricultural Products Primary Processing Machinery**			
农产品初加工动力机械	(万台)	Agricultural Products Primary Processing Power Machinery	(10000 units)	100.20	100.41
	(万千瓦)		(10000 kW)	902.46	916.01
农产品初加工作业机械	(万台)	Agricultural Products Primary Processing Operating Machinery	(10000 units)	52.11	52.38
六、农田基本建设机械	**(万台)**	**Farmland Capital Construction Machinery**	**(10000 units)**	**4.44**	**4.47**
	(万千瓦)		(10000 kW)	291.44	293.69
七、其他机械		**Other Machinery**			
#农用航空器	(架)	Agricultural Aircraft	(unit)	7566	10129

注：部分指标统计口径、指标名称进行提升和更名。

a)Some indicators have been updated and renamed with statistical caliber and indicator names.

13−15 各市主要农业机械年末拥有量(2021年)

Number of Major Agricultural Machinery at the Year-end by Region(2021)

地区 Region	农业机械总动力(千瓦) total power of agricultural machinery (kW)	#拖拉机及配套机械 Tractors and related machinery			#谷物联合收割机 Combine Harvester	
		拖拉机 Tractor		拖拉机配套农具 Tractor Supporting Tools		
		(台) (unit)	(千瓦) (kW)	(部) (unit)	(台) (unit)	(千瓦) (kW)
全省总计 Total	**111860715**	**2450109**	**44963852**	**4401391**	**336120**	**18189059**
济南市 Jinan	5701072	73759	1815035	125205	16838	906154
青岛市 Qingdao	7572981	210358	3778933	446112	18048	1099541
淄博市 Zibo	2471018	18678	782294	42050	6196	511703
枣庄市 Zaozhuang	3278707	38868	1318991	124166	12907	911371
东营市 Dongying	2752649	53122	1364733	124504	9460	511437
烟台市 Yantai	7914215	284371	3321542	360122	9930	509862
潍坊市 Weifang	10826356	177987	3922586	285562	27790	1776666
济宁市 Jining	9954809	109864	3106729	222226	38980	1511902
泰安市 Tai'an	5534833	92233	1954206	168118	21996	877234
威海市 Weihai	5039845	258218	2530335	542609	5482	215888
日照市 Rizhao	2912371	145840	1384002	501979	2738	143907
临沂市 Linyi	8317210	474277	5517294	639048	18481	993891
德州市 Dezhou	12779171	254536	5199181	304766	43952	2395218
聊城市 Liaocheng	10762845	83734	2979503	153048	36695	1903233
滨州市 Binzhou	5105107	80419	2100637	137341	21779	1030857
菏泽市 Heze	10937526	93845	3887851	224535	44848	2890196

13-16 各市地类面积(2020年)
Land Category Area by Region(2020)

单位:公顷 (hectare)

地 区	Region	农用地 Agricultural Land	#耕地 Cultivated Land	#水浇地 Irrigated Land	#园 地 Garden Land	#牧草地 Grazing and Pasture Land
全省总计	**Total**	**11697673**	**6409531**	**4642245**	**1264409**	**10**
济南市	Jinan	757429	342289	268186	102050	
青岛市	Qingdao	811447	432091	230374	81771	
淄博市	Zibo	438400	157886	114527	79093	
枣庄市	Zaozhuang	343050	203405	118864	50015	
东营市	Dongying	477709	217284	152323	5273	10
烟台市	Yantai	1091902	352037	130016	329543	
潍坊市	Weifang	1161529	657625	431054	95296	
济宁市	Jining	766355	502917	384848	26880	
泰安市	Tai'an	590784	280810	186280	69411	
威海市	Weihai	453347	162712	26154	67732	
日照市	Rizhao	418767	179841	42779	45408	
临沂市	Linyi	1337329	624697	276715	230376	
德州市	Dezhou	818158	631263	631127	9839	
聊城市	Liaocheng	670227	510919	510876	18537	
滨州市	Binzhou	629481	387877	376318	37213	
菏泽市	Heze	931760	765878	761802	15974	

注：数据来源于2020年度国土变更调查。
a)The data in this table come from the 2020 National Land Changing Survey.

13-17 各市灌溉面积

Irrigated Area by Region

单位：千公顷 (1000 hectares)

地 区	Region	有效灌溉面积 Effective Irrigated Area		#当年实灌 Irrigated in the Year		林地灌溉面积 Irrigated Area of Forest Lands		果园灌溉面积 Irrigated Area of Orchard	
		2020年	2021年	2020年	2021年	2020年	2021年	2020年	2021年
全省总计	**Total**	**5293.56**	**5329.30**	**4689.09**	**4572.91**	**236.08**	**248.11**	**366.48**	**353.11**
济南市	Jinan	293.98	289.78	265.34	277.82	10.14	13.71	10.87	8.64
青岛市	Qingdao	328.88	328.78	280.70	270.93	16.37	16.37	29.26	29.26
淄博市	Zibo	127.44	127.53	126.91	127.00	5.19	4.83	40.43	40.43
枣庄市	Zaozhuang	171.17	171.17	131.52	122.93	3.56	3.56	9.65	9.65
东营市	Dongying	196.56	196.56	184.01	170.77	9.97	9.97	5.36	5.36
烟台市	Yantai	247.08	246.43	213.21	207.76	7.16	7.12	74.04	72.17
潍坊市	Weifang	534.51	541.93	350.74	358.91	32.29	33.22	44.08	37.63
济宁市	Jining	475.83	477.23	459.65	456.30	14.58	14.58	8.40	8.40
泰安市	Tai'an	248.81	250.24	242.93	237.06	5.91	6.52	15.49	15.32
威海市	Weihai	129.02	129.02	95.71	95.71	1.05	1.05	19.32	19.32
日照市	Rizhao	114.83	101.98	56.04	62.88	6.91	6.39	14.21	11.23
临沂市	Linyi	365.17	360.59	305.03	295.66	34.46	33.80	32.34	31.76
德州市	Dezhou	523.78	525.08	517.24	462.93	28.60	39.13	17.01	18.46
聊城市	Liaocheng	510.76	510.10	505.76	505.10	9.31	9.07	16.72	16.05
滨州市	Binzhou	379.35	382.99	342.39	344.00	11.64	9.83	8.39	8.38
菏泽市	Heze	646.39	689.89	611.91	577.15	38.95	38.96	20.91	21.05

13-18 各市农村电气化和农业化学化情况(2021年)

Rural Electrification and Agriculture Chemicals by Region(2021)

单位：吨 (ton)

地 区	Region	农用化肥施用量(实物量) Consumption of Chemical Fertilizer (physical volume)	氮肥 Nitrogenous Fertilizer	磷肥 Phosphate Fertilizer	钾肥 Potash Fertilizer	复合肥 Compound Fertilizer	农用化肥施用量(折纯量) Consumption of Chemical Fertilizer (convert to pure volume)	氮肥 Nitrogenous Fertilizer	磷肥 Phosphate Fertilizer
全省总计	**Total**	**11114128**	**3447743**	**1464082**	**870677**	**5331627**	**3710289**	**1045314**	**323179**
济南市	Jinan	674551	236912	111808	49673	276158	199919	56438	21096
青岛市	Qingdao	668480	114775	45411	40322	467972	248971	30749	9664
淄博市	Zibo	248506	70340	28462	14818	134886	79440	20054	5909
枣庄市	Zaozhuang	541662	177538	26198	26794	311131	182512	53856	5785
东营市	Dongying	223186	52576	18386	6530	145695	83380	17957	4789
烟台市	Yantai	916215	257475	102890	93534	462316	320332	88049	25708
潍坊市	Weifang	1087614	189648	77608	70911	749447	401845	62593	18589
济宁市	Jining	950018	298257	145717	84764	421280	334075	99563	34609
泰安市	Tai'an	539802	138318	58891	48603	293991	178838	32037	13121
威海市	Weihai	315012	102154	36338	36821	139699	93294	26438	8047
日照市	Rizhao	246828	59512	23708	21513	142095	77021	17216	6744
临沂市	Linyi	1028974	354549	96594	103723	474108	299720	83618	21479
德州市	Dezhou	913632	382258	150804	60050	320521	290324	116277	33012
聊城市	Liaocheng	900511	318626	163118	63342	355425	315965	106613	36926
滨州市	Binzhou	515466	196425	54119	30509	234413	185046	64519	15720
菏泽市	Heze	1343669	498380	324029	118770	402490	419606	169336	61981

注：本表农村用电量数据来源于国网山东电力公司。
a)The data of rural electricity consumption in this table come from State Grid Shandong Electric Power Company.

13-18 续表 continued

单位:吨 (ton)

地 区	Region	钾 肥 Potash Fertilizer	复合肥 Compound Fertilizer	农用塑料薄膜使用量 Plastic Film Consumption	地 膜 使用量 Film Consumption	农 用 柴油量 Diesel Consumption	农 药 施用量 Pesticides Consumption	地 膜 覆盖面积 (公顷) Film Coverage (hectare)	农村用电量 (万千瓦时) Electricity Consumption in Rural Area (10000 kW·h)
全省总计	**Total**	**296966**	**2044830**	**259678**	**91599**	**1222315**	**108230**	**1610536**	**5077556**
济南市	Jinan	17015	105369	11709	4517	47472	2961	69085	452059
青岛市	Qingdao	15179	193379	16975	7219	138363	5107	133242	442451
淄博市	Zibo	4998	48478	5268	1220	15134	3524	18007	181073
枣庄市	Zaozhuang	9002	113870	7804	2783	14398	2836	35417	144584
东营市	Dongying	2503	58131	2403	1404	17869	2200	28097	403656
烟台市	Yantai	34169	172407	9227	6039	144512	14725	109846	540835
潍坊市	Weifang	27784	292880	71686	12160	112804	9878	176686	385515
济宁市	Jining	31965	167938	11538	7663	79406	10935	130183	221484
泰安市	Tai'an	15511	118169	9311	4116	41155	5165	71167	291405
威海市	Weihai	13389	45420	3065	1861	220861	7143	29747	350570
日照市	Rizhao	7137	45924	6059	3688	101954	2634	68324	218556
临沂市	Linyi	30116	164507	36779	12161	74440	10393	232766	579431
德州市	Dezhou	19271	121763	15784	7105	55070	8885	159748	475595
聊城市	Liaocheng	22133	150293	22813	5595	61026	7427	110171	127259
滨州市	Binzhou	10934	93874	5682	2691	27874	5274	57865	109021
菏泽市	Heze	35860	152428	23574	11378	69977	9143	180183	154063

主要统计指标解释

农林牧渔业总产值 指以货币表现的农、林、牧、渔业全部产品和对农林牧渔业生产活动进行的各种支持性服务活动的价值总量，它反映一定时期内农林牧渔业生产总规模和总成果。1957年以前的农林牧渔业总产值中包括了厩肥和农民自给性手工业(如农民自制衣服、鞋、袜，自己从事粮食初步加工等)。1958 年及以后，林业中增加了村及村以下竹木采伐产值；牧业中取消了厩肥产值；副业中取消了农民自给性手工业产值，增加了村及村以下办的工业产值；渔业中增加了海洋捕捞水产品产值。1980 年及以后，在副业中增加了农民家庭兼营工业商品部分的产值。从 1984 年起村及村以下工业产值划归工业。从 1993 年起取消副业，将野生动物的捕猎划入牧业，野生植物采集和农民家庭兼营商品性工业划归农业。从 2003 年起，执行新的国民经济行业分类标准，农林牧渔业总产值中包括了农林牧渔服务业产值。(2017国民经济行业分类标准中将“农林牧渔服务业”改为“农林牧渔专业及辅助性活动”)。林业中增加了森林采运业产值。农业中取消了家庭兼营商品性工业产值，将野生林产品的采集划归林业。

农林牧渔业总产值的计算方法通常是按农、林、牧、渔业产品及其副产品的产量分别乘以各自单位产品价格求得；少数生产周期较长，当年没有产品或产品产量不易统计的，则采用间接方法匡算其产值；然后将四业产品产值及农林牧渔专业及辅助性活动产值相加即为农林牧渔业总产值。

粮食产量 指日历年度内生产的全部粮食数量。按收获季节包括夏收粮食、早稻和秋收粮食，按作物品种包括谷物、豆类和薯类。其产量计算方法：谷物按脱粒后的原粮计算，豆类按去豆荚后的干豆计算；薯类(包括甘薯和马铃薯，不包括芋头和木薯)1964 年以前按每 4 公斤鲜薯折 1 公斤粮食计算，从 1964 年开始改为按 5 公斤鲜薯折 1 公斤粮食计算；城市郊区作为蔬菜的薯类(如马铃薯等)按鲜品计算，并且不作粮食统计。1989 年以前全国粮食产量数据主要靠全面报表取得，1989 年开始使用抽样调查数据。

棉花产量 指全社会的产量。包括春播棉和夏播棉。产量按皮棉计算。不包括木棉。

油料产量 指全部油料作物的生产量。包括花生、油菜籽、芝麻、向日葵籽、胡麻籽（亚麻籽）和其他油料。不包括大豆、木本油料和野生油料。花生以带壳干花生计算。

水产品产量 指人工养殖的水产品和天然生长的水产品的捕捞量。包括海水的鱼类、虾蟹类、贝类和藻类以及内陆水域的鱼类、虾蟹类和贝类，不包括淡水生植物。水产品产量是通过各级水产和统计部门逐级上报取得数据。1995 年及以前，贝类中牡蛎按鲜肉计算；蚶、蛤、蛙按 5 斤鲜品折 1 斤计算。1996 年以后则统一按鲜品计算。

猪、牛、羊肉产量 指当年出栏并已屠宰、除去头蹄下水后带骨肉(即胴体重)的重量。包括全社会范围内的产量。由于畜牧业产品年报数据与普查数据之间存在一定的差距，

根据国家统计局有关文件精神，从 2000 年起，对畜牧业年报数据与普查数据进行衔接。

期初(末)畜禽存栏头(只)数 指报告期初(末)农村各种合作经济组织和国营农场、农民个人、机关、团体、学校、工矿企业、部队等单位以及城镇居民饲养的大牲畜、猪、羊、家禽（鸡、鸭、鹅）等畜禽的存栏数。数据上报方式及数据调整情况同猪、牛、羊肉产量。

农作物播种面积 指实际播种或移植有农作物的面积。凡是实际种植有农作物的面积，不论种植在耕地上还是种植在非耕地上，均包括在农作物播种面积中。在播种季节基本结束后，因遭灾而重新改种和补种的农作物面积，也包括在内。它是反映我国耕地面积利用情况的一个重要指标。目前，农作物播种面积主要包括粮食、棉花、油料、糖料、麻类、烟叶、蔬菜和瓜类、药材和其他农作物九大类。

有效灌溉面积 指具有一定的水源，地块比较平整，灌溉工程或设备已经配套，在一般年景下，当年能够进行正常灌溉的耕地面积。在一般情况下，有效灌溉面积应等于灌溉工程或设备已经配备，能够进行正常灌溉的水田和水浇地面积之和。它是反映我国耕地抗旱能力的一个重要指标。

农用化肥施用量 指本年内实际用于农业生产的化肥数量，包括氮肥、磷肥、钾肥和复合肥。化肥施用量要求按折纯量计算数量。折纯量是指把氮肥、磷肥、钾肥分别按含氮、含五氧化二磷、含氧化钾的百分之百成分进行折算后的数量。复合肥按其所含主要成分折算。公式为：

折纯量=实物量×某种化肥有效成分含量的百分比

农业机械总动力 指主要用于农、林、牧、渔业的各种动力机械的动力总和。包括耕作机械、排灌机械、收获机械、农用运输机械、植物保护机械、牧业机械、林业机械、渔业机械和其他农业机械〔内燃机按引擎马力折成瓦(特)计算、电动机按功率折成瓦(特)计算〕。不包括专门用于乡、镇、村、组办工业、基本建设、非农业运输、科学试验和教学等非农业生产方面用的动力机械与作业机械。这个指标的统计数据主要来源于农机部门。

Explanatory Notes on Main Statistical Indicators

Gross Output Value of Farming, Forestry, Animal Husbandry and Fishery refers to the total value of products of farming, forestry, animal husbandry and fishery, and total value of services rendered to support farming, forestry, animal husbandry and fishery activities. It reflects the total scale and results of agricultural production during a given period. Prior to 1957, China's gross agricultural output value included barnyard manure and handicraft products for self consumption (clothes, shoes, stockings, and initial grain processing undertaken by peasants). Since 1958, cutting and felling of bamboo and trees by villages and other cooperative organizations under villages have been included in forestry; value of barnyard manure has been excluded from animal husbandry; self consumed handicrafts has been excluded from sideline occupations, while the output value of industries run by villages and cooperative organizations under village had been included in sideline occupations and the output value of fish catches by motor fishing boats has been added to fishery. Since 1980, the value of handicraft products made for sale by individuals in households had been added to sideline occupations. Since 1984, industries run by villages and under villages have been included in the sector of industry. Since 1993, the subdivision of sideline occupations has been canceled, and the hunting of wild animals has been classified into animal husbandry, and the gathering of wild plants and commodity industry run by rural household have been included in farming. A new industrial classification of economic activities was introduced in 2003. Under the new classification, value of services to farming, forestry, animal husbandry and fishery is included in the gross output value of agriculture, (In the 2017 National Economic Industry Classification Standard, Farming, forestry, animal husbandry and fishery service was changed to Farming, forestry, animal husbandry and fishery professions and auxillary activities).value of wood felling and transport is included in forestry, value of industrial output by rural households is not included in agriculture, and the collection of wild forest products is taken from agriculture and included in the forestry. The first agriculture census of China revealed some discrepancy between the production of animal products from the annual reports and that from the census. Efforts were made by the Rural Socio economic Survey Organization of NBS to adjust the output value of animal husbandry to make the figures from the annual reports consistent with the census data.

Gross output value of agriculture is obtained by first multiplying the output of each product or by product by its price, resulting in the output value of each single item. For a small number of products, annual output of which is not available or difficult to get due to the long production (growing) process involved, the output value is estimated through an indirect approach. The sum of output value of all products of farming, forestry, animal husbandry, fishery and output value of agriculture, forestry, animal husbandry and fishery specialty and auxiliary activities then equal to the gross output value of agriculture.

Grain Output refers to the total output of grains produced within a calendar year. It includes summer crops, early rice and autumn crops by harvest seasons; and covers cereals, beans and tubers by type of crops. Output of cereals cover husked grain only. Output of beans refers to dry beans without pods. The output of tubers (sweet potatoes and potatoes, not including taros and cassava) are converted with the ratio of 4:1, i.e. 4 kilograms of fresh tubers were equivalent to 1 kilogram of grain before 1964. Since 1964 the ratio has been changed to 5:1. Tubers consumed as vegetables (such as potatoes) in cities and suburbs are calculated as fresh vegetables and their output is not included in the output of grain. Data on grain production before 1989 were obtained through the comprehensive statistical reporting system. Since 1989, data from sample surveys are used.

Cotton Output refers to the cotton production in the whole country including cotton sown in spring and in autumn. Output is measured as the weight of ginned cotton. Ceiba is not included.

Output of Oil-bearing Crops refers to the total production of oil bearing crops of various kinds, including peanuts, (dry, in shell) rapeseeds, sesame, sunflower seeds, flax seeds, and other oil bearing crops. Soybeans, oil bearing woody plants, and wild oil bearing crops are not included.

Output of Aquatic Products refers to catches of both artificially cultured and naturally grown aquatic products, including fish, shrimps, crabs and shellfish in sea and inland water as well as seaweed. Freshwater plants are not included. Data on output of aquatic products are reported by aquatic product and statistical agencies level by level. Before 1995, among the shellfish, the oyster was counted as fresh meat; 5 kilograms of ark shell, clams and frogs are equivalent to 1 kilogram of fresh aquatic products; they are all counted as fresh aquatic products since 1996.

Output of Pork, Beef, and Mutton refers to the meat of slaughtered hogs, cattle, sheep and goats with head, feet, and offal taken away. Data refers to the production of the whole country. The first agriculture census of China in 1996 revealed some discrepancy between the production of animal products from the annual reports and that from the census. Efforts were made by the Rural Socio economic Survey Organization of NBS to adjust the output value of animal husbandry to make the figures from the annual reports consistent with the census data. Since 1999, NBS conducted sample survey for the major animal husbandry products, such as hogs, cattle, sheep and goats and fowls, and the data from sample surveys are used as national finalized data. Those products, which are not covered by the sample survey, are still reported by statistical agencies level by level.

Number of Livestock or Poultry in Stock at Beginning (or End) refers to the total number of large animals, pigs, sheep, fowls, （chicken,duck,goose） etc. raised by rural cooperative organizations, state farms, rural individuals, government agencies, schools, industrial and mining enterprises, army, and urban residents at the beginning (or end) of the reference period. Data reporting system and data adjustment are the same as that in the output of pork, beef and mutton.

Sown Area of Crops refers to area of land sown or transplanted with crops regardless of being in cultivated area or non cultivated area. Area of land re sown due to natural disasters is also included. This is an important indicator that can reflect the utilization condition of the cultivated land in China. At present, the sown area of crops mainly include the following 9 categories of crops: grain, cotton, oil bearing crops, sugar crops, fiber crops, Tobacco, Vegetables and melons, medicinal materials and other farm crops.

Irrigated Area refers to areas that are effectively irrigated, i.e. level land, which has water source and complete sets of irrigation facilities to lift and move adequate water for irrigation purpose under normal conditions. Under normal conditions, irrigated area is the sum of watered fields and irrigated fields where irrigation systems or equipment have been installed for regular irrigation purpose. This important indicator reflects drought resistance capacity of the cultivated land in China.

Consumption of Chemical Fertilizers in Agriculture refers to the quantity of chemical fertilizers applied in agriculture in the year, including nitrogenous fertilizer, phosphate fertilizer, potash fertilizer, and compound fertilizer. The consumption of chemical fertilizers is required in calculation to convert the gross weight into weight containing 100% effective component (e.g. 100% nitrogen content in nitrogenous fertilizer, 100% phosphorous pent oxide contents in phosphate fertilizer, 100% potassium oxide contents in potash fertilizer). Compound fertilizer is converted with its major component. The formula is:

Volume of effective component=physical quantity×effective component of certain chemical fertilizer (%)

Total Power of Farm Machinery refers to total mechanical power of machinery used in farming, forestry, animal husbandry, and fishery, including ploughing, irrigation and drainage, harvesting, transport, plant protection, stock breeding, forestry and fishery. The power of internal combustion engines is required to convert horsepower into watts and the power of electric motors is required to be converted into watts. Machinery employed for non agricultural purposes, such as the machines used in township run and village run industry, construction, non agricultural transport, scientific experiments and teaching, is excluded. Data are mainly from agricultural machinery agencies.

第14篇

工　业

Industry

简 要 说 明

一、本篇资料的主要内容

本篇资料反映全省规模以上工业生产和效益基本情况，主要包括规模以上工业、国有控股工业、外商投资和港澳台投资工业、非公有制工业的主要经济指标、相关的财务分析指标和主要工业产品产量等方面的内容。

二、本篇资料的统计范围

本篇资料中规模以上工业企业的统计范围：2007 年至 2010 年为年主营业务收入 500 万元及以上的工业法人单位；从 2011 年开始，为年主营业务收入 2000 万元及以上的工业法人单位。

三、本篇资料的来源

本篇资料主要来源于工业统计年报，由省统计局工业统计处整理提供。

四、数据使用注意事项

2018 年以来规模以上工业企业主要指标数据与往年数据之间存在不可比因素，其主要原因是：（一）根据统计制度，每年定期对规模以上工业企业调查范围进行调整。每年有部分企业达到规模标准纳入调查范围，也有部分企业因规模变小而退出调查范围，还有新建投产企业、破产、注（吊）销企业等变化。（二）加强统计执法，对统计执法检查中发现的不符合规模以上工业统计要求的企业进行了清理，对相关基数依规进行了修正。（三）加强数据质量管理，剔除跨地区、跨行业重复统计数据。根据国家统计局开展的企业组织结构调查情况，对企业集团（公司）跨地区、跨行业重复计算进行了剔重。（四）“营改增”政策实施后，服务业企业改交增值税且税率较低，工业企业逐步将内部非工业生产经营活动剥离，转向服务业，使工业企业财务数据有所减小。

Brief Introduction

I. Content

Data in this chapter show the basic condition of industrial enterprises above designated size in Shandong, mainly including the output of major industrial products and major economic and relevant financial indicators of industrial enterprises. Industrial enterprises include enterprises above designated size, state-holding enterprises, foreign funded enterprises, enterprises with funds from Hong Kong, Macao and Taiwan, Non-public Industrial Enterprises.

II. Scopes of Statistics

The scopes of industrial enterprises above designated size were: all industrial enterprises with revenue from principal business over 5 million yuan from 2007 to 2010; and all industrial enterprises with revenue from principal business above 20 million yuan since 2011.

III.Source of Data

Data in this chapter are based on the annual report of industrial statistics and are prepared and provide by the Division of Industry Statistics of Shandong Provincial Bureau of Statistics.

Ⅳ. Data Usage Notes

Since 2018，Data of main indicators of industrial enterprises above designated size are not comparable with previous years, the reasons are as following: (1) According to the statistical system, the investigation scope of industrial enterprises above designated size should be adjusted regularly every year. Every year, some enterprises meet the scale criteria to be included in the scope of investigation, some enterprises withdraw from the scope of investigation because of the smaller scale, and there are other changes: new enterprises, bankruptcy, annotation (cancellation) enterprises, etc. (2) Strengthening of statistical law enforcement, cleaning up enterprises found in the inspection of statistical law enforcement that do not meet the standard of industrial statistics above designated size, and amending the relevant cardinality in accordance with regulations. (3) Strengthening data quality management and eliminating duplicated statistical data across regions and across industries. According to the latest survey of organizational structure of enterprises carried out by the National Bureau of Statistics, the repeated calculation of enterprise groups (companies) across regions and industries is weighed. (4) After the implementation of the program to replace the business tax with a value-added tax, the value-added tax was paid by the service enterprises and the tax rate was lower. The industrial enterprises gradually stripped off the internal non-industrial production and operation activities and turned to the service industry, which reduced the financial data of the industrial enterprises.

14-1 规模以上工业企业主要经济指标(2021年)

Main Economic Indicators of Industrial Enterprises above Designated Size(2021)

单位:亿元 (100 million yuan)

类 别	Category	企业单位数(个) Number of Enterprises (unit)	资产总计 Total Assets	流动资产合计 Total Current Assets	负债合计 Total Liabilities
总 计	**Total**	**33057**	**111501.60**	**59617.18**	**68192.56**
一、按登记注册类型分	**by Status of Registration**				
内资企业	**Domestic Funded Enterprises**	**30346**	**91860.60**	**48702.42**	**57438.57**
国有企业	State-owned Enterprises	270	4765.41	1155.36	3126.79
集体企业	Collective-owned Enterprises	68	109.53	68.50	66.57
股份合作企业	Cooperative Enterprises	27	32.45	21.47	19.09
联营企业	Joint Ownership Enterprises	10	29.96	11.81	25.08
有限责任公司	Limited Liability Corporations	5402	35918.99	18101.88	23331.25
股份有限公司	Share-holding Corporations Limited	736	18309.23	8618.95	9348.83
私营企业	Private Enterprises	23829	32683.59	20720.54	21513.00
其他企业	Other Enterprises	4	11.44	3.91	7.97
港、澳、台商投资企业	**Enterprises with Funds from Hong Kong, Macao and Taiwan**	**865**	**10958.82**	**5383.61**	**6158.56**
外商投资企业	**Foreign Funded Enterprises**	**1846**	**8682.18**	**5531.16**	**4595.42**
二、按轻重工业分	**by Light & Heavy Industry**				
轻工业	Light Industry	11448	23432.55	13487.13	13201.17
重工业	Heavy Industry	21609	88069.05	46130.05	54991.38
三、按企业规模分	**by Enterprise Size**				
大型企业	Large-sized Enterprises	682	51524.11	24663.79	29384.73
中型企业	Medium-sized Enterprises	2752	25456.68	14938.98	16149.24
小微企业	Small-sized and Micro-sized Enterprises	29623	34520.80	20014.42	22658.59
四、按工业门类分	**by Industries**				
采矿业	Mining	373	7679.03	2748.44	5142.45
制造业	Manufacturing	31076	86612.80	51945.67	51591.15
电力、热力、燃气及水的生产和供应业	Production and Supply of Electric,Heat, Gas and Water	1608	17209.77	4923.08	11458.96
五、按行业大类分	**by Sector**				
煤炭开采和洗选业	Mining and Washing of Coal	121	4434.09	2087.21	2985.80
石油和天然气开采业	Extraction of Petroleum and Natural Gas	11	1556.31	84.69	1057.61
黑色金属矿采选业	Mining of Ferrous Metal Ores	62	381.26	168.73	260.43
有色金属矿采选业	Mining of Non-ferrous Metal Ores	44	880.43	233.49	576.38
非金属矿采选业	Mining and Processing of Nonmetal Ores	124	307.36	132.90	147.60
开采专业及辅助性活动	Mining Specialties and Auxiliary Activities	10	119.38	41.30	114.55
其他采矿业	Mining of Other Ores	1			
农副食品加工业	Processing of Food from Agricultural Products	2788	4316.46	2925.28	2898.77
食品制造业	Manufacture of Foods	820	1640.81	928.19	965.44
酒、饮料和精制茶制造业	Manufacture of Wine, Drinks and Refined Tea	184	1055.56	616.73	586.77
烟草制品业	Manufacture of Tobacco	4	342.69	244.92	112.82
纺织业	Manufacture of Textile	1803	2376.71	1381.05	1302.75
纺织服装、服饰业	Manufacture of Textile Wearing Apparel and Finery	704	1015.02	506.74	605.93

14-1 续表 1 continued

单位:亿元 (100 million yuan)

类别	Category	企业单位数(个) Number of Enterprises (unit)	资产总计 Total Assets	流动资产合计 Total Current Assets	负债合计 Total Liabilities
皮革、毛皮、羽毛及其制品和制鞋业	Manufacture of Leather, Fur, Feather & Its Products and Footwear	236	201.87	142.02	140.70
木材加工及木 竹、藤、棕、草制品业	Processing of Timbers, Manufacture of Wood, Bamboo, Rattan, Palm, and Straw Products	2300	660.30	404.19	455.31
家具制造业	Manufacture of Furniture	304	204.99	131.01	147.00
造纸及纸制品业	Manufacture of Paper and Paper Products	563	2631.62	1191.72	1879.34
印刷和记录媒介复制业	Printing, Reproduction of Recording Media	343	286.69	171.14	166.60
文教、工美、体育和娱乐用品制造业	Manufacture of Culture, Education,Arts and crafts, Sport and Entertainment Goods	642	570.45	383.94	314.56
石油、煤炭及其他燃料加工业	Processing of Oil, Coal and Other Fuel	279	7035.31	4554.12	5142.98
化学原料和化学制品制造业	Manufacture of Chemical Raw Material and Chemical Products	2481	11853.75	5787.43	6924.66
医药制造业	Manufacture of Medicines	592	4452.63	2507.14	1790.44
化学纤维制造业	Manufacture of Chemical Fiber	87	344.61	174.79	177.12
橡胶和塑料制品业	Manufacture of Rubber and Plastic	1544	3241.67	1977.64	1992.75
非金属矿物制品业	Manufacture of Non-metallic Mineral Products	3730	5738.24	3653.57	3511.70
黑色金属冶炼及压延加工业	Manufacture and Processing of Ferrous Metals	411	5768.23	2913.91	3704.15
有色金属冶炼及压延加工业	Manufacture & Processing of Non-ferrous Metals	534	4837.88	2622.34	2524.56
金属制品业	Manufacture of Metal Products	2215	3189.00	2033.83	2018.74
通用设备制造业	Manufacture of General Purpose Machinery	2228	4722.09	3155.14	2489.58
专用设备制造业	Manufacture of Special Purpose Machinery	2024	4611.86	3250.09	2689.38
汽车制造业	Manufacture of Automotive	1432	4721.47	3196.89	2943.42
铁路、船舶、航空航天和其他运输设备制造业	Manufacture of Railroad,Marine,Aerospace and Other Transportation Equipment	329	2071.65	1361.53	1308.64
电气机械及器材制造业	Manufacture of Electrical Machinery & Equipment	1233	3918.14	2338.50	2184.11
计算机、通信和其他电子设备制造业	Manufacture of Computer, Communications and Other Electronic Equipment	706	3956.74	2835.78	2188.12
仪器仪表制造业	Manufacture of Measuring Instrument	330	504.02	376.10	222.43
其他制造业	Other Manufacture	53	48.91	33.00	34.03
废弃资源综合利用业	Comprehensive Utilization of Waste	135	223.85	102.86	122.34
金属制品、机械和设备修理业	Metal Products, Machinery and Equipment Repair Industry	42	69.60	44.10	46.00
电力、热力的生产和供应业	Production and Supply of Electric Power and Heat Power	992	14701.67	3953.27	9884.63
燃气生产和供应业	Production and Supply of Gas	316	982.11	427.52	600.06
水的生产和供应业	Production and Supply of Water	300	1525.98	542.28	974.26

14-1　续表 2 continued

单位:亿元 (100 million yuan)

类　　别	Category	营业收入 Business Revenue	营业成本 Business Cost	利润总额 Total Profits	全部从业人员年平均人数(万人) Annual Average of Employed Persons (10 000 person)
总　　计	**Total**	**103804.16**	**89817.40**	**5394.75**	**554.91**
一、按登记注册类型分	**by Status of Registration**				
内资企业	**Domestic Funded Enterprises**	**88092.30**	**76377.92**	**4304.20**	**466.38**
国有企业	State-owned Enterprises	3840.91	3510.22	75.11	17.27
集体企业	Collective-owned Enterprises	138.20	113.37	3.95	1.02
股份合作企业	Cooperative Enterprises	37.14	28.72	2.95	0.33
联营企业	Joint Ownership Enterprises	18.29	13.72	1.96	0.10
有限责任公司	Limited Liability Corporations	31711.64	27237.65	1473.67	139.70
股份有限公司	Share-holding Corporations Limited	13077.22	10666.88	1064.97	61.66
私营企业	Private Enterprises	39258.47	34799.29	1680.11	246.23
其他企业	Other Enterprises	10.44	8.08	1.47	0.06
港、澳、台商投资企业	**Enterprises with Funds from Hong Kong, Macao and Taiwan**	**6977.00**	**5947.59**	**592.68**	**35.14**
外商投资企业	**Foreign Funded Enterprises**	**8734.86**	**7491.89**	**497.88**	**53.38**
二、按轻重工业分	**by Light & Heavy Industry**				
轻工业	Light Industry	23724.48	19917.89	1285.37	199.23
重工业	Heavy Industry	80079.69	69899.51	4109.38	355.67
三、按企业规模分	**by Enterprise Size**				
大型企业	Large-sized Enterprises	44432.00	37696.27	2981.92	187.92
中型企业	Medium-sized Enterprises	25897.91	22503.34	1189.29	146.31
小微企业	Small-sized Enterprises	33474.25	29617.79	1223.54	220.67
四、按工业门类分	**by Industries**				
采矿业	Mining	2864.56	2031.91	231.78	31.79
制造业	Manufacturing	93421.60	80648.11	5003.16	492.98
电力、热力、燃气及水的生产和供应业	Production and Supply of Electric,Heat, Gas and Water	7518.01	7137.38	159.81	30.13
五、按行业大类分	**by Sector**				
煤炭开采和洗选业	Mining and Washing of Coal	1260.89	827.08	169.87	17.50
石油和天然气开采业	Extraction of Petroleum and Natural Gas	772.85	561.17	7.20	6.84
黑色金属矿采选业	Mining of Ferrous Metal Ores	414.48	327.69	44.43	1.95
有色金属矿采选业	Mining of Non-ferrous Metal Ores	144.76	100.03	-8.26	2.67
非金属矿采选业	Mining and Processing of Nonmetal Ores	124.98	78.57	18.02	1.12
开采专业及辅助性活动	Mining Specialties and Auxiliary Activities	146.39	137.23	0.49	1.71
其他采矿业	Mining of Other Ores				
农副食品加工业	Processing of Food from Agricultural Products	8014.40	7532.69	139.93	43.55
食品制造业	Manufacture of Foods	1664.59	1335.16	126.85	14.73
酒、饮料和精制茶制造业	Manufacture of Wine, Drinks and Refined Tea	637.20	492.49	40.98	5.29
烟草制品业	Manufacture of Tobacco	382.81	108.21	24.35	0.57
纺织业	Manufacture of Textile	2403.41	2184.21	56.36	32.49
纺织服装、服饰业	Manufacture of Textile Wearing Apparel and Finery	735.23	637.17	27.90	16.48

14-1 续表 3 continued

单位:亿元 (100 million yuan)

类 别	Category	营业收入 Business Revenue	营业成本 Business Cost	利润总额 Total Profits	全部从业人员年平均人数(万人) Annual Average of Employed Persons (10 000 person)
皮革、毛皮、羽毛及其制品和制鞋业	Manufacture of Leather, Fur, Feather & Its Products and Footwear	255.53	234.87	0.73	3.88
木材加工及木 竹、藤、棕、草制品业	Processing of Timbers, Manufacture of Wood, Bamboo, Rattan, Palm, and Straw Products	1496.49	1399.55	33.40	11.84
家具制造业	Manufacture of Furniture	255.89	222.73	7.28	3.90
造纸及纸制品业	Manufacture of Paper and Paper Products	1968.40	1704.93	135.29	10.27
印刷和记录媒介复制业	Printing, Reproduction of Recording Media	294.09	250.83	11.20	3.63
文教、工美、体育和娱乐用品制造业	Manufacture of Culture, Education,Arts and crafts, Sport and Entertainment Goods	698.09	592.01	36.45	8.40
石油、煤炭及其他燃料加工业	Processing of Oil, Coal and Other Fuel	11979.54	10368.62	356.10	10.09
化学原料和化学制品制造业	Manufacture of Chemical Raw Material and Chemical Products	11813.64	9819.02	1222.55	37.11
医药制造业	Manufacture of Medicines	2928.87	1738.24	461.82	22.99
化学纤维制造业	Manufacture of Chemical Fiber	178.17	153.76	9.69	1.40
橡胶和塑料制品业	Manufacture of Rubber and Plastic	2684.70	2326.72	99.28	25.70
非金属矿物制品业	Manufacture of Non-metallic Mineral Products	4688.68	3892.27	340.31	32.13
黑色金属冶炼及压延加工业	Manufacture and Processing of Ferrous Metals	8305.09	7745.61	277.33	14.77
有色金属冶炼及压延加工业	Manufacture & Processing of Non-ferrous Metals	7076.26	6427.65	422.09	13.45
金属制品业	Manufacture of Metal Products	3837.57	3448.73	112.94	25.67
通用设备制造业	Manufacture of General Purpose Machinery	3487.97	2837.38	243.67	32.61
专用设备制造业	Manufacture of Special Purpose Machinery	3244.86	2624.79	223.57	28.58
汽车制造业	Manufacture of Automotive	5459.15	4879.52	172.26	33.31
铁路、船舶、航空航天和其他运输设备制造业	Manufacture of Railroad,Marine,Aerospace and Other Transportation Equipment	1111.50	949.61	52.67	8.58
电气机械及器材制造业	Manufacture of Electrical Machinery & Equipment	2926.21	2476.48	140.07	18.86
计算机、通信和其他电子设备制造业	Manufacture of Computer, Communications and Other Electronic Equipment	4236.68	3748.51	179.06	26.06
仪器仪表制造业	Manufacture of Measuring Instrument	347.16	243.21	35.02	4.21
其他制造业	Other Manufacture	50.59	44.17	1.99	0.68
废弃资源综合利用业	Comprehensive Utilization of Waste	214.15	193.28	9.40	0.97
金属制品、机械和设备修理业	Metal Products, Machinery and Equipment Repair Industry	44.72	35.69	2.63	0.79
电力、热力的生产和供应业	Production and Supply of Electric Power and Heat Power	6390.48	6174.71	85.99	24.07
燃气生产和供应业	Production and Supply of Gas	855.26	748.49	53.59	2.56
水的生产和供应业	Production and Supply of Water	272.26	214.19	20.23	3.51

14-2 规模以上国有控股工业企业主要经济指标(2021年)
Main Economic Indicators of State-holding Industrial Enterprises above Designated Size (2021)

单位:亿元 (100 million yuan)

类 别	Category	企业单位数(个) Number of Enterprises (unit)	资产总计 Total Assets	流动资产合 计 Total Current Assets	负债合计 Total Liabilities
总 计	**Total**	**1935**	**36301.69**	**14891.59**	**23224.97**
一、按隶属关系分	**by Type of Ownership**				
中央企业	Central Enterprises	362	12267.81	3455.67	7619.35
地方企业	Local Enterprises	1573	24033.88	11435.92	15605.62
二、按轻重工业分	**by Light & Heavy Industry**				
轻工业	Light Industry	258	2560.49	1406.14	1365.61
重工业	Heavy Industry	1677	33741.19	13485.44	21859.36
三、按企业规模分	**by Enterprise Size**				
大型企业	Large-sized Enterprises	172	23939.55	9161.00	14514.16
中型企业	Medium-sized Enterprises	393	6285.71	3042.17	4417.91
小微企业	Small-sized and Micro-sized Enterprises	1370	6076.42	2688.43	4292.91
四、按工业门类分	**by Industries**				
采矿业	Mining	140	6985.35	2382.24	4700.33
制造业	Manufacturing	1093	18363.60	10124.91	11078.03
电力、热力、燃气及水的生产和供应业	Production and Supply of Electric,Heat, Gas and Water	702	10952.73	2384.43	7446.60
五、按行业大类分	**by Sector**				
煤炭开采和洗选业	Mining and Washing of Coal	68	4234.70	1956.12	2866.27
石油和天然气开采业	Extraction of Petroleum and Natural Gas	10	1551.97	84.62	1053.80
黑色金属矿采选业	Mining of Ferrous Metal Ores	12	158.55	45.49	70.95
有色金属矿采选业	Mining of Non-ferrous Metal Ores	20	792.91	199.25	529.70
非金属矿采选业	Mining and Processing of Nonmetal Ores	29	139.63	63.42	72.12
开采专业及辅助性活动	Mining Specialties and Auxiliary Activities	1			
其他采矿业	Mining of Other Ores				
农副食品加工业	Processing of Food from Agricultural Products	42	107.76	56.47	80.09
食品制造业	Manufacture of Foods	31	126.96	66.49	63.99
酒、饮料和精制茶制造业	Manufacture of Wine, Drinks and Refined Tea	31	484.99	276.32	241.53
烟草制品业	Manufacture of Tobacco	4	342.69	244.92	112.82
纺织业	Manufacture of Textile	11	59.10	31.00	41.97
纺织服装、服饰业	Manufacture of Textile Wearing Apparel and Finery	13	33.63	18.45	19.31

14-2 续表 1 continued

单位:亿元 (100 million yuan)

类　别	Category	企业单位数(个) Number of Enterprises (unit)	资产总计 Total Assets	流动资产合　计 Total Current Assets	负债合计 Total Liabilities
皮革、毛皮、羽毛及其制品和制鞋业	Manufacture of Leather, Fur, Feather & Its Products and Footwear				
木材加工及木 竹、藤、棕、草制品业	Processing of Timbers, Manufacture of Wood, Bamboo, Rattan, Palm, and Straw Products	6	15.31	6.08	10.46
家具制造业	Manufacture of Furniture				
造纸及纸制品业	Manufacture of Paper and Paper Products	12	487.62	224.22	373.42
印刷和记录媒介复制业	Printing, Reproduction of Recording Media	18	34.51	21.76	16.43
文教、工美、体育和娱乐用品制造业	Manufacture of Culture, Education,Arts and crafts, Sport and Entertainment Goods	4	15.81	12.92	20.66
石油、煤炭及其他燃料加工业	Processing of Oil, Coal and Other Fuel	27	1669.07	897.77	1065.61
化学原料和化学制品制造业	Manufacture of Chemical Raw Material and Chemical Products	111	3460.60	1193.89	2062.49
医药制造业	Manufacture of Medicines	38	483.96	267.78	185.96
化学纤维制造业	Manufacture of Chemical Fiber	8	111.88	43.94	52.53
橡胶和塑料制品业	Manufacture of Rubber and Plastic	30	209.08	118.27	146.41
非金属矿物制品业	Manufacture of Non-metallic Mineral Products	200	1256.49	639.06	791.22
黑色金属冶炼及压延加工业	Manufacture and Processing of Ferrous Metals	21	1277.32	372.70	783.09
有色金属冶炼及压延加工业	Manufacture & Processing of Non-ferrous Metals	32	581.43	355.61	376.19
金属制品业	Manufacture of Metal Products	49	255.48	174.28	178.13
通用设备制造业	Manufacture of General Purpose Machinery	82	1670.33	1062.05	767.11
专用设备制造业	Manufacture of Special Purpose Machinery	87	1021.51	734.13	783.12
汽车制造业	Manufacture of Automotive	56	1566.30	1149.61	1041.04
铁路、船舶、航空航天和其他运输设备制造业	Manufacture of Railroad,Marine,Aerospace and Other Transportation Equipment	35	1506.34	988.71	965.64
电气机械及器材制造业	Manufacture of Electrical Machinery & Equipment	65	513.38	326.91	321.03
计算机、通信和其他电子设备制造业	Manufacture of Computer, Communications and Other Electronic Equipment	47	896.68	708.20	492.35
仪器仪表制造业	Manufacture of Measuring Instrument	16	124.19	104.10	53.43
其他制造业	Other Manufacture	2			
废弃资源综合利用业	Comprehensive Utilization of Waste	9	26.23	14.11	18.05
金属制品、机械和设备修理业	Metal Products, Machinery and Equipment Repair Industry	6	15.44	10.84	6.61
电力、热力的生产和供应业	Production and Supply of Electric Power and Heat Power	446	9339.05	1841.35	6440.50
燃气生产和供应业	Production and Supply of Gas	82	438.20	138.64	249.17
水的生产和供应业	Production and Supply of Water	174	1175.49	404.44	756.94

14-2 续表 2 continued

单位：亿元 (100 million yuan)

类 别	Category	营业收入 Business Revenue	营业成本 Business Cost	利润总额 Total Profits	全部从业人员年平均人数（万人） Annual Average of Employed Persons (10 000 person)
总 计	**Total**	**25823.10**	**21854.14**	**1443.08**	**104.00**
一、按隶属关系分	**by Type of Ownership**				
中央企业	Central Enterprises	9891.44	8358.62	385.69	34.77
地方企业	Local Enterprises	15931.65	13495.52	1057.39	69.23
二、按轻重工业分	**by Light & Heavy Industry**				
轻工业	Light Industry	1692.77	1134.51	141.51	11.35
重工业	Heavy Industry	24130.33	20719.63	1301.57	92.65
三、按企业规模分	**by Enterprise Size**				
大型企业	Large-sized Enterprises	17491.13	14622.56	1248.92	67.40
中型企业	Medium-sized Enterprises	5279.51	4623.33	67.97	23.05
小微企业	Small-sized Enterprises	3052.46	2608.25	126.18	13.55
四、按工业门类分	**by Industries**				
采矿业	Mining	2242.40	1545.82	181.91	27.27
制造业	Manufacturing	18556.45	15432.93	1301.19	54.26
电力、热力、燃气及水的生产和供应业	Production and Supply of Electric,Heat, Gas and Water	5024.25	4875.40	-40.01	22.46
五、按行业大类分	**by Sector**				
煤炭开采和洗选业	Mining and Washing of Coal	1094.88	704.66	155.74	15.49
石油和天然气开采业	Extraction of Petroleum and Natural Gas	771.51	560.35	6.86	6.83
黑色金属矿采选业	Mining of Ferrous Metal Ores	98.40	58.55	23.62	0.97
有色金属矿采选业	Mining of Non-ferrous Metal Ores	94.55	68.98	-14.04	2.26
非金属矿采选业	Mining and Processing of Nonmetal Ores	43.67	22.09	9.28	0.21
开采专业及辅助性活动	Mining Specialties and Auxiliary Activities				
其他采矿业	Mining of Other Ores				
农副食品加工业	Processing of Food from Agricultural Products	223.44	214.39	0.86	0.86
食品制造业	Manufacture of Foods	98.95	75.65	9.48	0.80
酒、饮料和精制茶制造业	Manufacture of Wine, Drinks and Refined Tea	328.06	257.02	26.66	2.38
烟草制品业	Manufacture of Tobacco	382.81	108.21	24.35	0.57
纺织业	Manufacture of Textile	52.94	47.15	0.29	0.73
纺织服装、服饰业	Manufacture of Textile Wearing Apparel and Finery	11.11	8.34	0.89	0.28

14−2 续表 3 continued

单位:亿元 (100 million yuan)

类　　别	Category	营业收入 Business Revenue	营业成本 Business Cost	利润总额 Total Profits	全部从业人员年平均人数(万人) Annual Average of Employed Persons (10 000 person)
皮革、毛皮、羽毛及其制品和制鞋业	Manufacture of Leather, Fur, Feather & Its Products and Footwear				
木材加工及木 竹、藤、棕、草制品业	Processing of Timbers, Manufacture of Wood, Bamboo, Rattan, Palm, and Straw Products	8.12	7.96	-0.72	0.10
家具制造业	Manufacture of Furniture				
造纸及纸制品业	Manufacture of Paper and Paper Products	136.66	114.41	32.57	0.73
印刷和记录媒介复制业	Printing, Reproduction of Recording Media	28.01	21.32	2.32	0.43
文教、工美、体育和娱乐用品制造业	Manufacture of Culture, Education,Arts and crafts, Sport and Entertainment Goods	3.95	3.74	-0.43	0.08
石油、煤炭及其他燃料加工业	Processing of Oil, Coal and Other Fuel	3532.55	2781.91	138.61	3.14
化学原料和化学制品制造业	Manufacture of Chemical Raw Material and Chemical Products	2945.59	2291.58	559.63	6.85
医药制造业	Manufacture of Medicines	228.22	130.69	31.63	2.36
化学纤维制造业	Manufacture of Chemical Fiber	39.75	31.30	7.62	0.35
橡胶和塑料制品业	Manufacture of Rubber and Plastic	120.15	109.08	-3.68	1.24
非金属矿物制品业	Manufacture of Non-metallic Mineral Products	754.68	569.54	103.42	4.31
黑色金属冶炼及压延加工业	Manufacture and Processing of Ferrous Metals	1740.38	1585.50	68.05	3.22
有色金属冶炼及压延加工业	Manufacture & Processing of Non-ferrous Metals	1383.21	1321.53	17.42	1.84
金属制品业	Manufacture of Metal Products	340.96	303.04	14.64	1.61
通用设备制造业	Manufacture of General Purpose Machinery	856.62	678.85	96.00	4.33
专用设备制造业	Manufacture of Special Purpose Machinery	564.77	483.14	5.84	3.87
汽车制造业	Manufacture of Automotive	2422.03	2226.02	72.33	5.63
铁路、船舶、航空航天和其他运输设备制造业	Manufacture of Railroad,Marine,Aerospace and Other Transportation Equipment	743.41	634.12	46.08	3.45
电气机械及器材制造业	Manufacture of Electrical Machinery & Equipment	359.15	316.50	7.41	1.81
计算机、通信和其他电子设备制造业	Manufacture of Computer, Communications and Other Electronic Equipment	1145.22	1030.66	31.72	2.37
仪器仪表制造业	Manufacture of Measuring Instrument	65.57	47.50	6.31	0.59
其他制造业	Other Manufacture				
废弃资源综合利用业	Comprehensive Utilization of Waste	24.37	21.80	0.76	0.10
金属制品、机械和设备修理业	Metal Products, Machinery and Equipment Repair Industry	12.48	9.39	0.86	0.22
电力、热力的生产和供应业	Production and Supply of Electric Power and Heat Power	4547.43	4474.19	-68.68	18.58
燃气生产和供应业	Production and Supply of Gas	294.00	251.56	23.40	1.04
水的生产和供应业	Production and Supply of Water	182.82	149.64	5.26	2.84

14-3 规模以上外商投资和港澳台商投资工业企业主要经济指标(2021年)

Main Economic Indicators of Industrial Enterprises above Designated Size with Funds from Foreign Countries (Territories),Hong Kong,Macao and Taiwan(2021)

单位:亿元 (100 million yuan)

类　别	Category	企业单位数(个) Number of Enterprises (unit)	资产总计 Total Assets	流动资产合计 Total Current Assets	负债合计 Total Liabilities
总　计	**Total**	**2711**	**19641.00**	**10914.77**	**10753.98**
一、按轻重工业分	**by Light & Heavy Industry**				
轻工业	Light Industry	1159	5858.71	3305.17	3136.57
重工业	Heavy Industry	1552	13782.28	7609.60	7617.41
二、按企业规模分	**by Enterprise Size**				
大型企业	Large-sized Enterprises	151	11646.69	6032.31	6609.66
中型企业	Medium-sized Enterprises	505	4044.02	2619.06	2098.91
小微企业	Small-sized and Micro-sized Enterprises	2055	3950.28	2263.39	2045.41
三、按工业门类分	**by Industries**				
采矿业	Mining	11	1976.70	775.32	1347.41
制造业	Manufacturing	2471	15242.59	9547.55	8190.48
电力、热力、燃气及水的生产和供应业	Production and Supply of Electric,Heat, Gas and Water	229	2421.70	591.90	1216.09
四、按行业大类分	**by Sector**				
煤炭开采和洗选业	Mining and Washing of Coal	4	1933.85	757.37	1323.50
石油和天然气开采业	Extraction of Petroleum and Natural Gas				
黑色金属矿采选业	Mining of Ferrous Metal Ores	4	27.77	10.83	19.96
有色金属矿采选业	Mining of Non-ferrous Metal Ores	2			
非金属矿采选业	Mining and Processing of Nonmetal Ores	1			
开采专业及辅助性活动	Mining Specialties and Auxiliary Activities				
其他采矿业	Mining of Other Ores				
农副食品加工业	Processing of Food from Agricultural Products	293	1088.27	773.74	696.04
食品制造业	Manufacture of Foods	113	538.36	341.52	295.24
酒、饮料和精制茶制造业	Manufacture of Wine, Drinks and Refined Tea	38	168.39	101.81	69.20
烟草制品业	Manufacture of Tobacco				
纺织业	Manufacture of Textile	98	232.51	142.87	113.71
纺织服装、服饰业	Manufacture of Textile Wearing Apparel and Finery	102	470.75	161.38	284.43

14-3 续表 1 continued

单位:亿元 (100 million yuan)

类别	Category	企业单位数(个) Number of Enterprises (unit)	资产总计 Total Assets	流动资产合计 Total Current Assets	负债合计 Total Liabilities
皮革、毛皮、羽毛及其制品和制鞋业	Manufacture of Leather, Fur, Feather & Its Products and Footwear	26	36.72	26.21	27.29
木材加工及木 竹、藤、棕、草制品业	Processing of Timbers, Manufacture of Wood, Bamboo, Rattan, Palm, and Straw Products	17	30.40	20.59	30.08
家具制造业	Manufacture of Furniture	33	33.14	23.42	20.54
造纸及纸制品业	Manufacture of Paper and Paper Products	55	1061.56	480.48	703.64
印刷和记录媒介复制业	Printing, Reproduction of Recording Media	27	51.65	34.82	24.70
文教、工美、体育和娱乐用品制造业	Manufacture of Culture, Education,Arts and crafts, Sport and Entertainment Goods	81	110.03	71.21	48.39
石油、煤炭及其他燃料加工业	Processing of Oil, Coal and Other Fuel	11	146.61	98.08	129.30
化学原料和化学制品制造业	Manufacture of Chemical Raw Material and Chemical Products	170	1237.80	709.35	612.00
医药制造业	Manufacture of Medicines	71	1358.54	717.77	519.70
化学纤维制造业	Manufacture of Chemical Fiber	12	31.29	19.93	12.87
橡胶和塑料制品业	Manufacture of Rubber and Plastic	118	581.30	357.29	274.23
非金属矿物制品业	Manufacture of Non-metallic Mineral Products	125	471.62	300.93	161.46
黑色金属冶炼及压延加工业	Manufacture and Processing of Ferrous Metals	15	901.97	588.60	551.86
有色金属冶炼及压延加工业	Manufacture & Processing of Non-ferrous Metals	21	1096.78	526.94	592.06
金属制品业	Manufacture of Metal Products	130	343.02	213.52	187.59
通用设备制造业	Manufacture of General Purpose Machinery	193	577.09	413.78	252.03
专用设备制造业	Manufacture of Special Purpose Machinery	144	875.70	675.20	446.84
汽车制造业	Manufacture of Automotive	202	1589.56	1091.10	839.04
铁路、船舶、航空航天和其他运输设备制造业	Manufacture of Railroad,Marine,Aerospace and Other Transportation Equipment	48	375.50	260.55	228.83
电气机械及器材制造业	Manufacture of Electrical Machinery & Equipment	102	461.40	287.70	238.95
计算机、通信和其他电子设备制造业	Manufacture of Computer, Communications and Other Electronic Equipment	187	1257.70	1022.86	776.31
仪器仪表制造业	Manufacture of Measuring Instrument	22	80.80	64.91	35.19
其他制造业	Other Manufacture	6	13.48	8.18	9.44
废弃资源综合利用业	Comprehensive Utilization of Waste	6	10.67	6.56	6.45
金属制品、机械和设备修理业	Metal Products, Machinery and Equipment Repair Industry	5	9.97	6.26	3.07
电力、热力的生产和供应业	Production and Supply of Electric Power and Heat Power	117	1921.77	393.01	929.92
燃气生产和供应业	Production and Supply of Gas	73	378.27	162.51	219.18
水的生产和供应业	Production and Supply of Water	39	121.66	36.38	66.99

14-3 续表 2 continued

单位:亿元 (100 million yuan)

类　别	Category	营业收入 Business Revenue	营业成本 Business Cost	利润总额 Total Profits	全部从业人员年平均人数(万人) Annual Average of Employed Persons (10 000 person)
总　计	**Total**	**15711.86**	**13439.49**	**1090.56**	**88.52**
一、按轻重工业分	**by Light & Heavy Industry**				
轻工业	Light Industry	4863.52	4016.16	399.68	37.70
重工业	Heavy Industry	10848.34	9423.33	690.88	50.83
二、按企业规模分	**by Enterprise Size**				
大型企业	Large-sized Enterprises	7528.54	6368.84	615.38	38.32
中型企业	Medium-sized Enterprises	4438.22	3798.09	324.88	28.32
小微企业	Small-sized Enterprises	3745.11	3272.56	150.30	21.88
三、按工业门类分	**by Industries**				
采矿业	Mining	352.97	201.53	76.84	4.62
制造业	Manufacturing	14592.25	12514.96	947.11	81.17
电力、热力、燃气及水的生产和供应业	Production and Supply of Electric,Heat, Gas and Water	766.65	723.00	66.61	2.73
四、按行业大类分	**by Sector**				
煤炭开采和洗选业	Mining and Washing of Coal	328.02	182.48	74.58	4.46
石油和天然气开采业	Extraction of Petroleum and Natural Gas				
黑色金属矿采选业	Mining of Ferrous Metal Ores	17.42	15.05	0.38	0.07
有色金属矿采选业	Mining of Non-ferrous Metal Ores				
非金属矿采选业	Mining and Processing of Nonmetal Ores				
开采专业及辅助性活动	Mining Specialties and Auxiliary Activities				
其他采矿业	Mining of Other Ores				
农副食品加工业	Processing of Food from Agricultural Products	1540.93	1436.98	24.38	7.83
食品制造业	Manufacture of Foods	473.74	365.85	42.86	3.72
酒、饮料和精制茶制造业	Manufacture of Wine, Drinks and Refined Tea	137.44	104.00	12.66	1.38
烟草制品业	Manufacture of Tobacco				
纺织业	Manufacture of Textile	207.24	181.68	5.02	3.37
纺织服装、服饰业	Manufacture of Textile Wearing Apparel and Finery	144.89	127.82	0.67	3.60

14-3 续表 3 continued

单位：亿元 (100 million yuan)

类别	Category	营业收入 Business Revenue	营业成本 Business Cost	利润总额 Total Profits	全部从业人员年平均人数(万人) Annual Average of Employed Persons (10 000 person)
皮革、毛皮、羽毛及其制品和制鞋业	Manufacture of Leather, Fur, Feather & Its Products and Footwear	41.80	38.76	-2.42	1.20
木材加工及木 竹、藤、棕、草制品业	Processing of Timbers, Manufacture of Wood, Bamboo, Rattan, Palm, and Straw Products	22.86	21.47	-0.58	0.25
家具制造业	Manufacture of Furniture	31.67	27.68	0.14	0.66
造纸及纸制品业	Manufacture of Paper and Paper Products	552.85	458.12	59.99	2.17
印刷和记录媒介复制业	Printing, Reproduction of Recording Media	54.40	45.60	2.73	0.55
文教、工美、体育和娱乐用品制造业	Manufacture of Culture, Education,Arts and crafts, Sport and Entertainment Goods	107.50	89.28	4.47	1.94
石油、煤炭及其他燃料加工业	Processing of Oil, Coal and Other Fuel	218.51	190.42	4.68	0.40
化学原料和化学制品制造业	Manufacture of Chemical Raw Material and Chemical Products	1281.00	1087.16	92.41	3.46
医药制造业	Manufacture of Medicines	828.21	540.99	182.87	5.47
化学纤维制造业	Manufacture of Chemical Fiber	29.85	24.05	3.04	0.19
橡胶和塑料制品业	Manufacture of Rubber and Plastic	413.92	339.26	26.43	3.48
非金属矿物制品业	Manufacture of Non-metallic Mineral Products	355.14	276.36	45.81	2.59
黑色金属冶炼及压延加工业	Manufacture and Processing of Ferrous Metals	1366.09	1269.28	59.44	1.43
有色金属冶炼及压延加工业	Manufacture & Processing of Non-ferrous Metals	858.51	788.19	32.81	0.94
金属制品业	Manufacture of Metal Products	437.71	373.25	33.10	3.18
通用设备制造业	Manufacture of General Purpose Machinery	620.90	508.86	45.08	4.34
专用设备制造业	Manufacture of Special Purpose Machinery	774.44	639.91	49.76	4.30
汽车制造业	Manufacture of Automotive	1735.80	1490.80	106.32	8.06
铁路、船舶、航空航天和其他运输设备制造业	Manufacture of Railroad,Marine,Aerospace and Other Transportation Equipment	194.32	166.24	7.59	1.99
电气机械及器材制造业	Manufacture of Electrical Machinery & Equipment	560.18	468.10	46.07	3.12
计算机、通信和其他电子设备制造业	Manufacture of Computer, Communications and Other Electronic Equipment	1501.83	1379.97	51.14	10.31
仪器仪表制造业	Manufacture of Measuring Instrument	62.93	42.31	8.68	0.50
其他制造业	Other Manufacture	13.25	11.98	0.48	0.40
废弃资源综合利用业	Comprehensive Utilization of Waste	11.20	10.34	0.63	0.04
金属制品、机械和设备修理业	Metal Products, Machinery and Equipment Repair Industry	13.14	10.27	0.84	0.30
电力、热力的生产和供应业	Production and Supply of Electric Power and Heat Power	416.27	421.36	40.71	1.35
燃气生产和供应业	Production and Supply of Gas	319.83	281.88	19.08	1.14
水的生产和供应业	Production and Supply of Water	30.55	19.75	6.83	0.23

14-4　规模以上非公有制工业企业主要经济指标(2021年)

Main Economic Indicators of Non-public Industrial Enterprises above Designated Size(2021)

单位:亿元　　(100 million yuan)

类　别	Category	企业单位数(个) Number of Enterprises (unit)	资产总计 Total Assets	流动资产合计 Total Current Assets	负债合计 Total Liabilities
总　计	**Total**	**30613**	**70242.58**	**42086.06**	**42381.16**
一、按轻重工业分	**by Light & Heavy Industry**				
轻工业	Light Industry	11032	19207.12	11297.73	10951.43
重工业	Heavy Industry	19581	51035.46	30788.33	31429.73
二、按企业规模分	**by Enterprise Size**				
大型企业	Large-sized Enterprises	469	25369.57	14218.31	13851.10
中型企业	Medium-sized Enterprises	2258	18097.10	11304.58	11096.82
小微企业	Small-sized and Micro-sized Enterprises	27886	26775.91	16563.17	17433.23
三、按工业门类分	**by Industries**				
采矿业	Mining	215	572.89	290.78	383.66
制造业	Manufacturing	29540	63707.58	39402.91	38268.96
电力、热力、燃气及水的生产和供应业	Production and Supply of Electric,Heat, Gas and Water	858	5962.12	2392.37	3728.54
四、按行业大类分	**by Sector**				
煤炭开采和洗选业	Mining and Washing of Coal	50	156.93	95.40	96.28
石油和天然气开采业	Extraction of Petroleum and Natural Gas	1			
黑色金属矿采选业	Mining of Ferrous Metal Ores	46	190.99	107.10	174.33
有色金属矿采选业	Mining of Non-ferrous Metal Ores	17	48.70	14.70	28.43
非金属矿采选业	Mining and Processing of Nonmetal Ores	91	159.93	65.43	73.67
开采专业及辅助性活动	Mining Specialties and Auxiliary Activities	9	11.79	7.96	7.05
其他采矿业	Mining of Other Ores	1			
农副食品加工业	Processing of Food from Agricultural Products	2706	4005.67	2734.58	2684.40
食品制造业	Manufacture of Foods	781	1488.69	848.12	884.90
酒、饮料和精制茶制造业	Manufacture of Wine, Drinks and Refined Tea	145	469.90	296.72	313.72
烟草制品业	Manufacture of Tobacco				
纺织业	Manufacture of Textile	1771	2145.56	1250.36	1121.14
纺织服装、服饰业	Manufacture of Textile Wearing Apparel and Finery	686	967.64	477.68	582.35

14-4 续表 1 continued

单位:亿元 (100 million yuan)

类 别	Category	企业单位数（个）Number of Enterprises (unit)	资产总计 Total Assets	流动资产合计 Total Current Assets	负债合计 Total Liabilities
皮革、毛皮、羽毛及其制品和制鞋业	Manufacture of Leather, Fur, Feather & Its Products and Footwear	235	200.65	141.14	139.53
木材加工及木 竹、藤、棕、草制品业	Processing of Timbers, Manufacture of Wood, Bamboo, Rattan, Palm, and Straw Products	2293	642.65	395.93	443.16
家具制造业	Manufacture of Furniture	304	204.99	131.01	147.00
造纸及纸制品业	Manufacture of Paper and Paper Products	543	2105.33	956.07	1481.24
印刷和记录媒介复制业	Printing, Reproduction of Recording Media	319	244.08	144.21	144.77
文教、工美、体育和娱乐用品制造业	Manufacture of Culture, Education,Arts and crafts, Sport and Entertainment Goods	632	546.85	366.19	291.41
石油、煤炭及其他燃料加工业	Processing of Oil, Coal and Other Fuel	243	4605.58	3180.20	3628.37
化学原料和化学制品制造业	Manufacture of Chemical Raw Material and Chemical Products	2305	7902.92	4352.06	4604.03
医药制造业	Manufacture of Medicines	542	3879.89	2175.77	1577.50
化学纤维制造业	Manufacture of Chemical Fiber	75	201.41	104.35	108.80
橡胶和塑料制品业	Manufacture of Rubber and Plastic	1501	2973.60	1832.59	1823.26
非金属矿物制品业	Manufacture of Non-metallic Mineral Products	3468	4278.29	2898.18	2654.19
黑色金属冶炼及压延加工业	Manufacture and Processing of Ferrous Metals	386	4470.59	2527.44	2905.40
有色金属冶炼及压延加工业	Manufacture & Processing of Non-ferrous Metals	490	3572.14	1953.40	1950.96
金属制品业	Manufacture of Metal Products	2128	2837.33	1792.92	1769.50
通用设备制造业	Manufacture of General Purpose Machinery	2121	2882.58	1974.84	1629.78
专用设备制造业	Manufacture of Special Purpose Machinery	1912	3532.37	2472.31	1871.81
汽车制造业	Manufacture of Automotive	1362	3006.14	1956.39	1835.71
铁路、船舶、航空航天和其他运输设备制造业	Manufacture of Railroad,Marine,Aerospace and Other Transportation Equipment	290	527.95	350.27	320.84
电气机械及器材制造业	Manufacture of Electrical Machinery & Equipment	1132	2331.14	1571.37	1341.77
计算机、通信和其他电子设备制造业	Manufacture of Computer, Communications and Other Electronic Equipment	652	3031.56	2107.60	1686.85
仪器仪表制造业	Manufacture of Measuring Instrument	311	375.30	269.43	166.46
其他制造业	Other Manufacture	51	39.39	28.68	26.67
废弃资源综合利用业	Comprehensive Utilization of Waste	124	190.78	85.12	100.11
金属制品、机械和设备修理业	Metal Products, Machinery and Equipment Repair Industry	32	46.61	27.98	33.33
电力、热力的生产和供应业	Production and Supply of Electric Power and Heat Power	513	5109.21	1990.88	3180.62
燃气生产和供应业	Production and Supply of Gas	224	514.85	272.70	334.69
水的生产和供应业	Production and Supply of Water	121	338.05	128.79	213.23

14-4　续表 2 continued

单位:亿元　　(100 million yuan)

类　别	Category	营业收入 Business Revenue	营业成本 Business Cost	利润总额 Total Profits	全部从业人员年平均人数(万人) Annual Average of Employed Persons (10 000 person)
总　计	**Total**	**74022.35**	**64582.16**	**3726.92**	**430.99**
一、按轻重工业分	**by Light & Heavy Industry**				
轻工业	Light Industry	21001.65	17925.19	1090.24	179.64
重工业	Heavy Industry	53020.70	46656.97	2636.68	251.36
二、按企业规模分	**by Enterprise Size**				
大型企业	Large-sized Enterprises	24713.19	21158.09	1617.17	110.32
中型企业	Medium-sized Enterprises	19818.45	17249.58	1040.92	117.88
小微企业	Small-sized Enterprises	29490.71	26174.50	1068.82	202.79
三、按工业门类分	**by Industries**				
采矿业	Mining	542.84	444.94	30.35	3.53
制造业	Manufacturing	71135.62	62020.39	3494.83	420.52
电力、热力、燃气及水的生产和供应业	Production and Supply of Electric,Heat, Gas and Water	2343.88	2116.83	201.73	6.95
四、按行业大类分	**by Sector**				
煤炭开采和洗选业	Mining and Washing of Coal	142.16	109.97	9.52	1.50
石油和天然气开采业	Extraction of Petroleum and Natural Gas				
黑色金属矿采选业	Mining of Ferrous Metal Ores	287.26	250.38	13.97	0.67
有色金属矿采选业	Mining of Non-ferrous Metal Ores	28.35	23.51	-0.80	0.27
非金属矿采选业	Mining and Processing of Nonmetal Ores	76.53	54.07	7.25	0.88
开采专业及辅助性活动	Mining Specialties and Auxiliary Activities	7.00	6.04	0.04	0.18
其他采矿业	Mining of Other Ores				
农副食品加工业	Processing of Food from Agricultural Products	7544.18	7097.77	129.93	41.13
食品制造业	Manufacture of Foods	1532.06	1234.20	115.39	13.65
酒、饮料和精制茶制造业	Manufacture of Wine, Drinks and Refined Tea	285.23	217.33	14.03	2.67
烟草制品业	Manufacture of Tobacco				
纺织业	Manufacture of Textile	2169.68	1975.24	51.42	29.41
纺织服装、服饰业	Manufacture of Textile Wearing Apparel and Finery	714.28	621.39	26.51	15.74

14-4 续表 3 continued

单位:亿元 (100 million yuan)

类别	Category	营业收入 Business Revenue	营业成本 Business Cost	利润总额 Total Profits	全部从业人员年平均人数(万人) Annual Average of Employed Persons (10 000 person)
皮革、毛皮、羽毛及其制品和制鞋业	Manufacture of Leather, Fur, Feather & Its Products and Footwear	253.93	233.27	0.95	3.81
木材加工及木 竹、藤、棕、草制品业	Processing of Timbers, Manufacture of Wood, Bamboo, Rattan, Palm, and Straw Products	1487.19	1390.46	34.11	11.72
家具制造业	Manufacture of Furniture	255.89	222.73	7.28	3.90
造纸及纸制品业	Manufacture of Paper and Paper Products	1802.28	1564.74	102.15	9.29
印刷和记录媒介复制业	Printing, Reproduction of Recording Media	258.57	223.25	8.38	3.08
文教、工美、体育和娱乐用品制造业	Manufacture of Culture, Education,Arts and crafts, Sport and Entertainment Goods	688.01	583.86	35.85	8.13
石油、煤炭及其他燃料加工业	Processing of Oil, Coal and Other Fuel	7548.29	6794.49	184.85	6.21
化学原料和化学制品制造业	Manufacture of Chemical Raw Material and Chemical Products	8434.61	7170.56	622.15	28.79
医药制造业	Manufacture of Medicines	2639.98	1581.94	413.58	20.19
化学纤维制造业	Manufacture of Chemical Fiber	125.95	110.93	2.19	1.01
橡胶和塑料制品业	Manufacture of Rubber and Plastic	2504.61	2164.71	100.71	23.90
非金属矿物制品业	Manufacture of Non-metallic Mineral Products	3791.24	3211.81	215.90	26.79
黑色金属冶炼及压延加工业	Manufacture and Processing of Ferrous Metals	6519.20	6116.72	209.25	11.42
有色金属冶炼及压延加工业	Manufacture & Processing of Non-ferrous Metals	5082.40	4568.55	365.06	9.77
金属制品业	Manufacture of Metal Products	3437.74	3094.49	97.19	23.31
通用设备制造业	Manufacture of General Purpose Machinery	2516.82	2067.05	141.50	27.47
专用设备制造业	Manufacture of Special Purpose Machinery	2646.46	2113.40	216.37	24.28
汽车制造业	Manufacture of Automotive	2912.71	2534.85	101.99	26.31
铁路、船舶、航空航天和其他运输设备制造业	Manufacture of Railroad,Marine,Aerospace and Other Transportation Equipment	340.75	290.53	5.62	4.91
电气机械及器材制造业	Manufacture of Electrical Machinery & Equipment	2051.48	1728.12	106.40	14.75
计算机、通信和其他电子设备制造业	Manufacture of Computer, Communications and Other Electronic Equipment	3061.79	2690.90	146.60	23.53
仪器仪表制造业	Manufacture of Measuring Instrument	277.85	192.60	28.67	3.58
其他制造业	Other Manufacture	47.32	41.58	1.74	0.65
废弃资源综合利用业	Comprehensive Utilization of Waste	176.60	160.02	7.38	0.68
金属制品、机械和设备修理业	Metal Products, Machinery and Equipment Repair Industry	28.55	22.93	1.70	0.43
电力、热力的生产和供应业	Production and Supply of Electric Power and Heat Power	1721.03	1578.46	159.94	4.89
燃气生产和供应业	Production and Supply of Gas	536.12	475.52	27.68	1.42
水的生产和供应业	Production and Supply of Water	86.73	62.85	14.11	0.64

14-5 规模以上工业企业主要财务分析指标(2021年)

Main Financial Indicators of Industrial Enterprises above Designated Size(2021)

类 别	Category	资产负债率(%) Assets-Liability Ratio (%)	成本费用利润率(%) Ratio of Profits to Cost (%)	流动资产周转率(次) Ratio of Turnover Working Capitals (time)
总 计	**Total**	**61.16**	**5.52**	**1.74**
在总计中:国有控股企业	of which:State-holding Enterprises	63.98	6.09	1.73
一、按登记注册类型分	**by Status of Registration**			
内资企业	**Domestic Funded Enterprises**	**62.53**	**5.19**	**1.81**
国有企业	State-owned Enterprises	65.61	2.04	3.32
集体企业	Collective-owned Enterprises	60.77	2.96	2.02
股份合作企业	Cooperative Enterprises	58.85	8.62	1.73
联营企业	Joint Ownership Enterprises	83.68	12.08	1.55
有限责任公司	Limited Liability Corporations	64.96	4.98	1.75
股份有限公司	Share-holding Corporations Limited	51.06	8.99	1.52
私营企业	Private Enterprises	65.82	4.47	1.89
其他企业	Other Enterprises	69.62	16.55	2.67
港、澳、台商投资企业	**Enterprises with Funds from Hong Kong, Macao and Taiwan**	**56.20**	**9.05**	**1.30**
外商投资企业	**Foreign Funded Enterprises**	**52.93**	**6.06**	**1.58**
二、按轻重工业分	**by Light & Heavy Industry**			
轻工业	Light Industry	56.34	5.75	1.76
重工业	Heavy Industry	62.44	5.45	1.74
三、按企业规模分	**by Enterprise Size**			
大型企业	Large-sized Enterprises	57.03	7.29	1.80
中型企业	Medium-sized Enterprises	63.44	4.87	1.73
小微企业	Small-sized and Micro-sized Enterprises	65.64	3.78	1.67
四、按工业门类分	**by Industries**			
采矿业	Mining	66.97	9.51	1.04
制造业	Manufacturing	59.57	5.71	1.80
电力、热力、燃气及水的生产和供应业	Production and Supply of Electric,Heat, Gas and Water	66.58	2.09	1.53
五、按行业大类分	**by Sector**			
煤炭开采和洗选业	Mining and Washing of Coal	67.34	16.41	0.60
石油和天然气开采业	Extraction of Petroleum and Natural Gas	67.96	1.12	9.13
黑色金属矿采选业	Mining of Ferrous Metal Ores	68.31	12.25	2.46
有色金属矿采选业	Mining of Non-ferrous Metal Ores	65.47	-5.54	0.62
非金属矿采选业	Mining and Processing of Nonmetal Ores	48.02	17.85	0.94
开采专业及辅助性活动	Mining Specialties and Auxiliary Activities	95.95	0.33	3.54
其他采矿业	Mining of Other Ores			
农副食品加工业	Processing of Food from Agricultural Products	67.16	1.77	2.74
食品制造业	Manufacture of Foods	58.84	8.27	1.79
酒、饮料和精制茶制造业	Manufacture of Wine, Drinks and Refined Tea	55.59	7.06	1.03
烟草制品业	Manufacture of Tobacco	32.92	15.66	1.56
纺织业	Manufacture of Textile	54.81	2.40	1.74
纺织服装、服饰业	Manufacture of Textile Wearing Apparel and Finery	59.70	3.93	1.45

14-5 续表 continued

类 别	Category	资 产 负债率 (%) Assets-Liability Ratio (%)	成本费用 利 润 率 (%) Ratio of Profits to Cost (%)	流动资产 周 转 率 (次) Ratio of Turnover Working Capitals (time)
皮革、毛皮、羽毛及其制品和制鞋业	Manufacture of Leather, Fur, Feather & Its Products and Footwear	69.70	0.29	1.80
木材加工及木 竹、藤、棕、草制品业	Processing of Timbers, Manufacture of Wood, Bamboo, Rattan, Palm, and Straw Products	68.96	2.29	3.70
家具制造业	Manufacture of Furniture	71.71	2.95	1.95
造纸及纸制品业	Manufacture of Paper and Paper Products	71.41	7.19	1.65
印刷和记录媒介复制业	Printing, Reproduction of Recording Media	58.11	3.94	1.72
文教、工美、体育和娱乐用品制造业	Manufacture of Culture, Education,Arts and crafts, Sport and Entertainment Goods	55.14	5.51	1.82
石油、煤炭及其他燃料加工业	Processing of Oil, Coal and Other Fuel	73.10	3.33	2.63
化学原料和化学制品制造业	Manufacture of Chemical Raw Material and Chemical Products	58.42	11.47	2.04
医药制造业	Manufacture of Medicines	40.21	18.35	1.17
化学纤维制造业	Manufacture of Chemical Fiber	51.40	5.70	1.02
橡胶和塑料制品业	Manufacture of Rubber and Plastic	61.47	3.83	1.36
非金属矿物制品业	Manufacture of Non-metallic Mineral Products	61.20	7.82	1.28
黑色金属冶炼及压延加工业	Manufacture and Processing of Ferrous Metals	64.22	3.45	2.85
有色金属冶炼及压延加工业	Manufacture & Processing of Non-ferrous Metals	52.18	6.30	2.70
金属制品业	Manufacture of Metal Products	63.30	3.04	1.89
通用设备制造业	Manufacture of General Purpose Machinery	52.72	7.46	1.11
专用设备制造业	Manufacture of Special Purpose Machinery	58.31	7.33	1.00
汽车制造业	Manufacture of Automotive	62.34	3.26	1.71
铁路、船舶、航空航天和其他运输设备制造业	Manufacture of Railroad,Marine,Aerospace and Other Transportation Equipment	63.17	4.93	0.82
电气机械及器材制造业	Manufacture of Electrical Machinery & Equipment	55.74	4.97	1.25
计算机、通信和其他电子设备制造业	Manufacture of Computer, Communications and Other Electronic Equipment	55.30	4.40	1.49
仪器仪表制造业	Manufacture of Measuring Instrument	44.13	11.07	0.92
其他制造业	Other Manufacture	69.58	4.03	1.53
废弃资源综合利用业	Comprehensive Utilization of Waste	54.65	4.56	2.08
金属制品、机械和设备修理业	Metal Products, Machinery and Equipment Repair Industry	66.09	6.25	1.01
电力、热力的生产和供应业	Production and Supply of Electric Power and Heat Power	67.23	1.31	1.62
燃气生产和供应业	Production and Supply of Gas	61.10	6.66	2.00
水的生产和供应业	Production and Supply of Water	63.85	7.85	0.50

14-6 规模以上国有控股工业企业主要财务分析指标(2021年)

Main Financial Indicators of State-holding Industrial Enterprises above Designated Size(2021)

类 别	Category	资产负债率 (%) Assets-Liability Ratio (%)	成本费用利润率 (%) Ratio of Profits to Cost (%)	流动资产周转率 (次) Ratio of Turnover Working Capitals (time)
总 计	**Total**	**63.98**	**6.09**	**1.73**
一、按隶属关系分	**by Type of Ownership**			
中央企业	Central Enterprises	62.11	4.34	2.86
地方企业	Local Enterprises	64.93	7.14	1.39
二、按轻重工业分	**by Light & Heavy Industry**			
轻工业	Light Industry	53.33	10.23	1.20
重工业	Heavy Industry	64.79	5.83	1.79
三、按企业规模分	**by Enterprise Size**			
大型企业	Large-sized Enterprises	60.63	7.91	1.91
中型企业	Medium-sized Enterprises	70.28	1.36	1.74
小微企业	Small-sized and Micro-sized Enterprises	70.65	4.33	1.14
四、按工业门类分	**by Industries**			
采矿业	Mining	67.29	9.68	0.94
制造业	Manufacturing	60.33	7.81	1.83
电力、热力、燃气及水的生产和供应业	Production and Supply of Electric,Heat, Gas and Water	67.99	-0.77	2.11
五、按行业大类分	**by Sector**			
煤炭开采和洗选业	Mining and Washing of Coal	67.69	17.54	0.56
石油和天然气开采业	Extraction of Petroleum and Natural Gas	67.90	1.07	9.12
黑色金属矿采选业	Mining of Ferrous Metal Ores	44.75	32.96	2.16
有色金属矿采选业	Mining of Non-ferrous Metal Ores	66.80	-13.25	0.47
非金属矿采选业	Mining and Processing of Nonmetal Ores	51.65	29.21	0.69
开采专业及辅助性活动	Mining Specialties and Auxiliary Activities			
其他采矿业	Mining of Other Ores			
农副食品加工业	Processing of Food from Agricultural Products	74.32	0.39	3.96
食品制造业	Manufacture of Foods	50.40	10.67	1.49
酒、饮料和精制茶制造业	Manufacture of Wine, Drinks and Refined Tea	49.80	8.77	1.19
烟草制品业	Manufacture of Tobacco	32.92	15.66	1.56
纺织业	Manufacture of Textile	71.02	0.56	1.71
纺织服装、服饰业	Manufacture of Textile Wearing Apparel and Finery	57.43	8.48	0.60

14-6 续表 continued

类　别	Category	资产负债率(%) Assets-Liability Ratio (%)	成本费用利润率(%) Ratio of Profits to Cost (%)	流动资产周转率(次) Ratio of Turnover Working Capitals (time)
皮革、毛皮、羽毛及其制品和制鞋业	Manufacture of Leather, Fur, Feather & Its Products and Footwear			
木材加工及木 竹、藤、棕、草制品业	Processing of Timbers, Manufacture of Wood, Bamboo, Rattan, Palm, and Straw Products	68.34	-8.11	1.33
家具制造业	Manufacture of Furniture			
造纸及纸制品业	Manufacture of Paper and Paper Products	76.58	24.62	0.61
印刷和记录媒介复制业	Printing, Reproduction of Recording Media	47.60	9.00	1.29
文教、工美、体育和娱乐用品制造业	Manufacture of Culture, Education,Arts and crafts, Sport and Entertainment Goods	130.70	-10.06	0.31
石油、煤炭及其他燃料加工业	Processing of Oil, Coal and Other Fuel	63.84	4.85	3.93
化学原料和化学制品制造业	Manufacture of Chemical Raw Material and Chemical Products	59.60	22.64	2.47
医药制造业	Manufacture of Medicines	38.42	15.98	0.85
化学纤维制造业	Manufacture of Chemical Fiber	46.95	22.12	0.90
橡胶和塑料制品业	Manufacture of Rubber and Plastic	70.02	-2.95	1.02
非金属矿物制品业	Manufacture of Non-metallic Mineral Products	62.97	15.81	1.18
黑色金属冶炼及压延加工业	Manufacture and Processing of Ferrous Metals	61.31	4.06	4.67
有色金属冶炼及压延加工业	Manufacture & Processing of Non-ferrous Metals	64.70	1.29	3.89
金属制品业	Manufacture of Metal Products	69.73	4.50	1.96
通用设备制造业	Manufacture of General Purpose Machinery	45.93	12.42	0.81
专用设备制造业	Manufacture of Special Purpose Machinery	76.66	1.04	0.77
汽车制造业	Manufacture of Automotive	66.47	3.09	2.11
铁路、船舶、航空航天和其他运输设备制造业	Manufacture of Railroad,Marine,Aerospace and Other Transportation Equipment	64.11	6.52	0.75
电气机械及器材制造业	Manufacture of Electrical Machinery & Equipment	62.53	2.09	1.10
计算机、通信和其他电子设备制造业	Manufacture of Computer, Communications and Other Electronic Equipment	54.91	2.84	1.62
仪器仪表制造业	Manufacture of Measuring Instrument	43.02	10.55	0.63
其他制造业	Other Manufacture			
废弃资源综合利用业	Comprehensive Utilization of Waste	68.81	3.25	1.73
金属制品、机械和设备修理业	Metal Products, Machinery and Equipment Repair Industry	42.80	7.47	1.15
电力、热力的生产和供应业	Production and Supply of Electric Power and Heat Power	68.96	-1.46	2.47
燃气生产和供应业	Production and Supply of Gas	56.86	8.59	2.12
水的生产和供应业	Production and Supply of Water	64.39	2.87	0.45

14-7 规模以上非公有制工业企业主要财务分析指标(2021年)

Main Financial Indicators of Non-public Industrial Enterprises above Designated Size(2021)

类 别	Category	资产负债率 (%) Assets-Liability Ratio (%)	成本费用利润率 (%) Ratio of Profits to Cost (%)	流动资产周转率 (次) Ratio of Turnover Working Capitals (time)
总 计	**Total**	**60.34**	**5.30**	**1.76**
一、按轻重工业分	**by Light & Heavy Industry**			
轻工业	Light Industry	57.02	5.45	1.86
重工业	Heavy Industry	61.58	5.24	1.72
二、按企业规模分	**by Enterprise Size**			
大型企业	Large-sized Enterprises	54.60	7.02	1.74
中型企业	Medium-sized Enterprises	61.32	5.57	1.75
小微企业	Small-sized and Micro-sized Enterprises	65.11	3.74	1.78
三、按工业门类分	**by Industries**			
采矿业	Mining	66.97	6.05	1.87
制造业	Manufacturing	60.07	5.18	1.81
电力、热力、燃气及水的生产和供应业	Production and Supply of Electric,Heat, Gas and Water	62.54	8.74	0.98
四、按行业大类分	**by Sector**			
煤炭开采和洗选业	Mining and Washing of Coal	61.35	7.40	1.49
石油和天然气开采业	Extraction of Petroleum and Natural Gas			
黑色金属矿采选业	Mining of Ferrous Metal Ores	91.28	5.18	2.68
有色金属矿采选业	Mining of Non-ferrous Metal Ores	58.37	-2.74	1.93
非金属矿采选业	Mining and Processing of Nonmetal Ores	46.06	10.97	1.17
开采专业及辅助性活动	Mining Specialties and Auxiliary Activities	59.83	0.61	0.88
其他采矿业	Mining of Other Ores			
农副食品加工业	Processing of Food from Agricultural Products	67.01	1.75	2.76
食品制造业	Manufacture of Foods	59.44	8.15	1.81
酒、饮料和精制茶制造业	Manufacture of Wine, Drinks and Refined Tea	66.76	5.50	0.96
烟草制品业	Manufacture of Tobacco			
纺织业	Manufacture of Textile	52.25	2.43	1.74
纺织服装、服饰业	Manufacture of Textile Wearing Apparel and Finery	60.18	3.84	1.50

14−7 续表 continued

类别	Category	资产负债率(%) Assets-Liability Ratio (%)	成本费用利润率(%) Ratio of Profits to Cost (%)	流动资产周转率(次) Ratio of Turnover Working Capitals (time)
皮革、毛皮、羽毛及其制品和制鞋业	Manufacture of Leather, Fur, Feather & Its Products and Footwear	69.54	0.38	1.80
木材加工及木 竹、藤、棕、草制品业	Processing of Timbers, Manufacture of Wood, Bamboo, Rattan, Palm, and Straw Products	68.96	2.36	3.76
家具制造业	Manufacture of Furniture	71.71	2.95	1.95
造纸及纸制品业	Manufacture of Paper and Paper Products	70.36	5.94	1.89
印刷和记录媒介复制业	Printing, Reproduction of Recording Media	59.31	3.33	1.79
文教、工美、体育和娱乐用品制造业	Manufacture of Culture, Education,Arts and crafts, Sport and Entertainment Goods	53.29	5.50	1.88
石油、煤炭及其他燃料加工业	Processing of Oil, Coal and Other Fuel	78.78	2.64	2.37
化学原料和化学制品制造业	Manufacture of Chemical Raw Material and Chemical Products	58.26	7.98	1.94
医药制造业	Manufacture of Medicines	40.66	18.18	1.21
化学纤维制造业	Manufacture of Chemical Fiber	54.02	1.78	1.21
橡胶和塑料制品业	Manufacture of Rubber and Plastic	61.31	4.18	1.37
非金属矿物制品业	Manufacture of Non-metallic Mineral Products	62.04	6.04	1.31
黑色金属冶炼及压延加工业	Manufacture and Processing of Ferrous Metals	64.99	3.31	2.58
有色金属冶炼及压延加工业	Manufacture & Processing of Non-ferrous Metals	54.62	7.64	2.60
金属制品业	Manufacture of Metal Products	62.36	2.91	1.92
通用设备制造业	Manufacture of General Purpose Machinery	56.54	5.93	1.27
专用设备制造业	Manufacture of Special Purpose Machinery	52.99	8.80	1.07
汽车制造业	Manufacture of Automotive	61.07	3.62	1.49
铁路、船舶、航空航天和其他运输设备制造业	Manufacture of Railroad,Marine,Aerospace and Other Transportation Equipment	60.77	1.67	0.97
电气机械及器材制造业	Manufacture of Electrical Machinery & Equipment	57.56	5.41	1.31
计算机、通信和其他电子设备制造业	Manufacture of Computer, Communications and Other Electronic Equipment	55.64	5.01	1.45
仪器仪表制造业	Manufacture of Measuring Instrument	44.35	11.34	1.03
其他制造业	Other Manufacture	67.71	3.78	1.65
废弃资源综合利用业	Comprehensive Utilization of Waste	52.47	4.34	2.07
金属制品、机械和设备修理业	Metal Products, Machinery and Equipment Repair Industry	71.50	6.37	1.02
电力、热力的生产和供应业	Production and Supply of Electric Power and Heat Power	62.25	9.27	0.86
燃气生产和供应业	Production and Supply of Gas	65.01	5.43	1.97
水的生产和供应业	Production and Supply of Water	63.08	19.34	0.67

14-8 2008-2021年规模以上工业增加值
Value Added of Industry Enterprises above Designated Size From 2008 to 2021

类 别	Category	2008 工业增加值比上年增长(%) Growth Rate(%)	2009 工业增加值比上年增长(%) Growth Rate(%)	2010 工业增加值比上年增长(%) Growth Rate(%)	2011 工业增加值比上年增长(%) Growth Rate(%)	2012 工业增加值比上年增长(%) Growth Rate(%)	2013 工业增加值比上年增长(%) Growth Rate(%)
全省总计	**Total**	**13.8**	**14.9**	**15.0**	**14.0**	**11.4**	**11.3**
在总计中:轻工业	of which:Light Industry	13.2	12.1	12.9	11.9	11.2	10.2
重工业	Heavy Industry	14.1	16.2	16.1	15.1	11.5	11.8
在总计中:国有企业	of which:State-owned Enterprises	4.6	4.6	13.2	15.7	6.1	5.3
集体企业	Collective-owned Enterprises	8.3	17.8	9.9	11.5	10.5	10.6
股份制企业	Cooperative Enterprises	15.1	16.0	15.6	14.6	12.3	12.3
外商及港澳台商投资企业	Enterprises with Funds from Foreign Countries,Hong Kong, Macao and Taiwan	14.1	11.0	14.1	11.1	7.8	10.3
在总计中:国有控股企业	of which:State-holding Enterprises	8.2	4.7	12.5	6.1	3.7	4.8
在总计中:大中型工业企业	of which:Large and Medium-sized Enterprises	8.7	9.1	13.3	11.0	8.0	9.5

注:本表增幅按快报可比价计算。
a)Data in this table are calculated at constant prices of the express report.

14-8 续表 continued

类 别	Category	2014 工业增加值比上年增长(%) Growth Rate(%)	2015 工业增加值比上年增长(%) Growth Rate(%)	2016 工业增加值比上年增长(%) Growth Rate(%)	2017 工业增加值比上年增长(%) Growth Rate(%)	2018 工业增加值比上年增长(%) Growth Rate(%)	2019 工业增加值比上年增长(%) Growth Rate(%)	2020 工业增加值比上年增长(%) Growth Rate(%)	2021 工业增加值比上年增长(%) Growth Rate(%)
全省总计	**Total**	**9.6**	**7.5**	**6.8**	**6.9**	**5.2**	**1.2**	**5.0**	**9.6**
在总计中:轻工业	of which:Light Industry	8.5	7.4	5.5	6.9	0.5	-4.7	4.2	16.3
重工业	Heavy Industry	10.1	7.5	7.5	6.9	7.4	3.1	5.3	7.4
在总计中:国有企业	of which:State-owned Enterprises	-0.2	-0.5	-2.6	8.5	13.6	7.4	2.5	11.8
集体企业	Collective-owned Enterprises	5.7	4.2	4.4	6.6	-7.7	-10.5	-11.3	-28.9
股份制企业	Cooperative Enterprises	10.3	7.8	7.4	7.1	4.7	0.8	4.6	10.6
外商及港澳台商投资企业	Enterprises with Funds from Foreign Countries,Hong Kong, Macao and Taiwan	9.0	7.5	5.6	7.0	9.2	1.4	7.4	5.2
在总计中:国有控股企业	of which:State-holding Enterprises	2.8	-1.9	4.5	9.3	9.1	3.8	3.5	5.7
在总计中:大中型工业企业	of which:Large and Medium-sized Enterprises	8.1	5.8	7.2	7.8	7.3	-0.6	6.0	8.6

14-9 按行业分规模以上工业增加值构成
Its Composition of Industry Enterprises above Designated Size by Sector

类　　别	Category	2020 增加值占规模以上工业比重(%) Composition (%)	2020 工业增加值比上年增长(%) Growth Rate (%)
全省总计	**Total**	**100.0**	**5.0**
采矿业	**Mining**	**6.6**	**2.8**
煤炭开采和洗选业	Mining and Washing of Coal	3.1	1.4
石油和天然气开采业	Extraction of Petroleum and Natural Gas	1.9	0.5
黑色金属矿采选业	Mining of Ferrous Metal Ores	0.6	13.7
有色金属矿采选业	Mining of Non-ferrous Metal Ores	0.5	7.0
非金属矿采选业	Mining and Processing of Nonmetal Ores	0.2	-2.5
开采专业及辅助性活动	Mining Specialties and Auxiliary Activities	0.3	20.9
其他采矿业	Mining of Other Ores		
制造业	**Manufacturing**	**83.4**	**5.7**
农副食品加工业	Processing of Food from Agricultural Products	4.8	4.0
食品制造业	Manufacture of Foods	1.7	10.5
酒、饮料和精制茶制造业	Manufacture of Wine, Drinks and Refined Tea	0.9	-11.7
烟草制品业	Manufacture of Tobacco	1.7	7.6
纺织业	Manufacture of Textile	2.3	-4.5
纺织服装、服饰业	Manufacture of Textile Wearing Apparel and Finery	1.0	-13.2
皮革、毛皮、羽毛及其制品和制鞋业	Manufacture of Leather, Fur, Feather & Its Products and Footwear	0.2	-22.5
木材加工及木 竹、藤、棕、草制品业	Processing of Timbers, Manufacture of Wood, Bamboo, Rattan, Palm, and Straw Products	1.1	6.6
家具制造业	Manufacture of Furniture	0.3	-2.8
造纸及纸制品业	Manufacture of Paper and Paper Products	1.7	12.2
印刷和记录媒介复制业	Printing, Reproduction of Recording Media	0.3	4.3
文教、工美、体育和娱乐用品制造业	Manufacture of Culture, Education,Arts and crafts, Sport and Entertainment Goods	0.8	1.3
石油、煤炭及其他燃料加工业	Processing of Oil, Coal and Other Fuel	7.6	1.8
化学原料和化学制品制造业	Manufacture of Chemical Raw Material and Chemical Products	10.2	6.6
医药制造业	Manufacture of Medicines	4.5	3.4
化学纤维制造业	Manufacture of Chemical Fiber	0.1	-10.9
橡胶和塑料制品业	Manufacture of Rubber and Plastic	2.5	6.9
非金属矿物制品业	Manufacture of Non-metallic Mineral Products	5.5	1.6
黑色金属冶炼及压延加工业	Manufacture and Processing of Ferrous Metals	5.8	7.7
有色金属冶炼及压延加工业	Manufacture & Processing of Non-ferrous Metals	4.3	-5.3
金属制品业	Manufacture of Metal Products	2.7	10.0
通用设备制造业	Manufacture of General Purpose Machinery	4.1	6.0
专用设备制造业	Manufacture of Special Purpose Machinery	4.4	14.6
汽车制造业	Manufacture of Automotive	6.5	23.6
铁路、船舶、航空航天和其他运输设备制造业	Manufacture of Railroad,Marine,Aerospace and Other Transportation Equipment	1.3	-1.1
电气机械及器材制造业	Manufacture of Electrical Machinery & Equipment	2.5	9.4
计算机、通信和其他电子设备制造业	Manufacture of Computer, Communications and Other Electronic Equipment	3.7	10.5
仪器仪表制造业	Manufacture of Measuring Instrument	0.5	7.4
其他制造业	Other Manufacture	0.1	38.7
废弃资源综合利用业	Comprehensive Utilization of Waste	0.2	-36.2
金属制品、机械和设备修理业	Metal Products, Machinery and Equipment Repair Industry	0.1	41.4
电力、热力、燃气及水的生产和供应业	**Production and Supply of Electric,Heat,Gas and Water**	**10.0**	**1.3**
电力、热力生产和供应业	Production and Supply of Electric Power and Heat Power	8.6	0.9
燃气生产和供应业	Production and Supply of Gas	0.8	1.1
水的生产和供应业	Production and Supply of Water	0.6	7.9

14-9 续表 continued

类 别	Category	2021 增加值占规模以上工业比重(%) Composition (%)	2021 工业增加值比上年增长(%) Growth Rate (%)
全省总计	**Total**	**100.0**	**9.6**
采矿业	**Mining**	**6.3**	**-0.1**
煤炭开采和洗选业	Mining and Washing of Coal	3.1	2.4
石油和天然气开采业	Extraction of Petroleum and Natural Gas	1.5	-1.7
黑色金属矿采选业	Mining of Ferrous Metal Ores	0.8	12.5
有色金属矿采选业	Mining of Non-ferrous Metal Ores	0.4	-47.2
非金属矿采选业	Mining and Processing of Nonmetal Ores	0.3	
开采专业及辅助性活动	Mining Specialties and Auxiliary Activities	0.3	1.0
其他采矿业	Mining of Other Ores		
制造业	**Manufacturing**	**83.3**	**10.1**
农副食品加工业	Processing of Food from Agricultural Products	4.2	9.1
食品制造业	Manufacture of Foods	2.1	31.2
酒、饮料和精制茶制造业	Manufacture of Wine, Drinks and Refined Tea	0.9	13.6
烟草制品业	Manufacture of Tobacco	1.6	6.7
纺织业	Manufacture of Textile	2.3	10.3
纺织服装、服饰业	Manufacture of Textile Wearing Apparel and Finery	0.9	13.4
皮革、毛皮、羽毛及其制品和制鞋业	Manufacture of Leather, Fur, Feather & Its Products and Footwear	0.2	10.0
木材加工及木 竹、藤、棕、草制品业	Processing of Timbers, Manufacture of Wood, Bamboo, Rattan, Palm, and Straw Products	1.3	18.4
家具制造业	Manufacture of Furniture	0.3	20.1
造纸及纸制品业	Manufacture of Paper and Paper Products	1.6	12.6
印刷和记录媒介复制业	Printing, Reproduction of Recording Media	0.3	20.4
文教、工美、体育和娱乐用品制造业	Manufacture of Culture, Education,Arts and crafts, Sport and Entertainment Goods	0.8	22.7
石油、煤炭及其他燃料加工业	Processing of Oil, Coal and Other Fuel	8.0	3.3
化学原料和化学制品制造业	Manufacture of Chemical Raw Material and Chemical Products	12.8	19.3
医药制造业	Manufacture of Medicines	4.5	10.6
化学纤维制造业	Manufacture of Chemical Fiber	0.1	15.9
橡胶和塑料制品业	Manufacture of Rubber and Plastic	2.7	6.9
非金属矿物制品业	Manufacture of Non-metallic Mineral Products	5.5	10.0
黑色金属冶炼及压延加工业	Manufacture and Processing of Ferrous Metals	4.7	-9.4
有色金属冶炼及压延加工业	Manufacture & Processing of Non-ferrous Metals	3.9	1.1
金属制品业	Manufacture of Metal Products	3.3	25.4
通用设备制造业	Manufacture of General Purpose Machinery	4.1	10.5
专用设备制造业	Manufacture of Special Purpose Machinery	4.1	12.4
汽车制造业	Manufacture of Automotive	5.1	-5.8
铁路、船舶、航空航天和其他运输设备制造业	Manufacture of Railroad,Marine,Aerospace and Other Transportation Equipment	0.9	-17.2
电气机械及器材制造业	Manufacture of Electrical Machinery & Equipment	2.4	9.8
计算机、通信和其他电子设备制造业	Manufacture of Computer, Communications and Other Electronic Equipment	3.7	31.6
仪器仪表制造业	Manufacture of Measuring Instrument	0.5	8.9
其他制造业	Other Manufacture	0.1	10.2
废弃资源综合利用业	Comprehensive Utilization of Waste	0.3	31.5
金属制品、机械和设备修理业	Metal Products, Machinery and Equipment Repair Industry	0.2	44.6
电力、热力、燃气及水的生产和供应业	**Production and Supply of Electric,Heat,Gas and Water**	**10.4**	**11.7**
电力、热力生产和供应业	Production and Supply of Electric Power and Heat Power	9.0	11.0
燃气生产和供应业	Production and Supply of Gas	0.8	19.4
水的生产和供应业	Production and Supply of Water	0.6	12.8

14-10 各市规模以上工业企业主要经济指标(2021年)

Main Economic Indicators of Industrial Enterprises above Designated Size by Region(2021)

单位:亿元 (100 million yuan)

地区	Region	企业单位数(个) Number of Enterprises (unit)	资产总计 Total Assets	流动资产合计 Total Current Assets	负债合计 Total Liabilities	营业收入 Business Revenue	营业成本 Business Cost	利润总额 Total Profits	全部从业人员年平均人数(万人) Annual Average of Employed Persons (10 000 person)
全省总计	**Total**	**33057**	**111501.60**	**59617.18**	**68192.56**	**103804.16**	**89817.40**	**5394.75**	**554.91**
济南市	Jinan	2543	8494.19	5224.97	5113.89	8492.55	7270.71	408.38	40.98
青岛市	Qingdao	4280	12950.41	8028.77	7351.40	11542.95	9838.36	578.03	68.90
淄博市	Zibo	1958	5924.15	3205.50	3436.47	6071.01	5003.44	394.86	31.32
枣庄市	Zaozhuang	841	2139.74	1090.43	1319.76	1600.86	1303.65	128.45	13.91
东营市	Dongying	895	8708.91	4784.25	6386.04	8891.40	7832.35	180.05	26.04
烟台市	Yantai	2421	11349.97	5688.07	6612.20	9094.80	7867.51	588.15	51.89
潍坊市	Weifang	3872	10852.53	6447.48	6794.71	11019.19	9589.66	515.14	68.47
济宁市	Jining	2195	7138.18	3304.99	4361.23	4700.30	3924.86	303.51	37.27
泰安市	Tai'an	1225	4252.91	2422.96	2972.14	2758.81	2292.20	153.61	22.05
威海市	Weihai	1214	4350.25	2563.82	2167.31	2916.78	2256.47	234.98	29.18
日照市	Rizhao	899	4537.31	2480.73	3052.94	4465.04	4063.47	203.23	13.81
临沂市	Linyi	3771	5880.10	3501.30	3862.79	6373.28	5644.22	184.63	41.75
德州市	Dezhou	1685	3521.60	1770.09	2032.16	3678.34	3130.76	245.77	23.81
聊城市	Liaocheng	1542	4328.42	2413.24	2841.55	4465.55	3973.98	195.24	21.27
滨州市	Binzhou	1494	9087.19	4463.30	5379.52	9208.76	8352.87	637.02	29.83
菏泽市	Heze	2218	3551.66	1559.02	2013.79	5291.97	4605.17	354.53	23.21

14-11 各市规模以上国有控股工业企业主要经济指标(2021年)

Main Economic Indicators of State-holding Industrial Enterprises above Designated Size by Region(2021)

单位:亿元 (100 million yuan)

地 区	Region	企业单位数(个) Number of Enterprises (unit)	资 产 总 计 Total Assets	流动资产合 计 Total Current Assets	负债合计 Total Liabilities	营业收入 Business Revenue	营业成本 Business Cost	利润总额 Total Profits	全部从业人员年平均人数(万人) Annual Average of Employed Persons (10 000 person)
全省总计	**Total**	**1935**	**36301.69**	**14891.59**	**23224.97**	**25823.10**	**21854.14**	**1443.08**	**104.00**
济南市	Jinan	252	3536.81	1948.35	2362.73	3635.12	3250.35	92.47	11.11
青岛市	Qingdao	226	4635.12	2749.80	2831.59	3909.85	3328.95	219.40	11.93
淄博市	Zibo	122	1290.18	580.53	710.95	1360.33	1064.06	82.17	5.95
枣庄市	Zaozhuang	112	1078.10	517.28	715.28	564.11	414.32	65.70	4.78
东营市	Dongying	63	2424.00	477.44	1774.29	1914.55	1521.70	5.70	9.33
烟台市	Yantai	173	4657.79	1545.40	3056.50	3359.53	2927.63	310.84	8.39
潍坊市	Weifang	138	2866.73	1558.67	1649.48	1936.60	1609.81	148.88	7.12
济宁市	Jining	180	3649.47	1524.22	2460.94	1475.01	1170.41	96.57	13.27
泰安市	Tai'an	124	1905.95	1055.82	1484.96	633.65	538.31	26.70	5.09
威海市	Weihai	72	771.17	341.70	494.04	256.79	226.91	0.23	2.44
日照市	Rizhao	50	895.73	309.60	626.25	811.67	714.07	45.08	1.31
临沂市	Linyi	107	838.50	333.99	512.84	446.36	377.85	20.63	2.59
德州市	Dezhou	68	770.39	264.69	390.52	719.03	583.34	91.96	2.13
聊城市	Liaocheng	76	965.41	415.17	577.65	758.21	624.37	78.45	3.17
滨州市	Binzhou	83	708.50	282.85	506.84	443.79	387.05	10.31	1.88
菏泽市	Heze	85	873.77	317.84	575.45	365.91	247.23	58.81	2.29

14-12 各市规模以上外商和港澳台商投资工业企业主要经济指标(2021年)
Main Economic Indicators of Industrial Enterprises with Funds from Foreign Countries (Territories), Hong Kong,Macao and Taiwan by Region(2021)

单位:亿元 (100 million yuan)

地　区	Region	企业单位数(个) Number of Enterprises (unit)	资产总计 Total Assets	流动资产合计 Total Current Assets	负债合计 Total Liabilities	营业收入 Business Revenue	营业成本 Business Cost	利润总额 Total Profits	全部从业人员年平均人数(万人) Annual Average of Employed Persons (10 000 person)
全省总计	**Total**	**2711**	**19641.00**	**10914.77**	**10753.98**	**15711.86**	**13439.49**	**1090.56**	**88.52**
济南市	Jinan	146	1343.25	839.51	679.82	1164.36	937.05	115.52	6.09
青岛市	Qingdao	817	2661.26	1829.37	1323.39	2952.78	2492.97	186.33	19.94
淄博市	Zibo	112	804.71	381.27	436.75	599.84	500.20	33.79	4.06
枣庄市	Zaozhuang	44	175.77	92.31	91.96	141.04	120.08	6.09	1.61
东营市	Dongying	44	383.50	273.89	278.75	366.26	321.71	17.40	0.77
烟台市	Yantai	471	3150.75	2114.83	1697.07	3300.46	2911.47	145.37	18.01
潍坊市	Weifang	248	1613.63	878.42	976.69	1148.48	982.82	91.96	6.76
济宁市	Jining	108	2592.32	1006.04	1642.29	673.05	481.54	95.14	7.64
泰安市	Tai'an	59	320.72	189.19	188.02	252.85	204.13	24.70	1.21
威海市	Weihai	257	847.84	499.29	339.97	626.42	487.88	63.76	7.56
日照市	Rizhao	92	1278.07	826.02	757.80	1743.75	1591.67	85.94	2.98
临沂市	Linyi	109	1040.75	737.95	618.03	734.75	590.96	37.98	4.66
德州市	Dezhou	75	292.40	139.64	146.11	266.80	242.14	6.77	1.97
聊城市	Liaocheng	37	1060.43	526.66	590.97	604.13	535.85	36.88	1.21
滨州市	Binzhou	46	399.26	145.67	231.04	334.74	306.75	6.37	1.82
菏泽市	Heze	44	463.88	256.04	194.20	618.47	508.76	111.29	1.69

14-13 各市规模以上非公有制工业企业主要经济指标(2021年)

Main Economic Indicators of Non-public Industrial Enterprises above Designated Size by Region(2021)

单位:亿元 (100 million yuan)

地 区	Region	企业单位数(个) Number of Enterprises (unit)	资产总计 Total Assets	流动资产合计 Total Current Assets	负债合计 Total Liabilities	营业收入 Business Revenue	营业成本 Business Cost	利润总额 Total Profits	全部从业人员年平均人数(万人) Annual Average of Employed Persons (10 000 person)
全省总计	**Total**	**30613**	**70242.58**	**42086.06**	**42381.16**	**74022.35**	**64582.16**	**3726.92**	**430.99**
济南市	Jinan	2243	4753.51	3156.53	2661.86	4702.13	3894.45	305.05	28.48
青岛市	Qingdao	3994	7073.14	4727.35	3900.51	6983.18	5960.00	326.14	54.05
淄博市	Zibo	1775	4386.08	2498.08	2545.30	4480.55	3735.87	306.34	24.08
枣庄市	Zaozhuang	715	927.71	524.54	542.05	960.28	831.70	50.15	8.86
东营市	Dongying	784	5275.77	3678.98	4008.05	5903.05	5381.83	121.55	14.59
烟台市	Yantai	2181	5712.93	3691.62	3135.72	4943.18	4263.90	224.58	39.93
潍坊市	Weifang	3698	7853.69	4805.90	5075.66	8936.04	7852.32	355.19	60.40
济宁市	Jining	2004	3460.53	1762.20	1885.94	3202.77	2739.12	203.01	23.57
泰安市	Tai'an	1072	2200.99	1262.43	1413.66	2022.08	1685.08	110.82	15.93
威海市	Weihai	1113	3449.52	2144.15	1616.80	2576.24	1957.77	228.01	25.79
日照市	Rizhao	827	3531.26	2113.65	2351.38	3574.15	3273.88	160.17	11.95
临沂市	Linyi	3642	4937.72	3097.45	3276.30	5827.62	5182.35	159.80	38.61
德州市	Dezhou	1600	2718.12	1491.87	1619.12	2939.12	2529.70	152.95	21.43
聊城市	Liaocheng	1450	3232.33	1918.83	2220.64	3596.83	3246.94	114.57	16.94
滨州市	Binzhou	1387	8062.25	3977.86	4695.10	8461.01	7696.60	614.26	25.64
菏泽市	Heze	2128	2667.04	1234.63	1433.08	4914.13	4350.67	294.31	20.74

14-14 各市规模以上工业企业主要财务分析指标(2021年)

Main Financial Indicators of Industrial Enterprises above Designated Size by Region(2021)

单位：% (%)

地区	Region	资产负债率 Assets-Liability Ratio	成本费用利润率 Ratio of Profits to Cost	流动资产周转率(次) Ratio of Turnover Working Capitals (time)
全省总计	**Total**	**61.16**	**5.52**	**1.74**
济南市	Jinan	60.20	5.06	1.63
青岛市	Qingdao	56.77	5.30	1.44
淄博市	Zibo	58.01	7.14	1.89
枣庄市	Zaozhuang	61.68	8.76	1.47
东营市	Dongying	73.33	2.18	1.86
烟台市	Yantai	58.26	6.85	1.60
潍坊市	Weifang	62.61	4.95	1.71
济宁市	Jining	61.10	6.91	1.42
泰安市	Tai'an	69.88	5.91	1.14
威海市	Weihai	49.82	8.66	1.14
日照市	Rizhao	67.29	4.75	1.80
临沂市	Linyi	65.69	2.99	1.82
德州市	Dezhou	57.71	7.19	2.08
聊城市	Liaocheng	65.65	4.55	1.85
滨州市	Binzhou	59.20	7.28	2.06
菏泽市	Heze	56.70	7.27	3.39

14-15 各市规模以上国有控股工业企业主要财务分析指标(2021年)
Main Financial Indicators of State-holding Industrial Enterprises above Designated Size by Region(2021)

单位：% (%)

地 区	Region	资 产 负债率 Assets-Liability Ratio	成本费用 利 润 率 Ratio of Profits to Cost	流动资产 周 转 率 (次) Ratio of Turnover Working Capitals (time)
全省总计	**Total**	**63.98**	**6.09**	**1.73**
济 南 市	Jinan	66.80	2.64	1.87
青 岛 市	Qingdao	61.09	6.10	1.42
淄 博 市	Zibo	55.10	6.97	2.34
枣 庄 市	Zaozhuang	66.35	13.47	1.09
东 营 市	Dongying	73.20	0.35	4.01
烟 台 市	Yantai	65.62	9.95	2.17
潍 坊 市	Weifang	57.54	8.50	1.24
济 宁 市	Jining	67.43	7.16	0.97
泰 安 市	Tai'an	77.91	4.39	0.60
威 海 市	Weihai	64.06	0.09	0.75
日 照 市	Rizhao	69.92	5.96	2.62
临 沂 市	Linyi	61.16	4.87	1.34
德 州 市	Dezhou	50.69	14.85	2.72
聊 城 市	Liaocheng	59.83	11.44	1.83
滨 州 市	Binzhou	71.54	2.49	1.57
菏 泽 市	Heze	65.86	20.02	1.15

14-16 规模以上工业主要产品产量(2021年)
Output of Major Industrial Products above Designated Size(2021)

名 称		Item		生产量 Output
铁矿石原矿量	(万吨)	Ironstone in Original Iron Ores	(10 000 tons)	2452.8
原 盐	(万吨)	Salt	(10 000 tons)	742.8
小麦粉	(万吨)	Wheat Flour	(10 000 tons)	1749.8
大 米	(万吨)	Rice	(10 000 tons)	46.3
精制食用植物油	(万吨)	Refined Edible Vegetable Oil	(10 000 tons)	558.9
鲜、冷藏肉	(万吨)	Frozen,Fresh Meat	(10 000 tons)	1001.4
配合饲料+混合饲料	(万吨)	Formula Feed & Mixed Feed	(10 000 tons)	2917.8
速冻米面食品	(万吨)	Quick-frozen Food	(10 000 tons)	3.7
方便面	(万吨)	Instant Noodles	(10 000 tons)	13.8
乳制品	(万吨)	Milk Products	(10 000 tons)	242.6
液体乳	(万吨)	Liquid Milk	(10 000 tons)	226.8
罐 头	(万吨)	Canned Food	(10 000 tons)	64.1
酱 油	(万吨)	Soy Sauce	(10 000 tons)	51.2
发酵酒精(折96度,商品量)	(万千升)	Fermenting Alcohol	(10 000 kiloliter)	69.6
饮料酒	(万千升)	Liquor	(10 000 kiloliter)	501.5
白酒(折65度,商品量)	(万千升)	White Spirit	(10 000 kiloliter)	23.7
啤 酒	(万千升)	Beer	(10 000 kiloliter)	461.3
葡萄酒	(万千升)	Wine	(10 000 kiloliter)	8.1
饮料	(万吨)	Drinks	(10 000 tons)	538.2
碳酸饮料	(万吨)	Carbonated Drinks	(10 000 tons)	100.0
包装饮用水	(万吨)	Bottled Drinking Water	(10 000 tons)	184.8
果汁蔬菜汁类饮料	(万吨)	Juice and Vegetable Juice Beverage	(10 000 tons)	101.0
冷冻饮品	(万吨)	Frozen Drinks	(10 000 tons)	8.4
卷 烟	(亿支)	Cigarettes	(100 million pieces)	1280.4
化学纤维用浆粕	(万吨)	Chemical Fiber Pulp	(10 000 tons)	6.3
化学纤维	(万吨)	Chemical Fiber	(10 000 tons)	77.1
粘胶短纤维	(万吨)	Viscose Staple Fiber	(10 000 tons)	9.7
合成纤维	(万吨)	Synthetic Fiber	(10 000 tons)	37.0
锦纶纤维	(万吨)	Nylon Fiber	(10 000 tons)	8.0
涤纶纤维	(万吨)	Polyester Fiber	(10 000 tons)	19.0
腈纶纤维	(万吨)	Acrylic Fiber	(10 000 tons)	2.7
丙纶纤维	(万吨)	Polypropylene Fiber	(10 000 tons)	3.0
纱	(万吨)	Yarn	(10 000 tons)	375.5
布	(亿米)	Cloth	(100 million m)	41.9
棉 布	(亿米)	Cotton Cloth	(100 million m)	35.0
棉混纺布(混纺交织布)	(亿米)	Cotton Blended Cloth	(100 million m)	3.8
化学纤维短纤布	(亿米)	Chemical Fiber Cloth	(100 million m)	3.0
印染布	(亿米)	Printed Fabric	(100 million m)	40.2
绒线(毛线)	(万吨)	Knitting Wool	(10 000 tons)	3.7
毛机织物(呢绒)	(万米)	Wool Fabric	(10 000 m)	3703.5
亚麻布	(万米)	Ramie and Flax Cloth	(10 000 m)	802.3
帘子布	(万吨)	Cord Fabric	(10 000 tons)	11.5

14-16 续表 1 continued

名称		Item		生产量 Output
服 装	(万件)	Garments	(10 000 pieces)	200105.1
梭织服装	(万件)	Woven Garments	(10 000 pieces)	70853.8
羽绒服	(万件)	Down Wear	(10 000 pieces)	972.6
西服套装	(万件)	Suits	(10 000 pieces)	853.6
衬 衫	(万件)	Shirts	(10 000 pieces)	1979.2
针织服装	(万件)	Knitted Clothing	(10 000 pieces)	129251.3
轻 革	(万平方米)	Leather	(10 000 sq.m)	3654.0
皮革鞋靴	(万双)	Shoes	(10 000 pairs)	3363.3
天然毛皮服装	(万件)	Natural Fur Apparel	(10 000 units)	5.8
人造板	(万立方米)	Manmade Plates	(10 000 cu.m)	6722.2
胶合板	(万立方米)	Plywood	(10 000 cu.m)	4478.3
纤维板	(万立方米)	Fiberboard	(10 000 cu.m)	1306.4
刨花板	(万立方米)	Flakeboard	(10 000 cu.m)	506.3
人造板表面装饰板(人造板)	(万立方米)	Secondary Processing Decorative Plates	(10 000 cu.m)	2846.9
实木地板(木地板)	(万平方米)	Solid Wood Floor	(10 000 sq.m)	9.1
复合木地板	(万平方米)	Engineered Wooden Floor	(10 000 sq.m)	1292.0
家 具	(万件)	Furniture	(10 000 units)	5341.1
木质家具	(万件)	Wood Furniture	(10 000 units)	3910.2
金属家具	(万件)	Metal Furniture	(10 000 units)	380.3
软体家具(包括床垫、沙发)	(万件)	Soft Furniture	(10 000 units)	217.6
纸 浆	(万吨)	Paper Pulp	(10 000 tons)	550.1
机制纸及纸板	(万吨)	Machine-made Paper and Paperboards	(10 000 tons)	2473.9
未涂布印刷书写用纸	(万吨)	Uncoated Writing Printing Paper	(10 000 tons)	147.8
新闻纸	(万吨)	Newsprint	(10 000 tons)	21.2
纸制品	(万吨)	Paper Products	(10000 tons)	466.4
瓦楞纸箱(纸箱)	(万吨)	Corrugated Box	(10000 tons)	191.9
硫酸(折100%)	(万吨)	Sulfuric	(10 000 tons)	590.7
盐酸(含量31%以上)	(万吨)	Hydrochloric Acid(content of more than 31%)	(10 000 tons)	89.5
烧碱(折100%)	(万吨)	Caustic	(10 000 tons)	1044.4
离子膜法烧碱(折100%)	(万吨)	Ionic Membrane Caustic	(10 000 tons)	927.9
碳酸钠(纯碱)	(万吨)	Soda Ash	(10 000 tons)	415.2
合成氨	(万吨)	Synthetic Ammonia	(10 000 tons)	656.8
农用氮、磷、钾化学肥料总计(折纯)	(万吨)	Chemical Fertilizer	(10 000 tons)	397.4
氮 肥(折含N 100%)	(万吨)	Nitrogen Fertilizer	(10 000 tons)	384.3
尿 素(折含N 100%)	(万吨)	Urea	(10 000 tons)	359.1
磷肥(折合P2O5 100%)	(万吨)	Phosphate Fertilizer	(10 000 tons)	2.3

14-16 续表 2 continued

名　　称		Item		生产量 Output
化学农药原药(折有效成分100%)	(万吨)	Chemical Pesticide	(10 000 tons)	29.2
杀虫剂原药	(万吨)	Insecticides Pesticide	(10 000 tons)	6.5
杀菌剂原药	(万吨)	Fungicides Pesticide	(10 000 tons)	1.1
除草剂原药	(万吨)	Herbicide Pesticide	(10 000 tons)	17.3
乙　烯	(万吨)	Ethylene	(10 000 tons)	261.5
纯　苯	(万吨)	Benzene	(10 000 tons)	162.1
精甲醇	(万吨)	Extracted Methanol	(10 000 tons)	379.0
冰醋酸	(万吨)	Acetic Acid	(10 000 tons)	164.2
涂料	(万吨)	Paint	(10 000 tons)	99.1
初级形态的塑料	(万吨)	Primary Plastic	(10 000 tons)	880.3
聚丙烯树脂	(万吨)	Polypropylene Colophony	(10 000 tons)	167.8
聚氯乙烯树脂	(万吨)	PVC Colophony	(10 000 tons)	260.3
合成橡胶	(万吨)	Synthetic Rubber	(10 000 tons)	145.5
合成纤维单体	(万吨)	Synthetic Fiber Monomer	(10 000 tons)	19.0
合成纤维聚合物	(万吨)	Synthetic Fiber Polymers	(10 000 tons)	26.8
合成洗涤剂	(万吨)	Synthetic Detergents	(10 000 tons)	66.0
中成药	(万吨)	Traditional Chemical Medicine	(10 000 tons)	12.8
橡胶轮胎外胎	(万条)	Tires	(10 000 tires)	40820.3
子午线轮胎外胎	(万条)	Radial Tires	(10 000 tires)	36755.4
塑料制品	(万吨)	Plastic Articles	(10 000 tons)	360.6
塑料薄膜	(万吨)	Plastic Film	(10 000 tons)	84.3
农用薄膜	(万吨)	Agricultural Film	(10 000 tons)	10.4
泡沫塑料	(万吨)	Foam	(10 000 tons)	11.9
塑料人造革、合成革	(万吨)	Plastic leather and synthetic leather	(10 000 tons)	2.3
日用塑料制品	(万吨)	Plastic Products for Daily Use	(10 000 tons)	22.6
硅酸盐水泥熟料	(万吨)	Portland Cement Clinker	(10 000 tons)	8759.4
窑外分解窑水泥熟料	(万吨)	Decomposition Kiln Clinker	(10 000 tons)	8233.8
水　泥	(万吨)	Cement	(10 000 tons)	16444.7
商品混凝土	(万立方米)	Concrete	(10 000 cu.m)	24965.6
水泥混凝土排水管	(千米)	Cement and Concrete Drain Pipes	(1 000 m)	3663.3
水泥混凝土压力管	(千米)	Cement and Concrete Pressure Pipes	(1 000 m)	1148.9
水泥混凝土电杆	(万根)	Cement Concrete Poles	(10 000 units)	56.1
预应力混凝土桩	(万米)	Prestressed concrete piles	(10 000 m)	1526.1
砖(折标准砖)	(亿块)	Brick	(100 million units)	52.2
瓦	(亿片)	Tile	(100 million units)	0.4
天然大理石建筑板材	(万平方米)	Natural Marble Building Block	(10 000 sq.m)	456.8
天然花岗石建筑板材	(万平方米)	Natural Granite Building Block	(10 000 sq.m)	862.8

14-16　续表 3 continued

名　　称		Item		生产量 Output
粉末冶金零件	(万吨)	Sintered Metal Products	(10 000 tons)	7.6
工业锅炉	(蒸发量吨)	Industrial Boilers	(evaporation ton)	41915.1
电站用汽轮机	(万千瓦)	Turbine Power Plant	(10 000 kW)	109.3
金属切削机床	(万台)	Metal-cutting Machine Tools	(10 000 units)	6.2
金属成形机床	(万台)	Metal Forming Machine	(10 000 units)	0.6
数控金属成形机床	(台)	CNC Metal Forming Machine	(units)	1277
铸造机械	(万台)	Casting Machinery	(10 000 units)	6.1
起重机	(万吨)	Lifting Equipment	(10 000 tons)	61.4
输送机械	(万吨)	Conveyer	(10 000 tons)	8.8
泵	(万台)	Pumps	(10 000 units)	175.0
气体压缩机	(万台)	Gas Compressor	(10 000 units)	1281.8
阀　门	(万吨)	Valves	(10 000 tons)	49.0
液压元件	(万件)	Hydraulic Components	(10 000 units)	2238.8
气动元件	(万件)	Pneumatic Components	(10 000 units)	994.7
滚动轴承	(亿套)	Rolling Bearings	(100 million units)	4.5
减速机	(万台)	Reducer	(10 000 units)	64.5
风　机	(万台)	Fans	(10 000 units)	72.7
包装专用设备	(台)	Packaging Special Equipment	(unit)	15405
矿山专用设备	(万吨)	Special Equipment for MIne	(10 000 tons)	67.4
挖掘、铲土运输机械	(台)	Mining and Shoveling Transport Machinery	(unit)	187754
压实机械	(台)	Compacting Machinery	(unit)	20257
水泥专用设备	(吨)	Cement Special Equipment	(ton)	16107.1
混凝土机械	(台)	Concrete Machinery	(unit)	58167
金属冶炼设备	(吨)	Metal Smelting Equipment	(ton)	73561.5
金属轧制设备	(吨)	Metal Rolling Equipment	(ton)	10195.0
饲料生产专用设备	(台)	Specialized Feed Processing Machinery	(unit)	439
印刷专用设备	(吨)	Printing Special Equipment	(ton)	3801.9
大型拖拉机	(台)	Large Tractors	(unit)	51222
中型拖拉机	(台)	Medium Tractors	(unit)	142574
小型拖拉机	(万台)	Small Tractors	(10 000 units)	5.4
收获机械	(台)	Harvesting Machinery	(unit)	74615
棉花加工机械	(台)	Cotton Processing Equipment	(unit)	1989
环境污染防治专用设备	(台(套))	Special Equipment for Environmental Protection	(unit)	155894
大气污染防治设备	(台(套))	Air Pollution Control Equipment	(unit)	25901
水质污染防治设备	(台(套))	Water Pollution Control Equipment	(unit)	73230
铁路货车	(辆)	Railway Freight Wagons	(unit)	3119

14-16 续表 4 continued

名 称		Item		生产量 Output
汽 车	(万辆)	Motor Vehicles	(10 000 units)	107.3
轿车	(万辆)	Cars	(10 000 units)	6.8
客车	(万辆)	Buses	(10 000 units)	5.1
载货汽车	(万辆)	Trucks	(10 000 units)	71.6
改装汽车	(万辆)	Modified Cars	(10 000 units)	14.2
民用钢质船舶	(万载重吨)	Civil Steel Vessels	(10 000 dwts)	354.3
电动自行车	(万辆)	Electric Bicycle	(10000 units)	88.8
发电机组	(万千瓦)	Power Generation Equipment	(10 000 kW)	578.1
汽轮发电机组	(万千瓦)	Steam Turbogenerator	(10 000 kW)	299.3
交流电动机	(万千瓦)	AC Motors	(10 000 kW)	2303.3
变压器	(万千伏安)	Transformers	(10 000 KVA pm)	28930.2
高压开关板	(面)	High Voltage Switch Plate	(unit)	28237
低压开关板	(万面)	Low Voltage Switch Plate	(10 000 units)	18.7
通信及电子网络用电缆	(万对千米)	Cable for Communications and Electronic Network	(10 000 couples·km)	32.4
电力电缆	(万千米)	Power Cable	(10 000 km)	139.4
光缆	(万芯千米)	Fire Optic Cable	(10 000 cores·km)	1157.8
绝缘制品	(吨)	Insulation Products	(ton)	31528.9
原电池及原电池组(非扣式)	(亿只)	Primary Cells and Batteries	(100 million units)	29.3
电光源	(万只)	Light Bulbs	(10 000 units)	31720.4
灯具及照明装置	(万套(台、个)	Lamps and Lighting Fixtures	(10 000 units)	7389.7
家用洗衣机	(万台)	Household Washing Machines	(10 000 units)	734.8
家用电冰箱	(万台)	Household Refrigerators	(10000 units)	888.8
家用冷柜(家用冷冻箱)	(万台)	Household Freezers	(10000 units)	781.9
房间空气调节器	(万台)	Air Conditioners	(10000 units)	1207.8
家用吸排油烟机	(万台)	Vacuum Cleaners	(10000 units)	256.5
家用电热水器	(万台)	Electric Water Heater	(10000 units)	544.2
电饭锅	(万个)	Electric Cookers	(10000 units)	46.8
电焊机	(万台)	Welders	(10000 units)	32.9
电子计算机整机	(万台)	Computers	(10000 units)	119.6
显示器	(万台)	Display	(10000 units)	152.9
打印机	(万台)	Printers	(10000 units)	952.9
电话单机	(万部)	Telephone Sets	(10000 units)	73.9
移动通信手持机(手机)	(万台)	Mobile Telephones	(10000 units)	531.6
彩色电视机	(万台)	Color Television Sets	(10000 units)	1986.7
半导体分立器件	(亿只)	Discrete Semiconductor Devices	(100 million units)	651.8

主要统计指标解释

工　业　指从事自然资源的开采，对采掘品和农产品进行加工和再加工的物质生产部门。具体包括：(1)对自然资源的开采，如采矿、晒盐等(但不包括禽兽捕猎和水产捕捞)；(2)对农副产品的加工、再加工，如粮油加工、食品加工、缫丝、纺织、制革等；(3)对采掘品的加工、再加工，如炼铁、炼钢、化工生产、石油加工、机器制造、木材加工等，以及电力、自来水、煤气的生产和供应等；(4)对工业品的修理、翻新，如机器设备的修理、交通运输工具(如汽车)的修理等。

工业统计调查单位为独立核算法人工业企业。

独立核算法人工业企业指从事工业生产经营活动的单位。独立核算法人工业企业应同时具备以下条件：①依法成立，有自己的名称、组织机构和场所，能够承担民事责任；②独立拥有和使用资产，承担负债，有权与其他单位签订合同；③独立核算盈亏，并能够编制资产负债表。

国有控股企业　即原来的国有及国有控股企业。国有企业(即原全民所有制工业或国营工业)指企业全部资产归国家所有，并按《中华人民共和国企业法人登记管理条例》规定登记注册的非公司制的经济组织。包括国有企业、国有独资公司和国有联营企业。1957年以前的公私合营和私营工业，后均改造为国营工业，1992年改为国有工业，这部分工业的资料不单独分列时，均包括在国有企业内。国有控股企业是对混合所有制经济的企业进行的“国有控股”分类。它是指这些企业的全部资产中国有资产(股份)相对其他所有者中的任何一个所有者占资(股)最多的企业。该分组反映了国有经济控股情况。

本年鉴中涉及的企业登记注册类型：

国有企业　指企业全部资产归国家所有，并按《中华人民共和国企业法人登记管理条例》规定登记注册的非公司制的经济组织。不包括有限责任公司中的国有独资公司。

集体企业　指企业资产归集体所有，并按《中华人民共和国企业法人登记管理条例》规定登记注册的经济组织。是社会主义公有制经济的组成部分。包括城乡所有使用集体投资举办的企业，以及部分个人通过集资自愿放弃所有权并依法经工商行政管理机关认定为集体所有制的企业。

股份合作企业　指以合作制为基础，由企业职工共同出资入股，吸收一定比例的社会资产投资组建，实行自主经营，自负盈亏，共同劳动，民主管理，按劳分配与按股分红相结合的一种集体经济组织。

联营企业　指两个及两个以上相同或不同所有制性质的企业法人或事业单位法人，按自愿、平等、互利的原则，共同投资组成的经济组织。

有限责任公司　指根据《中华人民共和国公司登记管理条例》规定登记注册，由两个以上，五十个以下的股东共同出资，每个股东以其所认缴的出资额对公司承担有限责任，公司以其全部资产对其债务承担责任的经济组织。

有限责任公司包括国有独资公司以及其他有限责任公司。

股份有限公司　指根据《中华人民共和国企业法人登记管理条例》规定登记注册，其全部注册资本由等额股份构成并通过发行股票筹集资本，股东以其认购的股份对公司承担有限责任，公司以其全部资产对其债务承担责任的经济组织。

私营企业　指由自然人投资设立或由自然人控股，以雇佣劳动为基础的营利性经济组织。包括按照《公司法》《合伙企业法》《私营企业暂行条例》规定登记注册的私营有限责任公司、私营股份有限公司、私营合伙企业和私营独资企业。

港、澳、台商投资企业　指企业注册登记类型中的港、澳、台资合资、合作、独资经营企业和股份有限公司之和。

外商投资企业　指企业注册登记类型中的中外合资、合作经营企业、外资企业和外商投资股份有限公司之和。

“三资”企业系指港、澳、台商投资企业和外资企业的简称。

轻工业　指主要提供生活消费品和制作手工工具的工业。按其所使用的原料不同，可分为两大类：(1)以农产品为原料的轻工业，是指直接或间接以农产品为基本原料的轻工业。主要包括食品制造、饮料制造、烟草加工、纺织、缝纫、皮革和毛皮制作、造纸以及印刷等工业；(2)以非农产品为原料的轻工业，是指以工业品为原料的轻工业。主要包括文教体育用品、化学药品制造、合成纤维制造、日用化学制品、日用玻璃制品、日用金属制品、手工工具制造、医疗器械制造、文化和办公用机械制造等工业。

重工业　指为国民经济各部门提供物质技术基础的主要生产资料的工业。按其生产性质和产品用途，可以分为下列三类：(1)采掘(伐)工业，是指对自然资源的开采，包括石油开采、煤炭开采、金属矿开采、非金属矿开采等工业；(2)原材料工业，指向国民经济各部门提供基本材料、动力和燃料的工业。包括金属冶炼及加工、炼焦及焦炭、化学、化工原料、水泥、人造板以及电力、石油和煤炭加工等工业；(3)加工工业，是指对工业原材料进行再加工制造的工业。包括装备国民经济各部门的机械设备制造工业、金属结构、水泥制品等工业，以及为农业提供的生产资料如化肥、农药等工业。

根据上述划分原则，修理业中以重工业产品为修理作业对象的划为重工业，反之划为轻工业。

工业增加值　指工业企业在报告期内以货币表现的工业生产活动的最终成果。

工业增加值有两种计算方法：一是生产法，即工业总产出减去工业中间投入加上应交增值税；二是收入法，即从收入的角度出发，根据生产要素在生产过程中应得到的收入份额计算，具体构成项目有固定资产折旧、劳动者报酬、生产税净额、营业盈余，这种方法也称要素分配法。本年鉴中的工业增加值是以生产法计算的。

生产法工业增加值的计算方法为：

工业增加值=工业总产出−工业中间投入+应交增值税

(1)工业总产出：指工业企业在一定时期内工业生产活动的总成果。工业总产出包括：成品生产价值，对外加工费收入，自制半成品、在产品期末期初差额价值。1995年后用新规定计算的工业总产值代替。

(2)工业中间投入：指工业企业在工业生产活动中消耗的外购物质产品和对外支付的服务费用。服务费用包括支付给物质生产部门(工业、农业、批发零售贸易业、建筑业、运输邮电业)的服务费用和支付给非物质生产部门(如保险、金融、文化教育、科学研究、医疗卫生、行政管理等)的服务费用。工业中间投入的确定须遵循以下原则：必须从外部购入的，并已计入工业总产出的产品和服务价值；必须是本期投入生产，并一次性消耗掉(包括本期摊销的低值易耗品等)的产品和服务价值。

资产总计　指企业拥有或控制的能以货币计量的经济资源，包括各种财产、债权和其他权利。资产按流动性分为流动资产、长期投资、固定资产、无形资产、递延资产和其他资产。该指标根据企业会计“资产负债表”中“资产总计”项目的期末数增列。

流动资产合计　资产满足以下条件之一应归为流动资产：(1）预计在一个正常营业周期中变现、出售或耗用，主要包括存货、应收账款等；(2）主要为交易目的而持有；(3）预计在资产负债表日起一年内（含一年）变现；(4）自资产负债日起一年内，交换其他资产或清偿负债的能力不受限制的现金或现金等价物。包括货币资金、应收票据、应收账款、存货等项目。来源于会计“资产负债表”中“流动资产合计”项目的期末余额数。

负债合计　指企业所承担的能以货币计量，将以资产或劳务偿付的债务，偿还形式包括货币、资产或提供劳务。负债一般按偿还期长短分为流动负债和长期负债。根据会计“资产负债表”中“负债合计”的年末数填列。

营业收入　指企业经营主要业务和其他业务所确认的收入总额。营业收入包括“主营业务收入”和“其他业务收入”。来源于会计“利润表”中“营业收入”项目的本年累计数。

营业成本　指企业经营主要业务和其他业务所发生的成本总额。包括企业（单位）在报告期内从事销售商品、提供劳务等日常活动发生的各种耗费。包括“主营业务成本”和“其他业务成本”。来源于会计“利润表”中“营业成本”项目的本年累计数。

利润总额　指企业生产经营活动的最终成果，是企业在一定时期内实现的盈亏相抵后的利润总额(亏损以“−”号表示)，它等于营业利润加上补贴收入加上投资收益加上营业外净收入再加上以前年度损益调整。

从业人员平均人数　是指报告期内每天拥有的从业人员人数。其计算公式为：

$$季平均人数=\frac{季内各月平均人数之和}{3}$$

$$月平均人数=\frac{报告月内每天实有人数之和}{报告月日历日数}$$

$$年平均人数=\frac{年内各月平均人数之和}{12}$$

资产负债率　该指标既反映企业经营风险的大小，也反映企业利用债权人提供的资金从事经营活动的能力。计算公式为：

$$资产负债率(\%)=\frac{负债总额}{资产总额}\times 100\%$$

资产与负债均为报告期期末数。

成本费用利润率　反映企业投入的生产成本及费用的经济效益，同时也反映企业降低成本所取得的经济效益。计算公式为：

$$成本费用利润率(\%)=\frac{利润总额}{成本费用总额}\times 100\%$$

公式中：成本费用总额为产品销售成本、销售费用、管理费用、财务费用之和。

流动资产周转率　指一定时期内流动资产完成的周转次数，反映投入工业企业流动资金的周转速度。计算公式为：

$$流动资产周转率=\frac{产品销售收入}{全部流动资产平均余额}$$

公式中：全部流动资产平均余额为期初和期末的流动资产之和的算术平均值。

Explanatory Notes on Main Statistical Indicators

Industry refers to the material production sector which is engaged in extraction of natural resources and processing and reprocessing of minerals and agricultural products, including (1) extraction of natural resources, such as mining, salt production (but not including hunting and fishing); (2) processing and reprocessing of farm and sideline produces, such as rice husking, flour milling, wine making, oil pressing, silk reeling, spinning and weaving, and leather making; (3) manufacture of industrial products, such as steel making, iron smelting, chemicals manufacturing, petroleum processing, machine building, timber processing; water and gas production and electricity generation and supply; (4)repairing of industrial products such as the repairing of machinery and means of transport (including cars).

Units of industrial statistics survey corporate industrial enterprises with independent accounting system.

Corporate industrial enterprises with independent accounting system refer to enterprises engaging in industrial production activities, which meet the following requirements: (1)They are established legally, having their own names, organizations, location, able to take civil liability; (2)They possess and use their assets independently, assume liabilities, and are entitled to sign contracts with other units; (3)They are financially independent and compile their own balance sheets.

State-holding Enterprises refer to state owned enterprises plus state holding enterprises. State owned enterprises (originally known as state run enterprises with ownership by the whole society) are non corporate economic entities registered in accordance with the Regulation of the People's Republic of China on the Management of Registration of Legal Enterprises, where all assets are owned by the state. Included in this category are state owned enterprises, state funded corporations and state owned joint operation enterprises. Joint state private industries and private industries, which existed before 1957, were transformed into state run industries since 1957, and into state owned industries after 1992. Statistics on those enterprises are included in the state owned industries instead of grouping them separately. State holding enterprises is a sub classification of enterprises with mixed ownership, referring to enterprises where the percentage of state assets (or shares by the state) is larger than any other single share holder of the same enterprise. This sub classification illustrates the control of the state over a particular industry.

Enterprises covered in the industrial statistics in the Yearbook include following categories by their registration:

State-owned Enterprises refer to non-corporation economic units where the entire assets are owned by the state and which have registered in accordance with the Regulation of the People ' s Republic of China on the Management of Registration of Corporate Enterprises. Excluded from this category are sole state funded corporations in the limited liability corporations.

Collective-owned Enterprises refer to economic entities registered in accordance with the Regulation of the People's Republic of China on the Management of Registration of Legal Enterprises, where assets are owned by collectively. Collective enterprises constitute an integral part of the socialist economy with public ownership. They include urban and rural enterprises invested by collectives, and some enterprises registered in industrial and commercial administration agency as collective units where funds are pulled together by individuals who voluntarily give up their right of ownership.

Share-holding Cooperative Enterprises refer to economic units set up on cooperative basis, with funding partly from members of the enterprise and partly from outside investment, where the operation and management is decided by the members who also participate in the production, and the distribution of income is based both on work (labour input) and on shares (capital input).

Joint Operation Enterprises refer to economic units that are established by joint investment by two or more corporate enterprises or institutions of the same or different types of ownership on voluntary, equal and mutual beneficial basis.

Limited Liability Corporations refer to economic units registered in accordance with the Regulation of the People's Republic of China on the Management of Registration of Corporations, with capitals from 2 to 49 investors, each investor bears limited liability to the corporation depending on his/her holding of shares, and the corporation bears liability to its debt to the maximum of its total assets.

Share-holding Corporations Ltd. refer to economic units registered in accordance with the Regulation of the People's Republic of China on the Management of Registration of Corporate Enterprises, with total registered capitals divided into equal shares and raised through issuing stocks. Each investor bears limited liability to the corporation depending on the holding of shares, and the corporation bears liability to its debt to the maximum of its total assets.

Private Enterprises refer to economic units invested or controlled (by holding the majority of the shares) by natural persons who hire labours for profit making activities. Included in this category are private limited liability corporations, private share holding corporations Ltd., private partnership enterprises and private sole investment enterprises registered in accordance with the Corporation Law, Partnership Enterprise Law and Tentative Regulation on Private Enterprises.

Enterprises with Funds from Hong Kong, Macao and Taiwan refers to all industrial enterprises registered as the joint venture, cooperative, sole (exclusive) investment industrial enterprises and limited liability corporations with funds from Hong Kong, Macao and Taiwan.

Foreign Funded Enterprises refers to all industrial enterprises registered as the joint venture, cooperative, sole (exclusive) investment industrial enterprises and limited liability corporations with foreign funds.

Enterpries with Hong Kong, Macao, Taiwan and foreign fund refer to all the enterpries with funds from Hong Kong Macao and Taiwan and foreign funded enterprises.

Light Industry refers to the industry that produces

consumer goods and hand tools. It consists of two categories, depending on the materials used:

(1) Industries using farm products as raw materials. These are branches of light industry which directly or indirectly use farm products as basic raw materials, including the manufacture of food and beverages, tobacco processing, textile, clothing, fur and leather manufacturing, paper making, printing, etc.

(2) Industries using non farm products as raw materials. These are branches of light industry which use manufactured goods as raw materials, including the manufacture of cultural, educational articles and sports goods, chemicals, synthetic fiber, chemical products for daily use, glass products for daily use, metal products for daily use, hand tools, medical apparatus and instruments, and the manufacture of cultural and clerical machinery.

Heavy Industry refers to the industry which produces capital goods, and provides various sectors of the national economy with necessary material and technical basis. It consists of the following three branches according to the purpose of production or the use of products:

(1) Mining, quarrying and logging industry refers to the industry that extracts natural resources, including extraction of petroleum, coal, metal and non metal ores.

(2) Raw materials industry refers to the industry that provides various sectors of the national economy with raw materials, fuels and power. It includes smelting and processing of metals, coking and coke chemistry, chemical materials and building materials such as cement, plywood, and power, petroleum refining and coal dressing.

(3) Manufacturing industry refers to the industry that processes raw materials. It includes machine building industry which equips sectors of the national economy, industries of metal structure and cement products, industries producing means of agricultural production, such as chemical fertilizers and pesticides.

According to the above principle of classification, the repairing trades, which are engaged primarily in repairing products of heavy industry are classified into heavy industry while these engaged in repairing products of light industry are classified into light industry.

Value-added of Industry refers to the final results of industrial production of industrial enterprises in money terms during the reference period.

Industrial value added can be calculated by two approaches: the production approach, i.e. gross industrial output value minus intermediate input plus value added tax, and the income approach, i.e. income for various factors used in the course of production, including depreciation of fixed assets, remuneration of labourers, net of production tax, and operating surplus. Value added of industry in the Yearbook is calculated by production approach as following:

Value added of industry=gross industrial outputindustrial intermediate input+value added tax

(1)Gross industrial output: refers to the total achievements of industrial production during a given period. Gross industrial output includes value of finished products, income from external processing, and value of change in semi finished products at the end and at the beginning of the reference period. Since 1995, it was substituted by the gross industrial output value by new method.

(2) Industrial intermediate input: refers to purchased goods and paid services consumed during the industrial production of enterprises. Fees paid for services include fees paid for the services provided by material production sectors (industry, agriculture, wholesale and retail trade, construction, transport, post and telecommunications) and by non material production sectors (insurance, banking, culture, education, scientific research, health and medical care, public administration, etc.). The determination of industrial intermediate input follows the principle that the goods and services must be purchased from outside and included in the gross industrial output, and that the goods and services are inputted into production and consumed (include low value consumables) during the reference period..

Total Assets refer to all economic resources, in monetary terms, that is owned or controlled by enterprises, including properties, creditors equity and other economic rights of all forms. Classified by the degree of equitability, total assets include circulating assets, long term investment, fixed assets, intangible assets and deferred assets, and other assets. Data on this indicator can be obtained by the year end figures of total assets in the Assets and Liability Table of accounting records of enterprises.

Total Current Assets refer to the assets that meet one of the following requirements: (1) expected to be cashed, sold or used in a normal operation cycle, mainly including inventory and accounts receivable; (2) be owned for trading purpose mainly; (3) expected to be cashed in one year (including one year) from the day of the Balance Sheet; (4) unlimited cash or cash equivalents that can be exchanged with other assets or being capable of settling debts during one year since the day of the Balance Sheet. Included are monetary capital, notes receivable, accounts receivable and inventories. Data on this indicator can be obtained from the year-end figures of total current assets in the Balance Sheet of accounting records.

Total Liabilities refer to payable liabilities of enterprises that have to repay in terms of money, assets or labour services. In terms of payment, it can be divided into liquid liabilities and long term liabilities. Data on this item is obtained from the ending figures on total liabilities from the Assets and Liability Table from the enterprises.

Business Revenue refers to the total revenue recognized by an enterprise in its principal business and other business operations. Business revenue includes " revenue from principal Business" and " revenue from other business". It comes from this year's cumulative report of "business revenue" items from the "income statement".

Business Cost refers to the total cost incurred by an enterprise in its principal business and other business operations. It includes various expenditures incurred by enterprises (units) in their daily activities of selling goods and providing labour services during the reporting period. It includes "Cost of principal business" and "Cost of other business". It comes from this year's cumulative report of "operating cost" items from the "income statement".

Total Profits refer to the final achievements of production and operation of the enterprises, represented by the total profits after deducting losses (loss is expressed by the negative figure). It is the sum of profits from operation, income from subsidies, investment earnings, net income from activities other than operation, and adjustment of profits and losses of previous years.

Average Annual Number of Employed Persons Employed persons refer to all those who are employed in enterprises and receive remunerations therefrom, including currently working employees, retirees who are re employed, teachers of local run schools, as well as foreigners, staff from Hong Kong, Macao and Taiwan, part time employees and persons with second job who are employed by the enterprise, and employees of other units temporarily working in the enterprises, but excluding former employees who left the enterprise with their employment records still kept by the enterprises.

Average number of employed persons refers to the number of employees everyday during the reference period, calculated with the following formula:

$$\text{Monthly average number} = \frac{\text{sum of actual employees everyday in reference month}}{\text{number of calendar dates in reference month}}$$

$$\text{Quarterly average number} = \frac{\text{sum of monthly average number in reference quarter}}{3}$$

$$\text{Annual average number} = \frac{\text{sum of monthly average number in reference year}}{12}$$

Ratio of Debts to Assets reflect both the operation risk and the capability of the enterprise in making use of the capital from the creditors. It is calculated as follows:

$$\text{Ratio of Debts to Assets (\%)} = \frac{\text{total debts}}{\text{total assets}} \times 100\%$$

Both assets and debts are figures at the end of the reference period.

Ratio of Profits to Total Industrial Costs refers to the ratio of profits realized in a given period to the total costs in the same period, which reflects the economic efficiency of input cost and is calculated as follows:

$$\text{Ratio of Profits to Total Industrial Cost (\%)} = \frac{\text{total profits}}{\text{total costs}} \times 100\%$$

Total costs in the above formula is the sum of cost of products sold, marketing cost, management cost and financial cost.

Ratio of Turnover of Working Capitals refers to the number of times of turnover of working capital in a given period of time, which reflects the speed of the turnover of working capital of industrial enterprises, and is calculated as follows:

$$\text{Ratio of Turnover of Working Capital} = \frac{\text{sales revenue of products}}{\text{average balance of total working capital}}$$

In the above formula, average balance of total working capital refers to the arithmetic mean of the sum of working capital at the beginning and at the end of the reference period.

第15篇

建筑业

Construction

简 要 说 明

一、本篇资料的主要内容

本篇资料反映了全省建筑业基本情况，主要包括建筑业总产值、从业人员、建筑企业生产指标、财务指标等方面的内容。

二、本篇资料的来源

本篇资料来源于建筑业统计年报，由省统计局投资处整理提供。

Brief Introduction

I. Content

Data in this chapter show the basic conditions of the construction industry in Shandong Province, mainly including the gross output value of construction, number of employed persons, major production indices and financial indicators.

II. Source of Data

Data in this chapter are based on the annual report of construction industry, and are prepared and provided by the Division of Investment and Construction Statistics of Shandong Provincial Bureau of Statistics.

15-1 主要年份建筑业总产值

Gross Output Value of Construction Enterprises in Major Years

单位:亿元 (100 million yuan)

年 份 Year	总 计 Total	#国有经济 State-owned Construction Enterprises	中 央 Central	地 方 Local
1957	1.32	1.32	0.67	0.65
1962	1.20	0.99	0.44	0.55
1965	2.51	1.66	0.53	1.13
1970	3.02	1.76	0.76	1.00
1975	7.24	4.66	2.27	2.39
1978	11.34	7.62	2.54	5.08
1979	11.96	8.14	2.62	5.52
1980	14.26	9.76	4.01	5.75
1981	13.42	9.41	4.98	4.43
1982	14.50	9.46	4.41	5.05
1983	15.89	10.45	4.56	5.89
1984	23.07	16.25	8.62	7.63
1985	31.21	22.05	12.21	9.84
1986	34.71	24.44	14.87	9.57
1987	40.91	28.67	17.51	11.16
1988	49.38	33.34	20.04	13.30
1989	55.24	37.94	22.36	15.71
1990	58.89	40.60	24.27	16.33
1991	71.40	47.77	27.40	20.38
1992	98.66	61.86	32.81	29.05
1993	141.14	93.32	46.57	46.75
1994	206.42	133.92	78.70	55.22
1995	257.95	163.73	92.25	71.48
1996	593.90	198.27	101.45	96.82
1997	652.59	228.26	112.47	115.79
1998	702.64	279.97	104.79	135.25
1999	770.80	248.19	113.14	135.05
2000	820.52	249.48	120.37	129.11
2001	986.49	246.45	94.37	152.08
2002	1153.24	254.86	86.30	168.56
2003	1485.89	331.17	126.80	204.37
2004	1969.01	657.70	302.85	354.85
2005	2509.17	782.56	365.49	417.07
2006	2791.81	799.34	370.15	429.19
2007	3289.05	977.26	459.81	517.45
2008	3842.52	963.53	478.23	485.30
2009	4579.15	1136.65	599.49	537.16
2010	5496.59	1368.34	704.30	664.04
2011	6482.90	1680.49	920.80	759.69
2012	7281.33	1811.97	968.40	843.57
2013	8467.67	1984.39	1068.93	915.46
2014	9313.45	2197.68	1242.32	955.36
2015	9378.54	2322.58	1323.14	999.45
2016	10087.43	2564.51	1463.21	1101.30
2017	11477.80	2936.38	1698.82	1237.56
2018	12898.29	3656.71	2169.51	1487.19
2019	14269.29	4288.38	2598.34	1690.04
2020	14947.30	4824.41	2927.95	1896.46
2021	16412.05	5261.21	3185.86	2075.35

注:1.1995年前数据不含县以下集体施工企业部分。2.从2004年开始国有经济含国有控股。

a) Before 1995, data in this table don't include the data of enterprises of collective owned ones under county level.

b) Since 2004,state-owned enterprises include state-controlled ones.

15-2 主要年份计算建筑业劳动生产率的平均人数

Average Number of Employed Persons in Construction Enterprises for calculating the Labor Productivity in Major Years

单位:万人 (10 000 persons)

年份 Year	总计 Total	#国有经济 State-owned Construction Enterprises	中央 Central	地方 Local
1957	4.21	4.21	2.14	2.07
1962	6.48	4.91	2.13	2.78
1965	7.35	4.77	1.52	3.25
1970	10.31	5.76	2.66	3.10
1975	18.81	11.33	5.36	5.97
1978	25.20	16.21	5.40	10.81
1979	26.00	16.96	6.24	10.72
1980	26.91	18.07	8.91	9.16
1981	28.55	19.20	11.07	8.20
1982	27.36	17.52	9.00	8.71
1983	27.88	18.02	6.42	11.55
1984	33.93	22.26	9.37	12.93
1985	40.53	26.89	13.13	13.67
1986	38.57	24.69	15.17	9.67
1987	39.34	24.50	14.97	9.62
1988	40.48	24.88	14.74	10.08
1989	38.90	22.86	13.63	10.83
1990	38.15	21.83	11.65	10.18
1991	39.72	23.83	12.51	11.32
1992	45.10	23.44	11.66	11.78
1993	52.78	29.57	11.87	17.70
1994	66.22	37.17	20.10	17.07
1995	66.84	35.32	14.91	20.40
1996	188.02	40.96	14.82	26.14
1997	175.78	40.49	14.39	26.10
1998	169.11	38.59	11.28	27.30
1999	164.95	33.56	10.86	22.70
2000	171.94	31.80	10.27	21.53
2001	181.07	29.15	8.15	21.00
2002	183.56	23.08	4.57	18.50
2003	210.11	29.43	8.50	20.93
2004	238.91	53.85	16.50	37.35
2005	249.81	48.93	16.21	32.72
2006	282.30	59.04	27.76	31.28
2007	288.40	51.78	17.36	34.42
2008	300.24	44.74	18.32	26.42
2009	305.99	42.81	17.99	24.82
2010	344.88	54.00	25.20	28.80
2011	307.56	45.07	21.18	23.89
2012	270.26	38.87	18.57	20.30
2013	305.01	44.17	23.15	21.02
2014	332.49	48.78	25.04	23.74
2015	310.73	43.10	21.65	21.45
2016	322.58	40.56	19.74	20.82
2017	349.15	50.42	27.55	22.87
2018	351.84	55.48	30.96	24.52
2019	345.09	55.71	29.03	26.68
2020	305.91	54.27	28.33	25.94
2021	306.86	59.99	35.11	24.88

注:1.1995年前数据不含县以下集体施工企业部分。2.从2004年开始国有经济含国有控股。

a) Before 1995, data in this table don't include the data of enterprises of collective owned ones under county level.

b) Since 2004, state-owned enterprises include State-controlled ones.

15-3 建筑业企业生产指标(2021年)
Main Production Indicators of Construction Enterprises(2021)

类 别	Category	企业个数(个) Number of Enterprises (unit)	建筑业总产值(万元) Gross Output Value (10 000 yuan)	竣工产值(万元) Value of Projects Completed (10 000 yuan)	签定合同额(万元) Value of Contracts (10 000 yuan)	#上年结转 Carryover of Last Year
总 计	**Total**	**9297**	**164120460**	**69352354**	**345178115**	**143548051**
#国有及国有控股企业	State-owned and State-controlled Enterprises	652	52612116	14547462	149801859	69304071
一、按登记注册类型分	**Grouped by Registration Status**					
内资企业	Domestic Funded	9284	163454006	68990683	344389169	143148591
国有企业	State-owned	207	3094753	1083150	5434271	2448748
集体企业	Collective-owned	240	2410366	1563455	5195640	2759105
股份合作企业	Stock-holding Cooperation	28	483446	52184	1716941	676166
有限责任公司	Company with Limited Liabilition	1425	72979598	27099155	163041154	70513703
股份有限公司	Stock-holding Company limited	120	13113745	4485105	43919286	18123078
私营企业	Private-owned	7253	71284977	34690575	124905834	48551755
其他企业	Others	11	87121	17059	176042	76035
港、澳、台商投资企业	Funded from Hong Kong,Macao and	5	336501	268538	412545	285640
外商投资企业	Foreign Funded	8	329954	93133	376401	113821
二、按国民经济行业分	**by Sector**					
房屋建筑业	Building	4042	97372997	48342892	201171191	88105683
土木工程建筑业	Civil Engineering	2717	46450410	12342571	117758712	48927114
建筑安装业	Construction Installation	1137	12655220	5744398	16058824	3994129
建筑装饰、装修和其他建筑业	Building Decoration and Others	1401	7641833	2922493	10189388	2521126
#建筑装饰和装修业	Building Decoration	1089	6099093	2181126	8048391	2006013

15-3 续表 1 continued

类别	Category	企业个数（个） Number of Enterprises (unit)	建筑业总产值（万元） Gross Output Value (10 000 yuan)	竣工产值（万元） Value of Projects Completed (10 000 yuan)	签定合同额（万元） Value of Contracts (10 000 yuan)	#上年结转 Carryover of Last Year
三、按企业资质等级分	**by Qualification Criteria**					
施工总承包	Construction Contract	6450	149710765	63143890	323649625	138670263
特 级	Special Grade	50	56682662	23698577	145528607	63034755
一 级	First Grade	528	53825258	22091897	112098723	50818619
二 级	Second Grade	2133	25483766	11824826	43246313	17435043
三级及以下	Third Grade and below	3739	13719080	5528590	22775982	7381846
专业承包	Professional Contract	2847	14409695	6208464	21528490	4877789
一 级	First Grade	473	7085472	3027342	11052454	2324828
二 级	Second Grade	1433	4615647	1993443	6654142	1603481
三级及以下	Third Grade and below	941	2708576	1187679	3821894	949480
四、按控股情况分	**by Share Holding**					
#国有控股	State-controlled	651	52594315	14544462	149784013	69300650
#集体控股	Collective-controlled	422	8163569	4239183	16195352	7862015
#私人控股	Private-controlled	7853	94095305	46080779	160644764	58994195
#港澳台商、外商控股	Hong Kong, Macao , Taiwan and forei holding enterprises	7	52507	23676	53602	11840

15-3 续表 2 continued

类 别	Category	房屋建筑施工面积(平方米) Floor Space of Buildings under Construction (sq.m)	房屋建筑竣工面积(平方米) Floor Space of Buildings Completed (sq.m)	年末从业人员(人) Staff Employed (person)
总 计	**Total**	**950118646**	**240181963**	**2706455**
#国有及国有控股企业	State-owned and State-controlled Enterprises	215204332	26397028	463097
一、按登记注册类型分	**Grouped by Registration Status**			
内资企业	Domestic Funded	948279039	238526867	2695580
国有企业	State-owned	4336903	629557	43368
集体企业	Collective-owned	20542485	7513706	63597
股份合作企业	Stock-holding Cooperation	826231	224859	7063
有限责任公司	Company with Limited Liabilition	416669908	81640159	1004001
股份有限公司	Stock-holding Company limited	70757598	17761753	185952
私营企业	Private-owned	435045496	130748868	1389955
其他企业	Others	100418	7965	1644
港、澳、台商投资企业	Funded from Hong Kong,Macao and	1161370	1322720	4703
外商投资企业	Foreign Funded	678237	332376	6172
二、按国民经济行业分	**by Sector**			
房屋建筑业	Building	864190918	215452839	1776773
土木工程建筑业	Civil Engineering	45829853	10041526	501757
建筑安装业	Construction Installation	30322962	7682674	300879
建筑装饰、装修和其他建筑业	Building Decoration and Others	9774913	7004924	127046
#建筑装饰和装修业	Building Decoration	8772510	5381305	104691

15-3 续表 3 continued

类 别	Category	房屋建筑施工面积（平方米） Floor Space of Buildings under Construction (sq.m)	房屋建筑竣工面积（平方米） Floor Space of Buildings Completed (sq.m)	年末从业人员（人） Staff Employed (person)
三、按企业资质等级分	**by Qualification Criteria**			
施工总承包	Construction Contract	910246063	218570160	2432030
特 级	Special Grade	414048602	84704654	688595
一 级	First Grade	264431497	69338648	854945
二 级	Second Grade	176766285	47176786	573742
三级及以下	Third Grade and below	54999679	17350072	314748
专业承包	Professional Contract	39872583	21611803	274425
一 级	First Grade	24986763	10966892	115132
二 级	Second Grade	11255822	8590801	86941
三级及以下	Third Grade and below	3629998	2054110	72352
四、按控股情况分	**by Share Holding**			
#国有控股	State-controlled	214610942	26297028	462977
#集体控股	Collective-controlled	63339165	17077203	178706
#私人控股	Private-controlled	613833380	178874441	1845427
#港澳台商、外商控股	Hong Kong, Macao , Taiwan and foreign holding enterprises	2480	2480	807

15-4 建筑业主要财务指标(2021年)
Major Financial Indicators of Construction Enterprises(2021)

单位:万元 (10 000 yuan)

类别	Category	年初存货 Inventory at Beginning of year	流动资产 Liquid Assets	固定资产原价 Fixed Assets Original Price	在建工程 Project under Constr-uction	资产合计 Total Assets	流动负债 Liquid Liabilities
总 计	**Total**	**27330811**	**162064832**	**16043021**	**1890997**	**193281314**	**139666512**
#国有及国有控股企业	State-owned and State-controlled Enterprises	5972472	64320296	5424224	520926	78513338	59992701
一、按登记注册类型分	**Grouped by Registration Status**						
内资企业	Domestic Funded	27312301	160765742	15927446	1885790	191799625	138626025
国有企业	State owned	1716054	14807502	1119540	130532	17791871	14133500
集体企业	Collective-owned	403110	2475633	246063	18348	2797500	2102619
股份合作企业	Stock-holding Cooperation	31128	249592	22993	728	274755	238038
有限责任公司	Company with Limited Liabilition	12155335	78793384	7091729	795581	95218159	70992875
股份有限公司	Stock holding Company limited	701058	6586429	889579	24289	7978091	4889207
私营企业	Private owned	12283701	57816916	6547720	916311	67699363	46245455
其他企业	Others	21915	36285	9822		39887	24330
港、澳、台商投资企业	Funded from Hong Kong,Macao and	10991	482232	5257	16	498286	419417
外商投资企业	Foreign Funded	7520	816858	110318	5190	983403	621071
二、按国民经济行业分	**by Sector**						
房屋建筑业	Building	16211640	79792319	6687911	983507	92654618	65520794
土木工程建筑业	Civil Engineering	8199493	66060422	7520815	713700	82047899	61056651
建筑安装业	Construction Installation	1889627	8785064	995125	64146	10012362	7247261
建筑装饰、装修和其他建筑业	Building Decoration and Others	1030051	7427027	839170	129644	8566435	5841806
#建筑装饰和装修业	Building Decoration	799043	5855496	429529	107409	6619495	4510429

15-4 续表 1 continued

单位:万元 (10 000 yuan)

类别	Category	年初存货 Inventory at Beginning of year	流动资产 Liquid Assets	固定资产原价 Fixed Assets Original Price	在建工程 Project under Construction	资产合计 Total Assets	流动负债 Liquid Liabilities
三、按企业资质等级分	**by Qualification Criteria**						
施工总承包	Construction Contract	24804320	146975825	13996945	1674553	175660783	127641141
特 级	Special Grade	4922392	46309175	2666501	272645	56056378	42730152
一 级	First Grade	9589576	53223586	4817238	501700	62132743	46230275
二 级	Second Grade	7282504	31148047	4221693	529463	37822464	25858193
三级及以下	Third Grade and below	3009848	16295017	2291513	370745	19649198	12822521
专业承包	Professional Contract	2526492	15089007	2046077	216444	17620531	12025371
一 级	First Grade	1033286	6839560	545274	60023	7627675	5495883
二 级	Second Grade	829197	5105050	799821	113138	6107573	4084395
三级及以下	Third Grade and below	664009	3144397	700981	43282	3885284	2445093
四、按控股情况分	**by Share Holding**						
#国有控股	State-controlled	5972472	64320296	5424224	520926	78513338	59992701
#集体控股	Collective-controlled	2848129	10971952	1300402	97380	12837017	9684931
#私人控股	Private-controlled	18490327	86529649	9236883	1267484	101600760	69743368
#港澳台商、外商控股	Hong Kong, Macao , Taiwan and foreign holding enterprises	8133	154782	79442	5207	240629	164153

15-4 续表 2 continued

单位:万元 (10 000 yuan)

类 别	Category	非流动负债 Non-current liabilities	负债合计 Total Liabilities	所有者权益 Creditors' Equity	主营业务收入 Revenue from Principal Business	主营业务成本 Cost of Principal Business
总 计	**Total**	**6204388**	**148264290**	**45017024**	**156292513**	**143905859**
#国有及国有控股企业	State owned and State controlled Enterprises	3829587	64317028	14196310	57451348	52926005
一、按登记注册类型分	**Grouped by Registration Status**					
内资企业	Domestic Funded	6186794	147180955	44618669	155688734	143372375
国有企业	State-owned	593308	14858900	2932971	7779402	7017483
集体企业	Collective-owned	21027	2204400	593099	1936735	1803007
股份合作企业	Stock-holding Cooperation	883	239311	35445	191859	175461
有限责任公司	Company with Limited Liabilition	4140208	75926254	19291905	77880855	71713197
股份有限公司	Stock-holding Company limited	352797	5302894	2675198	7943748	7248773
私营企业	Private-owned	1078571	48624754	19074609	59904349	55368814
其他企业	Others		24443	15444	51785	45640
港、澳、台商投资企业	Funded from Hong Kong,Macao	15128	434545	63741	319242	292664
外商投资企业	Foreign Funded	2466	648790	334614	284538	240820
二、按国民经济行业分	**by Sector**					
房屋建筑业	Building	2620706	69558995	23095623	85979938	79788306
土木工程建筑业	Civil Engineering	3337539	65061796	16986103	50472557	46144128
建筑安装业	Construction Installation	120333	7457015	2555347	12044670	11154003
建筑装饰、装修和其他建筑业	Building Decoration and Others	125810	6186484	2379951	7795348	6819422
#建筑装饰和装修业	Building Decoration	99592	4798677	1820818	6030684	5259828

15-4 续表 3 continued

单位:万元 (10 000 yuan)

类 别	Category	非流动负债 Non-current liabilities	负债合计 Total Liabilities	所有者权益 Creditors' Equity	主营业务收入 Revenue from Principal Business	主营业务成本 Cost of Principal Business
三、按企业资质等级分	**by Qualification Criteria**					
施工总承包	Construction Contract	5949026	135681807	39978975	140542748	130056678
特 级	Special Grade	2008793	44782037	11274341	56438161	52412616
一 级	First Grade	1867910	48548502	13584241	46471852	43338530
二 级	Second Grade	1246547	27910774	9911690	23908332	21841388
三级及以下	Third Grade and below	825776	14440494	5208704	13724402	12464145
专业承包	Professional Contract	255362	12582483	5038048	15749766	13849181
一 级	First Grade	65506	5652743	1974931	7535350	6577355
二 级	Second Grade	114119	4286325	1821247	5026827	4483802
三级及以下	Third Grade and below	75737	2643414	1241870	3187589	2788024
四、按控股情况分	**by Share Holding**					
#国有控股	State-controlled	3829587	64317028	14196310	57451348	52926005
#集体控股	Collective-controlled	463457	10344488	2492529	8872247	8195154
#私人控股	Private-controlled	1908342	73354260	28246501	89861663	82717704
#港澳台商、外商控股	Hong Kong, Macao , Taiwan and foreign holding enterprises	3003	167156	73474	86298	46531

15-4 续表 4 continued

单位：万元 (10 000 yuan)

类 别	Category	主营业务税金及附加 Taxes and Other Charges on Principal Business	销售费用 Sales Expenses	管理费用 Management Expenses	财务费用 Financial Expenses	利润总额 Total Profits
总 计	**Total**	**767453**	**294966**	**5302142**	**1105004**	**4521939**
#国有及国有控股企业	State-owned and State-controlled Enterprises	165044	59921	1488665	365176	1808702
一、按登记注册类型分	**Grouped by Registration Status**					
内资企业	Domestic Funded	757570	291860	5284335	1096561	4494869
国有企业	State-owned	29704	7628	274484	70900	257698
集体企业	Collective-owned	21593	4502	66353	7641	52127
股份合作企业	Stock-holding Cooperation	3954	285	6977	2671	4994
有限责任公司	Company with Limited Liabilition	300297	95408	2253798	529750	2526839
股份有限公司	Stock-holding Company limited	66711	11959	270050	58113	248924
私营企业	Private-owned	335072	172078	2411971	427466	1401740
其他企业	Others	239		704	20	2546
港、澳、台商投资企业	Funded from Hong Kong,Macao	1027	9	9058	5943	6250
外商投资企业	Foreign Funded	8856	3097	8748	2500	20820
二、按国民经济行业分	**by Sector**					
房屋建筑业	Building	474750	75180	2221443	610236	2605937
土木工程建筑业	Civil Engineering	165178	111344	2021190	421877	1512498
建筑安装业	Construction Installation	78545	65319	569932	35115	213964
建筑装饰、装修和其他建筑业	Building Decoration and Others	48980	43122	489578	37776	189541
#建筑装饰和装修业	Building Decoration	41279	33085	354151	27271	153985

15-4 续表 5 continued

单位:万元 (10 000 yuan)

类别	Category	主营业务税金及附加 Taxes and Other Charges on Principal Business	销售费用 Sales Expenses	管理费用 Management Expenses	财务费用 Financial Expenses	利润总额 Total Profits
三、按企业资质等级分	**by Qualification Criteria**					
施工总承包	Construction Contract	674788	180702	4207206	1021236	4126143
特　级	Special Grade	186327	35774	943844	337574	1927421
一　级	First Grade	210891	37763	1329298	365745	1259830
二　级	Second Grade	173605	42468	1122387	218732	628332
三级及以下	Third Grade and below	103965	64697	811678	99185	310560
专业承包	Professional Contract	92665	114264	1094936	83768	395797
一　级	First Grade	41107	47718	375433	25964	188915
二　级	Second Grade	29342	35629	384129	39053	130562
三级及以下	Third Grade and below	22216	30917	335375	18752	76320
四、按控股情况分	**by Share Holding**					
#国有控股	State-controlled	165044	59921	1488665	365176	1808702
#集体控股	Collective-controlled	57333	11789	419005	56968	223365
#私人控股	Private-controlled	544473	223081	3387137	682263	2469039
#港澳台商、外商控股	Hong Kong, Macao , Taiwan and foreign holding enterprises	450	175	6848	453	21133

15-5 各市建筑业主要生产指标(2021年)

Main Production Indicators of Construction Enterprises by Region(2021)

地 区 Region	企业个数(个) Number of Enterprises (unit)	建筑业合同(万元) Value of Construction Contracts (10 000 yuan)	#上年结转合同额 Carryover of Last Year	建筑业总产值(万元) Gross Output Value of Construction (10 000 yuan)	竣工产值(万元) Value of Construction Completed (10 000 yuan)	房屋建筑施工面积(平方米) Floor Space under Construction (sq.m)	房屋建筑竣工面积(平方米) Floor Space Completed (sq.m)	年末从业人员(人) Employees at year-end (person)
全省总计 Total	**9297**	**345178115**	**143548051**	**164120460**	**69352354**	**950118646**	**240181963**	**2706455**
济南市 Jinan	1182	113215099	49330365	41260343	13373476	194100032	37295693	422688
青岛市 Qingdao	799	74054954	34545600	32972735	11684026	219063666	45085485	492379
淄博市 Zibo	538	18610194	6001244	11295631	6185762	73307622	21717247	252822
枣庄市 Zaozhuang	289	5420029	1709888	3349909	1200019	21489332	6618640	80713
东营市 Dongying	348	5417424	1842464	2908618	1686703	8588160	2771485	52626
烟台市 Yantai	916	12598908	4144956	8483718	4389085	41188471	16228671	152620
潍坊市 Weifang	641	19395365	7856048	11171502	6274125	84933513	23207230	154674
济宁市 Jining	1109	15598701	7253372	7726273	3086071	55317013	12971968	174107
泰安市 Tai'an	418	18685422	6036096	11697338	5429073	20981714	8209434	271326
威海市 Weihai	519	6320226	2570347	3531072	1567639	26520926	4907534	48039
日照市 Rizhao	397	9352665	4563018	4975665	1612175	17779349	4264765	57736
临沂市 Linyi	623	20221168	6101904	11973719	6022472	93962906	26445445	269334
德州市 Dezhou	314	7998800	3141564	3712661	1986541	32573953	11387070	76140
聊城市 Liaocheng	410	8130086	3942935	3290835	1896666	28945504	7025394	74924
滨州市 Binzhou	343	4668311	2335625	2395820	1322623	13738038	4538197	40073
菏泽市 Heze	451	5490761	2172625	3374620	1635898	17628447	7507705	86254

15-6 各市建筑业主要财务指标(2021年)

Financial Indicators of Construction Enterprises by Region(2021)

单位:万元 (10 000 yuan)

地区	Region	流动资产 Liquid Assets	固定资产原价 Fixed Assets Original Price	在建工程 Projects under Construction	资产合计 Total Assets	流动负债 Liquid Liabilities	非流动负债 Non-current liabilities	负债合计 Total Liabilities
全省总计	**Total**	**162064832**	**16043021**	**1890997**	**193281314**	**139666512**	**6204388**	**148264290**
济南市	Jinan	39517609	2678923	302566	47761850	36706547	1525413	38401588
青岛市	Qingdao	27867867	2253431	414425	33170360	24784614	1378772	26400456
淄博市	Zibo	7558247	1080083	68515	8791462	5850822	85509	6046004
枣庄市	Zaozhuang	4325911	546040	32103	5314774	3673172	87126	3956927
东营市	Dongying	5027106	623445	36672	5892937	4471427	99133	4640515
烟台市	Yantai	9599618	1446897	245819	11503423	7417024	382434	8004297
潍坊市	Weifang	10843248	1276694	91140	12610775	8048618	675318	9011939
济宁市	Jining	10051496	1006975	103080	11502130	7342516	639404	8220491
泰安市	Tai'an	7351140	781819	65209	8449238	6561160	153519	6838705
威海市	Weihai	4745485	653252	85251	5603664	3899442	180139	4189951
日照市	Rizhao	6916038	730187	84537	8438185	6351707	232192	6642949
临沂市	Linyi	12215801	962962	111082	14904950	10959968	187877	11331583
德州市	Dezhou	4636970	579759	14363	5474479	3717881	86338	3865098
聊城市	Liaocheng	3561385	418578	66300	4275548	3051653	204989	3287780
滨州市	Binzhou	3367484	550472	145535	4230514	3193378	64586	3333467
菏泽市	Heze	4479427	453504	24399	5357025	3636584	221641	4092542

15-6 续表 continued

单位:万元 (10 000 yuan)

地区	Region	所有者权益 Owner's Equity	实收资本 Paid-in Capitals	主营业务收入 Revenue from Principal Business	主营业务成本 Cost of Principal Business	主营业务税金及附加 Taxes and Other Charges on Principal Business	管理费用 Management Expenses	财务费用 Financial Expenses	利润总额 Total Profits
全省总计	**Total**	**45017024**	**24948909**	**156292513**	**143905859**	**767453**	**5302142**	**1105004**	**4521939**
济南市	Jinan	9360262	5440547	42217623	38936683	133203	1208115	160972	1359403
青岛市	Qingdao	6769904	3592883	29929352	27789189	92927	795435	214657	735710
淄博市	Zibo	2745458	1384624	9615420	8987949	85134	292700	41982	217659
枣庄市	Zaozhuang	1357847	724768	3272718	2982308	37107	120376	14107	113047
东营市	Dongying	1252422	910270	3330501	3080919	17853	169377	43845	45910
烟台市	Yantai	3499126	1885882	8183132	7280978	77293	374375	87651	349650
潍坊市	Weifang	3598836	1566910	9400438	8600546	69862	401835	92978	390514
济宁市	Jining	3281640	2011899	7153898	6656558	36525	354162	58351	159410
泰安市	Tai'an	1610533	1192959	10995378	10511056	67768	273997	45922	94097
威海市	Weihai	1413713	726033	3408107	3088807	15997	199600	26597	89772
日照市	Rizhao	1795236	1027076	4669304	4191779	24166	182426	68653	149362
临沂市	Linyi	3573367	1521205	10769022	9611645	51447	373853	130512	478487
德州市	Dezhou	1609381	732609	3788642	3321583	15351	191109	32172	117687
聊城市	Liaocheng	987768	791647	3431176	3196808	13505	155320	32079	37412
滨州市	Binzhou	897047	690461	2539387	2354341	11479	95659	12838	69205
菏泽市	Heze	1264482	749137	3588416	3314712	17838	113803	41688	114616

主要统计指标解释

建筑业统计单位 指从事房屋、构筑物建造和设备安装活动的法人企业。建筑业法人企业应具有建筑业资质并能够独立核算，同时其应具备以下条件：①依法成立，有自己的名称、组织机构和场所，能够承担民事责任；②独立拥有和使用资产，承担负债，有权与其他单位签订合同；③独立核算盈亏，能够编制资产负债表。

建筑业总产值 是以货币形式表现的建筑业企业在一定时期内生产的建筑业产品和提供的服务的总和。建筑业总产值包括：

⑴建筑工程产值：指列入建筑工程预算内的各种工程价值。

⑵安装工程产值：指设备安装工程价值，不包括被安装设备本身的价值。

⑶其他产值：建筑业总产值中除建筑工程、安装工程以外的产值。包括房屋构筑物修理产值、非标准设备制造产值、总包企业向分包企业收取的管理费以及不能明确划分的施工活动所完成的产值。

a.房屋构筑物修理产值：指房屋和构筑物修理所完成的产值，但不包括被修理房屋、构筑物本身价值和生产设备的修理产值。

b.非标准设备制造产值：指加工制造没有定型的非标准生产设备的加工费和原材料价值(如化工厂、炼油厂用的各种罐、槽，矿井生产统一使用的各种漏斗、三角槽、阀门等)以及附属加工厂为本企业承建工程制作的非标准设备的价值。

房屋建筑施工面积 指在报告期内施过工的全部房屋建筑面积，包括本期新开工的房屋面积、上期施工跨入本期继续施工的房屋面积、上期停缓建在本期恢复施工的房屋面积、本期竣工的房屋面积及本期施工后又停缓建的房屋面积。

房屋建筑竣工面积 指在报告期内房屋建筑按照设计要求全部完工，达到了使用条件，经验收鉴定合格，正式移交使用单位的房屋建筑面积。

Explanatory Notes on Main Statistical Indicators

Statistical Unit in Construction refers to corporate enterprise engaged in the construction of buildings and structures and in the installation of equipment. A corporate construction enterprise should have qualification certificates with independent accounting system, and should meet the following 3 requirements: a) being set up in line with relevant legal basis, having its full name, organization and location, and capable of taking civil liabilities; b) independently possessing and using its assets and assuming its liabilities, and entitled to sign contracts with other institutions; and c) making independent accounts of its profits and losses, and capable of compiling its own balance sheet.

Gross Output Value of Construction refers to total of construction products and services, expressed in money terms, produced or rendered by construction and installation enterprises during a given period of time. It includes:

(1)Output value of construction projects, that is the value of projects covered by the project budgets;

(2)Output value of installation projects, that is the value of the installation of equipment, (excluding the value of the equipment to be installed);

(3)Output value of others, that is the output value of construction industry excluding that of construction projects and installation projects. It includes: output value of repair of buildings and structures; output value of non standard equipment manufacturing; overhead expenses received by contracted enterprises to the sub contracted enterprises and the completed output value of construction activities that have no clear definition.

a. Output value of repair of buildings and structures, that is the value created through the repairs of buildings or structures, but does not include the value of buildings or structures being repaired and the value of the repair of production equipment;

b. Output value of manufactured non standard equipment, that is the value of non standard production equipment including raw materials and manufacturing cost made for the construction project (i.e., chemical plant; kettles or tanks used by refineries; various fillers, triangle tanks, valves used by mines), and the output value of equipment manufactured by subsidiary workshops.

Floor Space of Buildings under Construction refers to floor space of buildings under construction during the reference period, including newly started buildings, buildings started earlier and continued during the reference period, and buildings suspended earlier but restarted during the reference period, buildings completed during the reference period, and buildings under construction and then suspended during the reference period.

Floor Space of Buildings Completed refers to the floor space of buildings that are completed in the reference period in accordance with the requirements of the design, up to the standard for putting them into use, and have been checked and accepted by concerned departments as qualified ones.

第16篇

服务业

Service Enterprises

简 要 说 明

一、本篇资料的主要内容

本篇资料主要反映规模以上服务业的财务状况。据国家统计报表制度，2012 年规模以上服务业年报首次纳入“一套表”联网直报系统。

二、本篇资料的来源

本篇资料来源于规模以上服务业年报数据，由省统计局服务业处整理提供。

Brief Introduction

I. Content

Data in this chapter reflect the basic information, financial condition, employed persons, labor remuneration and E-commerce transactions of some service enterprises above designated size. According to the National Statistical Reporting System, some service enterprises above designated size have been integrated into the "network reporting" system since 2012.

II. Source of Data

Data in this chapter are based on the yearly statistics report of some service enterprises above designated size and are prepared and compiled by the Division of comprehensive Service Statistics of Shandong Provincial Bureau of Statistics.

16-1 规模以上服务业企业主要财务状况(2021年)

Main Financial Indicators of Service Enterprises above the Designated(2021)

单位:亿元　　(100 million yuan)

项　目	Item	2021	2021年比2020年增长(%) Growth Rate in 2021 Over 2020(%)
资产总计	Total Assets	44450.27	11.8
负债合计	Total Liabilities	24464.46	13.5
营业收入	Business Revenue	12753.81	27.6
营业成本	Business Costs	10685.16	29.9
税金及附加	Tax and Extra Charges on Business	71.06	24.0
销售费用	Sales Expenses	360.33	9.8
管理费用	Management Expenses	947.23	16.0
财务费用	Financial Expenses	396.08	19.7
营业利润	Business Profits	703.22	11.6
利润总额	Total Profits	755.83	7.3
所得税费用	Income Taxes Payable	158.66	22.8
应付职工薪酬	Total Wages Payable	2088.32	16.1
应交增值税	Value-added Tax Payable	250.65	21.1

注:增速按可比口径计算。
a)The growth rates are calculated on comparable coverage.

16-2 规模以上服务业企业分登记注册类型财务状况(2021年)

Financial Indicators of Service Enterprises above Designated Size by Registration Type(2021)

单位:万元 (10 000 yuan)

类　别	Category	企业单位数(个) Number of Industrial Enterprises (unit)	资产总计 Total Assets	负债合计 Total Liabilities
全省总计	**Provincial Total**	**11353**	**444502739**	**244644642**
按登记注册类型分	**by Status of Registration**			
内资企业	**Domestic Funded Enterprises**	**11041**	**419131857**	**232940133**
国有企业	State-owned Enterprises	494	78881749	45612783
集体企业	Collective-owned Enterprises	56	842230	676579
股份合作企业	Cooperative Enterprises	11	68082	32142
联营企业	Joint Ownership Enterprises	4	160380	113125
有限责任公司	Limited Liability Corporations	3037	262358388	139019570
股份有限公司	Share-holding Corporations Limited	239	31636602	15421237
私营企业	Private Enterprises	7056	43855528	31260668
其他企业	Other Enterprises	144	1328899	804028
港、澳、台商投资企业	**Enterprises with Funds from Hong Kong, Macao and Taiwan**	**114**	**11400616**	**6796792**
合资经营企业(港或澳、台资)	Joint-ventures Enterprises	45	3004772	1301076
合作经营企业(港或澳、台资)	Cooperative Enterprises	1	69155	16994
港澳台商独资经营企业	Enterprises with Sole Investment	64	4275336	1746742
港澳台商投资股份有限公司	Share-holding Corporations Ltd. With Funds from Hong Kong, Macao and Taiwan	4	4051352	3731980
其他港澳台投资企业	Other Enterprises			
外商投资企业	**Foreign Funded Enterprises**	**198**	**13970266**	**4907717**
中外合资经营企业	Joint-venture Enterprises	71	3767796	1246614
中外合作经营企业	Cooperation Enterprises	4	13535	6491
外资企业	Enterprises with Sole Foreign Funds	112	9000906	3026551
外商投资股份有限公司	Share-holding Corporations Ltd. With Foreign Investment	7	933749	496446
其他外商投资企业	Other Enterprises	4	254280	131614

16-2 续表 1 continued

单位:万元 (10 000 yuan)

类 别	Category	营业收入 Business Revenue	营业成本 Business Costs	税金及附加 Tax and Extra Charges on Business
全省总计	**Provincial Total**	**127538106**	**106851617**	**710631**
按登记注册类型分	**by Status of Registration**			
内资企业	**Domestic Funded Enterprises**	**115265869**	**97261155**	**655417**
国有企业	State-owned Enterprises	8198365	6733009	59657
集体企业	Collective-owned Enterprises	195355	138276	4943
股份合作企业	Cooperative Enterprises	50640	17684	622
联营企业	Joint Ownership Enterprises	16789	8569	122
有限责任公司	Limited Liability Corporations	53070051	45336675	374401
股份有限公司	Share-holding Corporations Limited	8720212	6702650	46843
私营企业	Private Enterprises	44268953	37787538	167220
其他企业	Other Enterprises	745505	536755	1608
港、澳、台商投资企业	**Enterprises with Funds from Hong Kong, Macao and Taiwan**	**5235485**	**4231610**	**25411**
合资经营企业(港或澳、台资)	Joint-ventures Enterprises	1293035	956145	6402
合作经营企业(港或澳、台资)	Cooperative Enterprises	16088	14411	82
港澳台商独资经营企业	Enterprises with Sole Investment	2373057	1754476	16225
港澳台商投资股份有限公司	Share-holding Corporations Ltd. With Funds from Hong Kong, Macao and Taiwan	1553305	1506578	2702
其他企业	Other Enterprises			
外商投资企业	**Foreign Funded Enterprises**	**7036752**	**5358852**	**29803**
中外合资经营企业	Joint-venture Enterprises	2210063	1658559	6690
中外合作经营企业	Cooperation Enterprises	5287	2508	345
外资企业	Enterprises with Sole Foreign Funds	3864042	2929318	20636
外商投资股份有限公司	Share-holding Corporations Ltd. With Foreign Investment	434979	283521	1307
其他企业	Other Enterprises	522381	484946	825

16-2 续表 2 continued

单位:万元 (10 000 yuan)

类别	Category	销售费用 Selling Expenses	管理费用 Management Expenses	财务费用 Financial Expenses	营业利润 Business Profits
全省总计	**Provincial Total**	**3603258**	**9472289**	**3960820**	**7032172**
按登记注册类型分	**by Status of Registration**				
内资企业	**Domestic Funded Enterprises**	**3139908**	**8699443**	**3887802**	**5607119**
国有企业	State-owned Enterprises	149076	716286	853049	669352
集体企业	Collective-owned Enterprises	6543	47311	993	-55
股份合作企业	Cooperative Enterprises	19529	8775	90	2524
联营企业	Joint Ownership Enterprises	93	510	5141	2372
有限责任公司	Limited Liability Corporations	1289212	3864181	2454847	2270439
股份有限公司	Share-holding Corporations Limited	283122	587115	254004	1253667
私营企业	Private Enterprises	1357121	3336966	313713	1373389
其他企业	Other Enterprises	35213	138300	5965	35431
港、澳、台商投资企业	**Enterprises with Funds from Hong Kong, Macao and Taiwan**	**259638**	**271061**	**112252**	**325008**
合资经营企业(港或澳、台资)	Joint-ventures Enterprises	31401	56800	24364	217585
合作经营企业(港或澳、台资)	Cooperative Enterprises		291	527	776
港澳台商独资经营企业	Enterprises with Sole Investment	157555	162234	24982	237247
港澳台商投资股份有限公司	Share-holding Corporations Ltd. With Funds from Hong Kong, Macao and Taiwan	70682	51737	62378	-130600
其他企业	Other Enterprises				
外商投资企业	**Foreign Funded Enterprises**	**203712**	**501784**	**-39234**	**1100045**
中外合资经营企业	Joint-venture Enterprises	32623	157853	10479	326520
中外合作经营企业	Cooperation Enterprises	1521	1191	47	69
外资企业	Enterprises with Sole Foreign Funds	134044	316717	-53739	661068
外商投资股份有限公司	Share-holding Corporations Ltd. With Foreign Investment	26958	17052	3900	96607
其他企业	Other Enterprises	8565	8971	79	15782

16-2 续表 3 continued

单位:万元 (10 000 yuan)

类 别	Category	利润总额 Total Profits	所得税费用 Income Taxes Payable	应付职工薪酬 Total Wages Payable	应交增值税 Value-added Tax Payable
全省总计	**Provincial Total**	**7558281**	**1586624**	**20883188**	**2506488**
按登记注册类型分	**by Status of Registration**				
内资企业	**Domestic Funded Enterprises**	**6083695**	**1274201**	**19198142**	**2256058**
国有企业	State-owned Enterprises	770100	111982	1512600	145590
集体企业	Collective-owned Enterprises	5106	2840	52580	4693
股份合作企业	Cooperative Enterprises	2704	171	6063	1138
联营企业	Joint Ownership Enterprises	2655	801	1948	854
有限责任公司	Limited Liability Corporations	2574549	709210	10202031	1160687
股份有限公司	Share-holding Corporations Limited	1268740	172408	1492967	165217
私营企业	Private Enterprises	1429253	273749	5690388	769892
其他企业	Other Enterprises	30588	3039	239565	7987
港、澳、台商投资企业	**Enterprises with Funds from Hong Kong, Macao and Taiwan**	**337666**	**148944**	**740992**	**133773**
合资经营企业(港或澳、台资)	Joint-ventures Enterprises	216244	47168	113413	21755
合作经营企业(港或澳、台资)	Cooperative Enterprises	1772	448	232	2
港澳台商独资经营企业	Enterprises with Sole Investment	241160	132923	351613	104362
港澳台商投资股份有限公司	Share-holding Corporations Ltd. With Funds from Hong Kong, Macao and Taiwan	-121510	-31595	275734	7655
其他企业	Other Enterprises				
外商投资企业	**Foreign Funded Enterprises**	**1136920**	**163479**	**944055**	**116657**
中外合资经营企业	Joint-venture Enterprises	355688	77147	319009	21012
中外合作经营企业	Cooperation Enterprises	209	292	1748	187
外资企业	Enterprises with Sole Foreign Funds	667928	67229	560394	86698
外商投资股份有限公司	Share-holding Corporations Ltd. With Foreign Investment	97179	17111	45216	960
其他企业	Other Enterprises	15916	1699	17686	7800

16−3 规模以上服务业企业分控股情况财务状况(2021年)

Financial Indicators of Service Enterprises above Designated Size by Holding Type(2021)

单位:万元 (10 000 yuan)

类别	Category	企业单位数(个) Number of Industrial Enterprises (unit)	资产总计 Total Assets	负债合计 Total Liabilities	营业收入 Business Revenue	营业成本 Business Costs
全省总计	**Provincial Total**	**11353**	**444502739**	**244644642**	**127538106**	**106851617**
按控股情况分	**by Holding Type**					
国有控股	State-holding	1924	344709381	180853283	52757330	44907055
集体控股	Collective-holding	327	9661437	6617217	4445540	3465138
私人控股	Private-holding	8743	71753631	49945865	61388276	51709712
港澳台商控股	Holdings form Hong Kong, Macao and Taiwan	99	5874520	2619757	3259189	2471893
外商控股	Foreign-holding	149	11621746	4106351	5183236	3978936
其他	Others	91	799331	436425	436555	276639

16−3 续表 1 continued

单位:万元 (10 000 yuan)

类别	Category	税金及附加 Tax and Extra Charges on Business	销售费用 Selling Expenses	管理费用 Management Expenses	财务费用 Financial Expenses	营业利润 Business Profits
全省总计	**Provincial Total**	**710631**	**3603258**	**9472289**	**3960820**	**7032172**
按控股情况分	**by Holding Type**					
国有控股	State-holding	356217	1079357	3548311	3286185	3541353
集体控股	Collective-holding	43150	140185	504505	85574	181879
私人控股	Private-holding	261583	2001615	4664602	595031	2174982
港澳台商控股	Holdings form Hong Kong, Macao and Taiwan	21629	184210	228396	38253	280489
外商控股	Foreign-holding	26646	165403	392718	-46286	805391
其他	Others	1199	29261	112719	1922	19894

16-3 续表 2 continued

单位：万元 (10 000 yuan)

类　别	Category	利润总额 Total Profits	所得税费用 Income Taxes Payable	应付职工薪酬 Total Wages Payable	应交增值税 Value-added Tax Payable
全省总计	**Provincial Total**	**7558281**	**1586624**	**20883188**	**2506488**
按控股情况分	**by Holding Type**				
国有控股	State-holding	3865699	836222	10394400	1018154
集体控股	Collective-holding	199967	38899	876359	112952
私人控股	Private-holding	2352778	468448	8301361	1131020
港澳台商控股	Holdings form Hong Kong, Macao and Taiwan	283407	144241	436626	118198
外商控股	Foreign-holding	840063	96684	706561	104455
其他	Others	15024	1938	144183	8361

16-4 规模以上服务业企业分行业财务状况(2021年)
Financial Indicators of Service Enterprises above Designated Size by Sector(2021)

单位：万元 (10 000 yuan)

行　业	Category	企业单位数(个) Number of Industrial Enterprises (unit)	资产总计 Total Assets	负债合计 Total Liabilities	营业收入 Business Revenue
全省总计	**Provincial Total**	**11353**	**444502739**	**244644642**	**127538106**
按行业分	**Grouped by Sector**				
交通运输、仓储和邮政业	Transport, Storage and Postal Services	3621	190416812	105249727	60313396
信息传输、软件和信息技术服务业	Information Transmission, Software and Information Technology Services	912	35130372	17270680	21128349
房地产业	Real Estate	921	32505266	21345901	4391806
租赁和商务服务业	Leasing and Business Services	2462	102040988	55431502	18360734
科学研究和技术服务业	Scientific Research and Technical Services	1610	21132163	10940575	12508603
水利、环境和公共设施管理业	Management of Water Conservancy, Environment and Public Facilities	409	48224742	24670543	4343006
居民服务、修理和其他服务业	Households' service, Repair and Other Services	362	1307472	901767	1045087
教育	Education	203	1635048	1162817	800072
卫生和社会工作	Health and Social Work	398	4397188	2982764	2718639
文化、体育和娱乐业	Culture, Sports and Entertainment	455	7712689	4688365	1928414

16-4 续表 1 continued

单位:万元 (10 000 yuan)

行 业	Category	营业成本 Business Costs	税金及附加 Tax and Extra Charges on Business	销售费用 Selling Expenses	管理费用 Management Expenses
全省总计	**Provincial Total**	**106851617**	**710631**	**3603258**	**9472289**
按行业分	**Grouped by Sector**				
交通运输、仓储和邮政业	Transport, Storage and Postal Services	55586608	219443	747514	2794628
信息传输、软件和信息技术服务业	Information Transmission, Software and Information Technology Services	15351646	69924	1175611	1363438
房地产业	Real Estate	3142773	89927	224946	676865
租赁和商务服务业	Leasing and Business Services	15664384	153478	527449	1597569
科学研究和技术服务业	Scientific Research and Technical Services	9148061	76117	348102	1567594
水利、环境和公共设施管理业	Management of Water Conservancy, Environment and Public Facilities	3205352	56611	62847	407460
居民服务、修理和其他服务业	Households' service, Repair and Other Services	804700	4254	72824	124536
教育	Education	521587	3765	76187	173298
卫生和社会工作	Health and Social Work	2063223	6208	147212	422581
文化、体育和娱乐业	Culture, Sports and Entertainment	1363285	30904	220566	344320

16-4 续表 2 continued

单位:万元 (10 000 yuan)

行 业	Category	财务费用 Financial Expenses	营业利润 Business Profits	利润总额 Total Profits
全省总计	**Provincial Total**	**3960820**	**7032172**	**7558281**
按行业分	**Grouped by Sector**			
交通运输、仓储和邮政业	Transport, Storage and Postal Services	2121379	1903284	2137849
信息传输、软件和信息技术服务业	Information Transmission, Software and Information Technology Services	43836	2356482	2429108
房地产业	Real Estate	398387	500483	552793
租赁和商务服务业	Leasing and Business Services	804828	881777	1020619
科学研究和技术服务业	Scientific Research and Technical Services	63189	915930	967548
水利、环境和公共设施管理业	Management of Water Conservancy, Environment and Public Facilities	435925	355653	395150
居民服务、修理和其他服务业	Households' service, Repair and Other Services	2507	43380	49886
教育	Education	12003	15423	7248
卫生和社会工作	Health and Social Work	35999	36471	29963
文化、体育和娱乐业	Culture, Sports and Entertainment	42767	23289	-31883

16-4 续表 3 continued

单位:万元 (10 000 yuan)

行业	Category	所得税费用 Income Taxes Payable	应付职工薪酬 Total Wages Payable	应交增值税 Value-added Tax Payable
全省总计	**Provincial Total**	**1586624**	**20883188**	**2506488**
按行业分	**Grouped by Sector**			
交通运输、仓储和邮政业	Transport, Storage and Postal Services	649961	7466133	893763
信息传输、软件和信息技术服务业	Information Transmission, Software and Information Technology Services	413102	3445455	515071
房地产业	Real Estate	127433	1230704	172999
租赁和商务服务业	Leasing and Business Services	136307	3458479	380202
科学研究和技术服务业	Scientific Research and Technical Services	143083	2928222	337903
水利、环境和公共设施管理业	Management of Water Conservancy, Environment and Public Facilities	72606	585046	122310
居民服务、修理和其他服务业	Households' service, Repair and Other Services	9898	246553	24753
教育	Education	8182	312418	14807
卫生和社会工作	Health and Social Work	19770	800415	7378
文化、体育和娱乐业	Culture, Sports and Entertainment	6283	409764	37302

16-5 各市规模以上服务业企业财务状况(2021年)
Financial Indicators of Service Enterprises above Designated Size by Region(2021)

单位:万元 (10 000 yuan)

地区	Region	企业单位数(个) Number of Industrial Enterprises (unit)	资产总计 Total Assets	负债合计 Total Liabilities	营业收入 Business Revenue	营业成本 Business Costs	税金及附加 Tax and Extra Charges on Business	销售费用 Selling Expenses
全省总计	**Total**	**11353**	**444502739**	**244644642**	**127538106**	**106851617**	**710631**	**3603258**
济南市	Jinan	2250	168769790	87350227	34395045	28089074	170787	1221337
青岛市	Qingdao	2510	86039889	49309142	38033693	33298067	161031	802445
淄博市	Zibo	613	23176721	13173413	5229298	4286092	47990	123094
枣庄市	Zaozhuang	262	4770800	2789674	1436709	1139274	8537	46392
东营市	Dongying	437	12256613	7839057	5702760	5051757	64488	80826
烟台市	Yantai	823	26492962	16503309	8065699	6696596	59686	205264
潍坊市	Weifang	615	29353172	11148684	5082870	4076268	29104	182553
济宁市	Jining	740	10647817	6932315	5169411	4310465	26283	188745
泰安市	Tai'an	301	6795754	4104337	2435178	1972726	9963	87500
威海市	Weihai	321	6097094	3649692	2243007	1823980	16011	90571
日照市	Rizhao	363	30687854	18034928	5439171	4445436	31550	52255
临沂市	Linyi	735	10454470	7743397	4842444	3806608	29509	205070
德州市	Dezhou	306	4789226	2644519	2195437	1858064	18793	74843
聊城市	Liaocheng	348	9432628	6419681	2644009	2304634	12393	63180
滨州市	Binzhou	351	5582806	2778062	2027439	1653594	15220	63513
菏泽市	Heze	378	9155143	4224205	2595937	2038982	9289	115670

16-5 续表 continued

单位：万元 (10 000 yuan)

地 区	Region	管理费用 Management Expenses	财务费用 Financial Expenses	营业利润 Business Profits	利润总额 Total Profits	所得税费用 Income Taxes Payable	应付职工薪酬 Total Wages Payable	应交增值税 Value-added Tax Payable
全省总计	**Total**	**9472289**	**3960820**	**7032172**	**7558281**	**1586624**	**20883188**	**2506488**
济 南 市	Jinan	2958107	1339384	2019134	2121001	418281	7341480	864196
青 岛 市	Qingdao	2173568	776995	2097486	2132540	412445	4745633	532470
淄 博 市	Zibo	437126	196770	345418	349706	36954	891340	105378
枣 庄 市	Zaozhuang	134526	40014	52752	71470	12083	231005	42572
东 营 市	Dongying	416161	136708	10472	71107	57609	1417298	113793
烟 台 市	Yantai	650998	293031	346823	380128	102519	1316446	127669
潍 坊 市	Weifang	439849	178943	726278	763480	160391	800456	117446
济 宁 市	Jining	351337	133923	223673	266954	54970	652458	116110
泰 安 市	Tai'an	228245	54238	139436	153435	21510	450744	53428
威 海 市	Weihai	217417	50297	101712	105091	29562	441407	45966
日 照 市	Rizhao	301421	414703	388844	444249	103903	605468	74183
临 沂 市	Linyi	491654	118556	216769	235309	70541	699406	116713
德 州 市	Dezhou	154509	36081	62947	83212	10786	295428	60583
聊 城 市	Liaocheng	167049	90284	12427	41699	24744	356334	57367
滨 州 市	Binzhou	159310	27264	109328	138092	24395	311852	42792
菏 泽 市	Heze	191013	73629	178675	200808	45931	326435	35820

主要统计指标解释

规模以上服务业 辖区内年营业收入 2000 万元及以上服务业法人单位。包括：交通运输、仓储和邮政业，信息传输、软件和信息技术服务业，水利、环境和公共设施管理业三个门类和卫生行业大类。

辖区内年营业收入 1000 万元及以上服务业法人单位。包括：租赁和商务服务业，科学研究和技术服务业，教育三个门类，以及物业管理、房地产中介服务、房地产租赁经营和其他房地产业四个行业小类。

辖区内年营业收入 500 万元及以上服务业法人单位。包括：居民服务、修理和其他服务业，文化、体育和娱乐业两个门类，以及社会工作行业大类。

Explanatory Notes on Main Statistical Indicators

The statistical coverage of some service enterprises above designated size The corporative enterprises with annual revenue from business above 20 million yuan of some services business, including three sectors of transport, storage and postal services, information transmission, software and information technology services, management of Water Conservancy, Environment and Public Facilities, and one major categories of health services.

The corporative enterprises with annual revenue from business above 10 million yuan of some services business, including three sectors of leasing and business services, scientific research and technical services, education, and four sub-categories of property management ,real estate agent services, real estate lease operation and other real estate,etc.

The corporative enterprises with annual revenue from business above 5 million yuan of some services business, including two sectors of households' service, repair and other services, culture, sports and entertainment services, and one major categories of social services .

第17篇

运输和邮电

Transport, Post and Telecommunication Services

简 要 说 明

一、本篇资料的主要内容

本篇资料反映了全省交通运输业和邮电通讯业发展的基本状况，主要包括交通设施基本情况、客货运量及周转量、交通运输企业主要技术经济指标、沿海主要港口货物吞吐量、邮政和电信基本情况、地方交通和营业性运输车辆、民用汽车拥有量等方面的内容。

二、本篇资料的来源

本篇资料中，交通运输资料分别来源于济南铁路局、山东省地方铁路局、省交通厅、省公安厅交警总队，邮电通信业资料来源于省通信管理局和省邮政局。

本篇资料由省统计局服务业处整理提供。

Brief Introduction

I. Content

Data in this chapter cover mainly the basic conditions of the development of transport, post and telecommunications in Shandong Province, including the basic conditions of transport, the freight traffic and passenger traffic accomplished by various means, major financial indices of related enterprises, cargo handled at principal sea ports, the possession of the transport equipment and the basic conditions of post and telecommunication services.

II. Source of Data

Data in this chapter are provided by Jinan Railway Board, Shandong Local Railway Board, Shandong Communications Department, and Traffic Police General Brigade of Shandong Public Security Department. Data on post and telecommunication services are provided by Shandong Communication Administration and Shandong Post Bureau.

Data in this chapter are prepared and compiled by the Division of Comprehensive Service Statistics of Shandong Provincial Bureau of Statistics.

17-1 主要年份运输线路长度

Length of Transport Routes in Major Years

单位：公里 (km)

年份 Year	铁路通车里程 Length of Railways in operation	公路通车里程 Length of Highways in Operation	#晴雨通车 In Operation Regardless of Weather	内河通航里程 Length of Navigable Inland Waterways	#通机动船 In Operation for Motor Vessels
1949	887	3152	65	1082	
1952	954	7669	170	1459	409
1955	956	9070	667	1459	409
1957	1154	13425	2115	1642	1063
1962	1168	15766	4189	2179	1353
1965	1208	22176	5669	1827	1310
1970	1276	29159	12666	1821	1629
1975	1275	31712	20212	1876	1764
1976	1386	32978	21645	2118	1802
1977	1386	33629	23636	2343	1811
1978	1385	34244	25289	2403	1880
1979	1388	35139	26106	1972	1953
1980	1411	35311	26544	1970	1736
1981	1582	35292	27284	1849	1712
1982	1565	35504	27875	1859	1722
1983	1565	35722	28480	1859	1722
1984	1569	35935	29427	1859	1725
1985	1572	36327	30250	1840	1706
1986	2041	37005	31286	1840	1706
1987	2042	37530	32468	1840	1706
1988	2042	38759	34057	1840	1706
1989	2042	39783	35557	1840	1706
1990	2041	40772	37015	1840	1706
1991	2042	41937	39081	1891	1780
1992	2048	43134	40612	1891	1780
1993	2048	46033	43992	1891	1780
1994	2048	50225	48385	1891	1780
1995	2048	54243	52702	1891	1780
1996	2620	57271	55882	1891	1780
1997	2721	59260	58028	1414	1302
1998	2658	64145	63142	1414	1302
1999	2677	67847	67055	1476	
2000	2672	70686	70038	1476	
2001	2709	71128	70701	1476	
2002	2709	74029	73665	1476	
2003	3236	76266	75948	1012	
2004	3348	77768	77483	1012	
2005	3402	80132	79854	1012	
2006	3405	204911	203363	1012	
2007	3379	212236	211279	1012	
2008	3329	220687	219525	1012	
2009	3620	226693	225235	1012	
2010	3833	229858	228906	1150	
2011	4177	233189	232264	1150	
2012	4306	244586	243779	1150	
2013	4397	252785	252066	1150	
2014	4546	259514	259031	1150	
2015	4863	263447	262986	1150	
2016	4882	265720	265265	1150	
2017	5115	270590	270150	1150	
2018	5676	275642	275344	1150	
2019	5972	280325	280186	1150	
2020	6881	286814	286741	1117	
2021	7198	288143	283469	1117	

注：1. 2006年起，村道纳入公路通车里程。2. 自2020年起，铁路相关数据含地方铁路。
a)Length of highways includes that of village-level highways since 2006.b)The data of railways includes the local railways since 2020.

17-2 主要年份旅客运量及周转量

Passenger Traffic and Turnover Volume in Major Years

年 份 Year	客运量 (万人) Passenger Traffic (10 000 Persons)	铁 路 Railways	公 路 Highways	水 路 Waterways	周转量 (百万人公里) Passenger Turnover (million Passenger-km)	铁 路 Railways	公 路 Highways	水 路 Waterways
1949	928	846	82		1368	1287	81	
1952	1196	938	251	7	1553	1365	180	8
1955	1775	1086	678	11	2229	1786	438	5
1957	3019	1872	1128	19	3002	2427	565	10
1962	7590	5923	1599	68	7664	6690	933	41
1965	4566	2457	2077	32	3664	2699	953	12
1970	5725	2454	3240	31			1445	14
1975	7084	3202	3844	38	6676	4708	1953	15
1976	7614	3233	4239	52	6996	4791	2189	16
1977	8679	3522	5103	54	7702	5127	2560	15
1978	9431	3467	5897	67	8448	5535	2895	18
1979	10857	3431	7338	88	9373	5950	3403	19
1980	12208	3586	8532	90	10624	6769	3839	16
1981	12682	3600	8994	88	11365	7272	4077	16
1982	13109	3695	9322	92	12283	7788	4477	18
1983	14839	3792	10942	102	14237	8954	5264	19
1984	17309	4071	13125	113	17058	10615	6423	20
1985	19772	4073	15565	134	20357	12433	7901	23
1986	26459	4005	22311	143	24671	13895	10752	24
1987	25209	4212	20811	186	27316	15608	11680	28
1988	29035	4447	24297	291	32412	17974	14402	36
1989	30718	3905	26419	344	32286	16552	15693	41
1990	29798	3303	26136	359	30138	14830	15255	53
1991	31940	3286	28240	405	32620	15873	16598	96
1992	33920	3244	30145	486	35164	17043	18002	119
1993	33634	3346	29693	595	34068	17785	16114	169
1994	34592	3587	30253	627	35627	18273	17126	222
1995	36425	3414	32317	694	35097	17418	17449	230
1996	39199	2854	35611	734	35344	15317	19696	331
1997	43218	3071	39234	913	40060	17277	22347	436
1998	50904	3223	46467	868	45229	18327	24599	483
1999	59350	3670	54817	863	51828	20568	28846	414
2000	66128	3840	61466	822	54873	22180	32358	335
2001	70497	3723	65787	987	59432	23373	35573	486
2002	74626	3566	69948	1112	64294	24644	39173	477
2003	75492	3324	71053	1115	61769	22024	39223	522
2004	89388	3857	84290	1241	74799	26696	47545	558
2005	98485	3952	93178	1355	82778	28268	53910	600
2006	109472	4757	103298	1417	93014	32223	60128	663
2007	123963	5127	117309	1527	106879	34039	72022	818
2008	213387	5470	205917	2000	141867	36694	104569	604
2009	234234	5806	226134	2294	158713	37993	119723	997
2010	248720	6041	240044	2635	164471	42135	121151	1185
2011	250469	6609	241457	2403	172751	45872	125691	1188
2012	264935	7650	254711	2574	183196	50951	130995	1250
2013	269391	8484	258327	2580	189285	54995	133137	1153
2014	73582	9508	62052	2022	114056	61734	51141	1181
2015	59625	10666	46960	1999	112745	64444	47137	1164
2016	62727	11904	48823	2000	116882	68442	47240	1200
2017	64536	13388	49111	2037	122676	73365	48104	1207
2018	66613	14525	50044	2044	126935	76302	49357	1276
2019	67317	15722	49581	2014	127981	77287	49256	1439
2020	30096	9797	19475	824	59517	43191	15931	395
2021	28350	12164	15139	1047	70560	52392	17783	385

注:1.2008年起,公路、水路数据改用全国公路水路运输量专项调查数据(以下相关表同)。

2.交通运输部2014年修订了公路、水运运输量统计试行方案，统计口径发生了变化(以下相关表同)。

3.2020年起，铁路客货运量、周转量为济南局、北京局、郑州局在山东省内数据，口径为国家铁路(以下相关表同)。

a)Since 2008, data on highways and waterways are based on the National Special Highway and Waterways Survey(The same as the following tables).

b)The pilot statistical investigation program on passenger traffic and turnover was revised in 2014,and the statistical scope was adjusted(The same as the following tables).

c)The railway passenger and freight volume and turnover refer to the data of Jinan Bureau,Beijing Bureau and Zhengzhou Bureau in Shandong Province,the caliber is national railway(The same as the following tables).

17-3 主要年份货物运量及周转量

Freight Traffic and Turnover Volume in Major Years

年 份 Year	货运量 (万吨) Freight Traffic (10 000 tons)	铁 路 Railways	公 路 Highways	水 路 Waterways	周转量 (百万吨公里) Freight Turnover (million ton-km)	铁 路 Railways	公 路 Highways	水 路 Waterways
1949	547	381	166	0.2	1245	1178	66	1
1952	1802	640	1029	133	3711	3346	154	211
1955	3305	895	2013	397	4919	4359	246	344
1957	4558	1238	2973	347	6923	6190	327	406
1962	4500	1801	2419	280	8106	7309	421	376
1965	7544	2821	4339	385	11929	10721	750	458
1970	10081	3911	5693	477	19167	17346	1186	635
1975	14598	4214	9781	603	22198	18947	2374	877
1976	17320	4904	11732	684	24062	20096	2942	1024
1977	21484	5365	15255	864	27326	22293	3865	1168
1978	22964	5940	16128	896	31005	25746	4060	1199
1979	22536	5951	15748	837	31586	26540	3634	1113
1980	22086	5687	15629	770	31329	26087	4005	1237
1981	20496	5306	14427	763	31941	26332	4093	1516
1982	21641	5415	15413	813	35160	28400	4937	1823
1983	23726	5655	17216	855	38996	30966	5787	2243
1984	25310	6035	18389	886	41974	33250	6505	2219
1985	27371	6403	20105	863	48431	37342	8139	2468
1986	32299	6789	24619	893	57599	44618	10287	2694
1987	36012	7072	28008	932	64533	49069	12231	3234
1988	39866	7322	31670	874	72723	53851	15325	3547
1989	43098	7934	34331	833	78996	58657	16612	3727
1990	41443	8012	32654	777	77845	58546	15705	3594
1991	44145	8372	34587	1186	81402	59694	16660	5047
1992	47676	8609	37684	1381	87617	62750	18931	5936
1993	51250	9023	40820	1407	92257	63127	20444	8687
1994	57187	9259	46485	1443	101437	66744	23069	11625
1995	66546	9256	55669	1621	112655	69857	26397	16401
1996	70664	10226	58270	2168	122849	71385	30559	20895
1997	72780	10368	60340	2072	126093	73323	31915	20855
1998	76813	10224	64716	1867	118753	65877	34322	18513
1999	80212	10553	67696	1956	127304	73588	35350	18330
2000	92483	11253	76778	4452	403315	79964	40575	282776
2001	99464	12426	81574	5464	467545	84815	41143	341587
2002	107454	13624	89714	4116	304075	92525	46009	165541
2003	117712	17167	95900	4645	342906	107157	50987	184762
2004	132036	17862	106887	7287	478309	111109	59606	307594
2005	147999	18338	120455	9206	558286	121908	71182	365196
2006	167511	19126	136750	11635	665521	151159	84510	429852
2007	198507	19923	163959	14625	642854	131151	106926	404777
2008	247489	20872	216604	10013	1010234	134133	511792	364309
2009	284463	19596	251587	13280	1095569	134139	604502	356928
2010	298055	18056	264366	15633	1174705	144775	621680	408250
2011	314962	19711	279380	15871	1258364	152606	662435	443323
2012	330270	19814	296752	13704	1099119	149384	705922	243813
2013	344401	19043	311812	13546	1026088	138910	749888	137290
2014	260983	16792	230018	14172	817690	123808	571138	122744
2015	258444	15786	227934	14724	833415	107728	587699	137988
2016	281557	16745	249752	15060	879552	113668	607143	158741
2017	322564	17853	288052	16659	962225	121363	665022	175840
2018	349481	18710	312807	17964	995988	126468	685968	183552
2019	304732	20850	266124	17758	1007631	143456	674620	189555
2020	308627	23189	267230	18208	1034063	156609	678440	199014
2021	333420	22895	291196	19329	1200214	168212	751761	280241

注：2019年起，公路货运量采用全国公路货运量专项调查数据。与以往不可比(以下相关表同)。

a)The highway freight volume adopts the special survey data of national highway freight volume since 2019,and not comparable with the previous (the same as in the following tables).

17-4 沿海主要港口货物吞吐量
Volume of Freight Handled in Major Coastal Ports

单位:万吨 (10 000 tons)

港口名称	Seaport	1995	2000	2005	2010	2015	2016	2017	2018	2019	2020	2021
总　计	**Total**	**10594**	**16025**	**38401**	**86421**	**134218**	**142856**	**151571**	**161512**	**161064**	**168881**	**178158**
青岛港	Qingdao	5103	8661	18679	35012	49749	51463	51149	54250	57736	60459	63029
烟台港	Yantai	1361	1964	4506	15033	33027	35407	40058	44308	38632	39935	42337
日照港	Rizhao	1452	2674	8421	22597	36082	38286	40189	43763	46377	49615	54117
威海港	Weihai	379	658	1532	2407	7324	7554	7806	5570	3730	3863	4273

17-5 交通运输企业主要技术经济指标
Major Technical and Economic Indicators of Transportation Enterprises

类　别	Category	2015	2016	2017	2018	2019	2020	2021
铁路运输	**Railway Transport**							
货车周转时间 (天)	Turning Around Time of Freight Locomotives (day)	2.0	2.0	1.8	1.7	1.5	1.5	1.5
货车全周转距离 (公里)	Turning Around Length of Freight Locomotives (km)	432	434	435	419	419	411	407
货车中转距离 (公里)	Transfer Length of Freight Locomotives (km)	190	199	220	216	222	226	228
平均一日装车数 (车)	Daily Loading Coach (coach)	7081	7778	8316	8921	10072	10936	10937
平均一日卸车数 (车)	Daily Unloading Coach (coach)	8461	9111	9592	10696	12119	12903	13938
货车静载重 (吨)	Static Load of Freight Locomotives (ton)	61.1	58.8	58.9	57.5	56.8	57.6	57.1
货运机车日产量 (万总重吨公里)	Average Daily Ton-kilometers of Freight Locomotives (10 000 tonkm)	131.7	138.2	146.7	149.5	156.2	164.5	162.9
内燃机车每万吨公里耗油 (公斤)	Oil Consumption of Diesel Locomotives per 10000 Ton-km (kg)	33.4	34.9	35.8	38.0	38.6	47.5	49.7
沿海水运船舶	**Coastal Waterways Transport**							
全部船舶净载重量 (万吨)	Static Load of Vessels (10 000 tons)	1755	1909	1810	1659	1713	1681	1552
码头泊位 (个)	Berths in Ports (unit)	556	567	581	597	596	607	616
最大靠泊能力 (万吨)	Maximum Capacity on Berths (10 000 tons)	30	30	30	40	40	40	40
年综合通过能力 (万吨)	Integrated Capacity (10 000 tons)	67089	72097	78820	85866	90823	95179	100247
旅客吞吐量 (万人)	Passenger Handled (10 000 persons)	1378	1404	1446	1461	1480	637	694

17-6 1978-2021年邮政基本情况

Basic Conditions of Post Services from 1978 to 2021

年 份 Year	邮政局总计 (处) Post &Telecommunication offices (unit)	#设在农村 in Rural Area	邮路总长度 (万公里) Length of Postal Routes (10 000 km)	函 件 (万件) Letters (10 000 pcs)	报刊期发数 (万份) Issue of Newspapers and Magazines (10 000 copies)
1978	2349	2048		15532	542
1979	2348	2042	22.6	16336	613
1980	2363	2057	22.5	17324	775
1981	2363	2052	22.8	17540	859
1982	2371	2050	4.2	17340	946
1983	2384	2048	4.2	17434	1131
1984	2415	2060	4.4	18958	1572
1985	2516	2153	4.7	21930	2017
1986	2531	2174	5.0	23745	1743
1987	2540	2176	5.2	26940	1888
1988	2576	2196	5.3	28884	1777
1989	2608	2210	5.3	30043	1176
1990	2647	2233	5.8	29486	1047
1991	2672	2247	5.7	28001	1174
1992	2699	2267	6.7	28266	1326
1993	3259	2492	8.5	32966	1247
1994	4180		9.7	35920	982
1995	4080	3400	10.5	38789	1180
1996	3727	3013	13.4	35112	1020
1997	5397		15.1	32859	996
1998	5382		15.1	33114	1147
1999	4414	3497	18.5	35138	1568
2000	3011	2255	17.0	32878	1701
2001	3040	2225	15.9	31400	1324
2002	3012	2193	16.5	51496	972
2003	3007	2166	15.7	58220	1152
2004	3009	2118	16.2	50087	716
2005	3025	2118	17.3	24075	823
2006	3043	2105	17.0	44356	703
2007	3046	2086	17.4	47157	763
2008	2934	2080	17.7	46362	823
2009	2862	2030	18.1	52074	868
2010	2840	1991	6.8	53963	1618
2011	2851	2012	6.6	46014	796
2012	2856	2022	7.3	45663	976
2013	2861	2022	7.3	42389	914
2014	2870	2044	7.6	29233	976
2015	2870	2049	8.0	18787	943
2016	2878	2041	10.0	10328	837
2017	2880	2054	45.2	6978	1151
2018	2873	2063	40.8	6369	854
2019	2889	2060	44.3	6263	921
2020	3005	2037	26.9	4341	904
2021	2979	2009	41.6	3796	726

17-7 1978-2021年电信业务总量

Business Volume of Telecommunication Services from 1978 to 2021

年份 Year	电信业务总量(万元) Business Volume of Telecommunication Services (10 000 Yuan)	电报(万份) Telegraph (10 000 copies)	长话电路(路) Lines of Long-distance Calls (line)	长途电话(万次) Long-distance Calls (10 000 times)	市内电话(万户) Local Telephones (10 000 subscribers)	农村电话(万户) Rural Telephones (10 000 subscribers)
1978	10058	588	1082	1308	6.3	3.8
1979	10515	632	1177	1428	7.1	4.3
1980	11030	711	1282	1525	7.5	4.4
1981	11291	789	1415	1532	8.0	4.5
1982	11629	805	1532	1649	8.5	4.6
1983	12529	917	1653	1789	9.4	4.8
1984	13751	908	1929	1963	10.7	5.1
1985	16186	1132	2190	2325	12.1	5.2
1986	17735	1203	2638	2569	13.4	5.5
1987	20719	1519	3341	2984	15.2	5.9
1988	27124	1918	4392	3987	18.5	6.4
1989	32153	1812	5694	4693	22.3	6.9
1990	39401	1634	7436	5800	26.5	7.3
1991	103322	1651	12675	8724	32.9	8.1
1992	156134	1673	18422	16978	45.8	9.5
1993	274917	1412	32615	32273	69.6	12.8
1994	404027	987	47589	52719	84.8	19.2
1995	537135	667	40634	55755	165.8	46.1
1996	697719	458	54179	61409	227.0	80.0
1997	957400	324	67834	79719	283.5	128.6
1998	1338886	226	98760	97077	346.7	179.6
1999	1411800	202	163381	96553	413.8	283.8
2000	1865000	178	222500	96010	547.0	559.0
2001	2300200	138	108000	101682	661.0	827.0
2002	2759820		135000	99470	790.0	950.0
2003	3325632		268530	149245	1008.0	1085.0
2004	4846250		510000	121275	1314.0	1198.0
2005	6754670		290996	152883	1410.9	1275.7
2006	9286877		462662	148631	1380.5	1256.7
2007	11799357		350028	157152	1377.6	1211.5
2008	14262026		413082	124858	1398.4	1053.7
2009	15867854		1238400	123510	1291.3	965.0
2010	19209000				1193.5	829.6
2011	7236000				1087.6	809.0
2012	7976000				1101.3	786.8
2013	8637000				1032.2	712.2
2014	10678489				879.3	538.9
2015	12531166				773.2	343.9
2016	8633818				678.2	292.2
2017	14947602				639.0	245.0
2018	36519157				618.1	228.3
2019	57866070					
2020	72000713					
2021	10020067					

注：2021年起，电信业务总量按上年不变价格计算。
a)The business volume of telecommunication services was calculated at last year constant prices since 2021.

17-8 邮电业务基本情况

Basic Conditions of Post and Telecommunication Services

类 别		Category		2016	2017	2018	2019	2020	2021
邮电业务总量	(亿元)	Business Volume of Telecommunication Services	(100 million yuan)	1165.0	1887.7	4180.3	6499.7	8193.8	1644.8
函 件	(万件)	Letters	(10 000 pcs)	10328	6978	6369	6263	4341	3796
特快专递	(万件)	Express Mail Services	(10 000 pcs)						
报刊期发数	(万份)	Issue of Newspapers and Magazines	(10 000 copies)	837	1151	854	921	904	726
年末移动电话用户	(万户)	Number of Mobile Telephone Subscribers at Year-end	(10 000 subscribers)	9594.5	9943.9	10569.6	10785.5	10907.1	11248.5
#4G移动电话用户	(万户)	3G Mobile Phone Subscribers	(10 000 subscribers)	4647.5	6242.6	7294.2	8112.7	8450.1	7134.1
固定电话年末用户	(万户)	Number of Fixed Telephone Subscribers at Year-end	(10 000 subscribers)	970.4	884.0	846.3	1185.2	1125.2	1107.4
#城市电话用户	(万户)	Urban Fixed Telephone Subscribers	(10 000 subscribers)	678.2	639.0	618.1			
农村电话用户	(万户)	Rural Telephone Subscribers	(10 000 subscribers)	292.2	245.0	228.3			
邮政所	(处)	Post Offices	(unit)	2878	2880	2873	2889	3005	2979
邮路总长度	(公里)	Length of Postal Routes	(km)	104002	452268	408336	442719	269210	416064
国际互联网总网民数	(万人)	Number of Internet Subscribers	(10 000 persons)	5207					
互联网宽带接入用户	(万户)	Number of Internet Broad Band Subscribers	(10 000 subscribers)	2366.5	2588.7	2884.8	3186.1	3445.6	3863.7
移动互联网用户	(万户)	Number of Mobile Internet Subscribers	(10 000 persons)	7391.2	8508.0	9552.3	8855.3	8761.3	9368.0

注：2021年邮电业务总量按上年不变价格计算(以下相关表同)。

a) The business volume of post and telecommunication services of 2021 was calculated at 2020 constant prices. The same applies to the relevant following tables.

17-9 各市邮电业务基本情况(2021年)

Basic Conditions of Post and Telecommunication Services by Region (2021)

地 区	Region	邮电业务总量(亿元) Business Volume of Post and Telecommunication Services (100 million yuan)	邮政业务总量(亿元) Business Volume of Post Services (100 million yuan)	电信业务总量(亿元) Business Volume of Telecommunication Services (100 million yuan)	移动电话用户数(万户) Number of Mobile Telephone Subscribers (10 000 subscribers)	固定电话用户数(万户) Number of Fixed Telephone Subscribers (10 000 subscribers)	互联网宽带接入用户(万户) Number of Internet Broad Band Subscribers (10 000 subscribers)
全省总计	**Total**	**1644.8**	**642.8**	**1002.0**	**11248.5**	**1107.4**	**3863.7**
济 南 市	Jinan	225.8	89.3	136.5	1228.8	162.5	477.9
青 岛 市	Qingdao	224.3	88.0	136.3	1295.3	159.0	455.1
淄 博 市	Zibo	67.0	20.0	47.0	531.4	68.7	171.9
枣 庄 市	Zaozhuang	51.6	18.9	32.7	389.9	38.3	139.1
东 营 市	Dongying	35.3	8.1	27.2	282.6	33.4	99.8
烟 台 市	Yantai	107.2	35.2	72.0	864.2	91.2	296.5
潍 坊 市	Weifang	143.1	55.4	87.7	1056.5	101.3	329.3
济 宁 市	Jining	106.2	37.4	68.9	829.3	68.6	272.1
泰 安 市	Tai'an	63.7	20.7	43.0	562.3	54.2	185.5
威 海 市	Weihai	53.5	19.2	34.3	402.6	43.5	139.7
日 照 市	Rizhao	42.5	15.0	27.4	316.9	28.1	113.2
临 沂 市	Linyi	209.1	113.4	95.7	1097.1	77.4	378.8
德 州 市	Dezhou	78.7	37.1	41.7	547.2	46.6	190.3
聊 城 市	Liaocheng	80.0	33.3	46.6	591.4	55.1	196.6
滨 州 市	Binzhou	51.5	15.9	35.6	418.9	37.0	152.3
菏 泽 市	Heze	102.2	35.9	66.3	834.2	42.5	265.5

17－10 各市公路情况(2021年)

Basic Conditions of Highways by Region (2021)

单位:公里 (km)

地 区	Region	公路里程 Length of Highways	等级公路里程 Expressway and Class I to IV Highways	二级及二级以上公路合计 Second Class and Above	高速公路里程 Length of Expressway	公路密度(公里/百平方公里) Road Density (km/100 sq.km)
全省总计	**Total**	**288143**	**288123**	**46636**	**7477**	**184**
济南市	Jinan	18191	18191	2926	728	178
青岛市	Qingdao	15355	15355	4283	859	136
淄博市	Zibo	11387	11387	1840	208	191
枣庄市	Zaozhuang	9357	9357	1646	275	205
东营市	Dongying	9357	9357	1336	237	109
烟台市	Yantai	19749	19749	4364	668	142
潍坊市	Weifang	29165	29165	5239	577	181
济宁市	Jining	21226	21205	3335	439	190
泰安市	Tai'an	16701	16701	2549	475	215
威海市	Weihai	7219	7219	1958	235	124
日照市	Rizhao	10244	10244	1822	222	191
临沂市	Linyi	31405	31405	4782	687	183
德州市	Dezhou	21780	21780	2548	501	210
聊城市	Liaocheng	21250	21250	2272	474	244
滨州市	Binzhou	17339	17339	2590	367	179
菏泽市	Heze	28418	28418	3146	523	234

17－11 各市地方交通旅客运输量(2021年)

Passenger Transport Volume of Local Traffic by Region (2021)

地 区	Region	客运量(万人) Passenger Traffic (10 000persons)	公路 Highways	水运 Waterways	周转量(百万人公里) Passenger-Kilometers (million passenger-km)	公路 Highways	水运 Waterways
全省总计	**Total**	**16186**	**15139**	**1047**	**18168**	**17783**	**385**
济南市	Jinan	2070	2024	45	3964	3961	3.7
青岛市	Qingdao	4460	4340	119	2905	2893	12.8
淄博市	Zibo	177	177		290	290	
枣庄市	Zaozhuang	253	212	41	465	464	1.5
东营市	Dongying	244	239	4	518	517	0.8
烟台市	Yantai	2340	1897	443	2066	1732	333.5
潍坊市	Weifang	830	830		1103	1103	
济宁市	Jining	945	855	89	1228	1224	4.3
泰安市	Tai'an	1076	1075	1	681	681	
威海市	Weihai	775	491	284	821	793	27.7
日照市	Rizhao	181	164	16	269	268	0.8
临沂市	Linyi	758	755	3	997	996	0.2
德州市	Dezhou	203	203		361	361	
聊城市	Liaocheng	1173	1173		1188	1188	
滨州市	Binzhou	162	162		378	378	
菏泽市	Heze	541	541		935	935	

17-12 各市地方交通货物运输量(2021年)

Freight Transport Volume of Local Traffic by Region (2021)

地 区	Region	货运量(万吨) Volume of Freight Traffic (10 000tons)	公路 Highways	水运 Waterways	周转量(百万吨公里) Freight Turnover (million ton-km)	公路 Highways	水运 Waterways
全省总计	**Total**	**310525**	**291196**	**19329**	**1032002**	**751761**	**280241**
济南市	Jinan	24780	24669	112	58602	57741	861
青岛市	Qingdao	31475	28407	3068	256788	66292	190496
淄博市	Zibo	18411	18411		45454	45454	
枣庄市	Zaozhuang	10484	9717	767	20629	17537	3092
东营市	Dongying	7753	7689	65	17562	17313	249
烟台市	Yantai	23610	19216	4394	58052	42881	15171
潍坊市	Weifang	31360	27108	4252	92227	64100	28127
济宁市	Jining	33957	30405	3552	87121	71059	16062
泰安市	Tai'an	7741	7715	27	17847	17740	107
威海市	Weihai	8376	6583	1793	32653	18606	14046
日照市	Rizhao	8804	7920	884	31438	20503	10935
临沂市	Linyi	36908	36908		145991	145991	
德州市	Dezhou	15006	15006		30403	30403	
聊城市	Liaocheng	21197	21197		61199	61199	
滨州市	Binzhou	14451	14171	280	40155	39604	551
菏泽市	Heze	16211	16076	135	35880	35336	543

17-13 各市民用汽车拥有量(2021年)

Possession of Private Vehicles by Region(2021)

单位:辆 (Unit)

地 区	Region	民用汽车总计 Total	载客汽车 Passenger Vehicles	大型 Large	中型 Medium	小型 Small	微型 Minicar
全省总计	**Total**	**27368108**	**24066356**	**128494**	**35611**	**23633817**	**268434**
济南市	Jinan	3015711	2757969	15272	3591	2718619	20487
青岛市	Qingdao	3362506	3023577	21301	5835	2969733	26708
淄博市	Zibo	1290173	1162897	6763	2538	1145079	8517
枣庄市	Zaozhuang	1011052	912954	4126	1128	895208	12492
东营市	Dongying	848181	753949	3961	1769	743354	4865
烟台市	Yantai	1984350	1795904	10622	3933	1766424	14925
潍坊市	Weifang	2817693	2423659	11830	3217	2382155	26457
济宁市	Jining	1880619	1570164	10151	2050	1533692	24271
泰安市	Tai'an	1008520	893555	6173	1479	878609	7294
威海市	Weihai	937473	830616	5228	2233	818969	4186
日照市	Rizhao	825241	714345	3809	769	701515	8252
临沂市	Linyi	3117095	2634209	7734	2794	2571595	52086
德州市	Dezhou	1274109	1129130	4232	1163	1110456	13279
聊城市	Liaocheng	1311038	1131627	5848	788	1110074	14917
滨州市	Binzhou	1119496	969150	4763	844	954392	9151
菏泽市	Heze	1564851	1362651	6681	1480	1333943	20547

注:民用汽车不含三轮汽车和低速载货汽车。其他汽车指专项作业车。
a)Civil vehicles don't include three-wheeled vehicles and low-speed trucks.Other vehicles refer to special operation vehicles.

17-13 续表 continued

单位:辆 (Unit)

地区	Region	载货汽车 Trucks	大型 Large	中型 Medium	小型 Small	微型 Minicar	其他汽车 Others
全省总计	**Total**	**3173936**	**994551**	**56284**	**2121802**	**1299**	**127816**
济南市	Jinan	242302	51530	3778	186889	105	15440
青岛市	Qingdao	325163	85604	10256	229177	126	13766
淄博市	Zibo	120822	37624	1733	81088	377	6454
枣庄市	Zaozhuang	95204	33748	1185	60259	12	2894
东营市	Dongying	87079	26426	1055	59559	39	7153
烟台市	Yantai	181249	46295	4985	129923	46	7197
潍坊市	Weifang	381364	91803	9208	280223	130	12670
济宁市	Jining	297161	143880	2640	150547	94	13294
泰安市	Tai'an	110810	29075	2201	79529	5	4155
威海市	Weihai	102570	16561	1532	84468	9	4287
日照市	Rizhao	106690	27716	1105	77785	84	4206
临沂市	Linyi	471503	186922	9956	274537	88	11383
德州市	Dezhou	138645	40725	1393	96483	44	6334
聊城市	Liaocheng	173259	76387	1345	95479	48	6152
滨州市	Binzhou	145274	49615	1701	93944	14	5072
菏泽市	Heze	194841	50640	2211	141912	78	7359

17-14 各市私人汽车拥有量(2021年)

Possession of Private Vehicles by Region (2021)

单位:辆 (Unit)

地区	Region	汽车总计 Total	载客汽车 Passenger Vehicles	大型 Large	中型 Medium	小型 Small	微型 Minicar
全省总计	**Total**	**24425583**	**22459030**	**2374**	**13643**	**22198015**	**244998**
济南市	Jinan	2696874	2537374	784	1464	2515615	19511
青岛市	Qingdao	2919669	2738949	163	1586	2717786	19414
淄博市	Zibo	1166134	1094217	112	1371	1084448	8286
枣庄市	Zaozhuang	748443	692551	54	415	683314	8768
东营市	Dongying	757337	707152	65	510	702216	4361
烟台市	Yantai	1809543	1689300	31	1598	1673087	14584
潍坊市	Weifang	2620913	2327453	312	1790	2299423	25928
济宁市	Jining	1645874	1495385	195	637	1470759	23794
泰安市	Tai'an	930639	853660	36	645	845769	7210
威海市	Weihai	857968	783242	161	810	778245	4026
日照市	Rizhao	750001	678303	21	310	670089	7883
临沂市	Linyi	2788268	2520128	186	1210	2472631	46101
德州市	Dezhou	1110868	1027086	112	343	1015034	11597
聊城市	Liaocheng	1163117	1078432	50	257	1063614	14511
滨州市	Binzhou	1004794	916450	31	280	907396	8743
菏泽市	Heze	1455141	1319348	61	417	1298589	20281

注：私人汽车不含登记在个人名下三轮汽车和低速载货汽车。

a)Total vehicles don't include three-wheeled vehicles and low-speed trucks.

17-14 续表 continued

单位:辆 (Unit)

地 区	Region	载货汽车 Trucks	大 型 Large	中 型 Medium	小 型 Small	微 型 Minicar	其他汽车 Others
全省总计	**Total**	**1904514**	**106537**	**22394**	**1774886**	**697**	**62039**
济 南 市	Jinan	153514	13309	1207	138979	19	5986
青 岛 市	Qingdao	176187	1791	1754	172569	73	4533
淄 博 市	Zibo	68845	2169	611	65990	75	3072
枣 庄 市	Zaozhuang	54431	3459	382	50580	10	1461
东 营 市	Dongying	47858	1824	380	45633	21	2327
烟 台 市	Yantai	117464	9555	2268	105617	24	2779
潍 坊 市	Weifang	286034	31289	5406	249245	94	7426
济 宁 市	Jining	142861	13524	693	128568	76	7628
泰 安 市	Tai'an	74721	4251	924	69541	5	2258
威 海 市	Weihai	73166	5895	679	66585	7	1560
日 照 市	Rizhao	69685	2285	360	66972	68	2013
临 沂 市	Linyi	261100	10804	5662	244564	70	7040
德 州 市	Dezhou	80524	447	342	79706	29	3258
聊 城 市	Liaocheng	81418	1579	277	79518	44	3267
滨 州 市	Binzhou	85487	2487	684	82303	13	2857
菏 泽 市	Heze	131219	1869	765	128516	69	4574

17-15 各市公路营业性运输车辆(2021年)
Transport Vehicles in Operation by Region (2021)

单位:辆 (Unit)

地 区	Region	汽 车 Vehicles	客 车 Passenger Vehicles	货 车 Trucks
全省总计	**Total**	**1392201**	**17957**	**1374244**
济 南 市	Jinan	66944	2632	64312
青 岛 市	Qingdao	124945	2861	122084
淄 博 市	Zibo	56079	576	55503
枣 庄 市	Zaozhuang	53576	332	53244
东 营 市	Dongying	32689	528	32161
烟 台 市	Yantai	61104	1696	59408
潍 坊 市	Weifang	120432	1488	118944
济 宁 市	Jining	185065	1077	183988
泰 安 市	Tai'an	44208	857	43351
威 海 市	Weihai	22760	867	21893
日 照 市	Rizhao	37463	570	36893
临 沂 市	Linyi	260144	1423	258721
德 州 市	Dezhou	58293	489	57804
聊 城 市	Liaocheng	115603	1008	114595
滨 州 市	Binzhou	76038	494	75544
菏 泽 市	Heze	76858	1059	75799

注:公路营运载客汽车不包括在公路运输管理部门管理并注册登记为公共汽车和出租汽车的车辆。数据来源于交通部门。

a)Passenger vehicles do not include those managed by department of highway transportation and registered as buses and taxis.The data comes from the transportation department.

17-16 按行业分企业信息化及电子商务情况(2021年)

行业	Industry	企业数(个) Number of Enterprises (unit)	期末使用计算机数(台) Computers Used at the End of Period (unit)
全省	**Total**	**88436**	**3435073**
采矿业	Mining	347	91335
制造业	Manufacturing	30375	1338053
电力、热力、燃气及水生产和供应业	Production and Supply of Electricity, Heat, Gas and Water	1587	145129
建筑业	Construction	9738	353581
批发和零售业	Wholesale and Retail Trades	24197	422006
交通运输、仓储和邮政业	Transport, Storage and Post	3593	211228
住宿和餐饮业	Hotels and Catering Services	3380	53319
信息传输、软件和信息技术服务业	Information Transmission, Software and Information Technology Services	901	272952
房地产业	Real Estate	8471	171801
租赁和商务服务业	Leasing and Business Services	2429	89441
科学研究和技术服务业	Scientific Research and Technical Services	1605	160907
水利、环境和公共设施管理业	Management of Water Conservancy, Environment and Public Facilities	408	15471
居民服务、修理和其他服务业	Service to Households, Repair and Other Services	360	6661
教育	Education	201	32333
卫生和社会工作	Health and Social Service	397	44749
文化、体育和娱乐业	Culture, Sports and Entertainment	447	26107

注：有电子商务交易活动的企业是指通过计算机网络开展电子商务销售或电子商务采购的企业。

Informatization and E-Commerce of Enterprises by Industrial Sector (2021)

每百人使用计算机数(台) Computers Used Per 100 Persons (unit)	企业拥有网站数(个) Websites of Enterprises (unit)	每百家企业拥有网站数(个) Websites Per 100 Enterprises (unit)	有电子商务交易活动 With E-Commerce Transactions		电子商务销售额(万元) Sales of E-Commerce (10 000 yuan)	电子商务采购额(万元) Purchases of E-Commerce (10 000 yuan)
			企业数(个) Enterprises (unit)	比重(%) Proportion (%)		
32	**41834**	**47**	**13120**	**14.8**	**171455255**	**91155729**
29	158	46	13	3.7	463588	47413
27	19330	64	4929	16.2	99203535	48021823
48	721	45	156	9.8	567190	4553504
17	4094	42	702	7.2	1749860	2590274
52	7683	32	3382	14.0	53271757	30448754
38	1257	35	540	15.0	5918915	3405681
25	1123	33	1470	43.5	705074	8050
119	827	92	281	31.2	8197204	1385603
42	3355	40	588	6.9	40763	39306
22	1091	45	397	16.3	902105	237330
79	1151	72	297	18.5	94579	385213
11	173	42	63	15.4	30550	5002
14	146	41	53	14.7	71236	20106
101	150	75	23	11.4	52589	1287
56	309	78	75	18.9	12801	3300
68	266	60	151	33.8	173511	3084

a) Enterprises with E-Commerce Transactions refers to those enterprises which performed sales or purchases through internet.

17-17　各市企业信息化及电子商务情况(2021年)

地　区	Region	企业数 (个) Number of Enterprises (unit)	期末使用计算机数 (台) Computers Used at the End of Period (unit)	每百人使用计算机数 (台) Computers Used Per 100 Persons (unit)
全省总计	**Total**	**88436**	**3435073**	**32**
济 南 市	Jinan	11865	746797	46
青 岛 市	Qingdao	13200	634955	44
淄 博 市	Zibo	5563	193060	27
枣 庄 市	Zaozhuang	2260	70036	26
东 营 市	Dongying	2802	154839	33
烟 台 市	Yantai	6904	282375	32
潍 坊 市	Weifang	7751	325214	31
济 宁 市	Jining	6751	172168	25
泰 安 市	Tai'an	3566	117247	18
威 海 市	Weihai	3227	140230	32
日 照 市	Rizhao	2629	87171	32
临 沂 市	Linyi	7521	166171	23
德 州 市	Dezhou	3422	98332	27
聊 城 市	Liaocheng	3531	81164	21
滨 州 市	Binzhou	3188	86154	21
菏 泽 市	Heze	4256	79160	19

注：有电子商务交易活动的企业是指通过计算机网络开展电子商务销售或电子商务采购的企业。

Informatization and E-Commerce of Enterprises by Region (2021)

企业拥有网站数(个) Websites of Enterprises (unit)	每百家企业拥有网站数(个) Websites Per 100 Enterprises (unit)	有电子商务交易活动 With E-Commerce Transactions		电子商务销售额(万元) Sales of E-Commerce (10 000 yuan)	电子商务采购额(万元) Purchases of E-Commerce (10 000 yuan)
		企业数(个) Enterprises (unit)	比重(%) Proportion (%)		
41834	**47**	**13120**	**14.8**	**171455255**	**91155729**
6386	54	1327	11.2	23225392	10114798
7052	53	6413	48.6	60272009	41265379
2697	49	742	13.3	10626756	8788805
1035	46	157	6.9	790084	267094
1453	52	331	11.8	16399095	1144886
3440	50	644	9.3	12844548	8092937
3908	50	537	6.9	13943408	10647263
2940	44	434	6.4	1246654	894472
1633	46	242	6.8	1072598	573109
1684	52	273	8.5	2050631	1330123
1232	47	196	7.5	1342774	835204
1925	26	465	6.2	4099406	942944
1911	56	322	9.4	4770726	298700
1510	43	239	6.8	4461735	1970294
1375	43	343	10.8	6245392	2118186
1653	39	455	10.7	8064048	1871537

a) Enterprises with E-Commerce Transactions refers to those enterprises which performed sales or purchases through internet.

主要统计指标解释

铁路营业里程 又称营业长度(包括正式营业和临时营业里程)，指办理客货运输业务的铁路正线总长度。凡是全线或部分建成双线及以上的线路，以第一线的实际长度计算；复线、站线、段管线、岔线和特殊用途线以及不计算运费的联络线都不计算营业里程。该指标可以反映铁路运输业基础设施的发展水平，也是计算客货周转量、运输密度和机车车辆运用效率等指标的基础资料。

公路里程 指在一定时期内实际达到《公路工程\[WTBZ\]技术标准 JTJ01-88》规定的等级公路，并经公路主管部门正式验收交付使用的公路里程数。包括大中城市的郊区公路以及通过小城镇街道部分的公路里程和桥梁、渡口的长度，不包括大中城市的街道、厂矿、林区生产用道和农业生产用道的里程。两条或多条公路共同经由同一路段，只计算一次，不得重复计算里程长度。该指标可以反映公路建设的发展规模，也是计算运输网密度等指标的基础资料。

内河航道里程 也称内河通航里程，指在一定时期内，能通航运输船舶及排筏的天然河流、湖泊水库、运河及通航渠道的长度。包括全年季节性通航累计三个月以上的航道，不包括仅供零散流放竹、木排的河道。该指标可以反映内河水运网的规模、水平和发展情况。

货(客)运量 指在一定时期内，各种运输工具实际运送的货物(旅客)数量。该指标是反映运输业为国民经济和人民生活服务的数量指标，也是制定和检查运输生产计划、研究运输发展规模和速度的重要指标。货运按吨计算，客运按人计算。货物不论运输距离长短、货物类别，均按实际重量统计。旅客不论行程远近或票价多少，均按一人一次客运量统计；半价票、小孩票也按一人统计。

货物(旅客)周转量 指在一定时期内，由各种运输工具运送的货物(旅客)数量与其相应运输距离的乘积之总和。该指标可以反映运输业生产的总成果，也是编制和检查运输生产计划，计算运输效率、劳动生产率以及核算运输单位成本的主要基础资料。计算货物周转量通常按发出站与到达站之间的最短距离，也就是计费距离计算。计算公式为：

$$货物（旅客）周转量=\Sigma（货物（旅客）运输量\times 运输距离）$$

铁路货车平均静载重 指铁路货车在始发站静止状态下平均每车装载的货物重量，用以分析货车完成装车时车辆载重力的利用情况。计算公式为：

$$货车平均静载重=\frac{货物发送吨数}{装车数}$$

铁路货运机车日产量 指在一定时期内，平均每台货运机车在一昼夜内所完成的总重吨公里数，包括载运货物的重量和车辆本身的自重。该指标从时间和牵引能力两方面反映了机车运用效率。计算公式为：

$$货运机车平均日产量=\frac{货运总重吨公里数}{货运机车台日数}$$

沿海主要港口货物吞吐量 指经水运进出沿海主要港区范围，并经过装卸的货物数量，包括邮件及办理托运手续的行李、包裹以及补给运输船舶的燃、物料和淡水。货物吞吐量按货物流向分为进口、出口吞吐量，按货物交流性质分为外贸货物吞吐量和国内贸易货物吞吐量。货物吞吐量的货类构成及其流向，是衡量港口生产能力大小的重要指标。

民用汽车拥有量 指报告期末，在公安交通管理部门按照《机动车注册登记工作规范》，已注册登记领有民用车辆牌照的全部汽车数量。汽车拥有量统计的主要分类：根据汽车结构分为载客汽车、载货汽车及其他汽车；根据汽车所有者不同分为个人(私人)汽车、单位汽车；根据汽车的使用性质分为营运汽车、非营运汽车；根据汽车大小规格不同载客汽车分为大型、中型、小型和微型，载货汽车分为重型、中型、轻型和微型。

邮电业务总量 指以价值量形式表现的邮电通信企业为社会提供各类邮电通信服务的总数量。邮电业务量按专业分类包括函件、包件、汇票、报刊发行、邮政快件、特快专递、邮政储蓄、集邮、公众电报、用户电报、传真、长途电话、出租电路、无线寻呼、移动电话、分组交换数据通信、出租代维等。计算方法为各类产品乘以相应的平均单价(不变价)之和，再加上出租电路和设备、代用户维护电话交换机和线路等的服务收入。该指标综合反映了一定时期邮电业务发展的总成果，是研究邮电业务量构成和发展趋势的重要指标。计算公式为：

$$邮电业务总量=\Sigma（各类邮电业务量\times 不变单价）+出租代维及其他业务收入=邮政业务总量+电信业务总量$$

移动电话用户 指通过移动电话交换机进入移动电话网、占用移动电话号码的各类电话用户。包括签约用户和智能网预付费用户。一个移动电话号码统计为一户。

互联网上网人数 指平均每周使用互联网至少 1 小时的中国公民人数。

本地电话用户 指接入本地电信运营商固定电话网上的电话用户。包括：住宅用户、单位用户、公用电话用户等。按电话用户位置又分为市内电话用户和农村电话用户。1997 年以前，“市内电话用户”是指接入县城及县以上城市

的电话网上的电话用户；“农村电话用户”是指接入县邮电局农话台及县以下农村电话交换点，以县城为中心(除市话用户外)联通县、乡(镇)、行政村、村民小组的用户。从1997年起，电话用户数分组调整为以用户所在区域划分为“城市电话用户”和“乡村电话用户”，与过去的按市内电话和农村电话划分方法不同。而电话用户总数、电话机总部数统计范围不变。

城市电话用户 指直辖市、省辖市、地级市、县级市的市区、市郊区及县城(包括县人民政府所在地的县城关区或行政建制相当于县人民政府所在地的镇)范围内接入局用交换机的电话用户数，包括分布在农村地区的独立工矿区、林区、驻军等电话用户数。

农村电话用户 指按行政区划属于城市范围以外的乡(镇)、村的电话用户数。

Explanatory Notes on Main Statistical Indicators

Length of Railways in Operation refers to the total length of the trunk line under passenger and freight transportation (including both full operation and temporary operation). The calculation is based on the actual length of the first line even if this line has a full or partial double track or more tracks, excluding double tracks, station sidings, tracks under the charge of stations, branch lines, special purpose lines and the non payable connecting lines. The length of railways in operation is an important indicator to show the development of the infrastructure for the railway transport, and also the essential data to calculate volume of passenger freight transport, traffic density and utilization efficiency of the locomotives and carriages.

Length of Highways refers to the length of highways which are built in conformity with the grades specified by the highway engineering standard formulated by the Ministry of Communications,and have been formally checked and accepted by the departments of highways and put into use. The length of highways includes that of the suburb highways at large and medium sized cities, highways passing through streets at small cities and towns, and also the length of bridges and ferries. It does not include the length of streets in big and medium sized cities and highways built for the production purpose at factories, mines, forest areas and agricultural areas. If two or more highways go the same section of the way, the length of the section is only calculated for once and no duplication is allowed. The length of highways is an important indicator to show the development of the highway construction and to provide essential information to calculate the transport network density.

Length of Navigable Inland Waterways it is an indicator reflecting the size and development of inland water network, it refers to the length of the natural rivers, lakes, reservoirs, canals, and ditches open to navigation during a given period, which enables the transport by ships and rafts. It includes the channels open to navigation for over an accumulative 3 months in a year, yet this does not include the river courses, which are only used to float odd logs and bamboo rafts. This indicator can reflect the scale, level and development situation of the inland waterway network.

Freight (Passenger) Traffic refers to the volume of freight (passenger) transported with various means. Freight transport is calculated in tons and passenger traffic is calculated in the number of persons. Despite the type of freight and traveling distance, the freight transport is calculated in the actual weight of the goods: and despite the traveling distance and ticket price, the passenger traffic is calculated by the principle that one person can be counted only once in one travel. The passengers who travel with a half price ticket or a child ticket is also calculated as one person. The freight (passenger) traffic provides a quantitative measure to show how the transport industry serves the national economy and people, and is also an important indicator for planning the transport industry and for studying the development scale and speed of the transport industry.

Freight Ton kilometers (Passenger kilometers) refer to the sum of the products of the volume of transported cargo (passengers) multiplying by the transport distance. It is an important indicator to reflect the achievement of transportation industry. Normally, the shortest distance between the departure station and the destination station (i.e., the payable distance) is the basis to calculate the freight ton kilometers. This is an important indicator to show the total results of the transport industry, to prepare and examine the transport plan and to measure the efficiency, the labour productivity and the unit cost of transport.The formula is as follows:

$$\begin{matrix}\text{Freight ton - kilometres} \\ \text{(passenger - kilometres)}\end{matrix} = \sum \begin{matrix}\text{freight} \\ \text{(passenger)traffic}\end{matrix} \times \begin{matrix}\text{distance of} \\ \text{transportation}\end{matrix}$$

Static Load of Freight Cars refers to the average cargo weight as loaded by each freight car under the static condition at the departure station. It is used to show the utilization extent of the loading capacity of the freight cars. The formula is:

$$\begin{matrix}\text{Static load (ton)} \\ \text{of freight car}\end{matrix} = \frac{\text{tonnage of goods dispatched}}{\text{number of freight cars loaded}}$$

Average Daily Haul of Freight Locomotives refers to the average total ton kilometers accomplished by each freight transport locomotive over day and night during a given period of time. It includes both the weight of the goods carried and the dead weight of the train itself. It is a comprehensive indicator reflecting the locomotive efficiency in terms of both time and the pulling force.

$$\begin{matrix}\text{Average daily haul of} \\ \text{freight transport locomotive} \\ \text{(ton - kilometre)}\end{matrix} = \frac{\text{Total ton - kilometres of freight}}{\text{Daily number of freight transport locomotive}}$$

Volume of Freight Handled in Major Coastal Ports refers to the volume of cargo passing in and out the harbor area of the major coastal ports and having been loaded and unloaded. The volume includes that of the postal matters, registered luggage and fuels, materials and fresh water as supplies of the ships. The volume of freight handled may be classified by direction of flow as freight for import and freight for export, or by nature of cargo as freight for domestic trade and freight for foreign trade. As an important indicator, the volume of freight handled by type of cargo and by main flow direction reflects the production capacity of ports.

Possession of Civil Motor Vehicles refer to the total numbers of vehicles that are registered and received vehicles license tags according to the Work Standard for Motor Vehicles Registration formulated by transport management office under department of public security at the end of reference period. They are divided into following categories according to the structure of motor vehicles: passenger vehicles, trucks and others; and private vehicles and vehicles for units use according to ownerships; working vehicles and non working vehicles according to kind of usage; large passenger vehicles, medium passenger vehicles, small passenger vehicles and mini passenger vehicle, heavy trucks, light heavy trucks, light trucks and mini trucks according to sizes of vehicles.

Business Volume of Post and Telecommunications refers to the total amount of post and telecommunication services, expressed in value terms, provided by the post and telecommunications departments for the society. Post and telecommunication services can be classified as letters, parcels, remittance, issue of newspapers and magazines, fast mail service, express mail service, savings deposits, stamps for collection, public and individual telegraph service, facsimiles, long distance telephone service, leasing of telephone lines, urban paging service, mobile telephone service, data transfer and transmission, etc. The accounting approach is to multiply the service products of all types with their average unit price (constant price) to get sum of business value, plus income from other services such as leasing of telephone lines and equipment, maintenance of telephone switchboards and lines on behalf of customers. This indicator reflects the overall results of post and telecommunications service during a given period, and is important to study the composition of business service and the development of post and telecommunications service.

The formula is as follows:

Business volume of post and telecommunications
=∑(Transaction of post and telecommunication services
×price[constant price])
+Income from leasing, maintenance and other services
= business volume of postal service
+ business volume of telecommunications service

Mobile Telephone Subscribers refer to the persons who own mobile telephone numbers and are connected with the mobile telephone communication network through the mobile telephone switchboards, including contracted subscribers and pre paid subscribers for intelligent network. One mobile telephone is taken as a subscriber.

Internet Users refer to the number of Chinese citizens who use Internet at least for one hour each week.

Local Telephone Subscribers refer to subscribers that are connected to the local telecommunication service provider through fix line network, including household subscribers, institutional subscribers and public telephones. They are also classified as city subscribers and rural subscribers according to locations. Before 1997, city subscribers referred to those connected to city telephone networks in county towns and cities, while village subscribers referred to those connected to village telephone stations at and below counties. Since 1997, the classification of telephone subscribers was modified on the basis of physical location of the subscribers as urban telephone subscribers and rural telephone subscribers, which is different from the previous classification of categorizing local telephones and rural telephones, while the definition of total subscribers and total number of telephones remain unchanged.

Urban Telephone Subscribers refer to number of telephone subscribers, located at municipalities, cities under the jurisdiction of province, cities at prefecture level, downtown and suburb of city at county level town and county towns (including country towns where county government located, and towns of county level according to the administrative organizational system), that are connected to the public line telephone network, including rural mineral area, forest area, military area.

Rural Telephone Subscribers refer to telephone subscribers, located at counties (towns) and villages outside the range of cities according to administrative jurisdiction.

第
18
篇

批发和零售业、住宿和餐饮业

Wholesale, Retail, Hotels and Catering Services

简　要　说　明

一、本篇资料的主要内容

本篇资料反映全省市场发展情况、批发和零售业、住宿和餐饮业经营情况和效益情况等，主要包括批发和零售业商品流转情况及财务状况、住宿和餐饮业经营情况及财务状况、社会消费品零售总额等内容。

二、本篇资料的来源

本篇资料中除特别注明外，其余均来自限额以上批发和零售业、住宿和餐饮业年报资料和定期报表统计资料。

本篇资料由省统计局贸易处整理提供。

Brief Introduction

I. Content

Data in this chapter are supposed to show the development of Shandong's domestic market, wholesale and retail trade, hotels and catering services, mainly including the circulation of commodities in the wholesale and retail trade, the financial indices of related businesses and the total retail sales of consumer goods.

II. Source of Data

Except the data specifically noted, all data in this chapter are based on the annual report of wholesale, retail, hotels and catering services and periodic statistical statements.

Data in this chapter are prepared and compiled by the Division of Trade and External Economic Relations Statistics of Shandong Provincial Bureau of Statistics.

18−1 批发和零售业情况

Basic Conditions of Wholesale and Retail Trades

指　标		Item		2016	2017	2018	2019	2020	2021
批发和零售业		**Wholesale and Retail Trades**							
法人企业	（个）	Number of Corporation Enterprises	(unit)	16894	16865	15695	15617	21036	24740
年末从业人数	（万人）	Engaged Persons at Year-end	(10 000 persons)	96.0	90.1	82.5	74.3	78.9	81.9
商品购进额	（亿元）	Total Purchases	(100 million yuan)	29289.7	29812.8	30902.8	35945.1	45047.6	64852.2
#进口额	（亿元）	Imports	(100 million yuan)	765.7	872.6	769.5	1189.6	1671.7	2423.8
商品销售额	（亿元）	Total Sale	(100 million yuan)	32129.2	32944.0	34878.2	40037.2	48585.3	68119.2
#出口额	（亿元）	Exports	(100 million yuan)	895.5	1042.4	1233.0	1370.1	1409.2	1787.7
期末商品库存额	（亿元）	Total Stock at Year-end	(100 million yuan)	1686.3	1903.5	1961.1	2003.6	2479.5	3203.8
批发业		**Wholesale Trade**							
法人企业	（个）	Number of Corporation Enterprises	(unit)	8217	8310	8298	9938	15036	18293
年末从业人数	（万人）	Engaged Persons at Year-end	(10 000 persons)	38.0	35.1	32.6	32.3	37.7	40.1
商品购进额	（亿元）	Total Purchases	(100 million yuan)	19803.3	21821.3	24409.3	30080.8	38989.8	57869.4
#进口额	（亿元）	Imports	(100 million yuan)	680.2	796.0	676.8	1058.9	1549.3	2295.6
商品销售额	（亿元）	Total Sales	(100 million yuan)	21625.3	24016.9	27161.1	33144.5	41723.0	60197.3
#出口额	（亿元）	Exports	(100 million yuan)	892.2	1039.5	1230.8	1364.0	1407.4	1785.7
期末商品库存额	（亿元）	Total Stock at Year-end	(100 million yuan)	1001.3	1156.7	1183.3	1304.3	1783.1	2470.4
零售业		**Retail Trade**							
法人企业	（个）	Number of Corporation Enterprises	(unit)	8677	8555	7397	5679	6000	6447
年末从业人数	（万人）	Engaged Persons at Year-end	(10 000 persons)	59.0	55.1	50.0	42.0	41.2	41.7
商品购进额	（亿元）	Total Purchases	(100 million yuan)	9486.4	7991.5	6493.6	5864.3	6057.8	6982.8
#进口额	（亿元）	Imports	(100 million yuan)	85.5	76.6	92.8	130.7	122.4	128.2
商品销售额	（亿元）	Total Sales	(100 million yuan)	10503.9	8927.2	7717.1	6892.7	6862.3	7921.8
#出口额	（亿元）	Exports	(100 million yuan)	3.3	2.9	2.2	6.1	1.7	2.0
期末商品库存额	（亿元）	Total Stock at Year-end	(100 million yuan)	684.9	746.8	777.8	699.3	696.3	733.4
年末零售营业面积	（万平方米）	Business Area of Retail at Year-end	(10 000 sq.m)	3097.0	2908.0	2968.0	3043.9	3138.5	3241.6

18-2 限额以上批发和零售业商品购进、销售、库存总额(2021年)

单位:万元

指 标 名 称	Indicator	法人单位(个) Corporate Unit (unit)
总 计	**Total**	**24740**
一、批发业	**Wholesale Trade**	**18293**
1.按登记注册类型分	by Status of Registration	
内 资	Domestic Funded Enterprises	18029
国 有	State-owned	179
集 体	Collective-owned	9
股份合作	Cooperative	6
联营企业	Joint Ownership	5
有限责任公司	Limited Liability Corporations	2270
股份有限公司	Share-holding Corporations Ltd.	120
私营企业	Private Enterprises	15393
其 他	Others	47
港澳台商投资企业	Enterprises with Funds from Hong Kong,Macao and Taiwan	100
与港澳台商合资经营	Joint-venture	30
与港澳台商合作经营	Cooperative	1
港澳台商独资	Sole Investment	62
港澳台商投资股份有限公司	Share-holding Corporations Ltd. with Sole Investment	3
其他港澳台投资企业	Others	4
外商投资企业	Foreign Funded Enterprises	164
中外合资经营	Joint-venture	45
中外合作经营	Cooperative	4
外资企业	Sole Foreign Investment	104
外商投资股份有限公司	Share-holding Corporations Ltd. with Foreign Investment	3
其他外商投资企业	Others	8
2.按国民经济行业分(GB/T 4754-2017)	by Sector	
农、林、牧产品批发业	Wholesale of Farm Produce and Livestock Products	981
食品、饮料及烟草制品批发	Wholesale of Food, Beverages and Tobaccos	1524
纺织、服装及家庭用品批发	Wholesale of Textiles, Garments and Daily Consumer Articles	1051
文化、体育用品及器材批发	Wholesale of Culture, Sports Appliances and Equipments	396
医药及医疗器材批发	Wholesale of Medicines and Medical Appliances	966
矿产品、建材及化工产品批发	Wholesale of Mineral Products, Building Materials and Chemical Products	10257
机械设备、五金产品及电子产品批发	Wholesale of Machinery, Hardware and Electronic Equipment	2710
贸易经纪与代理	Trade Broker and Agency	57
其他批发业	Other Wholesale not Classified Elsewhere	351

Total Purchases,Sales and Inventory of Enterprises above Designated Size of Wholesale and Retail Trades(2021)

(10 000 yuan)

购进总额 Total Purchases Value	#进 口 Import	销 售 总 额 Total Sale Value 合 计 Total	批 发 Wholesale	#出 口 Export	零 售 Retail	年末库存总 额 Inventory (year-end)
648522341	**24238194**	**681191867**	**598417641**	**17876504**	**82774226**	**32038224**
578694466	**22956116**	**601973489**	**593209496**	**17856896**	**8763993**	**24704054**
550145520	20658382	571475505	564032062	15775453	7443442	23152529
23205406	607628	24453312	24395696	114429	57616	1206900
144306		156790	156046		744	6971
170911	265	215436	215436	5678		3922
555825		559943	555114		4829	68977
202695584	9200633	208795972	205359485	4683611	3436487	7397928
12242393	636504	12734410	11912634	478231	821777	1000926
310894119	10213353	324296075	321180632	10493505	3115442	13461808
236976		263567	257020		6547	5097
10589999	1637468	11104201	11028750	1791887	75450	923154
3756768	526243	3808459	3804604	198050	3855	117634
5662		9990	9990			117
6158886	1108679	6619552	6619540	1593699	12	789697
352334	2111	346608	275166		71443	7866
316351	436	319593	319451	138	141	7840
17958948	660265	19393783	18148683	289555	1245100	628371
5673904	493347	5719967	5719295	42210	672	328071
71952	2898	76512	75941	6871	571	9719
11848031	164020	12897170	11971799	224331	925372	279098
325148		654749	336263		318486	11468
39913		45385	45385	16144		16
17824598	1423763	18343969	18218970	342897	124999	1328460
36202637	2479128	41766147	40203658	1378517	1562489	2820225
25497623	522904	26782577	25897183	3303451	885394	1122606
9999975	232047	10413617	9448443	527635	965174	692285
23938524	347209	26942639	26744886	319040	197752	1879115
413002432	15726652	422446312	418672004	5921136	3774308	13486276
42440739	1121327	44690395	43661047	5377425	1029348	3000723
3770055	908677	3908917	3849463	419457	59454	152996
6017883	194410	6678917	6513842	267337	165075	221369

18-2 续表

单位:万元

指 标 名 称	Indicator	法人单位(个) Corporate Unit (unit)
二、零售业	**Retail Trade**	**6447**
1.按登记注册类型分	by Status of Registration	
内 资	Domestic Funded Enterprises	6295
国 有	State-owned	53
集 体	Collective-owned	30
股份合作	Cooperative	17
联营企业	Joint Ownership	2
有限责任公司	Limited Liability Corporations	1089
股份有限公司	Share-holding Corporations Ltd.	87
私营企业	Private Enterprises	5002
其 他	Others	15
港澳台商投资企业	Enterprises with Funds from Hong Kong,Macao and Taiwan	81
与港澳台商合资经营	Joint-venture	11
与港澳台商合作经营	Cooperative	1
港澳台商独资	Sole Investment	66
港澳台商投资股份有限公司	Share-holding Corporations Ltd. with Sole Investment	1
其他港澳台投资企业	Others	2
外商投资企业	Foreign Funded Enterprises	71
中外合资经营	Joint-venture	19
中外合作经营	Cooperative	2
外资企业	Sole Foreign Investment	44
外商投资股份有限公司	Share-holding Corporations Ltd. With Foreign Investment	5
其他外商投资企业	Others	1
2.按国民经济行业分(GB/T 4754-2017)	by Sector	
综合零售	Integrated Retail	706
食品、饮料及烟草制品专门零售	Retail of Food, Beverages and Tobaccos	468
纺织、服装及日用品专门零售	Special Retail of Textiles, Garments and Daily Consumer Articles	254
文化、体育用品及器材专门零售	Retail of Culture, Sports Appliances and Equipments	251
医药及医疗器材专门零售业	Retail of Medicines and Medical Appliances	368
汽车、摩托车、零配件和燃料及其他动力销售	Retail of Motor Vehicles, Motorcycles,Parts,Fuel and Other Power	2996
家用电器及电子产品专门零售业	Special Retail of Household Electric Appliances and Electronic Products	785
五金、家具及室内装修材料专门零售	Special Retail of Hardware, Furniture and Decoration Materials	234
货摊、无店铺及其他零售业	Non-shop and Other Retails	385

continued

(10 000 yuan)

购进总额 Total Purchases Value	#进口 Import	销售总额 Total Sale Value 合计 Total	 批发 Wholesale	 #出口 Export	 零售 Retail	年末库存总额 Inventory (year-end)
69827874	**1282079**	**79218379**	**5208146**	**19608**	**74010233**	**7334170**
62275775	1038852	70306651	4224137	19523	66082515	6500235
743115		788522	3171		785351	63843
134892		142303	6012		136291	9846
77755		79318	385		78933	11209
14474		16445			16445	372
20150257	298945	22418726	1854301	13012	20564425	1962795
5621290	48856	7729194	758879		6970315	397792
35511129	691052	39093412	1597952	6511	37495460	4053598
22864		38731	3437		35294	781
3470529	75670	3930469	118003	85	3812466	478169
498632		553261	2000		551261	74575
77016		101226			101226	7936
2825092	73463	3210101	116003	85	3094098	390967
31201		29293			29293	854
38588	2208	36589			36589	3836
4081570	167557	4981258	866006		4115252	355766
612431	18377	765632	78072		687560	205716
57370		56920			56920	4644
2478735	149180	2979181	494997		2484184	120384
932122		1178614	292937		885677	25022
912		912			912	
13888786	53196	17352098	1161598		16190500	1555807
1371246	18738	1612030	101764		1510266	164652
1769368	9051	2268783	330721	13012	1938062	498889
1385357	505	1524841	86490	1876	1438351	572908
3475418	16880	4014214	167448		3846766	539243
35305362	1104561	38838595	2146954	833	36691641	3023695
3906655	16691	4135208	222591	85	3912617	378251
523003	8584	635774	71228	1516	564546	63202
8202680	53874	8836838	919353	2285	7917485	537524

18-3 限额以上批发和零售业企业财务状况(2021年)

单位:万元

指标名称	Indicator	企业数(个) Number of Enterprises (unit)
总　　计	**Total**	**24740**
一、批发业	**Wholesale Trade**	**18293**
1.按登记注册类型分	by Status of Registration	
内　资	Domestic Funded Enterprises	18029
国　有	State-owned	179
集　体	Collective-owned	9
股份合作	Cooperative	6
联营企业	Joint Ownership	5
有限责任公司	Limited Liability Corporations	2270
股份有限公司	Share-holding Corporations Ltd.	120
私营企业	Private Enterprises	15393
其　他	Others	47
港澳台商投资企业	Enterprises with Funds from Hong Kong,Macao and Taiwan	100
与港澳台商合资经营	Joint-venture	30
与港澳台商合作经营	Cooperative	1
港澳台商独资	Sole Investment	62
港澳台商投资股份有限公司	Share-holding Corporations Ltd. with Sole Investment	3
其他港澳台投资企业	Others	4
外商投资企业	Foreign Funded Enterprises	164
中外合资经营	Joint-venture	45
中外合作经营	Cooperative	4
外资企业	Sole Foreign Investment	104
外商投资股份有限公司	Share-holding Corporations Ltd. with Foreign Investment	3
其他外商投资企业	Others	8
2.按国民经济行业分(GB/T 4754-2017)	by Sector	
农、林、牧产品批发业	Wholesale of Farm Produce and Livestock Products	981
食品、饮料及烟草制品批发	Wholesale of Food, Beverages and Tobaccos	1524
纺织、服装及家庭用品批发	Wholesale of Textiles, Garments and Daily Consumer Articles	1051
文化、体育用品及器材批发	Wholesale of Culture, Sports Appliances and Equipments	396
医药及医疗器材批发	Wholesale of Medicines and Medical Appliances	966
矿产品、建材及化工产品批发	Wholesale of Mineral Products, Building Materials and Chemical Products	10257
机械设备、五金产品及电子产品批发	Wholesale of Machinery, Hardware and Electronic Equipment	2710
贸易经纪与代理	Trade Broker and Agency	57
其他批发业	Other Wholesale not Classified Elsewhere	351

注：限额以上批发零售企业中，由于包含了部分视同法人单位，因此财务指标数据资产≠负债+所有者权益(以下相关表同)。

Financial Indicators of Enterprises above Designated Size of Wholesale and Retail Trades(2021)

(10 000 yuan)

年末资产负债 Assets and Liabilities at Year-end						损益及分配 Losses,Profits and Distribution	
流动资产合计 Total Working Capitals	固定资产原价 Original Value of Fixed Assets	本年折旧 Depreciation in the Year	资产合计 Total Assets	负债合计 Total Liabilities	所有者权益合计 Total Owner's Equities	营业收入合计 Business Revenue	主营业务收入 Revenue from Principal Business
233999097	**21648756**	**1361165**	**289518719**	**233730408**	**55203007**	**610262014**	**603460183**
203195222	**13152794**	**805556**	**246626818**	**198416665**	**46929678**	**540044100**	**535033104**
185265015	12186262	749734	224255689	184539838	38379582	512530548	507644230
8086453	595929	20350	9217785	6776000	2394167	21379865	21329780
122604	16749	613	167782	152888	14894	140618	139787
206739	31949	1683	258670	213576	45095	181525	181525
125768	1248	-530	126381	62805	63576	495622	494834
68934358	5439373	263663	89402927	66878797	22334247	186479254	185129412
15300674	668006	38949	19018230	17297364	1716770	11581259	11020325
92415463	5422533	424455	105975212	93097632	11782908	292024146	289101195
72958	10474	551	88702	60776	27926	248259	247371
10459795	387067	23308	13514650	9496898	4017014	10246066	10209629
6383056	165482	10271	8384113	5429127	2954891	3436039	3431501
14746	4868	-110	16105	12810	3295	8841	8841
3560030	176341	10168	4226602	3561599	664361	6173634	6141868
287853	32691	2862	660319	336296	324023	344712	344712
214111	7685	116	227512	157066	70445	282841	282708
7470412	579465	32514	8856479	4379928	4533081	17267486	17179244
1599853	74982	9376	1749092	1305680	499942	5084680	5071154
17518	11363	519	23570	21061	2509	69093	69093
4770782	387752	19939	5436091	2226265	3209826	11508865	11451634
1064883	105186	2656	1626047	820428	805620	563402	545931
17376	183	25	21678	6494	15184	41446	41432
5958266	1067774	38247	8318243	6573201	1735322	17281513	17177128
14236566	2093677	102230	17381345	11714199	5597126	38484495	38103785
13495286	565126	30047	15916519	13347940	2562758	24504456	24236190
4058853	480143	21025	5956135	4277266	1668931	9507480	8811120
17075010	1008799	75331	19627532	15955221	3660582	23833668	23717286
124613363	6450755	353243	151023394	123972319	25928384	376704508	373697223
20739419	1309604	171144	25029719	19750546	5249506	40568563	40197224
1107133	16081	1074	1143701	989110	154587	3600731	3598637
1911329	160835	13215	2230231	1836864	372482	5558687	5494509

a) Of enterprises above designated size of wholesale and retail trades, the financial data have the problem of total assets ≠ liabilities + total owner's equities, because some of them are regarded as legal entities(the same as in the following tables).

18-3 续表 1

单位:万元

指标名称	Indicator	企业数(个) Number of Enterprises (unit)
二、零售业	**Retail Trade**	**6447**
1.按登记注册类型分	by Status of Registration	
内 资	Domestic Funded Enterprises	6295
国 有	State-owned	53
集 体	Collective-owned	30
股份合作	Cooperative	17
联营企业	Joint Ownership	2
有限责任公司	Limited Liability Corporations	1089
股份有限公司	Share-holding Corporations Ltd.	87
私营企业	Private Enterprises	5002
其 他	Others	15
港澳台商投资企业	Enterprises with Funds from Hong Kong,Macao and Taiwan	81
与港澳台商合资经营	Joint-venture	11
与港澳台商合作经营	Cooperative	1
港澳台商独资	Sole Investment	66
港澳台商投资股份有限公司	Share-holding Corporations Ltd. with Sole Investment	1
其他港澳台投资企业	Others	2
外商投资企业	Foreign Funded Enterprises	71
中外合资经营	Joint-venture	19
中外合作经营	Cooperative	2
外资企业	Sole Foreign Investment	44
外商投资股份有限公司	Share-holding Corporations Ltd. With Foreign Investment	5
其他外商投资企业	Others	1
2.按国民经济行业分(GB/T 4754-2017)	by Sector	
综合零售	Integrated Retail	706
食品、饮料及烟草制品专门零售	Retail of Food, Beverages and Tobaccos	468
纺织、服装及日用品专门零售	Special Retail of Textiles, Garments and Daily Consumer Articles	254
文化、体育用品及器材专门零售	Retail of Culture, Sports Appliances and Equipments	251
医药及医疗器材专门零售业	Retail of Medicines and Medical Appliances	368
汽车、摩托车、零配件和燃料及其他动力销售	Retail of Motor Vehicles, Motorcycles,Parts,Fuel and Other Power	2996
家用电器及电子产品专门零售业	Special Retail of Household Electric Appliances and Electronic Products	785
五金、家具及室内装修材料专门零售	Special Retail of Hardware, Furniture and Decoration Materials	234
货摊、无店铺及其他零售业	Non-shop and Other Retails	385

continued

(10 000 yuan)

年末资产负债 Assets and Liabilities at Year-end						损益及分配 Losses,Profits and Distribution	
流动资产合计 Total Working Capitals	固定资产原价 Original Value of Fixed Assets	本年折旧 Depreciation in the Year	资产合计 Total Assets	负债合计 Total Liabilities	所有者权益合计 Total Owner's Equities	营业收入合计 Business Revenue	#主营业务收入 Revenue from Principal Business
30803875	**8495962**	**555609**	**42891902**	**35313744**	**8273329**	**70217913**	**68427079**
27990974	7151121	458420	38300241	32264659	6546389	61907676	60391947
345997	66732	7089	459606	380916	73377	724463	703903
53680	19217	820	71983	54802	17180	126732	125860
27455	17181	854	44203	30726	13477	71313	71285
1120	1157	52	2298	493	1806	14591	14554
8077436	2495423	156528	11372024	8972913	2384163	19963946	19433401
5886061	1461589	54845	8562097	7893684	1273817	5967869	5634832
13583239	3079761	238054	17711081	14876321	2760424	35010600	34384019
15986	10061	178	76950	54804	22146	28162	24093
1081947	479468	56379	1473232	1022583	450649	3648223	3550423
113409	54622	3822	184618	136505	48114	506218	489041
56255	23032	15938	63349	40280	23069	73252	73252
895012	400313	36544	1206191	838625	367566	3009754	2929645
9835	1053	15	10370	948	9421	25923	25923
7436	449	59	8704	6225	2479	33075	32563
1730954	865373	40810	3118428	2026502	1276291	4662015	4484709
354530	161121	10218	554655	349246	205409	697289	676485
37488	21199	1421	46154	17208	28947	56608	53315
908700	425691	18531	1572948	1230739	342758	2839817	2717033
427077	256289	10614	940209	426090	699177	1067736	1037877
3159	1074	26	4462	3220		565	
11023673	4179117	248890	16321270	13633964	2640013	14148716	13328165
1005873	252460	13410	1303501	966582	336077	1502939	1472317
1148794	158902	17572	1534489	1054374	481009	1993429	1963892
750496	122129	8165	927497	635308	279053	1411756	1393133
1849196	163438	14044	2356267	1913864	443318	3710901	3668388
10791829	3043314	220829	15215258	12868006	3143836	35393188	34692070
1844083	182124	7745	2226521	1943326	281219	3402227	3358794
317446	119264	7923	539716	364379	173958	580545	572963
2072485	275213	17031	2467383	1933940	494848	8074213	7977358

18-3 续表 2

单位:万元

指标名称	Indicator	营业成本 Cost of Business
总　计	**Total**	**581994162**
一、批发业	**Wholesale Trade**	**519962786**
1.按登记注册类型分	by Status of Registration	
内　资	Domestic Funded Enterprises	493337072
国　有	State-owned	20376561
集　体	Collective-owned	130919
股份合作	Cooperative	173807
联营企业	Joint Ownership	488770
有限责任公司	Limited Liability Corporations	179323949
股份有限公司	Share-holding Corporations Ltd.	10767635
私营企业	Private Enterprises	281839838
其　他	Others	235593
港澳台商投资企业	Enterprises with Funds from Hong Kong,Macao and Taiwan	9896207
与港澳台商合资经营	Joint-venture	3398420
与港澳台商合作经营	Cooperative	6381
港澳台商独资	Sole Investment	5904607
港澳台商投资股份有限公司	Share-holding Corporations Ltd. with Sole Investment	308976
其他港澳台投资企业	Others	277823
外商投资企业	Foreign Funded Enterprises	16729507
中外合资经营	Joint-venture	4923401
中外合作经营	Cooperative	57299
外资企业	Sole Foreign Investment	11157412
外商投资股份有限公司	Share-holding Corporations Ltd. with Foreign Investment	553625
其他外商投资企业	Others	37770
2.按国民经济行业分(GB/T 4754-2017)	by Sector	
农、林、牧产品批发业	Wholesale of Farm Produce and Livestock Products	16829107
食品、饮料及烟草制品批发	Wholesale of Food, Beverages and Tobaccos	33890619
纺织、服装及家庭用品批发	Wholesale of Textiles, Garments and Daily Consumer Articles	23028090
文化、体育用品及器材批发	Wholesale of Culture, Sports Appliances and Equipments	8847133
医药及医疗器材批发	Wholesale of Medicines and Medical Appliances	21213135
矿产品、建材及化工产品批发	Wholesale of Mineral Products, Building Materials and Chemical Products	368860008
机械设备、五金产品及电子产品批发	Wholesale of Machinery, Hardware and Electronic Equipment	38392251
贸易经纪与代理	Trade Broker and Agency	3523492
其他批发业	Other Wholesale not Classified Elsewhere	5378950

continued

(10 000 yuan)

损益及分配 Losses,Profits and Distribution							工资、福利、增值税 Wages,Welfare and Value Added Tax	
税金及附加 Taxes and Other Charges on Business	销售费用 Expenses on Sales	管理费用 Expenses on Management	财务费用 Expenses on Finance	营业利润 Profits from Business	利润总额 Total Profits	所得税费用 Income Tax Expense	应付职工薪酬 (本年贷方累计发生额) Payroll payable (Cumulative amount of credits)	应交增值税 Value Added Tax Payable
1961226	**13948987**	**6863403**	**2390068**	**5229874**	**6610986**	**1256351**	**6497584**	**3933264**
1727382	**8842244**	**4658151**	**1972024**	**4705029**	**6018572**	**1035434**	**3943336**	**3212263**
1696634	8439454	4416722	1889389	4236106	5545167	962650	3743580	3111182
318981	132337	204157	48553	209503	226718	74643	179130	154384
276	1510	12310	5445	-9817	-8470	35	9978	2172
184	476	3284	2570	1736	-1744	48	2412	156
408	841	1696	134	3859	3859	965	967	884
1027254	2634630	1550764	799451	2411659	3486144	505987	1572253	1124115
25800	459004	126975	108722	181638	191786	39782	208632	121221
323210	5207307	2514897	924026	1432557	1641715	340628	1766166	1707212
521	3351	2641	488	4972	5160	563	4043	1037
15240	108837	117637	63637	342644	343202	31860	67932	46504
2393	12680	14850	20493	278437	280725	2409	6334	6210
57	1002	769	569	64	58		161	471
11921	79882	87267	37185	58438	55676	25511	42983	32826
713	12646	13296	4262	6560	6586	3781	16999	6367
157	2627	1455	1128	-855	157	160	1456	631
15508	293953	123792	18998	126279	130203	40923	131874	54577
5393	70860	25157	12750	40236	41494	7202	29863	16801
95	3841	3473	462	3624	3695	792	2860	354
8453	188245	80633	7731	73625	78785	30864	82323	34442
1513	29691	13666	-1914	7308	4742	1747	15614	2625
54	1317	864	-31	1487	1488	318	1164	356
8382	179028	149099	154715	27532	60088	15768	115219	16588
1180874	1336656	933581	106178	1158249	1152423	312504	1007249	507250
41405	844927	345928	87010	210731	219508	50026	400904	216793
11062	265594	174255	43775	187850	193636	18016	215027	29743
56108	1459501	540375	153474	393627	398675	87697	490943	344465
320775	3582308	1771355	1178472	2404650	3624120	459000	1066891	1492164
78775	1018188	669774	215547	336318	349494	84749	583017	372874
1976	36432	12240	18494	8371	10144	2373	11945	4195
28026	119611	61544	14359	-22299	10484	5300	52142	228191

18-3 续表 3

单位:万元

指标名称	Indicator	营业成本 Cost of Business
二、零售业	**Retail Trade**	**62031377**
1.按登记注册类型分	by Status of Registration	
内　资	Domestic Funded Enterprises	54907660
国　有	State-owned	651600
集　体	Collective-owned	111656
股份合作	Cooperative	62491
联营企业	Joint Ownership	13915
有限责任公司	Limited Liability Corporations	17642213
股份有限公司	Share-holding Corporations Ltd.	5193642
私营企业	Private Enterprises	31209898
其　他	Others	22246
港澳台商投资企业	Enterprises with Funds from Hong Kong,Macao and Taiwan	3129968
与港澳台商合资经营	Joint-venture	450288
与港澳台商合作经营	Cooperative	60981
港澳台商独资	Sole Investment	2565589
港澳台商投资股份有限公司	Share-holding Corporations Ltd. with Sole Investment	22003
其他港澳台投资企业	Others	31108
外商投资企业	Foreign Funded Enterprises	3993749
中外合资经营	Joint-venture	534938
中外合作经营	Cooperative	48710
外资企业	Sole Foreign Investment	2451030
外商投资股份有限公司	Share-holding Corporations Ltd. with Foreign Investment	958568
其他外商投资企业	Others	504
2.按国民经济行业分(GB/T 4754-2017)	by Sector	
综合零售	Integrated Retail	11612595
食品、饮料及烟草制品专门零售	Retail of Food, Beverages and Tobaccos	1291437
纺织、服装及日用品专门零售	Special Retail of Textiles, Garments and Daily Consumer Articles	1587545
文化、体育用品及器材专门零售	Retail of Culture, Sports Appliances and Equipments	1215009
医药及医疗器材专门零售业	Retail of Medicines and Medical Appliances	2981080
汽车、摩托车、零配件和燃料及其他动力销售	Retail of Motor Vehicles, Motorcycles,Parts,Fuel and Other Power	32637003
家用电器及电子产品专门零售业	Special Retail of Household Electric Appliances and Electronic Products	3139314
五金、家具及室内装修材料专门零售	Special Retail of Hardware, Furniture and Decoration Materials	478341
货摊、无店铺及其他零售业	Non-shop and Other Retails	7089055

continued

(10 000 yuan)

损益及分配 Losses,Profits and Distribution							工资、福利、增值税 Wages,Welfare and Value Added Tax	
税金及附加 Taxes and Other Charges on Business	销售费用 Expenses on Sales	管理费用 Expenses on Management	财务费用 Expenses on Finance	营业利润 Profits from Business	利润总额 Total Profits	所得税费用 Income Tax Expense	应付职工薪酬（本年贷方累计发生额） Payroll payable (Cumulative amount of credits)	应交增值税 Value Added Tax Payable
233843	**5106743**	**2205252**	**418045**	**524845**	**592413**	**220917**	**2554248**	**721000**
197950	4320562	1954212	387862	437322	505335	172448	2293038	641495
1979	46435	19134	6477	5413	6258	2131	31014	22793
660	4258	8882	912	801	1340	261	6941	1933
326	4819	3387	425	99	146	77	3292	722
34	487	290	24	459	459	103	354	195
63058	1528743	512604	119601	182603	199632	66479	690392	204024
23578	518695	222075	36498	66422	71605	9281	232070	52922
108212	2215232	1186485	221831	181071	225369	94073	1326984	358829
104	1893	1356	2095	455	525	44	1991	78
19401	288011	67229	7504	127279	128660	34451	114005	36109
2835	18461	11449	3452	20006	20267	5186	12050	5602
119	10352	142	125	1567	1356	339	2865	190
16172	257488	53743	4016	103019	104273	28125	97012	30069
262	1091	860	-128	2427	2501	625	685	133
14	618	1037	39	260	264	176	1393	114
16493	498170	183810	22680	-39755	-41581	14018	147206	43397
3918	78508	81436	1806	10541	17158	5138	56119	14234
655	5437	1680	-775	876	984	245	4178	521
9609	323657	81688	14301	-41814	-47025	10862	63161	23594
2311	90569	18989	7348	-9401	-12742	-2215	23748	5043
1		17		43	44	-12		5
78757	1521628	742148	116629	245381	269996	69317	826717	162867
4300	84523	60243	6849	49111	52139	9781	68428	18033
8584	264696	102281	11620	34681	40077	10867	109016	36341
14410	96879	49932	6376	29194	31474	4510	66460	13277
13788	487509	211864	23708	1318	6287	10277	326832	54018
92851	1508821	730007	222882	292516	311982	89050	911422	337272
4605	174177	118904	16490	-43417	-42728	2493	108314	21613
3025	50027	45183	6570	-4595	-2396	1222	26590	9310
13524	918484	144690	6922	-79344	-74418	23402	110469	68268

18-4 各市限额以上批发和零售业商品购进、销售、库存总额(2021年)

Total Purchases,Sales and Inventory of Enterprises above Designated Size of Wholesale and Retail Trades by Region(2021)

单位：亿元 (100 million yuan)

地 区	Region	法人单位(个) Corporate Unit (unit)	年末从业人数(万人) Persons Employed at Year-end (10 000 person)	购进总额 Total Purchases Value	#进口 Import	销售总额 Total Sale Value 合计 Total	批发 Wholesale	#出口 Export	零售 Retail	年末库存总额 Inventory (year-end)
全省总计	**Total**	**24740**	**81.9**	**64852.2**	**2423.8**	**68119.2**	**59841.8**	**1787.7**	**8277.4**	**3203.8**
济南市	Jinan	4562	16.2	11031.2	221.7	11607.8	9892.3	271.9	1715.5	577.2
青岛市	Qingdao	3824	13.0	16562.2	1388.4	17109.6	15347.4	592.1	1762.2	795.9
淄博市	Zibo	1935	4.7	3752.9	130.8	3993.3	3607.2	51.5	386.1	136.9
枣庄市	Zaozhuang	572	1.8	749.2	5.6	814.2	669.7	30.9	144.5	38.3
东营市	Dongying	913	2.3	4684.8	30.8	4728.0	4529.1	51.6	199.0	309.1
烟台市	Yantai	1828	7.5	4107.5	119.1	4443.7	3754.6	162.5	689.1	260.7
潍坊市	Weifang	1704	6.3	4063.0	66.8	4470.1	3810.2	173.1	659.9	186.3
济宁市	Jining	1915	5.7	2565.1	37.5	2779.7	2363.5	59.8	416.2	134.9
泰安市	Tai'an	1227	3.1	2391.2	32.0	2526.3	2301.2	16.0	225.2	78.9
威海市	Weihai	576	3.3	1263.8	204.9	1377.3	942.0	73.1	435.3	64.1
日照市	Rizhao	745	1.9	3515.4	80.7	3623.1	3483.1	53.4	139.9	100.5
临沂市	Linyi	1851	6.0	3073.2	53.6	3284.8	2727.7	100.3	557.1	187.8
德州市	Dezhou	731	2.7	1119.1	4.3	1234.0	968.7	12.4	265.3	50.8
聊城市	Liaocheng	862	2.3	1862.5	24.2	1941.9	1722.3	45.1	219.6	58.3
滨州市	Binzhou	712	2.3	2795.6	19.7	2742.5	2549.1	84.9	193.4	167.7
菏泽市	Heze	783	2.6	1315.6	3.6	1442.9	1173.6	9.1	269.2	56.3

18-5 各市限额以上批发和零售业财务状况(2021年)

Financial Indicators of Enterprises above Designated Size of Wholesale and Retail Trades by Region(2021)

单位:亿元 (100 million yuan)

地 区	Region	企业数(个) Number of Enterprises (unit)	流动资产合计 Total Working Capitals	固定资产原价 Original Value of Fixed Assets	本年折旧 Depreciati-on in the Year	资产合计 Total Assets	负债合计 Total Liabilities	所有者权益合计 Total Owners' Equities	营业收入合计 Business Revenue	主营业务收入 Revenue from Principal Business
全省总计	**Total**	**24740**	**23399.9**	**2164.9**	**136.1**	**28951.9**	**23373.0**	**5520.3**	**61026.2**	**60346.0**
济南市	Jinan	4562	4101.5	359.6	22.7	5069.6	3859.1	1202.8	10358.7	10259.8
青岛市	Qingdao	3824	5653.9	340.3	20.5	6610.9	5444.4	1202.2	15295.9	15199.6
淄博市	Zibo	1935	1210.7	183.2	9.4	2044.5	1503.9	513.5	3610.9	3566.8
枣庄市	Zaozhuang	572	303.4	37.4	2.4	376.2	285.8	78.1	731.7	722.0
东营市	Dongying	913	1692.3	121.3	11.0	1898.8	1700.1	176.1	4226.3	4104.1
烟台市	Yantai	1828	1679.3	185.5	11.7	2066.2	1634.2	436.5	4007.1	3962.8
潍坊市	Weifang	1704	1459.6	214.3	13.0	1904.3	1612.3	289.9	3973.2	3879.8
济宁市	Jining	1915	832.7	128.2	8.6	1086.6	819.9	242.0	2506.7	2480.5
泰安市	Tai'an	1227	561.0	69.9	5.1	847.7	495.6	351.7	2263.3	2251.9
威海市	Weihai	576	645.8	76.1	4.9	976.4	683.3	293.1	1249.3	1226.9
日照市	Rizhao	745	998.7	83.4	3.9	1222.8	1100.9	111.7	3254.1	3229.1
临沂市	Linyi	1851	1084.0	109.2	6.8	1256.4	1035.3	234.5	2961.5	2922.9
德州市	Dezhou	731	390.8	91.4	5.8	519.8	405.8	116.3	1111.4	1096.0
聊城市	Liaocheng	862	384.6	41.0	2.5	436.3	337.1	101.0	1738.6	1730.1
滨州市	Binzhou	712	2089.7	74.9	5.2	2240.0	2148.4	84.1	2503.7	2487.8
菏泽市	Heze	783	311.8	49.1	2.7	395.3	306.9	86.9	1233.8	1225.7

18-5 续表 continued

单位:亿元 (100 million yuan)

地 区	Region	营业成本 Cost of Business	税金及附加 Taxes and Other Charges on Business	销售费用 Expenses on Sales	管理费用 Expenses on Manage-ment	财务费用 Expenses on Finance	营业利润 Profits from Business	利润总额 Total Profits	所得税费用 Income Tax Expense	应付职工薪酬(本年贷方累计发生额) Payroll payable (Cumulative amount of credits)	应交增值税 Value Added Tax Payable
全省总计	**Total**	**58199.4**	**196.1**	**1394.9**	**686.3**	**239.0**	**523.0**	**661.1**	**125.6**	**649.8**	**393.3**
济南市	Jinan	9794.7	29.0	291.7	141.9	40.9	90.3	195.7	26.9	143.3	65.9
青岛市	Qingdao	14667.7	31.7	331.2	141.6	46.0	102.8	110.2	32.8	137.8	85.6
淄博市	Zibo	3441.9	11.5	102.4	49.4	23.0	13.0	19.8	5.0	34.9	34.0
枣庄市	Zaozhuang	679.3	5.6	23.7	12.0	2.4	9.6	10.4	2.8	12.4	7.0
东营市	Dongying	4138.4	6.9	40.4	27.2	17.6	1.3	3.9	2.8	15.5	11.5
烟台市	Yantai	3734.9	16.2	131.4	53.3	18.9	61.3	62.8	11.8	62.3	39.5
潍坊市	Weifang	3771.8	17.9	86.7	55.8	18.9	35.1	38.9	7.6	49.5	36.6
济宁市	Jining	2337.4	12.2	76.4	36.4	9.0	43.1	45.8	8.8	32.8	21.0
泰安市	Tai'an	2175.8	8.2	35.1	20.7	6.5	47.9	48.2	4.7	19.8	16.2
威海市	Weihai	1149.7	6.0	50.3	26.5	7.5	15.0	18.4	3.8	25.7	7.6
日照市	Rizhao	3169.7	6.6	29.3	21.5	16.9	6.2	8.3	4.3	11.7	12.8
临沂市	Linyi	2807.9	15.1	72.1	38.7	11.0	18.2	17.8	5.6	38.2	19.5
德州市	Dezhou	1047.5	6.7	27.1	16.2	5.6	8.8	8.2	2.3	16.9	9.2
聊城市	Liaocheng	1682.2	6.2	25.8	15.2	4.2	5.8	6.1	1.9	16.2	8.1
滨州市	Binzhou	2446.1	6.1	32.2	14.5	7.4	51.9	54.0	1.1	15.1	9.9
菏泽市	Heze	1154.5	10.2	39.1	15.5	3.2	12.7	12.8	3.4	17.6	8.9

18-6 限额以上住宿和餐饮业情况
Basic Conditions of Hotels and Catering Services

指　　标	Item	2016	2017	2018	2019	2020	2021
住宿和餐饮业	**Hotels and Catering Services**						
法人企业 (个)	Number of Corporation Enterprises (unit)	3138	3010	2700	2466	2810	3475
年末从业人数 (万人)	Engaged Persons at Year-end (10 000 persons)	23.1	22.6	20.0	19.3	19.2	21.5
营业额 (亿元)	Business Revenue (100 million yuan)	561.5	494.6	386.9	385.9	349.4	480.3
#餐费收入 (亿元)	From Meals (100 million yuan)	381.2	320.3	240.8	242.7	227.9	317.9
年末餐饮营业面积(万平方米)	Business Area of Catering Services at Year-end(10 000 sq.m)	485.2	486.9	448.8	799.4	854.0	966.5
住宿业	**Hotels**						
法人企业 (个)	Number of Corporation Enterprises (unit)	1081	1144	1099	1089	1183	1403
年末从业人数 (万人)	Engaged Persons at Year-end (10 000 persons)	10.1	10.3	9.2	9.1	8.3	8.7
营业额 (亿元)	Business Revenue (100 million yuan)	227.8	213.1	170.9	171.0	139.3	184.7
#客房收入 (亿元)	From Hotel Rooms (100 million yuan)	101.7	102.8	85.3	85.3	69.7	96.3
餐费收入 (亿元)	From Meals (100 million yuan)	105.9	91.8	67.5	67.7	53.8	67.5
客房数 (万间)	Number of Room (10 000 rooms)	21.5	17.4	21.8	17.4	22.7	26.3
床位数 (万位)	Number of Beds (10 000 beds)	31.1	28.2	33.6	27.5	36.4	41.0
年末餐饮营业面积(万平方米)	Business Area of Catering Services at Year-end (10 000 sq.m)	173.2	182.4	179.1	453.1	486.7	541.7
餐饮业	**Catering Services**						
法人企业 (个)	Number of Corporation Enterprises (unit)	2057	1866	1601	1377	1627	2072
年末从业人数 (万人)	Engaged Persons at Year-end (10 000 persons)	13.0	12.3	10.9	10.2	10.8	12.8
营业额 (亿元)	Business Revenue (100 million yuan)	333.7	281.5	216.0	215.0	210.1	295.6
#餐费收入 (亿元)	From Meals (100 million yuan)	275.3	228.5	173.3	175.1	174.2	250.4
年末餐饮营业面积(万平方米)	Business Area of Catering Services at Year-end (10 000 sq.m)	312.0	304.5	269.7	346.3	367.3	424.8

18-7 限额以上住宿和餐饮业经营情况(2021年)
Business of Hotels and Catering Services above Designated Size(2021)

指标名称	Indicator	法人单位(个) Corporate Unit (unit)	从业人数(人) Employed Persons (person)
总 计	**Total**	**3475**	**214973**
一、住宿业	**Hotels**	**1403**	**87096**
1.按登记注册类型分	by Status of Registration		
内 资	Domestic Funded Enterprises	1378	83903
国 有	State-owned	85	13527
集 体	Collective-owned	9	545
股份合作	Cooperative	3	192
联营企业	Joint Ownership		
有限责任公司	Limited Liability Corporations	284	29057
股份有限公司	Share-holding Corporations Ltd.	12	743
私营企业	Private Enterprises	984	39684
其 他	Others	1	155
港澳台商投资企业	Enterprises with Funds from Hong Kong,Macao and Taiwan	14	2410
与港澳台商合资经营	Joint-venture	4	838
与港澳台商合作经营	Cooperative		
港澳台商独资	Sole Investment	9	1234
港澳台商投资股份有限公司	Share-holding Corporations Ltd. with Sole Investment		
其他港澳台投资企业	Others	1	338
外商投资企业	Foreign Funded Enterprises	11	783
中外合资经营	Joint-venture	6	585
中外合作经营	Cooperative		
外资企业	Sole Foreign Investment	2	122
外商投资股份有限公司	Share-holding Corporations Ltd. With Foreign Investment	2	58
其他外商投资企业	Others	1	18
2.按国民经济行业分(GB/T 4754-2017)	by Sector		
旅游饭店	Tourist Hotels	633	62610
一般旅馆	General Hotels	706	21729
民宿服务	Homestay Service	12	202
露营地服务	Campground Service		
其他住宿业	Other Accommodation Services	52	2555

18-7 续表 1 continued

指标名称	Indicator	法人单位(个) Corporate Unit (unit)	从业人数(人) Employed Persons (person)
二、餐饮业	**Catering Services**	**2072**	**127877**
1.按登记注册类型分	by Status of Registration		
内 资	Domestic Funded Enterprises	2038	116545
国 有	State-owned	37	4064
集 体	Collective-owned	4	122
股份合作	Cooperative	2	82
联营企业	Joint Ownership	1	153
有限责任公司	Limited Liability Corporations	298	26956
股份有限公司	Share-holding Corporations Ltd.	9	1189
私营企业	Private Enterprises	1686	83965
其 他	Others	1	14
港澳台商投资企业	Enterprises with Funds from Hong Kong,Macao and Taiwan	17	4880
与港澳台商合资经营	Joint-venture	9	960
与港澳台商合作经营	Cooperative		
港澳台商独资	Sole Investment	8	3920
港澳台商投资股份有限公司	Share-holding Corporations Ltd. with Sole Investment		
其他港澳台投资企业	Others		
外商投资企业	Foreign Funded Enterprises	17	6452
中外合资经营	Joint-venture	5	366
中外合作经营	Cooperative		
外资企业	Sole Foreign Investment	12	6086
外商投资股份有限公司	Share-holding Corporations Ltd. with Foreign Investment		
其他外商投资企业	Others		
2.按国民经济行业分	by Sector		
正餐服务	Dinner service	1640	90573
快餐服务	Fast Food Service	250	23060
饮料及冷饮服务	Beverages and cold drinks service	51	1694
餐饮配送及外卖送餐服务	Catering Delivery and Takeout Service	116	9358
其他餐饮业	Other Catering Services	15	3192

18-7 续表 2 continued

单位:万元 (10 000 yuan)

指标名称	Indicator	营业额 Business Revenue	客房收入 Revenue from Hotel Rooms	餐费收入 Revenue from Meals	商品销售收入 Revenue from Commodities	其他收入 Other Revenue
总 计	**Total**	**4803206**	**1218916**	**3178958**	**109407**	**295925**
一、住宿业	**Hotels**	**1847304**	**962970**	**675122**	**30685**	**178527**
1.按登记注册类型分	by Status of Registration					
内 资	Domestic Funded Enterprises	1764299	926958	642493	29217	165631
国 有	State-owned	250133	90002	118102	7421	34609
集 体	Collective-owned	10014	4292	4133	104	1485
股份合作	Cooperative	4274	1261	2837	1	175
联营企业	Joint Ownership					
有限责任公司	Limited Liability Corporations	629235	290248	253725	11966	73296
股份有限公司	Share-holding Corporations Ltd.	15044	6840	7465	287	452
私营企业	Private Enterprises	853778	533600	255251	9314	55613
其 他	Others	1821	715	981	126	
港澳台商投资企业	Enterprises with Funds from Hong Kong,Macao and Taiwan	62139	24108	27927	1136	8969
与港澳台商合资经营	Joint-venture	15904	6877	6409	338	2281
与港澳台商合作经营	Cooperative					
港澳台商独资	Sole Investment	37919	13827	17488	310	6293
港澳台商投资股份有限公司	Share-holding Corporations Ltd. with Sole Investment					
其他港澳台投资企业	Others	8317	3403	4030	488	395
外商投资企业	Foreign Funded Enterprises	20865	11905	4702	332	3927
中外合资经营	Joint-venture	11758	6807	3332	176	1445
中外合作经营	Cooperative					
外资企业	Sole Foreign Investment	5221	2127	547	124	2423
外商投资股份有限公司	Share-holding Corporations Ltd. With Foreign Investment	3464	2586	791	30	57
其他外商投资企业	Others	422	385	32	2	2
2.按国民经济行业分 (GB/T 4754-2017)	by Sector					
旅游饭店	Tourist Hotels	1309577	566299	573722	23992	145564
一般旅馆	General Hotels	483374	362927	84437	5981	30029
民宿服务	Homestay Service	5347	3721	1259	275	92
露营地服务	Campground Service					
其他住宿业	Other Accommodation Services	49006	30023	15703	438	2842

18-7 续表 3 continued

单位:万元 (10 000 yuan)

指标名称	Indicator	营业额 Business Revenue	客房收入 Revenue from Hotel Rooms	餐费收入 Revenue from Meals	商品销售收入 Revenue from Commodities	其他收入 Other Revenue
二、餐饮业	**Catering Services**	**2955902**	**255946**	**2503836**	**78722**	**117398**
1.按登记注册类型分	by Status of Registration					
内 资	Domestic Funded Enterprises	2569486	252566	2132664	70969	113286
国 有	State-owned	63344	20163	36849	790	5542
集 体	Collective-owned	2674	1162	1512		
股份合作	Cooperative	1861	813	794	26	229
联营企业	Joint Ownership	1452		1452		
有限责任公司	Limited Liability Corporations	662869	70511	519115	21577	51667
股份有限公司	Share-holding Corporations Ltd.	17688	3286	11863	414	2125
私营企业	Private Enterprises	1819260	156631	1560743	48163	53723
其 他	Others	337		337		
港澳台商投资企业	Enterprises with Funds from Hong Kong,Macao and Taiwan	97001	3095	85355	4590	3962
与港澳台商合资经营	Joint-venture	31622.7	2784	23338	3273	2228
与港澳台商合作经营	Cooperative					
港澳台商独资	Sole Investment	65378	311	62017	1317	1734
港澳台商投资股份有限公司	Share-holding Corporations Ltd.					
其他港澳台投资企业	with Sole Investment					
外商投资企业	Foreign Funded Enterprises	289415	285	285817	3163	150
中外合资经营	Joint-venture	5924	25	5858	41	
中外合作经营	Cooperative					
外资企业	Sole Foreign Investment	283491	260	279959	3122	150
外商投资股份有限公司	Share-holding Corporations Ltd.					
其他外商投资企业	with Foreign Investment					
2.按国民经济行业分(GB/T 4754-2017)	by Sector					
正餐服务	Dinner service	1958292	255120	1558422	43733	101017
快餐服务	Fast Food Service	662180	478	638121	17880	5701
饮料及冷饮服务	Beverages and cold drinks service	74712		69111	4278	1323
餐饮配送及外卖送餐服务	Catering Delivery and Takeout Service	215654	347	194577	12589	8141
其他餐饮业	Other Catering Services	45064		43605	243	1216

18-8 各市限额以上住宿和餐饮业经营情况(2021年)

Business of Hotels and Catering Services above Designated Size by Region (2021)

地区	Region	法人单位(个) Corporation Unit (unit)	从业人数(人) Persons Employed (person)	营业额(万元) Business Revenue (10000 yuan)	客房收入 Revenue from Hotel Rooms	餐费收入 Revenue from Meals	商品销售收入 Revenue from Commodi-ties	其他收入 Other Revenue
全省总计	**Total**	**3475**	**214973**	**4803206**	**1218916**	**3178958**	**109407**	**295925**
济南市	Jinan	702	42700	994854	246141	656574	18611	73528
青岛市	Qingdao	765	48976	1414271	306258	1007364	29808	70841
淄博市	Zibo	222	9601	225329	55320	144540	13244	12224
枣庄市	Zaozhuang	78	3610	57143	22982	29384	1394	3383
东营市	Dongying	69	5473	128313	33328	74287	2944	17754
烟台市	Yantai	283	18495	429927	117120	284682	4369	23756
潍坊市	Weifang	222	14367	297533	77892	189806	8925	20909
济宁市	Jining	301	13014	226883	69119	146985	2791	7987
泰安市	Tai'an	114	8952	146687	44598	89092	6005	6992
威海市	Weihai	136	14940	262517	57167	177989	6581	20780
日照市	Rizhao	73	4220	83599	29053	50834	879	2834
临沂市	Linyi	148	9940	195626	52797	118647	7905	16278
德州市	Dezhou	73	4636	77029	25737	43872	1285	6135
聊城市	Liaocheng	95	5803	91327	28680	51525	2814	8309
滨州市	Binzhou	82	4801	81974	22912	55214	912	2936
菏泽市	Heze	112	5445	90195	29812	58165	940	1278

18-9 限额以上住宿和餐饮业财务状况(2021年)

单位:万元

指 标 名 称	Indicator	企业数(个) Number of Enterprises (unit)
总 计	**Total**	**3475**
一、住宿业	**Hotels**	**1403**
1.按登记注册类型分	by Status of Registration	
内 资	Domestic Funded Enterprises	1378
国 有	State-owned	85
集 体	Collective-owned	9
股份合作	Cooperative	3
联营企业	Joint Ownership	
有限责任公司	Limited Liability Corporations	284
股份有限公司	Share-holding Corporations Ltd.	12
私营企业	Private Enterprises	984
其 他	Others	1
港澳台商投资企业	Enterprises with Funds from Hong Kong,Macao and Taiwan	14
与港澳台商合资经营	Joint-venture	4
与港澳台商合作经营	Cooperative	
港澳台商独资	Sole Investment	9
港澳台商投资股份有限公司	Share-holding Corporations Ltd. With Sole Investment	
其他港澳台投资企业	Others	1
外商投资企业	Foreign Funded Enterprises	11
中外合资经营	Joint-venture	6
中外合作经营	Cooperative	
外资企业	Sole Foreign Investment	2
外商投资股份有限公司	Share-holding Corporations Ltd. with Foreign Investment	2
其他外商投资企业	Others	1
2.按国民经济行业分(GB/T 4754-2017)	by Sector	
旅游饭店	Tourist Hotels	633
一般旅馆	General Hotels	706
民宿服务	Homestay Service	12
露营地服务	Campground Service	
其他住宿业	Other Accommodation Services	52

Financial Indicators of Enterprises above Designated Size of Hotels and Catering Services(2021)

(10 000 yuan)

年末资产负债 Assets and Liabilities at Year-end						损益及分配 Losses,Profits and Distribution	
流动资产合计 Total Working Capitals	固定资产原价 Original Value of Fixed Assets	本年折旧 Depre-ciation in the Year	资产合计 Total Assets	负债合计 Total Liabilities	所有者权益合计 Total Owner's Equities	营业收入合计 Business Revenue	主营业务收入 Revenue from Principal Business
3923191	**5867119**	**249357**	**9428725**	**7791940**	**1660126**	**4616869**	**4505208**
2337023	**3856022**	**150126**	**5485766**	**4654250**	**853174**	**1773256**	**1716407**
2211506	3471806	140025	5124487	4350632	793275	1694748	1640838
287753	847651	24929	824596	428717	395878	240042	233547
6053	28584	1666	20045	17865	2180	9409	9242
14198	4515	105	20035	18385	1650	4134	4134
1018191	1271157	53796	2065496	1783184	282124	606434	586138
14095	62826	2007	46752	49033	-2281	14605	14009
870546	1254238	57446	2144873	2047941	116540	818407	792053
671	2835	77	2691	5507	-2816	1717	1717
88971	345250	8117	277007	218280	60965	58923	58475
47001	84348	1470	74742	101103	-26361	15262	15029
36632	260432	6590	196635	109995	88879	35845	35630
5337	470	56	5630	7183	-1553	7816	7816
36547	38967	1984	84272	85338	-1066	19586	17095
33917	34225	1551	78682	81177	-2495	10967	10821
1160	3774	309	3328	2965	363	4935	2595
1185	207	26	1425	1201	224	3280	3280
285	762	99	837	-5	842	403	398
1840011	3398042	119652	4502247	3646670	876405	1255711	1213134
393425	346433	21913	787447	763031	25246	462898	451574
6977	14152	589	26301	25132	1169	6325	5189
96611	97395	7973	169771	219417	-49646	48323	46510

18-9 续表 1

单位:万元

指 标 名 称	Indicator	企业数(个) Number of Enterprises (unit)
二、餐饮业	**Catering Services**	**2072**
1.按登记注册类型分	by Status of Registration	
内 资	Domestic Funded Enterprises	2038
国 有	State-owned	37
集 体	Collective-owned	4
股份合作	Cooperative	2
联营企业	Joint Ownership	1
有限责任公司	Limited Liability Corporations	298
股份有限公司	Share-holding Corporations Ltd.	9
私营企业	Private Enterprises	1686
其 他	Others	1
港澳台商投资企业	Enterprises with Funds from Hong Kong,Macao and Taiwan	17
与港澳台商合资经营	Joint-venture	9
与港澳台商合作经营	Cooperative	
港澳台商独资	Sole Investment	8
港澳台商投资股份有限公司	Share-holding Corporations Ltd. With Sole Investment	
其他港澳台投资企业	Others	
外商投资企业	Foreign Funded Enterprises	17
中外合资经营	Joint-venture	5
中外合作经营	Cooperative	
外资企业	Sole Foreign Investment	12
外商投资股份有限公司	Share-holding Corporations Ltd. with Foreign Investment	
其他外商投资企业	Others	
2.按国民经济行业分(GB/T 4754-2017)	by Sector	
正餐服务	Dinner service	1640
快餐服务	Fast Food Service	250
饮料及冷饮服务	Beverages and cold drinks service	51
餐饮配送及外卖送餐服务	Catering Delivery and Takeout Service	116
其他餐饮业	Other Catering Services	15

continued

(10 000 yuan)

年末资产负债 Assets and Liabilities at Year-end						损益及分配 Losses,Profits and Distribution	
流动资产合计 Total Working Capitals	固定资产原价 Original Value of Fixed Assets	本年折旧 Depre-ciation in the Year	资产合计 Total Assets	负债合计 Total Liabilities	所有者权益合计 Total Owner's Equities	营业收入合计 Business Revenue	#主营业务收入 Revenue from Principal Business
1586167	**2011097**	**99231**	**3942959**	**3137690**	**806952**	**2843612**	**2788801**
1490835	1854479	93789	3621331	2798801	824213	2471914	2419131
88490	165604	8407	250255	131842	118413	61319	58870
1313	1955	212	2286	1402	884	2610	2610
5139	8452	24	9238	7747	907	1691	1523
450	1031	45	1510	25	1485	1370	1370
411630	820410	30465	1282522	715614	568093	635828	620711
33648	25662	-603	61355	62335	-980	16602	16168
950047	831343	55232	2014007	1879778	135311	1752173	1717557
118	22	8	158	58	100	322	322
62251	105812	4986	171461	237078	-65617	91490	89467
55389	82616	3553	125743	180500	-54757	29448	27715
6862	23197	1433	45718	56579	-10860	62043	61752
33082	50806	456	150167	101811	48356	280208	280203
4670	1156	85	5352	5671	-319	5699	5699
28412	49650	371	144815	96141	48675	274509	274504
1289462	1844729	88792	3343633	2709906	635606	1890432	1842917
149075	131763	6636	393346	300432	92858	633248	629938
32375	6772	668	50006	29962	19906	70561	70065
86389	25376	2825	124439	72700	51739	205512	202022
28867	2458	310	31534	24691	6844	43860	43860

18-9 续表 2

单位:万元

指 标 名 称	Indicator	营业成本 Cost of Business
总　计	**Total**	**2403242**
一、住宿业	**Hotels**	**774097**
1.按登记注册类型分	by Status of Registration	
内 资	Domestic Funded Enterprises	751826
国 有	State-owned	88092
集 体	Collective-owned	2783
股份合作	Cooperative	1958
联营企业	Joint Ownership	
有限责任公司	Limited Liability Corporations	283842
股份有限公司	Share-holding Corporations Ltd.	6088
私营企业	Private Enterprises	368360
其　他	Others	704
港澳台商投资企业	Enterprises with Funds from Hong Kong,Macao and Taiwan	18334
与港澳台商合资经营	Joint-venture	2918
与港澳台商合作经营	Cooperative	
港澳台商独资	Sole Investment	13908
港澳台商投资股份有限公司	Share-holding Corporations Ltd. with Sole Investment	
其他港澳台投资企业	Others	1508
外商投资企业	Foreign Funded Enterprises	3937
中外合资经营	Joint-venture	1565
中外合作经营	Cooperative	
外资企业	Sole Foreign Investment	508
外商投资股份有限公司	Share-holding Corporations Ltd. With Foreign Investment	1668
其他外商投资企业	Others	196
2.按国民经济行业分(GB/T 4754-2017)	by Sector	
旅游饭店	Tourist Hotels	539168
一般旅馆	General Hotels	211341
民宿服务	Homestay Service	2262
露营地服务	Campground Service	
其他住宿业	Other Accommodation Services	21326

continued

(10 000 yuan)

损益及分配 Losses,Profits and Distribution							工资、福利、增值税 Wages,Welfare and Value Added Tax	
税金及附加 Taxes and Other Charges on Business	销售费用 Expenses on Sales	管理费用 Expenses on Management	财务费用 Expenses on Finance	营业利润 Profits from Business	利润总额 Total Profits	所得税费用 Income Tax Expense	应付职工薪酬(本年贷方累计发生额) Payroll payable (Cumulative amount of credits)	应交增值税 Value Added Tax Payable
34345	**1344917**	**1024600**	**114979**	**-278073**	**-243714**	**16243**	**1195037**	**62198**
20843	**597870**	**559681**	**63024**	**-217538**	**-202068**	**2575**	**519616**	**28415**
18421	575274	522639	57706	-206353	-191244	2006	494602	27036
3393	107483	79684	-2222	-30218	-25340	620	100529	4988
55	5759	2790	-3	-2105	-1904	6	2669	261
15	971	1266	195	-271	-225		947	104
8297	201968	201918	28828	-95959	-91304	214	188570	8885
235	3819	6442	160	-2343	-2198	19	3412	317
6422	254533	228584	30743	-73766	-69046	1147	197385	12464
4	743	1954	5	-1692	-1228		1091	16
2126	13802	29578	3095	-7688	-7640	567	20250	1059
562	5591	8173	26	-1870	-1790		6561	305
1551	5641	18094	3002	-6165	-6255	567	11652	652
13	2570	3311	67	347	404		2037	103
296	8794	7465	2223	-3497	-3184	2	4765	320
263	5825	6067	2206	-5330	-5018		3767	78
31	2905	229	13	1251	1241		523	216
1	50	1034	2	525	536	1	401	2
1	13	135	2	57	57		73	25
18068	437768	408442	48569	-167580	-154791	2220	401435	21846
2000	140662	129421	9687	-34595	-31605	316	104565	6007
9	1955	1231	648	233	149	2	1002	44
767	17485	20587	4120	-15597	-15822	36	12614	518

18-9 续表 3

单位:万元

指标名称	Indicator	营业成本 Cost of Business
二、餐饮业	**Catering Services**	**1629145**
1.按登记注册类型分	by Status of Registration	
内 资	Domestic Funded Enterprises	1443262
国 有	State-owned	33180
集 体	Collective-owned	1621
股份合作	Cooperative	508
联营企业	Joint Ownership	1321
有限责任公司	Limited Liability Corporations	379404
股份有限公司	Share-holding Corporations Ltd.	8406
私营企业	Private Enterprises	1018676
其 他	Others	146
港澳台商投资企业	Enterprises with Funds from Hong Kong,Macao and Taiwan	38421
与港澳台商合资经营	Joint-venture	13678
与港澳台商合作经营	Cooperative	
港澳台商独资	Sole Investment	24743
港澳台商投资股份有限公司	Share-holding Corporations Ltd. with Sole Investment	
其他港澳台投资企业	Others	
外商投资企业	Foreign Funded Enterprises	147462
中外合资经营	Joint-venture	1972
中外合作经营	Cooperative	
外资企业	Sole Foreign Investment	145490
外商投资股份有限公司	Share-holding Corporations Ltd. With Foreign Investment	
其他外商投资企业	Others	
2.按国民经济行业分(GB/T 4754-2017)	by Sector	
正餐服务	Dinner service	1037562
快餐服务	Fast Food Service	361867
饮料及冷饮服务	Beverages and cold drinks service	30872
餐饮配送及外卖送餐服务	Catering Delivery and Takeout Service	165340
其他餐饮业	Other Catering Services	33504

continued

(10 000 yuan)

损益及分配 Losses,Profits and Distribution							工资、福利、增值税 Wages,Welfare and Value Added Tax	
税金及附加 Taxes and Other Charges on Business	销售费用 Expenses on Sales	管理费用 Expenses on Management	财务费用 Expenses on Finance	营业利润 Profits from Business	利润总额 Total Profits	所得税费用 Income Tax Expense	应付职工薪酬(本年贷方累计发生额) Payroll payable (Cumulative amount of credits)	本年应交增值税 Value Added Tax Payable
13502	**747047**	**464919**	**51955**	**-60535**	**-41646**	**13668**	**675420**	**33783**
13039	626219	428938	41836	-81044	-63388	7357	569521	28678
464	15635	19960	-103	-4708	-3780	376	23600	1577
19	295	520	106	69	71		599	48
3	734	429	41	-24	-14	2	447	32
	7	87	-1	-44	-15		540	
6193	165605	116745	10628	-25576	-19690	2281	150259	8546
233	3687	5646	22	-1355	675	4	5438	613
6128	440096	285550	31144	-49422	-40658	4694	388568	17862
	160			16	23		69	
296	42362	10292	7504	-5919	-4744	-487	27121	412
280	12664	6013	6000	-7682	-6523		5856	-125
16	29698	4279	1504	1763	1779	-487	21266	537
167	78465	25690	2615	26429	26486	6799	78778	4693
4	3402	683	20	-372	-369	1	1425	17
163	75064	25007	2595	26800	26855	6798	77354	4676
11399	520455	379473	44960	-103882	-84836	4597	453076	22537
1659	176440	55076	5824	33334	32507	6518	148494	7111
26	32775	4511	74	3202	3235	1437	22737	892
354	13410	21166	985	5023	5741	986	40018	2720
64	3967	4693	113	1789	1707	131	11095	522

18-10 各市限额以上住宿和餐饮业财务状况(2021年)

Financial Indicators of Enterprises above Designated Size of Hotels and Catering Services by Region(2021)

单位:万元 (10 000 yuan)

地 区	Region	企业数(个) Number of Enterprises (unit)	流动资产合计 Total Working Capitals	固定资产原价 Original Value of Fixed Assets	本年折旧 Deprecia-tion in the Year	资产合计 Total Assets	负债合计 Total Liabilities	所有者权益合计 Total Owners' Equities	营业收入合计 Business Revenue	主营业务收入 Revenue from Principal Business
全省总计	**Total**	**3475**	**3923191**	**5867119**	**249357**	**9428725**	**7791940**	**1660126**	**4616869**	**4505208**
济南市	Jinan	702	902072	946073	44593	1696080	1464689	238828	966927	938891
青岛市	Qingdao	765	1032755	1196089	43912	2010551	1706633	315881	1354785	1339324
淄博市	Zibo	222	95501	150719	6623	196673	211123	-14450	216473	211883
枣庄市	Zaozhuang	78	56703	202957	8925	221733	182671	40550	55414	53007
东营市	Dongying	69	101976	158461	6656	299423	293017	5290	120681	112184
烟台市	Yantai	283	270963	797213	26268	920641	716264	203831	408855	397543
潍坊市	Weifang	222	266126	282686	13628	524821	543649	-18279	284188	273703
济宁市	Jining	301	277492	469532	17709	770822	486438	284403	218312	216871
泰安市	Tai'an	114	116940	237960	9056	412627	362121	53583	141532	137120
威海市	Weihai	136	267637	403647	26741	735888	681934	52164	251617	246841
日照市	Rizhao	73	59410	82633	6539	144246	152570	-8324	79609	78481
临沂市	Linyi	148	177157	525167	19231	750520	335262	415575	186044	182915
德州市	Dezhou	73	54825	119446	4962	187642	140433	47282	73734	71785
聊城市	Liaocheng	95	106305	92481	5750	200408	205749	-3774	93402	83016
滨州市	Binzhou	82	83835	121428	4424	220655	216833	3630	79159	77943
菏泽市	Heze	112	53493	80628	4341	135998	92552	43937	86137	83702

18-10 续表 continued

单位:万元 (10 000 yuan)

地 区	Region	营业成本 Cost of Business	税金及附加 Taxes and Other Charges on Business	销售费用 Expenses on Sales	管理费用 Expenses on Management	财务费用 Expenses on Finance	营业利润 Profits from Business	利润总额 Total Profits	所得税费用 Income Tax Expense	应付职工薪酬(本年贷方累计发生额) Payroll payable (Cumulative amount of credits)	应交增值税 Value Added Tax Payable
全省总计	**Total**	**2403242**	**34345**	**1344917**	**1024600**	**114979**	**-278073**	**-243714**	**16243**	**1195037**	**62198**
济南市	Jinan	452670	5705	326184	216200	12806	-43683	-37429	1953	250511	12257
青岛市	Qingdao	713498	7990	379547	286223	28042	-42908	-35194	9856	354601	16916
淄博市	Zibo	125277	1003	56956	39701	2668	-9908	-7787	330	42232	3483
枣庄市	Zaozhuang	29489	577	13921	17028	970	-7428	-6985	63	14712	989
东营市	Dongying	57502	1771	41674	26615	6141	-11469	-9128	74	27490	2548
烟台市	Yantai	226416	4002	93208	84842	8890	-22581	-19257	1553	90030	5496
潍坊市	Weifang	145447	2683	89618	59544	8479	-19805	-17968	485	77869	3366
济宁市	Jining	128722	1702	48613	63376	10826	-29379	-25101	258	58081	2740
泰安市	Tai'an	72073	1192	41286	32586	5667	-15818	-12352	165	40528	2283
威海市	Weihai	137399	2878	78528	58829	10941	-35706	-35336	506	75861	3108
日照市	Rizhao	36747	252	26406	21732	2966	-7716	-9211	67	22909	1025
临沂市	Linyi	92834	1687	57862	53168	8482	-26725	-23860	554	46590	2802
德州市	Dezhou	35247	1122	24370	15518	668	11364	11904	59	19983	1704
聊城市	Liaocheng	54282	557	26627	17161	3193	-7503	-7483	101	26678	1268
滨州市	Binzhou	46354	547	17976	17816	2601	-9011	-8914	66	22859	1011
菏泽市	Heze	49286	678	22142	14262	1641	205	387	153	24103	1203

18-11 亿元以上商品交易市场情况(2021年)

Basic Statistics on Commodity Exchange Markets of Turnover above 100 Million Yuan (2021)

类　别	Category	市场数量(个) Number of Markets (unit)	摊位数(个) Number of Booths (unit)	年末出租摊位数(个) Number of Booths Rented at Year End (unit)	年末营业面积(平方米) Operating Area at Year End (sq.m)	成交额(亿元) Turnover (100 million yuan)
总　计	**Total**	**385**	**303616**	**258952**	**32845352**	**9053.9**
一、按市场类别分组	**Grouped by Market Category**					
综合市场	Comprehensive Markets	79	91739	76587	6163640	1357.5
生产资料综合市场	Means of production Comprehensive Markets	3	2046	2024	133376	25.8
工业消费品综合市场	Industrial consumer products Comprehensive Markets	21	39974	33404	2511239	636.4
农产品综合市场	Farmer Produces Comprehensive Markets	31	22041	19418	1416711	343.6
其他综合市场	Other Comprehensive Markets	24	27678	21741	2102314	351.7
专业市场	Special Markets	306	211877	182365	26681712	7696.4
生产资料市场	Means of Production Markets	59	28500	24660	8750058	3031.6
农业生产用具市场	Agricultural Tools Markets	1	84	84	80000	1.5
农用生产资料市场	Agricultural Production Markets					
煤炭市场	Coal and Charcoal Markets					
木材市场	Wood Markets	6	1689	1619	733868	112.2
建材市场	Building Materials Markets	18	12181	10956	1840938	342.7
化工材料及制品市场	Chemical Materials and Products Markets	1	875	780	110000	685.6
金属材料市场	Metal Materials Markets	25	8373	6166	5503114	1745.0
机械设备市场	Mechanical Device Markets	5	3976	3742	390002	122.1
其他生产资料市场	Other Means of Production Markets	3	1322	1313	92136	22.4
农产品市场	Agricultural Products Markets	93	72151	63409	7561483	2414.7
粮油市场	Grain and Oil Markets	8	2630	1914	363542	151.2
肉禽蛋市场	Meat, Poultry and Eggs Markets	3	2385	2022	77060	13.0
水产品市场	Aquatic Products Markets	21	15425	11629	906148	756.3
蔬菜市场	Vegetables Markets	39	38079	35347	4574698	795.2
干鲜果品市场	Dried and Fresh Melons and Fruits Markets	16	8960	8553	1201670	533.0
棉麻土畜、烟叶市场	Cotton ,Hemp,Local Livestock and Tobacco Markets					
其他农产品市场	Other Agricultural Products Markets	6	4672	3944	438365	165.9
食品、饮料及烟酒市场	Food, Beverages, Tobacco, and Liquor Markets	11	9760	8560	678010	178.4
食品饮料市场	Food and Beverage Markets	5	5782	5759	295580	91.8
茶叶市场	Tea Markets	2	800	620	90000	15.5
烟酒市场	Tobacco and Liquor Markets	1	360	275	16000	27.0
其他食品饮料及烟酒市场	Other Food, Beverages, Tobacco, and Liquor Markets	3	2818	1906	276430	44.1
纺织、服装、鞋帽市场	Textile, Garments, Footgear, and Hats Markets	36	37160	32553	1548926	540.3
布料及纺织品市场	Fabrics and Textile Markets	5	2191	1874	196900	52.9
服装市场	Clothing Markets	20	27821	23914	935170	436.5
鞋帽市场	Shoes and Hats Markets	4	2165	2001	68736	36.4
其他纺织服装鞋帽市场	Others	7	4983	4764	348120	14.5
日用品及文化用品市场	Daily Use and Cultural Goods Markets	13	11219	9714	694930	352.7
小商品市场	Merchandise Markets	8	8720	7347	481530	284.2
箱包市场	Case and Bag Markets	1	150	150	8400	1.4

18−11 续表 continued

类别	Category	市场数量(个) Number of Markets (unit)	摊位数(个) Number of Booths (unit)	年末出租摊位数 Number of Booths Rented at Year End	年末营业面积(平方米) Operating Area at Year End (sq.m)	成交额(亿元) Turnover (100 million yuan)
玩具市场	Toy Markets	1	600	590	60000	15.6
文具市场	Stationery Markets	1	580	480	60000	4.7
图书、报刊市场	Books, Newspapers and Magazines Markets	1	149	147	25000	11.2
音像制品及电子出版物市场	Video products and E-journal Markets					
体育用品市场	Sports Goods Markets					
其他日用品及文化用品市场	Other Daily Use and Cultural Goods Markets	1	1020	1000	60000	35.6
黄金、珠宝、玉器等首饰市场	Gold,Jewelry,Jade Markets	1	809	475	500000	125.4
电器、通讯器材、电子设备市场	Electrical Appliances, Communication Appliances, Electronic Equipment Markets	6	3002	2643	264700	70.7
家电市场	Household Appliances Markets	2	1071	1065	165000	53.4
通讯器材市场	Communication Appliances					
照相、摄像器材市场	Camera Equipment Markets					
计算机及辅助设备市场	Computers and Auxiliary Equipment Markets	4	1931	1578	99700	17.3
其他电器、通讯器材、电子设备市场	Others					
医药、医疗用品及器材市场	Medicine,Medical Supplies and Equipment Markets	1	1022	836	61420	8.5
中药材市场	Chinese Medicine Markets	1	1022	836	61420	8.5
其他医药、医疗用品及器材市场	Others					
家具、五金及装饰材料市场	Furniture,Hardware,and Decorative Materials Markets	46	32737	26362	3836078	368.1
家具市场	Furniture Markets	14	6585	5527	1075218	60.2
装饰材料市场	Decoration Materials Markets	17	9689	7845	1223302	102.8
灯具市场	Lamps Markets	1	970	956	150000	31.8
厨具、盥洗设备市场	Kitchen Utensils and Washing Equipment Markets	1	275	221	18000	1.6
五金材料市场	Hardware Materials Markets	8	8235	5749	558149	84.7
其他装修市场	Others	5	6983	6064	811409	87.0
汽车、摩托车及零配件市场	Automobile, Motorcycle and Spare Parts Markets	30	7888	6055	1823157	432.7
汽车市场	Automobile Markets	20	3858	2890	1576223	336.5
摩托车市场	Motorcycle Markets					
机动车零配件市场	Motor Vehicle Spare Parts Markets	10	4030	3165	246934	96.3
花、鸟、鱼、虫市场	Flowers,Birds,Fish,Insects Markets	2	3405	3405	720000	121.6
花卉市场	Flower Markets	2	3405	3405	720000	121.6
鸟市场	Bird Markets					
观赏鱼市场	Ornamental Fish Markets					
其他花鸟鱼虫市场	Others					
旧货市场	Second Hand Markets					
古玩、古董、字画市场	Antique,Antiques,Calligraphy and Painting Markets					
邮票、硬币市场	Stamps,Coins Markets					
其他旧货市场	Other Second Hand Markets					
其他专业市场	Others	8	4224	3693	242950	51.7
二、按营业状态分组	**Grouped by Operating Status**					
1.常年营业	Perennial operating	372	295162	251164	31511568	8704.0
2.季节性营业	Seasonal operating	13	8454	7788	1333784	349.9
3.其他	Others					
三、按经营方式分组	**Grouped by Operating Mode**					
1.以批发为主	Wholesale	275	236032	199289	26539662	8327.7
2.以零售为主	Retail	110	67584	59663	6305690	726.2
四、按经营环境分组	**Grouped by Operating Environment**					
1.露天式	Open Air	90	47907	41297	9731179	2139.0
2.封闭式	Closed	253	224519	191655	20296522	6151.9
3.其他	Others	42	31190	26000	2817651	763.1

18-12 亿元以上商品交易市场成交情况(2021年)

Basic Statistics on Commodity Exchange Markets of Turnover above 100 Million Yuan(2021)

类　　别	Category	年末出租摊位数(个) Number of Booths Rented at Year end (unit)	全年成交额(亿元) Turnover (100 million yuan)
合　计	**Total**	**258952**	**9053.9**
1.粮油、食品类	Grain、Oil and Food	93957	3083.1
#粮油类	Grain and Oil	7051	274.0
肉禽蛋类	Meal,Poultry and Eggs	8619	347.9
水产品类	Aquatic Products	18678	841.3
蔬菜类	Vegetables	35950	904.4
干鲜果品类	Dried and Fresh Fruits	19303	632.1
2.饮料类	Beverages	2690	57.9
3.烟酒类	Tobacco and Liquor	2902	55.6
4.服装、鞋帽、针、纺织品类	Clothing, Shoes, Hats and Textiles	49556	743.3
(1)服装类	Clothing	31226	445.9
(2)鞋帽类	Shoes and Hats	9149	130.2
(3)针、纺织品类	Knitwear and Textiles	9181	167.2
5.化妆品类	Cosmetics	2635	88.4
6.金银珠宝类	Gold,Silver and Jewelry	1072	135.7
7.日用品类	Articles for Daily Use	16047	403.8
#可穿戴智能设备	Wearable smart device	295	1.8
8.五金电料类	Hardware & Electrical Materials	10743	178.6
9.体育、娱乐用品类	Sports & Recreational Articles	1299	16.7
#照相器材类	Cameras and Related Equipments	35	0.1
10.书报杂志类	Newspapers and Magazines	253	13.5
11.电子出版物及音像制品类	E-journals and Video Products	96	1.7
12.家用电器和音像器材类	Household Appliances and Video Appliance	3678	95.1
#能效等级为1和2级的商品	Products with energy efficiency levels 1 and 2	45	0.3
#智能家用电器和音像器材	Smart home appliances and audiovisual equipment	55	0.2
13.中西药材品类	Traditional Chinese and Western Medicines	978	11.5
#西药类	Western Medicines	55	0.6
中草药及中成药类	Traditional Chinese Medicines	853	8.6
14.文化办公用品类	Cultural and Offices Appliances	5446	76.8
#计算机及其配套产品	Computers and Auxiliary Equipments	1438	17.1
15.家具类	Furniture	8607	111.5
16.通讯器材类	Communication Appliances	946	15.8
#智能手机	Smart phone	53	0.5
17.煤炭及制品类	Coal and Related Products	7	0.5
18.木材及制品类	Wood and Wooden Products	2580	141.6
19.石油及制品类	Petroleum and Related Products	172	157.3
20.化工材料及制品类	Chemical Materials and Related Products	1205	537.9
#化肥类	Fertilizers	50	1.0
21.金属材料类	Metal Materials	6983	1698.3
22.建筑及装潢材料类	Building and Decoration Materials	19745	506.3
23.机电产品及设备类	Mechanical & Electrical Products	6231	164.3
#农机类	Agricultural Machineries	119	2.1
24.汽车类	Automobiles	6405	445.8
#新能源汽车	New energy vehicles	502	10.3
25.种子饲料类	Seeds and Feedstuff	278	1.6
26.棉麻类	Cotton and Hemp	90	1.2
27.其他类	Others	14351	310.2

18-13 各市亿元以上商品交易市场情况(2021年)

Basic Statistics on Commodity Exchange Markets of Turnover above 100 Million Yuan by Region(2021)

地 区	Region	市场数量(个) Number of Markets (unit)	摊位数(个) Number of Booths (unit)	年末出租摊位数 Number of Booths Rented at Year End	年末营业面积(平方米) Operating Area at Year End (sq.m)	成交额(万元) Turnover (10 000 yuan)
全省总计	**Total**	**385**	**303616**	**258952**	**32845352**	**90538940**
济南市	Jinan	27	19497	18270	1704153	6598846
青岛市	Qingdao	58	40124	36732	4143984	13737184
淄博市	Zibo	13	12304	10360	967530	8858425
枣庄市	Zaozhuang	15	17448	12591	888406	1498582
东营市	Dongying					
烟台市	Yantai	17	19313	13075	1793774	3749210
潍坊市	Weifang	27	23970	22900	4226140	8599173
济宁市	Jining	13	12907	12584	1794837	4278281
泰安市	Tai'an	7	11906	10322	3148510	7112485
威海市	Weihai	4	2909	2880	206692	422827
日照市	Rizhao	8	10179	7169	653102	1317112
临沂市	Linyi	70	48355	44970	4997424	16340311
德州市	Dezhou	43	20915	16131	2642125	3350273
聊城市	Liaocheng	15	16388	14495	2219456	6394326
滨州市	Binzhou	7	4138	3547	590590	5378797
菏泽市	Heze	61	43263	32926	2868629	2903108

18-14 连锁门店及配送中心分布情况(2021年)

Distribution of Stores and Distribution Centers of chain stores of Wholesale and Retail Trades and Hotel and Catering Services(2021)

单位：个 (unit)

地 区	Region	门店总数 Number of Stores	直营店数 Under Direct Management	加盟店数 Through License Arrangement	配送中心数 Distribution Centers	自 有 Under Direct Management
合 计	**Total**	**21388**	**18414**	**2974**	**156**	**138**
批发和零售业	**Wholesale and Retail Trades**	**20447**	**17588**	**2859**	**149**	**131**
北 京	Beijing	9	7	2		
天 津	Tianjin	7	2	5		
河 北	Hebei	259	18	241		
山 西	Shanxi	12	2	10		
内蒙古	Inner Mongolia	9	5	4		
辽 宁	Liaoning	12	6	6		
吉 林	Jilin	5	2	3		
黑龙江	Heilongjiang	7	1	6		
上 海	Shanghai	4	4			
江 苏	Jiangsu	42	14	28		
浙 江	Zhejiang	20	6	14		
安 徽	Anhui	25	3	22		
福 建	Fujian	8	3	5		
江 西	Jiangxi	5	3	2		
山 东	Shandong	19823	17456	2367	149	131
济 南	Jinan	2641	2422	219	24	14
青 岛	Qingdao	3942	3574	368	30	27
河 南	Henan	82	17	65		
湖 北	Hubei	24	22	2		
湖 南	Hunan	6	1	5		
广 东	Guangdong	8	4	4		
海 南	Hainan	2	2			
重 庆	Chongqing	7	1	6		
四 川	Sichuan	21	3	18		
贵 州	Guizhou	5	1	4		
云 南	Yunnan	22	1	21		
陕 西	Shanxi	14	1	13		
甘 肃	Ganshu	4	1	3		
宁 夏	Ningxia	2	1	1		
新 疆	Xinjiang	3	1	2		
住宿和餐饮业	**Hotel and Catering Services**	**941**	**826**	**115**	**7**	**7**
北 京	Beijing	1	1		1	1
辽 宁	Liaoning	6	6			
上 海	Shanghai	1	1			
江 苏	Jiangsu	1	1			
安 徽	Anhui	2	2			
山 东	Shandong	922	807	115	5	5
济 南	Jinan	279	274	5	1	1
青 岛	Qingdao	240	189	51	2	2
河 南	Henan	2	2			
湖 南	Hunan	1	1			
广 东	Guangdong	1	1			
海 南	Hainan				1	1
西 藏	Tibet	1	1			
陕 西	Shanxi	2	2			
青 海	Qinghai	1	1			

注：本表数据是指总部设在山东的连锁企业的门店及配送中心的分布情况。
a)Data in this table refers to the distribution of stores and distribution centers of chain stores that headquarters in Shandong.

18-15 批发和零售业连锁经营情况(2021年)

指标	Item	连锁总店(总部)数(个) Number of chain head stores (unit)	合计 Total
总计	**Total**	**200**	**20447**
一、按行业分组	**by Sector**		
批发业	Wholesale Trade	10	3054
零售业	Retail Trade	190	17393
二、按登记注册类型分组	**by Status of Registration**		
内资企业	Domestic Funded Enterprises	194	19649
国有企业	State-owned Enterprises	6	224
集体企业	Collective-owned Enterprises	2	19
股份合作企业	Cooperative Enterprises	2	72
联营企业	Joint Ownership Enterprises		
有限责任公司	Limited Liability Corporations	75	5627
股份有限公司	Share-holding Corporations Limited	18	6149
私营企业	Private Enterprises	90	7514
其他企业	Other Enterprises	1	44
港、澳、台商投资企业	Enterprises with Funds from Hong Kong, Macao and Taiwan	2	439
合资经营企业(港或澳、台资)	Joint-ventures Enterprises	1	209
合作经营企业(港或澳、台资)	Cooperative Enterprises		
港、澳、台商独资经营企业	Enterprises with Sole Investment	1	230
港、澳、台商投资股份有限公司	Share-holding Corporations Ltd. With Funds from Hong Kong,Macao and Taiwan		
其他港澳台投资企业	Others		
外商投资企业	Foreign Funded Enterprises	4	359
中外合资经营企业	Joint-venture Enterprises	2	252
中外合作经营企业	Cooperation Enterprises	1	2
外资企业	Enterprises with Sole Foreign Funds		
外商投资股份有限公司	Share-holding Corporations Ltd. With Foreign Investment	1	105
其他外商投资企业	Others		
三、按连锁零售业态分组	**by Business Categories**		
便利店	Convenience Store	4	498
折扣店	Discount store		
超　市	Supermarket	29	1789
大型超市	Large supermarket	8	261
仓储会员店	Warehouse club stores		
百货店	Department store	10	1056
专业店	Professional store	131	15776
其中：加油站	In:Gas Station	20	4813
专卖店	Specialty store	13	806
家居建材商店	Home-furnishings store		
厂家直销中心	Factory Outlet Center		
其　他	Others	5	261

Business of chain operation of Wholesale and Retail Trade(2021)

门店总数(个) Number of Stores(unit)		年末零售营业面积(平方米) Operational Area(sq.m)			年末从业人员数(人) Engaged Persons(person)		
直营店 Under Direct Management	加盟店 Through License Arrangement	合计 Total	直营店 Under Direct Management	加盟店 Through License Arrangement	合计 Total	直营店 Under Direct Management	加盟店 Through License Arrangement
17588	**2859**	**29087079**	**17682204**	**11404875**	**177436**	**166887**	**10549**
2984	70	725877	720957	4920	27703	27542	161
14604	2789	28361202	16961247	11399955	149733	139345	10388
17018	2631	28551674	17162867	11388807	171517	161232	10285
224		102751	102751		2949	2949	
19		200400	200400		637	637	
55	17	264750	257738	7012	1718	1616	102
5067	560	3245593	3212161	33432	44853	41814	3039
4555	1594	23386730	12132799	11253931	83923	78454	5469
7054	460	1348385	1253953	94432	37363	35688	1675
44		3065	3065		74	74	
439		125432	125432		2700	2700	
209		62700	62700		1549	1549	
230		62732	62732		1151	1151	
131	228	409973	393905	16068	3219	2955	264
24	228	312325	296257	16068	2141	1877	264
2		12120	12120		614	614	
105		85528	85528		464	464	
270	228	50370	34302	16068	1431	1167	264
1770	19	2255339	2247447	7892	31078	30972	106
261		2305961	2305961		16503	16503	
573	483	8392424	8358482	33942	43185	42145	1040
14228	1548	15768249	4518311	11249938	77890	72487	5403
3702	1111	14541533	3321544	11219989	30296	25867	4429
326	480	56393	31925	24468	4574	1599	2975
160	101	258343	185776	72567	2775	2014	761

18-15 续表 1 continued

指标	Item	连锁门店商品购进额(万元) Total Purchases of chain store(10000 yuan)		
		合计 Total	直营店 Under Direct Management	加盟店 Through License Arrangement
总计	**Total**	**20283729**	**19831397**	**452331**
一、按行业分组	**by Sector**			
批发业	Wholesale Trade	6141782	6134691	7091
零售业	Retail Trade	14141946	13696706	445240
二、按登记注册类型分组	**by Status of Registration**			
内资企业	Domestic Funded Enterprises	19628522	19208854	419668
国有企业	State-owned Enterprises	271574	271574	
集体企业	Collective-owned Enterprises	65373	65373	
股份合作企业	Cooperative Enterprises	140916	137975	2941
联营企业	Joint Ownership Enterprises			
有限责任公司	Limited Liability Corporations	5125514	5075163	50351
股份有限公司	Share-holding Corporations Limited	11872354	11672116	200238
私营企业	Private Enterprises	2151512	1985375	166138
其他企业	Other Enterprises	1278	1278	
港、澳、台商投资企业	Enterprises with Funds from Hong Kong, Macao and Taiwan	179017	179017	
合资经营企业(港或澳、台资)	Joint-ventures Enterprises	86734	86734	
合作经营企业(港或澳、台资)	Cooperative Enterprises			
港、澳、台商独资经营企业	Enterprises with Sole Investment	92283	92283	
港、澳、台商投资股份有限公司	Share-holding Corporations Ltd. With Funds from Hong Kong,Macao and Taiwan			
其他港澳台投资企业	Others			
外商投资企业	Foreign Funded Enterprises	476190	443527	32664
中外合资经营企业	Joint-venture Enterprises	207171	174507	32664
中外合作经营企业	Cooperation Enterprises	87332	87332	
外资企业	Enterprises with Sole Foreign Funds			
外商投资股份有限公司	Share-holding Corporations Ltd. With Foreign Investment	181687	181687	
其他外商投资企业	Others			
三、按连锁零售业态分组	**by Business Categories**			
便利店	Convenience Store	92008	59344	32664
折扣店	Discount store			
超市	Supermarket	3742849	3738553	4296
大型超市	Large supermarket	1365688	1365688	
仓储会员店	Warehouse club stores			
百货店	Department store	3096815	3079313	17502
专业店	Professional store	10768431	10565603	202828
其中：加油站	In:Gas Station	7276932	7094196	182736
专卖店	Specialty store	529720	485573	44146
家居建材商店	Home-furnishings store			
厂家直销中心	Factory Outlet Center			
其他	Others	688217	537322	150896

18-15 续表 2 continued

指 标	Item	连锁门店商品销售额(万元) Sale Value of chain store(10000 yuan) 合 计 Total	直营店 Under Direct Management	加盟店 Through License Arrangement
总 计	**Total**	**25214513**	**24695548**	**518965**
一、按行业分组	**by Sector**			
批发业	Wholesale Trade	6200677	6192748	7928
零售业	Retail Trade	19013836	18502800	511037
二、按登记注册类型分组	**by Status of Registration**			
内资企业	Domestic Funded Enterprises	24471450	24001258	470192
国有企业	State-owned Enterprises	423404	423404	
集体企业	Collective-owned Enterprises	107160	107160	
股份合作企业	Cooperative Enterprises	149677	146469	3207
联营企业	Joint Ownership Enterprises			
有限责任公司	Limited Liability Corporations	5499890	5444214	55677
股份有限公司	Share-holding Corporations Limited	15905300	15645263	260037
私营企业	Private Enterprises	2384400	2233130	151271
其他企业	Other Enterprises	1619	1619	
港、澳、台商投资企业	Enterprises with Funds from Hong Kong, Macao and Taiwan	192475	192475	
合资经营企业(港或澳、台资)	Joint-ventures Enterprises	101174	101174	
合作经营企业(港或澳、台资)	Cooperative Enterprises			
港、澳、台商独资经营企业	Enterprises with Sole Investment	91301	91301	
港、澳、台商投资股份有限公司	Share-holding Corporations Ltd. With Funds from Hong Kong,Macao and Taiwan			
其他港澳台投资企业	Others			
外商投资企业	Foreign Funded Enterprises	550589	501816	48773
中外合资经营企业	Joint-venture Enterprises	267676	218903	48773
中外合作经营企业	Cooperation Enterprises	101226	101226	
外资企业	Enterprises with Sole Foreign Funds			
外商投资股份有限公司	Share-holding Corporations Ltd. With Foreign Investment	181687	181687	
其他外商投资企业	Others			
三、按连锁零售业态分组	**by Business Categories**			
便利店	Convenience Store	117838	69064	48773
折扣店	Discount store			
超 市	Supermarket	4159978	4154890	5088
大型超市	Large supermarket	1792875	1792875	
仓储会员店	Warehouse club stores			
百货店	Department store	6491561	6441076	50486
专业店	Professional store	11510527	11277858	232669
其中：加油站	In:Gas Station	7685143	7475591	209552
专卖店	Specialty store	469041	419486	49555
家居建材商店	Home-furnishings store			
厂家直销中心	Factory Outlet Center			
其 他	Others	672694	540298	132396

18-16 住宿和餐饮业连锁经营情况(2021年)

指标名称	Indicator	连锁总店或总部数(个) Number of chain head stores (unit)	门店总数(个) Number of Stores (unit)
总计	**Total**	**21**	**941**
一、按行业分组	**by Sector**		
住宿业	Hotel Services	3	50
餐饮业	Catering Services	18	891
二、按登记注册类型分组	**by Status of Registration**		
内资企业	Domestic Funded Enterprises	17	428
国有企业	State-owned Enterprises	1	30
集体企业	Collective-owned Enterprises		
股份合作企业	Cooperative Enterprises		
联营企业	Joint Ownership Enterprises		
有限责任公司	Limited Liability Corporations	6	220
股份有限公司	Share-holding Corporations Limited	3	42
私营企业	Private Enterprises	7	136
其他企业	Other Enterprises		
港、澳、台商投资企业	Enterprises with Funds from Hong Kong, Macao and Taiwan	3	143
合资经营企业(港或澳、台资)	Joint-ventures Enterprises		
合作经营企业(港或澳、台资)	Cooperative Enterprises		
港、澳、台商独资经营企业	Enterprises with Sole Investment	3	143
港、澳、台商投资股份有限公司	Share-holding Corporations Ltd. With Funds from Hong Kong, Macao and Taiwan		
其他港澳台投资企业	Others		
外商投资企业	Foreign Funded Enterprises	1	370
中外合资经营企业	Joint-venture Enterprises		
中外合作经营企业	Cooperation Enterprises		
外资企业	Enterprises with Sole Foreign Funds	1	370
外商投资股份有限公司	Share-holding Corporations Ltd. With Foreign Investment		
其他外商投资企业	Others		

Business of chain operation of Hotels and Catering Services(2021)

直营店 Under Direct Management	年末从业人员(人) Engaged Persons (person)	直营店 Under Direct Management	年末餐饮营业面积(平方米) Operational Area (sq.m)	直营店 Under Direct Management	客房数(间) Number of rooms (room)	直营店 Under Direct Management	床位数(个) Number of Beds (unit)	直营店 Under Direct Management
826	**24319**	**22400**	**545845**	**512571**	**12720**	**12490**	**19020**	**18689**
45	1100	1059	1250	1200	5315	5085	7502	7171
781	23219	21341	544595	511371	7405	7405	11518	11518
324	14620	13201	393320	365046	12720	12490	19020	18689
30	156	156	6300	6300				
220	2454	2454	42289	42289	4330	4330	6031	6031
37	9595	9554	296082	296032	7866	7636	12249	11918
37	2415	1037	48649	20425	524	524	740	740
132	4402	3902	43424	38424				
132	4402	3902	43424	38424				
370	5297	5297	109101	109101				
370	5297	5297	109101	109101				

18-16 续表

指 标 名 称	Indicator	餐位数(位) Number of Diningseats (unit)	直营店 Under Direct Management
总　计	**Total**	**104495**	**94008**
一、按行业分组	**by Sector**		
住宿业	Hotel Services	1780	1740
餐饮业	Catering Services	102715	92268
二、按登记注册类型分组	**by Status of Registration**		
内资企业	Domestic Funded Enterprises	62487	53500
国有企业	State-owned Enterprises	1800	1800
集体企业	Collective-owned Enterprises		
股份合作企业	Cooperative Enterprises		
联营企业	Joint Ownership Enterprises		
有限责任公司	Limited Liability Corporations	27932	27932
股份有限公司	Share-holding Corporations Limited	19396	19356
私营企业	Private Enterprises	13359	4412
其他企业	Other Enterprises		
港、澳、台商投资企业	Enterprises with Funds from Hong Kong,Macao and Taiwan	11887	10387
合资经营企业(港或澳、台资)	Joint-ventures Enterprises		
合作经营企业(港或澳、台资)	Cooperative Enterprises		
港、澳、台商独资经营企业	Enterprises with Sole Investment	11887	10387
港、澳、台商投资股份有限公司	Share-holding Corporations Ltd. With Funds from Hong Kong, Macao and Taiwan		
其他港澳台投资企业	Others		
外商投资企业	Foreign Funded Enterprises	30121	30121
中外合资经营企业	Joint-venture Enterprises		
中外合作经营企业	Cooperation Enterprises		
外资企业	Enterprises with Sole Foreign Funds	30121	30121
外商投资股份有限公司	Share-holding Corporations Ltd. With Foreign Investment		
其他外商投资企业	Others		

continued

连锁门店商品购进额(万元) Total Purchases of chain store (10000 yuan)	直营店 Under Direct Management	统一配送商品购进额 Centralized Purchases and Delivery	连锁门店营业额(万元) Bussiness Revenue of chain store (10000 yuan)	直营店 Under Direct Management	餐费收入 From Meals	直营 Under Direct Management
194084	**175167**	**151563**	**637116**	**573473**	**557574**	**495289**
226	226	226	17552	16184	196	186
193858	174941	151337	619565	557289	557378	495103
114427	97641	71906	316842	260301	243466	188282
2762	2762		5957	5957	5957	5957
28345	28345	22940	65071	65071	52604	52604
58190	58190	31635	170073	168705	112005	111995
25131	8344	17330	75741	20568	72900	17727
15493	13362	15493	77120	70019	70954	63853
15493	13362	15493	77120	70019	70954	63853
64164	64164	64164	243154	243154	243154	243154
64164	64164	64164	243154	243154	243154	243154

18-17 主要年份社会消费品零售总额
Retail Sale of Consumer Goods in Major Years

单位:亿元 (100 million yuan)

年 份 Year	社会消费品零售总额 Retail Sale of Consumer Goods	按所在地分 by Location			按行业分 by Sector				
		市 City	县 County	县以下 Under County Level	批发和零售业 Wholesale and Retail Trades	住宿和餐饮业 Hotels and Catering Services	制造业 Manufacturing	农业生产者 Agricultural Producers	其他行业 Other Sectors
1949	6.23				3.92	0.63	1.68		
1952	19.01				13.23	1.92	3.21	0.53	0.12
1957	26.00				21.86	1.08	2.19	0.51	0.45
1962	30.49				25.39	1.37	1.98	1.60	0.15
1965	33.85				29.92	1.83	1.35	0.60	0.15
1970	40.94				36.53	1.37	1.87	0.95	0.22
1975	60.32				51.98	2.72	2.85	1.54	1.22
1978	79.73	23.39	21.14	35.19	68.40	3.65	4.57	2.34	0.77
1979	92.22	27.46	23.10	41.66	78.38	4.25	6.09	2.64	0.86
1980	114.01	32.36	27.78	53.86	94.61	5.03	10.00	3.38	0.99
1981	131.47	35.84	34.40	61.23	107.10	5.82	13.42	3.53	1.60
1982	141.48	41.63	34.22	65.64	112.90	7.64	14.12	4.82	2.00
1983	162.14	47.85	37.49	76.80	127.67	9.83	16.93	5.16	2.55
1984	189.08	66.58	37.98	84.52	147.25	11.23	20.57	6.16	3.87
1985	227.03	84.16	46.50	96.38	173.62	13.86	25.27	8.94	5.34
1986	261.64	96.22	54.18	111.25	194.85	15.48	31.38	12.32	7.61
1987	300.69	119.11	58.69	122.89	217.34	18.16	41.14	14.91	9.14
1988	392.37	164.12	73.40	154.85	287.09	22.88	49.85	20.50	12.05
1989	430.74	199.91	72.75	158.09	315.80	23.93	49.86	26.34	14.81
1990	460.13	218.97	79.19	161.96	338.02	25.07	50.24	30.41	16.38
1991	536.03	263.90	86.76	185.36	392.19	30.67	59.41	35.48	18.28
1992	653.23	336.37	99.77	217.08	471.87	37.56	77.87	44.17	21.76
1993	875.00	476.00	123.37	275.63	610.75	52.50	124.25	67.37	20.13
1994	1183.67	655.75	168.08	359.84	795.42	85.23	139.67	111.27	52.08
1995	1532.39	891.85	171.62	468.92	991.45	125.65	188.49	153.24	73.55
1996	1833.77	1085.59	187.04	561.14	1173.62	161.37	232.89	168.71	97.19
1997	2117.72	1304.52	207.54	605.67	1348.99	184.24	264.72	220.24	99.53
1998	2400.27	1471.36	230.43	698.48	1497.77	223.22	307.23	254.43	117.62
1999	2659.30	1632.81	255.29	771.20	1672.70	260.61	319.12	281.89	124.98
2000	2988.30	1846.77	286.88	854.66	1900.56	310.78	328.72	304.80	143.43
2001	3291.04	2040.44	319.23	931.36	2119.43	362.02	329.10	322.52	157.97
2002	3652.03	2308.08	339.64	1004.30	2410.34	427.29	321.38	325.03	167.99
2003	4114.01	2637.09	415.51	1061.41	3398.18	518.36			197.47
2004	4653.79	2921.00	517.90	1214.89	3909.20	581.50			163.09
2005	5366.71	3386.04	598.29	1382.38	4502.52	675.75			188.44
2006	6212.32	3954.01	692.84	1565.47	5203.03	796.62			212.66
2007	7328.39	4672.93	826.82	1828.64	6135.16	956.52			236.71
2008	8977.22	5698.86	1044.43	2233.93	7845.43	895.96			235.83
2009	10293.79	6693.07	1197.16	2403.56	8616.39	1393.50			283.89
2010	12028.30								
2011	13939.83								
2012	15785.25								
2013	17703.85								
2014	19706.36								
2015	21550.95								
2016	23482.07								
2017	25527.94								
2018	27480.28								
2019	29251.18								
2020	29248.05								
2021	33714.54								

注:1.自2010年起，社会消费品零售总额由按所在地、按行业分组调整为按经营地、按消费形态分组。
2.2020年，根据第四次经济普查结果，对1993－2019年社会消费品零售总额及分组数据进行了修订。

a)Since 2010,the group of Retail Sale of Consumer Goods has been adjusted from grouping by location and industry to grouping by business location and consumption form.

b)Figures of total retail sales of consumer goods of 1993-2019 are revised according to the result of the fourth national economic census in 2020.

18-18 各市社会消费品零售总额(2021年)
Retail Sale of Consumer Goods by Region(2021)

地 区	Region	绝对额（亿元） Amount (100 million yuan)					比上年增长（%） Growth Rate (%)				
		社会消费品零售总额 Total Retail Sales of Consumer Goods	按经营地分 by Operation Place		按消费形态分 by Consumption Pattern		社会消费品零售总额 Total Retail Sales of Consumer Goods	按经营地分 by Operation Place		按消费形态分 by Consumption pattern	
			城镇 Urban	乡村 Rural	商品零售 Retail Sales	餐饮收入 Catering Income		城镇 Urban	乡村 Rural	商品零售 Retail Sales	餐饮收入 Catering Income
全省总计	**Total**	**33714.54**	**28080.98**	**5633.56**	**29886.32**	**3828.22**	**15.3**	**15.3**	**15.2**	**14.4**	**22.4**
济南市	Jinan	5126.10	4536.60	589.50	4390.05	736.05	14.7	14.9	13.4	13.8	20.5
青岛市	Qingdao	5975.43	4933.65	1041.78	5347.32	628.11	14.8	14.9	14.6	14.1	21.3
淄博市	Zibo	1308.89	1151.24	157.65	1164.09	144.80	15.4	15.3	16.4	14.9	19.3
枣庄市	Zaozhuang	1041.72	826.59	215.13	931.03	110.69	16.0	15.6	17.9	15.1	24.8
东营市	Dongying	756.89	645.63	111.26	645.05	111.84	15.8	15.5	18.8	15.7	16.7
烟台市	Yantai	3232.26	2546.65	685.61	2888.14	344.12	15.4	15.7	14.4	13.5	34.9
潍坊市	Weifang	2781.46	2289.14	492.32	2466.67	314.79	16.4	16.6	15.5	15.5	30.0
济宁市	Jining	2459.59	2092.69	366.90	2211.17	248.42	15.6	15.7	15.2	14.5	28.1
泰安市	Tai'an	1161.80	966.68	195.12	1041.55	120.25	13.6	13.7	13.5	13.0	19.1
威海市	Weihai	1347.61	1145.03	202.58	1206.79	140.82	15.5	15.9	13.5	13.9	32.3
日照市	Rizhao	654.89	519.88	135.01	593.47	61.42	12.0	10.2	19.5	11.2	20.7
临沂市	Linyi	2931.07	2412.27	518.80	2594.00	337.07	15.9	15.5	18.9	15.1	31.8
德州市	Dezhou	1279.56	1059.10	220.46	1138.81	140.75	14.8	12.9	25.1	14.3	20.7
聊城市	Liaocheng	917.55	718.92	198.63	812.03	105.52	14.5	14.6	14.3	14.4	16.8
滨州市	Binzhou	823.34	659.88	163.46	746.78	76.56	14.7	14.9	13.7	14.2	19.1
菏泽市	Heze	1916.39	1577.03	339.36	1709.38	207.01	17.0	17.1	16.7	15.8	35.8

主要统计指标解释

社会消费品零售总额 指企业（单位、个体户）通过交易直接售给个人、社会集团非生产、非经营用的实物商品金额，以及提供餐饮服务所取得的收入金额。个人包括城乡居民和入境人员，社会集团包括机关、社会团体、部队、学校、企事业单位、居委会或村委会等。

商品购进额 指从本企业以外的单位和个人购进（包括从国外直接进口）作为转卖或加工后转卖的商品金额（含增值税）。本指标反映批发和零售业从国内外市场上购进商品的总价。

商品购进包括：(1) 从工农业生产者、批发和零售业、住宿和餐饮业、出版社或报社的出版发行部门和其他服务业等企事业单位和个体经营户购进的商品；(2) 从机关社会团体购进的商品；(3) 从海关、市场管理部门购进的缉私和没收的商品；(4) 从居民收购的废旧商品等。

不包括：(1) 企业为本单位自身经营用，不是作为转卖而购进的商品，如材料物资、包装物、低值易耗品、办公用品等；(2) 未通过买卖行为而收入的商品，如接受其他部门移交的商品、借入的商品、收入代其他单位保管的商品、其他单位赠送的样品、加工回收的成品等；(3) 经本单位介绍，由买卖双方直接结算，本单位只收取手续费的业务；(4) 销售退回和买方拒付货款的商品；(5) 商品溢余；(6) 期货交易商品。

商品销售额 指对本单位以外的单位和个人出售的商品金额（包括售给本单位消费用的商品，含增值税），在批发和零售业中，本指标反映在国内市场上销售商品以及出口商品的总价。

商品销售包括：(1) 售给个人和社会集团消费用的商品；(2) 售给农业、工业、建筑业、服务业等国民经济各行业用于生产、经营用的商品，包括售予批发和零售业作为转卖或加工后转卖的商品；(3) 对国（境）外直接出口的商品。

商品销售不包括：(1) 未通过买卖行为付出的商品，如因机构变动移交给其他企业单位的商品、借出的商品、归还受其他单位委托代保管的商品、付出的加工原料和赠送给其他单位的样品等；(2) 促销返券所销售的、不计入营业收入的商品；(3) 经本单位介绍，由买卖双方直接结算，本单位只收取手续费的业务；(4) 未发生所有权转移的商品预付卡销售，如加油卡；(5) 汽车维修、电话卡销售等服务性经济活动；(6) 购货退回的商品；(7) 商品损耗和损失；(8) 出售本单位自用的废旧物资；(9) 期货交易商品；(10) 自来水供应企业、电力企业、天然气供应企业提供的水、电、气。

期末商品库存额 对于批发和零售业法人单位和个体经营户，是指报告期末取得所有权的全部商品金额（含增值税）；对于批发和零售业产业活动单位，是指报告期末实际在库且归属法人具有所有权的全部商品金额（含增值税）。这个指标反映批发和零售业的商品库存情况，以及对市场商品供应的保证程度。

库存商品包括：(1) 存放在本单位（如门市部、批发站、采购站、经营处）的仓库、货场、货柜和货架中的商品；(2) 挑选、整理、包装中的商品；(3) 已记入购进而尚未运到本单位的商品，即发货单或银行承兑凭证已到而货未到的商品；(4) 寄放他处的商品，如因购货方拒绝付款而暂时存在购货方的商品；(5) 委托其他单位代销（未作销售或调出）尚未售出的商品；(6) 代其他单位购进尚未交付的商品。

库存商品不包括：(1) 所有权不属于本单位的商品，如商品已作销售但买方尚未取走的商品，代替他人保管、运输、加工的商品，代其他单位销售（未做购进或调入）而未售出的商品；(2) 委托外单位加工的商品（包括本单位所属加工厂和其他生产单位加工生产尚未收回成品的商品）；(3) 外贸企业代理其他单位从国外进口，尚未付给订货单位的商品；(4) 代国家储备部门保管的商品。

库存商品金额可以采用进价或售价进行核算。采用进价核算的商品，应按商品进货原则（或实际采购成本）计算期末库存；采用售价核算的商品，应按商品的售价计算期末库存。购入的商品，在商品到达验收入库后计算期末库存（对已记入购进尚未运到的商品，也可计算期末库存）；对于月终尚未开出承兑商业汇票的入库商品，按应付给供货单位的价款暂估计算期末库存；年度终了，凡已转入库存和已作销售的进口商品，属于国外以离岸价格成交、有应付未付国外运保费的，应先估计期末库存，委托其他单位代销的商品包括在期末库存中；委托外单位加工的商品，在发出商品时作减少期末库存，当加工商品收回时增加期末库存（包括商品进货原价、加工费用、加工税金等）。

营业额 指住宿和餐饮业单位在经营活动中，因提供服务或销售商品等取得的全部收入（含增值税），收入主要来源于提供客房、餐费服务、商品销售和其他服务，如商务服务。不包括多产业法人企业附营的其他行业产业活动单位的餐费收入、商品销售收入等各项收入。

客房收入 指住宿和餐饮业单位在经营活动中因提供住宿服务取得的收入（含增值税）。不包括多产业法人企业附营的其他行业产业活动单位的客房收入。

餐费收入 指本单位为顾客提供就餐服务取得的收入（含增值税）。包括：经烹饪、调制加工后出售的各种食品，如主食、炒菜、凉拌菜等的收入。不包括多产业法人企业附营的其他行业产业活动单位的餐费收入。

亿元商品交易市场 指年成交额在亿元及以上的商品交易市场。商品交易市场是指经有关部门和组织批准设立，有固定场所、设施，有经营管理部门和监管人员，若干市场经营者入内，常年或实际开业三个月以上，集中、公开、独立地进行生活消费品、生产资料等现货商品交易以及提供相关服务的交易场所，包括各类消费品市场、生产资料市场等。

连锁总店（总部） 负责连锁企业资源（商号、商誉、经营模式、服务标准、管理模式等）的开发、配置、控制或使用等功能的企业核心管理机构。连锁经营是指经营同类商品或服务，使用统一商号的若干店铺，在同一总店（总部）的管理下，采取统一采购或特许经营等方式，实现规模效益的组织形式，包括直营连锁、特许连锁和自愿连锁三种形式。系统内企业，如新华书店、烟草公司、石油公司等，应注意是否具备连锁经营特征，如果不具备连锁经营特征，则不能纳入连锁统计范畴。

直营连锁：是指连锁店铺由连锁公司全资或控股开设，在总部的直接控制下，开展统一经营的连锁经营形式。

特许连锁：是指拥有注册商标、企业标志、专利、专有技术等经营资源的企业（特许人），以合同形式将其拥有的经营资源许可其他经营者（被特许人）使用，被特许人按合同约定在统一的经营模式下开展经营，并向特许人支付特许经营费用的连锁经营形式。

自愿连锁：是指若干个店铺或企业自愿组合起来，在不改变各自资产所有权关系的情况下，以同一个品牌形象面对消费者，以共同进货为纽带开展的连锁经营形式。

Explanatory Notes on Main Statistical Indicators

Total Retail Sales of Consumer Goods refers to the amount obtained by enterprises (units, self-employed individuals) through direct sales of non-production and non-business physical commodity to individuals, social institutions, and revenue from providing catering services. Individuals include rural and urban households, population from abroad, social institutions include government agencies, social organizations, military units, schools, institutions, neighbourhood (village) committees.

Total Purchases of Commodities refer to the total value of purchases of commodities by enterprises (establishments) from other establishments or individuals (including direct import from abroad) for the purpose of re-selling, either with or without further processing of the commodities purchased. The commodities include: (1) commodities purchased from agricultural and industrial producer, wholesaler, retailer, publishing house and other enterprises, institutions and individual operators of service business; (2) commodities purchased from institutions and social groups; (3) confiscated goods purchased from the customs authorities or market management agencies; (4) second-hand goods and wastes purchased from residents; The commodities exclude (1) commodities purchased by enterprises (establishments) for use in their own business operation, commodities obtained without buying or selling procedures such as materials, consumable goods of low value, office appliance, etc. (2) received goods without trading, such as goods handed over from others, borrowed goods, preserved goods for others, donated goods from others, processed and retrieved goods, etc. (3) goods of direct settlement between buyer and seller with handling fees introduced by others, (4) goods returned or refused to pay by the buyer, (5) excessive goods, (6) futures trading commodities.

Total Sales of Commodities refer to value of commodities sold by the establishments to other establishments and individuals (including goods sold for self consumption, including the value-added tax). The commodities include: (1) commodities sold to individuals and social groups for their consumption; (2) commodities sold to establishments in all industries for their production and operation, including agriculture, industry, construction, and catering services including commodities sold to wholesale and retail establishments for re-selling, with or without further processing; and (3) commodities for direct export to abroad. Excluded are (1) extended commodities without trading, such as goods handed over to other enterprises and institutions because of the change of organizations, lent goods, returned goods preserved for others, extended processing materials and samples donated to others, (2) goods sold by coupon rebates that are not included in business income, (3) goods of direct settlement between buyer and seller with handling fees introduced by others, (4) prepaid cards for goods without transfer of ownership, such as gas cards, (5) Service-oriented economic activities such as automobile maintenance and telephone card sales, (6) goods returned after purchase, (7) damaged and spoiled goods, (8) waste and used goods of self use, (9) futures trading commodities, (10) water, electricity and gas supplied by water supply enterprises, electric power enterprises and natural gas supply enterprises.

Total Stock of Commodities For the legal entities and self-employed individuals engaged in wholesale and retail trade, it refers to total value (including VAT) of commodities possessed at the end of the reference period; and for wholesale and retail establishments, it refers to the value (including VAT) of all commodities actually in stock and owned by their legal persons at the end of reference period. The commodities in stock includes: (1) commodities located in storage, garages, counters, and shelves of operating places of wholesale and retail trades (such as sale stores, wholesale centres, procurement stations and operating offices); (2) commodities in the process of being selected, sorted, and packed; (3) commodities not arrived but recorded as purchase in the account, i.e. commodities not arrived but payment receipts for the commodities from the sellers or the banks arrived; (4) commodities deposited in other places rather than places mentioned above, for instance: commodities in the hold of purchasers temporarily due to the refusal of payment; (5) commodities entrusted to other units to sell but not sold yet; (6) commodities purchased for other units but not delivered yet. Commodities not included as stock are those not owned by the enterprises (units), commodities on commission for processing, imported commodities of agency of foreign trade enterprise but not yet delivered to ordering units and finally those put in stock on behalf of the state reserves units.

The amount of inventory goods can be calculated using the purchase price or the selling price. In order to calculate the ending stocks at purchase price, the principle of accounting on the basis of actual purchase cost should be adopted; and to calculated the ending stocks at selling price, the principle of accounting on the basis of selling price adopted. Goods purchased should be calculated when they are delivered, checked and put in storage (for the goods purchase but not delivered, they are also included in the ending stocks). For the goods in storage and without commercial acceptance, the ending stocks are calculated at the price provided by the suppliers; at the end of the year, all the imported goods in storage or sold, which are transacted at F.O.B. prices and have not been paid the premiums payable, should be calculated as ending stocks, including the goods entrusted other units to sell. When the goods entrusted other units to manufacture are delivered, the ending stocks should be reduced; when it delivered back, the ending stocks increased (including purchase price, processing cost, processing taxes, etc.).

Business Revenue refers to the total income that the hotels and catering services enterprise received from providing services or selling commodities through business activities, including income from hotels, catering services, selling of commodities (including VAT) and other services. It excludes the income provided by the industrial units in other industries of this corporate enterprise.

Income from hotel rooms refers to the income of hotel and catering services provided by the enterprise in the hotel and catering service industry. It excludes the room income provided by the industrial units in other industries of this corporate enterprise.

Income from catering services refers to the income that the enterprise received by providing catering services, including selling of cooked or prepared foods, such as stable food, cooked dishes or cold dishes. It excludes the income provided by the industrial units in other industries of this corporate enterprise.

Volume of Transaction at Large Commodity Markets (with transaction value over 100 million yuan) refers to the commodity markets with an annual transaction at and above 100 million. The commodity market refers to the markets approved and managed by related departments, where there are fixed sites, facilities, managers and administration offices, where there are a certain number of traders to operate for three month and above or all the year, where the commodities including the articles for daily consumption and capital goods and services are traded in a centralized, independent and open way. Such market includes markets of daily goods and market of capital goods, etc.

Chain Enterprise (also called chain stores or chain corporations) refer to the core leading stores responsible for development, allocation, administration and utilization of resources (name of stores, brand of stores, operation model, service standard, management way, etc.) of chain stores. Chain stores refers to the stores engaged in providing homogeneous commodities or services, with the central leadership of head store (headquarters) and guided by common policies, conduct centralized purchase and distributed selling of commodities, in order to gain better efficiency through standardized operation. The chain stores include regular chain stores, franchise chain stores and voluntary chain stores. In-system enterprises, such as Xinhua Bookstore, Tobacco Company, and Oil Company, should pay attention to whether they have the characteristics of chain operation. If they do not have the characteristics of chain operation, they cannot be included in the chain statistics category.

Chain stores have 3 categories:

a) Chain stores under direct management: These are formal chain stores invested or controlled by the headquarters. They operate under the direct and unified management from the headquarters. Adopting a direct management approach, the headquarters give orders and control all retail stores, which follow completely the directives from the headquarters. Large monopolized commercial companies develop and expand their business through purchasing, merging, direct investment and controlling of shares.

b) Chain stores through special permit: Through contracts, chain stores (or their owners) obtain licenses from the headquarters to use designated trade marks, names, operation know how, and to sell the commodity developed by the headquarters. Under this arrangement, each store in the chain is an independent legal entity and operates under the guidance from the headquarters.

c) Chain stores through voluntary arrangement: Under this arrangement, all stores operate together under the guidance of the headquarters, while maintaining their status of independent legal entities with full ownership of their assets. They use the same store name, sign contracts with the headquarters concerning purchase, sale, publicity, etc. and operate under the contract. They are free to engage in other activities which are not bounded in the contract. They could join or leave the chain on voluntary basis.

第19篇

教育和科技

Education, Science and Technology

简 要 说 明

一、本篇资料的主要内容

本篇资料反映了全省教育和科技事业基本情况。教育部分主要包括高等教育、中等教育、初等教育、成人高等教育、职业教育、幼儿园等方面基本情况；科技部分主要包括科技成果、专利、规模以上工业科技活动和全社会科技活动情况。

二、本篇资料的来源

1.教育部分中，技工学校的资料来源于省人力资源和社会保障厅，其他资料来源于省教育厅。

2.科技部分中，科技成果资料来源于省科学技术厅，专利资料来源于省市场监督管理局，规模以上工业企业科技活动和全社会科技活动资料来源于省统计局统计年报。

本篇资料由省统计局人口处（社科处）整理提供。

Brief Introduction

I. Content

Data in this chapter show the basic conditions of education and technology. Data on education show the development of higher education, secondary education, primary education, vocational education and kindergartens. Data on technology show the basic conditions of scientific and technological achievements and prizes, number of patent applications examined and granted, scientific and technological activities of industrial enterprises above designate size and basic conditions of R&D institutions.

II. Source of Data

(1)Data on the basic conditions of technical schools are provided by Shandong Human Resources and Social Security Department and other data on education are provided by Shandong Provincial Education Department.

(2)Data on scientific and technological are provided by Department of Science and Technology of Shandong Province. Data on patents are provided by S Shandong Provincial Department of Market Regulatory Authority. Data on scientific and technological activities come from the annual report of scientific and technological activities, which is provided by Shandong Provincial Bureau of Statistics.

Data in this chapter are provided and compiled by the Division of Urbanization,Population and Employment Statistics（by the Division of Social,Science and Culture Industry Employment Statistics）of Shandong Provincial Bureau of Statistics.

19-1 各级各类学校基本情况(2021年)

Basic Statistics on Education Institutions(2021)

项　目	Item	学校数(所) Number of Schools (unit)	招生数(人) New Enrollment (person)	在校学生数(人) Total Enrol -lment (person)	毕业生数(人) Graduates (person)	教职工数(人) Teachers and Staff (person)	专任教师(人) Full-time Teachers (person)
高等教育	**Higher Education**						
研究生培养机构	Institutions Providing Postgraduate Programs	**35**	**53567**	**149077**	**34454**		
普通高校	Regular Institutions of Higher Education	32	53426	148701	34364		
科研机构	Research Institutions	3	141	376	90		
普通高等学校	Regular Institutions of Higher Education	**153**	**780954**	**2429912**	**617855**	**177805**	**129888**
本科院校	Universities with Full Undergraduate Courses	70	422348	1466422	358701	121998	87741
#独立学院	Non-university Tertiary	4	8935	33123	9064	1836	1540
#职业本科	Bachelor of Vocational Studies	3	19519	56536	7545	3369	2839
专科(高职)院校	Colleges with Specialized Courses	83	358606	963490	259152	55807	42147
#高等职业学校	Vocational and Technical Colleges	75	328232	881783	236117	51079	38690
成人高等教育	Institutions of Higher Education for Adult	11	451062	906118	280241	1140	702
中等教育	**Secondary Education**						
高中阶段教育	Senior Secondary Education						
普通高中	Regular Senior Secondary Schools	723	628796	1826401	539843	196816	155902
中等职业学校	Vocational Secondary Education	400	293603	839144	221047	60026	53576
技工学校	Technical Schools	194	169851	442034	104221	32647	26284
初中阶段教育	Junior Secondary Education						
普通初中	Regular Junior Secondary Schools	3296	1247046	3881202	1094495	389605	316086
初等教育	**Primary Education**						
普通小学	Regular Primary Schools	9458	1379227	7558069	1257272	410021	468276
特殊教育学校	**Special Education**	155	8637	51777	7930	6847	6063
学前教育	**Pre-school Education**	25203	1156647	3893098	1235255	424852	269592

注：1.研究生机构的学生数据为硕士研究生和博士研究生数据；2.普通高等学校的学生数据为普通本专科学生数据，按学校类型归类；3.成人高等教育学生数含普通高校开展的成人高等教育学生数；4.专任教师按教育层次归类。

a) Data on students of Institutions Providing Postgraduate Programs refers to graduate students and doctoral students.

b) Data on students of Regular Institutions of Higher Education refers to undergraduates.

c) Data on students of Higher Adult Education including those in both Institutions of Higher Education for Adult and Regular Institutions of Higher Education.

d) Full-time teachers classified according to the academic level of their students.

19-2 主要年份普通高等教育基本情况

Basic Statistics on Higher Education in Major Years

年 份 Year	学校数 (所) Number of Schools (unit)	招生数 (人) New Enrollment (person)	在校学生数 (人) Total Enrollment (person)	毕业生数 (人) Graduates (person)	教职工数 (人) Teachers and Staff (person)	专任教师 (人) Full-time Teachers (person)
1949	7	1405	3969	70	1908	484
1952	7	2777	6753	1703	3684	1024
1955	7	3280	8915	1825	3397	1471
1957	7	3122	12532	1686	4518	2114
1962	26	3496	26001	7148	10144	4318
1965	16	5621	22164	6102	9156	3898
1970	16			9162	10185	4526
1975	21	7366	17582	6033	13858	5601
1976	22	8896	21340	6072	15035	5941
1977	27	13192	25735	7203	17712	7028
1978	34	19712	38390	7015	20202	7855
1979	35	12856	44771	5364	23544	9478
1980	35	14402	51427	7684	26130	10347
1981	37	14160	59645	6311	27512	10379
1982	37	15765	51794	23993	30381	12065
1983	41	19827	55276	16806	31535	12943
1984	47	24862	66429	13563	33591	13919
1985	49	32745	83567	16159	36383	14974
1986	49	30211	92422	21183	39009	15951
1987	50	32972	95891	29428	41620	16716
1988	50	35714	101281	30869	43990	17585
1989	51	34308	103928	31766	46037	18162
1990	49	35023	105822	33104	46704	18377
1991	49	36067	107093	34500	46839	17825
1992	51	57878	130188	34994	47483	18059
1993	51	57918	151758	33935	48156	18405
1994	49	55036	156639	50457	49537	19460
1995	49	55611	160398	52083	50829	19932
1996	49	56544	169184	47835	51490	20079
1997	48	56950	175920	50141	50374	20414
1998	49	62994	187473	51477	50261	20581
1999	52	82410	213679	49612	49624	21252
2000	58	124817	303826	49687	54910	24764
2001	65	183553	449360	69583	64362	30902
2002	75	218719	583601	94697	72408	37412
2003	85	273894	761417	117253	84391	45457
2004	97	327452	946124	166959	93653	53847
2005	104	400573	1171284	224611	109920	64636
2006	109	445034	1338122	268384	121167	74676
2007	111	453479	1440378	355735	128761	81889
2008	114	514176	1534009	411143	134072	87432
2009	128	501082	1592974	431598	136753	89734
2010	133	495722	1631373	444003	139100	91413
2011	139	497292	1645589	472882	142698	94621
2012	137	498621	1658490	474266	142370	96058
2013	140	527539	1698545	475858	142240	98685
2014	142	580763	1796665	464076	143939	101380
2015	143	595646	1900612	474195	147035	104724
2016	144	624408	1995880	509142	150345	107748
2017	145	612660	2015345	571220	154311	110807
2018	145	629065	2040793	585871	158526	112717
2019	146	741661	2183944	577980	164932	117609
2020	152	729927	2291481	605379	172041	124215
2021	153	780954	2429912	617855	177805	129888

注：普通高等教育学生数据为普通本专科数据，含部分成人高校举办的高职班。

a)Data on higher education student is about normal university and technological university, with some held in adult colleges of higher vocational education.

19-3 主要年份中等专业教育基本情况

Basic Statistics on Vocational Secondary Education in Major Years

年 份 Year	学校数 (所) Number of Schools (unit)	招生数 (人) New Enrollment (person)	毕业生数 (人) Graduates (person)	在校学生数 (人) Total Enrollment (person)	教职工数 (人) Teachers and Staff (person)	专任教师 (人) Full-time Teachers (person)
1949	34	4784	1778	13738	1207	441
1950	48	7734	4292	14206	1663	709
1951	80	11179	4855	21918	3372	1307
1952	171	33756	5223	50175	6845	2744
1953	76	8478	23488	33516	4916	1812
1954	69	9478	9812	32458	4509	1807
1955	58	7738	11553	25336	3707	1477
1956	90	30047	9403	45706	6522	2573
1957	86	7972	12089	40738	6112	2742
1958	394	106779	15584	129494	8704	4537
1959	487	58777	21286	110617	11394	4955
1960	474	79722	32699	143184	15798	7893
1961	198	10395	22687	65735	12433	6008
1962	85	585	16909	23599	6072	2797
1963	79	9685	13814	18942	5883	3312
1964	94	15282	6751	27420	6086	2769
1965	275	35768	2242	72974	9197	4850
1966	158	2831	3403	50097	9128	4310
1967	160	2810	11544	41288	9159	4388
1968	155	11861	28731	24411	9461	4328
1969	128	2107	10537	15956	8410	3942
1970	126	2648	12356	6238	8121	3997
1971	135	18497	11758	12823	7776	5403
1972	140	9746	1313	11581	8756	3773
1973	122	16377	1980	25717	8366	3771
1974	129	18963	9440	34035	10175	4434
1975	144	21442	15786	40798	11378	5038
1976	178	23328	19908	44345	13296	5522
1977	176	23195	29665	33142	14004	5649
1978	189	25961	9006	49466	14814	6158
1979	195	26574	2882	75484	16080	6792
1980	203	28137	35212	68593	17617	7898
1981	165	27797	32661	63864	18563	8115
1982	174	29235	26782	66640	20482	9204
1983	179	31570	21413	77601	21503	9775
1984	188	33597	27166	84125	22539	10184
1985	208	45163	30024	100176	24511	11333
1986	227	44130	31422	114039	27320	12807
1987	214	40120	36247	103128	26820	12846
1988	225	44606	33551	114168	28985	14522
1989	230	48407	28370	134515	29314	14719
1990	236	48634	35423	148504	31634	16000
1991	240	52092	45259	155092	31842	15617
1992	234	55353	52088	158309	32857	15972
1993	241	77875	51360	185062	34354	16769
1994	243	89643	50801	222551	35066	17526
1995	244	95442	58680	258801	36084	18211
1996	255	105468	78496	289827	38030	19898
1997	252	112348	90545	311161	38458	20291
1998	254	114956	99483	327031	39160	20949
1999	251	122331	106740	344062	39274	21311
2000	243	93493	103629	333184	37241	20409
2001	200	92215	110827	310508	28002	15607
2002	165	115941	111333	314135	27005	15369
2003	154	94625	64046	256655	23630	13761
2004	145	87889	65953	260276	21621	12771
2005	134	86044	75076	257161	20406	12193
2006	130	90432	79902	264456	20563	12634
2007	135	98634	92275	283231	20985	13223
2008	130	93217	83077	271905	20308	13224
2009	124	99212	88355	271993	19981	13093

19-4 主要年份普通中学基本情况

Basic Statistics on Senior and Junior Secondary Education in Major Years

年 份 Year	学校数 (所) Number of Schools (unit)	招生数 (万人) New Enrollment (10 000 persons)	毕业生数 (万人) Graduates (10 000 persons)	在校学生数 (万人) Total Enrollment (10 000 persons)	教职工数 (人) Teachers and Staff (person)	专任教师 (人) Full-time Teachers (person)
1949	66	1.08	0.34	3.89	3431	1585
1952	189	6.12	0.99	10.44	10170	4507
1955	218	6.74	5.08	17.51	14778	6756
1957	1004	17.64	6.20	33.99	24369	14054
1962	1247	15.04	12.77	43.21	37062	21542
1965	6166	34.06	11.67	80.74	53914	37339
1970	13938	103.39	58.50	188.13	122751	100261
1975	14621	172.20	113.98	305.11	200906	161092
1976	19822	263.31	127.48	437.85	275864	228657
1977	20171	260.62	161.35	522.33	330445	277784
1978	17361	210.68	218.75	478.22	318128	264663
1979	16322	176.14	192.39	418.22	304551	246035
1980	14646	144.10	107.90	407.91	309538	247920
1981	12974	125.17	117.55	361.45	296240	233102
1982	11160	119.41	106.37	328.57	271664	212707
1983	9971	112.21	86.35	315.39	256926	200957
1984	9175	115.88	85.31	334.42	257968	201521
1985	9038	123.80	96.87	356.32	268321	209202
1986	8259	125.02	105.22	376.19	283726	220304
1987	7877	125.52	116.95	379.54	297083	232958
1988	7474	125.17	120.41	373.53	307364	241845
1989	6997	123.30	118.61	363.74	315494	245260
1990	6699	125.60	115.14	367.30	324027	249459
1991	6310	129.17	115.30	372.98	329927	253428
1992	5897	132.87	115.58	382.49	335020	258308
1993	5640	139.14	115.88	395.28	337259	260896
1994	5429	154.67	116.82	427.15	345640	268514
1995	5073	167.06	118.14	470.46	358301	279301
1996	4820	169.69	122.97	512.22	375463	294849
1997	4693	178.19	141.95	541.38	392365	310926
1998	4635	201.28	159.91	571.54	404824	322785
1999	4586	222.20	164.88	620.43	414538	333884
2000	4575	234.18	167.96	678.60	430754	350353
2001	4684	220.94	188.59	702.18	451014	359665
2002	4648	201.65	205.62	689.17	461898	369664
2003	4606	192.94	222.82	654.34	468627	374811
2004	4569	192.32	213.80	628.34	473687	379100
2005	4404	179.71	207.29	592.49	470584	377133
2006	4175	164.60	196.70	554.04	462298	372370
2007	4039	162.49	191.02	520.31	454920	370255
2008	3893	160.54	172.88	502.14	445545	367658
2009	3750	160.24	158.65	499.34	442447	372550
2010	3645	164.12	156.89	501.07	438787	372082
2011	3569	161.83	157.80	501.58	462765	376760
2012	3522	159.88	153.20	492.64	464942	376819
2013	3464	158.53	156.04	488.48	466088	382340
2014	3461	153.58	153.73	486.06	471653	386923
2015	3446	151.12	156.01	479.93	475798	390059
2016	3504	160.35	157.62	482.41	484579	397471
2017	3560	164.39	151.42	494.85	502004	410339
2018	3671	164.26	148.46	509.93	515123	419903
2019	3791	176.10	157.56	528.13	536931	435808
2020	3920	187.62	166.72	548.68	558935	453428
2021	4019	187.58	163.43	570.76	586421	471988

注：专任教师按照教师教授学生层次归类。
a)Full-time teachers classified according to the academic level of their students.

19-5 主要年份技工学校基本情况
Basic Statistics on Technical Schools in Major Years

年 份 Year	学校数(所) Number of Schools (unit)	招生数(人) New Enrollment (person)	毕业生数(人) Graduates (person)	在校学生数(人) Total Enrollment (person)	教职工数(人) Teachers and Staff (person)	专任教师(人) Full-time Teachers (person)
1953	1	150		150	25	15
1955	2	452	150	802	206	72
1957	6	1525	452	2300	614	213
1962	19	1274	906	5188	2078	688
1965	18	2336	1381	6662	1214	503
1970	6		452		639	106
1975	26	3407	1700	5652	1751	345
1976	26	3144	1704	5841	2204	435
1977	29	6083	5421	6414	3189	735
1978	64	13669	301	19651	7042	1563
1979	72	11673	4950	26632	7055	1951
1980	94	15698	9854	32208	8974	2978
1981	100	9323	11190	29605	9749	3474
1982	103	9379	12857	25953	10154	3474
1983	106	10698	11562	24343	10560	3508
1984	119	12851	8624	28302	11215	3732
1985	134	16748	9219	35163	14142	3423
1986	163	22069	10035	47114	19968	3928
1987	206	28114	11281	63839	22647	5390
1988	236	40381	16036	87832	26382	5996
1989	256	40821	22402	105330	27843	7088
1990	266	42429	28654	118605	19084	10084
1991	279	44081	39679	122591	33739	11210
1992	290	46436	39628	128557	37579	12233
1993	302	55920	42320	142660	37222	12853
1994	306	67812	45358	165989	39351	13424
1995	312	70251	65457	169023	38891	13948
1996	312	77595	62981	185253	37747	13778
1997	305	74054	65310	192675	35160	14059
1998	305	55668	59292	188493	33806	14035
1999	302	50896	71460	161531	28871	14531
2000	279	48008	66546	137718	24484	14066
2001	278	53283	55769	132122	23152	16060
2002	249	83186	49634	165386	22190	13072
2003	244	105896	46247	212811	20684	13371
2004	249	121444	58834	274432	21370	14607
2005	229	138505	78091	325924	22049	15058
2006	197	148625	98239	357648	22309	16211
2007	200	159954	110278	385325	26744	23586
2008	197	161000	121000	415000	24700	18847
2009	196	147000	140300	396200	24963	19378
2010	209	136995	133615	397719	18183	14962
2011	208	149407	123404	381503	24379	21050
2012	213	154546	113066	401207	29909	21451
2013	207	144165	121782	369922	30860	23977
2014	203	128007	108046	329473	29404	23000
2015	194	131550	98154	318182	29228	22613
2016	194	133600	89629	335348	29133	22908
2017	194	129109	103815	332634	29294	22565
2018	181	135184	96351	329897	29388	22525
2019	181	151122	91679	355409	29438	22294
2020	181	173803	95962	405418	29943	23573
2021	194	169851	104221	442034	32647	26284

19-6 主要年份小学基本情况

Basic Statistics on Primary Schools in Major Years

年 份 Year	学校数 (所) Number of Schools (unit)	招生数 (万人) New Enrollment (10 000 persons)	毕业生数 (万人) Graduates (10 000 persons)	在校学生数 (万人) Total Enrollment (10 000 persons)	教职工数 (人) Teachers and Staff (person)	专任教师 (人) Full-time Teachers (person)
1949	27476	64.85	5.92	193.00	47640	45710
1952	55096	138.44	15.52	453.75	130791	122107
1955	52171	91.05	19.65	432.74	135050	126975
1957	52337	90.99	43.32	490.88	153512	146366
1962	58670	125.37	40.61	487.56	185043	180870
1965	143202	289.83	44.92	966.72	322560	316441
1970	79041	206.71	138.66	813.58	331613	296931
1975	82327	240.58	143.75	1091.22	401530	390571
1976	78698	215.88	208.06	1059.68	403562	391905
1977	78137	220.55	198.87	1035.87	399653	388337
1978	79375	234.57	181.42	1041.84	395247	384540
1979	78828	219.38	164.83	1040.06	407704	393271
1980	78796	211.68	155.64	1041.70	418828	402739
1981	78829	197.06	154.84	1017.62	417223	400449
1982	77893	190.23	159.74	978.73	414849	395455
1983	76610	184.50	160.87	946.26	414753	393013
1984	74314	176.38	160.80	927.50	410443	387448
1985	71062	167.67	164.07	894.06	405550	379751
1986	65447	161.76	158.81	870.41	412879	384564
1987	64095	152.42	158.86	844.87	421864	394296
1988	63006	156.57	154.47	830.01	432249	404509
1989	62321	162.45	149.77	823.19	439419	408468
1990	61845	158.09	144.84	818.21	446395	414653
1991	59976	156.99	143.85	815.15	447368	414924
1992	56885	163.94	141.97	826.21	450396	416662
1993	54009	185.75	145.75	853.57	448575	415928
1994	50824	206.15	153.03	895.54	448601	414912
1995	47068	205.33	154.07	940.36	456568	422989
1996	40458	194.37	152.29	971.86	463651	429345
1997	37377	183.70	155.59	990.19	468548	434671
1998	34480	146.34	173.92	951.34	467987	435156
1999	29453	116.04	191.40	870.72	451063	418828
2000	26017	104.48	195.12	774.88	440161	408200
2001	21342	101.36	176.17	699.19	422905	390374
2002	19590	107.26	144.10	662.59	414600	383816
2003	18303	107.86	128.24	642.78	410968	380066
2004	16943	110.17	124.69	627.80	410264	378793
2005	15871	104.27	113.31	615.37	410394	377729
2006	14611	107.18	101.69	623.02	415117	381673
2007	14064	111.46	103.87	634.01	420353	386641
2008	13503	104.61	107.48	632.98	420552	387957
2009	12858	101.78	109.47	626.81	421057	389962
2010	12405	111.30	110.26	629.25	417504	387453
2011	12047	119.40	106.82	644.07	393612	386280
2012	11573	109.55	106.16	627.67	387203	382562
2013	11151	115.69	103.30	625.98	383692	387312
2014	10770	124.70	101.02	648.47	378886	389080
2015	10404	124.43	98.92	674.63	379239	396368
2016	10027	123.91	107.15	691.31	386405	408856
2017	9738	126.98	110.96	708.47	391838	421877
2018	9674	129.64	111.52	725.97	392333	430702
2019	9646	127.86	117.75	738.56	396465	442729
2020	9619	129.63	125.16	743.29	400114	454285
2021	9458	137.92	125.73	755.81	410021	468276

注：专任教师按照教师教授学生层次归类，包含九年一贯制和十二年一贯制学校中从事小学教育的专任教师。

a)Full-time teachers classified according to the academic level of their students,including the primary education section of the nine-year and twelve-yea primary-secondary schools.

19−7　1985−2021年成人高等教育基本情况

Basic Statistics on Adult Education from 1985 to 2021

年份 Year	学校数 (所) Number of Schools (unit)	招生数 (人) New Enrollment (person)	毕业生数 (人) Graduates (person)	在校学生数 (人) Total Enrollment (person)	教职工数 (人) Teachers and Staff (person)	专任教师 (人) Full-time Teachers (person)
1985	53	41358	14543	85909	7918	3677
1986	55	38305	18626	119123	9514	4417
1987	58	30789	30352	110258	8900	3847
1988	53	43784	35680	101606	10179	4137
1989	53	43386	30687	115753	11552	4754
1990	53	32580	29317	114764	12745	5164
1991	54	26409	40382	104560	12669	4926
1992	51	49078	41748	105427	12883	5017
1993	53	71210	31104	149282	12648	5257
1994	53	81379	30786	196381	13048	5872
1995	53	61032	55764	198934	13159	6037
1996	53	59850	65204	194454	13308	6495
1997	53	65775	74017	185029	14096	6925
1998	46	73618	61603	198780	13023	6557
1999	40	87117	61611	221161	14335	7131
2000	40	82423	70810	219977	14090	7084
2001	34	103165	57373	255775	13911	6841
2002	29	111023	69723	316605	11797	6182
2003	27	128242	79518	373086	9877	5300
2004	24	132313	107645	268112	11056	6247
2005	24	108707	118379	258521	11481	6683
2006	24	95858	34999	295189	12775	7516
2007	23	106857	97584	297085	12627	7537
2008	22	152713	93079	355307	7390	4840
2009	21	136048	105081	377343	6240	4142
2010	18	133191	110347	388741	4225	2946
2011	17	147677	144703	386481	3951	2731
2012	17	166515	120404	428180	4286	2917
2013	11	165522	128297	459803	2843	1982
2014	11	178737	147592	485274	2259	1544
2015	11	163012	161377	484493	2200	1493
2016	11	179199	167440	502274	1604	1082
2017	11	157559	279185	375102	1580	1048
2018	11	233966	181058	426995	1479	970
2019	11	292911	158662	556026	1257	785
2020	11	414972	223507	742379	1248	777
2021	11	451062	280241	906118	1140	702

注：自2001年起成人高等学历教育统计口径调整为不含电大普通专科班及高职。

a)After 2001,adult higher education exclude regular specialized courses and vocational education.

19-8 研究生教育基本情况

Basic Statistics on Postgraduate Education

项　目		Item		2015	2016	2017	2018	2019	2020	2021
一、培养单位数	**（个）**	**Institutions Providing Postgraduate Programs**	**(unit)**	**33**	**33**	**33**	**33**	**34**	**34**	**35**
高等学校	（个）	Regular Institutions of Higher Education	(unit)	30	30	30	30	31	31	32
科研单位	（个）	Research Institutions	(unit)	3	3	3	3	3	3	3
二、招生数	**（人）**	**Enrollment**	**(person)**	**27548**	**28543**	**35564**	**37796**	**40675**	**50518**	**53567**
攻读博士学位	（人）	Study for Doctor's Degree	(person)	2025	2109	2312	2663	3022	3346	3726
高等学校	（人）	Regular Institutions of Higher Education	(person)	2025	2109	2312	2663	3022	3346	3726
科研单位	（人）	Research Institutions	(person)							
攻读硕士学位	（人）	Study for Master's Degree	(person)	25523	26434	33252	35133	37653	47172	49841
高等学校	（人）	Regular Institutions of Higher Education	(person)	25473	26384	33198	35041	37558	47035	49700
科研单位	（人）	Research Institutions	(person)	50	50	54	92	95	137	141
三、在校生数	**（人）**	**Total Enrollment**	**(person)**	**77630**	**82055**	**91908**	**102531**	**114618**	**131563**	**149077**
攻读博士学位	（人）	Study for Doctor's Degree	(person)	8913	9322	10060	10835	11895	13391	15001
高等学校	（人）	Regular Institutions of Higher Education	(person)	8913	9322	10060	10835	11895	13391	15001
科研单位	（人）	Research Institutions	(person)							
攻读硕士学位	（人）	Study for Master's Degree	(person)	68717	72733	81848	91696	102723	118172	134076
高等学校	（人）	Regular Institutions of Higher Education	(person)	68569	72582	81694	91499	102461	117847	133700
科研单位	（人）	Research Institutions	(person)	148	151	154	197	262	325	376
四、毕业生数	**（人）**	**Graduates**	**(person)**	**23192**	**24137**	**24755**	**26286**	**27640**	**32795**	**34454**
攻读博士学位	（人）	Study for Doctor's Degree	(person)	1494	1591	1529	1569	1712	1716	1861
高等学校	（人）	Regular Institutions of Higher Education	(person)	1494	1591	1529	1569	1712	1716	1861
科研单位	（人）	Research Institutions	(person)							
攻读硕士学位	（人）	Study for Master's Degree	(person)	21698	22546	23226	24717	25928	31079	32593
高等学校	（人）	Regular Institutions of Higher Education	(person)	21652	22500	23175	24647	25881	31006	32503
科研单位	（人）	Research Institutions	(person)	46	46	51	70	47	73	90

19-9 各市中等职业学校基本情况(2021年)

Basic Statistics on Secondary Vocational Schools by Region (2021)

地 区	Region	学校数(所) Schools (unit)	招生数(人) New Enrollment (person)	毕业生数(人) Graduates (person)	在校学生数(人) Total Enrollment (person)	专任教师数(人) Full-time Teachers (person)
全省总计	**Total**	**400**	**293603**	**221047**	**839144**	**53576**
济南市	Jinan	41	20604	17249	63819	4040
青岛市	Qingdao	52	27244	25327	90220	6942
淄博市	Zibo	18	10009	7668	28577	2413
枣庄市	Zaozhuang	18	14059	10462	40593	1794
东营市	Dongying	9	9025	6910	25714	1415
烟台市	Yantai	29	16899	15008	48000	4445
潍坊市	Weifang	32	31919	21000	84802	5790
济宁市	Jining	19	19964	14681	57026	3242
泰安市	Tai'an	14	14284	10637	40111	2587
威海市	Weihai	18	8244	5666	21343	2024
日照市	Rizhao	12	9737	8001	31471	1729
临沂市	Linyi	31	36456	26522	104176	5102
德州市	Dezhou	31	16626	13574	47162	3255
聊城市	Liaocheng	16	18178	10403	48311	2957
滨州市	Binzhou	19	11398	8522	32252	2382
菏泽市	Heze	41	28957	19417	75567	3459

注：不含技工学校数据。
a)Data in the table excludes that on Technical Schools.

19-10 各市普通中学情况(2021年)

Basic Statistics on Secondary Schools by Region (2021)

地 区	Region	普通高中 Senior Secondary Schools					普通初中 Junior Secondary Schools				
		学校数(所) Schools (unit)	招生数(人) New Enrollment (person)	毕业生数(人) Graduates (person)	在校学生数(人) Total Enrollment (person)	专任教师数(人) Full-time Teachers (person)	学校数(所) Schools (unit)	招生数(人) New Enrollment (person)	毕业生数(人) Graduates (person)	在校学生数(人) Total Enrollment (person)	专任教师数(人) Full-time Teachers (person)
全省总计	**Total**	**723**	**628796**	**539843**	**1826401**	**155902**	**3296**	**1247046**	**1094495**	**3881202**	**316086**
济南市	Jinan	63	50299	45816	147496	12209	269	82717	77029	259282	23378
青岛市	Qingdao	85	52780	37866	151923	13223	260	93084	85359	294018	26298
淄博市	Zibo	37	28056	29366	89654	7732	155	39550	40937	161902	16064
枣庄市	Zaozhuang	29	27689	21995	74548	5753	114	66252	50487	185278	12638
东营市	Dongying	16	14755	13513	43175	3985	89	22018	22946	87786	8966
烟台市	Yantai	47	27833	27604	85016	9110	226	52164	49699	211497	21280
潍坊市	Weifang	64	62753	53573	181191	18270	311	89503	109981	300757	27792
济宁市	Jining	47	56733	45296	150008	11478	290	116551	101924	359991	28078
泰安市	Tai'an	40	26724	34758	95479	8787	171	53922	48332	209074	17863
威海市	Weihai	17	11555	9005	32702	3734	94	24291	21336	95895	8962
日照市	Rizhao	18	17809	16856	57813	4837	86	33628	30106	97841	8454
临沂市	Linyi	68	68465	58852	212046	16574	323	186706	127434	510168	36010
德州市	Dezhou	34	41085	33768	117284	9775	176	68868	67276	203953	16844
聊城市	Liaocheng	49	47554	37366	131168	10286	219	104934	78463	293485	19825
滨州市	Binzhou	40	22615	21859	70255	6690	137	38464	40963	112757	10805
菏泽市	Heze	69	72091	52350	186643	13459	376	174394	142223	497518	32829

注：专任教师按照教师教授学生层次归类。
a)Full-time teachers classified according to the academic level of their students.

19−11 各市小学基本情况(2021年)

Basic Statistics on Primary Schools by Region (2021)

地 区	Region	学校数(所) Schools (unit)	招生数(人) New Enrollment (Person)	毕业生数(人) Graduates (person)	在校学生数(人) Total Enrollment (person)	专任教师数(人) Full-time Teachers (person)
全省总计	**Total**	**9458**	**1379227**	**1257272**	**7558069**	**468276**
济南市	Jinan	641	120445	82164	610438	38467
青岛市	Qingdao	676	117741	92980	630538	39199
淄博市	Zibo	274	51126	39500	220015	16562
枣庄市	Zaozhuang	501	57715	66034	357185	22706
东营市	Dongying	103	29781	22188	127842	8884
烟台市	Yantai	292	66779	52184	296995	20260
潍坊市	Weifang	687	119931	89036	606239	41619
济宁市	Jining	1055	115958	119821	640040	42314
泰安市	Tai'an	485	67522	54304	321164	21511
威海市	Weihai	98	26746	23928	130757	8465
日照市	Rizhao	253	42188	33823	211074	12840
临沂市	Linyi	1335	197121	187919	1088769	58650
德州市	Dezhou	674	75688	69395	438172	28663
聊城市	Liaocheng	698	96287	107342	618527	37208
滨州市	Binzhou	270	50002	38875	276880	17479
菏泽市	Heze	1416	144197	177779	983434	53449

注：专任教师按照教师教授学生层次归类。
a)Full-time teachers classified according to the academic level of their students.

19−12 各市幼儿园基本情况(2021年)

Basic Statistics on Kindergartens by Region (2021)

地 区	Region	幼儿园数(所) Number of Kindergartens (unit)	入园(班)幼儿数(人) Entrants (person)	在园(班)幼儿数(人) Enrolment (person)	离园(班)幼儿数(人) Graduates (person)	专任教师数(人) Full-timeTeachers (person)
全省总计	**Total**	**25203**	**1156647**	**3893098**	**1235255**	**269592**
济南市	Jinan	2227	117649	369201	110012	26344
青岛市	Qingdao	2518	103562	367883	103557	28265
淄博市	Zibo	766	46203	158352	47337	11183
枣庄市	Zaozhuang	788	39560	117069	47862	6746
东营市	Dongying	382	26065	92537	24749	7807
烟台市	Yantai	949	51310	187444	60984	13443
潍坊市	Weifang	2082	104429	375077	104203	26711
济宁市	Jining	2354	126483	364118	114212	21264
泰安市	Tai'an	1383	53356	203967	65316	16061
威海市	Weihai	349	23325	79835	25583	6221
日照市	Rizhao	700	37775	129040	40937	8798
临沂市	Linyi	3456	160946	517052	163846	35284
德州市	Dezhou	1982	58634	217735	73380	16519
聊城市	Liaocheng	1214	61752	214019	71590	14071
滨州市	Binzhou	872	46588	163219	46350	11539
菏泽市	Heze	3181	99010	336550	135337	19336

19－13　各市特殊教育基本情况(2021年)

Basic Statistics on Special Education by Region(2021)

地　区	Region	学校数(所) Schools (unit)	招生数(人) New Enrollment (person)	毕业生数(人) Graduates (person)	在校学生数(人) Total Enrollment (person)	专任教师数(人) Full-time Teachers (person)
全省总计	**Total**	**155**	**8637**	**7930**	**51777**	**6063**
济南市	Jinan	13	664	658	3901	505
青岛市	Qingdao	15	977	827	4910	676
淄博市	Zibo	9	446	440	2109	422
枣庄市	Zaozhuang	6	336	329	2226	171
东营市	Dongying	3	121	78	853	101
烟台市	Yantai	9	400	394	2618	335
潍坊市	Weifang	13	677	785	4315	512
济宁市	Jining	12	1005	741	5631	448
泰安市	Tai'an	5	418	399	2247	268
威海市	Weihai	4	146	154	1075	179
日照市	Rizhao	8	321	380	2026	209
临沂市	Linyi	16	1242	967	7877	877
德州市	Dezhou	13	588	539	3618	364
聊城市	Liaocheng	9	537	621	3598	363
滨州市	Binzhou	8	260	239	1796	232
菏泽市	Heze	12	499	379	2977	401

注：专任教师按照教师教授学生层次归类。

a) Full-time teachers classified according to the academic level of their students.

19-14 各市中小学教职工情况(2021年)

Basic Statistics on Teachers and Staff of Primary and Secondary Schools by Region (2021)

单位:人 (person)

地区	Region	普通中学教职工 Teachers and Staff of Secondary Schools	普通中学专任教师 Full-time Teachers of Secondary School Students	小学教职工 Teachers and Staff of Primary Schools	小学专任教师 Full-time Teachers of Primary School Students
全省总计	**Total**	**586421**	**471988**	**410021**	**468276**
济南市	Jinan	48163	35587	30165	38467
青岛市	Qingdao	46282	39521	36702	39199
淄博市	Zibo	28124	23796	14245	16562
枣庄市	Zaozhuang	22581	18391	21604	22706
东营市	Dongying	15874	12951	6870	8884
烟台市	Yantai	38197	30390	16312	20260
潍坊市	Weifang	59828	46062	33807	41619
济宁市	Jining	47445	39556	39293	42314
泰安市	Tai'an	31882	26650	18656	21511
威海市	Weihai	16156	12696	6859	8465
日照市	Rizhao	15819	13291	11454	12840
临沂市	Linyi	62360	52584	52291	58650
德州市	Dezhou	32665	26619	26077	28663
聊城市	Liaocheng	38374	30111	33942	37208
滨州市	Binzhou	24437	17495	13662	17479
菏泽市	Heze	58234	46288	48082	53449

注：专任教师按照教师教授学生层次归类,小学专任教师含有一贯制学校中从事小学教育的专任教师。

a) Full-time teachers are classified according to the academic level of their students, primary full-time teachers including the ones engaged in primary education in general secondary school.

19-15 各市普通中小学专任教师学历情况(2021年)

Basic Statistics on Education of Teachers and Staff of Primary and Secondary Schools by Region (2021)

单位:人 (person)

地 区	Region	普通高中专任教师 Full-time Teachers of Senior Secondary Schools	#本科及以上 With Undergraduate Education or Higher	普通初中专任教师 Full-time Teachers of Junior Secondary Schools	#本科及以上 With Undergraduate Education or Higher	普通小学专任教师 Full-time Teachers of Regular Primary Schools	#本科及以上 With Undergraduate Education or Higher
全省总计	**Total**	**155902**	**154363**	**316086**	**290392**	**468276**	**369629**
济南市	Jinan	12209	12205	23378	22717	38467	33735
青岛市	Qingdao	13223	13221	26298	25954	39199	35910
淄博市	Zibo	7732	7702	16064	15851	16562	15399
枣庄市	Zaozhuang	5753	5664	12638	11955	22706	19054
东营市	Dongying	3985	3969	8966	8315	8884	7165
烟台市	Yantai	9110	9057	21280	20463	20260	18173
潍坊市	Weifang	18270	18180	27792	26544	41619	35782
济宁市	Jining	11478	11379	28078	24326	42314	28819
泰安市	Tai'an	8787	8710	17863	15937	21511	15645
威海市	Weihai	3734	3713	8962	8813	8465	8059
日照市	Rizhao	4837	4826	8454	7874	12840	10983
临沂市	Linyi	16574	16239	36010	33560	58650	45838
德州市	Dezhou	9775	9617	16844	14091	28663	18925
聊城市	Liaocheng	10286	10166	19825	17294	37208	27218
滨州市	Binzhou	6690	6633	10805	9825	17479	13600
菏泽市	Heze	13459	13082	32829	26873	53449	35324

注：专任教师按照教师教授学生层次归类。

a)Full-time teachers classified according to the academic level of their students.

19-16 各市幼儿园、特殊教育专任教师学历情况(2021年)
Basic Statistics on Education of Teachers and Staff of Kindergartens and Special Education(2021)

单位：人 (person)

地　区	Region	幼儿园专任教师 Full-time Teachers of Kindergartens	#本科及以上 With Undergraduate Education or Higher	特殊教育专任教师 Full-time Teachers of Special Education	#本科及以上 With Undergraduate Education or Higher
全省总计	**Total**	**269592**	**70819**	**6063**	**4952**
济 南 市	Jinan	26344	8614	505	443
青 岛 市	Qingdao	28265	10742	676	628
淄 博 市	Zibo	11183	3916	422	407
枣 庄 市	Zaozhuang	6746	1963	171	150
东 营 市	Dongying	7807	4610	101	93
烟 台 市	Yantai	13443	3837	335	290
潍 坊 市	Weifang	26711	9067	512	464
济 宁 市	Jining	21264	3361	448	365
泰 安 市	Tai'an	16061	3083	268	234
威 海 市	Weihai	6221	2916	179	173
日 照 市	Rizhao	8798	1744	209	148
临 沂 市	Linyi	35284	4518	877	602
德 州 市	Dezhou	16519	2995	364	227
聊 城 市	Liaocheng	14071	3436	363	254
滨 州 市	Binzhou	11539	3399	232	203
菏 泽 市	Heze	19336	2618	401	271

注：专任教师按照教师教授学生层次归类。
a)Full-time teachers classified according to the academic level of their students.

19-17 1978-2021年重要科技成果数量

Major Achievements in Science and Technology from 1978 to 2021

单位:项 (unit)

年份 Year	成果数量 Number of Achievements	#农业 Agriculture	#工业 Industry	国际领先先进水平 Advanced Internationally	国内领先先进水平 Advanced nationally
1978	652	116	443	19	283
1979	456	90	261	21	149
1980	657	195	396	25	210
1981	704	169	485	29	201
1982	732	153	516	35	298
1983	977	209	660	26	378
1984	997	196	730	21	420
1985	1196	277	758	41	566
1986	1337	183	933	75	634
1987	1525	264	964	92	838
1988	1786	300	1104	118	1045
1989	1957	325	1220	135	1081
1990	2112	375	1246	150	1148
1991	2488	541	1405	175	1503
1992	2668	57	1265	327	1538
1993	2858	605	1418	372	1745
1994	3113	696	1487	416	2131
1995	3251	702	1524	466	2272
1996	3388	709	1599	471	2353
1997	3507	737	1517	456	2678
1998	3558	614	1515	724	2516
1999	3688	557	1270	744	2737
2000	3728	575	1289	599	2861
2001	3112	494	1138	506	2439
2002	3018	452	1117	486	2371
2003	2896	433	1071	466	2276
2004	3028	454	1120	485	2392
2005	2408	320	539	534	1741
2006	2313	338	630	448	1742
2007	2346	330	704	543	1662
2008	2330	301	677	592	1618
2009	2364	306	849	751	1412
2010	2367	391	751	676	1316
2011	2379	305	723	647	1296
2012	2393	338	853	609	1349
2013	2332	297	866	681	1067
2014	2955	440	1095	817	1146
2015	3011	385	1019	967	1212
2016	3016	421	919	762	1095
2017	2537	363	796	610	973
2018	1791	232	451	416	682
2019	2552	316	807	735	957
2020	2342	338	673	485	988
2021	2908	329	754	638	1002

19−18 科技成果情况

Basic Statistics on Science and Technology

单位：项 (unit)

类 别	Category	2015	2016	2017	2018	2019	2020	2021
一、国家级科技成果奖励成果	**National Scientific and Technical Award**	**33**	**31**	**19**	**25**	**32**	**31**	
国家技术发明奖	National Technology Invention Award	5	7	3	4	5	6	
国家自然科学奖	State Natural Science Award	2			3	1	1	
国家科技进步奖	The State Scientific and Technological Progress Award	26	23	16	17	26	24	
国际合作奖	International Cooperation Award		1		1			
二、省级重要科技成果	**Important Scientific and Technical Award**	**3011**	**3016**	**2537**	**1791**	**2552**	**2342**	**2908**
三、省科学技术奖	**Provincial Science and Technology Award**							
自然科学奖	Natural Science Award	13	11	17	24	29	39	45
技术发明奖	Technological Invention Award	13	12	7	13	13	15	11
科技进步奖	Scientific and Technological Progress Award	112	112	122	157	199	215	243
四、专利情况	**Patent Applications**							
申请量	Number of Patent Applications	193220	212911	204861	238795	263407	369349	
其中发明专利	Inventions	93475	88359	67773	75817	69511	87330	
授权量	Number of Patent Applications Granted	98101	98093	100522	132382	146481	238778	329838
其中发明专利	Inventions	16881	19404	19090	20338	20652	26745	36345

注：1.2017年以前，专利申请量是指国家知识产权局受理的专利申请数量；从2017年开始，是指国家知识产权局受理的按规定缴足申请费符合进入初步审查阶段条件的专利申请数量。2021年起，国家知识产权局不再发布专利申请量数据。(下表同)

2.科技部科技奖励评审工作周期调整为两年一次或五年两次，国家级科技成果奖励成果数据统计频次相应调整，无2021年度数据。

a)Before 2017,the amount of patent application refers to the number of patent applications accepted by the State Intellectual Property Office;from 2017, it refers to the amount of application fees paid by the State Intellectual Property Office and the number of patent applications that have entered the preliminary examination stage.Since 2021, the State Intellectual Property Office has stopped publishing data on the amount of patent applications. The same applies to the following relevant tables.

b) Since the review frequency of scientific and technical award by MOST was adjusted to once every two years or twice every five years, the statistical frequency of National Scientific and Technical Award is adjusted accordingly. Annual data for 2021 are not available.

19−19 各市国内三种专利授权数（2021年）
Patents Granted by Region (2021)

单位：件 (piece)

地区	Region	申请授权数合计 Number of Patents Application Granted	发明 Inventions	实用新型 Utility Models	外观设计 Designs
总计	**Total**	**329838**	**36345**	**264072**	**29421**
济南市	Jinan	61767	8208	49784	3775
青岛市	Qingdao	75652	10210	58831	6611
淄博市	Zibo	16301	1389	13706	1206
枣庄市	Zaozhuang	7681	649	6364	668
东营市	Dongying	8614	1603	6702	309
烟台市	Yantai	21917	2487	17686	1744
潍坊市	Weifang	28888	3523	22421	2944
济宁市	Jining	17059	1468	14316	1275
泰安市	Tai'an	9708	839	8217	652
威海市	Weihai	13461	1005	11180	1276
日照市	Rizhao	6989	515	6024	450
临沂市	Linyi	19283	1669	14125	3489
德州市	Dezhou	12137	619	9794	1724
聊城市	Liaocheng	11007	920	9097	990
滨州市	Binzhou	9921	872	8381	668
菏泽市	Heze	9453	369	7444	1640

19-20 R&D经费支出情况(2021年)

单位：万元

类 别	Category	R&D经费内部支出合计 Internal Expenditure on R&D	基础研究支出 Basic Research	应用研究支出 Applied Research
总 计		**19446588**	**737455**	**1193994**
一、按行业分	**by Sector**			
农、林、牧、渔业	Agriculture,Forestry,Animal Husbandry and Fishing	23597	151	655
采矿业	Mining	418464	28712	55771
制造业	Manufacturing	15259876	30714	346138
电力、燃气及水的生产和供应业	Production and Supply of Electric Power and Heat Power	243469	217	10230
建筑业	Construction	597076	1920	59471
批发和零售业	Wholesale and Retail Trade	2573		
交通运输、仓储和邮政业	Traffic,Transport,Storage and Post	45674		342
住宿和餐饮业	Hotels and Catering Services			
信息传输、软件和信息技术服务业	Information Transfer, Software and Information Technology Services	466013		4432
金融业	Financial Intermediation	1870		57
房地产业	Real Estate			
租赁和商务服务业	Leasing and Business Services	10333		101
科学研究和技术服务业	Scientific Research and Technical Service	1310598	206729	254610
水利、环境和公共设施管理业	Management of Water Conservancy,Environment and Public Facilities	18187		1343
居民服务、修理和其他服务业	Households Services, Repair and Other Services			
教 育	Education	916811	384749	431208
卫生和社会工作	Health and Social Work	128146	84258	29608
文化、体育和娱乐业	Culture,Sports and Entertainment	3900	5	27
公共管理、社会保障和社会组织	Public management and Social Organization			
国际组织	International Organization			
二、按地区分	**by Region**			
济南市	Jinan	3067049	267574	386592
青岛市	Qingdao	3547948	244788	248964
淄博市	Zibo	1194271	18137	68284
枣庄市	Zaozhuang	306570	7857	27525
东营市	Dongying	809049	28834	43268
烟台市	Yantai	1731898	48797	55158
潍坊市	Weifang	1499827	18719	69592
济宁市	Jining	806575	27968	29343
泰安市	Tai'an	725904	19770	76366
威海市	Weihai	832726	3398	13486
日照市	Rizhao	682504	994	39549
临沂市	Linyi	1127486	16422	39425
德州市	Dezhou	999525	5495	27003
聊城市	Liaocheng	808556	13977	25902
滨州市	Binzhou	1003459	11252	29283
菏泽市	Heze	303241	3473	14256

注：农林牧渔业、金融业数据为2009年R&D资源清查数据。

Basic Statistics On Expenditure on R&D(2021)

(10 000 yuan)

试验发展支出 Experimental Development	政府资金 Government Appropriation Funds	企业资金 Self-raised Funds by Enterprises	境外资金 Foreign funds	其他资金 Other Funds	R&D经费外部支出合计 External expenditure on R&D	对境内研究机构的支出 Expenditure On Domestic Research Institutions	对境内高等学校支出 Expenditure On Domestic colleges and universities	对境内企业支出 Expenditure On Domestic Enterprises	对境外支出 Expenditure On Overseas
17515140	**1732299**	**17505480**	**19320**	**189490**	**1129405**	**219550**	**126789**	**651780**	**113363**
22792	3770	19784		44	1105	861	245		
333981	6108	410710		1646	38324	10544	12189	15571	20
14883024	369924	14850403	10487	29061	781399	131161	68735	471861	109642
233022	726	242328		415	47411	5755	10118	31539	
535684	905	595934	197	40	9539	2581	4442	2517	
2573	497	2077			114	114			
45332	106	45523		46	22533	388	1825	20319	
461580	24027	441956		30	56571	582	298	55691	
1813		1870							
10232	487	9846			1431	574	24	833	
849259	727007	497641	7749	78202	122585	53191	10922	41357	3262
16844	97	18085		5	701	191	75	435	
100854	506926	331850	872	77163	46328	13048	17856	11008	345
14280	91499	33798	10	2838	883	514	61	215	94
3869	221	3674	5		481	46		434	
2412882	628440	2388214	3730	46665	269410	26124	27058	167562	31330
3054196	545005	2919743	13858	69343	279755	85368	42270	133561	18347
1107850	84899	1098169	43	11160	52662	31825	3762	16782	271
271188	9672	294451	1	2446	6694	2564	1201	2929	
736947	5052	802876	36	1085	32654	12110	10841	8849	854
1627943	153259	1572131	331	6177	75477	11680	6437	51993	5366
1411515	60396	1433198	114	6119	163383	7344	9813	125531	20694
749264	62483	735873		8219	68817	6268	3737	28875	29697
629768	31152	693608	236	907	20009	8224	3419	7343	1024
815842	17516	813466	346	1397	28354	6386	4417	15334	2217
641961	24809	653526		4169	14792	3308	1183	10017	176
1071640	31465	1087868		8153	64445	4447	2218	54872	2903
967027	23448	969756		6320	20640	7347	4650	8623	21
768678	34593	758925	1	15037	13563	2531	1098	9513	421
962925	13799	987168	624	1868	10867	1431	3262	6164	9
285513	6311	296506		424	7886	2593	1423	3832	37

a)Data on Financial Intermediation , Agriculture, Forestry, Animal Husbandry and Fishery come from the result of R&D resource inventory of 2009.

19－21　R&D人员情况（2021年）

Basic Statistics On R&D Personnel(2021)

类　别	Category	有研究与试验发展活动单位数(个) Number of Units with Research and Development Activities (unit)	研究与试验发展人员(人) Research and Development Personnel (person)	全时人员 Full-time Personnel	非全时人员 Part-time Personnel
总　计		**17397**	**695945**	**468712**	**227232**
一、按行业分	**by Sector**				
农、林、牧、渔业	Agriculture,Forestry,Animal Husbandry and Fishing	27	848	594	254
采矿业	Mining	144	22155	10895	11260
制造业	Manufacturing	15175	498085	359844	138241
电力、燃气及水的生产和供应业	Production and Supply of Electric Power and Heat Power	328	9228	5543	3685
建筑业	Construction	257	20579	13368	7211
批发和零售业	Wholesale and Retail Trade	11	150	98	52
交通运输、仓储和邮政业	Traffic,Transport,Storage and Post	61	2205	885	1320
住宿和餐饮业	Hotels and Catering Services				
信息传输、软件和信息技术服务业	Information Transfer, Software and Information Technology Services	277	14207	10828	3379
金融业	Financial Intermediation	1	133	37	96
房地产业	Real Estate				
租赁和商务服务业	Leasing and Business Services	44	781	607	174
科学研究和技术服务业	Scientific Research and Technical Service	705	37498	27207	10291
水利、环境和公共设施管理业	Management of Water Conservancy,Environment and Public Facilities	40	617	397	220
居民服务、修理和其他服务业	Households Services, Repair and Other Services				
教　育	Education	233	77400	32113	45287
卫生和社会工作	Health and Social Work	78	11507	5962	5543
文化、体育和娱乐业	Culture,Sports and Entertainment	16	552	334	219
公共管理、社会保障和社会组织	Public management and Social Organization				
国际组织	International Organization				
二、按地区分	**by Region**				
济南市	Jinan	1455	99150	65097	34052
青岛市	Qingdao	2617	126288	90346	35942
淄博市	Zibo	1156	48234	33061	15173
枣庄市	Zaozhuang	451	14045	9048	4997
东营市	Dongying	394	20812	13712	7100
烟台市	Yantai	1506	62899	44642	18257
潍坊市	Weifang	1756	68192	47854	20338
济宁市	Jining	1386	40983	27447	13537
泰安市	Tai'an	523	25350	14713	10637
威海市	Weihai	784	32287	23358	8929
日照市	Rizhao	565	17458	10529	6929
临沂市	Linyi	1480	36057	23391	12666
德州市	Dezhou	780	30549	18689	11860
聊城市	Liaocheng	799	22016	15053	6963
滨州市	Binzhou	1011	34222	22745	11476
菏泽市	Heze	732	17404	9028	8376

19-22 R&D人员折合全时当量情况（2021年）

Basic Statistics On Full-time Equivalent of R&D Personnel(2021)

单位：人年 (man-year)

类别	Category	R&D人员折合全时当量 Full-time Equivalent of R&D Personnel	基础研究人员 Basic Research Personnel	应用研究人员 Applied Research Personnel	试验发展人员 Experimental Development Personnel
总计		**447642**	**29228**	**38192**	**380222**
一、按行业分	**by Sector**				
农、林、牧、渔业	Agriculture,Forestry,Animal Husbandry and Fishing	695	7	41	646
采矿业	Mining	12113	2780	2640	6693
制造业	Manufacturing	332185	762	9664	321759
电力、燃气及水的生产和供应业	Production and Supply of Electric Power and Heat Power	5081	7	224	4850
建筑业	Construction	14193	84	1773	12337
批发和零售业	Wholesale and Retail Trade	76			76
交通运输、仓储和邮政业	Traffic,Transport,Storage and Post	1129		24	1105
住宿和餐饮业	Hotels and Catering Services				
信息传输、软件和信息技术服务业	Information Transfer, Software and Information Technology Services	10069		192	9877
金融业	Financial Intermediation	28		12	16
房地产业	Real Estate				
租赁和商务服务业	Leasing and Business Services	513		5	508
科学研究和技术服务业	Scientific Research and Technical Service	27929	3955	6249	17726
水利、环境和公共设施管理业	Management of Water Conservancy,Environment and Public Facilities	384		30	353
居民服务、修理和其他服务业	Households Services, Repair and Other Services				
教育	Education	35851	18351	14736	2764
卫生和社会工作	Health and Social Work	7079	3282	2600	1196
文化、体育和娱乐业	Culture,Sports and Entertainment	319		2	316
公共管理、社会保障和社会组织	Public management and Social Organization				
国际组织	International Organization				
二、按地区分	**by Region**				
济南市	Jinan	61894	10273	10343	41279
青岛市	Qingdao	83263	6929	6311	70022
淄博市	Zibo	31030	988	2107	27935
枣庄市	Zaozhuang	9133	249	1041	7843
东营市	Dongying	13155	2817	575	9764
烟台市	Yantai	40857	1742	2130	36986
潍坊市	Weifang	46562	1182	3421	41959
济宁市	Jining	27408	1383	2035	23990
泰安市	Tai'an	19247	963	4388	13896
威海市	Weihai	20517	91	812	19615
日照市	Rizhao	10637	127	678	9832
临沂市	Linyi	22385	672	984	20729
德州市	Dezhou	17315	560	818	15936
聊城市	Liaocheng	13947	666	709	12572
滨州市	Binzhou	20781	391	930	19460
菏泽市	Heze	9513	197	910	8406

19−23 规模以上工业企业R&D经费支出情况（2021年）

单位：万元

类 别	Category	R&D经费内部支出合计 Internal Expenditure on R&D	基础研究支出 Basic Research
总 计		**15653402**	**59643**
一、按企业规模分	**by Enterprise Size**		
大型企业	Large-sized Enterprises	7465268	45147
中型企业	Medium-sized Enterprises	3502092	11225
小型企业	Small-sized Enterprises	4553758	2991
微型企业	Micro-enterprises	132285	279
二、按登记注册类型分	**by Status of Registration**		
内资企业	Domestic Funded Enterprises	13652695	56523
国有企业	State-owned Enterprises	175035	
集体企业	Collective-owned Enterprises	22219	
股份合作企业	Cooperative Enterprises	4059	
联营企业	Joint Ownership Enterprises	367	
有限责任公司	Limited Liability Corporations	4722429	15533
股份有限公司	Share-holding Corporations Limited	2950902	34444
私营企业	Private Enterprises	5777683	6546
其他企业	Other Enterprises		
港、澳、台商投资企业	Enterprises with Funds from Hong Kong, Macao and Taiwan	791815	1045
合资经营企业(港或澳、台资)	Joint-ventures Enterprises	279307	1045
合作经营企业(港或澳、台资)	Cooperative Enterprises	3114	
港、澳、台商独资经营企业	Enterprises with Sole Investment	331982	
港、澳、台商投资股份有限公司	Share-holding Corporations Ltd. With Funds from Hong Kong, Macao and Taiwan	176772	
其他港澳台投资企业	Other Enterprises with Funds from Hong Kong,Macao and Taiwan	640	
外商投资企业	Foreign Funded Enterprises	1208892	2076
中外合资经营企业	Joint-venture Enterprises	650593	250
中外合作经营企业	Cooperation Enterprises	47452	
外资企业	Enterprises with Sole Foreign Funds	318570	264
外商投资股份有限公司	Share-holding Corporations Ltd. With Foreign Investment	191188	1562
其他外商投资企业	Other Foreign Funded Enterprises	1090	
三、按工业行业大类分	**by Sector**		
采掘业	**Mining**	**418464**	**28712**
煤炭开采和洗选业	Mining and Washing of Coal	155968	
石油和天然气开采业	Extraction of Petroleum and Natural Gas	80128	28532
黑色金属矿采选业	Mining of Ferrous Metal Ores	57959	
有色金属矿采选业	Mining of Non-ferrous Metal Ores	57910	58
非金属矿采选业	Mining and Processing of Nonmetal Ores	9877	
开采专业及辅助性活动	Mining Specialties and Auxiliary Activities	56623	122
其他采矿业	Mining of Other Ores		
制造业	**Manufacturing**	**14991468**	**30714**
农副食品加工业	Processing of Food from Agricultural Products	661599	1084
食品制造业	Manufacture of Foods	233187	7165
酒、饮料和精制茶制造业	Manufacture of Wine, Drinks and Refined Tea	68330	1007
烟草制品业	Manufacture of Tobacco	875	
纺织业	Manufacture of Textile	331810	502
纺织服装、服饰业	Manufacture of Textile Wearing Apparel and Finery	64264	46
皮革、毛皮、羽毛及其制品和制鞋业	Manufacture of Leather, Fur, Feather & Its Products and Footwear	48706	
木材加工及木 竹、藤、棕、草制品业	Processing of Timbers, Manufacture of Wood, Bamboo, Rattan, Palm, and Straw Products	113432	
家具制造业	Manufacture of Furniture	27803	543

Expenditures of Industrial Enterprises above Designated Size on R&D(2021)

（10 000yuan）

应用研究支出 Applied Research	试验发展支出 Experimental Development	政府资金 Government Appropriation Funds	企业资金 Self-raised Funds by Enterprises	境外资金 Foreign funds	其他资金 Other Funds	R&D经费内部支出占营业收入比重（%） Ratio of Expenditure on R&D to Business Revenue (%)
391747	**15202012**	**298711**	**15331898**	**10487**	**12305**	**1.51**
181848	7238272	147771	7303499	6230	7767	1.68
89433	3401433	80331	3417229	2419	2113	1.35
116603	4434163	68103	4481675	1839	2141	1.48
3863	128143	2507	129495		283	0.50
368680	13227492	270936	13361599	8194	11965	1.55
2430	172606	1596	172285		1154	0.46
2359	19859		15988	6230		1.61
	4059	59	4001			1.09
	367		367			0.20
158099	4548798	97936	4617211	540	6741	1.49
37547	2878912	78338	2871545		1019	2.26
168246	5602891	93007	5680202	1424	3051	1.47
4590	786180	14317	776473	770	255	1.13
3229	275033	5431	273867		9	0.71
	3114		3114			2.20
1316	330666	810	330306	770	97	1.66
44	176728	8076	168546		150	1.72
	640		640			1.46
18477	1188339	13458	1193826	1524	84	1.38
4352	645991	6001	644400	172	20	1.57
11060	36392	2084	45368			1.53
1134	317171	1723	315431	1352	64	0.81
1931	187695	3581	187607			6.57
	1090	70	1020			0.22
55771	**333981**	**6108**	**410710**		**1646**	**1.46**
45784	110184	4572	151246		150	1.24
1293	50303	140	79236		752	1.04
6747	51212		57410		549	1.40
1141	56711	140	57770			4.00
807	9070	807	8874		196	0.79
	56502	450	56173			3.87
325746	**14635008**	**291877**	**14678861**	**10487**	**10243**	**1.60**
16991	643524	8846	652141		611	0.83
6513	219509	5041	228029	69	48	1.40
1026	66297	2983	65180	167		1.07
304	572		835		40	0.02
8897	322411	2758	328968		84	1.38
1309	62910	630	63635			0.87
281	48425	140	48566			1.91
4357	109075	991	112227		214	0.76
116	27144	15	27788			1.09

19－23 续表

单位：万元

类 别	Category	R&D经费内部支出合计 Internal Expenditure on R&D	基础研究支 出 Basic Research
造纸及纸制品业	Manufacture of Paper and Paper Products	287644	
印刷和记录媒介复制业	Printing, Reproduction of Recording Media	57026	5
文教、工美、体育和娱乐用品制造业	Manufacture of Culture, Education,Arts and crafts, Sport and Entertainment Goods	123051	2
石油、煤炭及其他燃料加工业	Processing of Oil, Coal and Other Fuel	635458	587
化学原料和化学制品制造业	Manufacture of Chemical Raw Material and Chemical Products	1672771	533
医药制造业	Manufacture of Medicines	1170535	7655
化学纤维制造业	Manufacture of Chemical Fiber	55805	
橡胶和塑料制品业	Manufacture of Rubber and Plastic	658575	
非金属矿物制品业	Manufacture of Non-metallic Mineral Products	549566	142
黑色金属冶炼及压延加工业	Manufacture and Processing of Ferrous Metals	1035962	4067
有色金属冶炼及压延加工业	Manufacture & Processing of Non-ferrous Metals	972812	297
金属制品业	Manufacture of Metal Products	643889	488
通用设备制造业	Manufacture of General Purpose Machinery	1075919	999
专用设备制造业	Manufacture of Special Purpose Machinery	1080349	650
汽车制造业	Manufacture of Automotive	826516	
铁路、船舶、航空航天和其他运输设备制造业	Manufacture of Railroad,Marine,Aerospace and Other Transportation Equipment	379257	1302
电气机械及器材制造业	Manufacture of Electrical Machinery & Equipment	884841	258
计算机、通信和其他电子设备制造业	Manufacture of Computer, Communications and Other Electronic Equipment	1086069	3382
仪器仪表制造业	Manufacture of Measuring Instrument	199596	
其他制造业	Other Manufacture	9565	
废弃资源综合利用业	Comprehensive Utilization of Waste	28112	
金属制品、机械和设备修理业	Metal Products, Machinery and Equipment Repair Industry	8147	
电力、热力、燃气及水的生产和供应业	**Production and Supply of Electric, Heat,Has and Water**	**243469**	**217**
电力、热力的生产和供应业	Production and Supply of Electric Power and Heat Power	210369	30
燃气生产和供应业	Production and Supply of Gas	20377	
水的生产和供应业	Production and Supply of Water	12723	187
四、按地区分	**by Region**		
济南市	Jinan	1704514	4960
青岛市	Qingdao	2300523	2792
淄博市	Zibo	1012513	
枣庄市	Zaozhuang	264782	
东营市	Dongying	772634	28653
烟台市	Yantai	1421182	383
潍坊市	Weifang	1405790	
济宁市	Jining	701179	937
泰安市	Tai'an	659149	7800
威海市	Weihai	801688	1770
日照市	Rizhao	617551	60
临沂市	Linyi	1055938	7528
德州市	Dezhou	936617	321
聊城市	Liaocheng	750938	1076
滨州市	Binzhou	958155	1869
菏泽市	Heze	290249	1493

continued

（10 000yuan）

应用研究支出 Applied Research	试验发展支出 Experimental Development	政府资金 Government Appropriation Funds	企业资金 Self-raised Funds by Enterprises	境外资金 Foreign funds	其他资金 Other Funds	R&D经费内部支出占营业收入比重（%） Ratio of Expenditure on R&D to Business Revenue (%)
913	286732	2100	285544			1.46
807	56214	582	56443			1.94
3954	119095	1158	121768		125	1.76
37233	597637	275	635182			0.53
34823	1637415	32420	1640296		55	1.42
9525	1153355	61462	1108552		521	4.00
3487	52318	1370	54435			3.13
11205	647370	4001	649971	13	4591	2.45
10451	538974	13193	536052		321	1.17
56107	975787	2814	1033145		3	1.25
17602	954912	5200	967611			1.37
7329	636071	5351	637022	204	1312	1.68
21782	1053138	25457	1048776	1246	441	3.08
27544	1052155	18702	1061219		429	3.33
10658	815858	7563	817413	322	1218	1.51
1655	376300	14716	364368	172		3.41
12620	871963	9842	868524	6243	232	3.02
12530	1070157	35271	1048747	2052		2.56
1158	198438	28247	171349			5.75
	9565	199	9366			1.89
4325	23787	545	27567			1.31
245	7902	4	8143			1.82
10230	**233022**	**726**	**242328**		**415**	**0.32**
9240	201099	597	209358		415	0.33
156	20222		20377			0.24
835	11701	129	12593			0.47
47377	1652176	61734	1641288	170	1321	1.45
18106	2279624	62625	2227402	9079	1417	1.99
14935	997577	18096	993962		454	1.67
17721	247062	3033	261704		45	1.65
38698	705283	3149	768547	36	903	0.87
20255	1400545	27906	1392953	195	129	1.56
36331	1369459	25615	1379319		855	1.28
13630	686612	16597	684441		141	1.49
55653	595695	12081	646518	39	511	2.39
9616	790303	13655	787219	346	469	2.75
29100	588391	7712	609829		10	1.38
31142	1017268	14315	1041081		543	1.66
18281	918015	14331	917267		5020	2.55
6741	743122	9490	741448			1.68
20579	935706	4824	952644	623	65	1.04
13582	275174	3549	286278		423	0.55

19-24 规模以上工业企业R&D人员情况（2021年）

单位：人

类 别	Category	研究与试验发展人员 Research and Development Personnel
总 计		**529468**
一、按企业规模分	**by Enterprise Size**	
大型企业	Large-sized Enterprises	189276
中型企业	Medium-sized Enterprises	130134
小型企业	Small-sized Enterprises	204126
微型企业	Micro-enterprises	5932
二、按登记注册类型分	**by Status of Registration**	
内资企业	Domestic Funded Enterprises	465002
国有企业	State-owned Enterprises	5966
集体企业	Collective-owned Enterprises	1398
股份合作企业	Cooperative Enterprises	259
联营企业	Joint Ownership Enterprises	17
有限责任公司	Limited Liability Corporations	145034
股份有限公司	Share-holding Corporations Limited	84813
私营企业	Private Enterprises	227515
其他企业	Other Enterprises	
港、澳、台商投资企业	Enterprises with Funds from Hong Kong, Macao and Taiwan	26029
合资经营企业(港或澳、台资)	Joint-ventures Enterprises	11554
合作经营企业(港或澳、台资)	Cooperative Enterprises	150
港、澳、台商独资经营企业	Enterprises with Sole Investment	8264
港、澳、台商投资股份有限公司	Share-holding Corporations Ltd. With Funds from Hong Kong, Macao and Taiwan	6031
其他港澳台投资企业	Other Enterprises with Funds from Hong Kong,Macao and Taiwan	30
外商投资企业	Foreign Funded Enterprises	38437
中外合资经营企业	Joint-venture Enterprises	18631
中外合作经营企业	Cooperation Enterprises	577
外资企业	Enterprises with Sole Foreign Funds	13330
外商投资股份有限公司	Share-holding Corporations Ltd. With Foreign Investment	5789
其他外商投资企业	Other Foreign Funded Enterprises	110
三、按工业行业大类分	**by Sector**	
采掘业	**Mining**	**22155**
煤炭开采和洗选业	Mining and Washing of Coal	11797
石油和天然气开采业	Extraction of Petroleum and Natural Gas	4249
黑色金属矿采选业	Mining of Ferrous Metal Ores	1436
有色金属矿采选业	Mining of Non-ferrous Metal Ores	2343
非金属矿采选业	Mining and Processing of Nonmetal Ores	609
开采专业及辅助性活动	Mining Specialties and Auxiliary Activities	1721
其他采矿业	Mining of Other Ores	
制造业	**Manufacturing**	**498085**
农副食品加工业	Processing of Food from Agricultural Products	23127
食品制造业	Manufacture of Foods	14059
酒、饮料和精制茶制造业	Manufacture of Wine, Drinks and Refined Tea	3855
烟草制品业	Manufacture of Tobacco	120
纺织业	Manufacture of Textile	23553
纺织服装、服饰业	Manufacture of Textile Wearing Apparel and Finery	5761
皮革、毛皮、羽毛及其制品和制鞋业	Manufacture of Leather, Fur, Feather & Its Products and Footwear	2519
木材加工及木 竹、藤、棕、草制品业	Processing of Timbers, Manufacture of Wood, Bamboo, Rattan, Palm, and Straw Products	5096
家具制造业	Manufacture of Furniture	1596

Basic Statistics On R&D Personnel of Industrial Enterprises above Designated Size(2021)

(person)

本年度参加项目人员 Personnel involved in the project current year	科技管理和服务人员 Technology management and service personnel	全时人员 Full-time Personnel	非全时人员 Part-time Personnel
492984	**36484**	**376282**	**153186**
178022	11254	137564	51712
121259	8875	90241	39893
188179	15947	144995	59131
5524	408	3482	2450
432676	32326	330266	134736
5606	360	4093	1873
1309	89	843	555
237	22	211	48
17		14	3
134211	10823	99100	45934
80206	4607	65805	19008
211090	16425	160200	67315
24386	1643	17176	8853
10846	708	6932	4622
131	19	119	31
7686	578	6058	2206
5698	333	4047	1984
25	5	20	10
35922	2515	28840	9597
17493	1138	14194	4437
559	18	488	89
12329	1001	9324	4006
5437	352	4738	1051
104	6	96	14
20592	**1563**	**10895**	**11260**
10891	906	4961	6836
3953	296	3069	1180
1341	95	697	739
2195	148	1281	1062
550	59	247	362
1662	59	640	1081
463979	**34106**	**359844**	**138241**
21087	2040	15667	7460
13114	945	9814	4245
3625	230	2664	1191
107	13	46	74
21341	2212	16894	6659
5439	322	3761	2000
2249	270	1728	791
4800	296	2769	2327
1468	128	982	614

19-24 续表

单位：人

类 别	Category	研究与试验发展人员 Research and Development Personnel
造纸及纸制品业	Manufacture of Paper and Paper Products	9857
印刷和记录媒介复制业	Printing, Reproduction of Recording Media	3208
文教、工美、体育和娱乐用品制造业	Manufacture of Culture, Education,Arts and crafts, Sport and Entertainment Goods	8313
石油、煤炭及其他燃料加工业	Processing of Oil, Coal and Other Fuel	9997
化学原料和化学制品制造业	Manufacture of Chemical Raw Material and Chemical Products	49365
医药制造业	Manufacture of Medicines	32322
化学纤维制造业	Manufacture of Chemical Fiber	1658
橡胶和塑料制品业	Manufacture of Rubber and Plastic	24604
非金属矿物制品业	Manufacture of Non-metallic Mineral Products	27094
黑色金属冶炼及压延加工业	Manufacture and Processing of Ferrous Metals	13845
有色金属冶炼及压延加工业	Manufacture & Processing of Non-ferrous Metals	14318
金属制品业	Manufacture of Metal Products	23376
通用设备制造业	Manufacture of General Purpose Machinery	44288
专用设备制造业	Manufacture of Special Purpose Machinery	39654
汽车制造业	Manufacture of Automotive	31189
铁路、船舶、航空航天和其他运输设备制造业	Manufacture of Railroad,Marine,Aerospace and Other Transportation Equipment	11285
电气机械及器材制造业	Manufacture of Electrical Machinery & Equipment	27782
计算机、通信和其他电子设备制造业	Manufacture of Computer, Communications and Other Electronic Equipment	34641
仪器仪表制造业	Manufacture of Measuring Instrument	9493
其他制造业	Other Manufacture	576
废弃资源综合利用业	Comprehensive Utilization of Waste	776
金属制品、机械和设备修理业	Metal Products, Machinery and Equipment Repair Industry	758
电力、热力、燃气及水的生产和供应业	**Production and Supply of Electric, Heat,Has and Water**	**9228**
电力、热力的生产和供应业	Production and Supply of Electric Power and Heat Power	7117
燃气生产和供应业	Production and Supply of Gas	1029
水的生产和供应业	Production and Supply of Water	1082
四、按地区分	**by Region**	
济南市	Jinan	43040
青岛市	Qingdao	79871
淄博市	Zibo	38519
枣庄市	Zaozhuang	11592
东营市	Dongying	18680
烟台市	Yantai	51934
潍坊市	Weifang	60932
济宁市	Jining	34618
泰安市	Tai'an	20461
威海市	Weihai	30538
日照市	Rizhao	14548
临沂市	Linyi	32507
德州市	Dezhou	25501
聊城市	Liaocheng	18580
滨州市	Binzhou	31613
菏泽市	Heze	16534

continued

(person)

本年度参加项目人员 Personnel involved in the project current year	科技管理和服务人员 Technology management and service personnel	全时人员 Full-time Personnel	非全时人员 Part-time Personnel
9255	602	6413	3444
3016	192	2138	1070
7556	757	5855	2458
9333	664	5009	4988
46026	3339	35228	14137
30582	1740	25919	6403
1539	119	1139	519
22944	1660	17528	7076
24887	2207	18024	9070
12828	1017	8694	5151
12804	1514	9918	4400
21717	1659	16381	6995
41414	2874	31346	12942
37230	2424	30037	9617
29196	1993	23233	7956
10687	598	9178	2107
25883	1899	20704	7078
32835	1806	29207	5434
9036	457	8002	1491
545	31	481	95
710	66	597	179
726	32	488	270
8413	**815**	**5543**	**3685**
6507	610	4221	2896
901	128	537	492
1005	77	785	297
40364	2676	32225	10815
73770	6101	61519	18352
35939	2580	27793	10726
10816	776	7997	3595
17503	1177	12677	6003
48763	3171	38814	13120
57613	3319	44506	16426
32558	2060	23946	10672
19331	1130	12440	8021
28056	2482	22328	8210
13534	1014	9314	5234
30405	2102	21522	10985
23531	1970	16821	8680
17653	927	13820	4760
27800	3813	21871	9742
15348	1186	8689	7845

19-25 规模以上工业企业R&D人员折合全时当量情况（2021年）
Full-time Equivalent of R&D Personnel of Industrial Enterprises above Designated Size(2021)

单位：人年 (man-year)

类别	Category	R&D人员折合全时当量 Full-time Equivalent of R&D Personnel	基础研究人员 Basic Research Personnel	应用研究人员 Applied Research Personnel	试验发展人员 Experimental Development Personnel
总计		**349379**	**3549**	**12528**	**333302**
一、按企业规模分	**by Enterprise Size**				
大型企业	Large-sized Enterprises	129999	3111	5082	121806
中型企业	Medium-sized Enterprises	86062	301	3384	82377
小型企业	Small-sized Enterprises	129758	129	3966	125663
微型企业	Micro-sized Enterprises	3561	8	96	3457
二、按登记注册类型分	**by Status of Registration**				
内资企业	Domestic Funded Enterprises	308352	3494	11753	293105
国有企业	State-owned Enterprises	3841		118	3723
集体企业	Collective-owned Enterprises	1137		123	1014
股份合作企业	Cooperative Enterprises	183			183
联营企业	Joint Ownership Enterprises	12			12
有限责任公司	Limited Liability Corporations	93898	389	5242	88266
股份有限公司	Share-holding Corporations Limited	62083	2991	1677	57415
私营企业	Private Enterprises	147199	115	4593	142491
其他企业	Other Enterprises				
港、澳、台商投资企业	Enterprises with Funds from Hong Kong, Macao and Taiwan	15883	2	286	15595
合资经营企业(港或澳、台资)	Joint-ventures Enterprises	7372	2	174	7197
合作经营企业(港或澳、台资)	Cooperative Enterprises	104			104
港、澳、台商独资经营企业	Enterprises with Sole Investment	4953		106	4847
港、澳、台商投资股份有限公司	Share-holding Corporations Ltd. With Funds from Hong Kong, Macao and Taiwan	3436		7	3429
其他港澳台投资企业	Other Enterprises with Funds from Hong Kong, Macao and Taiwan	18			18
外商投资企业	Foreign Funded Enterprises	25144	53	489	24603
中外合资经营企业	Joint-venture Enterprises	13030	22	163	12845
中外合作经营企业	Cooperation Enterprises	407		104	302
外资企业	Enterprises with Sole Foreign Funds	8628	7	110	8511
外商投资股份有限公司	Share-holding Corporations Ltd. With Foreign Investment	3015	24	111	2880
其他外商投资企业	Other Foreign Funded Enterprises	64			64
三、按工业行业大类分	**by Sector**				
采掘业	**Mining**	**12113**	**2780**	**2640**	**6693**
煤炭开采和洗选业	Mining and Washing of Coal	6011		2522	3489
石油和天然气开采业	Extraction of Petroleum and Natural Gas	2853	2750	33	70
黑色金属矿采选业	Mining of Ferrous Metal Ores	735		53	682
有色金属矿采选业	Mining of Non-ferrous Metal Ores	1646	24	31	1592
非金属矿采选业	Mining and Processing of Nonmetal Ores	265		2	263
开采专业及辅助性活动	Mining Specialties and Auxiliary Activities	603	6		597
其他采矿业	Mining of Other Ores				
制造业	**Manufacturing**	**332185**	**762**	**9664**	**321759**
农副食品加工业	Processing of Food from Agricultural Products	13876	32	776	13068
食品制造业	Manufacture of Foods	8940	152	289	8499
酒、饮料和精制茶制造业	Manufacture of Wine, Drinks and Refined Tea	2430	60	166	2203
烟草制品业	Manufacture of Tobacco	60		20	40
纺织业	Manufacture of Textile	14690	80	619	13991
纺织服装、服饰业	Manufacture of Textile Wearing Apparel and Finery	3463	20	76	3367
皮革、毛皮、羽毛及其制品和制鞋业	Manufacture of Leather, Fur, Feather & Its Products and Footwear	1466		32	1434
木材加工及木 竹、藤、棕、草制品业	Processing of Timbers, Manufacture of Wood, Bamboo, Rattan, Palm, and Straw Products	3218	8	187	3023
家具制造业	Manufacture of Furniture	839	9	6	824

19-25 续表 continued

单位：人年 (man-year)

类别	Category	R&D人员折合全时当量 Full-time Equivalent of R&D Personnel	基础研究人员 Basic Research Personnel	应用研究人员 Applied Research Personnel	试验发展人员 Experimental Development Personnel
造纸及纸制品业	Manufacture of Paper and Paper Products	6037		178	5859
印刷和记录媒介复制业	Printing, Reproduction of Recording Media	2162	1	34	2128
文教、工美、体育和娱乐用品制造业	Manufacture of Culture, Education,Arts and crafts, Sport and Entertainment Goods	5413		154	5259
石油、煤炭及其他燃料加工业	Processing of Oil, Coal and Other Fuel	6077	46	325	5706
化学原料和化学制品制造业	Manufacture of Chemical Raw Material and Chemical Products	34072	20	1145	32907
医药制造业	Manufacture of Medicines	22719	154	479	22086
化学纤维制造业	Manufacture of Chemical Fiber	1100		143	957
橡胶和塑料制品业	Manufacture of Rubber and Plastic	16424		415	16010
非金属矿物制品业	Manufacture of Non-metallic Mineral Products	17073	6	552	16516
黑色金属冶炼及压延加工业	Manufacture and Processing of Ferrous Metals	7873	41	603	7228
有色金属冶炼及压延加工业	Manufacture & Processing of Non-ferrous Metals	9556	3	359	9194
金属制品业	Manufacture of Metal Products	15586	13	315	15258
通用设备制造业	Manufacture of General Purpose Machinery	30120	18	540	29561
专用设备制造业	Manufacture of Special Purpose Machinery	27228	30	700	26498
汽车制造业	Manufacture of Automotive	19882		378	19504
铁路、船舶、航空航天和其他运输设备制造业	Manufacture of Railroad,Marine,Aerospace and Other Transportation Equipment	8092	39	72	7981
电气机械及器材制造业	Manufacture of Electrical Machinery & Equipment	19263	6	373	18883
计算机、通信和其他电子设备制造业	Manufacture of Computer, Communications and Other Electronic Equipment	26613	28	577	26008
仪器仪表制造业	Manufacture of Measuring Instrument	6569		113	6456
其他制造业	Other Manufacture	447			447
废弃资源综合利用业	Comprehensive Utilization of Waste	429		30	399
金属制品、机械和设备修理业	Metal Products, Machinery and Equipment Repair Industry	470		5	466
电力、热力、燃气及水的生产和供应业	**Production and Supply of Electric, Heat, Has and Water**	**5081**	**7**	**224**	**4850**
电力、热力的生产和供应业	Production and Supply of Electric Power and Heat Power	3853	1	193	3660
燃气生产和供应业	Production and Supply of Gas	606		16	591
水的生产和供应业	Production and Supply of Water	621	6	16	599
四、按地区分	**by Region**				
济南市	Jinan	28712	142	1260	27309
青岛市	Qingdao	54064	70	734	53259
淄博市	Zibo	25808		538	25270
枣庄市	Zaozhuang	8079		826	7253
东营市	Dongying	12065	2756	304	9005
烟台市	Yantai	35234	20	796	34418
潍坊市	Weifang	43159		1948	41211
济宁市	Jining	23391	8	1338	22045
泰安市	Tai'an	13887	88	1490	12308
威海市	Weihai	19609	35	473	19101
日照市	Rizhao	8748	12	268	8468
临沂市	Linyi	20353	169	603	19581
德州市	Dezhou	14820	11	344	14466
聊城市	Liaocheng	12417	24	199	12194
滨州市	Binzhou	19917	167	583	19167
菏泽市	Heze	9118	48	823	8247

19-26 按行业分规模以上工业企业新产品开发及生产情况(2021年)

New Products Development and Production of Industrial Enterprises above Designated Size by Industrial Sector(2021)

行业	Sector	新产品项目数(项) New Products (unit)	开发新产品经费(万元) Expenditure on new products Development (10 000 yuan)	新产品销售收入(万元) Sales Revenue of New Products (10 000 yuan)
总计	**Total**	**83641**	**17475012**	**275403023**
煤炭开采和洗选业	Mining and Washing of Coal	206	71654	203800
石油和天然气开采业	Extraction of Petroleum and Natural Gas	246	40212	292
黑色金属矿采选业	Mining of Ferrous Metal Ores	81	37912	436901
有色金属矿采选业	Mining of Non-ferrous Metal Ores	93	8444	166403
非金属矿采选业	Mining and Processing of Nonmetal Ores	43	5104	42254
开采专业及辅助性活动	Mining Specialties and Auxiliary Activities	90	39763	12537
其他采矿业	Mining of Other Ores	1	24	
农副食品加工业	Processing of Food from Agricultural Products	3376	646946	10850192
食品制造业	Manufacture of Foods	2052	311304	4680916
酒、饮料和精制茶制造业	Manufacture of Wine, Drinks and Refined Tea	539	112165	1465248
烟草制品业	Manufacture of Tobacco	43	5217	875103
纺织业	Manufacture of Textile	2424	429505	5492280
纺织服装、服饰业	Manufacture of Textile Wearing Apparel and Finery	668	72264	1263147
皮革、毛皮、羽毛及其制品和制鞋业	Manufacture of Leather, Fur, Feather & Its Products and Footwear	262	52694	600966
木材加工及木 竹、藤、棕、草制品业	Processing of Timbers, Manufacture of Wood, Bamboo, Rattan, Palm, and Straw Products	969	107082	1342076
家具制造业	Manufacture of Furniture	298	32730	400312
造纸及纸制品业	Manufacture of Paper and Paper Products	1169	400663	7324154
印刷和记录媒介复制业	Printing, Reproduction of Recording Media	605	65569	768443
文教、工美、体育和娱乐用品制造业	Manufacture of Culture, Education,Arts and crafts, Sport and Entertainment Goods	1373	170182	2210688
石油、煤炭及其他燃料加工业	Processing of Oil, Coal and Other Fuel	843	605495	17281876
化学原料和化学制品制造业	Manufacture of Chemical Raw Material and Chemical Products	7900	2060204	37808072
医药制造业	Manufacture of Medicines	6025	1254793	13232810
化学纤维制造业	Manufacture of Chemical Fiber	228	48809	526662
橡胶和塑料制品业	Manufacture of Rubber and Plastic	3893	736596	11505027
非金属矿物制品业	Manufacture of Non-metallic Mineral Products	5368	786541	9232929
黑色金属冶炼及压延加工业	Manufacture and Processing of Ferrous Metals	1345	1000041	17093782
有色金属冶炼及压延加工业	Manufacture & Processing of Non-ferrous Metals	1570	981725	19120439
金属制品业	Manufacture of Metal Products	4811	695534	12175445
通用设备制造业	Manufacture of General Purpose Machinery	8767	1238578	16706589
专用设备制造业	Manufacture of Special Purpose Machinery	9042	1226158	14892189
汽车制造业	Manufacture of Automotive	5013	1122158	24295768
铁路、船舶、航空航天和其他运输设备制造业	Manufacture of Railroad,Marine,Aerospace and Other Transportation Equipment	1677	437978	6435325
电气机械及器材制造业	Manufacture of Electrical Machinery & Equipment	5352	1021131	13257925
计算机、通信和其他电子设备制造业	Manufacture of Computer, Communications and Other Electronic Equipment	3386	1195847	20982949
仪器仪表制造业	Manufacture of Measuring Instrument	2130	226020	1587348
其他制造业	Other Manufacture	116	11394	130222
废弃资源综合利用业	Comprehensive Utilization of Waste	180	29354	382694
金属制品、机械和设备修理业	Metal Products, Machinery and Equipment Repair Industry	85	9937	64346
电力、热力生产和供应业	Production and Supply of Electric Power and Heat Power	1132	146356	355518
燃气生产和供应业	Production and Supply of Gas	127	21234	127396
水的生产和供应业	Production and Supply of Water	113	9699	72001

19－27 高技术制造业R&D活动及新产品开发情况

Statistics on R&D Activities and New Products Development in High-tech Manufacturing Industry

行　业	Industry	有R&D活动的企业数（个） Number of Enterprises with R&D Activities (unit)		R&D人员折合全时当量（人年） Full-time Equivalent of R&D Personnel (man year)		R&D经费内部支出（万元） Internal Expenditure on R&D (10 000 yuan)	
		2020	2021	2020	2021	2020	2021
合　计	**Total**	**1067**	**1338**	**44598**	**62205**	**2307305**	**2718772**
医药制造业	Medical and Pharmaceutical Products	400	446	16684	22719	1027460	1170535
航空、航天器及设备制造业	Aviation and Aircrafts Manufacturing	8	7	252	361	6314	6167
电子及通信设备制造业	Electronic and Communication Equipment	337	475	15532	22865	719914	890528
计算机及办公设备制造业	Electronic Computers and Office Equipment	34	49	3905	5730	253290	261638
医疗仪器设备及仪器仪表制造业	Medical Treatment Instruments and Meters	280	353	8133	10377	294300	384717
信息化学品制造业	Manufacture of Electronic Chemicals	8	8	92	153	6028	5187

19－27 续表 continued

行　业	Industry	专利申请数（件） Patent Applications (piece)		拥有发明专利（件） Patents in Force (piece)		新产品开发项目数（项） New Products (units)		新产品开发经费支出（万元） Expenditure on New Products Development (10 000 yuan)	
		2020	2021	2020	2021	2020	2021	2020	2021
合　计	**Total**	**14146**	**17170**	**17307**	**22209**	**9933**	**13497**	**2245843**	**2981907**
医药制造业	Medical and Pharmaceutical Products	3869	3805	6197	6844	4692	6025	948989	1254793
航空、航天器及设备制造业	Aviation and Aircrafts Manufacturing	42	29	86	60	64	83	6954	9046
电子及通信设备制造业	Electronic and Communication Equipment	5122	7636	6910	10439	2388	3281	729063	987859
计算机及办公设备制造业	Electronic Computers and Office Equipments	1517	1539	1468	1712	503	693	235205	284434
医疗仪器设备及仪器仪表制造业	Medical Treatment Instruments and Meters	3565	4082	2630	3095	2253	3343	319234	432560
信息化学品制造业	Manufacture of Electronic Chemicals	31	79	16	59	33	72	6398	13215

注：本表的数据口径为规模以上工业企业。

a)Data in this table cover industrial enterprises above designated size.

19−28 高技术制造业基本情况

Statistics on Production and Management in High-tech Manufacturing Industry

项　　目	Item	2016	2017	2018	2019	2020	2021
生产经营情况	**Production Operation**						
企业数　（个）	Number of Enterprises　(unit)	2207	2141	1979	1564	1718	1807
从业人员年平均人数　（万人）	Annual Average Number of Persons Engaged　(10 000 persons)	75.0	72.8	63.1	54.2	55.8	58.9
营业收入　（亿元）	Revenue from Principal Business　(100 million yuan)	12263.5	12206.8	7065.4	5910.6	6741.6	7935.4
利润　（亿元）	Profits　(100 million yuan)	952.7	948 2	621.8	478.8	682.2	744.3
R&D及相关活动情况	**R&D and related Activities**						
有R&D活动的企业数　（个）	Number of Enterprises with R&D Activities　(unit)	904	1001	898	865	1067	1338
R&D人员全时当量　（人年）	Full-time Equivalent of R&D Personnel　(man year)	51955	51057	49617	35706	44598	62205
R&D经费内部支出　（亿元）	Internal Expenditure on R&D　(100 million yuan)	222.5	250.6	226.6	195.9	230.7	271.9
新产品开发经费　（亿元）	Expenditure on New Products Development　(100 million yuan)	222.1	262.6	218.3	202.5	224.6	298.2
专利申请数　（件）	Number of Patent Applications Examined　(unit)	13983	17187	17712	11074	14146	17170
拥有发明专利数　（件）	Number of Invention Patents　(unit)	12298	17553	19986	18387	17307	22209
固定资产投资情况	**Investment in Fixed Assets**						
施工项目数　（个）	Number of Projects Under Construction　(unit)	1828					
#新开工项目数　（个）	Number of New Projects　(unit)	1287					
全部建成或投产项目数　（个）	Number of Projects Completed or Put into Use　(unit)	1249					
投资额　（亿元）	Investment　(100 million yuan)	1866.6					
新增固定资产　（亿元）	New Added Fixed Assets　(100 million yuan)	1041.5					

注：1.生产经营情况的数据口径为规模以上工业企业。2.从2015年起高技术制造业汇总范围包括信息化学品制造业。

a)Data on production operation cover industrial enterprises above designated size.

b)Data on high-tech manufacturing Industry include manufacture of electronic chemical since 2015.

主要统计指标解释

普通高等学校 指按照国家规定的设置标准和审批程序批准举办的，通过全国普通高等学校统一招生考试，招收高中毕业生为主要培养对象，实施高等教育的全日制大学、独立设置的学院和高等专科学校、高等职业学校和其他机构。

成人高等学校 指按照国家规定的设置标准和审批程序批准举办的，通过全国成人高等学校统一招生考试，招收具有高中毕业或同等学历的在职从业人员为主要培养对象，利用函授、业余、脱产等多种形式对其实施高等学历教育的学校。包括职工高等学校、农民高等学校、管理干部学院、教育学院、独立函授学院、广播电视大学、其他机构等。其他机构是承担国家成人招生计划任务不计校数的机构。

研究与试验发展(R&D) 指在科学技术领域，为增加知识总量，以及运用这些知识去创造新的应用进行的系统的创造性的活动，包括基础研究、应用研究、试验发展三类活动。国际上通常采用 R&D 活动的规模和强度指标反映一国的科技实力和核心竞争力。

基础研究 指为了获得关于现象和可观察事实的基本原理的新知识(揭示客观事物的本质、运动规律，获得新发现、新学说)而进行的实验性或理论性研究，它不以任何专门或特定的应用或使用为目的。其成果以科学论文和科学著作为主要形式。用来反映知识的原始创新能力。

应用研究 指为获得新知识而进行的创造性研究，主要针对某一特定的目的或目标。应用研究是为了确定基础研究成果可能的用途，或是为达到预定的目标探索应采取的新方法(原理性)或新途径。其成果形式以科学论文、专著、原理性模型或发明专利为主。用来反映对基础研究成果应用途径的探索。

试验发展 指利用从基础研究、应用研究和实际经验所获得的现有知识，为产生新的产品、材料和装置，建立新的工艺、系统和服务，以及对已产生和建立的上述各项作实质性的改进而进行的系统性工作。其成果形式主要是专利、专有技术、具有新产品基本特征的产品原型或具有新装置基本特征的原始样机等。在社会科学领域，试验发展是指把通过基础研究、应用研究获得的知识转变成可以实施的计划(包括为进行检验和评估实施示范项目)的过程。人文科学领域没有对应的试验发展活动。主要反映将科研成果转化为技术和产品的能力，是科技推动经济社会发展的物化成果。

研究与试验发展人员 指参与研究与试验发展项目研究、管理和辅助工作的人员，包括项目(课题)组人员，企业科技行政管理人员和直接为项目(课题)活动提供服务的辅助人员。反映投入从事拥有自主知识产权的研究开发活动的人力规模。

研究与试验发展人员全时当量 指全时人员数加非全时人员按工作量折算为全时人员数的总和。例如：有两个全时人员和三个非全时人员(工作时间分别为 20%、30%和 70%)，则全时当量为 2+0.2+0.3+0.7=3.2 人年。为国际上比较科技人力投入而制定的可比指标。

R&D 经费内部支出合计 指调查单位用于内部开展 R&D 活动（基础研究、应用研究和试验发展）的实际支出。包括用于 R&D 项目（课题）活动的直接支出，以及间接用于 R&D 活动的管理费、服务费、与 R&D 有关的基本建设支出以及外协加工费等。不包括生产性活动支出、归还贷款支出以及与外单位合作或委托外单位进行 R&D 活动而转拨给对方的经费支出。

专　利 是专利权的简称，是对发明人的发明创造经审查合格后，由专利局依据专利法授予发明人和设计人对该项发明创造享有的专有权。包括发明、实用新型和外观设计。反映拥有自主知识产权的科技和设计成果情况。

发　明 指对产品、方法或者其改进所提出的新的技术方案。是国际通行的反映拥有自主知识产权技术的核心指标。

Explanatory Notes on Main Statistical Indicators

Regular Institutions of Higher Learning refer to educational establishments set up according to the government evaluation and approval procedures, enrolling graduates from senior secondary schools and providing higher education courses and training for senior professionals. They include full time universities, colleges, high professional schools, high professional vocational schools and others.

Institutions of Higher Learning for Adults refer to educational establishments, set up in line with relevant rules approved by the government, enrolling staff and workers with senior secondary school or equivalent education, and providing higher education courses in many forms of correspondence, spare time, or full time for adults. Professionals thus trained receive a qualification equivalent to graduates studying regular courses at regular universities, colleges and professional colleges. Institutions of higher learning for adults include schools of high education for staff and workers, schools of high education for peasants, colleges for management cadres, pedagogical colleges, independent correspondence colleges, Radio and TV universities and other educational establishments. Other educational establishments are responsible for enrolling adult students but not covered in the number of schools.

Research and Development (R&D) refers to systematic and creative activities in the field of science and technology aiming at increasing the knowledge and using the knowledge for new application. R&D includes 3 categories of activities: basic research, applied research and experiments and development. The scale and intensity of R&D are widely used internationally to reflect the strength of S&T and the core competitiveness of a country in the world.

Basic Research refers to empirical or theoretical research aiming at obtaining new knowledge on the fundamental principles of phenomena of observable facts to reveal the nature and law of movement of objects and to acquire new discoveries or new theories. Basic research takes no specific or designated application as the aim of the research. Results of basic research are mainly released or disseminated in the form of scientific papers or monographs. This indicator reflects the original innovation capacity of knowledge.

Applied Research refers to creative research aiming at obtaining new knowledge on a specific objective or target. Purpose of the applied research is to identify the possible use of results from basic research, or to explore new (fundamental) methods or new approaches. Results of applied research are expressed in the form of scientific papers, monographs, fundamental models or invention patents. This indicator reflects the exploration of ways to apply the results of basic research.

Experiments and Development refer to systematic activities aiming at using the knowledge from basic and applied researches or from practical experience to develop new products, materials and equipment, to establish new production process, systems and services, or to make substantial improvement on the existing products, process or services. Results of experiment and development activities are embodied in patents, exclusive technology, and monotype of new products or equipment. In social sciences, experiment and development activities refer to the process of converting the knowledge from basic or applied researches into feasible programmes (including conduct of demonstration projects for assessment and evaluation). There are no experiment and development activities in the science of humanities. This indicator reflects the capability of transferring the results of S&T into technique and products, which is the materialized measurement of S&T pushing forward the economic and social development.

R&D Personnel refer to persons engaged in research, management and supporting activities of R&D, including persons in the project teams, persons engaged in the management of S&T activities of enterprises and supporting staff providing direct service to the research projects. This indicator reflects the size of personnel engaged in R&D activities with independent intellectual property.

Full time Equivalent of R&D Personnel refers to the sum of the full time persons and the full time equivalent of part time persons converted by workload. For instance, if there are 2 full time persons and 3 part time workers (20%, 30% and 70% of working hours respectively on R&D activities), the full time equivalent is 2+0.2+0.3+0.7=3.2 person years. This is an internationally comparable indicator of input of personnel in S&T activities.

Total Internal Expenditure of Funds on R&D refers to the real expenditure of surveyed units on their own R&D activities(basic research, application study, test and development)including direct expenditure on R&D activities,expenditure on capital construction and material processing by others.Excluding the expenditure on production activities,return of loan,and fee transferred to coopertated and entrusted agencies on R&D activities.

Patent is an abbreviation for the patent right and refers to the exclusive right of ownership by the inventors or designers for the creation or inventions, given from the patent offices after due process of assessment and approval in accordance with the Patent Law. Patents are granted for inventions, utility models and designs. This indicator reflects the achievements of S&T and design with independent intellectual property.

Inventions refer to the new technical proposals to the products or methods or their modifications. This is universal core indicator reflecting the technologies with independent intellectual property.

第20篇

文化、体育和卫生

Culture, Sports and Health

简 要 说 明

一、本篇资料的主要内容

本篇资料反映了全省文化、体育和卫生基本情况。文化部分主要包括文化、文物、广播、电视、档案、报纸杂志出版、图书出版等方面的发展状况。体育部分主要包括运动员、教练员、裁判员发展人数等情况。卫生部分主要包括卫生机构及其人员、床位数、县及县以上医院诊疗人次数、入院人数等基本情况。

二、本篇资料的来源

1.文化部分中，艺术事业、图书馆事业、群众文化事业的资料来源于省文化和旅游厅，广播电视资料来源于省广播电视局，电影有关资料来源于省电影局，新闻出版有关资料来源于省新闻出版局，档案馆有关资料来源于省档案馆。

2.体育部分的资料来源于省体育局。

3.卫生部分的资料来源于省卫健委。

本篇资料由省统计局人口处（社科处）整理提供。

Brief Introduction

I. Content

Data in this chapter show the basic conditions of culture,sports and health. Data on culture show the basic conditions on arts, cultural relics, broadcasting, television, archives and publication. Data on sports mainly include the number of athletes, coaches and referees. Data on health include the number of institutions, personnel, hospital beds.

II. Source of Data

(1)Data on the causes of arts, libraries, mass culture are provided by the Department of Culture and Tourism of Shandong Provincet. Data on broadcasting and television are provided by Shandong Provincial Administration of Radio and Television. Data on film are provided by Shandong Provincial Administration of Film. Data on news and publication are provided by Shandong Provincial Administration of Press and Publication. Data on archives and publication are provided by Shandong Provincial Archives Administration.

(2)Data on sports are provided by Shandong Provincial Physical Culture Administration.

(3)Data on public health are provided by Shandong Provincial Department of Health.

In this chapter, data are prepared by the Division of Urbanization,Population and Employment Statistics（by the Division of Social,Science and Culture Industry Employment Statistics）of Shandong Provincial Bureau of Statistics.

20-1 主要年份文化、文物事业基本情况

Number of Institutions for Culture and Cultural Relics of Major Years

年 份 Year	文化(艺术)馆 Cultural Centre		文化站 Cultural Station		艺术表演团体 Art Performance Groups	
	机构数 (个) Number (unit)	人 数 (人) Personnel (person)	机构数 (个) Number (unit)	人 数 (人) Personnel (person)	机构数 (个) Number (unit)	人 数 (人) Personnel (person)
1949	39				46	
1952	166		139		113	
1957	134		283		175	
1962	130		500		180	
1965	141	1261	6	10	176	9923
1970	137	1601			154	9599
1975	151	1891	887	944	157	12709
1976	150	1979	1644	1803	157	13396
1977	155	2110	1988	2185	156	13557
1978	155	2151	2103	2196	155	13219
1979	155	2138	2104	2163	155	12896
1980	155	2251	2117	2197	156	12562
1981	156	2420	2099	2218	157	11930
1982	155	2490	2107	2268	157	11280
1983	155	2609	2102	2172	157	10584
1984	154	2590	2132	2204	159	9922
1985	157	2818	2198	2230	158	9317
1986	159	2940	2276	2292	149	9177
1987	157	2849	2345	2410	139	7751
1988	159	3043	2423	2787	127	7344
1989	159	3140	2452	2643	123	6992
1990	159	3127	2482	2666	119	6703
1991	156	3100	2504	2783	120	6640
1992	156	3129	2481	2798	120	6657
1993	157	3145	2454	2862	119	6430
1994	157	3197	2387	2882	118	6448
1995	158	3265	2363	3117	118	6170
1996	159	3237	2466	3286	118	6090
1997	158	3264	2482	3177	118	6148
1998	158	3252	2494	3339	118	6170
1999	158	3194	2493	3293	117	6077
2000	159	3055	2422	3304	118	5943
2001	159	2975	1912	2943	121	5990
2002	156	2935	1866	3019	121	6030
2003	157	2968	1792	3022	120	5988
2004	159	3136	1783	3190	118	5995
2005	158	2982	1768	3166	117	6066
2006	158	3058	1857	3330	118	6250
2007	157	3012	1826	3715	119	6163
2008	156	3025	1826	3754	119	6254
2009	158	3115	1867	4593	118	6279
2010	158	3055	1855	4543	119	6268
2011	160	3086	1828	4643	116	6163
2012	158	3033	1821	4987	104	5722
2013	159	3062	1807	4915	103	5557
2014	158	3047	1811	5181	104	5728
2015	157	3034	1814	5534	104	5368
2016	157	3006	1816	5262	103	5651
2017	157	2978	1815	5334	105	5689
2018	157	2950	1819	5329	105	5539
2019	157	2864	1815	5581	104	5665
2020	158	2887	1821	5628	103	5381
2021	158	2974	1821	6194	101	5237

20-1 续表 continued

年 份 Year	剧 场(院) Theaters		图 书 馆 Libraries		博 物 馆 Museums	
	机构数 (个) Number (unit)	人 数 (人) Personnel (person)	机构数 (个) Number (unit)	人 数 (人) Personnel (person)	机构数 (个) Number (unit)	人 数 (人) Personnel (person)
1949	5		3			
1952	15		3			
1957	44		40			
1962	129		84			
1965	128	755	27	257	7	183
1970	83	600	12	193	5	155
1975	81	592	43	436	8	211
1976	71	577	62	564	9	237
1977	76	658	66	621	9	246
1978	75	661	80	737	10	298
1979	77	705	88	876	10	310
1980	71	627	88	924	10	317
1981	72	649	89	1004	9	268
1982	71	667	89	1075	15	338
1983	61	660	89	1131	17	364
1984	65	678	92	1240	19	380
1985	62	705	99	1338	23	488
1986	123	2193	101	1486	30	527
1987	119	2310	105	1613	36	763
1988	116	2388	111	1780	40	876
1989	118	2413	113	1796	40	979
1990	117	2516	115	1876	41	1021
1991	121	2736	118	1956	45	1141
1992	120	2772	122	2055	45	1215
1993	119	2837	126	2178	52	1329
1994	118	2878	126	2256	54	1418
1995	115	2783	130	2318	56	1462
1996	111	2727	131	2359	54	1522
1997	107	2652	131	2471	54	1562
1998	107	2577	131	2536	56	1422
1999	107	2544	133	2555	57	1663
2000	105	2473	133	2506	59	1633
2001	105	2444	136	2503	66	1611
2002	104	2434	140	2559	70	1566
2003	104	2353	140	2573	73	1634
2004	95	2088	142	2633	72	1684
2005	94	1881	145	2690	75	1723
2006	95	2098	143	2624	76	1770
2007	92	1937	145	2640	87	1915
2008	90	1827	147	2606	96	2064
2009	82	1640	150	2669	111	2307
2010	91	1904	149	2680	114	2456
2011	93	2134	150	2697	120	2787
2012	93	2083	150	2647	178	4353
2013	93	1719	153	2760	194	4748
2014	93	1734	153	2730	243	5369
2015	92	1632	154	2750	312	6310
2016	93	1602	154	2828	393	7152
2017	100	1821	154	2877	485	7976
2018	106	1902	154	2843	517	8059
2019	93	1732	154	2816	541	8319
2020	87	1712	154	2904	577	8871
2021	82	1618	153	2995	629	10114

20-2 文化、文物机构人员情况(2021年)

Number of Institution and Personnel in Culture and Culture Relics(2021)

项目	Item	机构数(个) Number of Institutions (unit)	人员数(人) Number of Employed Persons (person)
总计	**Total**	**19437**	**104958**
文化	Culture	2695	29081
公有制艺术表演团体	Public Arts Performance Troupes	101	5237
公有制艺术表演场馆	Public Arts Centers	82	1618
艺术展览创作机构	Art exhibition and Creation Institutions	82	608
公共图书馆	Public Libraries	153	2995
群众文化服务业	Mass Culture	1979	9168
艺术馆、文化馆	Cultural and Art Centers	158	2974
文化站	Cultural Stations	1821	6194
文化和旅游部门教育机构	Culture Education	4	691
文化和旅游科研机构	Art Research	4	139
文化和旅游行政主管部门	Administrative department of culture	159	6098
其他文化和旅游机构	Other cultural institutions	131	2527
文物	Cultural Relics	795	13815
文物保护管理机构	Agency of Relics Preservation	85	2675
文物科研机构	Scientific and Research Historical Relics Agency	10	310
博物馆	Museums	629	10114
其他文物机构	Other cultural relics institutions	71	716
文化市场经营机构	Business Units Dealing in Culture Market	15947	62062
娱乐场所	Place of entertainment	2064	12990
互联网上网服务营业场所(网吧)	Internet service establishments (Internet bar)	10724	9869

注：文化市场经营机构含互联网上网服务营业场所和娱乐场所。
a) Business units dealing in culture market include internet service and entertainment venues.

20-3 各市文化、文物事业基本情况(2021年)

Basic Statistics on Culture and Cultural Relics by Region (2021)

地区	Region	公共图书馆数(个) Public Libraries (unit)	公共图书馆藏书量(万册) Total Collections (10 000 volumes)	艺术表演团体(个) Performance Troupes (unit)	艺术表演场所(个) Art Performance Places (unit)	文化馆(群众艺术馆)(个) Cultural (Mass Art) Centers (unit)	文化站(个) Cultural Stations (unit)	文化事业费(万元) Total Cultural Expenditures (10 000 yuan)	文物事业费(万元) Total Cultural Relics Expenditures (10 000 yuan)	博物馆(个) Museums (unit)
全省总计	**Total**	**153**	**7526**	**101**	**82**	**158**	**1821**	**530152**	**130724**	**629**
济南市	Jinan	13	902	9	7	13	161	45324	11026	58
青岛市	Qingdao	11	896	8	7	11	137	52374	10204	105
淄博市	Zibo	9	340	3	5	9	88	20907	11593	70
枣庄市	Zaozhuang	7	189	1	2	7	64	9981	3835	22
东营市	Dongying	6	336	2	2	6	40	18069	1198	10
烟台市	Yantai	14	688	10	5	16	155	34574	11766	42
潍坊市	Weifang	12	792	6	2	13	118	32006	11273	62
济宁市	Jining	12	321	12	10	12	156	45941	15662	54
泰安市	Tai'an	7	204	4	5	7	88	15462	4723	47
威海市	Weihai	5	459	4	2	6	73	21180	4009	10
日照市	Rizhao	5	169	1	2	5	53	16671	1981	16
临沂市	Linyi	13	405	4	6	13	161	49651	9132	56
德州市	Dezhou	12	217	6	7	12	133	22163	2215	16
聊城市	Liaocheng	8	169	5	7	9	136	18270	3575	17
滨州市	Binzhou	8	264	9	2	8	90	16835	2530	20
菏泽市	Heze	10	228	11	7	10	168	17296	4597	21

注：全省数据含省本级数据。
a)Provincial data include provincial level data.

20-4 电影基本情况

Basic Statistics on Film

项目		Item		2017	2018	2019	2020	2021
电影剧本(梗概)备案公示数量	(部)	Number of Filing and Publicity of Movie Scripts	(unit)	194	198	109	135	173
电影完成片数量	(部)	Number of Completed Films	(unit)	51	42	57	46	77
农村公益电影放映队数量	(个)	Number of Movie Charity Projection Teams in Rural Areas	(unit)	3717	3838	4191	3983	4310
农村公益电影放映场次	(万场)	Number of Movie Charity Projection in Rural Areas	(10 000 stages)	83	80	78	73	79
城市影院银幕数量	(块)	Number of Movie Screens in City Cinemas	(piece)	2712	3159	3592	3697	4336
城市电影观影人次	(万人)	Number of Movie Viewers in City Cinemas	(10 000 persons)	7189	7769	8095	2854	6354
城市电影票房收入	(亿元)	City Movie Box Office	(100 million yuan)	22.9	26.0	28.8	10.0	25.0

20-5 广播电视基本情况

Basic Statistics on Radio and Television Stations

项目		Item		2017	2018	2019	2020	2021
广播		**Radio**						
广播节目综合人口覆盖率	(%)	Radio Coverage Rate of the Population	(%)	99.1	99.1	99.1	99.5	99.5
广播节目套数	(套)	Number of Radio Programs	(set)	162	181	172	171	171
广播节目制作时间	(万小时)	Length of Radio Programs Produced	(10 000 hours)	56.0	55.9	59.1	59.7	58.2
公共广播节目播出时间	(万小时)	Length of Public Radio Programs Broadcasted	(10 000 hours)	94.5	97.0	102.4	103.0	102.9
对外广播节目播出套数	(套)	Number of International Radio Programs Broadcasted	(set)	1	1			
对外广播节目播出时间	(万小时)	Length of International Radio Programs Broadcasted	(10 000 hours)	0.1	0.1			
广播节目播出语言种类	(种)	Kinds of Languages of Radio Programs Broadcasted	(kind)	1	1	1	1	1
电视		**Television**						
电视节目综合人口覆盖率	(%)	TV Coverage Rate of Population	(%)	98.9	99.1	99.1	99.6	99.6
有线广播电视用户数	(万户)	Number of Users of Cable Radio and TV	(10 000 households)	1765.7	1684.2	1579.2	1570.6	1550.0
有线广播电视入户率	(%)	Popularization Rate of Cable Radio and TV	(%)	55.9	53.0	49.2	47.9	45.4
电视节目套数	(套)	Number of TV Programs	(set)	251	261	259	259	267
电视节目制作时间	(万小时)	Length of TV Programs Produced	(10 000 hours)	25.8	24.4	24.0	20.8	19.3
公共电视节目播出时间	(万小时)	Length of Public TV Programs Broadcasted	(10 000 hours)	133.8	141.8	142.4	144.8	147.9
电视节目播出语言种类	(种)	Kinds of Languages of TV Programs Broadcasted	(kind)	3	3	3	2	2
对外电视节目播出套数	(套)	Number of International TV Programs Broadcasted	(set)	1	1	1	1	1
对外电视节目播出时间	(万小时)	Length of International TV Programs Broadcasted	(10 000 hours)	0.9	0.9	0.9	0.9	0.3
广播电视技术及其他		**TV Technology and Others**						
广播电视总收入	(亿元)	Revenue of Radio and TV	(100 million yuan)	172.9	170.3	172.7	174.1	234.5
广播电视从业人员数	(万人)	Staff and Workers of Radio and TV	(10 000 persons)	5.9	5.3	5.3	5.5	5.9
中、短波转播发射台	(座)	Transmission and Relaying Stations of Medium and Short Wave Broadcast	(unit)	31	30	30	25	25
调频、电视转播发射台	(座)	Relaying Stations and TV Transmission of Frequency Modulation Broadcasting	(unit)	204	201	198	192	181
微波实有站	(座)	Microwave Stations	(unit)	27	32	34	34	35

20-6 图书、期刊和报纸出版情况(2021年)

Number of Books,Magazines and Newspapers Published (2021)

类　别	Item	种数(种) Number of Publications (kind)	总印数(万册、万份) Total Printed Copies (10 000 Copies)
图书总计	**Books**	**15591**	**58014.45**
马列主义、毛泽东思想	Marxism-Leninism, Mao Zedong Thought	16	3.39
哲学	Philosophy	98	41.28
社会科学总论	General Social Sciences	64	77.67
政治、法律	Politics and Law	216	759.21
军事	Military Affairs	21	6.55
经济	Economics	195	64.53
文化、科学、教育、体育	Culture, Science, Education and Sports	10913	52001.88
语言、文字	Languages	154	122.40
文学	Literature	2020	3333.39
艺术	Arts	311	147.12
历史、地理	History and Geography	637	1033.87
自然科学总论	General Natural Sciences	12	4.25
数理科学、化学	Mathematics and Chemistry	83	37.46
天文学、地球科学	Astronomy and Geology	85	34.25
生物科学	Biology	55	28.67
医学、卫生	Medicine and Health Care	222	100.99
农业科学	Agricultural Science	39	8.66
工业技术	Industrial Technology	342	166.74
交通运输	Transportation	35	8.07
航空、航天	Aeronautics and Aerospace	1	0.10
环境科学	Environmental Science	19	11.31
综合性图书	General Books	53	22.66
图片(不使用《中国标准书号》)	Picture (not subject to CSBN)		
期刊总计	**Magazine**	**267**	**6445.28**
综　合	Synthesis	17	253.78
哲学社会科学	Philosophy and Social Science	72	2329.80
自然科学技术	Natural Science and Technology	132	301.00
文化教育	Culture and Education	30	2754.98
文学艺术	Literature and Arts	16	805.72
画　刊	Pictorial		
少　儿	Children's Books	6	3164.71
报纸总计	**Newspaper**	**124**	**148140.93**
综合报	Synthetical Newspaper	39	120440.07
专业报	Special Newspaper	22	18915.85
生活服务报	Life Service Newspaper	15	3301.58
读者对象报	Reader Object Newspaper	4	4595.80
高校校报	College Newspaper	44	887.63

20-7 档案馆基本情况(2021年)

Statistics on Archive Institution(2021)

项目	Item	总计 Total	国家综合档案馆 National Comprehensive Archive	省级 Provincial Level	市地级 City Level	县级 County Level
档案馆 (个)	Number of Institutions (unit)	207	159	1	16	142
现有专职人数 (人)	Number of Personnel (person)	2764	2309	90	440	1779
档案馆面积 (平方米)	Floor Space of Archives Institution (sq.m)	1007442	842873	49230	261541	532102
馆藏档案	Number of Archives					
全宗 (个)	Whole Volume (unit)	24422	24185	378	4803	19004
案卷 (卷)	Files (volume)	24805243	15768803	782188	3956852	11029763
中华人民共和国成立前档案案卷	Before 1949 Files	362538	348927	10462	329325	9140
中华人民共和国成立后档案案卷	After 1949 Files	24442906	15420077	771726	3627520	11020831
馆藏资料 (册)	Number of Material Stored (volume)	2780209	2700277	114649	606168	1979460
档案资料利用情况	Use of Archiver					
利用档案 (卷(件)次)	Number of Archives Used (volume-times)	1567263	1014069	67789	236925	709355
利用资料 (册次)	Number of Material Used (volume-times)	22903	19526	77	5561	13888
利用档案人次 (人次)	Number of Persons Using Material (person-times)	713703	300386	13987	31579	254820
开放案卷 (卷)	Opening Archives (volume)	5377580	1155791		456519	699200
开放档案目录(案卷级) (万条)	Catalog of Opening Archives (Files) (10 000 units)	492. 59	93.30		42.40	50.90

注：开放案卷、开放档案目录，省级仅有“文件级”的数据，故该两项为空。

a)Catalog of opening archives: only "file level" data is available at the provincial level, so the two items are empty.

20-7 续表 continued

项目	Item	国家专门档案馆 National Special Archives	部门档案馆 Depart-ment Archives	大型企业档案馆 Enterprise Archive Institution	省、部属事业单位档案馆 Province and Ministry Archive Institution
档案馆 (个)	Number of Institutions (unit)	21	2	5	20
现有专职人数 (人)	Number of Personnel (person)	285	8	21	141
档案馆面积 (平方米)	Floor Space of Archives Institution (sq.m)	103253	3276	18072	39968
馆藏档案	Number of Archives				
全宗 (个)	Whole Volume (unit)	11	1	169	56
案卷 (卷)	Files (volume)	6801356	100729	651725	1482630
中华人民共和国成立前档案案卷	Before 1949 Files	13465			146
中华人民共和国成立后档案案卷	After 1949 Files	6787891	100729	651725	1482484
馆藏资料 (册)	Number of Material Stored (volume)	24492	3403	18414	33623
档案资料利用情况	Use of Archiver				
利用档案 (卷(件)次)	Number of Archives Used (volume-times)	336175	7045	18502	191472
利用资料 (册次)	Number of Material Used (volume-times)	2600	92	148	537
利用档案人次 (人次)	Number of Persons Using Material (person-times)	309000	345	3059	100913
开放案卷 (卷)	Opening Archives (volume)	3838158			383631
开放档案目录(案卷级) (万条)	Catalog of Opening Archives (Files) (10 000 units)	370.29		5.60	23.40

20-8 等级运动员、教练员、裁判员发展人数
Basic Statistics on Athletes, Coaches and Referees

单位:人 (person)

项 目	Item	2015	2016	2017	2018	2019	2020	2021
等级运动员	**Number of Athletes and Referees in Grades**	**4006**	**4304**	**2908**	**3356**	**6500**	**4201**	**5151**
国际运动健将	International Master of Sportsmen	21	14	9	16	6	5	1
运动健将	Master of Sportsmen	134	178	137	174	94	147	57
一 级	First Grade Sportsmen	907	771	742	809	2051	618	1009
二 级	Second Grade Sportsmen	2944	3341	2020	2357	4438	3403	4084
聘任教练员	**Employed Coaches**	**134**	**97**	**105**	**127**	**165**	**130**	**258**
国家级	National Coaches			1	2	2	1	13
高 级	Senior Coaches	18	6	10	40	35	10	41
一 级	First Grade Coaches	39	32	27	43	54	28	73
二 级	Second Grade Coaches	59	52	55	35	62	69	94
三 级	Third Grade Trainers	18	7	12	7	12	22	37
等级裁判员	**Number of Referees in Grades**	**3630**	**2038**	**2524**	**4454**	**5003**	**1804**	**5383**
国际级	International Referees					4		29
国家级	National Referees	2				21	3	117
一 级	First Grade Referees	745	75	196	508	605	551	1065
二 级	Second Grade Referees	2883	1963	2328	3946	4373	1983	4172

20−9 分项目分技术等级运动员发展人数（2021年）

Certified Athletes by Type of Sports and Technical Grade(2021)

单位：人 (person)

项 目	Item	合 计 Total	国际级运动健将 International Master of Sportsmen	运动健将 Master of Sportsmen	一级运动员 First Grade Sportsmen	二级运动员 Second Grade Sportsmen
合计	**Total**	**5151**	**1**	**57**	**1009**	**4084**
田径	Track and Field Events	1943		1	103	1839
游泳	Swimming	725	1	7	129	588
跳水	Diving	1		1		
体操	Artistic Gymnastics	1		1		
蹦床	Trampoline					
花样滑冰	Figure skating	6			2	4
滑板	Skate	5			1	4
越野滑雪	Cross country skiing	1		1		
举重	Weightlifting	34			5	29
拳击	Boxing	72		1	16	55
摔跤	Wrestling	208			44	164
中国式摔跤	Chinese Wrestling	5			5	
柔道	Judo	116			22	94
跆拳道	Taekwondo	38			17	21
自行车	cycling					
场地自行车	track cycling	82			45	37
公路自行车	Road Cycling	30			16	14
山地自行车	Mountain biking	15			5	10
BMX小轮车	Bicycle Motocross	17		1	10	6
BMX泥地竞速	BMX mud racing					
击剑	Fencing	47		1	10	36
马术	Equestrian	10			1	9
现代五项	Modern Pentathlon	3			3	
射击	Shooting	63		1	39	23
射箭	Archery	35			13	22
赛艇	Rowing	171		7	48	116
皮划艇	Canoe Kayak					
帆船	Sailing	33			19	14
帆板	Windsurfing					
皮划艇静水	Canoe Sprint	137		8	30	99
皮划艇激流回旋	Canoe slalom	27			8	19
公开水域游泳	Open water swimming	1				1
足球	Football					
篮球	Basketball	292			59	233
篮球三人制	Threesome basketball	52			36	16
排球	Volleyball	107		18	39	50
沙滩排球	Beach Volleyball	19			9	10
乒乓球	Table Tennis	95		1	37	57
羽毛球	Badminton	35		3	12	20
网球	Tennis	108			6	102
手球	Handball	90				90
棒球	Baseball	48			10	38
垒球	Softball	40			10	30
短道速滑	Short-track Speed Skating	14			8	6
技巧	Acrobatic Gymnastics	3			3	
武术	Wushu					
围棋	Weiqi	5			1	4
象棋	Chinese chess	10			3	7
国际象棋	Chess					
仿真类模型	Simulation class model	1				1
登山	Mountain Climbing					
攀岩	Rock Climbing	48			21	27
摩托车	Motorcycle					
铁人三项	Triathlon	16		2	8	6
高尔夫球	Golf ball	20			7	13
橄榄球	Rugby	101			77	24
橄榄球15人制	15-a-side rugby	82			36	46
健美	Bodybuilding	1			1	
健美操	Aerobics	33			32	1
艺术体操	Rhythmic Gymnastics	1			1	
散打	Sanda	60				60
空手道	Karate	17		2	1	14
冲浪	Surfing	2		1	1	
武术套路	Wushu routine	25				25

20-10 体育系统机构人员情况（2021年）

Number of Institutions and Engaged Persons of Physical Education System(2021)

单位：个、人 (unit,person)

指 标	Item	省级 Provincial Level		地级 Prefectural Level		县级 County Level	
		机构 Institutions	人员 Persons	机构 Institutions	人员 Persons	机构 Institutions	人员 Persons
总 计	**Total**	**33**	**3680**	**74**	**3271**	**241**	**4536**
独立行政机关	Independent Administrative Agencies of Government	1	49	14	312	8	113
合并行政机关	Combined Administrative Agencies of Government			2	23	79	1027
竞技体校	Competitive Sports Schools			1	111	15	629
其他事业单位	Other Institutions	12	330	22	420	98	2042
本科院校	Colleges	1	649				
企业	Companies			2	38		
少儿体育运动学校(业余体校)	Spare-time Sports Schools			4	242	21	358
体育场馆	Stadiums and Gymnasiums	1	127	12	524	3	22
体育科研机构	Sport Scientific Research Institutions	1	49	1	12		
体育类民办非企业	People-run Non-enterprise Sport Units						
体育运动学校	Physical Education and Sport Schools	1	109	14	1479	6	107
体育中学	Sport Middle Schools			1	69	11	238
训练基地	Training Bases	1	28	1	41		
运动项目管理部门(优秀运动队)	Sports Events Managing Agencies	15	2339				
其他机构	Other Institutions						

20-11 卫生总费用

Total Health Expenditure

年份 Year	卫生总费用(亿元) Total Health Expenditure (100 million yuan)	政府卫生支出 Government Health Expenditure		社会卫生支出 Social Health Expenditure		个人现金卫生支出 Out-of-pocket Health Expenditure		人均卫生总费用(元) Per Capita Health Expenditure (yuan)	卫生总费用占GDP比重(%) Health Expenditure as Percentage of GDP (%)
		绝对数(亿元) Level (100 million yuan)	占卫生总费用比重(%) As Percentage of Health Expenditure (%)	绝对数(亿元) Level (100 million yuan)	占卫生总费用比重(%) As Percentage of Health Expenditure (%)	绝对数(亿元) Level (100 million yuan)	占卫生总费用比重(%) As Percentage of Health Expenditure (%)		
1998	195.71	30.66	15.67	56.62	28.93	108.43	55.40	221.44	2.79
1999	227.96	31.96	14.02	58.05	25.46	137.96	60.52	256.63	3.04
2000	271.98	34.96	12.85	67.16	24.69	169.85	62.45	302.30	3.26
2001	301.92	39.60	13.12	90.42	29.95	171.89	56.93	333.94	3.28
2002	353.46	48.42	13.70	96.92	27.42	208.13	58.88	389.19	3.44
2003	399.68	59.13	14.79	117.92	29.50	222.64	55.70	438.01	3.31
2004	448.60	69.68	15.53	136.31	30.39	242.61	54.08	488.67	2.99
2005	542.13	83.83	15.46	168.77	31.13	289.53	53.41	586.21	2.93
2006	650.10	108.89	16.75	219.95	33.83	321.26	49.42	698.36	2.94
2007	801.02	148.01	18.48	272.91	34.07	380.10	47.45	855.15	3.08
2008	987.17	193.19	19.57	359.72	36.44	434.26	43.99	1048.25	3.18
2009	1163.20	254.02	21.84	428.68	36.85	480.51	41.31	1228.26	3.43
2010	1345.30	327.40	24.34	497.02	36.95	520.88	38.72	1403.13	3.43
2011	1648.65	425.10	25.78	616.02	37.37	607.53	36.85	1710.70	3.63
2012	1928.88	498.38	25.84	726.42	37.66	704.09	36.50	1991.65	3.86
2013	2245.97	571.45	25.44	874.71	38.95	799.80	35.61	2307.49	4.11
2014	2484.16	619.70	24.95	1039.50	41.84	824.97	33.21	2537.60	4.18
2015	2844.96	722.22	25.39	1213.99	42.67	908.75	31.94	2889.11	4.52
2016	3354.70	813.19	24.24	1536.92	45.81	1004.59	29.95	3372.70	4.93
2017	3570.82	842.49	23.59	1679.35	47.03	1048.99	29.38	3568.74	4.92
2018	4140.82	917.10	22.15	1982.61	47.88	1241.11	29.97	4121.35	5.41
2019	4284.04	961.00	22.43	2060.05	48.09	1262.99	29.48	4254.18	6.03
2020	4823.41	1169.79	24.25	2235.99	46.36	1417.63	29.39	4750.85	6.60

20-12 卫生事业基本情况

Basic Statistics of Health Institutions

年 份 Year	卫生机构数 (个) Number of Health Institutions (unit)	#医 院、卫生院 Hospitals and Township Hospitals	卫生机构床位数 (万张) Number of Beds (10 000 sets)	#医 院、卫生院 Hospitals and Township Hospitals	卫生技术人员数 (万人) Medical Technical Personnel (10 000 persons)	#执业(助理)医师 Licensed (Assistant) Doctors
1949	288	112	0.3	0.3	2.6	1.8
1952	1879	223	1.8	0.9	3.9	2.0
1955	4620	221	2.1	1.1	6.0	2.9
1957	10235	232	2.4	1.5	7.3	3.3
1962	19460	349	4.9	3.4	9.0	4.3
1965	16336	502	5.4	3.8	8.9	4.4
1970	6173	2155	6.2	5.7	7.9	3.7
1975	7092	2336	9.3	8.6	12.4	5.0
1976	7438	2402	10.2	9.4	13.6	5.2
1977	8003	2420	11.1	10.3	14.4	5.5
1978	8389	2453	12.0	11.1	15.0	5.7
1979	8731	2541	12.5	11.6	16.1	6.2
1980	8908	2552	12.7	11.7	16.9	6.2
1981	9448	2565	12.9	11.8	17.9	6.9
1982	9830	2583	13.2	12.0	18.7	7.3
1983	9965	2597	13.5	12.2	19.3	7.6
1984	9972	2626	14.1	12.8	19.8	7.7
1985	10304	2623	14.7	13.4	20.5	8.0
1986	10399	2659	15.3	13.9	21.3	8.3
1987	10634	2690	16.2	14.7	22.1	8.7
1988	10475	2767	16.8	15.2	22.8	9.2
1989	10707	2975	17.2	15.5	23.4	10.4
1990	11040	3037	17.7	16.0	24.1	10.7
1991	11141	3066	18.2	16.5	24.1	10.5
1992	10865	3097	18.7	17.1	24.7	10.6
1993	10881	3096	19.5	17.7	25.8	11.1
1994	10654	3134	19.9	18.1	26.4	11.5
1995	10463	3104	20.0	18.2	27.1	11.9
1996	11968	3139	20.0	18.7	28.7	12.8
1997	10993	3151	20.7	19.4	29.4	13.0
1998	11008	3170	20.8	19.6	30.1	13.3
1999	14611	3151	21.3	20.1	30.8	13.9
2000	17118	3150	21.5	20.3	31.5	14.5
2001	17348	3000	21.8	20.7	31.8	14.9
2002	17500	2980	22.1	21.0	32.2	15.4
2003	16025	2929	21.8	20.8	31.1	13.4
2004	16574	2891	23.2	21.6	32.3	13.9
2005	16788	2922	25.1	23.5	32.5	14.1
2006	17016	2942	25.9	24.3	33.7	14.6
2007	15337	3075	28.3	26.5	34.6	15.0
2008	14973	3008	32.0	29.7	37.6	16.0
2009	15094	3024	34.7	32.1	40.6	16.9
2010	16496	3099	38.2	35.1	44.1	17.8
2011	68275	3135	41.6	37.8	48.2	18.6
2012	68840	3188	47.3	43.0	53.0	20.1
2013	75475	3426	49.0	44.6	59.8	23.2
2014	77066	3491	50.0	45.9	60.4	23.1
2015	77435	3556	51.9	47.7	61.9	23.7
2016	77050	3643	54.3	49.8	64.3	24.5
2017	79099	4108	58.5	53.8	68.9	26.5
2018	81512	4219	60.8	56.0	73.9	29.0
2019	83661	4203	63.0	58.1	78.3	31.5
2020	84870	4202	64.7	59.9	81.4	32.9
2021	85716	4194	67.4	62.3	85.3	34.3

注：1.自2011年，医疗卫生机构数含村卫生室。2.自2013年，医疗卫生机构数含部分计划生育技术服务机构。
a)Since 2011, the number of health institutions include village health room.
b)Since 2013 ,the data of health institutions include technical service centers for birth control.

20-13 医院工作状况

Basic Statistics of Hospitals above County Level

项目	Item	2016	2017	2018	2019	2020	2021
机构数 (个)	Number of Medical Units (unit)	2019	2450	2579	2615	2640	2654
诊疗人次数 (万人次)	Number of Patients Treated (10 000 person-times)	20363	22518	23295	24961	22155	26023
#门诊急诊人次数 (万人次)	Out-Patients and Emergency Patients (10 000 person-times)	19799	21831	22606	24240	21445	25184
#死亡人数 (人)	Casualties (person)	25060	29188	27655	29766	33146	37336
观察室收容病人数 (万人次)	Number of Inpatients (10 000 person-times)	229	262	216	183	139	162
#死亡人数 (人)	Casualties In-Patient (person)	4312	4108	5056	4737	3935	4675
健康检查人数 (万人)	Number of People Having Physical Checkup (10 000 persons)	1172	1287	1367	1481	1476	1713
本年入院人数 (万人)	Hospital Admissions (10 000 persons)	1298	1412	1447	1498	1340	1490
本年出院人数 (万人)	Number of People Discharged from Hospitals (10 000 persons)	1293	1408	1445	1491	1338	1485
本年住院病人手术人次数 (万人次)	Number of Operations on Inpatients (10 000 person-times)	330	381	396	431	436	523
年底实有病床数 (张)	Beds Owned by Hospitals at the Year-end (set)	400077	441012	460690	481391	498935	522326
实际开放总床日数 (万床日)	Total Number of Beds Used at Midnight (10 000 bed-days)	13925	15073	15769	16457	17177	17990
平均每日开放病床数 (张)	Average Number of Beds Used Every Day (set)	381505	412962	432014	450867	469322	492863
实际占用总床日数 (万床日)	Total Number of Beds Occupied (10 000 bed-days)	11812	12572	13015	13278	12199	13532
出院者占用总床日数 (万床日)	Total Number of Beds for Patients Discharged (10 000 bed-days)	11565	12157	12666	12883	11845	13077
病床周转次数 (次)	Turnover of Beds (time)	33.9	34.1	33.4	33.1	28.5	30.1
病床工作日 (日)	Days of Beds in Use (day)	309.6	304.4	301.3	294.5	259.9	274.6
病床使用率 (%)	Utilization Rate of Beds (%)	84.8	83.4	82.5	80.7	71.0	75.2
出院者平均在院日数 (日)	Average Hospitalization Period (day)	8.9	8.6	8.8	8.6	8.9	8.8

20-14 各类医疗卫生机构基本情况(2021年)

Basic Statistics on Medical Institutions(2021)

医疗机构分类	Institutions	机构数(个) Number of Institutions (unit)	床位数(张) Number of Beds (set)	卫生技术人员(人) Number of Medical Personnel (person)	执业(助理)医师 Licensed (Assistant) Doctors	注册护士 Registered Nurse	诊疗人次数(万人次) Visit (10 000 times)
总计	**Total**	**85716**	**673920**	**853225**	**342910**	**376498**	**67153**
医院	**Hospital**	**2654**	**522326**	**533449**	**189074**	**267072**	**26023**
综合医院	General Hospital	1447	342288	375354	134124	188955	19593
中医医院	Traditional Chinese Medicine Hospital	347	73528	79713	30103	36197	3607
专科医院	Specialized Hospital	729	93664	70268	22042	37828	2536
基层医疗卫生机构	**Basic Medical Institutions**	**82062**	**122246**	**256407**	**131782**	**85704**	**38406**
社区卫生服务中心(站)	Health Service Center for Community	2406	19309	41738	17321	16462	4897
卫生院	Health Centers	1540	100605	99292	41373	32438	8482
村卫生室	Village clinic	52940		26321	23635	2526	17724
门诊部	Outpatient Department	1869	1497	22282	10843	9421	900
诊所、卫生所、医务室	Infirmaries and Clinics	23307	835	66774	38610	24857	6403
专业公共卫生机构	**Specialized Public Health Institutions**	**780**	**26632**	**57748**	**20474**	**21525**	**2692**
疾病预防控制中心	Center for Disease Control and Prevention	192		10190	4779	851	
专科疾病防治院(所、站)	Specialized Disease Prevention &Treatment Institution	86	5733	3885	1366	1564	202
健康教育所(站、中心)	Health Education Institute	1		5	3	1	
妇幼保健院(所、站)	Women and Children Care Agencies	161	20835	38041	13677	17700	2386
急救中心(站)	First-Aid Center	19	64	421	114	235	104
采供血机构	Pick and Supply Blood Institution	27		2110	407	1115	
卫生监督所(中心)	Medical Supervision Institution	150		2811			
计划生育技术服务机构	Institutions of Technical Service for Family Planning	144		285	128	59	
其他机构	**Other Institutions**	**220**	**2716**	**5621**	**1580**	**2197**	**31**
疗养院	Sanatorium	14	2716	1297	445	635	31
临床检验中心	Clinical Laboratory Center	53		1218	172	82	

20-15 各市卫生事业基本情况(2021年)

Statistics on Health Service by Region(2021)

地 区	Region	卫生机构数(个) Number of Health Institutions (unit)	医院 Hospitals	疾病预防控制机构数 Sanitation Stations	妇幼保健机构 Maternity and Child Care Center	床位数(张) Beds (set)	医院 Hospitals	卫生机构人员(人) Health Care Institutions personnel (person)	卫生技术人员(人) Medical Technical Personnel (person)	执业(助理)医师 Licensed (Assistant) Doctors	注册护士 Nurses
全省总计	**Total**	**85716**	**2654**	**192**	**161**	**673920**	**522326**	**1055684**	**853225**	**342910**	**376498**
济南市	Jinan	7515	279	14	15	72832	62887	131269	108401	42474	49446
青岛市	Qingdao	8574	346	41	12	67748	57911	115880	97043	39969	44078
淄博市	Zibo	4715	154	9	8	34199	26515	54617	45380	18618	19340
枣庄市	Zaozhuang	2702	85	7	7	25970	19977	37017	30978	11718	15158
东营市	Dongying	1807	70	6	7	13696	12033	25239	21723	8822	9677
烟台市	Yantai	6090	191	15	15	43340	34032	70345	56015	23059	23561
潍坊市	Weifang	8433	251	17	14	67601	51654	95587	78450	31913	35385
济宁市	Jining	7281	212	12	12	56964	43575	89703	71663	27837	32901
泰安市	Tai'an	4665	105	8	7	35303	27244	54169	42803	16636	19166
威海市	Weihai	2629	77	5	5	18944	14826	31251	25518	10403	11135
日照市	Rizhao	2489	64	5	5	17881	13032	29117	22962	9035	10040
临沂市	Linyi	8210	228	14	14	73907	52098	101278	80039	30545	35452
德州市	Dezhou	5468	120	12	12	28191	19530	47732	38067	16907	15092
聊城市	Liaocheng	6095	133	9	9	34524	26057	52656	42438	17490	17472
滨州市	Binzhou	3192	103	8	9	26724	20160	36820	30774	12729	13547
菏泽市	Heze	5851	236	10	10	56096	40795	83004	60971	24755	25048

注:1.医院中不包括卫生院。2.本表内数字包括诊所、卫生保健所、医务室的机构、人员数。3.妇幼保健机构包括妇幼保健院、所、站。
a)Number of hospitals exclude the township hospitals.b)Data in this table include the number of clinics,health care centers,medical staff.
c)Maternity and child care centers include centers on different level.

主要统计指标解释

医疗卫生机构 指从卫生计生行政部门取得《医疗机构执业许可证》，或从民政、工商行政、机构编制管理部门取得法人单位登记证书，为社会提供医疗保健、疾病控制、卫生监督服务或从事医学科研和医学在职培训等工作的单位。医疗卫生机构包括医院、基层医疗卫生机构、专业公共卫生机构、其他医疗卫生机构。

医院 包括综合医院、中医医院、中西医结合医院、民族医院、各类专科医院和护理院，不包括专科疾病防治院、妇幼保健院和疗养院。

卫生人员 指在医院、基层医疗卫生机构、专业公共卫生机构及其他医疗卫生机构工作的职工，包括卫生技术人员、乡村医生和卫生员、其他技术人员、管理人员和工勤人员。一律按支付年底工资的在岗职工统计，包括各类聘任人员(含合同工)及返聘本单位半年以上人员，不包括临时工、离退休人员、退职人员、离开本单位仍保留劳动关系人员、本单位返聘和临聘不足半年人员。

卫生技术人员 包括执业医师、执业助理医师、注册护士、药师(士)、检验技师(士)、影像技师(士)、卫生监督员和见习医(药、护、技)师(士)等卫生专业人员。不包括从事管理工作的卫生技术人员(如院长、副院长、党委书记等)。

床位数 指年底固定实有床位(非编制床位)，包括正规床、简易床、监护床、正在消毒和修理床位、因扩建或大修而停用的床位，不包括产科新生儿床、接产室待产床、库存床、观察床、临时加床和病人家属陪侍床。

总诊疗人次数 指所有诊疗工作的总人次数，统计界定原则为：①按挂号数统计，包括门诊、急诊、出诊、预约诊疗、单项健康检查、健康咨询指导（不含健康讲座）人次。患者一次就诊多次挂号，按实际诊疗次数统计，不包括根据医嘱进行的各项检查、治疗、处置工作量以及免疫接种、健康管理服务人次数；②未挂号就诊、本单位职工就诊及外出诊（不含外出会诊）不收取挂号费的，按实际诊疗人次统计。

Explanatory Notes on Main Statistical Indicators

Health Care Institutions refer to the units which have been qualified the Certification of Health Care Institution issued by the administration of public health, or qualified the Certification of Corporate Unit issued by the administration of civil affairs, the administration for industry and commerce, or the commission office for public sector reform, and which engage in medical care, disease prevention and control, health supervision and inspection, medicine research and health education, etc, including: hospitals, primary-level medical and health care institutions, public health centers, and so on.

Hospitals include polyclinics, traditional Chinese therapeutics and western therapeutics, ethical hospitals, various specialty hospitals and nursing hospitals, exclusive of women and children care agencies, special disease prevention and curing agencies.

Health Care Employees refer to the employees engaged in hospitals, primary-level medical and health care institutions, and other medical and health institutions, including medical technical personnel, rural doctors and hygienists, other technical personnel, administrative staff and handymen. The data is based on the year end payroll, including all kinds employees (contract workers) and rehired retired staff, and excluding temporary workers, retired personnel, resigned personnel, personnel who have left the institution but kept labor relations, and rehired personnel on duty less than six months.

Medical Technical Personnel refers to the professional staff engaged in health care, including licensed doctors, licensed assistant doctors, registered nurses, pharmacists, and laboratory technicians, imaging technicians, health care supervisors, and intern doctors ,pharmacists, nurses, and technicians and so on, excluding the personnel engaged in managerial jobs, such as presidents, vice presidents or party secretaries.

The Number of Beds refer to the number of fixed existing beds which include regular beds, simple beds, care beds, beds being disinfected or fixed and beds not in use because of expansion and housing repairs, excluding neonatal beds, beds for expectant mothers, stored beds, observation beds, temporarily added beds and accompanying beds.

Total Visits refer to all the people visiting health institutions. The data is based on the registration number, including outpatients, emergency treatments, home visits, appointment clinics, health examinations and health counseling, and also on the number of people on medical treatment unregistered in and out of their units, with excluded the number of people on medical device for physical checkup, treatment, disposal workload, immunization and health management.

第21篇

公共管理和社会服务

Public Management and Social Services

简 要 说 明

一、本篇资料的主要内容

本篇资料反映了全省民政、司法、测绘、标准计量、质检和残疾人事业发展情况。

二、本篇资料的来源

1.民政部分的资料来源于省民政厅、省退役军人事务厅、省法院。

2.司法部分的资料来源于省司法厅、省检察院、省高院。

3.测绘部分的资料来源于省自然资源厅。

4.交通、火灾部分资料来源于省公安厅、省应急厅。

5.标准计量、质检部分的资料来源于省市场监管局。

6.残联资料来源于山东残疾人联合会。

本篇资料中，测绘和标准计量部分由省统计局综合处加工整理，其他各部分资料由省统计局人口处（社科处）整理提供。

Brief Introduction

I. Content

Data in this chapter show the basic conditions of civil affairs, legal and judicial affairs, surveying and mapping, standard measuring ,quality inspection and work for persons with disabilities .

II. Source of Data

(1)Data on civil affairs are provided by Shandong Provincial Department of Civil Affairs,Provincial Department of Retired Military Affairs and Provincial Department of Court.

(2)Data on legal and judicial affairs are provided by Shandong Provincial Department of Justice, Provincial Department of Procuratorate and Provincial Department of High Court.

(3)Data on surveying and mapping are provided by the Department of Nature and Resources of Shandong Province.

(4) Data on traffic and fire are provided by Shandong Provincial Department of Public Security and Provincial Department of Emergency.

(5)Data on standard measuring are provided by Shandong Provincial Department of Market Regulatory Authority .

(6)Data on Disabled persons are from the Shandong Disabled Persons Federation.

In this chapter, data on surveying are prepared by the Division of Comprehensive Statistics of Shandong Provincial Bureau of Statistics. Other data are prepared by the Division of Urbanization,Population and Employment Statistics（by the Division of Social,Science and Culture Industry Employment Statistics）of Shandong Provincial Bureau of Statistics.

21-1 民政事业基本情况
Basic Statistics on Civil Affairs

项　目		Item		2017	2018	2019	2020	2021
一、民政事业支出情况		**Civil Affairs Expenditures**						
民政事业费总支出	(万元)	Total Operating Expenses For Civil Affairs	(10 000 yuan)	3394553	3209887	1691003	2147802	2542677
基本建设支出	(万元)	Capital expenditures	(10 000 yuan)	66800	57604	56021	99174	101162
二、社会救助情况		**Social Relief**						
城镇居民最低生活保障人数	(人)	Number of Urban Residents for Minimum Livelihood Guarantee	(person)	237786	159119	132837	122978	108845
城镇最低生活保障支出	(万元)	Expenditures by Urban Residents for Minimum Livelihood Guarantee	(10 000 yuan)	126638	94895	82403	93355	95218
农村最低生活保障人数	(人)	Number of Rural residents for Minimum Livelihood Guarantee	(person)	1815546	1171327	1177686	1352566	1349399
农村最低生活保障支出	(万元)	Expenditures by Rural residents for Minimum Livelihood Guarantee	(10 000 yuan)	520892	413789	418351	608367	747980
农村特困供养人数	(人)	Rural Poor of Dependents	(person)	210461	223680	241442	324540	329213
三、社会组织情况		**Social Organization**						
社会组织个数	(个)	Total	(unit)	48727	51269	56022	60247	63687
社会团体	(个)	Social Groups	(unit)	17657	17533	18153	18473	19274
民办非企业	(个)	Private Non-Enterprise	(unit)	30903	33536	37657	41532	44129
基金会	(个)	Foundation	(unit)	167	200	212	242	284
四、社会事务情况		**Social Affairs**						
孤儿数	(人)	Number of Orphans	(person)	16072	10818	9479	8184	7940
儿童收养登记数	(件)	Number of Adoption Registration of Children	(case)	1662	1318	1143	1067	1411
殡葬类单位数	(个)	Number of Funeral and Interment Enterprises	(unit)	178	179	199	225	205
火化炉数	(台)	Number of Cremators	(set)	542	569	582	567	572
全年处理遗体数据	(具)	Cremated Remains During the Year	(bodies)	627723	659823	674830	692940	714755
五、基层自治组织情况		**Primary-Level Self-Governing Bodies**						
村民委员会	(个)	Villagers ' Committee	(unit)	74167	69599	69546	58868	54621
居民委员会	(个)	Residents ' Committee	(unit)	6828	7386	7594	7552	6840
六、福利彩票情况		**Welfare Lottery**						
销售额	(亿元)	Sales	(100 million yuan)	151.5	152.9	136.0	91.9	90.4
全省各级留用公益金	(亿元)	At All Levels In the Province Retained the Community Chest	(100 million yuan)	21.8	22.1	20.2	14.6	14.8

注：2019年开始民政事业费支出不再包含退役军人安置、优待抚恤、减灾救灾、医疗救助等资金支出。

a)Form 2019,total operating expenses for civil affairs does not contain some capital expenditures of veteran placement,preferential treatment,disaster reduction and relief,medical support.

21-2 婚姻登记情况
Basic Statistics on Marriages and Divorces

项目		Item		2017	2018	2019	2020	2021
一、国内登记结婚		**Domestic Marriage Registration**						
准予登记结婚	(对)	Registered Marriage	(couple)	625812	599034	532960	487448	462535
#恢复结婚	(对)	Resuming of Marriage	(couple)	13368	13706	8774	7552	7380
初婚人数	(人)	First Marriage	(person)	901747	839568	723525	668971	641630
再婚人数	(人)	Number of Remarriage	(person)	349877	358500	342395	305925	283440
男性	(人)	Male	(person)	162598	167142	159052	141555	130620
女性	(人)	Female	(person)	187279	191358	183343	164370	152820
二、涉外登记结婚		**Marriage Registration Concerning Foreigners, Overseas** Chinese and Hong Kong, Macao and Taiwan residents						
准予登记结婚	(对)	Registered Marriage	(couple)	1122	1316	1559	466	396
准予登记结婚人数	(人)	Number of Persons Registered	(person)	2244	2632	3118	932	792
内地居民	(人)	Mainland resident	(person)	1111	1313	1529	465	396
男性	(人)	Male	(person)	499	700	973	237	143
女性	(人)	Female	(person)	612	613	556	228	253
港澳居民	(人)	Compatriots in Hong Kong and Macao	(person)	27	30	36	18	27
台湾居民	(人)	Compatriots in Taiwan	(person)	145	127	146	50	62
华侨	(人)	Overseas Chinese	(person)	24	28	38	5	5
外国人	(人)	Foreigners	(person)	937	1134	1369	394	302
三、离婚登记		**Divorce Registration**						
法院受理离婚案件	(件)	Divorce Case Handled	(unit)	114869	115692	107613	102472	109325
准予登记离婚总数	(对)	Number of Registered Divorce	(couple)	272501	274497	284561	259610	187157
民政部门办理离婚	(对)	Divorces Handled through Civil Administration Departments	(couple)	220424	224524	237355	214479	135268
#涉外及华侨、港澳台居民登记离婚	(对)	Divorces Concerning Foreigners,Overseas Chinese, Hong Kong, Macao and Taiwan residents	(couple)	172	192	186	91	55
法院调解离婚	(对)	Divorces through Law Court Mediation	(couple)	35425	35404	33024	32117	39956
法院判决离婚	(对)	Divorces through Law Court Judgment	(couple)	16652	14569	14182	13014	11933

21−3 养老服务机构和设施情况（2021年）

Statistics on Old-age Care Institutions and Facilities(2021)

年 份 地 区	Year Region	养老机构和设施数量（个） Number of Old-age Care Institutions and Facilities (unit)	养老机构数量 Number of Old-age Care Institutions	养老设施数量 Number of Old-age Care Facilities	养老床位数量（个） Number of Beds in Old-age Care Institutions (unit)	年末收养人数（人） Number of persons who are cared in Old-age Care Institutions at the End of the Year (person)
全　省	**Total**	**19240**	**2380**	**16860**	**648604**	**172838**
济南市	Jinan	3760	148	3612	62896	10551
青岛市	Qingdao	1269	296	973	51559	21665
淄博市	Zibo	1223	153	1070	31591	11214
枣庄市	Zaozhuang	519	118	401	25034	6605
东营市	Dongying	426	53	373	12833	2802
烟台市	Yantai	1722	248	1474	69622	18318
潍坊市	Weifang	962	168	794	41842	13154
济宁市	Jining	1176	222	954	67779	14248
泰安市	Tai'an	1384	114	1270	40553	5402
威海市	Weihai	1693	160	1533	49472	16503
日照市	Rizhao	811	51	760	16469	2962
临沂市	Linyi	933	118	815	38059	11425
德州市	Dezhou	541	119	422	24425	8382
聊城市	Liaocheng	486	107	379	31452	9158
滨州市	Binzhou	906	102	804	36918	7817
菏泽市	Heze	1429	203	1226	48100	12632

21-4 律师、公证工作基本情况

Basic Statistics on Lawyers and Notarization

项目		Item		2014	2015	2016	2017	2018	2019	2020	2021
律师工作		**Lawyers**									
律师事务所	(个)	Number of Law Offices	(unit)	1512	1629	1796	1931	2029	2165	2290	2434
国资所	(个)	State-owned	(unit)	41	37	35	33	25	22	19	17
合伙所	(个)	Partnership	(unit)	1021	1079	1173	1276	1399	1551	1688	1859
个人所	(个)	Initiated by Individual	(unit)	450	513	588	622	605	592	583	558
执业律师	(人)	Number of Lawyers	(person)	18405	20043	22043	24437	26986	29960	31468	33960
专职律师	(人)	Full-time Lawyers	(person)	17147	18726	20601	22715	24478		27242	29454
兼职律师	(人)	Part-time Lawyers	(person)	568	615	624	656	676		910	747
公证工作		**Notarization**									
公证处	(个)	Number of Notary Offices	(unit)	158	157	157	157	158	160	161	160
公证员	(人)	Notaries	(person)	1040	1054	1017	2292	1037	1013	1012	1014
公证员助理	(人)	Assistant Notaries	(person)	518	528	569	714	827	905	1058	1058
办理各类公证事项	(万件)	Number of Notarized Affair	(10 000 units)	67.8	70.9	77.1	84.4	87.3	84.6	71.2	78.6

21-5 各市交通事故情况（2021年）

Basic Statistics on Traffic Accidents by Region (2021)

地区	Region	发生数（起） Number of Traffic Accidents (case)	死亡人数（人） Number of Deaths (person)	受伤人数（人） Number of Injuries (person)	直接财产损失（万元） Direct Property Losses (10 000 yuan)
全省总计	**Total**	**12660**	**3381**	**11553**	**6089.98**
济南市	Jinan	3318	447	3188	1206.82
青岛市	Qingdao	1734	307	1721	520.39
淄博市	Zibo	1019	261	867	498.05
枣庄市	Zaozhuang	263	108	221	70.59
东营市	Dongying	456	126	490	90.52
烟台市	Yantai	566	204	428	105.80
潍坊市	Weifang	904	289	843	716.47
济宁市	Jining	756	218	693	415.17
泰安市	Tai'an	462	193	396	185.45
威海市	Weihai	148	120	52	27.06
日照市	Rizhao	415	102	316	195.89
临沂市	Linyi	523	299	376	285.41
德州市	Dezhou	615	209	505	250.46
聊城市	Liaocheng	988	208	1065	457.16
滨州市	Binzhou	251	101	254	98.45
菏泽市	Heze	155	134	64	596.39

注：全省总计含省公安厅交通管理局五支队和直属公安局数据。

a) The number of total contains No.5 detachment of traffic administration bureau of Provincial Public Security Department and Public Security Bureau directly under.

21-6 火灾事故情况（2021年）
Basic Statistics on Fire Accidents(2021)

项 目	Item	合 计 Total	特 大 Extraordinarily Serious	重 大 Serious	较 大 Comparatively Serious	一 般 Ordinary
发 生 （起）	Fire Accidents (case)	85575			8	85567
死 亡 （人）	Deaths (person)	156			34	122
受 伤 （人）	Injuries (person)	109			1	108
直接经济损失 （万元）	Direct Economic Losses (10 000 yuan)	61312			195	61117
平均每起事故损失 （元）	Average Loss of Fire (yuan)	7165			24375	7143

注：根据应急管理部消防救援局统一部署，自2020年起，全国消防救援队伍实施“全口径”火灾统计，数据与以往不可比。
a)According to the unified deployment of the Fire Rescue Bureau of the emergency management department,from 2020,The national fire rescue team implements fire statistics of full caliber,and the data are not comparable with the previous.

21-7 各市火灾事故情况（2021年）
Basic Statistic on Fires by Region(2021)

地 区	Region	发生数（起） Number of Fire Accidents (case)	死亡人数（人） Number of Deaths (person)	受伤人数（人） Number of Injuries (person)	直接经济损失（万元） Direct Economic Losses (10 000 yuan)
全省总计	**Total**	**85575**	**156**	**109**	**61312.0**
济 南 市	Jinan	5907	24	11	6126.3
青 岛 市	Qingdao	7276	20	17	5704.8
淄 博 市	Zibo	4799	2	11	4898.8
枣 庄 市	Zaozhuang	3271	6	1	1568.3
东 营 市	Dongying	2879	14	7	3032.7
烟 台 市	Yantai	6682	9	15	3488.6
潍 坊 市	Weifang	8326	4	6	2971.1
济 宁 市	Jining	5451	6	6	2626.6
泰 安 市	Tai'an	3673	7	3	1807.7
威 海 市	Weihai	2379	6	5	2215.8
日 照 市	Rizhao	2070	9	7	3393.2
临 沂 市	Linyi	7822	19	8	9961.9
德 州 市	Dezhou	5995	9	1	5064.9
聊 城 市	Liaocheng	6620	5	2	4220.1
滨 州 市	Binzhou	6166	6	5	1604.9
菏 泽 市	Heze	6259	10	4	2626.3

21-8 人民检察院审查批准、决定逮捕犯罪嫌疑人和提起公诉被告人情况（2021年）

Arrests of Criminal Suspects and Defendants under Public Prosecution Approved by People's Procuratorate (2021)

案件分类	Category of Cases	批捕、决定逮捕合计 Total of Arrests		决定起诉合计 Total of Public Prosecutions	
		件 (case)	人 (person)	件 (case)	人 (person)
合　计	**Total**	**22492**	**29004**	**80124**	**103402**
公安、安全、监狱机关提请小计	Sub-total of Requests by Departments of State and Public Security and Prisons	22448	28969	79381	102525
危害国家安全案	Offences Against State Security	19	22	13	15
危害公共安全案	Offences Against Public Security	1902	1998	39685	39912
破坏社会主义市场经济秩序案	Offences Against Socialist Economic Order	2060	2797	4381	9323
侵犯公民人身、民主权利案	Offences Against Citizens' Personal and Democratic Rights	4887	5544	10012	11997
侵犯财产案	Offences Against Properties	7118	8621	13223	16910
妨害社会管理秩序案	Offences Against Social Management of Order	6451	9976	12053	24348
危害国防利益案	Offences Against National Defense	11	11	14	20
军人违反职责案	Offences on Dereliction of Duty by Servicemen				
职务犯罪案件小计	Sub-total of Cases Handled Directly by Procuratorate's Offices	25	35	743	877
贪污贿赂案	Offences on Corruption and Bribery	4	9	664	768
渎职侵权案	Offences on Abuse and Dereliction of Duty	21	26	79	109

21-9 人民法院审理一审案件情况

First Trial Cases by Courts

单位：件 (case)

年　份 Year	收　案 Cases Accepted	刑　事 Criminal	民　事 Civil	行　政 Administrative
2005	537098	41768	476405	18925
2006	530542	42175	468457	19910
2007	535832	43501	472368	19963
2008	603565	44935	534050	24580
2009	625334	45711	552631	26992
2010	652618	44885	578371	29362
2011	681311	48777	603837	28697
2012	711631	56597	629299	25735
2013	699878	54966	626509	18403
2014	730167	58763	655196	16208
2015	848676	63910	767974	16792
2016	848117	60802	769902	17413
2017	803382	63629	724970	14783
2018	926131	70425	838135	17571
2019	989818	87276	879704	22838
2020	1064382	64527	973955	25900
2021	1102277	80119	997867	24291

注：一审案件指人民法院按照诉讼级别管辖按第一审程序审理的案件。

a) First trial cases refer to cases accepted by people's courts according to the first trial proceedings.

21－10 各市测绘持证单位个数和人员情况(2021年)

Basic Statistics on Surveying and Mapping Departments by Region(2021)

地 区	Region	持证单位数(个) Departments with Certificate (unit)	#甲级 First-class	乙级 Second-class	测绘专业技术人员(人) Surveying and Mapping Technical Personnel (person)	#高级职称 Senior Title	中级职称 Intermediate Title	测绘服务总值(万元) Output Value (10 000 yuan)
全省总计	**Total**	**905**	**65**	**840**	**11723**	**1720**	**4753**	**641451**
济南市	Jinan	158	30	128	3809	624	1524	227181
青岛市	Qingdao	134	6	128	1547	348	621	108365
淄博市	Zibo	43	4	39	642	90	236	40216
枣庄市	Zaozhuang	25		25	199	13	92	4566
东营市	Dongying	58	5	53	630	93	248	60822
烟台市	Yantai	74	3	71	1013	123	419	53664
潍坊市	Weifang	67	3	64	652	65	232	23276
济宁市	Jining	50	2	48	408	53	169	13716
泰安市	Tai'an	42	2	40	443	49	192	20194
威海市	Weihai	32	2	30	323	27	155	14515
日照市	Rizhao	31	2	29	262	29	132	9720
临沂市	Linyi	54	3	51	569	73	219	21509
德州市	Dezhou	44	1	43	450	61	186	17195
聊城市	Liaocheng	33	1	32	253	15	125	8925
滨州市	Binzhou	22	1	21	181	18	65	7587
菏泽市	Heze	38		38	342	39	138	10000

21-11　残疾人事业基本情况

Basic Statistics on the Work for Persons with Disabilities

项　　目		Item		2021
康复		**Rehabilitation**		
视力残疾人接受基本康复服务	(人)	Basic Vision Rehabilitation Services for Persons with Disabilities	(person)	131720
0-6岁儿童	(人)	0-6 Years old Children	(person)	249
7-17岁儿童	(人)	7-17 Years old Children	(person)	1716
成人	(人)	Adult	(person)	129755
听力残疾人接受基本康复服务	(人)	Basic Rehabilitation Services for Persons with Hearing Disabilities	(person)	159400
0-6岁儿童	(人)	0-6 Years old Children	(person)	3095
7-17岁儿童	(人)	7-17 Years old Children	(person)	6039
成人	(人)	Adult	(person)	150266
肢体残疾人接受基本康复服务	(人)	Basic Rehabilitation Services for Persons with Physically Disabled	(person)	1017261
0-6岁儿童	(人)	0-6 Years old Children	(person)	5729
7-17岁儿童及成人	(人)	7-17 Years old Children and Adult	(person)	1011532
智力残疾人接受基本康复服务	(人)	Basic Rehabilitation Services for People with Mental Retardation	(person)	157179
0-6岁儿童	(人)	0-6 Years old Children	(person)	8780
7-17岁儿童及成人	(人)	7-17Years old Children and Adult	(person)	148399
精神残疾人接受基本康复服务	(人)	Basic Rehabilitation Services for persons with Mental Disabilities	(person)	183787
0-6岁孤独症儿童	(人)	0-6 Years old Autism Children	(person)	7041
7-17岁孤独症儿童	(人)	7-17 Years old Autism Children	(person)	5969
成年精神残疾人	(人)	Adults with Mental Disabilities	(person)	170777
残疾人康复机构	(个)	Rehabilitation of Persons with Disabilities	(unit)	1219
康复机构在岗人员	(万人)	Rehabilitation institutions Employed Personnel	(10 000 persons)	3.8
社区康复协调员	(万人)	Community Rehabilitation Coordinator	(10 000 persons)	4.7
教育		**Education**		
高等院校录取残疾考生	(人)	Admissions for Candidates with Disabilities in Colleges and Universities	(people)	1509
就业		**Employment**		
残疾人就业状况	(万人)	the Employment Situation of Persons with Disabilities	(10 000 persons)	52.8
按比例就业	(万人)	Proportional Employment	(10 000 persons)	7.1
集中就业	(万人)	Focus on Employment	(10 000 persons)	1.6
个体就业	(万人)	individual Employment	(10 000 persons)	3.0
公益性岗位就业	(万人)	Public Welfare Jobs Employment	(10 000 persons)	0.5
辅助性就业	(万人)	Accessible Employment	(10 000 persons)	0.3
农村种养殖	(万人)	Species Breeding in Rural Areas	(10 000 persons)	28.3
灵活就业	(万人)	Flexible Employment	(10 000 persons)	12.0
社会保障		**Social Security**		
残疾居民参加城乡社会养老保险	(万人)	Disabled Residents in Urban and Rural Social Endowment insurance	(10 000 persons)	186.4
其中重度残疾人	(万人)	Severe Disabilities	(10 000 persons)	93.4
托养服务机构	(个)	Fostering Services	(unit)	609
托养残疾人数	(万人)	Farmed Out the Number of Persons with Disabilities	(10 000 persons)	2.4
扶贫		**Poverty Alleviation**		
残疾人就业基地建设		the Disabled Poor Base Construction		
残疾人就业基地	(个)	Bases for Poverty Alleviation of Persons with Disabilities	(unit)	182
安置残疾人就业	(万人)	Disabled Employment	(10 000 persons)	0.5
扶持带动残疾人户数	(万户)	Support-Led Families of Persons with Disabilities	(10 000 households)	0.3
实用技术培训	(万人次)	Practical Techniques Training	(10 000 person-times)	1.8
维权		**Activist**		
处理残疾人来信	(件次)	Letter From Dealing with Persons with Disabilities	(piece-times)	367
接待残疾人来访	(人次)	Receiving Visiting Persons with Disabilities	(person-times)	2450
电话接听和处理残疾人反映问题	(件次)	Handled Phones Reflect the Problems of Persons with Disabilities	(piece-times)	12554

21-12 产品质量监督抽查情况(2021年)

Results of Sampling Check on the Quality of Products (2021)

项　目	Item	抽查企业 (家) Number of Enterprises Supervised (unit)	抽查产品 (批) Production Supervised (batch-time)	不合格产品 (批) Production Unqualified (batch-time)
合　计	**Total**	**6008**	**7942**	**722**
食品相关产品	Food related products	788	934	24
日用消费及纺织品	Consumer Goods and Textiles	730	1175	247
建筑与装饰装修材料	Building & Decoration Material	1262	1708	73
农业生产资料	Agricultural Means of Production	369	449	31
轻工产品	Light Industry Products	528	789	78
机械及安防产品	Machinery, Security and Protection Products	1350	1651	103
电子电器	Electronic and Electrical Appliances	384	542	127
电工及材料	Electrical Engineering and Materials	597	694	39

21-13 各市质量强省建设情况(2021年)

Statistics on Quality Province by Region (2021)

地 区	Region	国内注册商标期末有效量(件) The Volume of Domestically Registered Trademarks in Validity at the End of the Period (case)	马德里国际注册期末有效量(件) The Volume of Trademarks Registered Under the Madrid System in Validity at the End of the Period (case)	地理标志商标期末有效数(件) The Number of Geographical Indications in Validity at the End of the Period (case)	驰名商标期末实有数(件) The Actual Number of Famous Trademarks at the End of the Period (case)	年末累计省长质量奖(个) Shandong provincial governor Quality Award end to This Year (unit)	年末累计地理标志保护产品(个) Products Protected by Geographical Indications end to This Year (unit)
全省总计	**Total**	**2057493**	**9610**	**863**	**805**	**85**	**81**
济南市	Jinan	331760	859	42	78	14	7
青岛市	Qingdao	391532	4939	35	150	11	6
淄博市	Zibo	77689	155	52	69	5	3
枣庄市	Zaozhuang	52552	110	28	12	1	4
东营市	Dongying	32710	1481	45	22	7	1
烟台市	Yantai	128023	272	61	75	7	9
潍坊市	Weifang	168562	268	101	103	8	12
济宁市	Jining	86955	97	139	52	5	11
泰安市	Tai'an	60360	97	55	54		2
威海市	Weihai	61048	152	61	36	8	5
日照市	Rizhao	40907	99	41	7	2	3
临沂市	Linyi	271796	97	38	60	6	2
德州市	Dezhou	66482	143	24	30	1	1
聊城市	Liaocheng	86995	70	53	21	6	6
滨州市	Binzhou	54603	276	37	24	2	3
菏泽市	Heze	91562	486	51	12	2	6

21-14 各市标准化工作情况(2021年)
Statistics on Standardization by Region (2021)

单位：项 (unit)

地区	Region	制定国际标准数量 Number of Formulation International Standards		主导制定国家标准数量 Number of Leading Formulation National Standards		制修订地方标准数量 Number of Formulation or Revision Local Standards		标准化试点项目数量 Number of Standardization Project			
								国家级 National		省级 Provincial	
		本年度 This Year	累计 Accumul-ative	本年度 This Year	累计 Accumul-ative	本年度 This Year	累计 Accumul-ative	本年度 This Year	累计 Accumul-ative	本年度 This Year	累计 Accumul-ative
全省总计	**Total**	**30**	**252**	**134**	**1752**	**243**	**4540**	**51**	**482**	**141**	**1545**
省　直	Shengzhi		1	16	272	131	2432		3		10
济南市	Jinan	7	28	23	319	51	646	6	69	36	221
青岛市	Qingdao	9	122	33	538	15	253	2	55	8	107
淄博市	Zibo	3	19	10	146	5	78	3	29	7	79
枣庄市	Zaozhuang		2		5	1	44	2	13	5	57
东营市	Dongying	1	4	4	34	1	36	1	23	6	55
烟台市	Yantai	3	15	13	127	15	273	3	30	7	91
潍坊市	Weifang	2	10	7	74	4	118	4	55	8	101
济宁市	Jining			7	46		95	7	28	7	91
泰安市	Tai'an		2	3	55	4	296	3	28	6	77
威海市	Weihai		7	2	36	6	76	2	29	8	103
日照市	Rizhao		1	1	8	2	36	4	19	3	99
临沂市	Linyi	9	19	6	31		50	4	21	12	103
德州市	Dezhou		1	2	21	6	25		22	6	77
聊城市	Liaocheng	1	4	2	14	1	37	4	21	8	76
滨州市	Binzhou		1	5	18	1	30	4	34	8	109
菏泽市	Heze				8		15	2	20	6	89

主要统计指标解释

律　师　指依法取得律师执业证书，担任法律顾问，民事(刑事、行政)案件代理人、刑事案件辩护人、办理非诉讼业务，解答法律询问，代写法律事务文书等，为社会提供法律服务的人员。

公　证　指公证处根据当事人申请，依照事实和法律，按照法定程序制作的，具有法律效力的司法证明文书。

公证员　指在公证处工作的人员总称，包括公证处主任、副主任、公证员、公证员助理(助理公证员)和其他从事辅助性工作的人员。

公证员助理　指在公证机构中协助公证员完成公证执业活动中各项辅助性工作的专职人员。

批准逮捕　指人民检察院对公安机关、国家安全机关、监狱管理机关提出逮捕的犯罪嫌疑人进行审查，根据事实，依法做出逮捕决定。该指标主要反映人民检察院对提请逮捕犯罪嫌疑人进行审查后依法做出批准逮捕决定的情况。

决定逮捕　指人民检察院对直接立案侦查的案件，认为需要逮捕犯罪嫌疑人时，依据法律做出的逮捕决定。该指标主要反映人民检察院对直接受理的案件行使决定逮捕权的情况。

提起公诉　指人民检察院对公安机关移送起诉以及自行侦查终结移送起诉的案件，经审查认为犯罪嫌疑人符合法定的起诉条件而代表国家将其提交人民法院审判的一种诉讼活动。

Explanatory Notes on Main Statistical Indicators

Lawyers refer to professionals who have obtained a lawyer's practice certificate in accordance with the law, and act as legal advisers, agents in criminal or civil lawsuits, or defenders in criminal lawsuits, to handle non-litigious legal affairs, to advise on legal inquiries , to draft legal documents, or to provide the public with legal services.

Notarization refers to legally binding judicial notary documents, developed at the request of the interested party based on facts and the law following certain legal proceedings.

Notary Personnel refer to people working for notary offices including: directors, deputy directors, notaries, assistant notaries and other people providing assistance.

Assistant Notary refers to the full-time staff who assist the notary in the notary office to complete different auxiliary tasks of notarization.

Approval for Arrest refers to the decision made by the People's Procuratorates, in accordance with the law and relevant facts and after due investigation, to approve the arrest of the suspect(s) as proposed by the public security departments, state security departments or prisons authority. This indicator reflects approved arrests made by the People's Procuratorates that are proposed by related departments.

Decision on Arrest refers to decision made by the People's Procuratorates, in accordance with laws, to arrest the suspect(s) in the cases that are accepted and to be investigated by the People's Procuratorates. This indicator mainly reflects the decision on execution of the authority of arrests by the People's Procuratorates.

Initiation of Public Prosecution refers to the prosecution submitted to the People's Court for trial on behalf of the country by the People's Procuratorates, based on the fact that the suspect(s) is deemed to meet the legal requirements for prosecution after the People's Procuratorates have conducted investigations on the cases transferred by the public security organs.

第
22
篇

各县(市、区)主要经济指标

Main Indicators of Counties
(Cities and Districts at County Level)

简 要 说 明

一、本篇资料的主要内容

本篇资料反映了全省各县（市、区）经济社会事业发展基本情况，主要包括土地面积、生产总值、农业、金融、城乡居民收入和教育等方面的内容。

二、本篇资料的来源

本篇资料粮食数据、畜牧业数据和城乡居民人均可支配收入分别由山东调查总队农业调查处、农村调查处、居民收支调查处整理提供，其余资料由省统计局农村处、核算处整理提供。

Brief Introduction

I. Content

Data in this chapter show the development in society and economy of counties or cities on the county level, mainly including area, GDP, agriculture, banking, disposable income of rural and urban households, and education.

II. Source of Data

Grain data,Animal husbandry data and disposable income of rural and urban households in this chapter are provided respectively by the Division of Rural Surveys，the Division of Countryside Surveys and the Division of Residents' Income and Expenditure Surveys of NBS Survey office in Shandong. The rest of data are are provided by the Division of Countryside Statistics and National Accounts of Shandong Provincial Bureau of Statistics.

22-1 各县(市、区)主要经济指标(2021年)

Major Economic Indicators of Counties(Cities and Districts at County Level,2021)

地 区	Region	行政区域土地面积(平方公里) Area of Local land (sq.km)	地区生产总值(亿元) Gross Domestic Product (100 million yuan)	年末金融机构各项存款余额(万元) Deposit Balance of Financial Institution at Year-end (10 000 yuan)	住户存款余额(万元) Household Deposits (10 000 yuan)	年末金融机构各项贷款余额(万元) Loan Balance of Financial Institution at Year-end (10 000 yuan)
济南市	**Jinan**					
历下区	Lixia	101	2124.1			
市中区	Shizhong	281	1161.7			
槐荫区	Huaiyin	152	701.1			
天桥区	Tianqiao	259	660.0			
历城区	Licheng	1301	2741.9			
长清区	Changqing	1209	371.9	5405000	4056000	3300000
章丘区	Zhangqiu	1719	1120.4	10971985	7353031	8820589
济阳区	Jiyang	1099	267.5	3704317	2541603	2947943
莱芜区	Laiwu	1740	908.8	10222700		7838800
钢城区	Gangcheng	506	338.3			
平阴县	Pingyin	715	269.1	3006534	2156078	2093031
商河县	Shanghe	1162	208.5	2769684	2198571	1954147
青岛市	**Qingdao**					
市南区	Shinan	32	1400.6			
市北区	Shibei	66	1063.6			
黄岛区	Huangdao	2128	4368.5	27991800	12887700	27014200
崂山区	Laoshan	396	1011.1			
李沧区	Licang	99	601.2			
城阳区	Chengyang	584	1334.2	15743525		14205216
即墨区	Jimo	1921	1452.5	15124752	8628996	13096686
胶州市	Jiaozhou	1324	1456.3	12611500	7063340	11758800
平度市	Pingdu	3176	821.1	10231412	7560093	6420014
莱西市	Laixi	1568	625.5	6900008	4442722	6530726
淄博市	**Zibo**					
淄川区	Zichuan	960	519.5	7265781	5534060	3796775
张店区	Zhangdian	360	1098.6	23218543	12440435	20043731
博山区	Boshan	698	260.1	4386492	3751460	2052088
临淄区	Linzi	664	859.9	9858670	6782940	5440378
周村区	Zhoucun	307	266.7	4561116	3596742	2429837
桓台县	Huantai	509	674.0	5701959	3214282	4451730
高青县	Gaoqing	831	206.3	2372849	1873465	1838724
沂源县	Yiyuan	1636	315.5	3809700	2844639	2823979
枣庄市	**Zaozhuang**					
市中区	Shizhong	374	295.3	5714458	4021290	4557307
薛城区	Xuecheng	507	372.7	6076578	3628853	5534208
峄城区	Yicheng	637	164.6	1601042	1211678	1123776
台儿庄区	Taierzhuang	532	132.3	1410753	1095704	1158465

22-1 续表 1 continued

地 区	Region	行政区域土地面积(平方公里) Area of Local land (sq.km)	地区生产总值(亿元) Gross Domestic Product (100 million yuan)	年末金融机构各项存款余额(万元) Deposit Balance of Financial Institution at Year-end (10 000 yuan)	住户存款余额(万元) Household Deposits (10 000 yuan)	年末金融机构各项贷款余额(万元) Loan Balance of Financial Institution at Year-end (10 000 yuan)
山亭区	Shanting	1019	128.1	1510417	1193123	869959
滕州市	Tengzhou	1495	858.5	9447038	7169762	6868127
东营市	**Dongying**					
东营区	Dongying	1179	1693.3	26048500	12759428	19129200
河口区	Hekou	2267	418.2	3410218	2238057	1995377
垦利区	Kenli	2340	317.0	4427690	2697041	4184103
利津县	Lijin	1301	280.6	2918379	1617669	2297347
广饶县	Guangrao	1167	732.5	8320006	4474864	6005155
烟台市	**Yantai**					
芝罘区	Zhifu	181	1097.2			
福山区	Fushan	937	2397.9	26717950	8769835	19544580
牟平区	Mouping	1515	333.8	5232884	3866951	2793777
莱山区	Laishan	332	494.2	6737115	4089658	4713795
蓬莱市	Penglai	1204	489.7	5958302	4601649	3972033
龙口市	Longkou	941	1236.6	12721553	7424333	7606020
莱阳市	Laiyang	1731	479.2	6042561	4700068	2964448
莱州市	Laizhou	1949	701.3	9605200	7986440	3742779
招远市	Zhaoyuan	1432	749.4	7274624	5077835	3747749
栖霞市	Qixia	1793	272.7	3775636	3166074	1452388
海阳市	Haiyang	1916	459.6	5158689	4390167	3287392
潍坊市	**Weifang**					
潍城区	Weicheng	270	364.0			
寒亭区	Hanting	1301	607.2			
坊子区	Fangzi	896	261.9	3929612	2932595	2581497
奎文区	Kuiwen	193	1022.7			
临朐县	Linqu	1831	389.4	6410507	4798945	4414517
昌乐县	Changle	1101	405.3	5187569	3679707	4604455
青州市	Qingzhou	1561	676.8	10085420	8182231	6915936
诸城市	Zhucheng	2151	767.4	10280326	7461277	7853427
寿光市	Shouguan	1997	953.6	14311271	8710474	11030742
安丘市	Anqiu	1712	403.9	6549946	5066616	5448448
高密市	Gaomi	1527	614.6	7671847	5729349	6953381
昌邑市	Changyi	1628	527.9	5752951	4687552	3919213
济宁市	**Jining**					
任城区	Rencheng	884	956.6	23982375	12932703	24094872
兖州区	Yanzhou	650	807.4	5946746	4274711	3536681
微山县	Weishan	1738	428.5	3158977	2541836	1726473
鱼台县	Yutai	653	219.6	2293332	1872703	2018802

22-1 续表 2 continued

地 区	Region	行政区域土地面积（平方公里）Area of Local land (sq.km)	地区生产总值（亿元）Gross Domestic Product (100 million yuan)	年末金融机构各项存款余额（万元）Deposit Balance of Financial Institution at Year-end (10 000 yuan)	住户存款余额（万元）Household Deposits (10 000 yuan)	年末金融机构各项贷款余额（万元）Loan Balance of Financial Institution at Year-end (10 000 yuan)
金乡县	Jinxiang	888	245.8	3751013	3034517	2505773
嘉祥县	Jiaxiang	975	326.7	5065449	4263210	2866439
汶上县	Wenshang	889	250.5	3908000	3189700	2432700
泗水县	Sishui	1118	203.3	2803534	2354616	1627788
梁山县	Liangshan	961	268.1	5173117	4535661	2607960
曲阜市	Qufu	815	402.9	4688873	3595000	2888048
邹城市	Zoucheng	1617	960.6	11805151	5785382	9703353
泰安市	**Tai'an**					
泰山区	Taishan	337	528.8	9297600	5169800	7325200
岱岳区	Daiyue	1751	610.3	8642712	6213777	6580222
宁阳县	Ningyang	1124	274.1	4123955	3347401	2532324
东平县	Dongping	1340	238.6	4055200	3428417	2884489
新泰市	Xintai	1934	573.9	9015297	7336528	5704337
肥城市	Feicheng	1278	770.9	8126587	6150943	4256105
威海市	**Weihai**					
环翠区	Huancui	992	1482.2	28962084	15225337	23686422
文登区	Wendeng	1614	631.5	7598449	5802811	5653071
荣成市	Rongcheng	1555	1021.4	10778994	7439741	8162175
乳山市	Rushan	1660	328.8	5120918	4274191	2981408
日照市	**Rizhao**					
东港区	Donggang	1273	1014.8	19337937	9234519	23597014
岚山区	Lanshan	787	560.4	3211461	2436877	2529819
五莲县	Wulian	1497	211.9	3613054	2897700	2181208
莒 县	Juxian	1821	425.0	6898118	5539149	5346868
临沂市	**Linyi**					
兰山区	Lanshan	891	1334.1	31783543	16287602	36214903
罗庄区	Luozhuang	569	536.6	4697355	3182003	5657486
河东区	Hedong	834	630.4	8564505	4073000	8191965
沂南县	Yinan	1719	264.7	5506711	4483723	3506462
郯城县	Tancheng	1195	362.6	4211051	3548409	3066189
沂水县	Yishui	2414	503.7	6858489	5554472	4352059
兰陵县	Lanling	1724	316.8	5376020	4251657	4282890
费 县	Feixian	1660	469.7	4777590	3796327	3802743
平邑县	Pingyi	1823	279.2	4435539	3564384	3042770
莒南县	Junan	1751	339.4	6105268	4730873	4071905
蒙阴县	Mengyin	1602	195.9	3273810	2681677	2121389
临沭县	Linshu	1010	232.4	4020807	2794706	3389549

22-1 续表 3 continued

地 区	Region	行政区域土地面积(平方公里) Area of Local land (sq.km)	地区生产总值(亿元) Gross Domestic Product (100 million yuan)	年末金融机构各项存款余额(万元) Deposit Balance of Financial Institution at Year-end (10 000 yuan)	住户存款余额(万元) Household Deposits (10 000 yuan)	年末金融机构各项贷款余额(万元) Loan Balance of Financial Institution at Year-end (10 000 yuan)
德州市	**Dezhou**					
德城区	Decheng	538	802.7	15267266	9094838	10180309
陵城区	Lingcheng	1213	264.6	3139785	2612225	1521153
宁津县	Ningjin	833	273.8	3780420	3128595	1630094
庆云县	Qingyun	501	186.5	2106609	1477734	1436753
临邑县	Linyi	1016	305.1	3501500	2718400	1693200
齐河县	Qihe	1411	399.4	4255979	2970698	3421576
平原县	Pingyuan	1047	265.7	3111853	2592835	1294954
夏津县	Xiajin	882	226.6	2805112	2344972	1679227
武城县	Wucheng	751	205.1	2797887	2318413	1279736
乐陵市	Laoling	1173	274.9	3463894	2730791	2238484
禹城市	Yucheng	992	284.4	3539568	2607919	2654763
聊城市	**Liaocheng**					
东昌府区	Dongchangfu	1443	866.3	18442313	10150725	14739424
茌平区	Chiping	1003	345.8	4926718	3546751	2671728
阳谷县	Yanggu	1008	318.1	4923587	3853922	3290518
莘 县	Shenxian	1388	258.0	5006959	4463602	2326241
东阿县	Donge	727	168.5	2972419	2292533	1716980
冠 县	Guanxian	1161	247.3	4152103	3364096	2245448
高唐县	Gaotang	947	169.0	3196562	2690033	1781784
临清市	Linqing	951	269.3	5367800	4481275	2581821
滨州市	**Binzhou**					
滨城区	Bincheng	1040	745.9	14057700	6560400	12327700
沾化区	Zhanhua	2218	178.5	2149703	1459466	1380481
惠民县	Huimin	1363	228.9	3094569	2517989	1755508
阳信县	Yangxin	798	256.8	2175900	1685000	1780400
无棣县	Wudi	2094	388.1	3115933	2070387	2319377
博兴县	Boxing	900	441.9	5640378	3635869	4041028
邹平市	Zouping	1250	632.0	7436307	4803616	7071254
菏泽市	**Heze**					
牡丹区	Mudan	1415	963.3	16181594	9959609	13942403
定陶区	Dingtao	846	253.1	3366804	2877277	1875142
曹 县	Caoxian	1974	529.5	6377452	5401358	3573539
单 县	Shanxian	1647	397.0	5184671	4463003	3044568
成武县	Chengwu	998	176.7	3479773	3092688	1462181
巨野县	Juye	1308	396.5	5915224	5009935	3203702
郓城县	Yuncheng	1633	498.6	7179943	6438187	3293720
鄄城县	Juancheng	1032	277.4	4272932	3835221	1785110
东明县	Dongming	1370	484.5	4238218	3432509	2392339

22-1 续表 4 continued

地 区	Region	粮食面积(公顷) Area of Grain (hectares)	粮食产量(吨) Output of Grain (ton)	油料产量(吨) Output of Oil-bearing Crops (ton)	蔬菜产量(吨) Output of Vegetables (ton)	园林水果产量(吨) Output of Fruits (ton)	肉类总产量(吨) Output of Meat (ton)	奶类产量(吨) Output of Milk (ton)
济南市	**Jinan**							
历下区	Lixia							
市中区	Shizhong	3996	19050	12	2899	3737	2949	329
槐荫区	Huaiyin	2147	13160		11251	125	398	31
天桥区	Tianqiao	12374	70025	54	13738	8315	5599	1175
历城区	Licheng	19757	104134	1621	166985	119239	9762	8936
长清区	Changqing	44227	264462	17899	549528	58385	28998	69547
章丘区	Zhangqiu	107515	624821	5650	1861622	72911	45015	5921
济阳区	Jiyang	100814	622646	1785	1189918	22374	21147	37707
莱芜区	Laiwu	31475	194700	19946	1220409	110276	57497	1427
钢城区	Gangcheng	4321	24180	9550	208299	105602	26071	1066
平阴县	Pingyin	35270	196438	9412	673140	101186	29069	70357
商河县	Shanghe	121719	797090	28	1019838	16821	47072	224491
青岛市	**Qingdao**							
市南区	Shinan							
市北区	Shibei							
黄岛区	Huangdao	48285	261570	88535	587959	105260	56401	592
崂山区	Laoshan			171	8976	6269		
李沧区	Licang							
城阳区	Chengyang	905	5726	167	29045	17337	1858	5236
即墨区	Jimo	78113	445217	42909	657390	33881	72568	66009
胶州市	Jiaozhou	63382	389003	25272	1105858	57049	38746	5274
平度市	Pingdu	201721	1460114	100497	2958686	240443	149719	12056
莱西市	Laixi	87664	566113	81901	1269835	344988	186188	243318
淄博市	**Zibo**							
淄川区	Zichuan	13958	58208	819	28032	19239	13705	320
张店区	Zhangdian	4163	22485	141	36185	7161	5549	800
博山区	Boshan	5568	22648	839	58121	84917	3814	50
临淄区	Linzi	46319	334072	29	1064036	20599	37185	12700
周村区	Zhoucun	10418	54725	202	23161	7616	9600	1400
桓台县	Huantai	45907	344971	3	48690	4696	11118	5126
高青县	Gaoqing	81626	575318	273	432668	21499	36916	113221
沂源县	Yiyuan	9343	35242	12241	258722	858295	31423	300
枣庄市	**Zaozhuang**							
市中区	Shizhong	14249	76651	10910	163497	21187	17551	3123
薛城区	Xuecheng	38025	229963	5209	253787	14498	17596	925
峄城区	Yicheng	51067	285656	11839	656372	62881	29061	2704
台儿庄区	Taierzhuang	49909	290483	987	581481	16323	28913	23003

22-1 续表 5 continued

地 区	Region	粮食面积(公顷) Area of Grain (hectares)	粮食产量(吨) Output of Grain (ton)	油料产量(吨) Output of Oil-bearing Crops (ton)	蔬菜产量(吨) Output of Vegetables (ton)	园林水果产量(吨) Output of Fruits (ton)	肉类总产量(吨) Output of Meat (ton)	奶类产量(吨) Output of Milk (ton)
山亭区	Shanting	24284	147254	21047	220687	122792	24268	1033
滕州市	Tengzhou	106596	800831	30498	3604289	56482	47635	1041
东营市	**Dongying**							
东营区	Dongying	24728	131961	84	87505	9363	18865	7243
河口区	Hekou	24577	111246	341	28877	29819	54807	194710
垦利区	Kenli	56002	293571	158	57480	10193	69255	49455
利津县	Lijin	66667	352220	1267	204835	18593	72874	2515
广饶县	Guangrao	82280	476195		394227	6005	79674	122092
烟台市	**Yantai**							
芝罘区	Zhifu	48	271	102	18356	2777	193	269
福山区	Fushan	2356	13018	11713	78441	427569	19291	5535
牟平区	Mouping	19725	108961	34378	145928	728108	148532	17104
莱山区	Laishan	1887	11277	4463	45735	53005	346	101
蓬莱区	Penglai	8946	51711	20116	165426	1521620	62379	7785
龙口市	Longkou	15325	100125	6401	239757	540725	50427	24458
莱阳市	Laiyang	69813	418627	89899	534806	543603	131588	59078
莱州市	Laizhou	82999	529349	43855	432762	326234	119984	17306
招远市	Zhaoyuan	37641	218111	66638	141270	735055	51457	7731
栖霞市	Qixia	13503	80834	51550	169841	2091846	44041	5385
海阳市	Haiyang	50503	301096	86479	478952	464816	91575	8473
潍坊市	**Weifang**							
潍城区	Weicheng	10559	65239		109625	11397	7193	6383
寒亭区	Hanting	43991	277007	1158	299631	39066	31895	37469
坊子区	Fangzi	48600	306651	6836	628957	28968	45311	2592
奎文区	Kuiwen	1529	9272	150	700			
临朐县	Linqu	27840	167193	17263	282618	372147	101491	58039
昌乐县	Changle	36216	217909	37170	1374163	84431	88556	21326
青州市	Qingzhou	29365	178786	12	2005490	102452	125077	2966
诸城市	Zhucheng	126414	787265	45519	1053707	73596	206484	3259
寿光市	Shouguan	86550	594625	216	3797746	36350	187947	32417
安丘市	Anqiu	54938	332345	45448	2006157	138554	104586	8455
高密市	Gaomi	133822	881737	16462	758574	46821	148832	14391
昌邑市	Changyi	85428	540609	9209	748251	73865	98270	4183
济宁市	**Jining**							
任城区	Rencheng	64755	460089	104	313003	37504	13314	9392
兖州区	Yanzhou	46376	327844	2960	492818	9380	14207	3711
微山县	Weishan	50397	336053	1316	349460	4786	20643	1220
鱼台县	Yutai	48885	379873		720718	6767	18897	356

22-1 续表 6 continued

地 区	Region	粮食面积（公顷）Area of Grain (hectares)	粮食产量（吨）Output of Grain (ton)	油料产量（吨）Output of Oil-bearing Crops (ton)	蔬菜产量（吨）Output of Vegetables (ton)	园林水果产量（吨）Output of Fruits (ton)	肉类总产量（吨）Output of Meat (ton)	奶类产量（吨）Output of Milk (ton)
金乡县	Jinxiang	35595	224479	11827	2461194	48808	31399	7640
嘉祥县	Jiaxiang	102796	673956	1844	421256	19583	56990	3440
汶上县	Wenshang	100099	689504	6501	229667	13426	56695	66505
泗水县	Sishui	39263	246912	56867	641954	51681	67676	1236
梁山县	Liangshan	97909	615952	5980	843809	52357	82618	33008
曲阜市	Qufu	64176	439963	9207	147196	50996	48039	9727
邹城市	Zoucheng	69450	473499	51703	918991	93320	53567	2472
泰安市	**Tai'an**							
泰山区	Taishan	2109	15314	5	12844	5087	4071	9697
岱岳区	Daiyue	61371	454988	18862	1680204	123071	47617	57632
宁阳县	Ningyang	85287	603625	59072	863729	102668	73210	53920
东平县	Dongping	99914	626201	16187	613283	14406	34991	13027
新泰市	Xintai	52184	381371	87514	1369947	263583	94907	32864
肥城市	Feicheng	71011	490884	8115	1153483	79018	58823	85442
威海市	**Weihai**							
环翠区	Huancui	9702	52945	12809	76949	156542	14255	10995
文登区	Wendeng	38716	232820	61331	266446	315354	73879	3912
荣成市	Rongcheng	36689	218245	44053	225077	255689	29325	22740
乳山市	Rushan	36738	222680	80937	412868	472337	66511	3727
日照市	**Rizhao**							
东港区	Donggang	20800	137820	33122	110620	113988	43194	4301
岚山区	Lanshan	18801	125361	28239	147664	46063	35029	54271
五莲县	Wulian	34313	218799	71493	307178	130128	59873	
莒 县	Juxian	56867	389118	86278	595085	162959	132622	7248
临沂市	**Linyi**							
兰山区	Lanshan	30465	175193	18769	137424	74115	35896	10266
罗庄区	Luozhuang	27612	170666	10460	128255	7063	16242	25496
河东区	Hedong	45802	298670	17139	301784	37968	23214	879
沂南县	Yinan	58297	355483	77371	1134575	103579	213864	36144
郯城县	Tancheng	94208	723509	12312	646257	24080	71540	1519
沂水县	Yishui	48868	301135	80005	1003629	804485	126893	11778
兰陵县	Lanling	99262	669112	58959	3433378	95042	126140	19151
费 县	Feixian	50001	314586	79027	470535	280191	99698	7099
平邑县	Pingyi	46800	297056	63939	315534	290451	74334	355
莒南县	Junan	73445	428245	110800	322014	87233	187107	3773
蒙阴县	Mengyin	18131	130209	33613	195311	1289644	43686	
临沭县	Linshu	52139	316377	160737	165571	50439	77741	12009

22-1 续表 7 continued

地 区	Region	粮食面积（公顷）Area of Grain (hectares)	粮食产量（吨）Output of Grain (ton)	油料产量（吨）Output of Oil-bearing Crops (ton)	蔬菜产量（吨）Output of Vegetables (ton)	园林水果产量（吨）Output of Fruits (ton)	肉类总产量（吨）Output of Meat (ton)	奶类产量（吨）Output of Milk (ton)
德州市	**Dezhou**							
德城区	Decheng	32977	215042	95	89239	14639	13083	1352
陵城区	Lingcheng	131230	954085	171	594753	10584	76773	24739
宁津县	Ningjin	91443	641684	545	386781	10613	47509	5099
庆云县	Qingyun	42539	276973	93	148984	21694	33922	790
临邑县	Linyi	110324	781638	971	438096	8188	57617	10190
齐河县	Qihe	151390	1111998	1902	1094080	37825	98880	46760
平原县	Pingyuan	115178	837317	612	1243295	23410	100013	9172
夏津县	Xiajin	90342	610051	2442	272605	28094	90685	4078
武城县	Wucheng	88789	640019	3529	271853	15766	20851	6438
乐陵市	Laoling	117744	845045	18	361274	123342	63871	66261
禹城市	Yucheng	96814	702167	2065	1626927	9410	75312	90700
聊城市	**Liaocheng**							
东昌府区	Dongchangfu	110818	799791	3281	1234369	35889	93138	3055
茌平区	Chiping	106141	741001	1486	426777	20956	56915	3377
阳谷县	Yanggu	107670	781580	3438	1953639	47171	153249	11613
莘 县	Shenxian	115185	793428	10987	2790605	46049	123266	2640
东阿县	Donge	70187	490057	784	282148	21204	48756	1372
冠 县	Guanxian	102560	697084	7219	1408914	287936	89615	17290
高唐县	Gaotang	97143	669915	6117	274518	14954	52454	1454
临清市	Linqing	102994	706893	1097	752616	29623	36872	39985
滨州市	**Binzhou**							
滨城区	Bincheng	74134	456718	190	127294	11333	33485	35419
沾化区	Zhanhua	70865	408670	900	35845	309994	72204	12008
惠民县	Huimin	116242	762909	4859	1144357	89571	112892	5459
阳信县	Yangxin	68167	438435		191199	206353	123301	2045
无棣县	Wudi	74219	440736	1141	31439	118065	109882	851
博兴县	Boxing	75451	500369	109	149079	3214	33662	1040
邹平市	Zouping	108918	714139	456	73188	41482	79560	32557
菏泽市	**Heze**							
牡丹区	Mudan	130546	861566	22699	1168784	87583	79767	8074
定陶区	Dingtao	90513	613874	7153	790951	22585	39424	3590
曹 县	Caoxian	202562	1343040	34204	845841	38308	137311	131387
单 县	Shanxian	136851	903124	44235	1824484	135110	70799	12610
成武县	Chengwu	83744	556818	2552	1232796	24720	44322	1655
巨野县	Juye	102126	669787	9472	1550736	82016	61194	3076
郓城县	Yuncheng	167585	1113833	27720	1318661	49756	109333	4337
鄄城县	Juancheng	123279	817221	33084	365122	46540	74600	3120
东明县	Dongming	151867	997745	46479	624913	32046	95083	13228

22-1 续表 8 continued

地 区	Region	普通中学专任教师数（人）Full-time Teachers in Secondary Schools (person)	小 学专任教师数（人）Full-time Teachers in Primary Schools (person)	普通中学在校学生数（人）Total Enrollment in Secondary Schools (person)	小 学在校学生数（人）Total Enrollment in Primary Schools (person)	城镇居民人均可支配收入（元）Per Capita Disposable Income of Urban Households (yuan)	农村居民人均可支配收入（元）Per Capita Disposable Income of Rural Households (yuan)
济南市	**Jinan**						
历下区	Lixia	2862	4665	35064	81693	67893	
市中区	Shizhong	3282	4289	39187	68723	66270	
槐荫区	Huaiyin	1874	3075	22786	53192	59813	
天桥区	Tianqiao	2033	3244	23841	49875	58767	21150
历城区	Licheng	5954	6006	68018	96222	55484	25428
长清区	Changqing	2378	2151	24990	31150	46955	22607
章丘区	Zhangqiu	5598	4410	45167	62644	46329	26727
济阳区	Jiyang	2231	2241	30267	40031	37876	21240
莱芜区	Laiwu	4859	3148	56393	52435	41628	21506
钢城区	Gangcheng	1246	1046	12839	14980	48501	22808
平阴县	Pingyin	1661	1485	17596	19299	34294	18862
商河县	Shanghe	2239	2284	30660	40347	33201	18793
青岛市	**Qingdao**						
市南区	Shinan	2065	2299	24431	36452	69520	
市北区	Shibei	3108	3803	37679	65134	64112	
黄岛区	Huangdao	6690	6589	75843	118310	59249	26412
崂山区	Laoshan	954	1796	9855	27318	67591	29615
李沧区	Licang	1593	2469	18884	45910	63949	
城阳区	Chengyang	3665	4522	43656	82874	64738	28069
即墨区	Jimo	7952	5970	69903	86644	54372	26513
胶州市	Jiaozhou	4058	4266	50035	67606	53047	26305
平度市	Pingdu	5892	4745	59876	67906	51066	25196
莱西市	Laixi	4006	2476	41493	32479	51404	25875
淄博市	**Zibo**						
淄川区	Zichuan	3354	2232	34103	27628	47079	22769
张店区	Zhangdian	5349	4544	68486	73117	51853	26434
博山区	Boshan	2281	1293	21259	15639	45557	21584
临淄区	Linzi	3256	2028	34587	28340	51784	26542
周村区	Zhoucun	2024	1212	21171	16023	45059	22463
桓台县	Huantai	2688	1569	25950	21307	48400	24752
高青县	Gaoqing	1913	1397	20011	14025	38155	19636
沂源县	Yiyuan	3074	2141	28074	21916	45996	22287
枣庄市	**Zaozhuang**						
市中区	Shizhong	2892	3488	45495	60833	38664	20415
薛城区	Xuecheng	3386	3392	44442	55748	35401	18917
峄城区	Yicheng	2210	2354	33493	37460	33818	19527
台儿庄区	Taierzhuang	1602	1986	23916	31287	31284	16854

22-1 续表 9 continued

地 区	Region	普通中学专任教师数（人）Full-time Teachers in Secondary Schools (person)	小 学专任教师数（人）Full-time Teachers in Primary Schools (person)	普通中学在校学生数（人）Total Enrollment in Secondary Schools (person)	小 学在校学生数（人）Total Enrollment in Primary Schools (person)	城镇居民人均可支配收入（元）Per Capita Disposable Income of Urban Households (yuan)	农村居民人均可支配收入（元）Per Capita Disposable Income of Rural Households (yuan)
山亭区	Shanting	1776	2618	21333	33549	26031	16865
滕州市	Tengzhou	6525	8911	91147	138698	41705	20801
东营市	**Dongying**						
东营区	Dongying	5355	3864	63436	61283	57487	25525
河口区	Hekou	1231	933	10561	11009	53645	23188
垦利区	Kenli	1365	1068	13520	14652	52537	23252
利津县	Lijin	1696	1015	11008	10040	44663	21837
广饶县	Guangrao	3078	1846	31115	29700	50860	25747
烟台市	**Yantai**						
芝罘区	Zhifu	4165	2802	49786	49229	56587	
福山区	Fushan	3116	2880	38060	52128	55156	28031
牟平区	Mouping	1364	1458	11741	15503	52036	25551
莱山区	Laishan	1059	1182	11431	20097	62325	28361
蓬莱区	Penglai	2072	1551	18366	17767	54074	27138
龙口市	Longkou	2960	1846	31585	32266	57094	28101
莱阳市	Laiyang	3463	1980	32911	29948	41054	21011
莱州市	Laizhou	3777	2369	33262	29831	52194	26532
招远市	Zhaoyuan	2650	1330	23096	20008	53465	27038
栖霞市	Qixia	2358	1412	14516	11316	38563	19907
海阳市	Haiyang	2863	1484	25386	19645	51265	23907
潍坊市	**Weifang**						
潍城区	Weicheng	2228	1785	17571	36977	48425	25138
寒亭区	Hanting	3221	2317	22590	27892	44788	24023
坊子区	Fangzi	3451	2993	33711	33954	43846	23755
奎文区	Kuiwen	1743	3885	18076	65838	52040	
临朐县	Linqu	3620	3394	41748	59313	40379	22051
昌乐县	Changle	3866	2902	45715	39137	42144	23108
青州市	Qingzhou	4488	4060	36791	59881	45346	24323
诸城市	Zhucheng	5652	4257	60202	60636	47554	25725
寿光市	Shouguan	5632	5122	56415	75383	48487	26527
安丘市	Anqiu	4335	3375	52757	48102	40740	22626
高密市	Gaomi	4647	4024	50523	56581	45880	23355
昌邑市	Changyi	2619	2343	26435	30548	42646	24176
济宁市	**Jining**						
任城区	Rencheng	6975	6589	72189	69208	47377	21263
兖州区	Yanzhou	2516	2700	27811	39441	46274	23252
微山县	Weishan	2770	3182	28914	38764	37322	20281
鱼台县	Yutai	1730	2047	22876	30521	35386	19844

22-1 续表 10 continued

地 区	Region	普通中学专任教师数（人）Full-time Teachers in Secondary Schools (person)	小 学专任教师数（人）Full-time Teachers in Primary Schools (person)	普通中学在校学生数（人）Total Enrollment in Secondary Schools (person)	小 学在校学生数（人）Total Enrollment in Primary Schools (person)	城镇居民人均可支配收入（元）Per Capita Disposable Income of Urban Households (yuan)	农村居民人均可支配收入（元）Per Capita Disposable Income of Rural Households (yuan)
金乡县	Jinxiang	3555	3598	45205	49149	37524	21469
嘉祥县	Jiaxiang	4436	4378	68842	79680	35577	19941
汶上县	Wenshang	2808	3561	38895	56713	35842	20036
泗水县	Sishui	2237	3067	33027	40072	30235	16222
梁山县	Liangshan	3406	4172	54864	75000	35307	19586
曲阜市	Qufu	2808	2997	30235	40613	36457	20343
邹城市	Zoucheng	4896	5324	54414	80941	43216	21922
泰安市	**Tai'an**						
泰山区	Taishan	4654	2731	53899	56154	47992	22856
岱岳区	Daiyue	4280	3943	43698	51342	41299	20763
宁阳县	Ningyang	3324	3178	38029	38394	41278	20724
东平县	Dongping	3404	2532	39572	42552	36434	20192
新泰市	Xintai	6563	5583	81270	86787	42953	21667
肥城市	Feicheng	4437	3560	48066	47565	43714	22696
威海市	**Weihai**						
环翠区	Huancui	5273	4388	62393	71739	55816	24829
文登区	Wendeng	2672	1490	23011	20477	51234	27422
荣成市	Rongcheng	3030	1665	28602	27077	52209	27957
乳山市	Rushan	1721	922	14591	11464	45523	21818
日照市	**Rizhao**						
东港区	Donggang	4753	4630	56876	83030	40584	18756
岚山区	Lanshan	1595	1434	15214	21515	39901	20437
五莲县	Wulian	2579	1919	22575	26358	32105	19560
莒 县	Juxian	4788	4405	60989	80171	32571	19625
临沂市	**Linyi**						
兰山区	Lanshan	8901	9236	125379	233713	44709	18773
罗庄区	Luozhuang	4555	5355	67124	97347	44536	18655
河东区	Hedong	3997	5312	51000	93000	44046	18661
沂南县	Yinan	3849	3982	52700	63723	41676	17126
郯城县	Tancheng	3913	4925	55596	87840	42229	17681
沂水县	Yishui	4222	4597	53696	75645	43108	18294
兰陵县	Lanling	4924	5974	91978	141437	38683	18199
费 县	Feixian	3788	3867	49923	77666	43283	17529
平邑县	Pingyi	3381	4372	46918	83032	41962	17566
莒南县	Junan	3770	4661	41364	63405	39284	17020
蒙阴县	Mengyin	2365	2804	26018	44909	40602	16724
临沭县	Linshu	2617	2808	38441	47475	43801	17045

22-1 续表 11 continued

地 区	Region	普通中学专任教师数(人) Full-time Teachers in Secondary Schools (person)	小 学专任教师数(人) Full-time Teachers in Primary Schools (person)	普通中学在校学生数(人) Total Enrollment in Secondary Schools (person)	小 学在校学生数(人) Total Enrollment in Primary Schools (person)	城镇居民人均可支配收入(元) Per Capita Disposable Income of Urban Households (yuan)	农村居民人均可支配收入(元) Per Capita Disposable Income of Rural Households (yuan)
德州市	**Dezhou**						
德城区	Decheng	2211	3627	29895	81545	33498	19255
陵城区	Lingcheng	1765	2656	20788	33117	31691	18879
宁津县	Ningjin	1920	1906	26529	35753	31644	18607
庆云县	Qingyun	1966	2203	25489	36858	31281	17989
临邑县	Linyi	2943	2350	27842	33941	31900	19052
齐河县	Qihe	2046	2873	27456	38831	32429	19920
平原县	Pingyuan	1959	2384	21743	27201	32344	18919
夏津县	Xiajin	2490	2299	32130	37378	30947	18205
武城县	Wucheng	1809	1612	23536	29054	31698	18851
乐陵市	Leling	2990	3078	35550	47067	32152	19458
禹城市	Yucheng	2294	2278	26067	34313	32467	19506
聊城市	**Liaocheng**						
东昌府区	Dongchangfu	8165	10474	114404	162839	34017	17884
茌平区	Chiping	2362	2676	29979	47122	33481	17867
阳谷县	Yanggu	3574	4074	43528	58796	30820	17394
莘 县	Shenxian	5042	6176	76686	115792	29702	17863
东阿县	Donge	1787	1829	20642	26789	27076	17452
冠 县	Guanxian	3682	4906	55185	82657	31606	17197
高唐县	Gaotang	2126	2767	28977	41376	31844	17629
临清市	Linqing	3373	4306	55252	83156	31338	17347
滨州市	**Binzhou**						
滨城区	Bincheng	3782	4282	41296	66322	43016	21759
沾化区	Zhanhua	1625	1640	13502	20866	40267	20780
惠民县	Huimin	2450	2440	24501	35722	40429	19644
阳信县	Yangxin	2188	1898	24283	32500	39972	18928
无棣县	Wudi	1995	2244	22368	43520	40356	21183
博兴县	Boxing	2326	1989	21182	27518	42386	21529
邹平市	Zouping	3129	2986	35880	50434	42096	23686
菏泽市	**Heze**						
牡丹区	Mudan	6126	6681	87178	146547	35137	17304
定陶区	Dingtao	3091	3406	39907	59148	29611	16960
曹 县	Caoxian	6311	8814	103601	155428	31948	16695
单 县	Shanxian	5552	5777	75457	106832	30522	16735
成武县	Chengwu	3933	4083	54502	60912	30297	16893
巨野县	Juye	4816	5329	79762	111410	32624	17030
郓城县	Yuncheng	6273	6826	83369	115043	32210	17256
鄄城县	Juancheng	3703	4544	55238	83931	28855	16399
东明县	Dongming	4465	4737	61209	82027	30921	16734

附录1

全国各省（市、自治区）主要经济指标

Main Economic Indicators of the Whole Country by Region

简　要　说　明

一、本篇资料的主要内容

本篇资料反映了全国各省、自治区、直辖市经济社会发展基本情况，主要包括行政区划、人口、国内生产总值及其构成、财政、价格指数、居民生活、农业、工业、投资、建筑业、交通运输、国内贸易、进出口等方面的资料。

二、本篇资料的来源

本篇资料来源于中国统计出版社出版的《中国统计摘要 2022》，由省统计局综合处整理。

Brief Introduction

I. Content

Data in this chapter reflect the basic Socio-economic development of some provinces, mainly including divisions of administrative areas, population, GDP and its components, finance, price indices, livelihood, agriculture, industry, investment, construction industry, communications, domestic trade, exports and imports etc.

II. Source of Data

Data in this chapter come from China Statistics Abstract 2022 published by China Statistics Press and are prepared and compiled by the Division of Comprehensive Statistics of Shandong Provincial Bureau of Statistics.

附录 1-1 各地区行政区划(2021年底)

Divisions of Administrative Areas by Region(Year-end of 2021)

单位:个 (unit)

省级区划名称	Provinces, Autonomous Regions and Municipalities	地级区划数 Number of Regions at Prefecture Level	#地级市 Cities at Prefecture Level	县级区划数 Number of Regions at County Level	#市辖区 Districts under the Jurisdiction of Cities	#县级市 Cities at County Level	#县 Counties	#自治县 Autonomous Counties
全国总计	**National Total**	**333**	**293**	**2843**	**977**	**394**	**1301**	**117**
北京市	Beijing			16	16			
天津市	Tianjin			16	16			
河北省	Hebei	11	11	167	49	21	91	6
山西省	Shanxi	11	11	117	26	11	80	
内蒙古自治区	Inner Mongolia	12	9	103	23	11	17	
辽宁省	Liaoning	14	14	100	59	16	17	8
吉林省	Jilin	9	8	60	21	20	16	3
黑龙江省	Heilongjiang	13	12	121	54	21	45	1
上海市	Shanghai			16	16			
江苏省	Jiangsu	13	13	95	55	21	19	
浙江省	Zhejiang	11	11	90	37	20	32	1
安徽省	Anhui	16	16	104	45	9	50	
福建省	Fujian	9	9	84	31	11	42	
江西省	Jiangxi	11	11	100	27	12	61	
山东省	**Shandong**	**16**	**16**	**136**	**58**	**26**	**52**	
河南省	Henan	17	17	157	54	21	82	
湖北省	Hubei	13	12	103	39	26	35	2
湖南省	Hunan	14	13	122	36	19	60	7
广东省	Guangdong	21	21	122	65	20	34	3
广西壮族自治区	Guangxi	14	14	111	41	10	48	12
海南省	Hainan	4	4	25	10	5	4	6
重庆市	Chongqing			38	26		8	4
四川省	Sichuan	21	18	183	55	19	105	4
贵州省	Guizhou	9	6	88	16	10	50	11
云南省	Yunnan	16	8	129	17	18	65	29
西藏自治区	Tibet	7	6	74	8		66	
陕西省	Shaanxi	10	10	107	31	7	69	
甘肃省	Gansu	14	12	86	17	5	57	7
青海省	Qinghai	8	2	44	7	5	25	7
宁夏回族自治区	Ningxia	5	5	22	9	2	11	
新疆维吾尔自治区	Xinjiang	14	4	107	13	28	60	6
香港特别行政区	Hong Kong Special Administrative Region							
澳门特别行政区	Macao Special Administrative Region							
台湾省	Taiwan							

注:本表资料由民政部提供。

a)Data in this table are provided by the Ministry of Civil Affairs.

附录 1-1 续表 continued

单位：个 (unit)

省级区划名称	Provinces, Autonomous Regions and Municipalities	乡镇级区划数 Number of Regions at Township Level	#镇 数 Number of Towns	#乡 数 Number of Townships	#民族乡 Minority Autonomous Township	#街道办事处 Street Communities
全国总计	**National Total**	**38558**	**21322**	**8309**	**958**	**8925**
北京市	Beijing	343	143	35	5	165
天津市	Tianjin	252	125	3	1	124
河北省	Hebei	2254	1287	656	39	310
山西省	Shanxi	1278	631	430		217
内蒙古自治区	Inner Mongolia	1025	509	270	17	246
辽宁省	Liaoning	1354	640	201	54	513
吉林省	Jilin	958	426	181	28	351
黑龙江省	Heilongjiang	1316	565	336	52	415
上海市	Shanghai	215	106	2		107
江苏省	Jiangsu	1237	699	19	1	519
浙江省	Zhejiang	1364	618	258	14	488
安徽省	Anhui	1512	997	239	9	276
福建省	Fujian	1102	655	252	19	195
江西省	Jiangxi	1570	834	562	8	174
山东省	**Shandong**	**1825**	**1072**	**57**		**696**
河南省	Henan	2457	1178	606	12	673
湖北省	Hubei	1255	761	161	10	333
湖南省	Hunan	1943	1133	389	83	421
广东省	Guangdong	1609	1112	11	7	486
广西壮族自治区	Guangxi	1253	806	312	59	135
海南省	Hainan	218	175	21		22
重庆市	Chongqing	1031	625	161	14	245
四川省	Sichuan	3101	2016	626	83	459
贵州省	Guizhou	1509	831	314	192	364
云南省	Yunnan	1418	665	539	140	214
西藏自治区	Tibet	699	142	534	9	23
陕西省	Shaanxi	1316	973	17		326
甘肃省	Gansu	1356	892	337	32	127
青海省	Qinghai	404	140	222	28	42
宁夏回族自治区	Ningxia	242	103	90		49
新疆维吾尔自治区	Xinjiang	1142	463	468	42	210
香港特别行政区	Hong Kong Special Administrative Region					
澳门特别行政区	Macao Special AdministrativeRegion					
台湾省	Taiwan					

注：乡镇级总数包含河北省、新疆维吾尔自治区的各一个区公所。
a)Number of regions at townships level include one district office of Hebei and Xinjiang separately.

附录 1-2 地区生产总值、增长速度及构成(2021年)

Gross Domestic Product ,Growth Rate and Composition(2021)

地区	Region	地区生产总值(亿元) Gross Domestic Product (100 million yuan)	第一产业 Primary Industry	第二产业 Secondary Industry	第三产业 Tertiary Industry	地区生产总值比上年增长(%) Growth Rate (%)	构成(%) composition 第一产业 Primary Industry	第二产业 Secondary Industry	第三产业 Tertiary Industry
北京	Beijing	40269.6	111.3	7268.6	32889.6	8.5	0.3	18.0	81.7
天津	Tianjin	15695.0	225.4	5854.3	9615.4	6.6	1.4	37.3	61.3
河北	Hebei	40391.3	4030.3	16364.2	19996.7	6.5	10.0	40.5	49.5
山西	Shanxi	22590.2	1286.9	11213.1	10090.2	9.1	5.7	49.6	44.7
内蒙古	Inner Mongolia	20514.2	2225.2	9374.2	8914.8	6.3	10.8	45.7	43.5
辽宁	Liaoning	27584.1	2461.8	10875.2	14247.1	5.8	8.9	39.4	51.6
吉林	Jilin	13235.5	1553.8	4768.3	6913.4	6.6	11.7	36.0	52.2
黑龙江	Heilongjiang	14879.2	3463.0	3975.3	7440.9	6.1	23.3	26.7	50.0
上海	Shanghai	43214.9	100.0	11449.3	31665.6	8.1	0.2	26.5	73.3
江苏	Jiangsu	116364.2	4722.4	51775.4	59866.4	8.6	4.1	44.5	51.4
浙江	Zhejiang	73515.8	2209.1	31188.6	40118.1	8.5	3.0	42.4	54.6
安徽	Anhui	42959.2	3360.6	17613.2	21985.4	8.3	7.8	41.0	51.2
福建	Fujian	48810.4	2897.7	22866.3	23046.3	8.0	5.9	46.8	47.2
江西	Jiangxi	29619.7	2334.3	13183.2	14102.2	8.8	7.9	44.5	47.6
山东	**Shandong**	**83095.9**	**6029.0**	**33187.2**	**43879.7**	**8.3**	**7.3**	**39.9**	**52.8**
河南	Henan	58887.4	5620.82	24331.6	28934.9	6.3	9.5	41.3	49.1
湖北	Hubei	50012.9	4661.7	18952.9	26398.4	12.9	9.3	37.9	52.8
湖南	Hunan	46063.1	4322.9	18126.1	23614.1	7.7	9.4	39.4	51.3
广东	Guangdong	124369.7	5003.7	50219.2	69146.8	8.0	4.0	40.4	55.6
广西	Guangxi	24740.9	4015.5	8187.9	12537.5	7.5	16.2	33.1	50.7
海南	Hainan	6475.2	1254.4	1238.8	3982.0	11.2	19.4	19.1	61.5
重庆	Chongqing	27894.0	1922.0	11184.9	14787.1	8.3	6.9	40.1	53.0
四川	Sichuan	53850.8	5661.9	19901.4	28287.6	8.2	10.5	37.0	52.5
贵州	Guizhou	19586.4	2730.9	6984.7	9870.8	8.1	13.9	35.7	50.4
云南	Yunnan	27146.8	3870.2	9589.4	13687.2	7.3	14.3	35.3	50.4
西藏	Tibet	2080.2	164.1	757.3	1158.8	6.7	7.9	36.4	55.7
陕西	Shaanxi	29801.0	2409.4	13802.5	13589.1	6.5	8.1	46.3	45.6
甘肃	Gansu	10243.3	1364.7	3466.6	5412.0	6.9	13.3	33.8	52.8
青海	Qinghai	3346.6	352.7	1332.6	1661.4	5.7	10.5	39.8	49.6
宁夏	Ningxia	4522.3	364.5	2021.6	2136.3	6.7	8.1	44.7	47.2
新疆	Xinjiang	15983.6	2356.1	5967.4	7660.2	7.0	14.7	37.3	47.9

注：本表绝对数按当年价格计算，增长速度按不变价格计算。

a)Absolute figure are calculated at current prices,growth rate at constant prices.

附录 1-3 年末常住人口
Basic Statistics on National Population

单位:万人 (10 000 persons)

地 区	Region	2012	2013	2014	2015	2016	2017	2018	2019	2020	2021
全 国	**Total**	**135922**	**136726**	**137646**	**138326**	**139232**	**140011**	**140541**	**141008**	**141212**	**141260**
北 京	Beijing	2078	2125	2171	2188	2195	2194	2192	2190	2189	2189
天 津	Tianjin	1378	1410	1429	1439	1443	1410	1383	1385	1387	1373
河 北	Hebei	7262	7288	7323	7345	7375	7409	7426	7447	7464	7448
山 西	Shanxi	3548	3535	3528	3519	3514	3510	3502	3497	3490	3480
内蒙古	Inner Mongolia	2464	2455	2449	2440	2436	2433	2422	2415	2403	2400
辽 宁	Liaoning	4375	4365	4358	4338	4327	4312	4291	4277	4255	4229
吉 林	Jilin	2698	2668	2642	2613	2567	2526	2484	2448	2399	2375
黑龙江	Heilongjiang	3724	3666	3608	3529	3463	3399	3327	3255	3171	3125
上 海	Shanghai	2399	2448	2467	2458	2467	2466	2475	2481	2488	2489
江 苏	Jiangsu	8120	8192	8281	8315	8381	8423	8446	8469	8477	8505
浙 江	Zhejiang	5685	5784	5890	5985	6072	6170	6273	6375	6468	6540
安 徽	Anhui	5978	5988	5997	6011	6033	6057	6076	6092	6105	6113
福 建	Fujian	3841	3885	3945	3984	4016	4065	4104	4137	4161	4187
江 西	Jiangxi	4475	4476	4480	4485	4496	4511	4513	4516	4519	4517
山 东	**Shandong**	**9708**	**9746**	**9808**	**9866**	**9973**	**10033**	**10077**	**10106**	**10165**	**10170**
河 南	Henan	9532	9573	9645	9701	9778	9829	9864	9901	9941	9883
湖 北	Hubei	5781	5798	5816	5850	5885	5904	5917	5927	5745	5830
湖 南	Hunan	6590	6600	6611	6615	6625	6633	6635	6640	6645	6622
广 东	Guangdong	11041	11270	11489	11678	11908	12141	12348	12489	12624	12684
广 西	Guangxi	4694	4731	4770	4811	4857	4907	4947	4982	5019	5037
海 南	Hainan	910	920	936	945	957	972	982	995	1012	1020
重 庆	Chongqing	2975	3011	3043	3070	3110	3144	3163	3188	3209	3212
四 川	Sichuan	8085	8109	8139	8196	8251	8289	8321	8351	8371	8372
贵 州	Guizhou	3587	3632	3677	3708	3758	3803	3822	3848	3858	3852
云 南	Yunnan	4631	4641	4653	4663	4677	4693	4703	4714	4722	4690
西 藏	Tibet	315	317	325	330	340	349	354	361	366	366
陕 西	Shaanxi	3787	3804	3827	3846	3874	3904	3931	3944	3955	3954
甘 肃	Gansu	2550	2537	2531	2523	2520	2522	2515	2509	2501	2490
青 海	Qinghai	571	571	576	577	582	586	587	590	593	594
宁 夏	Ningxia	659	666	678	684	695	705	710	717	721	725
新 疆	Xinjiang	2253	2285	2325	2385	2428	2480	2520	2559	2590	2589

注:1.本表2011—2019年数据根据第七次全国人口普查数据修订。2.全国数据包括中国人民解放军现役军人数，但不包括香港、澳门特别行政区和台湾地区数据；分省数据中未包括中国人民解放军现役军人数。

a)The data in this table from 2011 to 2019 are revised based on the data of the seventh national census.

b)The military personnel were included in the national total population,but excluded in the regional total population.The national total population excluded the population of Hong Kong,Macao and Taiwan.

附录 1–4　固定资产投资(不含农户)增长速度

Investment in Fixed Assets growth rate

单位:%　　(%)

地　区	Region	2017	2018	2019	2020	2021
全国总计	**Total**	**7.2**	**5.9**	**5.4**	**2.9**	**4.9**
北　京	Beijing	5.3	-5.4	-2.5	2.2	4.9
天　津	Tianjin	0.5	-4.9	13.1	3.0	4.8
河　北	Hebei	5.3	5.7	6.5	3.2	3.0
山　西	Shanxi	6.3	5.7	9.3	10.6	8.7
内蒙古	Inner Mongolia	-7.2	-28.3	6.7	-1.5	9.8
辽　宁	Liaoning	0.1	3.9	0.3	2.6	2.6
吉　林	Jilin	1.4	1.4	-16.2	8.3	11.0
黑龙江	Heilongjiang	6.2	-4.7	6.3	3.6	6.4
上　海	Shanghai	7.2	5.2	5.1	10.3	8.0
江　苏	Jiangsu	7.5	5.5	5.1	0.3	5.8
浙　江	Zhejiang	8.6	7.2	10.0	5.4	10.8
安　徽	Anhui	11.0	11.8	9.2	5.1	9.4
福　建	Fujian	13.9	11.5	5.9	-0.4	6.0
江　西	Jiangxi	12.3	11.1	9.2	8.2	10.8
山　东	**Shandong**	**7.3**	**3.8**	**-8.2**	**3.6**	**6.0**
河　南	Henan	10.4	8.1	8.0	4.3	4.5
湖　北	Hubei	11.0	10.9	10.7	-18.8	20.4
湖　南	Hunan	13.1	10.0	10.1	7.6	8.0
广　东	Guangdong	13.5	10.7	11.1	7.2	6.3
广　西	Guangxi	12.8	10.7	9.6	4.2	7.6
海　南	Hainan	10.1	-12.5	-9.2	8.0	10.2
重　庆	Chongqing	9.5	7.0	5.6	3.9	6.1
四　川	Sichuan	10.6	10.2	8.6	2.8	5.9
贵　州	Guizhou	20.1	15.8	0.9	3.2	-3.1
云　南	Yunnan	18.0	11.6	8.5	7.7	4.0
西　藏	Tibet	23.8	9.9	-2.2	5.4	-14.2
陕　西	Shaanxi	14.6	10.4	2.5	4.1	-3.0
甘　肃	Gansu	-40.3	-3.9	6.6	7.8	11.1
青　海	Qinghai	10.5	7.3	5.0	-12.2	-2.9
宁　夏	Ningxia	3.0	-18.2	-10.3	4.0	2.2
新　疆	Xinjiang	20.0	-25.2	2.5	16.2	15.0

附录 1-5 房地产开发企业（单位）房屋施工、竣工面积和商品房销售面积

Floor Space of Buildings for Real Estate Development

单位：万平方米　　(10 000 sq.m)

地区	Region	房屋施工面积 Floor Space of Buildings under Construction		房屋竣工面积 Floor Space of Buildings Completed		商品房销售面积 Floor Space of Buildings Sold	
		2020	2021	2020	2021	2020	2021
全国总计	**Total**	**926759**	**975387**	**91218**	**101412**	**176086**	**179433**
北　京	Beijing	13919	14055	1546	1984	971	1107
天　津	Tianjin	12035	12628	1634	1893	1307	1435
河　北	Hebei	31408	35681	2367	2523	6028	6133
山　西	Shanxi	21938	24930	1481	2639	2685	3204
内蒙古	Inner Mongolia	15311	16395	841	1052	2046	1859
辽　宁	Liaoning	24003	25424	1848	2339	3743	3434
吉　林	Jilin	12341	13062	965	845	1831	1836
黑龙江	Heilongjiang	11262	10741	1438	968	1494	1348
上　海	Shanghai	15740	16628	2878	2740	1789	1880
江　苏	Jiangsu	67889	68480	11151	9141	15427	16552
浙　江	Zhejiang	56725	58819	6693	6387	10250	9991
安　徽	Anhui	44975	46813	5101	7013	9534	10461
福　建	Fujian	34557	34667	3804	4042	6607	6976
江　西	Jiangxi	23581	25220	2239	2517	6733	7676
山　东	**Shandong**	**79792**	**82772**	**9326**	**11374**	**13272**	**14273**
河　南	Henan	58438	62688	5413	6842	14101	13277
湖　北	Hubei	35419	37741	2647	3398	6588	7941
湖　南	Hunan	40757	42661	3964	4604	9437	9189
广　东	Guangdong	91642	94248	7764	8043	14908	14011
广　西	Guangxi	32184	34176	2129	2433	6729	6178
海　南	Hainan	8589	8939	687	475	752	889
重　庆	Chongqing	27368	26893	3774	4196	6143	6198
四　川	Sichuan	50756	54249	4546	4379	13258	13693
贵　州	Guizhou	26923	28750	862	916	5553	5586
云　南	Yunnan	25801	29148	1638	2541	4857	3881
西　藏	Tibet	945	945	28	88	93	141
陕　西	Shaanxi	28358	29978	1746	1770	4452	4260
甘　肃	Gansu	11328	13198	881	1463	1968	2224
青　海	Qinghai	2944	3399	154	160	470	386
宁　夏	Ningxia	5563	5607	772	1144	1095	1014
新　疆	Xinjiang	14268	16454	902	1502	1964	2399

附录 1-6　房地产开发企业(单位)投资和商品房销售额

Investment and Total Sale of Commercial Buildings of Enterprises for Real Estate Development

单位:亿元　　(100 million yuan)

地　区	Region	房地产开发投资额 Investment for Real Estate		商品房销售额 Total Sale of Commercial Buildings		#住　宅 Residential	
		2020	2021	2020	2021	2020	2021
全国总计	**Total**	**141442.9**	**147602.1**	**173612.7**	**181929.9**	**154567.0**	**162729.9**
北　京	Beijing	3938.7	4139.0	3656.8	4486.5	3131.3	4117.2
天　津	Tianjin	2608.5	2770.0	2113.6	2322.8	2001.0	2183.7
河　北	Hebei	4601.1	5023.9	4950.4	5052.9	4597.9	4814.3
山　西	Shanxi	1830.4	1945.2	1885.9	2170.9	1753.4	2030.1
内蒙古	Inner Mongolia	1176.5	1234.1	1365.5	1214.8	1242.6	1116.4
辽　宁	Liaoning	2978.9	2900.7	3366.3	3066.4	3114.1	2849.3
吉　林	Jilin	1460.8	1540.9	1381.5	1291.0	1238.2	1179.3
黑龙江	Heilongjiang	982.9	936.0	1064.2	858.1	946.1	751.9
上　海	Shanghai	4698.7	5035.2	6047.0	6788.7	5268.8	6104.9
江　苏	Jiangsu	13171.3	13477.4	19408.9	21361.3	18027.3	19626.1
浙　江	Zhejiang	11413.7	12389.1	17145.0	19052.2	15584.8	17172.8
安　徽	Anhui	7042.3	7263.2	7346.1	8143.2	6760.9	7514.6
福　建	Fujian	6026.8	6195.6	7497.7	8217.3	6343.3	7082.6
江　西	Jiangxi	2378.1	2528.8	5222.8	5894.1	4425.2	5110.0
山　东	**Shandong**	**9450.5**	**9819.7**	**11065.6**	**12155.6**	**10109.6**	**11044.1**
河　南	Henan	7782.3	7874.3	9364.4	8657.7	8402.5	7892.0
湖　北	Hubei	4888.9	6121.9	6087.9	7250.3	5447.3	6671.9
湖　南	Hunan	4880.4	5427.8	5947.1	6040.5	5223.6	5390.4
广　东	Guangdong	17312.7	17465.8	22572.5	22320.3	19829.6	19457.6
广　西	Guangxi	3845.6	3733.9	4251.5	3672.5	3803.6	3164.4
海　南	Hainan	1341.7	1379.6	1232.1	1559.2	1048.9	1179.6
重　庆	Chongqing	4352.0	4355.0	5071.3	5391.3	4293.2	4786.1
四　川	Sichuan	7315.3	7831.9	10394.3	10796.7	8767.0	9061.3
贵　州	Guizhou	3418.7	3383.1	3224.2	3243.9	2760.7	2713.4
云　南	Yunnan	4505.2	4309.9	3969.9	2962.5	3452.0	2524.7
西　藏	Tibet	165.5	142.0	83.9	121.7	72.0	97.5
陕　西	Shaanxi	4404.4	4441.0	4375.3	4146.3	3755.8	3762.1
甘　肃	Gansu	1355.6	1525.9	1293.4	1344.9	1205.4	1267.8
青　海	Qinghai	421.3	442.5	383.3	294.4	343.4	258.3
宁　夏	Ningxia	433.3	466.9	698.4	675.1	626.3	584.9
新　疆	Xinjiang	1260.9	1501.4	1145.8	1376.9	991.1	1220.3

附录 1-7 一般公共预算收入
General Public Budget Revenue

单位:亿元 (100 million yuan)

地 区	Region	2016	2017	2018	2019	2020	2021
地方总计	**Total**	**87239.4**	**91469.4**	**97903.4**	**101080.6**	**100143.2**	**111077.1**
北 京	Beijing	5081.3	5430.8	5785.9	5817.1	5483.9	5932.3
天 津	Tianjin	2723.5	2310.4	2106.2	2410.4	1923.1	2141.0
河 北	Hebei	2849.9	3233.8	3513.9	3739.0	3826.5	4167.6
山 西	Shanxi	1557.0	1867.0	2292.7	2347.7	2296.6	2834.6
内 蒙 古	Inner Mongolia	2016.4	1703.2	1857.6	2059.7	2051.2	2349.9
辽 宁	Liaoning	2200.5	2392.8	2616.1	2652.4	2655.8	2764.7
吉 林	Jilin	1263.8	1210.9	1240.9	1116.9	1085.0	1144.0
黑 龙 江	Heilongjiang	1148.4	1243.3	1282.6	1262.8	1152.5	1300.5
上 海	Shanghai	6406.1	6642.3	7108.1	7165.1	7046.3	7771.8
江 苏	Jiangsu	8121.2	8171.5	8630.2	8802.4	9059.0	10015.2
浙 江	Zhejiang	5302.0	5804.4	6598.2	7048.6	7248.2	8262.6
安 徽	Anhui	2672.8	2812.4	3048.7	3182.7	3216.0	3498.2
福 建	Fujian	2654.8	2809.0	3007.4	3052.9	3079.0	3383.4
江 西	Jiangxi	2151.5	2247.1	2373.0	2487.4	2507.5	2812.3
山 东	**Shandong**	**5860.2**	**6098.6**	**6485.4**	**6526.7**	**6559.9**	**7284.5**
河 南	Henan	3153.5	3407.2	3766.0	4041.9	4168.8	4347.4
湖 北	Hubei	3102.1	3248.3	3307.1	3388.6	2511.5	3283.3
湖 南	Hunan	2697.9	2757.8	2860.8	3007.1	3008.7	3250.7
广 东	Guangdong	10390.4	11320.3	12105.3	12654.5	12923.8	14103.4
广 西	Guangxi	1556.3	1615.1	1681.4	1811.9	1716.9	1800.1
海 南	Hainan	637.5	674.1	752.7	814.1	816.1	921.2
重 庆	Chongqing	2227.9	2252.4	2265.5	2134.9	2094.9	2285.5
四 川	Sichuan	3388.9	3578.0	3911.0	4070.8	4260.9	4773.3
贵 州	Guizhou	1561.3	1613.8	1726.9	1767.5	1786.8	1969.5
云 南	Yunnan	1812.3	1886.2	1994.3	2073.6	2116.7	2278.2
西 藏	Tibet	156.0	185.8	230.4	222.0	221.0	215.6
陕 西	Shaanxi	1834.0	2006.7	2243.1	2287.9	2257.3	2775.3
甘 肃	Gansu	787.0	815.7	871.1	850.5	874.6	1001.8
青 海	Qinghai	238.5	246.2	272.9	282.2	298.0	330.8
宁 夏	Ningxia	387.7	417.6	436.5	423.6	419.4	460.0
新 疆	Xinjiang	1299.0	1466.5	1531.4	1577.6	1477.2	1618.6

注:本表数据为地方财政本级收入。
a)Data in this table are the revenue of local governments.

附录 1-8　一般公共预算支出

General Public Budget Expenditure

单位:亿元　　(100 million yuan)

地　区	Region	2016	2017	2018	2019	2020	2021
地方总计	**Total**	**160351.4**	**173228.3**	**188196.3**	**203743.2**	**210583.5**	**211271.5**
北　京	Beijing	6406.8	6824.5	7471.4	7408.2	7116.2	7205.1
天　津	Tianjin	3699.4	3282.5	3103.2	3555.7	3151.4	3150.4
河　北	Hebei	6049.5	6639.2	7726.2	8309.0	9022.8	8854.5
山　西	Shanxi	3428.9	3756.4	4283.9	4710.8	5110.9	5048.1
内蒙古	Inner Mongolia	4512.7	4529.9	4831.5	5100.9	5270.2	5240.1
辽　宁	Liaoning	4577.5	4879.4	5337.7	5745.1	6014.2	5901.3
吉　林	Jilin	3586.1	3725.7	3789.6	3933.4	4127.2	3696.7
黑龙江	Heilongjiang	4227.3	4641.1	4676.8	5011.6	5449.4	5104.5
上　海	Shanghai	6918.9	7547.6	8351.5	8179.3	8102.1	8430.9
江　苏	Jiangsu	9982.0	10621.0	11657.4	12573.6	13681.6	14586.0
浙　江	Zhejiang	6974.3	7530.3	8629.5	10053.0	10082.0	11016.9
安　徽	Anhui	5523.0	6203.8	6572.1	7392.2	7473.6	7592.1
福　建	Fujian	4275.4	4684.2	4832.7	5077.9	5216.1	5210.9
江　西	Jiangxi	4617.4	5111.5	5667.5	6386.8	6674.1	6778.5
山　东	**Shandong**	**8755.2**	**9258.4**	**10101.0**	**10739.8**	**11233.5**	**11709.1**
河　南	Henan	7453.7	8215.5	9217.7	10163.9	10372.7	10419.9
湖　北	Hubei	6423.0	6801.3	7258.3	7970.2	8442.9	7937.3
湖　南	Hunan	6339.2	6869.4	7479.6	8034.4	8403.1	8364.8
广　东	Guangdong	13446.1	15037.5	15729.3	17297.9	17430.8	18222.7
广　西	Guangxi	4441.7	4908.6	5310.7	5851.0	6179.5	5810.2
海　南	Hainan	1376.5	1444.0	1691.3	1858.6	1972.5	1982.8
重　庆	Chongqing	4001.8	4336.3	4540.9	4847.7	4893.9	4835.1
四　川	Sichuan	8008.9	8694.8	9707.5	10348.2	11198.5	11215.6
贵　州	Guizhou	4262.4	4612.5	5029.7	5948.7	5739.5	5590.2
云　南	Yunnan	5018.9	5713.0	6075.0	6770.1	6974.0	6634.4
西　藏	Tibet	1588.0	1681.9	1970.7	2187.7	2210.9	2028.7
陕　西	Shaanxi	4389.4	4833.2	5302.4	5718.5	5930.3	6069.4
甘　肃	Gansu	3150.0	3304.4	3772.2	3951.6	4163.4	4025.9
青　海	Qinghai	1524.8	1530.4	1647.4	1863.7	1932.8	1872.0
宁　夏	Ningxia	1254.5	1372.8	1419.1	1438.3	1480.4	1428.3
新　疆	Xinjiang	4138.3	4637.2	5012.5	5315.5	5533.2	5309.2

注:本表数据为地方财政本级支出。
a)Data in this table are the expenditure of local governments.

附录 1-9　居民消费价格分类指数(2021年)

Consumer Price Indices by Category (2021)

(上年=100)　　(preceding year=100)

地区	Region	居民消费价格指数 General Index	食品烟酒 Food, Tobacco, Liquor	衣着 Clothing	居住 Residence	生活用品及服务 Daily Necessities and Services	交通和通信 Transportation and Communication	教育文化和娱乐 Recreation, Education and Culture	医疗保健 Medical Care	其他用品和服务 Other Supplies and Services
全　国	**Total**	**100.9**	**99.7**	**100.3**	**100.8**	**100.4**	**104.1**	**101.9**	**100.4**	**98.7**
北　京	Beijing	101.1	100.5	99.8	101.1	99.7	105.1	100.9	99.8	99.5
天　津	Tianjin	101.3	101.3	97.8	100.7	101.0	104.7	103.4	100.0	97.8
河　北	Hebei	101.0	100.9	99.3	100.2	99.7	104.5	101.2	100.3	99.3
山　西	Shanxi	101.0	100.4	100.3	100.4	100.4	104.4	102.6	99.5	98.1
内蒙古	Inner Mongolia	100.9	100.5	99.2	100.5	99.8	104.0	101.0	100.3	99.4
辽　宁	Liaoning	101.1	100.3	100.5	100.6	99.9	104.7	102.3	99.8	99.3
吉　林	Jilin	100.6	99.7	99.9	101.3	99.9	103.8	100.4	100.0	98.1
黑龙江	Heilongjiang	100.6	99.5	100.8	100.3	99.8	104.0	100.5	101.1	99.4
上　海	Shanghai	101.2	100.5	99.5	101.1	100.7	104.0	102.7	98.9	100.9
江　苏	Jiangsu	101.6	100.9	101.5	101.3	101.1	104.3	101.8	101.0	98.9
浙　江	Zhejiang	101.5	100.7	101.0	100.9	101.6	104.1	103.5	100.8	97.1
安　徽	Anhui	100.9	99.5	101.1	100.7	100.1	104.8	102.8	100.5	96.1
福　建	Fujian	100.7	98.9	101.5	101.3	100.7	103.7	102.0	100.0	96.3
江　西	Jiangxi	100.9	99.3	99.7	100.9	100.4	104.3	103.0	99.9	98.7
山　东	**Shandong**	**101.2**	**100.9**	**100.1**	**101.1**	**99.8**	**104.5**	**101.3**	**100.1**	**98.5**
河　南	Henan	100.9	100.2	99.4	100.7	100.0	102.8	103.5	100.4	98.2
湖　北	Hubei	100.3	98.5	100.0	100.0	100.4	104.0	102.4	100.1	97.7
湖　南	Hunan	100.5	98.0	100.7	101.2	100.3	104.8	101.0	100.7	97.9
广　东	Guangdong	100.8	99.4	100.3	101.0	100.6	104.4	101.8	100.2	98.5
广　西	Guangxi	100.9	98.8	101.0	100.8	100.4	102.7	103.7	102.4	99.7
海　南	Hainan	100.3	98.9	100.9	101.0	101.2	103.7	99.3	99.4	98.8
重　庆	Chongqing	100.3	97.8	101.4	100.4	100.7	104.7	101.7	99.6	97.3
四　川	Sichuan	100.3	98.0	99.8	100.3	100.6	104.1	100.9	101.9	100.1
贵　州	Guizhou	100.1	97.7	99.3	100.0	99.7	103.9	101.3	100.4	100.2
云　南	Yunnan	100.2	98.4	99.7	100.2	99.6	103.6	100.7	100.1	100.0
西　藏	Tibet	100.9	100.5	100.7	100.2	99.8	103.8	100.4	100.8	99.2
陕　西	Shaanxi	101.5	101.4	100.5	101.9	100.3	102.9	102.9	99.3	101.0
甘　肃	Gansu	100.9	100.3	100.0	101.1	100.3	103.8	100.6	100.2	100.5
青　海	Qinghai	101.3	100.1	101.0	101.3	99.9	103.7	102.0	102.2	98.8
宁　夏	Ningxia	101.4	101.5	99.0	100.8	100.7	104.1	101.5	101.7	98.5
新　疆	Xinjiang	101.2	100.7	102.0	101.2	100.4	104.5	99.9	100.2	99.3

附录 1-10 全体居民人均收支情况

Per Capita Income and Expenditure of All Households

单位:元 (yuan)

地区 Region	人均可支配收入 Per Capita Disposable Income						人均消费支出 Per Capita Consumption Expenditure					
	2016	2017	2018	2019	2020	2021	2016	2017	2018	2019	2020	2021
全国总计 Total	**23821**	**25974**	**28228**	**30733**	**32189**	**35128**	**17111**	**18322**	**19853**	**21559**	**21210**	**24100**
北　京 Beijing	52530	57230	62361	67756	69434	75002	35416	37425	39843	43038	38903	43640
天　津 Tianjin	34074	37022	39506	42404	43854	47449	26129	27841	29903	31854	28461	33188
河　北 Hebei	19725	21484	23446	25665	27136	29383	14248	15437	16722	17987	18037	19954
山　西 Shanxi	19049	20420	21990	23828	25214	27426	12683	13664	14810	15863	15733	17191
内蒙古 Inner Mongolia	24127	26212	28376	30555	31497	34108	18072	18946	19665	20743	19795	22658
辽　宁 Liaoning	26040	27835	29701	31820	32738	35112	19853	20463	21398	22203	20672	23831
吉　林 Jilin	19967	21368	22798	24563	25751	27770	14773	15632	17200	18075	17318	19605
黑龙江 Heilongjiang	19838	21206	22726	24254	24902	27159	14446	15578	16994	18112	17056	20636
上　海 Shanghai	54305	58988	64183	69442	72232	78027	37458	39792	43351	45605	42536	48879
江　苏 Jiangsu	32070	35024	38096	41400	43390	47498	22130	23469	25007	26697	26225	31451
浙　江 Zhejiang	38529	42046	45840	49899	52397	57541	25527	27079	29471	32026	31295	36668
安　徽 Anhui	19998	21863	23984	26415	28103	30904	14712	15752	17045	19137	18877	21911
福　建 Fujian	27608	30048	32644	35616	37202	40659	20168	21249	22996	25314	25126	28440
江　西 Jiangxi	20110	22031	24080	26262	28017	30610	13259	14459	15792	17651	17955	20290
山　东 Shandong	**24685**	**26930**	**29205**	**31597**	**32886**	**35705**	**15926**	**17281**	**18780**	**20427**	**20940**	**22821**
河　南 Henan	18443	20170	21964	23903	24810	26811	12712	13730	15169	16332	16143	18391
湖　北 Hubei	21787	23757	25815	28319	27881	30829	15889	16938	19538	21567	19246	23846
湖　南 Hunan	21115	23103	25241	27680	29380	31993	15751	17160	18808	20479	20998	22798
广　东 Guangdong	30296	33003	35810	39014	41029	44993	23448	24820	26054	28995	28492	31589
广　西 Guangxi	18305	19905	21485	23328	24562	26727	12295	13424	14935	16418	16357	18088
海　南 Hainan	20653	22553	24579	26679	27904	30457	14275	15403	17528	19555	18972	22242
重　庆 Chongqing	22034	24153	26386	28920	30824	33803	16385	17898	19249	20774	21678	24598
四　川 Sichuan	18808	20580	22461	24703	26522	29080	14839	16180	17664	19338	19783	21518
贵　州 Guizhou	15121	16704	18430	20397	21795	23996	11932	12970	13798	14780	14874	17957
云　南 Yunnan	16720	18348	20084	22082	23295	25666	11769	12658	14250	15780	16792	18851
西　藏 Tibet	13639	15457	17286	19501	21744	24950	9319	10320	11520	13029	13225	15343
陕　西 Shaanxi	18874	20635	22528	24666	26226	28568	13943	14900	16160	17465	17418	19347
甘　肃 Gansu	14670	16011	17488	19139	20335	22066	12254	13120	14624	15879	16175	17456
青　海 Qinghai	17302	19001	20757	22618	24037	25920	14775	15503	16557	17545	18284	19020
宁　夏 Ningxia	18832	20562	22400	24412	25735	27905	14965	15350	16715	18297	17506	20024
新　疆 Xinjiang	18355	19975	21500	23103	23845	26075	14066	15087	16189	17397	16512	18961

附录 1-11 城镇居民人均收支情况

Per Capita Income and Expenditure of Urban Households

单位:元 (yuan)

地 区 Region	人均可支配收入 Per Capita Disposable Income						人均消费支出 Per Capita Consumption Expenditure					
	2016	2017	2018	2019	2020	2021	2016	2017	2018	2019	2020	2021
全国总计 Total	**33616**	**36396**	**39251**	**42359**	**43834**	**47412**	**23079**	**24445**	**26112**	**28063**	**27007**	**30307**
北 京 Beijing	57275	62406	67990	73849	75602	81518	38256	40346	42926	46358	41726	46776
天 津 Tianjin	37110	40278	42976	46119	47659	51486	28345	30284	32655	34811	30895	36067
河 北 Hebei	28249	30548	32977	35738	37286	39791	19106	20600	22127	23483	23167	24193
山 西 Shanxi	27352	29132	31035	33262	34793	37433	16993	18404	19790	21159	20332	21966
内蒙古 Inner Mongolia	32975	35670	38305	40782	41353	44377	22744	23638	24437	25383	23888	27194
辽 宁 Liaoning	32876	34993	37342	39777	40376	43051	24996	25379	26448	27355	24849	28438
吉 林 Jilin	26530	28319	30172	32299	33396	35646	19166	20051	22394	23394	21623	24421
黑龙江 Heilongjiang	25736	27446	29191	30945	31115	33646	18145	19270	21035	22165	20397	24422
上 海 Shanghai	57692	62596	68034	73615	76437	82429	39857	42304	46015	48272	44839	51295
江 苏 Jiangsu	40152	43622	47200	51056	53102	57744	26433	27726	29462	31329	30882	36558
浙 江 Zhejiang	47237	51261	55574	60182	62699	68487	30068	31924	34598	37508	36197	42194
安 徽 Anhui	29156	31640	34393	37540	39442	43009	19606	20740	21523	23782	22683	26495
福 建 Fujian	36014	39001	42121	45620	47160	51141	25006	25980	28145	30946	30487	33942
江 西 Jiangxi	28673	31198	33819	36546	38556	41684	17696	19244	20760	22714	22134	24587
山 东 Shandong	**34012**	**36789**	**39549**	**42329**	**43726**	**47066**	**21495**	**23072**	**24798**	**26731**	**27291**	**29314**
河 南 Henan	27233	29558	31874	34201	34750	37095	18088	19422	20989	21972	20645	23178
湖 北 Hubei	29386	31889	34455	37601	36706	40278	20040	21276	23996	26422	22885	28506
湖 南 Hunan	31284	33948	36698	39842	41698	44866	21420	23163	25064	26924	26796	28294
广 东 Guangdong	37684	40975	44341	48118	50257	54854	28613	30198	30924	34424	33511	36621
广 西 Guangxi	28324	30502	32436	34745	35859	38530	17268	18349	20159	21591	20907	22555
海 南 Hainan	28453	30817	33349	36017	37097	40213	19015	20372	22971	25317	23560	27565
重 庆 Chongqing	29610	32193	34889	37939	40006	43503	21031	22759	24154	25785	26464	29850
四 川 Sichuan	28335	30727	33216	36154	38253	41444	20660	21991	23484	25367	25133	26971
贵 州 Guizhou	26743	29080	31592	34404	36096	39211	19202	20348	20788	21402	20587	25333
云 南 Yunnan	28611	30996	33488	36238	37500	40905	18622	19560	21626	23455	24569	27441
西 藏 Tibet	27802	30671	33797	37410	41156	46503	19440	21088	23029	25637	24927	28159
陕 西 Shaanxi	28440	30810	33319	36098	37868	40713	19369	20388	21966	23514	22866	24784
甘 肃 Gansu	25693	27763	29957	32323	33822	36187	19539	20659	22606	24454	24615	25757
青 海 Qinghai	26757	29169	31515	33830	35506	37745	20853	21473	22998	23799	24315	24513
宁 夏 Ningxia	27153	29472	31895	34328	35720	38291	20364	20219	21977	24161	22379	25386
新 疆 Xinjiang	28463	30775	32764	34664	34838	37642	21229	22797	24191	25594	22952	25724

附录 1-12　农村居民人均收支情况

Per Capita Income and Expenditure of Rural Households

单位:元　　(yuan)

地　区 Region	人均可支配收入 Per Capita Disposable Income						人均消费支出 Per Capita Consumption Expenditure					
	2016	2017	2018	2019	2020	2021	2016	2017	2018	2019	2020	2021
全国总计 Total	**12363**	**13432**	**14617**	**16021**	**17131**	**18931**	**10130**	**10955**	**12124**	**13328**	**13713**	**15916**
北　京 Beijing	22310	24240	26490	28928	30126	33303	17329	18810	20195	21881	20913	23574
天　津 Tianjin	20076	21754	23065	24804	25691	27955	15912	16386	16863	17843	16844	19286
河　北 Hebei	11919	12881	14031	15373	16467	18179	9798	10536	11383	12372	12644	15391
山　西 Shanxi	10082	10788	11750	12902	13878	15308	8029	8424	9172	9728	10290	11410
内蒙古 Inner Mongolia	11609	12584	13803	15283	16567	18337	11463	12184	12661	13816	13594	15691
辽　宁 Liaoning	12881	13747	14656	16108	17450	19217	9953	10787	11455	12030	12311	14606
吉　林 Jilin	12123	12950	13748	14936	16067	17642	9521	10279	10826	11457	11864	13411
黑龙江 Heilongjiang	11832	12665	13804	14982	16168	17889	9424	10524	11417	12495	12360	15225
上　海 Shanghai	25520	27825	30375	33195	34911	38521	17071	18090	19965	22449	22095	27205
江　苏 Jiangsu	17606	19158	20845	22675	24198	26791	14428	15612	16567	17716	17022	21130
浙　江 Zhejiang	22866	24956	27302	29876	31930	35247	17359	18093	19707	21352	21555	25415
安　徽 Anhui	11720	12758	13996	15416	16620	18372	10287	11106	12748	14546	15024	17163
福　建 Fujian	14999	16335	17821	19568	20880	23229	12911	14003	14943	16281	16339	19290
江　西 Jiangxi	12138	13242	14460	15796	16981	18684	9128	9870	10885	12497	13579	15663
山　东 Shandong	**13954**	**15118**	**16297**	**17775**	**18753**	**20794**	**9519**	**10342**	**11270**	**12309**	**12660**	**14299**
河　南 Henan	11697	12719	13831	15164	16108	17533	8587	9212	10392	11546	12201	14073
湖　北 Hubei	12725	13812	14978	16391	16306	18259	10938	11633	13946	15328	14472	17647
湖　南 Hunan	11930	12936	14093	15395	16585	18295	10630	11534	12721	13969	14974	16951
广　东 Guangdong	14512	15780	17168	18818	20143	22306	12415	13200	15411	16949	17132	20012
广　西 Guangxi	10359	11325	12435	13676	14815	16363	8351	9437	10617	12045	12431	14165
海　南 Hainan	11843	12902	13989	15113	16279	18076	8921	9599	10956	12418	13169	15487
重　庆 Chongqing	11549	12638	13781	15133	16361	18100	9954	10936	11977	13112	14140	16096
四　川 Sichuan	11203	12227	13331	14670	15929	17575	10192	11397	12723	14056	14953	16444
贵　州 Guizhou	8090	8869	9716	10756	11642	12856	7533	8299	9170	10222	10818	12557
云　南 Yunnan	9020	9862	10768	11902	12842	14197	7331	8027	9123	10260	11069	12386
西　藏 Tibet	9094	10330	11450	12951	14598	16932	6070	6691	7452	8418	8917	10577
陕　西 Shaanxi	9396	10265	11213	12326	13316	14745	8568	9306	10071	10935	11376	13158
甘　肃 Gansu	7457	8076	8804	9629	10344	11433	7487	8030	9065	9694	9923	11206
青　海 Qinghai	8664	9462	10393	11499	12342	13604	9222	9903	10352	11343	12134	13300
宁　夏 Ningxia	9852	10738	11708	12858	13889	15337	9138	9982	10790	11465	11724	13536
新　疆 Xinjiang	10183	11045	11975	13122	14056	15575	8277	8713	9421	10318	10778	12821

附录 1－13 农林牧渔业总产值及增长速度(2021年)

Gross Output Value and Growth Rate of Farming,Forestry, Animal Husbandry and Fishery(2021)

地 区	Region	农林牧渔业总产值(亿元) Gross Output Value (100 million yuan)	#农 业 Farming	#林 业 Forestry	#牧 业 Animal Husbandry	#渔 业 Fishery	农林牧渔业总产值比上年增长(%) Growth Rate (%)
全国总计	**Total**	**147013.4**	**78339.5**	**6507.7**	**39910.8**	**14507.3**	**7.9**
北 京	Beijing	269.5	123.0	88.8	46.3	4.4	2.8
天 津	Tianjin	509.3	258.4	9.5	142.5	80.9	2.1
河 北	Hebei	7018.7	3645.0	263.7	2239.5	298.0	7.1
山 西	Shanxi	2134.0	1223.1	159.8	624.4	9.1	9.9
内蒙古	Inner Mongolia	3815.1	1879.6	94.1	1755.3	29.8	5.1
辽 宁	Liaoning	4927.7	2222.5	120.9	1683.9	719.9	5.7
吉 林	Jilin	2972.3	1302.9	72.6	1454.3	54.4	7.5
黑龙江	Heilongjiang	6460.0	4099.5	208.0	1833.1	135.9	7.1
上 海	Shanghai	268.9	144.9	8.7	45.3	47.7	-6.7
江 苏	Jiangsu	8279.7	4426.1	178.2	1215.9	1833.5	4.3
浙 江	Zhejiang	3579.2	1697.9	168.3	402.7	1188.3	3.0
安 徽	Anhui	6004.3	2802.9	412.9	1810.9	621.7	9.3
福 建	Fujian	5201.0	1906.0	424.9	1059.9	1621.5	5.1
江 西	Jiangxi	3998.1	1796.3	398.9	1051.4	548.3	8.9
山 东	**Shandong**	**11468.0**	**5814.6**	**219.9**	**2904.2**	**1652.6**	**8.6**
河 南	Henan	10501.2	6564.8	134.1	2942.1	143.4	7.1
湖 北	Hubei	8296.4	3912.5	302.7	1990.2	1458.9	14.3
湖 南	Hunan	7662.4	3532.9	455.8	2542.5	570.8	10.4
广 东	Guangdong	8305.8	3951.1	495.4	1707.8	1747.3	7.1
广 西	Guangxi	6524.4	3690.7	538.1	1437.6	555.1	9.2
海 南	Hainan	2014.8	1049.6	118.3	327.7	435.2	5.1
重 庆	Chongqing	2935.6	1759.9	168.1	804.2	138.2	9.2
四 川	Sichuan	9383.3	5089.5	408.4	3305.3	327.8	7.5
贵 州	Guizhou	4692.0	3123.7	319.8	959.0	69.8	9.2
云 南	Yunnan	6351.8	3441.5	497.3	2113.3	112.4	10.4
西 藏	Tibet	255.3	115.3	4.0	129.3	0.3	5.6
陕 西	Shaanxi	4313.4	3035.6	100.0	917.8	35.0	6.7
甘 肃	Gansu	2439.5	1623.2	32.8	619.9	2.0	11.3
青 海	Qinghai	528.5	204.7	13.2	298.6	4.1	4.5
宁 夏	Ningxia	759.8	412.7	11.4	280.7	25.0	4.8
新 疆	Xinjiang	5143.1	3489.0	79.1	1265.7	35.9	8.8

注：本表绝对数按当年价格计算，增长速度按可比价格计算。

a)Absolute figures in this table are calculated at current prices while growth rate at constant prices.

附录 1-14 主要农产品产量(2021年)

Output of Major Agriculture Products(2021)

单位:万吨 (10 000 tons)

地区	Region	粮食 Grain	油料 Oil Crops	棉花 Cotton	蔬菜 Vegetables	水果 Fruits	肉类 Meat	#猪肉 Pork	#牛肉 Beef	#羊肉 Mutton	奶类 Milk
全国总计	**Total**	**68284.7**	**3613.2**	**573.1**	**77548.8**	**29970.2**	**8990.0**	**5295.9**	**697.5**	**514.1**	**3778.1**
北京	Beijing	37.8	0.5		165.6	48.8	4.4	2.6	0.4	0.2	25.8
天津	Tianjin	249.9	0.3	0.4	239.0	49.4	30.5	17.1	2.8	1.0	51.8
河北	Hebei	3825.1	118.4	16.0	5284.2	1445.1	464.3	265.7	55.8	33.9	501.9
山西	Shanxi	1421.2	15.5	0.1	976.3	974.9	135.4	88.4	9.0	10.4	135.7
内蒙古	Inner Mongolia	3840.3	213.9		993.7	190.8	277.3	67.4	68.7	113.7	680.0
辽宁	Liaoning	2538.7	116.2		1990.2	856.4	435.4	238.8	31.5	6.9	139.3
吉林	Jilin	4039.2	85.8		490.5	164.1	274.6	142.4	40.8	7.6	32.8
黑龙江	Heilongjiang	7867.7	13.6		725.4	184.3	300.4	184.8	50.7	15.0	501.0
上海	Shanghai	94.0	0.5		248.6	32.6	9.1	7.1	0.2	0.3	29.4
江苏	Jiangsu	3746.1	97.8	0.8	5856.6	969.1	306.5	175.2	2.8	6.6	64.9
浙江	Zhejiang	620.9	31.7	0.6	1933.6	722.6	103.6	65.2	1.7	2.4	18.6
安徽	Anhui	4087.6	167.1	2.9	2445.3	778.1	456.3	238.7	11.2	21.9	47.6
福建	Fujian	506.4	23.3		1686.5	810.3	286.5	124.3	2.6	2.3	20.0
江西	Jiangxi	2192.3	130.9	1.7	1730.6	744.6	345.0	238.5	16.7	2.9	8.4
山东	**Shandong**	**5500.7**	**285.9**	**14.0**	**8801.1**	**3032.6**	**819.3**	**355.9**	**61.3**	**33.0**	**288.4**
河南	Henan	6544.2	657.3	1.4	7607.2	2455.3	646.8	426.8	35.5	28.9	216.8
湖北	Hubei	2764.3	354.1	10.9	4299.8	1119.4	425.5	318.0	15.8	9.7	9.6
湖南	Hunan	3074.4	263.0	8.0	4268.9	1193.6	562.0	443.1	21.3	17.5	5.7
广东	Guangdong	1279.9	117.3		3855.7	1957.8	457.4	263.2	4.4	2.0	17.3
广西	Guangxi	1386.5	75.9	0.1	4047.5	3121.1	441.0	245.2	14.0	4.0	13.1
海南	Hainan	146.0	7.5		588.9	525.7	66.9	30.5	2.1	1.1	0.1
重庆	Chongqing	1092.8	68.5		2184.3	553.2	196.6	142.0	7.6	6.9	3.1
四川	Sichuan	3582.1	416.6	0.2	5039.1	1290.9	664.0	460.5	36.9	27.1	68.4
贵州	Guizhou	1094.9	94.9		3280.1	653.7	228.2	166.2	23.6	4.9	4.9
云南	Yunnan	1930.3	63.9		2748.9	1142.6	488.1	360.4	42.0	21.1	72.5
西藏	Tibet	106.2	4.6		89.5	3.0	27.4	1.3	20.5	5.1	53.7
陕西	Shaanxi	1270.4	58.3		2012.8	2141.1	128.0	97.6	9.0	10.2	161.9
甘肃	Gansu	1231.5	58.8	3.1	1655.3	883.8	135.3	64.1	27.0	33.5	67.5
青海	Qinghai	109.1	31.9		150.1	3.0	40.0	6.0	21.2	12.3	35.6
宁夏	Ningxia	368.4	4.8		533.0	262.8	35.3	9.1	11.8	11.5	280.5
新疆	Xinjiang	1735.8	34.6	512.9	1620.4	1659.5	198.7	49.9	48.5	60.4	221.9

注:水果产量含果用瓜。

a)Data of output of fruits include yield of melon and fruit.

附录 1-15 主要工业产品产量(2021年)

Output of Major Industrial Products(2021)

地区	Region	原油(万吨) Crude Petroleum Oil (10 000 tons)	发电量(亿千瓦时) Electricity (100 million kW·h)	生铁(万吨) Pig Iron (10 000 tons)	粗钢(万吨) Crude Steel (10 000 tons)	钢材(万吨) Steel (10 000 tons)	水泥(万吨) Cement (10 000 tons)
全国总计	**Total**	**19888.1**	**85342.5**	**86856.8**	**103524.3**	**133666.8**	**237810.8**
北京	Beijing		472.6			203.4	258.1
天津	Tianjin	3407.0	799.7	1818.4	1825.3	5991.7	632.0
河北	Hebei	544.6	3513.4	20203.0	22496.5	29559.4	11354.6
山西	Shanxi		3926.2	5988.4	6740.7	6173.9	5688.6
内蒙古	Inner Mongolia	42.1	6119.9	2347.4	3117.9	2957.6	3667.9
辽宁	Liaoning	1054.2	2257.6	7024.7	7502.4	7759.1	4938.9
吉林	Jilin	414.2	1025.7	1366.0	1538.9	1790.6	2125.3
黑龙江	Heilongjiang	2945.5	1200.5	846.5	960.6	951.4	2188.6
上海	Shanghai	50.9	1003.1	1391.0	1577.1	1941.4	444.0
江苏	Jiangsu	151.3	5968.9	10023.9	11925.0	15701.9	15402.1
浙江	Zhejiang		4222.5	794.8	1455.6	3451.8	13638.0
安徽	Anhui		3083.4	2911.6	3891.6	3820.3	15001.0
福建	Fujian		2950.8	1145.2	2535.5	3980.5	10131.0
江西	Jiangxi		1563.3	2315.6	2711.0	3480.9	10403.8
山东	**Shandong**	**2210.7**	**6210.3**	**7524.4**	**7649.3**	**10667.6**	**16617.5**
河南	Henan	234.7	3039.1	2746.7	3316.1	4336.0	11385.9
湖北	Hubei	53.2	3292.4	2624.4	3656.1	3852.1	11872.8
湖南	Hunan		1741.9	2177.4	2612.7	2979.7	10513.3
广东	Guangdong	1744.7	6306.2	2053.6	3178.3	5111.2	17084.3
广西	Guangxi	46.8	2081.9	3015.3	3660.9	5282.1	11432.9
海南	Hainan	37.3	391.2				1937.5
重庆	Chongqing		991.4	674.5	899.3	1310.5	6238.1
四川	Sichuan	9.2	4530.3	2092.0	2787.9	3496.2	14171.5
贵州	Guizhou		2368.4	375.4	461.9	811.2	9332.8
云南	Yunnan		3770.2	1711.6	2361.0	2646.4	11511.5
西藏	Tibet		112.8				991.6
陕西	Shaanxi	2552.8	2739.8	1136.3	1520.8	2097.4	6698.5
甘肃	Gansu	1029.1	1896.8	789.2	1059.0	1080.6	4478.2
青海	Qinghai	234.0	995.7	154.2	186.7	182.0	1107.1
宁夏	Ningxia	135.3	2082.9	457.6	596.3	582.3	1870.1
新疆	Xinjiang	2990.4	4683.6	1147.6	1299.9	1467.7	4693.4

附录 1-15 续表 continued

地　区	Region	布 (亿米) Cloth (100 million m)	家　用 电冰箱 (万台) Home Refrigerators (10 000 units)	农　用 化　肥 (万吨) Chemical Fertilizes (10 000 tons)	汽　车 (万辆) Motor Vehicles (10 000 sets)	程　控 交换机 (万线) Program Controlled Switchboards (10 000 lines)	移动通信 手持机 (万台) Mobile Communication Handsets (10 000 units)	微型计算机 设备 (万台) Microcomputer Equipments (10 000 units)
全国总计	**Total**	**502.0**	**8992.1**	**5543.6**	**2652.8**	**699.6**	**166151.6**	**46692.0**
北　京	Beijing				135.5		11624.5	647.3
天　津	Tianjin	0.4	15.0	56.0	74.0		4.6	0.2
河　北	Hebei	10.5		201.6	110.0	40.2	118.8	
山　西	Shanxi	0.2		383.3	11.9		2732.9	22.1
内蒙古	Inner Mongolia			395.0	5.4			
辽　宁	Liaoning	0.7	170.8	37.1	80.9	0.1	15.9	72.1
吉　林	Jilin	0.3		28.8	242.4			
黑龙江	Heilongjiang			73.6	7.6			
上　海	Shanghai	0.7		1.1	283.3		2892.2	3093.3
江　苏	Jiangsu	83.6	1372.1	178.7	77.6		4045.5	5472.2
浙　江	Zhejiang	123.4	537.3	80.8	99.4	67.7	3214.5	190.7
安　徽	Anhui	8.4	2381.4	210.2	150.3		96.6	3694.8
福　建	Fujian	83.2		66.7	34.3		2275.5	1369.7
江　西	Jiangxi	9.7	72.3	98.6	43.6		12322.7	1807.1
山　东	**Shandong**	**46.6**	**888.8**	**403.7**	**107.3**		**531.6**	**1.9**
河　南	Henan	19.3	278.9	359.0	52.8	0.4	15944.7	5.8
湖　北	Hubei	52.4	562.8	582.2	209.9		5622.3	2057.1
湖　南	Hunan	1.3		66.0	31.9		2352.0	300.9
广　东	Guangdong	27.2	2091.6	7.7	338.5	591.1	66965.4	5935.4
广　西	Guangxi	0.8	176.0	41.2	190.1	0.2	2337.9	224.3
海　南	Hainan			67.0	1.5			
重　庆	Chongqing	2.8	156.2	162.1	199.8		11158.3	10730.4
四　川	Sichuan	13.9	124.2	343.0	72.7		13137.2	9751.4
贵　州	Guizhou	0.5	162.0	336.7	8.8		2123.0	10.4
云　南	Yunnan			248.4	1.8		1483.9	1305.0
西　藏	Tibet							
陕　西	Shaanxi	8.2	2.7	166.4	80.1		4917.2	
甘　肃	Gansu			27.0				
青　海	Qinghai			494.3				
宁　夏	Ningxia	0.6		62.7				
新　疆	Xinjiang	7.0		365.1	1.6		234.5	

附录 1-16 规模以上工业主要经济指标(2021年)

Main Indicators on Economic Efficiency of Industrial Enterprises above Designated Size(2021)

单位:亿元 (100 million yuan)

地区	Region	资产总计 Total Assets	流动资产合计 Current Assets	负债合计 Total Liabilities	营业收入 Business Revenue	营业成本 Business Cost	利润总额 Total Profits
全国总计	**Total**	**1412880.0**	**723908.9**	**792289.9**	**1279226.5**	**1071247.1**	**87092.1**
北京	Beijing	60393.9	24700.9	26096.8	28054.0	21710.0	3664.9
天津	Tianjin	22897.8	11576.8	12386.3	22571.2	19334.6	1456.9
河北	Hebei	55395.6	27205.2	33720.3	52125.4	45918.9	2294.3
山西	Shanxi	55386.7	26513.2	39431.9	32396.2	25561.5	2949.9
内蒙古	Inner Mongolia	37260.6	13768.9	21219.2	23947.1	18271.5	3380.8
辽宁	Liaoning	42272.9	21287.0	25878.4	35214.2	29672.0	1699.6
吉林	Jilin	18846.1	8445.4	10258.0	14058.0	11608.6	1073.8
黑龙江	Heilongjiang	17732.9	8061.1	10653.1	11253.1	9336.7	515.2
上海	Shanghai	51746.2	30418.6	24912.9	44173.0	36026.8	3032.0
江苏	Jiangsu	149340.8	90383.5	79833.6	149920.7	126829.6	9358.1
浙江	Zhejiang	110368.5	62607.5	60931.7	97967.6	81918.3	6788.7
安徽	Anhui	48960.0	26305.7	27430.0	44775.9	38191.0	2669.9
福建	Fujian	46172.9	23691.0	23859.7	64743.0	55815.5	4353.3
江西	Jiangxi	30357.9	15472.9	16234.6	43976.7	37969.9	3122.4
山东	**Shandong**	**109712.9**	**58778.9**	**66996.9**	**102271.5**	**88711.2**	**5268.8**
河南	Henan	54479.5	26201.8	31194.6	54006.4	47301.5	2581.2
湖北	Hubei	46565.5	22506.8	24289.5	49215.7	41300.3	3189.5
湖南	Hunan	32485.2	15389.8	16219.6	42763.3	35350.4	2060.0
广东	Guangdong	169766.7	102873.7	95018.8	169785.1	141095.1	10927.6
广西	Guangxi	22802.3	11322.4	14509.5	21911.1	19081.5	1131.3
海南	Hainan	4281.6	1789.1	2472.1	2625.7	2052.8	212.1
重庆	Chongqing	24310.8	12872.2	13685.9	27118.9	22920.4	1877.5
四川	Sichuan	57922.3	25846.1	31904.3	52583.4	43160.9	4359.2
贵州	Guizhou	16452.9	7081.7	10291.4	9712.5	7563.3	1063.5
云南	Yunnan	24804.5	9518.8	13793.4	17359.5	13735.8	1211.0
西藏	Tibet	2139.1	487.7	1139.0	401.7	291.3	48.9
陕西	Shaanxi	40875.3	17900.9	22258.2	29585.6	22821.7	3605.1
甘肃	Gansu	12876.3	4953.1	7457.9	9601.7	8075.2	516.5
青海	Qinghai	6481.8	2200.7	4671.8	3186.7	2512.6	301.6
宁夏	Ningxia	11930.2	4042.7	7695.6	6491.2	5389.8	462.6
新疆	Xinjiang	27860.3	9704.8	15844.5	15430.4	11718.5	1916.1

注：本表为快报数据。
a):Data in this table are preliminary data.

附录 1-17 建筑业总产值和房屋建筑面积

Output Value of Construction and Floor Space of Buildings

地区	Region	总产值(亿元) Total Output Value (100 million yuan)		施工面积(万平方米) Floor Space of Buildings Under Construction (10 000 sq.m)		竣工面积(万平方米) Floor Space of Buildings Completed (10 000 sq.m)	
		2020	2021	2020	2021	2020	2021
全国总计	**Total**	**263947.0**	**293079.3**	**1494743.4**	**1575495.3**	**384819.8**	**408257.1**
北京	Beijing	12905.9	13987.7	88593.7	91154.8	9588.1	13254.5
天津	Tianjin	4388.2	4653.0	15234.5	18022.6	2453.4	2189.8
河北	Hebei	5948.1	6484.6	35081.6	35548.9	7316.0	8212.2
山西	Shanxi	5113.6	5677.7	19965.8	23316.4	4944.8	5048.0
内蒙古	Inner Mongolia	1134.4	1279.4	7016.7	7497.5	1411.0	1320.7
辽宁	Liaoning	3816.2	4044.9	16234.9	18129.7	4021.3	3459.0
吉林	Jilin	2005.8	2246.3	8447.3	8737.4	2892.8	3006.1
黑龙江	Heilongjiang	1206.4	1328.5	3285.4	3753.5	923.4	786.8
上海	Shanghai	8277.0	9236.4	53798.6	54802.9	8150.8	9232.4
江苏	Jiangsu	35251.6	38244.5	267407.7	273463.3	77802.9	74993.3
浙江	Zhejiang	20938.6	23011.0	180786.2	181956.4	40742.2	43302.4
安徽	Anhui	9365.1	10584.0	49377.0	53887.4	14441.8	14006.5
福建	Fujian	14117.8	15810.4	82579.1	87172.3	18202.3	19182.5
江西	Jiangxi	8649.2	9762.9	34235.5	35525.6	13911.9	14475.2
山东	**Shandong**	**14947.3**	**16412.0**	**86160.1**	**95011.9**	**21309.6**	**24018.2**
河南	Henan	13122.6	14192.0	65956.9	67394.3	19412.4	18988.6
湖北	Hubei	16136.1	19031.5	85268.2	94015.9	26559.5	33112.6
湖南	Hunan	11863.8	13280.1	67978.8	76367.9	21235.3	24029.1
广东	Guangdong	18429.7	21345.6	91890.6	105978.4	19264.2	24525.6
广西	Guangxi	5853.2	6699.6	28695.3	29484.2	8295.8	8596.7
海南	Hainan	391.4	447.1	1823.7	1700.3	299.5	475.8
重庆	Chongqing	8975.0	9943.0	38122.6	37895.2	14050.1	14162.0
四川	Sichuan	15612.7	17351.2	67655.2	72351.8	22572.8	23250.8
贵州	Guizhou	4080.2	4578.0	17167.5	17892.1	3951.7	4035.6
云南	Yunnan	6724.8	7336.6	20128.8	18747.2	6238.4	6648.6
西藏	Tibet	294.7	270.7	477.2	425.5	205.1	196.4
陕西	Shaanxi	8501.1	9176.4	37555.1	36561.9	7311.2	7164.9
甘肃	Gansu	2049.3	2270.3	10903.3	12419.0	2382.8	2341.4
青海	Qinghai	512.2	587.3	927.6	935.5	355.7	277.1
宁夏	Ningxia	641.8	681.5	2107.7	1989.7	757.0	839.9
新疆	Xinjiang	2693.1	3124.8	9881.0	13355.6	3816.2	3124.5

附录 1-18　建筑业主要效益指标(2021年)

Main Economic Indicators on Construction Enterprises(2021)

地区	Region	企业个数(个) Number of Enterprises (unit)	从事建筑业活动的从业人员平均人数(万人) Average Number of Employed Persons (10 000 persons)	按建筑业总产值计算的劳动生产率(元/人) Labor Productivity in Terms of Total Output Value (yuan/person)	人均竣工产值(元/人) Per Capita Output Value of Buildings Completed (yuan/person)	人均施工面积(平方米/人) Per Capita Floor Space of Buildings Under Construction (sq.m/person)	人均竣工面积(平方米/人) Per Capita Floor Space of Buildings Completed (sq.m/person)
全国总计	**Total**	**128746**	**6193.7**	**473191**	**217194**	**254.4**	**65.9**
北　京	Beijing	2518	218.5	640303	282065	417.3	60.7
天　津	Tianjin	2388	88.3	526910	171987	204.1	24.8
河　北	Hebei	3142	100.5	645244	278762	353.7	81.7
山　西	Shanxi	3733	122.8	462396	154534	189.9	41.1
内蒙古	Inner Mongolia	1026	24.5	521475	182283	305.6	53.8
辽　宁	Liaoning	5816	69.9	578784	217972	259.4	49.5
吉　林	Jilin	2801	37.5	598758	299817	232.9	80.1
黑龙江	Heilongjiang	2195	31.1	427852	147685	120.9	25.3
上　海	Shanghai	2362	121.4	760647	419933	451.3	76.0
江　苏	Jiangsu	11396	1035.3	369389	261398	264.1	72.4
浙　江	Zhejiang	8750	585.2	393185	206585	310.9	74.0
安　徽	Anhui	6834	198.6	533025	194050	271.4	70.5
福　建	Fujian	7758	490.9	322044	132909	177.6	39.1
江　西	Jiangxi	4663	181.7	537197	232050	195.5	79.6
山　东	**Shandong**	**9297**	**306.9**	**534836**	**226005**	**309.6**	**78.3**
河　南	Henan	8158	308.0	460835	199833	218.8	61.7
湖　北	Hubei	5077	250.0	761375	324678	376.1	132.5
湖　南	Hunan	3590	301.2	440841	225823	253.5	79.8
广　东	Guangdong	8501	393.0	543085	172710	269.6	62.4
广　西	Guangxi	2351	125.6	533283	253031	234.7	68.4
海　南	Hainan	271	6.6	674177	334117	256.4	71.8
重　庆	Chongqing	3500	227.9	436359	180882	166.3	62.2
四　川	Sichuan	7891	412.9	420179	183407	175.2	56.3
贵　州	Guizhou	1993	84.5	541463	172923	211.6	47.7
云　南	Yunnan	3770	162.3	452088	159844	115.5	41.0
西　藏	Tibet	410	4.6	586263	196521	92.1	42.5
陕　西	Shaanxi	3636	165.8	553355	180196	220.5	43.2
甘　肃	Gansu	2168	49.3	460361	180073	251.8	47.5
青　海	Qinghai	390	8.2	713397	221323	113.6	33.7
宁　夏	Ningxia	648	17.6	388333	220576	113.4	47.9
新　疆	Xinjiang	1713	62.9	497108	199891	212.5	49.7

附录 1-19 客运量和旅客周转量(2021年)
Passenger Traffic and Passenger-Kilometers(2021)

地 区	Region	客运量(万人) Passenger Traffic (10 000 persons)	#铁 路 Railways	#公 路 Highways	#水 运 Waterways	旅客周转量(亿人公里) Passenger Kilometers (100 million passenger km)	#铁 路 Railways	#公 路 Highways	#水 运 Waterways
全国总计	**Total**	**830257**	**261171**	**508693**	**16337**	**19758.2**	**9567.8**	**3627.5**	**33.1**
北 京	Beijing	36666	8607	28059		149.6	95.5	54.1	
天 津	Tianjin	12391	3406	8916	70	171.0	116.6	54.3	0.1
河 北	Hebei	15009	7931	7079		682.1	615.7	66.5	
山 西	Shanxi	11810	6454	5280	76	221.3	165.4	55.8	
内 蒙 古	Inner Mongolia	6283	3597	2686		164.8	130.6	34.2	
辽 宁	Liaoning	27408	7778	19362	268	431.4	333.5	96.1	1.9
吉 林	Jilin	13470	4216	9155	98	208.7	135.7	72.9	0.1
黑 龙 江	Heilongjiang	13480	4867	8477	135	190.2	133.5	56.6	0.1
上 海	Shanghai	11125	9284	1480	361	134.7	84.3	49.7	0.7
江 苏	Jiangsu	67295	21367	43789	2140	991.5	689.1	301.6	0.8
浙 江	Zhejiang	46355	18263	24246	3846	713.6	531.8	176.9	4.9
安 徽	Anhui	27563	11118	16284	161	753.6	605.6	147.8	0.2
福 建	Fujian	19614	8350	10522	742	314.0	238.6	74.5	0.8
江 西	Jiangxi	24304	9167	14978	159	603.9	506.0	97.7	0.2
山 东	**Shandong**	**29975**	**13790**	**15139**	**1047**	**706.8**	**525.1**	**177.8**	**3.9**
河 南	Henan	50717	13126	37388	203	985.3	691.2	293.7	0.4
湖 北	Hubei	33040	11627	21098	314	620.8	490.3	128.6	1.9
湖 南	Hunan	50660	12865	37031	764	857.7	660.6	195.4	1.7
广 东	Guangdong	53599	24452	27567	1580	940.9	670.4	266.0	4.5
广 西	Guangxi	27918	9088	18326	504	521.9	335.6	184.2	2.1
海 南	Hainan	8944	2771	4856	1317	89.9	44.7	42.4	2.8
重 庆	Chongqing	32754	6497	25647	610	281.2	157.8	120.4	3.0
四 川	Sichuan	60287	14073	45349	865	596.6	325.3	270.3	1.0
贵 州	Guizhou	25855	6481	19004	370	410.2	255.4	153.9	0.9
云 南	Yunnan	20582	5253	14973	357	283.4	144.7	138.0	0.6
西 藏	Tibet	939	327	612		30.2	15.4	14.8	
陕 西	Shaanxi	20587	7728	12794	66	435.5	333.4	102.0	0.1
甘 肃	Gansu	15494	4601	10813	79	335.9	269.1	66.7	0.1
青 海	Qinghai	2474	821	1590	63	85.0	57.2	27.7	0.1
宁 夏	Ningxia	3575	720	2713	141	55.9	29.0	26.8	0.1
新 疆	Xinjiang	16026	2543	13483		260.8	180.7	80.1	
不分地区	Not Classified by Region	44056				6529.7			

注：不分地区合计为民航完成数。
a)The total passenger traffic not classified by region refers to that completed by civil aviation.

附录 1-20 货运量和货物周转量(2021年)

Freight Traffic and Freight Ton-kilometers(2021)

地区	Region	货运量(万吨) Total (10 000 tons)	#铁路 Railways	#公路 Highways	#水运 Waterways	货物周转量(亿吨公里) Total (100 million ton-km)	#铁路 Railways	#公路 Highways	#水运 Waterways
全国总计	**Total**	**5298499**	**477372**	**3913889**	**823973**	**223600.4**	**33238.0**	**69087.7**	**115577.5**
北京	Beijing	23425	350	23075		1077.3	802.9	274.4	
天津	Tianjin	56435	11750	34527	10159	2677.6	553.6	672.7	1451.3
河北	Hebei	261208	29205	227203	4800	14769.5	5395.4	8650.1	724.0
山西	Shanxi	217623	102909	114698	16	6444.7	3218.9	3225.7	
内蒙古	Inner Mongolia	215975	83128	132847		4933.8	2715.3	2218.5	
辽宁	Liaoning	179238	23151	152596	3491	4524.7	1246.1	2719.5	559.1
吉林	Jilin	53587	5912	47675		2068.6	544.8	1523.8	
黑龙江	Heilongjiang	55116	12512	42086	519	1744.8	882.8	815.8	46.2
上海	Shanghai	154793	513	52899	101380	34074.6	18.9	1037.3	33018.3
江苏	Jiangsu	294678	9738	186708	98232	11788.6	357.5	3687.8	7743.3
浙江	Zhejiang	328041	5177	213653	109210	12937.5	271.0	2637.0	10029.5
安徽	Anhui	401415	7791	259044	134580	11068.0	826.9	3727.9	6513.3
福建	Fujian	166113	5112	110777	50224	10159.1	201.4	1233.2	8724.6
江西	Jiangxi	198685	4818	181024	12843	4884.7	570.4	3960.1	354.2
山东	**Shandong**	**342728**	**32203**	**291196**	**19329**	**12049.7**	**1729.7**	**7517.6**	**2802.4**
河南	Henan	255551	11563	226447	17541	10674.6	2384.5	7026.3	1263.7
湖北	Hubei	214762	5828	161310	47625	6742.9	1100.3	2196.2	3446.4
湖南	Hunan	224465	4771	198423	21272	2897.7	986.9	1461.2	449.6
广东	Guangdong	386540	11844	267489	107206	28031.5	362.5	2980.5	24688.5
广西	Guangxi	216168	9119	169019	38030	4882.0	772.7	1873.4	2235.9
海南	Hainan	27991	1100	7608	19282	8771.8	16.2	44.7	8710.9
重庆	Chongqing	144593	1946	121185	21462	3846.5	254.7	1155.8	2435.9
四川	Sichuan	184312	7535	171377	5400	3078.9	1024.4	1789.8	264.7
贵州	Guizhou	96989	7276	89154	560	1435.9	685.9	726.3	23.7
云南	Yunnan	135007	5342	129090	576	1868.3	482.8	1377.6	7.9
西藏	Tibet	4583	81	4502		150.1	31.2	118.9	
陕西	Shaanxi	160695	37894	122716	85	3945.0	2126.1	1818.7	0.3
甘肃	Gansu	76109	6444	69665		2887.3	1689.9	1197.4	
青海	Qinghai	17817	3735	14083		591.6	431.1	160.5	
宁夏	Ningxia	46929	9423	37506		812.2	234.5	577.7	
新疆	Xinjiang	73508	19199	54309		2000.1	1318.7	681.3	
不分地区	Not Classified by Region	83418			152	5780.8			83.5

注：1.不分地区合计中包括管道、民航等完成数。货运量和货物周转量的全国总计，等于分省数与不分地区中民航、管道运输数据之和。
a)The data not classified by region refers to pipelines, civil aviation ,etc.Ltd.The total freight traffic and freight ton-kilometers of China refers to the sum of the data classified by region and the data completed by civil aviation and pipelines.

附录 1-21 社会消费品零售总额

Total Retail Sale of Consumer Goods

单位:亿元 (100 million yuan)

地 区	Region	2020 社会消费品零售总额 Total Retail Sales of Consumer Goods	2020 增长 (%) Growth Rate (%)	2021 社会消费品零售总额 Total Retail Sales of Consumer Goods	2021 增长 (%) Growth Rate (%)
全 国	**National Total**	**391980.6**	**-3.9**	**440823.2**	**12.5**
北 京	Beijing	13716.4	-8.9	14867.7	8.4
天 津	Tianjin	3582.9	-15.1	3769.8	5.2
河 北	Hebei	12705.0	-2.2	13509.9	6.3
山 西	Shanxi	6746.3	-4.0	7747.3	14.8
内蒙古	Inner Mongolia	4760.5	-5.8	5060.3	6.3
辽 宁	Liaoning	8960.9	-7.3	9783.9	9.2
吉 林	Jilin	3824.0	-9.2	4216.6	10.3
黑龙江	Heilongjiang	5092.3	-9.1	5542.9	8.8
上 海	Shanghai	15932.5	0.5	18079.3	13.5
江 苏	Jiangsu	37086.1	-1.6	42702.6	15.1
浙 江	Zhejiang	26629.8	-2.6	29210.5	9.7
安 徽	Anhui	18334.0	2.6	21471.2	17.1
福 建	Fujian	18626.5	-1.4	20373.1	9.4
江 西	Jiangxi	10371.8	3.0	12206.7	17.7
山 东	**Shandong**	**29248.0**	持平	**33714.5**	**15.3**
河 南	Henan	22502.8	-4.1	24381.7	8.3
湖 北	Hubei	17984.9	-20.8	21561.4	19.9
湖 南	Hunan	16258.1	-2.6	18596.9	14.4
广 东	Guangdong	40207.9	-6.4	44187.7	9.9
广 西	Guangxi	7831.0	-4.5	8538.5	9.0
海 南	Hainan	1974.6	1.2	2497.6	26.5
重 庆	Chongqing	11787.2	1.3	13967.7	18.5
四 川	Sichuan	20824.9	-2.4	24133.2	15.9
贵 州	Guizhou	7833.4	4.9	8904.3	13.7
云 南	Yunnan	9792.9	-3.6	10731.8	9.6
西 藏	Tibet	745.8	-3.6	810.3	8.7
陕 西	Shaanxi	9605.9	-5.9	10250.5	6.7
甘 肃	Gansu	3632.4	-1.8	4037.1	11.1
青 海	Qinghai	877.3	-7.5	947.8	8.0
宁 夏	Ningxia	1301.4	-7.0	1335.1	2.6
新 疆	Xinjiang	3062.5	-15.3	3584.6	17.0

附录 1-22 货物进出口总额(按收发货人所在地分)
Total Volume of Imports and Exports (by Location of Importers/Exporters)

单位:亿美元 (100 million USD)

地区	Region	2016	2017	2018	2019	2020	2021
全国总计	**Total**	**36855.6**	**41071.6**	**46224.2**	**45778.9**	**46559.1**	**60514.9**
北京	Beijing	2823.5	3240.2	4124.9	4164.6	3364.8	4710.2
天津	Tianjin	1026.6	1129.2	1225.6	1066.5	1063.2	1325.7
河北	Hebei	466.8	498.6	539.0	580.4	644.7	838.1
山西	Shanxi	166.6	171.9	207.6	209.8	218.4	345.1
内蒙古	Inner Mongolia	116.4	138.7	156.9	159.4	152.2	191.2
辽宁	Liaoning	865.6	996.0	1146.0	1053.2	948.3	1194.8
吉林	Jilin	184.5	185.4	206.8	189.0	185.3	232.4
黑龙江	Heilongjiang	165.4	189.5	264.4	271.1	222.3	308.8
上海	Shanghai	4337.7	4762.0	5156.8	4939.1	5038.3	6286.0
江苏	Jiangsu	5093.0	5907.8	6639.1	6295.2	6428.3	8068.7
浙江	Zhejiang	3365.8	3779.1	4323.6	4472.2	4885.4	6410.9
安徽	Anhui	444.1	540.2	628.4	687.3	787.0	1071.0
福建	Fujian	1568.3	1710.2	1874.1	1931.1	2035.8	2855.0
江西	Jiangxi	400.3	443.4	481.9	508.9	580.3	770.8
山东	**Shandong**	**2343.6**	**2645.5**	**2924.0**	**2970.0**	**3202.1**	**4536.3**
河南	Henan	712.1	776.3	828.1	825.0	972.7	1271.0
湖北	Hubei	393.9	463.4	527.8	571.6	622.5	831.4
湖南	Hunan	262.4	360.3	464.7	628.5	706.8	927.1
广东	Guangdong	9553.0	10066.8	10844.6	10366.3	10240.2	12795.5
广西	Guangxi	476.3	578.8	623.0	682.2	704.1	917.0
海南	Hainan	113.5	103.7	127.3	131.5	135.9	228.7
重庆	Chongqing	627.5	666.0	790.2	839.5	941.8	1238.3
四川	Sichuan	493.1	681.1	899.2	984.0	1169.0	1473.2
贵州	Guizhou	57.0	81.6	76.0	65.7	79.1	101.3
云南	Yunnan	199.0	234.5	298.6	336.9	391.3	486.6
西藏	Tibet	7.8	8.6	7.2	7.0	3.1	6.2
陕西	Shaanxi	299.5	402.0	533.0	510.3	546.0	736.4
甘肃	Gansu	68.3	48.3	60.1	55.2	55.3	75.9
青海	Qinghai	15.3	6.6	7.3	5.4	3.3	4.8
宁夏	Ningxia	32.5	50.4	37.8	34.9	17.8	33.2
新疆	Xinjiang	176.4	205.7	200.0	237.1	213.7	243.0

附录 1-23 货物进出口总额(按境内目的地、货源地分)

Total Volume of Imports and Exports (by Destination and Origin of Goods in China)

单位:亿美元 (100 million USD)

地区	Region	2016	2017	2018	2019	2020	2021
全国总计	**Total**	**36855.6**	**41071.6**	**46224.2**	**45778.9**	**46559.1**	**60514.9**
北京	Beijing	1223.2	1216.2	1274.2	1122.8	1150.1	1576.0
天津	Tianjin	1069.7	1216.9	1417.4	1363.7	1257.7	1597.6
河北	Hebei	749.9	815.4	874.7	947.3	1000.8	1364.8
山西	Shanxi	188.4	207.9	246.5	228.6	219.9	366.0
内蒙古	Inner Mongolia	132.2	158.9	198.3	201.2	205.8	287.5
辽宁	Liaoning	961.3	1125.3	1340.8	1338.4	1182.6	1519.9
吉林	Jilin	192.4	197.9	215.4	192.4	195.9	243.8
黑龙江	Heilongjiang	139.4	167.1	237.4	248.8	205.3	288.1
上海	Shanghai	4046.1	4473.5	4858.6	4737.0	4787.8	6045.6
江苏	Jiangsu	5471.4	6364.9	7171.3	6785.3	6843.7	8663.8
浙江	Zhejiang	3434.5	3839.7	4414.5	4517.1	4650.4	6186.7
安徽	Anhui	409.7	509.9	594.0	637.8	752.2	1029.7
福建	Fujian	1368.0	1530.8	1728.3	1747.7	1721.0	2474.8
江西	Jiangxi	353.6	369.2	411.7	443.5	509.3	678.7
山东	**Shandong**	**2734.0**	**3162.9**	**3641.1**	**3587.6**	**3534.7**	**5322.0**
河南	Henan	741.1	813.7	874.9	880.0	1044.6	1364.8
湖北	Hubei	390.2	462.0	513.0	537.7	616.5	795.1
湖南	Hunan	231.5	300.1	354.6	421.0	478.6	571.4
广东	Guangdong	10601.2	11136.6	12112.5	11842.7	12062.1	14746.9
广西	Guangxi	439.1	526.0	607.3	653.3	667.0	1000.9
海南	Hainan	121.7	136.5	180.9	171.7	165.8	202.1
重庆	Chongqing	518.5	565.7	681.9	755.6	839.8	1090.9
四川	Sichuan	480.6	666.2	932.3	1044.0	1173.1	1422.0
贵州	Guizhou	52.0	81.2	83.6	69.3	74.8	102.1
云南	Yunnan	174.1	213.9	271.8	334.4	343.6	412.1
西藏	Tibet	5.9	6.1	6.4	6.2	2.8	6.3
陕西	Shaanxi	294.7	405.6	522.5	490.7	513.0	681.7
甘肃	Gansu	44.7	50.0	64.9	53.8	57.0	76.7
青海	Qinghai	5.2	4.5	5.8	4.9	3.1	4.0
宁夏	Ningxia	31.0	43.3	40.5	41.9	29.3	46.7
新疆	Xinjiang	250.0	303.9	347.0	372.8	270.7	346.4

附录 1-24 货物进出口总额(2021年)

Total Volume of Imports and Exports (2021)

单位:亿美元 (100 million USD)

地 区	Region	按收发货人所在地分 by Location of Importers/Exporters		按境内目的地、货源地分 by Destination and Origin of Goods	
		出口额 Exports	进口额 Imports	出口额 Exports	进口额 Imports
全国总计	**Total**	**33639.6**	**26875.3**	**33639.6**	**26875.3**
北 京	Beijing	946.4	3763.8	513.7	1062.3
天 津	Tianjin	599.7	726.0	573.5	1024.1
河 北	Hebei	469.0	369.2	669.9	694.9
山 西	Shanxi	211.4	133.7	246.0	120.0
内 蒙 古	Inner Mongolia	74.1	117.2	97.1	190.4
辽 宁	Liaoning	512.5	682.3	597.4	922.5
吉 林	Jilin	54.7	177.7	58.5	185.3
黑 龙 江	Heilongjiang	69.3	239.5	76.9	211.2
上 海	Shanghai	2433.1	3852.9	2024.5	4021.0
江 苏	Jiangsu	5035.4	3033.3	5053.6	3610.3
浙 江	Zhejiang	4661.2	1749.7	4586.6	1600.1
安 徽	Anhui	633.8	437.1	664.9	364.9
福 建	Fujian	1674.1	1180.9	1574.6	900.2
江 西	Jiangxi	568.2	202.5	477.9	200.8
山 东	**Shandong**	**2722.3**	**1813.9**	**2852.7**	**2469.3**
河 南	Henan	778.1	492.9	862.1	502.6
湖 北	Hubei	543.1	288.3	508.5	286.6
湖 南	Hunan	652.4	274.8	379.6	191.8
广 东	Guangdong	7819.1	4976.4	9023.2	5723.6
广 西	Guangxi	454.5	462.5	302.4	698.5
海 南	Hainan	51.5	177.2	45.6	156.4
重 庆	Chongqing	800.1	438.3	722.4	368.5
四 川	Sichuan	884.1	589.1	829.6	592.5
贵 州	Guizhou	75.4	25.9	72.9	29.1
云 南	Yunnan	273.5	213.1	194.2	217.9
西 藏	Tibet	3.5	2.7	4.0	2.3
陕 西	Shaanxi	397.3	339.2	384.8	296.9
甘 肃	Gansu	15.0	60.9	21.6	55.0
青 海	Qinghai	2.6	2.2	3.1	0.9
宁 夏	Ningxia	27.1	6.1	38.5	8.2
新 疆	Xinjiang	197.1	45.9	179.3	167.2

附录 1-25 外商投资企业进出口总额

Volume of Import and Export of Foreign-funded Enterprises

单位:万美元 (10 000 USD)

地区	Region	2020 进出口总额 Total	2020 出口额 Exports	2020 进口额 Imports	2021 进出口总额 Total	2021 出口额 Exports	2021 进口额 Imports
全国总计	**Total**	**179759020**	**93227385**	**86531635**	**217165345**	**115297908**	**101867437**
北京	Beijing	7832735	1949513	5883222	10429183	3463653	6965530
天津	Tianjin	5503326	2026901	3476425	6669858	2722053	3947805
河北	Hebei	859109	471967	387142	1281131	742419	538711
山西	Shanxi	1263027	836207	426820	1643489	1292816	350673
内蒙古	Inner Mongolia	92705	44414	48291	128286	63322	64963
辽宁	Liaoning	3660681	1578527	2082154	4525494	2045778	2479716
吉林	Jilin	921153	105030	816122	1090879	137583	953296
黑龙江	Heilongjiang	167678	76836	90842	175244	70761	104483
上海	Shanghai	32483346	11917931	20565416	38752139	14105413	24646726
江苏	Jiangsu	36109729	20235539	15874190	42395220	24149017	18246203
浙江	Zhejiang	7835808	4866946	2968862	10247404	6308205	3939199
安徽	Anhui	2214450	1256472	957978	2724049	1566514	1157535
福建	Fujian	5654720	3348399	2306320	6991097	4206724	2784373
江西	Jiangxi	1291600	756347	535253	1764230	994251	769979
山东	**Shandong**	**7075642**	**4379911**	**2695731**	**9092029**	**5828263**	**3263766**
河南	Henan	5989658	3558968	2430690	5877999	4500740	1377259
湖北	Hubei	1223451	667317	556134	1546194	804725	741469
湖南	Hunan	778977	375066	403910	823912	459211	364701
广东	Guangdong	40292326	24410960	15881366	48890765	29187473	19703292
广西	Guangxi	1127216	529414	597802	1594842	755354	839488
海南	Hainan	437789	230078	207711	504628	264645	239983
重庆	Chongqing	5043083	3432200	1610883	9431771	5152021	4279750
四川	Sichuan	8267110	4453731	3813379	5921455	4102573	1818882
贵州	Guizhou	35464	23486	11977	52482	31508	20974
云南	Yunnan	73908	33099	40809	62449	36603	25846
西藏	Tibet	2112	4	2108	670	42	628
陕西	Shaanxi	3470025	1638040	1831986	4474591	2269207	2205384
甘肃	Gansu	6970	1506	5464	9109	1973	7136
青海	Qinghai	643	602	42	525	525	
宁夏	Ningxia	30146	16730	13416	52994	30073	22921
新疆	Xinjiang	14435	5245	9190	11229	4461	6768

附录2

国际统计资料

International Statistical Data

简 要 说 明

一、本篇资料的主要内容

本篇资料反映了近年来世界主要国家经济社会事业发展基本情况，主要包括人口、土地面积、国内生产总值及其增长、农业、工业、国际贸易、直接投资、国际旅游、国际储备、外债、医疗卫生、互联网用户等方面的内容。

二、本篇资料的来源

本篇资料来源于中国统计出版社出版的《国际统计年鉴 2021》，由省统计局综合处整理。

Brief Introduction

I. Content

Data in this chapter show the social and economic indicators of other countries, mainly including population, territory, GDP, agriculture, industry, international trade, direct investment, international tourism, international reserve, international debts, public health, internet users, indicators on development of population and culture, and TOP500 of international companies, etc.

II. Source of Data

Data in this chapter come from International Statistical Yearbook 2021 published by China Statistics Press and are prepared and compiled by the Division of Comprehensive Statistics of Shandong Provincial Bureau of Statistics.

附录 2-1 中国主要指标居世界的位次
Ranking of China in the World in Terms of Main Indicators

资料来源：联合国贸发会议数据库、世界贸易组织数据库、世界银行WDI数据库、国际货币基金组织数据库。
Source: UNCTAD Database;WTO Database;World Bank WDI Database;IMF Database.

指　　标	Indicator	1978	1980	1990	2000	2010	2019	2020
国土面积	Surface Area	4	4	4	4	4	4	4
人　口	Population	1	1	1	1	1	1	1
国内生产总值	GDP	11	12	11	6	2	2	2
人均国民总收入①	GNI per capita ①	175(188)	177(188)	178(200)	141(207)	120(215)	71(192)	63(186)
货物进出口贸易总额	Foreign Trade Total	29	26	16	8	2	1	1
出口额	Exports	31	30	15	7	1	1	1
进口额	Imports	29	22	18	8	2	2	2
外商直接投资	Foreign Direct Investment Inflows	128	55	12	8	2	2	2
对外直接投资	Foreign Direct Investment Outflows	45	63	22	33	5	4	1
外汇储备	Foreign Exchange Reserves	38	36	10	2	1	1	1

注：①括号中所列为参加排序的国家和地区数。
Note:①The number in the parentheses indicates the number of countries or territories the order based on.

附录 2-2 中国主要指标占世界的比重
Major Indicators as Percentage of the World for China

资料来源：联合国贸发会议数据库、世界贸易组织数据库、世界银行WDI数据库、国际货币基金组织数据库、联合国FAO数据库。
Source: UNCTAD Database,WTO Database,World Bank WDI Database,IMF Database,FAO Database.
单位：%　　　　(%)

指　　标	Indicator	1978	1980	1990	2000	2010	2019	2020
国土面积	Surface Area	7.1	7.1	7.1	7.1	7.1	7.1	7.1
人　口	Population, Total	22.3	22.1	21.5	20.7	19.3	18.3	18.1
国内生产总值	GDP	1.7	1.7	1.6	3.5	8.3	16.3	17.4
货物进出口贸易总额	Foreign Trade Total	0.8	0.9	1.6	3.6	9.7	11.9	13.1
出口额	Exports	0.8	0.9	1.8	3.9	10.3	13.1	14.7
进口额	Imports	0.8	1.0	1.5	3.4	9.0	10.8	11.5
外商直接投资	Foreign Direct Investment Inflows		0.1	1.7	3.0	8.2	9.2	15.0
对外直接投资	Foreign Direct Investment Outflows			0.3	0.1	4.9	11.2	18.0
外汇储备	Foreign Exchange Reserves	0.5	0.6	3.3	7.7	30.1	25.8	25.0
稻谷产量	Rice Production	35.5	35.3	36.5	31.4	27.9	27.7	28.0
小麦产量	Wheat Production	12.1	12.5	16.6	17.0	18.0	17.4	17.6
玉米产量	Maize Production	14.2	15.8	20.0	17.9	20.8	22.7	22.4
大豆产量	Soybeans Production	10.0	9.8	10.1	9.6	5.7	4.7	5.5

附录 2-3 中国农业主要产品产量居世界的位次

Ranking of China in the World in Terms of Major Agricultural Products

资料来源：联合国FAO数据库。
Source: FAO Database.

项 目	Item	1978	1980	1990	2000	2005	2010	2019	2020
谷物	Cereals	2	1	1	1	1	1	1	1
肉类①	Meat,Total①	3	3	2	1	1	1	1	1
籽棉	Seed Cotton	2	2	1	1	1	1	1	1
大豆	Soybeans	3	3	3	4	4	4	4	4
花生	Groundnuts,with Shell	2	2	2	1	1	1	1	1
油菜籽	Rapeseed	2	2	1	1	1	1	2	2
甘蔗	Sugar Cane	10	10	4	3	3	3	4	3
茶叶	Tea	2	2	2	2	1	1	1	1
水果	Fruit	6	8	1	1	1	1	1	1

注：①1990年以前为猪、牛、羊肉产量的位次。
Note: ①Data refer to pork,beef and mutton prior to 1990.

附录 2-4 中国工业主要产品产量居世界位次

Ranking of China in the World in Terms of Major Industrial Products

资料来源：联合国统计月报数据库、联合国FAO数据库。
Source: UN Monthly Bulletin of Statistics Database,FAO Database.

项 目	Item	1978	1980	1990	2000	2005	2010	2019	2020
粗 钢	Crude Steel	5	5	4	1	1	1	1	1
煤	Coal	3	3	1	1	1	1	1	1
原 油	Crude Petroleum	8	6	5	5	5	4	6	6
发电量	Electricity	7	6	3	2	2	2	1	1
水 泥	Cement	4	4	1	1	1	1	1	1
化 肥	Fertilizer	3	3	3	1	1	1	1	1
棉 布	Woven Cotton Fabrics	1	1	1	2	2	1	1	1

附录 2-5 国土面积与人口密度
Country Area and Population Density

资料来源：世界银行WDI数据库。
Source: World Bank WDI Database.

国家或地区	Country or Area	国土面积（万平方公里）Surface Area(10 000 sq.km)	人口密度（人/平方公里）Population Density(persons/sq.km)		
		2018	2010	2018	2019
世　　界	**World**	**13454.3**	**53.3**	**58.4**	**59.0**
中　　国	China	960.0	141.9	147.8	148.3
中国澳门	Macao SAR, China		18121.7	19198.6	19466.4
孟加拉国	Bangladesh	14.8	1133.7	1239.7	1252.6
文　　莱	Brunei Darussalam	0.6	73.7	81.4	82.2
柬 埔 寨	Cambodia	18.1	81.1	92.1	93.4
印　　度	India	298.0	415.1	454.9	459.6
印度尼西亚	Indonesia	191.7	133.5	142.6	144.1
伊　　朗	Iran	174.5	45.3	50.2	50.9
以 色 列	Israel	2.2	352.3	410.5	418.4
日　　本	Japan	37.8	351.4	347.1	346.4
哈萨克斯坦	Kazakhstan	272.5	6.0	6.8	6.9
韩　　国	Korea, Rep.	10.0	509.8	529.2	530.2
老　　挝	Lao PDR	23.7	27.1	30.6	31.1
马来西亚	Malaysia	33.0	85.9	96.0	97.2
蒙　　古	Mongolia	156.4	1.8	2.0	2.1
缅　　甸	Myanmar	67.7	77.5	82.3	82.8
巴基斯坦	Pakistan	79.6	232.8	275.3	280.9
菲 律 宾	Philippines	30.0	315.1	357.7	362.6
中国香港	Hong Kong SAR, China	0.1	6689.7	7096.2	7149.9
新 加 坡	Singapore	0.1	7231.8	7953.0	8044.5
斯里兰卡	Sri Lanka	6.6	323.1	350.3	352.4
泰　　国	Thailand	51.3	131.5	135.9	136.3
越　　南	Viet Nam	33.1	283.7	308.1	311.1
埃　　及	Egypt	100.1	83.1	98.9	100.8
尼日利亚	Nigeria	92.4	174.0	215.1	220.7
南　　非	South Africa	121.9	42.2	47.6	48.3
加 拿 大	Canada	988.0	3.8	4.1	4.2
墨 西 哥	Mexico	196.4	58.7	64.9	65.6
美　　国	United States	983.2	33.8	35.7	35.9
阿 根 廷	Argentina	278.0	14.9	16.3	16.4
巴　　西	Brazil	851.6	23.4	25.1	25.3
委内瑞拉	Venezuela	91.2	32.2	32.7	32.3
捷　　克	Czech Rep.	7.9	135.6	137.7	138.2
法　　国	France	54.9	118.8	122.5	122.8
德　　国	Germany	35.8	234.6	237.3	237.8
意 大 利	Italy	30.2	201.5	202.9	200.6
荷　　兰	Netherlands	4.2	492.6	511.8	515.1
波　　兰	Poland	31.3	124.2	124.0	124.0
俄 罗 斯	Russia	1709.8	8.7	8.8	8.8
西 班 牙	Spain	50.6	93.2	93.7	94.3
土 耳 其	Turkey	78.5	94.0	107.0	108.4
乌 克 兰	Ukraine	60.4	79.2	77.0	76.6
英　　国	United Kingdom	24.4	259.4	274.7	276.3
澳大利亚	Australia	774.1	2.9	3.2	3.3
新 西 兰	New Zealand	26.8	16.5	18.6	18.9

附录 2-6 国内生产总值(现价美元)

Gross Domestic Product(USD)

资料来源：世界银行WDI数据库。
Source: World Bank WDI Database.

单位：亿美元 (100 million USD)

国家或地区	Country or Area	2000	2005	2010	2015	2019	2020
世　界	**World**	**337035**	**475709**	**661646**	**750274**	**874367**	**845780**
高收入国家	**High Income**	**276879**	**376916**	**454646**	**480199**	**549782**	**533994**
中等收入国家	**Middle Income**	**57950**	**95758**	**199863**	**263332**	**317096**	**304331**
中等偏下收入国家	**Lower Middle Income**	**14980**	**25406**	**51872**	**64398**	**77299**	**73288**
中等偏上收入国家	**Upper Middle Income**	**42970**	**70352**	**147990**	**198934**	**239797**	**231049**
中低收入国家	**Low and Middle Income**	**59006**	**97346**	**203058**	**267484**	**321574**	**308891**
东亚和太平洋	**East Asia and Pacific**	**17323**	**31067**	**78717**	**132785**	**171451**	**174430**
欧洲和中亚	**Europe and Central Asia**	**6997**	**16859**	**31113**	**30948**	**34916**	**32177**
拉丁美洲和加勒比	**Latin America and Caribbean**	**19808**	**24485**	**45473**	**46531**	**48416**	**40078**
中东和北非国家	**Middle East and North Africa**	**4531**	**6706**	**13288**	**13708**	**13107**	**11655**
南　亚	**South Asia**	**6304**	**10506**	**20608**	**27002**	**35969**	**33515**
撒哈拉以南非洲	**Sub-Saharan Africa**	**4005**	**7715**	**13846**	**16515**	**17705**	**16865**
低收入国家	**Low Income**	**1054**	**1593**	**3213**	**4169**	**4459**	**4583**
最不发达地区	**Least Developed Countries**	**2153**	**3441**	**6930**	**9541**	**11339**	**11327**
重债穷国	**Heavily Indebted Poor Countries**	**1700**	**2591**	**4991**	**6677**	**7919**	**8038**
中　国	China	12113	22860	60872	110616	142799	147227
中国香港	Hong Kong SAR, China	1717	1816	2286	3094	3630	3466
中国澳门	Macao SAR, China	68	122	282	451	552	
阿富汗	Afghanistan		62	159	199	193	198
阿尔巴尼亚	Albania	35	81	119	114	153	148
阿尔及利亚	Algeria	548	1032	1612	1660	1712	1452
安道尔	Andorra	14	32	34	28	32	
安哥拉	Angola	91	370	838	1162	894	623
安提瓜和巴布达	Antigua and Barbuda	8	10	11	13	17	14
阿根廷	Argentina	2842	1987	4236	5947	4454	3831
亚美尼亚	Armenia	19	49	93	106	137	126
阿鲁巴岛	Aruba	19	23	24	30		
澳大利亚	Australia	4152	6934	11461	13517	13966	13309
奥地利	Austria	1968	3160	3919	3818	4451	4309
阿塞拜疆	Azerbaijan	53	132	529	531	482	426
巴　林	Bahrain	91	160	257	311	385	
孟加拉国	Bangladesh	534	694	1153	1951	3026	3242
巴巴多斯	Barbados	31	38	45	47	52	44
白俄罗斯	Belarus	127	302	572	565	644	603
比利时	Belgium	2362	3856	4810	4621	5333	5153
伯利兹	Belize	8	11	14	17	20	18
贝　宁	Benin	35	66	95	114	144	157
百慕大	Bermuda	35	49	66	67	75	
不　丹	Bhutan	4	8	15	20	25	24
玻利维亚	Bolivia	84	95	196	330	409	367
波　黑	Bosnia and Herzegovinian	55	112	172	162	202	198
博茨瓦纳	Botswana	58	99	128	144	184	158
巴　西	Brazil	6554	8916	22089	18022	18778	14447
文　莱	Brunei Darussalam	60	95	137	129	135	120
保加利亚	Bulgaria	132	299	504	506	686	691
布基纳法索	Burkina Faso	30	61	101	118	160	174
布隆迪	Burundi	9	11	20	31	30	33
柬埔寨	Cambodia	37	63	112	180	271	253
喀麦隆	Cameroon	101	180	262	309	390	398
加拿大	Canada	7448	11731	16173	15565	17416	16440
佛得角	Cape Verde	5	10	17	16	20	17
中　非	Central African Rep.	9	13	21	17	22	23

附录 2-6 续表 1 continued

单位：亿美元 (100 million USD)

国家或地区	Country or Area	2000	2005	2010	2015	2019	2020
乍 得	Chad	14	66	107	110	113	101
海峡群岛	Channel Islands	64	88				
智 利	Chile	779	1230	2185	2439	2794	2529
哥伦比亚	Colombia	999	1456	2866	2935	3234	2713
科 摩 罗	Comoros	4	7	9	10	12	12
刚果(金)	Congo, Dem. Rep.	191	120	216	379	504	499
刚果(布)	Congo, Rep.	32	66	131	119	127	109
哥斯达黎加	Costa Rica	150	200	377	564	640	615
科特迪瓦	Cote D'Ivoire	107	171	249	458	585	613
克罗地亚	Croatia	216	454	599	495	608	560
古 巴	Cuba	306	426	643	871	1031	
塞浦路斯	Cyprus	100	184	257	198	249	238
捷 克	Czech Rep.	618	1371	2091	1880	2525	2453
丹 麦	Denmark	1642	2645	3220	3027	3476	3561
吉 布 提	Djibouti	6	7	11	24	33	34
多米尼克	Dominica	3	4	5	5	6	5
多米尼加	Dominican Rep.	243	358	539	712	889	788
厄瓜多尔	Ecuador	183	415	696	993	1081	988
埃 及	Egypt	998	896	2190	3294	3031	3631
萨尔瓦多	El Salvador	118	147	184	234	269	246
赤道几内亚	Equatorial Guinea	10	82	163	132	114	100
厄立特里亚	Eritrea	7	11	16			
爱沙尼亚	Estonia	57	141	195	229	310	307
埃塞俄比亚	Ethiopia	82	124	299	646	959	1076
法罗群岛	Faeroe Islands	11	17	23	25	31	
斐 济	Fiji	17	30	31	47	55	44
芬 兰	Finland	1257	2048	2492	2344	2688	2698
法 国	France	13622	21961	26426	24382	27289	26303
法属波立尼西亚	French Polynesia	34					
加 蓬	Gabon	51	96	144	144	169	156
冈 比 亚	Gambia	8	10	15	14	18	19
格鲁吉亚	Georgia	31	64	122	150	175	159
德 国	Germany	19431	28458	33964	33562	38883	38464
加 纳	Ghana	50	107	322	475	672	724
希 腊	Greece	1301	2478	2968	1953	2053	1894
格 陵 兰	Greenland	11	18	25	25		
关 岛	Guam		42	49	58	63	
危地马拉	Guatemala	193	268	407	622	770	776
几 内 亚	Guinea	30	29	69	88	135	157
几内亚比绍	Guinea-Bissau	4	6	8	10	14	14
圭 亚 那	Guyana	7	8	34	43	52	55
海 地	Haiti	69	70	117	149	143	134
洪都拉斯	Honduras	72	98	158	210	251	238
匈 牙 利	Hungary	472	1130	1319	1251	1635	1550
冰 岛	Iceland	90	169	138	175	249	217
印 度	India	4684	8204	16756	21036	28705	26230
印度尼西亚	Indonesia	1650	2859	7551	8609	11191	10584
伊 朗	Iran	1096	2265	4868	3850	2582	1917
伊 拉 克	Iraq	484	500	1385	1668	2224	1672
爱 尔 兰	Ireland	1000	2118	2217	2915	3991	4259
马 恩 岛	Isle of Man	16	30	59	71		
以 色 列	Israel	1327	1427	2340	3001	3947	4020
意 大 利	Italy	11438	18575	21340	18359	20049	18864
牙 买 加	Jamaica	90	112	132	142	158	138
日 本	Japan	49684	48315	57591	44449	51488	49754

附录 2-6 续表 2 continued

单位：亿美元 (100 million USD)

国家或地区	Country or Area	2000	2005	2010	2015	2019	2020
约　旦	Jordan	85	126	271	386	445	437
哈萨克斯坦	Kazakhstan	183	571	1480	1844	1817	1698
肯尼亚	Kenya	127	187	400	640	955	988
基里巴斯	Kiribati	1	1	2	2	2	2
韩　国	Korea, Rep.	5762	9349	11441	14658	16467	16305
科威特	Kuwait	377	808	1154	1146	1362	
吉尔吉斯斯坦	Kyrgyzstan	14	25	48	67	89	77
老　挝	Lao PDR	17	27	71	144	182	191
拉脱维亚	Latvia	79	170	239	272	341	335
黎巴嫩	Lebanon	173	215	384	499	520	334
莱索托	Lesotho	9	17	22	24	24	18
利比里亚	Liberia	9	9	20	32	31	30
利比亚	Libya	383	473	748	278	521	254
列支敦士登	Liechtenstein	25	37	51	63		
立陶宛	Lithuania	115	261	371	414	546	559
卢森堡	Luxemburg	213	373	532	577	711	733
马达加斯加	Madagascar	46	59	100	113	142	137
马拉维	Malawi	17	37	70	64	109	120
马来西亚	Malaysia	938	1435	2550	3014	3647	3367
马尔代夫	Maldives	6	12	26	41	56	40
马　里	Mali	30	62	107	131	173	174
马耳他	Malta	41	64	90	111	152	146
马绍尔群岛	Marshall Islands	1	1	2	2	2	
毛里塔尼亚	Mauritania	18	29	56	62	76	78
毛里求斯	Mauritius	47	65	100	117	140	109
墨西哥	Mexico	7079	8775	10578	11719	12689	10762
密克罗尼西亚	Micronesia, Fed.	2	3	3	3	4	
摩尔多瓦	Moldova	13	30	70	77	120	119
摩纳哥	Monaco	26	42	54	63	74	
蒙　古	Mongolia	11	25	72	117	140	131
黑　山	Montenegro	10	23	41	41	55	48
摩洛哥	Morocco	389	623	932	1012	1197	1129
莫桑比克	Mozambique	57	85	111	160	153	140
缅　甸	Myanmar	47	106	515	603	798	762
纳米比亚	Namibia	39	72	114	113	126	107
瑙　鲁	Nauru				1	1	
尼泊尔	Nepal	55	81	160	244	342	337
荷　兰	Netherlands	4164	6851	8466	7653	9102	9139
新喀里多尼亚	New Caledonia	27					
新西兰	New Zealand	526	1147	1465	1781	2129	2109
尼加拉瓜	Nicaragua	51	63	88	128	126	126
尼日尔	Niger	22	44	79	97	129	137
尼日利亚	Nigeria	694	1761	3615	4868	4481	4323
北马其顿	North Macedonia	38	63	94	101	125	123
挪　威	Norway	1712	3089	4288	3858	4055	3625
阿　曼	Oman	195	311	569	684	763	
巴基斯坦	Pakistan	820	1201	1772	2706	2782	2637
帕　劳	Palau	1	2	2	3	3	
巴拿马	Panama	123	164	294	541	668	529
巴布亚新几内亚	Papua New Guinea	35	49	143	217	248	236
巴拉圭	Paraguay	89	107	272	362	379	353
秘　鲁	Peru	517	761	1475	1898	2285	2020
菲律宾	Philippines	837	1074	2084	3064	3768	3615
波　兰	Poland	1722	3061	4798	4778	5959	5942
葡萄牙	Portugal	1183	1972	2379	1993	2395	2312

附录 2-6 续表 3 continued

单位：亿美元 (100 million USD)

国家或地区	Country or Area	2000	2005	2010	2015	2019	2020
波多黎各	Puerto Rico	617	839	984	1034	1049	1031
卡 塔 尔	Qatar	178	445	1251	1617	1758	1464
罗马尼亚	Romania	373	985	1663	1777	2497	2487
俄 罗 斯	Russia	2597	7640	15249	13635	16874	14835
卢 旺 达	Rwanda	21	29	61	85	104	103
圣基茨和尼维斯	Saint Kitts and Nevis	4	5	8	9	10	9
圣卢西亚	Saint Lucia	9	11	15	18	21	17
圣文森特和格林纳丁斯	Saint Vincent and the Grenadines	4	6	7	8	8	8
萨 摩 亚	Samoa	3	5	7	8	9	8
圣马力诺	San Marino	10	18	19	14	16	
圣多美和普林西比	Sao Tome and Principe		1	2	3	4	5
沙特阿拉伯	Saudi Arabia	1895	3285	5282	6543	7930	7001
塞内加尔	Senegal	60	111	161	178	233	249
塞尔维亚	Serbia	69	277	418	397	515	530
塞 舌 尔	Seychelles	6	9	10	14	16	11
塞拉利昂	Sierra Leone	6	17	26	42	41	39
新 加 坡	Singapore	961	1278	2398	3080	3744	3400
斯洛伐克	Slovakia	292	628	903	885	1051	1046
斯洛文尼亚	Slovenia	203	362	482	431	542	536
所罗门群岛	Solomon Islands	4	5	8	13	16	16
南 非	South Africa	1364	2578	3753	3176	3514	3019
西 班 牙	Spain	5969	11533	14207	11951	13930	12815
斯里兰卡	Sri Lanka	163	244	567	806	840	807
苏 丹	Sudan	123	265	656	645	323	261
苏 里 南	Suriname	9	18	44	51	42	38
斯威士兰	Swaziland	17	32	44	41	45	40
瑞 典	Sweden	2628	3922	4958	5051	5339	5411
瑞 士	Switzerland	2798	4205	6034	7021	7318	7522
叙 利 亚	Syrian Arab Republic	193	289				
塔吉克斯坦	Tajikistan	9	23	56	83	83	82
坦桑尼亚	Tanzania	134	184	320	474	611	624
泰 国	Thailand	1264	1893	3411	4013	5443	5018
巴 哈 马	The Bahamas	81	98	101	117	136	113
东 帝 汶	Timor-Leste	4	5	9	16	20	18
多 哥	Togo	15	23	34	42	72	76
汤 加	Tonga	2	3	4	4	5	
特立尼达和多巴哥	Trinidad And Tobago	82	160	222	250	232	215
突 尼 斯	Tunisia	215	323	441	432	392	392
土 耳 其	Turkey	2743	5063	7770	8643	7614	7201
土库曼斯坦	Turkmenistan	29	81	226	358	452	
图 瓦 卢	Tuvalu						
乌 干 达	Uganda	62	92	266	322	352	374
乌 克 兰	Ukraine	313	861	1360	910	1539	1556
阿 联 酋	United Arab Emirates	1043	1806	2898	3581	4211	
英 国	United Kingdom	16582	25328	24816	29328	28308	27077
美 国	United States	102523	130366	149921	182383	214332	209366
乌 拉 圭	Uruguay	228	174	403	533	612	536
乌兹别克斯坦	Uzbekistan	138	143	467	818	577	577
瓦努阿图	Vanuatu	3	4	7	7	9	9
委内瑞拉	Venezuela	1171	1455	3932			
越 南	Viet Nam	312	576	1159	1932	2619	2712
约旦河西岸和加沙	West Bank and Gaza	43	51	97	140	171	156
也 门	Yemen	97	167	309	424		
赞 比 亚	Zambia	36	83	203	213	233	193
津巴布韦	Zimbabwe	67	58	120	200	169	168

附录 2-7 人均国内生产总值

GDP per Capita

资料来源：世界银行WDI数据库。

Source: World Bank WDI Database.

单位：美元 (USD)

国家或地区	Country or Area	2000	2005	2010	2015	2019	2020
世　界	**World**	**5512**	**7305**	**9559**	**10223**	**11395**	**10909**
高收入国家	**High Income**	**25761**	**33913**	**39391**	**40444**	**45407**	**43953**
中等收入国家	**Middle Income**	**1252**	**1943**	**3825**	**4755**	**5480**	**5207**
中等偏下收入国家	**Lower Middle Income**	**613**	**955**	**1802**	**2075**	**2353**	**2200**
中等偏上收入国家	**Upper Middle Income**	**1968**	**3102**	**6307**	**8173**	**9589**	**9192**
中低收入国家	**Low and Middle Income**	**1177**	**1811**	**3538**	**4369**	**4998**	**4745**
东亚和太平洋	**East Asia and Pacific**	**954**	**1639**	**4004**	**6515**	**8189**	**8286**
欧洲和中亚	**Europe and Central Asia**	**1787**	**4301**	**7816**	**7546**	**8338**	**7657**
拉丁美洲和加勒比	**Latin America and Caribbean**	**4198**	**4856**	**8504**	**8241**	**8213**	**6733**
中东和北非国家	**Middle East and North Africa**	**1622**	**2200**	**3993**	**3766**	**3366**	**2942**
南　亚	**South Asia**	**453**	**692**	**1257**	**1543**	**1959**	**1805**
撒哈拉以南非洲	**Sub-Saharan Africa**	**602**	**1017**	**1593**	**1659**	**1600**	**1485**
低收入国家	**Low Income**	**272**	**357**	**625**	**714**	**688**	**689**
最不发达地区	**Least Developed Countries**	**328**	**462**	**828**	**1014**	**1097**	**1071**
重债穷国	**Heavily Indebted Poor Countries**	**360**	**477**	**800**	**930**	**988**	**976**
中　国	China	959	1753	4550	8067	10217	10500
中国香港	Hong Kong SAR, China	25757	26650	32550	42432	48354	46324
中国澳门	Macao SAR, China	15836	25183	52473	74839	86118	
阿富汗	Afghanistan		242	543	578	507	509
阿尔巴尼亚	Albania	1127	2674	4094	3953	5356	5215
阿尔及利亚	Algeria	1765	3113	4481	4178	3976	3310
安道尔	Andorra	21854	40064	40850	35771	40897	
安哥拉	Angola	557	1902	3588	4167	2810	1896
安提瓜和巴布达	Antigua and Barbuda	10872	12558	13049	14285	17113	14450
阿根廷	Argentina	7708	5110	10386	13789	9912	8442
亚美尼亚	Armenia	623	1644	3218	3607	4623	4267
阿鲁巴岛	Aruba	20618	23301	23514	28397		
澳大利亚	Australia	21679	33999	52022	56756	55057	51812
奥地利	Austria	24564	38403	46858	44178	50122	48328
阿塞拜疆	Azerbaijan	655	1578	5844	5500	4806	4214
巴　林	Bahrain	13636	17959	20722	22634	23443	
孟加拉国	Bangladesh	418	499	781	1248	1856	1969
巴巴多斯	Barbados	11268	13823	16056	16525	18148	15191
白俄罗斯	Belarus	1276	3126	6029	5949	6839	6411
比利时	Belgium	23042	36796	44142	40992	46414	44594
伯利兹	Belize	3364	3885	4271	4770	5079	4436
贝　宁	Benin	513	823	1037	1077	1220	1291
百慕大	Bermuda	56284	75882	101875	102006	117098	
不　丹	Bhutan	718	1228	2258	2753	3316	3122
玻利维亚	Bolivia	998	1034	1955	3036	3552	3143
波　黑	Bosnia and Herzegovinian	1468	2981	4636	4727	6120	6032
博茨瓦纳	Botswana	3522	5513	6435	6800	7971	6711
巴　西	Brazil	3750	4790	11286	8814	8897	6797
文　莱	Brunei Darussalam	18013	26105	35271	31164	31086	27466
保加利亚	Bulgaria	1621	3900	6812	7056	9828	9976
布基纳法索	Burkina Faso	256	458	648	653	787	831
布隆迪	Burundi	136	152	234	306	261	274
柬埔寨	Cambodia	301	474	786	1163	1643	1513
喀麦隆	Cameroon	652	1012	1287	1328	1507	1499
加拿大	Canada	24271	36383	47562	43596	46327	43258
佛得角	Cape Verde	1259	2099	3378	3043	3604	3064
中　非	Central African Rep.	251	331	488	377	468	477
乍　得	Chad	166	659	893	776	710	614
海峡群岛	Channel Islands	43383	58199				

附录 2-7 续表 1 continued

单位：美元 (USD)

国家或地区	Country or Area	2000	2005	2010	2015	2019	2020
智　　利	Chile	5075	7599	12808	13574	14742	13232
哥伦比亚	Colombia	2520	3414	6337	6176	6425	5333
科 摩 罗	Comoros	647	1069	1316	1243	1370	1403
刚果(金)	Congo, Dem. Rep.	405	218	334	497	581	557
刚果(布)	Congo, Rep.	1032	1835	3074	2448	2359	1973
哥斯达黎加	Costa Rica	3789	4676	8227	11643	12670	12077
科特迪瓦	Cote D'Ivoire	653	931	1213	1973	2276	2326
克罗地亚	Croatia	4842	10528	13949	11782	14944	13828
古　　巴	Cuba	2747	3787	5730	7694	9100	
塞浦路斯	Cyprus	14388	24959	31024	23408	28288	26624
捷　　克	Czech Rep.	6029	13431	19960	17830	23660	22932
丹　　麦	Denmark	30744	48800	58041	53255	59776	61063
吉 布 提	Djibouti	768	905	1343	2659	3415	3426
多米尼克	Dominica	4788	5161	6967	7597	8002	6527
多米尼加	Dominican Rep.	2869	3933	5555	6922	8282	7268
厄瓜多尔	Ecuador	1445	3002	4634	6124	6223	5600
埃　　及	Egypt	1450	1186	2646	3563	3019	3548
萨尔瓦多	El Salvador	2002	2429	2983	3706	4168	3799
赤道几内亚	Equatorial Guinea	1726	10963	17289	11283	8420	7143
厄立特里亚	Eritrea	308	389	501			
爱沙尼亚	Estonia	4071	10413	14663	17395	23397	23027
埃塞俄比亚	Ethiopia	124	162	342	641	856	936
法罗群岛	Faroe Islands	22652	36199	48541	52400	64225	
斐　　济	Fiji	2069	3628	3653	5391	6176	4882
芬　　兰	Finland	24285	39040	46460	42785	48678	48773
法　　国	France	22364	34760	40638	36638	40579	39030
法属波立尼西亚	French Polynesia	14324					
加　　蓬	Gabon	4136	6891	8849	7385	7767	7006
冈 比 亚	Gambia	594	666	861	661	778	787
格鲁吉亚	Georgia	750	1643	3233	4014	4698	4279
德　　国	Germany	23636	34507	41532	41087	46795	46208
加　　纳	Ghana	258	493	1299	1706	2210	2329
希　　腊	Greece	12043	22552	26691	18050	19151	17676
格 陵 兰	Greenland	19004	32490	43988	44536		
关岛	Guam		26596	31040	35829	37724	
危地马拉	Guatemala	1664	2069	2853	3995	4639	4603
几 内 亚	Guinea	363	322	672	769	1058	1194
几内亚比绍	Guinea-Bissau	309	436	558	603	749	728
圭 亚 那	Guyana	954	1106	4581	5577	6610	6956
海地	Haiti	812	767	1172	1389	1272	1177
洪都拉斯	Honduras	1093	1308	1904	2302	2574	2406
匈 牙 利	Hungary	4624	11201	13192	12707	16733	15899
冰　　岛	Iceland	32096	56795	43237	52952	68941	59270
印　　度	India	443	715	1358	1606	2101	1901
印度尼西亚	Indonesia	780	1263	3122	3332	4135	3870
伊　　朗	Iran	1670	3246	6600	4904	3115	2283
伊 拉 克	Iraq	2058	1856	4657	4688	5658	4157
爱 尔 兰	Ireland	26269	50914	48608	61988	80887	85268
马 恩 岛	Isle of Man	20323	37767	69767	85127		
以 色 列	Israel	21101	20586	30694	35814	43589	43611
意 大 利	Italy	20088	32043	36001	30230	33567	31676
牙 买 加	Jamaica	3392	4104	4704	4908	5369	4665
日　　本	Japan	39169	37813	44968	34961	40778	39539
约　　旦	Jordan	1652	2183	3737	4164	4405	4283
哈萨克斯坦	Kazakhstan	1229	3771	9070	10511	9813	9056
肯 尼 亚	Kenya	397	512	952	1337	1817	1838
基里巴斯	Kiribati	797	1215	1517	1543	1655	1671

附录 2-7 续表 2 continued

单位：美元 (USD)

国家或地区	Country or Area	2000	2005	2010	2015	2019	2020
韩 国	Korea, Rep.	12257	19403	23087	28732	31846	31489
科 威 特	Kuwait	18440	35591	38577	29870	32373	
吉尔吉斯斯坦	Kyrgyzstan	280	477	880	1121	1374	1174
老 挝	Lao PDR	325	476	1141	2135	2545	2630
拉脱维亚	Latvia	3358	7575	11380	13775	17794	17620
黎 巴 嫩	Lebanon	4492	4575	7762	7645	7584	4891
莱 索 托	Lesotho	436	843	1120	1146	1113	861
利比里亚	Liberia	307	295	513	710	622	583
利 比 亚	Libya	7143	8163	12065	4338	7686	3699
列支敦士登	Liechtenstein	74854	105399	141193	167313		
立 陶 宛	Lithuania	3293	7855	11988	14258	19555	19998
卢 森 堡	Luxemburg	48736	80290	104965	101376	114685	115874
马达加斯加	Madagascar	294	320	472	467	526	495
马 拉 维	Malawi	156	290	479	381	583	625
马来西亚	Malaysia	4044	5587	9041	9955	11414	10402
马尔代夫	Maldives	2235	3640	7077	9033	10626	7456
马 里	Mali	271	489	710	751	879	859
马 耳 他	Malta	10432	15888	21799	24922	30186	27885
马绍尔群岛	Marshall Islands	2273	2471	2846	3200	4073	
毛里塔尼亚	Mauritania	677	971	1611	1524	1679	1673
毛里求斯	Mauritius	3929	5283	8000	9260	11098	8623
墨 西 哥	Mexico	7158	8278	9271	9617	9946	8347
密克罗尼西亚	Micronesia, Fed.	2172	2358	2885	2907	3585	
摩尔多瓦	Moldova	441	1035	2438	2732	4494	4551
摩 纳 哥	Monaco	82365	124197	150738	165990	190513	
蒙 古	Mongolia	474	999	2643	3919	4340	4007
黑 山	Montenegro	1627	3675	6688	6517	8911	7686
摩 洛 哥	Morocco	1335	2018	2840	2875	3230	3009
莫桑比克	Mozambique	319	417	472	590	504	449
缅 甸	Myanmar	100	216	1018	1144	1477	1400
纳米比亚	Namibia	2186	3740	5395	4897	5037	4211
瑙鲁	Nauru			4752	8365	10983	
尼 泊 尔	Nepal	229	316	592	902	1195	1155
荷 兰	Netherlands	26149	41979	50950	45175	52476	52397
新喀里多尼亚	New Caledonia	12580					
新 西 兰	New Zealand	13641	27751	33677	38631	42755	41478
尼加拉瓜	Nicaragua	1007	1162	1504	2050	1927	1905
尼 日 尔	Niger	198	322	477	484	554	565
尼日利亚	Nigeria	568	1268	2280	2687	2230	2097
北马其顿	North Macedonia	1855	3037	4545	4843	6022	5888
挪 威	Norway	38131	66810	87694	74356	75826	67390
阿 曼	Oman	8601	12377	18713	16033	15343	
巴基斯坦	Pakistan	576	749	987	1357	1285	1194
帕 劳	Palau	7658	9627	10357	15876	14908	
巴 拿 马	Panama	4060	4917	8082	13630	15728	12269
巴布亚新几内亚	Papua New Guinea	602	749	1949	2679	2829	2637
巴 拉 圭	Paraguay	1664	1844	4359	5414	5381	4950
秘 鲁	Peru	1956	2729	5082	6229	7028	6127
菲 律 宾	Philippines	1073	1244	2217	3001	3485	3299
波 兰	Poland	4501	8022	12613	12578	15695	15656
葡 萄 牙	Portugal	11498	18773	22499	19242	23285	22437
波多黎各	Puerto Rico	16192	21959	26436	29763	32851	32291
卡 塔 尔	Qatar	29976	51456	67403	63039	62088	50805
罗马尼亚	Romania	1660	4618	8214	8969	12890	12896
俄 罗 斯	Russia	1772	5323	10675	9313	11498	10127
卢 旺 达	Rwanda	261	332	610	751	820	798
圣基茨和尼维斯	Saint Kitts and Nevis	9566	11679	15510	18029	19773	17436

附录 2-7 续表 3 continued

单位：美元 (USD)

国家或地区	Country or Area	2000	2005	2010	2015	2019	2020
圣卢西亚	Saint Lucia	5950	6949	8540	10094	11611	9276
圣文森特和格林纳丁斯	Saint Vincent and the Grenadines	3676	5070	6292	6922	7457	7298
萨摩亚	Samoa	1542	2590	3566	4074	4324	4067
圣马力诺	San Marino	36604	60901	60255	42663	47731	
圣多美和普林西比	Sao Tome and Principe		867	1090	1585	1988	2158
沙特阿拉伯	Saudi Arabia	9171	13791	19263	20628	23140	20110
塞内加尔	Senegal	617	998	1272	1219	1430	1488
塞尔维亚	Serbia	915	3720	5735	5589	7412	7666
塞舌尔	Seychelles	7579	11093	10805	14745	16199	11425
塞拉利昂	Sierra Leone	139	292	402	588	528	485
新加坡	Singapore	23852	29961	47237	55647	65641	59798
斯洛伐克	Slovakia	5413	11686	16751	16311	19273	19157
斯洛文尼亚	Slovenia	10201	18099	23510	20882	25943	25517
所罗门群岛	Solomon Islands	1018	1015	1604	2167	2344	2258
南非	South Africa	3032	5384	7329	5735	6001	5091
西班牙	Spain	14713	26419	30503	25732	29555	27063
斯里兰卡	Sri Lanka	870	1249	2800	3844	3852	3682
苏丹	Sudan	366	689	1490	1657	753	595
苏里南	Suriname	2012	3591	8256	9168	7261	6491
斯威士兰	Swaziland	1729	3084	4168	3680	3895	3415
瑞典	Sweden	29625	43437	52869	51545	51939	52259
瑞士	Switzerland	38952	56547	77117	84776	85335	87097
叙利亚	Syrian Arab Republic	1178	1572				
塔吉克斯坦	Tajikistan	138	341	750	978	891	859
坦桑尼亚	Tanzania	411	493	743	948	1086	1076
泰国	Thailand	2008	2894	5076	5840	7817	7189
巴哈马	The Bahamas	27098	30279	28444	31296	34863	28608
东帝汶	Timor-Leste	415	465	806	1333	1561	1381
多哥	Togo	303	407	534	571	893	915
汤加	Tonga	2091	2594	3528	4336	4903	
特立尼达和多巴哥	Trinidad And Tobago	6435	12327	16683	18214	16637	15384
突尼斯	Tunisia	2212	3193	4142	3862	3352	3320
土耳其	Turkey	4337	7456	10743	11006	9127	8538
土库曼斯坦	Turkmenistan	643	1704	4439	6433	7612	
图瓦卢	Tuvalu	1463	2185	3025	3198	4056	4143
乌干达	Uganda	262	334	819	844	794	817
乌克兰	Ukraine	636	1827	2965	2125	3663	3727
阿联酋	United Arab Emirates	33291	39365	33893	38663	43103	
英国	United Kingdom	28156	41933	39537	45039	42354	40285
美国	United States	36335	44115	48467	56863	65280	63544
乌拉圭	Uruguay	6875	5227	11992	15614	17688	15438
乌兹别克斯坦	Uzbekistan	558	547	1634	2615	1719	1686
瓦努阿图	Vanuatu	1471	1887	2839	2696	3102	2783
委内瑞拉	Venezuela	4842	5505	13825			
越南	Viet Nam	390	687	1318	2085	2715	2786
约旦河西岸和加沙	West Bank and Gaza	1476	1544	2557	3272	3657	3240
也门	Yemen	554	833	1335	1602		
赞比亚	Zambia	346	703	1489	1338	1305	1051
津巴布韦	Zimbabwe	563	477	948	1445	1156	1128

附录 2-8 三次产业对国内生产总值的贡献率

Share of the Contributions of the Three Strata of Industry to the Increase of GDP

资料来源：世界银行WDI数据库。
Source: World Bank WDI Database.
单位：% (%)

国家或地区	Country or Area	第一产业 Primary Industry		第二产业 Secondary Industry		第三产业 Tertiary Industry	
		2000	2020	2000	2020	2000	2020
中　国	China	5.4	9.4	41.5	43.3	53.1	47.3
孟加拉国	Bangladesh	26.2	16.1	24.0	29.2	49.8	54.8
文　莱	Brunei Darussalam	1.4	9.5	78.8	159.0	19.9	-68.5
柬埔寨	Cambodia	9.7	-3.3	57.0	17.2	33.2	86.0
印　度	India	-0.1	-8.7	42.7	33.4	57.3	75.3
印度尼西亚	Indonesia	6.6	-14.3	57.2	72.7	36.3	41.6
伊　朗	Iran	3.8	18.4	76.1	82.0	20.1	-0.4
以色列	Israel	1.2	3.5	29.5	12.4	69.3	84.1
日　本	Japan	4.5		28.7		66.9	
哈萨克斯坦	Kazakhstan	-3.1	-16.8	56.2	-63.1	46.9	179.9
马来西亚	Malaysia	7.6	2.8	60.0	41.1	32.4	56.1
蒙　古	Mongolia		-22.6		35.9		86.7
巴基斯坦	Pakistan	39.5	-132.7	6.2	160.2	54.3	72.4
菲律宾	Philippines	11.9	0.2	47.4	41.8	40.7	58.0
斯里兰卡	Sri Lanka	3.0	5.9	35.0	64.4	62.1	29.6
越　南	Viet Nam	17.4	13.5	50.6	53.0	32.0	33.5
埃　及	Egypt	-61.4	14.6	-304.0	7.6	465.4	77.8
尼日利亚	Nigeria	11.4	-28.4	63.3	67.6	25.3	60.8
南　非	South Africa	2.8	-5.8	31.4	52.9	65.8	52.9
加拿大	Canada	0.8	-2.2	34.9	33.7	64.3	68.5
墨西哥	Mexico	0.6	0.2	33.0	36.7	66.4	63.1
美　国	United States	3.7		26.7		69.6	
阿根廷	Argentina	24.5	7.0	104.8	26.6	-29.3	66.4
巴　西	Brazil	3.2	-3.0	32.0	21.9	64.8	81.1
委内瑞拉	Venezuela	9.6		50.2		40.2	
捷　克	Czech Rep.	2.1	-2.7	36.5	60.5	61.3	42.3
法　国	France	-0.5	0.0	30.5	27.2	69.9	72.8
德　国	Germany	-1.1	-0.2	40.9	45.7	60.2	54.6
意大利	Italy	-0.3	1.5	20.5	27.8	79.8	70.7
荷　兰	Netherlands	0.5	-0.2	19.5	13.4	80.0	86.8
波　兰	Poland	-0.1	-11.2	-8.1	65.4	108.2	45.8
俄罗斯	Russia	7.4	-0.3	46.3	43.2	46.3	57.1
西班牙	Spain	4.7	-1.1	29.8	21.4	65.5	79.8
土耳其	Turkey	10.4	37.7	27.3	25.2	62.3	37.1
乌克兰	Ukraine	16.6	39.5	58.7	22.7	24.7	37.8
英　国	United Kingdom	1.6	0.6	12.3	22.6	86.1	76.7
新西兰	New Zealand	6.9		8.5		84.5	

附录2-9 资本形成总额、消费支出及净出口对国内生产总值增长的贡献率

Share of the Contributions of Gross Capital Formation,Final Consumption Expenditure and External Balance on Goods and Services to the Increase of GDP

资料来源：世界银行数据库。
Source: World Bank Database.
单位：%　　(%)

国家或地区	Country or Area	资本形成总额 Gross Capital Formation		消费支出 Final Consumption Expenditure		净出口 External Balance on Goods and Services	
		2000	2020	2000	2020	2000	2020
中　　国	China	21.1		76.5		2.4	
中国香港	Hong Kong SAR, China		6.1		98.6		-4.7
孟加拉国	Bangladesh		19.2		106.1		-25.3
文　　莱	Brunei Darussalam		-519.8		-179.3		799.1
柬 埔 寨	Cambodia		17.4		51.4		31.2
印度尼西亚	Indonesia		92.8		52.6		-45.4
以 色 列	Israel	5.3	-12.1	59.4	233.2	35.3	-121.1
日　　本	Japan	34.9	25.3	60.7	56.3	4.4	18.4
韩　　国	Korea, Rep.		-16.7		164.3		-47.6
马来西亚	Malaysia		47.1		36.6		16.3
菲 律 宾	Philippines		95.2		46.4		-41.5
斯里兰卡	Sri Lanka		89.4		51.9		-41.3
越　　南	Viet Nam		36.7		19.1		44.1
尼日利亚	Nigeria		64.7		-268.8		304.2
南　　非	South Africa		65.1		62.3		-27.4
加 拿 大	Canada	32.0	45.9	53.6	66.6	14.4	-12.5
墨 西 哥	Mexico		46.7		88.1		-34.8
美　　国	United States	31.6	25.3	86.9	67.0	-18.5	7.7
阿 根 廷	Argentina		16.3		86.1		-2.5
巴　　西	Brazil		3.9		122.0		-25.8
捷　　克	Czech Rep.	77.3	49.0	18.6	42.7	4.1	8.4
法　　国	France	47.1	27.6	59.0	57.5	-6.1	15.0
德　　国	Germany	28.1	29.9	44.3	51.8	27.6	18.3
意 大 利	Italy	31.3	23.4	60.8	68.6	7.9	8.0
荷　　兰	Netherlands	7.9	32.1	62.9	69.8	29.2	-1.9
波　　兰	Poland		94.6		31.0		-25.6
西 班 牙	Spain	31.9	21.7	67.0	57.6	1.1	20.7
乌 克 兰	Ukraine		180.0		-10.3		-69.7
英　　国	United Kingdom	9.0	21.6	88.2	86.2	2.8	-7.9
新 西 兰	New Zealand	-13.4	-1640.1	47.1	1989.4	66.3	-249.3

附录 2-10 年中人口

Mid-year Population

资料来源：世界银行WDI数据库。
Source: World Bank WDI Database.

国家或地区	Country or Area	年中人口（万人） Mid-year Population (10 000 persons)				增长率(%) Growth Rate(%)
		2000	2005	2010	2020	2020
世　界	**World**	**611433.3**	**651174.8**	**692187.7**	**775284.1**	**1.0**
高收入国家	**High Income**	**107482.0**	**111142.3**	**115419.5**	**121493.0**	**0.3**
中等收入国家	**Middle Income**	**462823.2**	**492719.7**	**522545.9**	**584432.5**	**1.0**
中低收入国家	**Low and Middle Income**	**501532.0**	**537389.3**	**573924.3**	**650947.4**	**1.2**
低收入国家	**Low Income**	**38708.8**	**44669.5**	**51378.3**	**66514.9**	**2.7**
中　国	China	126264.5	130372.0	133770.5	140211.2	0.3
中国香港	Hong Kong SAR, China	666.5	681.3	702.4	748.2	-0.3
中国澳门	Macao SAR, China	42.8	48.3	53.8	64.9	1.4
阿富汗	Afghanistan	2078.0	2565.4	2918.6	3892.8	2.3
阿尔巴尼亚	Albania	308.9	301.1	291.3	283.8	-0.6
阿尔及利亚	Algeria	3104.2	3315.0	3597.7	4385.1	1.8
美属萨摩亚	American Samoa	5.8	6.0	5.6	5.5	-0.2
安道尔	Andorra	6.5	7.9	8.4	7.7	0.2
安哥拉	Angola	1639.5	1943.4	2335.6	3286.6	3.2
安提瓜和巴布达	Antigua and Barbuda	7.6	8.1	8.8	9.8	0.8
阿根廷	Argentina	3687.1	3889.3	4078.8	4537.7	1.0
亚美尼亚	Armenia	307.0	298.1	287.7	296.3	0.2
阿鲁巴岛	Aruba	9.1	10.0	10.2	10.7	0.4
澳大利亚	Australia	1915.3	2039.5	2203.2	2568.7	1.3
奥地利	Austria	801.2	822.8	836.3	891.7	0.4
阿塞拜疆	Azerbaijan	804.9	839.2	905.4	1011.0	0.9
巴　林	Bahrain	66.5	88.9	124.1	170.2	3.6
孟加拉国	Bangladesh	12765.8	13903.6	14757.5	16468.9	1.0
巴巴多斯	Barbados	27.2	27.6	28.2	28.7	0.1
白俄罗斯	Belarus	998.0	966.4	949.1	939.9	-0.2
比利时	Belgium	1025.1	1047.9	1089.6	1155.6	0.6
伯利兹	Belize	24.7	28.4	32.2	39.8	1.8
贝　宁	Benin	686.6	798.2	919.9	1212.3	2.7
百慕大	Bermuda	6.2	6.4	6.5	6.4	0.0
不　丹	Bhutan	59.1	64.9	68.6	77.2	1.1
玻利维亚	Bolivia	841.8	923.2	1004.9	1167.3	1.4
波　黑	Bosnia and Herzegovinian	375.1	376.5	370.5	328.1	-0.6
博茨瓦纳	Botswana	164.3	179.9	198.7	235.2	2.1
巴　西	Brazil	17479.0	18612.7	19571.4	21255.9	0.7
文　莱	Brunei Darussalam	33.3	36.5	38.9	43.7	1.0
保加利亚	Bulgaria	817.0	765.9	739.6	692.7	-0.7
布基纳法索	Burkina Faso	1160.8	1342.2	1560.5	2090.3	2.8
布隆迪	Burundi	637.9	736.5	867.6	1189.1	3.1
柬埔寨	Cambodia	1215.5	1327.3	1431.2	1671.9	1.4
喀麦隆	Cameroon	1551.4	1773.3	2034.1	2654.6	2.6
加拿大	Canada	3068.6	3224.4	3400.5	3800.5	1.1
佛得角	Cape Verde	42.8	46.3	49.3	55.6	1.1
开曼群岛	Cayman Islands	4.2	4.9	5.7	6.6	1.2
中　非	Central African Rep.	364.0	403.8	438.7	483.0	1.8
乍　得	Chad	835.6	1009.7	1195.2	1642.6	3.0
海峡群岛	Channel Islands	14.8	15.2	16.0	17.4	0.9
智　利	Chile	1534.2	1618.3	1706.3	1911.6	0.9
哥伦比亚	Colombia	3963.0	4264.8	4522.3	5088.3	1.1
科摩罗	Comoros	54.2	61.2	69.0	87.0	2.2
刚果(金)	Congo, Dem. Rep.	4710.6	5478.6	6456.4	8956.1	3.1
刚果(布)	Congo, Rep.	312.7	362.3	427.4	551.8	2.5
哥斯达黎加	Costa Rica	396.2	428.6	457.7	509.4	0.9
科特迪瓦	Cote D'Ivoire	1645.5	1835.5	2053.3	2637.8	2.5
克罗地亚	Croatia	446.8	431.0	429.5	404.7	-0.4

附录 2-10 续表 1 continued

国家或地区	Country or Area	年中人口（万人）Mid-year Population (10 000 persons)				增长率(%) Growth Rate(%)
		2000	2005	2010	2020	2020
古　巴	Cuba	1112.6	1126.2	1122.6	1132.7	-0.1
塞浦路斯	Cyprus	94.3	102.8	111.3	120.7	0.7
捷　克	Czech Rep.	1025.5	1021.1	1047.4	1069.9	0.3
丹　麦	Denmark	534.0	541.9	554.8	583.1	0.3
吉布提	Djibouti	71.8	78.3	84.0	98.8	1.5
多米尼克	Dominica	7.0	7.1	7.1	7.2	0.3
多米尼加	Dominican Rep.	847.1	909.7	969.5	1084.8	1.0
厄瓜多尔	Ecuador	1268.1	1382.6	1501.1	1764.3	1.5
埃　及	Egypt	6883.2	7552.4	8276.1	10233.4	1.9
萨尔瓦多	El Salvador	588.8	605.2	618.4	648.6	0.5
赤道几内亚	Equatorial Guinea	60.6	75.0	94.4	140.3	3.4
厄立特里亚	Eritrea	229.2	282.7	317.0		
爱沙尼亚	Estonia	139.7	135.5	133.1	133.1	0.3
埃塞俄比亚	Ethiopia	6622.5	7634.6	8764.0	11496.4	2.5
法罗群岛	Faeroe Islands	4.7	4.8	4.8	4.9	0.4
斐　济	Fiji	81.1	82.2	86.0	89.6	0.7
芬　兰	Finland	517.6	524.6	536.3	553.1	0.2
法　国	France	6091.3	6317.9	6502.8	6739.2	0.2
法属波立尼西亚	French Polynesia	24.1	25.9	26.6	28.1	0.6
加　蓬	Gabon	122.8	139.1	162.4	222.6	2.4
冈比亚	Gambia	131.8	154.4	179.3	241.7	2.9
格鲁吉亚	Georgia	407.7	390.2	378.7	371.4	-0.2
德　国	Germany	8221.2	8246.9	8177.7	8324.1	0.2
加　纳	Ghana	1927.9	2181.5	2478.0	3107.3	2.1
直布罗陀	Gibraltar	3.1	3.3	3.4	3.4	0.0
希　腊	Greece	1080.6	1098.7	1112.1	1071.6	-0.1
格陵兰	Greenland	5.6	5.7	5.7	5.6	0.3
格林纳达	Grenada	10.3	10.5	10.6	11.3	0.5
关　岛	Guam	15.5	15.8	15.9	16.9	0.9
危地马拉	Guatemala	1159.0	1294.8	1426.0	1685.8	1.5
几内亚	Guinea	824.1	911.0	1019.2	1313.3	2.8
几内亚比绍	Guinea-Bissau	120.1	134.5	152.3	196.8	2.4
圭亚那	Guyana	74.7	74.6	74.9	78.7	0.5
海　地	Haiti	846.4	919.5	994.9	1140.3	1.2
洪都拉斯	Honduras	657.5	745.9	831.7	990.5	1.6
匈牙利	Hungary	1021.1	1008.7	1000.0	975.0	-0.2
冰　岛	Iceland	28.1	29.7	31.8	36.6	1.6
印　度	India	105657.6	114761.0	123428.1	138000.4	1.0
印度尼西亚	Indonesia	21151.4	22628.9	24183.4	27352.4	1.1
伊　朗	Iran	6562.3	6976.2	7376.3	8399.3	1.3
伊拉克	Iraq	2349.8	2692.2	2974.2	4022.3	2.3
爱尔兰	Ireland	380.5	416.0	456.0	499.5	1.2
马恩岛	Isle of Man	7.7	8.0	8.5	8.5	0.5
以色列	Israel	628.9	693.0	762.4	921.7	1.8
意大利	Italy	5694.2	5796.9	5927.7	5955.4	-0.3
牙买加	Jamaica	265.5	274.0	281.0	296.1	0.4
日　本	Japan	12684.3	12777.3	12807.0	12583.6	-0.3
约　旦	Jordan	512.2	576.6	726.2	1020.3	1.0
哈萨克斯坦	Kazakhstan	1488.4	1514.7	1632.2	1875.4	1.3
肯尼亚	Kenya	3196.5	3662.5	4203.1	5377.1	2.3
基里巴斯	Kiribati	8.4	9.2	10.3	11.9	1.6
朝　鲜	Korea, Dem.	2292.9	2390.4	2454.9	2577.9	0.4
韩　国	Korea, Rep.	4700.8	4818.5	4955.4	5178.1	0.1
科威特	Kuwait	204.5	227.0	299.2	427.1	1.5
吉尔吉斯斯坦	Kyrgyzstan	489.8	516.3	544.8	659.2	2.1

附录2-10 续表 2 continued

国家或地区	Country or Area	年中人口（万人） Mid-year Population (10 000 persons)				增长率(%) Growth Rate(%)
		2000	2005	2010	2020	2020
老 挝	Lao PDR	532.4	575.2	624.9	727.6	1.5
拉脱维亚	Latvia	236.8	223.9	209.8	190.2	-0.6
黎 巴 嫩	Lebanon	384.3	469.9	495.3	682.5	-0.4
莱 索 托	Lesotho	203.3	199.6	199.6	214.2	0.8
利比里亚	Liberia	284.8	321.8	389.1	505.8	2.4
利 比 亚	Libya	535.8	579.9	619.8	687.1	1.4
列支敦士登	Liechtenstein	3.3	3.5	3.6	3.8	0.3
立 陶 宛	Lithuania	350.0	332.3	309.7	279.5	0.0
卢 森 堡	Luxemburg	43.6	46.5	50.7	63.2	2.0
马达加斯加	Madagascar	1576.7	1833.7	2115.2	2769.1	2.6
马 拉 维	Malawi	1114.9	1262.6	1454.0	1913.0	2.7
马来西亚	Malaysia	2319.4	2569.1	2820.8	3236.6	1.3
马尔代夫	Maldives	27.9	32.0	36.6	54.1	1.8
马 里	Mali	1094.6	1277.6	1504.9	2025.1	3.0
马 耳 他	Malta	39.0	40.4	41.5	52.5	4.1
马绍尔群岛	Marshall Islands	5.1	5.5	5.6	5.9	0.7
毛里塔尼亚	Mauritania	263.0	302.4	349.4	465.0	2.7
毛里求斯	Mauritius	118.7	122.8	125.0	126.6	0.0
墨 西 哥	Mexico	9890.0	10600.5	11409.3	12893.3	1.1
密克罗尼西亚	Micronesia, Fed.	10.7	10.6	10.3	11.5	1.1
摩尔多瓦	Moldova	292.4	288.8	286.1	261.8	-1.7
摩 纳 哥	Monaco	3.2	3.4	3.6	3.9	0.7
蒙 古	Mongolia	239.7	252.6	272.0	327.8	1.6
黑 山	Montenegro	60.5	61.4	61.9	62.2	0.0
摩 洛 哥	Morocco	2879.4	3045.6	3234.3	3691.1	1.2
莫桑比克	Mozambique	1771.2	2049.4	2353.2	3125.5	2.9
缅 甸	Myanmar	4672.0	4895.0	5060.1	5441.0	0.7
纳米比亚	Namibia	179.5	193.8	211.9	254.1	1.8
尼 泊 尔	Nepal	2394.1	2574.5	2701.3	2913.7	1.8
荷 兰	Netherlands	1592.6	1632.0	1661.5	1744.1	0.6
新喀里多尼亚	New Caledonia	21.3	23.2	25.0	27.2	0.2
新 西 兰	New Zealand	385.8	413.4	435.1	508.4	2.1
尼加拉瓜	Nicaragua	506.9	543.9	582.4	662.5	1.2
尼 日 尔	Niger	1133.2	1362.4	1646.4	2420.7	3.8
尼日利亚	Nigeria	12228.4	13886.5	15850.3	20614.0	2.5
北马其顿	North Macedonia	203.5	206.0	207.1	208.3	
北马里亚纳群岛	Northern Mariana Islands	5.7	5.7	5.4	5.8	0.6
挪 威	Norway	449.1	462.3	488.9	537.9	0.6
阿 曼	Oman	226.8	251.1	304.1	510.7	2.6
巴基斯坦	Pakistan	14234.4	16030.4	17942.5	22089.2	2.0
帕 劳	Palau	1.9	2.0	1.8	1.8	0.5
巴 拿 马	Panama	303.0	333.0	364.3	431.5	1.6
巴布亚新几内亚	Papua New Guinea	584.8	649.5	731.1	894.7	1.9
巴 拉 圭	Paraguay	532.3	582.4	624.8	713.3	1.2
秘 鲁	Peru	2646.0	2786.6	2902.8	3297.2	1.4
菲 律 宾	Philippines	7799.2	8632.6	9396.7	10958.1	1.3
波 兰	Poland	3825.9	3816.5	3804.3	3795.1	0.0
葡 萄 牙	Portugal	1029.0	1050.3	1057.3	1030.6	0.2
波多黎各	Puerto Rico	381.1	382.1	372.2	319.4	0.0
卡 塔 尔	Qatar	59.2	86.5	185.6	288.1	1.7
罗马尼亚	Romania	2244.3	2132.0	2024.7	1928.6	-0.4
俄 罗 斯	Russia	14659.7	14351.9	14284.9	14410.4	-0.2
卢 旺 达	Rwanda	793.4	884.0	1003.9	1295.2	2.5

附录2-10 续表 3 continued

国家或地区	Country or Area	年中人口（万人） Mid-year Population (10 000 persons)				增长率(%) Growth Rate(%)
		2000	2005	2010	2020	2020
萨摩亚	Samoa	17.4	18.0	18.6	19.8	0.7
圣马力诺	San Marino	2.7	2.9	3.1	3.4	0.2
圣多美和普林西比	Sao Tome and Principe	14.2	15.7	18.0	21.9	1.9
沙特阿拉伯	Saudi Arabia	2066.4	2381.6	2742.1	3481.4	1.6
塞内加尔	Senegal	979.8	1109.0	1267.8	1674.4	2.7
塞尔维亚	Serbia	751.6	744.1	729.1	690.8	-0.5
塞舌尔	Seychelles	8.1	8.3	9.0	9.8	0.9
塞拉利昂	Sierra Leone	458.5	564.6	641.6	797.7	2.1
新加坡	Singapore	402.8	426.6	507.7	568.6	-0.3
斯洛伐克	Slovakia	538.9	537.3	539.1	545.9	0.1
斯洛文尼亚	Slovenia	198.9	200.0	204.9	210.0	0.6
所罗门群岛	Solomon Islands	41.3	47.0	52.8	68.7	2.5
索马里	Somalia	887.2	1044.7	1204.4	1589.3	2.9
南非	South Africa	4496.8	4788.1	5121.7	5930.9	1.3
西班牙	Spain	4056.8	4365.3	4657.7	4735.2	0.5
斯里兰卡	Sri Lanka	1877.8	1954.5	2026.2	2191.9	0.5
苏丹	Sudan	2727.5	3095.0	3454.5	4384.9	2.4
苏里南	Suriname	47.1	49.9	52.9	58.7	0.9
瑞典	Sweden	887.2	903.0	937.8	1035.3	0.7
瑞士	Switzerland	718.4	743.7	782.5	863.7	0.7
叙利亚	Syrian Arab Republic	1641.1	1836.1	2136.3	1750.1	2.5
塔吉克斯坦	Tajikistan	621.6	678.9	752.7	953.8	2.3
坦桑尼亚	Tanzania	3349.9	3845.0	4434.7	5973.4	2.9
泰国	Thailand	6295.3	6541.6	6719.5	6980.0	0.3
巴哈马	The Bahamas	29.8	32.5	35.5	39.3	1.0
东帝汶	Timor-Leste	88.4	99.5	109.4	131.8	1.9
多哥	Togo	492.4	561.2	642.2	827.9	2.4
汤加	Tonga	9.8	10.1	10.4	10.6	1.1
特立尼达和多巴哥	Trinidad And Tobago	126.7	129.6	132.8	139.9	0.3
突尼斯	Tunisia	970.8	1010.7	1063.5	1181.9	1.1
土耳其	Turkey	6324.0	6790.3	7232.7	8433.9	1.1
土库曼斯坦	Turkmenistan	451.6	475.5	508.7	603.1	1.5
特克斯和凯科斯群岛	Turks and Caicos Islands	2.0	2.8	3.3	3.9	1.4
图瓦卢	Tuvalu	0.9	1.0	1.1	1.2	1.2
乌干达	Uganda	2365.0	2768.5	3242.8	4574.1	3.3
乌克兰	Ukraine	4917.7	4710.5	4587.1	4413.5	-0.6
阿联酋	United Arab Emirates	313.4	458.8	855.0	989.0	1.2
英国	United Kingdom	5889.3	6040.1	6276.6	6721.5	0.6
美国	United States	28216.2	29551.7	30932.7	32948.4	0.4
美属维尔京群岛	Virgin Islands(US)	10.9	10.8	10.8	10.6	-0.4
乌拉圭	Uruguay	332.0	332.2	335.9	347.4	0.3
乌兹别克斯坦	Uzbekistan	2465.0	2616.7	2856.2	3423.2	1.9
瓦努阿图	Vanuatu	18.5	20.9	23.6	30.7	2.4
委内瑞拉	Venezuela	2419.2	2643.2	2844.0	2843.6	-0.3
越南	Viet Nam	7991.0	8383.3	8796.8	9733.9	0.9
约旦河西岸和加沙	West Bank and Gaza	292.2	332.0	378.6	480.3	2.5
也门	Yemen	1740.9	2010.7	2315.5	2982.6	2.3
赞比亚	Zambia	1041.6	1185.6	1360.6	1838.4	2.9
津巴布韦	Zimbabwe	1188.1	1207.7	1269.8	1486.3	1.5

附录 2-11　万美元国内生产总值能耗(2017年不变价，PPP)

Energy Use per Ten Thousand USD of GDP (Constant 2017 PPP)

资料来源：世界银行WDI数据库。
Source:World Bank WDI Database.

单位：吨标准油/万美元　　(ton of oil equivalent per 10 000 USD)

国家或地区	Country or Area	2000	2005	2010	2013	2014	2015
世　界	**World**	**1.43**	**1.38**	**1.31**	**1.24**	**1.21**	
高收入国家	**High Income**	**1.28**	**1.19**	**1.12**	**1.04**	**1.02**	**0.98**
中等收入国家	**Middle Income**	**1.70**	**1.64**	**1.52**	**1.43**	**1.39**	
中　国	China	2.60	2.61	2.20	1.99	1.88	
中国香港	Hong Kong SAR, China	0.56	0.42	0.38	0.35	0.35	
孟加拉国	Bangladesh	0.74	0.72	0.72	0.66	0.65	
文　莱	Brunei Darussalam	1.04	0.87	1.23	1.13	1.35	
柬埔寨	Cambodia	1.89	1.22	1.36	1.24	1.24	
印　度	India	1.62	1.39	1.33	1.26	1.24	
印度尼西亚	Indonesia	1.29	1.19	1.06	0.91	0.90	
伊　朗	Iran	1.86	2.06	2.01	2.29	2.35	
以色列	Israel	0.97	0.89	0.90	0.79	0.74	0.74
日　本	Japan	1.12	1.06	1.02	0.90	0.87	0.85
哈萨克斯坦	Kazakhstan	2.33	2.03	2.04	2.02	1.82	
韩　国	Korea, Rep.	1.74	1.52	1.47	1.41	1.39	1.39
马来西亚	Malaysia	1.32	1.41	1.27	1.30	1.26	
蒙　古	Mongolia	2.21	2.02	1.94	1.76	1.67	
缅　甸	Myanmar	2.90	1.83	1.00	0.96	1.03	
巴基斯坦	Pakistan	1.39	1.29	1.21	1.14	1.10	
菲律宾	Philippines	1.15	0.89	0.73	0.68	0.68	
新加坡	Singapore	0.83	0.75	0.64	0.57	0.58	
斯里兰卡	Sri Lanka	0.75	0.66	0.53	0.44	0.45	
泰　国	Thailand	1.17	1.23	1.22	1.26	1.24	
越　南	Viet Nam	1.22	1.25	1.32	1.14		
埃　及	Egypt	0.76	0.97	0.85	0.82	0.80	
尼日利亚	Nigeria	2.36	1.90	1.53	1.46	1.38	
南　非	South Africa	2.20	2.14	2.03	1.85	1.92	
加拿大	Canada	2.22	2.00	1.74	1.66	1.66	1.61
墨西哥	Mexico	0.85	0.95	0.86	0.87	0.83	0.80
美　国	United States	1.61	1.44	1.32	1.23	1.22	1.16
阿根廷	Argentina	0.90	0.89	0.82	0.81	0.86	
巴　西	Brazil	0.92	0.92	0.91	0.92	0.95	
捷　克	Czech Rep.	1.60	1.45	1.27	1.19	1.14	1.07
法　国	France	1.04	1.03	0.95	0.90	0.85	0.85
德　国	Germany	0.95	0.93	0.85	0.79	0.74	0.75
意大利	Italy	0.70	0.73	0.69	0.64	0.61	0.62
荷　兰	Netherlands	1.00	1.01	0.97	0.89	0.83	0.80
波　兰	Poland	1.43	1.27	1.10	1.00	0.93	0.90
俄罗斯	Russia	2.90	2.27	2.01	1.93	1.87	
西班牙	Spain	0.86	0.86	0.73	0.71	0.69	0.69
土耳其	Turkey	0.78	0.68	0.74	0.64	0.63	0.64
乌克兰	Ukraine	3.63	2.68	2.36	1.96	1.98	
英　国	United Kingdom	0.97	0.86	0.77	0.69	0.63	0.61
澳大利亚	Australia	1.48	1.32	1.29	1.17	1.13	1.15
新西兰	New Zealand	1.35	1.10	1.12	1.10	1.13	1.08

附录 2-12 广义货币占国内生产总值比重

Broad Money (M2) as Percentage of GDP

资料来源：世界银行WDI数据库。
Source: World Bank WDI Database.
单位：% (%)

国家或地区	Country or Area	2000	2005	2010	2015	2018	2019	2020
中　国	**China**	**135.6**	**151.1**	**176.1**	**202.1**	**195.0**	**197.9**	**211.4**
中国香港	Hong Kong SAR, China	224.4	257.7	315.3	365.6	386.1	403.4	452.5
中国澳门	Macao SAR, China	156.2	139.3	107.5	131.4	145.9	154.5	356.2
孟加拉国	Bangladesh	30.6	47.4	58.7	64.5	64.3	63.7	66.7
文　莱	Brunei Darussalam	85.7	57.8	67.3	80.8	81.6	84.7	93.5
柬埔寨	Cambodia	13.0	19.3	41.6	72.4	100.7	107.7	
印　度	India	54.6	65.5	77.7	78.0	74.1	76.0	88.9
印度尼西亚	Indonesia	53.9	43.4	36.0	39.5	38.8	38.8	44.7
伊　朗	Iran	37.2	41.5	54.1	81.4			
以色列	Israel	81.1	97.5	74.5	83.8	85.2	86.8	
日　本	Japan	229.1	195.4	215.5	233.5	248.5	251.5	285.5
哈萨克斯坦	Kazakhstan	15.3	27.2	38.9	41.9	33.7	30.7	35.5
韩　国	Korea, Rep.	63.4	106.7	125.5	135.5	142.3	151.8	166.3
老　挝	Lao PDR	16.5	19.1	36.2				
马来西亚	Malaysia	122.7	125.0	129.6	132.8	125.1	123.1	137.8
蒙　古	Mongolia	21.1	37.5	48.0	43.4	60.1	55.9	65.5
缅　甸	Myanmar	31.5	21.6	23.6	45.4	52.0	55.4	68.6
巴基斯坦	Pakistan	34.8	45.5	52.5	53.3	58.0	59.0	62.1
菲律宾	Philippines	55.9	52.1	58.8	70.9	74.5	76.6	
新加坡	Singapore	103.2	103.3	123.3	122.9	118.8	123.8	152.6
斯里兰卡	Sri Lanka	38.4	41.7	32.6	52.5	61.1	63.0	
泰　国	Thailand	111.2	104.1	109.0	127.7	122.9	123.3	
越　南	Viet Nam	41.6	71.0	114.9	137.6	158.1	164.9	
埃　及	Egypt	76.7	97.1	80.7	78.0	81.8	77.2	84.5
尼日利亚	Nigeria	14.7	11.3	21.4	22.4	25.4	23.9	25.0
南　非	South Africa	52.7	67.0	75.8	73.5	72.8	74.1	82.8
加拿大	Canada	71.1	148.5					
墨西哥	Mexico	22.4	26.6	30.6	36.4	37.5	37.8	45.3
美　国	United States	68.5	72.5	85.2	88.8	89.0	92.8	111.3
阿根廷	Argentina	31.8	28.7	25.3	27.6			
巴　西	Brazil	46.5	60.1	74.2	88.1	93.7	95.8	111.5
委内瑞拉	Venezuela	19.8	23.7	32.2				
捷　克	Czech Rep.	60.6	55.2	69.1	77.7	83.1	82.5	92.3
波　兰	Poland	40.4	43.1	54.2	64.1	68.1	68.4	78.6
俄罗斯	Russia		33.4	51.4	61.8	59.1	59.1	70.4
土耳其	Turkey	33.5	38.7	52.9	52.4	53.2	58.7	67.5
乌克兰	Ukraine	18.6	44.0	55.4	50.0	35.9	36.2	44.1
英　国	United Kingdom	94.5	116.7	163.7	133.9	148.8	141.7	163.2
澳大利亚	Australia	67.7	78.5	100.7	113.2	113.5	122.6	137.1
新西兰	New Zealand	78.9	78.7	92.7	99.2	101.5	100.9	112.5

附录 2-13 生产者价格指数

Producer Price Indices

资料来源：联合国统计月报数据库。
Source: UN Monthly Bulletin of Statistics Database.

2010年=100 (2010=100)

国家或地区	Country or Area	2010	2015	2016	2017	2018	2019	2020
中国香港	**Hong Kong SAR, China**							
按供给组成分	by Components of Supply							
工业产品	Industrial Products	100.0	100.4	101.6	105.6	107.7	108.7	111.3
孟加拉国①	Bangladesh①							
按生产阶段分	by Stage of Processing							
中间产品	Intermediate Products	218.3						
按最终用途分	by End-Use							
消费品	Consumers' Goods	296.8						
投资用品	Capital Goods	280.8						
印　　度②	**India②**							
按供给组成分	by Components of Supply							
国内供应	Domestic Supply	100.0	110.8	108.0	114.1	119.0	121.2	121.7
农业产品	Agricultural Products	100.0	130.1	136.1	142.7	142.3	152.9	160.3
工业产品	Industrial Products	100.0	110.6	108.0	112.9	117.2	118.1	119.6
按生产阶段分	by Stage of Processing							
原材料	Raw Materials	100.0	120.8	124.3	130.2	133.0	141.2	144.5
印度尼西亚	**Indonesia**							
按供给组成分	by Components of Supply							
农业产品	Agricultural Products	100.0	129.8	133.0	136.4	140.7	143.2	146.6
工业产品	Industrial Products	100.0	134.6	137.7	141.1	144.8	147.5	149.6
伊　　朗	**Iran**							
按供给组成分	by Components of Supply							
国内生产	Domestic Production	63.9③	90.8⑧	95.3⑧	100.0⑧	110.0⑧		
农业产品	Agricultural Products	75.9③	92.4⑧	97.6⑧	100.0⑧	111.0⑧		
工业产品	Industrial Products	53.1③	96.9⑧	96.5⑧	100.0⑧	110.7⑧		
以 色 列	**Israel**							
按供给组成分	by Components of Supply							
工业产品	Industrial Products	100.0	104.8	101.0	102.5	105.9	104.7	99.5
日　　本④	**Japan④**							
按供给组成分	by Components of Supply							
国内供应	Domestic Supply	97.4	100.0	93.2	97.2	100.9	99.4	95.2
国内生产	Domestic Production	100.2	100.0	96.5	98.7	101.3	101.5	100.3
农业产品	Agricultural Products	93.4	100.0	102.5	107.6	109.8	108.9	107.9
工业产品	Industrial Products	99.1	100.0	97.0	98.9	101.1	101.3	100.4
进口产品	Import Products	88.1	100.0	83.6	92.7	99.7	94.4	84.7
按生产阶段分	by Stage of Processing							
原材料	Raw Materials	97.2	100.0	78.6	95.9	109.5	103.8	86.5
中间产品	Intermediate Products	96.3	100.0	93.4	97.4	101.6	100.6	97.2
按最终用途分	by End-Use							
消费品	Consumers' Goods	98.7	100.0	96.4	97.0	97.3	95.8	93.7
投资用品	Capital Goods	99.5	100.0	97.9	98.0	97.9	97.5	96.8
韩　　国④	**Korea, Rep.④**							
按供给组成分	by Components of Supply							
国内供应	Domestic Supply		100.0	97.3	101.4	104.5	104.7	102.3
国内生产	Domestic Production	101.8	100.0	96.8	101.1	103.3	102.5	100.8
农业产品	Agricultural Products	95.3	100.0	105.8	112.6	116.7	114.0	124.9
工业产品	Industrial Products	104.0	100.0	96.5	101.1	103.3	102.3	99.6
按生产阶段分	by Stage of Processing							
原材料	Raw Materials	126.4	100.0	84.7	104.0	119.4	118.8	99.3
中间产品	Intermediate Products	105.9	100.0	96.8	100.9	103.6	103.5	101.5
按最终用途分	by End-Use							
消费品	Consumers' Goods	98.0	100.0	99.2	100.1	100.3	100.5	99.7
投资用品	Capital Goods	100.2	100.0	101.5	100.4	100.2	102.6	103.8

附录 2-13 续表 1 continued

2010年=100 (2010=100)

国家或地区	Country or Area	2010	2015	2016	2017	2018	2019	2020
马来西亚	**Malaysia**							
按供给组成分	by Components of Supply							
国内供应	Domestic Supply	100.0	104.0					
国内生产	Domestic Production	100.0	102.2	101.1	108.0	106.7	105.2	102.4
进口产品	Import Products	100.0	107.7					
巴基斯坦	**Pakistan**							
按供给组成分	by Components of Supply							
国内供应	Domestic Supply	100.0	140.1	142.5	147.4	159.6		
农业产品	Agricultural Products	100.0	138.6	148.3	156.6	165.8		
菲 律 宾	**Philippines**							
按供给组成分	by Components of Supply							
国内供应	Domestic Supply	100.0	107.0	108.0	110.1	112.2	114.0	116.8
工业产品	Industrial Products	100.0	85.8					
新 加 坡	**Singapore**							
按供给组成分	by Components of Supply							
国内供应	Domestic Supply	100.0	86.8	80.7	86.4	92.0	89.0	81.3
国内生产	Domestic Production	100.0	89.9	85.0	88.2	92.1	89.0	82.9
进口产品	Import Products	100.0	86.2	81.7	86.4	90.7	89.7	83.4
泰 国	**Thailand**							
按供给组成分	by Components of Supply							
国内供应	Domestic Supply		100.0④	98.8④	99.5④	100.0④	99.3④	97.7④
按生产阶段分	by Stage of Processing							
原材料	Raw Materials	100.0	97.5	94.4	95.9	97.9	98.4	96.6
按最终用途分	by End-Use							
消费品	Consumers' Goods	100.0	109.5	109.7	106.2	105.1	109.3	110.7
投资用品	Capital Goods	100.0	101.1	100.5	99.6	97.8	95.6	93.6
埃 及⑤	**Egypt⑤**							
按供给组成分	by Components of Supply							
国内生产	Domestic Production	156.1	207.6	220.5			203.8	
农业产品	Agricultural Products	202.1	299.5	339.8			171.7	
按生产阶段分	by Stage of Processing							
原材料	Raw Materials	152.4	180.4	140.6			158.3	
中间产品	Intermediate Products	129.7	161.5	178.4			250.9	
按最终用途分	by End-Use							
消费品	Consumers' Goods	110.2	124.7	142.8			183.0	
投资用品	Capital Goods	140.6	171.9	178.5			231.5	
南 非⑥	**South Africa⑥**							
按供给组成分	by Components of Supply							
农业产品②	Agricultural Products②		113.1	131.6	132.2	134.0	131.6	137.8
工业产品	Industrial Products		118.0	126.3	132.5	139.7	146.2	149.9
按生产阶段分	by Stage of Processing							
中间产品	Intermediate Products		117.6	125.6	130.6	135.2	138.7	142.1
加 拿 大	**Canada**							
按供给组成分	by Components of Supply							
农业产品	Agricultural Products	100.0	130.2	124.8	125.9	124.3	125.1	128.0
工业产品	Industrial Products	100.0	110.3	93.5	96.4	100.2	100.0	99.6
按生产阶段分	by Stage of Processing							
原材料	Raw Materials	100.0	94.2	85.5	94.9	103.6	101.0	92.8

附录 2-13 续表 2 continued

2010年=100 (2010=100)

国家或地区	Country or Area	2010	2015	2016	2017	2018	2019	2020
墨西哥	**Mexico**							
按供给组成分	by Components of Supply							
国内供应	Domestic Supply	100.0	119.2	125.9	136.2	144.6	149.8	155.2
国内生产	Domestic Production	100.0	117.9	124.6	133.2	140.5	144.8	150.6
农业产品	Agricultural Products	100.0	119.6	130.6	140.3	144.7	147.4	154.3
工业产品	Industrial Products	100.0	118.6	128.1	136.6	143.3	148.1	157.1
进口产品	Import Products	100.0	105.3	104.2	106.8	110.6	110.8	109.9
按生产阶段分	by Stage of Processing							
中间产品	Intermediate Products	100.0	118.1	123.9	135.1	144.1	147.2	150.7
按最终用途分	by End-Use							
消费品	Consumers' Goods	100.0	120.2	126.4	135.4	142.2		
投资用品	Capital Goods	100.0	118.0	125.4	137.4	148.0	152.7	157.7
美国	**United States**							
按供给组成分	by Components of Supply							
国内生产	Domestic Production	100.0	103.1	100.4	104.8	109.4	108.2	105.3
农业产品	Agricultural Products	100.0	114.8	104.0	107.0	106.6	107.0	104.6
工业产品	Industrial Products	100.0	101.0	98.7	103.5	108.9	107.3	103.7
按生产阶段分	by Stage of Processing							
原材料	Raw Materials	100.0	89.1	81.7	89.8	94.3	87.6	79.0
中间产品	Intermediate Products	100.0	102.6	99.4	104.0	109.5	108.0	105.0
按最终用途分	by End-Use							
消费品	Consumers' Goods	100.0	108.1	106.5	110.6	114.7	115.0	112.4
投资用品	Capital Goods	100.0	107.1	107.6	108.6	110.4	112.8	114.0
阿根廷	**Argentina**							
按供给组成分	by Components of Supply							
国内供应	Domestic Supply	100.0						
国内生产	Domestic Production	100.0						
农业产品	Agricultural Products	100.0						
工业产品	Industrial Products	100.0						
进口产品	Import Products	100.0						
白俄罗斯	**Belarus**							
按供给组成分	by Components of Supply							
工业产品	Industrial Products	100.0	444.4	498.0	546.7	584.2	626.8	655.7
按生产阶段分	by Stage of Processing							
中间产品	Intermediate Products	100.0	478.1	533.8	593.2	639.1	689.3	732.4
按最终用途分	by End-Use							
消费品	Consumers' Goods	100.0	399.5	445.3	474.2	498.9	515.8	532.8
投资用品	Capital Goods	100.0	420.6	487.0	532.5	565.6	583.6	614.3
捷克	**Czech Rep.**							
按供给组成分	by Components of Supply							
农业产品	Agricultural Products	100.0	118.9	113.1	122.0	100.8	106.5	103.0
工业产品	Industrial Products	100.0	104.4	101.0	102.8	104.9	107.7	107.8
进口产品	Import Products	100.0	108.3	103.9	105.0	104.2	104.5	103.4
按生产阶段分	by Stage of Processing							
中间产品	Intermediate Products	100.0	106.8	103.9	106.3	108.7	109.6	107.9
按最终用途分	by End-Use							
消费品	Consumers' Goods	100.0	108.3	106.6	109.2	109.1	112.7	115.2
投资用品	Capital Goods	100.0	103.7	102.8	102.5	102.4	104.1	106.8
法国	**France**							
按供给组成分	by Components of Supply							
国内供应	Domestic Supply	100.0	102.1	99.2	101.8	104.6	104.8	101.6
农业产品	Agricultural Products	100.0	113.3	113.5	117.7	120.2	122.4	123.1
工业产品	Industrial Products	100.0	104.8	102.4	104.8	107.6	108.1	105.7
进口产品	Import Products	100.0	98.4	94.7	97.6	100.3	100.1	96.1
按生产阶段分	by Stage of Processing							
原材料	Raw Materials	100.0	98.6	88.2	96.6	108.8	107.7	91.0
中间产品	Intermediate Products	100.0	101.1	98.3	101.5	103.8	103.9	101.1
按最终用途分	by End-Use							
消费品	Consumers' Goods	100.0	105.5	104.9	105.5	105.1	105.5	106.1
投资用品	Capital Goods	100.0	101.4	100.8	101.2	101.7	102.7	103.7

附录 2-13 续表 3 continued

2010年=100 (2010=100)

国家或地区	Country or Area	2010	2015	2016	2017	2018	2019	2020
德　国	**Germany**							
按供给组成分	by Components of Supply							
农业产品	Agricultural Products	100.0	105.3	103.9	114.3	114.6	117.5	114.1
工业产品	Industrial Products	100.0	103.9	102.2	105.0	107.8	108.9	107.9
进口产品	Import Products	100.0	100.7	97.5	101.2		101.8	
按生产阶段分	by Stage of Processing							
中间产品	Intermediate Products	100.0	102.1	100.6	104.6	107.4	107.1	105.5
按最终用途分	by End-Use							
消费品	Consumers' Goods	100.0	108.1	108.8	112.1	112.8	114.7	116.1
投资用品	Capital Goods	100.0	104.1	104.7	105.9	107.3	108.9	110.0
意 大 利	**Italy**							
按供给组成分	by Components of Supply							
工业产品	Industrial Products	100.0	102.6	100.3	102.9	107.0	107.0	102.4
按生产阶段分	by Stage of Processing							
中间产品	Intermediate Products	100.0	103.8	102.6	105.5	107.6	107.5	106.8
按最终用途分	by End-Use							
消费品	Consumers' Goods	100.0	107.1	106.9	108.2	108.9	109.6	110.2
投资用品	Capital Goods	100.0	104.0	104.4	105.3	105.9	107.3	107.7
荷　兰	**Netherlands**							
按供给组成分	by Components of Supply							
工业产品	Industrial Products	100.0	100.9	98.4	102.7	105.9	107.7	104.8
按生产阶段分	by Stage of Processing							
中间产品	Intermediate Products	100.0	103.5	100.8	106.4	110.0	110.0	105.8
按最终用途分	by End-Use							
消费品	Consumers' Goods	100.0	109.1	110.1	113.6	113.7	116.9	120.2
投资用品	Capital Goods	100.0	105.2	106.2	108.0	109.3	116.5	118.6
波　兰	**Poland**							
按供给组成分	by Components of Supply							
工业产品	Industrial Products	100.0	106.1	106.0	111.1	114.2	115.5	114.9
按生产阶段分	by Stage of Processing							
原材料	Raw Materials	100.0	106.4	103.4	111.6	112.1①	116.7①	111.6
中间产品	Intermediate Products	100.0	108.6	108.9	113.3	117.5	118.6	117.2
按最终用途分	by End-Use							
消费品	Consumers' Goods	100.0	106.5	107.7	111.8	112.5	114.4	116.8
投资用品	Capital Goods	100.0	101.0	104.3	105.9	105.0	104.3	104.9
俄 罗 斯	**Russia**							
按供给组成分	by Components of Supply							
农业产品	Agricultural Products	100.0	148.5	142.3	150.3	148.2	160.2	161.3
工业产品	Industrial Products	100.0	153.8	160.5	172.7	193.7	197.6	190.2

附录 2-13 续表 4 continued

2010年=100 (2010=100)

国家或地区	Country or Area	2010	2015	2016	2017	2018	2019	2020
西 班 牙	**Spain**							
按供给组成分	by Components of Supply							
工业产品	Industrial Products	100.0	107.9	104.5	109.1	112.3	111.8	107.0
按生产阶段分	by Stage of Processing							
中间产品	Intermediate Products	100.0	105.8	104.3	107.8	110.6	110.3	108.3
按最终用途分	by End-Use							
消费品	Consumers' Goods	100.0	108.2	108.5	110.5	110.3	110.5	111.7
投资用品	Capital Goods	100.0	102.5	103.1	104.0	104.8	105.9	106.9
土 耳 其	**Turkey**							
按供给组成分	by Components of Supply							
农业产品	Agricultural Products	100.0	100.0④	103.0④	115.5④	128.9④	158.2④	181.66④
工业产品	Industrial Products	100.0	142.9	149.1	172.7	219.3	257.8	289.2
乌 克 兰⑦	**Ukraine⑦**							
按供给组成分	by Components of Supply							
农业产品	Agricultural Products		234.6	264.2		327.2	310.6	343.4
工业产品	Industrial Products		196.4	237.0	299.7	352.4	367.0	360.1
英 国	**United Kingdom**							
按供给组成分	by Components of Supply							
农业产品	Agricultural Products	100.0	104.1	102.9	116.6	119.8	117.0	120.1
工业产品	Industrial Products	100.0	106.6	100.2	104.1	107.7	109.2	108.2
进口产品	Import Products	100.0	98.6	105.1	112.1	114.5	116.1	114.7
按生产阶段分	by Stage of Processing							
原材料	Raw Materials	100.0	95.7	101.4	108.6	113.7	114.6	112.4
中间产品	Intermediate Products	100.0	106.3	100.1	103.6	108.2	110.4	110.5
按最终用途分	by End-Use							
消费品	Consumers' Goods	100.0	108.8	99.4	102.6	104.2	105.1	106.0
投资用品	Capital Goods	100.0	108.7	102.9	106.1	107.8	110.1	111.3
澳大利亚	**Australia**							
按供给组成分	by Components of Supply							
国内供应	Domestic Supply	100.0	109.2	110.2	111.8	113.9	115.9	116.1
国内生产	Domestic Production	100.0	109.3	110.4	112.6	114.5		
农业产品	Agricultural Products	100.0	127.1	131.4	133.3	134.9	144.4	155.3
工业产品	Industrial Products	100.0	107.4	106.8	110.2	116.0	119.9	121.1
进口产品	Import Products	100.0	110.5	110.7	108.5	111.3		
按生产阶段分	by Stage of Processing							
原材料	Raw Materials	100.0	110.6	111.0	113.8	118.8		
中间产品	Intermediate Products	100.0	110.7	111.3	114.2	118.9		
按最终用途分	by End-Use							
消费品	Consumers' Goods	100.0	110.9	111.9	113.9	115.7		
投资用品	Capital Goods	100.0	109.2	110.0	111.1	114.0		
新 西 兰	**New Zealand**							
按供给组成分	by Components of Supply							
农业产品	Agricultural Products	100.0	99.2	102.1	121.5	126.9	132.0	130.7
工业产品	Industrial Products	100.0	103.1	100.5	108.8	113.6	115.4	114.3
按生产阶段分	by Stage of Processing							
中间产品	Intermediate Products	100.0	105.1	105.6	110.4	114.3	117.5	117.5

注：①1988年7月1日至1989年6月30日为基期。②以2011—2012年为基期。③以2011财政年度(2011年3月21日—2012年3月20日)为基期。④以2015年为基期。⑤2004年7月1日至2005年6月30日为基期。⑥以2012年为基期。⑦以2005年为基期。⑧以2016财政年度(2016年3月21日—2017年3月20日)为基期。

Note: ①The base year is from 1 July 1988 to 30 June 1989.②The base year is 2011-2012.③The base year is fiscal year 2011(from 21 March 2011 to 20 March 2012).④The base year is 2015.⑤The base year is from 1 July 2004 to 30 June 2005.⑥The base year is 2012. ⑦The base year is 2005.⑧The base year is fiscal year 2016(from 21 March 2016 to 20 March 2017).

附录 2-14 居民消费价格指数
Consumer Price Indices

资料来源：世界银行WDI数据库。
Source: World Bank WDI Database.

2010年=100 (2010=100)

国家和地区	Country or Area	2014	2015	2016	2017	2018	2019	2020
中　国	China	113.3	114.9	117.2	119.1	121.6	125.1	128.1
中国香港	Hong Kong SAR, China	119.4	122.9	125.9	127.8	130.8	134.6	135.0
中国澳门	Macao SAR, China	125.6	131.3	134.4	136.1	140.2		
孟加拉国	Bangladesh	136.1	144.6	152.5	161.2	170.2	179.7	189.9
文　莱	Brunei Darussalam	100.4	99.9	99.7	98.4	99.4	99.0	100.9
柬 埔 寨	Cambodia	116.1	117.5	121.1	124.6	127.6		
印　度	India	140.9	147.9	155.2	160.3	166.7	172.9	184.3
印度尼西亚	Indonesia	124.4	132.3	137.0	142.2	146.7	151.2	154.1
伊　朗	Iran	256.0	288.0	308.8	333.7	393.8	550.9	
以 色 列	Israel	107.4	106.7	106.1	106.4	107.3	108.2	107.5
日　本	Japan	102.8	103.6	103.5	104.0	105.0	105.5	105.5
哈萨克斯坦	Kazakhstan	128.7	137.3	157.3	169.0	179.1	188.5	201.2
韩　国	Korea, Rep.	109.1	109.8	110.9	113.1	114.7	115.2	115.8
老　挝	Lao PDR	124.2	125.8	127.8	128.9	131.5	135.9	142.8
马来西亚	Malaysia	110.5	112.8	115.1	119.6	120.7	121.5	120.1
蒙　古	Mongolia	153.7	162.5	163.7	170.8	182.4	195.8	203.0
缅　甸	Myanmar	118.2	129.3	138.3	144.6	154.5	168.2	
巴基斯坦	Pakistan	141.7	145.3	150.8	156.9	164.9	182.3	200.1
菲 律 宾	Philippines	114.7	115.4	116.9	120.2	126.5	129.6	133.0
新 加 坡	Singapore	113.8	113.2	112.6	113.3	113.8	114.4	114.2
斯里兰卡	Sri Lanka	126.6	131.4	136.6	147.1	150.2	155.5	165.1
泰　国	Thailand	111.3	110.3	110.6	111.3	112.5	113.3	112.3
越　南	Viet Nam	143.6	144.6	148.4	153.6	159.1	163.5	168.8
埃　及	Egypt	142.1	156.8	178.4	231.1	264.4	288.6	303.1
尼日利亚	Nigeria	145.8	158.9	183.9	214.2	240.1	267.5	
南　非	South Africa	124.6	130.3	138.9	146.1	152.6	158.9	164.1
加 拿 大	Canada	107.5	108.7	110.2	112.0	114.5	116.8	117.6
墨 西 哥	Mexico	116.2	119.4	122.8	130.2	136.6	141.5	146.4
美　国	United States	108.6	108.7	110.1	112.4	115.2	117.2	118.7
阿 根 廷	Argentina							
巴　西	Brazil	126.9	138.4	150.5	155.7	161.4	167.4	172.8
委内瑞拉	Venezuela	348.2	772.0	2740.3				
捷　克	Czech Rep.	107.1	107.5	108.2	110.9	113.3	116.5	120.2
法　国	France	105.5	105.6	105.8	106.9	108.8	110.0	110.6
德　国	Germany	106.7	107.2	107.7	109.4	111.2	112.9	113.4
意 大 利	Italy	107.5	107.5	107.4	108.7	110.0	110.6	110.5
荷　兰	Netherlands	108.5	109.2	109.5	111.0	112.9	115.9	117.4
波　兰	Poland	109.1	108.1	107.4	109.6	111.6	114.1	118.0
俄罗斯	Russia	131.2	151.5	162.2	168.2	173.0	180.8	186.9
西 班 牙	Spain	107.0	106.5	106.3	108.4	110.2	111.0	110.6
土 耳 其	Turkey	135.7	146.1	157.4	175.0	203.5	234.4	263.2
乌 克 兰	Ukraine	121.4	180.5	205.6	235.3	261.1	281.7	289.4
英　国	United Kingdom	110.6	111.0	112.1	114.9	117.6	119.6	120.8
澳大利亚	Australia	110.4	112.0	113.5	115.7	117.9	119.8	120.8
新 西 兰	New Zealand	107.6	107.9	108.6	110.7	112.4	114.2	116.2

附录 2-15 主要农产品产量

Production of Major Farm Crops

资料来源：联合国FAO数据库。
Source:FAO Database.
单位：万吨 (10 000 tons)

国家或地区	Country or Area	谷物 Cereals,Total 2010	谷物 Cereals,Total 2020	国家或地区	Country or Area	稻谷 Rice,Paddy 2010	稻谷 Rice,Paddy 2020
世　界	**World**	**245794.7**	**299614.2**	**世　界**	**World**	**69444.9**	**75674.4**
中　国	China	49634.3	61551.8	中　国	China	19576.1	21186.0
美　国	United States	40112.6	43487.5	印　度	India	14396.3	17830.5
印　度	India	26783.8	33503.5	孟加拉国	Bangladesh	5006.1	5490.6
俄罗斯	Russia	5961.9	13003.8	印度尼西亚	Indonesia	5928.3	5464.9
巴　西	Brazil	7516.0	12556.8	越　南	Viet Nam	4000.6	4275.9
阿根廷	Argentina	3976.9	8657.3	泰　国	Thailand	3570.3	3023.1
印度尼西亚	Indonesia	7761.1	7714.9	缅　甸	Myanmar	3206.5	2510.0
加拿大	Canada	4612.2	6501.4	菲律宾	Philippines	1577.2	1929.5
乌克兰	Ukraine	3868.6	6434.2	巴　西	Brazil	1123.6	1109.1
孟加拉国	Bangladesh	5186.3	5996.0	柬埔寨	Cambodia	824.5	1096.0
法　国	France	6583.9	5685.0	美　国	United States	1102.7	1032.3
越　南	Viet Nam	4461.4	4732.1	日　本	Japan	1069.2	970.6
德　国	Germany	4403.9	4326.5	巴基斯坦	Pakistan	723.5	841.9
巴基斯坦	Pakistan	3481.1	4254.1	尼日利亚	Nigeria	447.3	817.2
土耳其	Turkey	3276.5	3718.5	尼泊尔	Nepal	402.4	555.1
墨西哥	Mexico	3492.5	3637.5	斯里兰卡	Sri Lanka	430.1	512.1
泰　国	Thailand	4093.4	3550.8	埃　及	Egypt	433.0	489.4
波　兰	Poland	2722.8	3486.5	韩　国	Korea,Rep.	581.1	471.3
埃塞俄比亚	Ethiopia	1838.0	3024.9	坦桑尼亚	Tanzania	265.0	452.8
尼日利亚	Nigeria	2465.0	2867.3	马达加斯加	Madagascar	473.8	423.2
缅　甸	Myanmar	3404.3	2755.3	老　挝	Lao PDR	307.1	368.7
菲律宾	Philippines	2214.9	2741.4	秘　鲁	Peru	283.1	343.7
西班牙	Spain	1988.0	2732.1	哥伦比亚	Colombia	198.8	342.4
澳大利亚	Australia	3346.5	2661.4	马　里	Mali	129.6	301.0
埃　及	Egypt	1946.5	2232.0	几内亚	Guinea	161.4	291.6
伊　朗	Iran	1959.7	2201.3	马来西亚	Malaysia	246.5	232.2
哈萨克斯坦	Kazakhstan	1211.6	2017.9	朝　鲜	Korea,Dem.	242.6	211.3
罗马尼亚	Romania	1671.3	1937.4	伊　朗	Iran	249.0	200.0
英　国	United Kingdom	2094.6	1896.2	中国台湾	Taiwan,China	145.1	175.1
南　非	South Africa	1470.1	1823.7	意大利	Italy	151.6	150.7
意大利	Italy	1850.3	1694.5	科特迪瓦	Côte d'Ivoire	120.6	148.1
匈牙利	Hungary	1226.9	1556.7	刚果(金)	Congo, Dem. Rep.	75.5	137.9
坦桑尼亚	Tanzania	864.3	1249.3	塞内加尔	Senegal	60.4	135.0
柬埔寨	Cambodia	901.9	1191.0	厄瓜多尔	Ecuador	170.6	133.7
塞尔维亚	Serbia	929.5	1147.2	阿根廷	Argentina	124.3	122.3
尼泊尔	Nepal	777.1	1093.6	乌拉圭	Uruguay	114.9	120.9
日　本	Japan	1145.5	1092.3	巴拉圭	Paraguay	31.5	118.8
马　里	Mali	533.9	1035.2	俄罗斯	Russian	106.1	114.2
丹　麦	Denmark	886.3	946.8	塞拉利昂	Sierra Leone	102.7	105.0
伊拉克	Iraq	436.2	888.5	土耳其	Turkey	86.0	98.0
保加利亚	Bulgaria	713.6	859.8	加　纳	Ghana	49.2	97.3
巴拉圭	Paraguay	497.6	843.3	多米尼加	Dominican Rep.	85.0	94.3
白俄罗斯	Belarus	674.2	840.4	西班牙	Spain	92.8	73.9
捷　克	Czech Rep.	688.2	812.7	圭亚那	Guyana	55.6	68.8
乌兹别克斯坦	Uzbekistan	747.4	712.2	哈萨克斯坦	Kazakhstan	37.3	55.7
立陶宛	Lithuania	279.7	654.5	玻利维亚	Bolivia	44.2	48.7
阿富汗	Afghanistan	595.7	602.6	尼加拉瓜	Nicaragua	45.4	47.7
瑞　典	Sweden	428.0	595.5	伊拉克	Iraq	15.6	46.4
尼日尔	Niger	526.4	587.8	阿富汗	Afghanistan	67.2	44.0
奥地利	Austria	486.7	565.0	委内瑞拉	Venezuela	90.0	42.9

附录 2-15 续表 1 continued

单位：万吨 (10 000 tons)

国家或地区	Country or Area	小麦 Wheat 2010	小麦 Wheat 2020	国家或地区	Country or Area	玉米 Maize 2010	玉米 Maize 2020
世 界	**World**	**64040.0**	**76092.6**	**世 界**	**World**	**85275.2**	**116235.3**
中 国	China	11518.1	13425.0	美 国	United States	31561.8	36025.2
印 度	India	8080.4	10759.0	中 国	China	17742.5	26067.0
俄 罗 斯	Russia	4150.8	8589.6	巴 西	Brazil	5536.4	10396.4
美 国	United States	6006.2	4969.1	阿 根 廷	Argentina	2266.3	5839.6
法 国	France	2330.0	3518.3	乌 克 兰	Ukraine	1195.3	3029.0
加 拿 大	Canada	3820.7	3014.4	印 度	India	2172.6	3016.0
乌 克 兰	Ukraine	2331.1	2524.8	墨 西 哥	Mexico	2330.2	2742.5
巴基斯坦	Pakistan	1685.1	2491.2	印度尼西亚	Indonesia	1832.8	2250.0
德 国	Germany	2378.3	2217.2	南 非	South Africa	1281.5	1530.0
阿 根 廷	Argentina	1967.4	2050.0	俄 罗 斯	Russia	308.4	1387.9
土 耳 其	Turkey	901.6	1977.7	加 拿 大	Canada	1204.3	1356.3
澳大利亚	Australia	1214.3	1500.0	法 国	France	1397.5	1341.9
伊 朗	Iran	2183.4	1448.0	尼日利亚	Nigeria	767.7	1200.0
英 国	United Kingdom	963.8	1425.8	罗马尼亚	Romania	904.2	1094.2
哈萨克斯坦	Kazakhstan	940.8	1243.3	埃塞俄比亚	Ethiopia	548.1	1002.2
波 兰	Poland	1487.8	965.8	巴基斯坦	Pakistan	370.7	846.5
罗马尼亚	Romania	717.7	900.0	匈 牙 利	Hungary	698.5	836.5
埃 及	Egypt	594.1	814.4	菲 律 宾	Philippines	637.7	811.9
意 大 利	Italy	581.2	675.5	塞尔维亚	Serbia	720.7	787.3
保加利亚	Bulgaria	685.0	671.6	埃 及	Egypt	704.1	750.0
乌兹别克斯坦	Uzbekistan	617.1	634.8	意 大 利	Italy	849.6	679.3
西 班 牙	Spain	274.9	623.8	坦桑尼亚	Tanzania	473.3	671.1
巴 西	Brazil	674.5	615.8	波 兰	Poland	199.4	669.5
匈 牙 利	Hungary	285.6	547.9	土 耳 其	Turkey	431.0	650.0
埃塞俄比亚	Ethiopia	453.2	518.5	巴 拉 圭	Paraguay	310.9	583.5
阿 富 汗	Afghanistan	374.5	512.1	泰 国	Thailand	486.1	480.6
捷 克	Czech Rep.	416.2	490.2	越 南	Viet Nam	460.7	456.0
丹 麦	Denmark	409.5	484.8	西 班 牙	Spain	332.5	421.4
伊 拉 克	Iraq	171.0	481.9	德 国	Germany	421.2	402.0
摩 洛 哥	Morocco	506.0	407.0	孟加拉国	Bangladesh	88.7	401.5
阿尔及利亚	Algeria	214.3	321.4	肯 尼 亚	Kenya	346.5	378.9
立 陶 宛	Lithuania	260.5	310.7	马 拉 维	Malawi	341.9	369.2
瑞 典	Sweden	367.7	298.7	马 里	Mali	135.6	351.7
墨 西 哥	Mexico	163.0	287.4	赞 比 亚	Zambia	279.5	338.7
叙 利 亚	Syrian Arab Republic	308.3	284.8	加 纳	Ghana	187.2	307.1
塞尔维亚	Serbia	173.9	284.8	保加利亚	Bulgaria	204.7	301.4
拉脱维亚	Latvia	98.9	266.0	尼 泊 尔	Nepal	185.5	283.6
白俄罗斯	Belarus	487.6	256.2	乌 干 达	Uganda	237.4	275.0
阿塞拜疆	Azerbaijan	155.7	218.5	克罗地亚	Croatia	206.8	243.1
尼 泊 尔	Nepal	118.5	213.3	奥 地 利	Austria	195.6	241.2
斯洛伐克	Slovakia	143.0	210.9	安 哥 拉	Angola	107.3	230.0
比 利 时	Belgium	127.2	181.9	朝 鲜	Korea, Dem.	168.3	221.4
奥 地 利	Austria	185.0	174.1	刚果(金)	Congo, Dem. Rep.	178.2	211.2
南 非	South Africa	151.8	165.3	喀 麦 隆	Cameroon	167.0	209.1
土库曼斯坦	Turkmenistan	147.7	132.0	缅 甸	Myanmar	135.4	204.1
突 尼 斯	Tunisia	140.2	130.3	布基纳法索	Burkina Faso	113.3	192.0
智 利	Chile	152.4	123.1	危地马拉	Guatemala	163.8	191.0
巴 拉 圭	Paraguay	192.1	109.5	斯洛伐克	Slovakia	92.1	164.3
摩尔多瓦	Moldova	82.2	104.2	莫桑比克	Mozambique	209.0	163.2
荷 兰	Netherlands	90.1	102.9	贝 宁	Benin	101.3	161.2

附录 2-15 续表 2 continued

单位：万吨 (10 000 tons)

国家或地区	Country or Area	大豆 Soybeans 2010	大豆 Soybeans 2020	国家或地区	Country or Area	根茎类作物 Roots and Tubers 2010	根茎类作物 Roots and Tubers 2020
世界	**World**	**26508.8**	**35346.4**	**世界**	**World**	**74571.3**	**84762.2**
巴西	Brazil	6875.6	12179.8	中国	China	14836.0	13394.7
美国	United States	9066.3	11254.9	尼日利亚	Nigeria	8731.2	11832.7
阿根廷	Argentina	5267.5	4879.7	印度	India	4573.2	5752.9
中国	China	1508.3	1960.0	刚果(金)	Congo, Dem. Rep.	3256.8	4276.1
印度	India	1273.6	1122.6	加纳	Ghana	2094.0	3173.6
巴拉圭	Paraguay	746.0	1102.4	泰国	Thailand	2245.7	2949.6
加拿大	Canada	444.5	635.9	巴西	Brazil	2925.7	2307.1
俄罗斯	Russia	122.2	430.8	印度尼西亚	Indonesia	2739.5	2154.7
玻利维亚	Bolivia	169.3	282.9	乌克兰	Ukraine	1870.5	2083.8
乌克兰	Ukraine	168.0	279.8	美国	United States	1943.3	2034.9
乌拉圭	Uruguay	179.3	199.0	俄罗斯	Russia	2114.1	1960.7
南非	South Africa	56.6	124.6	科特迪瓦	Cote D'Ivoire	784.1	1428.6
印度尼西亚	Indonesia	90.7	104.0	马拉维	Malawi	767.5	1409.5
意大利	Italy	55.3	100.6	坦桑尼亚	Tanzania	845.6	1307.5
塞尔维亚	Serbia	54.1	75.2	越南	Viet Nam	1026.7	1215.5
尼日利亚	Nigeria	36.5	60.0	德国	Germany	1014.3	1171.5
法国	France	14.0	40.7	安哥拉	Angola	1568.7	1095.6
罗马尼亚	Romania	15.0	35.4	孟加拉国	Bangladesh	823.7	985.2
赞比亚	Zambia	11.2	29.7	法国	France	666.1	869.2
克罗地亚	Croatia	15.4	26.6	喀麦隆	Cameroon	629.5	829.9
哈萨克斯坦	Kazakhstan	11.4	26.1	波兰	Poland	844.8	784.9
贝宁	Benin	6.3	25.4	柬埔寨	Cambodia	436.1	774.5
墨西哥	Mexico	16.8	24.6	贝宁	Benin	614.8	737.1
朝鲜	Korea, Dem.	35.0	23.0	秘鲁	Peru	560.2	734.1
日本	Japan	22.3	21.9	荷兰	Netherlands	684.4	702.0
埃塞俄比亚	Ethiopia	1.6	20.9	老挝	Laos	132.8	693.8
奥地利	Austria	9.5	20.5	莫桑比克	Mozambique	676.1	625.1
柬埔寨	Cambodia	15.7	18.0	乌干达	Uganda	517.1	605.3
马拉维	Malawi	7.3	18.0	埃及	Egypt	413.8	579.1
加纳	Ghana	14.6	17.7	英国	United Kingdom	605.6	552.0
匈牙利	Hungary	8.5	16.6	加拿大	Canada	544.1	529.5
土耳其	Turkey	8.7	15.5	白俄罗斯	Belarus	783.1	523.1
缅甸	Myanmar	25.5	14.5	土耳其	Turkey	454.9	520.0
伊朗	Iran	15.7	14.0	埃塞俄比亚	Ethiopia	236.1	511.4
斯洛伐克	Slovakia	2.4	13.2	巴基斯坦	Pakistan	361.3	493.7
哥伦比亚	Colombia	5.4	11.9	阿尔及利亚	Algeria	330.0	465.9
孟加拉国	Bangladesh	7.0	10.5	伊朗	Iran	427.5	447.5
德国	Germany	0.2	9.1	哥伦比亚	Colombia	439.8	433.2
韩国	Korea, Rep.	10.5	8.1	马达加斯加	Madagascar	438.8	420.5
乌干达	Uganda	2.7	7.5	赞比亚	Zambia	142.8	415.7
莫桑比克	Mozambique		7.5	哈萨克斯坦	Kazakhstan	255.5	400.7
越南	Viet Nam	29.9	6.5	布隆迪	Burundi	166.3	393.1
津巴布韦	Zimbabwe	5.7	6.0	比利时	Belgium	345.6	392.9
埃及	Egypt	4.3	5.0	卢旺达	Rwanda	381.3	366.4
布基纳法索	Burkina Faso	2.2	4.8	几内亚	Guinea	148.5	347.9
危地马拉	Guatemala	4.4	4.1	肯尼亚	Kenya	389.7	347.2
安哥拉	Angola	0.6	4.1	菲律宾	Philippines	291.6	339.9
尼泊尔	Nepal	2.2	3.8	巴拉圭	Paraguay	266.8	338.5
波斯尼亚和黑塞哥维那	Bosnia and Herzegovina	0.8	3.7	日本	Japan	355.5	332.4
摩尔多瓦	Moldova	11.1	3.3	尼泊尔	Nepal	267.5	329.1

附录 2-15 续表 3 continued

单位：万吨 (10 000 tons)

国家或地区	Country or Area	花生 Groundnuts,with Shell 2010	2020	国家或地区	Country or Area	油菜籽 Rapeseed 2010	2020
世　界	**World**	**4278.7**	**5363.9**	**世　界**	**World**	**5986.1**	**7237.6**
中　国	China	1564.4	1799.3	加拿大	Canada	1278.9	1948.5
印　度	India	826.5	995.2	中　国	China	1308.2	1400.0
尼日利亚	Nigeria	379.9	449.3	印　度	India	660.8	912.4
美　国	United States	188.6	278.2	德　国	Germany	569.8	352.7
塞内加尔	Senegal	128.7	179.7	法　国	France	481.5	329.7
缅　甸	Myanmar	137.0	164.7	波　兰	Poland	222.9	298.7
阿根廷	Argentina	61.1	128.5	俄罗斯	Russia	67.0	257.2
几内亚	Guinea	33.2	107.4	乌克兰	Ukraine	147.0	255.7
印度尼西亚	Indonesia	136.7	86.0	澳大利亚	Australia	190.7	229.9
乍　得	Chad	110.3	84.0	美　国	United States	111.2	157.6
坦桑尼亚	Tanzania	46.5	69.0	捷　克	Czech Rep.	104.2	124.5
巴　西	Brazil	26.1	65.1	英　国	United Kingdom	223.0	103.8
尼日尔	Niger	40.6	59.4	立陶宛	Lithuania	41.7	97.2
喀麦隆	Cameroon	53.6	50.0	匈牙利	Hungary	53.1	87.7
加　纳	Ghana	53.1	45.0	罗马尼亚	Romania	94.3	78.0
越　南	Viet Nam	48.7	42.5	白俄罗斯	Belarus	37.5	73.1
马拉维	Malawi	29.7	35.0	巴基斯坦	Pakistan	16.2	56.6
乌干达	Uganda	27.6	33.6	丹　麦	Denmark	58.0	56.0
刚果(金)	Congo, Dem. Rep.	38.8	31.5	拉脱维亚	Latvia	22.6	45.6
布基纳法索	Burkina Faso	34.0	27.0	斯洛伐克	Slovakia	32.2	44.6
马　里	Mali	31.4	26.0	孟加拉国	Bangladesh	22.2	35.8
安哥拉	Angola	11.5	23.2	伊　朗	Iran	14.6	34.0
科特迪瓦	Cote D'Ivoire	9.0	22.8	瑞　典	Sweden	27.6	33.9
土耳其	Turkey	9.7	21.6	保加利亚	Bulgaria	54.5	27.9
埃　及	Egypt	20.3	21.4	爱沙尼亚	Estonia	13.1	20.3
埃塞俄比亚	Ethiopia	7.2	20.5	西班牙	Spain	3.6	19.6
尼加拉瓜	Nicaragua	18.0	18.4	南　非	South Africa	3.7	16.7
贝　宁	Benin	15.4	17.3	智　利	Chile	4.4	15.4
中　非	Central African Rep.	14.0	13.9	哈萨克斯坦	Kazakhstan	10.9	15.3
赞比亚	Zambia	16.4	12.7	土耳其	Turkey	10.6	12.2
巴基斯坦	Pakistan	6.8	12.2	克罗地亚	Croatia	3.3	12.0
冈比亚	Gambia	13.8	11.0	乌拉圭	Uruguay	0.9	11.3
莫桑比克	Mozambique	15.8	10.3	奥地利	Austria	17.1	10.0
墨西哥	Mexico	8.1	10.1	瑞　士	Switzerland	6.8	8.8
津巴布韦	Zimbabwe	13.7	7.7	塞尔维亚	Serbia	2.4	7.4
孟加拉国	Bangladesh	5.3	6.0	巴拉圭	Paraguay	10.2	6.7
马达加斯加	Madagascar	3.0	5.9	意大利	Italy	5.0	4.9
塞拉利昂	Sierra Leone	8.1	5.9	摩尔多瓦	Moldova	4.5	4.7
中国台湾	Taiwan, China	6.5	5.4	爱尔兰	Ireland	2.8	4.4
南　非	South Africa	8.8	5.0	巴　西	Brazil	7.0	4.4
多　哥	Togo	4.6	4.5	阿根廷	Argentina	1.7	3.3
几内亚比绍	Guinea-Bissau	3.6	4.3	芬　兰	Finland	17.9	3.1
老　挝	Laos	5.1	4.2	比利时	Belgium	4.6	3.0
斯里兰卡	Sri Lanka	1.4	3.8	阿尔及利亚	Algeria	2.5	2.3
摩洛哥	Morocco	5.0	3.7	蒙　古	Mongolia	1.1	2.3
加　蓬	Gabon	2.0	3.6	埃塞俄比亚	Ethiopia	1.9	1.3
乌兹别克斯坦	Uzbekistan	0.8	3.2	希　腊	Greece	2.5	1.2
菲律宾	Philippines	3.0	2.9	波斯尼亚和黑塞	Bosnia and Herzegov	0.1	1.0
泰　国	Thailand	4.9	2.9	卢森堡	Luxembourg	1.6	0.9
玻利维亚	Bolivia	1.3	2.7	斯洛文尼亚	Slovenia	1.6	0.9

附录 2-15　续表 4　continued

单位：万吨　　(10 000 tons)

国家或地区	Country or Area	芝麻 Sesame Seed 2010	芝麻 Sesame Seed 2020	国家或地区	Country or Area	籽棉 Seed Cotton 2010	籽棉 Seed Cotton 2020
世　界	**World**	**407.5**	**680.4**	**世　界**	**World**	**6917.8**	**8311.3**
苏　丹	Sudan	24.8	152.5	中　国	China	1791.0	2950.0
缅　甸	Myanmar	78.7	74.0	印　度	India	1776.0	1773.1
坦桑尼亚	Tanzania	14.4	71.0	美　国	United States	947.4	973.7
印　度	India	89.3	65.8	巴　西	Brazil	295.0	707.0
尼日利亚	Nigeria	14.9	49.0	巴基斯坦	Pakistan	561.4	345.4
中　国	China	58.7	44.7	乌兹别克斯坦	Uzbekistan	344.3	306.4
布基纳法索	Burkina Faso	9.1	27.0	土 耳 其	Turkey	215.0	177.4
埃塞俄比亚	Ethiopia	32.8	26.0	阿 根 廷	Argentina	75.4	104.6
乍　得	Chad	12.6	20.2	布基纳法索	Burkina Faso	53.0	78.3
乌 干 达	Uganda	11.9	14.6	贝　宁	Benin	13.7	72.8
莫桑比克	Mozambique	6.3	13.2	墨 西 哥	Mexico	44.0	67.5
巴　西	Brazil	0.5	11.1	土库曼斯坦	Turkmenistan	128.6	63.6
巴基斯坦	Pakistan	3.1	10.2	科特迪瓦	Cote D'Ivoire	17.5	49.0
尼 日 尔	Niger	8.6	8.8	喀 麦 隆	Cameroon	19.0	44.6
喀 麦 隆	Cameroon	1.3	7.0	塔吉克斯坦	Tajikistan	31.1	40.1
墨 西 哥	Mexico	3.7	5.2	澳大利亚	Australia	93.9	37.3
阿 富 汗	Afghanistan	3.2	4.2	阿塞拜疆	Azerbaijan	3.8	33.7
埃　及	Egypt	4.6	3.8	哈萨克斯坦	Kazakhstan	24.0	32.7
巴 拉 圭	Paraguay	4.0	3.7	缅　甸	Myanmar	50.5	30.9
塞内加尔	Senegal	0.5	3.6	坦桑尼亚	Tanzania	26.7	30.2
马　里	Mali	1.3	3.5	尼日利亚	Nigeria	60.2	28.2
危地马拉	Guatemala	5.0	3.5	埃　及	Egypt	37.8	21.5
索 马 里	Somalia	2.6	3.4	埃塞俄比亚	Ethiopia	5.8	18.8
孟加拉国	Bangladesh	3.2	3.2	马　里	Mali	24.4	14.7
泰　国	Thailand	4.8	3.1	乍　得	Chad	6.4	14.5
柬 埔 寨	Cambodia	3.0	3.0	伊　朗	Iran	16.7	14.5
伊　朗	Iran	4.5	2.9	乌 干 达	Uganda	8.4	12.8
越　南	Viet Nam	1.7	2.8	南　非	South Africa	2.1	11.8
也　门	Yemen	2.5	2.2	多　哥	Togo	4.3	10.2
土 耳 其	Turkey	2.3	1.9	津巴布韦	Zimbabwe	15.0	9.3
委内瑞拉	Venezuela	1.5	1.5	叙 利 亚	Syrian Arab Republic	47.2	9.0
乌兹别克斯坦	Uzbekistan	0.4	1.3	莫桑比克	Mozambique	6.2	8.9
叙 利 亚	Syrian Arab Republic	0.5	1.2	阿 富 汗	Afghanistan	3.3	7.4
肯 尼 亚	Kenya	1.1	1.2	孟加拉国	Bangladesh	4.3	7.3
老　挝	Laos	1.0	1.1	吉尔吉斯斯坦	Kyrgyzstan	7.4	7.3
贝　宁	Benin	1.0	1.0	几 内 亚	Guinea	3.7	4.4
玻利维亚	Bolivia	1.0	1.0	赞 比 亚	Zambia	10.7	4.1
斯里兰卡	Sri Lanka	1.7	0.8	朝　鲜	Korea, Dem.	3.5	4.0
韩　国	Korea, Rep.	1.3	0.7	刚果(金)	Congo, Dem. Rep.	2.6	2.9
中　非	Central African Rep.	2.9	0.7	巴 拉 圭	Paraguay	1.5	2.9
伊 拉 克	Iraq	1.3	0.6	加　纳	Ghana	1.0	2.8
厄立特里亚	Eritrea	0.4	0.5	塞内加尔	Senegal	2.6	2.0
刚果(金)	Congo, Dem. Rep.	0.5	0.5	马 拉 维	Malawi	2.9	2.0
尼加拉瓜	Nicaragua	0.4	0.4	秘　鲁	Peru	6.4	1.9
海　地	Haiti	0.4	0.4	中　非	Central African Rep.	1.0	1.6
沙特阿拉伯	Saudi Arabia	0.5	0.4	以 色 列	Israel	1.8	1.5
哥伦比亚	Colombia	0.2	0.4	马达加斯加	Madagascar	1.4	1.5
塞拉利昂	Sierra Leone	0.3	0.3	也　门	Yemen	2.5	1.0
安 哥 拉	Angola	0.3	0.3	尼 日 尔	Niger	0.4	1.0
科特迪瓦	Cote D'Ivoire	0.3	0.3	哥伦比亚	Colombia	8.9	0.8

附录 2-15 续表 5 continued

单位：万吨 (10 000 tons)

国家或地区	Country or Area	甘蔗 Sugar Cane 2010	甘蔗 Sugar Cane 2020	国家或地区	Country or Area	甜菜 Sugar Beets 2010	甜菜 Sugar Beets 2020
世　界	**World**	**166940.9**	**186971.5**	**世　界**	**World**	**22830.2**	**25296.9**
巴　西	Brazil	71746.4	75711.7	俄罗斯	Russia	2225.6	3391.5
印　度	India	29230.2	37050.0	美　国	United States	2906.1	3049.8
中　国	China	11078.9	10812.1	德　国	Germany	2343.2	2861.8
巴基斯坦	Pakistan	4937.3	8100.9	法　国	France	3187.5	2619.5
泰　国	Thailand	6880.8	7496.8	土耳其	Turkey	1794.2	2302.6
墨西哥	Mexico	5042.2	5395.3	波　兰	Poland	997.3	1417.2
美　国	United States	2482.1	3274.9	埃　及	Egypt	784.0	1304.4
澳大利亚	Australia	3123.5	3028.3	中　国	China	929.6	1159.8
印度尼西亚	Indonesia	2660.0	2891.4	乌克兰	Ukraine	1374.9	915.0
危地马拉	Guatemala	2231.4	2835.0	荷　兰	Netherlands	528.0	669.1
哥伦比亚	Colombia	3253.9	2465.0	伊　朗	Iran	386.6	622.6
菲律宾	Philippines	1792.9	2439.9	英　国	United Kingdom	652.7	598.0
南　非	South Africa	1601.6	1822.0	比利时	Belgium	446.5	478.4
阿根廷	Argentina	1889.0	1804.6	白俄罗斯	Belarus	377.3	401.1
埃　及	Egypt	1570.9	1491.4	日　本	Japan	309.0	391.2
古　巴	Cuba	1160.0	1389.5	捷　克	Czech Rep.	306.5	367.1
缅　甸	Myanmar	925.0	1188.6	摩洛哥	Morocco	243.6	363.2
越　南	Viet Nam	1616.2	1153.5	丹　麦	Denmark	240.9	255.9
厄瓜多尔	Ecuador	834.7	1101.6	西班牙	Spain	353.5	243.3
秘　鲁	Peru	985.5	1046.9	奥地利	Austria	313.2	209.2
玻利维亚	Bolivia	640.3	1009.4	瑞　典	Sweden	197.4	202.7
尼加拉瓜	Nicaragua	489.4	858.5	塞尔维亚	Serbia	332.5	201.8
伊　朗	Iran	564.8	782.7	意大利	Italy	355.0	183.1
萨尔瓦多	El Salvador	512.7	769.4	瑞　士	Switzerland	130.2	142.4
巴拉圭	Paraguay	513.1	743.1	斯洛伐克	Slovakia	97.8	127.3
肯尼亚	Kenya	571.0	680.0	智　利	Chile	142.0	125.9
乌干达	Uganda	332.0	577.8	加拿大	Canada	50.8	106.7
斯威士兰	Eswatini	511.0	569.9	立陶宛	Lithuania	70.7	94.8
多米尼加	Dominican Rep.	457.7	531.7	匈牙利	Hungary	81.9	78.0
洪都拉斯	Honduras	444.4	503.0	罗马尼亚	Romania	83.8	77.8
赞比亚	Zambia	370.0	482.7	克罗地亚	Croatia	124.9	77.4
哥斯达黎加	Costa Rica	373.5	419.5	哈萨克斯坦	Kazakhstan	15.2	46.6
孟加拉国	Bangladesh	449.1	368.3	吉尔吉斯斯坦	Kyrgyzstan	13.9	44.9
坦桑尼亚	Tanzania	280.1	362.0	摩尔多瓦	Moldova	83.8	42.3
津巴布韦	Zimbabwe	269.2	359.0	芬　兰	Finland	54.2	42.2
尼泊尔	Nepal	259.3	340.0	阿塞拜疆	Azerbaijan	25.2	23.4
马拉维	Malawi	270.0	305.9	土库曼斯坦	Turkmenistan	18.0	19.5
马达加斯加	Madagascar	290.6	301.7	希　腊	Greece	88.9	8.9
巴拿马	Panama	222.9	277.9	突尼斯	Tunisia		8.6
莫桑比克	Mozambique	272.0	273.8	亚美尼亚	Armenia	2.6	5.5
毛里求斯	Mauritius	436.6	262.1	伊拉克	Iraq	2.0	3.2
委内瑞拉	Venezuela	684.2	261.9	哥伦比亚	Colombia	1.5	3.0
刚果(金)	Congo, Dem. Rep.	207.9	213.6	阿尔巴尼亚	Albania	4.0	2.7
科特迪瓦	Cote D'Ivoire	180.0	213.4	委内瑞拉	Venezuela	2.0	2.3
柬埔寨	Cambodia	36.6	212.3	巴基斯坦	Pakistan		1.7
斐　济	Fiji	175.1	172.6	马　里	Mali	0.4	0.8
海　地	Haiti	122.0	155.0	斯洛文尼亚	Slovenia		0.7
伯利兹	Belize	112.3	153.7	黎巴嫩	Lebanon	0.2	0.5
尼日利亚	Nigeria	100.9	151.7	阿富汗	Afghanistan	1.5	0.5
老　挝	Lao PDR	81.9	145.0	厄瓜多尔	Ecuador	0.4	0.4

附录 2-15 续表 6 continued

单位：万吨 (10 000 tons)

国家或地区	Country or Area	茶叶 Tea 2010	茶叶 Tea 2020	国家或地区	Country or Area	水果 Fruit Primary 2010	水果 Fruit Primary 2020
世　界	**World**	**461.1**	**702.4**	**世　界**	**World**	**73241.7**	**88702.7**
中　国	China	145.0	297.0	中　国	China	19510.0	24279.4
印　度	India	99.1	142.5	印　度	India	7640.9	10597.1
肯尼亚	Kenya	39.9	57.0	巴　西	Brazil	4155.7	3975.9
阿根廷	Argentina	9.2	33.5	土耳其	Turkey	1922.9	2415.3
斯里兰卡	Sri Lanka	33.1	27.8	墨西哥	Mexico	1705.9	2383.8
土耳其	Turkey	23.5	25.5	美　国	United States	2915.7	2374.8
越　南	Viet Nam	19.8	24.0	印度尼西亚	Indonesia	1563.5	2274.4
印度尼西亚	Indonesia	15.0	13.8	西班牙	Spain	1791.5	1947.1
缅　甸	Myanmar	9.5	12.6	伊　朗	Iran	1782.9	1896.4
泰　国	Thailand	6.7	9.8	意大利	Italy	1861.3	1782.8
孟加拉国	Bangladesh	6.0	9.0	菲律宾	Philippines	1618.9	1648.2
伊　朗	Iran	12.1	8.5	埃　及	Egypt	1231.3	1473.4
日　本	Japan	8.5	7.0	尼日利亚	Nigeria	1076.3	1153.0
乌干达	Uganda	4.9	6.3	越　南	Viet Nam	732.7	1061.7
马拉维	Malawi	5.2	4.8	哥伦比亚	Colombia	856.5	1052.2
坦桑尼亚	Tanzania	3.3	4.6	泰　国	Thailand	1039.5	1009.8
卢旺达	Rwanda	2.2	3.4	巴基斯坦	Pakistan	966.9	982.6
莫桑比克	Mozambique	2.9	3.4	法　国	France	904.4	888.7
尼泊尔	Nepal	1.7	2.4	厄瓜多尔	Ecuador	936.5	763.0
布隆迪	Burundi	3.8	1.6	乌干达	Uganda	474.9	745.8
中国台湾	Taiwan, China	1.7	1.4	南　非	South Africa	613.0	745.7
埃塞俄比亚	Ethiopia	0.8	1.0	阿根廷	Argentina	748.2	744.1
老　挝	Lao PDR	0.3	1.0	秘　鲁	Peru	494.1	737.6
马来西亚	Malaysia	2.0	0.9	阿尔及利亚	Algeria	444.8	705.5
巴布亚新几内亚	Papua New Guinea	0.6	0.6	危地马拉	Guatemala	432.9	689.9
喀麦隆	Cameroon	0.6	0.6	智　利	Chile	615.4	678.0
津巴布韦	Zimbabwe	1.1	0.4	刚果(金)	Congo, Dem. Rep.	406.9	674.8
刚果(金)	Congo, Dem. Rep.	0.2	0.3	喀麦隆	Cameroon	495.1	641.0
韩　国	Korea, Rep.	0.2	0.2	加　纳	Ghana	488.7	635.1
格鲁吉亚	Georgia	0.4	0.2	哥斯达黎加	Costa Rica	530.4	619.1
南　非	South Africa	0.2	0.2	俄罗斯	Russia	361.5	590.7
秘　鲁	Peru	0.3	0.2	乌兹别克斯坦	Uzbekistan	388.0	582.5
厄瓜多尔	Ecuador	0.2	0.1	多米尼加	Dominican Rep.	257.0	567.1
玻利维亚	Bolivia	0.1	0.1	坦桑尼亚	Tanzania	497.3	566.4
毛里求斯	Mauritius	0.1	0.1	摩洛哥	Morocco	429.7	558.7
赞比亚	Zambia	0.1	0.1	安哥拉	Angola	264.1	517.5
阿塞拜疆	Azerbaijan	0.1	0.1	孟加拉国	Bangladesh	391.8	502.7
萨尔瓦多	El Salvador	0.0	0.1	波　兰	Poland	278.9	450.0
危地马拉	Guatemala	0.1	0.1	希　腊	Greece	404.3	443.6
巴　西	Brazil	0.4		肯尼亚	Kenya	320.9	437.4
马达加斯加	Madagascar			马拉维	Malawi	113.0	371.4
俄罗斯	Russia			委内瑞拉	Venezuela	283.3	355.9
哥伦比亚	Colombia			澳大利亚	Australia	360.4	354.0
黑　山	Montenegro			阿富汗	Afghanistan	136.0	345.9
马　里	Mali			苏　丹	Sudan		326.3
塞舌尔	Seychelles			罗马尼亚	Romania	280.0	295.4
美属维尔京群岛	Virgin Islands(US)			日　本	Japan	345.5	293.0
阿尔巴尼亚	Albania			沙特阿拉伯	Saudi Arabia	215.5	291.4
斯洛文尼亚	Slovenia			科特迪瓦	Côte d'Ivoire	217.1	289.1
阿富汗	Afghanistan			哈萨克斯坦	Kazakhstan	135.3	286.4

附录 2-16 互联网网民占总人口比重

Individuals using the Internet as Percentage of Population

资料来源：世界银行WDI数据库。
Source: World Bank WDI Database.

单位：% (%)

国家或地区	Country or Area	2010	2015	2016	2017	2018	2019	2020
世　界	**World**	**28.9**	**40.9**	**43.8**	**46.3**	**49.9**	**56.7**	
高收入国家	**High Income**	**72.2**	**79.9**	**84.3**	**85.9**	**87.5**	**89.1**	
中等收入国家	**Middle Income**	**21.5**	**35.1**	**37.9**	**40.5**	**44.2**	**52.7**	
低收入国家	**Low Income**	**4.3**	**9.5**	**11.4**	**14.1**			
中　国	China	34.3	50.3	53.2	54.3	59.2	64.6	70.6
中国香港	Hong Kong SAR, China	72.0	84.9	87.5	89.4	90.5	91.7	92.4
中国澳门	Macao SAR, China	55.2	77.6	81.6	83.2	83.8	86.5	
孟加拉国	Bangladesh	3.7	8.3	9.2	10.3	11.5	12.9	
文　莱	Brunei Darussalam	53.0	71.2	90.0	94.9	95.0	95.0	
柬埔寨	Cambodia	1.3	18.0	32.4	32.9	65.0	78.3	78.8
印　度	India	7.5	14.9	16.5	18.2	20.1	41.0	
印度尼西亚	Indonesia	10.9	22.1	25.4	32.3	39.9	47.7	53.7
伊　朗	Iran	15.9	45.3	53.2	64.0	70.2	77.8	84.1
以色列	Israel	67.5	77.4	79.7	81.6	83.7	86.8	
日　本	Japan	78.2	91.1	93.2	91.7	91.3	92.7	
哈萨克斯坦	Kazakhstan	31.6	70.8	74.6	76.4	78.9	81.9	85.9
韩　国	Korea, Rep.	83.7	89.9	92.8	95.1	96.0	96.2	96.5
老　挝	Lao PDR	7.0	18.2	21.9	25.5			
马来西亚	Malaysia	56.3	71.1	78.8	80.1	81.2	84.2	89.6
蒙　古	Mongolia	10.2	22.5	22.3	23.7	47.1	51.1	62.5
缅　甸	Myanmar	0.3			23.6			
巴基斯坦	Pakistan	8.0	11.0	12.4	13.8	15.3	17.1	
菲律宾	Philippines	25.0					46.9	
新加坡	Singapore	71.0	79.0	84.5	84.5	88.2	88.9	75.9
斯里兰卡	Sri Lanka		12.1	15.1	21.3	26.0	29.0	35.0
泰　国	Thailand	22.4	39.3	47.5	52.9	56.8	66.7	77.8
越　南	Viet Nam	30.7	45.0	53.0	58.1	69.8	68.7	70.3
埃　及	Egypt	21.6	37.8	41.2	45.0	46.9	57.3	71.9
尼日利亚	Nigeria	11.5	24.5	25.7	28.0	31.9	33.6	
南　非	South Africa	24.0	51.9	54.0	56.2	62.4	68.2	
加拿大	Canada	80.3	90.0	91.2	92.7	94.6	96.5	
墨西哥	Mexico	31.1	57.4	59.5	63.9	65.8	70.1	72.0
美　国	United States	71.7	74.6	85.5	87.3	88.5	89.4	
阿根廷	Argentina	45.0	68.0	71.0	74.3			
巴　西	Brazil	40.7	58.3	60.9	67.5	70.4	73.9	
委内瑞拉	Venezuela	37.4						
捷　克	Czech Rep.	68.8	75.7	76.5	78.7	80.7	80.9	81.3
法　国	France	77.3	78.0	79.3	80.5	82.0	83.3	
德　国	Germany	82.0	87.6	84.2	84.4	87.0	88.1	89.8
意大利	Italy	53.7	58.1	61.3	63.1	74.4	76.1	
荷　兰	Netherlands	90.7	91.7	90.4	93.2	91.9	93.3	91.3
波　兰	Poland	62.3	68.0	73.3	76.0	77.5	80.4	86.8
俄罗斯	Russia	43.0	70.1	73.1	76.0	80.9	82.6	85.0
西班牙	Spain	65.8	78.7	80.6	84.6	86.1	90.7	93.2
土耳其	Turkey	39.8	53.7	58.3	64.7	71.0	74.0	77.7
乌克兰	Ukraine	23.3	48.9	53.0	58.9	62.6	70.1	
英　国	United Kingdom	85.0	92.0	94.8	90.4	90.7	92.5	94.8
澳大利亚	Australia	76.0	84.6	86.5	86.5			
新西兰	New Zealand	80.5	88.2	88.5	90.8			

附录 2-17 世界主要国家或地区货物进出口总额

Merchandise Imports and Exports by Country or Area

资料来源：世界贸易组织数据库。
Source: WTO Database.

单位：亿美元 (100 million USD)

国家或地区	Country or Area	2000	2005	2010	2015	2019	2020
世　界	**World**	**131015**	**212956**	**307421**	**332917**	**382988**	**353950**
中　国	China	4743	14219	29740	39530	45778	46469
中国香港	Hong Kong SAR, China	4167	5923	8421	10693	11127	11185
中国澳门	Macao SAR, China	52	70	65	119	128	129
孟加拉国	Bangladesh	153	232	470	744	984	860
文　莱	Brunei Darussalam	50	77	114	96	121	114
柬埔寨	Cambodia	33	70	119	218	351	362
印　度	India	939	2425	5766	6621	8104	6481
印度尼西亚	Indonesia	1090	1627	2934	2931	3390	3049
伊　朗	Iran	426	963	1667	1152	1075	930
以色列	Israel	691	877	1171	1261	1351	1195
日　本	Japan	8588	11108	14638	12730	14265	12759
哈萨克斯坦	Kazakhstan	139	452	911	765	951	837
韩　国	Korea, Rep.	3327	5457	8916	9633	10456	9801
老　挝	Lao PDR	9	14	38	93	121	113
马来西亚	Malaysia	1802	2560	3632	3759	4432	4240
蒙　古	Mongolia	12	22	62	85	137	129
缅　甸	Myanmar	40	57	134	283	367	347
巴基斯坦	Pakistan	199	414	592	663	737	678
菲律宾	Philippines	751	907	1100	1336	1883	1544
新加坡	Singapore	2723	4297	6627	6487	7500	6924
斯里兰卡	Sri Lanka	117	152	221	295	319	261
泰　国	Thailand	1309	2291	3762	4170	4825	4385
越　南	Viet Nam	301	692	1571	3277	5177	5454
埃　及	Egypt	199	354	794	849	999	868
尼日利亚	Nigeria	297	712	1282	949	1178	912
南　非	South Africa	597	1139	1882	1857	1976	1699
加拿大	Canada	5214	6829	7902	8402	9104	8044
墨西哥	Mexico	3458	4424	6085	7858	9280	8109
美　国	United States	20412	26338	32477	38179	42106	38392
阿根廷	Argentina	515	690	1250	1170	1142	972
巴　西	Brazil	1138	1962	3935	3702	4098	3762
委内瑞拉	Venezuela	497	797	1047	706	231	116
捷　克	Czech Rep.	611	1546	2596	2992	3782	3618
法　国	France	6666	9676	11348	10770	12256	10707
德　国	Germany	10490	17480	23137	23773	27234	25508
意大利	Italy	4793	7579	9344	8679	10127	9190
荷　兰	Netherlands	4514	7702	10907	10825	13443	12712
波　兰	Poland	808	1911	3378	3956	5319	5282
俄罗斯	Russia	1499	3692	6493	5344	6744	5715
西班牙	Spain	2714	4814	5814	5941	7068	6320
土耳其	Turkey	823	1903	2994	3646	3912	3889
乌克兰	Ukraine	285	704	1124	756	1107	1031
英　国	United Kingdom	6228	9154	10125	10959	11655	10380
澳大利亚	Australia	1354	2314	4143	3962	4926	4588
新西兰	New Zealand	272	479	620	709	819	761

附录 2-18　货物出口总额

Merchandise Export

资料来源：世界贸易组织数据库。
Source: WTO Database.

单位：亿美元 (100 million USD)

国家或地区	Country or Area	2000	2005	2010	2015	2019	2020
世　界	**World**	**64540**	**105103**	**153040**	**165581**	**190147**	**175829**
中　国	China	2492	7620	15778	22735	24995	25911
中国香港	Hong Kong SAR, China	2027	2921	4007	5105	5349	5488
中国澳门	Macao SAR, China	25	25	9	13	16	14
孟加拉国	Bangladesh	64	93	192	324	393	336
文　莱	Brunei Darussalam	39	62	89	64	70	65
柬埔寨	Cambodia	14	31	51	85	148	171
印　度	India	424	996	2264	2680	3243	2762
印度尼西亚	Indonesia	654	870	1578	1504	1677	1633
伊　朗	Iran	287	563	1013	703	657	542
以色列	Israel	314	428	584	641	585	496
日　本	Japan	4792	5949	7698	6249	7056	6414
哈萨克斯坦	Kazakhstan	88	278	600	460	573	464
韩　国	Korea, Rep.	1723	2844	4664	5268	5422	5125
老　挝	Lao PDR	3	6	17	37	58	61
马来西亚	Malaysia	982	1416	1986	2000	2382	2341
蒙　古	Mongolia	5	11	29	47	76	76
缅　甸	Myanmar	16	38	87	114	181	168
巴基斯坦	Pakistan	90	161	214	221	233	220
菲律宾	Philippines	381	413	515	588	709	638
新加坡	Singapore	1378	2296	3519	3516	3908	3625
斯里兰卡	Sri Lanka	54	63	86	105	119	101
泰　国	Thailand	690	1109	1933	2143	2463	2315
越　南	Viet Nam	145	324	722	1621	2643	2827
埃　及	Egypt	53	129	264	213	290	261
尼日利亚	Nigeria	210	505	840	502	625	345
南　非	South Africa	300	516	913	810	900	858
加拿大	Canada	2766	3605	3875	4101	4466	3907
墨西哥	Mexico	1664	2142	2983	3806	4607	4177
美　国	United States	7819	9011	12785	15026	16432	14316
阿根廷	Argentina	263	404	682	568	651	549
巴　西	Brazil	551	1185	2019	1911	2254	2099
委内瑞拉	Venezuela	335	557	657	373	172	50
捷　克	Czech Rep.	291	781	1330	1579	1991	1917
法　国	France	3276	4634	5238	5063	5710	4883
德　国	Germany	5518	9709	12589	13262	14894	13800
意大利	Italy	2405	3731	4473	4570	5377	4961
荷　兰	Netherlands	2331	4064	5743	5704	7086	6745
波　兰	Poland	317	894	1597	1991	2666	2711
俄罗斯	Russia	1050	2438	4006	3414	4199	3317
西班牙	Spain	1153	1926	2544	2823	3340	3070
土耳其	Turkey	278	735	1139	1510	1808	1695
乌克兰	Ukraine	146	342	515	381	501	492
英　国	United Kingdom	2832	3935	4202	4659	4697	4033
澳大利亚	Australia	639	1061	2126	1877	2710	2504
新西兰	New Zealand	133	217	314	344	395	389

附录 2-19 货币汇率(年平均价)

Exchange Rate (Period Average)

资料来源：世界银行WDI数据库。
Source: World Bank WDI Database.
单位：1美元合本币数 (local currency unit per US dollar)

国家或地区	Country or Area	2000	2005	2010	2015	2019	2020
中　国	**China**	**8.28**	**8.19**	**6.77**	**6.23**	**6.91**	**6.90**
中国香港	Hong Kong SAR, China	7.79	7.78	7.77	7.75	7.84	7.76
中国澳门	Macao SAR, China	8.03	8.01	8.00	7.98	8.07	7.99
孟加拉国	Bangladesh	52.14	64.33	69.65	77.95	84.45	84.87
文　莱	Brunei Darussalam	1.72	1.66	1.36	1.37	1.36	1.38
柬埔寨	Cambodia	3840.75	4092.50	4184.92	4067.75	4061.15	4092.78
印　度	India	44.94	44.10	45.73	64.15	70.42	74.10
印度尼西亚	Indonesia	8421.78	9704.74	9090.43	13389.41	14147.67	14582.20
伊　朗	Iran	1764.86	8963.96	10254.18	29011.49	42000.00	42000.00
以色列	Israel	4.08	4.49	3.74	3.89	3.56	3.44
日　本	Japan	107.77	110.22	87.78	121.04	109.01	106.77
哈萨克斯坦	Kazakhstan	142.13	132.88	147.36	221.73	382.75	412.95
韩　国	Korea, Rep.	1130.36	1024.33	1156.46	1130.95	1165.36	1180.27
老　挝	Lao PDR	7887.64	10655.17	8254.16	8127.61	8679.41	9045.79
马来西亚	Malaysia	3.80	3.79	3.22	3.91	4.14	4.20
蒙　古	Mongolia	1076.67	1205.25	1357.06	1970.31	2663.54	2813.29
缅　甸	Myanmar	6.52	5.82	5.63	1162.62	1518.26	1381.62
巴基斯坦	Pakistan	53.65	59.51	85.19	102.77	150.04	161.84
菲律宾	Philippines	44.19	55.09	45.11	45.50	51.80	49.62
新加坡	Singapore	1.72	1.66	1.36	1.37	1.36	1.38
斯里兰卡	Sri Lanka	77.01	100.50	113.06	135.86	178.74	185.59
泰　国	Thailand	40.11	40.22	31.69	34.25	31.05	31.29
越　南	Viet Nam	14167.75	15858.92	18612.92	21697.57	23050.24	23208.37
埃　及	Egypt	3.47	5.78	5.62	7.69	16.77	15.76
尼日利亚	Nigeria	101.70	131.27	150.30	192.44	306.92	358.81
南　非	South Africa	6.94	6.36	7.32	12.76	14.45	16.46
加拿大	Canada	1.49	1.21	1.03	1.28	1.33	1.34
墨西哥	Mexico	9.46	10.90	12.64	15.85	19.26	21.49
美　国	United States	1.00	1.00	1.00	1.00	1.00	1.00
阿根廷	Argentina	1.00	2.90	3.90	9.23	48.15	70.54
巴　西	Brazil	1.83	2.43	1.76	3.33	3.94	5.16
委内瑞拉	Venezuela	0.68	2.09	2.58	6.28		
捷　克	Czech Rep.	38.60	23.96	19.10	24.60	22.93	23.21
法　国	France	1.09	0.80	0.75	0.90	0.89	0.88
德　国	Germany	1.09	0.80	0.75	0.90	0.89	0.88
意大利	Italy	1.09	0.80	0.75	0.90	0.89	0.88
荷　兰	Netherlands	1.09	0.80	0.75	0.90	0.89	0.88
波　兰	Poland	4.35	3.24	3.02	3.77	3.84	3.90
俄罗斯	Russia	28.13	28.28	30.37	60.94	64.74	72.10
西班牙	Spain	1.09	0.80	0.75	0.90	0.89	0.88
土耳其	Turkey	0.63	1.34	1.50	2.72	5.67	7.01
乌克兰	Ukraine	5.44	5.12	7.94	21.84	25.85	26.96
英　国	United Kingdom	0.66	0.55	0.65	0.65	0.78	0.78
澳大利亚	Australia	1.72	1.31	1.09	1.33	1.44	1.45
新西兰	New Zealand	2.20	1.42	1.39	1.43	1.52	1.54

附录 2-20 外商直接投资

Foreign Direct Investment

资料来源：联合国贸发会议FDI数据库。
Source: UNCTAD FDI Database .
单位：亿美元 (100 million USD)

国家或地区	Country or Area	外商直接投资 FDI Inflows			对外直接投资 FDI Outflows		
		2000	2010	2020	2000	2010	2020
世 界	**World**	**13566.5**	**13937.3**	**9988.9**	**11624.9**	**13921.8**	**7398.7**
中 国	China	407.1	1147.3	1493.4	9.2	688.1	1329.4
中国香港	Hong Kong SAR, China	545.8	705.4	1192.3	540.8	862.5	1022.2
中国澳门	Macao SAR, China	0.0	28.3	35.1		-4.4	5.1
孟加拉国	Bangladesh	5.8	9.1	25.6		0.2	0.1
文 莱	Brunei Darussalam	5.5	4.8	5.8			
柬 埔 寨	Cambodia	1.5	14.0	36.2	0.1	0.2	1.3
印 度	India	35.9	274.2	640.6	5.1	159.5	115.6
印度尼西亚	Indonesia		137.7	185.8		26.6	44.7
伊 朗	Iran	1.9	36.5	13.4	0.1	2.4	0.8
以 色 列	Israel	69.6	69.8	247.6	33.4	80.0	58.6
日 本	Japan	83.2	-12.5	102.5	315.6	562.6	1157.0
哈萨克斯坦	Kazakhstan	12.8	115.5	38.8	0.0	78.9	-20.3
韩 国	Korea, Rep.	115.1	95.0	92.2	48.4	282.2	324.8
老 挝	Lao PDR	0.3	2.8	9.7	0.1	0.3	
马来西亚	Malaysia	37.9	90.6	34.8	20.3	134.0	28.3
蒙 古	Mongolia	0.5	16.9	17.2		0.6	0.3
缅 甸	Myanmar	0.9	66.7	18.3			
巴基斯坦	Pakistan	3.1	20.2	21.1	0.1	0.5	0.3
菲 律 宾	Philippines	22.4	13.0	65.4	1.3	29.4	35.3
新 加 坡	Singapore	147.5	574.6	905.6	68.5	354.1	323.8
斯里兰卡	Sri Lanka	1.8	4.8	4.3	0.0	0.4	0.1
泰 国	Thailand	34.1	145.5	-61.0	-0.2	79.4	167.2
越 南	Viet Nam	12.9	80.0	158.0		9.0	3.8
埃 及	Egypt	12.4	63.9	58.5	0.5	11.8	3.3
尼日利亚	Nigeria	13.1	61.0	23.9	1.7	9.2	-3.4
南 非	South Africa	8.9	36.4	31.1	2.7	-0.8	-19.7
加 拿 大	Canada	668.0	284.0	238.2	446.8	347.2	486.6
墨 西 哥	Mexico	182.5	271.4	290.8		145.6	65.3
美 国	United States	3140.1	1980.5	1563.2	1426.3	2777.8	928.1
阿 根 廷	Argentina	104.2	113.3	41.2	9.0	9.6	12.3
巴 西	Brazil	327.8	776.9	247.8	22.8	220.6	-258.1
委内瑞拉	Venezuela	47.0	15.7	9.6	5.2	24.9	-0.8
捷 克	Czech Rep.	49.9	61.4	62.9	0.4	11.7	31.4
法 国	France	275.0	138.9	179.3	1619.5	481.5	442.0
德 国	Germany	1982.8	656.4	356.5	570.9	1254.5	349.5
意 大 利	Italy	133.7	91.8	-3.9	66.9	326.9	103.6
荷 兰	Netherlands	638.5	-71.8	-1153.0			
波 兰	Poland	94.5	128.0	100.8	0.2	61.5	18.2
俄 罗 斯	Russia	26.5	316.7	96.8	31.5	411.2	63.1
西 班 牙	Spain	395.8	398.7	89.3	582.1	378.4	214.2
土 耳 其	Turkey	9.8	90.9	78.8	8.7	14.7	32.4
乌 克 兰	Ukraine	6.0	65.0	-8.7	0.0	7.4	0.8
英 国	United Kingdom	1153.0	582.0	197.2	2327.4	480.9	-334.1
澳大利亚	Australia	141.9	368.0	201.5	28.6	198.0	91.7
新 西 兰	New Zealand	13.5	-0.6	42.2	6.1	7.2	8.8

附录 2-21 外汇储备与黄金储备

Foreign Exchange and Gold Reserves

资料来源：国际货币基金组织IFS数据库。
Source: IMF IFS Database.

国家或地区	Country or Area	外汇储备（亿美元）Foreign Exchange (100 million USD)			黄金储备（万盎司）Gold Reserves(10000 fine troy ounces)		
		2000	2010	2020	2000	2010	2020
中　国	**China**	**1655.7**	**28473.4**	**32165.2**	**1270.0**	**3389.0**	**6264.0**
中国香港	**Hong Kong SAR, China**	**1075.4**	**2686.5**	**4916.3**	**6.7**	**6.7**	**6.7**
中国澳门	**Macao SAR, China**	**33.2**	**237.3**	**251.4**			
孟加拉国	Bangladesh	14.9	99.0	410.4	10.9	43.4	44.9
文　莱	Brunei Darussalam	3.6	12.1	33.6			14.6
柬埔寨	Cambodia	5.0	31.5	184.0	40.0	40.0	146.2
印　度	India	372.6	2678.1	5421.6	1150.2	1793.2	2175.5
印度尼西亚	Indonesia	282.8	899.7	1284.0	310.1	235.0	252.6
以色列	Israel	231.6	692.7	1712.4			
日　本	Japan	3472.1	10362.6	13127.9	2454.7	2460.2	2460.2
哈萨克斯坦	Kazakhstan	15.9	246.9	112.6	184.0	216.4	1247.0
韩　国	Korea, Rep.	958.6	2869.3	4301.2	43.9	46.4	335.8
老　挝	Lao PDR	1.4	7.3	13.2	1.7	28.5	
马来西亚	Malaysia	274.3	1023.2	1026.4	117.0	117.0	125.0
蒙　古	Mongolia	1.8	21.2	40.0	8.5	6.5	26.2
缅　甸	Myanmar	2.2	57.1	72.2	23.1	23.4	23.4
巴基斯坦	Pakistan	15.0	131.2	144.9	209.1	207.0	207.8
菲律宾	Philippines	129.7	539.9	964.7	722.8	495.4	607.0
新加坡	Singapore	795.1	2236.8	3593.4	409.6	409.6	409.6
斯里兰卡	Sri Lanka	9.8	66.3	51.9	33.6	34.6	21.5
泰　国	Thailand	319.3	1656.6	2460.3	236.7	320.0	495.0
越　南	Viet Nam	34.2	120.5	944.4			
埃　及	Egypt	129.1	323.5	334.2	243.2	243.1	257.9
尼日利亚	Nigeria	99.1	323.4	343.6	68.7	68.7	
南　非	South Africa	57.9	354.2	442.7	590.0	401.6	403.0
加拿大	Canada	290.2	448.9	768.2	118.4	10.9	
墨西哥	Mexico	351.4	1148.8	1841.8	24.9	22.7	386.0
美　国	United States	312.4	520.8	445.4	26161.1	26149.9	26149.9
阿根廷	Argentina	244.1	466.2	339.1	1.9	176.0	198.5
巴　西	Brazil	324.3	2805.7	3427.1	211.8	108.0	216.6
委内瑞拉	Venezuela	126.3	91.9		1024.0	1176.0	
捷　克	Czech Rep.	130.2	403.4	1641.3	44.6	40.8	30.5
法　国	France	321.1	362.1	551.6	9724.5	7830.1	7832.6
德　国	Germany	496.7	373.6	368.9	11151.9	10934.4	10810.6
意大利	Italy	224.2	356.8	465.9	7882.9	7882.9	7882.9
荷　兰	Netherlands	70.0	89.0	59.1	2931.5	1969.1	1969.1
波　兰	Poland	263.2	863.2	1385.1	330.6	330.9	735.2
俄罗斯	Russia	242.6	4329.5	4444.9	1235.9	2535.5	7390.0
西班牙	Spain	295.2	133.1	567.3	1682.9	905.4	905.3
土耳其	Turkey	223.1	790.5	483.9	373.9	373.3	2303.1
乌克兰	Ukraine	11.0	333.2	275.4	45.4	88.5	84.0
英　国	United Kingdom	341.6	493.3	1396.0	1567.3	997.5	997.6
澳大利亚	Australia	167.8	327.9	326.0	256.3	256.7	179.4
新西兰	New Zealand	36.2	151.3	120.1			

附录 2-22 研究与开发经费支出和公共教育经费支出占国内生产总值比重

Research and Development Expenditure and Public Spending on Education as Percentage of GDP

资料来源：世界银行WDI数据库。
Source: World Bank WDI Database.

单位：% (%)

国家或地区	Country or Area	研究与开发经费支出占国内生产总值比重 Research and Development Expenditure as of GDP			公共教育经费支出占国内生产总值比重 Public Spending on Education, Total as of GDP		
		2000	2010	2018	2000	2010	2018
世　界	**World**	**2.1**	**2.0**	**2.2**	**3.9**	**4.5**	**3.7**
高收入国家	**High Income**	**2.3**	**2.4**	**2.6**	**4.8**	**5.4**	**4.9②**
中等收入国家	**Middle Income**	**0.6**	**1.1**	**1.5**	**3.6**	**3.9**	**3.9**
中　国	China	0.9	1.7	2.1		3.8	
中国香港	Hong Kong SAR, Chi	0.5	0.7	0.9		3.5	3.8
中国澳门	Macao SAR, China		0.1	0.2	3.3	2.6	3.1
孟加拉国	Bangladesh				2.1	1.9①	1.3
文　莱	Brunei Darussalam			0.3	3.7	2.0	4.4④
柬埔寨	Cambodia			0.1③	1.7	1.5	2.2⑥
印　度	India	0.8	0.8	0.7	4.3	3.4	
印度尼西亚	Indonesia	0.1	0.1①	0.2		2.8	2.8
伊　朗	Iran		0.3	0.8②	4.0	3.7	3.7
以色列	Israel	3.9	3.9	4.9	6.1	5.5	6.1②
日　本	Japan	2.9	3.1	3.3			3.2②
哈萨克斯坦	Kazakhstan	0.2	0.2	0.1	3.3	3.5	2.9
韩　国	Korea, Rep.	2.1	3.3	4.5		4.7①	4.3④
老　挝	Lao PDR				1.5	1.7	
马来西亚	Malaysia	0.5	1.0	1.0	6.0	5.0	4.2
蒙　古	Mongolia	0.2	0.2	0.1	5.6	4.6	4.9
缅　甸	Myanmar	0.1		0.0②		0.9	2.0
巴基斯坦	Pakistan	0.1	0.4①	0.2②	1.8	2.3	2.5
菲律宾	Philippines		0.1①	0.2③	3.2	2.3	3.2
新加坡	Singapore	1.8	1.9	1.9②	3.3	3.1	2.6
斯里兰卡	Sri Lanka	0.1	0.1	0.1③		1.7	2.1⑥
泰　国	Thailand	0.2	0.2①	1.0②	5.3	3.5	3.0
越　南	Viet Nam			0.5②		5.1	4.1
埃　及	Egypt	0.2	0.4	0.7		3.5	
尼日利亚	Nigeria						
南　非	South Africa		0.7	0.8②	5.4	5.7	6.5
加拿大	Canada	1.9	1.8	1.6	5.4	5.4	1.5
墨西哥	Mexico	0.3	0.5	0.3	4.0	5.2	4.5②
美　国	United States	2.6	2.7	2.8		5.4①	
阿根廷	Argentina	0.4	0.6	0.5	4.6	5.0	4.8
巴　西	Brazil	1.0	1.2	1.2	3.9	5.6	6.3②
委内瑞拉	Venezuela		0.2	0.1④		6.9①	
捷　克	Czech Rep.	1.1	1.3	1.9	3.6	4.0	3.9②
法　国	France	2.1	2.2	2.2		5.7①	5.5②
德　国	Germany	2.4	2.7	3.1		4.9	4.9②
意大利	Italy	1.0	1.2	1.4	4.3	4.3	4.0②
荷　兰	Netherlands	1.8	1.7	2.2	4.6	5.5	5.2②
波　兰	Poland	0.6	0.7	1.2	5.0	5.1	4.6②
俄罗斯	Russia	1.0	1.1	1.0	2.9	4.1⑤	4.7②
西班牙	Spain	0.9	1.4	1.2	4.2	4.9	4.2②
土耳其	Turkey	0.5	0.8	1.0②	2.5		
乌克兰	Ukraine	1.0	0.8	0.5	4.2	7.4	5.4
英　国	United Kingdom	1.6	1.6	1.7	4.0	5.7	5.4②
澳大利亚	Australia	1.6	2.4	1.9②	4.9	5.6	5.1②
新西兰	New Zealand		1.3①	1.4②		7.0	6.3②

注：①2009年数据。②2017年数据。③2015年数据。④2016年数据。⑤2008年数据。⑥2018年数据。
Note:①Data refer to 2009.②Data refer to 2017.③Data refer to 2015.④Data refer to 2016.⑤Data refer to 2008.⑥Data refer to 2018.

附录 2-23 医疗支出占国内生产总值比重及人均医疗支出

Health Expenditure as Percentage of GDP and Health Expenditure per Capita

资料来源：世界银行WDI数据库。
Source: World Bank WDI Database.

国家或地区	Country or Area	医疗支出占国内生产总值的比重(%) Health Expenditure, Total as Percentage of GDP(%)			人均医疗支出(美元) Health Expenditure per Capita(USD)		
		2000	2010	2018	2000	2010	2018
世　界	**World**	**8.7**	**9.6**	**9.9**	**479.8**	**914.2**	**1111.1**
高收入国家	**High Income**	**9.5**	**11.6**	**12.5**	**2463.4**	**4648.0**	**5665.2**
中等收入国家	**Middle Income**	**5.1**	**5.0**	**5.4**	**63.9**	**192.7**	**286.1**
低收入国家	**Low Income**	**4.1**	**6.0**	**5.2**	**15.2**	**38.1**	**34.6**
中　国	China	4.5	4.2	5.4	42.1	186.5	501.1
孟加拉国	Bangladesh	2.0	2.5	2.3	8.6	20.8	41.9
文　莱	Brunei Darussalam	2.5	2.3	2.4	508.5	803.5	763.2
柬埔寨	Cambodia	6.5	6.9	6.0	19.7	54.3	90.6
印　度	India	4.0	3.3	3.5	18.5	45.1	72.8
印度尼西亚	Indonesia	1.9	3.0	2.9	16.2	92.5	111.7
伊　朗	Iran	4.7	6.8	8.7	80.9	445.7	484.3
以色列	Israel	6.8	7.0	7.5	1513.9	2234.9	3323.7
日　本	Japan	7.2	9.2	11.0	2740.7	4060.5	4266.6
哈萨克斯坦	Kazakhstan	4.2	2.7	2.9	51.0	249.3	275.9
韩　国	Korea, Rep.	3.9	5.9	7.6	474.0	1366.4	2542.8
老　挝	Lao PDR	4.3	2.9	2.2	14.4	35.0	57.1
马来西亚	Malaysia	2.5	3.2	3.8	111.3	292.0	427.2
蒙　古	Mongolia	4.9	3.7	3.8	27.0	98.8	155.1
缅　甸	Myanmar	1.7	1.9	4.8	4.3	19.6	59.2
巴基斯坦	Pakistan	2.9	2.6	3.2	15.6	25.3	42.9
菲律宾	Philippines	3.2	4.3	4.4	32.8	91.6	136.5
新加坡	Singapore	3.3	3.2	4.5	797.3	1496.8	2823.6
斯里兰卡	Sri Lanka	4.2	3.9	3.8	43.7	108.3	157.5
泰　国	Thailand	3.1	3.4	3.8	62.3	172.1	275.9
越　南	Viet Nam	4.8	6.0	5.9	18.9	78.6	151.7
埃　及	Egypt	4.9	4.2	4.9	73.7	113.2	125.5
尼日利亚	Nigeria	3.2	3.3	3.9	17.7	76.8	83.8
南　非	South Africa	7.4	7.4	8.3	225.5	543.4	526.0
加拿大	Canada	8.3	10.7	10.8	2007.9	5048.3	4994.9
墨西哥	Mexico	4.4	6.0	5.4	318.5	554.0	519.6
美　国	United States	12.5	16.3	16.9	4564.5	7930.2	10623.8
阿根廷	Argentina	8.5	9.4	9.6	708.8	985.0	1127.9
巴　西	Brazil	8.3	7.9	9.5	312.5	896.7	848.4
委内瑞拉	Venezuela	7.3	6.8	3.6	355.1	945.9	256.9
捷　克	Czech Rep.	5.7	6.9	7.6	342.9	1373.9	1765.6
法　国	France	9.6	11.2	11.3	2161.9	4598.3	4690.1
德　国	Germany	9.9	11.1	11.4	2344.4	4611.8	5472.2
意大利	Italy	7.6	8.9	8.7	1524.2	3217.7	2989.0
荷　兰	Netherlands	7.7	10.2	10.0	2028.2	5191.7	5306.5
波　兰	Poland	5.3	6.4	6.3	238.0	809.2	978.7
俄罗斯	Russia	5.0	5.0	5.3	95.4	566.1	609.0
西班牙	Spain	6.8	9.1	9.0	1005.3	2789.5	2736.3
土耳其	Turkey	4.6	5.0	4.1	199.5	539.3	389.9
乌克兰	Ukraine	5.3	6.8	7.7	35.1	202.3	228.4
英　国	United Kingdom	7.3	10.0	10.0	2054.2	3955.5	4315.4
澳大利亚	Australia	7.6	8.4	9.3	1638.8	4945.0	5425.3
新西兰	New Zealand	7.5	9.6	9.2	1053.9	3216.2	4037.5

附录3

统计公报和统计工作

Shandong Statistics Communique
and Shandong Statistical Undertaking

简 要 说 明

一、本篇资料的主要内容

本篇主要包括统计公报、统计工作综述和山东省统计局工作大事记。统计公报和统计工作综述综合反映全省经济社会发展概况和山东省统计工作情况；山东省统计局工作大事记按时间顺序记载了2021年山东省统计局发生的大事要事，包括局领导重要活动、方法制度改革、统计法制建设、统计基层基础建设、统计信息化建设、统计干部队伍建设等方面的内容。

二、本篇资料的来源

本篇资料由省统计局办公室和综合处整理提供。

Brief Introduction

I. Content

This chapter contains Bureau of Statistics Shandong Statistics Communique, Summary of Shandong Statistical Undertaking and Events of Shandong Provincial. Bureau of Statistics Shandong Statistics Communique and Summary of Shandong Statistical Undertaking comprehensively reflect the development of society and economy and show the achievements in statistics of Shandong Province. Events happened in 2021 of Shandong Statistical Bureau are recorded in time order, mainly including important activities of leaders, reform of statistical laws, development of primary-level statistical work, construction of information system, and training of statistics professionals, etc.

II. Source of Data

Data and files are provided by the Administrative Office and the Division of Comprehensive Statistics of Shandong Provincial Bureau of statistics.

2021 年山东省
国民经济和社会发展统计公报

山 东 省 统 计 局
国家统计局山东调查总队

2021 年，是中国共产党成立 100 周年，是全面迈入社会主义现代化新征程起步之年和“十四五”开局之年。全省上下坚持以习近平新时代中国特色社会主义思想为指导，深入落实习近平总书记对山东工作的重要指示要求，锚定“走在前列、全面开创”“三个走在前”总遵循、总定位、总航标，立足新发展阶段，完整、准确、全面贯彻新发展理念，主动服务和融入新发展格局，落实“六个一”发展思路、“六个更加注重”策略方法、“十二个着力”重点任务，更大力度统筹疫情防控和经济社会发展，更实举措做好“六稳”“六保”工作，全省经济稳中向好、进中提质，高质量发展步伐坚实有力，实现“十四五”良好开局。

一、综合

经济运行稳中向好。初步核算，全省实现生产总值 83095.9 亿元，按可比价格计算，比上年增长 8.3%。分产业看，第一产业增加值 6029.0 亿元，增长 7.5%；第二产业增加值 33187.2 亿元，增长 7.2%；第三产业增加值 43879.7 亿元，增长 9.2%。三次产业结构由上年的 7.4∶39.1∶53.5 调整为 7.3∶39.9∶52.8。

就业形势好于预期。城镇新增就业 124.2 万人，比上年增长 1.3%，完成年度目标的 112.9%。其中，失业人员再就业 45.1 万人，困难群体再就业 8.9 万人。城镇登记失业率 2.94%，比上年降低 0.16 个百分点。

物价水平温和可控。居民消费价格比上年上涨 1.2%。其中，消费品价格上涨 1.4%，服务项目价格上涨 1.0%；食品价格与上年持平，非食品价格上涨 1.5%。农产品生产者价格上涨 4.2%。工业生产者出厂价格上涨 10.3%，购进价格上涨 9.5%。

表 1　2021 年居民消费价格指数（以上年为 100）

指　标	全 省	城 市	农 村
居民消费价格指数	101.2	101.3	101.0
食品烟酒	100.9	101.1	100.1
粮食	101.1	101.8	99.8
鲜菜	109.0	107.8	112.9
猪肉	68.2	67.5	69.9
鸡蛋	116.5	114.7	120.7
鲜果	105.5	105.4	106.0
衣着	100.1	100.2	99.7
居住	101.1	101.0	101.6
生活用品及服务	99.8	99.8	100.0
交通通信	104.5	104.7	104.0
教育文化娱乐	101.3	101.3	101.1
健身活动	100.5	100.5	100.3
旅游	100.0	99.7	102.6
医疗保健	100.1	100.1	100.1
其他用品及服务	98.5	98.5	98.4
养老服务	101.0	100.7	102.0

人口总量平稳增长。年末常住人口 10169.99 万人。其中，0-14 岁人口占 18.42%，15-64 岁人口占 65.66%，65 岁及以上人口占 15.92%。常住人口城镇化率为 63.94%，比上年末提高 0.89 个百分点。全年出生人口 75.04 万人，出生率 7.38‰；死亡人口 74.83 万人，死亡率 7.36‰；人口自然增长率 0.02‰。

“六稳”“六保”落地见效。坚持精准高效调控经济运行，统筹推进实时监测报告、定期分析研判、政策集成供给、“四进”督导落实等系列工作举措，有效稳定市场预期，经济持续恢复发展。全面落实减税降费政策，新增减税降费超过 700 亿元。能源供给充足，原煤产量 9312.0 万吨；供应天然气 231.7 亿立方米，比上年增长 4.6%；净接纳省外电量 1187.4 亿千瓦时，增长 2.5%。产业链供应链保持稳定，行业增长面拓宽，规模以上工业 34 个大类行业增加值实现增长，增长面达 82.9%，比上年扩大 9.7 个百分点。基层运转保障有力，全年分配落实常态化直达资金 1630 亿元，支持实施 2.2 万个项目，超过 1 亿人次和 5 万户企业受益。

二、重点战略

动能转换加速突破。坚决淘汰落后产能，压减焦化产能 180 万吨，整合转移地炼产能 780 万吨。坚决改造提升传统动能，实施 500 万元以上工业技改投资项目 1.2 万个。裕龙岛炼化一体化等重大项目加快推进，万华百万吨乙烯项目达产。坚决培育壮大新动能，“四新”经济增加值占比为 31.7%，“四新”经济投资占比超过一半，达到 51.2%。高新技术企业总数突破 2 万家，比上年增长 38.2%，创历史新高。高新技术产业产值占规模以上工业产值的比重为 46.8%，比上年提高 1.7 个百分点。“十强”产业中，新一代信息技术、新能源新材料、高端装备产业增加值分别增长 17.1%、32.2%和 17.5%。光电子器件、半导体分立器件、集成电路、工业机器人等高端智能产品产量分别增长 73.1%、34.6%、65.2%和 38.7%。软件业务收入 7970.4 亿元，增长 29.3%。

乡村振兴有序推进。脱贫攻坚战取得全面胜利，新识别认定监测帮扶对象 1.56 万人，累计纳入 5.17 万人，全部落实针对性帮扶措施。产业集聚发展加快，累计创建国家级优势特色产业集群 4 个，现代农业产业园 11 个，特色农产品优势区 17 个，绿色发展先行区 2 个，农业产业强镇 78 个。农业经营主体培育壮大，累计培育家庭农场 10.4 万家，农民专业合作社 24.5 万户，农业产业化省级以上重点龙头企业 1133 家。休闲农业健康发展，累计创建中国美丽休闲乡村 63 个，全国休闲农业重点县 2 个。农村人居环境持续优化，排查农房 2345.9 万户，动态开展危房改造 1.7 万户，新增清洁取暖 208.4 万户，完成改厕 4.3 万户。

海洋强省建设扎实有力。海洋经济高质量发展，建成海水淡化工程 41 个，日产能达 45.1 万吨；新增国家级海洋牧场示范区 5 处，累计达到 59 处，占全国的 39.3%。沿海港口全年完成货物吞吐量 17.8 亿吨，集装箱吞吐量 3446 万标准箱，比上年分别增长 5.5%和 8.0%；集装箱航线、外贸航线总量分别达到 313 条和 221 条，航线数量和密度均居我国北方港口首位。海洋科技创新加速起势，累计建成全省技术协同创新中心 124 家，现代产业技术创新中心 156 家。省部共建国家海洋综合试验场（威海）挂牌运行，国家深海基因库、国家深海大数据中心、国家深海标本样品馆、中国海洋工程研究院落户青岛。海洋生态环境持续改善，积极处置各类生态自然灾害，打捞清理浒苔 181.4 万吨，治理互花米草面积 7600 公顷。

“两新一重”建设加力提速。大数据、工业互联网等新型基础设施建设扎实推进，建成并开通 5G 基站 10.1 万个，建设省级工业互联网平台 115 个，“上云用云”企业超过 35 万家。新型城镇化建设有序开展，紧扣智慧化、绿色化、均衡化、双向化，谋划布局 637 个新型城镇化重大工程、重大项目，高质量推进国家和省级城乡融合发展试验区建设。重大工程加速竣工，建成通车鲁南高铁曲阜至菏泽段、菏泽至兰考段（山东段）2 条高铁，改扩建京台高速德州至齐河（鲁冀界）段等 4 条高速公路，高铁、高速公路通车里程分别达到 2319 公里和 7477 公里。青岛港董家口港区液体化工码头等 6 个泊位竣工验收，万吨级以上深水泊位累计达到 358 个。

对外开放新高地加快形成。聚焦制度创新和特色产业发展，自贸实验区对标 CPTPP，加快建设联动创新区，形成 189 项制度创新成果，3 个片区特色产业培育成效明显。举办第二届跨国公司领导人青岛峰会、山东与世界 500 强连线等活动，签约重点外资项目 311 个，投资总额 351.2 亿美元。认定 5 家省级跨境电商平台、10 家产业园、20 家公共海外仓，全省跨境电商进出口、市场采购贸易出口“双过千亿元”。

绿色发展蹄疾步稳。可再生能源发电装机容量 5849.2 万千瓦，占电力装机容量的 33.7%，比上年提高 5.1 个百分点；光伏、生物质发电装机容量居全国首位。细颗粒物（$PM_{2.5}$）平均浓度 39μg/m^3，比上年改善 15.2%；环境空气质量综合指数 4.38，比上年改善 10.1%；优良天数平均比例 71.1%，比上年改善 2.3 个百分点；重污染天数平均 3.6 天，比上年改善六成。国控地表水考核断面（按153个计算）优良水体比例达到75.2%，比上年改善13.1个百分点，提升比例全国最高；近岸海域水质优良面积比例92.3%，比上年改善0.8个百分点。省控以上48条入海河流全部达到或优于四类。

区域发展更加协调。加快“一群两心三圈”建设，全力推动区域协调发展。省会、胶东、鲁南经济圈一体化稳步推进，三大经济圈分别实现生产总值31074.6亿元、35534.7亿元和16463.7亿元，按可比价格计算，比上年分别增长7.8%、8.3%和8.6%，对全省经济增长的贡献率分别为36.0%、43.2%和20.8%。济南、青岛合计实现生产总值25568.7亿元，增长7.8%，占全省生产总值的比重为30.8%，对全省经济增长的贡献率为29.5%。

三、改革与创新

重点领域改革纵深推进。国企改革三年行动扎实推进，三年整体任务完成占比超90%，省属企业通过混改引入社会资本289亿元，省属控股上市公司45家，资产证券化率超60%。农村改革稳步推进，全省流转承包地面积超过4400万亩，占家庭承包经营耕地面积的46%；农村集体产权制度改革成果巩固提升，8.6万个村集体经济组织与村党组织、村民委员会同步换届，累计发放农村集体资产股权质押贷款超过9亿元。医药卫生体制改革不断深化，常态化、制度化推进药品和医用耗材集中带量采购，大幅减轻群众就医用药负担。山东省第二批（鲁晋联盟）药品省级集采和第二批（鲁晋冀豫）医用耗材省级集采分别平均降价45.8%和70.8%，已累计为全省节约医药费134.7亿元。深入推进医保支付方式改革，在全国率先实现按疾病诊断相关分组（DRG）付费和按病种分值付费（DIP）改革区域全覆盖。扎实推进预算管理改革，出台深化预算管理制度改革实施方案，全面推行综合预算、零基预算、刚性预算、绩效预算、透明预算、可持续预算“六个预算”改革。

营商环境持续优化。实施优化营商环境创新突破行动，推动企业全生命周期服务集成改革，营商环境建设整体水平位列全国第一方阵。大力推进“双全双百”工程，创新推出70项“一链办理”主题集成服务，办事环节、申请材料、办理时限较之前均压减70%以上。全省依申请政务服务事项可网办率达90%以上，2767个事项实现全程无人工干预“秒批秒办”。开展电子证照应用专项行动，超过300类电子证照实现“亮证即用”。迭代升级“爱山东”APP，接入服务事项超过2万项，注册用户突破7000万。市场活力不断释放，年末实有各类市场主体1328.0万户，比上年增长12.0%。实有民营经济市场主体数量增长12.1%。新登记市场主体235.6万户，增长6.4%。

质量强省建设成效明显。年末有效注册商标205.7万件，比上年末增长27.8%。其中，驰名商标804件，地理标志商标850件。马德里国际注册商标9610件，增长3.8%。地理标志保护产品81个，中欧地理标志协定互认清单产品17个。年末累计批准创建山东省优质产品基地51个。44个品牌入围2021年“中国500最具价值品牌”榜单。评选制造业高端品牌培育企业290家、服务业高端品牌培育企业100家。开展重点领域标准建设，累计发布现行有效地方标准3432项，建设开展国家级、省级标准化试点示范项目577个和1460个。

创新动力显著增强。知识产权创造能力稳步提升，发明专利授权36345件，比上年增长35.9%；PCT国际专利申请量3244件。年末有效发明专利拥有量150776件，增长21.1%，每万人口有效发明专利量14.85件，增加2.45件。科技平台建设加快推进，建设6家山东省实验室，省级“政产学研金服用”创新创业共同体发展到31家；院士工作站数量达到444家。企业创新活力不断迸发，入库科技型中小企业2.9万家，居全国第3位。人才队伍不断壮大，享受国务院政府特殊津贴专家3510人、齐鲁首席技师1806人、高技能人才340万人、获得“山东惠才卡”人选7243人。

表2　2021年主要人才培养平台数量

指　　标	数量（个）
博士后科研工作站	351
博士后创新实践基地	366
国家级高技能人才培训基地	43
国家技能大师工作室	49
省级人力资源服务产业园	21
世界技能大赛省级集训基地	49
齐鲁技能大师特色工作站	120

四、农业

农业发展稳中有增。农林牧渔业产值 11468.0 亿元，按可比价格计算，比上年增长 8.6%。粮食再获丰收，粮食总产量 1100.1 亿斤，增加 10.8 亿斤，连续 8 年过千亿斤。

表 3　2021 年农林牧渔业产值及增长速度

指　标	产　值（亿元）	比上年增　长（%）
农林牧渔业	11468.0	8.6
农业	5814.6	4.3
林业	219.9	1.7
牧业	2904.2	21.1
渔业	1652.6	5.9
农林牧渔专业及辅助性活动	876.7	8.2

表 4　2021 年主要农产品产量及增长速度

指　标	产　量（万吨）	比上年增长（%）
粮食	5500.7	1.0
夏粮	2637.2	2.6
秋粮	2863.5	-0.5
棉花	14.0	-23.5
油料	285.9	-1.7
蔬菜及食用菌	8801.1	4.3
水果	3032.6	3.2
园林水果	1913.9	4.6

林牧渔业平稳发展。林地及非林地林木覆盖资源合计 400.2 万公顷，森林资源合计 330.1 万公顷，森林覆盖率 20.9%。猪牛羊禽肉产量 815.1 万吨，比上年增长 12.9%；禽蛋产量（不含小品种）455.4 万吨，下降 5.3%；牛奶产量 288.3 万吨，增长 19.4%。水产品总产量（不含远洋渔业产量）820.7 万吨，增长 3.9%。其中，海水产品产量 706.6 万吨，增长 4.0%；淡水产品产量 114.1 万吨，增长 3.3%。年末专业远洋渔船 563 艘。

现代农业发展基础稳固。引黄灌区农业节水工程稳步推进，累计完成投资 213 亿元，整治渠系 1.3 万公里，配套完善建筑物 1.6 万座、计量设施 2.6 万座，新增高效节水灌溉面积 390 万亩。高标准创建首批国家级水产健康养殖和生态养殖示范区 4 个。深入实施水产绿色健康养殖“五大行动”，重点培树 67 个骨干基地。农作物耕种收综合机械化率达到 89.7%，主要农作物良种覆盖率达到 100%，畜禽粪污综合利用率稳定在 90% 以上。

五、工业和建筑业

工业发展加速提质。全部工业增加值 27243.6 亿元，比上年增长 8.6%。规模以上工业增加值增长 9.6%，其中，装备制造业增加值增长 10.5%；高技术制造业增加值增长 18.5%，高于规模以上工业 8.9 个百分点。规模以上工业营业收入增长 18.0%，利润总额增长 20.9%。营业收入利润率为 5.2%，比上年提高 0.1 个百分点。全省重点调度的 120 种重点产品中，78 种产品产量比上年增长，增长面为 65.0%，比上年扩大 12.5 个百分点。民营工业企业发展活力不断增强，民营工业实现增加值比上年增长 11.3%，高于规模以上工业 1.7 个百分点。

表 5　2021 年规模以上工业主要产品产量及增长速度

指　标	单位	产量	比上年增长（%）
原煤	万吨	9312.0	-16.0
焦炭	万吨	3186.8	-11.0
天然气	亿立方米	6.2	7.8
原油	万吨	2227.7	-0.4
机制纸及纸板	万吨	2473.9	5.8
水泥	万吨	16444.7	4.0
平板玻璃	万重量箱	9074.9	13.3
光缆	万芯千米	1157.8	48.3
钢材	万吨	10667.6	-7.2
原铝	万吨	789.9	-2.0
锂离子电池	万只	26633.8	50.1
汽车	万辆	107.3	-8.5
工业机器人	套	9345.0	38.7
家用电冰箱	万台	888.8	6.8
家用洗衣机	万台	734.8	11.0
彩色电视机	万台	1986.7	11.9
电子计算机整机	万台	119.6	-18.1

建筑业实力增强。建筑业总产值 16412.0 亿元，比上年增长 9.8%。具有总承包或专业承包资质的有工作量建筑业企业 9297 家，比上年增加 1216 家。其中，国有及国有控股企业 652 家，增加 70 家。

表 6　2021 年建筑业总产值、增长速度及构成

指　标	总产值（亿元）	比上年增　长（%）	比重（%）
建筑业	16412.0	9.8	100.0
按资质分			
特级企业	5668.3	6.9	34.5
一级企业	6091.1	10.4	37.1
其　他	4652.6	12.7	28.4
按经济性质分			
国有及国有控股企业	5261.2	9.1	32.1
非国有企业	11150.8	10.2	67.9

六、服务业

服务业发展支撑有力。服务业实现增加值 43879.7 亿元，按可比价格计算，比上年增长 9.2%；占全省生产总值的比重为 52.8%;对经济增长的贡献率为 59.5%。规模以上服务业营业收入突破 1 万亿元，达到 1.2 万亿元，增长 23.7%，营业利润增长 7.0%。新产业新业态新商业模式表现亮眼，多式联运和运输代理业、互联网和相关服务、研究和试验发展、科技推广和应用服务业营业收入分别增长 88.0%、24.4%、26.9%和 37.2%。

旅游复苏提振强劲。接待游客 7.3 亿人次，旅游总收入 8278.6 亿元，分别比上年增长 26.6%和 37.5%。国家 A 级景区 1193 家，其中，5A 级景区 13 家。星级饭店 492 家，旅行社 2729 家。文旅融合发展再上新台阶，成功举办第二届山东省旅游发展大会、第五届山东文化和旅游惠民消费季和“山东人游山东”“好客山东游品荟”等活动。文旅促进消费取得新成效，发放文化和旅游惠民消费券 1.5 亿元，新增首批国家级夜间文旅消费集聚区 6 个、第二批国家级文旅消费示范试点市 3 个，国家级文旅消费试点市达到 7 个。乡村旅游发展势头良好，全国乡村旅游重点镇 3 个、全国乡村旅游重点村 7 个，山东省乡村旅游重点村 60 个、景区化村庄 285 个。

邮政电信持续向好。电信业务总量 1002.0 亿元，比上年增长 30.1%；邮政业务总量 642.8 亿元，增长 30.3%。快递业务量 56.0 亿件，增长 34.8%。全省电话用户总数为 12356.0 万户，其中移动电话用户 11248.5 万户。全省（固定）互联网宽带接入用户 3863.7 万户，增长 12.1%，其中 100M 以上用户占比达到 97.3%。移动互联网用户 9368.0 万户。固定宽带家庭普及率为 97.5 部/百户。移动基站总数达 60.9 万个。

交通运输稳步回升。铁路、公路、水路共完成客运量 2.8 亿人，比上年下降 5.8%；货运量 33.3 亿吨，增长 8.0%。铁路、公路、水路完成旅客周转量 705.6 亿人公里，比上年增长 18.6%；完成货物周转量 12002.1 亿吨公里，增长 16.1%。

表 7　2019 年客货运输量及增长速度

指　标	旅　客			
	运输量（亿人次）	比上年增长（%）	周转量（亿人公里）	比上年增长（%）
合 计	2.8	-5.8	705.6	18.6
铁 路	1.2	24.2	523.9	21.3
公 路	1.5	-22.3	177.8	11.6
水 路	0.1	27.0	3.9	-2.6

表 7　续表

指　标	货　物			
	运输量（亿吨）	比上年增长（%）	周转量（亿吨公里）	比上年增长（%）
合 计	33.3	8.0	12002.1	16.1
铁 路	2.3	-1.3	1682.1	7.4
公 路	29.1	9.0	7517.6	10.8
水 路	1.9	6.2	2802.4	40.8

七、固定资产投资

投资保持稳定增长。固定资产投资（不含农户）比上年增长 6.0%。三次产业投资构成为 1.9∶32.4∶65.7。重点投资领域中，民间投资增长 8.2%，占固定资产投资的比重为 65.2%，比上年提高 1.3 个百分点；制造业投资增长 13.1%，占固定资产投资的比重为 27.5%，比上年提高 1.7 个百分点;高新技术产业投资增长 11.6%，高于工业投资增速 1.8 个百分点。

房地产市场平稳运行。房地产开发投资 9819.7 亿元，比上年增长 3.9%。其中，住宅投资 7694.5 亿元，增长 5.5%。开发规模稳步提升，商品房施工面积突破 8 亿平方米，达 82771.7 万平方米，增长 3.7%。其中，住宅施工面积 60712.6 万平方米，增长 3.1%。商品房销售面积 14272.8 万平方米，增长 7.5%。其中，住宅销售面积 12632.0 万平方米，增长 6.1%。商品房销售

额 12155.6 亿元，增长 9.9%。其中，住宅销售额 11044.1 亿元，增长 9.2%。

八、消费市场

消费市场复苏提速。社会消费品零售总额 33714.5 亿元，比上年增长 15.3%。其中，餐饮收入 3828.2 亿元，增长 22.4%；商品零售 29886.3 亿元，增长 14.4%。城镇零售额 28081.0 亿元，增长 15.3%；乡村零售额 5633.5 亿元，增长 15.2%。

消费升级态势明显。传统消费品提档升级加速，限额以上体育娱乐用品、通讯器材、金银珠宝类零售额比上年分别增长 61.5%、54.3%和 69.7%。智能消费快速增长，限额以上可穿戴智能设备、智能家电、智能手机零售额分别增长 21.1%、26.0%和 64.6%。

线上消费高位运行。实现网上零售额 5409.1 亿元，比上年增长 17.8%。其中，实物商品网上零售额 4763.3 亿元，增长 16.5%；占社会消费品零售总额的比重为 14.1%，比上年提高 0.3 个百分点；拉动社会消费品零售总额增长 2.5 个百分点，比上年提高 0.5 个百分点。

九、开放型经济

对外贸易增长迅速。货物进出口总值 29304.1 亿元，比上年增长 32.4%。其中，出口 17582.7 亿元，增长 34.8%；进口 11721.4 亿元，增长 29.0%。出口商品中，机电产品出口 7585.6 亿元，增长 35.8%，占全省出口总值的比重为 43.1%。民营企业进出口 20875.0 亿元，增长 35.6%，占全省进出口总值的比重为 71.2%。

表 8　2021 年对主要国家和地区货物进出口总值及增长速度

国家和地区	进出口		出口		进口	
	总值（亿元）	比上年增长（%）	总值（亿元）	比上年增长（%）	总值（亿元）	比上年增长（%）
合计	29304.1	32.4	17582.7	34.8	11721.4	29.0
东盟	4308.8	42.7	2415.5	33.1	1893.3	57.2
欧盟	3339.3	37.3	2722.7	36.4	616.6	41.2
韩国	2887.6	24.3	2214.6	26.7	673.0	17.1
美国	2695.5	29.7	1746.8	31.0	948.7	27.2
日本	1821.5	16.5	1396.2	16.1	425.2	17.9

利用外资量稳质升。新设立外商投资企业 3064 家。实际使用外资 215.2 亿美元，比上年增长 21.9%。其中，制造业实际使用外资 65.4 亿美元，增长 72.9%；服务业实际使用外资 130.3 亿美元，增长 4.7%。

对外投资总体平稳。实际对外投资 69.8 亿美元，比上年下降 16.4%。对外承包工程完成营业额 93.1 亿美元，下降 1.2%。新签千万美元以上大项目 114 个，合同额 107.3 亿美元。

“一带一路”融入共建。对“一带一路”沿线国家和地区进出口 9376.0 亿元，比上年增长 40.8%。其中，出口 5418.4 亿元，增长 39.7%；进口 3957.6 亿元，增长 42.2%。实际对外投资 17.9 亿美元。对外承包工程完成营业额 58.8 亿美元，增长 5.6%。

十、财政金融

财政运行保障稳固。地方一般公共预算收入 7284.5 亿元，迈上 7000 亿元新台阶，比上年增长 11.0%。其中，税收收入 5476.0 亿元，增长 15.1%，占一般公共预算收入的比重为 75.2%。地方一般公共预算支出 11709.1 亿元，同口径增长 9.5%。其中民生支出占一般公共预算支出的比重达到 79%，教育、科技、社保、卫生、住房保障等支出增长较快。

金融市场稳健运行。社会融资规模增量 20831.7 亿元。年末金融机构本外币存款余额 130482.1 亿元，比上年增长 10.3%，比年初增加 12132.7 亿元。年末金融机构本外币贷款余额 111035.4 亿元，增长 13.4%，比年初增加 13154.8 亿元。其中，涉农贷款余额 32361.1 亿元，增长 9.4%，增加 3081.4 亿元；小微企业贷款余额 19751.4 亿元，增长 15.5%，增加 2681.6 亿元，其中普惠小微贷款余额 11069.8 亿元，增长 35.4%，增加 2893.3 亿元。绿色贷款余额 7979.2 亿元，增长 48.7%，增加 2600.6 亿元。

资本市场主体扩容。年末上市公司 371 家，全年新增 37 家。齐鲁股权交易中心、青岛蓝海股权交易中心挂牌企业分别达到 5447 家和 2016 家。私募基金管理机构 836 家，比上年增加 129 家，管理基金规模 3255.75 亿元，比上年增加 674.03 亿元。

保险业稳定向好。原保险保费收入（不含正在风险处置机构）2816.5 亿元，比上年增长 3.1%。其中，财产险公司原保险保费收入 786.7 亿元，增长 2.3%；人身险公司原保险保费收入 2029.8 亿元，增长 3.5%。承担各类风险责任金额 293.4 万亿元，增长 36.4%。赔付支出 977.9 亿元。农业保险保费收入 52.7 亿元，增长 27.7%，为 1479.2 万户（次）农户提供 1371.6 亿元的风险保障。

十一、民生保障

居民生活质量稳步提升。居民人均可支配收入 35705 元，比上年增长 8.6%。其中，城镇居民人均可支配收入 47066 元，增长 7.6%；农村居民人均可支配收入 20794 元，增长 10.9%。居民人均消费支出 22821 元，增长 9.0%。其中，城镇居民人均消费支出 29314 元，增长 7.4%；农村居民人均消费支出 14299 元，增长 12.9%。居民人均住房建筑面积 41.3 平方米。

表 9　2021 年全省居民人均收入、消费支出情况

指　标	绝对量（元）	比上年增长(%)
可支配收入	35705	8.6
工资性收入	20413	9.1
经营净收入	7593	9.0
财产净收入	2441	3.6
转移净收入	5257	8.4
消费支出	22821	9.0
食品烟酒	6196	7.6
衣着	1530	6.4
居住	4683	5.5
生活用品及服务	1716	9.3
交通通信	3496	16.4
教育文化娱乐	2729	15.0
医疗保健	2016	5.3
其他用品和服务	456	2.4

表 10　2021 年末每百户居民家庭主要耐用消费品拥有量

指　标	单位	数量
家用汽车	辆	52.4
摩托车	辆	21.3
洗衣机	台	99.5
电冰箱（柜）	台	103.9
彩色电视机	台	104.8
空调	台	135.8
热水器	台	96.6
洗碗机	台	2.1
固定电话	线	5.4
移动电话	部	242.0
其中：接入互联网	部	198.1
计算机	台	49.7
照相机	台	9.0
健身器材	台	4.5
空气净化器（含新风系统）	台	5.9

城市更新步伐加快。城市建设（不含轨道交通）完成投资 1481.7 亿元，比上年增长 6.5%。新增城市综合管廊 43.9 公里，设区市新增海绵城市面积 109.1 平方公里，新增集中供热面积 7468 万平方米。新增城市污水处理能力 82 万吨/日，新建改造雨水管网 1350 公里、污水管网 1593 公里，改造合流制管网 1042 公里，整治黑臭水体工程 104 条。新增垃圾无害化处理能力 5100 吨/日，城乡生活垃圾焚烧处理率达到 90%，所有县（市、区）全部启动垃圾分类。新建城市绿道 779 公里，新增综合性公园和专类公园 40 个、口袋公园 975 处。新公布历史文化街区 25 处、历史建筑 900 处。

社会保障扎实稳固。年末职工基本养老、基本医疗、失业、工伤、生育保险参保人数分别为 3226.7 万人、2435.6 万人、1542.7 万人、1921.9 万人和 1607.5 万人。居民基本养老保险和医疗保险参保人数分别为 4614.1 万人和 7296.7 万人。企业退休人员基本养老金月人均 3127.2 元。居民基本养老保险基础养老金最低标准提高到每人每月 150 元，居民基本医保财政补助和个人缴费最低标准分别由 550 元、280 元提高至 580 元、

320 元。医保电子凭证激活人数及开通应用定点医药机构分别为6056.9万人和6.2万家。跨省和省内异地就医住院联网即时结算医院4164家。失业保险金标准调整为1890元、1710元和1530元，1至4级工伤职工伤残津贴平均增长4.9%。城市最低生活保障人数10.9万人，月人均保障标准814元，比上年提高82元。农村最低生活保障人数134.9万人，月人均保障标准634元，比上年提高74元。养老机构2380处，养老机构床位40.3万张；护理型床位23.8万张，建有社区老年人日间照料中心3252处、农村幸福院11260处。

住房保障体系日趋完善。开工改造棚户区13.0万套，基本建成43.6万套，开工改造老旧小区65.6万户。开工保障性租赁住房7.5万套，筹集公租房1610套，发放住房租赁补贴5.6万户。住房公积金缴存1590.8亿元，发放贷款920.2亿元。

安全生产形势稳定。生产安全事故起数和死亡人数比上年分别下降26.4%和30.6%，亿元GDP生产安全事故死亡率0.0131，十万人工矿商贸企业就业人员生产安全事故死亡率0.67，道路交通万车死亡率1.03，煤矿百万吨死亡率0.042。

十二、社会事业

教育事业稳步发展。完成配套幼儿园整治2121所，全省新建改扩建幼儿园571所、中小学277所，分别新增学位15.1万个和34.0万个。中小学56人及以上大班额保持动态清零。全省新建乡村教师周转宿舍1.1万套，农村教师工作生活条件不断改善。新补充中小学教师3.7万人、公办幼儿园教师1.1万人，小学教育、初中教育、高中教育专任教师分别为46.8万人、31.6万人和15.6万人。中等职业学校专任教师5.4万人，普通高等学校专任教师13.1万人。优化高等教育布局结构，新设立1所高职院校。新增博士高校2所、硕士高校1所，新增10个博士学位授权点和114个硕士学位授权点。获得全国职业院校技能大赛金牌60枚、奖牌100枚，金牌数和奖牌数全国“双第一”。进一步深化教育国际交流与合作，新增中外合作办学机构4个、项目29个，总量分别达到21个、206个，机构加项目总量居全国第2位。获批全国首批海外“中文工坊”3所，数量居全国第一。

表11　2021年各类学校基本情况

指　　标	数量（个）	招生数（万人）	在校生数（万人）
研究生培养机构	35	5.4	14.9
普通高等教育	153	78.1	243.0
中等职业学校（不含技工学校）	400	29.4	83.9
技工学校	182	16.5	41.9
普通高中	723	62.9	182.6
普通初中	3296	124.7	388.1
普通小学	9458	137.9	755.8
特殊教育学校	155	0.9	5.2
幼儿园	25203	115.7	389.3

文化事业产业繁荣兴盛。承办第四届中国歌剧节、举办第十二届山东文化艺术节，开展“8个100庆祝建党100周年”“红色文化主题月”等系列活动，6部作品入选“庆祝中国共产党成立100周年全国优秀舞台艺术作品展演”。年末广播人口、电视人口综合覆盖率分别为99.51%和99.65%。城市、县城和乡镇影院672家，票房25.0亿元。公有制艺术表演团体103个，艺术表演场馆87个，博物馆639个，公共图书馆154个，群众艺术馆和文化馆158个，其中133个文化馆被命名为国家一级馆，数量居全国第一。美术馆58个，文化站1821个。出版各类图书21093种，报纸82种，期刊265种。国家级、省级文化产业示范园区（基地）分别为16个和171个。国家级、省级非遗代表性项目分别为186项和1073项。国家、省级重点文物保护单位分别为226处和1711处。

医疗卫生水平持续提升。年末医疗卫生机构8.6万所。其中，医院2660所，比上年末增加20所；基层医疗卫生机构8.2万所，增加0.1万所。58家疾控中心进行改扩建，超过半数的地市建成一所达到三级传染病医院标准的医疗机构，设立9个省级公共卫生事件应急救援区域中心。人均基本公共卫生服务经费补助标准由74元提高至79元。累计组建家庭医生服务团队3.2万个，签约居民4686.2万人。

体育事业全面推进。山东运动员东京奥运会勇夺7枚金牌、1枚银牌、3枚铜牌。第十四届全运会勇夺58

枚金牌、160枚奖牌，实现“四连冠”。县级“三个一”、乡镇“两个一”健身工程覆盖率分别提升至84.3%和82.4%，115所公共体育场馆免费或低收费开放。举办第十一届全民健身运动会，参与人数超过450万人次。在8个市试点举办800多场社区运动会，第二届云走齐鲁线上健步走比赛41万人参与。新创建7个国家级、27个省级体育产业示范基地和10个省级体育服务综合体，新增国家级体育旅游示范基地和精品线路4处、省级体育旅游精品线路22条。

灾害防御水平提升。启动重大气象灾害应急响应1123次，人工作业增加降水9.02亿立方米，减少雹灾损失4.37亿元。妥善应对M2.3级以上地震26次。

注：

1. 本公报中数据均为初步统计数，部分数据因四舍五入影响，存在总计与分项合计不等情况。

2. 全省生产总值、各产业增加值按现价计算，增长速度按可比价格计算。“十强”产业增长速度均按现价计算。

3. 规模以上工业企业指年主营业务收入2000万元及以上的工业法人企业。

4. 规模以上服务业企业：一是辖区内年营业收入2000万元及以上服务业法人单位，包括：交通运输、仓储和邮政业，信息传输、软件和信息技术服务业，水利、环境和公共设施管理业三个门类和卫生行业大类。二是辖区内年营业收入1000万元及以上服务业法人单位，包括：租赁和商务服务业，科学研究和技术服务业，教育三个门类，以及物业管理、房地产中介服务、房地产租赁经营和其他房地产业四个行业小类。三是辖区内年营业收入500万元及以上服务业法人单位，包括：居民服务、修理和其他服务业，文化、体育和娱乐业两个门类，以及社会工作行业大类。

5. 2021年，邮政、电信业务总量按2020年价格计算，与之前数据不可比。

6. 固定资产投资（不含农户）包括城镇和农村各种登记注册类型的企业、事业、行政单位以及城镇个体户计划总投资500万元及以上的建设项目投资，有开发经营活动的全部房地产开发经营业法人单位开发项目投资。

7. 限额以上批发业企业指年主营业务收入2000万元及以上的批发业企业，限额以上零售业企业指年主营业务收入500万元及以上的零售业企业，限额以上住宿和餐饮业企业指年主营业务收入200万元及以上的住宿和餐饮业企业。

8. 林业数据来源于2019年度森林资源管理“一张图”与“国土三调”成果融合。

2021年山东统计工作综述

2021年是党和国家历史上具有里程碑意义的一年，是山东迈入社会主义现代化建设新征程的起步之年。一年来，全省统计部门弘扬伟大建党精神，扎实开展党史学习教育，加快推进统计改革创新，持续深化基层基础建设，全面抓实数据质量管理，精准服务经济社会发展，统计工作开创新局面、取得新成效。省委、省政府对统计工作给予充分肯定。省委书记李干杰指出，2021年全省统计工作成效明显，为全省经济社会高质量发展提供了有力保障。省长周乃翔指出，全省统计系统紧紧围绕统筹疫情防控和经济社会发展大局，扎实开展重大普查调查，持续推进重点领域改革，全面提升统计服务水平，为宏观管理和科学决策提供了有力支撑。

一、全面从严治党向纵深发展

全省统计部门始终把政治建设放在第一位，将政治标准和政治要求贯穿统计全过程，不断增强“四个意识”、坚定“四个自信”、做到“两个维护”，牢记“国之大者”，提高政治判断力、政治领悟力、政治执行力。认真落实“第一议题”学习制度，自觉把习近平总书记重要讲话精神和中央要求落实到统计实践中，主动对标对表，确保政令畅通、令行禁止。各级统计局党组扎实开展党史学习教育，围绕四部《简史》和“七一”重要讲话、党的百年奋斗重大成就和历史经验的决议等规定书目及重要文献，精心组织各层级学习研讨，依托特色红色资源开展主题教育，发挥数据优势为群众办实事，推动学习教育走深走实。认真落实从严管党治党责任，深化党风廉政建设，定期排查风险隐患，经常开展警示教育，筑牢廉洁从政防线。强化机关作风建设，开展“五查五看”作风专项整治。强化模范机关和精神文明创建，省统计局荣获国家级、省级节能机关称号，持续保持全国文明单位荣誉。

二、重大普查调查进展顺利

一是圆满完成第七次全国人口普查。全省2000余个普查机构，50余万名普查指导员和普查员，克服疫情影响，攻坚克难、连续奋战，对50多万个普查小区、3700多万户家庭、1亿多人口进行了逐门逐户的访问登记，查清了全省人口数量、结构、分布、城乡住房等基本情况，获得了丰富翔实的数据。及时召开新闻发布会，发布人口普查公报，围绕重点指标开展宣传解读。召开总结表彰视频会议，表彰奖励大幅向基层倾斜。山东省普查数据质量得到国务院人普办事后质量抽查组充分肯定，普查工作得到国家统计局多次表扬，并在全国统计工作会上作典型发言。二是各项调查任务顺利完成。全省上下通力合作，圆满完成工业、投资、贸易、人口、社科、农村、能源、服务业等8个专业24项统计报表，以及1%人口抽样调查、“四下”单位抽样调查、部分行业事业单位调查、城市基本情况统计、统计用区划代码和城乡划分代码更新维护等重点调查工作。

三、统计数据质量不断提高

一是管控机制更加完善。修订统计数据质量管控体系，省、市、县、乡四级统计机构数据质量管理责任不断压实。扎实开展地区生产总值统一核算，建立季度核算数据对接评估机制，核算质量和数据公信力明显提升。二是现场核查持续加强。省统计局联合省“四进”攻坚工作组，对全省一套表调查单位和5000万元以上固定资产投资项目逐一核查，单位真实性达到100%，基础信息准确率达到90%，夯实了数据填报基础。省委书记李干杰作出批示予以肯定。坚持问题导向，采用市县全面自查、省级随机抽查等方式，开展钢铁焦化、重点行业投资、煤炭消费量、发电企业数据质量、企业研发填报资格及数据质量、化肥农药使用量等多项专项核查，统计数据质量进一步提升。三是纳统机制更加规范。创新推进应统尽统，印发《关于建立分类培育高质量纳统工作机制的通知》，明确各级各部门纳统职责任务；探索批发零售领域分散市场主体纳统模式；利用税务资料核实营业收入达到“四上”标准企业，全年全省新纳统单位近2万家，客观准确反映经济发展成果。

四、统计改革创新实现突破

一是谋划建设“七个工作体系”。坚持一体规划、分步实施，扎实推进“七个工作体系”建设，经过一年努力，搭建起了督查督办系统、统计信息综合服务平台、态势运行综合指标专区等“三个平台”，健全完善了数据质量管控、企业高质量纳统、经济形势分析、统计法治保障监督等“四个机制”，有效提升了统计工作质量。二是创新变革数据填报方式。探索变革源头数据采集方式，通过开发应用软件，变统计数据手工录入为程序自动转换，在全省联网直报企业中有计划、分类别推进企业财务报表与统计报表自动转换，全省90%以上“四上”企业实现报表自动转换，夯实了源头数据质量，提高了工作效率。三是稳妥推进制度方法改革。做好知识产权投资、劳动工资统计等改革，开展企业电子统计台账建设试点，参加全国服务消费统计试点，制定服务业统计改革发展方案，试编月度、季度服务业生产指数，探索“碳达峰”“碳中和”基础统计研究，制度方法科学性、有效性不断提高。

五、统计基层基础不断筑牢

一是基层基础建设年活动有序开展。突出加强力量、提升素质、制度建设等7个方面，细化24项措施，有序开展基层基础建设年活动，着力提升基层统计规范化水平。建立基层工作联系点制度，省统计局班子成员及各处室分别联系2个县、乡统计机构，指导解决实际问题。在济宁召开全省统计基层基础建设现场观摩会，交流推广基层典型经验和创新做法。二是统计技能提升工程全面实施。建立网络教育培训机制，围绕制度方法、报表填报、指标计算等内容制作80余节精品网课，组织全省统计业务人员在线学习测试。利用“山东统计大讲堂”开展业务轮讲，采用线上线下结合方式开展企业统计人员培训，推动统计人员干业务、比业务、精业务。三是延伸拓展统计人才培育。开展第二批全省基层统计人才培育工程评选，首次开展基层统计高级职称评审。

六、统计监督工作有效开展

一是科学监测经济社会发展。围绕全省重大战略规划部署，创新监测指标，扩展监测领域，开展新旧动能转换、“六稳六保”等15项重点监测。发挥社情民意调查桥梁作用，完成32项委托调查和自主调查，及时传递民情民声民意。二是强化统计督察。全面做好国家统计督察反馈意见整改，4方面11项问题全部整改到位。建立省级防范和惩治统计造假督察机制，对济宁、威海、德州、菏泽4市开展了首轮督察，推动优化统计环境。三是执法监督震慑有力。制定统计执法检查规范、统计行政处罚裁量基准，规范执法程序和违法行为处罚。与纪检监察机关、巡视机构建立案件处置协作配合机制。保持执法检查高压态势，全省执法检查企业4486家，依法处罚64家，处分处理责任人20余人，有效净化了统计生态。

七、统计服务质效创新提升

一是数据服务及时主动。紧跟领导决策需求，建立数据即时报送机制，每月6批次报送32项主要经济指标数据（季度40项）；建成“山东统计信息综合服务平台”，基于地理位置展示企业纳统情况，即时查询区域概况及综合指标；针对部门管理需求提供定制化服务，汇总形成涉及30多个部门的50余项数据清单，服务质效进一步提高。二是分析服务优质高效。聚焦全省经济高质量发展，坚持“打开数字”搞分析，全年撰写统计分析100余篇，获省领导批示160余次，统计信息得分在省“两办”分居第3位、第1位，10篇信息获国务院领导批示，充分发挥了参谋智囊作用。三是决策服务成果显著。聚焦山东经济高质量发展组织专题调研，为制定宏观政策提供咨询建议，撰写的《关于新时代山东高质量发展“十大需求”的初步思考》进入省委经济工作会议“扩需求十大行动”决策参考；深挖统计数据开展重点行业研究，《关于我省食品工业发展情况的分析报告》《提高教育质量增加学位供给》两篇分析报告获第一届省政府决策咨询奖。四是统计宣传广泛深入。举办“统计法治宣传月”“中国统计开放日”活动，生动开展庆祝建党100周年、全面建成小康社会、“十三五”发展成就主题宣传，统计社会影响力不断提升。

这些成绩的取得，是省委、省政府和国家统计局坚强领导的结果，是各级各部门大力支持的结果，是全省广大统计干部职工奋力拼搏的结果。全省统计系统将始终坚持以习近平新时代中国特色社会主义思想为指导，全面贯彻习近平总书记关于统计工作重要讲话指示批示精神，认真落实省委经济工作会议和全国统计工作会议精神，以党的政治建设为统领，强化统计数据质量管理，深化统计制度方法创新，提升统计规范化水平，有效发挥统计监督作用，为全省经济社会高质量发展提供坚实统计支撑，以优异成绩迎接党的二十大胜利召开。

2021 年山东省统计局大事记

1 月 1 日，省委书记刘家义，省委副书记、省长李干杰，省委常委、常务副省长王书坚分别对省统计局报送的《国务院第七次全国人口普查事后质量抽查组对我省人口普查数据质量给予充分肯定》作出批示。

1 月 4 日，省委副书记、省长李干杰对省统计局报送的《1-11 月“六保三促”工作目标完成情况的监测分析》作出批示。

1 月 6 日，省统计局党组书记、局长辛树人一行 4 人以“四不两直”方式到济南万达广场调研城市商业综合体纳统工作。

1 月 7 日，省统计局召开专题会议，传达学习省委统筹疫情防控和经济运行工作指挥部（扩大）会议精神，安排部署下步疫情防控重点工作。党组书记、局长辛树人主持会议并讲话。

1 月 18 日，省委书记刘家义，省委副书记、省长李干杰，省委常委、常务副省长王书坚分别对省统计局报送的《关于全国统计工作视频会议精神的汇报》作出批示。

1 月 19 日，省政府召开新闻发布会，通报 2020 年全省经济运行情况。省政府副秘书长、新闻发言人于成河介绍全年主要数据指标情况，省统计局副局长、新闻发言人陆万明出席发布会并回答记者提问。省发展改革委、省商务厅有关负责人出席发布会，介绍相关领域发展情况。

1 月 23 日，省委书记刘家义，省委副书记、省长李干杰，省委常委、常务副省长王书坚分别对省统计局报送的《关于 2020 年全省规模以上工业运行情况的汇报》作出批示。

1 月 26 日，省统计局召开 2020 年度党员领导干部民主生活会。省委第二十二督导组组长、省委老干部局副局长李学忠一行到会指导。

1 月 27 日，省委副书记、省长李干杰，省委常委、常务副省长王书坚分别对省统计局报送的《关于经济运行数据协调调度情况的汇报》作出批示。

1 月 27 日，省委副书记、省长李干杰对省统计局报送的《2020 年“六保三促”工作目标完成情况的监测分析》作出批示。

1 月 27 日，省委副书记、省长李干杰，省委常委、秘书长刘强对省统计局报送的《“十三五”期间我省企业入库纳统情况》作出批示。

1 月 29 日，省委副书记杨东奇莅临省统计局和山东调查总队调研指导工作。省委农办主任、省农业农村厅厅长李希信，省委副秘书长赵晓晖，省委办公厅综合一室主任侯立江等陪同调研。

2 月 3 日，省委书记刘家义，省委副书记、省长李干杰分别对省统计局报送的《关于 1 月份全省财政收支与用电量情况的汇报》作出批示。

2 月 5 日，省委第二巡视组向省统计局党组反馈巡视情况。省委巡视工作领导小组成员刘树军主持反馈会议，出席向省统计局党组领导班子反馈会议，省委第二巡视组组长丁信贤代表省委巡视组分别向辛树人和领导班子反馈了巡视情况。省统计局党组书记、局长辛树人就做好巡视整改工作表态发言。

2 月 5 日，省委书记刘家义，省委副书记、省长李干杰，省委副书记杨东奇，省委常委、常务副省长王书坚，副省长凌文、于国安，分别对省统计局报送的《深挖抓实区域伙伴协定红利 加快形成经济高质量发展新策源地》作出批示。

2 月 7 日，省统计局召开 2020 年度总结表彰会议。党组书记、局长辛树人主持会议并讲话。

2 月 10 日，省委常委、宣传部部长于杰对省统计局报送的《新动能领跑 大项目集聚 我省文化产业历经风雨吐芳华——2020 年山东省文化产业发展情况汇报》作出批示。

2 月 19 日，省委书记刘家义，省委副书记、省长李干杰，省委常委、常务副省长王书坚分别对全省统计工作作出批示。

2 月 22 日，省委副书记、省长李干杰对省统计局报送的《关于外省法人在鲁分支机构经营统计情况的汇报》作出批示。

2 月 24 日，山东省统计学会第八次会员代表大会在济南召开。会议选举产生山东省统计学会第八届理事会会长、副会长、秘书长、常务理事、理事及监事，表决通过了新修订的《山东省统计学会章程》。省社科联党组书记、副主席刘致福出席会议并致辞。省统计局党组书记、局长辛树人当选学会新一届理事会会长。

2 月 25 日，全省统计工作会议在济南召开。会议深入学习中央领导同志关于统计工作重要批示精神和省领导对全省统计工作批示要求，传达学习全国统计工作会议精神，总结2020年全省统计工作，研究部署2021年重点任务。省统计局党组书记、局长辛树人代表局党组作了题为《担当作为 砥砺奋进 努力谱写统计改革发展新篇章》工作报告。

3月5日，省委书记刘家义，省委常委、常务副省长王书坚分别对省统计局报送的《关于今年我省经济运行走势的初步预判》作出批示。

3月5日，省统计局召开国民经济核算方法专题培训会议。党组书记、局长辛树人出席会议并讲话。

3月8日，省委副书记、省长李干杰，省委常委、常务副省长王书坚分别对省统计局报送的《关于2020年我省新旧动能转换监测有关数据情况的汇报》作出批示。

3月12日，省统计局党组召开党组成员履行全面从严治党责任汇报会议，党组成员分别汇报2020年度履行全面从严治党责任情况。党组书记辛树人主持会议。

3月12日，省统计局党组与省纪委监委驻省统计局纪检监察组共同召开党风廉政建设专题会议，省统计局党组书记辛树人主持会议并讲话，省纪委监委驻省统计局纪检监察组组长李永进对党风廉政建设工作提出意见。

3月16日，省委书记刘家义对省统计局报送的《前2个月我省经济总体开端良好》作出批示。

3月17日至18日，国家发展改革委副主任兼国家统计局局长、党组书记宁吉喆一行到山东调研基层统计工作和经济形势。省委书记刘家义会见宁吉喆一行，省委副书记、省长李干杰在日照市一同调研。

3月22日，省统计局办公室印发《关于做好2021年统计普法宣传教育工作的通知》（鲁统办字〔2021〕9号）。

3月23日，省委书记刘家义，省委副书记、省长李干杰，省委副书记杨东奇，省委常委、常务副省长王书坚，副省长曾赞荣分别对省统计局报送的《关于国家统计局反馈我省公众生态环境满意度调查结果的汇报》作出批示。

3月24日，省委副书记、省长李干杰到省统计局调研，深入了解工业统计、GDP核算、统计数据生产流程等情况，剖析经济运行发展形势，对统计工作把关定向、明确任务、提出要求。

3月24日，省统计局召开2021年度全面从严治党暨党风廉政建设工作会议。传达学习十九届中央纪委五次全会、省纪委十一届六次全会主要精神，省统计局党组书记、局长辛树人作工作报告，省纪委监委驻省统计局纪检监察组组长李永进讲话。

3月24日，省统计局召开党史学习教育动员大会，党组书记、局长辛树人作动员讲话。

3月27日，省委常委、常务副省长王书坚对省统计局报送的《我省自备电厂1-2月发电量增速情况分析》作出批示。

3月27日，省委书记刘家义，省委副书记、省长李干杰，省委常委、常务副省长王书坚分别对省统计局报送的《关于宁吉喆同志在鲁调研期间对山东工作建议及对统计局工作要求的汇报》作出批示。

3月29日，省委书记刘家义，省委副书记、省长李干杰，省委常委、常务副省长王书坚，省委常委、秘书长刘强分别对省统计局报送的《关于做好我省统计督察反馈意见整改工作的汇报》作出批示。

3月31日，国家统计局第6统计督察组向山东省委、省政府反馈了统计督察意见。第6统计督察组组长，国家统计局党组成员、副局长鲜祖德通报督察意见，山东省委常委、常务副省长王书坚主持会议并对整改工作提出要求，第6统计督察组有关负责同志，山东省直有关部门负责同志参加会议。

4月2日，全省能源统计工作视频会议在济南召开。会议传达学习李干杰省长来省统计局调研座谈讲话精神和全省统计工作会议、全国能源统计工作视频会议精神，研究新形势下提高能源统计数据质量、优化能源统计服务水平的办法措施。省统计局党组成员、副局长周尊考出席会议并讲话。

4月8日，省委常委、常务副省长王书坚对省统计局报送的《关于我省统计督察反馈意见整改有关情况的汇报》作出批示。

4月8日，山东省统计局印发《关于积极推进联网直报企业财务报表自动有序转换生成统计报表工作的通知》（鲁统字〔2021〕17号），在全省联网直报企业推进财务报表统计数据自动生成工作，促进提高源头统计数据质量。

4月12日，省委副书记、省长李干杰主持召开省政府常务会议，研究国家统计督察反馈意见整改等工作。

4月12日，省委副书记、省长李干杰对省统计局报送的《关于一季度我省经济增长情况的汇报》作出批示。

4月12日，省统计局印发《2021年季度市级生产总值统一核算方案》（鲁统字〔2021〕18号）和《山东省统计局统计执法检查规范（试行）》（鲁统字〔2021〕21号）。

4月15日，全省统计督察整改工作部署电视会议在济南召开，省委常委、常务副省长王书坚出席会议并讲话。会议由省政府办公厅副主任宫志远主持，省统计局局长辛树人就统计督察整改工作方案和重点任务作了说明。省有关部门负责同志在主会场参加会议。

16市设分会场，各市市政府分管统计工作负责人和有关部门负责人参加会议。

4月15日，省第七次全国人口普查领导小组全体会议在济南召开，会议通报全省第七次全国人口普查工作情况，对下一步重点任务进行安排部署。省委常委、常务副省长、省第七次全国人口普查领导小组组长王书坚主持会议并讲话，省第七次全国人口普查领导小组全体成员参加会议。

4月16日，省统计局印发《山东省统计系统贯彻落实国家统计局统计督察反馈意见整改工作方案》(鲁统字〔2021〕24号)，部署推进全省统计系统统计督察整改工作。

4月18日，省委副书记、省长李干杰，省委常委、常务副省长王书坚分别对省统计局报送的《关于贯彻落实李干杰省长讲话精神和工作要求的报告》作出批示。

4月19日，省统计局办公室印发《山东省统计局数字山东建设重点任务攻坚推进工作方案》(鲁统办字〔2021〕15号)。

4月19日，省统计局办公室印发《关于开展发电企业数据质量核查的通知》(鲁统字〔2021〕25号)，对全省“四上”发电企业进行数据质量核查。

4月20日，全省统计系统统计督察整改工作视频会议在济南召开，省统计局党组书记、局长辛树人出席会议并讲话。会议由省统计局党组成员、副局长周尊考主持，省统计局领导班子成员，二级巡视员、两总师，各处室、事业单位主要负责人，各市统计局局长在主会场参加会议。16市设分会场，各市统计局领导班子成员及各科（处）室负责人参加会议。

4月20日，2021年全省一季度市级生产总值统一核算工作会议在济南召开。会议传达了李干杰省长在省统计局调研时的讲话精神和工作要求，总结2020年市级生产总值统一核算工作,对下步工作提出要求。省统计局党组书记、局长辛树人出席会议并讲话。

4月21日，省政府召开新闻发布会，通报2021年一季度全省经济运行情况。省政府副秘书长、新闻发言人于成河介绍一季度全省主要数据指标情况，省统计局副局长、新闻发言人陆万明出席发布会并回答记者提问。

4月21日，省统计局党组印发《2021年山东省统计局机关党的工作要点》《2021年山东省统计局党风廉政建设工作要点》《2021年山东省统计局精神文明建设工作要点》(鲁统党字〔2021〕18号)。

4月22日，省统计局办公室印发《统计工作推进落实体系建设方案》(鲁统办字〔2021〕16号)。

4月22日至23日，省统计局党组书记、局长辛树人一行赴潍坊青州市、寿光市调研涉农经济纳统工作。

4月25日，省统计局办公室印发《山东省统计局统计法治保障监督实施办法》(鲁统办字〔2021〕17号)，探索构建系统完整、协同高效、约束有力的现代化统计法治保障监督体系。

4月27日，省委副书记、省长李干杰，省委常委、常务副省长王书坚分别对省统计局报送的《当前我省投资运行态势及与苏浙粤相关比较分析》作出批示。

4月27日至28日，省统计局党组书记、局长辛树人一行赴淄博张店区、桓台县和高新区调研当前经济运行情况。

4月29日，省委副书记、省长李干杰，省委常委、常务副省长王书坚分别对省统计局报送的《关于季度GDP环比增速推算方法的说明》作出批示。

4月30日，省统计局办公室印发《关于做好2021年度统计执法检查工作的通知》(鲁统办字〔2021〕19号)，安排部署2021年度全省统计执法检查工作。

5月1日，省委书记刘家义，省委常委、常务副省长王书坚分别对省统计局报送的《关于一季度我省GDP增速拉动情况的汇报》作出批示。

5月6日，省统计局办公室印发《关于开展全省统计系统2021年网络安全检查工作的通知》(鲁统办函〔2021〕2号)，安排部署2021年度全省统计系统网络安全工作。

5月6日，省委副书记、省长李干杰在省统计局报送的《关于全面建成小康社会统计监测有关情况的报告》作出批示。

5月7日至8日，省统计局党组书记、局长辛树人一行赴济宁市调研经济运行情况和基层统计工作。

5月10日，山东省统计局承办的日喀则市统计系统业务培训班在济南开班。省统计局党组书记、局长辛树人，省政府副秘书长，省统计局党组副书记、副局长，省第九批援藏干部领队，日喀则市委副书记、常务副市长马金栋出席开班仪式并讲话。西藏自治区统计局党组成员、一级巡视员达顿主持开班仪式。培训班为期2周，日喀则市统计系统19名业务骨干参加培训。

5月10日，省统计局印发《山东省统计系统基层基础建设年实施方案》(鲁统字〔2021〕33号)，在全省统计系统开展基层基础建设年活动。

5月11日至13日，国家统计局社科文司副司长韩静一行，到山东枣庄、济南、威海3市调研医养结合产业发展情况。省统计局党组书记、局长辛树人陪同在济南调研。

5月12日，省委副书记、省长李干杰，省委常委、常务副省长王书坚分别对省统计局报送的《我省制造业竞争力总体水平较高分行业差异仍比较明显》作出批示。

5月14日，省统计局组织召开省直机关统计督察整改工作座谈会，总经济师宫照华介绍统计督察反馈意见情况，并就认真落实省委、省政府整改方案提出建议。省纪委监委机关、省委组织部、省发展改革委等28个部门（单位）参加会议。

5月17日至18日，国家统计局核算司副司长吕峰一行，到山东青岛市调研自然资源资产负债表编制和生态产品价值核算工作情况。省统计局党组书记、局长辛树人陪同调研。

5月21日，省政府召开新闻发布会，发布全省第七次全国人口普查主要数据。省统计局党组书记、局长辛树人介绍第七次全国人口普查主要数据情况，并回答记者提问。

5月24日至27日，省统计局到烟台市、淄博市实地督导国家统计督察反馈意见整改工作推进情况。

5月24日至28日，省统计局党史学习教育处级干部培训班在淄博市博山区举办。二级巡视员和全体处级干部（不含主持工作处长）参加培训。

5月25日，省委副书记、省长李干杰，省委常委、常务副省长王书坚分别对省统计局报送的《关于1-4月全省主要经济运行情况的汇报》作出批示。

5月27日，省统计局印发《山东省企业统计工作规范》（鲁统字〔2021〕35号），进一步夯实企业统计工作基础，提高企业统计工作规范化、制度化、科学化水平。

5月27日至28日，国家统计局农村司一级巡视员黄秉信一行2人，到山东潍坊市调研县域统计制度填报情况。省统计局二级巡视员姜西海陪同调研。

5月28日，副省长王心富对省统计局报送的《关于我省文化产业统计工作及文化产业发展情况的汇报》作出批示。

6月1日，国家统计局服务业统计司副司长赵庆河一行4人，到山东省调研服务业统计改革发展情况。省统计局党组成员、副局长陆万明参加座谈会。

6月1日至4日，国家统计局工业司副司长朱虹一行，到山东省泰安市、枣庄市调研工业经济运行形势。省统计局党组成员、副局长周尊考陪同调研。

6月3日，省委常委、常务副省长王书坚对省统计局报送的《关于全国统计对口援疆工作会议精神及贯彻落实工作的报告》作出批示。

6月3日至8日，省统计局党组书记、局长辛树人率队赴西藏调研对接统计援藏工作，并看望慰问山东统计系统援藏干部。局党组成员、副局长、人事处处长李涛，临沂市统计局主要负责同志等参加调研。西藏自治区人民政府副主席、日喀则市委书记张延清会见辛树人一行。西藏自治区统计局党组书记刘柏呈，党组成员、副局长马洪钧，山东省政府副秘书长、山东第九批援藏干部管理组组长、日喀则市委副书记、常务副市长马金栋，日喀则市委常委、常务副市长巴桑，西藏自治区统计局、日喀则市统计局、国家统计局日喀则调查队有关同志参加调研。

6月4日，省委常委、常务副省长王书坚对省统计局报送的《关于外省法人在鲁分支机构有关情况的汇报》作出批示。

6月6日，省委常委、常务副省长王书坚对省统计局报送的《关于统计督察整改工作进展情况的汇报》作出批示。

6月8日至9日，国家统计局统计执法监督局王康康一行2人，到山东省调研民间和涉外调查管理工作情况。省统计局党组成员、副局长周尊考会见调研组。

6月10日，省统计局印发《山东省统计系统网络安全检查工作方案》，安排部署全省统计系统网络安全检查工作。

6月10日，山东省副省长、烟台市委书记傅明先带队到省统计局调研，省统计局领导班子成员参加座谈。

6月11日，省统计局印发《山东省统计数据质量管控体系（2021修订稿）》（鲁统字〔2021〕40号），严格数据生产全流程管控。

6月17日，省委编办副主任李捷一行5人，到省统计局调研评估深化事业单位改革试点工作情况。省统计局党组成员、副局长、人事处处长李涛参加座谈。

6月17日至19日，国家统计局信息民调中心王海峰一行，到山东省对2021年上半年全国群众安全感调查质量进行巡查，并调研指导社情民意调查工作。省统计局党组成员、副局长周尊考陪同调研。

6月21日，省委副书记、省长李干杰对省统计局报送的《关于5月份全省第二批数据情况的汇报》作出批示。

6月23日，省统计局举行“光荣在党50年”纪念章颁发仪式暨老党员座谈会，局党组书记、局长辛树人出席会议，并向15名老党员颁发“光荣在党50年”纪念章。

6月23日，省统计局党组书记、局长辛树人带队赴省交通运输厅走访调研，交流上半年交通运输发展和统计工作情况。省交通运输厅党组书记、厅长孟庆斌参加座谈。

6月24日，省统计局召开党史学习教育专题党课会议，局党组书记、局长辛树人为全局干部职工作专题党课辅导。省委党史学习教育第十四巡回指导组组长刘鲁生出席会议。

6月25日，济南市委副书记边祥慧带领市发展改革委、市工业和信息化局、市住房城乡建设局、市商务局、市统计局、市考评办主要负责人到省统计局走访座谈。省统计局领导班子成员参加座谈。

6月29日，省统计局参加省直机关庆祝中国共产党成立100周年大合唱比赛决赛，局党组书记、局长辛树人，党组成员、副局长陆万明参加合唱。

7月2日，省统计局与山东社会科学院举行战略合作框架协议签署仪式。省统计局党组书记、局长辛树人，山东社会科学院党委书记郝宪印出席仪式并致辞，省统计局党组成员、副局长陈汉臻，山东社会科学院副院长杨金卫代表双方签署协议。

7月5日，省统计局召开网络教育培训工作推进会议。局党组书记、局长辛树人出席会议并讲话。局领导班子成员，二级巡视员，总师，各处室、各事业单位主要负责同志及相关工作人员参加会议。

7月5日，省统计局与省住房城乡建设厅召开座谈会，交流建筑市场形势和建筑业统计工作。省统计局党组成员、副局长陈汉臻，省住房城乡建设厅党组成员、副厅长王润晓参加座谈会。

7月6日，省统计局党组成员、副局长周尊考一行3人赴国网山东省电力公司调研，座谈交流上半年全省电力运行和电力统计工作。省电力公司副总工程师刘志清等参加座谈。

7月6日，省统计局办公室印发《山东省统计局大数据分析体系工作方案》(鲁统办字〔2021〕26号)，规范统计数据资源整理，深度挖掘统计数据信息，更好支撑经济形势分析研判需要。

7月6日，省统计局办公室印发《山东省统计局完善分析研判体系提升统计咨政能力工作方案》(鲁统办字〔2021〕27号)，统筹利用全局经济形势分析力量资源，深度挖掘专业形势分析成果，全力打造全局“一盘棋”经济形势分析研判格局。

7月7日至8日，国家统计局设管司副司长吕庆喆一行3人,到山东调研2021年制度修订和统计制度方法改革情况。省统计局党组成员、副局长陈汉臻陪同调研。

7月9日，省委常委、常务副省长王书坚对省统计局报送的《关于做好粗钢产量统计工作的汇报》作出批示。

7月12日，全省粗钢产量统计专项工作培训视频会议在济南召开。省统计局党组成员、副局长周尊考出席会议并讲话。全省涉及粗钢生产的12市及县(市、区)统计局分管局领导及工业科人员参加会议。

7月17日，省委书记刘家义，省委副书记、省长李干杰分别对省统计局报送的《关于2021年上半年各省（区、市）生产总值有关情况的汇报》作出批示。

7月19日至20日，2021年上半年全省市级生产总值统一核算工作会议在济南召开。会议传达国家统计局2021年上半年地区生产总值统一核算培训班精神，总结2020年以来市级地区生产总值统一核算工作进展情况。省统计局党组书记、局长辛树人出席会议并讲话。

7月22日，全省建筑业统计业务培训班在济南举办。培训班邀请国家统计局投资司建筑业处处长陈淑清授课。

7月27日至29日，全省统计系统党组中心组(扩大)理论学习读书班暨基层基础工作现场会议在济宁曲阜召开。会议深入学习贯彻习近平总书记在庆祝中国共产党成立100周年大会上的重要讲话精神，现场观摩并交流统计基层基础建设工作经验，研究部署下半年重点工作任务。省统计局党组书记、局长辛树人出席会议并讲话，济宁市委副书记、市长于永生到会致辞。

7月30日，省统计局党组印发《山东省统计局认真学习贯彻习近平总书记在庆祝中国共产党成立100周年大会上的讲话实施方案》(鲁统党字〔2021〕25号）和《山东省统计局精神文明建设三年行动计划(2021-2023年)》(鲁统党字〔2021〕26号)。

8月2日，省委书记刘家义，省委副书记、省长李干杰，省委常委、常务副省长王书坚分别对省统计局报送的《关于我省化肥农药统计工作及有关情况的汇报》作出批示。

8月2日，省委副书记、省长李干杰对省统计局报送的《上半年能耗大幅增长 节能压煤任务艰巨》作出批示。

8月3日，全省统计法治工作会议在济南召开。会议传达学习全国统计法治工作会议精神，总结2020年来全省统计法治工作情况，交流工作经验。

8月4日，省委书记刘家义，省委副书记、省长李干杰，省委常委、常务副省长王书坚，副省长凌文分别对省统计局报送的《定量分析表明我省制造业竞争力仍居全国前列》作出批示。

8月4日，省委常委、常务副省长王书坚对省统计局、国家统计局山东调查总队联合报送的《关于全国统计系统援藏工作会议精神及贯彻落实工作的报告》作出批示。

8月4日，省统计局党组书记、局长辛树人一行3人赴泰安调研当前经济运行形势和基层统计工作。

8月9日，省统计局党组书记、局长辛树人一行2人赴山东产业技术研究院调研。

8月11日，省委书记刘家义，省委常委、常务副省长王书坚，副省长李猛分别对省统计局报送的《关于上半年全省GDP增速产业拉动情况的汇报》作出批示。

8月11日，省统计局党组书记、局长辛树人一行4人到济南家居市场进行专题调研。

8月12日，省委书记刘家义，省委副书记、省长李干杰，省委常委、常务副省长王书坚，省委常委、秘书长刘强分别对省统计局报送的《关于涉农分散市场主体纳统工作有关情况的汇报》作出批示。

8月13日，省委书记刘家义，省委常委、常务副省长王书坚，副省长凌文分别对省统计局报送的《关于上半年国有经济统计监测情况的报告》作出批示。

8月19日，省统计局党组印发《中共山东省统计局党组关于开展“走在前列 全面开创 我在行动”主题活动 推进模范机关建设的实施方案》(鲁统党字〔2021〕29号)。

8月20日，省统计局召开全省一套表调查单位数据质量核查培训视频会议，对协助省“四进”攻坚工作组开展全省一套表调查单位核查工作进行动员部署，培训核查业务有关知识。

8月20日，省统计局召开统一核算专题会议。局党组书记、局长辛树人主持会议，并对统一核算工作进行安排部署。

8月24日，省委常委、常务副省长王书坚，副省长王心富分别对省统计局报送的《上半年我省文化产业统计分析汇报》作出批示。

8月25日，省委书记刘家义对省统计局报送的《用电结构变化凸显新旧动能转换成效》作出批示。

8月25日至26日，省统计局党组书记、局长辛树人一行4人到聊城调研当前经济运行形势和基层统计工作。

9月1日，省委副书记、省长李干杰对省统计局报送的《关于山东高质量发展的几点思考》作出批示。

9月1日至2日，省统计局党组书记、局长辛树人一行4人到德州市调研当前经济运行形势和基层统计站建设情况。

9月7日，省统计局召开保密工作培训会议。

9月7日，省统计局党组印发《中共山东省统计局党组关于进一步加强作风建设的意见》(鲁统党字〔2021〕32号)，进一步加强机关作风建设。

9月8日，省委书记刘家义，省委副书记、省长李干杰，省委常委、常务副省长王书坚分别对省统计局报送的《上半年我省民营经济健康发展》作出批示。

9月9日，省委副书记、省长李干杰对省统计局报送的《关于我省上半年新旧动能转换监测情况的汇报》作出批示。

9月16日，省委副书记、省长李干杰，省委常委、常务副省长王书坚分别对省统计局报送的《关于我省人口就业历史数据修订情况的汇报》作出批示。

9月24日，由山东省统计局、国家统计局山东调查总队与临沂市人民政府主办，临沂市统计局、国家统计局临沂调查队、莒南县人民政府承办的山东省暨临沂市第十二届“中国统计开放日”系列活动在莒南县山东省人民政府旧址成功举办。省统计局党组成员、副局长陆万明，国家统计局山东调查总队二级巡视员范坤文，临沂市人民政府副市长张玉兰出席现场活动并致辞。

9月25日，省委常委、常务副省长王书坚对省统计局报送的《关于社情民意调查工作调研情况的汇报》作出批示。

9月26日，省委副书记、省长李干杰，省委常委、常务副省长王书坚分别对省统计局报送的《关于德州1-8月投资增速波动情况的汇报》作出批示。

9月26日，省统计局印发《关于开展2021年山东省1%人口抽样调查的通知》(鲁统字〔2021〕70号)，部署2021年全省1%人口抽样调查工作。

9月27日，省统计局办公室印发《山东省统计系统业务轮讲实施方案》(鲁统办字〔2021〕37号)，部署开展全省统计系统业务轮讲活动。

9月27日至30日，省统计局党组书记、局长辛树人一行3人到潍坊、烟台、威海调研当前经济运行形势和基层统计站建设情况。

9月28日，省统计局办公室印发《山东省统计局关于推进服务业统计改革发展实施方案》(鲁统办字〔2021〕38号)，全面深化服务业统计改革，提高服务业统计现代化水平。

9月29日，省委常委、常务副省长王书坚对省统计局报送的《关于全省第七次全国人口普查工作的报告》作出批示。

9月30日，省统计局印发《关于进一步做好批发零售领域分散市场主体升规纳统工作的通知》(鲁统字〔2021〕71号)，积极推动批发零售领域分散市场主体升规纳统工作。

10月16日，省委书记李干杰，省委副书记、代省长周乃翔，省委常委、常务副省长王书坚分别对省统计局报送的《关于2020年我省研发情况的汇报》《关于2020年我省社会评价结果的汇报》《关于全省乡村振兴齐鲁样板监测情况的汇报》作出批示。

10月16日，省委书记李干杰对省统计局报送的《当前全省工业运行总体平稳 下行压力有所加大》作出批示。

10月19日，全省2021年1-3季度市级生产总值统一核算工作视频电话会议在济南召开。

10 月 20 日，经省政府同意，省统计局印发《关于印发 2020 年山东省社会评价结果的通知》（鲁统字〔2021〕75 号），通报全省 2020 年社会评价结果。

10 月 20 日至 22 日，国家统计局信息民调中心副主任李武一行 3 人，来我省巡查 2021 年全国卷烟零售客户满意度调查质量，并调研指导社情民意调查工作。

10 月 25 日，省政府新闻办召开发布会，通报前三季度全省经济运行情况。省政府副秘书长王贞军介绍有关情况，省统计局副局长、新闻发言人陆万明出席发布会并回答记者提问。

10 月 26 日，2021 年首期“山东统计大讲堂”在省统计局开讲，山东产业技术研究院院长、博士、研究员孙殿义作了题为《现代化产业创新发展的方向》的报告，省统计局党组书记、局长辛树人主持讲座。

11 月 1 日，省委书记李干杰，省委副书记、省长周乃翔，省委副书记杨东奇，省委常委、常务副省长王书坚，副省长孙继业、汲斌昌、李猛，省政府秘书长宋军继，分别对省统计局报送的《关于当前全省经济运行情况的汇报》作出批示。

11 月 1 日，省委书记李干杰，省委常委、常务副省长王书坚，省委常委、秘书长刘强，省政府秘书长宋军继，分别对省统计局报送的《关于我省制造业创新驱动高质量发展路径的课题调研报告》作出批示。

11 月 2 日至 4 日，省统计局党组书记、局长辛树人带领调研组赴临沂市调研经济形势和统计工作。

11 月 5 日，省统计局印发《关于开展企业研发创新数据质量核查工作的通知》（鲁统字〔2021〕79 号），落实国家统计局有关要求，在全省开展企业研发创新数据质量核查工作。

11 月 6 日，省委书记李干杰，省委常委、常务副省长王书坚分别对省统计局报送的《关于我省亿元及以上项目投资进展情况的汇报》作出批示。

11 月 8 日，省委常委、常务副省长王书坚对省统计局报送的《关于前三季度全省 GDP 增速产业拉动情况的汇报》作出批示。

11 月 9 日，省统计局印发《山东省统计行政处罚裁量基准》（鲁统字〔2021〕80 号），规范统计违法行为行政处罚自由裁量权。

11 月 11 日，省统计局党组书记、局长辛树人带队到市中区泺源街道永长街社区开展“双报到”活动。

11 月 12 日，省统计局召开党组（扩大）会议，传达学习中国共产党第十九届中央委员会第六次全体会议公报，研究贯彻落实意见。党组书记、局长辛树人主持会议并讲话，党组成员、二级巡视员、总经济师和有关处室负责同志交流发言。

11 月 12 日，省统计局党组印发《关于认真学习贯彻习近平总书记在深入推动黄河流域生态保护和高质量发展座谈会上的重要讲话精神和视察山东重要指示要求的通知》（鲁统党字〔2021〕36 号），全面部署贯彻落实习近平总书记重要讲话精神和重要指示要求。

11 月 16 日，省委书记李干杰，省委常委、常务副省长王书坚分别对省统计局报送的《关于加快发展高端生产性服务业的几点思考》作出批示。

11 月 16 日，省统计局利用“山东统计大讲堂”举办业务轮讲专题讲座。统计执法监督局局长管大炜以《统计法治工作概述》为题进行授课，局党组成员、副局长周尊考主持。

11 月 16 日，省统计局办公室印发《山东省统计法治宣传教育第八个五年规划（2021—2025 年）》（鲁统办字〔2021〕45 号），部署 2021—2025 年全省统计法治宣传教育工作。

11 月 17 日，省委常委、常务副省长王书坚对省统计局报送的《关于 1-10 月全省经济运行情况的报告》作出批示。

11 月，经山东省委、省政府批准，省统计局组织开展防范和惩治统计造假专项督察，随机抽取济宁、威海、德州、菏泽 4 市进行实地督察。

11 月，省统计局被山东省爱国卫生运动委员会办公室授予无烟党政机关。

11 月，省统计局被国家机关事务管理局、中共中央直属机关事务管理局、国家发展和改革委员会、财政部授予节约型机关。

11 月，省统计局被山东省机关事务管理局、山东省发展和改革委员会、山东省财政厅授予节约型机关。

12 月 1 日，省委常委、宣传部部长白玉刚对省统计局报送的《前三季度我省文化产业统计分析》作出批示。

12 月 6 日，省委常委、秘书长刘强对省统计局报送的《关于企业统计入库纳统的几点问题》作出批示。

12 月 8 日，全省第七次全国人口普查总结表彰视频会议在济南召开。会议表彰了山东省人口普查先进集体和先进个人，总结全省第七次全国人口普查工作。省委常委、常务副省长，省人口普查领导小组组长王书坚出席会议并讲话。省政府副秘书长、办公厅主任杨国强主持会议，省人口普查领导小组副组长、省人普办主任、省统计局局长辛树人汇报全省人口普查工作情况，省人力资源和社会保障厅副厅长周春艳宣读表彰决定。

12 月 9 日，山东省暨滨州市庆祝《中华人民共和国统计法》颁布 38 周年“统计法治宣传月”启动仪式在滨州市政文化广场举行。省统计局党组书记、局长辛树人出席活动并讲话，滨州市委副书记、市长宋永祥致辞。

12 月 10 日，省统计局党组书记、局长辛树人一行到济南市章丘区调研基层统计工作联系点工作情况和经济运行情况。济南市委副书记边祥慧，市委常委、副市长王宏志陪同有关活动。

12 月 15 日，省统计局印发《关于开展企业电子统计台账试点工作的通知》（鲁统字〔2021〕96 号），在泰山区、罗庄区、阳谷县开展相关试点工作。

12 月 17 日，省统计局印发《关于开展研发和劳动工资电子统计台账试点工作的通知》（鲁统字〔2021〕98 号），在部分县（市、区）开展试点工作。

12 月 23 日，省统计局印发《市、县级人民政府统计机构统计调查项目管理办法》（鲁统字〔2021〕99 号）。

12 月 23 日，省委书记李干杰，省委副书记、省长周乃翔，省委常委、常务副省长王书坚对省统计局报送的《关于一套表调查单位数据质量核查情况的报告》作出批示。

12 月 28 日，省统计局党组印发《关于加强机关纪委建设的意见》（鲁统党字〔2021〕38 号），对加强机关纪委工作作出安排部署。

12 月 28 日，省统计局党组印发《山东省统计局党支部标准化规范化建设提升工程实施方案》（鲁统党字〔2021〕39 号）。

12 月 31 日，省委副书记、省长周乃翔，省委常委、常务副省长王书坚对省统计局、国家统计局山东调查总队联合报送的《关于全国统计工作会议精神的汇报》作出批示，并对全省统计工作作出批示。